Presented to

School for

Central Terri

COMMISSIONER SAMUEL HEPBURN

A Geneva Series Commentary

THE PSALMS

A COMMENTARY ON

THE PSALMS

———

DAVID DICKSON

Two Volumes in One

THE BANNER OF TRUTH TRUST
78B Chiltern Street, London, W.1

First published 1653–5

First Banner of Truth Trust edition 1959

Reprinted 1965

PRINTED IN GREAT BRITAIN BY OFFSET LITHOGRAPHY BY
BILLING AND SONS LTD., GUILDFORD AND LONDON

DEDICATION TO THE FIRST VOLUME.*

TO

THE TRULY HONOURABLE AND RELIGIOUS LADIES,

MY LADY MARCHIONESS OF ARGYLE,

AND

MY LADY ANN CAMPBELL,

HER ELDEST DAUGHTER,

GRACE AND PEACE THROUGH JESUS CHRIST.

It is the good and wise way of God, in matters concerning this temporal life, to make manifest his bounty and kindness to all men, how unkind and wicked soever they be, and not leave himself without a witness against complainers; but in the matters of salvation, and things which belong to eternal life, he useth not to extend his special love so largely; for even the external means of saving knowledge are bestowed upon few nations and people, in comparison to the whole race of mankind. "He sheweth his word unto Jacob, and his statutes and his judgments unto Israel. He hath not dealt so with any nation, and *as for his* judgments they have not known them." And though the people be few to whom the offer of salvation is made, in comparison of the rest of the world; yet are they many in com-

---

* The following work was originally published, at different times, in three volumes, each containing a commentary on Fifty Psalms, with a Preface and Dedication—but as there does not appear any necessity for observing the same division, now that it is published collectively, all the Dedications and Prefaces are here printed together.

parison to those who find grace in the eyes of the Lord, to accept the offer of grace tendered unto them in Christ Jesus; " for many are called, but few chosen." And albeit it be true, that God's calling and election have place in all ranks and estates of persons, higher and lower, learned and unlearned, rich and poor; yet this grace stretcheth itself to many more of the meaner sort of the people, than of the wise, wealthy, and honourable in the world. " Ye see your calling, brethren, how that not many wise men after the flesh, not many mighty, not many noble are called." Therefore, so much the greater is the favour of God, which your souls have found, most honourable, that you are made some of those few, yea, after so comfortable a manner, that the daughter finding herself led by her mother's hand, in her tender youth unto Christ the Saviour, looketh on her as her mother twice; and the mother, having power and place to draw the veil of her daughter's virginal modesty, retiredness, and prudence, which concealeth much of the lustre of her accomplishments from the sight of others who stand at a greater distance, looketh upon her notable endowments and growing graces, as more than a recompense of all the pains sustained in bringing forth, and bestowed upon educating such a plant; a plant so well fitted for that which is most desirable in earth and heaven. And thus much I have reason to say, not only because it is my part, as I have occasion, to stir up parents to study to have their children timously engaged to the Lord, in hope to have the more early and abundant comfort by them in their own time ; but also because I have been witness of the Christian behaviour of both your ladyships, in no small trial of your faith and patience by the troubles of the times, both public and private, for a number of years together ; which experience hath now good use, to fit and prepare your honours for what further exercise true believers may be subject unto in this life, and for what this present time calleth unto all to be prepared for. As this condition is in all ages incident to the godly, it should not be looked upon, in our time, as some strange thing which has befallen us ; for it is the Lord's ordinary way of dealing with his children, by changes of their condition, outward and inward, by vicissitudes of straits and outgates, by interchange of crosses and comforts, and by much variety of several conditions, powerfully to train, advance, and settle their faith, and to increase the growth of all graces accompanying salvation in them; for what we cannot conceive at one lesson, because we are dull, he teacheth us by parts, in many and sundry instructions, all tending to bring us to a further measure of humiliation and self-denial, on the one hand, and of submission unto God and faith in Christ, on the other. And this way of God is made plain by the practice of the saints, and is laid open before us in the book of Psalms; whereof, at this time, I have only taken a third part to handle by way of essay, thereby to find the advice of judicious brethren, how to satisfy and edify the reader more in what remains to be handled, if God be pleased to give further employment and assistance in this service; and this which here is offered to the edification of the Lord's people, I have put forth under your honours' names, because of your constant affection to the study of the Scriptures, and respect to all the messengers of truth, and to me for the truth's cause, for which I will still remain,

Your honours' much obliged servant in the gospel,

DAVID DICKSON.

PREFACE TO THE FIRST VOLUME.

CHRISTIAN READER,

In this Essay on the Psalms, as in other like pieces, on some other books of Scripture, sent forth to the world from me, a part of my design is still the same, that hereby I may try, if it may be the Lord's will, to stir up some more able instruments to lay open briefly, in this mould, or any other they please better, the chief doctrines treasured up in the store-house of holy Scripture, whereby the Lord's people may be solidly informed in the knowledge, and established in the faith of true religion, by the most near and immediate way of drawing their light from the fountain of the Lord's own word: for this were a means, as I humbly conceive, to cut off many needless disputes wherewith the world is filled; a means to refute many errors which the ignorance of Scripture and of the power of God hath bred and fostered in the Christian church; a means to prevent many mistakes wherein well-meaning zeal ofttimes falleth, for lack of a brief introduction into the true sense and intent of places mistaken. And I am not altogether out of hope, that the Lord shall hearken to my desire, and set some of his servants to work, ere it be long, to entertain this motion, and to take a share also in the task. Meantime, I pray let my aim and endeavour be acceptable unto thee, and do not take exception that so much is left unsaid upon such pregnant passages of Scripture as I go through briefly, and that so much good matter is hinted at, and past by so quickly, and sometimes so abruptly; nor that the deductions of sundry doctrines from the ground pointed at in the text, are ofttimes not so convincingly cleared as you would. But take this consideration along with thee, that any longer insisting, either in explication of the grounds of the doctrines pointed at in the text, or in amplification of the doctrines deduced from the grounds, would have marred much the intended brevity of the mould, wherewith both the learned, and such as have less leisure to read longer discourses, possibly will be well pleased; mainly for this cause, that they are not much taken off their studies, or their other necessary employments, by this manner of writing. Remember also, that charitable censurers will perhaps be content when they perceive, that in this plainness and brevity, every reader shall quickly meet with good matter of meditation at least, whereby the smallest grains of sound truth, sown by this means among readers, may by God's blessing get root, watering, and increase in a good and honest heart: which blessing, that it may be very large, shall be the hearty prayer of,

            Thy servant in the work of the gospel,

                      DAVID DICKSON.

DEDICATION TO THE SECOND VOLUME.

TO THE RIGHT HONOURABLE

THE EARL OF EGLINTON,

MERCY AND PEACE THROUGH JESUS CHRIST.

My Right Noble Lord,

THE reason of my sending forth this piece under your lordship's name, is, that by this means I may pay home, before I die, the old debt which I owe to your lordship, and to your whole noble family, for countenancing and encouraging me openly in my ministry, all the while that I was in Irvine, near your lordship, full twenty years.

And the reason why I confess my debt now, and go about to discharge some part of it, at this time of your lordship's restraint in England, is, because when I call to mind the time of my restraint about some thirty years ago, (when the high commission court of prelates procured my confinement within a little village in the north, beyond Aberdeen, because I could not give them satisfaction by receiving the yoke of some popish ceremonies, imposed then upon the ministry,) I cannot forget how comfortable your lordship was to me then, and what pains and travel you endured, summer and winter, without wearying, until they who at that time had power to loose me from my confinement, being made sensible, some of them of the iniquity, and all of them of the inexpedience of keeping me in bonds, restored me to the free and full use of my ministry. Wherefore I esteem it a part of due gratitude, to do what in me lieth, to be comfortable to your lordship in this your present condition; and heartily pray to God, that your exercise and trouble may prove a means of your happiness. It is true, indeed, that happiness without these means were to be wished, if so it were God's pleasure; but unto God only (in whose hands alone it is to make men blessed, and in whose friendship and favour only, through Christ, men are really blessed,) it belongeth, as to choose the man to whom, so also to choose the means whereby, and the manner how, he will communicate the right and possession of true blessedness. If happiness were at men's wish and carving, no man would choose God for his chief good, nor God's way to bring his felicity about; for the multitude of men are still saying, " Who will shew us any good ?"

The good which God doth show unto them, and the way how, by reconciliation with himself and walking humbly and uprightly before him, they may have God to be their rich reward, is not the thing they love to have ; but corn, and wine, and oil, and whatsoever may best please their fleshly fancy, are their desire. And of this the Lord complaineth, " My people," saith he, " would not hearken to my voice, and Israel would none of me." And what was it which they preferred unto God ? They loved to have their own will in this world, whatsoever should befall them after death; they loved rather to have their own earthly desires satisfied, than to have the friendship of God : and their choice was given unto them to their own destruction. " So," saith the Lord, " I gave them over to their own heart's lust, and they walked in the counsel of their own heart." Few, when they look upon the course which the world runneth after, yea, very few, prefer the fellowship of God reconciled to them in Christ, before riches, honour, and sensual pleasure : for " Who will shew us any good ?" is that which many say. But, " Lord, lift thou up the light of thy countenance upon us," is the petition of the few opposed to the multitude ; and even those few godly would wish to go to heaven with ease, and to be free from trouble in their journey, if it were the Lord's will, as we may see in the prayer of Jabez, " who called on the God of Israel, saying, Oh that thou wouldest bless me indeed, and enlarge my coast, and that thine hand might be with me, and that thou wouldest keep me from evil, that it might never grieve me." But our loving and wise God, who knoweth perfectly what is fittest for every man, crosseth and correcteth those natural desires of his children. And howsoever he will now and then possibly grant the prayer of Jabez to some of his people, yet he hath appointed this to be the ordinary road-way to heaven, which the apostle pointeth thus forth to us; "we must through much tribulation enter into the kingdom of God."

And this course of carrying God's children through many afflictions, no ways hindereth their happiness; for how many soever their crosses be, yet this holdeth always fast, "Blessed is the man whom thou choosest, and causest to approach unto thee." If, therefore, by plurality of chastisements, the Lord shall draw, and drive them to seek remission of sins and reconciliation with himself, and the renewed sense thereof through Christ, and shall by the rod hedge them within the way of walking with him in a friendly communion: they lose nothing except their lusts, and gain eternal blessedness. And certainly, there are so many relics of natural corruption, such strong inclinations unto sin, so many actual outbreakings, and gross transgressions to be found in the most precious saints, that there is no wonder the Lord should visit their trespasses with the rod, and their iniquity with stripes; but all the wonder is, that he will not take his loving-kindness utterly from them. There is also so great need of loosing their affections from what seemeth love-worthy in this world; so great need of raising the hearts of the heirs of salvation unto the seeking of a kingdom which cannot be shaken, and of a crown incorruptible; as all reason doth call for the mixture of troubles with earthly comforts, lest the sweetness of temporary vanities should prove unto them poisonable. Moreover, the experience of the saints set down in Scripture, and especially in the Psalms, maketh it manifest, that by the variety of outward and inward troubles, the faith of God's children hath been tried, and trained to further strength. Their love, hope, and patience, and all other spiritual graces in them have been so fostered and augmented, that they have been made, joyfully and thankfully, to subscribe this truth, "Blessed is the man whom thou chastenest, O Lord, and teachest him out of thy law." This is the language of the Lord's present dispensation towards his people, and the lesson which his providence recommendeth to us all, that we may learn it to our good : whereunto if this piece shall contribute any thing for the edifying of those who shall be pleased to read it, and in special, if it shall be acceptable to your Lordship, this shall do much more than recompense the labour of

Your lordship's obliged servant in the gospel,

DAVID DICKSON.

PREFACE TO THE SECOND VOLUME.

CHRISTIAN READER,

THE acceptance which the former fifty psalms have found, doth give me encouragement sufficient to offer these other fifty to thy view also, and to promise the last fifty so soon as the Lord shall enable me. I am still sparing of thy time, and do strive to point forth, not all the doctrines which may be deduced from the words; but so many only as, being joined together and compared with the text, may give unto thee both the sense and the use thereof. It is not possible to express grave purposes sufficiently without a volume, nor to open mysteries in few words unto thy satisfaction, who canst not choose but wish to have more of the purpose, where-of thou lovest to hear much, and findest but a little of it hinted at. No sort of writing, except that of the Scripture, hath all perfections : but this advantage thou hast by this mould, thou shalt not read long till thou meet with matter worthy of thy meditation ; and whensoever thou meetest with a word spoken in season, or fit for thy condition, thou mayst close thy reading for the time, without losing any long dis-course, and feed upon what thou hast found till it be digested, and then return when thou wilt, and seek for as much as may be another morsel. For the reading of many diverse doctrines without some interlaced meditation, is like eating of marrow without bread, and cannot but cloy thee for the time, or give thee a surfeit of wholesome food: which evil, if it befall thee, may be helped for after time by short ejaculations of a word of prayer whilst thou are reading, according as the purpose calleth thee to seek the Lord's blessing unto that which thou readest; whose presence that thou mayst find comfortable, is the prayer of

Thy servant in the gospel,

DAVID DICKSON.

DEDICATION TO THE THIRD VOLUME.

TO THE RIGHT HONOURABLE

THE EARL OF CASSILS,

GRACE AND PEACE THROUGH CHRIST JESUS.

MY RIGHT NOBLE LORD,

ONE of the special motives of my resolution to follow this work in parcels, was the apparent hazard, that if, in this time of trouble and of my old age, I should have delayed to put forth some part of it till all had been ready, the whole might have been miscarried or marred, by some passage of providence which might have befallen me. But seeing it hath pleased the Lord to spare my life, and my health, and my liberty in his service, as I wanted not the example of grave authors before me to divide the whole book of the Psalms into three parts, and to dedicate every part to different persons; so I judged it good thrift, to take occasion thereby to testify my bounden duty and respect, to so many of the noble friends of Zion as I could overtake; and that with a mind to honour all the rest, who have put their shoulder to the work of settling religion and the kingdom of Christ among us: whose labours, albeit they should have

no other fruit in our time, than the right stating of the
question between us and all adversaries of the true doctrine,
worship, and discipline of Christ's house, as it is set down
in the Confession of Faith, in the Directory for Public Worship, and in the Rules of Government of Christ's Church,
drawn forth from scripture warrant; yet even that much is
worth all the expense of whatsoever is bestowed, by any or
all the Lord's worthies, upon religion. And howsoever the
Lord claimeth, and calleth for, the whole glory of this work
to himself alone, by staining the pride of the glory of all
instruments whereof he hath made use about it, as now appeareth, lest the glory due to himself, in all and every one
of the passages of promoting the same, should be eclipsed;
yet will he never utterly reject this service, nor disallow the
upright endeavours of his servants therein; but will in his
own time and way, both advance it, and bear witness to his
faithful servants in and about it, wheresoever he hath a mind
to keep house, or to reign as king in Zion. Yea, he will
also make it known to the world, that, as on the one hand
he will not want a visible kingdom in the world, though not
of this world; so, on the other hand, his kingdom shall
be so far from hindering the civil government of magistrates,
where it hath place, that, on the contrary, it shall be a
chief prop and pillar of every kingdom where it is received.

In this number of upright promoters of the kingdom of
Christ, your lordship hath been always looked upon, all the
time of our late troubles, as one very eminent: and I, since
my first admission into your lordship's acquaintance, have
observed your constant care and endeavour, as to know what
was the right in difficult questions, as also to hold it fast,
according to your power, after you had discovered it.
Which, as it may be your lordship's comfort, so is it your
commendation, and all men's duty to do the like, especially
in this dangerous time, wherein sins practised, and not repented of, are so severely and justly punished by God's
giving over the impenitent to the open professing and defending of their unrepented faults: for God in justice and
wisdom has suffered the hedges of his vineyard to be broken
down, and the holy discipline of his house to be set at

nought by all sorts of persons, that every spirit of error, having open way to come in at the breach, he might thereby try and exercise all his people, who stand in covenant with him by profession, and reclaim or punish such as live in error. And no wonder that he should do so : for when there is so little use made of the holy ordinances of religion ; when the Scriptures are either not read, or not esteemed ; when the form of godliness is separated from upright endeavour to feel and show forth the life and power of it ; when the grace of the gospel is turned into wantonness, and men are become so much the more bold to sin, as they hear much of the mercifulness of God ; when every divine truth is either not believed at all, or received only with human and temporary faith ; when Christ is looked upon by many only as a man, and not as God manifested in the flesh, nor as the eternal Son of God, who from everlasting was with God, and was God, co-worker in the creation with the Father and the Spirit ; when Christ is confessed to be Christ, but not employed as mediator, or, as if men had no need of him, not made use of in his offices ; when many cast open their souls unto, and seek after, another spirit than the Spirit of truth, the comforter, the Holy Ghost, who, according to the Scriptures, both wounds and heals the consciences of believers, and sanctifieth the heart and conversation of all them that come to God through Christ,—In this time, I say, when these and many other ungodly practices of men, walking after the imaginations of their own hearts, so abound ; what wonder is it that the Lord hath let loose so many unclean spirits, as no history can show more in so short a time, in any age, or in any place of the world ! By the ranging up and down of these spirits among us, God is about to make manifest the stability and sincerity of the faith of them who are approved, and to take trial of others, in whom such damnable practices, as by the doctrine of devils are now openly defended, will be found unrepented, whether, after they shall hear their ungodly pranks maintained and patronized by some sect-master, heretic, or schismatic, they will abhor such abominable doctrine, and repent their own former misdeeds, which have spoken the language of some of those vile errors ;

or whether they will justify their own faults, as their sect-masters teach them to do, either by despising all the ordinances, and lifting themselves above the same, or by rejecting the commands and cords of the moral law, will loose themselves from the obedience thereof, as if Christ had freed the believer from the command and authority of the law, no less than from the covenant and curse thereof; or by blaspheming the Scripture, will cry down the truth, and the use and power of it; or by calling every truth in question, will exempt themselves from the bonds of all religion; or will walk after the imagination of their own heart, and make their own conceits their oracle, their fancy their faith, and their lusts their God; or will, by opposing one or other of the persons of the Godhead, deny and separate the individual essence of one God in three persons; or by receiving the doctrine of some of those many lesser antichrists which are in the world, will incorporate themselves in the great mystical body of the one antichrist, spoken of in Scripture; or in a word, will, by rejecting the truth, and not receiving it in love, when it is offered, bring in upon themselves strong delusions, and give a powerful possession of themselves to the devil, whereby he may so rule in them, as to make them vent whatsoever hell can devise, to the dishonour of God, and the Christian religion, that all such may be damned, as for their not receiving the truth in love, so also for their taking pleasure in unrighteousness, according as the apostle prophesied should come to pass.

In such a time therefore as this is, wherein the Lord is manifesting who are of God, and who not, who know God, and who do not; who follow the Spirit of truth, and who are led by the spirit of error, and is deciphering them by this infallible mark which the apostle giveth, that the one give a believing and obediential ear to the penmen of holy Scripture, the other do not; what a mercy, yea, what an honour and happiness is it for the Lord's children, to make such use of a settled ministry, which is the great gift of Christ bestowed upon his church, as not to be carried about with every wind of doctrine, not to be led away with the error of the wicked, nor fall from their own steadfastness, but to grow in grace, and in the knowledge of our Lord and Saviour Jesus Christ! Which grace, and honour, and happiness, that it may not only continue with your lordship, but also be granted to all those that love our Lord Jesus Christ in sincerity, is the prayer of

Your lordship's ready servant in the gospel,

DAVID DICKSON.

PREFACE TO THE THIRD VOLUME.

CHRISTIAN READER,

In the two former parts of this work, I have spoken my mind to thee in relation to this Brief Explication of the Psalms: I will not here keep thee up in the entry of this last part, nor say any more unto thee save this, it is our bounden duty to bless Him that inhabiteth the praises of Israel, who will have all the mourners in Zion to be comforted, and who, as he hath prepared in this mountain to all people "a feast of fat things, a feast of wines on the lees, of fat things full of marrow, of wines on the lees well refined," by bestowing Christ and the unsearchable riches of his grace, upon every penitent who fleeth to him for delivery from sin and wrath; so hath he also prepared to every such soul the excellent songs of Zion, to increase their festival gladness; and for evidencing of his purpose to give unto them everlasting joy, after this life is ended, hath put into their hands, for their comfort in every condition, wherein they can be in this present life and valley of tears, this sweet-smelling bundle of psalms; wherein he hath made his works of mercy and of judgment the pledges of his promises for complete happiness unto them, and also of the utter overthrow and perdition of all their enemies, and hath appointed both mercy and judgment to be the matter, as of their joy, so of his own glory in the church, to be lifted up, as a sacrifice upon the altar

Christ Jesus, by the voice of his people, singing with grace to him, both alone and in company, and making melody in their hearts. Therefore, as in the changes of our own particular private condition, we have liberty to choose for our use such parts of the psalms as speak closest to our present case: so let us be bound in public meetings of the church to join with the congregation in singing every truth uttered by God's Spirit in the psalms, as we are directed by the minister and mouth of the meeting, for glorifying Him who hath done, promised, threatened, and taught whatsoever is therein expressed; remembering that his praises are the pillars of our faith: and that his joy is our strength; and that those calves of our lips are acceptable sacrifices to God through Jesus Christ, in and for whom,

I am thy servant in the work of the gospel,

DAVID DICKSON.

SHORT ACCOUNT

OF

THE LIFE OF THE AUTHOR.

MR DAVID DICK, or DICKSON, was the only son of John
Dick, or Dickson, merchant in Glasgow, whose father was an
old feuar and possessor of some lands in the barony of Fin-
try, and parish of St Ninians, called the Kirk of the Muir.
His parents were religious persons of considerable substance,
and many years married before they had this child, and he
was the only one ever they had, as I am informed. As he
was a Samuel asked of the Lord, so he was early devoted to
him and the ministry; yet afterwards the vow was forgot,
till providence by a rod and sore sickness on their son,
brought their sins to remembrance; and then he was put to
resume his studies which he had left, and at the university of
Glasgow he made very great progress in them.

Soon after he had received the degree of Master of Arts,
he was admitted regent, or professor of philosophy in that
college, where he was very useful in training up the youth in
solid learning; and with the learned principal Boyd of
Trochridge, the worthy Mr Robert Blair, and other pious
members of that learned society, his pains were singularly
blessed, in reviving decayed serious piety among the youth,
in that declining and corrupted time, a little after the impos-
ing of prelacy upon us.

By a recommendation of the General Assembly not long
after our reformation from popery, the regents were only to
continue eight years in their profession, after which such as

were found qualified, were licensed, and upon calls after trials, admitted to the holy ministry. By this constitution, this church came to be filled with ministers well seen in all the branches of useful learning. Accordingly Mr Dickson was, in 1618, ordained minister to the town of Irvine, where he laboured about twenty-three years.

That very year, the corrupt assembly at Perth agreed to the five notorious articles, palmed upon this church by the king and prelates. Mr Dickson had not much studied these questions, till the articles were imposed by this meeting. Then he closely examined them, and the more he looked into them, the more aversion he found to them; and when some time after by a sore sickness he was brought within view of death and eternity, he gave open testimony of their sinfulness.

When this came to take air, Mr James Law, archbishop of Glasgow, summoned him to appear before the high commission, January 29, 1622. Mr Dickson at his entrance to his ministry at Irvine, had preached upon 2 Cor. v. 11, the first part, "Knowing the terrors of the Lord, we persuade men;" when at this juncture he apprehended a separation, at least for a time, the Sabbath before his compearance, he chose the next words of that verse, " But we are made manifest unto God." Extraordinary power, and singular movings of affections, accompanied that parting sermon.

According to the summons, Mr Dickson appeared before the commission, the day named. His prudent carriage, the declinature he gave in, the railing of Archbishop Spottiswood thereupon, the sentence of deprivation and confinement to Turref passed upon him, with his Christian speech upon the intimation of it, are to be found in Mr Calderwood's history.

After much intercession with the bishops, and various turns in this affair, narrated by the last named historian, he got liberty to quit Turref, and returned to his longing flock, July, 1623, where his ministerial work was no more interrupted, until he was called to a more important station, as we shall hear.

At Irvine, Mr Dickson's ministry was singularly countenanced of God. Multitudes were convinced and converted; and few that lived in his day were more honoured to be instruments of conversion, than he. People under exercise and soul concern, came from every place about Irvine and attended upon his sermons, and the most eminent and serious Christians from all corners of the church, came and joined with him at his communions, which were indeed times of refreshing from the presence of the Lord of these amiable institutions: yea, not a few came from distant places, and settled in Irvine, that they might be under the drop of his ministry. Yet he himself used to observe, that the vintage of Irvine was not equal to the gleanings, and not once to be compared to the harvest at Ayr in Mr John Welch's time, when indeed the gospel had wonderful success in conviction, conversion, and confirmation.

Mr Dickson had his week day's sermon upon the Mondays, the market days then at Irvine. Upon the Sabbath evenings, many persons under soul distress, used to resort to his house after sermon, when usually he spent an hour or two in answering their cases, and directing and comforting those who were cast down, in all which he had an extraordinary talent; indeed he had the tongue of the learned, and knew how to speak a word in season to the weary soul. In a large hall he had in his house at Irvine, there would have been, as I am informed by old Christians, several scores of serious Christians waiting for him, when he came from the church. Those, with the people round the town, who came in to the market at Irvine, made the church as throng, if not thronger, on the Mondays, as on the Lord's day, by these week-day sermons. The famous Stewarton sickness was begun about the year 1630, and spread from house to house for many miles in the strath where Stewarton water runs, on both sides of it. Satan indeed endeavoured to bring a reproach upon the serious persons who were at this time under the convincing work of the Spirit, by running some, seemingly under serious concern, to excesses both in time of sermon, and in families. But the Lord enabled Mr Dickson, and other ministers who dealt with them, to act so prudent a part, that Satan's design was much disappointed, and solid serious practical religion flourished mightily in the west of Scotland about this time, under the hardships of prelacy.

About the year 1632, some of our Scots ministers, Mr Robert Blair, Mr John Livingston, &c., settled among the Scots in the north of Ireland, were remarkably owned of the Lord, and their ministry and communions about the Six Mile water, were made useful for reviving religion in the power and practice of it. The Irish prelates, at the instigation of ours, got them removed for a season, much against excellent Bishop Usher's mind. When silenced and come over to Scotland about the year 1638, Mr Dickson employed Messrs Blair, Livingston, and Cunningham, at his communion ; for this he was called before the high commission. He soon got rid of this trouble, the prelates' power being now on the decline.

I have some of Mr Dickson's sermons at Irvine taken from his mouth. They are full of solid substantial matter, very scriptural, and in a very familiar style, not low, but extremely strong, plain, and affecting. It is somewhat akin to Mr Rutherford's, in his admirable letters. I have been told by some old ministers, that scarce any body of that time came so near Mr Dickson's style and method in preaching, as the Rev. Mr William Guthrie, minister of Fenwick, who equalled, if not exceeded him here.

As Mr Dickson was singularly useful in his public ministrations, so I could give many instances of his usefulness more privately, both to Christians in answering their perplexing cases of conscience, and students who had their eye to the ministry, while he was at Irvine : his prudent directions, cautions, and encouragements, given them, were extremely useful and beneficial. I could also give examples of his usefulness to his very enemies, and the Lord's making what he spoke to one that robbed him on the road to Edinburgh of a considerable sum of money, the occasion of the poor youth's change of life, and at length of real conversion. The account of which I have from a worthy person, who had it from himself. But there is not room here to enlarge on these things.

It was Mr Dickson who brought the presbytery of Irvine to supplicate the council, 1637, for a suspension of a charge given to ministers to buy and use the service-book. At that time four supplications from different quarters, without any concert in the supplicants, met at the council-house door, to their mutual surprise and encouragement. These were the small beginnings of that happy turn of affairs, that and next years, of which it were to be wished we had fuller and better accounts than yet have been published.

In that great revolution, Mr Dickson bore no small share. He was sent to Aberdeen, with Messrs Henderson and Cant, by the Covenanters, to persuade that city and country about, to join in renewing the land's covenant with the Lord. This brought him to bear a great part in the debates with the learned doctors Forbes, Barron, Sibbald, &c. at Aberdeen, which being in print, I say no more of them.

When the king was prevailed with to allow a free General Assembly at Glasgow, November, 1638, Mr Dickson and Mr Bailey from the presbytery of Irvine, made a great figure there. In all the important matters before that grave meeting, he was very useful, but Mr Dickson signalized himself in a seasonable and prudent speech he had, when his majesty's commissioner threatened to leave the assembly. It is in mine eye, but too long to stand here, and too important and nervous to abridge. In the 11th session, December 5th, he had another most learned discourse against Arminianism, which I also omit.

The reports of the Lord's eminent countenancing Mr Dickson's ministry at Irvine, had, ere this time, spread through all this church; but his eminent prudence, learning, and holy zeal, came to be universally known, especially to ministers, from the part he bore in the assembly at Glasgow: so that he was almost unanimously chosen moderator to the next General Assembly at Edinburgh, August, 1639. Many of his speeches, and instances of his wise management at so critical a juncture, are before me in a MS. account of that assembly. In the 10th session, the city of Glasgow presented a call to him; but partly because of his own aversion, and the vigorous appearances of the earl of Eglinton and his loving people, and mostly from the remarkable usefulness of his ministry in that corner, the General Assembly continued him at Irvine.

But not long after, 1641, he was transported to be professor of divinity in the university of Glasgow, where he did great services to the church and interests of real religion, by training up many youths for the holy ministry. Notwithstanding his laborious work amongst them, he preached every Lord's day forenoon in the high church there; and got in, and I think, had for his colleague, the learned and zealous Mr Patrick Gillespie.

In the year 1643, the church laid a very great work on him, Mr Henderson, and Mr Calderwood, to form the draught of a directory for public worship, as appears by the acts of assembly. When the pestilence was raging at Glasgow, 1647, the masters and students of the university removed to Irvine, upon Mr Dickson's motion. There the holy and learned Mr Durham passed his trials, and was earnestly recommended by the professor to the presbytery and magistrates of Glasgow, and in a little time ordained minister to that city. Great was the friendship and familiarity between these two eminent lights of this church there; and among other effects of their familiar conversation, which still turned upon profitable subjects and designs, we have the Sum of Saving Knowledge, which hath been so often printed with our Confession of Faith and Catechisms. This, after several conversations, and thinking upon the subject and manner of handling it, so as it might be most useful to vulgar capacities, was by Messrs Dickson and Durham dictated to a reverend minister, who informed me, about the year 1650. It was the deed of these two great men, and though never judicially approven of by this church, deserves to be much more read and considered than I fear it is.

About this time, Mr Dickson had a great share in the printed pamphlets upon the unhappy debates betwixt the Resolutioners and Protesters. He was in his opinion for the public resolutions, and most of the papers upon that side were written by him, Mr Robert Bailey, and Mr Robert Douglas; as those upon the other side were written by Mr James Guthrie, Mr Patrick Gillespie, and a few others.

I have not inquired into the exact time when Mr Dickson was transported from the profession of divinity at Glasgow, to the same work at Edinburgh; but I take it to have been about this time. There he continued his laborious care of students of divinity, the growing hopes of a church; and either at Glasgow or Edinburgh most part of the presbyterian ministers, at least in the west, south, and east parts of Scotland, from the year 1640 to the happy revolution, were under his inspection. And from his Truth's Victory over Error, we may perceive his care to educate them in the form of sound words, and to ground them solidly in the excellent standards of doctrine agreed to by this church. May it still be the care and mercy of the church of Scotland, to preserve and hand down to posterity, the scriptural pure doctrine delivered by our first reformers to Mr Dickson and his contemporaries, and from him and the other great lights in his day handed down to us now upon the stage, without corruption and declining to right or left hand.

Mr Dickson continued at Edinburgh discharging his great trust with faithfulness and diligence, until the melancholy turn by the restoration of prelacy, upon king Charles's return; when, for refusing the oath of supremacy, he was with many other worthies turned out. His heart was broken with the heavy change on the beautiful face of this reformed church. He was now well stricken in years, his labour and work were over, and he was ripe for his glorious reward.

Accordingly in December, 1662, he fell extremely weak. Mr John Livingston, now suffering for the same cause with him, and under a sentence of banishment for refusing the foresaid oath, came to visit Mr Dickson on his death-bed. They had been intimate friends near fifty years, and now rejoiced together as fellow confessors. When Mr Livingston asked the professor how he found himself, his answer was, " I have taken all my good deeds and all my bad deeds, and cast them through each other in a heap before the Lord, and fled from both, and betaken myself to the Lord Jesus Christ, and in him I have sweet peace." Mr Dickson's youngest son gave my informer, a worthy minister yet alive, this account of his father's death. Having been very weak and low for some days, he called all his family together, and spoke in particular to each of them, and when he had gone through

them all, he pronounced the words of the apostolical blessing, 2 Cor. xiii. 14, with much gravity and solemnity ; and
then put up his hand and closed his own eyes, and without
any struggle or apparent pain, immediately expired in the
arms of his son, my brother's informer.

Mr Dickson married Margaret Roberton, daughter to
Archibald Roberton of Stonehall, a younger brother of the
house of Ernock, in the shire of Lanark. By her he had
three sons, John Dickson, clerk to the exchequer in Scotland ;
Mr Alexander Dickson, professor of the Hebrew tongue in
the university of Edinburgh ; and Mr Archibald Dickson,
who lived with his family in the parish of Irvine. By these
he hath left a numerous posterity.

It remains only now that I give some account of Mr
Dickson's writings and works, he hath left behind him in
print and MS., which speak when he is dead. He was concerned in, and I am ready to think one principal mover of,
that concert among several worthy ministers of this Church,
for publishing short, plain, and practical expositions upon
the whole Bible. I cannot recover all their names who were
engaged in this work, but I know Mr Robert Douglas, Mr
Rutherford, Mr Robert Blair, Mr G. Hutcheson, Mr James
Ferguson, Mr Alexander Nisbet, Mr James Durham, Mr
John Smith, and some others, had particular books of holy
Scripture allotted to them. The labours of the most of these
are published, and the works of others of them yet remain in
MS. Mr Dickson, with whom at present I am only con-
cerned, published, his Commentary on the Hebrews, 8vo ;—
On Matthew, 4to ;—On the Psalms, 8vo ;—On the Epistles,
Latin and English, 4to and folio ;—Therapeutica Sacra, or
Cases of Conscience Resolved, in Latin, 4to, in English, 8vo ;
—A Treatise of the Promises, 12mo, Dublin, 1630.—The
work entitled Truth's Victory over Error, was translated
from his Prælectiones in Confessionem Fidei, or heads of
his lectures delivered in the Divinity chair, and first published after his death, Lond. 1688, 12mo.

Besides these, he wrote a great part of the Answers to the
Demands, and Duplies to the Replies of the Doctors of Aberdeen, 4to, and some of the pamphlets in defence of the

public resolutions, as hath been observed; with some short poems on pious and serious subjects, which I am told have been very useful, when printed and spread among country people and servants; such as, "The Christian Sacrifice," "O Mother dear, Jerusalem!" and one somewhat larger, 8vo, 1649, entitled, "True Christian Love, to be sung with the common tunes of the Psalms." This is all of his I have seen in print.

Several of his MSS. remain unprinted. Besides some of his original letters, I have his "Preparatio Tyronis Concionaturi," which I suppose he dictated to his scholars at Glasgow. "Summarium Libri Jesaiæ;" his "Letter on the Resolutions;" his "First Paper upon the Public Resolutions;" his "Reply to Mr P. Gillespie and Mr James Guthrie;" his "No Separation of the well-affected from the Army." I am not sure but some of these may be in print, they are generally pretty large papers, of several sheets in writing. His sermons at Irvine upon 1 Tim. 1. 5, I have mentioned already. I doubt not but many more of his valuable papers are in the hands of others: such as his "Precepts for a Daily Direction of a Christian's Conversation." "The Grounds of the true Christian Religion," by way of catechism for his congregation of Irvine. "A Compend of his Sermons upon Jeremiah and the Lamentations, and the first Nine Chapters of the Epistle to the Romans." These I have not seen, but I know they are in the hands of ministers.

ROBERT WODROW

Eastwood, *Jan.* 5, 1726.

A COMMENTARY ON THE PSALMS

VOLUME I

A BRIEF EXPOSITION

OF THE

FIRST FIFTY PSALMS.

ALBEIT the Book of the Psalms be not composed after the manner of human writings, in some such method of parts as history or art could possibly prescribe; yet it is so digested in Divine Providence, as the order it hath is far better than human artifice could have given unto it: for the scope of this book being not only to teach us the grounds of divinity for our information, but also to direct us how to apply saving doctrines practically to ourselves, and to make use thereof for reformation of our affections and actions, and to help us by the example of the practice and exercise of God's dear children, to go after their footsteps, being led by this directory all along, as by the hand, unto the fruition of felicity, in higher and higher degrees thereof, till we be perfectly possessed of it in heaven. The Psalms, in relation to this scope, are so placed, as the first psalm having divided all men into two ranks, in order to the way of seeking felicity, giveth directions to us to choose, not the counsel of the wicked, but the word of God, for the rule whereby to walk unto true blessedness. And the second psalm giveth us God, in Christ, for a captain and leader to us, who is able to maintain his church, and all those who shall follow this rule, against all the opposition which can be made against them by the power and multitude of the wicked, who will not be bound by the bonds and cords (as they esteem) of this rule of the Lord's law. And the rest of the Psalms hold forth the examples of Christ and his followers, yoked in conflict with their persecutors for righteousness' sake; in all assaults making use of their covenant with God, and prevailing by his power, which upholdeth, directeth, comforteth them in all their troubles, and giveth victory and delivery unto them out of them all; to the intent that every one who shall choose to be truly blessed in the way prescribed of God, (who only can give and maintain felicity,) may resolve and prepare themselves for such a life as the saints have had in all generations before them; that is, a life mixed with crosses and sweet comforts; a life wherein they shall be put to make use of their faith in God by prayers, and shall not want for their answer in due time, matter of joy and praises to God; a life composed of variety of godly exercises, and alternating vicissitudes of conditions, as the bulk of this book representeth; but closing, as this bundle of psalms closeth, with six times pure praises, whereunto now and then the Lord frameth the heart of the believer with joy unspeakable and full of glory: that endless and uninterrupted thanksgiving and praise being reserved to the general assembly and full meeting of Christ, and all his redeemed ones, at the great day of our Lord's second coming.

BRIEF

EXPLICATION OF THE PSALMS.

PSALM I.

This Psalm teacheth, that no ungodly man is blessed, but the godly man only, v. 1, 2. Which is proved by three reasons: The first, because God blesseth the godly even in this life with grace to bring forth good works profitable to themselves and others, in every state of life, v. 3; but all that the wicked do for making themselves happy, shall be blasted, and found to be mere vanity, v. 4. Another reason is, because after this life the wicked shall be secluded from the presence of God and society of the godly, at the day of judgment, v. 5. The third reason, confirming both the former, is, because God approveth the way of the godly, and will make the end of the way of the ungodly destruction, v. 6.

1. *Blessed* is *the man that walketh not in the counsel of the ungodly, nor standeth in the way of sinners, nor sitteth in the seat of the scornful.*

2. *But his delight* is *in the law of the Lord, and in his law doth he meditate day and night.*

From the pronouncing of the godly man to be the blessed man, and not the ungodly, learn, 1. Though sin and misery abound among men, yet blessedness may be attained ; for God here pronounceth some to be blessed. 2. In relation to the seeking of blessedness, all men, within and without the visible church, are divided into godly men, that seek to be blessed in God's way ; and ungodly men, who seek blessedness, but not in God's way ; for so are they here all ranked. 3. To determine the question, who is the blessed man, is competent to God only, in whose hand alone it is to make a man blessed ; for here he taketh it upon him, to pronounce the godly man to *be the blessed man.* 4. The ungodly think themselves very wise in following the counsel of their own heart, and of others like themselves, that they may be blessed ; but this is not the way of the blessed man, *he walketh not in the counsel of the ungodly.* 5. The ungodly obstinately continue in the course of sinning, but the blessed man, if he be overtaken in a sin,

B

doth not defend his sin, nor persist in it : *he standeth not in the way of sinners.* 6. The ungodly may come to that height at length, as to mock godliness, as mere folly, and to scorn admonitions and reproofs : but the blessed man never hardeneth his heart so, as to mock piety in others, or instruction offered to himself, *he sitteth not in the seat of the scornful.* 7. The blessed man maketh the word of God in holy Scripture, to be his counsellor concerning the remedy of sin and misery, and to be the rule to walk by, till his blessedness be perfected ; for the Scripture to him, for the obedience of faith, is a law, and that fenced with supreme authority : *it is the law of the Lord.* 8. In that measure that a man is godly and blessed, he maketh the word of God, which holdeth forth the way of reconciliation with God, through the Messiah, Christ, the way of growing in communion with God through him, the matter of his chief delight, and contentment ; *his delight is in the law of the Lord.* 9. In that measure that a man delighteth in the law of the Lord, he verseth himself therein upon all occasions : *in his law doth he meditate day and night.*

3. *And he shall be like a tree planted by the rivers of water, that bringeth forth his fruit in his season : his leaf also shall not wither ; and whatsoever he doeth shall prosper.*

4. *The ungodly* are *not so : but* are *like the chaff which the wind driveth away.*

This is the first reason preving the godly man to be the only blessed man, and not the ungodly : hence learn, 1. In that measure a man studieth holy communion with God, by delighting and meditating in his word, he shall be fixed and furnished with the influence of Grace from Christ, for the entertaining of spiritual life in him ; *he shall be like a tree planted by the rivers of water.* 2. The man that maketh the word of God his delight, shall be made fruitful in every good work, as opportunity is offered to him ; *he shall be like the tree that bringeth forth his fruit in his season.* 3. This man shall be enabled to bear out a holy profession of his faith in, and obedience to God, in adversity, as well as in prosperity : *his leaf also shall not wither.* 4. Whatsoever duty or service to God this man goeth about, shall not want the assistance of God, nor success, nor accep-

tance at his hands ; *whatsoever he doeth shall prosper.*
5. The ungodly man, whatsoever he may seem to be before the world, yet he is destitute of all spiritual life, and alien from the fellowship of God's grace, unfit for every good work, ready when tempted hard, to quit his counterfeit profession of religion, and is cursed in all that he doth ; for what the blessed godly man is here said to be, the wicked is the contrary ; *the ungodly are not so.* 6. Whatsoever appearance of godliness, or temporal prosperity, or hope of happiness the ungodly man seemeth to have, it shall be found but counterfeit, and shall stand him in no stead in his greatest need : *the ungodly are like the chaff which the wind bloweth away.*

5. *Therefore the ungodly shall not stand in the judgment, nor sinners in the congregation of the righteous.*

The second reason, proving the godly man to be the blessed man, and not the ungodly, is a consequence of the first : whence learn, 1. Not only shall all that the ungodly man soweth to his fleshly felicity, prove chaff ; but also for his pains he shall answer to God in the day of judgment, and there be condemned ; for it is said, *therefore the ungodly shall not stand in the judgment.* 2. Howsoever the godly cannot enjoy one another's fellowship in this life, for many reasons ; yet at last they shall meet in a general assembly of all saints, in the full fellowship of God ; for there is a day of judgment to be, wherein they shall stand, and not be cast or condemned, but shall be fully absolved, and remain in the *standing congregation of the righteous.* 3. Albeit now the ungodly and godly do live together, mixed in one kingdom, city, incorporation, visible church, family, and bed possibly, yet there shall be a perfect separation at last, of the one from the other ; for sinners or (servants of sin) *shall not stand in the congregation of the righteous.*

6. *For the Lord knoweth the way of the righteous : but the way of the ungodly shall perish.*

The third reason confirmeth the former two : Whence learn, 1. Albeit there be no man that liveth and sinneth not, yet the godly man, being justified by faith, and careful to bring forth the fruits of faith, is not a sinner in God's esteem ; for he is here called righteous. 2. However there be many imperfections and failings of the godly man's ac-

tions, yet the course he keepeth, and way which he endeavoureth to walk in, is holy and acceptable to God; *for
the Lord knoweth* or approveth *the way of the righteous.*
3. Let the men of this world please themselves, and applaud
one another in their godless carriage; yet the end of their
course shall be everlasting destruction; *for the way of the
ungodly shall perish.*

PSALM II.

That this Psalm doth mainly, if not only, concern Christ, appeareth by
this: That it hath not so much as *David's* name in the inscription, albeit he did write it: and by Acts iv. 25, 26, where it is appropriated
to Christ. This Psalm hath two parts; in the former is set down the
stability of Christ's kingdom, against all the enemies thereof, v. 1, 2, 3.
First, because God the Father taketh part with his Son, against all his
enemies, and will establish Christ's kingdom, in spite of them all, v. 4,
5, 6. Secondly, because in the covenant of redemption, the Father
hath promised to the Son enlargement of his kingdom, and victory over
all his enemies, v. 7, 8, 9. In the latter part of the Psalm the prophet
delivereth the use of this doctrine in an exhortation to great and small
to repent of their sins, and to believe in Christ, v. 10, 11, 12.

1. *Why do the heathen rage, and the people imagine
a vain thing?*

2. *The kings of the earth set themselves, and the
rulers take counsel together, against the Lord, and
against his Anointed,* saying,

3. *Let us break their bands asunder, and cast away
their cords from us.*

The prophet showeth, that in vain shall Christ's enemies oppose his kingdom: whence learn, 1, That the
ungodly world, being strangers from the life of God, are
incensed in a mad mood against the church and kingdom
of Christ in the world, *the heathen rage,* saith he, to wit,
against the visible government of Christ in his visible church,
as appeareth, v. 2, 3. 2. Their opposition is altogether
unjust, without cause, and reasonless; for being asked,
they cannot render a reason *why.* 3. Though Christ's
enemies promise to themselves success in their opposition
to Christ, and that they shall surely overturn his kingdom,
yet shall their imaginations prove folly; they shall not prevail, *for they imagine a vain thing,* which is impossible to
be effectuated. 4. The chief instruments that Satan stirreth
up against Christ, to be heads and leaders to heathen and

godless people in opposing and persecuting Christ's kingdom and church, are the magistrates, rulers, and statesmen, that he may colour his malice with the shadow of authority and law ; *for the kings of the earth and rulers set themselves,* to wit, in opposition to him. In this attempt the great ones among men agree more easily together, than in any thing else ; they fix their resolutions, communicate their counsels, and conjoin their power ; *the kings of the earth set themselves, and the rulers take counsel together.* 6. Howsoever the persecutors of the church conceive themselves not to oppose God but men only, when they trouble his people and servants for righteousness, yet because the quarrel is the Lord's, therefore their opposition is declared here to be *against the Lord, and his Anointed,* or *his Christ,* who is distinguished here from the *Lord,* in regard of his incarnation, mediation, and offices, being otherwise, in respect of his Godhead, one in essence with the Father and the Holy Spirit. 7. Though the law and ordinances of God be most holy, most equitable, most harmless, yea, also most profitable : yet the wicked esteem of them, as they call them here, *bands and cords,* because they curb and cross their carnal wisdom and licentiousness of life. 8. It is not enough to the wicked to disobey and reject the law and ordinances of Christ for their own part, but they will also have them abolished, that God in Christ should not have a church at all, at least in their bounds, or where they have power. *Let us break their bands asunder and cast away their cords from us.*

4. *He that sitteth in the heavens shall laugh : the Lord shall have them in derision.*

5. *Then shall he speak unto them in his wrath, and vex them in his sore displeasure.*

6. *Yet have I set my King upon my holy hill of Zion.*

The first reason of the stability of Christ's kingdom is, because God scorneth men's opposing thereof, and will vex his enemies, and settle Christ's kingdom in his visible church, in the sight of his enemies : hence learn, 1. Though the church visible, and the ordinances of Christ be among the feet of potentates, and Christ's subjects want wisdom and power on earth, to defend themselves, yet their maintainer is *omnipotent* God, judge over all, *even he that sitteth in heaven.* 2. All the devices and conspiracies of men against Christ's kingdom, (how terrible soever to God's people) are but ridiculous and foolish attempts in God's sight ; *the King that sitteth in heaven, shall laugh at them all,* and expose them to mockery before men : *he shall have them in derision.* 3. After the Lord hath made manifest the intent of his enemies, and brought their foolish and mad purposes to light, he will not fail to manifest his mind, and just indignation against them ; for *then shall he speak to them in his wrath.* 4. The Lord hath his appointed time wherein he will arise, and vex the enemies of his church, partly by disappointing them of their hopes, and partly by inflicting sore plagues upon them *; then shall he vex them in his sore displeasure.* 5. When the Lord ariseth to judge the enemies of his church, then doth he give a further manifestation of his purpose to establish his church, and the visible kingdom of Christ, in the world, in spite of all opposition : *yet have I set my King upon my holy hill of Zion.* 6. Though all kings and kingdoms belong unto the Lord, yet he owneth the church (represented by the hill of Zion) and he owneth his Son Christ, the king thereof, in a special manner, as his peculiar property, wherein he glorieth more than in all his works ; therefore saith he, *I have set my King upon my holy hill ;* this is the speech of God the Father, speaking by his Spirit in the prophet concerning Christ his Son.

7. *I will declare the decree : the Lord hath said unto me, Thou* art *my Son, this day have I begotten thee.*

8. *Ask of me, and I shall give* thee *the heathen* for *thine inheritance, and the uttermost parts of the earth* for *thy possession.*

The second reason of the stability of Christ's kingdom is, the decreed agreement between God the Father and the Son in the covenant of redemption ; some articles whereof Christ by his prophet doth here reveal ; for this is the speech of Christ the Son of God, to be incarnate, speaking by his Spirit, concerning the stability of the church, and his kingdom over it : whence we learn, 1. The faith of the saints, in time of the persecution of the church, may, and should rest persuaded of the stability of the church, and of Christ's kingdom in it, because it is grounded upon the mysterious and unchangeable decree of God, which here is brought to light, *I will declare the decree*, saith Christ, not as yet incarnate. 2. It is Christ's office as Prophet, to reveal the secret counsel of the Trinity, being the substantial Word of the Father ; and who before the world was created, was with God, and was God, John i. 1. 2. *I will declare the decree,* saith the Son of God. 3. The Son of God as he is a person, concurring in the decree of establishing of the church, and kingdom of God in it, against all opposition ; so is he party contractor in the covenant of redemption : and as he is the promiser and undertaker, to pay the price of the redemption of his people ; so also is he the receiver of promises, made in favour of his church and kingdom. It is he to whom the Father directeth his promise concerning his church, *first and immediately ;* for the Son, in declaring the decree, saith, *the Lord said to me.* 4. It is one of the articles of the covenant of redemption, that the promised *seed of the woman,* the Redeemer of his people the promised seed of *Abraham,* the Messiah and Saviour of the elect, the promised son of *David,* and true king of *Israel* after his incarnation, shall not be disowned of the Father. But in and after his deepest humiliation and sufferings, as he shall be, and remain really the very Son of God, so shall he really at the set day, be acknowledged by the Father, to be the only begotten Son of God ; which day, is the day of the resurrection of Jesus Christ from the dead, as the apostle, Rom. i. 4, teacheth us, saying, *He was declared to be the Son of God with power by the resurrection from the dead.* For the resurrection of Jesus Christ was a real speech, saying to Christ in the audience of all the world, in effect as much as *I declare thee this day to be my Son, my only begotten Son, one in substance with me eternally.* 5. The declaration of the decree of the manifesting of Christ to be the Son of God, is a sufficient demonstration of the impregnable stability of the church, in spite of all the opposition of all the power in the world ; for to this very end is the decree of revealing Christ to be the Son of God, here declared. *Thou art my Son whom I have begotten,* is proof abundant ; for this is the rock whereupon Christ undertaketh to build his church, against which the gates of hell shall not prevail, Mat. xvi. 16, 18. and *who is he that overcometh the world,* saith John, *save*

he that believeth that Christ is the Son of God. 1 John
v. 5. 6. Another article of the covenant of redemption
here declared is, that after Christ's resurrection, and declaration of his formerly over-clouded Godhead, he should
continue in the office of his mediation and intercession ;
and by virtue of his paid ransom of redemption, call for
the enlargement of his purchased kingdom among the Gentiles : for this is the Father's compact with the Son, saying,
ask of me, and I will give thee the heathen. 7. The opposition which the world shall make to the kingdom of Christ,
shall not hinder the enlargement and spreading thereof ;
but by the intercession of Jesus Christ, *the heathen shall
be his inheritance, and the uttermost parts of the earth his
possession ;* not his by a short tack, or lease for some few
years, but a *lasting inheritance,* and constant *possession.*
8. The necessity of prayer is pointed out to all the Lord's
people by this, that the possession of the purchase which
our Lord hath made by his precious blood, is to be drawn
forth by a sort of *prayer and intercession* suitable to
Christ's person. *Ask of me,* saith the Father, *and I will
give thee the heathen, &c.*

9. *Thou shalt break them with a rod of iron, thou
shalt dash them in pieces like a potter's vessel.*

A third article of the covenant of redemption, is, a promise made to Christ, of full victory over all his, and his
church's enemies, ver. 9 ; wherein observe, 1. That
Christ shall not want enemies, who will not only for their
own parts, refuse salvation offered by him, and subjection
to be given to him ; but also will oppose him, and make
head against him, till he destroy them ; for these kings and
rulers spoken of ver. 2, 3, will not cease, *till he break them,
and dash them in pieces,* and these are here understood, as
repeated from ver. 1, 2, 3.

2. Though Christ's church be weak and unable to help
itself against persecution, yet Christ will own the quarrel,
and fight against all the enemies thereof himself, whereunto
he is sufficiently furnished, for *he shall break them, in pieces
with an iron rod.* 3. Though the enemies be numerous
and strong, being compared with the godly, whom they do
persecute, yet compared with Christ, or looked upon
by him, they are but weak, brittle, and naughty things.
Thou shalt dash them in pieces as a potter's vessel.

10. *Be wise now, therefore, O ye kings : be in-structed, ye judges of the earth.*

11. *Serve the Lord with fear and rejoice with trem-bling.*

12. *Kiss the Son, lest he be angry, and ye perish* from *the way, when his wrath is kindled but a little : blessed* are *all they that put their trust in him.*

This is the latter part of the Psalm, wherein the uses of the former doctrine are set down. Whence learn, 1. The more clear advertisement is given concerning the sin and danger of opposing Christ's kingdom, cause, work, or peo-ple ; the more wary should all men be, and namely potentates, as they love their places or souls, to eschew this evil ; for he hath said, *be wise now, therefore, O ye kings and judges of the earth.* 2. Though it may seem wisdom to make and execute laws in prejudice of Christ and his cause, rather then vent their malice without a pretence ; yet it is more wisdom to cease from opposition, and take laws from Christ ; for so the Lord doth reckon, saying, *be wise now, therefore, and instructed.* 3. If any be guilty of this sin and not as yet smitten for it, the goodness of God offereth to him mercy in time, and steppeth in timeously to take off the snares of flatterers, who use to harden men, and espe-cially great men, in this sin. *Be wise now,* saith the Lord, *O ye kings.* 4. It is no disparagement to the greatest monarchs (but a mean for them to eschew the wrath of God) to be subject to Christ Jesus, to stand in awe of him, to submit themselves to him, and promote his service to their power ; for the command to all, and to them in special, is *serve the Lord in fear.* 5. As there is matter of fear to Christ's subjects, lest they provoke him ; for there is matter of rejoicing for them to be under his government, and these two affections may well consist in his service : *rejoice in trembling :* yea there is no right rejoicing in any thing without some mixture of fear to offend him. 6. Because Christ Jesus the Son of God, is a lovely king, bringing righteousness and eternal life to all his true subjects, he should be submitted unto, and em-braced (when he offereth grace) very heartily : to this end, *kiss the Son,* or do him homage, is added ; for to kiss is a sign of religious adoration, Hos. xiii. 2, and a sign of homage and hearty subjection, Sam. x. 1. 7. Where

grace offered by Christ Jesus is refused, the refusing of
mercy shall procure more anger than all former sins ; *kiss
the Son lest he be angry.*   8. When Christ taketh a refusal
off a man, to whom grace is offered, wrath will follow, to
the cutting off of the refuser from all means of happiness,
both temporal, which he hunteth after ; and eternal, which
is offered in Christ unto him, and to the bringing upon
him utter perdition ; for it is said, *kiss the Son, lest he be
angry, and ye perish from the way of all possible salvation.*
9. Unspeakable must the wrath of God be, when it is
kindled fully, since perdition may come upon the *kindling
of it but a little.*   10. Remission of sin, delivery from
wrath, communion with God, and life everlasting, are the
fruits of embracing Christ, of closing in covenant with
Christ, and resting on Christ ; for *blessed are all they that
put their trust in him.*

PSALM III.

A Psalm of David when he fled from Absalom his son.

This Psalm holdeth forth a notable proof and benefit of faith in *David's*
experience ; who, when his own son *Absalom* rebelled against him, and
forced him to flee for fear of his life, first laid before the Lord his pitiful condition, v. 1, 2.   Secondly, he settled his faith on God, prayed,
and obtained a comfortable answer, was quiet and refreshed in soul and
body, and made confident against all fears possible, v. 3, 4, 5, 6.
Thirdly, he continueth in prayer, confirming his faith from former experience, v. 7.   And lastly, he giveth forth the use of his experience
to the church's edification in a general doctrine, v. 8.

From the inscription, learn, 1. How great calamity may
befall the best of God's children, and that from those persons
from whom they could least expect to be troubled : for
David was deserted of his own subjects, and chased from
his palace and royal state by his own son Absalom.   2.
Although the Lord do not follow the sins of his children
with vindictive justice, yet by the sharp rods of fatherly
correction, he can make his own children, and all the beholders of their scandalous sins, see how bitter a thing it is
to provoke him to wrath, as once David did.   3. Even
when sin hath drawn on judgment, God must be dealt with
for relief, no less than if it had been sent for trial only ; as
David doth in the case of the correcting and purging of
the pollution of his family, by the insurrection of his son
against him.

1. *Lord, how are they increased that trouble me?
many are they that rise up against me.*

2. *Many* there be *which say of my soul,* There is
no help for him in God. Selah.

From his laying before God his pitiful condition : learn
1. The man who believeth in God, hath an advantage above
whatsoever any ungodly man can have in the time of
trouble : he hath the Lord to go unto for comfort and
relief, of whose kindness he may make use, as David did
here, laying out his trouble before him, and saying, *Lord,
how are they increased that trouble me! &c.* 2. The world
counteth a man's case desperate, when they see no worldly
help for him. *Many say, there is no help for him in God.*
3. Merciless beholders of the corrections of God's children
for their sins, think and say also oft times, that God is following them with vindictive justice, and is destroying them
both in regard of their souls and bodies, &c., without mind
of mercy to them. *Many say of my soul, there is no help
for him in God.* 4. Temptation to despair of relief, doth
accompany unexpected and sad troubles ; and this is more
grievous than the trouble itself : therefore David presenteth this temptation before God in the last place, as the
heaviest part of his exercise, with a note of uplifting the
mind and voice. *Selah.*

3. *But thou, O Lord,* art *a shield for me, my glory,
and the lifter up of mine head.*

In the second place he showeth how he made use of faith
in prayer ; and what fruit he received thereby : whence
learn, 1. The nature of true faith is to draw the more near
to God, the more it be driven from him, *many say, no help
in God ; but thou art my shield.* 2. God is a counter-
comfort in all calamity, our shield in danger, our glory in
shame, *the lifter up of our head* in dejection. 3. As there
is relief in God out of all evil, so faith seeth in God sufficient help from all evil, and in special that the sword of the
enemy cannot be so near, but he can interpose himself, as
a *shield* to ward off the blow : *but thou, O Lord, art a
shield round about me, &c.;* yea, faith seeth in God matter
of rejoicing and gloriation in the midst of all the shame
and disgrace which men can cast upon the believer, and
can make a man say to God, *thou art my glory.* In a

word, faith seeth goodness and power in God to raise the believer out of the lowest condition wherein he can be. *Thou art the lifter up of my head.*

4. *I cried unto the Lord with my voice, and he heard me out of his holy hill. Selah.*

5. *I laid me down and slept; I awaked, for the Lord sustained me.*

6. *I will not be afraid of ten thousands of people that have set* themselves *against me round about.*

From the exercise of faith, and the fruits of it in these three verses, learn, 1. The conscience of seeking God by prayer is an ease to a man not only for the present time, while he is in prayer pouring out his heart, but refreshful also, when it is looked back upon : therefore by way of gratulation saith David here, *I cried to the Lord.* 2. Faith in a strait stirreth up affection and earnestness in prayer, and maketh the whole man to be taken up about it : *I cried to the Lord with my voice,* saith he. 3. The prayer of faith shall not want an answer, and the return thereof is worthy to be attended and marked, when it is obtained ; *I cried and he heard me.* 4. The prayer of faith trusteth God in Christ, as the propitiatory and mercy seat, and seeketh audience and answer only for Christ's cause, whose sacrifice, and mediation, and benefits were shadowed forth in the tabernacle : and the believer, as he should take heed that his prayer go up to God through Christ, so should he observe how it is answered and returned also through Christ, represented by the ark in the tabernacle, pitched on the holy hill of Zion : *he heard me also out of his holy hill.* 5. In the greatest extremity of danger, a believer may have his mind quieted, and his body refreshed also, after that in faith he hath had his recourse to God, and hath casten his care upon him : *I laid me down and slept* ; *I awaked.* 6. The quietness and settledness of a man's heart by faith in God, is another sort of work than the natural resolution of manly courage ; for it is the gracious operation of God's spirit upholding a man above nature, and therefore God ought to have all the glory of it : *the Lord sustained me.* 7. When the Lord will answer the believer to his comfort, he can not only satisfy him in the particular which he prayeth for, but also furnish him with

confidence against whatsoever evil can be apprehended by
him for time to come : *I will not be afraid of millions of
people that have set themselves against me round about.*
8. When faith finds itself welcome to God, it is able to
give a defiance to all adversaries ; more or fewer, weaker
or stronger enemies, all are alike despised : *I will not be
afraid of thousands of people.*

7. *Arise, O Lord, save me, O my God, for thou
hast smitten all mine enemies* upon *the cheek bone : thou
hast broken the teeth of the ungodly.*

In the third place, he continueth to pray against the evil
which might thereafter follow : whence learn, 1. Faith in
God is not a bragger, nor confident in the man's own
strength or imagination ; but humbly dependeth on God,
and continueth in prayer, so long as the danger remaineth ;
as David doth here, after delivery received. 2. The covenant of grace, wherein the believer is entered with God,
furnisheth him with confident prayer and hope of salvation :
save me, O my God. 3. When faith is fixed upon God
covenanted, then by-gone experiences come up as pin-
nings in the building of a wall, to bolster it up, and confirm
it ; *for thou hast smitten all mine enemies upon the cheek
bone, thou hast broken the teeth of the ungodly.* 4. God
smites the pride of persecutors with a shameful stroke, and
their beastly cruelty, with breaking their power ; *thou
hast smitten mine enemies on the cheek bone, thou hast
broken the teeth of the ungodly.*

8. *Salvation* belongeth *unto the Lord : thy blessing*
is *upon thy people. Selah.*

From the last part of the Psalm, wherein he giveth forth
from his own experience a general doctrine, for the comfort
of all the Lord's people, learn, 1. The use of the experience of the godly should be the confirmation of the faith
of all others, as well as of their own ; as here is seen.
2. The fruit of the Lord's putting his own in straits, is to
make them and all men see, that he hath ways of deliverance, more than they know of ; and that he will save his
own when men count their case desperate : for, *salvation* belongeth *to the Lord.* 3. Whatsoever mixture his
people find of crosses and comforts, or vicissitudes of
danger and delivery, adversity or prosperity ; still the

course of blessing of them standeth, which now and then they are forced to acknowledge to the Lord : *thy blessing is upon thy people.*

PSALM IV.

To the chief Musician on Neginoth. A Psalm of David.

Another experience of *David*, as an example of a Christian sufferer, unjustly persecuted and scorned for his piety, by his profane enemies; such as *Saul* and his courtiers were: wherein, first, he setteth down his prayer, v. 1. Then being comforted in God, he insulteth over his enemies, and glorieth in God's favour, v. 2, 3. Thirdly, he exhorteth his enemies to repentance and faith in God, v. 4, 5. Fourthly, he preferreth the blessedness of his estate above whatsoever the worldly man can enjoy, v. 6, 7, 8.

From the inscription of this Psalm, which is the first wherein mention is made of the chief musicians, or musical instruments : learn 1. The praise of God and the joy of his Spirit, allowed on his people, surpass all expression which the voice of words can make; for this was signified by the plurality, and diversity of musical instruments (some of them sounding by being beaten, some of them by being blown,) superadded to the voice of singing in the prædagogy of Moses. 2. Albeit the ceremonial, figurative, and religious use of musical instruments be gone, with the rest of the Levitical shadows, (the natural use of them still remaining :) yet the vocal singing of Psalms in the church is not taken away, as the practice and doctrine of Christ and his apostles make evident; and so the voice of a musician in the public worship still is useful. 3. The Psalms are to be made use of with discretion, as the matter of the Psalm, and edification of the worshippers may require. And in the public, it is the called minister of the congregation's place, to order this part of the worship with the rest ; for this, the direction of the Psalms to the chief musician giveth ground.

1. *Hear me when I call, O God of my righteousness : thou hast enlarged me when I was in distress ; have mercy upon me, and hear my prayer.*

From his prayer, learn, 1. Though there be many and divers troubles of the godly, yet there is but one God to give comfort and relief, and one way to draw it from God ; to wit, by prayer in faith : *hear me when I call.* 2. Albeit the conscience of much sin be opposed to the prayer of the believer, yet the everlasting righteousness of faith, (whereof the Lord is God, author, and maintainer for ever,) doth open the way to the suppliant, especially when he cometh to God in a righteous cause : *hear me, O God of my righteousness.* 3. Acknowledgment of by-past mercies in former experience is a good preparation for a new mercy, and a mean to strengthen our faith to receive it : *thou hast enlarged me when I was in distress, have mercy upon me, and hear my prayer.* 4. Faith is a good orator, and a noble disputer in a strait. It can reason from God's readiness to hear, *hear me when I call, O God :* and from the everlasting righteousness given to the man, in the justification of his person ; *O God of my righteousness :* and from God's constant justice in defending the righteousness of his servant's cause, *O God of my righteousness :* and from both present distresses and those that are by-past, wherein he hath been : and from by-gone mercies received ; *thou hast enlarged me when I was in distress :* and from God's grace, which is able to answer all objections from the man's unworthiness, or ill-deserving ; *have mercy upon me, and hear my prayer.*

2. *O ye sons of men, how long* will ye turn *my glory into shame ?* how long *will ye love vanity* and *seek after leasing ? Selah.*

3. *But know that the Lord hath set apart him that is godly for himself: the Lord will hear when I call unto him.*

In the next place, after comfort received, he triumpheth in God's good will over all his enemies : whence learn, 1. Though a godly man, when he is both persecuted for righteousness, and mocked for his piety, may hang his head in his trouble for a little, till he goes to God with his complaint ; yet after that he is comforted, he will be able to speak a word to his mockers, and holily to insult over them, time about ; as after prayer, David here turneth him to speak to the *sons of men.* 2. Mockers of piety, when pious men are under affliction, bewray themselves to be still in the state of nature, and destitute for the present of the spirit of regeneration : for David calleth them, in relation to their sinful condition, *O ye sons of men.*

3. Though faith in God, and calling on him in trouble, and innocency of life under persecution, be the highest commendation and glory of a man ; yet the wicked, (though oft convinced of God's goodness to such persons,) do not stand to reproach piety, as a matter of scorn, so oft as God doth suffer the godly to fall into calamity : *how long will ye turn my glory into shame?* 4. Mere natural men cannot be made wise, neither by the word of God, nor by experience in their own and others' persons, to consider that things of this earth, as temporary riches, honour, and pleasure, are nothing but vanity and deceiving lies, which promise something, and pay nothing but vexation of spirit, because of guiltiness and misery following upon the abuse of them : *how long will ye love vanity, and seek after leasing ?* 5. The most satisfactory revenge, which the godly can desire of their persecutors and mockers, is, to have them made converts, to have them recalled from the vanity of their way, and brought to a right understanding of what concerneth their salvation, whereunto the godly are ready to offer themselves admonishers of them, and instructors, as here the prophet doth : *O ye sons of men, how long ? &c. But know, &c.* 6. The cause of the world's despising of piety in the persons of God's afflicted children, is the gross ignorance of the precious privileges of the Lord's sincere servants : the world cannot think that the godly, in the midst of their calamities, are God's peculiar jewels, chosen and called out of the world, for honouring of God ; admitted to fellowship with God in this life, and appointed to dwell with him for ever. Therefore, *know,* saith David, as speaking to ignorants, *that God hath set apart for himself him that is godly.* 7. This is one of the privileges of the godly, that how oft soever they are put to their prayers, by trouble or temptation, so oft they get audience, upholding, comfort, and delivery ; as their crosses abound, so do their consolations ; as the prophet testifieth, saying, *the Lord will hear me when I call upon him.* 8. The experience of one of the saints concerning the verity of God's promises, of the certainty of the written privileges of the Lord's people, is a sufficient proof of the right which all his children have unto, and ground of hope for their partaking in the same mercies in their need ; therefore, David, to prove his general doctrine, set down in the first

part of the verse, saith, *the Lord will hear me when I call unto him.*

4. *Stand in awe and sin not : commune with your own heart upon your bed, and be still.   Selah.*

5. *Offer the sacrifices of righteousness, and put your trust in the Lord.*

In the third place, he exhorteth his enemies to repent-ance and faith in God; wherein as he laid down the course which they should keep, to wit, to have their judgment well informed in the principles of religion, in the former verse ; so here in this verse, he will have their heart and affections reformed : and in the following verse he will have their actions also reformed in relation to the duties of the first and second table, and their actions to flow from their faith in God.   Whence, learn, 1. Repentance is not real and sound, till the heart be affected with the sense of sin by-past, and fear of sinning hereafter, and be brought in subjection under the dreadful Majesty of God : therefore, after instruction, (v. 2, 3,) he saith here, *stand in awe and sin not.*   2. The means prescribed of God to make the heart sensible of its condition, is the serious and daily exa-mination of the conscience, posing it to answer all interro-gatories concerning the man's conformity to God's law, and that in secret in the night, without distraction : for a man had need to have all his wits about him, when he goeth to examine a deceitful thief : to this purpose, saith he, *com-mune with your hearts on your beds.*   3. The fruit of daily, serious examination of the conscience, concerning sin com-mitted, is, to make a man humble, quiet, and submissive to the Lord.   This he insinuateth in foretelling them that thus they *shall be still, or silent,* not opening the mouth to ex-cuse their sins, or to mock the godly.   As for reformation of their lives in relation to the law of God, (v. 5,) he teacheth, 1. That the formal discharge of the external cere-monies of religion will not prove a man to be a true convert, or a sincere penitent; but the true sacrifice of Christ's obe-dience unto the death, signified by the external sacrifices, must be looked unto; and the sacrifice of thanksgiving and well doing, and the dedication of the whole man, to the service of God, must testify the truth of repentance.   There-fore, in opposition to the external ceremonial sacrifice, he

commandeth to *offer the sacrifices of righteousness.* 2.
When a penitent hath for evidencing the sincerity of his
turning to God, brought forth fruit suitable to repentance,
he must not lay weight upon his works, but lay all his confidence upon God's free grace, who justifieth the true convert by faith only : therefore, after commanding them to
offer the sacrifices of righteousness, he directeth them, saying, *put your trust in the Lord.*

6. There be *many that say, who will show us* any
*good? Lord, lift thou up the light of thy countenance
upon us.*

7. *Thou hast put gladness in my heart, more than
in the time* that *their corn and their wine increased.*

8. *I will both lay me down in peace, and sleep : for
thou, Lord, only makest me dwell in safety.*

In the last place he commendeth his own blessed estate,
and to enforce the former exhortation, he compareth the
happiness which the worldling seeketh after, with spiritual joy which is granted to the godly, and preferreth the
last far before the other. Hence learn, 1. The blind worldlings, ignorant of what is truly good, are taken with insatiable wishing, and seeking for some earthly thing, whereby
they conceive they may be happy. Of those speaketh he,
saying, *there be many that say, Who will show us any
good.* 2. The truly godly join one with another, in seeking
their felicity in God's favour, and in the sense of his reconciliation, and not in seeking the worldly man's choice; for
in the opposition to the worldling's wishes, David, with the
rest of the godly, saith, *Lord, lift thou up the light of thy
countenance upon us.* 3. The comfort of God's Spirit, and
sense of a man's reconciliation with God in Christ, is
greater than any worldly joy can be, and is able to supply
the want of riches, honours, and pleasures worldly, and to
season, yea and swallow up the sense of poverty, disgrace,
and whatsoever other evil. This David testifieth by his own
experience, saying, *thou hast put gladness in my heart,
more than in the time that their corn and wine increased.*
4. Faith in God, as it bringeth joy, so also peace unspeakable, and passing understanding, in the midst of trouble.
This David's experience teacheth also : *I will both lay me
down in peace and sleep,* notwithstanding of all the opposi-

tion the sons of men made unto him. Whether God do give means of safety, or none at all which can be seen, preservation and safety is his gift, and the making a man observe the benefit of preservation is another gift also: wherefore, David giveth the glory of both unto God: *thou only makest me dwell in safety.*

PSALM V.

To the Chief Musician upon Nehiloth. A Psalm of David.

David, as a type of Christ, and one of the number of his afflicted followers, set forth in his affliction, as an example of exercise to others in after ages, doth pray for himself, and against his enemies, using sundry arguments to strengthen himself in his hope to be heard. First, from the grace of God bestowed on himself to use the means, v. 1, 2, 3. Secondly, from the justice of God against his wicked enemies, v. 4, 5, 6. Thirdly, from his own steadfast purpose and desire to continue in God's service, and to walk so uprightly, as the enemy shall not have advantange of him by his miscarriage, v. 7. 8. Fourthly, from the ripeness of sin in his adversaries, which prepared them for sudden destruction, v. 9, 10. Fifthly, from the certain hope of joy and defence, and spiritual blessing to be bestowed on himself and all believers, **out** of the free love and favour of God toward them, v. 11, 12.

1. *Give ear to my words, O Lord ; consider my meditation.*

2. *Hearken unto the voice of my cry, my King and my God: for unto thee will I pray.*

3. *My voice shalt thou hear in the morning, O Lord ; in the morning will I direct my prayer unto thee, and will look up.*

In his strengthening of his hope to be heard, from the grace of God bestowed on him, to use the means for obtaining a good answer, learn, 1. When the Lord giveth us a mouth to speak to him, there is ground of hope he will grant an ear to us; for so reasoneth David, *give ear to my words, O Lord.* 2. In time of trouble, the heart hath more to say to God, than words can utter ; and what a man cannot express, the Lord will take knowledge of it, no less than of his words ; this the prophet hopeth for, saying, *consider my meditation.* 3. When extremity of danger forceth a way to the Lord, the believer's necessity hath a voice, louder than his expressed words, and whereunto the Lord will give ear ; *hearken to the voice of my cry.* 4. It is a point of spiritual wisdom for the help of our faith, to take hold of those relations we have to God, whereby we may expect what we pray for, as David doth here, when we would have protection and delivery, saying ; *my King, and my God.* 5. Faith knoweth no other to pray unto for help, save God alone, nor any other way to be helped, save by perseverance in prayer ; *for unto thee will I pray,* saith he. 6. Resolved importunity in prayer must be joined with taking hold of the first and fittest opportunity offered for prayer : *my voice shalt thou hear in the morning, O Lord,* saith he. 7. Calling on God in trouble, with dependence on him, giveth hope of audience, and delivery by him, by way of a convincing syllogism, whereof the promise of delivery made to such as call on the name of the Lord in the day of trouble, is the first proposition; the conscience of resolved calling on him maketh the assumption or second proposition; and faith concludeth the expectation of deliverance ; for the prophet's reasoning is this in effect—whosoever they be that pray to the Lord in their trouble, thou wilt hear them : but I pray to thee, and resolve to continue praying ; therefore thou, O Lord, wilt hear me.

4. *For thou art not a God that hast pleasure in wickedness : neither shall evil dwell with thee.*

5. *The foolish shall not stand in thy sight : thou hatest all workers of iniquity.*

6. *Thou shalt destroy them that speak leasing : the Lord will abhor the bloody and deceitful man.*

In the second place, he reasoneth from the justice of God against his enemies: whence learn, 1. The worst qualities in the adversaries of the godly, furnish good matter of faith and hope to the believer to be rid of them : for this use doth David make of the wickedness of his enemies in these three verses. 2. Such as take pleasure in sin : *thou art not a God,* saith he, *that hast pleasure in wickedness :* and such as will not part with sin, God shall separate them from his company ; for it is said, *neither shall evil dwell with thee.* 3. Let wicked men seem never so wise politicians among men, yet shall they be found mad fools before God, selling heaven for trifles of the earth, holding war with the Almighty, and running upon their own destruction in their self-pleasing dreams, to the loss of their life and state, temporal and eternal ; for the *foolish*, saith he, *shall not stand in thy sight.* 4. Such as make iniquity their work, shall have the effects of God's hatred for their wages : for *thou hatest all the workers of iniquity.* 5. The enemies of God's people, while by slanders and lies they murder the innocent, draw upon themselves swift damnation from God : *thou shalt destroy them that speak leasing,* saith he. 6. Falsehood and cruelty, which are the characters of the foes of the godly, are abomination to the Lord, which he cannot endure : *thou wilt abhor the bloody and deceitful man.*

7. *But as for me I will come* into *thy house, in the multitude of thy mercy ;* and *in thy fear will I worship toward thy holy temple.*

8. *Lead me, O Lord, in thy righteousness, because of mine enemies : make thy way straight before my face.*

In the third place, he resolveth that whatever the enemy shall do, he will walk as God hath commanded him : with resolution to serve God in sincerity, as also a profession of hope to enjoy the society of his saints in God's public worship : and to this end he prayeth he may be kept straight in his walking, that the enemy might have nothing wherewith to reproach him. Hence learn, 1. Though the godly want not the conscience of their own sins, when they speak of the sins of their enemies, yet there is a difference between them and the wicked, in respect the godly are humbled in the sense of their sins, are brought to the acknowledgment of their need of mercy, and flee to God for having mercy, and to the *multitude of mercy*, as they see the multitude of their sins : and therefore saith he of himself, in opposition to the wicked, *but as for me, I will come into thy house, in the multitude of thy mercy.* 2. The faith which the godly have in the mercies of God, doth encourage them to follow the service of God ; and in some cases doth give them hope to be loosed from the restraints which hinder them from enjoying the public ordinances : *I will come into thy house, in the multitude of thy mercy.* 3. The right temper of the heart of a true worshipper, is fear before God : *in thy fear will I worship.* 4. Under the sense of sinfulness and unworthiness, faith must be supported by looking towards Jesus Christ, prefigured by the tabernacle and temple: *in thy fear*, saith he, *I will worship toward thy holy temple.* 5. When the godly are under trouble from their enemies, and under trial by other sorts of exercise, they are no less feared for their miscarriage and offending the Lord, than they are feared for what their enemies can do against them : therefore, *lead me, O Lord, in thy righteousness*, saith he. 6. So much the more as the godly are sensible of their own blindness, and weakness, and readiness, to go out of the right way ; so much the more do they call for, and depend upon God's directing of them. *Lead me*, saith he ; as one that seeth not, or as one who is not able to hold a right course, without a guide. 7. If the godly man take a sinful course, to be relieved from his trouble, the enemy is hardened in his wicked course, by this means to blaspheme the profession of piety, as mere hypocrisy, and so God is provoked to let the enemy prevail, because the miscarriage of the godly hath made way to him; for avoiding of which inconvenience, he prayeth, *lead me in thy righteousness because of my enemies.* 8. The deceitfulness of sin, the ignorance of what is expedient and lawful in a particular case, the mist of private affections, and the example of ill counsel of the world, are ready to make a man mistake the right way, except the Lord make clear what is his duty: therefore, saith he, *make thy way straight before my face.*

9. *For* there is *no faithfulness in their mouth; their inward part* is *very wickedness : their throat* is *an open sepulchre; they flatter with their tongue.*

10. *Destroy thou them, O God: let them fall by their own counsels : cast them out in the multitude of their transgressions, for they have rebelled against thee.*

In the fourth place he strengtheneth his hope to be helped, because his enemies' sins were ripe for judgment. Whence learn, 1. Among other motives to make the godly take heed of their carriage in time of trial, this is one; they have to do with a false world, and hollow-hearted men, who will make false pretences of what is not their intentions, and will make promise of what they mind not to perform, and will give none but rotten and poisonable advice, gilded with false flattery, and all to deceive the godly, and draw them in a snare. This is it, he saith, *for there is no faith-*

fulness in their mouth ; their inward part is very wickedness ; their throat is an open sepulchre; they flatter with their tongue ; and this is the nature of all carnal men, when it cometh to the point of defending God's cause in time of trial. 2. Though this prayer be not to be drawn in imitation against particular persons, by us who have not so infallible revelation of men's state before God ; yet is it a prophecy against all the irreconcilable enemies of God, and of his people, against whom the Spirit of God maketh imprecation here, saying, *destroy thou them, O God.* 3. There is no need of any other means to destroy the Lord's enemies, than their own devices: the very course they take to establish themselves will serve for their own ruin. *Let them fall,* saith he, *by their own counsel.* 4. The certain cause of the ruin of the persecutors of God's people, is the ripeness and full measure of their sins. *Cast them out,* saith he, *in the multitude of their transgressions.* 5. The opposing of truth, and of the ordinances of God, in the person of his servants who stand for the same, is not simply the opposing of mortal men, but the opposing of God, whose quarrel it is ; therefore saith he, *they have rebelled against thee.*

11. *But let all those that put their trust in thee rejoice : let them ever shout for joy, because thou defendest them : let them also that love thy name, be joyful in thee.*

12. *For thou, Lord, wilt bless the righteous; with favour wilt thou compass him, as* with *a shield.*

In the last place, he maketh prayer for all the godly, militant in this warfare with himself, that they may share together in the Lord's favour. Hence learn, 1. Persecution for righteousness is a cause common to all believers, wherein they should all join, and pray one of them for another, and seek for a joyful out-gate to each other in their own time; for this cause, after prayer against enemies, he saith, *but let all that trust in thee rejoice.* 2. The manifested care of God for his people, in protecting and delivering them from their enemies, is matter of exceeding joy to his people, because he is glorified herein, and his church is preserved : *let them ever shout for joy, because thou defendest them.* 3. Such believers as have gotten grace to love God's name, albeit it be not yet given unto them to suffer for his name, are allowed to share in the joy of victorious sufferers. *Let them also that love thy name*, saith he, *be joyful in thee.* 4. The person who is justified by faith, and studieth unto holiness, is an heir of God's blessing, whether he be less or more taken notice of by the world, whether entered in the conflict with persecutors or not : *For thou, O Lord, wilt bless the righteous.* 5. The favour and good will of God toward his own, is a strong and glorious defence to them ; it is a crowning shield,—a shield compassing a man round about like a glorious diadem,—a shield very handsome and strong which the believer ought to grip well, and hold fast, and manage warily, and oppose it to every assault of the adversary : a crowning shield, which circleth the man round about, and keepeth off the dint of the adversary's weapon, even when the pursued believer is not aware : *with favour wilt thou compass him as with a shield.*

PSALM VI.

To the Chief Musician on Neginoth upon Sheminith. A Psalm of David.

Another experience of David, useful to be known by all the children of God, who are subject to the like exercise ; wherein David, being under the sense of the Lord's heavy hand, upon his body and spirit, prayeth for the removal of self-wrath, v. 1, 2, 3. Next prayeth for the renewed feeling and experience of God's mercy towards him, laying forth his lamentable condition before the pitiful eye of God, v. 4, 5, 6, 7. After which, being heard and comforted, in the third place, he defieth and triumpheth over all his enemies, v. 8, 9.

1. *O Lord, rebuke me not in thine anger, neither chasten me in thy hot displeasure.*

2. *Have mercy upon me, O Lord, for I* am *weak ; O Lord, heal me for my bones are vexed.*

3. *My soul is also sore vexed : but thou, O Lord, how long ?*

From his prayer for removal of wrath, learn, 1. It is possible, that a true believer, who had been ofttimes refreshed with the sense of God's favour, may, by some sad exercise have his conscience so wakened to the sense of sin, as he can feel nothing but wrath, and fear of cutting off ; as this experience of David maketh manifest. 2. There is no relief in such case, save to set faith on work, whatso-

ever be felt or feared, and to seek mitigation and deliverance of God, as the prophet doth here. 3. Even the
fatherly wrath of God, and far more the apprehension of
hot displeasure of an angry judge, is insupportable to a
soul that knoweth God, and hath ever tasted of his favour
before: *rebuke me not in thy wrath*, saith he. 4. There is
as much ground of faith holden forth in the Lord's name,
Jehovah, (importing his unchangeable being, and his constancy in his promises,) as to ground a prayer upon it, for
obtaining the change of a man's case to the better, in the
hardest condition imaginable ; *O Lord*, or *O Jehovah*, saith
he, *rebuke me not in thy wrath*. 5. Though sense feel
wrath, and see nothing but hot displeasure, yet faith can
pierce through clouds, and bespeak mercy: *have mercy on
me, O Lord*, saith David, in the midst of this sad condition.
6. Though sin doth provoke anger, yet the misery and inability to subsist, presented unto God, is the object of
mercy, and a motive to faith to expect compassion : *have
mercy on me*, saith he, *for I am weak*. 7. When sin hath
drawn on sickness, or any other danger, let pardon of sin
be first sought, and after that, the removing of the stroke ;
for first, he saith, *have mercy on me*, and then, *heal me*.
8. The Lord can make the strongest and most insensible
part of a man's body, sensible of his wrath, when he
pleaseth to touch him ; for here David's *bones are vexed*.
9. Anguish of spirit and torment of conscience, is heavier
than any torture of body, as, *my soul is also vexed*, doth
import. 10. The Lord's apprehended absence in trouble,
and delaying to answer the supplicant, putteth a load above
a burden, and surpasseth all expression of words; for here
his speech is cut, *but thou O Lord, how long ?*

4. *Return, O Lord, deliver my soul: O save me for
thy mercies' sake.*

5. *For in death* there is *no remembrance of thee :
in the grave who shall give thee thanks ?*

6. *I am weary with my groaning ; all the night
make I my bed to swim: I water my couch with my
tears.*

7. *Mine eye is consumed because of grief; it waxeth
old because of all mine enemies.*

In the next place, he prayeth for a renewed sensible experience of God's mercy to him, because of his pitiful condition. Wherein learn, 1. A renewed glimpse of the Lord's countenance will satisfy a soul in the greatest distress: therefore David craveth this for a remedy of all his sorrow: *return, O Lord.* 2. If desertion continue, fear of perishing utterly doth present itself; as this prayer insinuateth: *O Lord, deliver my soul.* 3. The only time to spread the praise of God, by making mention of him before them that know him not, is the time of this life: *for in death there is no remembrance of thee.* 4. The Christian's love of life, should proceed from the love of honouring God in this life, (where it may enlarge God's glory, before them who may be profited by preaching his praise,) and should be preferred to our own contentment for a time in heaven, so long as God pleaseth to take service of us here. For this is the force of the prophet's reasoning, *in the grave who shall give thee thanks?* 5. Our place waiteth for us, and no man can take it over our head, while we on earth are enduring toil and trouble, to bring more to heaven with us. 6. A true desire and purpose to glorify God in this life, to the edifying of others, may give hope of some prolonging of life, and assurance of not perishing for ever: for David's hope to be heard doth run here upon this ground. 7. The most lasting, pressing, and piercing sorrow that ever soul felt, is from the sense of sin, and of God's displeasure for it, as the prophet's expression here doth give evidence. 8. The exercise of the godly under the sense of God's displeasure, may be very heavy, and of long continuance; the prophet is *weary with his groaning, and his eyes consumed with grief.* 9. No delay of comfort, no sense of sin, no fear of God's utter displeasure can be a reason to the believer to cease from prayer, and dealing with God for grace; for the prophet is *weary,* but giveth not over; only his condition is the matter of fresh mourning to him night and day, and pouring out of tears in the Lord's bosom: *all the night maketh he his bed to swim, and watereth his couch with his tears.* 10. The insulting of enemies over the godly when the Lord's hand is heavy upon them, because it reflecteth upon religion and upon God's glory, is a main ingredient in the sorrow of the godly: *David's* eye had waxen *old and dim with grief because of all his enemies.*

8. *Depart from me all ye workers of iniquity; for the Lord hath heard the voice of my weeping.*

9. *The Lord hath heard my supplication; the Lord will receive my prayer.*

10. *Let all mine enemies be ashamed and sore vexed: let them return and be ashamed suddenly.*

In the third place David defieth all his enemies, being comforted by the light of God's countenance, and lifted up in his spirit. Whence learn, 1. The Lord can shortly change the cheer of an humble supplicant, and raise a soul trembling for fear of wrath, to a triumphing over all sort of adversaries, and over all temptations to sin arising from them, for the return of the prophet's prayer maketh him say, now, *depart from me all ye workers of iniquity.* 2. The sacrifice of a contrite spirit, offered by a believer, the Lord will not despise; *for the Lord heard the voice of the prophet's weeping.* 3. The hearing of our prayer should be thankfully observed and made use of, for strengthening our faith in prayer afterward: for after the prophet hath said, *the Lord hath heard my supplication*, he addeth, *the Lord will receive my prayer.* 4. The enemies of the godly shall all of them be disappointed of their hopes, and ashamed for their attempts against them, and filled with vexation for their pains; for this prayer furnished by the Spirit, v. 10, to one of the godly against his wicked enemies, is a prophecy against all the rest of the enemies of the godly in all ages.

PSALM VII.

Shiggaion of David, which he sang unto the Lord, concerning the words of Cush, the Benjamite.

The prophet as a type of Christ mystical, and an example of Christians suffering, being slandered of treason against his prince, by one of the courtiers, first fleeth to God for delivery, v. 1, 2. Secondly, cleareth his innocence, v. 3, 4, 5. Thirdly, requesteth the Lord to judge between him and his enemies, v. 6, 7, 8, 9. And fourthly, in prayer is made confident, that the Lord will plead for him against his enemies, v. 10, 11, 12, 13, and will return their devised mischief against him, upon their own head, v. 14, 15, 16. Whereupon in the last place he promiseth praise to God for his righteous judgment, v. 17.

1. *O Lord my God, in thee do I put my trust: save me from all them that persecute me, and deliver me;*

2. Lest he tear my soul like a lion, rending it *in pieces while* there is *none to deliver;*

As to the first part, wherein he fleeth to God to be delivered from the bloody tongues of calumniators; learn, 1. It is a part of the exercise of Christ's servants, to be slandered as traitors to their lawful magistrates, as David was by Cush, a flattering courtier. 2. God who is able to clear the innocent, and to defend them from malice, is in this case to be run unto, and use is to be made of faith in him, and our covenant with him, for relief from all adversaries, as the prophet doth here. 3. If God do not interpose himself, for defence of his unjustly slandered servants, there is nothing to be expected from wicked enemies enraged, but merciless beastly cruelty, as is shown in David's experience.

3. O Lord my God, if I have done this; if there be iniquity in my hands;

4. If I have rewarded evil unto him that was at peace with me; (yea, I have delivered him that without cause is mine enemy;)

5. Let the enemy persecute my soul, and take it; *yea, let him tread down my life upon the earth, and lay mine honour in the dust. Selah.*

In the second place, wherein he cleareth his own innocence, learn, 1. Though innocence cannot exempt a man from being unjustly slandered, yet it will furnish him with a good conscience, and much boldness in the particular, before God; as here is seen, v. 3, 4. 2. The more a man doth render good for evil, the more confidence shall he have when he cometh to God; for innocence served David for this good use, that he had delivered Saul, who without cause was his enemy, v. 4. 3. He that is conscious of doing, or intending injury to his neighbour, will have his own conscience against him, in the time when he meeteth with a greater injury done to him, and in that case will be forced to justify God's righteousness against himself, as David's conditional prayer here importeth, v. 5.

6. Arise, O Lord, in thine anger, lift up thyself, because of the rage of mine enemies; and awake for me to the judgment that *thou hast commanded.*

7. So shall the congregation of the people compass

thee about: for their sakes therefore return thou on high.

8. *The Lord shall judge the people : judge me, O Lord, according to my righteousness, and according to mine integrity that is in me.*

9. *Oh let the wickedness of the wicked come to an end; but establish the just : for the righteous God trieth the hearts and reins.*

In the third place, he prayeth that God would judge between him and his enemies: whence learn, 1. Though the Lord for the trial and exercise of his children, sit still as it were for a time, when men are about to oppress them; yet will he in due time manifest himself to be no idle spectator of wrong, but a just defender of the oppressed, and avenger of the injurious, *he will arise in anger and lift up himself* 2. When our enemies are desperately malicious, and nothing can mitigate their fury; ¹et the consideration of God's justice mitigate our passion : *for he will arise in anger against them.* 3. There is no less just zeal in God, to defend his own oppressed people, than there is malice in the wicked, to wrong them : *for his rising in anger,* is here opposed *to the rage of the enemies.* 4. Albeit judgment against the oppressor be not at the first executed, yet God in his word hath given out sentence against them, and in his active providence, hath prepared means and instruments for execution thereof in due time; *when he shall awake to execute the judgment which he hath commanded,* or given order for. 5. When the Lord ariseth to judge his enemies, then the Lord's people will draw warmly unto him, and as it were, *compass him round about.* 6. In calling for justice upon the wicked enemies of God's people, we should not be led with private passion, or desire of revenge, but with desire of God's glory, and edification of his people : *for their sakes,* prayeth he, *return thou on high,* or ascend to thy tribunal seat. 7. Principles of religion, whereof we may have use in our exercises, should be solidly digested, that we may apply them readily to use, as need requireth, for strengthening of our faith, and prayer to God: for when the prophet hath settled his faith upon the doctrine of *God's judging and executing justice in favour of his people,* in the general, he applieth it to his own particular, saying, *judge*

me, O Lord. 8. When a man hath made peace with God
about all his sins, upon the terms of grace and mercy,
through the sacrifice of the mediator, he may in comparison with his injurious enemies, in a particular cause, appeal to God's justice to decide the controversy ; as here the
prophet doth, saying, *judge me according to my righteousness, O Lord, and mine integrity* that is *in me.* 9. When
a process hath been lying long before God, and the controversy between the godly and their persecutors is not yet decided, the godly may put in a bill for passing the decree,
and executing of the sentence, as here is done: *oh let the
wickedness of the wicked come to an end, &c.* 10. The upright man needs not to fear that his enemies shall obtain a
decree in their favour, or suspension, or reduction of the
sentence pronounced: *for the righteous God trieth the
heart and the reins.*

10. *My defence is of God, which saveth the upright
in heart.*

11. *God judgeth the righteous, and God is angry*
with the wicked *every day.*

12. *If he turn not, he will whet his sword; he hath
bent his bow, and made it ready.*

13. *He hath also prepared for him the instruments of
death; he ordaineth his arrows against the persecutors.*

14. *Behold, he travaileth with iniquity, and hath
conceived mischief, and brought forth falsehood.*

15. *He made a pit, and digged it, and is fallen into
the ditch* which *he made.*

16. *His mischief shall return upon his own head, and
his violent dealing shall come down upon his own pate.*

In the fourth place, is the answer of his prayer, viz., assurance given of delivery to him, and of judgment on his enemies ; whereupon the supplicant giveth thanks to God.
Whence learn, 1. The fruit of faith joined with a good conscience, is access to God in prayer, confidence, peace and
tranquillity of mind, mitigation of trouble, protection and
deliverance, as the prophet's experience here doth prove.
2. Victory granted unto faith, after wrestling with darkness,
is satisfactory to the soul of the godly, as if all that the believer did hope for were perfected ; for he is now clear to
say, *my defence is of God, &c.* 3. Whatsoever we think

in the time of temptation, neither justice against the wicked, nor mercy toward the godly is idle ; for God's word and works speak mercy to the one, and wrath to the other, every day ; all things are working for the one's good ; and for the other's damage continually ; *for God judgeth the righteous and is angry with the wicked every day.* 4. God delayeth the execution of his judgment on the wicked, to lead them to repentance ; for here *God hath whetted his sword to strike, if the wicked turn not.* 5. If repentance intervene not, the destruction of the wicked is inevitable : *If he turn not, the instruments of death are prepared, and the arrows directed towards the persecutors.* 6. It is a matter of no small pains that the sinner is put unto, to serve the devil, and his own corrupt affections, *he travaileth* as with a child ; he digs a pit, one of the hardest pieces of work to slaves. 7. When once the wicked hath conceived mischief, he cannot rest till he bring his purpose to action, but his sinful thoughts may be wrought in effect : *he conceiveth mischief and travaileth with iniquity.* 8. The adversary of God's people shall have no profit of all his labour, but shall be met with disappointment, *he bringeth forth falsehood,* and the evil which is most contrary to his hope and intention shall befall him : *He is fallen in the ditch which he made and his mischief shall return upon his own head, &c.* as a stone thrown up against heaven, returneth upon the head of him who threw it.

17. *I will praise the Lord according to his righteousness; and will sing praise to the name of the Lord most high.*

In the last place he promiseth praise, and closeth his song so. Whence learn, 1. The issue of the hardest exercise of the godly, is comfort to their souls, and praise to God, as here we see. 2. When faith is sensibly satisfied, and settled in assurance of what was promised, it will be glad and give thanks for what is to come, as if it were in possession already : so speaketh this conclusion, I will praise the Lord, and I will sing praise to the name of the Lord. 3. Let the party opposer of the godly be never so powerful and violent, and his place in the world never so high, faith may set to its seal, that God shall manifest himself a righteous judge in power and authority above the highest oppressing powers on earth : *I will sing praise to the name of the Lord most high.*

PSALM VIII.

To the chief Musician upon Gittith. A Psalm of David.

To the end the prophet may commend the glory of God's grace toward
man, he first admireth his glory in the works of creation and providence, which are able to stop the mouths of all blasphemous atheists,
ver. 1, 2 ; in the second place he admireth the Lord's love to man above
all other, even the most glorious creatures, v. 3, 4 ; thirdly, he setteth
out this grace of God to man, in the incarnation, humiliation, and exaltation of Christ for man's cause, and for restoring redeemed men
in Christ, to their right unto, and over the visible creatures, ver. 5, 6,
7, 8 ; and closeth the psalm, with the admiration of God's glory in all
the earth, ver. 9.

1. *O Lord our Lord, how excellent* is *thy name in
all the earth ! who hast set thy glory above the heavens.*
2. *Out of the mouth of babes and sucklings hast thou
ordained strength because of thine enemies, that thou
mightest still the enemy and the avenger.*

From his admiration of God's glory in the works of creation and providence, learn 1. The godly are not always
borne down with trouble ; sometimes they have liberty to
go, and delight themselves in the beholding of God's glory
and goodness towards themselves, as the whole psalm showeth. 2. The mystery of the glory of God, in his works
of creation and redemption, is such, as none, save the eye
spiritually illuminated by his Spirit, can see : and he that
seeth it, cannot but be ravished therewith, when he
discerneth it ; and none can sufficiently comprehend it, or take
it up fully, save God himself. Therefore the prophet
directeth his speech full of admiration, wholly to the Lord,
throughout all the psalm. 3. The glory of the Lord is
greatly sweetened unto the godly, in the time of their praising of his majesty, when they consider their own interest
in him as in their own property. Therefore saith he, *O
Lord our Lord, how excellent is thy name !* 4. No words
are sufficient to set out the glory of the Lord, not only as
it is in itself, but even as it is discovered to a spiritual understanding ; therefore by way of admiration, must he cry
out, *how excellent is thy name !* 5. The heavens and
celestial lights shining from above speak much of God's
glory, but in effect his glory is greater than they can hold
forth : for his glory is set above the heavens. 6. Albeit
the glory of the Lord filleth the world, yet hath he en-

emies of his glory, to wit, profane and godless persons, atheists, epicures, and persecutors of his people and truth ; for here are enemies spoken of, and avengers, opening blasphemous mouths against him, and his people, as if God, and his people, had injured them. 7. Not only the providence of God in new-born babes, framing them in the belly, providing nourishment unto them when they are born, and making them to suck the breasts ; but also the giving of saving knowledge to some of them, in their tender years, is able to refute all atheists and profane despisers of the glory of the Lord ; *for out of the mouth of babes and sucklings he hath ordained strength*, or strong conviction, to *still the enemy and the avenger*, and put him to silence. Matthew 21. 26.

3. *When I consider thy heavens, the work of thy fingers, the moon and the stars, which thou hast ordained.*

4. *What is man, that thou art mindful of him ? and the son of man, that thou visitest him ?*

From his admiration in God's respect, and love to man above all other creatures, learn, 1. The weakness and unworthiness of man, considered both in himself, and compared with his glorious creatures made for his use, commend the bounty of God to man, and make it a matter of great admiration. For when the prophet considereth the glorious heavens, &c. he asketh *what is man, &c.* 2. Man of all the creatures is most esteemed and taken care of by God ; for he is mindful of man, and daily visiteth him.

5. *For thou hast made him a little lower than the angels, and hast crowned him with glory and honour.*

6. *Thou madest him to have dominion over the works of thy hands ; thou hast put all* things *under his feet ;*

7. *All sheep and oxen, yea, and the beasts of the field ;*

8. *The fowl of the air, and the fish of the sea,* and whatsoever *passeth through the paths of the seas.*

In the third place, he looketh on man considered in his creation before the fall, and as he is in his head, Christ (who is God incarnate, humbled and exalted for man's cause after the fall), restored to what he lost by the fall. Whence

C

learn, 1. Look unto man in his creation, and God hath given him the place, in order of dignity, above all the creatures visible, next unto heavenly angels : *thou hast made him a little lower than the angels.* 2. Look unto man after his fall, restored by Christ unto his place, and in this respect he is established in that dignity to be next unto the glorious angels: *thou hast made him a little lower than the angels.* 3. Look unto man in our head Christ Jesus, God incarnate, and there man is wonderfully exalted in regard that for respect and love to man, the Man Christ being very God, is humbled unto the death of the cross. And in this sense doth the apostle, Heb. ii. 7, 9. take this place *thou madest him a little lower than the angels, for the suffering of death.* 4. Look unto man in Christ Jesus after his resurrection, and in his glorification ; *God hath crowned him with glory and majesty.* 5. It is no small point of dignifying man, that all believers have by Christ this title of heirship, with lawful use and possession of the creatures recovered and restored unto him : *thou madest him to have dominion over the works of thine hands.* 6. As there is nothing which may do man good service, which God hath not granted man dominion over, in and through Christ, so there is nothing can harm him, but he hath put under Christ's feet and under believers' feet in and through Christ, to wit, sin and Satan, and all our enemies, and death the last enemy ; *he hath put things under his feet,* as the apostle gathereth, 1 Cor. xv. 26. 7. Christ shall not lay down his kingdom which he hath in his church, and over all her enemies, till he hath put down all rule and authority, and power against him and his church, and have subdued all enemies under himself. *For he must reign till he hath put all things under his feet,* as the apostle collecteth, 1 Cor. xv. 25. 8. Nothing is excepted or exempted from being subject to Christ, as man ; no, not the holy angels (who are made ministering spirits, to serve believers) but only God, essentially considered, he only is excepted. *For he hath put all things under his feet ; but when he saith, all things are put under* him, it is *manifest that he is excepted who did put all things under* him, as the apostle proveth from this place, 1 Cor. xv. 27.

9. *O Lord our Lord, how excellent* is *thy name in all the earth !*

He closeth the psalm as he began it with admiration :

whence learn, 1. The praises of our Lord, and the excellency of our covenant right, and interest in him, are worthy again and again to be considered; and that God should be proclaimed Lord of us whom he hath lifted up to so high a dominion : therefore is this verse repeated again. 2. When a man hath begun to declare some reason of his wondering at the glory of God, manifested in the whole world, and specially in his church, he must give over the full explication of this glory, and close, as he began, with wondering still; as here the same exclamation of wondering at the excellency of God's glory concludeth the psalm as it began, *O Lord our Lord, how excellent is thy name in all the earth!*

PSALM IX.

To the chief Musician upon Muth-Labben. A Psalm of David.

Here is David's song of praise to God, first, for his own experience of God's goodness towards himself, and God's righteous judgment against his enemies, v. 1, 2 3, 4. Secondly, for the Lord's readiness to do the like work, in favour of all the godly, v. 5, 6, 7, 8, 9, 10. Thirdly he exhorteth the godly to praise God with him, v. 11, 12. Fourthly, he prayeth for his own delivery out of his present distress, v. 13, 14. Fifthly, he hath assurance of the overthrow of all his enemies, v. 15, 16, 17, 18. And last of all, for the execution of this overthrow, he heartily prayeth, v. 19, 20.

1. *I will praise thee, O Lord, with my whole heart; I will shew forth all thy marvellous works.*

2. *I will be glad and rejoice in thee : I will sing praise to thy name, O thou most High.*

3. *When mine enemies are turned back, they shall fall and perish at thy presence.*

4. *For thou hast maintained my right and my cause : thou sittest in the throne judging right.*

From the first part of this song of praise, learn, 1. The exercise of the saints in variety of troubles occasioneth the setting forth of the glory of God in all his attributes as in this psalm is shown. 2. When the heart is enlarged with the sense of God's goodness, the work of praising God will be more heartily undertaken, and a large heart will make a loosed tongue and an open mouth, to set forth his glory. David *will* now *praise the Lord with his whole heart.* 3. One work of God's wonderful goodness useth to call for an-

other that they may go forth together in each other's hands
to set forth his excellency; as here David *will show forth
all his wonderful works*.   4. A lover of the glory of God
cannot rest till he communicate with others what he
knoweth of the Lord's wonders: *he will show forth* (for
others' upstirring) *all the Lord's marvellous works*.   5. Not
any benefit or gift received of God, but God himself, and
his free favour is the matter of the believer's joy: David
will be glad and rejoice in God himself.   6. It is not enough
to have joy in our heart in the Lord, but it is his glory,
that the joy which we have in him, be openly known as occasion offereth : therefore *will* David *sing praises to the
name of the Lord most high*.   7. The way of giving God
the glory in every action, and in special of our victories
over our enemies, is to acknowledge him to be the chief
worker thereof, and the creatures to be but instruments by
whom he turneth the enemy back : for *the enemy falleth
and perisheth at his presence*.   8. As for time by-gone
God should have the glory of what is done, so must we consecrate the glory of what shall be done, and of what we
would have done altogether to the Lord : therefore also for
time to come David speaketh, *when mine enemies are turned
back*, (to wit, by thy power,) *they shall fall at thy presence*.
9. Were a cause never so right and just, it requireth God's
power for keeping it on foot : the justness of the cause
must not be relied on, but God must have the trust of the
cause, and the glory of maintaining it : David acknowledgeth *God the maintainer of his right and cause*.   10. What
judge soever shall condemn us unrighteously, there is a higher
judge to judge the cause over again, and the parties also :
who when he showeth himself, should be glorified in his
justice by us ; *thou sittest in the throne judging right*, saith
David, after he was condemned of the judges of the land.

5. *Thou hast rebuked the heathen, thou hast destroyed the wicked, thou hast put out their name for ever and
ever.*

6. *O thou enemy, destructions are come to a perpetual end ; and thou hast destroyed cities ; their memorial is perished with them.*

7. *But the Lord shall endure for ever : he hath prepared his throne for judgment.*

8. *And he shall judge the world in righteousness, he shall minister judgment to the people in uprightness.*

9. *The Lord also will be a refuge for the oppressed, a refuge in times of trouble.*

10. *And they that know thy name will put their trust in thee: for thou, Lord, hast not forsaken them that seek thee.*

In the second place, he foreseeth in the Spirit what shall become of all God's enemies, and adversaries of his people, and prophesieth concerning them, to the praise of God, and comfort of the godly, who were to live after his time : whence learn, 1. Although the conscience of the persecutors of God's people be silent in their security, yet shall God's judgment against them awake their conscience at last, whether they be enemies without the church, or within it ; yea, the Lord shall destroy them : *for thou, O Lord, hast rebuked the heathen, thou hast destroyed the wicked.* 2. Although the enemies have a great name in the world, yet shall their glory be blasted, and their renown vanish, as if it had never been heard of : for *thou, Lord, hast put out their name for ever and ever.* 3. The destructions of the Lord's people, and of their dwellings, intended by the wicked, shall be charged upon their enemies, though they have not executed and brought their malice to pass, even when the enemies themselves know and think, they have not attained their purpose : their intended *destructions shall come to a perpetual end.* 4. The time shall come, when the godly shall triumph over all their oppressors : yea, in the midst of the enemies' insolencies, the godly by faith may triumph over them, and say as here, *O thou enemy, destructions are come to a perpetual end.* 5. As the enemies of God's church have destroyed the earthly dwellings of the Lord's people ; so the Lord hath destroyed, and will *destroy their cities and their dwellings, and make their memorial cease with them.* 6. The reign of the wicked adversaries of God's people is very short, and in a few days they are cut off ; but *the Lord shall endure for ever,* to defend his people from age to age. 7. Courts of justice among men are not always ready to hear plaintiffs ; but the Lord holdeth court continually ; the taking in of no man's complaint is delayed so much as one hour, though thousands should come at once, all of them with sundry petitions : *he hath prepared his throne for judgment.* 8. Albeit in the courts of men justice be not always found, and very rarely in any matter concerning Christ; yet *the Lord shall judge the world in righteousness, and minister judgment to the people in uprightness :* the injuries done to his people shall be all of them righted by him. 9. Although the Lord's children have no residence, but be chased from place to place, and know not whither to go in the earth ; yet there is an open city of refuge unto them, where they shall find shelter : *for the Lord also will be a refuge to the oppressed.* 10. The Lord's relief which he giveth to his people, is reserved, till other inferior reliefs fail, till the godly man be humbled and emptied, and then will he help: *unto the oppressed he will be a refuge in time of trouble.* 11. The way of the Lord's helping and comforting his own people, is by lifting up the believer above any thing which can overtake him ; above the reach of all creatures ; *the Lord will be a high tower,* a high place as the word importeth, whence the believer may look down and despise what flesh can do unto him. 12. The ignorance of the Lord's goodness, mercy, truth, and other his attributes, is the cause of making so little use of God in prosperity, and so little believing in him in the time of trouble: for, *they who know his name, will trust in him.* 13. They to whom the spiritual knowledge of God is revealed, will certainly trust in him : and they that trust in him will *seek* him : and they that seek him, will find him to be what he is called: for the man *knowing God, trusting in God, and seeking God,* is the same here. 14. The Lord may for a time hide himself, or delay to manifest himself to a believer that seeketh him, (which he doth sometimes for the believer's trial, exercise, and profiting,) yet no age can give an instance of his rejecting such a supplicant : *for thou, Lord, hast not forsaken them that seek thee.* 15. As many experiences as are past of God's grace to believing supplicants before this day, so many confirmations of faith are given, and so many encouragements to all believers to seek his face in Christ : *for he never forsook them that sought him.*

11. *Sing praises to the Lord, which dwelleth in Zion : declare among the people his doings.*

12. *When he maketh inquisition for blood, he re-*

membereth them: he forgetteth not the cry of the humble.

In the third place, he exhorteth the rest of the godly to praise God with him; whence learn, 1. It is the duty of all believers to join themselves cheerfully in the setting forth the Lord's care over them, and whatsoever may make his lovely Majesty known to the world: for so he requireth the present precept and example,—*sing praises to the Lord.* 2. The only true God, and the right object of our joy and praises, is he who manifested himself to the church of the Jews of old; who gave his Scriptures and his ordinances to them; and among whom he took up his residence in Jerusalem, *in Zion*, in the temple, in the mercy seat, betwixt the cherubims, (which was a figure of the incarnation of the Son of God; in whom, as the only Mediator, is the trysting place between God and believers, for accepting their persons and worship,) for so doth the description of the true God here teach us: *sing praises to the Lord who dwelleth in Zion.* 3. The acts of the Lord for his people are so stamped with the impression of his divinity, that they are able to purchase glory to God even among the nations that are without the church, and to draw them to him: and so it is not a needless, fruitless, or hopeless work, to *declare his doings among the nations.* 4. If the Lord be pleased to honour himself with the martyrdom of any of his servants, it is not for disrespect to their persons, for they remain, even when dead, honourable in his estimation, and high in his affection; for *he remembereth them* in a special manner. 5. There is a time appointed of God for bringing to judgment every sin, and especially murder; and of all murders, to avenge most severely the slaughter of his servants, concerning whom it is here said, *when he maketh inquisition for blood, he remembereth them*: precious in his eyes is the death of his saints. 6. There is not a lost word in the earnest prayers of the humble believer, poured forth in the day of his necessity: every petition shall have a full answer, partly in this life, and partly in the life to come: for *God forgetteth not the cry of the humble.*

13. *Have mercy upon me, O Lord; consider my trouble* which I suffer *of them that hate me, thou that liftest me up from the gates of death!*

14. *That I may show forth all thy praise in the gates of the daughter of Zion: I will rejoice in thy salvation.*

In the fourth place, he cometh to his own particular and present case, and prayeth for a new experience of the truth formerly set down, believed, and sealed by him. Whence learn, 1. When new troubles befall experienced believers, they must betake them to their old refuge, and to the formerly blessed means of prayer; as here David doeth: *have mercy, O Lord, upon me.* 2. Never a word of merit should be in the mouth of a true believer; for, *have mercy on me, O Lord*, is David's only plea: any good in us, is but a sandy ground to build on. 3. It sufficeth a believer acquainted with God, to present before God the trouble he suffereth unjustly from his enemies, and to expect deliverance from the Lord's grace towards himself, and from his justice in relation to the adversary: for this is the argument here used, *consider my trouble which I suffer of them that hate me.* 4. Extreme danger of present death, should not dash nor discourage the believer to pray for deliverance, because experience hath proven, that the Lord *can lift a believer up from the gates of death.* 5. Life should not be loved so much for itself, as that we may glorify God in our life, and edify others in the knowledge of God; for deliverance from death is here asked of God, that he *may set forth all the praises of God in the gates* and most open places *of the daughter of Zion:* that is, in the audience of the people of God. 6. He gets a satisfactory answer: which teacheth us, that in a moment the Lord can persuade the supplicant of the grant of his prayer, and fill him with joy; as here in one breath, ere the prophet could close his prayer, he is made to joy in the salvation or deliverance which he was persuaded God was to give to him; *I will rejoice in thy salvation.*

15. *The heathen are sunk down in the pit* that *they made: in the net which they hid is their own foot taken.*

16. *The Lord is known* by *the judgment* which *he executeth: the wicked is snared in the work of his own hands. Higgaion. Selah.*

17. *The wicked shall be turned into hell,* and *all the nations that forget God.*

18. *For the needy shall not always be forgotten: the expectation of the poor shall* not *perish for ever.*

In the fifth place is set down, how with confidence of his own delivery, he is made sure of the overthrow of the enemy: whence learn, 1. Ordinarily, the delivery of the persecuted people of God is joined with the overthrow of their oppressors: and certainly, the wicked cannot take a readier way to ruin themselves, than to seek the overthrow of the Lord's church and people; for here, *the heathen are sunk down in the pit that they made;* andtheir crafty counsel against the godly, is the trap to take themselves in: *in the net which they hid, their own feet are taken.* 2. None of God's judgments, and specially none of those judgments whereby he pleads the cause of his church against her enemies, should be lightly looked upon; *for the Lord is known by the judgments which he executeth.* His judgments bear the impression of his wisdom and justice: so as the sin may be read written on the rod. 3. Amongst other manifestations of God's wisdom and justice in punishing his adversaries, this is one, the Lord makes the works of the wicked, and specially what they do against his people, to be the very means to undo them: *the wicked is snared in the work of his own hands.* 4. As the devices of the wicked come from hell, so they return thither, and draw the devisers with them: though they cry, Peace, peace, and put the fear of hell far from them, yet *all the wicked shall be turned into hell.* 5. As they who give themselves to sin, and specially enemies to peace, cast away the knowledge of God out of their mind and affection; so shall God cast them away far from his presence: *all the nations that forget God, shall be turned into hell.* 6. Albeit the Lord does not presently execute judgment on the godless oppressors of his people, yet for respect the Lord doth bear to his people, their destruction shall certainly come: *they shall go down to hell; for the needy shall not always be forgotten.* The cry of the needy and oppressed shall bring judgment upon the oppressors. 7. The Lord's people are an humbled people, afflicted, emptied, sensible of their need, driven to a daily attendance on God, daily begging of him, and living only upon the hope of what

is promised : for so are they here described needy, poor
supplicants, and expectants of the performance of what is
promised. 8. Albeit the Lord seems to lay aside the
prayers of the oppressed godly, and forget them : and albeit
the godly man's hope doth seem for a time vain, *yet shall
he not always be forgotten, nor his expectation perish for
ever,* and specially the expectation he hath of things everlasting, shall not be disappointed, but shall be satisfied *for
ever.*

19. *Arise, O Lord; let not man prevail; let the
heathen be judged in thy sight.*
20. *Put them in fear, O Lord;* that *the nations
may know themselves* to be but *men. Selah.*

In the last place he followeth his condemnatory sentence
of the wicked with prayer, that the Lord would put it in
execution, even in his own time. Whence learn, 1. The
Lord doth not so delay to execute judgment on the
oppressors of his people, but he may be entreated to make
speedy despatch, and as need requireth *to arise* and fall to
work. 2. The time of God's arising is, when the cause of
God which the godly maintain is like to be lost : *arise,
O Lord, let not man prevail.* There is his reason, why he
would have God to arise. 3. When God ariseth for the
godly, he maketh it appear, that they are his people, and
that their adversaries are in effect before him but heathen
and strangers for the inward covenant and commonwealth
of his people, whether they be within the visible church or
not ; for he prayeth, *let the heathen be judged in thy sight.*
4. So long as the Lord doth spare his adversaries, they
misknow themselves, and God also. Sin doth so besot
ignorant and graceless people, that they forget that they
are mortal, and that God is their judge. Therefore David
desireth, *that the nations may know themselves to be but
men.* 5. Where there is any hope or possibility of the
salvation of enemies, the godly man's desire is they should
be brought in subjection to God, and humbled before him ;
and that judgments might be so tempered as the enemy
might profit thereby, and God be glorified : *put them in
fear, that they may know themselves to be but men.*

PSALM X.

This Psalm wanteth an inscription, and that is God's wisdom, that being less restricted to a particular man's case, it may be of more general use, whensoever the godly find themselves in a condition whereunto this prayer may be suitable: and specially in time of general persecution. The prophet here complaineth to God and craveth justice against the persecutors of his people, because of the intolerable wickedness of the oppressor, ver. 1—11. Secondly, he prayeth for hastening of the delivery of the Lord's people, and for hastening of judgment upon the persecutors, for vindication of the glory of God's justice against his enemies, and of his mercy to his people, ver. 12—15. Thirdly, he professeth his confidence that he shall be heard, and so glorifieth God, ver. 16—18.

1. *Why standest thou afar off,* O Lord? why *hidest thou* thyself *in times of trouble?*

2. *The wicked in* his *pride doth persecute the poor : let them be taken in the devices that they have imagined.*

3. *For the wicked boasteth of his heart's desire, and blesseth the covetous,* whom *the Lord abhorreth.*

4. *The wicked, through the pride of his countenance will not seek* after *God: God* is *not in all his thoughts.*

5. *His ways are always grievous; thy judgments* are *far above out of his sight :* as for *all his enemies, he puffeth at them.*

6. *He hath said in his heart, I shall not be moved: for* I shall *never* be *in adversity.*

7. *His mouth is full of cursing, and deceit, and fraud : under his tongue* is *mischief and vanity.*

8. *He sitteth in the lurking places of the villages : in the secret places doth he murder the innocent*: *his eyes are privily set against the poor.*

9. *He lieth in wait secretly as a lion in his den: he lieth in wait to catch the poor : he doth catch the poor, when he draweth him into his net.*

10. *He croucheth,* and *humbleth himself, that the poor may fall by his strong ones.*

11. *He hath said in his heart, God hath forgotten : he hideth his face; he will never see* it.

In this complaint he speaketh to God after the manner of men, in the terms of sense, and as matters did seem to him in outward appearance. Whence learn, 1. How far contrary to the word of promise, may God's word and dispensation seem to speak : the word saith, *he will ever be with his own, and not forsake them ;* and here his dealing with them seemeth to say, *that he standeth afar off, and hideth himself in times of trouble.* Sense may sometime speak contrary to faith. 2. In this case the speech of sense is not to be subscribed, but the truth of the word should be relied upon ; and the objection made by sense, or suggestion against the word, is to be brought before the Lord in prayer, that it may be discussed : as here the prophet doth : *why standest thou afar off, &c.* 3. Observe how homely an humbled soul may be with God, and how far the Lord will be from mistaking of his people, when faith borroweth sense's tongue. The Lord will suffer such speeches and not take them in ill part, knowing that they proceed from faith and love, wrestling with sense ; yea, and he will suffer them to be registered in his book, as here we see, for prudent use-making of them, though they appear to challenge him, *for standing aloof, and hiding himself.* 4. Oftimes it cometh to pass, that the godly are in a mean condition in the world, when their adversaries are in high places and power, and so be able to oppress them as their underlings : *the wicked in his pride doth persecute the poor.* 5. In respect that pride disdaineth what is apparently good in a mean person, and overvalueth its own worth, therefore pride is easily coupled with oppression, and pride is able to raise persecution : *the wicked in his pride doth persecute the poor.* 6. What persecutors devise against God's people, may with good grounds be expected to turn to be a snare unto themselves. *Let them be taken in the devices they have imagined.* 7. All the politicians on earth cannot describe the vileness of the wicked, so well as the Spirit of the Lord doth point it out, for he setteth him forth. 1. He is an arrogant, self-confident man, threatening to bring to pass what he would have done, as if he were able in despite of God to effectuate it : *he boasts of his heart's desire.* 2. He accounts of no man, but such a one as by hook and crook is able to enhance honour and riches ; *he blesseth the covetous man.* 3. He valueth not what God judgeth of a man, whether he be a man whom God oveth and respects, or not ; he setteth his opinion in opposition to God's judgment of men, *he blesseth the man whom God abhorreth.* 4. The wicked man hath such a conceit of his own ability and perfection, as his countenance and carriage doth testify that he scorneth to employ God by prayer for any thing : *through the pride of his countenance he will not seek God.* 5. For the rule of his life, he consulteth not what may please or displease God, what may honour or dishonour God ; he troubles not himself with such thoughts: *God is not in all his thoughts* ; that is, as the Hebrew phrase doth mean, all his thoughts are, that there is no God : or none of his thoughts are upon God. 6. His ways are ever noisome, tending especially to hurt the godly : *his ways are always grievous* ; or as his ways prosper, they vex others. 7. He feareth not God's judgments, he believeth not that they shall ever come ; he putteth them far away in his conceit : yea, and what the Lord hath set down in his word, as his judgment, he apprehendeth it not ; he is not capable of spiritual wisdom: *the Lord's judgments are far above out of his sight.* 8. He neither feareth God nor man: *all his enemies he puffeth at them ;* as disdaining what they can do against him. 9. The wicked promise to themselves perpetuity of prosperity, and do not fear evil, to see a change to the worse ; *he assureth himself never to be moved, nor to be in adversity.* 10. For his words, he standeth not to blaspheme God, to lie, swear, and curse, if it may purchase him credit, and may help him to deceive others. *His mouth is full of cursing.* 11. His fair promises are but vanity ; and when he minds a mischief, he hides it with pretences of best intentions, *under his tongue is mischief and vanity.* 12. As thieves and cut-throats lie in wait about villages, to catch the straggling passengers, where there are few to help them, so do the wicked watch where they may oppress those who have few to do for them : *he sitteth in the lurking places of the villages, in secret places doth he murder the innocent.* 13. As an archer in the hunting of his prey, so doth the wicked mark and spy out a poor man, to take advantage of him: *his eyes are privily set against the poor.* 14. As a lion in his den, or some lurking place, lieth still till the prey come by, and then he leapeth out upon it, when he is able to take it : so doth the wicked dissemble his malice, till he be master over a man, and then doeth what he can against him ; *he lieth secretly in wait, as a lion.* 15. As a crafty hunter spread-eth his net for a prey, and miskenneth it, till the prey be entangled; so doth the wicked lay some device to catch the poor, and taketh him: *he doth catch the poor, when he draws him in his net.* 16. As the lion lieth low in the dust, as if he minded to do no harm at all; so do the wick-ed men pretend themselves the most reasonable men that can be, and most observant of law and equity, till by their power they may have their intent of the poor: *he croucheth and humbleth himself, that the poor may fall by him, or his associates.* 17. Present prosperity joined with impurity maketh him persuade himself that God will never take notice of him hereafter, or call him to account, or punish him: *he hath said in his heart, God hath for-gotten, he hideth his face, he will never see it.*

12. *Arise, O Lord; O God, lift up thine hand: forget not the humble.*

13. *Wherefore doth the wicked contemn God? he hath said in his heart, Thou wilt not require* it.

14. *Thou hast seen* it; *for thou beholdest mischief and spite, to requite* it *with thy hand: the poor com-mitteth himself unto thee; thou art the helper of the fatherless.*

15. *Break thou the arm of the wicked and the evil* man: *seek out his wickedness* till *thou find none.*

Thus he hath given the character of the enemies of God's people, and so made a ditty for them. Now in the second place, he prayeth against them, that their doom may be given out, and may be executed. Whence learn, 1. The more we see atheism in the wicked, the more we should draw near to God: and albeit the godly conceive God to lie off, and sit still from executing justice, the godly being tempted with the temptations which overcome the wicked, yet they must not yield to the temptation, but pray against it, as is here done; *arise, O Lord, lift up thy hand.* 2. The merciful respect and love which the Lord hath to his afflicted people, will not suffer his justice against these persecutors to be long quiet, *for he will not forget the humble.* 3. As the interest which God hath in his own people, engageth him to fall on their enemies; so the vindication also of his own glory from the contempt which they do to his name engageth him against them; for *wherefore doth the wicked contemn God, &c.?* 4. The god-less enemies of God's people deny God's providence, and deny God's justice; yet his people are comforted under their saddest sufferings by the Lord's seeing and marking thereof; for the godly say here, *thou hast seen it, and beholdest mischief.* 5. God's judgments on the wicked shall really refute the atheism of the wicked, and requite their opposition made to the godly. *He beholds mischief and spite to requite it with his hand.* 6. When a man hath laid forth his desires, and poured out his heart before God, he should quiet himself, and cast himself with his burden upon the Lord; for here *the poor committeth himself to God.* And when an humble believer hath cast his burden on the Lord, the Lord will not fail to take care of what he is trusted with, it is an engaging of God, that the poor hath committed himself to him. 7. As the Lord's office, custom, and nature is, so is his real work to do for them who employ him, and are not able to do for themselves; *he is the helper of the fatherless.* 8. The power of persecutors cannot be so great, but God shall weaken and break it, so as they shall not be able to trouble his people. *Break thou the arm of the wicked.* 9. Though the Lord reckons not with his enemies for their sins at first, yet he reckons for all at last; for less and for greater, for one and for all, and doth not pass a farthing of the debt of punishment unexacted: *but seeketh out their sins till he find none.* O how fearful a reckoning must it be, which the Lord maketh with the impenitent, who die unpardoned, and unreconciled with God, through the Mediator Christ Jesus!

16. *The Lord is King for ever and ever: the hea-then are perished out of his land.*

17. *Lord, thou hast heard the desire of the humble: thou wilt prepare their heart, thou wilt cause thine ear to hear.*

18. *To judge the fatherless and the oppressed, that the man of the earth may no more oppress.*

In the last place, the answer of the petition followeth, in a comfortable persuasion of the supplicant, concerning the grant thereof: whence learn, 1. That the prayer of the persecuted shall not be rejected, because the kingdom of

Christ in his church is perpetual: earthly kings cannot live still to help their friends, followers, or flatterers, or to persecute and molest God's church: but *Christ is the Lord and King for ever and ever*, to defend his people, and punish his foes. 2. The wicked within the visible church, howsoever they have the external privileges of God's people, yet if they continue unreconciled, and oppose piety, they shall be in God's estimation, and in the day of his judging them, counted as they are here called, heathen, and shall be separated from the fellowship of God and God's people, *the heathen shall perish out of his land*. 3. It is the Lord's way to exercise his children with trouble, till he humble them and make them sensible of the need of his help, till he turn their sense of need into a desire of his relief, and their desire into a prayer, and then he will in due time give answer: *Lord, thou hast heard the desire of the humble*. 4. Grace to pray, and the fixing of the heart in prayer on the Lord, is his gift, no less than the answer of the prayer: and where the Lord giveth the one grace, he will also give the other: *thou wilt prepare their heart, thou wilt cause thine ear to hear*. 5. When God beginneth to show his respect to the prayers of his people against their oppressors, then the helpless and weak servants of God shall have deliverance from the power of oppressors, and their oppressors shall not be able to do any more harm, when the Lord causeth his ear to hear their prayer: *the fatherless shall be judged*, yea declared righteous, absolved and delivered; *and the oppressor shall no more oppress*. 6. If there were no more comfort to the godly oppressed, yet this may suffice, that their life, inheritance, and happiness is in heaven; and that their oppressors, in opposition to them, are declared here, to be *but men of this earth*, whose portion is no better than what they have here in this world.

PSALM XI.

To the Chief Musician. A Psalm of David.

David, as an example of a Christian under the trial of his faith in time of trouble, and tempted to desperation, resisted the temptation, how desperate soever his condition seemed, v. 1, 2; and disputeth for the confirmation of his own faith, v. 3—7.

1. *In the Lord put I my trust: how say ye to my soul, Flee as a bird to your mountain?*

2. *For, lo, the wicked bend* their *bow, they make ready their arrow upon the string, that they may privily shoot at the upright in heart.*

Before the prophet dispute, and produce his reasons against the temptations unto unbelief, he asserteth and avoweth his faith, and presenteth the danger he is in, before God. Whence learn, 1. It is the surest method in our spiritual combat against Satan, and his fiery darts, to hold up the shield of faith, and to fix ourselves in resolution never to loose our hold of the Lord; as David doth here: *in the Lord put I my trust.* 2. Having once fixed our foot on the rock, we may the more effectually rebuke our adversaries, for mocking of our confidence: as David doth here, saying, *how say you to my soul, flee?* 3. God is a strong refuge to his own, whereunto they should fly like birds, chased to their strength, in all necessities, for he is our *rock* or *mountain.* 4. The wicked world scorn the godly man's confidence, and the avowing of his faith in God, when they see no visible help for him on earth. Take up your faith now, say they, when they see the man beset by apparently inextricable troubles, as here they say to David, *flee now as a bird to thy mountain.* 5. The believer is not stupid in time of danger, nor senseless of difficulties, when he asserteth his faith: *for lo,* saith he, *the wicked bend their bow,* they have me, as it were, under the aim of their shot. 6. The Lord for the exercise of the faith of his own, and for discovery of the plots of the wicked against them, and for showing his own glory in protecting them more clearly, suffereth the wicked to make all ready, even unto present execution of their cruelty, as here, *they make ready their arrow upon the string to shoot, &c.*

3. *If the foundations be destroyed, what can the righteous do?*

4. *The Lord* is *in his holy temple, the Lord's throne* is *in heaven: his eyes behold, his eyelids try, the children of men.*

5. *The Lord trieth the righteous; but the wicked, and him that loveth violence, his soul hateth.*

6. *Upon the wicked he shall rain snares, fire and brimstone, and an horrible tempest:* this shall be *the portion of their cup.*

7. *For the righteous Lord loveth righteousness; his countenance doth behold the upright.*

In the next place, he disputeth for the confirmation of his own faith by sundry reasons or several considerations.

The first reason to confirm his faith, is from the absurdity of the temptation, tending to the overturning of the very foundation of religion, whereunto, if the believer should yield, he is lost and gone. Whence learn, 1. Faith in God, and flying to him in all straits for relief, is the *foundation* of all religious and righteous persons, whereupon they build their hope and happiness solidly; for David had laid it for a foundation, that God was *a rock*, or mountain of refuge for men to flee unto in straits. 2. A temptation to mistrust God, and not to flee to him in all hazards, is most dangerous, and destructive of all true religion, for it is the destroying of the very foundations of righteousness and happiness; and the resisting of this temptation is so necessary, as in what measure it is yielded unto in that measure the righteous man is put to a stand, and to a comfortless perplexity, and should despair certainly if he went from it : for, *if the foundations be destroyed, what shall the righteous man do?* If it be in vain to fly to God, righteous men are lost men, which is absurd.

The next reason to confirm his faith is the establishment of a Mediator, set forth in the word of God, and other holy ordinances, concerning the covenant of grace, and the benefits of it, and duties required in it, all to be found in the Lord's holy temple, or tabernacle, representing Christ Jesus and his church, and the mutual relations between God and his people. Whence learn, 3. The way to refresh and strengthen faith, is to look to God in Christ the Mediator, reconciling the world to himself, according as he was shadowed forth in the temple of Jerusalem, and as he is still holden forth in the church, in his word and other ordinances. First and last, Christ is the trysting place, where God is constantly to be found on his mercy seat; for *the Lord in his holy temple* did speak so much to the church in typical terms.

4. The third reason is, because God is a perfect judge to take order in due time, both with them who oppose his work and people, and with those who will not make use of his mercy : *the Lord's throne is in heaven.* 5. The

Lord's knowledge of all men's carriage is perfect: *his eyes behold.* 6. When the Lord doth not make manifest by his work that he seeth men's carriage, but seemeth, as is were, to wink and close his eyes, he is then about to try the hearts of men, and to bring their thoughts to light: *his eye-lids* (when his eyes seem closed) *try the children of men.* 7. The troubles whereunto the Lord doth put his children in times of temptation, are not to be exposed as acts of displeasure, or mere justice, but as acts of wisdom and love, to try, exercise, and frame them to obedience. *The Lord trieth the righteous*; at such time as he sendeth trouble specially. 8. However he giveth the wicked and violent persecutor to have a seeming prosperity, while the godly are in trouble, yet that is no act of love to them: for *the wicked, and him that loveth violence, his soul hateth.* 9. All the seeming advantages which the wicked have in their own prosperity, are but means of hardening them in their ill course, and holding them fast in the bonds of their own iniquities, till God execute judgment on them: *upon the wicked he shall rain snares.* 10. Whatsoever be the condition of the wicked for a time, yet at length sudden, terrible, irresistible, and remediless destruction they shall not escape: *fire and brimstone, and an horrible tempest is the portion of their cup.*

The fourth reason for confirmation of his faith is from the Lord's love, settled upon his upright servants, in the midst of their troubles, while they suffer for righteousness' sake. Whence learn, 11. The respect that the Lord hath to the cause for which his servants suffer, hasteneth on, and fasteneth wrath upon their adversaries: for *the righteous Lord loveth righteousness*, is given as a reason of the sentence in the preceding verse. 12. Though clouds sometimes hide the expressions of the Lord's respect and love towards his people, yet still his love is set upon them; for *continually his countenance doth behold the upright.*

PSALM XII.

To the chief Musician upon Sheminith. A Psalm of David.

The prophet having observed, as is set down, v. 8, how wickedness lifteth up the head in all the land, when the places of power and trust come into the hands of naughty and vile men, giveth direction by his own example unto the godly; first, to have their recourse to God by prayer, while they are borne down by the wicked in such an ill time, v. 1, 2; and next how to comfort themselves by the word of God, pronouncing the sentence of justice upon all loose-tongued men, v. 3, 4; and promising delivery to the oppressed godly, and preservation of his church in all generations, v. 5—7. Howsoever, he suffers wicked men to bear rule sometimes, and wickedness to abound by that means, v. 8.

1. *Help, Lord; for the godly man ceaseth: for the faithful fail from among the children of men.*

2. *They speak vanity every one with his neighbour:* with *flattering lips,* and *with a double heart, do they speak.*

David finding no friend at court, nor any place or power, who either would speak a word in his favour, or give him any friendly counsel, turneth himself to God. Whence learn, 1. The face of the visible church may sometimes be so far defaced, that there cannot be a man found to show himself openly, for a good cause, as here is noted: *the godly man ceaseth, the faithful fail from among the children of men.* 2. In such a case God can and will supply the lack of friends and counsellors to his own, when they say to him, *help Lord; the Lord will help.* 3. At such a time, a godly person may not think upon seditious practices against those that are in lawful authority, but take himself to prayer; for David who had a fairer pretence for such a practice than any private man or men can have, because he was designed successor to the kingdom, goeth to God in this case, and crieth, *help Lord.*

He proveth the lack of godliness and faithfulness, because there was no upright, nor honest dealing among the people, but falsehood and flattery. Whence learn, 4. Where true godliness is out of request, the common bonds of neighbourhood, (including bonds of blood, alliance, and acquaintance,) will fail also, and every one will go about to deceive his neighbour; so that a man cannot trust what another saith: for *they speak vanity every one with his neighbour.* 5. When ungodly men intend most to deceive, then they are sure to speak fairest, giving pleasant words, with insinuation of respects in abundant compliments. They *speak vanity to their neighbour with flattering lips.* 6. Vain talk, cozening speeches, flattering words are unbeseeming honest men, and argue in so far as men affect them, ungodliness, unfaithfulness, and deceitfulness in a man; for when *with flattering lips they speak, with a double heart they speak.*

3. *The Lord shall cut off all flattering lips,* and *the tongue that speaketh proud things;*

4. *Who have said, With our tongue will we prevail; our lips* are *our own: who* is *Lord over us?*

He setteth down in the next place the comforts of the godly, which are three. The first is from God's justice in punishing calumniators of the godly, and proud boasters. Whence learn, 1. Although pickthanks, and flatterers of great men, in prejudice of the godly, hope to stand by their flattery, yet *the Lord shall cut off all flattering lips.* 2. Albeit men in power and place threaten to bring about great things against God's people, yet they shall not be able to do what they have said: *for God shall cut off also the tongue that speaketh proud things.* 3. Wicked men are confident, and assure themselves to double out their course by their falsehood, flattery, and calumnies against the godly; *they have said, With our tongue will we prevail.* 4. Wicked men make no conscience to use well the gifts which they have gotten of God; such as wit or language, or any other thing; for they say, *our lips are our own.* 5. Wicked men stand not in awe of God; they fear not punishment from him, for in effect they say, *who is Lord over us?* But we must learn from their faults three contrary lessons; to wit, 1. That nothing which we have is our own. But, 2. Whatsoever is given to us of God is for service to be done to him. 3. That whatsoever we do, or say, we have a Lord over us, to whom we must be answerable, when he calleth us to account.

5. *For the oppression of the poor, for the sighing of the needy, now will I arise, saith the Lord; I will set* him *in safety* from him that *puffeth at him.*

6. *The words of the Lord* are *pure words :* as *silver tried in a furnace of earth, purified seven times.*

7. *Thou shalt keep them, O Lord, thou shalt preserve them from this generation for ever.*

The second comfort of the godly in an ill time, is from the promise of God, to deliver the godly out of the hand of the wicked. Whence learn, 1. When the Lord hath exercised the godly for a while, with the oppression of the wicked, he will not fail to make manifest, that he hath heard their sad supplications, and seen their oppression ; *for the oppression of the poor, for the sighing of the needy, now will I arise, saith the Lord.* 2. The proud persecutor thinketh little of the godly, or any power that can defend him, but doth mock the hope he hath to be helped ; yet *God will set the godly in safety from him that puffeth at him.*

This promise the prophet commendeth to the church, as a precious truth which will be found forth-coming to the full, in experience. Whence learn, 3. To the end that the word of promise may be comfortable to us, till new experience comes, we must consider whose word it is, and that there is no vanity in promises, but all contained in them, shall be found very solid, like the refined silver, or gold, which is purged from all dross, and the oftener it is put in the fire, it is the more fair, and of greater value ; for *the words are the Lord's words, and pure words,* try-ed, true in his experience, *as silver tried in a furnace of earth seven times,* and clear from all dross.

The third comfort of the godly is from assurance given of the perpetuation of the church, and custody of it by God in all ages. Whence learn, 4. Let men persecute the godly as much as God pleaseth to suffer them, yet shall God preserve a church of godly persons at all times to the end of the world : *for God shall preserve the godly from this generation for ever.* 5. Albeit the discomforted godly, under persecutors, are not always able to draw presently comfort from this promise ; yet it is a truth which God will own, which God will keep in his hand to us, when we come to him, and which every believer must own, though no man should take it off his hand. Therefore doth David turn himself to God, in delivering this charter of the church's safety ; *thou,* saith he, *shalt keep them.*

8. *The wicked walk on every side, when the vilest men are exalted.*

In the close of the psalm, upon his own experience, he draweth up a general observation of what may be expected, when the most wicked are most advanced. Whence learn, 1. God sometimes so disposeth in his wisdom and justice, for punishing of wicked people, and exercising of the god-ly, that the places of government in a kingdom, are filled not with the best men, but with the *vilest of the sons of men ;* for in David's experience it was so, and he presupposeth it might fall to be so, that the vilest of men should be exalted. 2. The wickedness of the ungodly, in this case, breaketh forth most, and spreadeth itself among the subjects, being heartened thereunto by the ruler's toleration, connivance, or instigation, or example, and countenance ; *for when the vilest men are exalted, then the wicked walk on every side.* Turn you where you will, you shall meet with them, at such a time *as the vilest are exalted.*

PSALM XIII.

To the chief Musician. A Psalm of David.

Another Christian experience, wherein David under the sense of desertion, laying forth his lamentable case before the Lord, ver. 1, 2 ; prayeth for relief, ver. 3, 4 ; and by faith is refreshed and comforted, ver. 5. 6.

1. *How long wilt thou forget me, O Lord ? for ever ? how long wilt thou hide thy face from me ?*

2. *How long shall I take counsel in my soul,* having *sorrow in my heart daily ? how long shall mine enemy be exalted over me ?*

In laying forth his grief, he beginneth at his apparent desertion ; then speaking of the perplexity of mind, arising herefrom ; and last of all, he mentioneth the continuance of his outward trouble from his enemies. Whence learn, 1. Trouble outward and inward, of body and spirit, fightings without, and terrors within, vexations from heaven and earth, from God deserting and men pursuing, may fall upon a child of God at one time, and continue for a time long enough, as here ; *how long wilt thou forget me ? how long shall mine enemy be exalted over me ?* 2. When trouble is continued, and an appearance of means of delivery is not, and God both witholdeth inward and outward help, sense calleth this the Lord's *forgetting* and *hiding of his face*: *how long wilt thou forget me, and hide thy face?* 3. The Lord's children in their resolution for faith and patience, set to themselves a shorter period usually than the Lord doth, for making them have their perfect work ; therefore, when their hope is deferred, it makes their heart sick, and cry out, *How long ? how long ?* 4. When comfort trysteth not with our time, fear of eternal off-casting may readily slide in : and this fear, a soul acquainted with God, or that loveth him in any measure, cannot endure : *wilt thou forget me for ever?* saith he.   5. Whatsoever sense speaketh, or suggested temptations speak, faith will relate the business to the Lord, and expect a better speech from him : for in this condition the prophet goeth to God, saying, *How long, O Lord?*   6. A soul finding desertion, multiplieth consultations, falleth into perplexity, changeth conclusions, as a sick man doth his bed, falleth in grief, and cannot endure to live by its own finding, but runneth upon God for direction, as here we see it ; *how long shall I take counsel in my soul, having sorrow in my heart daily?*   7. The enemies taking advantage, (by the continuance of trouble upon the godly,) against his cause and religion, and against God, augmenteth both the grief and temptation of the godly ; *how long shall mine enemies be exalted over me?*

3. *Consider* and *hear me, O Lord my God : lighten mine eyes, lest I sleep the* sleep of *death ;*

4. *Lest mine enemy say, I have prevailed against him ;* and *those that trouble me rejoice when I am moved.*

Now followeth his prayer for some comfortable answer, lest both he should perish, and God be dishonoured : whence learn, 1. The edge of temptations is blunted, and grief assuaged, when the swelling of the soul venteth itself to God : and certainly complaints are then best eased, when they are dissolved in humble supplications, as here, *consider and hear me, O Lord my God.*   2. Albeit faith believeth that God considereth and heareth always, yet it cannot rest till it feel by some effect that he doth hear and consider, by his giving some real support, or help in need, according to covenant ; this is imported in his praying, and words of prayer, *consider, hear me.*   3. If the Lord think it not good to give an outward delivery, faith will be content of a glimpse of God's countenance for the present ; *lighten mine eyes,* saith he ; that is, let me have some immediate comfort to uphold me in the hope of my delivery.   4. It is a death to the godly man who hath seen him that is invisible, to be long without the sense of God's love :

sense of succumbing and perishing in trouble, doth in this case usually set upon the godly, as here, *lighten mine eyes lest I sleep the sleep of death.* 5. The enemies of the godly feed themselves with the trouble of the godly, and rejoice the more they see them in distress and discouragement; which two inconveniences the Lord useth to prevent, for he cannot endure long to see the pride and rejoicing of the enemy to feed itself on the miseries of his children; and this the prophet insinuateth, when he seeketh relief, *lest the enemy glory that he hath prevailed, &c.*

5. *But I have trusted in thy mercy; my heart shall rejoice in thy salvation.*

6. *I will sing unto the Lord, because he hath dealt bountifully with me.*

Here the prophet is raised up unto comfort by degrees : first he settleth himself upon the tried grounds of faith, then promiseth to himself deliverance, and thirdly, findeth comfort: whence learn, 1. Albeit we find not present relief or comfort when we pray, yet we must resolve to adhere to God by faith : when we have poured out our soul in his bosom by prayer, we must resolve to settle our feet on the ground of faith, before we can expect to be comforted : for here David relied on *God's mercy*, and ratifieth his former resolution and practice of resting on his mercy : *I have trusted on thy mercy.* 2. So soon as faith is fixed, and resolute to adhere to covenanted mercy, hope lifteth up the head, and this anchor of the tossed ship stayeth the soul from being driven ; the believer looketh out for God's salvation, by some way of delivery, which God thinks good to give, and assureth himself it shall come, and that he shall find joy in God's way of deliverance : *my heart*, saith he, *shall rejoice in thy salvation.* 3. When the believer is resolved to rest on God's mercy by faith, then followeth peace, at least, and readily more comfort of God's Spirit, than for the present he expected to have : yea, as much as shall satisfy him, and make him count himself richly dealt with, as here David acknowledgeth, saying, *he hath dealt bountifully with me.* 4. Fresh experience of favour from God, in the renewed sense of his good-will to a soul, is a matter of great joy in the midst of trouble ; and the right fruit of it is a renewed resolution cheerfully to praise God, as here we have the example, *I will sing unto the Lord, because he hath dealt bountifully with me.*

PSALM XIV.

To the Chief Musician.   A Psalm of David.

David, looking on the constitution of the visible Church, and seeing the great body of the people lying in their natural state, working iniquity and hating the truly godly amongst them, even to the death, verse, 1—3, comforteth the godly, first by the care the Lord hath of them, in pleading their cause against the ungodly, vers. 4—6, and next by giving hope of better days for the godly, when, after sore plagues come on that people, Christ should manifest himself unto them, vers. 7.

1. *The fool hath said in his heart,* There is *no God. They are corrupt; they have done abominable works;* there is *none that doeth good.*

2. *The Lord looked down from heaven upon the children of men, to see if there were any that did understand,* and *seek God.*

3. *They are all gone aside, they are* all *together become filthy;* there is *none that doeth good, no, not one.*

The prophet divideth all those who were in the visible church, into unregenerate men on the one hand, and God's true people converted inwardly unto him, on the other hand; and argueth all the unregenerate to be practically atheists, without God in the world, by the same proof whereby the apostle convinceth all men in nature, to be in the state of sin, Rom. iii. 13.   Whence learn, 1. Every man so long as he lieth unrenewed and unreconciled unto God (how wise soever, or of how great parts soever he may seem to be to himself or the world), is nothing in effect but a madman, running to his own destruction in losing his soul and eternal life, when he seemeth most to gain the world, therefore he is called *the fool.*   2. It is not heeded by God what a man's mouth saith of God, or of himself, but what his heart saith: *the fool hath said in his heart, There is no God.*   3. It is not the word, or outward profession, which truly exposeth the heart, but the current of a man's life and actions; for here it is proved, that the heart is full of atheism, by this that *they* are *corrupt* in their conversation, *and do abominable works.*   4. God is the only right judge of regeneration and unregeneration, and the only true searcher of the heart: it is *he who looketh down from heaven, to see if any of the sons of men*, or any in the state of nature, have any wisdom in them, or affection after God ; *if any of them have understanding, or seek after God;* for he that doth not seek God, hath no understanding, nor principle of spiritual life in him. 5. Whatsoever may be the odds among unrenewed men, some more, some less gross in their outbreaking, yet God pronounceth of them all *that they are all of them gone out of the way*, to wit, of holiness and happiness, *they are altogether become filthy ;* that is, all their actions, flowing forth from their corrupt hearts, are vile and loathsome in God's sight, and they are all in one rank in this, *there is none of them that doeth good ;* none of them, being unreconciled to God, do, or can do, any thing at all commanded of God, as commanded from right principles, and for right ends.

4. *Have all the workers of iniquity no knowledge ? who eat up my people* as *they eat bread, and call not upon the Lord.*

5. *There were they in great fear : for God* is *in the generation of the righteous.*

6. *Ye have shamed the counsel of the poor, because the Lord* is *his refuge.*

In the next place he comforteth the people of God, living in society of the visible church, with the unrenewed multitude. First, by this, that the Lord doth plead their cause against the ungodly. Whence learn, 1. That the nature of all unrenewed men, is to bear deadly enmity against those that are really God's people, and delight to undo the godly, as contemners of all that live not as they do : *they eat up my people as they eat bread,* saith the Lord. 2. The Lord owns the quarrel, and wrongs done to the godly, as done to him, in whomsoever his image is hated or persecuted : *they eat up my people,* saith he. 3. The causeless hatred of the godly is a most unreasonable thing, and argueth admirable stupidity in wicked men, who malign the innocent, by whose life they are admonished of their duty, and taught the way to felicity: *have all the workers of iniquity no knowledge ?* 4. The miskenning of God, and working of iniquity, and persecuting of the godly, are three

conjunct properties of a man in nature, not reconciled to
God: *for to be workers of iniquity, and eaters up of God's
people as bread, and not calling on God*, are put for the
marks and properties of the same sort of ungodly men.

Upon the challenge of the ungodly, the prophet inferreth
the consequence of certain and sad judgments to follow on
the wicked, because God is nearly concerned in the quarrel
of his people. Whence learn, 5. The persecution of piety
in the godly, provoketh God to inflict the most fearful and
most sudden judgments: *for therein specially were the ungodly put to fear, where they had no fear at all.* 6. The
near conjunction which God hath with the godly, is the
reason of the greatness of the sin of persecution of them for
godliness: for here it is given for a reason why *there* they
were in fear, why they were to tremble when God came to
avenge the oppression of the godly, which the wicked never
feared to be questioned: *because God is in the generation of
the righteous.* 7. Persecuting a man for piety, were it but
in jesting at a man, or mocking of him for piety, is the
turning of piety, which is a man's glory, into a matter of
reproach to him; and a means to drive him and others from
seeking of God: *you have shamed the counsel*, or resolution,
of the poor, when you scorn, because he hath made God his
refuge.

7. *Oh that the salvation of Israel were* come *out of
Zion! When the Lord bringeth back the captivity of
his people, Jacob shall rejoice*, and *Israel shall be glad.*

The next comfort of the godly, is from the hope of
Christ's coming, in whom the redressing of this evil, and of
all other, is to be found, for whose coming he wisheth. It
is true, the sending of deliverance unto the distressed people
of God in Saul's time, by bringing David to the kingdom,
was worthy to be wished for: but this could not fill up the
measure of the wish here stirred up by the Spirit. Therefore we must look to the substance in Christ, in whom this
wish and prayer hath full accomplishment, which in effect
is, *O that Christ the Saviour of Israel were come out of Zion.*
And this same wish closeth the fifty-third psalm also;
where salvations of Israel in the plural number is set down,
to note the perfection of salvation which cometh only by
Christ, at whom the very form of the Hebrew wishing doth

look, as pointing at the person which shall give all sort of
salvation to Israel, *who shall give;* now there was a coming of Christ in the flesh *unto Zion,* foretold by the Spirit,
Zech. ix. 9, and this is presupposed in this wish; for
Christ must be in Zion before he come out of it.   But not
by this coming were so many Israelites saved as here is wished for; not by this coming was the body of Israel brought
back from the captivity here prophesied.   There is also, Isaiah
ii. 3, a coming of Christ *out of Zion* to the *Gentiles;* and this
coming is presupposed here, before that Israel's captivity be
loosed.   There is, Isaiah lix. 20, compared with Rom. xi. 26,
a coming out of *Zion* for the bringing salvation to the body of
the now misbelieving nation of the captive Israelites, lying in
captivity, scattered among the Gentiles, and this is directly
prayed for, and longed after in this place: *O that the salvation
of Israel were come out of Zion,* even the time when the Lord
shall bring back the captivity of his people.   Paul, Rom. xi.
26, calleth this the Redeemer's coming *out of Zion,* in regard
of the time when, and the condition wherein Christ is to find
the Israelites, to wit, *out of Zion,* out among the Gentiles,
scattered among the Gentiles, to whom Christ came when he
left Judea.   And Isaiah calleth it a coming *to Zion,* in respect
to the benefit to be given to the Jews, who are designed oft by
Zion.   Whence learn, 1. Christ is the salvation of *Zion,* both
figuratively and properly called so, as well before he came as
after; for here he is looked on as the *salvation of Israel,*
in whom all our salvation, Jews or Gentiles, is founded.
2. Whosoever seeth him, (from how far off soever,) cannot
choose but long for a further manifestation of him, for perfecting of the blessedness of his people: *O that the salvation
of Israel were come out of Zion!*   3. It was revealed to
the prophets, that Christ was to come to the church of the
Jews, and from thence to manifest himself to the Gentiles,
casting off the Israelites for a time, scattering them among
the Gentiles, and then to come about again towards the
Jews in their scattering and captivity, without casting off
the Gentiles; and this last turn is in the prophet's eye,
and aimed at by the Spirit, when he wisheth that *the salvation of Israel were come out of Zion.*   4. It was revealed
also to the prophets, and to David, that before the constitution of the church of Israel should be freed from the
persecution of domestic enemies, vexing the hearts of the

godly, or delivered from such men's power, as are described, v. 1—3, that sore plagues were to be poured out upon that people, and that the Israelites were to be driven out of their own land, and led in captivities, as the words here, and Psalm liii. 6, import; for they who were to be brought back from captivity after Christ's coming out of Zion unto the Gentiles, are presupposed to be in captivity, when Christ cometh to give salvation unto them. 5. Because of the large pouring out of the Spirit upon the body of the converted Jews or Israelites, when the time shall come of their turning Christians, prophesied of here, and Isaiah lix. 20, and Rom. xi. 25, 26, as their mourning in repentance for the injuries done by them and their progenitors, to Jesus Christ, shall be as the mourning of Hadadrimmon, in the valley of Megiddon, Zech. xii. 10, 11; so here, joy in Jesus Christ reconciled unto them, shall be greater than any that ever that nation saw, whether in David's time, or Solomon's: for then *the Lord shall bring back the captivity of his people,* here prophesied of, to be under the time of the gospel, (whether by loosing their captivity bodily as well as spiritual, whether they shall return to their own land or not, or what the Scripture speaketh to this purpose, this place is not for the determining of it.) *Then Jacob shall rejoice, and Israel shall be glad, when the Saviour of Israel shall come out of Zion to them.*

PSALM XV.

A Psalm of David.

The prophet, for distinguishing of the true members of the church from those who were only outwardly professors, asketh of the Lord how the one may be known from the other, ver. 1, and receiveth answer to the question, ver. 2—5.

1. *Lord, who shall abide in thy tabernacle? who shall dwell in thy holy hill?*

The question is proposed about the marks of the sincere believers, the true covenanters with God, the true professors of true religion; they who shall not be cast out from the society of God's true church. Whence learn, 1. The tabernacle pitched by Moses, and the hill of Zion, where the tabernacle and the temple were at last settled, was a type of the true church, and of communion with God in Christ the

Mediator, a type of God incarnate, dwelling, and exercising all his offices in his church, and of the heavenly condition of his people called out of the world, and lifted up toward him, designed under the name of God's tabernacle, and
God's holy hill. 2. Some of those who profess to be of
this fellowship may be thrust out from it again, and debarred from all communion with God, when other some
shall remain in this state, and not be removed. For the
question is moved, What are the marks of the members of
the church invisible ? and who they are *who shall abide in
God's tabernacle, and dwell in his holy hill?* 3. Only the
Lord who searcheth the heart, can put the difference between the true and the false ; for this cause the question is
proposed to God, *Lord, who shall abide in thy tabernacle?*

2. *He that walketh uprightly, and worketh righteousness, and speaketh the truth in his heart.*

3. He that *backbiteth not with his tongue, nor doeth
evil to his neighbour, nor taketh up a reproach against
his neighbour.*

4. *In whose eyes a vile person is contemned ; but
he honoureth them that fear the Lord :* he that *sweareth to* his own *hurt, and changeth not.*

5. He that *putteth not out his money to usury, nor
taketh reward against the innocent. He that doeth
these* things *shall never be moved.*

The Lord answereth in the rest of the Psalm, by showing the fruits of faith manifested in obedience to God's
commands, both moral and judicial, in the sight of all men :
the sincerity of which faith and truth was to be certainly
known to God only, and to the conscience of every man's
self ; which was sufficient to satisfy the question, quieting
and comforting of the upright ones. Whence learn, 1.
The sincere endeavour of universal obedience in a man's
conversation, is a fruit and evidence of true faith, and a
mark of a true member of the church invisible ; *he walketh uprightly and doth righteousness.* 2. Another fruit of
true faith is conscience-making of what a man speaketh,
ruling his tongue so, as his heart and his tongue agree in
the truth : *he speaketh the truth from the heart.* 3. A
third fruit of unfeigned faith, is making conscience in all his
dealings, that he harm not his neighbour, neither in his

name, nor in his person, nor his goods : and making conscience not to receive readily a false report of his neighbour, when it is devised by another ; *he backbiteth not with
his tongue, nor doeth evil to his neighbour, nor taketh up a
reproach against his neighbour.* 4. A fourth fruit of sound
faith, is the low estimation of any worldly excellency wherewith a wicked man can be busked ; to whom, although the
godly, according to duty, will give civil honour, as his
place requireth, yet he counteth him a poor miserable man
for all his honour and wealth, because he walketh in a godless way : but where he seeth one that feareth God, he esteemeth highly of him in his heart, whatsoever external expressions thereof he find fit to give, because of the honourable way of holiness, wherein the godly walketh ; *for in his
eyes a vile person is contemned, but he honoureth him that
feareth the Lord.* 5. A fifth fruit of sound faith, is tender
respect to the name of God, and care to keep lawful promises, covenants, and oaths, whatsoever civil inconveniences
may follow upon the strict keeping of them ; *though he
swear to his own damage, he changeth not.* 6. A sixth
fruit and evidence of faith, is dispensing with commodity,
when God, by a special reason, calleth for so doing, albeit
otherwise a man might take reasonably more gain. Many
of such sort of cases occur in merchandise, and in exacting
rents and debts, as circumstances may teach, when and
where God calleth for most moderation. Such was the
judicial dispensing with commodity, put upon the Jews, for
loosing the yoke of a bought servant, being a Jew, at the
end of six years ; and quitting of houses and lands bought
from a Jew at the year of jubilee, how dear soever it cost
the buyer ; and not taking usury of a Jew ; wherein the
Jew was privileged above men of another country : for in
all these three particulars, it was lawful for the Jew to do
otherwise with other countrymen, to wit, in buying a servant from a stranger, and not letting him loose all his days,
and buying land from a stranger of another country, and
transmitting it to his own posterity, and taking usury of a
stranger, according to the rate which was acknowledged on
all hands to stand with equity ; which commodity, if an
Israelite did not dispense with towards an Israelite, it made
him short of this commendation of the true Israelite, *who
putteth not his money to usury.* 7. The seventh fruit and

evidence of faith, is freedom from bribery, with love of justice, which the believer will not pervert, to the detriment of the man who hath a good cause, for whatsoever bud or reward man can give him. This is the upright man's last property, *he taketh not a reward against the innocent.*

Having numbered out the evidences of a sound convert and true believer, who shall never be thrust out of God's fellowship, he concludeth, *that whosoever doeth these things,* or studieth to do them, *shall never be moved;* that is, he that shall evidence his faith in God, by a sincere endeavour to do the duties of the first and second tables of God's law, shall not be removed from God's house, but shall abide in his tabernacle, and dwell in Zion, in the fellowship of God and his saints for ever.

PSALM XVI.

Michtam of David.

David, in this Psalm, finding himself in the state of grace, prayeth for preservation in general, in relation to all dangers and evils of body and soul, and whatsoever other evil, from which a godly man, with allowance of God's word, might pray to be preserved. His only reason to assure himself to be heard, is, because he had gotten grace to trust in God; the sincerity of which trust in God, he proveth by sundry evidences, ver. 1—4. In the second place, he climbeth up to the comfort and joy of believing; and all the grounds of joy whereupon he goeth, serve both to confirm his faith and to give him assurance of the granting of his prayer, ver. 6—11.

1. *Preserve me, O God: for in thee do I put my trust.*

He findeth himself in a good condition, and all the prayers he prayeth, are, in one word, for preservation. Whence learn, 1. As our being, living, and moving natural, and our bringing into the spiritual and blessed estate of grace, is of the Lord, so is our keeping therein of the Lord also, and our duty is to acknowledge God in both, and to live unto, and pray for, his upholding of us, and not to lean upon our own wisdom, strength, or holiness; for David teacheth so to do; *preserve me, O God.* 2. The grace of God having granted to us lively faith, settled on God, is a sufficient ground of our hope, and assurance to persevere, and to be still preserved, for this is the reason whereby David confirmeth his prayer, *for in thee do I put my trust.*

D

2. *O* my soul, *thou hast said unto the Lord, Thou* art *my Lord: my goodness* extendeth *not to thee ;*

3. But *to the saints that* are *in the earth, and to the excellent, in whom* is *all my delight.*

Because he hath made his faith in God, the reason of his hope of perseverance, and of his having his prayer granted, he proveth the sincerity of his faith by five evidences or fruits thereof. Whence learn, 1. The first solid evidence of the sincerity of saving faith, is the testimony of the conscience, bearing witness to a man, that he hath laid hold on the covenant of grace, and hath chosen God for his protector and master, and that he is resolved to depend upon God, and to serve him, as David did, saying, *O my soul, thou hast said unto the Lord, Thou art my Lord.* 2. Another evidence of the sincerity of faith, is renunciation of all confidence in a man's own works, and the rejecting of all conceit of any possibility of merit at God's hand, who cannot be profited by our goodness ; for we have what we have of him, and can never put an obligation on him by any thing which we can do: *my goodness doth not extend to thee.* 3. A third fruit and evidence of faith, is love and kindness to the godly, and bestowing of our own goods for supplying their need, joined with a high estimation of their preciousness, above the godless world, and with pleasure-taking in their fellowship ; so reckoneth the prophet, saying, *my goodness extendeth not to thee, but to the saints that are on the earth, and to the excellent, in whom is all my delight :* where, by the way, let us observe, he knew no saints to whom he could be profitable, save only the saints who are *upon the earth.*

4. *Their sorrows shall be multiplied* that *hasten* after *another* god : *their drink-offerings of blood will I not offer, nor take up their names into my lips.*

A fourth fruit and evidence of faith, is, the hating of false religion, and counting all followers of idolatry, or worship of another god, than the true God, to be accursed ; such a hating of false religion as is accompanied with the discountenancing, open discrediting, and abhorring of all idol service, as David expresseth here in the whole verse. Whence learn, 1. Men, as they are naturally averse from following the true God and the true religion, so are they naturally bent to all idolatry, and zealous in following idols, and any false religion ; *they hasten after another god.* 2. The more men hasten after felicity in the way of idolatry, they have the worse speed ; for *their sorrows shall be multiplied that hasten after another God.* 3. The more madly the world run after idolatry, the more shall the faithful man testify his abomination thereof, as David doth. *Their drink-offerings of blood will I not offer,* nor take up *their names into my lips.* He cannot speak of them without disdain.

5. *The Lord is the portion of mine inheritance and of my cup : thou maintainest my lot.*

A fifth fruit and evidence of faith in God, is delight and satisfaction in, and resting on God, as all-sufficient for the believer's complete happiness, as the whole verse holdeth forth. Whence learn, 1. The believer hath as sure right unto God, as any man hath to the patrimony whereunto he is born ; or any tribe ever had to his share in the land of Canaan. *The Lord is the portion of his inheritance.* 2. The Lord is the believer's lot and share, when the world are seeking, some one, some another temporal good; *the Lord, and the light of his countenance,* is the believer's complete good ; whatsoever measure of earthly things is given to the godly beside, Levi's portion is his portion : *the Lord is the portion of his inheritance.* 3. The Lord is the believer's livelihood, and the furnisher of his daily bread ; *he is the portion of his cup.* 4. The Lord giveth himself to the believer for his felicity, as he also maintaineth the believer in the right unto, and possession of himself : *he maintaineth his lot;* and so, as the believer cometh to his right he hath unto God, not by his own purchase, but by spiritual birth-right, as a child of Christ by faith, or by free donation of this inheritance, received of God by faith ; so he may lay claim to God, and enjoy the possession of God, as firmly as his inheritance ; as fully as if God were his particular property and portion ; as sweetly as his daily food, and the portion of his domestic cup : and with as great quietness and security, as the immediate vassal of the mightiest monarch, being willing, able, and engaged most deeply to maintain his lot.

6. *The lines are fallen unto me in pleasant places; yea, I have a goodly heritage.*

In the second place he climbeth up to the joy of faith, arising from the certain persuasion, and present sense of his being in the state of grace. The reasons or grounds of his joy are six. The first reason of his joy, is founded upon the properties and self-sufficiency of God, compared to a *goodly* and pleasant *heritage*, which wanteth no commodity within itself. Whence learn, 1. Pleasure and profit, and all commodities of life, are abundantly to be found in God ; and whatsoever can be represented by any goodly heritage, lying in most pleasant places, is but a shadow of what is to be found in him, as the comparison taken from lower things here importeth. 2. The more the believer considereth what the Lord is, and what are his perfections, and what is the believer's own interest in God, the more is he satisfied, and ravished in the beholding of God, and his own felicity in him. No wonder, therefore, if David say, for the measuring out of this share to him, *that his lines are fallen out to him in pleasant places, &c.* 3. The believer hath liberty to appropriate God in a manner to himself, and in comparison with the share of the worldlings, to prefer his own portion above all others. This doth David, when he calleth God his *own pleasant places, and his own heritage.*

7. *I will bless the Lord, who hath given me counsel ; my reins also instruct me in the night-seasons.*

The second reason and ground of joy, is because God hath persuaded him to believe in the Messiah, or Christ to come, as is clear by the next verse, and that God hath taken the directing of him. Whence learn, 1. As it is the work of God only, to give effectual counsel to any man to believe in Christ ; so also the way of persuasion of a soul to trust in God, is a way of working, proper only to God ; for it maketh the man so free an agent, in the act of believing, as if God's work were counsel only, and the work of active persuasion so invincible, as the work is effectually wrought and infallibly : for he calleth the bestowing of saving faith, or grace to consent to the covenant of grace, a giving counsel : *he hath given me counsel.* 2. The glory of trusting in God, is not a matter of gloriation of the believer, in his own disposing of himself, but a matter of thanksgiving to God, and glorifying of him, who giveth the counsel to believe, and maketh the counsel to him effectual ; for David saith, *I will bless the Lord who hath given me counsel :* to wit, effectually ; for faith is not of ourselves, it is the gift of God, wherein flexanimous power and voluntary consent are sweetly joined together. 3. This mercy of powerfully persuading a soul to make choice of God, to close in covenant with him, and to trust in him, putteth a perpetual obligation of thanksgiving unto God upon the believer, to make him say in all time coming, and for ever, *I will bless the Lord, who hath given me counsel.* 4. With the gift of saving faith, or persuasive counsel to believe in God, is joined the sweet guiding and directing of the Lord's spirit, how to order the ways of the believer ; for here instruction of him in the night-season, is joined with the former mercy, and is made a reason of thanksgiving and blessing of God : for he addeth, *my reins also shall instruct me in the night-seasons.* 5. The framing of the will, desire, appetite, affections, inclinations, thoughts, and secret meditations, is so inward, secret, and deep a work, as the Spirit of God thinks good to express this his giving discretion secretly to David, in the terms of the teaching of the reins, because they are the most hidden parts of the body, and nearest to the back of any of the inward noble parts ; and because of the nature of the reins, which have much affinity with the affections, and have for their office the discretive purging of the blood, the natural furniture of life, *my reins also instruct me in the night-seasons.*

8. *I have set the Lord always before me : because he is at my right hand, I shall not be moved.*

The third reason and ground of joy, is the gift of the grace of God, making him always keep his eye (for getting assistance, direction, and comfort,) to good purpose upon Jesus Christ, the Lord, of whom this place is exposed, Acts ii. 25. Whence learn, 1. The duty of the believer, and the way for him to have and retain joy in the Lord, is to fix the eye of faith, always, in all estates, on the Mediator, the promised Messiah, the Lord Jesus, for direction, assistance, comfort, and delivery. For this was David's way, *I have set the Lord always before my face.* 2. Such as implore Jesus Christ for all things in all estates, shall be sure to have his effectual presence near hand to help him in time of need ; for *he is at such a man's right hand, at all times.* 3. Faith, kept in exercise by employing of Jesus Christ, may have assurance of perseverance, and enjoying constantly the state of grace: whatever alterations and commotions come, their state shall stand fixed ; they shall stand in grace; for upon this ground the prophet saith, *I shall never be moved.*

9. *Therefore my heart is glad, and my glory rejoiceth ; my flesh also shall rest in hope:*

A fourth reason of joy abounding in his heart, and breaking forth in his words, is his victory over death and the grave, by faith in Jesus Christ. Whence learn, 1. Faith in Christ is able not only to give peace that passeth understanding, but also to fill the heart with joy, and to make the tongue, which is a man's glory, above all other creatures, sometime to break forth in expressions of joy; for *therefore,* saith he, *my heart is glad, and my glory rejoiceth.* 2. So great victory over death and the grave is gotten by faith in Jesus Christ, that a believer can lay down his body in the grave, as in a bed, to rest it there, in hope of the resurrection ; and here an instance and example of it, *my flesh also shall rest in hope.*

10. *For thou wilt not leave my soul in hell ; neither wilt thou suffer thine Holy One to see corruption.*

The first reason of his joy is the assurance of the resurrection of Jesus Christ, his head, through whom he hopeth to be raised in his own order and time. Whence learn, 1. A believer is so nearly joined with Christ, that he may give to him the styles of what is nearest and dearest to him, and call him his very life and soul, as here David saith of Christ, who behoved to rise again, Acts ii. 25, *thou wilt not leave my soul* (or my life) *in the grave :* and by this means he also is assured of his own resurrection in due time ; for our life and soul is bound up in Christ, our life is hid with God in Christ, specially in respect of that wherein he standeth in our room, such as his suffering, rising, reigning, as our surety and attorney. 3. The body of Christ not only was to rise from the dead, but also could not so much as putrefy in the grave : for of Christ he saith, *thou wilt not suffer thy Holy One to see corruption.*

11. *Thou wilt show me the path of life : in thy presence is fulness of joy ; at thy right hand there are pleasures for evermore.*

The last ground and reason of his joy, is the assurance

he hath of blessedness and of eternal life; whence learn, 1. The believer who is fixed by faith on Christ, may be assured of his perseverance in the way leading to life : *thou wilt show me the way to life;* that is, thou wilt point out the way that I should walk in, thou wilt go alongst with me, and make me effectually find thy help, to walk in it. 2. The fruition of God's immediate presence is not like the joys of this world, which neither feed nor fill a man: but when we shall enjoy God's presence fully, we shall have full contentment, and complete felicity, for *in his presence is fulness of joy.* And the felicity of believers is not like the pleasures of this world, which pass away suddenly as a dream : but it endureth for ever. *At his right hand are pleasures for evermore.*

PSALM XVII.

A Prayer of David.

This psalm, according to the inscription thereof, is a *prayer of David*, mixed with sundry reasons for helping; wherein, first, he craveth, in general, justice in the controversy between him and his oppressors, ver. 1—4. Secondly, more specially he requesteth for a wise carriage of himself under this exercise, ver. 5, 6. Thirdly, prayeth for protection and preservation from his enemies, ver. 7—12. Fourthly, for disappointment to his enemies, and for delivery of himself from them, ver. 13, 14, and closeth comfortably in confidence of a good answer, and hope of satisfactory happiness, ver. 15.

1. *Hear the right, O Lord, attend unto my cry; give ear unto my prayer,* that goeth *not out of feigned lips.*

2. *Let my sentence come forth from thy presence; let thine eyes behold the things that are equal.*

3. *Thou hast proved mine heart; thou hast visited me in the night; thou hast tried me,* and *shalt find nothing: I am purposed* that *my mouth shall not transgress.*

4. *Concerning the works of men, by the word of thy lips I have kept* me from *the paths of the destroyer.*

The first part of the prayer is unto God, as a righteous judge, to hear his plaint, and to decide in his favour, according to his just cause, and righteous carriage in relation to his enemies : whence learn, 1. As righteous men are subject unto injuries and oppressions, as well as others are, and are driven by trouble to seek relief of God, as in this case ; it is a special comfort to have God, a righteous judge, to hear them, and a righteous cause to bring before him, that the man may say, *Hear the right, O Lord.* 2. The conscience of earnest and honest dealing with God, in the singleness of our heart, in prayer, is a good reason to help our faith in prayer, when we may say, We *cry* and *pray not with feigned lips.* 3. When we are unjustly condemned by men, we may appeal to God, and call the appellation, and seek and expect a more just sentence pronounced and executed by God ; we may say, *Let my sentence come forth from thy presence.* 4. Although men cast out our true defences, which we make against false libels, and do not respect equity ; yet God will take notice of the whole process, *his eyes will behold things that are equal.* 2. Sincerity of heart giveth boldness to a man to present himself to God, to be examined, after that the conscience, in its private trial of the man's carriage toward the adversary, hath, in the sight of God, absolved him ; as here the prophet, in relation to his carriage toward the oppressor, speaketh to God, *thou hast tried me in the night, and hast found nothing.* 6. Sincerity of carriage for time by-past, must be joined with a purpose of sincerity in time coming, that he may say with David, in relation to his part, *I am purposed that my mouth shall not transgress :* that is, not to speak a wrong word against him. Natural men's manner of dealing, when they are injured, is to recompense evil for evil ; for *the works of men* are to follow *the paths of the destroyer.* 8. There is no way to keep the children of God from these paths of the destroyer, when they are provoked to injuries, except in the fear of God, they look to what God's word directeth them to do. Thus did David escape an ill course, when his nature might have tempted him to it. *By the words of thy lips have I kept me from the paths of the destroyer.*

5. *Hold up my goings in thy paths,* that *my footsteps slip not.*

6. *I have called upon thee ; for thou wilt hear me, O God : incline thine ear unto me,* and *hear my speech.*

The second part of the prayer, wherein he requesteth for grace to be kept still in a righteous and holy way ; whence learn, 1. The most holy man, though he have stood fast formerly, is most feared to offend, and most suspicious of himself, and most earnest with God to be holden up, that he fall not in time to come; and giveth all the glory of his standing in a good cause unto God, as is evidently holden forth in this petition of David, *Hold up my goings in thy paths, that my footsteps slip not.* 2. The best way to have deliverance from, and victory over adversaries, is to keep a straight course of carriage in the fear of God; *going in God's paths;* that is, as God hath prescribed our way in his word. 3. Our prayer should be such, and so put up, as we may be sure to be heard; and when we have prayed unto God, according to his will, we may be confident of a good answer with David, *that he will incline his ear, and hear our speech.* 4. Confidence to be heard, must not slacken our hands in prayer, but hearten us to pray, as this example teacheth us.

7. *Show thy marvellous loving-kindness, O thou that savest by thy right hand them which put their trust in thee, from those that rise up* against them.

8. *Keep me as the apple of the eye; hide me under the shadow of thy wings.*

The third part of his prayer, is, for a merciful protection, and preservation from his enemies. Whence learn, 1. The believer must hold his eye in time of dangers and straits, especially upon God's good-will and kindness, as a counter-balance to all the malice of men: and here, though his straits were never so great, he shall read a possibility of wonders for his delivery, as here is seen: *show thy marvellous loving-kindness, O Lord.* Beside common favours, God hath other mercies in keeping for his own, and those are marked even with some wonderfulness, either in the time, or manner, or measure, or mean, or some other respect. 2. The Lord's power and his office of Saviourship, and his constant manner of dealing for believers, are the pillars of the persuasion of help to be had in God; so reasons David, saying, *O thou that savest with thy right hand them which put their trust in thee:* for God's nature, Christ's office, and his manner of dealing, are equivalent to promises, when they are looked unto by a believer. 3. Such as trouble unjustly them, of whom the Lord hath taken the maintenance, do in a sort engage God to be their party, and to defend his servants, *for they rise up against* not only God's servants, but against *God who saveth by his right hand.* 4. The care God hath of his poor children, that depend upon him, is unspeakable; and the tender love he beareth unto them, no one similitude can express, as plurality of similitudes, joined here, give evidence; for God's care of them is comparable to man's care *of the apple of his eye;* God's love to them is comparable to the love of the bird-mother toward her young ones, whom she warmeth, and *hideth under the shadow of her wings.* O wonderful goodness, and wisdom of God, who admitteth himself to be compared to such low similitudes, that he might lift up our faith above all objections of misbelief.

9. *From the wicked that oppress me,* from *my deadly enemies,* who *compass me about.*

10. *They are enclosed in their own fat: with their mouth they speak proudly.*

11. *They have now compassed us in our steps; they have set their eyes bowing down to the earth;*

12. *Like as a lion that is greedy of his prey,* and as *it were a young lion lurking in secret places.*

The reason of his prayer, is taken from the deadly malice of his enemies, v. 9; from their pride, v. 10; from their confidence, v. 11; from their beastly cruelty, v. 12. Whence learn, 1. The enemies of God's people are ordinarily wicked, oppressors, deadly enemies to them, proud of their wealth and power, boasters, crafty foxes, cruel lions : and the more of these evils break forth against God's people, the more should the dangers be laid before God ; not for information of him, but for the exoneration of our griefs, temptations, fears, and dangers before God, and laying of our care upon him : and so much the more also is vengeance on the enemy, and the delivery of the godly near hand ; and hopes of answering the prayers put up against them, are the more made certain, as the use of the wickedness of the enemy made by the prophet here teacheth.

13. *Arise, O Lord; disappoint him, cast him down: deliver my soul from the wicked,* which is *thy sword:*

14. *From men* which are *thy hand, O Lord, from men of the world* which have *their portion in* this *life, and whose belly thou fillest with thy hid* treasure : *they*

are full of children, and leave the rest of their substance *to their babes.*

The fourth part of the prayer is, for frustrating the intention of the enemy, and setting the supplicant free from
the danger. Whence learn, 1. When danger is most nigh,
God is more nigh, and he can shortly interpose himself, to
the overturning of the design of the enemy, and to the ruin
of the enemy himself: be can quickly *arise, and disappoint him, and cast him down.* 2. The power of the enemy
standeth in the Lord's employing him; he cannot strike,
except God strike by him; therefore he is called *God's
sword.* 3. The shortest way to be safe from what the
wicked can do, is prayer to God, to overrule him. Therefore saith David, *deliver my soul from the wicked, which is
thy sword.* 4. The Lord ordinarily for execution of wrath,
and for hard trials, and troubles of the godly, doth in his
providence make use of the wicked; *deliver me,* saith he,
from men which are thy hand. 5. The wicked neither
have, nor seek any felicity, but what may be had in this
life, *they are men of this world, and have their portion in
this life,* they need look for no more good than they find
in the world, and that is, *a poor,* and sorry happiness. 6.
The belly full of sensual lust, and rarest dishes, and best
meats which God's store-house can afford, is the height of
the happiness of a poor rich worldling. In his own person, it is all that God giveth him for his portion, and which
the fool hath chosen, even the *filling of his belly with
God's hid treasure,* or of some rare meat, which meaner
people cannot have, and therefore it is called *God's hid
treasure.* 7. All the felicity which the worldling can have,
in the point of honour and riches to himself, and his posterity, is worldly wealth while he liveth, and a number of
children to enjoy his wealth after him; whether they shall
live and inherit it, whether they shall prove wise men or
fools, he knoweth not; this is his all; for in God's favour
he hath no interest; heaven he hath nothing to do with;
and at the best, *they are full of children, and leave the rest
of their substance to their babes.*

15. *As for me, I will behold thy face in righteousness: I shall be satisfied, when I awake, with thy
likeness.*

He closeth his prayer comfortably, with the hope of true felicity in fellowship with God. Whence learn, 1. In the midst of whatsoever worldly trouble the godly can be, his hope is far better than the worldly man's possession; and the prophet here, for this cause, doth prefer his present condition being in danger daily of his life, to all his enemies' prosperity, saying, by way of opposition, *as for me, I will behold thy face.* 2. The enjoying of the presence, and sense of the loving-kindness of the Lord, is the felicity of the godly, in that measure they attain it; the hope whereof upholds the believer's heart in the darkest times of trouble. *As for me,* saith he, *I will behold thy face.* 3. The enjoying of God is proper only unto the man justified by faith, and endeavouring to live righteously; and it is righteousness with God, that such a man be brought to the enjoying of his hope, *I will behold thy face in righteousness,* saith he. 4. There is a sleep of deadness of spirit, out of which the shining of God's loving countenance awaketh a believer and reviveth the spirit of the contrite ones; and there is a sleep of death bodily, out of which the loving-kindness of the Lord shall awake all his own, in the day of the resurrection, when he shall so change them into the similitude of his own holiness and glorious felicity as they shall be fully contented for ever; and this first and second delivery out of all trouble, may every believer expect and promise to himself: *I shall be satisfied, when I awake, with thy likeness.*

PSALM XVIII.

To the chief Musician. A Psalm *of David, the servant of the Lord, who spake unto the Lord the words of this Song, in the day* that *the Lord delivered him from the hand of all his enemies, and from the hand of Saul. And he said:*

David in this psalm, as a type of Christ, and fellow partaker of the sufferings of Christ in his mystical members, and of deliveries and victories over his and their enemies, being now settled in the kingdom, praiseth God for his marvellous mercies; and as a type of Christ, he prophesieth of the enlargement and stability of his own kingdom, and of Christ's kingdom, represented thereby; and first obligeth himself thankfully to depend upon God, whatsoever enemies he shall have to deal with, v. 1—3. Secondly, he giveth a reason of his resolution, from the experience of the Lord's delivering of him out of his deepest distresses, v. 4—19. Thirdly, he amplifieth this mercy, acknowledging that this was a fruit of his faith, and righteous dealing with his party adversary; the like whereof every believer might expect, as well as he, for the time coming, by reason of this his by-gone large experience, from v. 20—30. Fourthly, he praiseth God in particular, for the experience he hath had in time by-gone in warfare, and victories in battle, to v. 43. Fifthly, as a type of Christ, he promiseth to himself the enlargement of his own kingdom, and prophesieth of the enlargement of Christ's kingdom among the Gentiles, for which he praiseth God unto the end of the psalm, v. 43—50.

In the inscription, he telleth the time, and occasion of his writing of this song, whence learn, 1. That after long trouble, the Lord will give his children rest at last, one way or other, and delivery from all their enemies, as here is given to David from Saul and all his enemies. 2. When the believer getteth relaxation from trouble, he should set himself to glorify God for his delivery, and give evidence of his thankfulness, as David doth in penning this song, when God delivered him. 3. It is a greater honour to be a real servant of the Lord in any calling, than to have the honour of being a king, not being his servant: so esteemed David when he made this inscription, *a psalm of David, the servant of the Lord.*

1. *I will love thee, O Lord, my strength.*

2. *The Lord is my rock, and my fortress, and my deliverer; my God, my strength, in whom I will trust; my buckler, and the horn of my salvation,* and *my high tower.*

3. *I will call upon the Lord,* who is *worthy to be praised: so shall I be saved from mine enemies.*

In the first part of the psalm, he settleth his resolution yet more to love God, to believe in him, and to worship him still in all difficulties, knowing by experience, this to be the way to be saved from all his enemies. Whence learn, 1. The chief fruit of faith, and end of God's mercies to us, is to grow in estimation of, and affection towards God: for so doth David, saying, *I will love thee, O Lord.* 2. Whatsoever a believer hath need of, that will the Lord supply; that will the Lord be himself unto him according to his need, as here he is David's strength in weakness; his rock of refuge, when he is pursued; his fortress, when besieged; and his deliverer when in extreme danger. 3. Experience of the Lord's faithfulness, and kindness to us, should confirm us in the covenant of grace, and strengthen our resolution to believe in him: for upon this account David calleth the Lord, *my God, my strength, in*

whom I will trust. 4. When the believer is yoked in fight
with whatsoever adversary, he shall be sure to have defence
in it, delivery out of it, and preservation after it.   Therefore doth David glory in God, as a buckler to be opposed
to all blows, and throws of darts from adversaries, as the
horn of his salvation, powerfully fighting for his delivery
and victory: and as his high tower, whence he might look
down, and despise all the wit, malice, and power of his
enemies.   5. Prayer and invocation of God, should be
always joined with praises and thanksgiving, and used as a
means, whereby faith may extract the good which it
knoweth is in God, and of which he hath made promise, *I
will call upon the Lord who is worthy to be praised.*
6. Delivery, safety, and peace may the believer expect, as
the answer of his invocation upon God: *so shall I be safe
from mine enemy.*

4. *The sorrows of death compassed me, and the
floods of ungodly men made me afraid.*

5. *The sorrows of hell compassed me about; the
snares of death prevented me.*

In the second part, he bringeth forth his experience,
whereby he was encouraged unto the foresaid duties:
whence learn, 1. Although the word of God be infinitely
sure, and true in itself, yet experience of the truth thereof,
helpeth much to strengthen our gripping thereof, and to
cherish hope, as here is declared.   2. The believer in his
exercise, may be put hard to it, and brought in sight of
apparent perishing of soul and body; while men seek his
life, God for a time hideth his face: for David felt deadly
fears, and extreme torment of soul, even *the sorrows of
death, the sorrows of hell, and the snares of death preventing him,* that he could not get free from them.

6. *In my distress I called upon the Lord, and cried
unto my God: he heard my voice out of his temple, and
my cry came before him,* even *into his ears.*

He hath set down the strait he was in; now he setteth
down the mean he used to be relieved, to wit, prayer to
God, as in covenant with him; and how he was mercifully
heard through Christ: whence learn, 1. No strait is such
but God can deliver out of it, no case is so desperate, as to
make prayer needless or useless: for David saith in his

deepest distress, *I called on the Lord.* 2. It is necessary not to give over, when help is delayed; yea, it is necessary to grow more fervent, and for this end to lay hold on the covenant of reconciliation, and upon God in covenant with us: for he addeth, *I cried to my God.* 3. By virtue of Christ's sacrifice, and his intercession, notice is taken of prayer graciously, and answer cometh to the believer; for he addeth, *he heard my voice out of his temple, and my cry came before him even into his ears;* he pointeth at the temple, in regard of the ark, and other figures representing Christ in his intercession for us in heaven.

7. *Then the earth shook and trembled; the foundations also of the hills moved and were shaken, because he was wroth.*

8. *There went up a smoke out of his nostrils, and fire out of his mouth devoured: coals were kindled by it.*

9. *He bowed the heavens also, and came down: and darkness was under his feet.*

10. *And he rode upon a cherub, and did fly; yea, he did fly upon the wings of the wind.*

11. *He made darkness his secret place; his pavilion round about him were dark waters and thick clouds of the skies.*

12. *At the brightness that was before him, his thick clouds passed; hail-*stones *and coals of fire.*

13. *The Lord also thundered in the heavens, and the Highest gave his voice; hail-*stones *and coals of fire.*

14. *Yea, he sent out his arrows, and scattered them; and he shot out lightnings, and discomfited them.*

15. *Then the channels of waters were seen, and the foundations of the world were discovered at thy rebuke, O Lord, at the blast of the breath of thy nostrils.*

The manner of his delivery is set down in comparative speeches, alluding to the most glorious manifestations which ever God gave of himself, in mount Sinai, or in the days of Joshua, or in the days of the Judges, or Samuel, all which glorious manifestations of God to his people, David esteemeth to be reacted in the wonderfulness of his delivery; so as he thinks he may justly compare the wonders shown in his preservation from his enemies, to any of, or to all

God's former wonders, in saving his people: Whence learn,
1. Although our natural stupidity, unbelief, and enmity
against God, extenuate the works of God's providence
about his children; yet the believer should look upon them
with a spiritual and discerning eye, and should so set them
forth to others, as David doth here. 2. The most sensible
mutations in heaven and earth, are not so observed by the
blind world, as a soul illuminate with spiritual light will
observe God's spiritual providence in his works towards
his people, and towards himself, as here David's example
showeth. 3. The history of the Lord's redeeming his
church, set down in Scripture, and by David alluded unto,
may be seen in God's particular dealing with his children,
as very like to the same, and as appendicles of the same
work repeated. This is imported in David's re-calling to
memory what is said, Exod. ix. 23, 24, and ix. 18; Josh.
x. 11; Judg. v. 4; 1 Sam. xii. 18, concerning the Lord's
manifesting of himself. 4. The terribleness of God coming
to judge his enemies, is a matter of consolation to the
believer, and of praise to God, as here is set down.

16. *He sent from above, he took me, he drew me out
of many waters.*

17. *He delivered me from my strong enemy, and from
them which hated me: for they were too strong for me.*

18. *They prevented me in the day of my calamity:
but the Lord was my stay.*

19. *He brought me forth also into a large place; he
delivered me, because he delighted in me.*

Now he draweth forth his delivery in lower comparisons,
and more proper words, for the more clear capacity of the
church; to wit, that God delivered him as one in peril of
drowning, v. 16; as helping a weak man from a strong
party, v. 17; as upholding a man circumvented, and ready
to fall and fail, v. 18; and setting a man free from all
danger, v. 19. Whence learn, 1. Our weakness in the
time of our delivery, commendeth God's power, as David's
delivery is magnified, because it was as a *drawing of him
out of many waters, where he was like to drown.* Whether
God use means or not in our deliveries, the work must ever
be ascribed to him alone: *he sent from above and took me
out.* 3. Power of adversaries will not hinder God's helping

hand; he can, and doth usually *deliver his own from them that are too strong for them.* 4. A soul sensible of God's merciful work, cannot satisfy itself with expressions about it. And as many new considerations as a believer hath of the circumstances of a mercy, so many new mercies doth he see; therefore is it that David repeateth the same work of deliverance in more and more new expressions, and cannot express himself in one word, with satisfaction to himself. 5. When a man is enclosed, and prevented from escaping out of trouble, faith would fail, and then despair should follow, if God did not interpose himself, and did not furnish strength in this difficulty. David being thus circumvented, saith, *but the Lord was my stay.* 6. The Lord doth not leave his work about his own, till he perfect it, but he completeth their delivery ere he cease, and crowneth his mercy with joy: to express this, David saith, *he brought me forth also into a large place.*

19. *He brought me forth also into a large place; he delivered me, because he delighted in me.*

20. *The Lord rewarded me according to my righteousness; according to the cleanness of my hands hath he recompensed me.*

21. *For I have kept the ways of the Lord, and have not wickedly departed from my God.*

22. *For all his judgments were before me, and I did not put away his statutes from me.*

23. *I was also upright before him, and I kept myself from mine iniquity.*

24. *Therefore hath the Lord recompensed me according to my righteousness, according to the cleanness of my hands in his eye-sight.*

The third part of the psalm, wherein he goeth on to amplify mercy sundry ways; and first, from the cause of it, which is the mere good-will and love of God. Whence learn, 1. That the cause of any mercy shown to us, is not to be found in us, but in God's free love; *he delivered me, because he delighted in me.* 2. The belief of God's love sweeteneth and commendeth the mercy exceedingly: the delivery here is great, but this word, *because he delighted in me,* is far more sweet, verse 20. There is another point of amplifying the mercy of his preservation and delivery, in the clearing of his innocency, and freeing him from the slanders of ingratitude, rebellion, treachery against his father-in-law, and his prince, which was the fruit of another grace of God, given unto him; to wit, righteousness and innocence, in relation to his enemies, ver. 20; and a study to keep God's commands, ver. 21; and the fear of God fastening him to God's statutes, ver. 22; and sincere and tender walking with God, and watching over the sin which did most beset him, ver. 23; where his delivery from his enemies, and clearing his innocence from calumnies, was a gracious reward, ver. 24. Whence learn, 1. In a good cause it is necessary we have a good carriage, lest we mar our cause, and our comfort also; for David studied *right-eousness and cleanness of hands*, in relation to his enemies, when he was most unjustly persecuted. 2. A godly beha-viour in a good cause shall not want fruit, for the free love of God rewarded David according to his righteousness. 3. The conscience of a godly behaviour in time of persecution is twice profitable: once under the trial and trouble it sup-porteth: again, after the delivery, the looking back upon it comforteth, as here is shown. 4. As we should at all times take heed to our conversation, so in special, when by persecution we are troubled for a good cause, for now we are upon the trial of our faith, patience, wisdom, and other graces, as David was, and should do as he doth here. 5. We have special rules of good behaviour set down in Da-vid's example. First, we must be sure to follow such ways as God's word alloweth, that we may say, *I have kept the ways of the Lord.* Secondly, if in our infirmity we be mis-carried at any time, we must not persist in a wrong course, but return to the way of God's obedience, that we may say, I have not wickedly departed from my God, neither in the point of belief, nor practical obedience. Thirdly, we must set all the commands of God, and his written judgments be-fore us, to be observed, one as well as another, and must have respect to God's threatened and executed judgments also, that we may say with David, *all his judgments were before me, and I did not put away his statutes from me.* Fourthly, we must study sincerity in our carriage, doing good actions well from right principles, and for the right end, that we may say, I was also upright before him. Fifthly, we must keep strict watch over our wicked nature, and most raging passions and affections, lest they break out ; that our conscience may not contradict us, when we say, I have kept myself from mine iniquity. 6. It is wisdom to join one mercy with another, in our reckoning, that we may say that we have gotten grace for grace, as David acknowledgeth; that as God had given him grace to study righteousness and innocence, *so had he recompensed* him *according to his righteousness.* 7. When the world would bury our innocence with slanders, it is lawful and expedient to defend our own good name, and to speak and write in defence of it, as David doth here.

25. *With the merciful thou wilt shew thyself merciful; with an upright man thou wilt shew thyself upright;*

26. *With the pure thou wilt shew thyself pure; and with the froward thou wilt shew thyself froward.*

27. *For thou wilt save the afflicted people; but wilt bring down high looks.*

From his own experience he draweth up a general doctrine, concerning the Lord's holy, just, and wise manner of dealing with all men, according to their carriage towards him. Whence learn, 1. The experiences which any of the saints have, of the effects of God's word, are proofs of the certainty of God's promises and threatenings, and pawns of the like effects to follow unto others; for here David draweth a general doctrine from his particular experience. 2. As a man would have a meeting from God, so must he study to behave himself toward God and man, for God's cause; for with the bountiful, merciful, upright, and pure, he will deal accordingly. 3. Whoever shall walk contrary to God, and strive with him, or will not submit themselves unto him, he shall walk contrary unto them, and punish them seven times more, because of their stubbornness ; for *toward the froward, he will shew himself froward.* 4. Albeit the godly be for a while afflicted, and the wicked prosper, yet after the affliction of the godly, salvation shall come to them; and after the prosperity, vain and proud gloriation of the wicked, their destruction shall follow, for he *will save the afflicted people, but will bring down high looks.*

28. *For thou wilt light my candle : the Lord my God will enlighten my darkness.*

From bygone experience he strengthens his own hope of further experience thereafter, as need should require. Whence learn, 1. Believers being delivered out of many bygone troubles, must not promise to themselves exemption from new troubles hereafter, but rather make themselves ready for new exercise, and more sad passages of God's dispensations towards them. For David presupposeth here, that he may, yea, and that he shall be thereafter in darkness, and want, for a while, the candle light of consolation. 2. As the godly man may expect crosses, so may he be sure also of as many consolations, and sweet seasonings of his troubles, and deliverances out of them ; so that he may say, both before trouble come, and in the midst of it, *the Lord will light my candle, and my God will enlighten my darkness.*

29. *For by thee I have run through a troop ; and by my God have I leaped over a wall.*

Here is another part of his experience, concerning his victories and good success in battle, the glory whereof he ascribes altogether to God. Whence learn, 1. Although the courage, valour, and success of all soldiers is from the Lord, yet only the believer giveth God the glory thereof, as David here. 2. Natural courage, and whatsoever measure a man may have of it, now and then may faint and fail altogether, when it meeteth with very strong opposition ; but the spiritual courage which is from faith, is from a more sure ground, and will not fail, when faith setteth it on, whatsoever be the apparent difficulty : for by faith in God David was made to *run through a troop,* or *leap over a wall,* into a town full of his enemies, with assurance of victory.

30. As for *God, his way is perfect : the word of the Lord is tried; he is a buckler to all those that trust in him.*

31. *For who is God save the Lord ? or who is a rock save our God?*

The fourth part of the psalm, wherein he praiseth the Lord expressly for what he had found in him, and in this he is a special type of Christ, in his conquest and victories. The reasons of his praising are four, set down in order. Whence learn, 1. The constant, equable, and old way of God's dealing with those that believe in him, is a matter of God's praise, and a reason why the experience of one believer may be a ground of hope for another, to find the like, because it is said here, *as for God, his way is perfect.* This is one reason of his praise, and of the believer's hope. 2. In all times bygone, experience hath proved the word of the Lord to be most solidly true; which serveth for the second reason of praising God, and grounding of our hope: *the word of the Lord is tried.* 3. There is none of the believers excepted from the benefit of his promises, which is a third reason of God's praise, and our hope, for *he is a buckler to all those that trust in him.* He is a defence which we may constantly carry along with us wherever we go, and make use of his power and love as of a buckler, in all conflicts. 4. A fourth reason of God's praise, and ground of our hope, is, that as there is no true religion, nor true faith, save one, so there is no true God save only one, whose true and tried word is with his true church and saints, who believe in him: *for who is God save the Lord? or who is a rock save our God?* 5. There is no fountain of comfort, or of strength, or delivery, save the Lord, of whom only all things have their being: *for who is God save the Lord?* 6. There is no ground to build our confidence and felicity upon, save God alone, who is in covenant through Christ with us: *Who is a rock save our God?*

32. It is *God that girdeth me with strength, and maketh my way perfect.*

33. *He maketh my feet like hinds' feet, and setteth me upon my high places.*

34. *He teacheth my hands to war, so that a bow of steel is broken by mine arms.*

35. *Thou hast also given me the shield of thy salvation; and thy right hand hath holden me up, and thy gentleness hath made me great.*

36. *Thou hast enlarged my steps under me, that my feet did not slip.*

He goeth on to reckon the furniture and ability for war, which the Lord gave to him. Whence learn, 1. The man of God must resolve to be a man of war, and to yoke with adversaries of one sort or other ; such as was David, and Christ, and his followers, represented by him. 2. The man whom the Lord sendeth out to fight his battles, he will arm

him completely from head to foot, he will gird him with
strength, and make his way plain and perfect ; he will
make his feet swift, he will furnish him with a retiring place
on high, he will furnish him with a bow of steel, and with
all arms offensive, and will enable him with more skill and
strength then to make use of them ; he will furnish him also
with *a shield of salvation,* which shall save him in effect :
and with all arms defensive, and uphold him by his right
hand, when he is like to be overcome ; and by his tender
care of him, will make him a great man, a valiant man of
war, and hold him on his feet, that he fall not in his service ; whereof David here hath experience in his warfare,
bodily and spiritual. 3. What God hath done for a man will
be better seen after the trouble is ended, than in the mean
time. The back-look upon the Lord's assistance is most
clear, as here David giveth the clearest count of God's assistance, when his experience is reviewed. 4. All the furniture of spiritual armour, in our spiritual warfare, which
here is chiefly aimed at, is only from the Lord ; for he,
even he only, is here declared the furnisher thereof, and without him the man is altogether weak, witless, and naked.

37. *I have pursued mine enemies, and overtaken
them ; neither did I turn again till they were consumed.*

38. *I have wounded them, that they were not able to
rise : they are fallen under my feet.*

39. *For thou hast girded me with strength unto the
battle : thou hast subdued under me those that rose up
against me.*

40. *Thou hast also given me the necks of mine enemies, that I might destroy them that hate me.*

Here he maketh mention of the victories which God gave
to him, as a type of Christ, over all his enemies. Whence
learn, 1. It was revealed to David, that as he himself had,
so also should Christ have many enemies, and should fight
against them, and prevail over them, and make all his followers victorious over them all; that he should pursue his
and their enemies, in every age, and *not turn again till they
shall be consumed,* as is ver. 37; *till he cast them down,
that they be not able to rise,* ver. 38; till he hath subdued
them all under his feet, and ours, ver. 39; till he have
taken them captives, and destroyed them, ver. 40. For

Christ's victories are common to him and his followers, in as far as their warfare is from him, and he is engaged to fight our battles for us, or by us, as he sees fit.

41. *They cried, but* there was *none to save* them ; even *unto the Lord, but he answered them not.*

42. *Then did I beat them small as the dust before the wind; I did cast them out as the dirt in the streets.*

In the type of some passages of some severe justice which David executed against his enemies, he setteth forth the certain destruction of Christ's enemies, in judgment merciless. Whence learn, 1. That whosoever look for release out of their trouble, and that not through Christ, shall have no release at all: *though they cry, there shall be none to save them.* 2. It may be some may think themselves friends to God, and God a friend to them, and pray to him, albeit they be enemies to Christ; but that prayer which is put up to God, without reconciliation made through Christ, shall be rejected. *Though they cry to the Lord, he shall not answer them.* 3. If men, pursued by Christ for their enmity against him, shall, not under the rod at least, turn to him, there remaineth nothing for them, but that they be utterly destroyed, and, as it were, *beaten as small as the dust.* 4. The obstinate enemies of Christ's kingdom shall perish shamefully, and as they have despised the blood of Christ, and of his servants, so shall the Lord despise them; he shall *cast them out as the dirt in the streets.*

43. *Thou hast delivered me from the strivings of the people;* and *thou hast made me the head of the heathen: a people* whom *I have not known shall serve me.*

44. *As soon as they hear of me they shall obey me : the strangers shall submit themselves unto me.*

In the fifth and last part of the psalm, he promiseth to himself the settling and enlargement of his own kingdom, and prophesieth also of Christ's kingdom represented thereby. Whence learn, 1. As was David's, so is Christ's kingdom, subject to intestine commotions, tumults, and dissensions; as in the one there were, so in the other have been, and will be contentions, and *strivings of the people*, raised by Satan, fostered by wicked hypocrites, and by the corruption of the Lord's children. 2. Such striving and dissension put our Lord's kingdom in a sort of hazard, if we look to second causes, so as there will be need of God's help for a delivery from it. But the kingdom of Christ shall stand for all that, notwithstanding these contentions, that it may still be said of his kingdom, as it is said here of the typical kingdom, and is prophesied of Christ's kingdom, *thou hast delivered me from the strivings of the people*. 3. To the prophet it was revealed, that Christ's kingdom was not to remain straitened within the bounds of Judea, but to be extended to the Gentiles, over whom Christ was to reign, and now hath a long time reigned: *the Father*, as he made David the type, so *hath he made Christ head of the heathen*. 4. The wickedness of a person or people, whose works have been most loathsome to the Lord, cannot hinder him to show mercy to them through Christ, when he pleaseth to convert them; for he hath said, *a people whom I have not known, shall serve me:* which hath ofttimes come to pass, and will yet more be seen effectually. 5. The word of the Lord is the sceptre of his kingdom, the sword whereby he subdueth his people to himself; *as soon as they hear of me*, saith the Lord, in the mouth of his type, and prophet, *they shall obey me*. 6. The more room the word gets in a man's heart, and the sooner it be believed and obeyed, after signification of God's will to him by his word, the more kindly is the conversion, and the more of the Lord's power is evidenced : as here is imported in, *as soon as they hear of me*. 7. When Christ subdueth nations to himself by his word, and converteth the elect, or his own redeemed ones: strangers in heart will come also outwardly unto the society of his church and kingdom, though feignedly: *the strangers shall submit themselves to me : feignedly*, as the word importeth. 8. Even this outward offer of submission to Christ's kingdom, made by strangers coming to the visible church, is not refused, but received *pro tanto*, and made a matter of glorifying of Christ : *the strangers shall feignedly submit themselves to me.* For it is no small glory to Christ that the majesty of his word and ordinances, maketh many stoop before him, who are not turned truly unto him. Meantime, albeit by entering into, and submitting to the external covenant, a man be admitted into the visible church, and outer court of God's house, yet not without real conversion is a man made a member of the invisible church, and admitted into the inner court of heaven.

45. *The strangers shall fade away, and be afraid out of their close places.*

He prophesieth what shall become of Christ's enemies at length. Whence learn, 1. As some strangers shall come into the outward fellowship of Christ's kingdom, so others of them shall remain professed strangers, and disaffected to his kingdom, and whether strangers within or without, shall continue to be strangers still, both of them shall perish : *for strangers shall fade away.* 2. Albeit Christ at first, may have many enemies and unfriends where he cometh to set up his kingdom, yet where and when he pleaseth to stay and keep up his kingdom, his open enemies shall grow fewer: *the strangers shall fade away :* to wit, where he minds to stay, and for that end thinks good to diminish them. 3. Whether the Lord be pleased to convert strangers or not, their strong holds (whether their high imaginations, or their earthly power) shall not be able to stand before him ; let him come to convert them outwardly or inwardly also, or destroy them as he shall be pleased, his terror shall affright them ; *for the strangers,* before him, *shall be afraid out of their close places.*

46. *The Lord liveth ; and blessed* be *my Rock ; and let the God of my salvation be exalted.*

47. It is *God that avengeth me, and subdueth the people under me.*

48. *He delivereth me from mine enemies ; yea, thou liftest me up above those that rise up against me : thou hast delivered me from the violent man.*

49. *Therefore will J give thanks unto thee, O Lord, among the heathen, and sing praises unto thy name.*

50. *Great deliverance giveth he to his king ; and sheweth mercy to his anointed, to David, and to his seed for evermore.*

He concludeth the psalm with thanksgiving, and praiseth the Lord for his personal preservation unto eternal life, v. 46, for overthrowing of his enemies, v. 47, for delivery of him from them, v. 47, 48, and in Christ's name he setteth forth the Lord's glory before the Gentiles, for the mercies following the kingdom of Christ, and his own kingdom, the type thereof, v. 49, 50. Whence learn, 1. The end of all our speeches, concerning what we have been employed into, and have done, or have had success in, should be to show forth the glory of God to others, and to offer praise and thanks to him : for this, *blessed be my rock, &c.*, is the end whereunto *David's* example driveth. 2. *Life*, and *blessed life, quickening life*, the only *fountain* of life, is the proper style of God, of whom most properly and deservedly we may say, *the Lord liveth.* 3. Because God is the fountain of all blessedness to angels and men; therefore should we acknowledge him, and proclaim him *blessed*, that the hearer may seek blessedness in him alone. 4. The perfection of God in himself, the out-letting of his goodness to the creature, his immutability in his love to his own, his making himself to be as it were the proper good of the believer by covenant, and his giving the certainty of salvation to the believer, established by covenant : these and other perfections should exalt the Lord highly in the estimation and affection of the believer, and make the believer heartily wish the Lord may be known to his praise : for this cause, saith the prophet, *the Lord liveth*, and *blessed be my Rock, and let the God of my salvation be exalted.* 4. David, as a type of Christ, in name and behalf of Christ, giveth unto God the glory of taking order with his enemies, for preserving and propagating his kingdom, and for the delivering his people from cruel persecutors. *It is God*, saith he, *that avengeth me, and subdueth the people under me. He delivereth me from mine enemies ; yea, thou liftest me up above those that rise up against me ; thou hast delivered me from the violent man.*

49. *Therefore will I give thanks unto thee, O Lord, among the heathen ; and sing praises unto thy name.*

Besides present praising of God, he promiseth to insist in praise and thanksgiving. This the apostle, Rom. xv. 9, showeth to be the speech of Christ, and a prophecy of the conversion of the Gentiles. Whence learn, 1. Beside all the victories given to the church in David's time, as a pledge of promises, it was foretold that the Gentiles should see many victories over the enemies of the church of Christ, after his coming, and that they should join with the Jews in thanksgiving to God for the same ; for upon account of the Lord's lifting up Christ above his adversaries and cruel persecutors, *thanks shall be given unto the Lord among the hea-*

then. 2. The sacrifice of praise offered up in the church, as it is the work of the saints in one respect, so it is the work of Christ in another respect; because he raiseth by his Spirit the song in their hearts, and offereth up the sacrifice of thanks unto the Father. For it is Christ who here saith, *I will give thanks unto thee, O Lord, among the heathen; and sing praises to thy name.*

50. *Great deliverance giveth he to his King : and sheweth mercy unto his anointed : to David and to his seed for evermore.*

David, as a type of Christ, giveth a reason of perpetual praising of God ; to wit, the constant course of God's mercies shown to him and his house, and to be shown to Christ, and his children and house, for evermore. Whence learn, 1. As difficulties, enemies, and dangers of the church, are many and great ; so shall their victories over these evils be great also ; *for great deliverance giveth he,* in a continual tract and course, as it were, one after another, as need is. 2. All the deliverances are given to Christ principally, and in him to his church, and particular souls through him ; for it is said, *great deliverance giveth he to his King.* 3. The choosing of a man for a service, shall, by the calling of him to it, and qualifying him for it, and sustaining him in it, be confirmed to him, and by the course of mercy following him in all his difficulties, which he shall meet with in his calling. Therefore significantly doth he say, *Great deliverance giveth he to his King,* to *David,* a chosen type, and to his anointed Christ, represented by him: *he sheweth mercy to his anointed,* Christ his seed. 4. It is mere mercy whereof Christ's followers, Christ's children and seed, stand in need : and mercy by course constantly shall follow them, not for a short time, but world without end ; for *the Lord sheweth mercy to David and his seed for evermore.*

PSALM XIX.

To the Chief Musician. A Psalm of David.

This psalm is a sweet contemplation of the glory of God's wisdom, power, and goodness, shining in the works of creation, v. 1—6, and of the glory of his holiness and rich grace, shining through his word and ordinances in his church, v. 7—10, whereof the prophet having proof, prayeth to have the right use and benefit, v. 11—14.

1. *The heavens declare the glory of God: and the firmament sheweth his handy work.*

Albeit the whole earth be full of the glory of the Lord, yet the prophet contenteth himself to pitch his meditations on the heavens alone, and the vicissitude of day and night, and upon the course of the sun's light: whence learn, 1. Albeit the glory of the Lord shine in all his works, yet any portion thereof will take up a man's meditation, when he beginneth to think upon it, as here the heavens are the prophet's theme and subject matter of meditation. 2. The invisible things of God, even his eternal power and Godhead, and glorious attributes of wisdom, and goodness, and majesty, are to be seen in the works of creation, from the beginning of the world: *the heavens declare the glory of God, and the firmament sheweth his handy work.* 3. Though his glory be shown to all men, yet it is the illuminate child of God that can observe it; for he that setteth it forth to others, doth it by the inspiration of the Lord's own Spirit: he is a prophet who here is stirred up to point unto us this lesson, most worthy of our observation. For in substance the heavens declare that they are not their own maker, but that they are made by one infinite, incomprehensible, omnipotent, everlasting, good, kind, and glorious God. And the firmament (taking it for the region of the air, and place of the stars) declares how curiously he can adorn the work of his hands, and how powerfully he can put glory abundant on the creature, though it have no matter in it to make it glorious.

2. *Day unto day uttereth speech, and night unto night sheweth knowledge.*

3. There is *no speech nor language* where *their voice is not heard.*

4. *Their line is gone out through all the earth, and their words to the end of the world. In them hath he set a tabernacle for the sun:*

He looketh next upon the vicissitude of night and day, and as he saw what the heavens gave him to read, so he hearkeneth and heareth what the day and the night did speak; and he compriseth all their speech in the doctrine of knowledge: whence learn, 1. The right observation of the vicissitude of the night and day, may give instruction unto us to be wise; *for day unto day*, in their revolution, *uttereth speech* to the observing ear; *and night unto night*, in their vicissitude *sheweth* to the understanding man *knowledge*. For in substance, the vicissitude of day after day, serveth to teach man that he liveth in time, and that his days are numbered, that his days go quickly away, and that time is precious, and cannot return when it is gone; and that so long as it shall last, it shall serve man to view the works of the Lord, and to go about his own necessary labours; and such like other speeches doth it speak : also the night saith, that man in himself is weak, and cannot endure long toiling in labour; that as some little short rest and recreation of the labourer is necessary, so it is prepared for him, that he may lie under a curtain, and sleep a while, and so be fitted for more work, if more time be lent unto him; and that he may now quietly examine, what he hath been doing, may commune with his heart and be still; and that if he do not what he hath to do in time, *the night cometh when no man can work :* by which and such like speeches men may learn knowledge. 2. There is no people nor country, but as much of the speech of the creature is spoken convincingly unto them, as may make them inexcusable; and albeit all do not learn wisdom, yet *the voice* of the works of creation and providence, *is every where* in some measure *heard : their line* and direction *is gone out through the earth.*

5. *Which* is *as a bridegroom coming out of his chamber,* and *rejoiceth as a strong man to run a race.*

6. *His going forth* is *from the end of the heaven, and his circuit unto the ends of it: and there is nothing hid from the heat thereof.*

He contracteth his thoughts from the highness of the heavens, and pitcheth upon the sun, and beholdeth God's glory in it. Whence learn, 1. All the glory to be seen in the sun belongeth unto the Lord; for he made it, and set it in its place, *as in a tabernacle,* for a time, so long as he hath use and service for it. 2. The beauty of the sun when it ariseth in the morning; the wonderful swift and regular motion of it, so tempered by the huge distance thereof from the earth, that it cannot be seen moving, when it is running in a circle in the heaven most swiftly : the constancy of the motion of it from day to day, from year to year, without

wearying or failing; the vast circle which it maketh every
twenty-four hours; the heat and virtue, and powerful operation upon all inferior creatures,—are all admirable, and
matter of manifesting the glorious perfection of God, who
made it, and moveth it; *as the bridegroom he riseth, compasseth the circle of heaven and earth, and nothing is hid
from the heat thereof.*

7. *The law of the Lord is perfect, converting the
soul: the testimony of the Lord is sure, making wise
the simple:*

8. *The statutes of the Lord are right, rejoicing the
heart: the commandment of the Lord is pure, enlight-
ening the eyes:*

9. *The fear of the Lord is clean, enduring for ever:
the judgments of the Lord are true and righteous altogether.*

10. *More to be desired are they than gold, yea, than
much fine gold; sweeter also than honey, and the honey-
comb.*

The next part of his contemplation, is concerning the
glory of the Lord declared in his word and Scripture; which
light, as it is more necessary for our blessedness than the
sun's light for our bodies, so he commendeth this point of
God's glory far above that which shineth in the work of
creation, from the perfection, efficacy, infallibility, and
sundry other properties of it. Whence learn, 1. The doctrine of life and salvation, set down to us in God's word, as
a law to us, and a rule of faith and obedience, needeth no
deck of human traditions; it is sufficient in itself, and
wanteth nothing necessary unto salvation; *for the law of the
Lord is perfect.* 2. No doctrine, no word save this divine
truth, set down in Scripture, is able to discover the sin and
misery of man, or the remedy and relief from it; no doctrine save this alone, can effectually humble a soul, and
convert it to God; or make a soul sensible of the loss it
hath by sin, and restore it to a better condition than is lost
by sin; for it is the property of this law or *doctrine, to be
converting of souls.* 3. Whosoever hearkeneth to this word,
shall be satisfied about what is the Lord's mind and will in
all matters of religion, concerning God's service, and man's
salvation; *for it is the testimony of the Lord,* wherein he

giveth forth his will, concerning what he approveth, and what he disalloweth. 4. This word being understood rightly, as it may be understood when it is compared with itself, one part of it with another, and other means also used, which God hath appointed, may be safely relied upon: it will not disappoint a man; *for the testimony of the Lord is sure.* 5. Albeit there be many deep mysteries in this word, which may exercise the greatest wits, yet for the points necessary for the salvation of every soul, it is so plain and clear, that it may be understood by persons of mean wits, and may make those who are otherwise dull of understanding, wise to salvation; for it is a *testimony making wise the simple.* 6. Nothing is commanded by God in his word, but that which the illuminate soul must subscribe unto, as equitable in itself, and profitable to us; *for the statutes of the Lord are right.* 7. The approving and following of the Lord's directions given to us in his word, is a sure mean to get comfort and joy raised in our conscience: *for the statutes of the Lord rejoice the heart.* 8. There is no mixture of error, no dross nor refuse doctrine, no deceit in the Lord's word; for *the commandment of the Lord is pure.* 9. By the word of God a man may clearly see himself in himself blind and naked, and wretched, and miserable, and by coming into the grace and mercy offered in the Messiah, Christ, may see himself entered in the only safe way of salvation. By the word of God a man may see every thing in its own colours; virtue to be virtue, and vice to be vice and vanity : *for the word illuminates the eyes.* 10. The way of worshipping, fearing, and serving God, set down in his word, is holy, and in substance the same in all generations, and always unalterable by man for ever. *The fear of the Lord is clean, enduring for ever.* 11. The doctrines set down in the word of God, are all of them decrees of the Almighty Lawgiver, given forth in his own court with authority uncontrollable; all of them are true and worthy to be obeyed; for the *judgments of the Lord are true, and righteous altogether.* 12. The word of God is able to enrich a man more than all the riches in the world, because it is able to bring him to an everlasting kingdom ; for God's judgments being as judicial sentences, to determine all necessary truths and controversies about saving truth, *are more to be desired than gold, yea, than much*

fine gold. **13.** There is more sweet comfort and true pleasure to be found in the Lord's word, than in any pleasant
thing in this world : *they are sweeter than honey, and the
honey-comb.*

11. *Moreover, by them is thy servant warned :* and
in keeping of them there is *great reward.*

The prophet subscribeth this commendation of God's
word, by his own experience, and seeketh to make good
use of it. Whence learn, 1. That man, of all other, is
most meet to commend the word of the Lord, who in himself hath felt the experience of the effects and good use
thereof, as the prophet's example showeth. 2. As the
word of God is able to make a man wise to salvation, so
also to make him prudent in his carriage, to eschew not
only sin, but also inconveniences, and to warn him of
snares, wherein he may fall by imprudence. For beside
all the former commendation, he addeth, *moreover by them
is thy servant warned.* 3. When a man hath said all he
can, in commendation of the word of God, he shall not be
able to say all, but must close in some general, because the
benefit of observing the Lord's statutes and commands,
passeth his reach ; for thus the prophet closeth, *in keeping of them* there is *great reward.*

12. *Who can understand* his *errors ? cleanse thou
me from secret* faults.

Lest he should seem to speak like one who seeks to be
justified by his works, he acknowledgeth himself a man
that cleaveth not to his own righteousness, but to the fountain of free grace, and to the expiation of sin made by
Christ, signified under the shadow of ceremonial cleansing.
Whence learn, 1. The most holy man, after conversion,
must make still use of the law for his humiliation, and for
driving of him to Christ continually : and when he compareth himself with the law of God, he will be forced to
blush and acknowledge himself and every other man unable
to condescend upon the particulars, and the multitude even
of his actual sins. Therefore saith he, *who can understand
his errors ?* 2. Sins of ignorance, sins passed out of memory, leave guiltiness upon the man, and must be counted for in heap at least : and mercy through the blood of
cleansing must be requested for, as here ; *cleanse thou me
from secret sins.*

13. *Keep back thy servant also from presumptuous* sins; *let them not have dominion over me : then shall I be upright, and I shall be innocent from the great transgression.*

He puts up another petition, to wit, That he may be preserved from presumptuous sins. Hence learn, 1. Holiest men are most sensible of their by-gone sins, and so also of their natural sinfulness and readiness to fall, whereof the prophet here is in fear, saying, *Keep back also thy servant from presumptuous sins.* 2. Even the regenerate, if the Lord do not keep them from temptation, or if he leave them in temptation, unto their own will and strength, they may fall into most scandalous sins, against the light of their conscience, and be slaves thereunto ; therefore prayeth he *to be kept back from presumptuous sins, and that God would not suffer such sins to have dominion over him ;* insinuating his own weakness, if God did not prevent, did not assist and help him to prevail against them. 3. Uprightness and integrity in God's obedience may stand with sins of infirmity and sins of ignorance, but cannot stand with presumptuous sins, against the light of conscience ; for if the Lord shall save him from presumptuous sins, *then,* he saith, *he shall be upright.* 4. Presumptuous sins, and letting sin reign in a man's mortal body, is the highway to the sin unto death, or sinning maliciously, with despite against God ; and he that makes conscience of secret sins, and is feared to fall into presumptuous sins, and fleeth to God to be cleansed from the one, and preserved from falling into the other, may be sure not to fall into the sin against the Holy Ghost. For the prophet having prayed to be cleansed from his secret sins, and kept back from presumptuous and reigning sins, assureth himself, *that so he shall be innocent from the great transgression.*

14. *Let the words of my mouth, and the meditation of my heart, be acceptable in thy sight, O Lord, my strength, and my redeemer.*

The third petition, is, for the acceptance of his service in his prayer, and purpose of heart. Whence learn, 1. As pardoning grace, and preventing grace, and restraining grace, must be prayed for ; so also powerful, sanctifying, or enabling grace, both for inward and outward service ;

E

yea, and grace accepting the service when it is offered, must be fought for by prayer from God. For as the prophet hath prayed for the former acts of grace, so also he prayeth here for the latter sort, saying, *let the words of my mouth and the meditation of my heart be acceptable.* 2. As all our prayers, and all our holy endeavours, and abilities to serve God, must be furnished unto us by our Redeemer, who is Jesus Christ; so also every other grace, and the acceptance of our persons and services, must come through him ; and we may look for all these by virtue of the covenant of grace, whereby Christ is made our strength and Redeemer in all respects : therefore layeth he all the weight on this, *O Lord, my strength, and my Redeemer.*

PSALM XX.

To the chief Musician. A Psalm of David.

This Psalm was dited to the church in form of a prayer for the kings of Israel, but with a special eye upon, and relation unto Christ, the King of Israel; in respect of whom this prayer is a prophecy, and a form of blessing of Christ, and praying for his kingdom, whereof the kingdom of Israel was a type, and the kings thereof are types of Christ. Not that the kingdom in every condition was figurative, or every king a type of him ; but as the priests being taken not severally, one by one, but together, shadowed forth, in something, Christ in the office of his priesthood; so the kings, not every one, but taken together, shadowed forth in something, Christ in his royal office, and their kingdom resembled his kingdom in his visible church in some things, and in his invisible church in other some things, leaving room to some persons, both among the priests and kings, to be more specially types than any of the rest in common, v. 1—5. After which the church's confidence to be heard is set down, and their gloriation in God over their enemies, with dependence on God for salvation in all difficulties and straits, v. 6—9.

1. *The Lord hear thee in the day of trouble; the name of the God of Jacob defend thee.*

2. *Send thee help from the sanctuary, and strengthen thee out of Zion.*

3. *Remember all thy offerings, and accept thy burnt-sacrifice. Selah.*

4. *Grant thee according to thine own heart, and fulfil all thy counsel.*

5. *We will rejoice in thy salvation, and in the name*

of our God we will set up our banners : the Lord ful-
fil all thy petitions.

From this prayer of the church for the king of Israel,
learn, 1. It is the duty of all the godly, wherever they live,
to pray for the welfare of their kings, rulers, and magistrates, as this example teacheth. 2. Greatest men, though
they be also gracious, are subject to trouble : for even the
best of the kings of Israel, and Christ typified by them,
were not exempted therefrom : *the Lord hear thee in the
day of trouble.* 3. It is the part of such as desire the prayers of others to be made for them, to pray also themselves,
were they never so great kings; and prayer must be counted their best weapons in trouble ; *the Lord hear thee,*
saith he, *in the day of thy trouble.* 4. No defence to be expected from God, but when he is looked upon and believed
in as he is manifested to us in his word; therefore he
saith, *the name of the God of Jacob defend thee.* Or, God,
who in his word hath revealed himself to Israel, and entered
in covenant to be his God, *defend thee.* 5. It is by virtue
of God's dwelling amongst men, and his taking on man's
nature in the person of Christ (represented by God's presence in *Zion* and the sanctuary), that help must be expected from God. Therefore, saith he, *the Lord send thee
help out of the sanctuary, and strengthen thee out of Zion.*
6. Kings, and all for whom the godly may pray with confidence, must be worshippers of God, believers in Christ, re-
liers upon the mercy of this only once offered sacrifice, represented by often repeated typical burnt-offerings ; for
this is imported in, *the Lord remember all thy offerings,
and accept thy burnt sacrifices.* For it is for Christ's sacrifice that we are accepted, and that any grace is granted
to us. 7. A believer in Christ, praying according to the
revealed will of God, ask what he will, it shall be granted ;
he who studieth to walk sincerely before God, studying to
do what is pleasant to God's heart, shall receive satisfactory
answers according to his own heart's wish. Upon this
ground the prayer goeth here, *the Lord grant thee according to thine own heart, and fulfil all thy counsel.* 8. Whosoever partaketh with Christ's subjects in trouble, shall
share with them also in the joy of their deliverance ; therefore it is said, *we will rejoice in thy salvation.* 9. When
it goeth well with the king, and chief magistrates, it goeth

the better with all the subjects; and the praise of delivery and welfare redoundeth to the glory of God, who is the fountain of all felicity; for, *in the name of our God, we shall set up our banners,* saith the church, if God shall be the king.

6. *Now know I that the Lord saveth his anointed: he will hear him from his holy heaven with the saving strength of his right hand.*

7. *Some trust in chariots, and some in horses; but we will remember the name of the Lord our God.*

8. *They are brought down and fallen; but we are risen, and stand upright.*

9. *Save, Lord: let the King hear us when we call.*

This is the church's confidence to be heard, and her gloriation in God, and dependence on God for salvation; whence learn, 1. A believer may be sure he hath his request granted, when he hath prayed according to God's will; in special when he prayeth for the safety of the church and kingdom of Christ. *I know,* saith he, *that the Lord saveth his anointed.* 2. He that seeketh God by the means appointed; in special, he who seeketh God, and help from him, through Christ, in whom the fulness of the Godhead dwelleth, shall have the grant of his prayer from heaven; for *help sought to come from the sanctuary,* ver. 2, *is granted from his holy heaven,* ver. 6. 3. Whatsoever be the straits of God's church, or any member thereof, faith seeth sufficiency in God to relieve out of it, and doth lay hold on it, for *he heareth with the saving strength of his right hand.* 4. Weak man cannot choose but have some confidence, without himself, in case of apparent difficulties; and natural men do look first to some earthly thing wherein they confide: *some trust in chariots, and some in horses,* some in one creature, some in another. 5. The believer must quit his confidence in these things, whether he have them, or want them, and must rely on what God hath promised in his word to do unto us: *but we will remember the name of the Lord our God.* 6. That which terrifieth the believer in the first assault of a temptation, before he go to his refuge, is contemned by the believer when he looks to the Lord, his true defence; chariots and horses when they are invading God's people are terrible; but now when the Lord is remembered, they are here set at nought in comparison. 7. The condition of the worldly man and of the enemies of God's people seems to be the better, at the first, and the condition of the church the worse; but a short resolution cometh, which determineth the question in the end; the standing of the ungodly is followed with a fall; and the low condition of the godly hath a better condition following upon it. The worldly man and enemy, is brought down, and falleth; but the godly are made to say, *we are risen and stand upright.* 8. True confidence strengthens itself by prayer: *Save, Lord.* 9. That which is prayed for in the type, is perfected in Christ, who is the truth; salvation is granted to all his subjects, whensoever they call; *let the King hear us when we call.* 10. And when the Lord is relied upon for safety, the means shall have the promised blessing. The kings of Israel were to be the more useful to the people when safety was sought from the Lord. First, they pray, *Save us,* and then, *let the King hear us when we call,* or implore him.

PSALM XXI.

To the chief Musician. A Psalm of David.

As the former psalm was a prayer for the preservation of the kingdom of Israel, in relation to the kingdom of Christ, represented by it, so this psalm is a form of thanksgiving unto God by the church, for blessing the kingdom of Israel, representing the blessing, and cause of thanksgiving, to be found in Christ and his kingdom; wherein a number of good things are set forth, heaped upon the King, ver. 1—7; and a number of miseries set forth, heaped on the head of his enemies, ver. 8—12; for both which the Lord is glorified, ver. 13. The reason why the former psalm and this are referred in so many particulars to Christ, is, because the verity of these things here spoken of is to be sought in Christ and his kingdom: for but in some few only of the kings, and in some few times of the kingdom only, was the shadow of what is here spoken of to be found, when the whole history is consulted.

1. *The king shall joy in thy strength, O Lord; and in thy salvation how greatly shall he rejoice!*

2. *Thou hast given him his heart's desire, and hast not withholden the request of his lips. Selah.*

3. *For thou preventest him with the blessings of goodness: thou settest a crown of pure gold on his head.*

4. *He asked life of thee,* and *thou gavest* it *him,* even *length of days for ever and ever.*

5. *His glory* is *great in thy salvation : honour and majesty hast thou laid upon him.*

6. *For thou hast made him most blessed for ever : thou hast made him exceeding glad with thy countenance.*

7. *For the king trusteth in the Lord ; and through the mercy of the most High he shall not be moved.*

The benefits bestowed on the king and his kingdom, are seven or eight, which are so many reasons of thanksgiving. The first is, joy in the king's heart, for strength and salvation given unto him. Whence learn, 1. As prayer is necessary, so also is thanksgiving ; and the offering of both to God, as it is our duty, so it is his due ; and as we should seek the concurrence of others in prayer, so should we seek their concurrence in praise ; and he that offereth prayer one day, shall have matter of praise to offer another day, as here we are taught. 2. Christ, and all his true subjects, are sure to be furnished with furniture of strength from God, for every employment, and to be delivered out of every danger by God, and to have joy and rejoicing in the experimental feeling thereof : for, *the king shall joy in thy strength, O Lord, and in thy salvation how greatly shall he rejoice!* This is the first reason of praise and thanks, for this first benefit. The second benefit bestowed on Christ, to be forth-coming to his true subjects, is this : satisfactory answers shall be given to all the articles of Christ's intercession, and all the articles of the saint's warrantable supplications. *Thou hast given him his heart's desire, and hast not withholden the request of his lips.* The third benefit is this : there shall be a ready out-giving of liberal gifts for Christ's subjects, and fruits of God's love, before the need thereof be felt, or observed ; *thou preventest him with the blessing of goodness.* The fourth benefit is right, and title, and possession given to Christ ; a name of glory, or the gift of a glorious kingdom, wherein Christ shall give all his subjects crowns of glory : *thou settest a crown of pure gold upon his head.* The fifth benefit is right to eternal life, as the fruit of Christ's intercession ; *he asked life of thee, and thou gavest it him, even length of days for ever and ever.* The sixth benefit given to Christ and his subjects, is growing honour, and growing weight of glory, a load of it, even before men ; for nothing can make men more glorious, even before the world, than God's owning them before the world, and putting respect upon them ; yea, and the world shall more and more see and admire the glory which God shall put upon Christ and his kingdom ; *his glory is great in thy salvation ; honour and majesty hast thou laid upon him.* The seventh benefit is a begun possession of everlasting blessedness and joy unspeakable ; partly from the feeling of the first fruits, partly from the hope of a full harvest ; for God will never make an end of blessing whom he will bless. *Thou hast made him* and his followers *most blessed for ever ; thou hast made him exceeding glad with thy countenance.* The eighth reason of thanksgiving, and the last benefit, in relation to the giving of what is good to Christ, and to his subjects, (among whom David and every one of the godly come in to share,) is the unchangeableness of God's mercy, and powerful love toward the believer, who hath closed in covenant with him, and trusteth in him. *He shall not be moved.* And why so ? *The king trusteth in the Lord.* What then ? The covenanted mercy of the most High is unchangeable, and maketh all blessedness fast to Christ and to every believer ; *through the mercy of the most High he shall not be moved.* Christ's kingdom in his person, and his subjects with him, shall stand when all the kingdoms of the earth shall stagger and fall.

8. *Thine hand shall find out all thine enemies ; thy right hand shall find out those that hate thee.*

9. *Thou shalt make them as a fiery oven in the time of thine anger ; the Lord shall swallow them up in his wrath, and the fire shall devour them.*

10. *Their fruit shalt thou destroy from the earth, and their seed from among the children of men.*

In the second place, there is a prophecy of God's vengeance on the enemies of Christ and his church, under the type of the enemies of David's kingdom. Whence learn, 1. All the enemies of Christ and his church shall be pursued by God, and overtaken, and none of them shall escape his hand, neither open enemies nor close lurking traitors. The Lord's hand shall find out all the King's enemies, and his right hand shall find out all those that hate him. 2. A ll the enemies of Christ and his kingdom, howsoever they may possibly be spared and forborn for a while, yet there is a set time for punishing them, here called the time of God's anger. 3. When the time is come, their judgment is inevitable, horrible, and completely full: *thou shalt make them as a fiery oven,* when the burning is extremely hot, the heat striking upon what is in it, from all hands, above, below, and about, on all hands, and the door closed from going out, or suffering any cool refreshment to come in. 4. There is no possibility to apprehend the horrible punishment of Christ's enemies: for after their casting into a fiery oven, they are set down here as fuel, to suffer what God's being incensed in anger, as a consuming fire swallowing them up, and devouring them in his incomprehensible wrath, importeth. 5. After the Lord's vengeance is come upon the enemies of Christ's kingdom, his curse shall follow the works of their hands, and upon whatsoever they sought to make themselves happy by in their life : and his vengeance shall follow upon their posterity, till he have rooted out their memorial from among men. *Their fruit shall he destroy from the earth, and their seed from amongst the children of men.*

11. *For they intended evil against thee ; they imagined a mischievous device,* which *they were not able* to perform :

For evidencing the Lord's justice, he giveth a reason of this from the design which the enemies have to root out the Lord's anointed, and his seed, ver. 11. Whence learn, 1. The malicious enemies of Christ's kingdom, (beside all the hatred they have shown, and evil which they have done) are still upon plots and designs to overturn Christ's kingdom and work: *they intended evil against thee.* The enemies of Christ's kingdom may possibly conceive they only oppose such as trouble men's interests, and not as they are the Lord's children ; yet it is found, that what they do against them, they do it against the Lord, because they do it against his children and subjects, for his cause and service. 2. Plot what the wicked please against Christ and his church, they shall not be able to accomplish their design or desire ; *they have imagined a mischievous device, which they are not able to perform.* 3. The evil which the wicked would do, and set themselves to do, shall be made their ditty, and the reason of their doom and destruction, as well as the evil which they have done, if they repent not. For *they in-tended*, is here given as the reason of the judgment.

12. *Therefore shalt thou make them turn their back,* when *thou shalt make ready* thine arrows *upon thy strings against the face of them.*

He cleareth their ditty and judgment yet more, vers. 12, teaching us, 1. That the Lord will suffer his enemies to manifest themselves in open opposition ofttimes, before he fall upon them : for here they are found in the posture of pursuers and opposers of God, setting their face against him when he cometh to execute judgment on them : *thou shalt make them turn their back.* 2. When God falleth upon his enemies to be avenged upon them, he useth to make them and the beholders see, that he hath set them up as a mark to shoot at : for *he will make ready his ar-rows,* one after another, *against the face of them.* 3. The Lord's wrath shall so meet his enemies in the teeth, where-soever they turn, that they shall be forced to forsake their pursuing of the church: *thou shalt make them turn their back.*

13. *Be thou exalted, Lord, in thine own strength :* so *will we sing and praise thy power.*

He closeth the psalm with giving glory to God, includ-ing also a prayer. Whence learn, 1. When the Lord's church is preserved from persecutors, then the Lord is ex-alted: *be thou exalted,* saith he. 2. When the church is delivered, it is not by her own strength, but by the power of the Lord : *be thou exalted in thine own strength.* 3. Albeit the godly be put to mourn for a time, yet when the Lord appeareth for them, they get matter of joy to them-selves, and praise to God. *So will we sing and praise thy power.*

PSALM XXII.

To the Chief Musician upon Aijeleth Shahar. A Psalm of David.

This psalm is a prophecy of Christ's deepest sufferings, whereof David's exercise is a type. The agony of spirit in Christ, and wrestling of David's faith as the type, is set down to ver. 22, and the victory and the outgate, to the end of the psalm. In the exercise there are three

conflicts between sense and faith. The first conflict, wherein the sense
of trouble is set down, ver. 1, 2, and faith's wrestling against it, ver.
3—5. The second conflict, wherein is the second assault of sense, ver.
6—8, and faith's wrestling against it, ver. 9—11. The third conflict,
wherein the third assault of sense is, ver. 12—18, and faith's wrestling
with it, ver. 19—21. ¶Then follows the victory, set forth, first in a promise of praise, ver. 22; secondly, in an exhortation to all the godly
to praise the Lord, with a reason from his experience, ver. 23, 24;
thirdly, in a renewed promise of praise and thanks, to the edification
of the church, ver. 25; fourthly, in a prophecy of the increase of God's
glory in the earth, as a fruit of Christ's suffering and victory, ver. 26
—31.

1. *My God, my God, why hast thou forsaken me ?*
why art thou so *far from helping me* and from *the
words of my roaring ?*

2. *O my God, I cry in the day time, but thou hearest not, and in the night* season, *and am not silent.*

In this exercise of David the type, and of Christ represented here, both agree in these four things. 1. Both
are under the sense of wrath, and of oppressing trouble ;
2. both are tempted to doubting and desperation ; 3. both
wrestle against the temptation, and against trouble, the occasion thereof ; and 4. both get the victory. But they
differ in these four things. First, in the measure of the
trouble; David's trouble was little in comparison of Christ's
trouble; David laid not down his life under trouble; but
Christ's trouble was incomparably more, and his soul made
heavy unto death, and the trouble took his life from him.
Secondly, in the manner of the trouble they differ ; for
David's trouble was only a probatory exercise, without vindictive wrath ; not a curse, but a cross for trying of him,
and training of him to believe against sense; which trouble
of his paid no debt, neither his own nor any others; but
Christ's trouble was a vindictive and avengeful punishment ;
for real wrath was against him, as he was bearing our sins,
and the bitter curse of the law was cast upon him : for he
was made a curse for us ; and his punishment paid our debt ;
and was expiatory and satisfactory to justice. Thirdly,
though both David and Christ were tempted to doubting
and desperation, yet David's temptation could not be sinless
because of his sinful imperfections, common to him and all
the rest of the godly; the temptation got some advantage of
him, because of the imperfection of his knowledge, faith,
love, and abilities ; and because of the power of the body of

original sin in him. But Christ's passive temptation was altogether sinless, and could not have any sin at all on his part; for albeit he was tempted in all things like unto us, yet it is said, *without sin*. Because, when the prince of this world, Satan, came and took essay of him, he found none of his own stuff in Christ: he had *nothing in him* to work upon; and it was impossible that sin could be in him, being the *Holy One of Israel our sanctifier, Holy Lord God almighty* and man also, in one person, Isaiah vi. 3. Job xii. 41. Fourthly, they differ in their wrestling and victory; for David wrestled not in his own strength, got not the victory in his own strength, but in and through Christ's strength, who gave David a taste only, or a smell rather, of the cup which he was to drink out unto the dregs, and with the dregs, and who helped him to wrestle by faith. But Christ wrestled and got the victory in his own strength, which is one with the strength of the Father; for he is Jehovah our righteousness. In all the psalm we shall look upon every passage, not so much as it concerneth David the type, as wherein it concerneth Christ the truth. In the first conflict of the sense of trouble with faith, learn from the words as they are Christ's words, 1. God is Christ's God; he being considered as God and man, in one person, entered in the covenant of redemption with the Father as Mediator and surety for men; that he shall satisfy justice, and do all the Father's will in behalf of the elect, and that God shall be his God, and the God of all the elect redeemed by him. Therefore doth he here say, *My God, my God*. 2. Faith, as it is a virtue giving perfect trust and credit unto God's promises made to his Son the Redeemer, is a part of that original holiness in the man Christ, and a point of his personal perfection, suitable to his employment. This faith he professeth while he saith, *My God, my God*. 3. Christ, as man lying under the curse of the law for us, was really deserted and forsaken for a time, in regard of all sensible consolation: for it behoved him to bear the wrath, or effects of wrath, due to our sins really, so far as might satisfy for us, and relieve us from wrath. It is true, the man Christ could no more be forsaken, in regard of the divine presence supporting him, than the personal union of the two natures could be dissolved. But in regard of sensible consolation, he was, by way of punishment for

our sins, and by way of cursing our sin in him, really in our
stead for a while deprived, as man, of the sense of the
comfort of his own Godhead. The sense of wrath filling
now the soul of the man to the brim, and running over ;
therefore speaks he of his forsaking, *Why hast thou forsaken
me ?* 4. As sense and reason can express themselves in
seeming contradictory terms, and yet without contradiction
can very well agree in their seeming opposite and inconsistent expressions : so can faith and sense express themselves in seeming contradictory terms, and yet very well
agree ; for as sense, and pain, and sickness, in the patient
can, in its own language and style of natural feeling, say to
the chirurgeon cutting and lancing the flesh, and to the
physician who hath given a bitter potion, *You have hurt me,
you have made me sick :* when indeed in the style of reason
and wit, he hath been healing the man, and recovering him
from sickness ;—so sense of sorrow, grief, pain, and affliction, desertion, and wrath, can speak in the terms of
natural feeling, that which may seem to cross, but doth not
indeed cross, faith speaking in the terms and language of
supernatural theological truth. Therefore, *My God, my God,*
spoken in the perfection of faith's language, can very well
agree with *Why hast thou forsaken me ? why art thou so
far from helping me, and from the words of my roaring ?*
spoken here in the language of perfect natural sense ; for
perfect faith, and perfect natural sense were in our Lord
Christ : very God and very man, completely holy. 5. Bitter was the cup of divine wrath which Christ did drink ;
great was the price our Redeemer paid to ransom us, when
the sense thereof drew forth of his Majesty such expressions. Thus faith and feeling may both speak, each
of them their own language to God in one breath, as
here they do. Now as these words are David's who had in
him sinful corruption of nature, learn, 1. Sense, and temptation, and corrupt nature, may represent God in his dispensations to his own children, as if he had forsaken altogether, and regarded not their hard condition, and would
not help, as here is shown in David's experience. 2. Faith
should correct sense, and refute temptations, and bridle affections, and not suffer their words to go forth, expressing
sense or appearance of doubting God's favour, till first faith
speak, and go before, and fasten its gripes on the covenant ;

as here faith goes foremost, and calleth the Lord, *My God,
my God,* before that sense utter a word. 3. At one time,
and in one exercise, these three may concur. 1. Desertion
in the point of comfort. 2. Growing trouble without help
seen.   And, 3. Apparent rejecting of prayer : and these
three joined together, set sore upon the faith of a child of
God ; for continuance of trouble is a sore temptation, albeit comfort be now and then mixed. Want of sensible comfort, mixed with trouble, doubleth the burden, and disquiet-
eth the mind much ; but to seem to lose labour in prayer
made for either help or comfort, is the heaviest part of the
exercise : *I cry day and night, and thou hearest not,* is
a sad condition. 4. In this case it is the best remedy to
lay the worst of our thoughts single before the Lord, and
to tell him whatsoever is suggested to us, and not to be
secretaries to Satan, but to reveal ourselves fully to God, and
fix ourselves on the covenant of grace, wherein we have
closed with him, yea, and to double and treble our gripes
of *My God.*

3. *But thou* art *holy,* O thou *that inhabitest the
praises of Israel.*

4. *Our fathers trusted in thee : they trusted, and
thou didst deliver them.*

5. *They cried unto thee, and were delivered : they
trusted in thee, and were not confounded.*

Now faith having spoken with sense, and grappled with
the temptation, speaketh alone, that it may prevail. Whence
learn, 1. Were temptations ever so black, faith will not
hearken to an ill word spoken against God, but will justify
God always ; this should be our part in time of greatest
perplexity, to say, *But thou art holy.* 2. It is wisdom for
a soul in a sad exercise, to take side and part with faith,
to gather arguments to strengthen it, to divert the mind
from thinking still on its calamity, and to set it upon the
contemplation of God's perfections in himself, and toward
us in his Gospel, and of the passages of his providence toward
his people, whereby he hath purchased constant praises
at their hands : in the right of which praises and possession whereof, God is resolved to keep himself and to dwell
therein as in a habitation wherein he delights to remain.
O thou that inhabitest the praises of Israel. 3. It is wis-

dom to look to the carriage of the godly in former times;
our fathers trusted in thee; to their trusting, and trusting in God constantly in their trouble; *they trusted in thee,
they trusted,* and the third time *they trusted*: and to look
upon their patient depending on God, doubling their diligence in calling on him; as their straits did grow, *they cried,
they trusted*: and to remember that they did never seek
God in vain, but every one of them were delivered, and not
confounded; for this direction is holden forth to us in this
example, which our Lord Jesus could well make use of for
our consolation, and whereof David made use for his own
upholding.

6. *But I* am *a worm and no man; a reproach of
men, and despised of the people.*

7. *All they that see me, laugh me to scorn: they
shoot out the lip, they shake the head,* saying,

8. *He trusted on the Lord, that he would deliver
him: let him deliver him, seeing he delighted in him.*

The second conflict, wherein the sense of trouble is set
forth as a new assaulting of faith. Whence learn, 1.
Never was any child of God before Christ under so much
misery as Christ was himself: his own heavens, his own
Father, his own Godhead, did hide their face and consolation
from him: our sins willingly taken on him, and God's
wrath pressed the weight of punishment with the full
power of justice, both upon his soul and body: those for
whom he died despised him; he himself being emptied
of all things which make men respected to the world, and
depressed lower than ever any man was, as a worm to
be trod upon, he was made a matter of common talk and
reproach in all men's mouths; set at naught by the
basest of the people; derided and scorned in his most holy
behaviour; sport and matter of laughter was made of
his sufferings; malice feeding itself with pleasure upon his
pain and misery, and expressing itself with the basest signs
of disgrace which disdain could devise, for flouting of him,
mocking of his saving doctrine, and faithful testimony given
unto it; insulting over him, as if he had been neither God's
Son, nor an honest man; and all this was counted little
enough for satisfaction to justice, exacting of him, as the
due punishment of our sins, whatsoever is imported in the
sad expression set down in the text. 2. As the more

misery the children of God are under, the more doth temptation make their misery seem weighty, for bearing down
their confidence in God : so the more that misery seemeth
to grow, and the world to turn their back on God's children in their trials, the more should they draw near to
God, and lay out their case before him, as here we are
taught by this example. 3. Let no man wonder to be despised of men, and mocked for religion, for so was the man
according to God's own heart ; and Christ our Lord was
mocked more than any in his sad sufferings. *Let God deliver him, seeing he delighted in him,* said his enemies.

9. *But thou* art *he that took me out of the womb;
thou didst make me hope* when I was *upon my mother's
breasts.*

10. *I was cast upon thee from the womb: thou* art
my God from my mother's belly.

11. *Be not far from me, for trouble* is *near; for*
there is *none to help.*

Here faith opposeth whatsoever the complaint could import to the prejudice of confidence, and laboureth to
strengthen itself by all arguments. Whence learn, 1. As
Satan maketh assault after assault against faith, upon new
representations of calamity and misery, so we should raise
bulwark after bulwark for defence; and after we have
looked upon other men's experiences before us, we should
recount our own experiences of God's care towards us, and
should make use of all that the Lord hath done unto us for
our strengthening ; for so doth this example teach us.
2. Albeit men in a fit of misbelief, will admit no proof of
God's respect unto them, except singularities, and will
question also special grace when it is given, yet the humbled believer is so wise as to make use of the most common
benefit which the man hath received from God for confirmation of his own faith ; even the ordinary work of our
conception, frame of body, birth, and education, may suffice us to draw in to God who made us, and hath done so
much for us (ere we could implore him, or do any thing for
ourselves,) as may encourage us to come to him, and seek
his favour, whatsoever objection can be made to the contrary, for this example teacheth us so to do. 3. Seeing the
Lord doeth many things for us, which in the time he doeth

them for us we do not observe, it is our duty to look upon
them afterwards, that they may furnish us with matter of
praise to God and faith in him ; for so doth this example
teach us. 4. Whatsoever instruments and means the Lord
maketh use of, the spiritual eye pierceth through them,
and looketh on God as worker of all things, for and upon
them from their cradle: *thou lookest me out of my mother's
womb.* 5. Children born within the covenant have God
for their God from their nativity, and may lay their reckoning so ; and whensoever they would draw near to God to
make use of the covenant, they may say, *Thou art my God
from my mother's belly.* 6. The approaching of trouble,
and nearness of danger, should draw us near to God : who
in an instant can interpose himself between us and the evil :
and the less help we have beside the Lord himself, the more
hope may we have to be helped by God. This is the prophet's plea, *be not far from me, for trouble is near, &c.*

12. *Many bulls have compassed me: strong* bulls *of
Bashan have beset me round.*

13. *They gaped upon me* with *their mouths,* as *a
ravening and a roaring lion.*

From v. 12—22, is the third conflict of sense with faith,
upon the consideration of the multitude, power, and cruelty
of his enemies, compared with his own infirmity, now
emptied of all strength to resist them ; and these are mixed
one with another. The enemy's terribleness is first set
forth, then his emptiness and weakness by turns, to v. 19 ;
unto all which faith opposeth itself, by prayer to God, to
v. 22. He compareth, v. 12, 13, his persecutors to *bulls,
many bulls,* strong, cruel, gaping, roaring, devouring lions.
Whence learn, 1. The persecutors of Christ and his people
are but beastly sensual bodies, sold to this present world,
and destitute of grace and humility : more like in their
rage to savage beasts than to rational men ; commonly also
they are men of riches and worldly power, fed and fat bulls,
and many in number, all of them ready for an ill turn, and
so cruel, that nothing less will satisfy them than blood and
slaughter, as they are here described. And no wonder
that Christ's servants shall find it so in their case, seeing
Christ himself and his servants before us have had experience of such enemies.

14. *I am poured out like water, and all my bones are out of joint: my heart is like wax; it is melted in the midst of my bowels.*

15. *My strength is dried up like a potsherd; and my tongue cleaveth to my jaws; and thou hast brought me into the dust of death.*

What the Lord wrought upon his body, and natural spirits, and strength, is here set down. Whence learn, 1. It was determined by God, that with outward persecution of Christ, by his cruel adversaries, the Father should bruise him and break him inwardly also, and punish him with all severity : for here his suffering is in body and mind, in flesh and bones, in his natural spirit and natural courage, in heart and whole strength, that in nothing he should be un-punished, wherein we sinners are found polluted : to the intent, that he being fully emptied, the ransom might be full ; he is *poured like water*, and emptied of all that the created human nature could furnish. The terror of divine justice and wrath did in a manner loose *all the joints of his body*, so that natural courage, before the dreadful avenger of sin, did fail, *his heart was made soft like wax* to receive and keep the impression of divine terror, till justice should be satisfied, and was dissolved like wax, in the point of resolu-tion to withstand it. It is *melted in the midst of his bowels*, his natural strength is dried, burnt up like a *potsherd*, baken in the fire ; his mouth was stopped from all defence and apology, for he was content to be holden as guilty, standing in our room, *therefore his tongue cleaved to his jaws*. And in a word, the hand of God exacteth the full price of him, and brings him down so, as there is not a bit of him free of the punishment ; *thou*, saith he, *hast brought me into the dust of death*. This, David had but a taste of in his deepest trouble. The verity and weight of this are to be found only in Christ, of whom this was prophesied, that it should come, and indeed is come, done and ended, and so it behoved to be.

16. *For dogs have compassed me; the assembly of the wicked have inclosed me; they pierced my hands and my feet.*

Again he bringeth forth his enemies' part, to show us that Christ's enemies were to prove but bloody dogs, when they should be let loose upon him, whom nothing but *Crucify him*, *crucify him*, could satisfy: and such will they be still who persecute his church. Next, to show, that although his enemies were to be the assembly of the visible church, for open profession, yet by rejecting his grace, and opposing him in God's sight and estimation, they were holden for the *assembly of the wicked*. Thirdly, to foreshow the death of the cross to be appointed for Christ, it is said, *they pierced my hands and my feet*.

17. *I may tell all my bones: they look* and *stare upon me.*

18. *They part my garments among them, and cast lots upon my vesture.*

Another, and further point of Christ's fore-prophesied suffering, is his nakedness on the cross, and the discovery of his lean body, being wasted with decreed sorrows, and the gazing of his enemies upon him hanging on the cross, and the parting of his garments among the soldiers, and the casting of lots for his upper garment, because it was woven, and could not be divided. Whence learn, 1. All that our Lord Jesus suffered, was before decreed and agreed upon, betwixt the Father and the Son, and foretold by Christ himself long before his incarnation, speaking by his Spirit in his prophets, as here appeareth by the description of our Lord's death and passion, so plainly and particularly as if it were a history, and not a prophecy. 2. Beside pain of body, leanness of flesh, with daily sorrows and trouble of spirit, the least disgrace done to our Lord, the least wrong, a look unto him, the least injury in the matter of his clothing, are all reckoned up in his sufferings, all counted up in the price of redemption, that there may be nothing inlacking in the punishment of our cautioner, whereby God's justice might be satisfied, or our consciences quieted, for the expiation of our sin, by his suffering in body, soul, fame, apparel, and every other thing else, wherein justice could overtake the guilty.

19. *But be not thou far from me, O Lord, O my strength, haste thee to help me.*

Unto this last assault, faith opposeth prayer for divine assistance, for strength to bear out, and for delivery, in all which he was heard. Whence learn, 1. Faith is made vic-

torious over all assaults, by opening of its temptations to
God, and putting up prayer to him for help, as here is seen.
2. If God shall not withdraw his sweet presence for supporting a soul, albeit it should not find his presence for
comforting of it, supporting presence may suffice in a time
of sad exercise: for this much did satisfy our God in his
agony: *be not thou far from me, O Lord.*   3. Faith findeth
God to be its strength when the believer is emptied of his
own strength; *O my strength,* saith David, the type, and
Christ as man by him represented.   4. As the haste of our
necessity doth require, we may without limitation request
the Lord to haste: *haste thee to help me.*

20. *Deliver my soul from the sword: my darling
from the power of the dog.*

21. *Save me from the lion's mouth: for thou hast
heard me from the horns of the unicorns.*

He prayeth to be delivered from the violent blood-shedder,
and bloody doggish persecutor, and from the cruel lion-like
oppressor, and then saith presently, that he is heard and
delivered from the power of the enemies which were setting
upon him as unicorns. Now concerning David, the matter
is clear; for he was delivered so from his enemies, that they
got not his life: but of Christ the question may be, how he
was delivered, seeing his life is taken: for answer, Christ
here doth say, that he was delivered; and so it was indeed;
for when he had paid the price, he was not holden by the
bonds of death, and the grave, but rose again the third day.
Whence learn, 1. Christ was no less delivered from dogs,
lions, unicorns, his persecuting enemies, by his resurrection after death, than if he had been taken out of their
hands, when they came to apprehend him in the garden ;
yea, this delivery out of the grave, was a far greater delivery than if he had not been slain at all: for then he had
delivered himself only, and not us: but now by the laying
down of his life, he hath discharged himself of his suretyship
for us, and delivered us with himself, and so hath saved
both himself and us; yea, by his rising out of the grave,
he is demonstrated more fully to be the Son of God, than by
any of his miraculous escapings out from the hands of the
multitude, when they were about to apprehend him: *thou
hast heard me,* that is, delivered me. 2. To get victory

over trouble, is a no less glorious delivery from trouble, than to be preserved from falling into trouble; yea, it is a more glorious delivery. For the troubles are broken, by falling on the believer, like waves of the sea on the rock, and the believer remaineth victor, and settled as a rock. 3. It is a notable argument of confidence to be heard by way of delivery, when a man can say he hath in extremity of danger prayed, and hath been heard as a supplicant: *save me, for thou hast heard me from the horns of the unicorns.*

22. *I will declare thy name unto my brethren: in the midst of the congregation will I praise thee.*

After the conflict, the victory and outgate by way of thanksgiving is set down, to the end of the psalm: wherein David's part is but a little shadow, and is swallowed up here in Christ's glory, shining in the fruits of his passion and resurrection. Learn from David's part, that delivery foreseen by faith, worketh in some sort the effects of the delivery past in effect; to wit, quietness, peace, joy, and thanksgiving; as here is to be seen. From Christ's part promising and prophesying of the fruits of his death and resurrection, learn 1. Christ, though he be God Almighty; yet by reason of his incarnation, for the redeemed's sake, he is not ashamed to call them *brethren.* 2. The preaching of the gospel of Christ's satisfaction for our sins by death, and of his resurrection for our justification, is matter of great praise to God and comfort to the redeemed: *I will declare,* saith Christ, *thy name to my brethren.* 3. In the right preaching of the gospel, the ministers are in effect but Christ's voice. Christ himself is the principal prophet and preacher: *for I,* saith he, *will declare thy name in the midst of the* great *congregation;* to wit, of the whole catholic church on earth.

23. *Ye that fear the Lord, praise him: all ye the seed of Jacob, glorify him; and fear him all ye the seed of Israel.*

24. *For he hath not despised nor abhorred the affliction of the afflicted; neither hath he hid his face from him; but when he cried unto him he heard.*

He exhorteth all that fear God, to praise and glorify God, because of Christ's victory, and God's hearkening un-

to his intercession made for the redeemed. Whence learn,
1. Such as are made partakers of the benefit of Christ's passion and resurrection, are chiefly called, and bound to praise
God for their redemption, and to fear God more and more,
that they may be more and more fitted to praise and glorify
him ; for of a sanctified mouth only will God accept praise.
*Ye that fear the Lord, praise him : all ye seed of Jacob,
glorify him; and fear him, all ye the seed of Israel.* 2. The
Father's hearkening unto Christ's intercession, and delivering
of him from our sin, and our deserved punishment laid upon
him, is the common benefit of all the redeemed, the matter
of their common thanksgiving and praise, and the matter
of their assurance of their delivery from sin and death ; of
the certainty of which delivery Christ's deliverance is both
a cause and a pawn : *for he hath not hid his face from
him, but when he cried, he heard him.* 3. Neither the
sense of a man's own meanness and despicableness, nor the
mean estimation that the world hath of him, will prejudge
him when he is a supplicant at the Lord's hand ; *for he
hath not despised, nor abhorred the afflictions of the afflicted.*

25. *My praise* shall be *of thee in the great congregation : I will pay my vows before them that fear him.*

He reneweth the promise of thanksgiving, which, as it
concerneth David, teacheth, 1. That the purpose of praising God, is no light motion in the hearts of his children,
when the Lord hath given them experience of his respect
to them ; but a fixed and solid resolution to set forth
the goodness of God before others. For here he receiveth his promise to praise. 2. The Lord, and the Lord
only, is the theme which the believer handleth in point
of praise ; no other subject of praise acknowledgeth he ;
my praise shall be of thee, &c. 3. The opportunity of
time, place, and persons, offered for praising of God,
ought to be taken, and made use of by every one, according
to their calling : *my praise shall be of thee in the great congregation.* 4. Duties, specially when lying upon us by vows
or oaths, ought to be the more heeded, and made conscience
of : *I will pay my vows before them that fear him.* As this
concerns Christ's undertaking, it teacheth, 1. The Son of
God, and promised Son of David, Christ Jesus, by all the
work of redemption, studieth, as to bring salvation to his

elect, so to honour the Father; saying here, *My praise shall be of thee in the great congregation.* 2. Albeit our Lord hath finished all his undertaking for the payment of the price and ransom of redemption, yet hath he not yet performed all which he hath undertaken for making use of his purchased salvation, unto the enlarging of the glory of his Father, and gathering into the great congregation all his redeemed ones to be worshippers of the Father in spirit and truth: but as he is still upon this work from generation to generation, so is he willing still to lie under this engagement and these vows, till he perform them to the full: *I will pay my vows before them that fear him.*

26. *The meek shall eat and be satisfied: they shall praise the Lord that seek him: your heart shall live for ever.*

He alludeth to the manner of offering peace-offerings, where the godly friends concurring in the thanksgiving, had a share in the feast of what was sacrificed. Whence learn, 1. The mercy bestowed upon one of the godly, serveth to refresh the souls of the rest: and in special there is a banquet prepared for the souls of the redeemed by the purchase of Christ's sacrifice, whereof the humbled believer is made partaker: *the meek shall eat, and be satisfied.* 2. Albeit the believer at all times do not find the sweetness of this feast, but be put to work after a meal received, put to fight after a feast, and made hungry after a new meal, and be made to pray for it, and to seek after the Lord in the use of the means, yet shall he eat again in due time, and be satisfied: *for they shall praise the Lord that seek him,* is as much as they that seek him, shall find so much as shall make them both to have cause of praising, and also in effect to praise him. 3. Whatsoever alterations or vicissitudes of things be in the condition of humble believers, seeking more and more communion with God, they may be sure of eternal life, beside what they get by way of earnest in this life; for the Spirit of the Lord, directing his speech to them, hath said, *Your heart shall live for ever.*

27. *All the ends of the world shall remember, and turn unto the Lord: and all the kindreds of the nations shall worship before thee.*

28. *For the kingdom* is *the Lord's; and he* is *the governor among the nations.*

Now followeth special prophecies of the enlargement of
Christ's kingdom, wherein the prophet by the Spirit of prophecy doth speak, and teach us, 1. That the calling of the
Gentiles after Christ's resurrection, was a concluded matter
with God, whereof he gave warning long before it came,
which though it be come to pass, yet not in so ample a measure as may be yet further expected ; because, for the making of these words yet more clearly seen to be fulfilled, it
shall come to pass, that *all the ends of the world shall remember.* 2. So long as men shall lie unconverted, they know
not what they are doing, they are as men sleeping or distracted, not making use of so much as the very principles
of truth, which, by the light of common reason from inspection of the creatures, may be learned, concerning the invisible things of God ; but when the light of Christ's gospel
shineth in upon their heart, they are made *to remember and
turn to the Lord.* 3. Such as are converted, make God
the object of their worship, embrace his ordinances, and
subject themselves to his laws and discipline ; *for they worship before him,* become subjects to him, and that by the
powerful subduing of them to himself: *for the kingdom is
the Lord's, and he is governor among the nations.*

29. *All* they that be *fat upon earth shall eat and
worship : all they that go down to the dust shall bow
before him ; and none can keep alive his own soul.*

30. *A seed shall serve him; it shall be accounted to
the Lord for a generation.*

31. *They shall come, and shall declare his righteousness unto a people that shall be born, that he hath
done* this.

A further clearing of this prophecy of Christ's kingdom
enlarged among the Gentiles. Whence learn, 1. That
kings, rulers, and magistrates shall have no cause of jealousy from Christ's kingdom, and his governing over nations ; for so many of them as shall embrace Jesus Christ,
not only may brook their places, honours, riches, and all
lawful benefits, wherein their fatness and worldly welfare
seem to consist; but also shall be made partakers of the
delicates of the Lord's house, which shall so satisfy their
souls, as they shall count his gospel their choice cheer, and
shall bless God for his consolations ; for it is promised to all

Christ's true subjects, who are in high place: *all they that be fat upon earth shall eat and worship.* 2. As the highest condition worldly shall not be hurt by obedience to Christ, but helped, for the benefit of the true believer; so believers in the meanest condition they can be in on earth, shall find relief, comfort, and making up of all their inlacks in Jesus Christ, and shall fall down and worship their rich and bountiful Lord: *all that go down to the dust shall bow before him.* 3. Whosoever shall not come to Christ to be saved by him, shall perish ; and they that come unto him, shall be forced to hold their salvation of him: *for none can keep alive his own soul*: this is the proper work of the only Saviour Jesus. 4. Albeit every particular person, in every nation and kingdom, be not converted unto Christ: yet so many persons of all ranks, out of all nations, shall be converted, as shall make evident Christ's power and sovereignty to conquer subjects to himself at his pleasure, even as many as may perpetuate his kingdom, and the succession of worshippers of him from one generation to another ; *for a seed shall serve him, it shall be accounted to the Lord for a generation :* he will make little reckoning of the rest, whom he converteth not. 5. Albeit there be little appearance of accomplishing prophecies and promises of the propagation of Christ's kingdom from age to age, yet the promise and prophecy shall be fulfilled : *they shall come,* who shall receive the doctrine of Christ's righteousness by faith in him, and *shall declare this righteousness* of faith, and God's faithfulness in promise-keeping, *to another generation, unto a people that shall be born.* 6. The whole work of redemption, converting of souls, comforting of souls, propagation of the doctrine of righteousness, and manifestation of God's glory thereby, shall from age to age be declared to be the work of God himself, which he doth by his instruments and means ; *they shall declare to their children* and successors, that *God hath done this* ; to wit, all that is spoken of here, or elsewhere in his word : *unto a people that shall be born, that he hath done this.*

PSALM XXIII.

A Psalm of David.

This Psalm is the expression of the prophet's confidence in God's grace, wherein, from the settling himself in the belief of our covenanted relation between God and him, he draweth sundry comfortable conclusions and confirmations of faith from it, concerning the Lord's furnishing every necessary good thing to him, v. 1, 2; for recovery of him from every evil condition, wherein he may fall, v. 3; and for assisting and comforting him in the greatest danger he could fall into, v. 4; and for making him blessed in despite of his enemies, v. 5; and for his continuing in God's grace and fellowship for ever, v. 6.

1. *The Lord is my shepherd, I shall not want.*

He layeth down for a ground his relation to God, and thence confirmeth his assurance to have the fruits thereof. Whence learn, 1. The Lord is content to demit himself to be compared unto any thing which may import his love, and respect, and care of his own: as here for our comfort he is pleased to be called a *shepherd.* 2. The grounds of our faith in God, making us to have right unto him by covenant, should be solidly laid ; and these being firmly laid, then comfortable conclusions may, and should be, drawn from thence, as here the prophet doeth. 3. In special, whatsoever sweet relation the believer standeth in with God, he may assure himself of all the fruits, and good, which that relation can import. As here having said, *the Lord is my shepherd*, he assureth himself then, *he shall not want ;* to wit, what such a shepherd seeth necessary for such a sheep.

2. *He maketh me to lie down in green pastures : he leadeth me beside the still waters.*

3. *He restoreth my soul : he leadeth me in the paths of righteousness for his name's sake.*

He goeth on numbering the benefits following from the foresaid relation, partly showing what experience he hath had, partly assuring himself what further to find. Whence learn, 1. As the shepherd provideth good and wholesome pasture for his sheep, and a place of safety and rest, with the commodity of all needful refreshment of calm running waters : so doth the Lord furnish the food of life to the believer with quiet rest, and satisfaction of timous consolation, by his Word and Spirit : *he maketh me lie down in green pastures, &c.* 2. It is possible through the evil that is in us, we may fall into decay of graces, into sicknesses of divers

sorts; yea, and that we may wander away from the shepherd,
and the society of the flock sometime. In which case we
should perish, if our careful Lord did not apply himself to
our necessities, to relieve us; for it is *he that restoreth
our soul*; it is he that reclaimeth us from our wanderings;
it is he that directeth us, and keepeth us from going on
still in by-paths: *he leadeth me*, saith he, *in the paths of
righteousness*. 3. It is not for any good we deserve, or
have done, or can do, for which he taketh such care of his
weak and foolish children. It is for the glory of his free
grace, constant love, and sworn covenant, even *for his own
name's sake.*

4 *Yea, though I walk through the valley of the shadow of death, I will fear no evil: for thou* art *with
me; thy rod and thy staff they comfort me.*

He presupposeth he may fall into new and harder troubles
than ever he fell into before, and yet hopes to be delivered
therefrom. Whence learn, 1. The believer in his best condition may not promise to himself immunity from trouble
or perils; but must prepare for the worst, even to be put
to extreme danger of perishing, and in such darkness as
were most like, and near (unto death) *to walk through the
valley of the shadow of death,* where sheep may fall into the
pit, or be fallen upon by every devouring beast in the dark.
2. The fruit of former delivery out of trouble, should encourage us to hope for deliverance out of whatsoever new
trouble we may fall into, as the prophet's example doth
teach. 3. Faith after a victory is very stout, and hath
warrant indeed to be so, and may and should resolve to be
stout by God's grace; howsoever, when trouble cometh,
which is the touchstone of the strength of faith, it may
discover weakness for a time: for here David saith, *I will
fear no evil, though I walk through the valley of the shadow of death.* 4. The consideration of God's covenanted
presence with his own in trouble, and of his power to protect and deliver them, and of his wisdom and goodness to
make his own profit by troubles, may and should comfort
the believer against the fear of perishing, in whatsoever
trouble; for David giveth this as a reason of not fearing
evil, *Thou art with me, thy rod and thy staff they comfort
me.*

5. *Thou preparest a table before me in the presence of mine enemies ; thou anointest my head with oil ; my cup runneth over.*

From the grounds of his faith, confirmed by experience, he seeth still satisfaction from God, who giveth the banquet to him, as it were, in his enemies' sight. Whence learn. 1. Albeit sometimes the believer may be put to hardship and hazard, for trying and training of his faith ; yet sometimes also the Lord will give him rich evidence of his love and kindness unto him, if not in both outward and inward benefits, yet at least in spiritual consolations comparable to a royal feast ; as here, *thou preparest a table before me.* 2. Although the enemies of the godly are not few, both bodily and spiritual, all concurring to mar the felicity of the Lord's children, yet shall they not be able to hinder their sense, now and then, of satisfactory blessedness maugre them all ; for as oft as God seeth fit, he giveth his own banquet *in the presence of his enemies.* 3. When it pleaseth the Lord to comfort a believer, and to give him the banquet, there is nothing wanting, during the time of the Lord's comfortable entertaining of him, which may strengthen him or rejoice him ; but as much given unto him sensibly, as may make him say, *thou anointest my head with oil, and my cup runneth over,* Psal. xcii. 10, and civ. 15.

6. *Surely goodness and mercy shall follow me all the days of my life ; and I will dwell in the house of the Lord for ever.*

He showeth that in his former speeches, he meant not of earthly benefits, although these also be worthy of acknowledgment and of thanksgiving for them ; but of spiritual mercies, by this, that he is assured of the continuance thereof, in this life and in the life to come. Whence learn. 1. The delight and satisfaction of the believer is not in any earthly portion, but in God's good-will and pity toward him ; God's goodness and mercy is the matter of his contentment. 2. An humble believer, who in his own eyes is like a weak, witless sheep, and yet doth follow the shepherd, may assure himself, from the covenant relation between God and him, of the constancy of God's good-will and actual outletting of liberal gifts of good things unto him, and of removing of evils, both of sin and of the fruits

of it, and be persuaded of his own perseverance in the way
to salvation, all the days of his life; for here is an instance
of it, *surely goodness and mercy shall follow me all the
days of my life.* 3. As a believer may be assured of the
constant course of God's love to follow him, and of his own
preserving in the way of life, so may he be persuaded of
eternal life, and everlasting communion with God in heaven.
And this perfecteth the felicity of the believer; and no less
can do it than this; *I will dwell in the house of the Lord
for ever.*

PSALM XXIV.

A Psalm of David.

The psalmist having in the first place set down God's Lordship in the
world, that he may thereby commend the special prerogative of the
true church, v. 1, 2, describeth, in the next place, the true citizens of this
spiritual kingdom, v. 3—6; and exhorteth, in the third place, all incorporations, and in special the visible church, to accept the offer of a
more entire communion with God in Christ, that they may enjoy the
spiritual privileges of the subjects of the invisible and spiritual kingdom, v. 7—10.

1. *The earth is the Lord's, and the fulness thereof;
the world, and they that dwell therein:*

2. *For he hath founded it upon the seas, and established it upon the floods.*

From the lordship and sovereignty of God over all the
world, learn, 1. The Lord's power and authority over the
saints, considered in their natural condition, is no less than
over the rest of the world, and the Lord is no more bound
to one than to another, laying aside the decree of his own
good-will and pleasure; *the earth is the Lord's and the fulness thereof; the world, and they that dwell therein.* 2. The
earth is as full of the riches of God's bounty towards man
as it can hold; and the standing miracle of the dry land,
lifted up contrary to the nature of that element, which is to
be under and not above, and much higher than the element
of water, is a standing evidence of God's power and care
employed to make a habitation for man: *for he hath founded the earth upon the seas, and established it upon the floods,*
commanding the element of water to go down below the
earth, as if it were the foundation thereof.

3. *Who shall ascend into the hill of the Lord? and who shall stand in his holy place?*

4. *He that hath clean hands, and a pure heart; who hath not lifted up his soul unto vanity, nor sworn deceitfully.*

5. *He shall receive the blessing from the Lord, and righteousness from the God of his salvation.*

6. *This* is *the generation of them that seek him, that seek thy face, O Jacob.   Selah.*

In the second place, he cometh to the special dominion of God and Christ in the church, and asketh for the marks and privileges of the true subjects of this kingdom. Whence learn, 1. God hath chosen a church out of all the earth, to be his peculiar people, with whom he may converse, and to whom he may give privilege of communion for ever with himself; he hath his own *holy and high hill,* he hath his own *holy place,* to wit, a holy universal church, represented by the *hill of Zion,* lifted up above the inferior valleys; he hath his holy tabernacle, where he giveth the signs of his presence, separate from the common multitude, and worldly affairs; *who shall ascend into the hill of the Lord? and who shall stand in his holy place?* He compareth the invisible church to a *hill* or *mountain,* and *the holy place,* because God's true church indeed for firmness, durableness, dignity above all other incorporations, and spiritual sublimity, is like a *hill* above the plain, lifted up above all the world, a holy society, wherein God delighteth to dwell. 2. Not every one who is a member of the visible church, but only true converts, who make up the invisible church, have the honour and happiness of ascending unto the spiritual use, end, meaning, and profit of the ordinances of God in his church, and of keeping constant communion with God in heaven, represented by standing in the *holy place.* Therefore, for stirring up of outward professors of religion, to examine themselves, lest they be mistaken and so perish, the question is here made to God to show *who shall ascend to his hill, and who shall stand in his holy place.* 3. The marks of a citizen of the invisible church and kingdom of God, are only such as God and a man's own conscience can soundly judge of; to wit, faith in God, manifested by endeavoured sanctity of thoughts, words, and deeds, by way of obedience to the first and second table in sincerity: for he must, after covenanting with God by faith which makes him a subject, study also cleanness of hands, or innocency of life, and that out of a pure heart, cleansed by the blood of sprinkling for justification, and by the clean water of begun sanctification; and therefore he must not any more look upon the deceitful baits of sin, with a longing desire to have them; for that were to *lift up his soul unto vanity.* Neither must he misregard an oath, whether in or after the taking of it; for that were to *swear deceitfully,* seeming to stand in awe of God when he doth not fear him at all. 4. Every believer who setteth himself to bring forth the fruits of his faith in obedience to God's law, shall have a gracious reward; *he shall receive the blessing from the Lord.* 5. The holy life of the true believer, is not the cause of his justification before God, by reason of the imperfection thereof, and impossibility to satisfy the law thereby; but he shall receive justification and eternal life, as a free gift from God, by virtue of the covenant of grace: therefore it is said here, that *he shall receive righteousness from the God of his salvation.* 6. Whosoever they be within the visible church, who have the marks of true covenanters, such as are here described, yea, whosoever are seeking God, to make them such; whosoever are seeking reconciliation with God, and communion with him, whether they be Jews or Gentiles, bond or free, male or female; they are the generation that shall ascend and dwell in God's holy place; for *this is the generation of them that seek him.* The generation that seek thy face, saith he to God. This is the true Jacob, the true heir of the promises.

7. *Lift up your heads, O ye gates; and be ye lift up, ye everlasting doors; and the King of glory shall come in.*

8. *Who* is *this King of glory? The Lord strong and mighty, the Lord mighty in battle.*

9. *Lift up your heads, O ye gates; even lift them up, ye everlasting doors; and the King of glory shall come in.*

10. *Who* is *this King of glory? The Lord of hosts, he* is *the King of glory. Selah.*

In the third place, having described those persons who

shall surely dwell in heaven with God, he exhorteth all the members of the visible church, to the intent they may receive righteousness and salvation from God (who is in covenant with his church), heartily to welcome Christ Jesus, the King of glory and Lord of hosts, dwelling in the midst of them in the tabernacle, shadowing forth and signifying his coming in the flesh, by his giving oracles from the ark of the covenant, defending them, feeding them, and fighting their battles, and at length in David's time ascending on mount Zion, he and the ark of the covenant triumphantly, to let them see in a shadow, how, after his great battles, foughten for our redemption, he should ascend to heaven, and make way for his subjects to come up after him, to dwell with him: he exhorteth, I say, patent doors to be made unto him, wherever he offereth himself to kingdoms, cities, incorporations, visible churches, families, and hearts of men in special. Whence learn, 1. The way to make men true converts, true believers, true saints, and inheritors of heaven, is to receive Christ heartily and honourably, to cast up doors in hearty consent of faith and love, like triumphant arches, for welcoming so glorious a conqueror to be their guest; *lift up your heads, O ye gates, &c.* 2. Whosoever shall receive the offer, and open the heart to him, he shall close covenant with him: *be ye lift up, ye everlasting doors, and the King of glory shall come in.* 3. He is an unknown•king till he be manifested to us; and such as are wise, when they hear of him, will seek to know him: *who is this King of glory?* will be their question. 4. Such as seek to know Christ, shall indeed have experimental knowledge of him: that he is able to save them to the uttermost, to work all their work for them, to defend them from their adversaries, and to give them complete victory; *he is the Lord strong and mighty, the Lord mighty in battle.* 5. We have need again and again to hear the offer of Christ's grace, and to be wakened up to observe Christ and his glory; need to be exhorted again and again to open our hearts wide to him: *lift up your heads, ye gates,* the second time. 6. Christ is indeed glorious, and a glorious king, in all the passages of redemption, and salvation of his people; albeit the ignorance and unbelief, and the crosses and troubles following his kingdom in this world, do obscure his glory to the carnal eye: and therefore no wonder, that men do often move the question about his kingdom and glory, asking, *who is the King of glory?* 7. Christ Jesus (whose ascension was prefigured by the ascending of the ark upon mount Zion, convoyed with David, and all Israel,) as he is true man, so he is also very God Almighty, one with the Father, and Holy Spirit, in his Godhead: for *the Lord of hosts he is the King of glory.*

PSALM XXV.

A Psalm of David.

In this psalm the prophet being in danger of his life by his enemies without, and troubled with the sense of sin within, maketh his prayer for relief from both, mixing meditation with prayer, along the psalm, for strengthening of his faith: so first he prayeth from v. 1 to 8, then meditateth, v. 8—10. In the third room he prayeth again, v. 11. In the fourth is a new meditation, v. 12—15. In the last room is a prayer from v. 16 to the end.

1. *Unto thee, O Lord, do I lift up my soul.*

2. *O my God, I trust in thee: let me not be ashamed; let not mine enemies triumph over me.*

3. *Yea, let none that wait on thee be ashamed: let them be ashamed which transgress without cause.*

In the entry of his prayer, he draweth his eye off all relief save God alone, and fixeth his trust upon him, and then prayeth. Whence learn, 1. It is necessary for a supplicant, if he would have help from God, to loose his confidence off all creature help, and set his eye and heart on God, as David here *lifteth up his soul to God.* 2. Faith in God, fixed on the covenant, giveth wings to the soul, as misbelief causeth it to sink: *O my God,* saith he, *I lift up my soul, I trust in thee.* 3. It is not enough to act faith in time of a strait; but it is profitable to observe also the least measure of faith bestowed on us, and to entertain it, were it never so little, and to avow it that it may be fixed when we go to pray: for, before David put up any petition, he prefixeth, *I lift my soul to thee, I trust in thee;* for otherwise the prayer of the supplicant can find no footing. 4. The believing supplicant shall never be disappointed of promised help; nor shall the hope and expectation of the enemies of God be satisfied: *he will not suffer the believer to be ashamed, nor the enemy long to triumph.* 5. The godly in their prayers are not selfish, nor suitors for singularities to be granted unto them, but are content, yea and desirous, that all other believers may share in their mercies: *yea, let none that wait for thee be ashamed,* saith he. 6. The godly shall not want enemies, albeit they give no offence to the world: for carnal hope and expectation to obtain worldly gain by opposing of the godly, may, and usually doth, set the wicked on work against them; but they that look to have advantage that way, shall be close disappointed; for the godly shall escape their snare, and they shall lose their hoped advantage, and shall gain to themselves nothing save shame and a mischief: for *let them be ashamed that transgress without a cause,* is an enduring petition, and a granted petition against them.

4. *Shew me thy ways, O Lord; teach me thy paths.*

5. *Lead me in thy truth, and teach me: for thou art the God of my salvation; on thee do I wait all the day.*

6. *Remember, O Lord, thy tender mercies and thy loving-kindnesses; for they* have been *ever of old.*

Here he prayeth for grace to behave himself holily under his exercise, and to have renewed experiences of mercies, such as he had felt formerly. Whence learn, 1. The understanding of the way how the Lord useth to deal with his children, serveth greatly for patient bearing of affliction; and the best way to eschew the snare of adversaries, is to carry ourselves holily. Therefore prayeth David four times to be instructed, and effectually taught and guided in the ways and paths of God's truth or faithful word. 2. Because the Lord in covenanting with us, taketh the work of our salvation in hand, not to lay it down till he hath perfected it; he alloweth his children, in all particular difficulties, to hold this ground, and constantly to expect the accomplishment thereof, whatsoever strait they fall into: and to wait for direction how to behave themselves, till it be perfected: for David giveth this for a reason of his prayer, *thou art the God of my salvation; on thee do I wait all the day long.* 3. Though the course of kindness and mercy seem to be interrupted by affliction and temporal desertion, and to be forgotten on God's part; yet faith must make use of experiences, and read them over unto God out of the register of a sanctified memory, as a recorder to him that

F

cannot forget: *remember thy tender mercies, O Lord, and thy loving-kindnesses.* 4. Mercies and kindnesses sometimes felt, may be, and should be, followed up unto the very fountain of eternal love and election from which they came ; so shall the channel be opened and run clear with fresh consolation so much the sooner ; *remember thy mercies to me, for they have been ever of old.*

7. *Remember not the sins of my youth, nor my transgressions : according to thy mercy remember thou me for thy goodness' sake, O Lord.*

He laboureth to have his sins removed, as the chief impediment of the granting of his prayer. Whence learn, 1. New afflictions may easily renew the sense of old sins, even from the time of youth, albeit forgiven of God, and forgotten by the believer, and the tempter can make use thereof against faith in the day of trouble ; in which case the believer without loss may read over blotted accounts, and renew petitions for pardon: *remember not,* saith David, *the sins of my youth, nor my transgressions.* 2. As God holdeth two courts in a man's conscience, concerning sin ; one of justice according to the law, or covenant of works ; another of mercy, according to the gospel, and covenant of grace offered in the Mediator, which is posterior to the other court ; wherein the man who hath glorified justice, and acknowledged his sin, and deserved perdition, is pardoned, for the ransom paid by the Messiah Christ Jesus the Mediator, to whom the sinner is fled for refuge. So the believer hath two reckonings with God, about his sins ; one according to justice, and another according to mercy ; and albeit the believer will never refuse to read, acknowledge, and subscribe again and again, the first reckoning to be just, yet he will not stand to that reckoning for payment, but will hold him to the last bargain of grace, and mercy, and goodness, which cleareth the claim of the first account: for this is David's practice here that the first account may be forgotten: *remember not the sins of my youth,* and that the last account and reckoning may stand, and be held in memory, saying, *according to thy mercy, remember thou me.* 3. For evidencing the stability of the account of mercy for pardoning of sin, the glory of God's goodness is laid in pawn in the covenant ; and that holdeth all fast unto the

believer: therefore, saith he, *remember, for thy goodness'
sake, O Lord.*

8. *Good and upright* is *the Lord; therefore will he
teach sinners in the way.*

9. *The meek will he guide in judgment; and the
meek will he teach his way.*

10. *All the paths of the Lord* are *mercy and truth
unto such as keep his covenant and his testimonies.*

In the second place, after praying, he falleth upon a meditation of the grace and good will of God to a believer,
and of his merciful dealing with him in every condition.
Whence learn, 1. In the secret exercise of the saints, a pause
may be usefully made in prayer, and a meditation, or soliloquy may be fallen upon, when the Lord doth fit matter for
fostering faith, and furthering of prayer, as here we may
in David's practice observe. 2. The goodness and faithfulness of God in his promises, and his readiness without respect of persons, to be gracious to every one who cometh
unto him, are the fountain of the believer's strength, hope,
and consolation ; *good and upright is the Lord,* is here a
well of comfort to the supplicant. 3. The conscience of
sin must not keep the believer back from confidence to b3
heard in his prayer, when he cometh to seek direction : for
from this ground, *that the Lord is good,* the prophet draweth
this consequence, *therefore will he teach sinners in the way.*
4. God's justice will not hinder his mercy to be bountiful,
nor will former breaking of commands prejudice the sinner, who, being weary of his wandering, doth seek to be
directed hereafter in the Lord's way ; *he will teach sinners
in the way.* 5. When by affliction a man is humbled, and
brought to submit himself to God, he shall not want a guide
to lead him out of his trouble, to direct his paths, till the
delivery come; for *God will guide the meek in judgment,*
most wisely and discreetly, as his good requireth, *and teach
him his way.* 6. The property of the believer, is to cleave
to the covenant and to what the Lord hath set down in his
word ; *they keep his covenant and his testimonies,* and will
not part with them whatsoever cometh. 7. Whosoever
hold fast the covenant of grace, and make conscience of
obeying God's word, they may be sure that all their troubles
and variety of exercise is nothing but God's way, to make

them partake of God's promises; for unto such *all the paths of the Lord are mercy and truth.*

11. *For thy name's sake, O Lord, pardon mine iniquity; for it* is *great.*

In the third place, having laboured to strengthen his faith, he falleth to prayer again, for remission of sin. Whence learn, 1. The conscience of sin will oftener assault our faith than once, and so oft as it assaulteth, it is to be answered with renewed prayer to God; *O God,* saith he, *pardon my iniquity.* 2. The honour of the Lord is engaged by covenant for remission of sin to the penitent believer, and the Lord counts it a glory to be merciful; therefore, saith he, *for thy name's sake pardon.* 3. Faith can make advantage of misbelief's arguments to retort them against it, and can plead for pardon from the very multitude and grievousness of sin; as here, *pardon my iniquity, for it is great.* For the greater sin is acknowledged to be, the more is the object of pardon made clear, because it cannot be paid for by the sinner; and the more is the Lord's pity letten forth, that the believer be sensible of the weight.

12. *What man* is *he that feareth the Lord?* him *shall he teach in the way* that *he shall choose.*

13. *His soul shall dwell at ease; and his seed shall inherit the earth.*

14. *The secret of the Lord* is *with them that fear him; and he will shew them his covenant.*

In the fourth place, there is another meditation of God's goodness to a believer, for strengthening of his faith yet further, wherein he layeth down three general promises, made to them that believe in God, and stand in awe to offend, ver. 12—14; and by way of syllogism he assumeth of himself, that he is a believer, whereupon he inferreth the conclusion, ver. 15. Whence learn, 1. The fear of God (importing care to serve God according to his word, and to stand in awe to offend him) is the necessary property of a true and lively believer; therefore it is made the believer's cognizance, and mark to discern him by: *what man is he that feareth the Lord?* 2. The believer walking in the fear of God, may expect from the Lord direction and light how to carry himself in all perplexities, so oft as he in his need shall seek it of God; for, in dubious cases, *God shall*

teach him in the way that he shall choose. 3. Albeit the
believer be put to trouble, and hard exercise, yet shall he
have place always with God, as a man reconciled to him,
and peace in his conscience also, as his good doth require,
and he shall have contentment in his lot; for, *his soul shall
dwell at ease.* 4. The surest way to transmit inheritances
to a man's children, and to make houses to stand, and, however matters go, for a man to be sure of the kingdom of
heaven, (signified by an inheritance in the land of Canaan)
is, that the parents fear God, and that the children do follow their footsteps, and fear God also; *for the seed of the
man fearing God shall inherit the land.* 5. The man that
feareth God, shall know more of God's mind than others
shall; he shall know the good and acceptable will of God
for his direction in dangerous controversies, and for his satisfaction about God's dispensations, both toward himself
and others, and for his consolation in all afflictions; *for the
secret of the Lord is with them that fear him.* 6. Albeit
the Lord's covenant with the visible church be open, and
plain in itself to all men, in all the articles thereof, yea, it
is a mystery to know the inward sweet fellowship which a
soul may have with God, by virtue of this covenant; and a
man fearing God shall know this mystery, when such as
are covenanters only in the letter, do remain ignorant thereof; for *to the fearers of God only* is this promise made,
that to them the Lord will shew his covenant.

15. *Mine eyes* are *ever toward the Lord; for he
shall pluck my feet out of the net.*

Having laid the ground of his reason in the former
verses, which is in sum this, to every believer God will be
gracious, as his need is, now he assumeth I am a believer;
for mine eyes are ever toward the Lord. Therefore to me
God will be gracious in my need, and so *pluck my feet out
of the net,* as my need now requireth. Whence learn, 1.
The believer can read his own name, and his own blessedness in the promises made to believers, and can draw out
the extract of God's decree of absolution, direction, consolation, and salvation, in his own favour; for where
the general is written, there all the particulars are also
written in effect: and so the believer may read his name
written in the book of life, as here David doth read

his own deliverance, in the charter of believers ; *mine eyes are ever toward the Lord, therefore he will pluck my feet out of the net.* 2. The believer is not a little helped to believe, and to draw sweet conclusions from inspired scripture, to strengthen himself by avowing himself to be a believer, or to have the true property of a believer, as here David doth, saying, *mine eyes are ever toward the Lord;* first, he avoweth his faith, and then draweth this conclusion from it, *he shall pluck my feet out of the net.* 3. To depend on God for the supply of all necessities, and for deliverance out of all straits, is the property of true faith: for the prophet, to prove himself a believer, and to have an interest in the mercies formerly set down, v. 12—14, saith, v. 15, *mine eyes are ever toward the Lord.* 4. Though the godly walk among snares, and nets, set by their enemies, bodily and spiritual, to entrap them, yet God will either direct their way, to eschew these snares and nets, or will pluck their feet out of them; for this is the prophet's comfort, *thou shalt pluck my feet out of the net.*

16. *Turn thee unto me, and have mercy upon me; for I* am *desolate and afflicted.*

17. *The troubles of my heart are enlarged : O bring thou me out of my distresses.*

After meditation, he concludeth his exercise with petitions for himself and for the church. The petitions for himself are six, in so many verses. In the first learn, 1. Natural sense and suggestion of Satan saith, that God doth turn his back on us, when he doth not sensibly, by outward works, show himself for us as we could wish; but faith maketh advantage of the temptation by adhering to God in time of a seeming desertion, and prayeth for his manifesting of himself unto us; *turn thee unto me, and have mercy upon me.* 2. A felt and acknowledged miserable, helpless, and desperate condition, is, to the believer, half a promise, and a whole reason to expect relief from God; *turn thee unto me, and have mercy on me, for I am desolate and afflicted*; and so also in his second petition, *the troubles of my heart are enlarged, O bring me out of my distresses.* As his troubles were multiplied and enlarged, his heart was straitened and his distresses multiplied, and this he bringeth for a reason of his hope to be brought out of these straits.

18. *Look upon mine affliction and my pain, and forgive all my sins.*

From the third petition learn, 1. How sad and fearful troubles a believing and beloved soul may be brought into, no words can sufficiently express: he is *desolate, afflicted, the troubles of his heart are enlarged;* he is in more distresses than one; he is in *affliction and pain,* which no eye can see, nor any beholder judge of, save God only; therefore saith he to God, *Look on my affliction and my pain.* 2. Sore trouble will waken up the conscience of sin afresh, and call to mind forgiven and buried sin; which new challenge cannot be answered but by prayer for a new application and intimation of remission of sins, as here; *forgive all my sins.*

19. *Consider mine enemies, for they are many; and they hate me with cruel hatred.*

20. *O keep my soul, and deliver me: let me not be ashamed; for I put my trust in thee.*

From the fourth and fifth petitions, relating to the hazard of his life from his bodily enemies, learn, 1. The multitude, power, rage and cruelty of the enemies of the Lord's people, are a ground of hope to the believer to be delivered from them; *consider my enemies, for they are many, &c.* 2. There is no surer evidence of deliverance, than faith in God, settled on a promise; *let me not be ashamed, for I put my trust in thee.*

21. *Let integrity and uprightness preserve me; for I wait on thee.*

The sixth petition is for the fruit of his innocent behaviour toward his enemies. Whence learn, 1. Albeit a man be burdened with the sense of many sins against God, yet he may have the conscience of innocency toward his enemies; and here a good conscience giveth great boldness before God to hope for delivery; *let integrity and uprightness preserve me.* 2. Integrity of life, or a good behaviour after prayer, is as needful as before it; yet neither integrity before nor after must be leaned upon, but God's goodness and mercy only; *let uprightness preserve me,* so David reasoneth, *for I wait on thee.*

22. *Redeem Israel, O God, out of all his troubles.*

He closeth his exercise with a prayer for the church. Whence learn, 1. It is the common lot of all the saints to be exercised with plurality of troubles; and as the troubles of each particular member should not swallow up the sense of the troubles of the church, but rather private troubles should make every one sensible of the like or greater troubles of the rest of the body; so should the delivery of the whole church be sought after, as our own, yea, and more than our own, and as our last petition; and, however the matter shall go with ourselves, let us pray, *redeem Israel, O Lord, out of all his troubles.*

PSALM XXVI.

David being oppressed by the judges of the land, his powerful adversaries, and being exiled from the house of God, he appealeth to God, the supreme judge, in the testimony of a good conscience, bearing him witness, first, of his endeavour to walk uprightly, as became a believer, ver. 1—3; and secondly, of his keeping himself from the contagion of the evil counsel, sinful courses, and example of the wicked, ver. 4, 5; thirdly, of his purpose still to behave himself holily and righteously, out of love to be partaker of the public privileges of the Lord's people in the congregation, ver. 6—8. Whereupon he prayeth to be free of the judgment coming on the wicked, ver. 9, 10. According as he was purposed to eschew their sins, ver. 11. And he closeth his prayer with comfort and assurance to be heard, ver. 12.

1. *Judge me, O Lord; for I have walked in mine integrity: I have trusted also in the Lord;* therefore *I shall not slide.*

2. *Examine me, O Lord, and prove me; try my reins and my heart.*

3. *For thy loving-kindness* is *before mine eyes; and I have walked in thy truth.*

From David's appellation from the unjust sentence of men against him in their courts and elsewhere, calumniating him, and burying him under slanders, from which God and his own conscience knew he was free; learn, 1. God's children may be, for a time unjustly in their cause and name, so borne down with calumnies by judges and others, that they must content themselves with the approbation of God, and of their own conscience, as David doth here. 2. When no remedy is seen on earth for God's oppressed children, remedy may be had from God, the supreme judge, who can redress all matters abundantly. This did David, when he said, *judge me, O Lord:* that is, do the part of a just judge to me, in this controversy between my adversaries and me. 3. He who appealeth to God, had need of a good cause and a good conscience for his carriage in it, that he may say with David, *I have walked in mine integrity.* 4. A good carriage in any controversy is then only comfortable and commendable when it is the fruit of faith in God : therefore David addeth, *I have trusted also in the Lord.* 5. He that in obedience to God doth carry himself righteously, may be assured he shall stand and prevail; for this conclusion doth the prophet draw from these grounds, saying, *I shall not slide.* 6. Not only must a man's hand be free from injuring his party, but his affections also : in which case the upright man is content the Lord should try him, and tell him what is wrong, that it may be amended hereafter; for here sincerity saith, *examine me and try my reins.* 7. Sincerity of behaviour may abide the trial of the conscience, and expect the approbation of God, when the word of God is the man's rule, and fear of interrupting the sense of sweet communion with God, is the awband to keep him to his rule, for so doth David prove his sincerity here : *for thy loving-kindness is before mine eyes, and I have walked in thy truth,* to wit, looking to thy precepts, threatenings, and promises.

4. *I have not sat with vain persons, neither will I go in with dissemblers.*

5. *I have hated the congregation of evil-doers; and will not sit with the wicked.*

The second part of the testimony of his conscience, that he hath rejected the course of wicked men, and their ill counsel, and that he would neither follow the way against his enemies which they followed against him, nor hearken to the evil advice which wicked men, under whatsoever pretence of good-will to him, did offer to him, for a sinful transaction or private revenge. Whence learn, 1. Though innocency may seem to make the godly a prey to their enemy, yet it will promote their cause more before God, and give greater contentment to the conscience than witty wicked plotting against witty and wicked enemies; for this doth David's example teach us. 2. A godly man may take the service of many in a case of law-businesses and civil matters, whose counsel he must refuse in a moral duty ; as when David's followers counselled him to slay the king when he had him in his power in the cave. In such a consultation or debate, he will not *sit* nor *go in with the wicked.* 3. He

that giveth ill counsel, whatsoever pretence of friendship
or advantage be made to commend the counsel which he
offereth, yet in that point he is a vain man and a dissembler.
So doth the prophet style him here. 4. It is necessary to
hate and abhor every wicked course, lest, if we do not hate
it but hearken unto it, we be drawn over to embrace it; *I
hate*, saith he, *the congregation of the evil-doers.*

6. *I will wash my hands in innocency: so will I
compass thine altar, O Lord ;*

7. *That I may publish with the voice of thanksgiving, and tell of all thy wondrous works.*

8. *Lord, I have loved the habitation of thy house,
and the place where thine honour dwelleth.*

The third part of the testimony of his conscience, is concerning his resolution to behave himself righteously and
godlily, out of love to honour God and to be the fitter for
worshipping God and serving him, as he should be employed. Whence learn, 1. The man whose hands are not clean
from injuries done to men, his conscience should tell him that
he is not meet to offer worship to God : and where guiltiness is, it should be taken away, lest the worship be refused; so resolveth David, *I will wash my hands in innocency, and so compass thine altar.* 2. Whatsoever was
the ceremony of the godly with their friends, in compassing
the altar with songs of praise when they offered their
peace-offerings, it yieldeth a fit direction for every worshipper, and offerer of prayer or praise to God, to do it with
an eye to Jesus Christ, the true altar that sanctifieth our offerings, and maketh our persons and services acceptable ; for
the compassing of the altar, with an eye on it, signified this
duty. 3. The Lord's mercies to his own are marvellous in effect, when all circumstances are well considered ; therefore
are they here called *wondrous works.* 4. To love the fellowship of the saints in the public worship of God, is a token
of our interest in God; and the conscience of this love is
refreshful, as here ; *Lord, I have loved the habitation of
thy house.* 5. The meetings of the church should be to
proclaim the Lord's glory in the exercise of all his ordinances; and where this is endeavoured, there will God
dwell, for such holy assemblies are the places where his
honour dwelleth, albeit many of the members of the church

be such before God as they were in Saul's time, whereunto this psalm relateth.

9. *Gather not my soul with sinners, nor my life with bloody men;*

10. *In whose hands is mischief, and their right hand is full of bribes.*

11. *But as for me, I will walk in mine integrity: redeem me, and be merciful unto me.*

Now he prayeth to be exempted from the company of the wicked in their punishment, seeing he hath gotten grace to resolve not to walk in their sin. Whence learn, 1. The Lord hath a harvest and a gleaning time also set, for cutting down and binding together, in the fellowship of judgments, God's enemies, who have followed the same course of sin-ning; for here we are given to understand, that God will *gather their souls*, and so will let none escape. 2. Such as separate themselves, not from the lawful society, but from the sinful ways, of the world, shall also be separate from the society of their punishment; the soul of the one and the other shall not be gathered together; *gather not my soul with sinners*. 3. Ungodly men will never stand to consent to the taking the life of the godly. If, by a fit of tempta-tion, they be put to it, a bribe, or fear, which is all one, will do the turn; for sinners here are declared bloody men, *in whose hands a mischief is, and their right hand is full of bribes*. 4. It is the mark of a wise and godly soul, not to be diverted from his God or godliness by the temptation of loss or gain, which overturneth the worldly man; for Da-vid resolveth, go others where they will, *as for me, I will walk in my integrity.* 5. A man so resolved, that is, who hath chosen God for his redeemer, and God's ways for his rule, may be sure to be borne through all difficulties, all troubles and temptations, and to meet with mercy in the course and close of his life; for David, after resolution of faith in God, and resolution honestly to endeavour obedience to God in his course, prayeth (which is as good as a promise to us), *redeem me, and be merciful to me.*

12. *My foot standeth in an even place; in the con-gregations will I bless the Lord.*

He closes the Psalm comfortably. Whence learn, 1. The believer, resolving obedience to God, and wrestling in prayer

with God, shall not want a comfortable answer; his conscience shall speak good to him, and God shall ratify the
testimony of it with his testimony : thus shall the man be
established in that sweet course of faith and obedience,
and have cause to say, *my foot stands in an even place.* 2.
Such a man may be assured to bless God effectually, for
the performance of promises, and that in good company,
either in this life, or in the next, or in both; and in this
life with assurance, he may say with David, *in the congregation will I bless the Lord.*

PSALM XXVII.

In this psalm David setteth down what use he had of his faith in God,
in the time of his trouble: and first, how he strengthened his faith,
v. 1—6, and next, how he prayed, upon the foresaid grounds, v. 7—
12 ; and thirdly, what advantage he had by believing in God, in the
time of his exercise, v. 13. Whereupon he exhorts all the godly to
follow his example, under hope to be helped, as he was helped, v. 14.

1. *The Lord is my light, and my salvation; whom
shall I fear? the Lord is the strength of my life; of
whom shall I be afraid?*

The grounds of strengthening of his faith are three.
The first is, that God by virtue of the covenant hath obliged himself to give direction and comfort in trouble, and deliverance out of it ; from which he inferreth, that he needeth not fear his enemies.   Whence learn, 1. When we are
to wrestle in prayer, against the doubts which trouble and
temptation may raise in our hearts to mar our confidence
in prayer, it is wisdom to arm ourselves by faith against
these doubts, before we pray, for so doth the prophet's example teach us.   2. He who is in covenant with God,
hath solid ground to expect from God direction and comfort in every trouble, and deliverance out of it ; for by virtue of the covenant of grace David saith, *the Lord is my
light and my salvation.*   3. When we have fastened our
faith on God, we may then with reason defy our enemies,
and say with the prophet, *of whom shall I be afraid?*   4.
When our enemies appear strong, and we know ourselves
to be but weak, we should oppose the Lord's strength to
our temptation, that we may resist all fear ; for so teacheth
David, *the Lord is the strength of my life, of whom shall I
be afraid ?*

2. *When the wicked, even mine enemies and my foes, came upon me to eat up my flesh, they stumbled and fell.*

The next ground of confidence is, that he had proof and experience of the fruit of the covenant, when he was in greatest danger of being overtaken by his enemies. Whence learn, 1. When the rage of the wicked against the godly doth break forth, then no less than the precious life of the godly can satisfy their beastly cruelty ; they hunger even to *eat their flesh.* 2. God can easily make the wicked, in their hottest pursuit of the godly, to come short of their purpose, as here, *to stumble and fall.* 3. Experience of God's power is very forcible to confirm our faith, and to erect our hope, as it did David's faith.

3. *Though an host should encamp against me, my heart shall not fear; though war should rise against me, in this will I be confident.*

After settling of his faith, he puts on a resolution to stand to his point, in resisting assaults of fears, from whatsoever temptation. Whence learn, 1. It is a mean to strengthen faith, to resolve by the grace of God to put faith in act, in whatsoever difficulty, and in a manner to lay hands on ourselves, to hold up this shield against whatsoever fiery darts, albeit possibly when it cometh to push of pike, we be not found so strong as we are stout, as here David doth. 2. The Lord being ours by covenant, and the Lord proved to be ours in experience, is warrant and reason sufficient for us to put on such a resolution; *though war be raised, in this* (that is, upon the foresaid ground) *will I be confident,* saith he.

4. *One thing have I desired of the Lord, that will I seek after ; that I may dwell in the house of the Lord, all the days of my life, to behold the beauty of the Lord and to enquire in his temple.*

A third ground of confidence, is the conscience of his purpose to study to have constant communion with God, in the use of the means, and the conscience of his very earnest desire to have the benefit of all the public ordinances, in the fellowship of the church. Whence learn, 1. Hearty resolution to subject ourselves to all God's ordinances, and to follow the appointed means of communion-keeping with God, is a sound mark of solid faith; and the conscience of this resolution, serveth much to confirm our confidence in God, if we can say with the prophet, *this one thing have I desired, &c.* 2. In the using of the means and ordinances of God's house, the glory of the Lord may be seen, counsel and direction in all things may be had, with comfort and spiritual delight to our souls; for in the ordinances David was to *behold the beauty of the Lord,* with delight, *and to enquire in his holy temple.* 3. The desire of communion with God, and love to his ordinances, where it is sincere, should have the chief place in the heart, above all earthly desires and delights whatsoever : *one thing have I desired.* 4. A sincere desire must not be suffered to go away, but should be pursued resolutely, and recommended to God daily ; *this I will still seek after,* saith he : and the means of communion with God in the public fellowship of the church must be constantly continued in, *even all the days of our life.*

5. *For in the time of trouble he shall hide me in his pavilion: in the secret of his tabernacle shall he hide me ; he shall set me up upon a rock.*

He giveth a reason of his so earnest a desire to have fellowship with God entertained by the use of all God's ordinances, because in this way he was sure that faith should draw all necessary comfort and protection from God, as need should require. Whence learn, 1. Faith keeping communion with God, findeth him all-sufficient in all necessities, to supply every inlack of the creature, where the believer standeth in need; *he will be a pavilion in warfare, and a hiding-place and rock of refuge,* that is, God will make a man as quiet by faith, in himself, as if there were no hazard ; *in the time of trouble he shall hide me in his pavilion : in the secret of his tabernacle, shall he hide me ; he shall set me up upon a rock.* 2. The godly cannot promise to themselves the influence of God's grace in time of need, otherwise than by following divine ordinances, both private and public, so far as they may be had ; for the prophet promiseth to himself this protection, as a fruit of his faith, fostered by the use of the ordinances, *I desire,* saith he, *to dwell in thy house, and to enquire in thy holy temple ; for in the time of trouble he shall hide me, &c.*

6. *And now shall mine head be lifted up above mine enemies round about me : therefore will I offer in his tabernacle sacrifices of joy ; I will sing, yea, I will sing praises unto the Lord.*

After this wrestling of faith, he obtaineth victory, and assurance of satisfaction to his desire, and the grant of all that he was to seek in his prayer. Whence learn, The Lord can give a believer assurance of what he would have, and make him so clear of the possession of the promise, as if it were in his hand ; as here the psalmist is sure to prevail over his enemies, sure to come to the temple even as he wished : *and now shall mine head be lifted up above mine enemies, I will offer sacrifices of joy in his tabernacle.*

7. *Hear, O Lord, when I cry with my voice : have mercy also upon me, and answer me.*

8. *When thou saidst, Seek ye my face ; my heart said unto thee, Thy face, Lord, will I seek.*

In the second place, having thus strengthened his faith, he entereth the lists with his present trouble and tempta-tions, and encountereth them by prayer to God upon the foresaid grounds, in three petitions. In the first he prayeth for the sensible experience of God's favour, as his present condition required ; wherein he strengthens his faith by three considerations. The first is, because he had gotten grace to close with the word of God, inviting him to seek what he sought, v. 8. Whence learn, 1. Confidence in God is diligent in prayer, and despiseth not the means whereby the mercy hoped for may be brought about ; but by prayer it maketh particular application of the Lord's good-will, offered to all, unto itself, that it may be helped in the present need, as here David doth : *hear me when I cry, have mercy on me, answer me.* 2. As the Lord's word encourageth us to seek things of God which, without a warrant, we durst not seek ; so, when we have gotten grace to embrace God's warrant given to us by precept or promise, we may ask with confidence to obtain : *hear me, answer me ;* why ? *when thou saidst, seek ye my face ; my heart answered, I will seek thy face, O Lord.*

9. *Hide not thy face far from me ; put not thy servant away in anger : thou hast been my help ; leave me not, neither forsake me, O God of my salvation.*

He meets here with an objection from his sins and mis-deservings, and prayeth it down, adding another consider-ation to confirm his faith from bygone experience of mer-cy, notwithstanding his unworthiness. Whence learn, 1. Though, when we would draw near to the Lord, sense of sin and unworthiness, and fear of wrath, fly in our throat, yet faith cleaving to God's goodness, and to the promises of mercy, and to our relation unto our God, may cry down the temptation: *hide not thy face, put not away thy servant in anger.* 2. The former experiences which we have had of God's being gracious to us, according to the tenor of the covenant of salvation, should confirm our faith, that God will never cast us off, nor any man that cannot endure to be separate from him: thus David reasons, *thou hast been my help, leave me not, neither forsake me, O God of my salvation.*

10. *When my father and my mother forsake me, then the Lord will take me up.*

A third consideration to confirm David's faith, is a nearer relation between God and David, than between David and his parents. Whence learn, that the bands between God and a believing soul are more strait and intimate, and more strong than any band, civil or natural, between him and any creature; and they are appointed to hold fast when natural bands fail, as here is asserted: *when my father and my mother forsake me, then the Lord will take me up.* This is for the first petition.

11. *Teach me thy way, O Lord, and lead me in a plain path, because of mine enemies.*

The second petition is for direction in a holy and wise carriage, that his enemies get no advantage against his be-haviour or person. Whence learn, 1. There is danger of desertion, or of God's leaving us to the will of our enemies, if we carry not a good cause in a lawful, holy, tender way; and therefore we had need to seek our direction from God, *to be taught in his way, and led in a plain path.* 2. Because the enemies of the godly are ready to calumniate their cause, and their intentions, and to take advantage to calumniate them upon the least occasion of a questionable practice, we had the more need to be circumspect, and to pray to be directed *in a plain path, because of our enemies.*

12. *Deliver me not over unto the will of mine ene-*

mies : for false witnesses are risen up against me, and such as breathe out cruelty.

The third petition is, to be delivered from the power of the enemy, prosecuting their false calumnies, and raging in cruelty. Whence learn, 1. The godly have reason to pray with submission, that they may not fall into the hands of men because of their cruelty, and to say to God, *deliver me not over unto the will of mine enemies.* 2. Because it is easy for the Lord to mitigate the enemies' fury, or to break their power, or to elude their craft and power; let us pray, *deliver,* and let God choose the way of delivery. 3. When the good cause of the godly and the persons also, are left to suffer both together, there is ground that God in that case will interpose himself in due time : for this is David's reason of hope to be helped, because false witnesses resolved to oppress him in name, and *breathers out of cruelty* were set to have his life, ever *rising against him :* and here he is a clear type and example of the suffering of Christ and his followers.

13. I had fainted, *unless I had believed to see the goodness of the Lord in the land of the living.*

14. *Wait on the Lord ; be of good courage, and he shall strengthen thine heart : wait, I say, on the Lord.*

In the third place, he cometh to show and to make use of the benefit he had by believing, that he may encourage others to follow his example in their trials. Whence learn, 1. Discouragement under trouble is a sort of quitting of our cause, and of all comfort in it; but faith keepeth a man close to his cause, and from being overcome with troubles ; it holds up his heart in his duty till the Lord send an outgate, wherein he were not able to subsist otherwise : *unless I had believed I had fainted.* 2. Our experiences of the good of believing in the time of straits, should be communicated to others, as our calling may suffer, to encourage them ; for so doth the prophet, saying, *wait on the Lord, and be of good courage.* 3. The striving to take courage from the ground of faith, shall be followed with strength from God to go under the trouble, and to find comfort now and then, and full delivery at last : *he shall comfort thy heart.* 3. Albeit the Lord let the trouble lie on, and strong temptations to increase, and grief of heart to grow, yet must we still wait ; for at the due time the outgate shall come: *wait, I say, on the Lord.*

PSALM XXVIII.

In the first part of this psalm we have the prophet's conflict against his
enemies, such as in the former psalm is to be seen, wherein he prayeth
for audience, ver. 1, 2, and delivery to himself, ver. 3, and that God
would vindicate his own justice against his disdainful enemies, ver. 4, 5.
In the latter part, the prophet having gotten comfort in his prayer,
doth glorify God, ver. 6, and strengthens his own and the rest of the
godly's faith, ver. 7, 8, and prayeth for a blessing to the church, ver. 9.

1. *Unto thee will I cry, O Lord my rock ; be not
silent to me : lest,* if *thou be silent to me, I become like
them that go down into the pit.*

2. *Hear the voice of my supplications, when I cry
unto thee, when I lift up my hands toward thy holy
oracle.*

In his conflict with trouble he runneth to God for a comfortable answer, with reasons to help his hope to be heard.
Whence learn, 1. It is good to pray in time of trouble, and
to be instant, and resolved to be instant ; for *unto thee will
I cry,* doth import these three. 2. A soul in great straits
is not able to suspend and want comfort long ; it must have
some comfortable answer, because of what God is unto it
by covenant,—*my rock, be not silent unto me.* 3. It bringeth
deadness of soul on a supplicant, when his prayer is not
taken off his hand, which albeit it be by no reason but a
consequence ill inferred from the Lord's not answering of
us, yet we are subject to this evil, and should pray to have
it prevented : *be not silent,* saith he, *lest I become like them
that go down into the pit.* 4. Though the heart be in
bonds in time of prayer under trouble, yet the Lord will
not despise the voice, nor the knees bowed, nor the hands
lifted up, nor the least expressions of a supplicant's desire
to be helped by him : *hear my voice when I cry, and the
lifting up of my hands,* saith he. 5. Seeking of God in
Christ, and trysting the fulness of the Godhead in the person of the Mediator, represented by the tabernacle and
oracle, answer all objections from the supplicant's unworthiness, and give encouragement to expect a good answer
from God ; for to this purpose doth he mention *his lifting
up of his hands towards the Lord's holy oracle.*

3. *Draw me not away with the wicked, and with
the workers of iniquity, which speak peace to their
neighbours, but mischief is in their hearts.*

Now he prayeth God would deliver him, and not deal with him as with an enemy. Whence learn, albeit there be sin in the godly, yet are they not workers of iniquity, nor treacherously disposed toward their neighbours, when they pretend to have friendship with them ; and therefore may the godly expect from God not to be dealt with as obstinately wicked and impenitent sinners ; for this he meaneth, saying, *draw me not away with the workers of iniquity, &c.*

4. *Give them according to their deeds, and according to the wickedness of their endeavours : give them after the work of their hands ; render to them their desert.*

5. *Because they regard not the works of the Lord, nor the operation of his hands, he shall destroy them, and not build them up.*

He prayeth now against his enemies, not out of private revenge, but being led with the infallible spirit of prophecy, looking through these men to the enemies of Christ and of his people in all ages. Whence learn, 1. Albeit imprecations must not be used against our own enemies, nor for any injury done to us, nor against any in hatred of their persons, nor against every enemy of God, but only against desperate sinners, and that in general, rather than with an eye to this man or that man in special, about whom we may be mistaken : yet the imprecation of the Spirit of God standing in the scripture, crieth still against obstinate sinners, although we cannot condescend particularly upon their names ; *God shall give them according to their deserts.* In the controversy between the godly and their enemies, not only doth God show by his word which party he alloweth, but also by the works of his providence, in favour of the godly and against their enemies, he doth give forth his mind, according to what he hath said in his word to be observed ; but when both these are misregarded, he will destroy the wicked, and not suffer them to carry on their purpose ; for, *because they regard not the works of the Lord, nor the operation of his hands, he shall destroy them, and not build them up.*

6. *Blessed* be *the Lord, because he hath heard the voice of my supplications.*

7. *The Lord* is *my strength and my shield: my heart trusted in him, and I am helped; therefore my heart greatly rejoiceth, and with my song will I praise him.*

8. *The Lord* is *their strength, and he* is *the saving strength of his anointed.*

The other part of the psalm, wherein he maketh use of the good answer given to him; first, honouring God for it ; then strengthening his own faith by it ; and thirdly, strengthening the faith of others also. Whence learn, 1. The believing supplicant shall not seek God in vain ; he shall not fail in due time to find such fruit, as shall make him bless and praise God for the answer ; for in the entry of the psalm it was, *be not silent to me, O Lord, lest I become like them that go down to the pit,*—and here, *blessed be the Lord, because he hath heard the voice of my supplication.* 2. What faith saith to God in wrestling, it shall be made to subscribe it victoriously and experimentally thereafter ; *my rock,* said he, *hear me,* v. 1 ; and here, *the Lord is my strength and my shield;* to furnish me within and without. 3. It is a good use made of experience, to confirm our faith thereby, and to commend the course of believing in God, as here David doth ; *my heart trusted in him, and I am helped.* 4. The joy of faith and of sense also, will be given sometime together to the godly, for the increasing of their joy, as here he showeth ; *therefore my heart greatly rejoiced.* 5. Albeit we must praise God in whatsoever condition we can be in ; yet spiritual rejoicing doth specially call for singing a psalm unto God ; *therefore with my song will I praise him,* saith he. 6. What the Lord is to one of the godly calling on him in the sense of need, he is unto them all the same: as he was David's *strength,* v. 7, so *is he their strength,* to wit, all his people's strength, v. 8. 7. All the blessings which believers get belong unto Christ, first as to the anointed of the Lord in chief, and to his servants as partakers of his anointing ; for the Lord *is the saving strength, or the strength of salvation to his anointed,* or to his Christ, and those that are true Christians, partakers *of his unction,* or holy Spirit: what concerneth David is but a shadow, and as one who is a partaker of the holy unction through Christ.

9. *Save thy people, and bless thine inheritance: feed them also, and lift them up for ever.*

He closeth his prayer with intercession for the church. Whence learn, 1. Such as find access in prayer to God for themselves, should speak also a word for his church, and pray, *Lord, save thy people.* 2. The privileges which the godly have are common to them all. The godly are all God's *people, his inheritance, his flock:* and as the benefits imported under these titles are common, so are the duties due from us to God, imported thereby, common also; and to be so studied, that we may discharge them, as we would find from God the benefits of protection and deliverance, as subjects whom he will save ; of being watered and warmed, as *his inheritance; fed and led on,* as his flock, and exalted over all our enemies, or being lifted up for ever.

PSALM XXIX.

David exhorteth princes and great men to humble themselves before God, and to worship him, as he hath commanded, in his public ordinances, v. 1, 2. First, because he is infinitely higher than they, and more terrible to all men, than they can be to their subjects or inferiors, as the uttering of his majesty and power by thunder maketh evident, v. 3—9. Secondly, because he offereth the means of saving knowledge, even all his ordinances, whereby men may heartily glorify him in their assemblies, v. 9. Thirdly, because he is an everlasting king and ruler of all the creatures, v. 10. And fourthly, because such as do humbly submit themselves to him, and worship him as his people should do, shall be furnished with abilities for every good work, and shall be abundantly blessed.

1. *Give unto the Lord, O ye mighty, give unto the Lord glory and strength.*

2. *Give unto the Lord the glory due unto his name ; worship the Lord in the beauty of holiness.*

He directeth his speech and exhortation to the potentates of the earth, that they may humble themselves before God, and give him the glory of all power, and authority, and excellency above themselves, and above all other creatures. Hence learn, 1. Of all men princes should be most careful to glorify God, and yet it is most rare to see them humble themselves before him: for natural corruption is as strong in them as in others: their education breedeth them to high and stately thoughts of themselves, their riches and power puff them up, and flatterers, ordinarily following them, make them forget themselves and God also; therefore are they here thrice exhorted to give glory to God. 2. It is most necessary that potentates humble themselves before God, and be particularly dealt with to that purpose, because their example and authority move many outwardly to submit to God, or stand out from his service: therefore he speaketh to them in their grandeur, *give glory to God, O ye mighty.* 3. As men are great in the world, so they are ready to think much of their own strength, of what their power is able to reach to, and what honour is due to them; but if they reckon right, *strength and glory belong to God.* And according as he is above them in power and excellency, so should he proportionably be magnified; *give unto the Lord glory and strength,* and *give unto the Lord the glory due unto his name.* 4. He will have no glory of men, but as he hath prescribed to men in his own ordinances, given forth in his word to his church: *worship him in the beauty of holiness,* that is, in the glorious sanctuary, the place of public meeting; beautiful indeed, not for timber or stones so much, as because the holy and beautiful means of grace to men, and God's worship showing forth his glory, was there to be found.

3. *The voice of the Lord is upon the waters: the God of glory thundereth; the Lord is upon many waters.*

4. *The voice of the Lord is powerful; the voice of the Lord is full of majesty.*

He proveth that strength and glory belong to the Lord, by one only work of thundering, and kindling fire in the midst of watery clouds, that he may make thunder in the conflict of water closing in the fire, and fire breaking through the clouds, how oft soever he pleaseth to show his power to the children of men. Whence learn, 1. Though the standing works of creation speak most of God, yet such is our foolishness, that we are least apprehensive of that which is daily seen, and a less work more rarely occurring will move more; as for example, the thunder or the eclipse of the sun or moon, will move more than the making of heaven and earth. 2. No work of the Lord is rightly taken up till he himself be looked unto, as the immediate worker of it: therefore he points out the sound of the thunder, as *the voice of the Lord upon many waters.* 3. Though the Lord should be observed as the worker of every work, yet not at first is he seen in his work to any purpose, till we by oftener reviewing his operation about it, be somewhat affected with his glory and power therein; therefore he repeateth the second time, *the God of glory thundereth;* and the third time, *the Lord is upon many waters.* 4. When the thunder or any work of God is well considered, some invisible thing of God will appear therein; as for example, his power and majesty will be evidenced in the thunder, for *the voice of the Lord is powerful and full of majesty.*

5. *The voice of the Lord breaketh the cedars; yea, the Lord breaketh the cedars of Lebanon.*

6. *He maketh them also to skip like a calf; Lebanon and Sirion like a young unicorn.*

7. *The voice of the Lord divideth the flames of fire.*

8. *The voice of the Lord shaketh the wilderness; the Lord shaketh the wilderness of Kadesh.*

9. *The voice of the Lord maketh the hinds to calve, and discovereth the forests; and in his temple doth every one speak of* his *glory.*

He insisteth in his subject, and showeth the effects thereof, on trees, v. 5 ; on mountains, v. 6 ; on the fire of the thunder, parting it in lightning, v. 7 ; on the waste wilderness, v. 8 ; on the beasts and woods where they haunt, v. 9. Whence learn, 1. That the stupidity and senselessness of man is greater than that of the brute creatures, which are all more moved with the thunder, than the hearts of men for the most part, as here may be seen in the comparison. 2. One work of God dwelt upon, shall show more of God than many of his works being slightly looked on, and passed over: as for example, this one of the thunder, considered with the effects, saith more than many ; yea, one sensible and understanding man, will discover more of God in one work of God, than many in their ordinary mood, either in that work, or in any other, or in all his works.

9. *The voice of the Lord maketh the hinds to calve, and discovereth the forests; and in his temple doth every one speak of* his *glory.*

He giveth a second reason of his exhortation to the

mighty, *to worship God in the beauty of holiness*, because
in his temple every one doth speak of his glory. Whence
learn, 1. The glory of the Lord is shown forth in all the
earth, and in all his works; but in his temple, in his church,
his works are holden forth expressly and fully, for there by
his word, his counsel is opened, his holiness, his goodness,
justice, mercy, and all his attributes are declared. Without the church, men are compelled to acknowledge glory
now and then, but in his church men do declare his glory
distinctly and willingly: *in his temple doth every one speak
of his glory*; all men there confess his praise, and every
thing in the temple holdeth forth something of Christ and
his benefits, to the glory of God's mercy; and this is more
than the world understandeth.

10. *The Lord sitteth upon the flood; yea, the Lord
sitteth King for ever.*

A third reason to move princes to give to God glory and
strength, is, because his kingdom reacheth to the ruling of
the waters, and because he is a king immortal. Whence
learn, 1. As the strength of the Lord appeareth in all his
works, so especially that he ruleth the raging sea, whereby
once he did drown the world, and now bindeth it up, that it
should do no more so again: *the Lord sitteth upon the floods*.
No king is king over every kingdom and king, but God is
King above all kings; no king is of long continuance, but
the Lord is the everlasting King, *he sitteth King for ever;*
and therefore every mighty man should do him homage, as
his King, his Lord, and supreme superior.

11. *The Lord will give strength unto his people; the
Lord will bless his people with peace.*

The last reason to move potentates to give all glory to
God, and to join with his people in glorifying him, is, because of the blessedness of his people, who worship him in
his holy temple. Whence learn, 1. The power of the Lord
is not against his people; but for his people, against his
and their enemies, *he giveth strength to his people*, to wit,
against their enemies, and for furnishing them to every
part of his service whereunto he calleth them. The Lord's
people do give the glory of power and strength to the Lord;
and the Lord will give strength to his people. 2. The true
worshippers of God, whatsoever may be their exercise in

the world, may be sure of reconciliation with him, and of true blessedness, *for the Lord will bless his people with peace.*

PSALM XXX.

A psalm and song at the dedication of the house of David.

David praiseth God for his late deliverance from the hand of Absalom, v. 1—3. And secondly, he exhorteth others to praise God also for his mercies, v. 4, 5. Thirdly, he confesseth his carnal security, and how he was corrected for it, v. 6, 7. Fourthly, he showeth how he prayed for mercy, v. 8—10. And fifthly, he praiseth the Lord for his gracious answer, v. 11, 12.

The inscription of the psalm showeth, that it was indited at the dedication of David's house, after it was polluted by Absalom's vileness with his father's concubines, as David's security and trouble after that herein described, giveth us to understand. Whence learn, 1. That no benefit or creature-comfort is lawful and pure to us, except it be sanctified by the word and prayer, except we dedicate ourselves and the creatures also to God's service; and more specially the dedication of a man's house with the ceremonies of the law, used about the dedication thereof, teacheth us to consider and to acknowledge before God, that we are the Lord's tenants at will, received by him in his lodgings, to be entertained by him during our abode on earth; it teacheth us also that our houses should be holy, both for the persons in our company, and for the exercise of religion therein daily, before and after our lawful daily refreshments and employments therein; and that the Lord only is the preserver of us, and of our houses, against what evil might otherwise befall us, by men, or devils, or any other accident; and that the house is polluted, especially when God is openly dishonoured therein: in which case we are to seek mercy to ourselves, and to our families, and to pray to God for the continuance of his guard about us, and his grace, to make a right use of our house hereafter, which is the substance of the old ceremonies used in dedication of a man's house.

1. *I will extol thee, O Lord; for thou hast lifted me up, and hast not made my foes to rejoice over me.*

2. *O Lord my God, I cried unto thee, and thou hast healed me.*

3. *O Lord, thou hast brought up my soul from the grave: thou hast kept me alive, that I should not go down to the pit.*

He praiseth God for a number of mercies concurring together in his deliverance out of the hazard of losing both his life and his kingdom. Whence learn, 1. The more the Lord exalts us, we should humble ourselves the more before him, and magnify his bounty : for David *will extol the Lord* here, *because the Lord had lifted him up.* 2. The disappointment of our enemies is a new mercy, beside our delivery from their cruelty, and a reason of thanksgiving to God, when he makes our foes not to rejoice over us. 3. When God seemeth to desert us, and expose us to hazards, readily our spirits grow sick, and deadness of spirit (with inability to go about any point in our calling, or of his service) seize on us; but when, after the prayer of faith grounded on the covenant, the Lord sendeth relief, it is a reviving of us again, as we see in David's case: *O my God, I cried unto thee, and thou hast healed me.* 4. Preservation from evil, and delivery out of evil, are mercies equivalent ; rescuing a man from instant death, should be looked upon as resurrection from death, and acknowledged so to be in our thanksgiving to God ; for David here saith, *The Lord hath brought up his soul from the grave, because he had kept him alive, that he should not go down into the pit.*

4. *Sing unto the Lord, O ye saints of his, and give thanks at the remembrance of his holiness.*

5. *For his anger* endureth but *a moment; in his favour* is *life; weeping may endure for a night, but joy* cometh *in the morning.*

The second part of the psalm, wherein he stirreth up others to praise God for his mercies. Whence learn, 1. Dwelling a while upon the consideration of mercies shown unto us, bringeth with it rejoicing in God, and a singing disposition, whereunto when we are once wakened and warned, we will think that one mouth to praise God is too little, as here we see in David, who not only praiseth God himself, but also setteth all the saints on work to the same purpose, saying, *sing to the Lord, all ye saints of his.* 2. Albeit we have no present sense of lately received remarkable mercies, yet bygone experiences of the Lord's faithfulness and holiness, should give matter of thanks and praise on all occasions, specially in the congregation, where his works are called to mind : *give thanks*, saith he, *at the remembrance of his holiness*. 3. Albeit we were not upon the thoughts of any particular experience, yet the known perfections of God should furnish matter, and in special, because howsoever we be sinful, and do provoke the Lord often, yet he, *as he is slow to anger,* so is he soon pacified, *his anger endureth but for a moment.* 4. When reckoning is rightly made, the tokens of God's displeasure are but for *a moment.* But the evidence of his favours to believers is a life-time, for in the midst of wrath he remembereth mercy ; and the tokens of his favour are far more than of his displeasure, and wrath soon goeth, and favour shineth latest, and is of longest continuance; wrath is but temporary at the longest, but favour endureth for ever : *his anger is but for a moment, but in his favour is life, yea life everlasting.* 5. When the Lord showeth himself angry at a soul, it is dark and cold night with it, and what can it do but weep or walk heavily in this case, when the bridegroom is as absent : *weeping may abide for a night.* 6. Unto the believer the longest winter night hath a change to the better following it : consolation is certain after a mournful condition ; *weeping may endure for a night, but joy cometh in the morning.*

6. *And in my prosperity I said, I shall never be moved.*

7. *Lord, by thy favour thou hast made my mountain to stand strong: thou didst hide thy face, and I was troubled.*

In the third place, he cometh to his late experience, which gave occasion and matter of this psalm ; he abused his prosperity, not remembering that because his standing was by grace, therefore he should have stood in awe, and feared to forget himself, and therefore he was chastised for it. Whence learn, 1. A child of God, after long trouble may have a time of outward rest and prosperity ; for example, David, whose troubles were many, acknowledgeth here that he was in prosperity. 2. As men in trouble do fear they shall never be rid of it, so when God granteth a change to the better, they think never to be so troubled

again; this fleshly security is a soul-sickness, attending prosperity, and the most holy men may easily be overtaken
with it; for David confesseth, *I said in my prosperity, I
shall never be moved.* 3. The consideration that our standing in any good condition, is of God's mere favour and
grace, should keep us in fear and trembling to offend, and
prevent our falling in carnal security. This David acknowledgeth for aggravating of his fault, *Lord, by thy favour
thou hast made my mountain strong.* 4. The Lord will
not suffer his own to lie still in carnal security, but will
withdraw the bolster and pillow of those benefits whereon
they sleep, and together with that, will withdraw also the
sweet sense of reconciliation, and put his own in trouble
to waken them: David's experience teacheth so much,
thou didst hide thy face, and I was troubled. 5. Men
understand the folly of their sinful way, and of their careless entertaining of God's favour, not so well in the time of
prosperity, as after they have smarted for their folly, and
have found the fruit of their forgetfulness of God, and of
their too much embracing and resting on prosperity, to be
nothing save sore and sad troubles, both bodily and spiritual; for this is taught us by the reckoning that David
now maketh, as a pilot discovering a rock, to forewarn
others to beware of security; and this reckoning is all after
his trouble, and after his victory also over it.

8. *I cried to thee, O Lord; and unto the Lord I
made supplication.*

9. *What profit is there in my blood, when I go
down to the pit? Shall the dust praise thee? shall it
declare thy truth?*

10. *Hear, O Lord, and have mercy upon me: Lord,
be thou my helper.*

In the fourth part of this psalm he showeth his recovery
out of his trouble, and out of his sinful security which
drew it on; he prayed, disputed, and dealt with God, till
the Lord delivered him. Whence learn, 1. As the fire
and the hammer, and the files serve to put off the rust
of iron, so doth affliction to rouse a godly soul out of security, and drive him to earnest prayer; for after trouble
is come, David crieth to the Lord. 2. Albeit a man hath
miscarried, and proved ungrateful to God in his prosperity,

and unmindful of his resolutions and promises made to God in his low estate, when he should come to prosperity; yet when trouble cometh to waken him up, and call him to a reckoning, he must not despair, nor sit down in discouragement in the conscience of huge guiltiness. But because the Lord is angry, and no remedy but God's grace, he must lay himself at God's feet a supplicant : *unto the Lord David made supplication.* 3. Faith in God is very argumentative, and will dispute well for the man's life, having the covenant of grace as a ground to go upon. It will take a reason to strengthen itself from God's nature, who doth not delight in the death of a penitent sinner, and a reason from no advantage unto justice, by the man's destruction, when justice may have satisfaction in the Redeemer, and the man may be saved also. *What profit is there in my blood, when I go down to the pit?* and a reason from the man's purpose to glorify God, to the edifying of others in his life, if he should be spared : from which mercy if he should be cut off, it would be better to him than death : *shall the dust praise thee? shall it declare thy truth?* 4. When faith hath said to God what it hath to say, it will wait for a good answer; will rely on his mercy, and expect relief from the Lord, as here David doth ; *hear, O Lord, have mercy on me, be thou my helper.*

11. *Thou hast turned for me my mourning into dancing: thou hast put off my sackcloth, and girded me with gladness.*

12. *To the end that* my *glory may sing praise to thee, and not be silent. O Lord my God, I will give thanks unto thee for ever.*

In the last part of the psalm he thankfully praiseth God, for granting unto him all he desired, and obligeth himself to a more careful carriage, and setting forth of God's glory. Whence learn, 1. It becometh the child of God to weep when he is beaten, and to humble himself in the exercise of prayer and fasting ; for David's *mourning* and *sackcloth,* showeth his exercise in his former trouble. 2. As security turneth all our joy into trouble, so sincere seeking of God in trouble, is the way to turn all our trouble into joy ; *thou hast turned for me all my mourning into dancing, &c.,* and great is that joy which a reconciled soul findeth in God, after renewed feeling of the interrupted sense of mercy.

3. A well-ordered tongue, watching all opportunities to glorify God, and edify others, is a main point of a man's excellency, not only above beasts,, but also above all men, who do not use their tongue for God, and for good to others. Therefore David calleth his tongue his glory. 4. The very intent of God's showing mercy to men, is to oblige them to give praise and glory to himself before the world ; *thou hast girded me with gladness,* saith he, *to the end my glory may sing praise to thee, and not be silent.* 5. The right use of our experiences of God's mercy to us, is first to fasten our faith in God, and to stand fast to the Lord's covenant made with us in Christ; next, after acknowledging that this is our duty, to be thankful to God to engage our hearts to the discharge thereof constantly. The first of these the prophet doth here by calling God, *the Lord my God ;* the next he doth in these words, *I will give thanks to thee for ever.*

PSALM XXXI.

To the chief musician. A psalm of David.

Another exercise of David, wherein he being in great danger to be taken by his enemies, prayeth for delivery, ver. 1—6. Secondly, he strengtheneth his faith by his by-gone experience, ver. 7, 8. Thirdly, in prayer he layeth out his lamentable condition before God, ver. 9—13. Fourthly, he wrestleth on in prayer for comfort and safety to himself, and confusion to his enemies, ver. 14—18. Fifthly, being delivered and comforted by a new experience of God's merciful preservation of him, he maketh good use of it, by praising God for it, and exhorteth the godly to love God and rely on him, ver. 19—24.

1. *In thee, O Lord, do I put my trust; let me never be ashamed : deliver me in thy righteousness.*

2. *Bow down thine ear to me ; deliver me speedily : be thou my strong rock, for an house of defence to save me.*

3. *For thou art my rock and my fortress : therefore, for thy name's sake, lead me, and guide me.*

From his interest in God, by covenant, he strengthens himself in prayer for delivery. Whence learn, 1. Faith avowed and maintained, furnisheth prayer, and giveth hope to be heard ; for David having first said, *In thee, O Lord, do I put my trust;* he subjoineth, *let me never be ashamed ;* for this much may a believer expect, that albeit he be put to hang down the head for a little, yet he shall not at last be ashamed. 2. As the Lord sendeth, in his wisdom, trouble after trouble upon a believer, so he sendeth, in his justice and faithfulness, promised delivery after delivery from oppressors: *deliver me in thy righteousness.* 3. Where the danger is pressing, and the affection is ardent, the petition may be repeated without babbling, and speedy help may be craved without limitation of God; and hearkening to a poor supplicant, as it were, with a bowed down ear, may be prayed for without abasing of God's majesty, as here, *bow down thine ear to me, deliver me speedily.* 4. Were there but a moment betwixt us and perishing, and our enemies, stronger than we, were ready to lay hands on us, faith seeth that God can interpose himself speedily, and lift us up above our enemies' reach: *be thou my strong rock, for a house of defence to save me.* 5. What the Lord is engaged to be unto us by covenant, we may pray and expect to find him in effect; *be thou my strong rock,* saith he, *for thou art my rock.* 6. When trouble and uncouth passages discover our ignorance, our blindness and weakness unto us, we have God engaged for his glory's cause to take care of us, and to bring us through; for the prayer of the believer is, *for thy name's sake lead me and guide me.*

4. *Pull me out of the net that they have laid privily for me; for thou* art *my strength.*

5. *Into thine hand I commit my spirit: thou hast redeemed me, O Lord God of truth.*

6. *I have hated them that regard lying vanities: but I trust in the Lord.*

He cometh more particularly to his danger, and prayeth for delivery, and strengthening his faith by sundry reasons. Whence learn, 1. As the children of this world are more wise in their generation, than the children of the light: so do they hunt and overtake the godly, by their crafty devices against him; *they laid their nets privily against* David, *and ensnared him.* 2. Though the godly be both weak and simple-witted, yet they have a wise and strong God to call upon, who is able to break the snare, and set his own free, whose help David imploreth here; *pull me out of the net, for thou art my strength.* 3. The way to quiet our minds, in the hazard of our mortal life, (which is soon and easily taken away, and we cannot ourselves preserve,) is to put our soul over on God's care and custody, *into his hands committing our spirits.* 4. The word of God, giving assurance to the believer of his redemption, is a ground sufficient to make him confidently commit his soul to God's keeping; for he may say with warrant, *thou hast redeemed me, O God of truth.* 5. Worldly men that believe not in God, have some other thing wherein they trust beside, as riches, friendship, their own wit, &c., which carnal confidences are but lying vanities, whereof the true believer must be aware, and hate the way of such as follow them; for David hated them that *regarded lying vanities, because he trusted in God.*

7. *I will be glad and rejoice in thy mercy: for thou hast considered my trouble; thou hast known my soul in adversities;*

8. *And hast not shut me up into the hand of the enemy: thou hast set my feet in a large room.*

In the next place, he strengtheneth his faith by his former experience, and promiseth himself after this present sorrow, joy and gladness, whereof he hath some present sense, stirred up by calling its memory his experience. Whence learn, 1. In the midst of trouble faith will furnish matter of joy, and promise to itself gladness, especially from the memory of by-past experiences of God's mercy; as here, *I will rejoice and be glad in thy mercy.* 2. When a believer is in adversity, the Lord will not misken him, he will make him know, that even then he hath an eye upon him, and friendly affections to him: *thou hast known my soul in adversity.* 3. Adversary powers shall not get their will of a fixed believer, but he shall have delivery from them, and victory over them, either temporally or spiritually, or both ways; for here is the experience of it, *thou hast not shut me up in the hand of the enemy, thou hast set my feet in a large room.* 4. The ground of our gladness, when we have found a proof of God's kindness to us, should not be in the benefit so much, as in the fountain of the benefit; for this giveth us hope to drink again of the like experience, from the fountain which did send forth that benefit. Therefore David says, *I will be glad and rejoice in thy mercy for ever.*

9. *Have mercy upon me, O Lord, for I am in*

trouble: mine eye is consumed with grief, yea, *my soul and my belly.*

10. *For my life is spent with grief, and my years with sighing: my strength faileth because of mine iniquity, and my bones are consumed.*

11. *I was a reproach among all mine enemies, but especially among my neighbours, and a fear to mine acquaintance: they that did see me without fled from me.*

12. *I am forgotten as a dead man out of mind: I am like a broken vessel.*

13. *For I have heard the slander of many; fear* was *on every side: while they took counsel together against me, they devised to take away my life.*

In the third place, he layeth out his lamentable condition in regard of perplexity of mind and decay of natural strength, by grief and sorrow of heart, and in regard of the contempt of his adversaries, and neglect of his friends, and hazard of his life, joined with the sense of God's displeasure for his sins, wherein he is a type of Christ suffering for our sins imputed to him, and an example of the hard exercise of the saints. Whence learn, 1. Great and·of long continuance may the troubles of the godly be, great may their grief and heaviness of heart be, before they get comfort, as the example of this meek man—so holy in his way, so subdued in his affections—showeth by sundry expressions. 2. Albeit the Lord needs no words to inform him of our condition, or to move his affection to his children in trouble, yet he hath appointed us, for evidencing our faith in him, and dependence upon him for relief, to come and tell him what aileth us; and indeed it is an ease to the godly heart to have the Lord to speak unto, and lay out their case before him, as here we see. 3. The conscience of sin joined with trouble is a load above a burden, and able to break a man's strength more than any trouble; for here he saith, *my strength faileth because of mine iniquity, and my bones are consumed.* 4. When the godly have many and powerful enemies, then their acquaintance and neighbours, and the multitude of the people will readily believe that all the misreports of them are true, and this maketh the grief of the godly the greater; as here, *I was a reproach among all mine enemies, but especially among my neighbours.* 5. When

G

the godly fall under persecution and trouble, their worldly friends, for fear of danger or burden by them, will turn their back on them, and forget acquaintance, yea, and natural bands with them also ; and then must the godly lean to God, and expect comfort from him. This is holden forth in this type of Christ, and example of believers under trials : *I am a fear to my acquaintance,* &c. 6. Long lying in trouble will make a man to be forgotten of his friends, as if he were dead, and make him to lose all estimation at their hands, as if there were no worth in him at all; *I am forgotten as a dead man out of mind, I am like a broken vessel.* 7. It is Satan's policy to draw great men and councillors of state into a disgust of the godly, because commonly what great men esteem of the godly, that passeth for current ; and it is Satan's policy first to load the godly with slanders, and then to persecute them to death ; *I heard the slanders of many, they took counsel together to take away my life.* 8. In a sharp trial, a soul may be assaulted with terrible temptations on all hands, and feel terror and fighting within and without : *fear,* saith he, *was on every side.*

14. *But I trusted in thee, O Lord: I said, Thou art my God.*

15. *My times are in thy hand: deliver me from the hand of mine enemies, and from them that persecute me.*

16. *Make thy face to shine upon thy servant: save me for thy mercies' sake.*

17. *Let me not be ashamed, O Lord; for I have called upon thee: let the wicked be ashamed, and let them be silent in the grave.*

18. *Let the lying lips be put to silence ; which speak grievous things proudly and contemptuously against the righteous.*

In the fourth place, he wrestles by faith for delivery and comfort in the mean time, till delivery come to himself and disappointment to his enemies. Whence learn, 1. It is the nature of faith, and it is the believer's duty, to oppose help from God unto all temptations, were they ever so many, as here David did : *but I trusted in thee, O Lord.* 2. Except we hold fast the grip of our covenant with God, and avow it before him, trust will fail and temptations readily prevail. Much use made David of the covenant in his strait: *I said, thou art my God.* 3. Faith can make good cheer of the general grounds of God's providence, by making application thereof to its present use. The dispensations of all men's comforts and troubles, life and death, are in God's hand, and not in men's power: *my times are in thy hand,* saith David. 4. Because all power is in God's hand, prayer to him will prevail more for delivery from enemies than any means besides: *deliver me from the hand of mine enemies, and them that persecute me.* 5. When the cloud of trouble hideth the Lord's favour, faith knoweth it may shine again, and therefore prayeth through the cloud for dissolving of it: *make thy face to shine upon me.* 6. As we must study to approve ourselves to be the Lord's servants, by studying obedience to him; so must we make grace, and nothing else save grace, the ground of our hope to be helped, comforted, or saved: *shine upon thy servant,* saith he, *save me for thy mercy's sake.* 7. As the humble prayer of the persecuted godly shall be granted and have effect; so the proud brags, coloured calumnies, and threatenings of slanderous and cruel adversaries, shall be shamefully refuted and disappointed; and if the enemies shall not timously cease to persecute, they shall be made to cease in their graves: *let me not be ashamed, for I have called upon thee; let the wicked be ashamed, and let them be silent in the grave: let the lying lips be put to silence, which speak grievous things proudly and contemptuously against the righteous.*

19. Oh *how great is* thy *goodness, which thou hast laid up for them that fear thee;* which *thou hast wrought for them that trust in thee before the sons of men !*

20. *Thou shalt hide them in the secret of thy presence from the pride of man ; thou shalt keep them secretly in a pavilion from the strife of tongues.*

21. *Blessed* be *the Lord; for he hath shewed me his marvellous kindness in a strong city.*

Comfort and deliverance being the answer of his prayer, he praiseth God, and stirreth up the godly to set their hearts on God, and trust in him at all times. Whence learn, 1. The bounty of the Lord to his own people, seen in the world, observed in the Lord's ordinary dispensations towards them, and felt in a man's own experience, is able to ravish the heart with admiration of the blessedness of God's people; as here, *Oh how great is thy goodness !* 2. Beside what consolation of spirit the Lord giveth to his own, the Lord sometimes will manifest so much respect in his providence to his servants, that not only the godly, but also they who are but children of men, will be forced to acknowledge the Lord's singular respect to them ; and beside what the Lord bestoweth, either inwardly or outwardly, upon his own, in this life, there is yet more laid up for afterwards, for completing the blessedness in the life to come : *how great is thy goodness which thou hast laid up for them that fear thee, which thou hast wrought for them that trust in thee before the sons of men!* 3. How great peace of conscience before God, and comfort in the Holy Ghost, the Lord can give a believer, when he hath to do with proud, open persecutors, and privily whispering slanderers! it is a secret and hid mystery to the worldly man : this David describeth in a similitude taken from warfare: *thou shalt hide them in the secret of thy presence from the pride of man, thou shalt keep them secretly in a pavilion, from the strife of tongues.* 4. As every believer, having gotten any experience of God's goodness, should read it as a particular proof of some general promise made to the godly ; so should he subscribe the truth of that promise, in favour of all believers, and bless God for his own particular experience of it ; for so doth the prophet here, saying, *he hath showed his kindness to me,* that is, how kind a God he is to his own, *as in a strong city;* that is, preserved me in the wilderness, as if I had been in the best fenced city in the world, furnished with men, victual, and ammunition in abundance.

22. *For I said in my haste, I am cut off from before thine eyes : nevertheless thou heardest the voice of my supplications when I cried unto thee.*

He confesseth the great distress he was in, and how weak his faith was under the temptation; this he to his own shame acknowledgeth, also, that he may give the greater glory to God. Whence learn, 1. The faith of the godly may be shaken, and the strongest faith may sometimes show its infirmity : *I said in my haste, I am cut off from before thine eyes.* 2. Though faith be shaken, yet it is fixed in the root, as a tree beaten by the wind, keeping strong gripe of good ground ; though faith seem to yield, yet it faileth not, and even when it is at the weakest it is uttering itself in some act as a wrestler; for here the expression of David's infir-

mity in faith is directed to God, and his earnest prayer joined
with it : *I am cut off from before thine eyes, yet thou heardest the voice of my supplications.* 3. Praying faith, how
weak soever, shall not be misregarded of God ; for *nevertheless,* saith he, *thou heardest the voice of my supplications.*
4. There may be in a soul at one time both grief oppressing
and hope upholding ; both darkness of trouble and the light
of faith : both desperate doubting and strong griping of
God's truth and goodness ; both a fainting and a fighting ;
a seeming yielding in the fight and yet a striving of faith
against all opposition ; both a foolish haste and a settled
stayedness of faith ; as here, *I said in my haste, &c.*

23. *O love the Lord, all ye his saints ; for the Lord
preserveth the faithful, and plentifully rewardeth the
proud doer.*

24. *Be of good courage, and he shall strengthen your
heart, all ye that hope in the Lord.*

Now he maketh farther use of his experience, in exhorting
all the godly to follow his example, encouraging them yet
with hope of like success. Whence learn, 1. The gracious
dealing of God with believers should glue their own hearts,
and all other saints' hearts that hear of it, unto God, in
faith and love : *O love the Lord, all ye his saints.* He putteth love for faith, because it is inseparable from faith ; and
faith worketh by love, and love proveth the sincerity of faith.
2. The faithful man shall not want an upholder, albeit he
had no friends : *for the Lord preserveth the faithful.* 3.
The proud man shall not want a pursuer, and one to be
avenged on him for his pride and oppression, though all the
world should let him alone: *for the Lord plentifully rewardeth the proud doer.* 4. Albeit opposition be made unto a
believer, yet must he resist every thing which might put
him back from trusting in God ; for it becometh a believer
to be stout: *be of good courage.* 5. Whoso aimeth at
courage in the Lord shall be furnished with strength to
double out his undertaking of faith : *be of good courage, and
he shall strengthen your heart.* 6. Hope, grounded on the
promise, must be fixed, that our courage may be founded,
not on ourselves but on the word of God: *be of good courage,
all ye that hope in the Lord.*

PSALM XXXII.

A psalm of David. Maschil.

David, in this psalm, describeth the blessedness of the man justified by faith, by way of general doctrine; set down, ver. 1, 2: which he cleareth by his own experience, ver. 3—5. Then he showeth the uses, both of the general doctrine and of his own experience; first, for inducing the godly to go to God by prayer, in trouble, ver. 6; secondly, for confirming of his own faith, ver. 7; thirdly, for teaching all men submission to God, and not to strive with him when he doth correct or exercise them, ver. 8, 9; fourthly, for believing in God in all conditions, ver. 10; and, fifthly, for making the Lord the joy and delight of the justified man.

Maschil is put in the inscription of the psalm, signifying instruction; to teach us, that the doctrine of justification by faith is a lesson which all men have need to learn, and to learn more and more solidly; because salvation and daily consolation, in all the exercises of a man's soul, dependeth on it.

1. *Blessed* is he whose *transgression* is *forgiven,* whose *sin* is *covered.*

2. *Blessed* is *the man unto whom the Lord imputeth not iniquity, and in whose spirit* there is *no guile.*

In the doctrine set down in these two verses, Learn, 1. That sin draweth on a debt which no man can satisfy; such a debt as a man must perish, if it be *not forgiven.* 2. Sin is a filthiness which neither God can behold, without abominating the sinner, nor the guilty conscience can look upon without horror, except it *be covered.* 3. Sin draweth on a guiltiness which may draw men to damnation, if it shall be *imputed.* 4. There is no justification of a sinner, by his good works, before God; but only by the forgiveness of his evil works, as the apostle, Rom. iv. 6—8, citing this place, proveth : *blessed is he whose transgression is forgiven.* 5. Justification by faith, or remission of sins, is accompanied with right unto salvation, because it is written, *blessed is the man whose transgression is forgiven.* 6. Justification by faith, or absolution from sin, is accompanied also with the upright endeavour of sanctification; for of the justified man it is said, *blessed is the man in whose spirit there is no guile.* 7. Albeit no man liveth and sinneth not, yet God hath a way to cleanse the conscience of the upright man, who honestly, and without guile, endeavoureth to walk before God, by bringing him to give account of his debt, and to acknowledge his filthiness and his guiltiness before God, and then, for Christ's sake, *forgiving him*, and with Christ's right-eousness *covering him*, and for Christ's mediation *not im-puting iniquity unto him*.

3. *When I kept silence, my bones waxed old, through my roaring all the day long:*

4. *For day and night thy hand was heavy upon me: my moisture is turned into the drought of summer. Selah.*

He declareth this doctrine by his own experience, how God's wrath never left pursuing of him, till he came to make use of this doctrine, acknowledging his sin and flee-ing to the benefit of remission of sin, for the blood of the Messiah, the Lamb slain from the beginning of the world, in the symbol of the expiatory sacrifice then daily offered for sin. Whence learn, 1 That man is fittest to speak of the doctrine of man's sin and misery, and of God's free grace and mercy, who hath felt the bitterness of sin and wrath, and the sweetness of God's grace by experience of God's pardon; therefore is this doctrine recommended to the church by David, who had felt both. 2. A justified man who knoweth the doctrine of justification by faith in Christ, possibly, yea readily, may forget to make use of this precious truth, when he hath most need of it, being under guiltiness and the pressure also of God's fatherly wrath for it; for David for a while being in this condition, was si-lent, and did not come to the acknowledgment of his sin, but was taken up only with the sense of the rod. 3. When the Lord is about to make his child sensible of his sins, and of the necessity of a free remission of them through the Mediator, he can awake the conscience of sin, by the sense of sad affliction, and can increase the heat of the furnace, and make his child roar for sorrow and pain, and thereby weaken his natural strength, and waste his spirits and his flesh, and his bones, and drive him to death's door, till he make use of the doctrine of justification, or remission of sin by faith in God the Redeemer. This was David's case; *when he kept silence, his bones waxed old. God's hand was heavy upon him night and day, and the sap of his body* was dried up as a piece of moist earth is dried *in the drought of summer.*

5. *I acknowledged my sin unto thee, and mine iniquity have I not hid. I said, I will confess my transgressions unto the Lord; and thou forgavest the iniquity of my sin. Selah.*

At last the Lord led him to the right remedy, pointed out the way unto him of humiliation, and confession of sin, and seeking of mercy, as it is prescribed in the word, and so he was relieved. Whence learn, 1. Before the Lord let his child go from under the rod, after he hath given him an essay of himself, and of his own way how unprofitable it is, he will bring him about to the right way of relief, as here we see. 2. The only way to quiet the conscience, to pacify wrath, and remove judgment, is ingenuously to confess sin, and to aggravate it sincerely, (laying aside extenuations, excuses, and subterfuges, for justifying of God's dealing with us, and for humiliation of our ownselves before him,) and to fly to God's mercy, laying out all before him, as before a gracious God, who doth pursue controversies with his own, only to the intent that they may make peace with him in the Mediator, and so be reconciled. So did David ; *he acknowledged his sin, and that unto God, he hid not his iniquity.* 3. Reconciliation with God, and renewing our peace is ready at hand, when we take the right way as is said, to be delivered ; for so soon as David resolved upon this course, and said *he would confess,* it followeth, *thou forgavest the iniquity of my sin.*

6. *For this shall every one that is godly pray unto thee in a time when thou mayest be found; surely in the floods of great waters they shall not come nigh unto him.*

The first use of this doctrine and of David's experience, is to teach others how to behave themselves in their trouble. Whence learn, 1. The doctrine of justification by gracious forgiving iniquity, is the ground of all the godly's approaches to God, and right worshipping of him ; for, to show the use of this doctrine, thus tried by experience, he saith, *every godly one shall pray unto thee.* 2. There is a time when God may be found, to wit, so long as God is offering grace and sparing extremity of wrath, which time men ought to lay hold on, not knowing how short while it may last : they shall pray *in a time when thou mayest be found.* 3. It is possible, that a godly man may be in the midst of the waters of sore troubles, and yet these troubles not come near unto him, because God can furnish the man an ark in Christ, whereby he shall swim above the deluge; and when God keepeth off trouble, that it proveth not hurtful, (much more when he maketh trouble a means of spiritual good to a man, and giveth the man true peace and contentment in himself,) it is verified what is promised here: *surely in the floods of great waters, they shall not come near him.*

7. *Thou* art *my hiding-place; thou shalt preserve me from trouble; thou shalt compass me about with songs of deliverance. Selah.*

From the second use wherein David confirmeth his own faith for time to come, learn 1. Experience of God's mercies bygone should fasten resolution to make use of faith hereafter in all troubles, as here. 2. The godly after one trouble, should prepare for another, after one delivery expect another, as here. 3. What God hath proved himself to be to us before, we may promise he shall be the same to us in effect hereafter, because he is that by covenant and promise to us, what in practice we have found him to be; for David reasoneth thus, *thou* art *my hiding place; thou shalt preserve me from trouble;* that is, I shall have no damage by trouble, as is said. A justified soul resolving to make use of God in every condition that can come unto him, according to the covenant, may promise to himself a comfortable outgate of all his troubles, and matter of praise and joy from God on all hands; yea, he may confidently say with David, *thou shalt compass me about with songs of deliverance.*

8. *I will instruct thee, and teach thee in the way which thou shalt go: I will guide thee with mine eye.*

9. *Be ye not as the horse, or as the mule, which have no understanding; whose mouth must be held in with bit and bridle, lest they come near unto thee.*

From the third use of teaching others to be wise by his example, learn 1. The right use of experience is to edify others as our calling requireth; when we are converted, we should strengthen our brethren; for this David doth, *I will instruct thee, &c.* 2. When we have heard how others have

been afflicted, we should be wiser, and take instruction by
their example, that we strive not with God, but submit
ourselves under his hand, acknowledge our sins, and seek
mercy of him: *be not as the horse or the mule.* 3. Whosoever will not submit unto God, and seek unto his favour,
shall find themselves so much the more hardly dealt with, as
horses and mules *are bound in with bit and bridle.*

10. *Many sorrows* shall be *to the wicked: but he
that trusteth in the Lord, mercy shall compass him
about.*

From the fourth use of maintaining a course of adhering to God in all conditions, because it shall be better with
the believer than with the wicked; learn, 1. There is no
advantage to be had by repining against God, only the multiplication of sorrows shall follow thereupon, sin upon sin,
wrath upon wrath, judgment upon judgment; and after
temporal evils, everlasting shall follow, *for many sorrows
shall be to the wicked.* 2. Not repining against God, taking with our chastisements, acknowledging of our sins in
our affliction; seeking God's mercy, and leaning unto
him,—putteth difference between the wicked and the godly ;
for here the believer is set in opposition to the wicked, and
to the man that is like a horse or mule; for he is called *the
man that trusteth in the Lord.* 3. Whatsoever temptation,
trouble, or opposition shall make assault against the believer; mercy shall make the defence, and shall give the
deliverance on all hands, *for mercy shall compass him about.*

11. *Be glad in the Lord, and rejoice, ye righteous:
and shout for joy,* all ye that are *upright in heart.*

From the last use of making God our joy and delight,
learn, 1. Such as understand the way of justification by
grace, and have fled to God for pardon of sin, and so are
justified, have great matter of rejoicing, and should make
conscience to rejoice in God; for to them it is said, *rejoice,
ye righteous.* 2. The justified man is no counterfeit in the
matter of religion, nor hypocrite in the matter of outward
obedience to the Lord's law: *he is a righteous man, he is
upright in heart.* 3. The matter of his joy and triumphing
is the Lord himself, his grace, his good-will, his covenant,
his promise, and constant kindness and mercy, for it is said
to them, *be glad in the Lord.*

PSALM XXXIII.

This psalm in God's providence hath no inscription, as also many others have none; that we may look upon holy Scriptures as altogether inspired of God, and not put price upon it for the writers thereof, whether their name be expressed or not. In it there is first an exhortation to praise God, v. 1—3, for his powerful, wise, and righteous government of all things in general, v. 4, 5; and more specially for his powerful guiding the works of creation, v. 6, 7. Secondly, an exhortation, as to praise God, so also to fear him, for his omnipotency and his powerful over-ruling and disappointing all the devices of men against his church, and his powerful executing all his own will, v. 8—11. Thirdly, a proclaiming the blessedness of the Lord's church and people, and of God's praises in reaching his providence over all the world, in favour of his people, v. 12—15. In special, for disappointing and evacuating all vain confidences of men, great and small, who do not trust in him, v. 16, 17, and taking care of such as fear him and trust in him, to deliver them from all evil, v. 18, 19. Fourthly, the use is set down which the godly make of this doctrine and song of praise.

1. *Rejoice in the Lord, O ye righteous; for praise is comely for the upright.*

2. *Praise the Lord with harp; sing unto him with the psaltery and an instrument of ten strings.*

3. *Sing unto him a new song, play skilfully with a loud noise;*

From the exhortation made to the godly to praise God, learn, 1. That to rejoice in God is a point of praising of him, for it is here expounded to be praise; *rejoice in the Lord,* saith he, *for praise is comely.* 2. Albeit all be bound to praise God, yet none will do it cheerfully and acceptably, save only the godly; *rejoice, ye righteous.* 3. There is no exercise more becoming the godly, than praising of God, whether we look to the object of the praise, which is God; or whether we look to their obligation above all people in the world; *for praise is comely to the upright.* 4. There is no exercise whereunto we have more need to be stirred up, than to praise; such is our dulness, and such is the excellency and necessity of the work, as the ceremonial use of musical instruments in the pedagogy of Moses did signify and import; the religious use whereof, albeit it be taken away with the rest of the ceremonial law, (the natural or civil use thereof remaining still the same, both before the ceremonial law and after it;) yet the thing signified, which is the bending all the powers of our soul and body to praise God, is not taken away : and this necessity of our up-stirring is imported in a threefold exhortation. 5. The praises of the Lord, being well considered, will yield continually new matter, and fresh delight in the work. *Sing unto him*, saith he, *a new song*.

4. *For the word of the Lord is right; and all his works are done in truth.*

5. *He loveth righteousness and judgment: the earth is full of the goodness of the Lord.*

From the arguments of praise taken from his good governing of all things in general, learn, 1. The powerful appointment of what is done in the world, and the execution thereof in effect, is most holy, just, and equitable, that the creatures are so ranked as they are, some of them superior, some inferior; some of them ruling, some of them serving; some of them stronger, some weaker; some of them agreeing to other, some of them disagreeing one from another; some of them feeding upon, and others of them made food and prey to others: all making up a harmony of well-ruled concords and discords, all is done well and equitable: for, *the word of the Lord is right, and all his works are done in truth.* 2. The Lord cannot but do justly, because his nature is such, *he loveth righteousness and judgment.* 3. There is no part of the world we can set our eyes upon, but speaketh praise to God for his bounty to his creatures, and specially to man; *the earth is full of the goodness of the Lord.*

6. *By the word of the Lord were the heavens made; and all the host of them by the breath of his mouth.*

7. *He gathereth the waters of the sea together as an heap; he layeth up the depth in storehouses.*

From the works of creation, learn, 1. The omnipotence and wisdom of God in creating heaven and earth, and all things of nothing; as they praise God, so also do they prove the power and righteousness of his governing them; *by the word of the Lord the heavens were made.* 2. How easy a thing it is to God to govern and guide the world well, appeareth by his making of all things at a word; *he made all the host of them by the breath of his mouth,* and it can cost him no more to uphold and rule them at his pleasure. 3. He is able to ward off whatsoever evil can befall us: *for he gathers the waters of the sea as an heap*, which would naturally overflow the earth. 4. He hath more bands over our heads to keep us in fear and awe before him, and amongst the rest, *he layeth up the deep in store-houses,* to let them loose when, and where, and how far he pleaseth.

8. *Let all the earth fear the Lord : let all the inhabitants of the world stand in awe of him :*

9. *For he spake and it was* done; *he commanded, and it stood fast.*

10. *The Lord bringeth the counsel of the heathen to nought: he maketh the devices of the people of none effect.*

11. *The counsel of the Lord standeth for ever, the thoughts of his heart to all generations.*

In the second place, he exhorteth us to praise, so also to fear him. Whence learn, 1. The right use of the works of creation, is, to take up how glorious and how dreadful the Creator of them is, and to beware to offend him : *let all the earth fear before the Lord.* 2. No man on earth is exempted from God's judgment, when he transgresseth God's law, albeit he be without the church : *let all the inhabitants of the world stand in awe of him.* 3. His omnipotence, manifested in framing and settling the frame of the world at a word, should move men to fear him ; for it is given for a reason to fear him, *because he spake, and it was done ; he commanded, and it stood fast.* 4. Such as fear not God, have many devices of their own how to make themselves blessed, and how to overturn his church and people ; but God disappointeth them of their design, both in the one and in the other ; *he bringeth the counsel of the heathen to nought, and he maketh the devices of the people of none effect,* and therefore all should fear him. 5. The whole work of the Lord's providence, from the beginning of the world to the end thereof, is all at once before his eyes, and all the Lord's work is deliberately fixed by him ; *the counsel of the Lord standeth for ever.* 6. The Lord goeth on in executing of his determinate resolution, from one generation to another, without being frustrated of his purpose in any thing, less or more at any time : *the counsel of the Lord standeth for ever, the thoughts of his heart to all generations.* 7. Such as follow God's direction, obey his revealed will, take the course set down by him in his word for their re-

conciliation with him, through the Messiah Christ, and set
his word before them, to be the rule of their faith and obedience, cannot be disappointed of what is promised by God
in his revealed will; *for the counsel of the Lord standeth for
ever, and the thoughts of his heart to all generations.*

12. *Blessed* is *the nation whose God* is *the Lord;*
and *the people* whom *he hath chosen for his own inheritance.*

13. *The Lord looketh from heaven; he beholdeth all
the sons of men.*

14. *From the place of his habitation he looketh upon
all the inhabitants of the earth.*

15. *He fashioneth their hearts alike; he considereth
all their works.*

In the third place, he showeth the blessedness of God's
people, in order to his praise who hath chosen them, and
who disposeth of all things to their behoof. Whence learn,
1. Of all the people on the earth, the Lord hath only entered into covenant with his church, to be their God in a
peculiar way ; for here, *there is a nation whose God is the
Lord.* 2. Such as do lay hold on God as their God, are
the only blessed people in the world ; for it is said, *blessed
is that nation whose God is the Lord.* 3. Such as, in the
sense of their own sin and misery, and consideration of the
vanity of all things beside God, have chosen God for their
God, to live in communion with him, have evidence of
their election ; for they are here called, *the people whom he
hath chosen.* 4. Such people, as is said, are that peculiar
portion of the world which God hath set apart for himself,
to draw the rent of his glory in the world by them, and
from them in a special way ; and whom he will keep in his
possession for ever, and not suffer himself to be bereft of
them : *for they are the people whom he hath chosen for his
inheritance.* 5. Though the church be the only inheritance
of God, yet the rest of the world is the object of his wise,
holy, and powerful providence, no less than the church :
*the Lord looketh down from heaven, and beholds all the sons
of men.* 6. There cannot be a plot on earth against God's
church, but God is privy to 'it, and knoweth it perfectly ;
for *from the place of his habitation, he looketh on all the inhabitants of the earth.* 7. The Lord cannot be ignorant

of the most secret devices of men, better or worse, because he is the Maker of the hearts of all men : *he fashioneth their hearts alike* (that is, the heart of one as well as of another), *he considereth all their works,* that he may make of them what he will. 8. Men had need to consider whereupon their heart is set, and what course they are upon, and what work they are about, for he knoweth the heart, *and considereth every man's work.*

16. *There is no king saved by the multitude of an host: a mighty man is not delivered by much strength.*

17. *An horse* is *a vain thing for safety: neither shall he deliver* any *by his great strength.*

18. *Behold, the eye of the Lord* is *upon them that fear him, upon them that hope in his mercy;*

19. *To deliver their soul from death, and to keep them alive in famine.*

Here he sets at nought all carnal confidence of men, that his people may neither fear their enemies, nor trust in their own furniture, and preferreth trusting in God to all carnal confidence whatsoever. Whence learn, 1. Trusting in means, (such as a man's strength, and the assistance of other men, or other creatures,) is an error so natural and fixed, as it hath need to bé refuted by God, who hath said, that they are a vain confidence to lean unto, which cannot deliver a man ; *there is no king saved by the multitude of an host ; a mighty man is not delivered by much strength ; and a horse is a vain thing for safety.* And the actual frustrating of men's hopes, to be helped by authority, strength, or external helps, should teach men not to lean to them, when they are making use of them. 2. The man that believeth in God, and feareth him, is in a more safe condition than the wicked in all their power and riches : *behold the eye of the Lord is upon them that fear him, and hope in his mercy, to deliver them.* 3. The whole perfection of a Christian life is comprised in these two,—trusting in God's mercy, and fearing him : for this is the description here of the elect and blessed man. 4. The godly cannot secure themselves from being brought into straits and necessities, but may be sure that God shall have a care of them in their necessities, and give them a blessed outgate out of them all ; *for his eye is on them, to deliver them from death, and to keep them alive in famine.*

20. *Our soul waiteth for the Lord: he* is *our help and our shield.*

21. *For our heart shall rejoice in him; because we have trusted in his holy name.*

22. *Let thy mercy, O Lord, be upon us, according as we hope in thee.*

In the last place is set down the use of this doctrine which the godly should make of it. Whence learn, 1. All the points of the Lord's praise, are props of the saints' faith and grounds of their hope, as this conclusion drawn from this song of praise doth show : *our soul waiteth for the Lord, &c.* 2. Every believer may rejoice, and promise to himself cause of rejoicing, through faith in his name ; *our hearts shall rejoice in him, because we have trusted in him.* 3. Faith always differenceth itself from presumption, by praying for what is promised ; *let thy mercy be upon us,* say the believers. 4. Because the hope of the godly is grounded upon God's promises, therefore it shall not be disappointed, *but God's mercy shall be on them, according as they hope in him.*

PSALM XXXIV.

A psalm of David, when he changed his behaviour before Abimelech ; who drove him away, and he departed.

In this psalm David praiseth God for his delivery from the king of Gath, and exhorteth others to praise God with him, for his experience of God's mercy, ver. 1—6. Then for making farther use of this mercy, he gives out general doctrines concerning God's protection and care of his children, with the uses thereof, ver. 7—10. Thirdly, he giveth counsel how to lead a blessed life, ver. 11—14. Fourthly, he enforceth his council by promises to the godly who obey God's counsel, and threatenings to the wicked man who obeyeth not, ver. 15—22.

From the inscription we learn, 1. That it is to good purpose to observe special mercies in a special manner, and to note the circumstances thereof as here is done. 2. And that men in a preposterous fear, flying from one danger may fall into another worse, as David did, when he fled into an unhallowed place, amongst God's enemies, for fear of Saul, he falleth into Abimelech or Achish's hands. 3. And that God pitieth the infirmity of his children, and gives success some whiles to weak and unthrifty shifts, as here when David changed his behaviour, he escaped. 4. That God can and doth dispose of men's hearts, as he hath a mind to work by them : for he did move the heart of Achish not to take notice of David, otherwise than of a distracted man.

1. *I will bless the Lord at all times : his praise* shall *continually* be *in my mouth.*

2. *My soul shall make her boast in the Lord : the humble shall hear* thereof, *and be glad.*

He promiseth here for his own part to praise God for the mercy received. Whence learn, 1. As no mercy should be misregarded ; so, notable mercies should be specially re-membered, and God blessed for the same. 2. It is a point of thankfulness, to take all occasions to speak of God to others ; *his praise shall be continually in my mouth.* 3. Whatsoever be our condition in ourselves, matter of glori-ation in God shall never be wanting to the believer, and this gloriation is a duty and a point of praising God; *my soul shall make her boast in the Lord* Only humble souls sensible of their own weakness are the people who reap benefit by God's mercies, bestowed on others and them-selves : *the humble shall hear and be glad.*

3. *O magnify the Lord with me, and let us exalt his name together.*

4. *I sought the Lord, and he heard me and delivered me from all my fears.*

He exhorteth others to praise God with him, magnifying him for his greatness, and exalting him for his highness. Whence learn, 1. The saints are obliged to help one an-other in praises as well as in prayer, albeit it cometh to pass that many do crave aid of others' prayers, who call not for their help to praise : for here it is, *let us exalt his name together.* 2. By prayer the Lord is sought and found, and it is no small matter of comfort to us, and glory to God, that our prayer is regarded : *I sought the Lord,* saith he, *and he heard me.* 3. The fear of what is like to be, should not hinder prayer; for the fears of the godly are not certain prophecies ; for God can deliver out of them all : *he delivered me out of all my fears.*

5. *They looked unto him, and were lightened; and their faces were not ashamed.*

6. *This poor man cried, and the Lord heard* him, *and saved him out of all his troubles.*

He is glad, and commendeth God's goodness to him for the fruit of this mercy to other believers. Whence learn, 1. One man's experience may be an encouragement to many to run to God for the like alms. This David fore-seeth shall be the fruit of God's mercy to him, when men, seeing him delivered, shall look to God, and take comfort and confidence by this means; *they looked on him*, that is, on David, and so may we on Christ, (represented by him,) and at the fulness of the Godhead dwelling in Christ: so they were lightened, and thus comforted in the midst of the darkness of their troubles: *and their faces were not ashamed*, because of confidence raised by this experience, that they should find the like mercy when they stood in need. 2. The way to make the best use of the example of God's mercy to any persons set down in Scripture, or which fall forth in our time, or are made certainly known to us any way, is to look upon them, not as they differ from us or our condition, but as they draw nearest in similitude to us, and unto the mean con-dition we are in, for so do the saints look on David, say-ing, not this rare saint David, or this great prophet David, or this holy man David, who was according to God's heart —but *this poor man* David *cried, and the Lord heard him, and saved him out of all his troubles.*

7. *The angel of the Lord encampeth round about them that fear him, and delivereth them.*

8. *O taste and see that the Lord is good: blessed is the man that trusteth in him.*

In the next place, are set down general doctrines concern-ing God's care of believers, to protect and feed them, and the uses thereof, to trust and fear God. Whence learn, 1. A right sight of God's dealing with a man's ownself will give him great light about the Lord's manner of deal-ing with others, his children, as here. 2. Though the godly walk among foes, and be in a continual warfare, yet they are well looked to and guarded: *the angel of the Lord encampeth round about them.* 2. The sense of God's mer-cy and goodness is the sweetest thing that ever was felt, and is able to season the bitterest cup that ever believer drank of: *taste and see that the Lord is good.* 4. By faith is the taste of this sweetness gotten, *for blessed is the man that trusts in him.* 5. All that the believer can attain to in this life of spiritual consolation, whether by faith or experience, sweetened with lively comforts of the holy Ghost, is but a taste in comparison of what is to be had hereafter, and yet that taste, O how sweet a joy unspeakable, and full of glory is it ! *O taste and see that the Lord is good.* 6. Affliction purgeth the taste of the believer, and a soul driven from all worldly helps, is fitted for exercising spiritual senses, as here we see David's taste is purged well after trouble. 7. As God is very communicative of his goodness, and offereth himself to men to be taken a proof of, so also gracious souls do wish and invite others to share with them in whatsoever grace the Lord doth bestow on them, as David doth here, saying to all, *O taste and see.* 8. Albeit this sweetness be not found at the first out-putting of faith, yet let faith rest on God and it shall feel in due time, for blessed is he that putteth his trust in God; yea, faith itself is a taste of that grace that is in God.

9. *O fear the Lord, ye his saints: for* there is *no want to them that fear him.*

10. *The young lions do lack, and suffer hunger: but they that seek the Lord shall not want any good* thing.

Another doctrine concerning God's care to feed and provide for all necessary furniture unto the believer, with the use thereof, which is to fear God. Whence learn, 1. True believers in God must study holiness for evidencing of their faith, for therefore are they called saints, and *his* saints. 2. The fear of the Lord is the property of the saints, whereby they are set on work to do what the Lord commandeth, and to forbear what he forbiddeth, and no bonds of inclination, counsel, example, laws, fear of shame, or punishment from men, are able to keep a man in order when he meeteth with a fit temptation to sin; but the fear of God restraineth the man both outwardly and inwardly, in secret and open, always, and everywhere; and whatsoever measure of holy fear the saints have attained unto, yet may they be exhorted, and must hearken unto exhortation, to grow in this grace; *O fear the Lord, ye his saints.* 3. Such as fear God need not to want any necessary furniture in God's service; *for there is no want to them that fear him.* 4. Proud oppressors, wealthy and potent princes, that trust in their own power, shall not be so sure of their

own standing and furniture, as the meanest of true believers are; *the lions do lack, and suffer hunger, but
they that seek the Lord shall not want;* though the godly
may want many earthly things, yet shall they have food and
raiment, *and shall not want any good thing.* 6. The
right sort of fearing God, and labouring for more and
more near communion with him, are inseparable properties
of the saints, for they that are called saints are called here
fearers of him and seekers of him also.

11. *Come, ye children, hearken unto me; I will
teach you the fear of the Lord.*

12. *What man is he that desireth life,* and *loveth*
many *days, that he may see good?*

13. *Keep thy tongue from evil, and thy lips from
speaking guile.*

14. *Depart from evil, and do good; seek peace, and
pursue it.*

In the third place, he giveth direction how a man shall
live blessedly; by evidencing the sincerity of the fear of
God in him, which is a grace inseparable from faith in
God, manifesting itself in obedience to his commands.
Whence learn, 1. There should be such mutual love and
respect between the teacher and the people taught, as is
between parents and children, yea, God in his servants offereth himself as a father, ready to instruct his visible
church as his children; *come, ye children,* saith he, *and
hearken unto me.* 2. The true fear of God is the way to
live blessedly in this life, where misery most aboundeth; and
this should be a motive to seek after this grace, for it is asked
here, *what man is he that desireth life?* &c., and then the
way to attain to it is set down in some particulars of the
fear of God, as the inseparable companions of faith in God.
3. The true fear of God must evidence itself by the fruits
thereof, such as are the ruling of man's tongue, and of the
rest of the outward man, eschewing whatsoever the Lord
forbids, and endeavouring every good duty which God
commandeth, and the keeping peace with all men so far as
in us lieth, for so doth the prophet's words bear; ver. 13,
14. This is the evidence of the fear of God in effect, when
such outward works proceed from inward principles of
saving grace.

15. *The eyes of the Lord* are *upon the righteous, and his ears* are open *unto their cry.*

16. *The face of the Lord* is *against them that do evil, to cut off the remembrance of them from the earth.*

In the last place, he presseth this doctrine by showing the privileges of the righteous, and the miserable state of the wicked, setting the one against the other thrice. In the first learn, 1. It is a good means to keep our hearts in the fear of God to consider the gain of godliness, and the damage and danger of wickedness, as here they are set in opposition. 2. Such as have their eye upon God and his word for righteousness and life, may be sure of the watchful eye of God on them for their direction in their way, their consolation in their grief, and deliverance out o f trouble ; for *the eyes of the Lord are upon the righteous.* 3. As the righteous lend their ears to God's word, to his promises and precepts, so the Lord lendeth his ear to their supplications and desires: *his ears are open to their cry.* 4. On the other hand, as the wicked who fear not God, set their face to do evil, and to transgress God's commands, so God shall set his face against them, to be avenged on them: *the face of the Lord is against them that do evil.* 5. The only happiness which the wicked man seeketh, is to have riches, honour, and pleasure in the earth, and to have his own name in estimation among men hereafter, and these things also, beside the loss of heaven, shall be taken from him, and his temporal life withal : for *the face of the Lord is set against them, to cut off their remembrance from the earth.*

17. The righteous *cry, and the Lord heareth, and delivereth them out of all their troubles.*

18. *The Lord* is *nigh unto them that are of a broken heart; and saveth such as be of a contrite spirit.*

19. *Many* are *the afflictions of the righteous: but the Lord delivereth him out of them all.*

20. *He keepeth all his bones : not one of them is broken.*

21. *Evil shall slay the wicked; and they that hate the righteous shall be desolate.*

Another opposition of the good appointed for the godly, and the evil appointed for the wicked. Whence learn, 1.

The Lord putteth the godly to trouble, and by trouble putteth them to their prayers, and delays answer till the need be great; and then they cry to the Lord, and he giveth evidence of his hearing, and sendeth deliverance: for *the righteous cry, and the Lord heareth, and delivereth them out of all their troubles.* 2. It is as true as it may seem strange, that the Lord will press his own so long with trouble till he break their heart, and kill their natural courage and confidence; for here are the godly described to be men of *a broken heart and contrite spirit.* 3. Though the Lord so break the natural confidence of his own, and so empty them, by trouble, of all conceit of their own worth, wisdom, or ability to deliver themselves out of trouble, that they may rely on God only; yet will he not withdraw himself from them, nor suffer them to perish in discouragement: *the Lord is near to them that are of broken heart, and saveth such as be of a contrite spirit.* 4. Though the righteous be the only men in the world whom God loveth best, yet will he not only not exempt them from trouble, but also will exercise them with multitudes and varieties of troubles from his own hand immediately, from Satan's temptations, from the malice of the wicked of the world, &c.: *many are the troubles of the righteous;* for thus will the Lord conform the redeemed to their Head—try, and train them up in faith, and patient submission to God's will; teach them to pray and wait on, and give proof of the sincerity of the grace given to them. 5. The godly are as oft delivered as they are troubled, either by removing the trouble, or by giving strength and patience to bear it, or comfort under it and certain hope of outgate from it, or by ending all troubles to them at once: *many are the afflictions of the righteous, but the Lord delivereth him out of them all.* 6. The Lord moderateth, weigheth, and measureth all the troubles of his own—what they shall suffer in their life and death—and leaveth it not to the will of the instruments of their trouble: *he keepeth all his bones : not one of them is broken.* This was true of Christ our Lord, of whom many things were prefigured and prophesied in the psalms, and in this among the rest: which showeth, that in the psalms, as the matter will suffer, Christ is much to be eyed, and more than David, of whom, at first, the same seem to speak chiefly. 7. As to the opposite state of the wicked, we learn, that the wickedness of the wicked is both the meritorious cause and the means of the wicked man's destruction : *for evil shall slay the wicked.* 8. It is the mark of a wicked man *to hate the righteous* for his righteousness; and so is it set down here. 9. He that hateth the righteous, or the image of God in his neighbour, shall be guilty of all the consequences of the enmity, and be destitute of comfort when he hath most need : *he that hateth the righteous shall be desolate.*

22. *The Lord redeemeth the soul of his servants; and none of them that trust in him shall be desolate.*

The third opposition between the righteous and the wicked, is in relation to what is said in the former verse. Whence learn, 1. The wicked shall perish in their sin, and for their sin, but the righteous shall not perish in their sins, nor for them : for *evil shall slay the wicked, but the Lord shall redeem the soul of his servants ;* to wit, out of sin and misery. 2. As the wicked are servants of sin, and serve an ill master, and get an ill reward ; so the godly are servants of righteousness, and have God for their master, and shall have delivery and salvation for their reward ; as the comparison here set down showeth. 3. As the wicked, who are destitute of faith in God, when they fall into trouble, want consolation ; so all the righteous, who are no other than sincere believers in God, shall have good company and consolation in all their trouble, and never be left alone : for *the haters of the righteous shall be desolate, but none of them that trust in God shall be desolate.*

PSALM XXXV.

A psalm of David.

This psalm is a representation of Christ's hottest contest with his adversaries, wherein they are about to do their worst against him, and his kingdom; and he denounceth the hottest wrath of God against them, for their everlasting overthrow, set forth under the shadow of David's contest with his irreconcilable enemies: wherein he prayeth God to arise for him, ver. 1—3, and take order with his despiteful enemies, ver. 4—8 ; which, as it may comfort the supplicant, so shall it serve also for God's glory, ver. 9, 10. A main reason for which petition is the unjust and ungrateful dealing of his enemies with him, ver. 11—16 ; whereupon he reneweth his petition the second time, ver. 17—19, pressing his former reason from the enemy's unjust and insolent disposition, ver. 20, 21; and then reneweth his petition the third time for himself, ver. 22—26, and for all the favourers of his cause, ver. 27, 28.

1. *Plead* my cause, *O Lord, with them that strive with me : fight against them that fight against me.*

2. *Take hold of shield and buckler, and stand up for mine help.*

3. *Draw out also the spear, and stop* the way *against them that persecute me; say unto my soul, I am thy salvation.*

From his petition for himself, learn, 1. Such as take part with God against his enemies, the Lord will take part with against their enemies: if any plead against the believer by verbal calumnies and slanders, the Lord will be their party: if any will oppose the godly with violence, the Lord will oppose them ; for this prayer of one of the godly is as good as a promise to all: *plead my cause, O Lord, with them that strive with me: fight against them that fight against me.* 2. There is defence in abundance to be found in God against whatsoever the enemy can do ; a shield and buckler in God's hand, when he pleaseth to stand up and help. 3. The Lord can terrify the enemy so that he dare not assault the man whom God pleaseth to defend, and hold him off with long weapons, giving the enemy some other thing to do than pursue his people: he can *draw out the spear, and stop the way against them that persecute the godly.* 4. He can quiet the hearts of his own in the midst of persecution, and make them fearless in persuading them of their salvation, everlasting at least ; and this may fully satisfy, if the Lord *say unto their soul, I am thy salvation.*

4. *Let them be confounded and put to shame that seek after my soul: let them be turned back and brought to confusion that devise my hurt.*

5. *Let them be as chaff before the wind: and let the angel of the Lord chase them.*

6. *Let their way be dark and slippery: and let the angel of the Lord persecute them.*

7. *For without cause have they hid for me their net* in *a pit,* which *without cause they have digged for my soul.*

8. *Let destruction come upon him at unawares; and let his net that he hath hid catch himself: into that very destruction let him fall.*

From his petition against his enemies, learn, 1. Shameful disappointment shall they find at length who intend to destroy the godly : *let them be confounded and put to shame that seek after my soul.* 2. Though the enemies of Christ and the godly advance in the prosecution of their hurtful devices; yet shall they be forced to retire with shame: *they shall be turned back and brought to confusion who devise their hurt.* 3. As the enemy hath pursued, so shall God's wrath pursue, chase, and drive him to perdition: *they shall be as the chaff before the wind.* 4. Albeit there were no earthly man to pursue Christ's enemies, yet avenging angels, or evil spirits, shall be let forth upon them and their families, to trouble them: *let the angel of the Lord chase them.* 5. The Lord shall put them to such straits as they shall not know what hand to turn to, what way to take, and in the way which they take they shall fall: *let their way be dark and slippery.* 6. When they fall into mischief, the hand of the Lord shall be stretched out against them: *let the angel of the Lord pursue them.* 7. Though the godly, by behaving themselves innocently, cannot eschew the persecution of the wicked; yet innocent behaviour is a great ease to the conscience of the godly, a matter of encouragement to them in their addresses to God, and a great aggreging of the ditty of the enemy; as here twice he saith, *without cause they hid their net.* 8. Though the enemies of the godly do plot secret devices against them, yet not so secret but God can give warning of it, and make it an errand for the godly to pray to him to disappoint the plot; as is here imported: *they have hid for me their net in a pit.* 9. The wicked know not how to be sure of their prey when they hunt for the life of the godly: *they prepare the net and set it; they hide it, and they hide it in a pit.* 10. When the enemies of God's people least expect harm, then shall mischief surprise them: *destruction shall come upon them unawares.* 11. The very course which the enemy taketh against God's church and people, shall be the nearest course to destroy themselves: *let his net that he hath hid catch himself: into that very destruction let him fall.*

9. *And my soul shall be joyful in the Lord: it shall rejoice in his salvation.*

10. *All my bones shall say, Lord, who is like unto thee, which deliverest the poor from him that is too strong for him, yea, the poor and the needy from him that spoileth him?*

He brings a reason of his prayer from the comfort which

he should have, and the glory which God should have, by
its answer. Whence learn, 1. It is a good reason to
strengthen our hope to be heard, when our comfort and
God's glory may both be promoted by the granting of our
desire, as here we find it. 2. The destruction of the enemies of the church is not a matter of rejoicing in men's
destruction, but of rejoicing in the Lord, and in his wise
manner of delivering his people : *my soul shall be joyful in
the Lord* : *it shall rejoice in his salvation.* 3. In the estimation of the godly, the tongue is too little to magnify the
Lord for his mercies; for their desire is, that all the powers
of the soul, and all the parts of the body, even the bones,
which are least sensible in their own kind, might praise
him : *all my bones shall say, &c.* 4. The Lord hath wonderful ways, other and more than ever man conceived, whereby he can deliver his own, in their lowest condition, from
their oppressors, when they are in the height of their power
and pride : *Lord, who is like unto thee, which deliverest the
poor from him that is too strong for him, &c.* 5. Though,
before deliverance come, faith hath cause to say all that
sense can say of God's praises after deliverance is come ;
yet, when sensible experience of a hoped delivery is come,
there is a more hearty and cheerful manner of expressing
the Lord's praises than can be before it come; as the pre-
mise of the prophet to say so and so, as is in the text, after
the delivery is come, doth import. 6. It is a sort of, as it
were, engaging of God to deliver, when the heart of the
believer engageth itself to glorify God after the delivery;
for here the prophet maketh use of this, promising praise
towards this end.

11. *False witnesses did rise up : they laid to my
charge* things *that I knew not.*

12. *They rewarded me evil for good,* to *the spoiling
of my soul.*

13. *But as for me, when they were sick, my clothing*
was *sackcloth : I humbled my soul with fasting ; and
my prayer returned into mine own bosom.*

14. *I behaved myself as though* he had been *my
friend* or *brother : I bowed down heavily, as one that
mourneth* for his *mother.*

15. *But in mine adversity they rejoiced, and gathered*

themselves together; yea, *the abjects gathered themselves together against me, and I knew* it *not; they did tear* me, *and ceased not :*

16. *With hypocritical mockers in feasts, they gnashed upon me with their teeth.*

He amplifieth that reason of his petition, taken from his enemies' carriage, by laying before God their falsehood and ingratitude. Whence learn, 1. The godly are subject, not only to be backbitten, and reduced privily, and slandered more openly ; but also to be charged unjustly before judges, and pursued criminally for their life without a cause, and to have false witness led against them, that they may be condemned under colour of law ; this was found in effect by David, and Christ represented by him. *False witnesses did rise up; they laid to my charge things that I knew not.* 2. No bonds of nature or humanity will bind up the wicked from persecuting the godly, even to death, how well soever the godly have deserved of them ; *they rewarded me evil for good, to the depriving me of my life.* 3. True love is best known, as by rejoicing at another's welfare, so by grieving for his grief ; *when they were sick, my clothing was sackcloth.* 4. Hearty prayer also for any man, is a token of unfeigned love to a man, specially when prayer and fasting are joined together for them : *I humbled my soul by fasting.* 5. When the expressions of grief, by words or tears in prayer for any, waken up the affection yet more to pray ardently for them; it is yet a farther token of unfeigned love of them for whom we pray. *My prayer,* saith he, *returned into my bosom;* which is as much as my expressions in prayer, in sighs, affectionate words and tears, affected my heart, Lament. iii. 49—51, with new motions of earnest dealing for them. 6. True Christians' affection to their enemies, is able to affect the soul as much to the seeking their welfare, and commiserating their misery, as the natural affection of a natural man can affect him toward friends and kinsfolk, in nearest natural relations unto him ; for David saith, *I behaved myself as though he had been my friend or brother; I bowed down heavily as one that mourneth for his mother.*

From the evil meeting which he received of his enemies, v. 15, 16, learn, 1. Many of those that pretend great friendship to the godly in time of prosperity, may not only turn their back upon them in time of adversity, but also turn to be their open enemies, and rejoice in their calamity ; *but in my adversity*, saith he, *they rejoiced.* 2. The troubles of the godly draw the wicked into a more near union amongst themselves, as it were congratulating one another in their sinful courses, and strengthening one another ; *they gather themselves together.* 3. Base rascals, who have nothing to commend them save merely their hatred of God's people and of their piety, will get respect amongst the enemies of Christ and of his people, for that very reason, because they hate the godly, and will be admitted into the fellowship of ringleading enemies ; *yea, the abjects gathered themselves together against me.* 4. In the meeting of the wicked among themselves, Christ and his followers have their name torn and rent in pieces continually, with calumnies and slanders, which possibly come not to their ears, half of them : *they gathered together, and I knew it not : they did tear me in pieces and ceased not.* 5. Sad taunts and scoffs of pretended holy men jeering at true piety, is no small part of the persecution of Christ, and of his followers ; for here amongst the rest are *hypocritical mockers.* 6. When the wicked without fear fill and stuff their belly in their feasting, in the time of the church's trouble: their scoffs and their jests, yea and their bloody expressions of cruelty against the godly, are the most relishing sauce of their banquets : *with hypocritical mockers in their feasts, they gnash upon me with their teeth.*

17. *Lord, how long wilt thou look on ? rescue my soul from their destructions, my darling from the lions.*

18. *I will give thee thanks in the great congregation : I will praise thee among much people.*

19. *Let not them that are mine enemies wrongfully rejoice over me; neither let them wink with the eye that hate me without a cause.*

20. *For they speak not peace ; but they devise deceitful matters against* them that are *quiet in the land.*

21. *Yea, they opened their mouth wide against me,* and *said, Aha, aha! our eye hath seen* it.

He repeateth his petition for delivery from his enemies the second time, and presseth the same reason taken from the insolent and cruel disposition of the enemy. Whence learn, 1. The time of trouble and persecution of the godly may continue much longer than the godly expected, in which case, as they must wait on patiently till the Lord put to his hand to relieve his church and punish their enemies; so they may ease their heart, in laying their earnest longing to be delivered before the Lord, and say, *Lord, how long wilt thou look on?* 2. As it is lawful to lament the Lord's seeming long delay to help us, so we must not complain too soon; for, before David uttereth this, *how long*, he is long in trouble, and in danger of his life, by unreasonable and beastly cruel men, and is altogether destitute of all means of relief, as his prayer testifieth ; *rescue my soul from their destructions, my darling from the lions.* 3. The godly, by faith in the deepest danger, may see their delivery in their saddest and darkest sorrow; yea, may behold the light of consolation coming ; in their banishment, may behold their liberty, and see their fellowship with the saints ; and, in the midst of complaints, may promise to themselves reasons of praise, and the payment of their vows made to God, as here we see in the midst of this sad condition the prophet saith, *I will give thee thanks in the great congregation : I will praise thee among much people.* 4. It augmenteth the grief of the godly, to see the wicked take advantage of their trouble, and mockers of religion rejoice over their sufferings in a good cause ; and they may heartily deprecate this evil, that it may not at least last long ; *let not those that are my enemies rejoice over me.* 5. The less cause of provocation of our enemies be given to them by us, the greater is the hope of delivery, and the readier shall be our help from God, and the less cause shall be to the enemy to wink with the eye, as witty well-pleased scoffers do, when they get their will; *neither let them wink with the eye,* saith he, *that hate me without a cause.* 6. Albeit godly men's quiet carriage in the land where they live, will not save them from the hostile speeches, and malicious plottings of their adversaries against them, yet shall their quiet behaviour speak to God for them, and against their enemies, and make a speedy mischief come upon them from the Lord ; for, to this purpose he saith, *they speak not peace, but they devise deceitful matters against them that are quiet in the land.* 7. The enemies of the church are a base generation, taking pleasure and sport in the miser-

ies of the godly, who do not injure them, yea, are a vain
and insolent generation, triumphing over the weakness of
the innocent when they are in low condition, and in the
case of suffering, which common humanity and ordinary
generosity abhorreth : *they opened their mouth wide against
me, and said, Aha, aha, our eye hath seen it.*

22. This *thou hast seen, O Lord : keep not silence :
O Lord, be not far from me.*

23. *Stir up thyself, and awake to my judgment,* even
unto my cause, my God and my Lord.

24. *Judge me, O Lord my God, according to thy
righteousness; and let them not rejoice over me.*

25. *Let them not say in their hearts, Ah, so would
we have it : let them not say, We have swallowed him
up.*

26. *Let them be ashamed, and brought to confusion
together, that rejoice at mine hurt : let them be clothed
with shame and dishonour that magnify* themselves
against me.

He reneweth his petition for himself and against his enemies the third time. Whence learn, 1. Such as feed their
eyes upon the miseries of the godly, the Lord shall not
wink at their wickedness, but make it appear, that he hath
marked their cruelty, that he may punish it exemplarily ;
for after the enemies' crying out, *our eye hath seen,* the
prophet addeth, *this thou hast seen, O Lord, be not silent.*
2. The hardest condition that can befall a believer, is a tolerable case and condition, if God draw near to his soul :
for all the remedy that David craveth, till the outgate come,
is, *O Lord, be not far from me.* 3. Though the Lord for a
time suffer his own to lie under foot oppressed, yet for his
justice' sake, and for his covenant's sake, he will justly
determine the controversy, and clear his own servants ; *he
will stir up himself to do judgment, and decide their cause.*
4. In the decision of the controversy between the godly
and their enemies, the cause of the godly shall get no wrong,
but be declared to be righteous, and the enemies shall have
no matter to rejoice in. *He shall judge the godly according to their righteousness, and shall not suffer the wicked
to rejoice over them.* 5. When the enemies of the church
have laid the last reckoning of the issue of their bloody

course against the godly, they shall see the matter go otherwise than they would, or expected, on both hands. They shall not have cause to say, *so would we have it,* or *we have swallowed them up.* They are too precious a morsel for them to devour. 6. Shame and confusion, dis-honour and disgrace, on all hands shall be upon one, and upon all Christ's enemies, who seek the detriment of his cause, and to have gain to themselves, by opposing him and his cause in his people's hand; for this prayer against them shall still speak effectually, *let them be ashamed and brought to confusion together, and let them be clothed with shame and dishonour, &c.*

27. *Let them shout for joy, and be glad, that favour my righteous cause; yea, let them say continually, Let the Lord be magnified, which hath pleasure in the prosperity of his servant.*

28. *And my tongue shall speak of thy righteousness,* and *of thy praise, all the day long.*

As David prayeth for himself, so he prayeth for all the favourers of his righteous cause, as the type of Christ, whose Spirit spake by him, for the edification of the church in all times coming. Whence learn, 1. It is one mark of god-liness amongst many others, to befriend the cause of Christ, and to further it in the person of his saints, suffering for righteousness, with their best affection; for here they are described by being *the favourers of their righteous cause.* 2. In the persecution of the godly for the cause of God's truth and true religion, all the godly are concerned; and as they partake of the sufferings with others under Christ the Head, so shall they partake of the joy of the victory and outgate, which shall be exceedingly joyful at last : *let them shout for joy, and be glad,* saith the type of Christ, *that do favour my righteous cause.* 3. The troubles of the godly are not so many but room is left sometimes for prosperity; for God *loveth the prosperity of his servants;* to wit, as it may conduce to his purpose and their good. 4. When any of the godly are delivered from their persecutors, all the rest of the godly are bound, as they understand it, to set forth the power of God, and his love and bounty, manifested and forthcoming to his people: *let them say continually, Let the Lord be magnified, which hath pleasure in the prosperity of his servants.* 5. Whatsoever opposition the enemies of

Christ and of the godly shall make, Christ shall keep up
the open profession of true doctrine, which manifesteth the
righteousness of God—leading men to eternal life, and bringing glory to God ; for this is the undertaking of the type,
and of Christ represented by him, after the hottest contest
between him and his wicked enemies : *my tongue shall speak
of thy righteousness, and of thy praise all the day long.*

PSALM XXXVI.

To the chief musician.   A psalm of David, the servant of the Lord.

This psalm hath three parts. In the first, David sets down the perverseness of the wicked in their sinful course and devices against the godly
and himself, ver. 1—4.   In the second, he comforts himself, and doth
settle his faith on the praises and properties of God, ver. 5—9.   In the
third, he prayeth in the behalf of God's children, and for himself, to
be delivered from the wicked, ver. 10—12.

From the inscription, learn, that to be a servant of the
Lord is an honour, and a privilege above all earthly privileges ; and by giving a sweet testimony to the conscience,
it doth season every condition of life, more than any earthly advantage can do.

1. *The transgression of the wicked saith within my
heart,* that there is *no fear of God before his eyes.*

2. *For he flattereth himself in his own eyes, until his
iniquity be found to be hateful.*

3. *The words of his mouth* are *iniquity and deceit:
he hath left off to be wise,* and *to do good.*

4. *He deviseth mischief upon his bed; he setteth
himself in a way* that is *not good; he abhorreth not
evil.*

From his observation of the carriage of the wicked ;
learn, 1.   Albeit all the world cannot be discerned to be
graceless and unconverted, yet the lewd life of some may
speak their being in the state of corrupt nature unconverted,
to the conscience of a discerning man ; *for the transgression of the wicked saith in my heart, that there is no fear of
God before his eyes.*   2. It is not the imperfection or short-
coming in the fear of God, but the being destitute of it altogether, that proveth a wicked man : *there is no fear of
God before his eyes.*   3. As a man that feareth God is
watchful over his own ways, and censorious of himself; so
the man that feareth not God is secure, and well-pleased

with his own doings ; *he flattereth himself in his own eyes*
4. As the man that feareth God laboureth to inform his
conscience well, that he may not commit iniquity ; so the
man that feareth not God, gulleth and deceiveth his own
conscience, till he have gotten the iniquity accomplished,
and it be now made open in its own colours ; *he flattereth
himself in his own eyes, till his iniquity worthy to be hated
be found, or his iniquity be found to be hateful.* 5. As the
man that feareth God will discern the sin in himself, whereof he is in danger, before any man perceive it ; so the man
that feareth not God, will not see his own sin, no not when
any that looks upon his way may see it ; *he flattereth himself in his own eyes, till his iniquity be found to be hateful.*
6. As the man that feareth God makes conscience of his
speeches, and will be loth to cover sin with vain pretences
and excuses, but rather will confess it ; so the man that
feareth not God will not stand, whatever pretence he
useth for doing iniquity, nor what excuse he maketh
for the iniquity, when it is done, for deceiving both
others and himself : *the words of his mouth are iniquity and deceit.* 7. As the man that feareth God, by all
means striveth that he may grow wiser and holier, so the
man that fears not God, will misregard and cast off the
means of wisdom and holiness ; *he hath left off to be wise,
and to do good;* whatsoever he seemed to have before, he
goeth back even from that more and more. 8. As the
man that feareth God, communeth with his heart upon his
bed, that he may not sin, no not in his heart ; so the man
that feareth not God, deviseth how he may plot and perform
sin willingly ; *he deviseth mischief on his bed.* 9. As the
man that feareth God abhorreth that which is evil, and laboureth to be sure that the way he is upon is good ; so the
man that feareth not God, taketh no farther notice of what
he doth, than what is most for his purpose ; and neither
abhorreth what he would be at, because it is evil, nor af-
fecteth it, because it is good ; but having digested his purpose by meditation and resolution, he goeth on obstinately ;
he setteth himself in a way that is not good; he abhorreth
not evil : and such were David's enemies, and such will be
the enemies of Christ and his people.

5. *Thy mercy, O Lord,* is *in the heavens;* and *thy
faithfulness* reacheth *unto the clouds.*

6. *Thy righteousness* is *like the great mountains;*

H

thy judgments are *a great deep : O Lord, thou preserv-est man and beast.*

7. *How excellent* is *thy loving-kindness, O God! therefore the children of men put their trust under the shadow of thy wings.*

8. *They shall be abundantly satisfied with the fat-ness of thy house ; and thou shalt make them drink of the river of thy pleasures.*

9. *For with thee is the fountain of life : in thy light shall we see light.*

The second part of the psalm, wherein David comfort-eth himself in God, and settleth his faith on the praise-worthy properties of God. Whence learn, 1. The turning of the believer's eye off the wickedness of adversaries, and looking to God's goodness and wise dispensation, will com-fort his heart against all that the enemy can do, and set him on work toward godliness, so much the more as he perceiveth atheism in them ; for when David had pointed out his enemy, he falleth to the praising of God, saying, *thy mercy, O Lord, is in the heavens.* 2. Albeit the car-riage of the wicked toward God and the godly doth tend to obscure God's glory in the point of justice toward the one, and point of mercy toward the other, yet the works of cre-ation, and the constant government thereof, shall bear wit-ness of the constancy of God's mercy, and faithfulness, and righteousness, and judgment, as here is shown. 3. Though the effects of God's mercy should not appear to the be-liever on earth, yet faith will see them in their fountain and cause ; *thy mercy, O Lord,* saith the believer, *is in hea-ven.* 4. Let God's works and his word be compared to-gether, and the truth of his promises and threatenings shall be so traced, and seem to be true, as shall satisfy us, and let us see so far till our eye can follow no farther ; *thy faithfulness reacheth unto the clouds.* 5. Whatsoever car-nal reason may judge of God's dispensations towards the godly and the wicked, yet his holiness and justice is firm and unchangeable ; *thy righteousness is like the great mountains.* 6. Albeit we cannot see through matters, nor reconcile cross cogitations, sometimes offered from the grounds of faith on the one hand, and from the effects of providence offered by sense on the other hand, yet must we remember that God is wiser than we, and his deep draughts are past finding out by us; *thy judgments are a great deep.* 7. This one consideration of God's course of kindness to his own creatures, making his sun to shine and his rain to fall on his enemies as on his friends, may quiet our mind concerning God's sparing for a time the wicked, and liberal dealing with them; *O Lord, thou preservest man and beast.* There is a course of common preservation and kindness running unto all. 8. Over and above common kindness, there is a more entire, special, and precious love and kindness toward believers in God, which is inexpressible and wanteth comparison; *how excellent,* or precious, *is thy loving-kindness, O God!* saith David, speaking of this. 9. The belief of God's readiness to let forth this love, may, and should, and doth animate men to draw near unto him, albeit they have as yet no experience of the fruits of it; *therefore the children of men that put trust under the shadow of thy wings.* 10. The Lord, without exception of any to whom he sendeth the gospel, and without exception of any within the visible church, doth offer to be reconciled through Christ Jesus to every man who shall fly into the propitiatory and mercy-seat erected in Jesus Christ, who is God incarnate, according as he was holden forth in the figure of the golden ark of the covenant, and the stretched forth wings of the cherubim, as is here said, *therefore the children of men put their trust under the shadow of thy wings.* 11. Such as do not give the lie to God when they find not at first what they hoped for, but indeed believe in his word, and wait on till he make his word good to them; such as do not tempt or take essay of God, as if they would see what believing may do, and then quit their gripes if their expectation be not answered—but indeed trust God upon his word, and resolve to die with the gripe in their hand of his freely offered covenant of grace in Christ, and of his promises made to them that fly to him for refuge,—shall be sure to be in more respect with God than common subjects. They shall be domestics of his house, of the household of faith, to whom God shall keep a table furnished for spiritual life unto them ; he shall make them now and then, when it is meet time for the hungry, to feed abundantly and to be satisfied ; *they that put their trust under the shadow of thy wings, shall be abundantly satisfied with the goodness of thy house.* 12. In the use of the means and holy ordinances of God given to his church, God shall make the man that indeed giveth him credit upon the word of his grace, sensibly feel the joy of the holy Spirit to be unspeakable and full of glory, and that there are greater contentments to be found for a man's soul in God, reconciled through Christ, than the world can yield beside; for, *thou shalt make them drink of the rivers of thy pleasures.* 13. Whatsoever can be found in the creature, even when God blesseth the use thereof to his own children, is but a drop from the ocean, is but a little water out of the well, in comparison of what a believer will see and feel to be in God reconciled through Christ; for, *with thee is the fountain of life.* 14. No light save the light of God's revealed word in the holy Scriptures for the mirror, no light but the light of God's Spirit illuminating the mirror, can make a man understand, or believe, or sensibly discern, the wisdom, comfort, and felicity which are held forth to his church in his ordinances, and felt in himself by experience; *in thy light,* saith he, *shall we see light.*

10. *O continue thy loving-kindness unto them that know thee; and thy righteousness to the upright in heart.*

11. *Let not the foot of pride come against me, and let not the hand of the wicked remove me.*

12. *There are the workers of iniquity fallen: they are cast down, and shall not be able to rise.*

The last part of the psalm, wherein he prayeth for all believers, himself being included, and then for himself in particular. Whence learn, 1. The true mark of a godly man standeth in the conjunction of faith in God with sincere study of obedience to him, for he is the man that knoweth God, and is upright in heart. 2. Albeit what the believer hath found in God by experience, he may expect it shall be continued unto him, both for his entertainment by God, and defence and deliverance in his righteous cause from his enemies; yet must he follow his confidence with prayer: *O continue thy loving-kindness unto them that know thee, and thy righteousness to the upright in heart.* 3. As we have no right to any benefit, but in so far as we are of the number of upright-hearted believers, so should we seek every benefit we would have, as being of this number, and as seeking that others may be sharers with us, as David doth before. 4. It is the Lord only who can divert proud persecutors, that they hurt not his children, and it is the Lord only who can keep his children in the course of faith and obedience, when the wicked employ their power against them. Therefore David prayeth, *let not the foot of pride come against me, and let not the hand of the wicked remove me.* 5. The ruin of the enemies of the godly is as certain as if it were already past, yea, faith may look upon it through the prospect of the word of God as if it were to be seen and pointed out to others to behold with their eyes; *there are the workers of iniquity fallen.* 6. The fall of the wicked is not like the fall of the godly, for though the godly fall sundry times, yet they recover their feet again; but a fall is prepared for the wicked, after which they shall not recover themselves; *they are cast down, and shall not be able to rise.*

PSALM XXXVII.
A Psalm of David.

This psalm tendeth to guard the godly against the ordinary temptations unto envy, emulation, fretting, and discouragement in the way of godliness, arising from the temporal prosperity of the wicked, and that by eight directions or counsels from the Lord; each of them is confirmed by reasons, most of which are comparisons of the blessed estate of the godly at the worst, with the estate of the wicked at their best. The first direction or counsel, v. 1, 2; the second, v. 3; the third, v. 4; the fourth, v. 5, 6; the fifth, v. 7; the sixth, v. 8—26; the seventh v. 27—33; the eighth direction, v. 34 to the end.

1. *Fret not thyself because of evil-doers, neither be thou envious against the workers of iniquity :*

2. *For they shall soon be cut down like the grass, and wither as the green herb.*

The first direction is to beware of fretting at, or envying of, the prosperity of the wicked, because their prosperity is but temporal. Whence learn, 1. Wicked men may be in a more prosperous condition in the world than the godly, and oftentimes, yea, and for the most part are; for this is presupposed here, as an ordinary temptation in all ages and places. 2. Albeit carnal reason, and suggestions of Satan and corrupt nature, from the prosperity of the wicked, and the ordinary troubles of the godly, furnish temptations unto the godly to be malcontents with God's dispensation, yet should the godly take heed that they be not overcome by, or yield in any sort to, this temptation : *fret not thyself because of evil-doers.* 3. As temptation to malcontentment maketh assaults, on the one hand, to render the godly weary of well-doing, so temptation to emulate the course of the wicked, and following their way, assault, on the other hand, but should no way get place : *neither be thou envious against the workers of iniquity.* 4. If it were well considered that all the prosperity of the wicked is but in things concerning the outward man, and that this prosperity is but temporal, and often of shorter continuance than a man's own brittle life, there should be no ground of envy found therein ; *for they shall soon be cut down like the grass, and wither as the green herb.*

3. *Trust in the Lord, and do good :* so *shalt thou dwell in the land, and verily thou shalt be fed.*

From the second point of God's counsel and direction, learn, 1. Holding fast the covenant of grace made with God, through Christ, and studying to bring out the fruits of faith, in obedience to God's command, is a sovereign remedy against malcontentment with a man's own condition, and against envying the wicked : *trust in the Lord, and do good.* 2. Continuance in the faith and obedience of God, whatsoever temptation we meet with, is the surest way to have God's blessing in this life, and to have heaven, represented by Canaan, after this life : *trust in the Lord, and do good, so shall thou dwell in the land.* 3. The upright believer in God is the only man that gets the right use of the creature, and into whose cup the true juice of God's benefits, being pressed out, is poured ; whose bread is dipped in oil, and in whom spiritual life is constantly entertained : *verily thou,* that art such a man, *shalt be fed.*

4. *Delight thyself also in the Lord ; and he shall give thee the desires of thine heart.*

From the third direction to ward off the temptation, learn, 1. The godly man hath warrant to make God the object of his delight, who, being reconciled to the believer through the Mediator, is become the believer's own, in whom he may continually rejoice ; but the object of the ungodly prosperous man's delight is but some creature, or temporal trifle ; for to the believer it is said, *delight thyself in the Lord.* 2. Though the believer be rich in his rights, yet he is slow to make use thereof, and hath need to be stirred up to take possession : *delight thyself.* 3. If the believer shall make use of his covenant right and interest in God, and set his affections upon him, he shall find such solid contentment and satisfaction in God, as he shall not envy the condition of the most prosperous wicked man in the world ; for it is said, *delight thyself in the Lord, and he will give thee the desires of thy heart.* And certainly the forgetting, or not hearkening to this direction, is the cause of our being malcontented with our lot, and of our envying the wicked.

5. *Commit thy way unto the Lord; trust also in him, and he shall bring* it *to pass:*

6. *And he shall bring forth thy righteousness as the light, and thy judgment as the noon-day.*

From the fourth direction, learn, 1. When we bear the burden of our own affairs ourselves, and are chastened with anxiety and want of success, and with envying the ungodly who prosper better than we do ; the best remedy is, first, to do our duty, as we are enabled, in the use of the means; then cast the care of the success over on God, as the plough-man doth when he hath harrowed his land, and let the burden of it rest on God, and let us not take it off him again, but put our mind to rest, resolved to take the harvest in good part, as he shall send it : *commit thy way unto the Lord, trust also in him.* 2. The man who followeth this direction shall come to speed best in his affairs, because God shall do that wherewith the man shall have reason to be satisfied, for that which he would have done, or what is better, shall be effected : *commit thy cause unto the Lord, and he shall bring it to pass.* 3. It is possible that the godly, following this counsel, may be misreported of, and both lose his labour and estimation among men, yet it shall not be long so ; for *God shall bring forth thy righteousness as the light.* 4. Albeit the godly and his cause may be obscured by a shorter or longer winter-night of trouble, as shall please God to appoint, yet shall he, and his cause and integrity, be found absolved by God in due time : *he shall bring forth thy judgment,* or decree of absolution, *as the noon-day.*

7. *Rest in the Lord, and wait patiently for him : fret*

not thyself because of him who prospereth in his way,
because of the man who bringeth wicked devices to pass.

From the fifth direction, learn, 1. The victory over the
temptation to envy the wicked is not gotten at first, nor by
carnal reason, but by faith in God, and patient waiting on
him : *rest on the Lord, and wait patiently for him.* 2. As
the temptation to fretting is very pressing, when we see the
wicked get so much of their will, so much of their purpose
brought to pass; so we have need to be pressed again and
again to resist this temptation : therefore is it said again,
fret not thyself because of him who prospereth in his way,
because of the man who bringeth wicked devices to pass.

8. *Cease from anger, and forsake wrath : fret not*
thyself in anywise to do evil.

The sixth direction is to curb this temptation, in case it
hath already defiled and fired a man's spirit, lest it break
out, and make the believer put forth his hand to iniquity.
Whence learn, 1. The insolence of the wicked is such, and
their provocation of the godly ofttimes so great, that their
spirits are much stirred and kindled with indignation and
thoughts of private revenge ; yet must not this passion prevail with the godly, but should be striven against : *cease from*
anger, and forsake wrath ; vengeance is the Lord's, he will
repay. 2. The godly should eschew the motions of fretting,
anger, or envy against the wicked ; and if anger enter, he
must cease from it : if it urge itself on him with pretences of
reason or violent impulse, he must *forsake it ;* but by any
means he must keep this temptation within doors, that it
drive him not to break forth to a completed sin in action
and doing wrong : *fret not thyself in anywise to do evil.*

9. *For evil-doers shall be cut off : but those that wait*
upon the Lord, they shall inherit the earth.

The prophet presseth this direction by sundry reasons ;
and in special, by six comparisons of the Lord's way and
purpose about the wicked and the godly, how prosperous
soever the wicked may be for a time, and howsoever the
godly may be afflicted and exercised for a time. The first
comparison is in this verse. Whence learn, 1. If any who
pretend to be godly shall, by the foresaid temptation, forsake the way of godliness and follow the way of the wicked,
they shall have the reward of the wicked for changing their

way : *for evil-doers shall be cut off.* 2. It is not the present
condition wherein men are which is to be looked to, but
what shall become of them at length ; for all the prosperity
of the wicked is blasted with this one sentence of the supreme
Judge : *evil-doers shall be cut off.* 3. Albeit the godly be
kept in some hardships for a time, as young heirs in their
minority ; yet shall their inheritance in heaven (represented
by the land of Canaan) be reserved unto them ; and, in the
meantime, by their heirship in Christ, they have solid right
to what portion in this world God alloweth them ; they have
the use thereof with a good conscience, and remain on the
earth as long as God hath service for them, however the
wicked would thrust them out of the world as unworthy of
it : and if they be banished out of one country, they know
that *the earth is the Lord's, and the fulness thereof,* and they
live more contentedly in that condition, than the wicked in
their nest : for *those that wait upon the Lord, they shall
inherit the earth.*

10. *For yet a little while, and the wicked* shall *not*
be : *yea, thou shalt diligently consider his place, and it*
shall *not* be.

11. *But the meek shall inherit the earth ; and shall
delight themselves in the abundance of peace.*

From the second comparison of the wicked and the godly,
learn, 1. We must not pass sentence suddenly, to absolve
their way who are prosperous, or condemn their way who
are crossed ; but we should wait upon God's word till God,
from heaven, manifest his judgment about both, which shall
not long be delayed in regard of the wicked ; *for yet a little
while, and the wicked shall not be : yea, thou shalt diligently
consider his place, and it shall not be.* 2. Submission unto
God's dispensation allayeth all troubles, and enlargeth the
good of every benefit ; and a good construction of God's
dealing with us bringeth much peace and quietness of mind
with it, and enricheth our portion : *the meek shall inherit
the earth ; and shall delight themselves in the abundance of
peace.*

12. *The wicked plotteth against the just, and gnasheth upon him with his teeth.*

13. *The Lord shall laugh at him ; for he seeth that
his day is coming.*

14. *The wicked have drawn out the sword, and have bent their bow, to cast down the poor and needy, and slay such as be of upright conversation.*

15. *Their sword shall enter into their own heart, and their bows shall be broken.*

The third comparison of the wicked and godly looseth a doubt, when the godly cannot get living in their mean condition, in presence of the wicked, but their life is also in peril by their plotting, for the effectuating the destruction of the godly. Whence learn, 1. The godly have not only to wrestle against the thriving condition of the wicked, but also with their deadly hatred ; *the wicked plot against the righteous, and gnasheth upon him with his teeth.* 2. The godly must make the Lord to be party against the wicked, and must oppose his justice, power, and wisdom to the enmity of the wicked ; for albeit the godly be forced to mourn at their threatening, yet their plotting and prattling against the godly, as if they could do any thing of themselves, is ridiculous ; *the Lord shall laugh at them.* 3. If the godly did consider of the wicked, as the word of the Lord speaketh of them, they might look upon their boasts, as on the brags of a man upon the scaffold, ready to be executed ; *for, God seeth his day is coming.* 4. The godly must resolve to bear the open violence also of the wicked, and to be made as butts for their arrows, and sheaths for their swords, which is more than their words ; for, *the wicked have drawn out the sword, and bent their bow.* 5. Before deliverance come unto the godly, they shall find themselves in a weak condition, for any thing they can do for themselves ; for here they are poor and needy, and the wicked thinks *to cast them down.* 6. Those are the truly godly, and the objects of the wicked's malice, who for their inward condition depend on God in the sense of their poverty and neediness, and withal are of *an upright conversation,* as they are here described. 7. When the wicked are most near to do a mischief to the Lord's people, then is a mischief most near unto them ; *their sword shall enter into their own heart, and their bows shall be broken.*

16. *A little that a righteous man hath is better than the riches of many wicked.*

17. *For the arms of the wicked shall be broken : but the Lord upholdeth the righteous.*

The fourth comparison of the godly and wicked, looseth another doubt about the wealth and power of the wicked. Whence learn, 1. The odds between men's living and means of livelihood stands not in more or less abundance of worldly goods, but in God's blessing, which because it accompanieth the provision of the godly, have they less or have they more ; therefore, *a little that one righteous man hath, is better than the riches of many wicked.* 2. The little something of the godly's provision is made to subsist for the poor man's standing, while the power and wealth of the wicked comes to nothing ; *for the arms of the wicked shall be broken : but the Lord upholdeth the righteous.*

18. *The Lord knoweth the days of the upright ; and their inheritance shall be for ever.*

19. *They shall not be ashamed in the evil time ; and in the days of famine they shall be satisfied.*

20. *But the wicked shall perish, and the enemies of the Lord* shall be *as the fat of lambs: they shall consume ; into smoke shall they consume away.*

From the fifth comparison of the godly and wicked, learn 1. The godly have two advantages above the wicked ; one in this life, another in the life to come. For the first, all the vicissitudes of dangers and daily necessities of the godly are taken notice of in a special way by God choosing and weighing to them exercises for their condition, moderating them in their measure and time, seasoning them with mixture of consolation, turning them to their best, furnishing all necessaries to bear out their exercises, and sending particular deliverances, one after another ; *for the Lord knows the days of the upright.* As for the next life, he hath reserved for them an inheritance of constant blessedness, never to be taken from them ; *their inheritance shall be for ever.* 2. Albeit the Lord will not exempt the godly from sharing in common calamities with the wicked, yet shall they have the evidences of God's favour to them in the time of trouble, and shall not be disappointed of the kindness promised by God and expected by them ; *they shall not be ashamed in the evil time.* 3. Whatsoever scant or inlack be of creature-comfort, the godly shall be supplied to their reasonable satisfaction ; *in the days of famine they shall be satisfied.* 4. When the wicked are most liberally dealt with, it is but a feeding

of them like beasts to the slaughter; all their glory shall vanish, and they themselves shall be destroyed in God's wrath:
*but the wicked shall perish, the enemies of the Lord shall be
as fat of lambs, they shall consume into smoke, they shall
consume away.*

21. *The wicked borroweth, and payeth not again:
but the righteous sheweth mercy, and giveth.*

22. *For* such as be *blessed of him shall inherit the
earth ; and* they that be *cursed of him shall be cut off.*

From the sixth comparison, learn, 1. In the midst of the
wicked man's wealth he is ofttimes wanting, as if he were a
poor man ; if he have much wealth, he hath much to do
with it, and many times is unable to defray his charges
without borrowing ; and when he has borrowed, he is either
unable or unwilling to pay again, and so is but a miserable
wretch with all he hath ; or he is a profuse prodigal and
deceiver of his creditors : *the wicked borroweth, and payeth
not again.* 2. On the contrary, the righteous man, by his
godly behaviour, manageth the little which God giveth him
so well, as he needeth not to borrow ; he wanteth not for
any good work which God calleth him unto, and is able to
supply others' necessities : *the righteous sheweth mercy, and
giveth.* 3. The blessing of God on the godly maketh the
odds betwixt them and the wicked, for it is to him as good
as the inheritance of the whole earth; but God's curse
rooteth the wicked man out of the earth ; for, *such,* saith
he, *as be blessed of him, shall inherit the earth; and they
that be cursed, shall be cut off.*

23. *The steps of a* good *man are ordered by the
Lord ; and he delighteth in his way.*

24. *Though he fall, he shall not be utterly cast down:
for the Lord upholdeth* him with *his hand.*

25. *I have been young, and* now *am old ; yet have I
not seen the righteous forsaken, nor his seed begging
bread.*

26. He is *ever merciful, and lendeth ; and his seed*
is *blessed.*

He closeth the confirmation of the sixth direction with
enumerating sundry privileges of the godly, of some whereof
he made observation in his own time. Whence learn, 1. The
privileges of the godly are so great as should content him,

albeit his outward prosperity and wealth be not such as he conceiveth the wicked to have ; for God teacheth the godly how to behave himself in his particular actions, prudently and holily ; *the steps of a good man are ordered of the Lord*, he approveth the course the godly man keepeth: *he delights in his way*. Though the godly man through infirmity fall into a sin, or by his sin draw a calamity on himself, yet the Lord recovereth him again : *though he fall, he shall not be utterly cast down ;* and that he perish not when he falleth, the Lord shall preserve him by holding a grip of him : *the Lord upholdeth him with his hand*. 2. Albeit the Lord will not exempt the godly from poverty, nor yet their seed ; albeit we presuppose the children be godly also, if he think it good to exercise them so, yet the Lord hath made the examples of such misery so rare, as a man of good years could observe few or none of them beggars; especially in the prophet's time, when God by external benefits was training his people to the hope of spiritual things, as David here testifieth. 3. It is a gift of God to use whatsoever a man receiveth of God, so as others be helped thereby : *the godly is ever merciful, and lendeth*. 4. The readiest way to bring a blessing to a man's house and posterity, is to be godly himself ; for, *the godly man's seed is blessed*.

27. *Depart from evil, and do good ; and dwell for evermore.*

28. *For the Lord loveth judgment, and forsaketh not his saints ; they are preserved for ever : but the seed of the wicked shall be cut off.*

29. *The righteous shall inherit the land, and dwell therein for ever.*

From the seventh direction and the reasons thereof, teaching how to guard against fretting at, and envying of, the prosperity of the wicked, learn, 1. To meet an injury with another injury, or to recompense evil for evil, or to forbear to do good where it is not deserved, is not the way to be blessed ; but, on the contrary, the way of possessing settled felicity is *to depart from evil, and to do good ; so shall a man dwell for ever*. 2. The love that the Lord beareth to righteousness, is the cause why it cannot but be well with the righteous ; for, *the Lord loveth judgment*. 3. The Lord may well exercise his children with trouble, yet he will not withdraw himself from them **in trouble,** but will stay with them, and bear them company, and save them to the utter-most: *he forsaketh not his saints; they are preserved for ever.* 4. As wickedness is the ready way to root out a man and his family from off the earth, so is righteousness the way to establish a man's family, and to bring himself to a solid habitation with God for ever; for, *the seed of the wicked shall be cut off. The righteous shall inherit the land, and dwell therein for ever;* that is, in heaven, signified by that land.

30. *The mouth of the righteous speaketh wisdom, and his tongue talketh of judgment.*

31. *The law of his God is in his heart; none of his steps shall slide.*

Because so much is spoken of the righteous man, he de-scribeth him by three properties; one in his words, another in his affections, a third in his deliberate actions and course of his ways and life. Whence learn, 1. The righteous man studieth in his speeches to glorify God, and edify those he speaketh to, and in all things he is truth's friend; *the mouth of the righteous speaketh wisdom, and his tongue talketh of judgment.* 2. For his affections, he loveth that which is commanded of God, and hateth that which is forbidden him, because God hath taken him into covenant with himself to be his man; *the law of God is in his heart.* 3. For his course of life, whatsoever temptation he meeteth with, to divert him from the faith and obedience of God, he will not choose another way than the law of his God; *none of his steps shall slide.*

32. *The wicked watcheth the righteous, and seeketh to slay him.*

33. *The Lord will not leave him in his hand, nor condemn him when he is judged.*

For clearing of the seventh direction, he answereth an objection from the persecutions which the righteous are sub-ject unto from the wicked. Whence learn, 1. Temporal blessings or benefits are not so promised to the godly, as that they shall be free from troubles, crosses, and persecu-tions; for the Lord, for his own glory, for edification of his church, for conviction of his enemies, and for perfect-ing his children in holiness, useth to suffer the wicked to hunt and persecute them, even to death; *the wicked watch-*

eth the righteous, and seeketh to slay him.   2. The wicked
may apprehend the righteous man's person, lay false accu-
sations to his charge, and bring him before judges, and not
get his will of him, to drive him from a righteous cause;
for, *the Lord will not leave him in his hand.*   3. Albeit the
righteous man by persecutions may be judged and condemned to death unjustly, yet may he be more than a conqueror through God that loveth him, and careth for him;
for God will not condemn him when he is judged; and that
may suffice him against whatsoever flesh can do to him.

34. *Wait on the Lord, and keep his way, and he
shall exalt thee to inherit the land: when the wicked
are cut off, thou shalt see it.*

35. *I have seen the wicked in great power, and
spreading himself like a green bay-tree:*

36. *Yet he passed away, and, lo, he was not; yea,
I sought him, but he could not be found.*

The eighth direction is to wait on God, and to keep his
way; serving, with the former direction, to guard the godly
man's heart against all the temptations of fretting, envy,
anger, and emulation, because of the wicked man's seemingly more prosperous condition in the world than his own;
and this direction is confirmed with five reasons.   Whence
learn, 1. He that believeth on God must not make haste,
nor judge rashly of matters as they seem for the present,
but must attend till God make his word good; *wait on the
Lord.*   2. True patient hope and waiting on God, must be
joined with the study of obedience to God's directions; *wait
on the Lord, and keep his way.*   3. Though the godly be
kept under for a while and humbled, yet God shall lift them
up to a satisfactory estate; *he shall exalt thee to inherit the
land.*   This promise is the first reason to move us to wait
on the Lord.   In every age some of the wicked shall be
made spectacles of God's threatened judgment, before the
eyes of the godly, to give assurance of his judgment; that
he shall overthrow all the rest in due time, and avenge on
them all the wrongs done by them unto the godly: *when
the wicked are cut off, thou shalt see it.*   And this is the
second argument to confirm the exhortation.   4. How the
wicked have seemed very glorious in the world for a while,
and shortly both they and their glory vanished, every man
in his own time should make his own remarks and obser-

vations, as the prophet showeth here, that he had his observations in his time, v. 35, 36. And this is the third reason
to confirm the direction taken from experience concerning
the wicked.

37. *Mark the perfect man, and behold the upright:
for the end of that man is peace.*

38. *But the transgressors shall be destroyed together; the end of the wicked shall be cut off.*

The fourth reason of the direction, is from the happy
close of the course of the godly, and the certain perdition
of the wicked. Whence learn, 1. The Lord gives so many
remarkable instances of the comfortable departure of the
godly out of this life, as may give assurance of the dying of
all the upright in God's favour; *mark the upright man,
for the end of that man is peace.* 2. Whether men be
witnesses or not of the departure of the wicked, one and
all of them die in a desperate condition; they are deprived
of heaven and earth, and perish, soul and body, at the ex-
piring of their breath; *transgressors shall be destroyed together; the end of the wicked shall be cut off.*

39. *But the salvation of the righteous is of the
Lord; he is their strength in the time of trouble.*

40. *And the Lord shall help them, and deliver them:
he shall deliver them from the wicked, and save them,
because they trust in him.*

The last reason to move men to wait on God, is from
his care of the godly. Whence learn, 1. How hard soever
the condition of the godly be, the Lord hath ways of his
own to preserve and save them; yea, the Lord is resolved
and hath passed his word that he will save them; *the salvation of the righteous is of the Lord.* 2. So long as God
is pleased to let righteous men's trouble continue, he will now
and then comfort them, and will enable them to bear their
trouble, when comfort is suspended; *he is their strength in
time of trouble.* 3. When the godly in their trouble feel
their own wants and weakness, he will furnish what in them
is lacking, till the delivery come; *the Lord shall help them,
and deliver them.* 4. Albeit many be the troubles of the
godly, especially from their wicked persecutors, yet by faith
in God they shall keep their conscience clean; their cause
they maintain whole, and shall have their souls safe, do

what their persecutors can ; *he shall deliver them from the wicked, and save them because they trust in him.*

PSALM XXXVIII.

A psalm of David, to bring to remembrance.

In this psalm, David, in trouble both of soul and body, as an example of the hardest exercises that Christ's followers can fall into, first, prayeth for the mitigation of his trouble, and removal of wrath, v. 1 ; and secondly, layeth out this sense of the trouble which he felt immediately from God, v. 2—8 ; thirdly, having put up his confused desires to God for prayers, in the sense of his inability to express himself, v. 9, 10, he lays out his sense of the grief and troubles which he felt from men, and endured with great patience, v. 11—14 ; fourthly, he sets down the wrestlings he had in prayer to God, because of his persecution by his adversaries, v. 15—20 ; and closeth the psalm, not having gotten comfort for the time, v. 21, 22.

From the inscription, learn, that exercises of conscience, the more heavy they have been, the more should they be remembered, and the passages thereof more carefully marked when the sense is most fresh, lest they pass without the fruit which may be had of them after delivery : for thus much are we taught by the inscription of this psalm, wherein it is entitled, *a psalm of David, to bring to remembrance.*

1. *O Lord, rebuke me not in thy wrath : neither chasten me in thy hot displeasure.*

From his prayer for mitigation of trouble and removal of wrath, learn, 1. It is consistent with God's fatherly love, and our sonship, to taste of fatherly wrath against our sins, as this place proveth. 2. Albeit it is not lawful for us to follow our natural desires in prayer, or to seek to be free of chastisement, yet we may seek mitigation of trouble, and tempering of our cup, so as we may digest it, and we may pray for the removal of fatherly wrath also ; *rebuke me not in thy wrath, nor chasten me in thy hot displeasure.*

2. *For thine arrows stick fast in me, and thy hand presseth me sore.*

3. There is *no soundness in my flesh because of thine anger ; neither* is there any *rest in my bones because of my sin.*

4. *For mine iniquities are gone over mine head; as an heavy burden they are too heavy for me.*

5. *My wounds stink, and are corrupt, because of my foolishness.*

6. *I am troubled; I am bowed down greatly; I go mourning all the day long.*

7. *For my loins are filled with a loathsome disease; and* there is *no soundness in my flesh.*

8. *I am feeble and sore broken: I have roared by reason of the disquietness of my heart.*

He giveth reason of his prayer from his pitiful case both in soul and body. Whence learn, 1. When it pleaseth the Lord to make his children sensible of their sins, and of his dreadful justice, he can make the tokens of his displeasure against sin piercing sharp, and pressing heavy; *thy arrows stick fast in me, and thy hand presseth me sore.* 2. Although the Lord should set us as a mark to shoot at, and lay the heaviest load of judgments on us for our sins; yet we must not seek the ease thereof, nor can we have ease from them, save by coming to God himself, to bemoan our misery, as this example teacheth us. 3. As the sense of trouble on our body, or any way else, will waken the conscience of sin; so the conscience of sin and feeling of wrath due for our sin, will make no small alteration on our very bodies; *there is no soundness in my flesh, because of thine anger, nor rest in my bones because of my sin.* 4. One sin will waken the memory of more sins, till they present themselves as an innumerable army; *my iniquities are gone over my head.* 5. How light soever sin may seem when it is committed, it will be found insupportably heavy, when God pursues for it; *as an heavy burden, they are too heavy for me.* 6. When the Lord smiteth the conscience for sin, the rod will not fail to make a wound, which shall have need of the cure of the physician, according to the bruise made by his hand, or deep piercing of his arrows; for after arrows and pressing hand, he mentions wounds more than one. 7. When a wounded spirit is not timously, by a right cure, bound up and healed, the wounds grow the longer the worse; the longer, the more guiltiness, filthiness, and perplexity of spirit grow; *my wounds stink and are corrupt.* 8. As through our inconsideration of our duty, and danger of sinning, we fall actually into sin, and draw upon ourselves wrath ; so by our inconsideration of the right remedy, we augment that measure of both ; *my wounds stink, and are corrupt; because of my foolishness.* 9. So long as the conscience of sin and sense of wrath kept on thereby last, the man's wit and his courage, and his countenance and his joy are smitten, both before God and men ; *I am troubled, I am bowed down greatly, I go mourning all the day long.* 10. To add to the pace, and to make the sense of sin more bitter, the Lord can lay his hand on the body, and make the loathsomeness of the sickness resemble the loathsomeness of the sin which drew it on, and to speak unto the conscience in its own language, the cause why it is sent unto him ; *for my loins are filled with a loathsome disease; and there is no soundness in my flesh.* 11. A wounded spirit will dash and beat down the stoutest heart it can meet with ; *I am feeble and sore broken.* 12. If the Lord pursue a man's conscience for sin, and intimate his displeasure against him, and continue this exercise for any time ; it will pass the man's power to hide or smother his grief, or hold in the expressions thereof ; *I have roared by reason of the disquietness of my heart.*

9. *Lord, all my desire* is *before thee; and my groaning is not hid from thee.*

10. *My heart panteth, my strength faileth me: as for the light of mine eyes, it also is gone from me.*

In the third place, that he may bring forth the trouble which he suffered from men, and his patience towards them, he presenteth his heart to God, as if it was full of confused desires, instead of explicit prayers, being now unable to express himself more largely. Whence learn, 1. As sin causeth wrath, and wrath sore strokes and sorrow ; so these evils looked upon, should waken desires to have them removed, and send us to seek the true remedy thereof in God, as here the psalmist doth. 2. As desires and groans, if they be presented to God, have their own speech, which we cannot express in time of confusion ; so should we account them, not as vanishing expressions of nature, but as prayers stirred up by God, and standing before him till they receive their answer ; *Lord, all my desire is before thee.* 3. It is not wrestling with trouble within ourselves, nor vent-

ing our grief as natural men, which can give us ease, but
pouring out our heart before the Lord which must do it;
all my desire is before thee. 4. The strength of faith in the
godly is not so great as to swallow up all infirmities; but
so great as to wrestle with them, and confess them to God,
who useth to supply his own with his strength and wise direction, when their own strength is evacuated, and the man
is before God humbled; for here even *David's heart panteth
and his strength faileth him, and the light of his eyes is gone
from him;* not so much in regard of the body's decay, as in
his spiritual condition, expressed in bodily terms; and thus
much for the troubles, which he felt immediately from God's
hand.

11. *My lovers and my friends stand aloof from my
sore, and my kinsmen stand afar off.*

12. *They also that seek after my life lay snares* for
me; *and they that seek my hurt speak mischievous things,
and imagine deceits all the day long.*

13. *But I, as a deaf* man, *heard not; and* I was *as
a dumb man* that *openeth not his mouth.*

14. *Thus I was as a man that heareth not, and in
whose mouth* are *no reproofs.*

From the troubles which he felt from men, learn, 1. A
wounded spirit is a disease which the natural man hath no
skill of, nor will to meddle with, but flieth from it, as from a
plague or pest; *my lovers and my friends stand aloof from
my sore.* 2. In time of sad affliction and narrow trial of
our faith, natural bonds between us and our kinsfolk will
shrink and fail us, so as we shall have little comfort in the
earth; *my kinsmen stand afar off.* 3. In time of sad exercises and hard trials, as friends may fail, so enemies may
make head; and, by craft and cruelty, by slander and cunning policy, open enmity and secret plotting, may conspire
against a man's fame, good cause, and life; *they also that
seek after my life, lay snares for me; and they that seek my
hurt, speak mischievous things, and imagine deceits all the
day long.* 4. The more emptied, afflicted, disconsolate, forsaken of friends, and pursued by foes, a man be; if he go to
God for reconciliation and relief, he hath ground of hope to be
helped, and to have God engaged to him so much the more;
for here David maketh this use of all his troubles, he layeth

all out before God. 5. It is possible, yea and ofttimes cometh to pass, that the godly have so many lies made of them, calumnies and slanders devised and vented against them by so many mouths, that they are not able to follow them, or to answer and refute them, but are forced to mis-ken them, and in patience hold themselves quiet till God make matters clear for them; *but I as a deaf man heard not, and as a dumb man opened not my mouth.* 6. When the godly, overloaden with a multitude of calumnies and a multitude of enemies backing them, sit down in patient silence, not seeing to what purpose they speak, they are taken readily as guilty, or as such who cannot refute the thing which is alleged of them, nor maintain the truth which they profess; and this is an addition unto all the rest of their trouble, as David importeth, saying: *thus was I as a man that heareth not, and in whose mouth are no reproofs.*

15. *For in thee, O Lord, do I hope : thou wilt hear, O Lord my God.*

16. *For I said,* Hear me, *lest* otherwise *they should rejoice over me : when my foot slippeth, they magnify* themselves *against me.*

17. *For I* am *ready to halt, and my sorrow* is *continually before me.*

18. *For I will declare mine iniquity ; I will be sorry for my sin.*

19. *But mine enemies* are *lively,* and *they are strong; and they that hate me wrongfully are multiplied.*

20. *They also that render evil for good are mine adversaries ; because I follow* the thing that *good* is.

In the fourth place, he setteth down his wrestling against his persecutors, seeking to destroy both him and his righteous cause. Hence learn, 1. It is a sore and high degree of the trial of the godly, when at one time God pursueth for sin, and friends withdraw from them in the duties of humanity, and persecutors are likely to destroy their lives, and withal suppress religion in their person by this means; and yet this hath been the case of many of God's children, and may be also, as this example teaches us ; yea, also our Lord Jesus' condition was like this, when he suffered for our sins. 2. Sore trials cannot be borne without holding fast the grip of

the covenant of grace ; for this fixeth faith, and strengtheneth
hope, and furnisheth patience in greatest troubles ; for David
rendereth this reason for his bearing patiently his foresaid
hard condition ; *in thee, O Lord, do I hope ; thou wilt hear,
O Lord, my God.* 3. If the covenant be holden fast, whereby we may warrantably call God our God, we may be, as it
were, surety to ourselves for a good answer from God ;
thou wilt hear me, O Lord my God. 4. When the enemies
of the godly in their righteous cause, are ready to triumph
over the godly and their cause, and the godly are like to be
discouraged, if the Lord help not, then the godly may be
sure the Lord will hear and help : for David giveth this as
a reason of his persuasion, that God would hear him, v. 15,
because the enemies otherwise would triumph, and he be
made to halt, and turn off the way, v. 16, 17 ; for in this
the Lord's glory is interested. 5. When the outward prosperous condition of the godly is changed, and their feet slip,
and the hand of the Lord lieth on sore without relaxation,
even they of strong faith are ready to be discouraged and
faint ; so weak are we in faith when a hard trial cometh ;
for, *when the enemy magnified himself against David ; when
his feet slipped, when his sorrow was continually before him,*
he confesseth he was ready to halt, to warn the godly, that
they might guard against this tentation. 6. To keep ourselves from fretting under trouble, it is expedient that we
compare our sins with God's fatherly chastisements of us, and
that we take course for remission of our sin, and turn the
sorrow raised by affliction into godly sorrow for sin ; for this
David resolved in his distress ; *I will declare mine iniquity, I
will be sorry for my sin.* 7. The Lord so disposeth of the
outward condition of the godly and the wicked in this life,
that the godly ofttimes have the mourning part, and the
wicked the rejoicing part, and that so much the more as
they see the head of the godly is borne down ; *I will be sorry
for my sin, but mine enemies are lively and strong.* 8. As it
is a matter of grief to see the affliction of the godly growing,
and the enemies growing in joy, and strength, and number ;
so it is a matter of comfort, that the enemies of the godly
are enemies without a just cause given to them ; *they that
hate me wrongfully, are multiplied.* 9. We must not leave
off the doing of what God requireth at our hands, albeit we
should have the hatred of the world ; for *David followed that*

which was good, albeit his adversaries for that very cause
did render to him evil for good.

21. *Forsake me not, O Lord: O my God, be not far
from me.*

22. *Make haste to help me, O Lord my salvation.*

He closeth the psalm with prayer, laying all his weight
on the covenant, not having gotten comfort for the time.
Whence learn, 1. We must not limit the Lord to give us
comfort and deliverance when we think we have greatest
need of it, but must leave our prayer at his feet, as the
prophet doth.   2. The believer must be so wary of leaning
to sense, that he must hold the grip of faith not only when
he misseth sense of comfort, but also when God's dispensation towards him, and his sense thereof, seem to speak most
contrary to faith: *forsake me not, O Lord: be not far from
me. Make haste to help me*, saith David's faith, when his
sense speaketh what his prayer here importeth; that is,
present perdition.   3. The bond of the covenant of grace
is able to bear the weight of the believer's heaviest burden,
and by virtue of it he may lay claim to God, as his own
God, and lay claim also to salvation in him; for, notwithstanding all the troubles and temptations set forth in this
psalm, the believer sustaineth all on this ground—*O my
God, O Lord my salvation:* and here is the victory of
faith.

PSALM XXXIX.

To the chief musician, even to Jeduthun.   A psalm of David.

Another such like hard exercise as in the former psalm, wherein David
acknowledgeth his infirmity in a passionate expression, when he was in
trouble, ver. 1—4; secondly, he recovered and comforted himself, ver.
5—7; thirdly, what was his prayer in this exercise, ver. 8—13.

1. *I said, I will take heed to my ways, that I sin
not with my tongue; I will keep my mouth with a
bridle, while the wicked is before me.*

2. *I was dumb with silence; I held my peace,* even
from good; and my sorrow was stirred.

3. *My heart was hot within me; while I was musing
the fire burned:* then *spake I with my tongue.*

4. *Lord, make me to know mine end, and the measure of my days, what it is;* that *I may know how frail
I am.*

The prophet, for fear of impatient expression in his trouble, resolved to keep silence in the audience of the wicked, but was not able to keep in his passionate wishing for death. Whence learn, 1. As it is the Lord's will that we should have the infirmities of the saints registered unto us, for our edification, as well as their virtues ; so it is his will, that, when the confession of our infirmity may profit others, we should not spare to let it be known, as this passage teacheth us. 2. Consciousness of our weakness, and of the unruliness of our tongues, ready to break forth in the time of temptation, should make us take better heed to ourselves, and to watch over our speech: *I said, I will take heed to my ways, that I sin not with my tongue.* 3. Because the wicked may take advantage of the godly's miscarrying in time of their trouble, it is the more needful to watch over our behaviour and words in their presence : *I will keep my mouth with a bridle, while the wicked is before me.* 4. When we are about to keep in our corruptions, and amend our faults by our own way of it, by our wisdom, strength, or resolutions, we do not eschew the evil we would eschew, and we also fall into a fault we were not aware of ; as here, instead of praying to God to direct one part of his speech after another, that he might speak prudently in the audience of the wicked, he did not speak at all ; he did not speak that which he might and should have spoken : *I was dumb with silence ; I held my peace, even from good.* 5. When grief is not rightly vented but suppressed, it is not thereby assuaged but rather increased : *I held my peace, and my sorrow was stirred.* 6. The power of sinful nature and enraged passion is such, that even when they are opposed by reason of strength of grace in us, they may easily overpower us, except God put to his hand to help us in the conflict : *my heart was hot within me : while I was musing the fire burned : then spake I with my tongue.* 7. It is a natural evil in man, when he is overcome by trouble in this life, to wish for death, expecting to be in a better condition by the change ; as the sick man expecteth ease by changing his bed ; and here, v. 4, we have the example of it. 8. The shortness of this life is a mitigation of the troubles thereof unto the godly, and the fear that life should continue longer than the afflicted man wisheth, augmenteth his trouble ; and this is the fountain of this passionate and curious wish :

Lord, make me to know mine end, and the measure of my days, what it is ; that I may know how frail I am.

5. *Behold, thou hast made my days as an hand-breadth, and mine age is as nothing before thee : verily every man at his best estate is altogether vanity. Selah.*

6. *Surely every man walketh in a vain shew ; surely they are disquieted in vain : he heapeth up riches, and knoweth not who shall gather them.*

7. *And now, Lord, what wait I for ? my hope is in thee.*

In the second place, not being answered in this curious question, but secretly checked for his impatient wish, he contents himself with the known truth, that this present life is but short, how long soever it shall last, and resolveth to wait on God's time patiently. Whence learn, 1. For tempering our condition, whatsoever it be, it should suffice us to know that, whether we be in prosperity or adversity, our time in this life is but short : *thou hast made my days as an hand-breadth, and mine age is as nothing before thee.* 2. Not in prosperity, but in adversity, is the uncertainty, weakness, emptiness, and vanity, of prosperity and things temporal, well seen ; for in trouble, says David, *verily every man at his best estate is altogether vanity.* 3. Whatsoever seemeth excellent in the eyes of natural men in this world, is but the shadow of what it seemeth : health, strength, prosperity, riches, pleasure, honour, dominion, power, authority, are but the shadows of things so named : *every man walketh in a vain shew.* 4. Too much care and anxiety about things of this life, is a sickness and folly : *surely they are disquieted in vain.* 5. Experience putteth a deep stamp of the truth upon a man's mind, and causes him to set his subscription unto it without hesitation : *verily, surely, surely,* is the seal of this truth here delivered after his experience. 6. The excessive care which men take to gather riches, this toiling and travailing, this spending of body, of wit and time, this frowning on some and fawning to others, this pleading and fighting with some and flattering of others, with other shifts by which men use to gather riches, (which they must leave behind them, and do not know to whom,) is a point of great folly and vanity in men : *he heapeth up riches, and knoweth not who shall gather them.* 7. The right use of the perceived vanity of all things under the sun, is, that we should be sent by that consideration unto God, to rest on him : *and now, Lord, what wait I for ?* 8. That which God hath promised in the life to come is only satisfactory and able to quiet a man's mind, and make him patiently wait on God in all his trouble: *what wait I for ? my hope is in thee.*

8. *Deliver me from all my transgressions ; make me not the reproach of the foolish.*

9. *I was dumb, I opened not my mouth ; because thou didst* it.

10. *Remove thy stroke away from me : I am consumed by the blow of thine hand.*

11. *When thou with rebukes dost correct man for iniquity, thou makest his beauty to consume away like a moth : surely every man is vanity. Selah.*

12. *Hear my prayer, O Lord, and give ear unto my cry ; hold not thy peace at my tears: for I* am *a stranger with thee, and a sojourner, as all my fathers* were.

13. *O spare me, that I may recover strength, before I go hence, and be no more.*

In the third place, he prayeth to be freed from his sins and the sense of God's wrath, using sundry reasons to help his faith. Whence learn, 1. Seeing sin plungeth us into all perplexities, and bringeth trouble after trouble upon us, the best cure of our trouble is to seek pardon for our sins : *deliver me from all my transgressions.* 2. The ungodly are fools, let them seem to themselves and others what they please ; for all their way and work is to make themselves miserable ; therefore the scripture calleth them *foolish.* 3. That the wicked get no advantage of us, so as by troubling us to drive us from the profession of righteousness, for which they persecute us, should be the main care of every believer under persecution ; for this is David's prayer : *make me not the reproach of the foolish.* 4. It is usual for us to see our duty, after we have sinned, better than before ; for, after experience of his falling, he resolveth it to be his duty not to speak an impatient word, but *to be silent, and not open his mouth ;* to wit, impatiently. 5. The consideration of God for our party, with whom we have to do in trouble, should humble us and make us quiet : David saith, he should not have openedh is mouth, *because thou, Lord, didst it.* 6. Prayer for removing the tokens of God's displeasure, especially after prayer for remission of sins, is not contrary to patience and silent submission under God's hand; for he prayeth also, *remove away thy stroke from me.* 7. When we feel the Lord's hand heavy upon us, we may bemoan ourselves to him, with submission to his will; for he pitieth us, and will lay no more on us than we are able to bear: *I am consumed by the blow of thy hand.* 8. The stoutest and strongest courage will soon be brought down by trouble of conscience; when God entereth into judgment with him, man falls down: *when thou with rebukes dost correct man for iniquity, thou makest his beauty to consume away like a moth: surely every man is vanity.* 9. When God seemeth to refuse to hear prayer, true faith will follow God with more fervent prayer, and crying, and tears, and not leave God without a good answer: *hear my prayer, O Lord, and give ear unto my cry; hold not thy peace at my tears.* 10. The more our hearts are alienated from this world and conversant with God by faith, the more we miss our country, our parents, our kinsmen on earth, and have our conversation in heaven; the more we may be assured that God shall avow himself to be our God: *I am a stranger with thee, and a sojourner.* 11. Entering ourselves heirs unto the godly, who lived before us in their estrangements from the world, and seeking after heaven, entitleth us unto their comforts also; *I am a sojourner, as all my fathers were.* 12. It is a usual temptation unto the godly in their trouble, that they shall never be relieved out of it in this life: *O spare me, before I go hence.* 13. The godly may pray for a little breathing before death, with submission, that they may the more quietly render up their spirits to God: *spare me, that I may recover strength, before I go hence, and be no more.* 14. If the Lord hearkeneth not to us when we would, let us leave our petition beside him till he answer it, as here the prophet doth.

PSALM XL.

To the chief musician. A psalm of David.

David, as a type of Christ in the whole psalm, and as an example of the exercise of the godly, giveth thanks for the experience of God's delivering him out of a notable trouble, v. 1—4. In the second place, he is led on in his thanksgiving to praise God for the great work of redemption by Christ the Son of God coming into the world, which is the fountain of all other mercies to the saints, v. 5—8. In the third place, David in type, and Christ in the accomplishment, giving account of his prophetical office, intercedeth and prayeth for the evidence of God's favour to himself personally and mystically considered, v. 9—13: and for disappointment of his enemies, v. 14, 15, and for the comfort of all the godly beholding his exercise and his delivery which he confidently doth expect, v. 16, 17.

1. *I waited patiently for the Lord, and he inclined unto me, and heard my cry.*

2. *He brought me up also out of an horrible pit, out of the miry clay, and set my feet upon a rock, and established my goings.*

3. *And he hath put a new song in my mouth, even praise unto our God: many shall see* it, *and fear, and shall trust in the Lord.*

4. *Blessed* is *that man that maketh the Lord his trust, and respecteth not the proud, nor such as turn aside to lies.*

In his thanksgiving, learn, 1. As the Lord of set purpose delayeth to answer the prayer of his own, and suspendeth to help them out of trouble for a time, that he may try and train their faith to a better measure; so the believer must resolve to wait on patiently; *I waited patiently for the Lord.* 2. Albeit waiting for the time is joined with languor and grief, yet the remembrance of it is sweet, and it wants not a blessing following it; *I waited, and he inclined to me, and heard my cry.* 3. The godly may be brought in their trouble to as desperate-like condition, as a man fallen into a horrible, deep, and dark pit, sinking in miry clay, out of which there is no appearance of relief: in which case, as the greatness of the danger commendeth the faith of him that calleth upon God, and waiteth for him; so doth it commend God's wisdom, power, goodness, and faithfulness in delivering the patient waiter. To this end saith the psalmist, *he brought me out of an horrible pit, and out of the miry clay.* 4. The man who dependeth on the Lord, when he is delivered out of trouble, is not left to himself; but the Lord's care attendeth him to guide him after his delivery; *he brought me out of the miry clay, and set my feet upon a rock, and established my goings.* 5. As it is a part of our duty to glorify God after every mercy, and in a special manner when the mercy is very notable : so it is a new gift of God to enable a man to give thanks and praise for the mercy received ; therefore it is put for a point of thanksgiving ; *he hath put a new song in my mouth.* 6. As the experience of God's mercy to one who is in cove-nant with God, is the encouragement of all believers: so should it be the common matter of praise unto God from them all, therefore he calleth the praises which he did sing *the praises of our God.* 7. The right observation of God's mercy to his children, especially when he will show himself eminently, is able to strike a man with much awe and rever-ence of God, who is fearful even in his praises ; *many shall hear and fear.* 8. Then do we make right observation of God's mercy to his children, when thereby we encourage ourselves to look for the like mercy, when we call for it in our need ; *many shall hear and fear, and trust in the Lord.* 9. As the preciousness of faith is not seen in the time of trial so well as after the victory ; so the fruit of it when it is seen is no less than true blessedness ; *blessed is the man who maketh the Lord his trust.* 10. All true believers are humble toward God, and of a high spirit against whatsoever cometh in competition with him, and will despise every man's way who regardeth not him: so the misbeliever is proud towards God and his truth, but a base subject of his own spirit and to lying vanities ; for the believer here is opposed to the *proud,* and to such *as turn aside to lies.*

5. *Many, O Lord my God,* are *thy wonderful works* which *thou hast done, and thy thoughts* which are *to us ward; they cannot be reckoned up in order unto thee:* if *I would declare and speak* of them, *they are more than can be numbered.*

In the second place he is led up to the consideration of God's wonderful care and providence about men, and in special to the work of redemption by Christ's coming into the world. Whence learn, 1. One of the Lord's wonder-ful works of providence well meditated upon, may and should lead us to the consideration of many other of his works of that kind ; *many, O Lord my God, are thy wonderful works, which thou hast done.* 2. The works of God's providence about us should lead us up to the counsel of God, to behold his care of us, his mind and purpose to us ward, who are brought into covenant with him, for confirming of our faith in him ; *many, O Lord my God, are thy thoughts which are to us ward.* 3. Albeit the Lord's deep thoughts and works of wonder about his own people, be unspeakable, unsearchable, and innumerable, yet must we not cease to look upon them, and speak of them in heap when we cannot attain to them in tale ; *they cannot be reckoned up in order to thee : if I should declare and speak of them, they are more than can be numbered.*

6. *Sacrifice and offering thou didst not desire; mine ears hast thou opened : burnt-offering and sin-offering hast thou not required.*

7. *Then said I, Lo, I come : in the volume of the book* it is *written of me.*

8. *I delight to do thy will, O my God : yea, thy law* is *within my heart.*

He condescends upon a particular which did not overcome his declaration and searching, to wit, the covenant of redemption between the Father and the Son coming into the world, some articles whereof he toucheth, as they are rehearsed by the Son speaking here by his Spirit. Whence learn, 1. The work of redemption by Christ, the covenant betwixt the Father and the Son about our redemption, the incarnation of the Son of God, and the course of the salvation of the redeemed, is one of the most wonderful things that ever was heard tell of, wherein so many wonderful works of God, so many wonderful thoughts of God about us concur, that they can neither be declared, nor numbered, nor set in order ; for this work here touched is set down for an instance of what was said in the former verse : now that this is spoken by Christ, the apostle, Heb. x. 5, 6, &c., showeth unto us. 2. Albeit sacrifices and oblations were appointed to be offered before Christ came, yet were they not acceptable in themselves, but in respect of the sacrifice of Christ signified by them ; not they, but Christ signified by them, could take away sin ; *sacrifices and offerings thou didst not desire, burnt-offerings and sin-offerings thou didst not require,* to wit, for any worth in themselves, or as real satisfactions for sin. 3. The ceremonial law was not to remain, but to be taken away when Christ came to offer himself, who was foreshadowed by the sacrifices and

Levitical ordinances; for, *sacrifices and oblations thou didst not desire, but mine ears thou hast opened;* which presupposeth *thou hast formed a body unto me,* as the apostle, Heb. x. 5. showeth ; and so the rejecting of the ceremonies, is at the incarnation, or at the forming of the body of Christ, and bringing the Son into the world. 4. The Son of God incarnate becomes voluntarily, a very capable, discreet, ready, and obedient servant to the Father for us : *mine ears hast thou opened,* to wit, for receiving of every command ; or *mine ears hast thou* bored, as the servant's ears were bored under the law, when he chose to stay still with his master in service, Exod. xxi. 5. 5. By offering of burnt-offering God was not satisfied for sin, but only by Christ's coming and offering himself a sacrifice once for all : *burnt-offering and sin-offering hast thou not required; then said I, lo I come,* saith Christ. 6. Both in the book of God's eternal decrees and in the book of holy scripture, this way of taking away the sins of men was established, as the only way to effect it ; for, that the seed of the woman by his suffering should bruise the head of the serpent was foretold by God, Gen. iii. 15. and Christ was the lamb slain in the representative sacrifices from the beginning of the world : *in the volume of the Book it is written of me.* 7. Jesus Christ, God incarnate, is in covenant with God the Father, that believers may be in covenant with God by this means also, therefore doth he call him, *O my God* : as our Lord, John, xx. 17, saith, I ascend to my Father and your Father, to my God and your God. 8. All Christ's sufferings and service done in our name for us, were most willingly and heartily undertaken and discharged by Christ ; *I delight to do thy will,* that is, as the apostle, Heb. x. 10, doth expound it, to perform whatever might sanctify us throughout for ever. 9. The way of our redemption by Christ's doing and suffering for us, is God's own device, his very will and pleasure ; and the obedience of Christ unto the very death of the ross done in our name unto the Father, hath pleased the Father fully ; *I delight to do thy will, O my God.* 10. The Son of God incarnate was perfectly holy, so as he could answer to the law completely, and give account of it to the Father ; *yea thy law is within my heart.* That these words may be applied to David, and made use of by every believer in their own degree and measure, there is no question : but

that they are principally and in the main intention to be
applied to Christ speaking of himself, the matter itself doth
evidence ; for who but he can ascribe to himself the accomplishing of what the typical sacrifices foreshadowed ? who
but he could satisfy for sin, which the sacrifices could not ?
Again the apostle Paul, Heb. x. 5, 6, &c., cleareth the
matter so, as no ground of doubting is left. In all the
psalm, let David be as the shadow, but let Christ be the substance.

9. *I have preached righteousness in the great congregation : lo, I have not refrained my lips, O Lord
thou knowest.*

10. *I have not hid thy righteousness within my heart ;
I have declared thy faithfulness and thy salvation : I
have not concealed thy loving-kindness and thy truth
from the great congregation.*

In the third place, as Christ hath given an account of
the execution of his priestly office, in expiation of sin, so
here he giveth account of his prophetical office, to make
way for his intercession. Whence learn, 1. Christ did not
only undertake to suffer for expiation of our sins, but also
he undertook to apply to his people, by preaching, the
fruits of his sufferings, for their righteousness and salvation, for justifying, sanctifying, and saving the redeemed ;
I have preached righteousness in the great congregation.
2. The way appointed for application of the grace purchased
to the redeemed, is preaching ; *I have preached righteousness in the great congregation,* in the visible church, and in
all confluences of the redeemed where opportunity is offered.
3. As Christ did not conceal what might save souls, but
communicated it carefully, so should they who are trusted
by him to preach without fear sincerely, as they will be able
to answer God, proclaim it : *I have not refrained my lips,
O Lord, thou knowest.* 4. The true way of justification
of sinners by faith, is a jewel so precious and necessary for
poor souls, that it should not be concealed ; *I have not hid
thy righteousness within my heart.* 5. One sermon on this
subject is not sufficient, it is necessary to make this mystery
plain, how by faith in Christ the man that flieth to him is
justified from his sins, and saved according to the covenant
passed between the suffering Mediator and God the faithful

promiser, to justify and save by his own way ; *I have de-clared thy faithfulness and thy salvation.* 6. The way of righteousness and salvation purchased unto believers by Jesus Christ, is very solid and complete ; for, first, this way of forgiving sins unto us, because of the satisfaction made by Christ for us in his obedience unto the Father, even unto the death of the cross, is of God's own devising, and his free gift; therefore, as it is called the righteousness of God, Rom. iii. 21, 22 ; so here it is called God's righteousness ; *O Lord, I have not hid thy righteousness.* And the salva-tion or eternal life annexed to this imputed and gifted righteousness bestowed upon the embracer of it, is also of God's devising, and his free gift, therefore it is also called his salvation ; *I have declared thy salvation.* Next, the cer-tainty and ground of the believer's assurance that this right-eousness and salvation are made fast unto him, are the truth and faithfulness of God, obliging himself to make good this way of justification and salvation by the covenant of redemption made between the Father and the Son our Mediator, as in the promises of the covenant of grace, is set down in scripture; which can no more disappoint the believer, than the truth and faithfulness of God can fail ; *I have declared thy faithfulness and thy salvation.* And, last of all, the fountain, spring, and rise, and unchangeable ground of righteousness and salvation, purchased by the re-demption made by Jesus Christ, and applied to us by faith in him, is the mere good-will and pleasure of God : the free grace, the free love and bounty of God, without any de-serving of the redeemed ; *I have not concealed thy loving-kindness and thy truth from the great congregation.* This indeed is a solid ground. 7. The plain preaching, de-claration, and manifestation of this gospel, with the grounds thereof, are able, by the blessing of God, to persuade a trembling soul to lay itself over upon Jesus Christ, and to rest upon the unchangeable truth and kindness of God of-fered to every poor humble sinner, without exception, for the preaching of these things, not refraining the lips, not hiding this precious and saving truth, the declara-tion and not concealing of it, is given up here for the suffi-ciency of means to apply the purchased righteousness and sal-vation by Christ to the redeemed ; and this execution of Christ's prophetical office hath been faithfully performed by

I

him, not only in his personal preaching in the days of his flesh,
but also in his ministers, both befoe his incarnation and
since, which also shall be continued from generation to
generation, to the end of the world, maugre all opposition :
for Christ shall be able to make no less perfect account of
his other offices than of the kingly office, when he shall
give up the kingdom to his Father.   8. What may concern David here as the type of Christ, or as one of the servants of Christ, we take up in one word, which is this :—
the more faithful preachers are to declare the gospel to
the salvation of souls, the more confidence and comfort shall
the testimony of their conscience afford to them in the day
of their trouble, when they come before God : as the prophet here by experience findeth.

11. *Withhold not thou thy tender mercies from me,
O Lord: let thy loving-kindness and thy truth continually preserve me.*

12. *For innumerable evils have compassed me about ;
mine iniquities have taken hold upon me, so that I am
not able to look up : they are more than the hairs of
mine head : therefore my heart faileth me.*

13. *Be pleased, O Lord, to deliver me : O Lord,
make haste to help me.*

Christ having given account of his performance of what
was undertaken, intercedeth for the promised mercies to
his mystical body and to himself, as standing in the room of
the ransomed, wherein David, as the type of Christ, and as
a member of Christ's mystical body, hath his own place.
Whence learn, 1. Because the price of redemption is holden
here as fully paid, and nothing is left unpaid by Christ,
therefore the application of the purchased mercy must be
granted ; for Christ, here speaking, having declared his
performance of his part of the covenant, from v. 6, to v.
11, doth now require the performance of promised kindness
and mercy to him and his mystical body : saying, *withhold
not thy tender mercies from me, O Lord: let thy loving-
kindness and thy truth continually preserve me ;* and this is
a standing petition of the Mediator, in favour of his afflicted
mystical body in all generations. 2. The unchangeableness
of God's loving-kindness, and truth of promises made in his
covenant, are solid grounds of assurance that the Lord will

not withhold his tender mercies from the afflicted believer ; for, upon this ground do the parts of his petition run : *with- hold not thy tender mercies from me, and let kindness and truth continually preserve me.* 3. Albeit the troubles which are inflicted be drawn on by sin, and be the effects of just wrath for sin, yet are they also the object of tender mercies, when the afflicted present both their troubles and their sins, which deserved them, before God's merciful eye ; for here a reason of hoping for tender mercy, is brought from both trouble and sin lying on ; *for innumerable evils have compassed me about, and mine iniquities have taken hold on me.* 4. By virtue of the intercession of Christ, every be- liever may take up the same supplication in Christ's name, and present it in his own behalf unto God, in the time of trouble and necessity ; for, since David might make this use of it, as one of the members of the mystical body, so may all the rest of believers also ; because Christ the Mediator owneth all the sins of all his redeemed ones as his own, as made his by consent to have them imputed unto him, and hath borne the punishment thereof so much as may and doth satisfy justice for them. Therefore Christ in behalf of his redeemed ones, and every believer in Christ for that re- spect may expect continual preservation by the loving-kind- ness and truth of God laid in pawn for it by the covenant, when they have recourse to God in the time when trouble and guiltiness both set on at once ; for the reason of the prayer is so conceived, as it may fit both the Mediator inter- ceding for his mystical body, and every wearied soul also who is fled to God through Christ by faith in him, that he may find his outgate and deliverance in, with, and for Christ : *let thy loving-kindness and thy truth continually preserve me ; for innumerable evils have compassed me about, mine iniqui- ties have taken hold on me.* 5. Nothing can so empty a man, and lay him low, and fill him with confusion of face, as his sin pursuing him : *mine iniquities have taken hold upon me, so that I am not able to look up.* 6. When all that is a man's own, as natural strength, wit, or courage, faileth, yet God doth not fail, and faith doth not fail : *for here when it is come to this, my heart faileth me,* faith stands up, and in prayer pleadeth for mercy and kindness for this very reason, because the heart faileth. 7. As the strait is great, and the burden heavy, and the creature weak, so are the delivery and help near at hand: *be pleased, O Lord, to deliver me : O Lord, make haste to help me.*

14. *Let them be ashamed and confounded together that seek after my soul to destroy it ; let them be driven backward, and put to shame, that wish me evil.*

15. *Let them be desolate for a reward of their shame that say unto me, Aha, aha !*

From this part of his prayer, which is against his ene-mies, learn, 1. As the Lord, for the intercession of Christ, will not fail to help his people in trouble, so will he not miss to disappoint and bring mischief upon the enemies of his people, how many and how strong soever they be : *let them be confounded together and ashamed that seek after my soul to destroy it.* 2. Not only the open persecutors of the godly, but all their ill-willers and unfriends, who could be content to see evil come upon God's church, shall be punished with the open adversaries: *they shall be driven backward, and put to shame, that wish them evil.* 3. The mocking of the godly, and putting them to shame, is the shame indeed of the mockers, and not of the godly, upon whom, in their suf-ferings, the spirit of glory resteth, and therefore shall the wicked scorners bear their own shame and their punishment : *let them be desolate for a reward of their shame, that say unto me, Aha, aha !*

16. *Let all those that seek thee rejoice and be glad in thee : let such as love thy salvation say continually, The Lord be magnified.*

17. *But I am poor and needy ; yet the Lord thinketh upon me : thou art my help and my deliverer ; make no tarrying, O my God.*

From this prayer, that the rest of the godly may have comfort by his delivery, which delivery he confidently ex-pecteth, learn, 1. As every mercy to every believer giveth a proof of God's readiness to show the like mercy to all be-lievers when they stand in need, so should every mercy shown to any of the number, being known to the rest, be made the matter and occasion of magnifying the Lord ; *let all those that seek thee rejoice and be glad in thee.* 2. The godly, whose property it is to be partakers of the affliction of Christ with others, and to seek God, and to wait for the Lord's way of delivery, and to love the safety of his people, shall have reason to rejoice and praise God continually for new evidences of his mercy to his own : *let all those that seek thee rejoice and be glad in thee : let such as love thy salvation say continually, the Lord be magnified.* 3. It is a usual condition of the godly, before they be delivered out of any difficulties, to be made once sensible of their own weakness, emptiness, and necessities, as here; *I am poor and needy.* 4. It is an ordinary exercise of the afflicted, to be despised of the world, and contemned ; and this also is a temptation to move them to mistake their own condition before God ; for so doth the psalmist propound the matter before God ; *but,* saith he, *I am poor and needy.* 5. Whatsoever the world, or sense and false suggestions say of the afflicted, yet faith gives ground of assurance that our base and mean condition is so far from making us loathsome to God, that, on the contrary, the lower we are brought the more we are in his heart and estimation ; *yet the Lord thinketh upon me ;* and God's respecting us may easily make up our loss of respect among men. 6. When the believer hath fastened his faith, he may expect shortly his relief; *thou art my help and my deliverer,* saith he, and then, *make no tarrying, O my God.*

PSALM XLI.

To the chief musician. A psalm of David.

David as a type of Christ, and one of his afflicted followers, after prayer comforteth himself against the uncharitable judgment, which the wicked had of him in his affliction, v. 1—4. In the second place, he complaineth of his enemies' cursed disposition against him, and prayeth to be delivered out of his trouble, v. 5—10. In the third place, he is answered comfortably, and praiseth God for it, v. 11—13.

1. *Blessed* is *he that considereth the poor: the Lord will deliver him in time of trouble.*

2. *The Lord will preserve him, and keep him alive;* and *he shall be blessed upon the earth : and thou wilt not deliver him unto the will of his enemies.*

3. *The Lord will strengthen him upon the bed of languishing: thou wilt make all his bed in his sickness.*

4. *I said, Lord, be merciful unto me : heal my soul · for I have sinned against thee.*

That he may comfort the godly in their afflictions, and correct the common judgment of the world concerning afflicted people, he giveth a reason for which it is safe to judge charitably of every man who humbleth himself before God in his affliction. Whence learn, 1. Albeit it be usual for the world to judge all them that are afflicted to be plagued of God in wrath, yet it is a blessed course to study to frame our hearts to a wise and discreet judging of other men's estates, by looking to a man's behaviour in his trouble, and to judge charitably of the man who is contrite, and humbleth himself before God in his afflictions; *blessed is he that considereth the poor,* or giveth comfort and instruction to the weak. 2. It is a blessed thing for a man afflicted and humbling himself before God to judge charitably of his own condition, as well as of another's condition in the like case; for, *blessed is he that considereth the poor,* is so set down as it is applicable to the patient in affliction judging of himself; no less than to the beholder of another in affliction: and, for confirmation of this, he giveth six reasons of comforting the afflicted and humbled man, and confirming the charitable beholder and judger of him as a fellow sufferer with him. 3. The afflicted and humble man shall be delivered out of his trouble, be what it may be; *the Lord will deliver him in time of trouble.* This is the first reason of the comfort, and withal a reason of confirmation and encouragement of him that judgeth wisely of the afflicted. 4. The Lord hath a way of delivery, not only from trouble, that a man fall not into it, and not only of delivering from trouble by removing of the trouble, but also a way of delivery, when the trouble is yet remaining; to wit, by sustaining the man, comforting him, saving him from any harm by the trouble, giving him good by the trouble, quieting his mind by patient submission unto God under the trouble, &c. *The Lord will deliver him in time of trouble*: and this is branched out in particulars in the verses following, as so many reasons of comfort, and charitable judging of his own condition and others. 5. Albeit the godly be brought very low, yet shall he not perish, *the Lord will preserve him and keep him alive;* and this is the second reason of comfort; albeit he faint, and have soul-faintings now and then, yet shall spiritual life be kept in him. 6. None of the godly man's afflictions shall hinder or take away his begun blessedness, even in this world ; *he shall be blessed on the earth :* and this is the third reason of comfort ; if it may be for God's glory and the man's good, this temporal life shall be preserved, and evidences of God's blessing shall be seen upon him. 7. No persecutor shall drive the godly man from his point, and make him forsake God, or the way of godliness; if he slip in a step, God shall raise him up again ; *thou wilt not deliver him to the will of his enemies :* and this is the fourth reason of his comfort. 8. The Lord will strengthen the godly to bear whatsoever trouble he putteth on him : *the Lord will strengthen him on the bed of languishing :* and this is the fifth reason of his comfort. 9. The Lord shall mitigate and moderate all the afflictions of the godly, and ease him under his trouble, as tenderly as when a sick person's bed is made the best way that can be for his ease ; *thou shalt make all his bed in his sickness :* and this is the sixth reason of his comfort. 10. The man who may look for all these consolations, and may be judged of charitably, whether it be himself, or another, is the man who in the sense of his sins, humbleth himself before the Lord, especially when he is afflicted and flieth to God's mercy ; first, to have sins pardoned, and next to have his trouble removed, as God seeth it fit for his salvation. This is pointed out in David's behaviour under his trouble, of set purpose, that he may give the character of the Lord's poor man, to whom the foresaid comforts belong, and of whose estate a good construction is to be made ; *I said, Lord be merciful to me, heal my soul, for I have sinned against thee.*

5. *Mine enemies speak evil of me ; when shall he die, and his name perish?*

6. *And if he come to see me, he speaketh vanity : his heart gathereth iniquity to itself; when he goeth abroad, he telleth it.*

7. *All that hate me whisper together against me : against me do they devise my hurt.*

8. *An evil disease, say they, cleaveth fast unto him : and now that he lieth, he shall rise up no more.*

6. *Yea, mine own familiar friend, in whom I trusted, which did eat of my bread, hath lifted up his heel against me.*

10. *But thou, O Lord, be merciful unto me, and raise me up, that I may requite them.*

From his complaint against his enemies, set down in the second place, learn, 1. Evil speeches against the godly will be taken notice of by God, and made a part of the wicked's duty ; *mine enemies speak evil of me.* 2. The malice of the enemies of godliness is such against the godly, as nothing but their utter overthrow and rooting out from the earth of such a sort of people can satisfy them ; *when shall he die, and his name perish,* say they. 3. The godly have to do, not only with open enemies, but with secret false dissemblers also, who will profess friendship with fair words, when they are following the way of malice, from whose falsehood there is no refuge more than from the force of the open enemy, save to fly to God, the Judge of all oppressed people ; *if he come to see me, he speaketh vanity ;* many fair words, but none of them true. 4. The end of the wicked man's pretended kindness to the godly, and of his insinuating himself into their fellowship, is, that he may make observation of something in their behaviour, or condition, or speeches, whereof he may make advantage against them ; *if he cometh to see me, his heart gathereth iniquity to itself ; when he goeth abroad he telleth it.* 5. Albeit the wicked can do no more against the godly than God will permit to be done for the godly man's exercise and good, yet many are the consultations which the wicked have, that they may hurt and destroy the godly ; *all that hate me whisper together against me, against me do they devise my hurt.* 6. When the godly fall into straits, the wicked judge that the godly shall never get out of their trouble, and in this hope refresh themselves ; *an evil disease cleaveth fast unto him, and now that he lieth, he shall rise no more.* 7. The lot appointed to Christ, and to all the true members of his mystical body as well as to David, is to find in the time of their trials a hard meeting in the world from the wicked, how many bonds soever of nature, friendship, familiarity, or obligations of the wicked unto the godly intervene, which otherwise might require better offices ; *yea, mine own familiar friend in whom I trusted, which did eat of my bread, hath lifted up his heel against me.* 8. We must not dwell upon our miseries in time of trouble, as if we had nothing to do, save to weep and mourn, but we should turn ourselves to God, and pray to him for mercy, and expect a delivery, as the psalmist doth here; *but thou, O Lord, be merciful to me, and raise me up.* 9. Albeit it be not fit for every believer to resolve requiting their persecutors and enemies, as it was fit to David as a magistrate, and to Christ who is King of kings, here represented by him, to resolve vengeance, and to execute the same also against their enemies ; yet every believer may be assured of this, that what injuries are done to Christ in his person, Christ shall requite. his persecutors; for he, in his mystical members, shall never be so borne down, but he shall be raised up again as he was raised up personally after his personal suffering. *Raise me up, that I may requite them.*

11. *By this I know that thou favoures tme, because mine enemy doth not triumph over me.*

12. *And as for me, thou upholdest me in mine integrity, and settest me before thy face for ever.*

13. *Blessed* be *the Lord God of Israel from everlasting, and to everlasting. Amen, and Amen.*

In the last part of the psalm is his thanksgiving, presupposing that the psalm was drawn up after the delivery from the trouble which is set forth in the former part. Whence learn, 1. Albeit external deliveries from enemies, and success external do not always serve for marks of God's favour, (for an ill man in an ill cause may have success for a time;) yet when the man is reconciled to God, and the cause which the reconciled man defendeth against his persecutors, is the Lord's cause, in this case; if God shall give to his servant either spiritual victory, that the enemy prevail not so over him as to drive him from his righteous cause, or external victory, and deliverance also from the power of the adversary, together with the spiritual victory ; in this case, I say, the word and work of God concurring, give evidence not only of God's favouring the man's person, but also of his favouring the man's cause and carriage in the cause, so as he may say, *by this I know that thou favourest me, because mine enemy triumpheth not over me.* 2. Uprightness is a special means to bring a man through difficulties, and whatsoever infirmities the believer be subject unto, he shall not want comfort, if he keep conscience of integrity, uprightness, and sincerity ; for this is the psalmist's rejoicing, when he looks back upon his former exercise under trouble ; *as for me, thou upholdest me in mine integrity.* 3. The wise wrestler with temptations is made at length to see and acknowledge by the experience he hath of himself and of God's help in time of temptation, that all the glory of his standing and bearing out in trouble for righteousness, belongeth to the Lord ; *thou upholdest me in mine integrity.* 4. Experience of God's gracious bearing out of a believer in time of trial, serveth for a good argument to make him confident of the continuance of God's favour to him for ever ; yea, after experiences and victory, God useth to give some measure of persuasion of his everlasting love toward them that have overcome ; as here, *thou settest me before thy face for ever.* 5. He that gets a sight of God's love to him, may knit God's felt favour in effect with God's everlasting love decreeing to show favour, and his everlasting love communicating itself to him, and performing the decrees of love touching him, and may behold the course of everlasting blessings running from eternity before the world, to everlasting after the world ; and the believer having seen it, should acknowledge this with praise and thanksgiving ; as here, *blessed be the Lord God of Israel, from everlasting to everlasting.* 6. He that seeth the course of God's love to himself, seeth God's love in conjunction with the rest of the Lord's people also, who are joined in the same covenant with him unto God in Christ ; *blessed be the Lord God of Israel,* says the psalmist, now when he will bless God for his own particular mercy. 7. Fresh experiences of God's love in a particular trial, especially when the soul is lifted up to the eternal original and everlasting endurance of it, will make a soul heartily, with all his strength, give everlasting praise to God, and seal it affectionately again and again ; *blessed be the Lord God of Israel from everlasting to everlasting, amen, and amen.*

PSALM XLII.

To the chief musician, Maschil, for the sons of Korah.

In this psalm David showeth what was his longing after the fellowship of the saints in their public worship and service of God, in the time of his banishment, by the persecution of Saul, v. 1—4, and how he wrestled with discouragements, by checking himself for it, and by praying to God, whereby he was erected unto hope and confidence to be answered, v. 5—11.

1. *As the heart panteth after the water-brooks, so panteth my soul after thee, O God.*

2. *My soul thirsteth for God, for the living God: when shall I come and appear before God?*

3. *My tears have been my meat day and night, while they continually say unto me, Where is thy God?*

4. *When I remember these* things, *I pour out my soul in me: for I had gone with the multitude; I went with them to the house of God, with the voice of joy and praise, with a multitude that kept holy-day.*

He setteth down his sad condition in his banishment, especially when he remembered the solemn assembly of God's people at the temple, and saw himself, either in the wilderness or among the heathen, deprived of the use of public ordinances. Whence learn, 1. It is not a bare formal use of the ordinances, but communion with God himself, which the lively believer seeketh after, in the use of public ordinances: *my soul panteth after thee, O God.* 2. Spiritual affections, when they are raised, and, by delay or by outward restraint, are kept off from satisfaction, are comparable, in measure or in point of sincerity, to the kindly appetite of natural food: *as the hart panteth after the water-brooks, so panteth my soul after thee, O God.* 3. Worshippers of the true God find, and may more and more find, lively refreshments to their souls in him; the experience whereof kindleth their desire for renewing them by such means as they have found satisfying before; *my soul thirsteth for God, for the living God.* 4. Because the assemblies of the church, for the exercises of religion, are the trysting-places, where God showeth himself to his people; therefore, lovers of God are hearty lovers of the public ordinances, and most desirous to frequent them for that cause: *when shall I come and appear before God?* 5. It is not enough for the wicked to see the godly in affliction, except they impute the misery of the godly unto their religion, and insult them, either as atheists, false worshippers, or hypocritical people, forsaken of God: *they continually say unto me, Where is thy God?* 6. To find Satan, wicked men, and God's dispensations, seeming to speak rejection from God, and to see the glory of the true religion, and a man's own interest in God, called in question, and thrust through with fiery darts of insulting enemies; is a matter indeed of great grief, and sufficient to render all creature comforts tasteless to a godly soul: *my tears have been my meat day and night,*

while they continually say unto me, Where is thy God? **7.**
As they who have had most of the means of grace may
have scarcity of them ere all be done ; so no one will take the
inlack of them more heavily than they who have reaped
most spiritual benefit by them : *when I remember these things,
I pour out my soul in me.* **8.** The saints should be so far
from separation from the fellowship of the visible church,
in the public exercises of holy ordinances, albeit they know
certainly that all are not sound professors who are to join
with them, that it should be their joy to have multitudes
partaking in the use, at least of some, of the public means,
and such as were not publicly scandalous, joining in all the
ordinances whereby God might be openly honoured, and
his elect among them might, in his own time, be converted ;
for David *went with the multitude, and that to the house of God,
with the voice of joy and praise, and with a multitude that kept
holy-day.* And this was at the time when king Saul and his
courtiers were joined in the public ordinances with him,
and with Jonathan, and other such godly persons. Now,
what the constitution of the church visible was in Saul's days,
in regard to the hypocrisy of professors, known to David,
sundry of his psalms make evident ; and yet, for all that, he
wisheth to have the like occasion of worshipping God again,
and accounteth highly of what he sometimes enjoyed.

5. *Why art thou cast down, O my soul? and* why
*art thou disquieted in me? hope thou in God ; for I
shall yet praise him* for *the help of his countenance.*

In the second part of the psalm, he wrestleth with discouragements ; and the conflicts are four. In the first he
laboureth to comfort himself three ways ; first, by checking
himself for his dejection of spirit and disquietude ; next, by
stirring up the grace of God in himself, namely, faith and
hope ; thirdly, by application of the word of promise made
unto him for strengthening both, to bear him out till the
Lord should manifest his promised kindness. Whence learn,
1. When sore troubles, instead of humbling a man, press him
down unto dejection and discouragement of mind ; it is a
gracious man's part to check himself for this reasonless fit
of unbelief, and to put his conscience to answer for yielding
so far to the temptation : *why are thou cast down, O my
soul?* 2. Misbelief, in a child of God, is followed by restlessness of spirit, as a chastisement drawn on by that sin,

for which disquieting of himself the man may justly be challenged also, and will not be able to give a reason for it: *why art thou disquieted within me?* 3. The only means of remedying discouragements and unquietness of mind, is to set faith on work to go to God and take hold on him, and to cast anchor within the vail, hoping for, and expecting, relief from him: *hope thou in God.* 4. The believer, in the midst of trouble, may promise to himself new experience of God's kindness and consolation, by delivery out of it; and to God he may promise praises: *I shall yet praise him for the help of his countenance.*

6. *O my God, my soul is cast down within me: therefore will I remember thee from the land of Jordan, and of the Hermonites, from the hill Mizar.*

In the second conflict he turneth him to God, and layeth the case of his discouraged heart before him, labouring to make use of old experience. Whence learn, 1. Albeit a dejected and disconsolate soul may and should deal with itself rationally, to recover itself, yet can it not do it effectually; but, as a man sick and weak, and fallen from his bed, calleth for help, so must it call to God, and lay out its case before him, that he may recover it: *O my God, my soul is cast down within me.* 2. Albeit the power of making the means effectual be not in us but in the Lord's hands, yet must we not cease to use the means rationally still, whereby the Lord useth to convey his efficacious power, and to call to mind experiences, as a good means for recovering ourselves: *O my God, my soul is cast down within me; therefore will I remember thee from the land of Jordan:* that is, I will aim at comforting myself by remembering what I have found by experience, in several places of Judea, of thy goodness to me; and I will look to the Holy Land and to the temple, the place where thy gracious presence is vouchsafed, and where thine honour dwelleth.

7. *Deep calleth unto deep at the noise of thy water-spouts: all thy waves and thy billows are gone over me.*

In the third conflict, wherein the very remembrance of bygone experience, which even now was made use of to comfort him, kindleth afresh his grief, learn, 1. Though using the right and appointed means to comfort us should seem to us to have a contrary effect to what we intended, and to increase our grief by our using them, yet still must we wrestle, using one mean after another, mixing prayer with all other means, as David doth here, saying, *deep calleth unto deep at the noise of thy water-spouts.* 2. As the noise of rain from the clouds causeth a noise in the inferior waters and floods ; as the raising of brooks raiseth the rivers, and all shut themselves into a sea; and as the waves of the sea call one upon another to follow the former at the back ; so, one grief wakeneth another, one temptation strengtheneth another, one affliction augmenteth another, till a sea of troubles, raised by a storm, be like to overwhelm the man: *all thy waves and thy billows are gone over me.*

8. Yet *the Lord will command his loving-kindness in the day-time, and in the night his song* shall be *with me,* and *my prayer unto the God of my life.*

9. *I will say unto God my rock, Why hast thou forgotten me ? why go I mourning because of the oppression of the enemy ?*

To oppose this new assault, faith puts forth itself the third time, promising to the wrestler what God hath promised to the believer; whereupon he resolveth to plead his cause more hardly, and ply God yet again with prayer more earnestly, that he may prevail. Whence learn, 1. Faith seeth in God's word, and in bygone evidence of his truth manifested in his word, as it were a written order and commission, ready to be given forth in acts of providence, for satisfying the believer with so much fresh experience as may fill him day and night with a sense of God's love and songs of praise: *yet the Lord will command his loving-kindness in the day-time, and in the night his song shall be with me.* 2. The care of our life, bodily, spiritual, and everlasting, lieth upon God, by virtue of his covenant with us to keep it, to feed it and renew it in all the decays thereof, till it be possessed of unchangeable blessedness; the belief whereof is a ground of perseverance in prayer: *my prayer shall be unto the God of my life.* 3. Faith may improve its right before God, and plead that the believer be not rejected, and may regret any appearance, which is offered to sense, of rejection : *I will say unto God, Why hast thou forgotten me ?* 4. The believer, in his complaints, must not weaken his own faith, but weaken his unbelief rather, and to this end should fasten his faith ere he complain : *I will say unto God, My rock—* there faith is fastened ; then followeth the complaint—*why hast thou forgotten me? why go I mourning because of the oppression of the enemy?*

10. As *with a sword in my bones, mine enemies re-proach me; while they say daily unto me, Where* is *thy God?*

11. *Why art thou cast down, O my soul? and why art thou disquieted within me? hope thou in God; for I shall yet praise him,* who is *the health of my counte-nance, and my God.*

In the fourth conflict, which he hath chiefly with the mockers of his religion, his cause, and his trust in God, learn, 1. The sharpest part of a believer's trial and afflic-tion is, when, in his person, religion and God's glory is mocked; this cruel sort of persecution pierceth deepest in his heart, because it tends to drive the man to desperation, and to make religion and faith in God out of request: *as with a sword in my bones, mine enemies reproach me.* 2. Continuance of the reproach of godliness, and of the inso-lence of mockers scorning religion in the afflicted man's face, in the time when it seemeth that his affliction speaketh desperation of relief, greatly increaseth the power of the temptation and the godly man's grief: *a sword in my bones, while they say daily unto me, Where is thy God?* 3. As the battle against discouragements and unbelief useth to be oftener renewed even after the believer hath gotten the vic-tory once and again, and as the wrestler's weakness useth oftener to be made evident; so the same means and wea-pons must be oftener used, and we must not be weary to fight on; for, *why art thou cast down, O my soul,* is now repeated as before; the misbelief, and disquietness drawn on by misbelief, must be yet again rebuked : *why art thou disquieted within me?* faith and hope must be set on work against all the disappearances of help : *hope thou in God;* we must, as it were, be surety to ourselves for God's promises made to us, that they shall be performed : *I shall yet praise him.* 4. As when the Lord withdraweth both the outward tokens of his favour and his inward consolation for a time, the countenance of the godly cannot but be heavy, cast down, and look sad, like a man that is sick; so, when God returneth to comfort and to own his own, either both in-wardly and outwardly, or inwardly only, the man's face looketh cheerful : *he is the health of my countenance.* 5.

Although the Lord, for a time, shall neither remove the outward affliction nor inwardly give comfort, yet faith will sustain itself upon the covenant, and lay its whole weight upon it, and may do it confidently ; for it will not sink under the man nor under his burden : *he is my God.*

PSALM XLIII.

This psalm tendeth to the same purpose with the former; for David in exile complaineth of his persecutors, and prayeth for delivery, and regretteth his sad condition, ver. 1, 2; prayeth for restitution unto the liberty of the public ordinances, promising to praise God at his returning cheerfully, ver. 3, 4; and wrestleth with his discouragements, as he did in the former psalm, ver. 5.

1. *Judge me, O God, and plead my cause against an ungodly nation : O deliver me from the deceitful and unjust man.*

2. *For thou art the God of my strength : why dost thou cast me off? why go I mourning because of the oppression of the enemy ?*

From his complaint and prayer against his enemies learn, 1. As the godly have usually enemies powerful, many, crafty and cruel, oppressing them for righteousness, so they want not an impartial judge, who is sufficient to take order with their adversaries, to whom they may and should address themselves in their affliction, as David doth here : *judge me, O Lord, and plead my cause against an ungodly nation.* 2. The cruelties and falsehood, and fair pretences, whereby the enemies palliate their cruel purposes, are more dangerous than their professed cruelty ; from which no wisdom, except divine direction, can save a man ; *O! deliver me from the deceitful and unjust man.* 3. What the oppressed church, or particular believer wanteth, God hath and will be forthcoming for the believer's use and benefit, as his need shall be, to uphold him by it, and comfort him, and deliver him, and bless him ; *for, thou art the God of my strength.* 4. Although the Lord be all in all to us by covenant, yet for our good and his own glory he may so exercise us, as we may want possession for a time of what we have in promise ; and seem also to be thrust out of our right ; in which case if we shall once fix our faith, we shall have liberty to dispute our right against all temptations, and to express the sense of our condition unto God without being mistaken, as here David doth, saying (not before, but after the fixing of his faith ;) *why dost thou cast me off ? why go I mourning for the oppression of the enemy ?*

3. *O send out thy light and thy truth : let them lead me, let them bring me unto thy holy hill, and to thy tabernacles.*

4. *Then will I go unto the altar of God, unto God my exceeding joy : yea upon the harp will I praise thee, O God, my God.*

From this prayer and promise of thanksgiving, learn, 1· No temptation unto discouragement, nor seeming desertion should divert the believer from pursuing his desire of relief, but rather kindle his affection in prayer ; *O send out thy light.* 2. Comfort, deliverances from troubles, and performance of promises, when they most disappear, are kept in store for us, and fast locked up, to be let forth to us in due time ; *O send out thy light and thy truth.* 3. Direction how to conduct ourselves till we obtain our desires, and observation of the steps of God's providence, bringing us to the possession of promised mercies, are necessary preparations for the mercy which we seek, and should be prayed for as mercies in order preceding that particular which we should have ; *let them lead me; let them bring me unto thy holy hill.* 4. Spiritual grief must have spiritual comfort ; godly sorrow for distance from God and want of the comfortable use of his ordinances, admits of no comfort, save a comfort of that kind ; for David longeth more to have the free use of the public ordinances, than to have the kingdom ; therefore saith he, *let them bring me to thy holy hill and to thy tabernacles.* 5. The first thing a soul is to attend to in his address to God, is the means of expiation of his sin, and that is Christ represented by the altar, offering himself a ransom for the sinner, and sanctifying the person of the offerer, and the worship and service of the man that comes to God through him ; *then will I go to the altar of God.* 6. This way of making address to God by Christ, gives present access to God, and peace to the soul of him who draws near this way ; *thus I will go to God.* 7. God laid hold upon through Christ, furnishes not only peace, but unspeakable joy also to the believer ; yea, God reconciled through Christ, is the life of the believer's gladness ; *I*

will go to God, my exceeding joy. 8. As is the longing of the soul after God, when it is at a distance from
him : so are the consolation and satisfaction which it findeth
after renewed access ; and as the supplicant is earnest for
renewed sense of fellowship, so he purposeth that the
praises of God shall be hearty, at the receiving of that which
he longed for, and also that his faith shall be stronger by
the fastening of the bond of the covenant between him and
God more strongly : *I will praise thee with the harp, O my
God.*

5. *Why art thou cast down, O my soul ? and why
art thou disquieted within me ? hope in God : for I
shall yet praise him,* who is *the health of my countenance, and my God.*

He closeth this psalm as the former one, setting faith and
hope on work to wrestle with discouragement. Whence
learn, 1. The strongest believer may be overtaken with fits
of dejection and discouragement ; for this champion findeth
his soul cast down. 2. A praying soul, believing in God
through Christ, hath no reason of dejection and discouragement, whatever reason of humiliation he may have ; *why
art thou cast down, O my soul ?* 3. It is a sanctifying means
for wrestling out of discouragement, to dispute misbelief to
the door, or to dispute ourselves out of melancholy by reason taken from the Lord's word ; and it is wisdom to get
the conscience to be our friend, when the mind and the
heart are in a wrong temper in this case ; it is necessary to
take God's part against misbelief, and unwarrantable unquietness, and to dispute both his cause and our own against
temptations ; *why art thou disquieted within me ?* 4. No
rest to a troubled and disquieted spirit, but by casting anchor on the Rock, and hoping in God ; *hope thou in God.*
5. Hope cannot raise itself in trouble, but by the grip of
a promise ; *hope in God, for I shall yet praise him.* 6.
Though faith be in darkness, yet it will see afar off ; as soon
as it puts the prospect of the covenant of grace to its eye,
it discerneth the proper remedy of present evils to be in
God, and the good it would be at, coming along unto it,
and is as sure of it, as if it were in possession : *he is the
health of my countenance, and my God.*

PSALM XLIV.

To the chief musician, for the sons of Korah.   Maschil.

The Church, under heavy persecution, first strengtheneth her faith in God before she enter upon her lamentation, ver.1—8.   In the second place, she layeth forth her sad sufferings under the hands of cruel persecutors, v. 9—16.   In the third, she professeth her constant adherence unto God, and avoweth his truth for time by-past, and her purpose to continue for time to come, v. 17—22.   In the last place, they pray unto the Lord to arise and relieve them from their cruel persecutors, for the glory both of his justice and mercy, v. 23—25.

From the inscription, learn, seeing the canon of the whole Hebrew bible is commended to us by Christ and his Apostles, as the undoubted word of God, and the undoubted Scriptures given by inspiration of the Holy Spirit to the holy men of God, the writers thereof, as kept entire and not vitiated by the Jews, (whose honour for preserving faithfully the oracles of God committed unto them, is unstained, Rom. 4, 2.) We are not to trouble ourselves about the name of the writer, or time of writing of any part thereof ; especially because God of set purpose concealeth the name, sundry times, of the writer, and the time when it was written, that we look in every book, more to the inditer of it, than to the writer of it ; and that the use of any exercise of any of the saints set down therein, might be so much the more large, as the consideration of particular circumstances of time and persons, (whereunto it might seem only to be applied) were laid aside ; for this psalm, wanting the name of the writer, and time of the writing of it also, is looked upon by the Apostle, Rom. 8, 36, not only as an experience of the church before us, but also as a prophecy of the martyrdom of Christians under the gospel, and as encouragement to stand constant in the faith in hottest persecutions.

1. *We have heard with our ears, O God, our fathers have told us,* what *work thou didst in their days, in the times of old.*

2. How *thou didst drive out the heathen with thy hand, and plantedst them ;* how *thou didst afflict the people, and cast them out.*

3. *For they got not the land in possession by their own sword, neither did their own arm save them ; but thy right hand, and thine arm, and the light of thy countenance, because thou hadst a favour unto them.*

For the confirmation of their faith, they lay forth three arguments. The first is from the Lord's mighty work in driving out the Canaanites and planting their fathers in Canaan, made mention of in holy Scripture. Whence learn,

1. The information which the Scripture giveth us of God's working for his people, is as sure, and should be so looked upon by us, as if the people of God who lived in the days when these works were done, and who were eye witnesses thereof, should also rise up from the dead, when the Scriptures are read, and testify unto us, saying, of these things we were eye witnesses, and we tell them unto you for unquestionable truths ; for thus much do these words import: *we have heard with our ears, O God, our fathers have told us what thou didst in their days.* 2. The Scripture keepeth the declarations of God's work and will so fresh, and clean, and pure from the mixture, and superfluity, and imperfection of human tradition, that God will own it as his own proper testimony, when we bring it before him : *our ears have heard, O God, what thou didst in the times of old.* 3. God's old works have new use in all ages, for the furtherance of believers' faith, patience and comfort : *we have heard what thou didst in times of old,* say the saints now in trouble, and standing in need of experience of the like works of God for them. 4. Albeit comparison of by-gone better times with ours, augmenteth grief and temptation at first ; yet when they are well looked upon in their end and use, they serve to comfort us, and confirm our faith, as here the persecuted Kirk's use-making of the like condition of the Lord's people before them teacheth us. 5. Although families and nations were rooted in a land, like old oak trees, and were very long possessors of it ; yet God can drive them out of it, by what instruments soever he pleaseth to do it ; the work of vanquishing nations, and subduing them, and casting them out, is the Lord's work : *thou didst drive out the heathen with thy hand.* And so is the planting of a people in a land, or continuing families in succession ; *thou plantedst our fathers, and castedst out the people.* 6. The Lord's part in a work is best seen, when man's part and all that he, as an instrument, hath done, or could have done, is all declared null ; being considered as separate from God, who moved the instruments, and wrought by them what he pleased ; *they got not the land in possession by their own sword, &c.* 7. The

fountain of all good which is done to, or by the church, is only the mere favour of God and his good pleasure ; that they are an incorporation, a church planted, fostered, defended so long, watered, spared so long, all is free favour ; *neither did their own arm save them, but thy right hand, &c., because thou hadst a favour unto them.* 8. When God showeth the light of his countenance to a people or person, he will also show his power for them ; *thy arm and the light of thy countenance, gave them the land in possession.* These two go together.

4. *Thou art my King, O God: command deliverances for Jacob.*

The second argument for confirmation of the church, is from the relation between God and her ; *thou art my King, O God, &c.* Whence learn, 1. Trouble maketh faith thirsty, and teacheth the believer to make use of his right and interest, and relations between God and him, which otherwise possibly might have lien idle in his coffer ; yea, and faith by trouble is made wise to choose out the relation which serveth most for its present use ; *thou art my king, O God.* 2. Relations between God and his people, stand constantly in adversity, as well as in prosperity. The godly in persecution have God for a king to come unto, from whom they may expect all the benefits which subjects can expect from a potent king ; as here the church saith to God, however thou thinkest it fit to put us under the feet of persecutors, yet *thou art my king, O God.* 3. Whatsoever be the particular condition of any member of the church, his prayer should be put forth for the whole body ; specially when the persecution is of the whole ; *command deliverance for Jacob.* 4. It will cost the Lord but a word to deliver his people : let him give out order, and it shall be effected ; the church craveth no more, but *command deliverance.*

5. *Through thee will we push down our enemies ; through thy name will we tread them under that rise up against us.*

6. *For I will not trust in my bow, neither shall my sword save me.*

7. *But thou hast saved us from our enemies, and hast put them to shame that hated us.*

8. *In God we boast all the day long, and praise thy name for ever. Selah.*

The third argument to confirm their faith, is the conscience of their sincere purpose to give God the glory of
enabling them unto all duties, whereunto he has promised
to enable them. Whence learn, 1. The believer may promise to himself whatsoever God hath promised unto him.
Hath God promised to give his own people the victory over
their enemies ? then the believer may promise to himself he
shall overcome his persecutors, and through God's strength
be more than a conqueror over them : *through thee will we
push down our enemies.* If the enemy make head against
them after a defeat, the believer may say, *through thy name
will we tread them under that rise up against us.* 2. The
less confidence we have in ourselves, or in any thing besides
God, the more evidence have we of the sincerity of our faith
in God : *for I will not trust in my bow, neither shall my
sword save me.* 3. It is a proof of sincerity of faith, to
give God as much credit for time to come, as he hath gained
to himself by the evidencing of his truth in time by-gone :
*my sword shall not save me : but thou hast saved us, and
therefore through thee will we push down our enemies.* 4.
Whosoever hateth the Lord's people, shall be forced to think
shame of their enmity one day : *thou hast put them to shame
that hated us.* 5. The glory which we give to God in prosperity, we should give him the same in our adversity ; change
of times and dispensations should not change his glory, nor
our confidence in him. Though the church be under foot
of men, the church's God is above all : *in God will we boast
all the day long, and praise thy name for ever.*

9. *But thou hast cast off, and put us to shame ; and
goest not forth with our armies.*

10. *Thou makest us to turn back from the enemy ;
and they which hate us spoil for themselves.*

11. *Thou hast given us like sheep* appointed *for
meat ; and hast scattered us among the heathen.*

12. *Thou sellest thy people for nought, and dost not
increase* thy wealth *by their price.*

13. *Thou makest us a reproach to our neighbours, a
scorn and a derision to them that are round about us.*

14. *Thou makest us a by-word among the heathen, a
shaking of the head among the people.*

15. *My confusion* is *continually before me, and the shame of my face hath covered me,*

16. *For the voice of him that reproacheth and blasphemeth; by reason of the enemy and avenger.*

Having thus fastened a resolution to believe constantly in God, the psalmist layeth forth the lamentable condition of the church before God, with the temptation that assaulteth his people in their suffering. Whence learn, 1 It can stand with the constant love of God to his people, to put them to so hard exercises by variety of troubles, as he may seem not only to break off his former course of kindness towards them, but also to cast them off, and turn against them, by sending sore judgments on them, which ordinarily speak unto human sense wrath, and utter wrath : *thou hast cast off;* yea, and they may seem disappointed of their hoped for protection and assistance from God : *thou hast put us to shame :* and may lose heart and hand when they go to battle against their enemies in a good cause : *thou goest not forth with our armies*; v. 9, and be put to flight in battles, and made a spoil to their despiteful enemies ; *thou makest us turn back from our enemies, and they that hate us spoil for themselves,* v. 10; and, being destitute of human help for recovery, may seem to be left in the hand of the enemy, to dispose of them as it may seem to his pleasure : *thou hast given us like sheep for meat.* And albeit all believers cannot be cut off, yet we may lose the face of a church or congregation : *thou hast scattered us among the heathen,* v. 11, and may be made underlings and slaves to oppressors with no apparent advantage to the Lord's glory, but seeming loss rather : *thou sellest thy people for nought, and dost not increase thy wealth with their price,* v. 12 ; and may be deprived, not only of the common duties of humanity, which may be expected of neighbours, but also be disdained by them, mocked and reproached by them : *thou makest us a reproach to our neighbours, a scorn and derision to them that are about us,* v. 13 ; and, in a word, may be the most despised people under heaven ; which, as it is the just punishment of the scandalous carriage of the visible church, when they make God's name to be reproached among idolaters and heathen people ; is also the sharpest trial and temptation of the truly godly that can be : *thou makest us a byword among the heathen, a shaking of the head among the people,* v. 14. Learn also, 2. As God's presence, manifested among his people, and for them in the sight of the world, makes them the most famous, wise, courageous, prosperous, and blessed people in the world : so when God, being provoked by the wicked behaviour of his professed people, leaveth them, withdraweth his protection from them, and showeth himself angry at them, they become foolish and feeble sheep, a despicable and a disdained people above all others : *we turn back from the enemy. Thou hast given us as sheep appointed for meat, a reproach, a scorn, a by-word.* 3. Whatsoever calamity cometh upon us, howsoever, and for whatsoever cause, we may safely take God for the worker of all our woe ; albeit the meritorious cause be in ourselves, the inflicting of the calamity is of the Lord ; for there is no trouble in the city which the Lord will not avow himself to be the inflicter of ; for here the prophet puts all upon God : *thou hast done it,* five or six times. 4. When the visible church hath drawn misery on herself, and God hath inflicted calamities justly on her, it is safer to go to God, and lay before him all his work of justice, and the misery which lieth on us, than to keep it within our breasts, or tell it of him to others ; he that hath wounded us is only able to heal us, so this example teacheth us to do. 5. When the visible church is visited with sad calamities, the true members thereof are partakers of the trouble, and sorrow, and shame of that condition : *my confusion is continually before me,* saith the psalmist. 6. It is not very soon that the church is delivered out of her trouble, when once she falleth into it ; there is a time wherein it is continued : *my confusion is continually before me, and the shame of my face hath covered me,* v. 15. 7. When the enemy reproacheth religion and righteousness, because of the calamity of the godly, the more is spoken of God's respect to the godly and their cause, the more the enemy reproacheth and putteth the godly to shame ; and so, while God's dispensation seemeth to speak the contrary, it seemeth to be but their own confusion for the godly to speak of God, or godliness and the righteousness of their cause. This is a sad case ; *the shame of my face hath covered me, for the voice of him that reproacheth and blasphemeth ; by reason of the enemy and the avenger,* v. 16.

17. *All this is come upon us ; yet have we not for-*

*gotten thee ; neither have we dealt falsely in thy cove-
nant.*

18. *Our heart is not turned back ; neither have our
steps declined from thy way.*

19. *Though thou hast sore broken us in the place of
dragons, and covered us with the shadow of death.*

20. *If we have forgotten the name of our God, or
stretched out our hands to a strange god ;*

21. *Shall not God search this out? for he knoweth
the secrets of the heart.*

22. *Yea, for thy sake are we killed all the day long ;
we are counted as sheep for the slaughter.*

In the third place, the godly profess, for all that is said,
their steadfastness in the profession of their faith for which
they were persecuted. Whence learn, 1. It is the duty of
the Lord's people, whatsoever trouble or persecution they
shall fall into, to be steadfast in the profession of the true religion, and in every point of controverted truth : *all this is
come upon us, yet have we not forgotten thee.* 2. As the
maintaining of controverted truth must flow from faith
in God and love to him, entertaining the affectionate remembrance of God's kindness, whatsoever change of dispensation they shall feel ; so the passing from a point of
truth in time of trouble, is a forgetting of God, who is but
hiding himself for a while, till the trial be perfected : therefore say the faithful, *all this is come upon us, yet have we
not forgotten thee.* 3. As the Lord hath been pleased to
enter into covenant with his church, and to make the covenant a sanctified means for keeping his people more steadfast
in their duty ; so should his people make conscience of keeping covenant made with God, and of remaining steadfast in
the maintenance of every duty whereunto they stand bound
therein, that, when they give account thereof, they may say
with comfort, *we have not dealt falsely in thy covenant.* 4.
Covenants which people make for adhering to the true religion, and to moral duties commanded in God's word, are
not of the nature of human covenants, wherein man and
man are the parties, and God only judge and witness, but are
such covenants as God is also a party therein, to whom a
people is so much the more engaged, as they are sworn to
keep his law, and therefore such covenants are called God's

covenant : *we have not dealt falsely in thy covenant.* 5. No excuse from hazard of trouble, or persecution, can guard the conscience, to shift or pass from the covenant of God ; nothing can make us give a comfortable account of our carriage in relation to the covenant, save upright and straight dealing before God : *we have not dealt falsely in thy covenant,* v. 17. 6. The Lord can procure more honour to himself in the time of the persecution of his scattered people, by the constancy of his martyrs and suffering saints, in their open profession and maintenance of his truth before their persecutors, than when the visible church lived in prosperity, and scandalized their neighbours by their ill behaviour, as this experience of scattered Israel maketh evident. 7. A good conscience much sweeteneth affliction in the time of trial, as here appeareth. 8. It is necessary for making a man constant in the outward profession of truth in the time of persecution, that his heart be established by grace, that his heart be fixed, trusting in the Lord: these shall be borne through who may say, *our heart is not turned back.* 9. It is necessary to watch over our several actions, lest by little and little in particular passages we be drawn aside from our walking with a straight foot toward the gospel ; and lest the heart be stolen away by little and little from the truth ; therefore these two must be joined together in our endeavour ; *that neither our heart be turned back, neither our steps decline from the Lord's way,* v. 18. 10. Albeit the Lord, for perfecting the full trial of the faith of his people, should put them in the power of most cruel tyrants, and in daily danger of losing their life; yet should they choose to suffer all extremity of torments, and death itself, rather than to depart from the truth ; for so did the Lord's approved witnesses before us: *though God did break them sore in the place of dragons, and cover them with the shadow of death,* v. 19. 11. In the time of trial concerning religion, two sorts of sins are to be eschewed. The one is the passing from any point of the truth of doctrine or divine ordinances ; the other is the practising of any point of false worship of another institution than what is the Lord's; whether under pretence of offering it to the true God, or with profession unto another God; for both these are to be eschewed, because the first sort of sin is a forgetting of the name of God, the other is *a stretching out of our hands to a strange god.*

12. The Lord, who searcheth the depth of a man's heart, will make special search for corrupters of religion, and depravers of divine doctrine, worship, or ordinances, and all sorts of idolatry, whatsoever excuses or pretences be used for the colouring or covering of the same : *if we have forgotten the name of our God, or stretched out our hands to another god, shall not God search this out ?* v. 20. 13. In time of persecution for religion, nothing can counterbalance the terrors and allurements of the persecutors, and make a man steadfast in the cause of God, save the fear of God, and love to God settled in the heart ; for the reason of the saints' steadfastness in this psalm is, *because God would have searched out their sin,* if they had done otherwise ; for *he knoweth the secrets of the hearts,* v. 21. 14. Such as resolve to bear out the profession of the truth, must resolve to give their life for the maintenance of it : *we are killed all the day long.* 15. It is ordinary for the world to hate the servants of God and true saints, more for their faithfulness to God, and uprightness in his service, than for any other cause : *for thy sake are we killed.* 16. It is mercy to us, that when God might punish us for our sins, he maketh our correction honourable, and our troubles to be for a good cause : *for thy sake are we killed.* 17. Although all the hours of the day the persecutors were taking and killing some of our brethren, the saints, for their faith in God and fidelity in his service ; yet that must not divert the rest from following the truth, and professing true religion ; how long soever the Lord continue the persecution and our trouble for his cause, we should resolve constantly to endure to the end : *yea, for thy sake are we killed all the day long,* v. 22.

23. *Awake, why sleepest thou, O Lord? arise, cast us not off for ever.*

24. *Wherefore hidest thou thy face, and forgettest our affliction, and our oppression ?*

25. *For our soul is bowed down to the dust; our belly cleaveth unto the earth.*

26. *Arise for our help, and redeem us, for thy mercies' sake.*

In the last part of the psalm, the psalmist in behalf of the church prayeth to be delivered from the cruelty of persecutors;

and, being in bitterness of spirit for anguish and grief, venteth his present sense of God's dispensation, yet corrected by
faith.   Whence learn, 1. Albeit the Lord who watcheth over
Israel be most vigilant for every one of his children, and
never slumbereth nor sleepeth, but is still upon his work, his
glorious work of preparing his jewels for eternal life, even
when he putteth his people in the furnace of affliction by
hottest persecution, (for then in special he is about to glorify
himself and his saints also in the trial of their precious faith,
and is bringing to the view of men and angels, that he hath
a people who love him better than their own lives, and who
will endure any misery rather than deny any point of his
truth committed unto them ;) yet such is the strength of natural senses and affections, such is the partiality of self-love
in carnal disputation about God's providence, when he putteth his people to so sad sufferings for no fault done to their
persecutors ; and such is the power of Satan's temptations,
helped on by human infirmity and perturbation of passions,
that God is looked on as if he misregarded the case of his own
people, and took no more care of them than a sleeping man
doth of his business ; and this is imported in this expression,
awake, why sleepest thou, O Lord ?   2. Faith doth not allow
nor subscribe unto carnal sense, but in presenting the objections thereof unto God, really refuteth them ; first, in
that by prayer it goeth to God, who is the hearer of the most
secret sighs of supplicants, at whatsoever time, night or day,
or in whatsoever place opened up unto him ; secondly, by
intreating him to refute the slander and calumny which carnal sense and suggested temptations put upon him: *awake,
arise ;* that is, let it be seen by the manifesting of thy justice
and mercy, as thou usest to do by thy open working for us,
that thou takest notice of our sufferings, and of our persecutor's violence ; thirdly, by avowing that such misregarding of his own cause and servants, as sense and temptation
vented, is inconsistent with his nature, covenant, promises, and
practices towards his people ; for, *why sleepest thou,* is as
much as, it is not possible that thou sleepest ; and why here
is not a word of quarrelling, but a word of denying, that any
reason can be given for such a thought, as God sleepeth ;
fourthly, by avowing faith and hope of God manifesting himself in due time, for deciding of the controversy between them
and their persecutors ; for what he prayeth for, he believeth

to obtain. His prayer being according to the revealed will of God : and *awake, why sleepest thou, O Lord,* is as much as I believe, Lord, that thou wilt indeed let us and the world see that thou art not sleeping in all this our hard sufferings for thy sake, and therefore I pray thee show thyself early. 3. As temptation, if it cannot fasten upon us any thought of God's careless misregarding of us in our sad sufferings, yet will it suggest suspicions of God's wrath, indignation, hatred, rejection, and reprobation of us ; so faith will study to dispel this mist, and quench this fiery dart by prayer also ; *cast us not off for ever ;* giving assurance, that albeit there were wrath in their exercise, yet it shall be but for a short time, and shall not be perpetual. 4. As temptation, if it cannot fasten upon us suspicion of God's hatred of us, and of his purpose to cast us off for ever ; yet it will suggest that God is pursuing us for some sin which we know not of, that he is wroth with us in suffering persecutors to prevail and to oppress us, (when in the mean time he is glorifying himself, and his truth in us, edifying others by our constancy in such a point of truth, and by our patience in bearing the cross, to the advantage both of the present age and posterity :) so faith must study to dispel this mist also, and to quench this fiery dart as well as the former, by rejecting this to be the cause ; for it is no token of God's pursuing sin in wrath, when God giveth us grace, not only to believe in him, but also to suffer for his name's sake, and the gospel's ; when he maketh us to be his public martyrs and witnesses for his truth, some in one degree of martyrdom, some in another ; when he maketh the Spirit of glory and of God to rest upon us, and so blesseth us, that when on the persecutor's part he is evil spoken of, he is on our part glorified. This, I say, is no token of wrath, no token of pursuing us for our sins. Therefore albeit sense calls this a hiding of his face, yet faith will not admit these causes which might import wrath : for, *wherefore hidest thou thy face,* is in the terms of faith, as much as, albeit it be true that we have sinned, and *thou seemest to hide thy face,* yet I cannot admit this thought, that this thy dealing with us is in wrath ; I see no reason why I should expound thy dispensation so ; yea, the very question *wherefore,* importeth that the psalmist cannot condescend upon any suggested reason of this sort, to prove the hiding of God's face, as sense would say ; and therefore he expecteth the Lord will show forth tokens of his love and good-will to them in due time. 5. As when these temptations are refuted by faith, long-lasting trouble meeting with infirm flesh holdeth up the complaint of poor frail man, not being able to endure trouble long, weak nature is ready to think that it is forgotten or laid aside, and striketh still upon its own string of lamentation, whatsoever faith speaketh to the contrary, whether it have reason or not ; so faith must do its office, and that is, when it cannot stop complaining, it must lay forth before God in prayer the lamenter and his lamentation, to find pity ; *why forgetteth thou our affliction, and our oppression ?* 6. All the reason that a poor perse-cuted and afflicted person can bring from himself, to plead pity when he lamenteth his case to the Lord, is his own weak-ness, emptiness, low condition, near-drawing to discourage-ment, fainting, and dying ; for, *our soul is bowed down to the dust.* 7. The godly soul under persecution, resolveth never to yield to the will of the persecutors, nor quit the Lord's cause, but to lie supplicant at God's feet from day to day, and there to die, if it be his will to delay or deny outward re-lief. Thus much the gesture of the supplicant speaks ; *our belly cleaveth to the earth.* 8. Though the believer find no reason in himself of his prayer for relief, yet he findeth rea-sons sufficient to give him hope in God : as, first, the Lord's sovereign power and place to help such weak creatures as come to him in their need ; *arise for our help, arise a help for us ;* secondly, the office of a redeemer, wherewith he clothed himself in the Messiah Christ Jesus; in the paction of whose redemption, and payment of the price of it, and be-gun and perfected accomplishment of it, every believer hath undoubted interest and right unto all particular deliveries out of all straits, as branches and appendices of the great re-demption of their souls unto eternal life. And this is hinted at in these words; *arise for our help, and redeem us ;* thirdly, the purchased, promised, and constantly running forth, and offered mercy of God to believers, looseth all objections and doubts arising from our sins, unworthiness, and ill-deserving; for, *redeem us for thy mercies' sake,* importeth so much.

PSALM XLV.

To the chief musician upon Shoshannim, for the sons of Korah, Mas-
chil. A song of loves.

Laying aside what useth to be spoken here of Solomon's marrying Pharaoh's daughter, and of some typical things therein, (tending to the ex-
tenuation of Solomon's fault,) as conjectural and serving nothing to the
advantage of that marriage, presuppose the conjecture held, both concerning the occasion, and also what might seem typical in it; because
similitudes taken from, and types made of, what thing soever God pleaseth, serve to make clear what the Spirit will have taken up about Christ,
or about any spiritual antitype; but doth not serve to make clear the
thing resembled by the antitype, from being sinful, as, by the type of
Agar, and of the brazen serpent, and of Jonah's punishment, and sundry other similitudes and parables set down in Scripture appeareth.
But we are sure this psalm is a song, describing the mystical marriage
of the Messiah, Christ Jesus our Lord, and his church, wherein Christ the
bridegroom is praised, ver. 1—9:—and the church his spouse is instructed in her duty to him, ver. 10—15;—and the end of the song declared
to be the everlasting praise of Christ, ver. 16, 17.

Concerning the inscription, that this psalm is altogether
spiritual and holy, appeareth, first, by this, that it is directed to the public minister of God's worship, to be made publicly use of in God's public praises: *to the chief musician,
for the sons of Korah;* secondly, it is entitled Maschil, a song
to give instruction to the church of God, concerning the
majesty and the grace of the kingdom of Christ, and the duty
of the church, and the spiritual blessings of the believers;
thirdly, it is a part of divine scripture, ranked among the
psalms, and acknowleged by the church of the Old Testament
for such; fourthly, the testimony of the apostle, applying
it directly as the word and speech of the Father to the Son
of God, Christ Jesus, Heb. i. 8; fifthly, the matter and
words of the psalm, which cannot be verified in any person
save in Jesus Christ alone; sixthly, the plurality of loves here
spoken of, to show unto the reader the excellency of the love
of Christ, or the love of God to us in Christ Jesus; wherein
the perfection of all loves that ever were heard tell of, is sur-
passed; *it is a song of loves.*

1. *My heart is inditing a good matter; I speak of the
things which I have made touching the king; my tongue
is the pen of a ready writer.*

This verse is a commendation given to this song by the
Spirit of God, by way of preface. 1. It is a good matter.
2. It is inspired; the Spirit of the Lord making the heart
filled with his presence, to be boiling in the inditing of it.

3. It is of Christ the King.   **4.** It is the poem of the inspired prophet, made ready to express what is furnished by the
Spirit, for the edification of the church in all ages. Whence
learn, 1. The knowledge of the love of Christ to his church,
and of his espousing her, is the sweetest subject, the matter of the most glad tidings that ever sinners heard of, and
worthy indeed to be called a good matter. 2. The heart, acquainted with this sweet and saving knowledge, will be more
ready to communicate what it knoweth, than able to express
itself ; the heart will be as a spring well, a boiling pot, according to the measure of the Lord's presence in it.   3.
The theme of the praises of the believing soul is Christ's
person, clothed with offices for the salvation of souls; for
the main subject of the song is touching the king.   4. When
the heart is full of gracious affection, the tongue will be loosed to praise God, so as others may be edified : out of the abundance of the heart, the mouth will speak heartily; *my tongue
is the pen of a ready writer.*

2. *Thou art fairer than the children of men; grace
is poured into thy lips: therefore God hath blessed thee
for ever.*

3. *Gird thy sword upon* thy *thigh,* O most *Mighty,
with thy glory and thy majesty.*

4. *And in thy majesty ride prosperously, because of
truth, and meekness,* and *righteousness; and thy right
hand shall teach thee terrible things.*

5. *Thine arrows* are *sharp in the heart of the King's
enemies;* whereby *the people fall under thee.*

6. *Thy throne,* O *God,* is *for ever and ever: the
sceptre of thy kingdom* is *a right sceptre.*

7. *Thou lovest righteousness, and hatest wickedness:
therefore God, thy God, hath anointed thee with the oil
of gladness above thy fellows.*

8 *All thy garments* smell *of myrrh, and aloes,* and
*cassia, out of the ivory palaces, whereby they have made
thee glad.*

9. *Kings' daughters* were *among thy honourable women : upon thy right hand did stand the queen in gold
of Ophir.*

In the description of the excellency of Christ, the very
true Son of God, there are set down sundry points of glory.

1. No beauty among men is comparable to the beauty of Christ, who is not only the fairest of ten thousand for wisdom and holiness, and whatsoever virtue can be named, as he is man; but also, as he is God, he is the resplendency of his Father's glory, the Holy One of Israel, of whose glory the whole earth is full, by whose beautiful righteousness and power the deformity of sin and misery of his own is taken away in part, and shall be removed fully; therefore justly is it said of him, *thou art fairer than the children of men.* 2. Christ, by the doctrine which he delivereth, is able not only to discover sin and misery, and the true way of delivery from the same by grace, and to direct a man in the way of salvation by grace, but also graciously and powerfully to persuade a man to embrace it: *grace is poured into thy lips.* 3. Christ, as man, is furnished, abundantly and above measure, for communicating the blessing to his hearers invincibly and infallibly, and for making his doctrine effectually powerful to salvation to whomsoever he will; for *therefore*, or to this purpose, *God hath blessed him forever.* 4. Christ is furnished to subdue and conquer and bring in so many as he pleaseth under subjection unto his kingdom; he hath his *sword*, even the rod of his mouth, his word, which is sharper than any two-edged sword, which no man can withstand. 5. He goeth not abroad to conquer or subdue without this his sword, which is his word; it is always with him ready to be drawn forth, and to be thrust into the soul and conscience of the hearer with whom he mindeth to deal: *his sword is girded upon his thigh.* 6. Christ is almighty, and so able to make good all that he speaketh, and to make his word of precept, promise, and threatening effectual unto the errand for which it is sent: *he is most mighty.* 7. Where he is pleased to open his word and to discover himself what he is, they that sit in darkness see a great light of his own glory as God; a shining light, a glorious light, making open the deep counsel of God and mystery of men's salvation: *gird thy sword upon thy thigh, O most mighty, with thy glory.* 8. Where he pleaseth to show himself, there the stateliness of a mighty monarch is seen, the sovereignty of the rule of heaven and earth is seen, able to shake with fear and awe of his greatness; with his *glory* there is *majesty*, or stately magnificence. 9. The wheels of Christ's chariot, whereupon he rideth when

K

he goeth to conquer and subdue new converts to his kingdom, are *majesty, truth, meekness, righteousness,* manifested in the preaching of his gospel; *majesty,* when the stately magnificence of his person and offices is declared; *truth,* when certainty of all that he teacheth in Scripture is known; *meekness,* when his grace and mercy are offered to rebels; and *righteousness,* when justification by faith in his name is clearly set forth. 10. Christ goeth no voyage in vain, he cometh not short of his intent and purpose, but doth the work for which he cometh, preaching the gospel: *in his majesty, truth, meekness, and righteousness he rideth prosperously.* 11. Christ can do what he will; he can do terrible things, to make his enemies tremble and his friends reverence him with holy fear, having omnipotency in him to work by, as ready as a man hath his right hand to employ; let him but will to have any thing done, and it shall be done; he hath not long to advise what he is able to do, as men consult with their ability whether they be so powerful as to effect what they intend or would have done: *thy right hand shall teach thee terrible things.* 12. Albeit he needeth no admonition to do what he is doing or will do, yet loveth he to have his children furthering the advancement of his kingdom, showing unto him what they would have done, and praying unto him that his kingdom may more and more come, as the form of speech indited by the Holy Spirit importeth: *gird thy sword, ride thou prosperously, &c.* 13. Christ in his conquest is to meet with his enemies, of whom some will openly oppose him, some will feignedly profess subjection, but will not heartily submit themselves unto him, but stand aloof and at a distance, being far from him in their hearts when with their lips they draw near hand unto him; both these are here called *the King's enemies.* 14. Such as do not draw near unto him in their heart, he can and will send messengers of wrath unto their heart, *threatenings* which shall be executed, *terrors* which shall be followed with judgments, and *judgments* which shall end in their destruction, sudden and unexpected; how many or how strong soever they seem to be, they shall not stand before him nor be able to hinder his conquest: *thine arrows are sharp in the heart of the King's enemies,* whereby *the people fall under thee.* 15. Christ Jesus, the promised Messiah, was revealed to the church of Israel to be the very true eternal God, that their faith and ours might have satisfaction, and a solid ground to rest upon, in the all-sufficiency and infinite worthiness of the promised Redeemer; as the apostle, Heb. i. 8, confirmeth unto us, citing to this purpose this very text, *thy throne, O God, is for ever and ever.* 16. Christ shall not want a church, from generation to generation; let persecutors do their worst, he shall reign as King, and sit on his throne in his church, giving forth his laws, and executing them, oppose him who will: *thy throne, O God, is for ever and ever.* 17. The sceptre of Christ's kingdom, which is the gospel, or the word of God in Scripture, whereby he gathereth his subjects and ruleth them, and the manner of his governing his people by the rules of his law and discipline, are most just and equitable; a righteous sceptre, whereby the subjects may be instructed in all righteousness, and may be justified and made righteous: *the sceptre of thy kingdom is a right sceptre.* 18. The holiness and righteousness of Jesus Christ, both as he is God and as he is God incarnate, are so essential to his person and employment, that his rule of government and administration of his affairs in his kingdom cannot be but right, as for direction, so also for rewards to them who obey his direction, and punishments of the disobedient: *thou lovest righteousness and hatest iniquity.* 19. As Christ is very God, so is he very man in all things, except sin, like unto us whom he calleth, Psal. xxii. 22, and Heb. ii. 12, *his brethren,* and here his *fellows,* sharemen and partakers of all that is given to him, and joint-heirs with him, Rom. viii. 17, and by reason of making covenant in our name with the Father, and by assuming our nature, according to the tenor of the covenant, God becometh his God and our God, and he, in our name, as man, receiveth the gifts of the Holy Spirit without measure, for fitting him, as he is man, to manage his kingdom in righteousness effectually ; for it is said, *therefore,* or to that intent, *God, thy God, hath anointed thee with the oil of gladness.* 20. The gifts and graces of the Holy Spirit, spoken of here in terms of oil, (employed for figuring men's furnishing unto their calling, and enabling of kings and priests unto their offices, and employed also in the entertainment of honourable guests invited to a feast,) are so bestowed on believers, joint-heirs with Christ, as Christ is not degraded from his sovereignty

by his partners' exaltation ; for of Christ it is said, *thy God
hath anointed thee with the oil of gladness above thy fellows.*
21. As the attendants of great persons are refreshed by the
smell of their ointments and perfumed garments, so are
Christ's attendants refreshed with the consolations of Christ's
Spirit perfuming all his outward ordinances, wherein, as in
his garments, he showeth forth himself to his church more
comfortably than any perfume or odoriferous spice can set
forth : *all thy garments smell of myrrh and aloes and cassia.*
22. Not only the heavens, where God showeth forth his
glory to souls of just men made perfect, but also all the
places where his honour dwelleth, all the meetings of his
church where he showeth himself in his ordinances to a
spiritual eye, are all of them most glorious and stately
palaces ; for there is the temple of the Holy Ghost, and
there is the beauty of holiness, whence cometh forth the
smell of his graces in his ordinances, as *out of ivory palaces.*
23. It is savoury and well-pleasing to Christ when his people
find pleasure in him and are refreshed by his blessing upon
the public ordinances ; for *thereby they have made thee glad,*
saith the psalmist to Christ. 24. Albeit the catholic church,
consisting of true converts or real saints, be but the one
and only true spouse of Christ, yet particular visible churches,
consisting of saints by calling, by obligation, by profession,
and common estimation, their own or others ; some of them
being true saints indeed in the spirit, some of them but
counterfeits and saints in the letter only, are in number
many, as they are dispersed for time and place wherein they
live, and make up sundry incorporations and ecclesiastic
consociations in parishes, towns, countries, and kingdoms,
as the Lord giveth them occasion, opportunity, or possibility, to make use of one another for communion of saints ;
in this respect, I say, they are many, and therefore the true
spouse, the true church, consisting of true converts, (whose
praise is of God, to whom only they are certainly known,
and not of men,) being but one, is compared to the queen ;
but the particular churches, whose collections and consociations are known to men, being many, are compared to
ladies of honour which serve the queen; of this sort it is here
prophesied, that the most renowned cities, countries, pro-
vinces, and kingdoms, should be professed attendants of
Christ the bridegroom's honour, and professed servants of

his church, and promoters of the honour, estate, and welfare of his spouse: *kings' daughters among thy honourable women.* 25. Albeit our Lord will allow a place of honour and room in his own court unto visible churches, in their several consociations, greater and smaller, for that service which they may do in order to the gathering in of the elect into the inner court of nearest spiritual communion with him, yet it is the universal invisible church which he counteth his spouse; she is the queen who hath access unto him, to be in highest honour beside him: *upon thy right hand did stand the queen.* 26. As the whole society of true saints reverently attend the will of the Lord, that every one of them in their place may honour the Lord; so are they all highly honoured of the Lord, and adorned with whatsoever may make them glorious; for the ornaments put on by Christ, such as adoption, justification, sanctification, with all other relations tending to their felicity, are here compared to the finest gold: *the queen doth stand at his right in gold of Ophir.*

10. *Hearken, O daughter, and consider, and incline thine ear; forget also thine own people, and thy father's house;*

11. *So shall the King greatly desire thy beauty; for he is thy Lord, and worship thou him.*

12. *And the daughter of Tyre* shall be there *with a gift;* even *the rich among the people shall entreat thy favour.*

13. *The King's daughter is all-glorious within; her clothing is of wrought gold.*

14. *She shall be brought unto the King in raiment of needle-work: the virgins her companions that follow her shall be brought unto thee.*

15. *With gladness and rejoicing* shall *they* be *brought: they shall enter into the King's palace.*

This is the other part of the psalm wherein the Spirit of the Lord speaketh to the true church militant, and directeth her in her duty; and encourageth her by sundry inducements to follow the Lord's direction. Whence learn, 1. As because there is spiritual love and respect between God and his church, therefore the covenant and the spiritual communion between Christ and his church are compared to a marriage; so, because the derivation of all spiritual life, grace, and motion which the church hath, is from God, and dependeth on him ; therefore the church is compared to a daughter; *hearken, O daughter,* and ver. 13, she is called *the King's daughter.* 2. The way and order of bringing the church to her duty, is by hearing of his word, consideration of what is taught, and subjection of her spirit to the obedience of faith ; *hearken, O daughter, and consider, and incline thine ear.* 3. Because even the true members of the church, whose praise is not of men but of God, are in this life entangled in affection to their old ways and corruption of manners ; therefore every one hath need to renounce and forget more and more his old lusts and enticements of the world, which is a very true fruit, and necessary evidence of their hearing in faith ; *forget also,* saith he, *thine own people, and thy father's house.* 4. The more we renounce and abandon our lusts and sinful inclinations in obedience to God, the more are we beautified with holiness, and are acceptable to God in our endeavours ; *forsake thy father's house, so shall the King greatly desire thy beauty.* 5. Christ hath all right unto our service, and by creation, redemption, and covenant, we are absolutely bound to serve and honour him in all things; *he is thy Lord, and worship thou him.* 6. When the church honoureth Christ he will honour her, and make the noble and potent in the world submit themselves to her and seek communion with her, and to esteem the meanest true member of the church, more blessed than riches or honour can make any man ; *the daughter of Tyre shall be there with a gift : the rich among the people shall entreat thy favour.* 7. The glory of the true kirk, and of every true member thereof is in things spiritual, not discernible by the uptaking of the natural man ; for what is outwardly professed, is inwardly studied unto sincerity by them who worship God in spirit and in truth ; and the graces wherewith she is adorned, as knowledge, faith, love, hope, zeal, courage, sobriety, patience, are not the object of outward beholders, but most beautiful in the eyes of a spiritual discerner, and in the eyes of Him that seeth in secret : *the King's daughter is all-glorious within.* 8. Whatsoever inherent graces the saints have, and how beautiful soever they be; yet they have need of a garment which may hide their imperfections, and beautify them before God; to wit, the imputed right-eousness of Christ, the husband of the church, who only hath this garment to sell, Rev. iii. 18; and though it be bought without money and without price, yet it is very rich, for whatsoever either nature or art can furnish to set it forth, is but a shadowing similitude of it; *her clothing is of wrought gold.* 9. Though the marriage of Christ and his church be bound up, and the hand-fastening be past, and tokens of love be given to the bride, yet the full solem-nity of the complete marriage is delayed till a set time, that the particular members and the whole church may be per-fected. The time of the bride's being brought to a constant habitation with Christ, is at the Lord's appointed time; to wit, at the death of every particular saint, and of the whole church together at the day of our Lord's second coming; the day is coming, wherein *she shall be brought unto the King.* 10. Albeit now there be many imperfections of the saints, which Christ's imputed righteousness hideth, yet in the day of the church's being brought into the pre-sence of God, to be with him for ever, she shall have no im-perfection, spot or wrinkle, or want of any thing which may perfect her glory in all respects. She shall put on immor-tality and incorruption, and her very body of flesh shall be made conformable to the glorious body of our Lord Jesus; *she shall be brought unto the King in raiment of needle work:* wherein the height of artifice and of nature's ma-terials are joined, as the fittest similitude which can express this inexpressible glory. 11. The same shall be the glori ous state of particular saints, and particular congregations, which shall be of the whole church universal; whereof as every true congregation and particular saint therein is a part, and have contributed their service in their time to the good of the whole church, as handmaids to their mistress: so shall they share in the glorious reward; *the virgins, her companions shall be brought unto thee,* saith the psalmist unto Christ. 12. Great shall be the joy of men and angels in the general meeting of the whole church, all being gathered together by the angels, who have lived from the beginning of the world to the ending thereof, and all re-ceived into the fellowship of God in blessedness to endure for ever; *with gladness and rejoicing shall they be brought, they shall enter into the King's palace.*

16. *Instead of thy fathers shall be thy children, whom thou mayest make princes in all the earth.*

17. *I will make thy name to be remembered in all generations: therefore shall the people praise thee for ever and ever.*

The two last verses may be applied both to the bride the true militant church, and to the bridegroom Christ Jesus, the King of saints. As it is applied to the church, learn, 1. The saints have no ground of gloriation in their progenitors according to the flesh, of whom they draw nothing but what is polluted with sin; but all the glory of the church is rather in her children which she bringeth forth by the gospel unto God: *instead of thy fathers shall be thy children.* 2. What any member of the church seemeth to lose in the world by forsaking thereof and coming to Christ, it is made up to them by Christ in spiritual respects, if not also in temporal blessings when God seeth fit; *instead of thy fathers shall be thy children.* 3. The true children of the church are indeed the excellent ones of the earth, and princes indeed, wherever they live, in comparison of all other men who are but the beastly slaves of Satan; *thy children are princes in all the earth.* 4. The true church shall be honourable, and honoured by her kindly children in all generations, because of the estimation which God putteth upon her in his holy Scripture; *I will make thy name to be remembered in all generations: therefore the people shall praise thee.*

These verses may also be applied more pertinently to the bridegroom Christ Jesus, for whose praise the whole psalm is composed, ver. 1. Of whom only the words can be verified fully, as only capable of what is ascribed directly to the person spoken unto here, and cannot be well ascribed to Solomon and Pharaoh's daughter in their marriage; because partly Solomon's marriage with outlandish women is marked among his faults, and so can hardly be esteemed to be honoured with this song delivered to the church for her perpetual instruction; partly because in the inscription there is not so much as mention of Solomon's name, either as type or resemblance of this marriage of Christ and his church; and partly also because what is here spoken, hath little typical verity answering to it in the history of Scripture concerning Solomon's marriage, or children of Pharaoh's daughter. And lastly, this song is set down not in a typical manner, but in a simple similitude of the marriage of a king and queen indefinitely, whose marriage useth to be the most glorious of all earthly marriages, and fittest to lead us up to that incomparably glorious spiritual marriage of Christ and his church. In which consideration, from these words, learn, 1. Christ draweth not glory from his progenitors according to his flesh, but giveth being, and gracious being, to such as he regenerateth by his word and Spirit, to be his children; and so it may be said to Christ, *instead of thy fathers shall be thy children.* 2. The excellency of Christ's children, and their princely disposition above the rest of mankind unregenerate, is of Christ's making; he only it is, of whom properly it may be said, *thou shalt make thy children princes in all the earth;* for, *he hath made us kings and priests to God and his Father.* 3. By the Spirit that indited this psalm, and all other Scriptures, Christ's name shall be holden forth and remembered from age to age, while the world lasteth : *I will make thy name,* saith the Spirit, *to be remembered to all generations.* 4. Christ's espousing unto himself a church, and gathering more and more from age to age by his word and Spirit unto it, his converting souls, and bringing them into the fellowship of his family, and giving unto them princely minds and affections wherever they live, are large matters of growing and everlasting glory unto his majesty; for in regard of this point, and what is said before in this psalm, he addeth as the close of all, *therefore shall the people praise thee.*

PSALM XLVI.

To the chief musician, for the sons of Korah. A song upon Alamoth.

After some notable delivery of the church from her enemies, the Lord's people confirm themselves in their resolution to trust in God, and not to be afraid of trouble, because of his comfortable presence among them, which is like unto a river of continual refreshment, as late experience gave evidence, v. 1—6 ; and exhort all men in the world to observe this his late work, and make use of it for their humiliation, v. 7—10, as the church maketh use of it for confirmation, v. 11.

1. *God* is *our refuge and strength, a very present help in trouble :*

2. *Therefore will not we fear, though the earth be removed, and though the mountains be carried into the midst of the sea ;*

3. Though *the waters thereof roar* and *be troubled,* though *the mountains shake with the swelling thereof. Selah.*

From bygone experience of God's defending his church, the Lord's people strengthen themselves in the faith of God's word, concerning the care of his people; and from this ground guard their heart against the fear of all possible trouble in time coming. Whence learn, 1. Faith in God's word and profession of it, are made much more vigorous and lively after experience of the verity thereof; for the church believed this truth before this late delivery, but now after this fresh experience they are animated to set to their seal to it more confidently, saying, *God is our refuge.* 2. Albeit the church were destitute of all human strength within herself, and were forsaken, yea and pursued by all kings and princes, yet hath she God for a retiring place, and for furnishing of what is sufficient for her subsistence; *God is our refuge and strength.* 3. Albeit the Lord will not exempt his people from trouble, yet he will be near them in time of trouble; and when their weakness is discovered to them, then he will help them, and will not delay his help too long, but will give help in time of need effectually; for God is to his people *a very present help in trouble.* 4. Nothing can guard the heart of God's people against the terror of possible, or imminent troubles, save faith in God; for here the Lord's people, having fixed their faith, make this inference, *therefore will we not fear.* 5. The terror of apparent trouble, is the touchstone of confidence in God, and then is faith fixed, when it doth look upon the greatest dangers and troubles that can be imagined, with resolution to adhere to God, and to that truth which persecutors oppose, whatsoever may come: *we will not fear, though the earth be removed.* 6. Albeit the whole frame of the world were changed, and the work of creation were either dissolved or confounded, which shall be in effect at the last day; yet faith findeth footing and ground to stand upon in God himself; *we will not fear, though the*

*mountains be carried into the midst of the sea, though the
waters thereof roar and be troubled, though the mountains
shake with the swelling thereof. Selah.*

4. There is *a river, the streams whereof shall make
glad the city of God, the holy* place *of the tabernacles
of the most High.*

5. *God is in the midst of her; she shall not be moved: God shall help her,* and that *right early.*

The church looketh upon the Lord's word and ordinances, joined with the blessing of his Spirit among them,
as upon a sufficient consolation against whatsoever trouble
can be imagined. Whence learn, 1. Although there be
many particular persons in the Lord's church militant, and
many particular congregations as there were many habitations in Jerusalem, and many tabernacles at the time of the
solemn feast, when all the Lord's people were gathered together to the keeping thereof; yet they are all one church
universal, one kingdom of God, one city, compact together
in the union of one sealed covenant, one true faith, and
one Spirit; the plurality *of the tabernacles of God* doth make
but *one city of God* here. 2. Albeit trouble without comfort may fall on men who know not God; yet to believers
within the church there can no trouble come, wherein the
true citizens may not find consolation and joy to uphold
them against all causes of sorrow; *there is a river, the
streams whereof make glad the city of God.* 3. The consolations which God furnishes to all who will make use of
them within the church, are not like the consolations which
the world can afford, which are in all respects insufficient
to overcome trouble; but the consolations of God are abundant, constantly running, ready at hand, and able to make
a man a conqueror over trouble effectually, and to make him
rejoice in the Lord in the midst of trouble; for this is imported in the similitude of refreshing water; *there is a
river, the streams whereof shall make glad the city of God.*
4. God will never forsake his people who seek after him,
but where they are following his ordinances in any measure
of sincerity, there will he be: *God is in the midst of her.* 5.
As the consolation of the church, so also the stability of the
church, and continuance of it from generation to generation, dependeth upon God's settled residence therein: *God*

is in the midst of her, she shall not be moved. 6. God's presence among his people will not exempt them from trouble, but from perdition in trouble : he will not exempt the bush from burning, but from being consumed ; *for God shall help her.* 7. Albeit the Lord does not appear at the point of time when we would, yet shall he come and help in time of need most timously ; *God shall help her, and that right early.*

6. *The heathen raged, the kingdoms were moved ; he uttered his voice, the earth melted.*

7. *The Lord of hosts is with us ; the God of Jacob is our refuge. Selah.*

He cleareth the doctrine delivered, by a late experience of God's taking order with the enemies of the church, at the time when they in great confluence and power made assault against her. Whence learn, 1. It is no small indignation which the world beareth against the Lord's kingdom, his people, and work among them : nor is it any mean power, from which the church is in danger to suffer hardship; but fury in the height of it, and force in the farthest extent of it, may she expect to encounter with : *the heathen raged, the kingdoms were moved.* 2. It is not the worldly power of the Lord's people which can sustain the assault of their raging enemies, but God must prove party to her oppressors ; therefore here the Lord interposeth himself for his people ; *the Lord uttered his voice.* 3. It shall not cost the Lord any business to despatch the enemies of his people ; let him show himself a little, let him but say the word, and they are gone ; as snow before the sun, or fat cast into the fire, so are they consumed ; *he uttered his voice, the earth melted.* 4. Any one experience of the Lord's working for his church, may suffice to confirm the faith of his people concerning his perpetual presence in his church, for assistance of his people in their difficulties ; for, from this one experience he draweth the inference ; *the Lord of hosts is with us.* 5. What the Lord is in wisdom, power, and other attributes, that may the church apply to herself, and be sure to have the fruit of it as her need requireth ; if hosts of heathen and huge great armies of whole kingdoms be against his church, yet still we may be sure that God the Lord of armies will stand up against them, and for his church : *the Lord of hosts is with us.* 6. The covenant of

God made with the church in former ages is good enough
security for the church in after ages, for obtaining whatsoever benefit his covenant includeth; *the God of Jacob is our
refuge*; yea, the right made to the incorporation of the
church, is as good security for the use of every particular believer, as if it were made personally to every member by
name; and therefore, as wise citizens reckon whatsoever they
can claim by their town charter, no less to belong to them
than their own private possessions : so whatsoever the believer can claim by virtue of the great charter made to the
church, he should reckon it as sure to be his, as if his proper
name had been specified in the promises; for, *the God of
Jacob is our refuge*, is thus much; because God is undoubtedly the God of Jacob, and his children's refuge, he must
undoubtedly be our God, who are members of that incorporation, and our refuge.

8. *Come, behold the works of the Lord, what desolations he hath made on the earth.*

9. *He maketh wars to cease unto the end of the earth ;
he breaketh the bow, and cutteth the spear in sunder ;
he burneth the chariot in the fire.*

10. *Be still, and know that I* am *God : I will be
exalted among the heathen, I will be exalted in the
earth.*

11. *The Lord of hosts* is *with us : the God of Jacob is our refuge. Selah.*

In the latter part of this psalm, he exhorts all men to
make use of this deliverance given to the church for their
humiliation, confidence in God, and consolation. Whence
learn, 1. When God worketh works of wonder in favour of
his church, most men mark not the Lord's doing; such is
the dulness and stupidity, ingratitude, misbelief, and perverseness of men, either thinking little of his work, or ascribing the praise to instruments, or some other thing besides
God; so that there is need to call unto men, and set them to
their duty; *come and behold the works of the Lord*. 2.
Wonderful calamities doth God pour out upon the enemies
of his people, when he entereth into judgment with them;
for what they intended to do to his people, he doth unto
them; *behold what desolations he hath made in the earth*.
3. When it seemeth good to the Lord, he can give peace

universally to his church, and awhile's breathing from the troubles of outward enemies: *he maketh wars to cease to the ends of the earth.* 4. Long preparations for war, arms and ammunition which have been made with great labour and expenses against his church, the Lord can soon give a short account of them, and make them useless when he pleaseth; *he breaketh the bow, and cutteth the spear in sunder, he burneth the chariot in the fire.* 5. Because men cannot understand what they are doing, or what is their duty, so long as their passions are aloft, so long as their minds are tumultuous, busied about many things, and distracted from what is most necessary; it is good for people, from time to time, to gather in their straying thoughts, to silence their passions and perturbations, and humbly compose themselves for observation of whatsoever God requireth of them: *be still, and know that I am God.* 6. It is better for men to be wise and acknowledge the Lord by the words of his instruction, than to leave their lesson to be learned by doleful experience and danger of destruction; *be still, and know that I am God.* 7. There is not so ready a way for the Lord's people to quiet their mind against the fear of trouble and persecution of men, as to settle their faith about God's taking care of his people and of his own cause, and of his mind declared against his and their enemies; *be still, and know that I am God.* 8. The Lord will not be at a loss by the opposition of his enemies; he will not fail to enlarge his glory, the more that men go about to suppress it; he will make an inroad upon his adversaries' lands, and make them know himself to be God, either to their conversion, or confusion and destruction; *I will,* saith he, *be exalted among the heathen.* 9. How little notice soever be taken of the majesty of God ofttimes in the visible church, and always without the church he be misregarded, yet will he see to his glory, not only in the church, but also among the enemies of the church; and not only among such as have actually invaded his people, but also among them far and near that have taken no notice either of him or of his people : *I will be exalted in the earth.* 10. Whatsoever manifestation of God's power be made in the world by his judgment against his enemies who know him not; yet he is ever doing for his church, and not against her : *the Lord of hosts is with us.* 11. The church of God, or believers, need not

care how many be against them, seeing they have more for
them than can be against them; to wit, God and all the
creatures at his command : *the Lord of hosts is with us.*
12. The strength of the church stands in her renouncing
her own and fleeing unto God's strength, and not in opposing their enemy by strong hand, but by betaking themselves
to God : *the God of Jacob is our refuge.* 13. We have need
to make God the ground of our confidence, and to make
our communion with God the ground of our comfort; for
God is sufficient for us against every evil, and God is sufficient unto us for furnishing every good; and we have need
to fix and settle our grounds, by oftener subscription of this
truth, and oftener avowing of it : *the Lord of hosts is with
us, the God of Jacob is our refuge,* is repeated.

PSALM XLVII.

To the chief musician.   A psalm for the sons of Korah.

This psalm is a prophecy of the enlargement of Christ's kingdom, and of
the conjunction of Jews and Gentiles in one body under Christ their
Head and Lord, delivered by way of exhortation to Jews and Gentiles,
joyfully to praise the God and Saviour of his people, Jesus Christ, on
whom the psalmist looketh as now ascended into heaven triumphantly,
after the full payment made of the price of redemption, and as going
about the gathering in of the redeemed Gentiles, till he bring in the
fulness of them into one church with the Jews.   The exhortation is
prefixed, ver. 1, and repeated, ver. 6, 7.   The reasons of the exhortation to a joyful praising of him are seven.   The first, ver. 2; the second,
ver. 3; the third, ver. 4; the fourth, ver. 5; the fifth, ver. 7; the sixth,
ver. 8; the seventh, ver. 9.

1. *O clap your hands, all ye people ; shout unto God
with the voice of triumph :*

From the exhortation to Jews and Gentiles, joyfully to
praise the Redeemer, learn, 1. Christ's kingdom and the
benefits thereof belong to more nations than one, for in him
the redeemed in all the nations of the earth are blessed :
clap your hands, all ye people, or, *all ye nations,* saith the
Lord.   2. The kingdom of Christ coming to a people, or
family, or person, is matter of chief joy to them, because
thereby delivery cometh from sin, Satan, and misery, and
sure mercies of righteousness, peace, and joy in the Holy
Ghost, with eternal life, brought to them, and therefore just
reason to say to them to whom Christ cometh, *O clap
your hands, shout unto God with the voice of triumph.*   3.

Our joy and our victory over all our enemies, which Christ
hath purchased and bringeth to all believers in every nation,
are the matter of Christ's praise, and declare that he is
God, who, having in his manhood suffered, wrestled against
sin, Satan, death, hell, and the curse of the law, did, by the
power of his Godhead, prevail before he brought joy to the
Gentiles. Thus much the words of the exhortation import;
for his triumph presupposeth his victory, and his victory
presupposeth his battle before he overcame, and the commanding of the Gentiles *to clap their hands and shout*, and
to shout *with the voice of triumph*, presuppose their interest in the victory; and, while they are bidden shout to *God*,
the triumpher, who, in all this psalm, is the Redeemer,
Christ (as shall appear hereafter), it imports that the Redeemer is God, and howsoever he is God inseparably from
the Father and the Holy Spirit, yet here he is distinctly to
be looked on in his person; and howsoever he is inseparably
to be praised with the Father and Holy Spirit, yet here he is
distinctly to be praised for this his work of victorious redemption of sinners; therefore it is said with distinct relation
to his person, *shout unto God with the voice of triumph*.

2. *For the Lord most High is terrible: he is a great
King over all the earth.*

From the first reason of the joyful praising of Christ,
taken from his sovereign majesty over all the world, learn,
1. That the Redeemer, the victorious triumpher, is the Lord
very God, essentially *Jehovah, the Lord most high.* 2. Christ
is able both to keep his subjects in subjection by his rod and
corrections, and to take order with his enemies also, how
high soever they be: *the Lord most high is terrible.* 3.
Christ hath right and just title to erect a church in what
country and kingdom he pleaseth, without asking any man's
license, and to set up among his subjects the profession of
his name, and practice of all his ordinances pertaining to
the exercise of religion, in doctrine, worship, and ecclesiastic
government of his subjects: *he is a great King over all the
earth.*

3. *He shall subdue the people under us, and the nations under our feet.*

From the second reason for joyfully praising Christ, taken
from the increasing of his own kingdom, and the exalting
of all his subjects above the rest of the world, learn, 1. The

true church of Christ may, from age to age, promise to herself addition of new subjects, or bringing down of their enemies under their feet; for, as the true church in the prophet's time might say, so may also every true church say after them, *he shall subdue the people under us, and the nations under our feet.* 2. If it will not please the Lord at such a time as men would wish, to execute judgment on their enemies, nor yet to convert them, and make them additional subjects to his kingdom, yet shall he not fail to make his own people victorious over their opposition, power, and persecution, and more than conquerors in this respect : *he shall subdue the people under us, and the nations under our feet.*

4. *He shall choose our inheritance for us, the excellency of Jacob, whom he loved. Selah.*

From the third reason of Christ's praise, taken from the care he hath for sustentation and welfare of his subjects, learn, 1. As God, by allotting earthly Canaan for the inheritance of his people, testified his care to provide for them both earthly sustenance and an enduring substance for their spiritual subsistence represented thereby; so will he provide for the sustenance of all his subjects in all ages, both bodily and spiritual : *he shall choose our inheritance for us.* 2. As he is most loving of us, and more wise to make choice of what is good for us than we ourselves are; so will he employ his wisdom and love in carrying out unto us our lot, measure, portion, and inheritance : *he shall choose our inheritance for us,* and not leave it to our carving. 3. The main part of the inheritance of Christ's subjects is no earthly thing, but his very best blessing, such as he gave to Jacob above Esau : *their inheritance shall be the excellency of Jacob.* 4. The fountain of Christ's care for all his subjects, is common to them and to Jacob, and that is his love : *the excellency of Jacob whom he loved, shall be their inheritance. Selah.*

5. *God is gone up with a shout, the Lord with the sound of a trumpet.*

From the fourth reason of Christ's praise, taken from his glorious triumphing over all his enemies and ours when he ascended to heaven, learn, 1. " He that ascended, what is it but that he also descended first into the lower parts of the earth? he that descended is the same also that ascended up

far above all heavens, that he might fill all things," Eph. iv. 9.
That is, Christ, being very God, descended, in humbling
himself to take on him the shape of a servant, and when he
had perfected the work of redemption, ascended in our nature, the same very person still, very God, which descended;
for *God is gone up with a shout.* 2. As the ark of the covenant, the figure of Christ, after the victory gotten over the
chief enemies of the church, ascended up to Zion and God's
presence; so Christ, after victory obtained over his chief
enemies on the cross, ascended triumphantly into heaven:
*God is gone up with a shout, Jehovah with the sound of a
trumpet.*

6. *Sing praises to God, sing praises; sing praises
unto our King, sing praises.*

7. *For God* is *the King of all the earth; sing ye
praises with understanding.*

The exhortation given to all people to praise Christ for
the work of redemption, is repeated, and directed to the
church of the Jews more particularly, with a fifth reason of
praise, taken from a nearer conjunction between Christ and
them, than between him and any other nation. Whence
learn, 1. Albeit the Lord showeth his glory in the works of
creation, and is shining daily in the works of providence
also; yet in the work of redemption, conversion, and salvation of souls, his glory is manifested far more; for here,
praise, praise, praise, and the fourth time *praise* is called
for. 2. When believers in Jesus Christ consider how he
abased himself to assume our nature, how he paid the ransom for us as surety, how he encountered and fought with
all our enemies, and, being victorious in our name, ascended
in our nature with the shout of victory and sound of the
trumpet of the triumpher, they cannot choose but see reasons
for praising joyfully the glorious Godhead of Jesus Christ,
and of singing praises to him as God again and again. 3.
Of all nations of the earth the Jews have the first place,
privilege, and prerogative, most bonds with and interests in
Jesus Christ; for he delivered them out of Egypt, settled
them in Canaan, held house among them in a tabernacle,
answered them by oracle out of the ark of the covenant, the
type of his incarnation, took upon him to be their king and
sanctifier, the Holy One of Israel, their Redeemer, took of
them his human nature, and was born a Jew, therefore had

the prophet good reason to say to the church of the Jews, *sing praises to our King, sing praises ;* and in this song may all they join with the Jews who have embraced Jesus for their king. 4. Christ is so king over the Jews, as he also extendeth his kingdom over all the earth, not only in regard of his power in a common manner, but in regard of his special grace gathering in subjects out of all parts of the world, till he have the full number brought in and saved; he, he only, is the true catholic king : *for God is the King of all the earth.* 5. As none can praise God, or praise Christ sincerely, who do not understand the reasons for which they should praise; so he that praiseth understandingly, cannot choose but praise affectionately, therefore, saith he, *sing ye praises with understanding.*

8. *God reigneth over the heathen : God sitteth upon the throne of his holiness.*

From the sixth reason of Christ's praise, taken from the keeping a church among the Gentiles for gathering the redeemed out of all tongues and languages, and reigning among them as king of saints, and author of holiness, learn, 1. To the end that faith may find footing and a rock to rest upon, we must, in all the promises, works, and praises of Christ, still remember that as he is now very man, so is he also eternally God, and that no man reasonably or with understanding can praise him as the redeemer and perfecter of what is spoken of him in Scripture, except he acknowledge him to be God; therefore is Christ eight times in this psalm called God, beside the ascribing unto him works proper to God only; and twice he is called by the incommunicable name of Jehovah the Lord; and in this verse Godhead is twice acknowledged in him, as King of the church among the Gentiles : *God reigneth over the heathen, God sitteth upon the throne of his holiness.* 2. Because the sum of Christ's kingdom is holiness, and his work is to teach, prescribe, and command holiness, to take away sin, and powerfully to apply and work in his own redeemed ones holiness, and to continue in his actual governing of his subjects, till he have made all and every one of the redeemed perfectly holy; therefore is his throne in a special manner called the throne of holiness : *God sitteth upon the throne of his holiness.*

9. *The princes of the people are gathered together,*

even *the people of the God of Abraham ; for the shields
of the earth* belong *unto God : he is greatly exalted.*

From the seventh reason of Christ's praise, taken from his
converting great men of the earth (as kings and princes),
and bringing them to the obedience of the faith and union
with the true church, learn, 1. Albeit ofttimes it is seen,
that not many rich, noble, or potent are called; yet God for
his own glory is, from time to time, bringing in some of
them, and when it may glorify his name, shall bring in and
perfect what is promised and prophesied here: *the princes of
the people are gathered together.* 2. It is a point of Christ's
praise in the conversion of men, that his omnipotency maketh
men voluntary subjects, and to come in to him as by invincible
power on his part, so also deliberately with a free election, and
hearty consent of will on the converted man's part : the
princes of the people and excellent ones in the earth, of whatsoever rank, converted unto Christ, are voluntary people; for
the original suffereth also this reading : *the voluntary of the
people are gathered together.* 3. The church of the Jews is
the mother church, whereof Abraham and the godly Jews,
yea, and Christ himself were members; the church of the Jews
is the olive-tree, whereinto all the converts of the Gentiles
are ingraffed, gathered, and made one people with Abraham
and the faithful among the Jews : *the princes of the people
are gathered together, the people of the God of Abraham.* 4.
The unity of the church standeth in the union of the Spirit,
under the service of the only true God and in conjunction
with his people; for the union of Jew and Gentile *is the
gathering together of the princes of the people to the God of
Abraham.* 5. As there is a necessity of the union of Jews and
Gentiles in one visible Christian church, because it is promised
and prophesied that it shall be so; so there is reason to wish
for the more evident union of them, that they may be as eminently consociate as ever the Christian churches were, either
in the Apostles' time, or in the Christian emperors' time, in
a general assembly or œcumenical council; because there is
at least a possibility of an œcumenical council, or a general
assembly of Jews and Gentiles in this world under Christ
their King. This place makes it plain, because after it is
foretold that there shall be such a union of all the people of
the God of Abraham, Jews and Gentiles, as *their princes
shall be gathered together,* he takes away the chief ground

of a great objection which may be made from the discord and
disagreement of the princes of the world; some of them being averse altogether from the Christian religion, some of
them from the true religion of Christ, and all of them almost
dissenting one from another, and warring one against another; whereby now for many years the gathering of an œcumenical council hath not been possible.   He meeteth this objection in the text, saying, *for the shields of the earth belong
unto God*, that is, the hearts and power of all the kings of the
earth are in the Lord's hand, and he hath the disposing of
shields, armies, and ammunition, with all their commanders
and rulers in the world, and therefore can make them serviceable for the nearest conjunction and union of his visible
church, which can be for his glory in this world, as he sees
fit, how and when he will.   6. When all is said of Christ's
praise that man can express of him, there is no possibility to
attain the full or satisfactory setting forth of his glory as it
deserveth; but men must content themselves to set sail, and
to rest in the general, that Christ is and shall be very highly
glorified; for so the psalmist closeth, saying after all, *he is
greatly exalted.*

PSALM XLVIII.

A song and psalm for the sons of Korah.

In this psalm the Lord is magnified for all his mercies bestowed on his
church, resembled by Jerusalem, v. 1—3. And in special for a late
mercy manifested in a passage of his care to preserve Jerusalem, a type
of the church universal, against the assault of mighty kings, ver. 4—6.
The uses of which mercies are set down, in number seven; the first, v. 7;
the second, v. 8 ; the third, v. 9 ; the fourth, v. 10; the fifth, v. 11;
the sixth, v. 12, 13; the seventh, v. 14.

1. *Great* is *the Lord, and greatly to be praised in
the city of our God,* in *the mountain of his holiness.*

2. *Beautiful for situation, the joy of the whole earth,*
is *mount Zion,* on *the sides of the north, the city of the
great King.*

3. *God is known in her palaces for a refuge.*

In the first place, he declareth his purpose to give God
the praise of whatsoever is commendable in Jerusalem, or
done unto it, or wrought for it.   Whence learn, 1. As God
shows his greatness and glory in all his works, and specially

in his care for, respect unto, and operation in his church;
so should he have glory and praise from his church, for and
from all his works, but specially for his care of her : *great
is the Lord, and greatly to be praised in the city of our God.*
2. As it is the benefit of Jerusalem, and of his church represented thereby, to be united and governed in a regular
incorporation; so it is a matter of God's praise that he
maketh his visible church above all other incorporations and
societies of men in the world to be his city, with which he
will be in covenant, and wherein he will manifest his holy
name; therefore Jerusalem, and the church represented by
her, is here called, *the city of our God, and the mountain of
his holiness.* 3. Whatsoever could commend Jerusalem for
situation in point of pleasantness, commodity, strength, or
stateliness; all is but a shadow of the glory of the Lord's
church, and in particular, as the joy of the whole land depended on Jerusalem's welfare, and this city did adorn all
Judea, and the great King's palace adorned her; so the
church is the joy of the whole earth, by holding out to all
the light of saving doctrine, and showing the authority,
power, wisdom, and grace of Christ; who is her great King,
and who beautifieth her, for the illumination of the blind,
dark world : *beautiful for situation, the joy of the whole
earth is mount Zion, on the sides of the north, the city of the
great King.* 4. As the walls, houses, and palaces of Jerusalem were not the strength of the citizens, but God was
her strength, as they had learned by experience; so worldly
strength is not the confidence of God's church, but God
only, who defendeth her by his power : *God is known in her
palaces for a refuge.*

4. *For, lo, the kings were assembled, they passed by
together.*

5. *They saw it, and so they marvelled ; they were
troubled, and hasted away.*

6. *Fear took hold upon them there, and pain, as of
a woman in travail.*

He confirmeth what he hath spoken, by a late experience
of deliverance from the invasion of mighty kings, gathered
to besiege and destroy Jerusalem. Whence learn, 1. The
Lord by experience, from time to time, maketh manifest his
care to defend his church against most mighty oppressors,

who use to combine themselves together, when they mind to overthrow the church : *for, lo, the kings were assembled.* 2. Many imaginations are in the heads of adversaries when they are plotting the ruin of God's church, which, when they are about to execute, vanish and prove presumptuous and vain apprehensions of their own ability, and of the church's weakness : *when the kings were assembled, they passed by together.* They found themselves unable to effect what they intended and hoped to bring to pass. 3. When the strait cometh, and the church is in danger, then the Lord showeth himself for her, and against her enemies, and makes men see his interest in his church; now, when the kings were assembled, they perceived themselves mistaken wonderfully : *they saw it, so they marvelled.* 4. Such as come to bring trouble to God's church, come to catch trouble to themselves : when kings assembled to trouble God's people, *they saw, and marvelled, and were troubled.* 5. If the enemies of the church could foresee their own foul retreat, they would not advance, or make assault against the church; for now when they saw matters as they were indeed, *they were troubled, and hasted away.* 6. Besides the mischief which God bringeth upon the church's enemies, when he begins to plead by way of judgment against them, he sendeth terror on them also, a messenger of the ill tidings to forewarn them that worse shall yet befall them : *fear took hold upon them there.* 7. Heart and hand, courage and strength, counsel and resolution fail a man, when he seeth God to be his party, and to be prevailing against him : *fear took hold on them, and pain as a woman in travail;* sudden, unexpected, sore, and inevitable, is their destruction when it cometh.

7. *Thou breakest the ships of Tarshish with an east wind.*

The first use they make of this experience is this, they are led up by it to see and acknowledge God's power in all the world, to take order with, and destroy whomsoever he will. Whence learn, 1. No power can stand before God, and none can escape his hand; go whither they will, he can arm some of his creatures against them, both by land and sea : *thou breakest the ships of Tarshish with an east wind.* 2. One work of the Lord's justice or power against his ene-

mies, and one experience of his merciful defending his
church, should lead his people to acknowledge his sovereign
power and omnipotence over all, whereby he, having all
creatures at his disposal, can secure his people from all
quarters, and destroy all that shall rise against them; for
this speech saith this in substance : thou, who hast scattered
the armies of kings who had invaded us, hast power in all
the world by sea and land to overtake thy enemies; for, *thou
breakest the ships of Tarshish with an east wind.*

8. *As we have heard, so have we seen in the city of
the Lord of hosts, in the city of our God : God will
establish it for ever. Selah.*

The second use is this : by this experience we perceive
that the Lord will keep his promise to his church, and preserve her for ever. Whence learn, 1. They that believe the
word of God, and mark his works foretold in the word, shall
see and find by experience the event thereof to answer to the
prediction; and, having their faith so confirmed, they should
say, *as we have heard, so have we seen in the city of the
Lord.* 2. The mercies of the Lord bestowed on his church
for her defence and continuance, flow from his covenanting
with his church; for the reason of the mercy now bestowed
is, *because the city of the Lord of hosts is the city of our God.*
3. Albeit all kingdoms and commonwealths be subject to
destruction, and have their certain limits and periods; yet
the church, the kingdom of Christ, the city of God, shall
endure throughout all generations, and the gates of hell
shall not prevail over it : *God shall establish it for ever.*

9. *We have thought of thy loving-kindness, O God,
in the midst of thy temple.*

A third use is the acknowledgment of the sweet fruit of
their former patient depending upon God's kindness in the
use of public ordinances, and now they perceive by this
late experience it was not vain. Whence learn, 1. They
that believe God's loving-kindness in the time when there
are apparent signs of his wrath, and patiently depend on
him in the use of holy ordinances, shall not be frustrate of
their expectation, as here the psalmist acknowledgeth. 2. As
it is a good thing patiently to wait on God's loving-kindness
in the use of the means, when troubles and dangers come;
so it is a good thing for the godly, after receiving the fruit

of their faith, hope, and patience, to observe the grace gotten of God, which made them to meditate upon and look unto his loving-kindness, and so to strengthen themselves in their resolutions to follow this blessed course hereafter, as the faithful do here : *we have thought of thy loving-kindness, O God, in the midst of thy temple.*

10. *According to thy name, O God, so* is *thy praise unto the ends of the earth : thy right hand is full of righteousness.*

A fourth use is their gladness because of the increase of God's glory by this his late mercy towards them, wherever it should be mentioned. Whence learn, 1. Whatsoever God giveth himself out for, that will he be found to be answerable unto in effect, even to all his holy and magnificent attributes: *according to thy name, O God, so is thy praise.* 2. The manifestation of God's name by preaching of his word cometh to many, who will not subscribe all to be true that is said of him; but afterward, when he maketh his word good, to the comfort of his people and overthrow of his enemies, men will be forced to say of him, that he is as good as his word, and that his works loose his word laid in pawn for performance of it: *according to thy name, O God, so is thy praise unto the ends of the earth.* 3. The Lord's power is not idle, but constantly working in equity and justice for performance of promises and threatenings, for defending his people, and punishing his enemies: *thy right hand is full of righteousness.*

11. *Let mount Zion rejoice, let the daughters of Judah be glad, because of thy judgments.*

A fourth use is to stir up all good people to rejoice, because God hath pleaded their cause against their enemies. Whence learn, 1. It becometh all men to be glad to see God glorify himself in deciding controversies equitably; but most of all the people of God, who have the present benefit thereof, and in whose favour controversies between them and their enemies are decided : *let mount Zion rejoice, and let the daughters of Judah be glad.* 2. Albeit it be lawful for God's people to rejoice when the enemies are punished; yet had they need to take heed to their spirit, that their joy be not fleshly, for satisfaction gotten to their vindictive passions; but spiritual, for the declaration of God's kindness to his people, and just indignation at the wickedness of their malicious persecutors: *let them be glad, because of thy judgments.*

12. *Walk about Zion, and go round about her : tell the towers thereof.*

13. *Mark ye well her bulwarks, consider her palaces ; that ye may tell* it *to the generation following.*

The sixth use of this late experience of the church's delivery, is to observe the impregnable defence of the church, shadowed forth by the walls of Jerusalem, for the encouraging of God's people in all ages, and cautioning all men to beware of attempting to do her wrong in time coming. Whence learn, 1. The church of God is so well guarded by God's wisdom, power, good-will, and justice, as with a wall of fire, that all the strength to be observed in the walls and towers of earthly Jerusalem are but shadows; for, *walk about Zion, and go round about her, and tell the towers thereof*, is no other thing than look through the type, and consider God's protection represented thereby. 2. When a type is to be studied, observation particularly may and should be made of whatsoever in it may lead us further in upon the right uptaking of the antitype resembled thereby: *walk about, go round about ; mark ye well her bulwarks, consider her palaces ;* for in God, or in God's attributes, something answerable to all these will be found. 3. What light the Lord furnisheth concerning himself and his church, which may glorify God, and serve posterity for their edification, should be transmitted to them : *mark ye well, that ye may tell it to the generation following.*

14. *For this God is our God for ever and ever : he will be our guide even unto death.*

The seventh and last use of this experience of the church, is consolation in God to God's people in every hard case, and encouragement to them against all future fears, because God is the same constantly to his people in all ages as the late experience of the church had given proof. Whence learn, 1. The great Maker of heaven and earth, and Redeemer of his people is one and the same for ever, both in himself and towards those that believe in him; *this God is our God.* 2. God is still in covenant with his church, and with all the members thereof, as well in one age as in another; now, as of old; for, *this God is our God for ever and ever.*   3. God will guide them whose God he is, when they seek his counsel out of desire to follow it, and he will not lay down the conducting and governing of those who have committed themselves unto him, but will guide them constantly all the days of their life; *he will be our guide, even unto death.*

PSALM XLIX.

To the chief musician.   A psalm for the sons of Korah.

This psalm sets forth the gloriation of a believer in the grace of God, and in his blessed condition, wherein he is lifted up above all the wealthy and honourable men in the world who are not reconciled unto God: and this the psalmist delivereth out of his own feeling and experience. And, first, because it is a main matter and worthy of all acceptation, he maketh a preface to his gloriation, v. 1—4.   Then he cometh out with it, making his boast in God, that by faith in God he was so secured against sin and misery that they should not be able to mar his happiness, v. 5.   Thirdly, he preferreth his blessedness above whatsoever wealth or riches could yield to man, v. 6—10, and above whatsoever dominion over fair lands, or honour among men could yield to any man, either living or after his death, either to himself or to any of his posterity, v. 11—14.   Fourthly, he giveth reason of his gloriation, because, being justified by faith, and at peace with God, he was sure of delivery from every evil, and to be received out of his grave into glory and fellowship with God, v. 15.   Fifthly, he guards every true believer against every temptation which might disquiet him, when he seeth himself and other godly persons in outward trouble, and the wicked in prosperity, v. 16—20.

1. *Hear this, all ye people ; give ear, all ye inhabitants of the world :*

2. *Both low and high, rich and poor, together.*

3. *My mouth shall speak of wisdom ; and the meditation of my heart shall be of understanding.*

4. *I will incline mine ear to a parable ; I will open my dark saying upon the harp.*

The preface calleth to the hearer for attention, faith, and affection to this excellent mystery which he is to deliver unto all men, concerning the blessedness of the believer above all other men in the world.   Whence learn, 1. A prepared and sanctified ear is necessary for heavenly doctrine, and people had great need to be stirred up to take knowledge of the excellency of it; *hear this, all ye people, give ear.*   2. The doctrine of salvation, of faith, and of consolation against sin and misery, concerneth all people in the world to know;

*give ear, all ye inhabitants of the world, both low and high,
rich and poor, together.* 3. That is true wisdom and understanding, which maketh men wise unto salvation, and
which maketh them truly blessed in this life; and this wisdom is not the birth of man's brain, but is revealed in the
word of the Lord, delivered to his church by the holy men
of God in holy scripture; *my mouth shall speak of wisdom,
and the meditation of my heart shall be of understanding.*
4. As it is necessary for the preacher's encouragement to
believe what he preacheth; so is it a great inducement to the
people to hear God's word from him who speaketh God's
word, because he believeth and subjecteth his spirit to the
Lord's word, as the prophet doth here; *I will incline my ears
to a parable.* 5. The doctrine of true blessedness, and the
mystery of man's salvation manifested in the Scripture, far
transcendeth the carnal wisdom of the world; the excellency
of the gospel unto the natural man, is a *parable and dark
saying: I will declare my dark saying on the harp.* 6.
How dark and difficult soever the mystery of the gospel be
to the carnal world; yet to the man of experience it is plain,
sweet, and comfortable; and a man of experience as he is
best seen in that matter, so is he most willing, heartily to
communicate it to others : *I will open,* saith he, *my dark
saying upon the harp;* intimating his delight in the doctrine.

5. *Wherefore should I fear in the days of evil,* when
the iniquity of my heels shall compass me about ?

After this preface he uttereth his parable and dark saying,
the substance whereof is this : I am so persuaded of the favour of God now reconciled to me by the blood of the covenant, that neither do I need to fear by-past sins, nor any
trouble which can come on me hereafter : and this I say, to
let all men know that this blessedness may be attained by
every man, who shall acknowledge his sins and embrace the
offers of grace made by God with his directions unto life, as
I have done. Whence learn, 1. What God has spoken in
his word of the blessedness of the man that is justified by
faith, every true believer may find, and may attain to be
fully assured of his perseverance unto eternal life; for here
is a proof and example of it in the psalmist's person. 2. This
doctrine of the unspeakable peace of the believer reconciled
to God through the blood of the covenant, is a point of truth

which the world is ignorant of, and hardly will believe: no wonder therefore he before called it, and here uttereth it, as *a parable and dark saying.* 3. A believer after reconciliation, must neither exempt himself from danger of sinning, nor from giving daily account of his carriage unto God, not from challenges for sin, nor from ordinary chastisements for sin, nor from heavy troubles and ill days which he may meet with; whether by God's immediate hand for his correction, or by the persecutors of godliness for his further trial, exercise, and training of faith; for here the psalmist presupposes that evil days will come: he presupposeth that every sin or iniquity of every action and passage of his life, shall leave behind it an impression of guiltiness to be taken notice of thereafter, like the print of a man's foot when he lifts his heel and walketh forward; he presupposeth after remission of sin, after the daily exercise of repentance, after frequent intimation made of remission of sin, and that oftener from day to day repeated, a man may be brought back in the day of trouble to an account for altogether, and old reckonings may be raked up again by the troubled conscience, and by the accuser of the brethren, and that God will be ruling the business for the further glory of the riches of his grace, and the further good of his exercised child; for here the psalmist foreseeth, and speaketh of his looking for days of evil, and of the iniquity of his heels compassing him about, as what shall or may befall him. 4. Faith in the Messiah Jesus Christ, is able to make a man, not only at length triumph over sin and misery, over the curse of the law, and condemnation, or trouble and persecution, but also before trouble come in humble and solid confidence to be fearless for what can come, and to look all possible evils out of countenance; *wherefore should I fear in the days of evil, &c.* 5. Albeit it be possible when it cometh to push of pike, and when the man is yoked in the conflict with troubles from without, and challenges for his sins within, that the strongest in faith may find himself not a little afraid; yet when he considereth the ground laid down for settling his faith, to wit, the truth of the covenant, the merit of the Mediator's sacrifice, and the freedom, riches, and immutability of God's love and grace, with the psalmist he may confidently profess and acknowledge, that he has no reason to be feared for what Satan or conscience may threaten him with;

for this also is imported in *wherefore should I fear in the days of evil, when the iniquity of my heels shall compass me about?* which is as much as if he had said, Whatsoever may be my weakness, and exercise in trial; yet I know there is no just reason why I should fear condemnation, or be debarred from the possession of full blessedness, by whatsoever possibly can come unto me.

6. *They that trust in their wealth, and boast themselves in the multitude of their riches ;*

7. *None* of them *can by any means redeem his brother, nor give to God a ransom for him :*

8. *(For the redemption of their soul is precious, and it ceaseth for ever ;)*

9. *That he should still live for ever, and not see corruption.*

10. *For he seeth* that *wise men die, likewise the fool and the brutish person perish, and leave their wealth to others.*

In the third place, the believer preferreth this his blessed condition to whatsoever either riches or honour or any earthly thing can yield to any man. Whence learn, 1. The blessedness of the believer and the glory of faith are best seen, when the vanity of all earthly happiness and worldly gloriation in any thing beside God is discovered and compared with the condition of the believer, therefore are *they that trust in their wealth* brought in comparison with the believer here. 2. In whatsoever men count their felicity to stand, in that they put their confidence, and do glory in it, as here is presupposed : they that count riches their happiness *trust in their wealth, and boast themselves in the multitude of their riches.* 3. The weakness of all worldly things to make a man blessed best appears when death cometh; for when the time thereof is come, no rich man can help himself, nor yet, joining his with his brother's riches, can help his brother, either by lengthening his life and suspending death temporal, or by recovering him from death when he dies : *none can by any means redeem his brother.* 4. All men are God's prisoners of war, his captives, and liable by justice to death temporal and eternal ; and there is no delivery from death, whether temporal or eternal, but by paying a ransom unto God, which is impossible for a mere man to pay :

none can give to God a ransom for his brother. 5. We are not redeemed with silver or gold, or any perishing thing; our ransom must be of greater value than a mere man can pay, that is a man, and no more : *the redemption of a man's soul is precious,* and it ceaseth for ever. 6. Not so much as this worldly life can be perpetuated, by whatsoever wealth, or riches, or human ability can do; far less can the life of God, and that blessedness in heaven be purchased by any mere man : *none can redeem his brother, that he should still live for ever and not see corruption.*

11. *Their inward thought* is, that *their houses* shall continue *for ever,* and *their dwelling-places to all gene- rations : they call* their *lands after their own names.*

12. *Nevertheless, man* being *in honour abideth not : he is like the beasts* that *perish.*

13. *This their way is their folly ; yet their posterity approve their sayings. Selah.*

14. *Like sheep they are laid in the grave ; death shall feed on them ; and the upright shall have dominion over them in the morning ; and their beauty shall con- sume in the grave from their dwelling.*

He compareth the gloriation of the believer with the con- dition of those who are not only rich, but also honourable, and lords of great rents, fair lands, houses and heritages ; and he preferreth the blessedness of the believer to their con- dition also. Whence learn, 1. Albeit experience teaches that death is common to men of all ranks, wise and foolish, rich and poor; yet men are so besotted, as when they see this, they do not consider that they should not place their happi- ness in any thing, wherefrom they may be separated by death : *the worldly man seeth the wise man die, and also the foolish.* He sees also that many rich men leave their goods, they know not to whom : *they leave their wealth to others :* and yet for all this their seeing the mortality and the folly of mortal men dying before them, they that survive a little do not draw wisdom from this observation, but dream they shall deceive death, and make themselves some way eternal; they think to perpetuate their name in their posterity by their heritages, and the honours of their great families : *their inward thought is, that their houses shall continue for ever, and their dwell- ing-places to all generations. They call their lands after their own names.* 2. The cause of this folly are his deceived heart, and vain conceits and imaginations, which by death are blown away : *their inward thought is to eternize themselves. Nevertheless, man being in honour abideth not,* or attains not his fancied eternity. 3. The blessedness of the wealthy, potent, and honourable man, as it is not permanent; so it leaves him in the dirt at length, and in no better case (if he hath no faith or saving knowledge) than a beast ! *nevertheless, man being in honour abideth not, he is like the beasts that perish.* 4. Though the men who are most able to purchase lands, and to transmit them to their posterity, are counted ordinarily the most wise men; yet when men spend their wit and care mainly about things of this present earth, the Lord pronounceth them to be fools : *their way is their folly.* 5. Though the observation of the folly of predecessors should make the posterity wise; yet few are found father-better, or father-wiser; but fools follow fools in a race, and folly will not want a patron so long as fools are gone before : *this their way is their folly, yet their posterity approve their sayings.* 6. A worldly man not reconciled to God, dieth as a foolish, sensual, and secure beast as he lived : *like sheep they are laid in the grave,* for they are death's prey, both soul and body : *death shall feed on them.* 7. The righteous man justified by faith, and studying to live righteously, albeit you look on him in the worst estate he can be in in the world, under poverty and persecution; yet he is in better condition than the richest and most honourable ungodly man in all the earth; and albeit this doth not appear in this dark world, to blind men that have not the light of God's word in them; yet at the resurrection it shall be seen, that the poor and mean just man shall be in a glorious condition above the worldling : *the upright shall have dominion over them in the morning.* 8. The whole glory of the worldly-minded man is shortly consumed so soon as he dieth, and then he changeth his lodging for the worse, the best days that ever he shall see are gone : *their beauty shall consume in their grave from their dwelling.*

15. *But God will redeem my soul from the power of the grave ; for he shall receive me. Selah.*

In the fourth place, he perfects the comparison, and gives a reason of his gloriation, whereof we heard, v. 5, the sum whereof is this : wealth and riches, nobility, honour and dominion among men can follow an ungodly man no farther than the grave, there all welfare doth forsake him for evermore: but as for me who am reconciled to God, justified, and in some measure sanctified, though I die, yet do I live in my soul, being kept by God till the day of complete redemption; and then my soul, being deprived only for a while of the body, shall have it restored again in the resurrection, and then soul and body both shall be fully redeemed and delivered from the power of the grave: for, as God hath received me into favour in this life, and shall receive my soul at death; so, at the time of the delivering of my body from the grave, he shall receive me, both soul and body, into his fellowship, and therefore my condition is better, how many days of evil soever I shall see in this life, than the condition of an ungodly man in the world, how wealthy, how honourable and apparently happy soever he be in this world; yea, I may justly glory over all ungodly men, and say yet again, *wherefore should I fear in the days of evil, when the iniquity of my heels shall compass me about; for God will redeem my soul from the power of the grave?* Whence learn, 1. Albeit the godly may be subject to mortality and the outward misery of this mortal life, common to him and the ungodly, yet here is the difference, he is sure of a deliverance from all misery; *but God shall redeem my soul*, saith he; which God will not do to the ungodly. 2. Hope of the resurrection is the godly man's chief consolation, and this was the hope of the saints before Christ came, as well as since: *God shall redeem my soul from the power of the grave.* 3. A believer hath good warrant to be persuaded, not only of his reconciliation with God in this life, but also of the receiving of his soul after this life into the fellowship of the glory of God, both in soul and body, at the resurrection: *God shall redeem my soul from the power of the grave; for he shall receive me. Selah.*

16. *Be not thou afraid when one is made rich, when the glory of his house is increased;*

17. *For when he dieth he shall carry nothing away; his glory shall not descend after him:*

18. *Though while he lived he blessed his soul; and men will praise thee, when thou doest well to thyself.*

L

19. *He shall go to the generation of his fathers ; they shall never see light.*

20. *Man that is in honour, and understandeth not, is like the beasts that perish.*

In the last part, by way of exhortation to make use of this doctrine, he guardeth every believer against every temptation which may arise from the prosperity of the wicked, and the hardship of the godly in this life. Whence learn, 1. It is a temptation which shaketh the faith of the godly sometimes, when they see the flourishing prosperity of the wicked, and their own daily affliction; but this should not move the godly, nor make them suspect themselves to be in a wrong course, and the ungodly in a better way : *be not thou afraid when one is made rich.* 2. The consideration of the shortness both of our temporal calamity and of the ungodly man's prosperity, both which end at death, is the way to evercome the foresaid temptation; for, *when he dieth, he shall carry nothing away, his glory shall not descend after him.* It is not so with the godly, whose glory and happiness meet him at death. 3. A man's own self-deceiving heart, measuring all happiness by a man's present outward condition in the world, and hearkening to the flattery of fools about him, who use to curry the favour of the wealthy, and love to have the like condition themselves, is the cause why the miserable man is kept still in a golden dream, as if he were happy : *though while he lived he blessed his soul ; and men will praise thee when thou dost well to thyself;* that is, when thou takest a life of it while thou mayest have it; yet he and they are altogether deceived. 4. The ungodly at their death shall go the way the ungodly went before them, to the place of darkness and disconsolation, being separate from God and his saints, and from all blessedness, and shall never have comfort in their miserable estate for ever: *he shall go to the generation of his fathers :* and what shall become of such wretches? *they shall never see light ;* that is, they shall never see the meanest appearance of any joy or comfort. 5. It is not honour, but want of understanding, want of saving faith and wisdom to provide for eternal life, that puts man down from his excellence, and debarreth him from blessedness : *man that is in honour, and understandeth not,* is the man here set at nought, and declared to be far from true blessedness. 6. Whatsoever natural excellence be in man above the beasts; yet sin hath put him so far down, that, except he get saving knowledge of God, and be reconciled to him, he is in no better condition, at least when he dieth, than a beast: *man that is in honour, and understandeth not, is like the beast that perisheth.*

PSALM L.

A psalm of Asaph.

This psalm is a citing of the visible church before God, the Judge of all the earth, (who at last shall judge all flesh in the day of judgment, and take vengeance on the wicked,) to compear before the tribunal of God, now in time while mercy may be had, timously to consider the Lord's controversy against the sinners in his church, that they may repent and be saved. And, first, the dreadfulness of the judgment is set down, v. 1—3. Secondly, the citation of the party, that is, the visible church, with the witnesses, v. 4—6. Thirdly, there is a challenge of self-work-justiciaries, legalists, and formal ceremonialists, who rested upon outward good behaviour, and upon the outward discharge of the ordinances, as if the sacrifices of the law, or any performance of external duties, had been sufficient to expiate sin, and justify a man, v. 7—13. Fourthly, there is a direction unto them how to come off their legal righteousness and carnal way of worship, and to turn themselves to the right way of worshipping God in spirit and truth, v. 14, 15. Fifthly, there is a challenge of those who were grossly wicked, v. 16—21. And lastly, there is a direction also to them to repent, and to give God glory in time, with an encouragement to the upright believers to go on their way, v. 22, 23.

1. *The mighty God, even the Lord, hath spoken, and called the earth, from the rising of the sun unto the going down thereof.*

2. *Out of Zion, the perfection of beauty, God hath shined.*

3. *Our God shall come, and shall not keep silence : a fire shall devour before him, and it shall be very tempestuous round about him.*

From the description of the terror of the Lord coming to judge his visible church, for the slighting of the means of salvation, and looseness of life and conversation, learn, 1. As the Lord is to judge the whole world one day, so in a special and most exact manner will he judge those that draw near to him in the profession of true religion, as this whole psalm holdeth forth. 2. This advantage have they who live in the visible church, they are warned of the judgment ere it come; for, as many other places of Scripture, so this

psalm is an express warning piece to the church to prepare
for judgment.   3. The terrible process of the day of God's
severe judgment being well meditated upon, is a special
means to waken men's consciences to take course about
their sins in time, that they may be pardoned, and their
ersons reconciled, which is the scope of the whole doctrine
delivered in this psalm.   4. The mystery of the great and
terrible day of general judgment is to be learned from the
Scriptures, and express predictions thereof in God's word,
the authority, weight, certainty, and efficacy whereof flows
from, and depends upon God Almighty only : *the mighty
God*, even *the Lord hath spoken.*   5. God Almighty, the
sovereign Judge of all the earth, hath appointed that all
who ever took life, in whatsoever time or place they have
lived in the world, shall compear before his majesty in the
appointed time : *the Lord hath spoken, and called the earth,
from the rising of the sun unto the going down thereof.*   6.
The true visible church, where God's ordinances are set up
as he hath appointed, where his word is purely preached, is
the most beautiful thing under heaven, and there is God's
glory set forth and manifested more clearly than in all the
Lord's handiwork beside in heaven or earth; therefore is the
place of the Lord's temple here so highly commended, and
Zion called the perfection of beauty, because of the glory of
God sundry ways revealed there: *out of Zion God hath
shined*, saith he, in regard to the clear manifestation of his
will, specially in the matter now in hand about the day of
judgment.   7. Men will take no heed unto what the word
of the Lord declareth, till the authority, supremacy, omnipotency, and justice of God the Judge be apprehended by
them, and the great day of his terrible judgment be looked
upon as a thing which shall most certainly come to pass at
the time appointed; therefore is it said, *our God shall come,
and shall not keep silence.*   8. So many as are reconciled
with God, and have closed uprightly with him in the covenant of grace, may look upon the day of judgment without
terror or perplexity; yea, and with comfort and confident hope
to find the Judge gracious to them, according to the tenor of
the covenant, even their God : *our God*, saith the prophet,
shall come.   9. Look how fearful and terrible the Lord
showed himself at the giving out of the law, no less terrible
shall he be in the execution thereof, in the day of judging

all those whose sins shall be found not pardoned before: *a fire shall devour before him, and it shall be very tempestuous about him.*

4. *He shall call to the heavens from above, and to the earth, that he may judge his people.*

5. *Gather my saints together unto me; those that have made a covenant with me by sacrifice.*

6. *And the heavens shall declare his righteousness: for God* is *judge himself. Selah.*

In the second place, he sets down the citation, and summoning of officers, parties, and witnesses, to make all ready for the judging of all the world, but in special of the people who have given up their name to God and have made a covenant with him, and professed themselves to be his people; all of them shall find at last, that they have had to do with a righteous judge. Whence learn, 1. In the great day of the last judgment, heaven and earth, and all the elements shall be moved to render up all they have received in custody unto that day; *the Lord shall call to the heavens from above, and to the earth.* 2. We need not question how all the dead shall be raised, how souls shall be reunited to their bodies, how they shall all be gathered together, and how such great things shall come to pass; one word resolves all; *he shall call to the heavens and to the earth.* For as at a word all were made: so at a word when he shall call and give out the order for compearance, the dead shall be raised, and all shall compear; good angels and wicked spirits, all men, good and evil, young and old, every reasonable and understanding creature in heaven and earth, by his almighty power, shall be made quickly to present themselves; *he shall call,* is sufficient to effect whatsoever he will. 3. What will be the course the Judge shall follow regarding those who have not heard of him, or who have heard of him and lived without the church, is not the main matter which the Lord's people should inquire about; but this is their part to know, to wit, what concerneth themselves; therefore doth the Lord say no more here, but, *he shall call to the heavens and to the earth, that he may judge his people.* 4. All who are in covenant with God, every member of the visible church are saints by calling; God alloweth this stile upon them because they are dedicated and consecrated to him, since they are all by special vow obliged to be saints; all make profession of their purpose to be such; all claim for themselves, and will have allowed unto them by others, the estimation of God's people, what-soever be their deserving; therefore, saith he, *gather my saints together unto me.* 5. At how great a distance so-ever, whether of time or place, God's people by profession have lived in this world, all of them shall be assembled at length to the judgment of that great day; some to the judgment of absolution, some to the judgment of condem-nation, good and bad, all shall be gathered before the Judge at once; *gather my saints together unto me.* 6. The Lord shall not want officers, sergeants, and servants sufficient for this work; he hath angels innumerable, who shall effect what he giveth order unto them for; *gather ye my saints together.* 7. The external covenant with God, is the ground of the title and honour of saintship, and church membership; whosoever are in visible covenant with God, are called, by his allowance, *his saints*; for so here he ex-poundeth whom he calleth *his saints*, even all those *who have made a covenant with him by sacrifice.* 8. No cove-nant can be made with God without the interposing of, or professed respect unto a sacrifice, according as the Lord did teach his people in the type and shadow of the ceremon-ial sacrificing; for, as God by appointing a sacrifice to be offered by his people would have every covenanter to ac-knowledge and profess that he was worthy to die for his sins, and that it behoved him to fly to a surety to die for him, (even to the promised Messiah Jesus Christ, that Lamb of God which was slain from the beginning of the world, to take away the sins of the world;) and to consecrate himself wholly to God's service; so the Lord requireth still the same things of every covenanter, from every one of his peo-ple; and whosoever profess their accepting of the condi-tions of the covenant, are called those that have made *a covenant with God by sacrifice.* 9. In that general judg-ment, the wise framing of the world, the constant course of governing it, the appointing of the seasons of summer and winter, spring and harvest, the making of the sun to shine and the rain to fall upon all, and the furnishing all with food and good things, shall be witnesses for God's part to-ward all men, and so *the heavens shall declare his right-*

cousness. 10. No man shall be injured or suffer wrongfully that day; yea, all men shall have wrongs done to them repaired, all rewards shall be given according as the word of the Lord hath said; *for God is judge himself. Selah.*

7. *Hear, O my people, and I will speak ; O Israel, and I will testify against thee : I* am *God,* even *thy God.*

Having now foretold his people, that there shall be certainly a great day of judging all men, and specially his covenanted people; he entereth here into a friendly manner of controversy with his visible church or professed people, that they might repent and find mercy in time, before they were brought to a tribunal of severe justice. And first, he useth a preface, directing his speech to such as were of a better outward behaviour than the worst, to wit, such as trusted in their own works, and specially in the external sacrifices and ceremonies of the law, without looking to the end and intent thereof; as if by those external sacrifices their sins had been expiated, and God fully satisfied for them. Whence learn, 1. A people settled upon the dregs of their carnal customs, in security and presumption, cannot be moved to enter into consideration of their ways, or into suspicion of their dangerous condition, except the Lord show himself to them, and rip up their conscience; therefore saith he to them, *hear, O my people, and I will speak.* 2. Albeit the Lord suffereth such as are without the church, strangers to the covenant and commonwealth of Israel, to lie still in their sins; yet will he debate his quarrel against his own people, which is no small mercy : *O Israel, I will testify against thee.* 3. The covenant made with God, joined with his absolute sovereignty, lays double bonds upon God's people for the obedience of faith, obliging them not to seek salvation otherwise than he teacheth us, but to worship and serve him as he appointeth; for, *I am God, even thy God,* saith the Lord. 4. Whatsoever quarrel the Lord has against his people for not keeping covenant made with him; yet so long as there is hope of repentance, he will not dissolve the covenant, but will offer the benefit thereof unto them; for when the Lord hath said, *I will testify against thee,* he addeth, *I am God, even thy God,* v. 11.

8. *I will not reprove thee for thy sacrifices, or thy burnt-offerings,* to have been *continually before me.*

9. *I will take no bullock out of thy house*, nor *he-goats out of thy folds:*

10. *For every beast of the forest is mine*, and *the cattle upon a thousand hills.*

11. *I know all the fowls of the mountains; and the wild beasts of the field* are *mine.*

12. *If I were hungry, I would not tell thee: for the world* is *mine, and the fulness thereof.*

13. *Will I eat the flesh of bulls, or drink the blood of goats?*

After the preface, the Lord passeth by the reproof for much neglect, even in the external performances of outward ordinances, and challengeth only their relying upon the outward work, and their putting a sort of merit upon their work, as if they minded to render God obliged to them by their outward performances. Whence learn, 1. Albeit there be just reason to challenge men for coming short of their duty in the discharge of outward ordinances; yet when that is not the main fault, or when the mending of that fault will not satisfy God, he will waive that challenge for the present, and fasten upon their chief sins: *I will not reprove thee for thy sacrifices, or thy burnt-offerings which should have been continually before me.* 2. As men are ordinarily little sensible of their omissions of duties, so are they ready to overvalue their outward performances, and to think that what they do in this kind shall be very acceptable to God, as the carnal Israelites, here challenged, conceived their bullocks *and goats out of their houses or folds* should have been esteemed by God, as of as much worth as they who offered them put upon them. 3. That which is most esteemed by men, without allowance of God, is abomination to God: such were the external sacrifices of carnal Israelites, who rested upon the offering of external sacrifices, without looking to that only true sacrifice of the Mediator represented thereby: *I will take no bullock out of thy house, nor he-goat out of thy fold.* 4. It is a disease of foolish man to think with himself that God is obliged to him when he offereth unto God any part of his goods, although in the mean time a man hath nothing but what God hath given him, and which is the Lord's by primitive right: *every beast of the forest is mine, and the cattle upon a thousand hills.* 5. Albeit all men pro-

fess that they acknowledge God to be owner of all the creatures, because he hath made them all; yet their practice
many ways bewrayeth their heart-ignorance on this point,
and that they have need to be taught this lesson from God :
*I know all the fowls of the mountains, and the wild beasts of
the field are mine.* 6. Unrenewed men cannot choose but
have gross conceptions of God, and to think of him after
their own fancy, as the carnal Israelites conceived that a fat
sacrifice was as acceptable to God as a fat dinner was to
themselves; but God is not like man, and standeth in no
need of supply from man or from any of his creatures; all
of them have their being and dependence on God, to dispose
of them, and bestow them on whom he will, at his pleasure :
he is not hungry ; and put the case he had a mind to serve
himself of any of the creatures, yet he needs not employ man
for that effect; for, *the earth is the Lord's and the fulness
thereof.* 7. The Lord disdaineth the fleshly conceits which
men have, to satisfy his justice for their sins by any thing
that man can offer unto him, as imaginations unbeseeming
a reasonable man : *will I eat the flesh of bulls, or drink the
blood of goats ?*

14. *Offer unto God thanksgiving ; and pay thy vows
unto the most High :*

15. *And call upon me in the day of trouble; I will
deliver thee, and thou shalt glorify me.*

In the third place, he exhorteth them to forsake this carnal way of seeking salvation, and setteth them upon the right
course of true blessedness and spiritual service.　Whence
learn, 1. The way of salvation and of God's worship is spiritual, and may possibly be resembled and furthered by external bodily exercises, but does not stand on things external;
and to speak it more particularly, God will have the man
whose person and service he will accept, to be sensible of
his own want of every good thing, and inability to furnish
to himself any thing which he lacketh, to acknowledge God
only to be the all-sufficient fountain of grace and of every
good donation, to seek what he hath need of from God, to
depend upon his grace when he hath sought it, and to return the praise of God's free and gracious gift unto him
when he hath received it; for all this is presupposed and
imported in this offering of thanks : *offer unto God thanksgiving;* to wit, for every point and passage of his undeserved

favour: and this he calleth for, because this offering of the sacrifice of praise and thanks was more acceptable to God than their ceremonial sacrifices of slain beasts. 2. God will have the man whose person and service he will accept, to make conscience of all his lawful vows made unto God, in special of his covenant vow, made for giving God the obedience of faith all the days of his life, which vow true worshippers are wont upon sundry occasions solemnly to renew: *offer unto God thanksgiving, and pay thy vows unto the most high God.* 3. Were a man ever so faithful and upright in the Lord's service, yet he is not exempted from trouble, for reasons concerning God's glory, good of the person troubled, and benefit of others; this the Lord holdeth forth in preparing their minds, by making mention unto believers *of a day of trouble.* 4. Among other ends of the Lord's sending trouble, this is one; to cause the believer, in the sense of his need, to make use of his covenant with God, and by faith to draw near to him in prayer for help and relief in due time: *call upon me in the day of thy trouble.* 5. The true believer and depender upon the sure and rich grace of God, cannot possibly fall into any trouble out of which he shall not be delivered, but, whatsoever evil come, he may, by praying to God, yea, he shall be delivered: *call upon me in the day of trouble, I will deliver thee.* What more absolute promise can be made to a believing supplicant? 6. A believing supplicant shall not only be graciously answered, and so have cause of praising God, but shall also have grace in effect to praise God: *and thou shalt glorify me.*

16. *But unto the wicked God saith, What hast thou to do to declare my statutes, or that thou shouldest take my covenant in thy mouth?*

17. *Seeing thou hatest instruction, and castest my words behind thee.*

18. *When thou sawest a thief, then thou consentedst with him, and hast been partaker with adulterers.*

19. *Thou givest thy mouth to evil, and thy tongue frameth deceit.*

20. *Thou sittest* and *speakest against thy brother ; thou slanderest thine own mother's son.*

21. *These* things *hast thou done, and I kept silence ; thou thoughtest that I was altogether* such an one *as*

thyself: but I will reprove thee, and set them *in order before thine eyes.*

In the fourth place, the Lord mercifully remonstrateth with the gross sinner and scandalous liver, for abusing this privilege of the covenant by his lewd conversation and secure atheism, that he, being convinced of his sin, might repent, and eschew the wrath which is to come. Whence learn, 1. To such as profess religion, and observe the outward ordinances thereof, and do not live scandalously, the Lord, howsoever he lets them know he is not well pleased with their way, yet speaketh unto them more mildly, because it is possible some beloved Laodiceans, young and unskilful true converts, may be guilty of no small measure of dead formality; but to such as live in gross scandalous sins, the Lord speaketh more roughly, calling them by the name of *wicked : but unto the wicked God saith.* 2. Such is the deceivableness of sin, and the deceit of the heart, and the power of Satan upon secure sinners, that they can without remorse of conscience profess the true religion, pretend to a covenant with God, and yet live loosely as pagans or atheists : *they take God's covenant in their mouth,* and meantime *hate instruction, and cast God's words behind them.* 3. Such as by their lewd conversation give an open affront to their religion, are so detestable to God, that he accounteth them wicked haters of reformation, contemners of Scripture, disgracers of their holy profession, and such as he will take no religious service from : *unto the wicked God saith, what hast thou to do to declare my statutes, or that thou shouldest take my covenant in thy mouth, seeing thou hatest instruction, and castest my words behind thee?* 4. Albeit men profane the covenant, and deserve to be thrust out of it as unworthy to have the benefit of it, or to be suffered any more to profess it; yet God will not give them up hastily, but will, after a friendly manner, declare to them their sin and misdeserving, that their conscience may be moved towards repentance : *what hast thou to do to take my covenant in thy mouth, seeing thou hatest instruction ?* 5. The man who casteth God's word behind him, cannot choose but serve a worse master, and be made slave to his lusts, and be led away to every sin, as temptation leadeth him; he will not stand to be a greedy thief and a filthy adulterer, v. 18, and to loose his tongue to all the evils whereunto the tongue can serve, v. 19, yea and to become unnatural to those to whom

he is bound in nearest bonds of blood, v. 20. 6. Such is the
Lord's patience, that he doth ofttimes endure very long horrible provocations of those that are in outward covenant with
him, so that by his long-suffering he may lead them to repentance : *these things thou didst, and I kept silence.* 7.
When men profit not by the means which should lead them
to repentance, they grow worse for the means, more secure
and hardened in their ill ways, and more godless in all respects : *thou thoughtest I was altogether such a one as thyself.*
8. Such as live a loose life with a profession of religion under the shining light of God's word, keep not their consciences quiet, otherwise than by transforming God into an
idol after their own fancy, and by feigning him to be what he
is not, and not to be what he declareth himself to be : *thou
thoughtest that I was altogether such a one as thyself ;*
that is to say, *no more displeased with thy ways than thou
thyself wast.* 9. Although the Lord keep silence for a time,
yet he will at length let the sinner know by his word and rods,
how displeased he is at sin ; *but I will reprove thee,* saith the
Lord. 10. Sins forgotten, cast behind back, and cast together in confusion by the secure sinner, shall, in the day of
God's reckoning, be brought to remembrance with time, place,
and other circumstances, and so presented to the consci nce,
as the sinner shall not be able to look aside from his fearful
accusation and ditty : *I will set them in order before thine
eyes.*

22. *Now consider this, ye that forget God, lest I tear*
you *in pieces, and* there be *none to deliver.*

23. *Whoso offereth praise glorifieth me : and to him
that ordereth* his *conversation* aright *will I shew the salvation of God.*

In the last place, the Lord being loath to dissolve the covenant, or to destroy those that are in the visible church, how
wicked soever, exhorteth them to repentance while it is time,
before he cast them off utterly, and so showeth them the way
of returning home to him, as he also encourageth such as are
sincere worshippers of him to go on. Whence learn, 1. The
Lord's controversy with his people and threatening of wrath
upon them, carry much love and mercy in their bosom ; it
is admirable that such offers of grace and reconciliation are
made by God after so just and fearful challenges, as here we

read.　2. As the affectionate remembrance of God is an
awband to keep from sin, and a spur to all duties; and as
consideration of God's word is a means to waken the conscience and affect the heart with high and right thoughts of
God : so the forgetting of God, and consideration of what is
necessary, casts a man open to all sin, and makes way for his
destruction : *consider this, ye that forget God, lest I tear you
in pieces.*　3. If they who have gone far away from God,
haste not home unto him, they are likely to meet with merciless judgment, and to find no opportunity or time granted
as they could wish to repent : *consider, lest I tear you in
pieces, and there be none to deliver you.*　4. To set men on
work to promote the honour of God by worshipping him in
spirit, and to conform the outward actions of the body to the
rule of God's word, is the scope of all God's pleading with
his own people; for his controversy is closed with a direction
to all, *to glorify God, and to order their conversation aright.*
5. That man worshippeth God in spirit, who giveth him the
praise of his justice, in acknowledging his sins against God's
law and his ill deservings in the course of daily renewed repentance; and who giveth unto God the praise of his grace
and mercy, in flying to the refuge set before him in the gospel, in the course of daily renewed acts of faith in Christ; and
who giveth God the praise of his holiness, in studying daily
to mortify the lusts of the flesh by his Spirit, and to be renewed in his mind and affections; and in a word, who, in his
heart and affections studieth to give God the honour of all
his attributes, titles, or name, by whatsoever occasion manifested to him.　This is the worshipper of God in spirit and
truth, whom the Lord by all his dealing with his people is
seeking to form and gain to himself : *whoso offereth praise,
glorifieth me.*　6. Sincere endeavour to worship God in spirit,
is best seen in a man's care to conform his life and bodily actions to the rule of God's word; for with *glorifying God* he
joineth-here, *ordering his conversation aright.*　7. Whosoever shall set himself to be God's servant in spirit and truth,
shall find God to be his Saviour to the uttermost, how godless soever, how vile soever he hath been.　If he shall prepare himself against the dreadful day of judgment, by receiving the offer of grace in Jesus Christ, with all the fulness
of the salvation of God in him, and in Christ's strength shall
study to bring forth the fruits of his faith in a blameless con-

versation, he shall undoubtedly be saved : for God hath said, *whoso offereth the sacrifice of praise, glorifies me, and to him who ordereth his conversation aright, will I shew the salvation of God.* Amen, Amen.

PSALM LI.

To the chief musician. A psalm of David, when Nathan the prophet came unto him, after he had gone in to Bathsheba.

The psalmist, in the sad sense of his guiltiness, prayeth for remission of sin, with an eye to the Lord's large mercy, v. 1, 2, and followeth his petition with a deep and hearty confession of his sinfulness, v. 3—6. He prayeth the second time for remission of sin, with an eye toward the blood of the Messiah, v. 7, and followeth it with another petition for comfort to his afflicted spirit, v. 8. He prayeth for remission of sins the third time, v. 9, and followeth it with another petition for renewed comfort of the Holy Spirit, and for removal of felt wrath, with a promise of making use thereof, to the edification of God's people, v. 10—13. He prayeth for remission of sin the fourth time, namely of that particular sin wherewith for the present his conscience was most troubled, v. 14 ; and he followeth it with another petition to fit him for a more spiritual and sincere manner of serving God hereafter, renouncing all confidence in the external ceremonies of the law, v. 15—17. And last of all, he prayeth for mercy to the church, v. 18, 19.

From the inscription, learn, 1. How soon the most mortified lust may be kindled, and break forth like fire in the embers when it meeteth with powder; how frail the strongest of the saints are in themselves, when they are tempted to sin; and what need he who standeth hath to take heed lest he fall; for the holy prophet, the sweet singer of Israel, is here foully defiled by *his going in to Bathsheba.* 2. How fast asleep in sin even the most watchful watchman may fall, and that he cannot at all awake of himself, till God of his grace (who in love pursueth fugitives) by some means of his own choosing, stir up his conscience, as here is evidenced in the case of the psalmist, who lay still secure in his sin till Nathan the prophet came to him. 3. How faithful ministers ought to be in their proper charges, reproving sin, even in the greatest personages, when God calleth them unto it, and how acceptable their reproof should be to the honest heart : as David's seer, Nathan the prophet's coming unto David and rebuking him after the open knowledge of his sin, and David's acceptance of this office at his hands, and the honourable mention made of his fidelity here, teach us. 4. How little a true penitent hesitateth to shame himself, when his sin hath dishonoured God, and he seeth that the confession of it may glorify God; and how far the penmen of holy Scripture differ in this point from the writers of human histories, as David, in the inscription of this psalm, giveth proof.

1. *Have mercy upon me, O God, according to thy loving-kindness; according to the multitude of thy tender mercies blot out my transgressions.*

2. *Wash me thoroughly from mine iniquity, and cleanse me from my sin.*

In this first affectionate prayer for remission of sins, learn, 1. As the conscience, till it be awakened by God, cannot apprehend how displeasant sin is to God; how it meriteth wrath, and how insupportable a burden it is to the sinner, when he is charged with it; so, after it is wakened, it can see no refuge till it consider that mercy may be had in God, and then the more it is pressed by the law, or fear of wrath, the more it seeketh after God's mercy, as here we see: *have mercy on me, O God.* 2. The consideration of the Lord's loving-kindness and readiness to forgive the sinner that cometh unto him, should keep the sinner (how grievous soever his offence hath been) from running away from him, yea should give him hope to meet with mercy, whatsoever may be his demerits: *have mercy upon me, O God, according to thy loving-kindness.* 3. Sin is a debt obliging a man to a penalty which he cannot pay; but it must be forgiven, otherwise he perisheth : as *blot out my transgressions* importeth. 4. All doubts arising from the multitude of sins forgiven before, and from the abuse of many mercies already received, and from the deep deservings of many heinous sins, are solved, when God's loving-kindness and the multitude of the mercies of God are opposed to these doubts and fears, and are put in the balance over against them; *according to thy loving-kindness, according to the multitude of thy tender mercies blot out my transgressions.* 5. When a saint now justified doth any thing against the law of God, his sin is so far from being extenuated or made less, that, on the contrary, it is multiplied so much the more, and found to have in it a plurality of sins, when rightly considered : *blot out,* saith he in the plural number, *my transgressions.* 6. Sin, as it bindeth a man over to punishment, till he be forgiven; so it defileth a man, and puts an abominable deformity on him, which his enlightened conscience cannot look upon without loathing, till it be, by pardon and purging, washed away : *wash me, and cleanse me from mine iniquity and my sin.* 7. The pollution of sin goes through the whole powers of the soul and body, which have been serviceable to it; through mind, will, affections, senses, bodily and all; and nothing can quiet the soul here, except it find pardoning mercy, and sanctifying mercy following all the foul footsteps of sin, and doing away the filthiness thereof : *wash me thoroughly, and cleanse me.*

3. *For I acknowledge my transgressions : and my sin is ever before me.*

4. *Against thee, thee only, have I sinned, and done this evil in thy sight ; that thou mightest be justified when thou speakest, and be clear when thou judgest.*

5. *Behold, I was shapen in iniquity ; and in sin did my mother conceive me.*

6. *Behold, thou desirest truth in the inward parts ; and in the hidden part thou shalt make me to know wisdom.*

Here he maketh confession of his sin and sinfulness, and aggravateth his guiltiness from the very root of original sin, and subscribeth whatsoever God hath spoken in the Scripture, of man's sinful nature and deserved punishment, approving himself unto God for the sincerity of his confession. Whence learn, 1. Whosoever would have mercy and pardon of his sin from God, must acknowledge his sin and debt, and must take part with God, and with justice against himself, because the psalmist here giveth this for a reason of his hope of pardon : *for I acknowledge my transgression.* 2. Albeit God hath pardoned sin to a penitent soul, and albeit his ministers have made declaration of the pardon to him; yet the conscience will not pronounce the sentence of absolution, but still present the sin as unpardoned, till God quieteth it by his immediate intimation; for David, after Nathan had told him from the Lord that his iniquity was pardoned, still findeth the conscience pursuing for the guilt : *my sin is ever before me.* 3. The dividing of the grant of pardon from the effectual intimation thereof unto the conscience, is done in God's wisdom and mercy towards his child for good;

for here it ripeneth repentance, and bringeth forth this deep confession : *I acknowledge mine iniquity, and my sin is ever before me.* 4. It is most suitable for true repentance, to pitch upon some particular sin, in the vileness whereof the evil of other sin may be taken up and lamented: *against thee have I done this evil* : he meaneth the particular whereof Nathan charged him in the matter of Uriah. 5. The material injury and hurt of a sinful action may resolve upon a creature; but the formal obliquity of the action resolveth upon the law or command of God, and upon his sovereign authority which gave the law : *against thee, thee have I sinned.* 6. If the injury done to the creature, could be severed from the offence done to God, the conscience would not be so much troubled for the first, as for the last; or if the injury done to God against so many obligations, be compared with the injury done to the creature; the injury done to God is so high as it comprehendeth all the challenge which the creature could make for its part, and leaveth nothing to the creature to say besides : therefore, saith he, *against thee, thee only, have I sinned, and done this evil in thy sight.* 7. Albeit no man should challenge for a wrong done by one man to another, and in particular for a wrong done to a subject by a prince or ruler, yet will the Lord challenge for it, and bring the man to an account for it : *against thee, thee only, have I sinned.* 8. How closely soever the circumstances of a sinful action be conveyed, that men should not see the vileness thereof, yet before God all the matter is plain : *I have done this evil in thy sight,* saith he. 9. The conscience rightly wakened to the sense of sin, cannot but justify what God hath spoken in his word of man's sinfulness, and of the demerit of sin, and of whatsoever God hath done, or shall do in punishing : for David maketh this deep confession of sin against himself, *that God may be justified when he speaketh, and clear when he judgeth.* 10. Although presumptuous man will not stand to examine, judge, and pass sentence upon God and his words and works, yet shall no man be able to bear a blot upon God; but every conscience, when awake, shall be found to blame the man, and to justify God in all his words and proceedings, as David is forced to blame himself here; *that God may be justified when he speaketh, and clear when he judgeth.* 11. As original sin is common to all men by

natural propagation, so is it not abolished out of the most
holy in this life; and as it is found to show itself in the
children of God by actual transgressions, so must the evil
thereof be acknowledged by them, and that not to extenuate
but to aggravate their sin, as David showeth here, saying,
*behold, I was shapen in iniquity, and in sin did my mother
conceive me.* 12. No confession of sin, or any other part
of God's worship, giveth ease to the mind, or is acceptable
to God, except it be done in sincerity and truth, and when
it is done in spirit and truth, it is acceptable to God, and
giveth ease to the conscience; behold, saith David after his
deep confession, *thou desirest truth in the inward parts.* 13.
The last operation of God's grace in us, is worthy to be observed, acknowledged, and made use of, as an evidence that
God hath some work in us, wherein he taketh pleasure : behold, saith David to God, *thou desirest, or delightest in
truth in the inward parts.* 14. When a man hath found
some spark of grace in himself, he may expect to find yet
more grace from God, as David, after this experience of
grace given to him to make a sincere confession of his sin,
expecteth that God shall effectually teach him more wisdom,
or wise behaviour in his sight. *In the hidden parts thou wilt
make me to know wisdom ;* that is, thou wilt make my conscience judge yet more impartially of my native sinfulness,
and wilt teach me to walk more circumspectly before thee,
in the sense of my fulness.

7. *Purge me with hyssop, and I shall be clean;
wash me, and I shall be whiter than snow.*

8. *Make me to hear joy and gladness ; that the bones*
which *thou hast broken may rejoice.*

He prayeth for remission of sin the second time, with an
eye to the blood of the Messiah Christ, and joineth with it,
a petition for comfort to his afflicted spirit. Whence learn,
1. No less loathsome than leprosy is the sight of sin, when
it is looked upon as unpardoned; and nothing less than the
blood of Christ signified by the blood of the clean bird slain
to cleanse the leper, can purge a man of it, for David looketh unto the manner of cleansing the leper, as it is set down,
Levit. xiv. Where two birds were taken, and one of them
slain, the living bird, being dipped with hyssop in the blood
of the slain bird, was let fly away, to signify the leprous

sinner's deliverance from perdition by the blood of the pure
sacrifice of Jesus Christ : *purge me with hyssop*, saith he.
2. Whatsoever application of Christ's blood in justification
of his person, hath been made to a man, it hindereth not
but rather openeth a way unto the renewed acts of application thereof, according as new sins draw on new guiltiness : for here justified David prayeth to be yet again purged with hyssop. 3. Renewed acts of remission of sin granted, by new application of the virtue of Christ's blood,
cleanse the conscience of the guilt of sin, and clear the
man before God's justice : *purge me with hyssop, and I
shall be clean*, saith he. 4. Howsoever remission of guilt
for Christ's sake be inseparable from the imputation of
righteousness for Christ's sake, yet may these two be distinguished, and distinctly looked upon for the believer's comfort; for here David, looking on the removing of the guiltiness of sin by Christ's death, saith, *purge me with hyssop,
and I shall be clean;* and looking upon the imputation of Christ's righteousness, or obedience even unto the
death, he saith, *wash me and I shall be whiter than snow*.
Now, that these two branches of mercy are distinguishable,
may appear from this, that, as to be delivered from eternal
torment is one benefit, (supposing that a man were annihi-
lated in his escape from it,) and to be not only freed from
eternal torment, but also made blessed by the gift of eternal
life, is another and a greater benefit; so, deliverance from
the guilt of sin, in relation to the removing of punishment,
is one thing, and the assignation of Christ's righteousness,
in relation to eternal life, is another thing; and both these
two benefits are purchased by Christ's perfect obedience unto
death, and are holden forth, Levit. xiv; for, after the delivery of the leper from death, figured and symbolized by
the letting go of the living bird dipped in the blood of the
slain bird, the clothing of the leper with righteousness is
figured and symbolized, by the washing of the man and putting clean clothes upon him. Now, it is not the man's inherent personal sanctification, (which, in every man, is joined
with much pollution,) that maketh him clean, but the imputation of Christ's righteousness; this maketh him *whiter
than snow*. 5. As we must not neglect the ordinances of
God, but must use them carefully for obedience unto God,
and for strengthening our faith; so we must not rest upon

them, but search for the signification, substance, and end of
them, which is Christ; as here David seeketh perfect pardon by Christ's blood, and perfect purging and cleansing
through him, under the terms of *purging with hyssop and
washing.*   6. The grief and torment which follow sin, and
are felt by a wounded spirit, are greater, even in the children of God, in the time of their repentance, than ever the
pleasure of sin was to them, as David showeth here, who
speaketh of his vexation and wounded spirit, as of the most
painful trouble which can befall the body; for, by *the bones
which thou hast broken,* he meaneth the chastisement of his
spirit inflicted by God.   7. Nothing can heal this wound of
the spirit save the hand that made it; nothing but God's
effectual application of his word of grace and pardon to the
guilty sinner can do it; for David will not rest with what
Nathan had spoken, till God speak the same effectually unto
him : *make me to hear joy and gladness.*   8. As there is
no sorrow so deep as the sense of God's displeasure, so there
is no joy so refreshing as the inward consolation of God's
Spirit; for David's broken bones will rejoice if God speak
peace to his soul : *make me to hear joy and gladness, that
the bones which thou hast broken may rejoice.*

9. *Hide thy face from my sins, and blot out mine
iniquities.*

10. *Create in me a clean heart, O God; and renew
a right spirit within me.*

11. *Cast me not away from thy presence; and take
not thy Holy Spirit from me.*

12. *Restore unto me the joy of thy salvation; and
uphold me with thy free Spirit:*

13. *Then will I teach transgressors thy ways; and
sinners shall be converted unto thee.*

He prayeth for remission of sin the third time, v. 9, and
joineth therewith a petition for rectifying his sad condition;
first, by renovation of that grace which was decayed, and,
as it were, lost, in his sense, v. 10; secondly, by preventing
his deserved and dreaded separation from God and from
communion with his Spirit, v. 11; thirdly, by repairing and
restoring his former gracious condition, and settling him
therein by the Spirit of adoption, v. 12; and then he promiseth to make good use thereof for the comfort and edifi-

cation of other sinners, v. 13. Whence learn, 1. Sin is soon committed, and guiltiness and misery soon drawn on, but not soon and easily removed; many a cry to God may be uttered, in the sense of the felt displeasure of God and fear of more and more evil following it, before the soul feel freedom from it; as this frequently repeated petition for pardon, and those expressions here set down make evident. 2. Earnestness of affection maketh frequent repetition not to be babbling, and when that which most presseth us is most insisted on by us in our prayer, it is no vain repetition or idle multiplication of words, as may here be seen. 3. Sin, seen in its own shape, is a loathsome sight to God, and horrible to the sinner; which loathsome sight nothing can remove save the Lord's voluntarily forgiving it, and his not setting it before his own face to be punished in severe justice : *hide thy face from my sins.* 4. As one sin wakeneth up the consciousness of many other sins, so nothing can quiet the conscience about any one sin, except both it and all other sins be forgiven; therefore, saith he, *blot out all mine iniquities.* 5. A sincere penitent is no less desirous of renovation and sanctification than he is of forgiveness of sin; for, with *blot out mine iniquities,* he joineth, *create in me a clean heart, and renew a right spirit within me.* 6. Albeit sin against the conscience, in a renewed man, defileth it thoroughly, and defaceth the work of the Holy Spirit, openeth the floodgate of natural corruption, to the pollution of the whole frame of a holy heart, openeth the way unto, and strengtheneth the work of, an evil and deluding spirit; yet no principle of grace in the renewed man is able to remove this evil, but the removing of it must be by the immediate work of God's own omnipotent hand. This work is no less than creation; therefore, saith he, *create in me a clean heart, and renew a right spirit within me ;* that is, it is not in my power to clear my conscience and my polluted heart, or to set my perverted spirit in a right frame again; but thy creating and renewing power, which borroweth nothing from the creature, must do it; *create in me,* importeth this. 7. Albeit a renewed soul cannot be utterly cast off from God, nor bereft utterly of saving grace once bestowed on him; yet, if he grieve the Lord's Spirit by presumptuous sinning, his assurance of standing in God's favour may be mightily endangered, and he put in fear of losing the possession of what is behind of the saving work of God's Spirit in him, especially when he considereth that his provocation deserveth no less at God's hand; therefore, saith he, *cast me not away from thy presence, and take not away thy Holy Spirit from me.* 8. Nothing is so terrible to a renewed soul, which hath been sometimes sensible of God's favour and sure of the presence of his Spirit, as to be shut out from God's favour, and severed from the communion of his Spirit, as this prayer testifieth : *cast me not away, &c.* 9. As a believer may come to assurance of his own salvation, and when he keepeth a good conscience, may sweetly rejoice therein; so when he seeth that the pleasure of sin hath marred this joy unto him, he cannot rest or be quiet till he recover the assurance he had, and his wonted joy be joined therewith : *restore unto me the joy of thy salvation.* 10. The godly, by their fall, should learn sensibly to acknowledge their own weakness, and their need of the supporting strength of God's Spirit, and to account the bonds of his Spirit, keeping them in order and in obedience, to be their only freedom. Therefore David, after prayer to have the joy of God's salvation restored unto him, fearing lest he should lose it again if he were left to himself, addeth another prayer, *uphold me with thy free Spirit.* 11. As the end of seeking mercy to ourselves should be this, that we may be enabled to be instruments of glorifying God, and saving others; so the sensible feeling of mercy which is sought after greatly encourageth a man to the work : *then will I teach transgressors thy ways.* *Then*, that is, when the joy of God's salvation is restored to me, and I confirmed somewhat in the grace of God. 12. As the way which God keepeth in manifesting his justice against transgressors, and his mercy to self-condemned sinners flying to him in Christ, is not known by nature to sinners, so long as they go on in their evil course, or before they be effectually taught to know both; so, none are so fit to teach and persuade them of this mystery as those who, by frequent experience, are acquainted with the ways of God : *then will I teach transgressors thy ways.* 13. The communicating the knowledge and experience of God's justice and mercy, according to every man's place and calling, is a good means of converting others who know no such thing : *I will teach others thy ways, and sinners shall be converted unto thee.*

14. *Deliver me from blood-guil'iness, O God, thou*

*God of my salvation ; and my tongue shall sing aloud
of thy righteousness.*

He prayeth the fourth time for remission of sin, and particularly of that fearful and bloody transgression in the
matter of Uriah, which now troubleth his conscience most.
Whence learn, 1. As the conscience passeth to particulars,
in the midst of confused challenges for multitudes of sins;
so, it presseth some particulars more eagerly than others,
according as it is set on work, as here the guiltiness in the
matter of Bathsheba and Uriah presseth David : *deliver me
from blood-guiltiness.* 2. Though sin seem pleasant at the
beginning, yet at length it is found a devouring enemy, from
which none can deliver a soul save God alone: *deliver me
from blood-guiltiness, O God.* 3. Upon the general grounds
of the covenant of grace made with us for salvation through
Christ, must a soul seek to have particular mercies: *deliver
me, thou God of my salvation.* 4. The righteousness of God,
which standeth in the remission of sin and imputation of
Christ's obedience unto us, through faith, according to God's
promise, is the matter of our joy and song of praise to God :
which song a soul being in thraldom by felt guiltiness can
hardly sing, but after the intimation of pardon will sing it
cheerfully : *deliver me from blood-guiltiness, then shall my
tongue sing aloud of thy righteousness.*

15. *O Lord, open thou my lips; and my mouth shall
shew forth thy praise.*

16. *For thou desirest not sacrifice, else would I give
it ; thou delightest not in burnt-offering.*

17. *The sacrifices of God* are *a broken spirit: a
broken and a contrite heart, O God, thou wilt not despise.*

He pursueth this fourth petition for remission of sin, with
a request for enlarging his heart, and furnishing him with
matter and ability for praising God; wherein he sincerely
renounceth all confidence in external ceremonies of the law,
or in any thing else which he could perform. Whence learn,
1. Howsoever proud spirits think that they can do any thing
they please in God's service, yet a humbled soul under exercise, knoweth that it is God who giveth both to will and to
do of his good pleasure; such a man knoweth that the habit
of grace is a gift, and the bringing of the habit into exercise

is another gift; he knoweth that when one hath gotten grace to will to praise God, he must have grace to put this will to act effectually: this the psalmist acknowledgeth and prayeth, *open thou my lips, and my tongue shall show forth thy praise.* 2. Whatsoever holy ordinances and outward services God prescribeth to his church, are not required for satisfaction of his justice, nor are they the main thing he is pleased with, but they are means only to lead men to himself in Christ, in whom only justice findeth satisfaction, and man findeth strength to go about the worship, that so God himself may have all the praise of our services: therefore David giveth it for a reason of his former petition, *for thou desirest not,* or thou hast not pleasure in, *sacrifice.* 3. That which God aimeth at we should most desire, and what he is well pleased with we should most endeavour after: *thou desirest not sacrifice, else would I give it.* 4. The main design of the sacrifices under the law was, that a man under the sense of sin and deserved judgment, and inability to satisfy for his faults, should come and empty himself before God, and rely only on the one propitiatory sacrifice, represented in those external sacrifices: *the sacrifices of God are a broken spirit;* that is, the right way of sacrificing is, that a man's spirit be emptied of its own self-confidence when it cometh to offer unto God the external sacrifices which otherwise God regardeth not. 5. The man who most renounceth his own works, worth, or merits, and despiseth all his own doings, as a broken earthen vessel, is most acceptable in his approaches to God's free grace in the Mediator: *a broken and a contrite heart, O God, thou wilt not despise;* and that not for any worth in the matter of contrition, but because by contrition is expelled all conceit of self-worth, and so the man is most fit for receiving grace and free pardon from God.

18. *Do good in thy good pleasure unto Zion: build thou the walls of Jerusalem.*

19. *Then shalt thou be pleased with the sacrifices of righteousness, with burnt-offering, and whole burnt-offering: then shall they offer bullocks upon thine altar.*

In the last verse David prayeth for the Lord's people; that what breach had been made in the walls of God's protection about them, by his sins and theirs, might be repaired; and God more holily and heartily worshipped, both by himself and by them, in time coming. Whence learn, 1. As every true member of the church should bear in heart the condition of the body, and offer it up to God, whatsoever be the man's own private condition; so in special he that hath by his sins provoked God to withdraw his protection from the incorporation wherein he is, should most earnestly intercede for the good of the body, as David doth here: *do good in thy good pleasure unto Zion, build thou the walls of Jerusalem.* 2. The rich grace of God, his free love and unchangeable good-will to his people, are the cause of all the welfare of the church: *do good in thy good pleasure unto Zion.* 3. Whosoever have been most instrumental in the building of God's church, must some way be emptied of the glory of this work, that it may be all ascribed unto God alone, who is the only builder of his own church; as David here emptieth himself of this honour and ascribeth it to God, saying, *build thou up the walls of Jerusalem.* 4. When God poureth out upon his people his Spirit of grace and supplication, and other proper effects of his good-will to them, then, and not till then, are they fit to do him service acceptably: *do good in thy good pleasure to Zion, then shalt thou be pleased with the sacrifices, &c.* 5. No sacrifice is acceptable to God save the sacrifices of righteousness; now the sacrifices of righteousness are, first, the propitiatory sacrifice of Christ, whereunto every believer must have respect, as offered in his name, when he cometh to God; and next, the sacrifices of thankfulness and new obedience, offered up by virtue of Christ's sacrifice, to be accepted. The first sort of sacrifice was represented most specially by burnt-offering, and whole burnt-offering; and the other sort by peace-offerings and other oblations: *then shalt thou be pleased with the sacrifices of righteousness, with burnt-offering, and whole burnt-offering; then shall they offer bullocks upon thine altar.*

PSALM LII.

To the chief musician, Maschil. A psalm of David, when Doeg the Edomite came and told Saul, and said unto him, David is come to the house of Ahimelech.

The scope of the psalmist is to show that Doeg, his enemy, had no reason to glory in the favour of the court, purchased by his false and cruel calumnies against him and the Lord's priests, which he proveth by four reasons; first, because God's kindness could not be taken away by Doeg's cruel calumnies, ver. 1; secondly, because God would root Doeg out of the world for his wicked calumnies, ver. 2—5; thirdly, because Doeg would be made a laughing-stock and matter of derision to the godly, ver. 6, 7; fourthly, because maugre his malice, David should be blessed as a believer in God, and a true worshipper of him, ver. 8; whereupon, he concludeth with praise to God, ver. 9.

From the inscription, learn, 1. It is no new policy of wicked men to seek to be great in court and in the favour of princes, by maligning the godly and fostering the displeasure of princes against them; for Doeg of old climbed into court this way. 2. Such practices are most suitable to false brethren; for this Doeg is an Edomite, of the posterity of Esau. 3. When the wicked come to be in power and credit with kings for their very enmity against God's people, it is a narrow trial, and a sore temptation to the godly, as here, in David's case with Doeg, is to be seen. 4. In this case there is nothing so needful as to go to God for direction and consolation; for so David did, and came back with a *maschil*, or psalm, for instruction to himself and others. 5. It is no advantage to a malicious calumniator, to pretend that he told nothing but the truth, and told no more than what he saw; for it is true that David came to the house of Ahimelech, but the telling of this to Saul imported much mischief in the matter, even all the evil which happened, and all this is laid on Doeg, presupposing he had said no more than is expressed here, that is, that he told Saul *David is come to the house of Ahimelech.*

1. *Why boastest thou thyself in mischief, O mighty man ? the goodness of God endureth continually.*

David chargeth Doeg with the vanity of his gloriation, that he was now made so mighty a man, for his ill service done against the Lord's servants, and refuteth his folly, because he could not take the kindness of God from the godly so easily as he might steal their good estimation from them among men. Whence learn, 1. Prosperity and success following upon a wicked course, hide the sin and mischief which is in it from the sinner; as we see here, how the favour which foolish Doeg found at court for his calumniating David and the Lord's priests, puffed him up. 2. There is small reason for a wicked man to glory in his wickedness, whatsoever profit or preferment it may bring to him, for, after examination he will not be able to give a reason of his vain boasting : *why boastest thou thyself of thy mischief, O thou mighty man ?* 3. Albeit the wicked think that God forgetteth his simple and weak servants, yet it is not so; and albeit the Lord altereth the exercise of the godly, and changeth their prosperity into adversity, yet he changeth not his affection to them; this remaineth fast for ever, whatsoever may appear to the carnal spectator of the Lord's dealing with his people : *the goodness of God endureth continually.* 4. So long as God's unchangeable kindness endureth, the wicked have no cause to exult over the godly, nor have the godly cause to faint or be discouraged, for this goodness of God David opposeth, both to Doeg's boasting, and to his own temptation: *the kindness of the Lord endureth for ever.*

2. *Thy tongue deviseth mischiefs ; like a sharp razor, working deceitfully.*

3. *Thou lovest evil more than good,* and *lying rather than to speak righteousness. Selah.*

4. *Thou lovest all devouring words, O* thou *deceitful tongue.*

The next argument for refuting Doeg's folly, is, because this cruel calumny would bring God's vengeance on Doeg, and root him out of all felicity; and here he first sets down his ditty in these three verses, before he sets down his doom, v. 5. Whence learn, 1. The tongue, when it is abused, is a world of wickedness, setting the world on fire, as itself is set on fire from hell by Satan : for, whatsoever mischief the devil can suggest, or a wicked heart can devise, the tongue will serve to vent; therefore is the tongue charged with devising mischief : *thy tongue deviseth mischief.* 2. The smooth convey of a wicked device, hideth not the mischief of it from God's sight, nor extenuateth the man's fault, but rather helpeth on the mischief more cunningly and powerfully : *like a sharp razor, working deceitfully.* 3. When a man speaketh no more of a tale of his neighbour, but what may serve to the man's hurt and prejudice, and keepeth up the relation of that part of the tale which might clear the man's innocence, or might give a right construction of his actions; albeit that part of the tale told be true, if all the rest of the tale had been told with it, yet, being told alone as if it were the full history, *it is evil, it is false lying.* It is a murdering and devouring speech, and full of deceit, and argueth the speaker to be such a one as Doeg was, in this particular at least, to whom David saith, *thou lovest evil more than good, and lying rather than to speak righteousness; thou lovest all-devouring words, O thou deceitful tongue.* 4. The more design, deliberation, and affection there is in a sin; the heavier is the guilt, and the challenge for it more just. *Doeg's devising mischief, Doeg's choosing evil and not good; choosing lying, and not righteousness; loving these evil and all-devouring words,* make his ditty most fearful.

5. *God shall likewise destroy thee for ever : he shall take thee away, and pluck thee out of* thy *dwelling-place, and root thee out of the land of the living. Selah.*

Now followeth his doom : Whence learn, 1. As any wicked man is instrumental for bringing temporal destruction on the godly, so is he instrumental in drawing everlasting destruction upon himself from God's hand : *God shall likewise destroy thee for ever.* 2. He that seeketh to settle himself, to enlarge himself, to root himself in the earth, and to prolong his standing in the world, by wrong means; and in special, by hurting the godly, and their good name and cause, shall find the event quite contrary to his desire, design, and expectation, as Doeg did, whose doom was destruction, for his evil offences done at court against David and the Lord's ministers : *God shall take thee away, and pluck thee out of thy dwelling-place, and root thee out of the land of the living.*

6. *The righteous also shall see, and fear, and shall laugh at him :*

7. *Lo,* this is *the man* that *made not God his strength ; but trusted in the abundance of his riches,* and *strengthened himself in his wickedness.*

The third argument of refutation of Doeg's vain boasting, is, that his wisdom should appear ridiculous folly, and his boasting the matter of his shame and disgrace. Whence learn, 1. The notable enemies of God's children and servants may expect to be notably punished, and that they who saw their sin, shall see also God's vengeance on them :. *the righteous shall see it.* 2. As the godly are the only wise observers of God's work, and the dispensation of his mercy and justice; so also are they the only persons who gain spiritual advantage thereby : *the righteous shall see it, and fear.* 3. As the good of godliness is seen and felt by the godly in their own experience of God's blessing upon themselves, so is it seen and observed also in the contrary evils which befall the ungodly : *lo, this is the man that made not God his strength,* say they, *but trusted in the abundance of his riches, and strengthened himself in his wickedness.*

8. *But I* am *like a green olive-tree in the house of God : I trust in the mercy of God for ever and ever.*

The fourth argument for refutation of Doeg's foolish boasting, is because, I, saith David, shall flourish in God's favour, in despite of Doeg. Whence learn, 1. Whatsoever may befall the godly by the malice of their enemies, it shall not diminish their felicity; when their enemies are running to their own destruction, it shall be well with the godly, they may be persuaded of it, for the psalmist's example encourageth to it : *but I am like a green olive-tree.* 2. As the olive-tree, being planted in a fertile ground, draweth in moisture, whereby it is nourished and groweth up: so the believer, being planted in the church, draweth spirit and life from God by holy ordinances, whereby he groweth up : *I am like a green olive tree in the house of God.* 3. The wisdom of the godly, and the ground of their true blessedness is this, they make fast work of their everlasting felicity by faith in God, and this maketh them like green olives all the days of their life : *for I trust in the mercy of God for ever and ever,* is given here for a reason of his happy growing in the house of God.

9. *I will praise thee for ever, because thou hast done it : and I will wait on thy name ; for it is good before thy saints.*

He closeth the psalm comfortably, with resolution to praise God, and to depend upon him. Whence learn, 1. Victory over temptations obtained by faith, is very glorious; for faith maketh a man as sure of what is to come, as if it were perfected, and filleth him with praise for the certain hope of the performance of promises : *I will praise thee for ever,* saith David, *because thou hast done it.* 2. Faith being solidly fixed, bringeth forth hope and quiet expectation of what is promised : *I will wait on thy name.* 3. As the Christian patience of one of the saints, is a matter of good example and great encouragement unto all the rest that behold it: so the consideration of the good which may redound to others, who shall be witnesses of our patient attending upon God, should stir us up to this duty of patient hope in God: *I will wait on thee, for it is good before thy saints.*

PSALM LIII.

To the chief musician upon Mahalath, Maschil. A psalm of David.

As in the fourteenth psalm, so here David comforteth himself and the rest of the godly in their sad sufferings which they felt from godless men, lying in the miserable condition of nature, v. 1—3. The grounds of comfort are three; the first, because God was engaged in the sufferings of his own, and would plead their controversy against the wicked, v. 4; the next, because God's judgments were to come on all the persecutors of the godly, v. 5; and the third, because there is hope of the full salvation of the godly in Christ, v. 6. Comparing this psalm with psalm xiv, wherein the enmity of the wicked against the godly, and the comfort of the godly in that case, are the same in this place, as those set down there, we learn, that as the godly men may fall oftener than once, in one case, under one and the same temptation, some sort of hard exercise and grief: so may they and should they make use of the same comforts, and bring to memory the same doctrines for that end, as the church is taught to do, psalm xiv, and here in this psalm.

1. *The fool hath said in his heart,* There is *no God. Corrupt are they, and have done abominable iniquity :* there is *none that doeth good.*

2. *God looked down from heaven upon the children of men, to see if there were* any *that did understand, that did seek God.*

3. *Every one of them is gone back ; they are altogether become filthy :* there is *none that doeth good, no, not one.*

From the description of the miserable condition wherein the world and every unrenewed man within the church visible lie, learn, 1. All the unrenewed persons are fools before God, how wise soever they may seem to men. 2. All unrenewed men are, inwardly in their affections and resolutions, atheists in effect, and such as do not regard God in any thing; whatsoever they may seem to themselves or others outwardly, *they say in their heart,* There is no God. 3. All unrenewed men are altogether rotten in their principles and motives of action: *they are corrupt.* 4. The actions of the unrenewed will be found abomination before God, and will prove them to be corrupt : *they have done abominable iniquity.* 5. Among all unrenewed men, whether without or within the visible church, not one man shall be found to have done so much as one good action, which can stand for good in God's account : *there is none that doeth good.* 6. The truth of this doctrine is put to trial and proof by God himself, and sentence is pronounced of all men's natural averseness from God, and impotency to do good : *God looked down from heaven upon the children of men, to see if there were any that did good, and he found none.* 7. As it is impossible that those can do any good, or be wise, who seek not God; so the proof and trial of this naughtiness of all men, so long as they lie in nature unrenewed, are found by their not *understanding, nor seeking of God : the Lord looked to see if there were any that did understand, that did seek God.* 8. Every man by nature is a revolter from God, and from the state wherein once God made man : *every one of them is gone back.* 9. There is nothing clear and unpolluted in soul or body of the unrenewed man, but the longer he liveth in nature, the viler is he : *they are altogether become filthy.* 10. Seeing all men by nature are concluded under sin, without exception, *and there is none that doeth good, no, not one;* it is no wonder that the image of God, appearing in his children, be ill entertained by natural men, and that God's children expect no good fruits from such ill trees as all men are by nature; for this doctrine is delivered to quiet the hearts of the godly, when they are molested by the men of this world. It should yield comfort to the godly to behold the miserable condition wherein all men are by nature, and themselves called forth from this miserable estate and converted; for this doctrine offereth ground for comparison, and for consolation.

4. *Have the workers of iniquity no knowledge ? who eat up my people as they eat bread : they have not called upon God.*

The first direct argument for the comforting of the godly under their persecution by the wicked among whom they live, is, that God considereth their case, and will plead their cause. Whence learn, 1. The Lord observeth every point of enmity which the world carrieth against his people; he taketh their case to heart, and will plead their cause; and this is a solid ground of comfort to his people in all their sufferings : *have the workers of iniquity no knowledge ? that eat up,* &c.   2. The grounds of difference between the unrenewed and the renewed or reconciled, offered in this opposition of the one sort to the other, are these : first, the unrenewed, all of them are called *workers of iniquity ;* but they that are reconciled, although they are not free from sin, yet they are not counted by God to be the workers of iniquity.   Again, the Lord acknowledgeth the regenerate, and calleth them *his own people ;* but disclaimeth the other, as in effect not his people, but his enemies.   And lastly, the unregenerate *do not call upon God,* to wit, in earnest, or in truth; but the regenerate, by the opposition made, are presupposed here to call on God, and to depend upon him in truth.   3. Nothing maketh more evident the blindness and beastly besotting of the conscience of sinners, than the persecuting of the saints; it will not suffice the ungodly to live a godless life themselves, except they malign and most unreasonably oppose piety in others: *have the workers of iniquity no knowledge? that they eat up my people as they eat bread.*   4. To vex, bear down, and destroy the godly, is as great a pleasure to the wicked, as to eat their meat : *they eat up my people as they eat bread.*

5. *There were they in great fear,* where *no fear was : for God hath scattered the bones of him that encampeth* against *thee: thou hast put* them *to shame, because God hath despised them.*

The next ground of comfort to the godly against persecution, is, because God's judgments shall overtake the troublers of God's people, when they least fear it.   Whence learn, 1. As persecution cauterizeth the conscience, and maketh it senseless of sin; so also it maketh the persecutors fearless of judgment, when they eat up the people of God as bread without fear : *for there,* saith he, *no fear was.*   2. The more secure a sinner is, and in special a persecutor of God's people, the more terrible shall his wakening be, when God's judgment cometh on him : *there were they in great fear, where no fear was.*   3. The enemies of God's church make it their study and main work to overthrow the godly, and to compass them, as it were, by way of laying siege about them, that they escape not : *they encamp against thee,* saith

the psalmist, speaking as it were to every one of God's people.   4. Wrath pursueth the persecutor, both living and
dead, and ceaseth not to follow him so long as there is any
thing of him capable of punishment; for God not only raiseth
the siege, and destroyeth the enemy, and consumeth his flesh,
but also he hath *scattered the bones of him that encampeth
against thee.* 5. When there is nothing left of the persecutor's substance unpunished in the world, the wrath of
God pursueth his name and memorial; and the wrong done
to the innocent is the persecutor's greatest disgrace: *thou
hast put them to shame.* 6. As true honour, and the con-
ferring of respect from men upon any, are the gifts of God,
who honoureth them that honour him; so deserved shame
and disgrace for sin committed, when poured out as the
effect of God's justice, make them who dishonour him to be
lightly esteemed : *thou hast put them to shame, because God
hath despised them.*

6. *Oh that the salvation of Israel were come out of
Zion ! When God bringeth back the captivity of his
people, Jacob shall rejoice, and Israel shall be glad.*

The last ground of comfort to the persecuted godly, is
the hope of complete salvation to the church of God, and
of every true member thereof in Christ. Whence learn, 1.
There is no solid consolation against persecution, or any
other grievance, save in the salvation which is to be had in
Christ : *he is the Saviour and salvation of Israel.* 2. As
Christ's coming to accomplish salvation part by part, in his
own order and time, is most certainly to be believed and
hoped for : so is it most earnestly to be wished, longed after, and prayed for : as the example of the Lord's people
here (longing for his coming to *Zion*, in his incarnation and
manifestation of his grace; and then in the spreading forth
of his grace and salvation out of *Zion* to Gentiles and Jews)
teacheth us : *O that the salvation of Israel was come out of
Zion.* 3. As the captivity of God's people remaineth in
any degree and measure, which may make Christ's coming
to be so much the more desirable, and to be the object of
wishes and matter of prayer; so shall every sort and degree
of captivity at last be removed from God's people, till redemption be completely fulfilled; God shall bring back the
captivity of his people.   4. As of all people, who ever had

M

the name of God's people, the miseries and captivities of the
Israelites, because of their provocation against God, have
been the most conspicuous and signal: so of all the people
on the earth, and of all the nations which have been honoured
with the title of *God's people*; the deliverance of Israel from
captivity shall be most eminently and conspicuously comfortable; for, *when God shall bring back the captivity of his
people, then Jacob shall rejoice and Israel shall be glad.*

PSALM LIV.

*To the chief musician, on Neginoth, Maschil. A psalm of David,
when the Ziphim came and said to Saul, doth not David hide himself with us ?*

David being betrayed by the Ziphim; first, maketh his prayer to God
for delivery, v. 1, 2; secondly, he strengtheneth his faith by some reasons, v. 3; thirdly, he is confident of his own delivery, and of God's
judgment on the Ziphim, whereunto he subscribes, v. 4, 5; and, last
of all, he promiseth praise to God for his own assured deliverance,
v. 6, 7.

From the inscription, learn, 1. Particular straits and
particular deliveries should be particularly remarked: as
David here remembereth the danger he was in by the
treachery of the Ziphim. 2. Mighty men will find readily
more friends in an evil cause, than the godly find in a good
one : as Saul hath the Ziphim to offer their service to his
cruelty, when David was in straits. 3. The wicked are
very hearty to do an ill action, and glad to find occasion
for it : *doth not David,* say they, *hide himself with us ?* as
if this had been good and blessed news.

1. *Save me, O God, by thy name, and judge me by
thy strength.*

2. *Hear my prayer, O God ; give ear to the words
of my mouth.*

From David's prayer, learn, 1. The godly can never
be so surprised with trouble, but they may fly to God for
delivery, as David doth here; and it is a rare virtue not
to forget this relief in depth of distress. 2. When men
believe that God is all-sufficient and answerable for what is
spoken of him, they have great encouragement to go to
him in difficulty; *save me by thy name,* saith David. God's
name gave him ground to pray and hope for deliverance.

3. Albeit no man should rashly call God to give judgment, yet in a good cause, against a strong party, an upright man may call for and expect assistance from God : *judge me by thy strength*, saith he. 4. In fervent prayer, the very voice hath use; as with the supplicant to express his earnestness, and his faith in God, and to stir him up and hold him fixed to his supplication; so with God also, for it is an express invocation of him, and a sign of dependence upon him, and of expectation of a good answer from him; *hear my prayer, O God, give ear unto the words of my mouth.*

3. *For strangers are risen up against me ; and oppressors seek after my soul : they have not set God before them. Selah.*

The reasons supporting his faith in his prayer, are taken from the unkindness, unnaturalness and cruelty, not only of his countrymen, but also of his father-in-law and his old acquaintance, slippery courtiers, who some time professed friendship. Whence learn, 1. No strangers are more strange than they who cast off the bands of civility and nature, whereby they were bound : false countrymen, false brethren, false friends, false alliance, are those of whom men may expect least in their need, for David findeth such men to be his greatest enemies : *strangers are risen up against me*, saith he. 2. When they who should protect a man, do him most wrong, God will hear the plaints put up against such men : *oppressors seek after my soul*, or life. 3. When the fear of God is laid aside, there is nothing to be expected of the godless man but the worst of evils which he is able to do; there is no awband to restrain him : for *they have not set God before them.* 4. The less hope there be of man's mercy, the more hope is of God's help; the more unkind and cruel men be, who should be friends, the more may the Lord's kindness and comfort be expected for supply of inlacks, as here the drift of David's argument holdeth forth.

4. *Behold, God* is *mine helper : the Lord* is *with them that uphold my soul.*

5. *He shall reward evil unto mine enemies : cut them off in thy truth.*

In the third place, he is assured of help to himself and to his friends, and of vengeance to his enemies. Whence learn,

1. Fervent prayer hath readily a swift answer, and some-times wonderfully swift, even before a man have ended speech, as here David findeth in experience : *behold,* saith he, *God is my helper.* 2. The sight of faith is very clear, and piercing through all clouds; when God holds forth the light of his Spirit to it, it can demonstrate God present in an in-stant, ready to help in greatest straits : *behold, God is my helper.* 3. There is more joy in God's felt presence, than grief in felt trouble; for, *behold, God is my helper,* is more comfort than his friends' unkindness, and strangers' malice were grievous. 4. Such as comfort and help a man in time of his temptation, are not only helpers unto him in the mat-ter of his temporal life, but also instruments to save his soul, which by temptations is like to be drawn into sin, and so to destruction; for David saith of such men, *they uphold my soul.* 5. Such as take part with the persecuted saints, God will take part with : *the Lord is with them that uphold my soul.* 6. As God is a friend to the friends of his dis-tressed children, so he is a foe to their foes; and their foes shall smart for their enmity in due time : *he shall reward evil to my enemies.* 7. The doom of the wicked enemies of God's children, is set down in God's word; his truth is the wicked man's terror, and the godly man's strength : *cut them off in thy truth.* 8. Albeit we may not without clear warrant pray against particular persons, yet we may sub-scribe to God's word set down in Scripture against his ob-stinate enemies, and our enemies for his cause : *cut them off in thy truth.*

6. *I will freely sacrifice unto thee ; I will praise thy name, O Lord, for* it is *good.*

7. *For he hath delivered me out of all trouble ; and mine eye hath seen* his desire *upon mine enemies.*

In the last place, he promiseth praise to God for the cer-tainty he had of his deliverance, whereof he was no less as-sured than if he had seen it with his eyes. Whence learn, 1. Promised and hoped for deliverance is able to affect the heart, as a mercy present and already past, as here it doth David : *I will sacrifice to thee, and praise thee.* 2. Readi-ness of heart to glorify God, and liberty of spirit, with oc-casion granted to praise him for a benefit, are other new benefits superadded and greatly to be esteemed, as David accounteth it : *I will freely sacrifice unto thee, and praise thy name, for it is good ;* that is, not only is thy name good, but to have a heart sincerely to serve thee, and liberty to express thy praise before others, is good.   3. An action is good, when it is done because it is a good action, and is not gone about for by ends : *I will praise his name, for it is good,* saith he.   4. In experience of one.delivery man may have a foresight of a full delivery out of every evil or trouble wherein he can fall, as here David speaketh of hopes for full delivery : *he hath delivered me out of all troubles.* 5. The same light of God's word, made lively by God's Spirit, is able to show a man, both the destruction of his wicked enemies, and his own deliverance from them; and as a man may rejoice, in God's mercy towards himself, so also may he rejoice in God's justice against his enemies, provided he be free of private revenge : *mine eye hath seen thy judg-ments upon mine enemies.*

PSALM LV.

To the chief musician on Neginoth, Maschil.   A psalm of David.

This psalm containeth this doctrine, That albeit Christ and his follow-ers may be in great straits by the treachery of their pretended friends, yet through God's favour they shall be delivered, as David felt in ex-perience.   The use of which doctrine is subjoined in the end of the psalm, which well agreeth with the psalmist's condition in the time of Absalom and Ahitophel's conspiracy.   The parts of the psalm we may make these three.   In the first is set down his sorrowful supplication, to v. 16 ; in the next, his comforting himself in the Lord for his deliver-er, to v. 22 ; in the third, use of this experience, in the last two verses. In his supplication he prayeth, in the first place, for a gracious hearing, because of the calumnies and cruelty of his enemies, v. 1—3.   In the next place, he setteth down his pitiful condition of mind, v. 4—5, mak-ing him to wish to be far from the company of those conspirators who were combined against him, v. 6—8.   In the third place, he prayeth to God to confound their counsels, because the whole city was in an up-roar against him, seeking how to execute their mischievous plot, v. 9—11.   In the fourth place, he condescends upon a more particular reason of his prayer for confounding their counsels, because the plotter of the conspiracy had been most intimate in his familiarity, and deep upon his counsel, v. 12—14.   Whereupon, in the last place, by way of prayer he prophesieth of the curse of God to come upon them, v. 15. In the second part of the psalm he comforteth himself in God ; first, by his resolution constantly to depend upon God, and hopefully to pray, v. 16, 17; secondly, by his former experiences of deliverances granted to him before, v. 18; thirdly, because he was assured God would punish his enemies for their treacherous breach of covenant, and cloaking of their malicious designs with fair pretences and deep dissimulation,

v. 19—21. In the third part of the psalm are the uses of this experience, v. 22—23.

1. *Give ear to my prayer, O God; and hide not thyself from my supplication.*

2. *Attend unto me, and hear me : I mourn in my
complaint, and make a noise ;*

3. *Because of the voice of the enemy, because of the
oppression of the wicked : for they cast iniquity upon
me, and in wrath they hate me.*

From his address to God for relief in this, as in his other
sad conditions, learn, 1. Many grievances are the godly
subject unto, but in none of them all is there any ease for
them, till they go to God and lay out their case before him :
give ear to my prayer, O God. 2. As it is ease of heart
to supplicants to have any sign of the acceptance of their
supplication; so not to find access in prayer addeth much
weight to their trouble : *hide not,* saith he, *thyself from my
supplication.* 3. When a sad heart is fixed on God, and findeth what to say to him, it may expect that its words shall
not be misregarded of God, but punctually taken knowledge of : *attend unto me and hear me.* 4. Though a child
of God were ever so stout-hearted naturally, yet when God
exerciseth his spirit with trouble, he shall be made to weep
before God as a child, and must not be ashamed to be thus
humbled before him : *I mourn in my complaint,* saith he,
and make a noise. 5. A mourning supplicant shall neither
lose his prayers nor his tears; for, *I mourn,* is brought as
a reason of his hope that God shall *attend and hear him.*
6. When the godly fall into persecution and trouble from
men, their lives, their estate, and their good name, readily
come altogether to be in danger at once, as it befell David
when the conspirators made head against him; they traduced
his former government, as if he had been a wicked man,
and sought to bear him down, and to have his life : *because
of the voice of the enemy,* there is their railing; *because of
the oppression of the wicked,* there is their violent robbing
him of his estate; *they cast iniquity upon me,* there are their
slanderous traducings of him, and charging him with faults
falsely; *in wrath they hate me,* there is their cruel seeking
to kill him.

4. *My heart is sore pained within me ; and the terrors of death are fallen upon me.*

5. *Fearfulness and trembling are come upon me, and horror hath overwhelmed me.*

In this pitiful condition of mind, learn, 1. It is not a thing inconsistent with godliness to be much moved with fear in time of danger; natural affections are not taken away in conversion, but sanctified and moderated : *my heart is ore pained within me.* 2. Natural sagacity and courage re not sufficient to bear a man out in a great stress, for they will fail him; and if a man have not stronger supporters than his natural parts, he is undone; for here *the terrors of death are fallen upon me, and horror hath overwhelmed me.* 3. The godly have an advantage above all natural men : for when natural strength and courage fail them, they have nothing behind; but the godly have faith in God, to open a fountain of fresh supply of wisdom, courage, and strength to them, when all natural parts fail them; for, David being now emptied of natural strength, hath wisdom and strength to go to God, and hope of heart to be helped by him.

6. *And I said, Oh that I had wings like a dove !* for then *would I fly away, and be at rest.*

7. *Lo,* then *would I wander far off,* and *remain in the wilderness. Selah.*

8. *I would hasten my escape from the windy storm* and *tempest.*

Whereas he wished to have been out of the reach and society of such wicked enemies, learn, 1. When a man may escape a present hazard of life, with a good conscience, he may lawfully flee and eschew the danger, as David here wished he could have escaped: *O if I had wings, then would I fly away.* 2. A godly man may be in such peril as it seems to him he cannot without a miracle be delivered, as David saw no way to escape the conspiracy, save this way : *O that I had the wings of a dove*; and yet God may so dispose, as he may be delivered in an ordinary way, as here David was. 3. It is better to be in the wilderness in some cases, than to be in the company of the wicked : *lo, I would wander far off, and remain in the wilderness.* 4. The way to eschew the fury of a sudden insurrection of a tumultuous multitude, is not to come forth and appease them with words, but to decline their present fury by going out of the way, if God offer occasion : *I would hasten my escape from the windy storm and tempest.*

9. *Destroy, O Lord,* and *divide their tongues : for I have seen violence and strife in the city.*

10. *Day and night they go about it upon the walls thereof : mischief also and sorrow* are *in the midst of it.*

11. *Wickedness* is *in the midst thereof; deceit and guile depart not from her streets.*

In the third place, he prayeth to confound the counsel of his enemies, because they had put the whole city in confusion, and set the citizens upon a course of cruelty and violence. Whence learn, 1. A visible church may sometimes be in so sinful a condition, as a godly man shall not know what to do, or to whom he may have recourse, or where to hide himself; as here the condition of the holy city, the city of Jerusalem is described. 2. The prayers of the godly are more able to disappoint the plots of cruel enemies, than all human policy : *destroy, O Lord, and divide their tongues.* 3. The believer should make use of such courses as God hath taken before for disappointing wicked enterprises, for supporting his faith in his need, as here David maketh use of God's dissolving the conspiracy of Corah, Dathan, and Abiram, and of the proud enterprise of the wicked in building Babel: *destroy, O Lord, and divide their tongues.* 4. A man should be very sure, that such as he prayeth against, and complaineth of unto God, are in a wicked condition, and upon a mischievous course; for David giveth for a reason of his imprecation, that he had *seen violence and strife in the city,* the rulers of the city diligently watching for his life to do mischief ; *day and night going about the walls, mischief, sorrow, wickedness, deceit, guile in the midst of it, and openly avowed in the streets.*

12. *For* it was *not an enemy that reproached me ; then I could have borne* it : *neither* was it *he that hated me* that *did magnify himself against me ; then I would have hid myself from him :*

13. *But* it was *thou, a man mine equal, my guide, and mine acquaintance.*

14. *We took sweet counsel together,* and *walked unto the house of God in company.*

In the fourth place, he condescendeth upon a more special reason of his imprecation, because Ahitophel and other
like traitors, (fit types of Judas) had treacherously abused
their trust and familiarity which they had with him, whose ingratitude grieved him more than the injuries of others.
Whence learn, 1. It is not a strange thing for the godly to
find such as should be their friends become their greatest
foes, especially in a good cause; this David's experience
maketh evident. 2. The worst that a professed enemy can
do against the godly in a good cause, is more tolerable than
treachery against us, or the forsaking of us by a professed
friend; for that importeth a reproach in the party forsaken,
as having a bad cause, or being unworthy to be assisted :
*it was not an enemy that reproached me, then I could have
borne it.* 3. The injuries of a suspected enemy, are not
so unavoidable before they be done, nor so piercing when
they are done, as the injuries of one whom a man sus-
pecteth not, or as the injuries done to us by a professed
and trusted friend : *neither was it he that hated me, then
I could have hid myself from him.* 4. The disappointing
of us by a friend in a good cause, much more the open
opposition, and most of all the treachery of a trusted friend
against us in a good cause, carry with them a vilifying and
despising of our person and cause, and import our ill deserving at his hand, our ill carriage in the cause, and our
deserving to be forsaken; and say in effect, that the false
friend or traitor hath reason to be avenged on us, and to oppose us in that cause; and what can be heavier to a godly
persecuted person ? for this is a very exalting of the traitor
against us : *neither was it he that hated me, that did magnify
himself against me.* 5. Amongst many friendly neighbours,
it has been the custom of godly and wise men, to choose out
some to be their most intimate friends, whom they would use
most familiarly and freely, whose counsel they would take,
and most readily follow : *it was thou, O man, mine equal, my
guide, and my acquaintance.* 6. To find a godly and wise
man with whom we may be free in all cases of mind or conscience into which we may fall, to whom we may freely open
our mind, and be strengthened by him in the service of God,
is a notable refreshment, and part of happiness and contentment : *we took sweet counsel together, and walked unto the
house of God in company.* 7. A godly and wise man may

be deceived in his choice by the close carriage of a hypocrite, who, because he hath no sound principles of steadfastness in a good cause, may both disappoint his friend, and deceive himself also, and so do that which he did not at first intend to do. This disappointment to the godly is a very heavy
affliction : *but it was thou, O man, mine equal, my guide.*

15. *Let death seize upon them,* and *let them go down
quick into hell : for wickedness* is *in their dwellings,*
and *among them.*

From his prophetical imprecation against his enemies,
such as Ahitophel was to David and Judas to Christ, and
such like, together with their followers and accomplices,
learn, 1. Swift destruction is the reward of the enemies of
God's servants, and specially of treacherous apostates from a
good cause, as Ahitophel's and Judas's latter end gave example : *let death seize upon them, and let them go down quick
into hell.* 2. Such as give entertainment and lodging unto
wickedness, shall have hell for their lodging, where wickedness lodgeth; for here it is given for a reason why the wicked
shall go down to hell : *because wickedness is in their dwellings, and among them.* 3. What the Lord hath revealed to
be his righteous decree, the godly may warrantably subscribe
unto it : *let death seize on them, &c.*

16. *As for me, I will call upon God; and the Lord
shall save me.*

17. *Evening, and morning, and at noon, will I pray,
and cry aloud ; and he shall hear my voice.*

In the second part of the psalm he comforteth himself in
his resolution constantly to depend on God, and his confidence
to find access in worship. Whence learn, 1. The right use
of God's judgments on the wicked for their wickedness is to
draw near to God, to worship him and depend upon him, as
David here resolved : *as for me, I will call upon God.* 2. A
man may be sure to be saved in drawing near to the Lord,
whatsoever shall befall the wicked : *I will call on God, and
the Lord shall save me.* 3. He who resolveth to live upon
God's good-will and bounty, and hopeth to be saved at last,
must resolve also to be constant, fervent, and importunate in
his daily worship and attendance on God : *evening and morning will I pray, and cry aloud.* 4. As it is needful upon
all occasions to watch unto prayer, and to entertain a frame

of spirit fit for supplication : so is it fit for giving ourselves
more specially and fully to this work, to have (albeit not
fixed canonic hours,) yet set times every day, at or about
which we may follow religious worship, such as are *morning*,
evening and noon, or any other time most fitting for the
work, all circumstances being compared; as here David's resolution and example teach us.

18. *He hath delivered my soul in peace from the
battle that was against me; for there were many with
me.*

His next encouragement is taken from the experiences of
former deliveries given to him by God. Whence learn, 1.
We make good use of experiences, when we stir up ourselves
thereby, to believe the more in God, and to call on him in all
conditions, as David here giveth this, *he hath delivered my
soul*, as a reason of his former resolution. 2. In the midst
of war, the Lord can keep a man as safe as in the time of
peace, and in extreme perils preserve him from danger : *he
hath delivered my soul in peace from the battle that was
against me.* 3. He that depends upon God in the time of
trouble, albeit he had a host against him, yet hath he more
with him when God is with him, than can be against him :
he hath delivered my soul, for there are many with me.

19. *God shall hear, and afflict them, even he that
abideth of old. Selah. Because they have no changes,
therefore they fear not God.*

20. *He hath put forth his hands against such as be at
peace with him; he hath broken his covenant.*

21. The words *of his mouth were smoother than butter, but war* was *in his heart: his words were softer
than oil, yet* were *they drawn swords.*

His third encouragement is taken from assurance, that
God should punish his enemies for their godless security,
breach of covenant, and deep dissimulation. Whence learn,
1. Upon the complaint of the oppressed servants of God, not
only are they delivered themselves, but also their enemies are
punished : *God shall hear and afflict them.* 2. God's eternity and immutability is a sufficient ground of the manifestation of his mercy to his own people, and his justice against
their enemies from generation to generation : *God shall hear
me, and afflict them, even he that abideth of old.* Selah.

3. The more gently the Lord deals with the wicked in not exercising them with so many crosses, outward and inward, as
he doth his own, the more godless are they, the more secure
are they; and the more godless and secure they are, the more
certainly is their vexation coming : *he will afflict them sore ;
because they have no changes, therefore they fear not God.* This
is one reason of the Lord's pursuing the wicked. **4.** Whoever
he be that maketh a breach in the peace between himself and
others, shall have God for his party, who shall not fail to
afflict the peace-breaker; he shall afflict them, especially the
chief ringleaders, *who have put forth their hands against
such as be at peace with them :* and this is another reason of
the Lord's punishing the enemies of his people.   **5.** The
Lord will make a quarrel, and pursue for the breach of covenant in special, because this is a most solemn confirmation
of peace, and one which God hath special interest to see
performed, or the breach of it punished : *he has broken his
covenant ;* and this is the third reason of God's punishing
false brethren, pretended friends to God's people, but in effect most pernicious foes.   **6.** The bosom enemies of the
church, and underminers of the Lord's people, and of his
work in their hands, make fairest pretences; when their
vilest plots are in hand, then they are at Hail Master, and
offering kisses, then they are about to betray : *the words of
his mouth were smoother than butter, but war was in his
heart ; his words were softer than oil, yet were they drawn
swords ;* and this vile dissimulation is the fourth reason of
the Lord's avenging the persecution of false brethren.

22. *Cast thy burden upon the Lord, and he shall sustain thee: he shall never suffer the righteous to be moved.*

23. *But thou, O God, shalt bring them down into the
pit of destruction: bloody and deceitful men shall not
live out half their days ; but I will trust in thee.*

The use of this experience the psalmist setteth forth;
first by giving counsel to the oppressed to cast their burden
upon the Lord, when they are over-burdened, and by making promises for encouraging them thereto; secondly, by
giving assurance of the perdition of the treacherous enemies
of the church; thirdly, by setting forth his own resolution
to keep confidence in God.   Whence learn, 1. The use
of the experience which godly persons have had, of comfort

in and delivery out of trouble, is the encouragement of us to take the same course which the godly followed before us, by seeking our relief in God only : *cast thy burden on the Lord.* 2. Whosoever repose with confidence on God in their weighty troubles, shall never sink under them; *cast thy burden on the Lord, and he shall sustain thee.* 3. Though the godly be troubled and tossed, yet because they continue to seek God, and to walk in the way of righteousness, they shall never be driven from their anchor-hold, they shall not be loosed at the root; their building shall be found still in its own place, upon the rock : *he shall never suffer the righteous to be moved.* 4. As on the one hand the Lord shall uphold the believer, how low soever he shall be brought, that he perish not: so shall the Lord still bring down the wicked to perdition, how high soever, how fixed soever his state appear; believe this who will : *God will not suffer the righteous to be moved, but thou, O God, shalt bring them down into the pit of destruction.* 5. Treacherous and cruel adversaries of the Lord's people shall be cut off before they accomplish their bloody plots; they shall never die full of days, but wrath shall take them away when they would least : *bloody and deceitful men shall not live half their days.* 6. Whether such as trouble the godly live longer or shorter, they will cause trouble to the godly, so long as they live; and the only rest that godly hearts can have against all the trouble they feel or fear from their enemies, or otherwise, is to stay themselves on the Lord; for so resolveth the psalmist : *but I will trust in thee,* saith he, and so closeth.

PSALM LVI.

To the chief musician upon Jonath-Elem-Rechokim, Michtam of David, when the Philistines took him in Gath.

David flying from Saul to the country of the Philistines, (as we read, 1 Sam. xxi. 13.) is apprehended, prayeth to God, and is delivered. There are two parts of the psalm. In the former part there are three conflicts of David's faith with his trouble and temptation, and three victories. The first conflict is in prayer, laying forth his enemies' carriage against him, v. 1, 2 ; and his first victory by faith, v. 3, 4. The second conflict in his complaint he maketh against his enemies, v. 5, 6; and his second victory by faith, v. 7. His third conflict is by laying forth his mournful condition before God, with hope to be regarded, v. 8 ; and his third and greatest victory by faith, v. 9—11. In the latter part of the psalm is David's obligation thankfully to acknowledge his merciful delivery, with a petition for grace to persevere in the course of obedience, under God's protection, v. 12, 13,

From the inscription, learn, 1. When once God's children are entered on their trials, they meet with new and unexpected difficulties, as David here flying from one ene-my, falls into the hands of another. 2. Those means of safety which God's children devise themselves, readily prove snares; David flying out of the holy land, falleth into the hands of his adversaries : *the Philistines took him in Gath.*

1. *Be merciful unto me, O God; for man would swallow me up : he fighting daily oppresseth me.*

2. *Mine enemies would daily swallow me up ; for* they be *many that fight against me, O thou most High.*

His first wrestling in prayer is with the check of his con-science, whether for his daily sins, or in particular for cast-ing himself in so apparent danger as to have ventured with-out probable security, to seek shelter among the enemies of the people of God, whose blood he himself had shed abund-antly; for this rashness or other sins he beggeth mercy, and layeth out before God the pressing temptation from Saul and his countrymen's cruelty, which drove him to this poor shift. Whence learn, 1. There is no fence for challenges of conscience for by-gone sins meeting with trouble drawn on by our folly, but flying to the mercy and rich grace and pity of God, as David doth here: *be merciful to me, O God.* 2. When all men and means fail us, and we see none but wolves and lions ready to devour us, there is hope of help in God's mercy; *be merciful to me, O God, for man would swallow me up.* 3. Continued temptations, and renewed dangers, overset the strength of a frail man, till he go to God to have relief from the temptation, or new strength: *he fighting daily oppresseth me.* 4. Whatsoever inconven-iences the godly fall into by flying from persecution, they are all charged justly upon the persecutor, and the chief authors of their trouble: *he fighting daily oppresseth me,* saith David of Saul, who drove him to these straits. 5. Bloody persecutors follow hard after the chase of God's servants, without intermission, as dogs or lions after their prey; with as great desire to have their blood, as hungry beasts have after their food; *mine enemies would daily swallow me up.* 6. One ringleader in the persecution of the godly, will find a multitude follow him; *many are they that fight against me.* 7. There is one above all, who can and will take order with all the enemies of his people, who only can ease their hearts when they complain of their foes : *many are they that fight against me, O thou most High.*

3. *What time I am afraid, I will trust in thee.*

4. *In God I will praise his word ; in God I have put my trust : I will not fear what flesh can do unto me.*

Here faith gets the victory, by setting God's word against all difficulties, within or without him, whereupon the psalmist defieth what man can do unto him. Whence learn, 1. Albeit the godly be not so stout in their trials, as not to feel their own infirmity, or not to be afraid, yet they are kept from fainting in their fear, by faith in God : *what time I am afraid, I will trust in thee.* 2. Albeit faith doth not always put forth itself, yet when fear assaulteth most, then faith in God most evidently manifesteth its force; for then especially by directing the man's eye towards God, it settleth a troubled mind, strengtheneth weak courage, and relieveth the oppressed heart : *what time I am afraid, I will trust in thee.* 3. The experience of the sweet fruit of faith endeareth the Lord to a soul, and strengtheneth a man to the employing of faith, come what can, as David's affectionate resolution here teacheth us : *what time I am afraid, I will trust in thee.* 4. Faith groweth valiant in fight; albeit it begin like a coward, and stagger in the first conflict, yet it groweth stout and triumphant and pulls its adversaries under foot : *in God I have put my trust, I will not fear what flesh can do unto me.* 5. When faith prevaileth fear ceaseth, and all opposition of enemies is despised : *I will not fear what flesh can do unto me.* 6. The best hold that faith can have of God, is to take him by his word : however his dispensation seem to be; this will give satisfaction at length; for, *in God I will praise his word,* is as much as, albeit he withhold comfort and deliverance from me, so that I cannot find what I would, yet let me have his word, and I will give him the glory of all his attributes.

5. *Every day they wrest my words: all their thoughts*
are *against me for evil.*

6. *They gather themselves together, they hide them-*
selves, they mark my steps, when they wait for my soul.

His second conflict is with the malice of his crafty and
cruel enemies; of whom he complained that they miscon-
strued his actions, words, and deeds, as smelling only of
treason and rebellion, whether he remained in the country
or fled out of it, and whatsoever expressions fell from him,
at any time, for his own clearing, all was wrested to another meaning. 2. They devised, each of them, how to
bring mischief upon him. 3. What they could not make
out severally they sought to ripen by consulting. 4. They
covered all their plots with fair pretences, and dissembled
their intentions. 5. They observed narrowly every one of
his steps, to make out something against him in their observations, for which it might seem justice to kill him. 6.
They thought to double their course by more and more
iniquity against him, for which he prayeth the Lord to execute justice against them. Whence learn, 1. Let the godly
say or do whatsoever they can, how justly, how innocently
soever they carry themselves, yet their adversaries will put
another face upon their words and deeds than what is right:
every day they wrest my words. 2. The persecutors of.
God's people spend their wits in devising some harm or
other against them: *all their thoughts are against me for*
evil. 3. What the wicked cannot make out against the
godly by themselves severally, they labour to make out by
mutual counsel and concurrence: *they gather themselves*
together. 4. Though the wicked reveal themselves, one to
another, in their plots and designs against the godly, yet
before others they use to put a veil over their malice, and
some fair pretence on what they intend to do: *they hide*
themselves. 5. The wicked take occasion to forge their
pretences from observation of some passage of the carriage
of the godly, that they may make them odious and cut
them off: *they mark my steps, they wait for my soul.*

7. *Shall they escape by iniquity? in* thine *anger cast*
down the people, O God.

The second victory of faith is in the psalmist's foresight
of the punishment of his enemies approaching, howsoever

they feared no such thing. Whence learn, 1. Sinners see no way to hide the mischief of their actions save by doing more mischief, and in special by colouring their injuries with calumnies against the persons they injure, and by pretending law for what they do : *they think to escape by iniquity.* 2. Howsoever the wicked may by false pretences deceive themselves and others like them, and so escape man's punishment, yet shall they not eschew the vengeance of God, but rather be so much the more liable to it, as they multiply iniquity to hide iniquity : *shall they escape by their iniquity?* *cast them down.* 3. Neither high place, nor multitude of people following wicked men in an evil course against God's servants, shall save them from the wrath of God: *in thine anger cast down the people, O God.*

8. *Thou tellest my wanderings: put thou my tears into thy bottle:* are they *not in thy book?*

The third conflict, wherein he layeth out his mournful condition before God, with hope to find pity. Whence learn, 1. When faith hath gotten victory, it will find new assaults; though faith overcome a temptation, the tempter will make head again; though faith overcome one temptation, another will enter the lists and set on, as conflict after conflict here maketh evident. 2. Many a tear may the godly shed before their trial be ended, when once it is begun, and many uncouth paths may they tread who are forced to fly the cruelty of persecutors, before they find rest ; multitude of *wanderings* had David, and large *measure of tears* shed he, before he was delivered. 3. The looking back upon many and long-continued troubles, laid together in a heap, or put in order one after another, musters terribly, and makes a great assault against a man's faith and patience, as here the multitude of David's wanderings and tears showed themselves together before him. 4. God hath so great compassion on his servants in trouble that he reckoneth even the steps of their wanderings and pilgrimage, and numbereth all their tears, and keepeth the count thereof, as it were in a register; and therefore every troubled servant of God, when he looks upon his sufferings, should look upon God also taking as particular notice of his troubles as he himself can do: *thou tellest my wanderings : put thou my tears into thy bottle : are they not in thy book ?*

9. *When I cry* unto thee, *then shall mine enemies
turn back: this I know; for God* is *for me.*

10. *In God will I praise* his *word; in the Lord will
I praise* his *word.*

11. *In God have I put my trust: I will not be afraid
what man can do unto me.*

In these verses we behold the third and complete victory
of faith. Now the psalmist is confident to rout all his
enemies by prayer, and to defy all mortals by faith in God's
word. Whence learn, 1. Laying forth our cares and fears
before God in prayer, is the way to get a satisfactory delivery by faith before the bodily delivery come: *when I cry
unto thee, then shall mine enemies turn back.* 2. Faith goeth
upon solid grounds, and is not a fallible conjecture but a
sure knowledge: *this I know,* saith he. 3. A reconciled
man, praying to God in a good cause for victory over his
persecutors, may be assured that God will own his quarrel
and give him the victory: *this I know, because God is for
me.* 4. The special attribute of God wherewith faith meeteth, and whereby it attaineth unto, rest and contentment in
God, is his truth and fidelity to his promises: *in God I will
praise his word;* albeit there be no appearance of performance, God's word is sure enough to fix upon. 5. The grounds
of faith are the more sweet and satisfactory the more they
are examined and compared with their effects; for David is
not content once to say, *in God will I praise his word;* but
with comfort and confidence he reneweth his commendation
of God's word, and the benefit he hath by it: *I will not be
afraid what man can do unto me.* 6. As it is necessary for
our justification to believe in God, so is it necessary for our
consolation to observe that we have believed; for then may
we promise to ourselves all the blessedness which belongs to
the believer: *in God I have put my trust, I will not be afraid;*
for when we thus resolutely set our seal to God's truth, believing, and asserting our belief: then he setteth his seal to
our faith, in comforting and relieving us.

12. *Thy vows* are *upon me, O God: I will render
praises unto thee.*

13. *For thou hast delivered my soul from death:* wilt
not thou deliver *my feet from falling, that I may walk
before God in the light of the living?*

In the latter part of the psalm, having now obtained delivery in his spirit by faith, he obliges himself to thankfulness, wishing to be preserved and enabled of God for that end. Whence learn, 1. As God puts the duty of glorifying him upon the supplicant, when he promiseth delivery to him; so may the supplicant put the obligation of glorifying God upon himself, when he is praying for delivery out of his trouble, as David giveth us to understand he did, while he saith, *thy vows are upon me.* 2. An honest heart is no less desirous to perform the duty of praise to God after delivery, than he was ready to make his vow and promise before his delivery; yea, the consciousness of the twofold obligation is a burden upon his spirit, till he go about the payment of his twice due debt: *thy vows are upon me, O God, I will render praises to thee.* 3. As deep dangers serve to discover our weakness and our need of God's help; so a well-seen danger maketh clear the greatness of the delivery, and the greatness of the delivery deciphers the wisdom, power, and goodness of God to us, and our obligation to him: *I will render praises unto thee, for thou hast delivered my soul from death.* 4. The right use of bypast dangers and deliveries is to prepare for new dangers and difficulties, (for when one danger is past all perils are not past;) to renounce our own wisdom and strength, as insufficient to preserve us from ruin either of soul or body; to give up ourselves to God's guiding and preservation; and to depend upon God, and steadfastly hope to be directed and preserved by him : all this is imported in David's words, *thou hast delivered my soul from death, wilt thou not preserve my feet from falling?* 5. The end of our desires to have deliveries and benefits from God should be, that we may spend our life, and the gifts bestowed upon us, sincerely in the service of God, for the edification of his people : *wilt thou not preserve my feet from falling, that I may walk before God in the light of the living?*

PSALM LVII.

To the chief musician, Al-taschith, Michtam of David, when he fled from Saul in the cave.

This psalm of David, as many others of his psalms, representeth the condition of his spirit, both in the time of his trouble and after his delivery from it: what was his exercise in the cave, and what was his condition after he was delivered out of that danger, whereof we read 1 Sam. xxiv. There are two parts of this psalm: the first containeth his prayer for deliverance, which is pressed by six arguments, all serving to strengthen his faith. The first is, because he trusted in God, ver. 1; the second, because he resolved to insist in prayer till he was heard, ver. 2; the third, because he hoped certainly to find signal delivery from this extraordinary danger, ver. 3; the fourth, because his enemies were beastly cruel, ver. 4; the fifth, because this mercy might contribute much to the glorifying of God, ver. 5; the sixth is from the low condition whereunto his spirit is brought, by their crafty and cruel pursuit of him, ver. 6. In the rest of the psalm is his thanksgiving, consisting of five parts: the first is the acknowledgment of the mercy and delivery granted, ver. 6; the next is his fixed resolution to praise God for it, ver. 7; the third is the upstirring of tongue and hand, and the whole man, to praise God, ver. 8; the fourth is a promise to transmit the knowledge of God's mercy to other nations, ver. 9; the fifth is the acknowledgment of the glory of this mercy, with a wish that it might be more and more seen and acknowledged by giving new experience of it, ver. 10, 11.

From the inscription, learn, That the godly may be involved in a deadly danger, (as David was, when he fled from Saul in the cave,) and yet not perish. Now he was as a man ready to be buried quick; for the cave was as a grave, and the army of Saul at the mouth of the cave, was as the grave-stone: let, then, the army of Saul only know that he is there, and keep him in, and he is gone; yet God blinded them, brought David out, and so delivered him.

1. *Be merciful unto me, O God, be merciful unto me ; for my soul trusteth in thee : yea, in the shadow of thy wings will I make my refuge, until* these *calamities be overpast.*

From the psalmist's prayer for deliverance, and first argument taken from his trusting in God, learn, 1. The only refuge of a man in trouble is the mercy of the Lord; be it sin, be it misery, be it peril, or pressing evil; in mercy only is the relief of one and all sad conditions : and in this case must a soul double its petition in the Lord's bosom : *be merciful unto me, O God, be merciful unto me.* 2. As it is not trouble simply which maketh prayer to be fervent, but solid faith pressed with trouble, which doubleth petitions unto God; so where faith in trouble fleeth unto God it cannot but speed : *be merciful, O God, for I trust in thee.* The force of the reason is, The Lord cannot forsake the soul which hath committed itself to him. 3. The Lord offereth relief and protection in Christ to miserable sinners, in as warm a manner as the similitude of a hen gathering her chickens, or the type of stretching the wings of the cherubim about the mercy-seat could express; and faith clingeth no less warmly to this offer in time of straits, than this similitude importeth: *yea, in the shadow of thy wings will I make my refuge.* 4. The use of God's protection and warm love is best known in time of trouble, and faith is also best set on work, to make use of God's love and protection in time of trouble: *in the shadow of thy wings will I make my refuge, until these calamities be overpast.*

2. *I will cry unto God most High ; unto God that performeth* all things *for me.*

From the second argument which he useth for strengthening his faith, learn, 1. Faith in God and invocation of his name, are graces inseparable; and resolution to persevere in believing is inseparable from resolution to persevere in praying unto God : and he that findeth in his heart such resolutions, may also be confident to speed in his requests made to God; for as the psalmist resolved to believe in the former verse, so here he addeth, *I will cry unto God,* and hereby expecteth that God shall be merciful unto him. 2. It is needful for the supplicant in his straits, to keep in sight the Lord's supremacy and omnipotency, for encouraging himself in hope to speed : *I will cry to God most High,* saith he. 3. The consideration of the Lord's constant going on in the perfecting of the work of grace, which once he beginneth graciously in us or for us, serveth much to strengthen our faith in prayer : *I will cry to God, who performeth all things for me.*

3. *He shall send from heaven, and save me* from *the reproach of him that would swallow me up. Selah. God shall send forth his mercy and his truth.*

From the third argument and prop of his prayer, taken from his hope to be helped, learn, 1. Albeit faith see no help on earth, yet it looketh for help in heaven; and if ordinary means fail, it assureth itself of God's working wonders for perfecting his promises : *he shall send from heaven and save me.* 2. The godly man's making God his refuge, is a matter of mocking to the wicked; which mocking God will certainly refute, by making the godly find the fruit of their flying to him : *he will save me from the reproach of him that would swallow me up.* 3. The mercy and truth of God, whereupon faith fixeth itself, remove all impediments, and set on work all the means of the salvation of the believer, and that effectually : *God shall send forth his mercy and his truth.*

4. *My soul* is *among lions ;* and *I lie* even among *them that are set on fire,* even *the sons of men, whose teeth* are *spears and arrows, and their tongue a sharp sword.*

From the fourth reason of his prayer, taken from the beastly cruelty of his enemies, learn, 1. The condition of the people of the Lord in this world may be ofttimes like sheep in peril of their lives, compassed about with ravenous beasts: *my soul is among lions.* 2. Yea, they may be so desolate, as having no assistance from without themselves to fly or fight, they shall be forced, like darned birds chased by the hawk, or like bound sheep, to clap close to the ground : *I lie,* saith he, *among them.* 3. The desolate condition of the godly moveth not their persecutors to pity: deadly malice is most ready then to break forth and devour : *I lie even among them that are set on fire.* 4. Graceless men, destitute of the fear of God, are fit enough instruments for the persecution of God's children and his dear servants, if they be no more, but in nature, *even the children of men.* 5. The slanders, mockings, lies, calumnies, reproaches, and aspersions, cast upon the godly by godless men, are no little part of their cruel persecution, of cutting and piercing the Lord's people very deeply : *whose teeth are spears and arrows, and their tongue a sharp sword.*

5. *Be thou exalted, O God, above the heavens ;* let *thy glory* be *above all the earth.*

From the fifth reason of his petition, learn, 1. When the godly are borne down, and the wicked carry all matters before them, the glory of the Lord is obscured and eclipsed in some sort among men; therefore saith he, *be thou exalted, O God.* 2. In what measure God's children are helped by him, and his enemies are borne down, in that measure is he gloriously manifested to be the Ruler of heaven and earth : *be thou exalted above the heavens, and thy glory above all the earth.* 3. However the wicked obscure the glory of the Lord, and how little evidence soever God's children see of his appearing for their relief; yet they ought to glorify him in their heart, and not only believe his sovereign power able to set all things in order, but also to profess their hope, that he shall manifest himself from heaven, to be Lord over all his enemies and adverse powers of tne world : *be thou exalted above the heavens, and thy glory above all the earth.*

6. *They have prepared a net for my steps ; my soul is bowed down : they have digged a pit before me, into the midst whereof they are fallen* themselves. *Selah.*

From the last reason of his supplication, learn, 1. That the wicked use great sleight and subtilty to overtake the godly in some snare or other : *they have prepared a net for my steps.* 2. The godly man's strength will soon fail him in time of straits, if the Lord give not supply : yea, the Lord, for the clearer manifestation of his glory, both before the godly, and before the wicked, suffereth his children to come to so low a condition of spirit, that they are ready to succumb if he help not : *my soul is bowed down.* 3. When the enemies are at the highest of their plots, and the godly at the lowest step of their humiliation, then is the Lord's time to turn the chase, and to fall upon his enemies; and that ofttimes by the very same means whereby they were about to make all fast for their own power, and the oppression of the godly: *they have digged a pit before me, into the midst whereof they are fallen themselves.* And this last sentence is the first of his thanksgiving, in acknowledging the Lord's wonderful mercy and justice, in changing upside down the scales of his low condition, and the enemy's lofty persecution on a sudden.

7. *My heart is fixed, O God, my heart is fixed ; I will sing and give praise.*

In the rest of the psalm he prosecuteth his thanksgiving, and this is the second part of it, wherein he professed his fixed purpose to praise the Lord for his delivery. Whence learn, 1. Renewed sense of God's favour, and fresh experience of his mercy towards his children, and of his justice against his and their enemies, much refresheth, quieteth, and settleth the hearts of his people, and confirmeth their faith : *my heart is fixed.* 2. It is a part of our thanksgiving unto God, to acknowledge the fruit of his gracious working for us, felt upon our spirits, whensoever our hearts are cheered up by him after any sad exercise : *my heart is fixed, O God, my heart is fixed.* 3. As it is needful to labour on the heart, that it may be fitted and prepared, fixed and bended, for God's worship; so in special, for the work of praise, whereunto naturally we are most dull and indisposed; then shall the work go on more cheerfully : *my heart is fixed, I will sing and give praise.*

8. *Awake up, my glory ; awake, psaltery and harp : I* myself *will awake early.*

From the third part of his thanksgiving, wherein he stirs up himself, by all means, within and without himself, to set forth his sense of God's mercy, and glory in bestowing it, learn, 1. A well-employed tongue for praising God, and edifying others, is indeed a man's commendation and glory above other creatures; therefore David, directing his speech towards his tongue, after the manner of orators, affectionately speaking, saith, *awake, my glory.* 2. Albeit the abolition of the ceremonial law hath taken away the room which musical instruments once had in the stately, public, instituted worship of God in the congregation; yet neither is the natural private use thereof taken away, nor the signification of that typical ordinance to be forgotten, to wit, that we of ourselves are dull and unapt to holy things, and that the Lord's praises are above our power to reach or express; and that we should stir up all the faculties of our souls unto this holy service, as David here insinuateth to be the moral signification thereof; for, after he hath said, *awake, psaltery and harp,* he subjoineth, *I myself will awake.* 3. As he who in earnest is wakened up to glorify and praise God, will find himself short in abilities to discharge this work of praise; so will he find the choicest time of the day, when the body is best refreshed, most deservedly bestowed upon this exercise : *I myself will awake early.*

9. *I will praise thee, O Lord, among the people ; I will sing unto thee among the nations :*

From the fourth part of this thanksgiving, wherein he promiseth to let all the world know the mercy bestowed upon him, learn, 1. The Spirit of God, who inditeth this scripture, made his penman know that the Gentiles should have the use of his psalms : *I will praise thee among the people.* 2. David was a type of Christ in sufferings, spiritual exercises, and in receiving deliveries; for this promise is fulfilled in Christ, and this undertaking is applied unto Christ, Rom. xv. 9. 3. We seriously mind the praise of God when, according to our place, we labour to make others also know God, as we know him: *I will praise thee among the people.*

10. *For thy mercy is great unto the heavens, and thy truth unto the clouds.*

11. *Be thou exalted, O God, above the heavens: let thy glory be above all the earth.*

From the last part of his thanksgiving, wherein the psalmist confesseth that the excellency of the glory of God transcendeth his reach and capacity, and that he can follow it no further than by wishing the Lord to glorify himself, learn, 1. The matter of the joy of the saints, and of their sweetest songs, is the goodness of God, which appointed and promised such and such mercies unto them, and the faithfulness of God, which bringeth to pass his gracious purpose and promises made unto them: *for thy mercy is great, and thy truth,* saith he. 2. There is no possibility of taking up the greatness of God's mercy and truth; they reach so far as our sight cannot overtake them: *thy mercy is great unto the heavens,* where mortal eyes cannot come to see what is there, *and thy truth unto the clouds,* through which man's eye cannot pierce. 3. Seeing the Lord's glory is greater than heaven or earth can contain, and God himself only can manifest his own glory, it is our part when we have said all we can for glorifying God, to pray to him to glorify himself, and to make it appear to all, that his glory is greater than heaven or earth can comprehend: *be exalted above the heavens, and let thy glory be above all the earth.*

PSALM LVIII.

To the chief musician Al-taschith, Michtam of David.

The psalmist, being oppressed by the calumnies of the courtiers of king Saul, and by the senators of the courts of justice, who should have provided against the oppression of the subjects, chargeth them, in the first part of this psalm, as most guilty of injustice done to him, v. 1—5. In the second part, he prayeth against them, that God would execute judgment upon them, v. 6—8. And, in the third part, he pronounceth the sentence of their deserved destruction, v. 9—11. From this experience of the prophet, we may see what strong parties and hard opposition the godly may meet with in the defence of a good cause, and how necessary it is in such trials to exercise our faith, and to exalt God above all opposite powers, that we may be borne out, and get consolation and victory in the Lord.

1. *Do ye indeed speak righteousness, O congregation ? do ye judge uprightly, O ye sons of men ?*

2. *Yea, in heart ye work wickedness ; ye weigh the
violence of your hands in the earth.*

3. *The wicked are estranged from the womb; they
go astray as soon as they be born, speaking lies.*

4. *Their poison is like the poison of a serpent :* they
are *like the deaf adder,* that *stoppeth her ear;*

5. *Which will not hearken to the voice of charmers,
charming never so wisely.*

In the last part David chargeth the council and senate,
or congregation of the judges; first, with not giving out
righteous decrees or sentences, v. 1; secondly, with their
obstinate, violent, oppressing decrees, v. 2; thirdly, with
their inveterate wickedness and falsehood from the womb,
v. 3; fourthly, with their incorrigible wickedness, which they
will not for any admonition or advice amend, v. 4, 5. Whence
learn, 1. There is a congregation of rulers, whose office it is
to administer justice to the people, who presuppose they are
the supreme court, in authority and place above the body of
the people; yet are they subject to God's challenge, which
he sendeth unto them by the hand of his messengers when
they do wrong, as here we see : *do ye indeed speak righteousness, O congregation ?* 2. When the just cause of the righteous cometh before the Judge, whosoever be pursuer, were
he as great a party as king Saul pursuing David, the Judge
should defend the righteous, and absolve him, without fearing man's face; and if he do not he shall be called to a reckoning for it before God : *do ye judge uprightly, O ye sons of
men ?* 3. The Lord looketh to the affections, purposes, and
conclusions of a man's heart, and what ill action a man is
resolved to do; for that is a done work before God : and the
man is so much the more guilty, as his sin is deliberate : *yea,
in heart you work wickedness.* 4. A wicked judge hesitates
not to give out a decree for as much oppression as he is able
to put in execution : *you weigh the violence of your hands in
the earth.* And when he is thus oppressing men, he will
labour to seem to make his decree no less agreeable to the
law, than the equal scales of the merchant's balance answer
in a just weight, one to another : *you weigh the violence of
your hands.* 5. An unrenewed man is a born stranger to

God, to good men, and all goodness: *the wicked are estranged from the womb.* 6. Men's wicked actions prove the wickedness of nature; or men's original sin augmenteth the ditty and condemnation of unrenewed men for their actual sins: *they are estranged from the womb,* is here made a part of their challenge. 7. Error and falsehood are kindly sins to men; they break out early, continue long, and draw on guiltiness the longer the more : *they go astray as soon as they be born, speaking lies.* 8. There is as great natural enmity in the wicked against the godly, as there is in serpents against mankind, and they are as ready to vent their deadly hatred against them, as serpents are to spue forth their deadly venom: *their poison is like the poison of a serpent.* 9. That which filleth up the measure of the sins of the wicked is this, they are obdured in their sins, incorrigible, and will not receive instruction, admonition, or correction from the word of God : *they are like the deaf adder that stoppeth her ear.* 10. Albeit Holy Scripture useth to compare the best things in some points with the worst things, for clearing the purpose in hand by a similitude; yet doth it not therefore justify the wicked thing by borrowing a similitude from it, as here the admonition and reproof of sinners are compared to the charming of an adder: and yet for that comparison the damnable sin of charming is not the less damnable, nor is the duty of reproof and admonition of sinners the worse or less laudable for the comparison: for it is a challenge : *they are like the deaf adder that stoppeth her ear, which will not hearken unto the charmer, charming never so wisely.*

6. *Break their teeth, O God, in their mouth ; break out the great teeth of the young lions, O Lord.*

7. *Let them melt away as waters* which *run continually :* when *he bendeth* his bow to shoot *his arrows, let them be as cut in pieces.*

8. *As a snail* which *melteth, let* every one of them *pass away ;* like *the untimely birth of a woman,* that *they may not see the sun.*

In the second part of this psalm David maketh imprecation against them, by special warrant of the Spirit of God, who indited this psalm to him, that judgment might be executed against them unto destruction. Whence learn, 1. The Lord shall in due time disable the wicked from doing the harm they intend to do against God's people; for this prayer is a prophecy and promise to the church's comfort : *break their teeth, O God, in their mouth.* 2. Were the wicked ever so potent and resolute to execute their cruelty, God shall break their power in pieces : *break out the great teeth of the young lions, O Lord.* 3. When once God entereth into judgment with the enemies of his people, he shall bring upon them a constant daily consumption and wasting of their power and abilities, till they be abolished : *let them melt away like mater that runs continually.* 4. The chief plots of the wicked shall miscarry in the very point of their putting them in execution : *when he bendeth his bow to shoot his arrows, let them be as cut in pieces.* 5. How strong soever the foundation of the enterprises of the wicked against the godly seem to themselves to be, yet the event shall prove them to be weak, feeble, and effectless devices : *as a snail which melteth, let them pass away, as the untimely birth of a woman, that they may not see the sun.*

9. *Before your pots can feel the thorns, he shall take them away as with a whirlwind, both living, and in his wrath.*

10. *The righteous shall rejoice when he seeth the vengeance; he shall wash his feet in the blood of the wicked.*

11. *So that a man shall say, Verily, there is a reward for the righteous: verily he is a God that judgeth in the earth.*

In the last part of the psalm, David pronounceth the sentence of deserved destruction upon the wicked and unrighteous potentates, oppressors of the godly, as an answer from God to the former imprecation against them, and that for the consolation of the godly, and clearing of God's justice among men. Whence learn, 1. Howsoever the ungodly hope to procure for themselves good cheer by their works of iniquity, and rejoice a while in their hopes, yet before they find any ripe satisfaction by their ill deeds, suddenly they are destroyed, and as it were swallowed up quickly, and taken away by the fierce wrath of God against them : *before your pots can feel the thorns, he shall take them away as with a whirlwind, both living and in his wrath.* 2. It is lawful for the godly to rejoice in God's justice against the obstinate enemies of his people, provided their joy be indeed in God's

justice; not in the destruction of the creature, but in the manifestation of God's just avenging hand : *the righteous shall
rejoice when he seeth the vengeance.* 3. The punishment of
the wicked should teach the Lord's people to be more holy
in all their ways, for this is one of the ends of God's punishing the wicked in their sight : *the righteous shall wash his
feet in the blood of the wicked.* 4. When the Lord executeth
judgment against the wicked, then men who knew not what
to think of God's providence, when they saw the godly oppressed and the wicked high in power, shall come to a right
judging of matters : *so that a man shall say, Verily there
is a reward for the righteous.* 5. No man serveth God for
nought; in following the course of friendship with God, and
walking in obedience unto him, fruit certainly will be found :
verily there is a reward for the righteous. 6. Albeit the
Lord setteth not down his court for executing justice so soon
as men would, yet he fails not to show himself ruler of the
affairs of men and a righteous judge, as to relieve the oppressed, so also to take order with oppressors : *verily he is a
God that judgeth in the earth.*

PSALM LIX.

*To the chief musician, Al-taschith, Michtam of David, when Saul sent,
and they watched the house to kill him.*

David, in present danger of his life by Saul, (who having David inclosed
within the city and within his own house, thought surely to have killed
him, as we read, 1 Sam. xix. 11,) prayeth to God for deliverance, v. 1, 2;
and as a reason for his prayer, maketh a complaint against his enemies,
v. 3, 4. In the next place, he prayeth the second time for delivery to
himself and judgment against his enemies, v. 5, and complaineth of
them the second time, v. 6, 7. In the third place, he declareth his confidence of being delivered, v. 8—10. In the fourth place, he maketh
imprecation against his enemies for their wickedness, v. 11—15. And,
in the last place, he promiseth thanks to God for his delivery, whereof
he was assured before it came, v. 16, 17.

From the inscription, learn, 1. No common bands of nature or civil relations can secure the godly from the persecution of the wicked : for Saul, David's father-in-law, sendeth to kill David. 2. God's children cannot be in so great
straits, nor the vigilance of the wicked to overtake the godly
be so great in a strait, but God can deliver a supplicant;
they watched the house to kill him, yet he escaped, and wrote
this psalm : by what means he escaped he doth not tell here,

for he attributeth the delivery to God, from whom he sought it by prayer.

1. *Deliver me from mine enemies, O my God; defend me from them that rise up against me.*

2. *Deliver me from the workers of iniquity, and save me from bloody men.*

From his prayer, learn, 1. Whatsoever means God shall offer for escaping out of a trouble, prayer is our best weapon against our enemies, the best of all means, and first of all to be used for a delivery: *deliver me from mine enemies.* 2. Time of trouble and difficulty compelleth believers to make use of the covenant of grace, and of God's friendship and power for their deliverance: *O my God, defend me from them that rise up against me.* 3. When wicked, powerful, and bloodthirsty men turn persecutors of the godly, no power but divine can be looked to for relief: *deliver me from the workers of iniquity, and save me from bloody men.*

3. *For, lo, they lie in wait for my soul: the mighty are gathered against me; not for my transgression, nor for my sin, O Lord.*

4. *They run and prepare themselves without my fault: awake to help me, and behold.*

From his complaint against his enemies, and reason of his prayer, learn, 1. Desperate-like dangers, arising from the power and craftiness of enemies, must not discourage the godly, but sharpen their prayer to God, with whom are power and wisdom to deliver them: *for lo, they lie in wait for my soul.* 2. It is no new thing, to see them who are in greatest power, the chief in the persecution of God's children: *the mighty are gathered together against me.* 3. A good conscience, especially in the particular for which a man is pursued, giveth greatest comfort in the time of trouble: *not for my transgression nor my sin, O Lord.* 4. Albeit the persecutors of the godly cannot find a fault in them, for which they may pursue them; yet will they devise some challenge, and make a great business to accomplish their design: *they run and prepare themselves not for my fault.* 5. The Lord will let the plot go on, and the danger of the godly grow, as if he minded not to take notice of it, that he may first put his children to prayer, and then appear in the fit time: *awake to help me, and behold.*

5. *Thou therefore, O Lord God of hosts, the God of Israel, awake to visit all the heathen : be not merciful to any wicked transgressors.   Selah.*

6. *They return at evening : they make a noise like a dog, and go round about the city.*

7. *Behold, they belch out with their mouth : swords are in their lips ; for who* (say they) *doth hear ?*

For his repeated prayer and complaint presented the second time, learn, 1. In time of straits we should set our eyes most upon those providences of God, which most serve to strengthen our faith, especially such as hold forth his power, and good-will to employ his power for us : *thou therefore, O Lord God of hosts, the God of Israel, awake.* 2. Counterfeit professors and professed pagans are in effect all one before God, and the counterfeit professor will be as ready an instrument to persecute the godly as a professed enemy; for so are Saul and his followers named here : *awake to visit all the heathen.* 3. Although the Lord bear with the wicked a while, he will at last take order with hypocrites and obstinately malicious transgressors : *awake to visit all the heathen, be not merciful to any wicked transgressor.* 4. From the time that persecutors have once resolved cruelty, they cease not to pursue their purpose, but like bloody dogs, they run to and fro till they catch their prey; they are busy all the day, and set watches in the night to hurt the man they would have : *they return at evening, they make a noise like a dog, and go round about the city.* 5. Resolved obstinacy in sin taketh away all remorse of conscience, all fear of God and shame before men, and maketh men openly avow their wickedness; yea and their cruel hearts will vent their bloody purpose, when they think they are sure to accomplish their design : *behold, they belch out with their mouth, swords are in their lips ; for who, say they, will hear ?*

8. *But thou, O Lord, shalt laugh at them ; thou shalt have all the heathen in derision.*

9. *Because of his strength will I wait upon thee : for God is my defence.*

10. *The God of my mercy shall prevent me : God shall let me see my desire upon mine enemies.*

In the third place, the psalmist declareth his confidence

to be delivered, and maketh use of his faith for keeping up his heart under his trouble. Whence learn, 1. The first fruit of an humble prayer, is a spiritual delivery of a man's oppressed spirit, granted unto him by faith and assurance of an outgate; as here and many times elsewhere appeareth. 2. When faith seeth God to be a friend, it scorneth all opposition of whatsoever enemies, few or many, all is one to the clear-sighted believer : *but thou, O Lord, shalt laugh at them; thou shalt have all the heathen in derision.* 3. How weak soever the believer may find himself, and how powerful soever he perceive his enemies to be, it is all one to him, he hath no more to do, but to put faith on work and wait till God work; because of his strength, that is, the enemies' strength; *I will wait upon thee,* saith he to the Lord, *for God is my defence.* 4. When faith gets up the head, it seeth its own deliverance and the overthrow of the enemy, both at once in the proper cause thereof, to wit, the fountain of over-running mercy, engaged unto it by covenant : *the God of my mercy.* There is the fountain of *everlasting mercy,* whereof God is called God, because he is the believer's God for ever, and therefore the Lord of all mercy, consolation, and salvation to the believer : *he,* saith he, *shall prevent me ;* that is, he shall give manifest deliverance before I succumb : it shall come sooner than I could set it a time. Then, for his enemies, he saith, *God shall let me see my desire upon mine enemies ;* to wit, what I could lawfully desire, or what should satisfy me.

11. *Slay them not, lest my people forget: scatter them by thy power; and bring them down, O Lord our shield.*

12. For *the sin of their mouth,* and *the words of their lips, let them even be taken in their pride ; and for cursing and lying* which *they speak.*

13. *Consume* them *in wrath ; consume* them, *that they* may *not* be ; *and let them know that God ruleth in Jacob unto the ends of the earth. Selah.*

14. *And at evening let them return ;* and *let them make a noise like a dog, and go round about the city.*

15. *Let them wander up and down for meat, and grudge if they be not satisfied.*

In the fourth place, David prayeth to God to glorify himself in the manner and measure of his just judgment on his obstinate enemies; which in effect is a prophecy of the punishment of the persecutors of the righteous, and of the wrath to come upon the enemies of Christ,'of whom David in his trouble and unjust sufferings was a type. Whence learn, 1. Sometimes the Lord will delay cutting off wicked enemies of his people, for a curse to them and a benefit to his people : *slay them not, lest my people forget.* 2. The Lord's people are subject to forget the Lord's doing for them, and punishing their enemies, except he renew the evidence of the care he hath of them, by often renewed, or long-continued judgment on their enemies, whose misery is more to them, by lingering judgments in the sight of men, than if they were cut off suddenly : *slay them not, lest my people forget.* 3. In praying against our wicked enemies that persecute us, we must take heed that we be found pleading, not our own particular revenge, but the common cause of the church and the Lord's quarrel : *slay them not, lest my people forget ; scatter and bring them down, O Lord, our shield.* It is the good of the Lord's people, and the glorifying of God which is in his eye. 4. Albeit the Lord cuts not off at first the troublers of his church, but suffers them to live for the exercise of his people; yet it is mercy worthy to be prayed for, if God disable them and break their power, that they prevail not over the righteous : *scatter them by thy power, and bring them down, O Lord our shield.* 5. Albeit the persecutors accomplish not their purpose against the righteous; yet their pride, their brags, their lies, their slanders, their curses against the godly, are a sufficient ditty for damnation and wrath to come upon them : *for the sin of their mouth, and the words of their lips, let them even be taken in their pride, and for cursing and lying which they speak.* 6. After the keeping alive of the wicked for a time, to the increasing of their misery, at length utter destruction cometh upon them : *consume them in wrath, consume them, that they may not be.* 7. By the judgments of God upon the adversaries of his people, the knowledge of his sovereignty over, and kingly care for, his church is made more known to the world, the increase of which glory of the Lord should be the scope of the prayers of the saints against their foes : *and let them know that God ruleth in Jacob unto the ends of the earth.* 8. It is suitable to God's justice and no

N

strange thing to see such as have been messengers, servants, officers of persecuting powers, or searchers out of the godly, as beagles or blood-hounds, made beggars, vagabonds, and miserable spectacles of God's wrath before they die, roving to and fro like hungry and masterless dogs : *at evening let them return, and let them make a noise like a dog, and go round about the city ; let them wander up and down for meat, and grudge if they be not satisfied.*

16. *But I will sing of thy power ; yea, I will sing aloud of thy mercy in the morning : for thou hast been my defence and refuge in the day of my trouble.*

17. *Unto thee, O my strength, will I sing : for God* is *my defence,* and *the God of my mercy.*

In the last place, David promiseth thanksgiving for the mercy which he felt in the day of his trouble, and fixeth his faith on God, as his merciful protector and only strength, whereon he was to lean in every condition wherein he could fall. Whence learn, 1. Whatsoever mischief fall upon the wicked, the Lord's children, whom they malign, shall have reason to rejoice and praise God for supporting them in their trials, and delivering them out of troubles : *but I will sing of thy power.* 2. When the godly compare the Lord's putting difference between them and the rest of the wicked world, pitying them and pardoning their sins, when he justly punisheth the sins of others, they cannot but rejoice, and proclaim God's mercy with earnest affection : *yea I will sing aloud of thy mercy in the morning.* 3. The shining light of one late experience of God's care of a man, serveth to bring to remembrance, and to illuminate the whole course of God's by past care and kindness to him, and to raise a song of joy and praise to God for altogether : *for thou hast been my refuge and defence in the day of trouble.* 4. What God hath been unto us, being looked on rightly, may serve to certify what God is unto us, what he shall be to us, and what we may expect of him: for from *thou hast been my defence and my refuge,* he inferreth hope of joyful experience of the same mercy for time to come : *unto thee, O my strength, will I sing.* 5. When a man is sure of God's being engaged to him by good-will and covenant, and proof given for letting out to him protection and mercy, as his soul needeth, he cannot but have a heart full of joy, and a mouth full of joyful praises unto God: *unto thee, O my strength, will I sing, for God is my defence, and the God of my mercy.*

PSALM LX.

To the chief musician upon Shushan-eduth, Michtam of David, to teach; when he strove with Aram-naharaim, and with Aram-zobah, when Joab returned, and smote of Edom in the valley of Salt twelve thousand.

This psalm is a prayer for the victory of Israel over their enemies, indited unto the prophet when Israel was fighting with the Syrians and Edomites. It may be divided into three parts. In the first part the psalmist prayeth for help more largely, ver. 1—5; in the second, David is made confident of the victory, ver. 6—10; in the third, he repeateth his prayer more briefly, and his confidence of his having the victory, ver. 11, 12.

From the inscription learn, 1. The children of God must not think it strange to be put to wrestling, striving, and fighting for a promised kingdom, before they be settled in possession, as David was; yea, the church of Christ must expect such like exercises; for this psalm is given to the public ministers of the church for use in all ages. 2. The church must make use of her prayers as well when she is furnished with a regular army as when she wanteth bodily arms, as David teacheth the church here. 3. There is hope of victory, when God, by prayer, is more relied upon than the army in the field; for, with the psalmist the mention of the victory of the Lord's host is set down and the slaughter of the enemy recorded: *that Joab smote of Edom twelve thousand.*

1. *O God, thou hast cast us off, thou hast scattered us, thou hast been displeased; O turn thyself to us again.*

Of the larger prayer there are three branches. The first is for reconciliation with God, v. 1; the second for reparation of the decayed state of the kingdom, v. 2, 3; the third, for delivery and victory in the conflict with the enemy, v. 4, 5.

In the first branch of his prayer the psalmist acknowledgeth bygone judgments as the fruit of God's displeasure, and of the people's provocation of God to wrath, and so he prayeth that God would turn again and be reconciled to his people. Whence learn, 1. Terrible evils may befall the Lord's people, or the visible church, when they, by their sin, provoke him to wrath, as was seen in the time of the Judges and in Saul's time: *O God, thou hast cast us off, hou hast scattered us.* 2. When God plagueth a whole kingdom, or the body of the visible church, it is not a matter of simple exercise or trial, (as when he bringeth trouble on some of his dear servants in the time of their upright carriage,) but it is for their sins and provocation of the eyes of his glory : *thou hast been displeased.* 3. Such as would have plagues removed must acknowledge their sin, and seek to be reconciled with God; and in this way may they expect to find favour : *O turn thyself to us again.* 4. Whatsoever sins the visible church and incorporation of professors have committed against God, or whatsoever injuries they have done against the godly, in assisting persecuting powers against them; yet the godly must not only not separate from them, but must also be ready to receive them into favour, be reconciled to them, forgive their former injuries, join in church and camp-fellowship with them, being reconciled, by compassion share with them in calamities, intercede with God for them as for themselves, as being all of one incorporation; as David, the type of Christ's moderate and merciful governing, and a pattern to all the godly, forgave those that persecuted him, fought against him under king Saul, and stood longest out against him when Saul was dead : for David here saith with and for the people, *O God, thou hast scattered us; O turn thyself again to us.*

2. *Thou hast made the earth to tremble; thou hast broken it : heal the breaches thereof; for it shaketh.*

3. *Thou hast shewed thy people hard things : thou hast made us to drink the wine of astonishment.*

When Saul reigned, all things went wrong; the wicked abounded, vile men were exalted, and God plagued the land; therefore, in the second branch of his prayer, he prayeth for restoration of the dejected state of the kingdom : the calamities whereof he layeth forth, both before and after the petition. Whence learn, 1. When people will not stand in awe of God and fear him, he will strike them with the fear of his wrath and sense of sore judgments : *thou hast made the earth to tremble.* 2. War, and in special civil and intestine war, is most able to ruin a kingdom, and, like an earthquake, to make ruptures and breaches in it to the renting of it in pieces : *thou hast made the earth to tremble, thou hast broken it.* 3. It is a Christian and royal virtue to seek the union of the subjects among themselves, and to remove divisions of the kingdom, without the removing whereof the state can never be settled; but it is a divine power to work this union effectually, therefore David prayeth to God for it: *heal the breaches thereof, for it shaketh.* 4. When people will not see nor take knowledge of their sins against God, and their bounden duties to him, he will let them see sa spectacles of bloody wars, foreign and intestine: *thou hast shewed thy people hard things.* 5. When people have be-sotted themselves in their sin, and have not believed what God hath threatened against them, no wonder they know not what hand to turn them to, and be stricken with asto-nishment in the execution of his judgments, which, when they fall upon a people, either suddenly or more heavily than they could have expected, put men's minds in confusion, as if they were drunk; for sudden, sore, and lasting judg-ments confound the thoughts of secure sinners, so as they can make little use of the word of God, or of their wit, or any other means of relief, more than a drunken man over-charged with wine: *thou hast made us to drink the wine of astonishment.*

4. *Thou hast given a banner to them that fear thee, that it may be displayed because of the truth. Selah.*

5. *That thy beloved may be delivered, save* with *thy right hand, and hear me.*

In the third branch of his prayer, David seeketh delivery and victory over the enemy, and that because God had begun to give some hope of changing the face of affairs, by raisi...g a banner in David's hand for the Lord's cause and people. Whence learn, 1. When the godly are oppressed, the truth of religion and of God's promises is prostrated, like a fallen standard; and when God raiseth up instruments for their protection and comfort, as here he did in bringing David to the kingdom, it is like the lifting up of an ensign in the hand of a valiant standard-bearer: *thou hast given a banner to them that fear thee.* 2. It is on the godly's account that mercy is shown to a whole land: *thou hast given a banner to them that fear thee.* 3. When the godly get up their head, all their endeavour, according to the utmost of their power, should be to advance true religion and the practice of it: *thou hast given a banner, that it may be displayed, because of the truth.* 4. As nothing is respected by God in a land so much as his elect that fear him; so, nothing can encourage us to seek and hope for mercy to a land, so much as the Lord's love to them that fear him it: *that thy beloved may be delivered,* save. 5. When God hath begun to appear for his church, then in special should we follow a begun blessing, with prayer that God would work out the benefit: *thou hast given a banner to them that fear thee; that thy beloved may be delivered, save.* 6. Whatsover difficulties appear in the way of the church's delivery, we must oppose the omnipotency of God to them all, and sustain our faith in prayer by looking to his love towards his church and power to do for her: *that thy beloved may be delivered, save with thy right hand, and hear me.*

6. *God hath spoken in his holiness; I will rejoice: I will divide Shechem, and mete out the valley of Succoth.*

7. *Gilead is mine, and Manasseh is mine; Ephraim also is the strength of mine head; Judah is my lawgiver;*

In the second part of the psalm is set down David's confidence to have the victory over his enemies, and to have his kingdom both settled at home, v. 6, 7, and enlarged abroad, v. 8—10.

By David's prayer, the word of promise, that he should be established king, is made evident to him, whereupon he is comforted and made confident of the accomplishment thereof in all points. Whence learn, 1. As faith helpeth up prayer, so by prayer faith is settled and strengthened, as here is evidenced. 2. The word of promise is a more sure evidence than begun possession, for David was not so sure of his kingdom now, because he had begun to reign, as *because God had spoken.* 3. The word of God is rested on and rejoiced in, when it is received as his word, when his holiness is taken as a pledge of performance: *God hath spoken in his holiness; I will rejoice.* 4. Whatsoever resteth unperfected, of what is promised to us by God, shall be fully put in our possession, as David here assureth himself to exercise the supreme government in those parts of his kingdom, on the one or other side of Jordan, which yet were not brought into subjection or settled under him: *I will divide Shechem, and mete out the valley of Succoth, &c.* 5. What-

soever strength or increase of number the kingdom of Israel
was to have from the plurality of tribes and their strength,
yet the union of the sons of Abraham and stability of the
kingdom of Israel, consisted in their joint subjection to the
lawgiver and government of Judah, out of which tribe Christ
came, who is the true lawgiver and king of Israel, towards
whom the church of old was to direct its eye through its
typical governors: *Judah is my lawgiver.*

8. *Moab is my wash-pot; over Edom will I cast out
my shoe : Philistia, triumph thou because of me.*

9. *Who will bring me* into *the strong city ? who will
lead me into Edom ?*

10. Wilt *not thou, O God,* which *hadst cast us off?
and* thou, *O God,* which *didst not go out with our
armies ?*

Here David is assured by the Lord's word, not only of
the establishment of his kingdom at home, but also of the
enlarging of it abroad, by the subduing of such as had been
enemies to Israel before. Whence learn, 1. When the Lord
uniteth his people under the government of Judah, and
giveth them grace to take the true ruler of the tribe of
Judah for their lawgiver, then shall the enemies of Israel
be brought low, and either used contemptibly, as they sometimes used the Lord's people, or else shall profess themselves
happy in their subjection to the King of Israel; for, after
David, as the type of Christ, had indited a song to the church,
wherein they should acknowledge Judah their lawgiver, then
he, as the type of Christ, giveth them to sing this also:
Moab is my wash-pot ; that is, the Moabites shall serve me
in the basest service I shall put them to: *over Edom will I cast
out my shoe ;* that is, I shall subdue them and trample them
under my feet as I pass through them: *Philistia, triumph
thou because of me;* that is, instead of thy triumphing over
my people, thou shalt be made to profess thy joy to be under
my government. 2. The believer, when he promiseth to
himself great things, must neither be senseless of the difficulties of opposition which he is to meet with, nor of his
own inability to overcome difficulties; but, being sensible of
both, must look to God for assistance and strength to overcome; for, when David considered the strength of the fenced
royal cities of the enemy, he saith, *who will bring me into*

*the strong city? who will lead me into Edom? wilt not thou,
O God?* 3. It is God's absence from, or gracious presence
with, a people, which maketh the success of the wars of his
people against their enemies worse or better, and their bad
success in former time, or bypast judgment on them; for
sin must be so far from marring the confidence of a people
turning home to God, and seeking to find help from him,
that, on the contrary, the judgments inflicted upon them
in their impenitency, serving for confirmation of the threatenings of God's word, and evidence of his justice, must be
made arguments of confirmation of faith in God's promises
of merciful assistance, when they are turned towards God;
for so reasoneth David: *who will bring me into Edom? wilt
not thou, O God, which hadst cast us off? and thou, O God,
which didst not go out with our armies?*

11. *Give us help from trouble: for vain is the help
of man.*

12. *Through God we shall do valiantly: for he* it is
that *shall tread down our enemies.*

In the last place, he briefly resumeth his prayer and
confidence to be heard. Whence learn. 1. The certainty
of hope should not make us the more slack, but rather the
more earnest and fervent in prayer ; for, after this professed assurance, David insisteth in prayer : *give us help from
trouble.* 2. Seeing God only is the strength and furniture
of his people, and he cannot endure that they should rely
upon any means which they may and must use, but upon
himself only; therefore the less confidence we put in the
creature, the more may we be confident of help from God :
give us help from trouble, for vain is the help of man. 3.
A self-denying and humbled believer may go with courage
and hope of success to the use of the means, and may encounter with whatsoever opposition of enemies: *through God
we shall do valiantly.* 4. Praise of the valour and gallan-
try of victorious soldiers must not separate betwixt God and
the victor: but whatsoever God doth in us or by us, must
be no less wholly ascribed unto God, than if he had done
all the work without us; for, both the valour of the instrument, and the victory, are the works of the Lord. The
motions of the body and soul of the victor are the work
and upstirring of God within him; and the operation and

effects wrought by the instrument, are the works of God, without the victor: *for he it is that shall tread down our enemies.*

PSALM LXI.

To the chief musician upon Neginah. A psalm of David.

David now in his exile maketh his address to God in a sad condition, v. 1—3; is comforted in the Lord, and persuaded of his present and future happiness, v. 4, 5; and of the perpetuity of the kingdom of Christ, represented by him, to the comfort of all Christ's subjects in all ages, v. 6—8.

1. *Hear my cry, O God; attend unto my prayer.*

2. *From the end of the earth will I cry unto thee, when my heart is overwhelmed: lead me to the Rock that is higher than I.*

3. *For thou hast been a shelter for me,* and *a strong tower from the enemy.*

In his sad supplication David prayeth for a comfortable receiving of his request, and a comfortable rest of his soul on God himself through Christ, hoping to be heard because he was resolved to look toward God and to continue praying, whatsoever condition of spirit he should be in, and in whatsoever part he should be; and also because he had experience of God's help in his straits in former times. Whence learn, 1. The best expedient for a sad soul, is to run to God by prayer for comfort, and to insist earnestly, albeit God should seem not to attend: *hear my cry, O God, attend unto my prayer.* 2. When the godly are driven from their country and fellowship with the saints, and from exercise of public ordinances, no wonder they fall into perplexity of spirit; for David, forced to flee to *the ends of the land,* finds his heart *overwhelmed within him.* 3. It is exile indeed to be secluded from the liberty of public ordinances, and it is our home to be where God is publicly worshipped; for David counteth himself cast out *unto the ends of the earth,* when he is debarred from the temple of the Lord. 4. Albeit a man were ever so far banished from the free society of the church, and communion with God's people in ordinances, yet he is still within cry unto God : *from the ends of the earth will I cry unto thee.* 5. There is a rock of refuge for safety and comfort to the exiled and perplexed saint, which is able to supply all wants, and to sweeten all sorrows; and this is the rock of God's felt friendship in Christ from heaven, represented by the visible rock of *Zion*, where the tabernacle and mercy-seat were situate, the appointed trysting place, where God received the prayers of his people, and answered them from heaven; when David could not come to the typical mount or rock, he prayeth to have access to the thing signified : *lead me to the rock that is higher than I.* 6. Sensible and comfortable communion with God, is a mystery spiritual, which man's wisdom or power cannot discover, nor bring unto him: but God himself must reveal, and must renew the revealing of himself to a soul in trouble, and must make a man's soul apply itself to him powerfully, else a man cannot feel this comfortable fellowship with God, more than a blind man can find out what is removed from him, or a weak child can go not being led, or a man can reach up to a steep high place, not being lifted up unto it. Therefore must the Lord himself draw us near to himself, and lift us up to himself : *lead me to the rock that is higher than I.* 7. This spiritual felt communion with God is able to put a man far from the reach of any enemy, and maketh a soul quietly to rest itself from fear of trouble, how great soever the external danger can be, as David many times felt by experience : *for thou hast been a shelter unto me, and a strong tower from the enemy.* 8. A believer's resolution for depending on God and praying to him in hardest conditions, and his present use-making of former experiences, as they serve much for strengthening his faith in prayer; so they are the nearest means that can be for coming by a renewed sensible comfort, as here we see: for David resolveth, *from the ends of the earth I will cry ;* and prayeth, *lead me to the rock ;* and saith, *thou hast been a strong tower to me ;* and so comfort followeth quickly after this preparation, as the next verse showeth.

4. *I will abide in thy tabernacle for ever; I will trust in the covert of thy wings. Selah.*

5. *For thou, O God, hast heard my vows : thou hast given me the heritage of those that fear thy name.*

Here he is comforted in his exile, and made to be at home in his spirit, by reason of the present sense of God's favour to him, and of his confirmed hope in the performance of the promises made unto him. Whence learn, 1. The Lord can give such satisfaction to a sad heart in the time of its trouble, that the trouble may turn to be no trouble, even while it lieth on still, as here is to be seen in David's comfort, who speaketh as if he were restored, while he is yet in exile. 2. Spiritual consolations in temporal troubles, give satisfaction to a soul both for the present and for time to come, for everlasting happiness: *I will abide in thy tabernacle for ever:* his hope is, that not only shall he be restored to the fellowship of the saints, at the tabernacle in Jerusalem, but also that he shall be in God's company in heaven, represented by the tabernacle, and that for ever. 3. True consolation standeth not in earthly things, but in things heavenly, and things having nearest relation thereto; for David's comfort was not so much that he should be brought to the kingdom, as that he should be brought to the tabernacle, and to heaven by that means : *I will abide in thy tabernacle.* 4. Sincerity setteth no term-day to God's service, or to the seeking of communion with him : *I will abide in thy tabernacle for ever.* 5. The ground of all spiritual consolations is in the mercy and grace of God offered to us in Christ, represented by the wings of the cherubim stretched out over the mercy-seat; there faith findeth a rest and solid ground able to furnish comfort abundantly : *I will trust in the covert of thy wings.* 6. Access to God in prayer, and approbation of the conscience, and the sincere pouring forth of the heart melting with present felt sense of God's love, strengthen greatly the assurance of everlasting communion with God : *for thou, O God, hast heard my voice.* 7. As spiritual comfort in time of trouble granted to a believer, is indeed the earnest of everlasting life, so should they, to whomsoever the earnest is given, make reckoning that by this earnest the inheritance is confirmed to them by way of possession begun : *thou hast given me the heritage of those that fear thy name.* 8. The inheritance of the chief of God's servants, and of the meanest and weakest of them, is one; the right of every believer is alike good, albeit the hold laid upon the right by all is not alike strong: and what the strongest of the godly believe for their own consolation and salvation, the weakest may believe the same to belong to every believer that feareth God, as David doth here : *thou hast given me the heritage of those that fear thy name.*

6. *Thou wilt prolong the king's life;* and *his years as many generations.*

7. *He shall abide before God for ever : O prepare mercy and truth,* which *may preserve him.*

8. *So will I sing praise unto thy name for ever, that I may daily perform my vows.*

In the third place, the psalmist prophesieth, not simply of the stability of the kingdom in his own person and posterity, but under the type; namely, he speaketh of the perpetuity of the kingdom of Christ the true king of Israel; for which end he prayeth that mercy and truth may be forthcoming to subjects of Christ, that his kingdom may be prolonged; and so David in his time, and all the saints in their time, may joyfully praise God continually. Whence learn, 1. It is not unusual with God, together with present consolation and the light of future salvation in Christ, to reveal also and give assurance of great things concerning Christ's kingdom, as here and elsewhere in the Scripture is to be seen : *thou wilt prolong the king's life, and his years as many generations.* 2. The glory of Christ, and the perpetuity of his kingdom are every subject's good and comfort; for this is comfort to David, that Christ shall live for ever : *that he shall abide before God for ever.* 3. The kingdom of Christ, and government of his subjects in his church, shall be allowed of God, and be protected of God, and blessed of God for ever, however it be opposed by men in the world : *he shall abide before God for ever.* 4. The perpetuity of Christ's kingdom, and preservation of his subjects in this life, till they be possessed of heaven, is by the merciful remedying of the misery and removing of the sin which they are subject unto, and by performing what he hath promised and prepared through Christ to bestow upon them : *O prepare mercy and truth, which may preserve him.* 5. The best retreat that can be made, after wrestling and victory over troubles, are prayer and praises; as here David after his exercises prayeth, *O prepare mercy and truth ;* and then saith, *unto thee will I sing.* 6. As the main matter of our vows is the moral duty of rejoicing in God and hearty praising him; so renewed experience of God's mercy and truth towards his people in Christ, is the main matter of our joy in him, and praise unto him : *O prepare mercy and truth, &c. so will I sing praise unto thy name, that I may daily perform my vows.*

PSALM LXII.

To the chief musician, to Jeduthun.   A psalm of David.

This psalm is the issue of a sore conflict and inward combat, which David felt from the strong opposition of his irreconcileable adversaries, and from the lasting troubles which he sustained by their persecution, and by his friends forsaking him, whereby he was puzzled what to think or what to do: at length faith in God giveth him victory, and maketh him first to break forth in avowing his faith and hope in God, v. 1, 2; next, to insult over his enemies as dead men, because of their sinful course, v. 3, 4; thirdly, to strengthen himself in his faith and hope, v. 5—7; fourthly, to exhort all men to trust in God, and to depend on him, for reasons set down, v. 8, 9; and not to trust in oppression and robbery, for reasons set down, v. 10—12.

1. *Truly my soul waiteth upon God: from him* cometh *my salvation.*

2. *He only* is *my rock and my salvation;* he is *my defence; I shall not be greatly moved.*

From this abrupt beginning of the psalm, declaring that David hath had a sore disputation and wrestling with temptations within him, and out of which this is the first coming forth, learn, 1. Albeit strong faith be put to a conflict when trouble and temptations abound, yet when it looketh on God and his promises, it gets the victory, and putteth the soul to a submissive attendance on God, and a quiet hope of complete deliverance: *truly my soul waiteth upon God; from him cometh my salvation.* 2. Then is faith well tried and approved, when, being stript of all supporters except God, it contenteth itself with him alone, as all-sufficient: *he only is my rock and my salvation.* 3. Faith findeth as many answers in God's sufficiency, as temptations can make objections against it: *he is my rock and my salvation: he is my defence.* 4. As a man resolveth to believe and follow the course of sound faith, so he may assure himself of establishment and victory over all temptations, notwithstanding his own weakness: *I shall not be greatly moved,* David concludeth, from his resolution to rest on God.

3. *How long will ye imagine mischief against a man? ye shall be slain, all of you : as a bowing wall* shall ye be, and as *a tottering fence.*

4. *They only consult to cast* him *down from his excellency ; they delight in lies : they bless with their mouth, but they curse inwardly.   Selah.*

In the second place, David insulteth over his enemies, and

layeth before them the danger of their wicked ways. Whence
learn, 1. So soon as a man hath fastened himself on God, he
may reckon with all adverse powers, and insult over them;
for the seeing of God's help discovers to the believer the vanity of all opposition : *how long will ye imagine mischief
against a man ?* 2. As the godly, when they fall under persecution, may lie long under it, and must resolve patience
all the while on the one hand; so, on the other hand, persecutors are unreasonably carried on in the course of persecution, like mad men, who cannot give over the pursuit,
albeit they see God against themselves and with the godly
whom they pursue: *how long will ye imagine mischief against
a man ?* 3. Persecutors shall not have their will against the
godly, but by their persecution shall draw upon themselves
complete, sudden, and irrecoverable destruction : *ye shall be
slain, all of you, as a bowing wall, and a tottering fence ;*
that is, you shall perish suddenly, as when a bowing wall and
tottering fence rush to the ground in a moment. 4. As
standing fast in the faith and service of God in a good cause,
is the excellency of the believer; so is it the eye-sore of his
adversaries, which they of all things can least endure in the
godly; and therefore chiefly bend all their wit and forces, to
break them off their holy carriage and course : *they only consult to cast him down from his excellency.* 5. Not truth and
light, but darkness, error, falsehood, and deceit, are the
pleasure of the wicked : *they delight in lies.* 6. When the
wicked intend their worst against the godly, then will they
speak fairest words to them, to see whether by falsehood or
force they can prevail most, to draw them off their good
course : *they bless with their mouth, but they curse inwardly.*

5. *My soul, wait thou only upon God ; for my expectation is from him.*

6. *He only is my rock and my salvation : he is my
defence; I shall not be moved.*

7. *In God is my salvation and my glory : the rock
of my strength, and my refuge, is in God.*

In the third place, David strengtheneth his faith and his
hope, that he may be able to endure trouble till the sin of the
wicked be ripe, and their judgment be executed. Whence
learn, 1. Our resolution patiently to keep silence in waiting
on God, and our putting the resolution to practice, differ :

our practising is so short of our resolution, that we had need
to be stirred up, and to stir up ourselves to our duty. And
as Satan is still moving new perturbations; so have we need
of, and must study to have, new confirmations : *my soul,
wait thou only upon God.* 2. They that expect their help
from God, must not expect help from any other airth, no not
when they shall use all means lawful for their delivery; but
the success must be, without haste-making, patiently waited
for from God alone : *wait thou only on God, for my expectation is from him.* 3. The grounds of confidence are able
to abide new assaults, and must be brought forth and aver-
red, so oft as they are opposed : for here unto the new
stirrings of the same temptations, he opposeth this over
again : *he only is my rock : he is my defence and my salvation.* And whereas he said before, I shall not be greatly
moved; now he saith more confidently, *I shall not be moved :*
and yet more he triumphs in the Lord : *he is my salvation
and glory ;* which he speaketh in regard of hope to have all
good which he needed. And lastly, in regard of supply, in
whatsoever wants, and delivery from all evil, he saith, *he is
the rock of my strength, and my refuge is in God :* and so
his faith settleth itself, and temptations are overcome.

8. *Trust in him at all times ; ye people, pour out
your heart before him : God is a refuge for us. Selah.*

9. *Surely men of low degree are vanity, and men of
high degree are a lie : to be laid in the balance, they
are altogether lighter than vanity.*

In the fourth place, the psalmist exhorteth all men to
place confidence upon God, partly because God is able to
give deliverance, as a place of refuge, and partly because
men, whether great or small, few or many, cannot but deceive and disappoint the man that trusteth in them. Whence
learn, 1. The duty of comforted and victorious believers, is
to communicate the fruit of their experience, for strengthening their brethren, and edification of others, as their calling
permitteth them, as David doth here : *trust in him at all
times, ye people.* 2. Whatsoever condition, how hard soever, we fall into, the grace of God and grounds of confidence in God must not be lost, but always made use of :
trust in him at all times. 3. As a guilty conscience, heavy
trouble, misbelief and suspicion of God's good-will, lock up

the heart in sorrow; so any measure of faith in God, going to him by prayer, easeth the heart and layeth the burden of grief down before the Lord : *ye people pour out your heart before him : God is a refuge to us.* 4. The way to place our confidence in God, is to lift our confidence off all creatures, and in special off men of superior or inferior ranks : and the way to lift our confidence off the creature, is to consider the inability of men to help us, except God make them do it; and that, without God, they are nothing worth to us : *men of low degree are vanity.* 5. Whosoever trust on men, higher or lower, are sure to be disappointed in their expectation, and of whatsoever man's help can promise : and, if we will not be deceived, the voice of God and experience of his saints may give us certainty of the truth of the doctrine; for out of experience David saith, *surely men of low degree are vanity, &c.* 6. Carnal confidence is not only unable to help a man, when he hath most need, but also bringeth damage unto him, and makes him to find God in his jealousy an adversary and just judge to plague and curse him; and so if the matter be well weighed, creature-help, and creature-comfort, when it is relied upon, is worse than no help : *being laid in the balance, they are altogether lighter than vanity.*

10. *Trust not in oppression, and become not vain in robbery : if riches increase, set not your heart* upon them.

11. *God hath spoken once ; twice have I heard this, that power* belongeth *unto God.*

12. *Also unto thee, O Lord,* belongeth *mercy : for thou renderest to every man according to his work.*

The other part of the exhortation forbiddeth trust in oppression, or riches, or power, or greatness of place, because God disposeth of all things as he pleaseth, showing mercy to such as trust in him, and rendering to every man according to his work.   Whence learn, 1. There are many more idols than one to draw away a man's heart from God; for, when trusting in men of high degree and low degree is cast down, then oppression, robbery, and riches stand up, and take God's room in the heart, as here we see.   2. It is more hard to divert a man from confidence in himself, and what is in his own power, then to draw him from confidence in men of higher or lower degree. Therefore, after casting down carnal confidence in men, high or low; he dischargeth confidence in whatsoever a man is able to do of himself, as might, and riches, and authority of high place: *trust not in oppression; if riches increase, &c.* 3. Whosoever is confident, by his own strength and might, to debate his business against any man, and to do his adversaries two wrongs for one, shall find himself to have disobeyed God, and to have been proud in a matter of nothing: *trust not in oppression, become not vain in robbery.* 4. It may stand with godliness and trusting in God, to be rich; but not to have our heart set upon riches, either to gather or keep them, either to rejoice in them, or be proud because of them: *if riches increase, set not thy heart thereon.* 5. Nothing is able to settle man's confidence in God, and to keep his heart from idols, or carnal confidence in creatures, or to bear in upon others this twofold duty, save the powerful impression of the unchangeable word of God; therefore saith he, *God hath spoken once.* 6. Albeit one testimony of Scripture for a ground of faith, or rule of life, rightly considered, be abundantly sufficient to settle our faith in that point, and to warrant our obedience; yet God will inculcate that truth oftener, and have us receive it oftener, and more firmly; and as it is the Lord's kindness to us and care of us, to cause his once spoken word to be often repeated to us, oftener cleared and confirmed unto us by repeated experimental evidence of the certainty thereof: so it is our duty, to receive it more and more heartily, so oft as it is repeated and inculcated, to meditate on and consider it, and to take a deeper and a deeper impression from it: *God hath spoken once, twice have I heard it.* 7. The possession of authority and power to do all and every thing, is the Lord's only: and as for the power of the creature, it is but lent and derived to it, at God's pleasure. The creature can neither hurt us, nor help itself or us, but as God is pleased to use it as an instrument: *twice have I heard this, that power belongeth to God.* 8. To induce a soul to trust in God only, it is necessary, that it so look to his power, as it looks to his mercy, and lay hold on both: faith hath need of both, as of two wings, to carry it up to God above all vain enticements, and terrors, and temptations, and as props whereon to settle and fix itself jointly: *also unto thee, O Lord, belongeth mercy.* 9. As the man that puts his trust in God, and studieth to obey his word, shall find God's mercy to pardon his transgression, and God's power to sustain him in all his difficulties, and to perform all the promises made to his servants: so the man that trusts not in God, but in himself, or in some creature without himself, thinking to work his own happiness by his own ways, shall find the fruit of his wicked course according as God hath forewarned : *for thou renderest to every man according to his works.*

PSALM LXIII.

A psalm of David, when he was in the wilderness of Judah.

We have in this psalm David's exercise in his banishment, when he was hiding himself from Saul in the wilderness of Judah ; wherein are set down his lingering and prayer after the benefit of public ordinances, v. 1, 2; and the fruits of a gracious and comfortable answer given to his prayer, in number four. The first is a resolution to follow spiritual duties, and in special to praise God, v. 3 ; to be a constant supplicant depending on God, v. 4; to take his contentment in God and in his praises, v. 5, 6 ; and joyfully to trust in God's mercy, v. 7. The second fruit is the acknowledgment of God's power, sustaining him in his adherence unto God, practised by him for time past, and purposed for time to come, v. 8. The third fruit is confidence of the destruction of his enemies, v. 9, 10. The fourth is assurance that he shall receive the kingdom promised unto him, to the confusion of all such as slandered him as a traitor.

From the inscription, learn, 1. Such of God's children as dwell most stately and commodiously among their neighbours, may be driven sometimes to hide themselves in a wilderness, as David was. 2. Banishment from among friends cannot banish a man from God, but may serve rather to drive him toward God. 3. Troubles are grievous when they are present, but may prove a matter of a joyful song, when called to remembrance : *a psalm of David, when he was in the wilderness of Judah.*

1. *O God, thou art my God ; early will I seek thee : my soul thirsteth for thee, my flesh longeth for thee in a dry and thirsty land, where no water is ;*

2. *To see thy power and thy glory, so as I have seen thee in the sanctuary.*

From this prayer learn, 1. The Lord is the only ease of a distressed mind, and there is no speedier relief than to

go to God in prayer, as the psalmist did, saying, *O God.*
2. When we would speak unto God to purpose, we should
fasten our hold on the covenant : *O God, thou art my God.*
3. Troubles will sharpen a man in the use of the means,
and rouse him out of sluggish security : *early will I seek
thee.* 4. It is good to fasten duties on ourselves by resolution, and to strengthen our resolution by showing it to the
Lord : *early will I seek thee.* 5. A lively soul will be no
less desirous of spiritual comfort from God than the body
for natural food after long fasting; *my soul thirsteth for thee.*
6. Spiritual affections, when they are strong, will affect the
body with impressions answerable thereto; *my flesh longeth
after thee.* 7. It is a barren place to a godly soul, where
the public exercises of religion cannot be had; for this cause
mainly David called the wilderness *a dry and thirsty land,*
where no water is. 8. Because the power and glory of God
are nowhere so clearly seen as in public ordinances, therefore should the ordinances be loved and earnestly sought
after; that we may find communion with God in them: *my
soul thirsteth to see thy power and thy glory.* 9. The more
good a man hath found in the public exercises of religion,
the more will he esteem them, and, in special, when he is
deprived of them: *my soul thirsts to see thy power and glory,*
so as I have seen thee in thy sanctuary.

3. *Because thy loving-kindness is better than life, my
lips shall praise thee.*

4. *Thus will I bless thee while I live : I will lift up
my hands in thy name.*

5. *My soul shall be satisfied as* with *marrow and
fatness ; and my mouth shall praise* thee *with joyful
lips ;*

6. *When I remember thee upon my bed, and meditate
on thee in the* night-*watches.*

7. *Because thou hast been my help, therefore in the
shadow of thy wings will I rejoice.*

Here the Lord giveth to his servant a gracious answer,
and sweeteneth his condition in the wilderness, making him
no less glad than ever he was in the public exercise of religion, by granting him the comfort of his Holy Spirit, as
the fruits of the answer to his prayer make manifest. The
first whereof is shown in sundry holy resolutions to praise

the kindness of God, to bless God, to call on his name in all conditions, to possess contentment in God, and to trust in him. Whence learn, 1. When a man who loveth the public ordinances is debarred from them, and maketh use of private exercises of religion, God can and will supply unto him what he wanteth, and be a little sanctuary unto him, as here appeareth. 2. The felt kindness of God, and shedding abroad of his love in the heart of a believer, is joy unspeakable and glorious, able to supply all wants unto him, and to sweeten all troubles unto him, and to give him more comfort than what is most comfortable in this world; yea, to make life itself, without the feeling, or hope of feeling, this love, to be little worth to him : *thy loving-kindness is better than life.* 3. Rich experiences of the felt love of God, in the use of means, deserve to be brought forth to the praise of God when it may glorify him: *because thy loving-kindness is better than life, my lips shall praise thee.* 4. One proof of God's loving-kindness towards us is reason abundant for us to bless God for ever thereafter, and to acknowledge him the fountain of blessings, even to ourselves, whatsoever change of dispensations we shall meet with : *thus will I bless thee while I live.* 5. As our assurance of God's love unto us, and of his purpose to bless us, serveth to prepare us for straits and difficulties hereafter; so also it helpeth us to pray to God with confidence of being helped, into whatsoever change of condition we may afterwards fall : *thus will I bless thee while I live, I will lift up my hands in thy name ;* to wit, as a man engaged to depend upon thee, to call upon thee as my need requireth, and a man particularly encouraged by thee, and confirmed by experience from thy former helping of me, that I shall have a good answer from thee, who hast manifested thyself unto me by thy word and works. 6. The spiritual life of the soul hath its own food as well as the bodily life of nature; and the life of the godly is not so barren, so sad and uncomfortable, as the world believeth. They have their hidden manna and the water of life, solid and satisfactory consolations and joy in the Holy Spirit, wherewith strangers intermeddle not, of which joys the sweetest morsel of delicate banquets is but a shadow : *my soul shall be satisfied as with marrow and fatness.* 7. Such as hunger and thirst after communion with God in Christ, and resolve to spend their life in God's service, may promise to themselves that they shall feel sweet satisfaction in this course, and with David say, *my soul shall be satisfied as with marrow.* 8. Spiritual joys are not like carnal joys, which end in sadness, but they terminate in glorifying, and make the very outward man partaker of the benefit; therefore the psalmist addeth, *and my mouth shall praise thee with joyful lips.* 9. The way to find spiritual refreshment, is, beside public ordinances, to give ourselves to spiritual exercises in secret, at such times as our necessities, civil and natural, may best spare, and then and there to recall to mind what we have heard, seen, or felt of God's word or working, and to keep up our thoughts upon this holy subject by prayer, soliloquy, and meditation, as David showeth to us the example: *when I remember thee upon my bed, and meditate on thee in the night-watches.* 10. As one experience should call another to remembrance, so the calling of experiences to our memory should lead and encourage us, in all conditions, joyfully to make use, by faith, of God's standing offer of grace for us in Christ, shadowed forth by the wings of the cherubim stretched out always over the mercy-seat : *because thou hast been my helper, therefore in the shadow of thy wings will I rejoice;* for here, and here only, is the remedy of all sin and misery.

8. *My soul followeth hard after thee: thy right hand upholdeth me.*

From the second fruit of the gracious answer given to David's prayer; that is, from his giving the glory of the acts of grace which he did, unto God the furnisher thereof, learn, 1. The Lord useth to exercise the souls of his own children with a sense of desertion, and withdrawing of his presence one way or other. This is presupposed in David's *following after the Lord,* when he felt him withdrawing himself, as it were. 2. A believer in God cannot endure a thought of separation from God, nor forbear to seek after God, when he misseth his presence, but will use all means to recover the sense of his presence which he hath felt before : *my soul followeth hard after thee.* 3. It is our wisdom to reflect upon and acknowledge the grace of God in us, and review the acts of our faith and love toward God, for our own strengthening, as David doth here, saying, *my soul followeth hard after thee.* 4. Although the exercise of gracious habits be our act, yet the enabling us to bring our acts forth is the Lord's work, who giveth us both to will and to do of his own good pleasure; and as it is our duty to acknowledge this, so it is the fruit of our feelings of God's help to profess it : *my soul followeth hard after thee;* but by what power, strength, and furniture doth he this? *thy right hand upholdeth me.*

9. *But those* that *seek my soul, to destroy* it, *shall go into the lower parts of the earth.*

10. *They shall fall by the sword; they shall be a portion for foxes.*

The third fruit of the answer to David's prayer, is assurance given that his enemies shall be destroyed, for it is revealed to him that Saul would be slain by the sword; he knew by revelation that his carcass would lie in the fields, a prey for foxes and wild beasts. Whence learn, 1. The deadly and irreconcilable enemies of God's people, hating them for a good cause, draw destruction on themselves: *those that seek my soul to destroy it, shall go down to the lower parts of the earth.* 2. It is agreeable to God's justice that bloody enemies of God's people be punished by their bloody enemies; God can stir up the wicked against the wicked, to avenge the wrongs done to his children: *they shall fall by the sword, they shall be a portion for the foxes.* 3. The Lord, to ease the hearts of his oppressed children, sometimes maketh them foresee beforehand the destruction of his adversaries, whether by teaching them in an ordinary way to apply the general sentences of the Scripture unto them, or in a more special way revealing his mind, as he seeth fit, as here : *they shall fall by the sword, &c.*

11. *But 'the king shall rejoice in God; every one that sweareth by him shall glory: but the mouth of them that speak lies shall be stopped.*

The last fruit of David's prayer is assurance that he shall be king, that all the godly shall be comforted by this means, and that his righteousness shall be cleared against all the calumnies of the wicked. Whence learn, 1. Howsoever it may go hard with the righteous, and their enemies may prosper for a time, yet their lot shall be changed to the better at length; and when their enemies are borne down, their head shall be lifted up; and whatsoever is promised unto them, they may be as sure of it as if they had possession of it, yea they may style themselves by the title which God's word hath given unto them, as David doth in this particular, calling himself king now when he was a banished man in the wilderness of Judah : *the king shall rejoice*, saith he. 2. The true ground of a believer's joy is not the gift he receiveth from God, how great soever it may be, but the good-will of the giver, even God himself : *the king shall rejoice in God.* 3. Every true worshipper of God (whose property truly it is to fear the true God, and the cognizance of whose sincerity is his conscience-making of an oath,) shall have matter of gloriation, after a while's patient suffering in time of trial : *every one that sweareth by him shall glory.* 4. The borne-down righteousness of the godly, and of their cause, by the lies, slanders, and calumnies of the wicked, shall be brought to light in due time, and the wicked made ashamed of their lies: *the mouth of them that speak lies shall be stopped.*

PSALM LXIV.

To the chief musician. A psalm of David.

This psalm hath two parts. In the former is David's heavy complaint unto God against his deadly enemies, laid forth before God in sundry particular evidences of their malice, v. 1—6 ; and in the latter part is the Lord's comfortable answer unto him, by giving him assurance of God's judgment coming on them, to their own and others astonishment, and to the comfort of the godly, v. 7—10.

1. *Hear my voice, O God, in my prayer : preserve my life from fear of the enemy.*

2. *Hide me from the secret counsel of the wicked ; from the insurrection of the workers of iniquity :*

In his prayer David requested first in general, delivery of his life from the secret plotting and often practising of his enemies against him. Whence learn, 1. Present danger is able to force out cries to God, and such earnest prayers, poured out in extreme necessity, shall not want an answer: *hear my voice, O God, in my prayer.* 2. The danger cannot be so great, wherein help may not be had from God; he is so near to a supplicant, so powerful, and so ready to save the man who hath made God his refuge : *preserve my life from fear of the enemy.* 3. God can so overrule and outwit the devices of our enemies, that they shall either not light upon the mean whereby they might overtake us, or shall miss their intent in case their device be probable : *hide me from the secret counsel of the wicked.* 4. What the wicked cannot do against the righteous by craft, they will pursue with open violence; but God, as he is wiser in counsel, and able to befool them, so is he stronger in power and able to break them : *hide me from their insurrection.* 5. That we may have the greater confidence to be delivered from our enemies, we had need to be sure that we are in a good cause, and that our adversaries have a wrong cause : *hide me from the workers of iniquity.*

3. *Who whet their tongue like a sword,* and *bend* their bows to shoot *their arrows,* even *bitter words ;*

4. *That they may shoot in secret at the perfect : suddenly do they shoot at him, and fear not.*

5. *They encourage themselves* in *an evil matter : they commune of laying snares privily ; they say, Who shall see them ?*

6. *They search out iniquities ; they accomplish a diligent search : both the inward* thought *of every one* of them, *and the heart,* is *deep.*

Here David complaineth of his enemies, and layeth forth several degrees of their desperate wickedness before God, as so many arguments to strengthen his faith and hope for delivery from them. Whence learn, 1. The benefit of a good cause, and of a good conscience appeareth best in a strait, when nothing can help a man against his enemies save God alone, as here appeareth in David's case. 2. Calumnies and slanders against the godly are very cruel weapons; for not only hurt they the estimation of their good cause, and personal good behaviour, but they also stir up all men to take their lives : *they whet their tongue as a sword, and bend their bows to shoot their arrows, bitter words.* 3. There is no dread of a privy slander; a man is wounded ere he is aware, and no man's innocency or integrity of life can be a guard against the shot of a calumniator's tongue : *they shoot in secret at the perfect, suddenly do they shoot at him.* 4. Because God only can heal the wound of a slander, and sustain the man in the consciousness of his good cause and carriage, till he clear him; the righteous man must content himself to refer the matter to God, as David doth here. 5. Godless men are dangerous enemies; *for they fear not God*, and so have no powerful restraint within them from doing any mischief, and the more they sin, they acquire the greater boldness to sin more : *they encourage themselves in an evil matter.* 6. The wit and wickedness which is within themselves, will not suffice their devilish intention, therefore they seek all help they can find from without: *they commune of laying snares privily.* 7. They seek how they may overtake the man's person, after they have killed his good name and cause with calumnies and bitter aspersions. Yea, Satan so blindeth them, that they neither look to God, the avenger of such plots and practices, nor do they consider that God seeth them, and they think their pretences before men are so thick a covering, that no man can see through them: *they say, Who shall see them ?* 8. If there hath been any slander of the upright man's misdemeanour in any former time, which for the falsehood of it is evanished, they make search after it, to waken it up again; and if there be any possibility to devise new inventions, with any probability, they go about it busily, yea they search hell itself to find out how to bring a mischief upon the upright : *they search out iniquities, they accomplish a diligent search.* 9. Last of all, their wickedness is unsearchable, the uncontrolled bent of their wicked wit and will, assisted with what Satan can suggest, furnish, and stir up—all is employed—and it is hard to say whether their wit or will be most wicked, or draw nearest to hell; but of both it may be truly affirmed, that *both the thoughts of every one of them, and the heart is deep.*

7. *But God shall shoot at them* with *an arrow ; suddenly shall they be wounded.*

8. *So they shall make their own tongue to fall upon themselves : all that see them shall flee away.*

9. *And all men shall fear, and shall declare the work of God ; for they shall wisely consider of his doing.*

10. *The righteous shall be glad in the Lord, and shall trust in him ; and all the upright in heart shall glory.*

In the latter part of the psalm is set down David's prayer and confidence of justice to be executed against his enemies, and mercy to be shown to him, and to all the godly.

Whence learn, 1. The godly want not a friend to avenge their quarrel : God will shoot against wicked archers and not miss the mark : *but God shall shoot at them ; with an arrow shall they be wounded.* 2. Where desperate malice is seen, there sudden mischief may be foreseen; it shall light upon the malicious : *suddenly shall they be wounded.* 3. The wicked adversaries of God's people are destroyers of themselves by their opposition unto them; for as they thought to do unto God's children, God doth to them : *so they shall make their own tongue fall upon themselves.* 4. Sometimes God will make the wicked spectacles of his judg-ment to the affrightment of all that know them and see their plague : *all that see them shall flee away.* 5. The judgment of the wicked should be all men's lesson; and all sorts of people shall learn, by their plagues, to know God's justice and terror : *and all men shall fear and declare the works of God.* 6. Not every spectator of God's work giv-eth glory to God, but they only who compare his word with his works, and through the veil of means and instruments look to God the righteous judge of the world : *they shall declare the work of God, for they shall consider wisely of his doing.* 7. When woe and wrack come upon the wicked, then joy and comfort come to the godly, not so much for the damage of the wicked, as for the manifestation of the glory of God : *the righteous shall be glad in the Lord.* 8. As the Lord's mercies confirm the faith of the righteous, so also do the works of his justice : *they shall be glad in the Lord, and shall trust in him.* 9. The delivery of one of the godly, is a pledge of the like delivery to all in the like case: and as one, so all and every one of the righteous and upright in heart shall triumph at length over all enemies, and make their boast of God : *all the upright in heart shall glory.*

PSALM LXV.

To the chief musician. A psalm and song of David.

This psalm is all of God's praises. The proposition that he is to be praised, is set down, v. 1. The reasons of his praise unto the end, are nine. The first whereof is, because he heareth prayer, v. 2 ; the second, because he mercifully pardoneth sins, v. 3; the third, because of his gracious purpose and powerful prosecution of the decree of election of his own redeemed ones, v. 4 ; the fourth, because of his defending his church in all places, v. 5; the fifth, from the strength manifested in framing and settling the mountains, v. 6; the sixth, from the wise and powerful overruling of all unruly and raging creatures, v. 7; the seventh, from his preventing troubles, which are coming to his church, by terrifying all nations at beholding the tokens of his displeasure against the enemies of his people, v. 8; the eighth argument is taken from the joyful peace, granted sometimes to his people, v. 8; the ninth argument of God's praise, is from the rich plenty of all necessary food from year to year, which God provideth for maintenance of man and beast, and specially of his people Israel in their land, v. 9—13.

1. *Praise waiteth for thee, O God, in Zion : and unto thee shall the vow be performed.*

From the proposition concerning his purpose to spend this psalm only in praising God, learn, 1. Although prayer and praises always agree well, yet some time may call for praises and the work of praise only, and may take up the whole man for a time, as here. 2. How mournful soever a condition the Lord's people may be in, yet God is preparing matter thereby for his own glory; *praise waiteth for thee.* And whatsoever matter of praise be seen, or whatsoever measure of praise be given unto God by his people, more is due to him, and more is making ready for him : *praise waiteth for thee.* 3. Although the rest of the world be senseless of God's benefits, yet his church must set about the work of his praise, and shall be enabled to give him praise: *praise waiteth for thee, O God, in Zion.* 4. As it is the duty of every man, who seeketh deliverance from trouble, or any other benefit from God, to oblige himself to praise God for it: so it is the Lord's manner to gain to himself praise by granting prayers, and to purchase the performance of promised praises unto him: *unto thee shall the vow be performed.*

2. *O thou that hearest prayer, unto thee shall all flesh come.*

From the first reason of the Lord's praise, learn, 1. The hearing and granting of prayer are the Lord's property, and his usual practice, and his pleasure, and his nature, and his glory : *O thou that hearest prayer !* 2. The readiness of the Lord to hear prayer, openeth the door of access to all sorts of people, who are sensible of their own frailty and necessities, and know his readiness to relieve them : Gentiles as well as Jews shall come unto him; *O thou that hearest prayer ! all flesh shall come unto thee.*

3. *Iniquities prevail against me :* as for *our trans-gressions, thou shalt purge them away.*

From the second reason of the Lord's praise, learn, 1. Sin is a sore adversary, and many times prevails over us, and draws troubles on us, which make us know the ill of it better than we knew before committing it: *iniquities prevail against me.* 2. Whatsoever be the sins of the people we live amongst, let us make special account of our own guilti-ness in the point of confession, as David doth here, when he saith, *iniquities prevail against me.* 3. Our sins should be looked upon, not to chase us from God, but to humble us, and drive us to seek pardon and purgation from the Lord, whose free grace only can take sins away; *iniquity prevails over me : but as for our transgressions, thou shalt purge them away.* 4. The holy prophets and penmen of Scrip-ture have no grounds of hope for pardon of sin, save those which are common to the meanest of God's people; for Da-vid in his confession cometh in by himself alone, aggravating his own sins most : *iniquities prevail against me,* saith he; but, in hope of pardon, he joineth with the rest of God's people, saying, *as for our transgressions, thou shalt purge them away.*

4. *Blessed* is the man whom *thou choosest, and caus-est to approach* unto thee, that *he may dwell in thy courts : we shall be satisfied with the goodness of thy house,* even *of thy holy temple.*

From the third reason of the Lord's praise, learn, 1. God hath made election of some out of the rest of mankind, on whom he effectually bestoweth blessedness : *blessed is the man whom thou choosest.* 2. All those whom God effectu-ally calleth, and reconcileth and draweth into communion and society with himself, are elected and blessed persons : *blessed is the man whom thou choosest, and causest to ap-proach unto thee.* 3. It is the free good-will of God which putteth the difference among men, and maketh some to be partakers of blessedness, and not others : *blessed is the man whom thou choosest.* 4. The power and glory of the work of conversion, reconciliation, and drawing near to God, for communion with him, of so many as are converted, are the Lord's power and glory no less than election is his free choice and glory : *blessed is the man whom thou choosest,* and whom *thou causest to approach unto thee.* 5. The man elected, effectually called, reconciled and drawn into society with God, is a true member of his church, a constant member thereof in this life, and one who shall be a member of the church triumphant, in the life to come, and so effectually blessed; *he shall dwell in thy courts,* saith the text in the original. 6. Whatsoever is sufficient for begetting and entertaining the life of grace and of true blessedness in God's elect, is to be found by means of public ordinances in the church of God: *we shall be satisfied with the goodness of thy house, even of thy holy temple.* 7. Whosoever find in themselves the proper effects or consequents of election in special, a powerful drawing of them to the covenant with God, and to a nearer and nearer approach unto God, in the way of obedience to the public ordinances of his house; may be assured of their election, of their effectual calling, of their blessedness, and of their interest in all the goodness of God's house, to their full contentment; for, after the general doctrine, he applieth, *we shall be satisfied with the goodness of thy house, even of thy holy temple.*

5. By *terrible things in righteousness wilt thou answer us, O God of our salvation;* who art *the confidence of all the ends of the earth, and of them* that are *afar off* upon *the sea.*

The fourth reason of the Lord's praise is taken from the defending of his church in all ages and places, and saving of his people, by giving terrible answers to their prayers against their enemies, for the performance of his own word, and confirmation of the faith of his own people, in whatsoever part of the earth, unto the end of the world. Whence learn, 1. As the love of God to his people exempteth not them from the molestation of enemies, because the Lord will have the faith of his people by this means exercised, and them put to pray unto him, and complain of the injuries done unto them; so his love to them will not suffer their prayers to want an answer in their troubles, to the amazement of their adversaries: *by terrible things wilt thou answer us.* 2. In the Lord's relieving his people and destroying their enemies, he will have the work looked upon as the performance of his word, wherein he hath promised to be a friend to the friends of his people, and a foe to their foes: *by terrible things in righteousness wilt thou answer us.* 3. The reason of particular deliveries of God's people from their enemies, is, because these deliveries are append-ices of the covenant of grace, established for giving to them everlasting life: *thou wilt answer us, O God of our salva-tion.* 4. What the Lord hath promised and done to his church of old, is a sufficient ground of confidence to the people of God, in all times and places, to expect and find the like mercy unto that which they of old expected and found; *O God of our salvation, the confidence of all the ends of the earth, and of them that are afar off upon the sea;* that is, thy people, whether dwelling on the continent, or in isles, or sailing on the sea.

6. *Which by his strength setteth fast the mountains; being girded with power:*

The fifth reason of the Lord's praise is his strong power, whereby he is able to do all things, as appeareth by his framing and settling the mountains. Whence learn, 1. The power of God manifested in the work of creation, is a prop to the faith of his people to believe the promises, and a pledge of the performance thereof unto them: *by his strength he setteth fast the mountains.* 2. Whatsoever great work the Lord hath done, he is able and ready to do a greater work, if need be, for his people: *he is girded with power.*

7. *Which stilleth the noise of the seas, the noise of their waves, and the tumult of the people.*

From the sixth reason, taken from his wise and powerful overruling all commotions of unruly creatures of whatso-ever sorts, learn, 1. There is nothing so turbulent, and raging, and reasonless in the whole world, which God doth not rule and bridle, and make quiet as he pleaseth: *he stilleth the noise of the seas, the noise of their waters.* 2. As the commotions of people, their seditions, their insur-rections and conspiracies against God's people within and without the visible church, are no less raging and reason-less than are the commotions of the sea; so God hath the ruling of them as well as of the seas, and by his *stilling the noise of the seas, the noise of the waters thereof,* he giveth an evidence of his power and purpose to bridle the fury and rage of reasonless men who threaten trouble and destruction to his people : *he stilleth their waves, and the tumult of the people.*

8. *They also that dwell in the uttermost parts are afraid at thy tokens: thou makest the outgoings of the morning and evening to rejoice.*

From the seventh reason of God's praise, taken from the affrighting of all the world by his judgments against the enemies of the people, lest they should attempt the like, learn, 1. As the Lord can still the tumults of the people, when they rage most; so he can by his terror prevent their commotions against his church, by showing them his terrible judgments executed on others, which are the tokens of the power of his displeasure against all who shall dare to be adversaries to his people : *they also that dwell in the uttermost parts, are afraid at thy tokens.*

The eigthth reason of God's praise, is from the joyful tranquillity and peace, which he, when he pleaseth, giveth to his people, after he has settled their enemies' rage and power against them. Whence learn, as the Lord sometimes exerciseth his people with trouble and persecution from their enemies; so also he can, and doth give them some breathing times, some comfortable seasons, as it were fair days, from morning to evening; yea, sundry full fair days, one after another, so that his people are made to rejoice before him from day to day; *thou makest the outgoings of the morning and evening to rejoice.*

9. *Thou visitest the earth, and waterest it: thou greatly enrichest it with the river of God, which is full of water : thou preparest them corn, when thou hast so provided for it.*

10. *Thou waterest the ridges thereof abundantly; thou settlest the furrows thereof; thou makest it soft with showers ; thou blessest the springing thereof:*

11. *Thou crownest the year with thy goodness; and thy paths drop fatness.*

12. *They drop* upon *the pastures of the wilderness , and the little hills rejoice on every side.*

13. *The pastures are clothed with flocks ; the val-*

leys also are covered over with corn; they shout for joy, they also sing.

The ninth reason of the Lord's praise, is from his plentiful furnishing of food yearly for man and beast, but in special for his making the promised land fruitful unto his people Israel, when he shall give them rest from their enemies, and peace therein, after their being exercised with troubles. What may be prophetical, in this whole psalm, as touching the Israelites, we will not here inquire; nor how far the prophet looked beyond his own and Solomon's time, when he said, *praise waiteth for thee in Zion, &c.* Only, hence learn general doctrines, 1. The Lord's blessing the ground, and making it fruitful, is his coming as it were to visit: *thou visitest the earth, and waterest it.* 2. God's providence is then best seen, when particular parts are looked upon, one after another; *thou waterest it, thou enrichest it, thou preparest them corn, &c.* 3. The sending of timely rain and plenty of it, and after that abundance of victual, should not be slightly passed over, but well and carefully marked: for the husbandry is all the Lord's: *thou preparest them corn, when thou hast so provided for it.* 4. Second causes, and the natural course of conveying benefits unto us, are not rightly seen, except when God, the first and prime cause, is seen to be nearest unto the actual disposing of them for producing the effect: *thou waterest the ridges thereof abundantly, &c., thou blessest the springing thereof.* 5. From the one end of the year to the other God hath continual work about the bringing forth of the fruits of the ground, and gloriously perfecteth it once a-year : *thou crownest the year with thy goodness.* 6. Every one of the footsteps of God's providence, for the provision of his people's food, hath its own blessing, as appeareth in the profitable use of the straw and stubble and chaff, and multiplication of the seed : *thy paths drop fatness.* 7. The Lord hath a care to provide food, not only for man, but also for beasts; and not only for tame beasts, which are most useful for man, but also for wild beasts in the wilderness; making his rain fall on all parts of the ground : *they drop upon the pastures of the wilderness, and the little hills rejoice on every side.* 8. Albeit temporal benefits be inferior to spiritual, yet because unto God's children they be appendices of the spiritual, they are worthy to be taken notice of, and God should be praised for them; as here the psalmist showeth, praising God for spiritual blessings, in the beginning of the psalm, and here, in the end, for temporal benefits. 9. The plurality of God's creatures, and the comparison of God's benefits set before our eyes, are the scale, music book, and noted lessons of the harmony and melody which we ought to have in our hearts, in praising him : yea, these benefits begin and take up the song in their own kind, that we may follow them in our kind: *the pastures are clothed with flocks, the valleys also are covered over with corn, they shout for joy, they also sing.*

PSALM LXVI.

To the chief musician. A song or psalm.

This psalm being all of praises, may be divided into three parts. In the first, the psalmist exhorteth all the earth to praise God, v. 1—4, and that because of the works which God did of old for his people, v. 5, 6, and because he is able to do the like when he pleaseth, v. 7. In the second part, he exhorts the church of Israel living with him in that age, to praise God for the late experience of God's goodness towards them, in the delivery granted to them out of their late trials, troubles, and sore vexations, v. 8—12. In the third place, the prophet expresseth his own purpose of thankfulness unto God for the large experience which he had in particular of God's mercies to himself, from v. 13, to the end.

1. *Make a joyful noise unto God, all ye lands :*
2. *Sing forth the honour of his name ; make his praise glorious.*

From this urgent exhortation to praise God, learn, 1. As the duty of praise is most necessary, and most spiritual, so are we more dull and indisposed thereto than to any other spiritual exercise, and had need to be stirred up thereunto; therefore, saith he, *make a noise, sing forth, &c.* 2. The prophets of old had it revealed to them, that the Gentiles should be brought to the knowledge of God, and made to worship him, as, *make a joyful noise unto God, all ye lands*, importeth. 3. The praise of the Lord is a task for all the world to be employed about, and a duty whereunto all are bound; for all see his works, and hold what they have of him, but specially those that hear of him by his word, to whom most specially the word speaketh : *make a joyful noise, all ye lands.* 4. Men ought to go about the work of praising God so cheerfully, so wisely, and so avowedly, that they

O

who hear his praise spoken of, may understand his majesty, magnificence, goodness, power, and mercy : *make a noise unto God, sing forth the honour of his name, make his praise glorious.*

3. *Say unto God, How terrible art thou in thy works! through the greatness of thy power shall thine enemies submit themselves unto thee.*

4. *All the earth shall worship thee, and shall sing unto thee ; they shall sing to thy name. Selah.*

Here the psalmist, as the Lord's penman, furnisheth to the hearers matter and words for praising God, and prophesieth that the fulness of the Gentiles shall concur in his worship, and take part in the song of his praise. Whence learn, 1. Because we can do nothing of ourselves in this work of the Lord's praise, God must furnish to us matter and words: *say unto God, How terrible, &c.* 2. As the work of the praise of God should be done in love, confidence, sincerity, and in his own strength, so may it be directed to him immediately, and that without flattery; (otherwise than men are praised) for praise properly is due to God only, and no man can speak of him, except in his own audience : *say unto God, How terrible art thou in thy works!* 3. The works of the Lord, every one of them being rightly studied, are able to affright us by discovering the incomparable, dreadful, and omnipotent majesty of the worker thereof : *how terrible art thou in thy works!* 4. When the Lord is pleased to let forth his judgments on his adversaries, and to let them see what he can do, none of them dare stand out against him; and, if they be not converted, yet will they be forced to feign submission unto him : *through the greatness of thy power shall thine enemies submit themselves to thee.* 5. Over and above what is already accomplished of this prophecy concerning the conversion of the Gentiles, a higher measure is yet to be expected in the bringing in of that number of them which the Scripture calleth the " fullness of the Gentiles," and the making all the kingdoms of the earth to become the Lord's, and his Son Christ's; for this word must be fulfilled in a greater measure than yet is come to pass : *all the earth shall worship thee ; they shall sing unto thee ; they shall sing unto thy name.* Which word importeth the revealing of the glad tidings of Jesus Christ unto them, their joyful acceptation of the gospel, and glorifying of God for it. 6. As it is the Lord's glory to have many praising him, so should it be the joy of all that love him, now to foresee the success of Christ's kingdom, as well as it was of old, when it was the church's song: *all the earth shall worship thee.*

5. *Come and see the works of God:* he is *terrible* in his *doing toward the children of men.*

6. *He turned the sea into dry*-land: *they went through the flood on foot; there did we rejoice in him.*

7. *He ruleth by his power for ever; his eyes behold the nations: let not the rebellious exalt themselves. Selah.*

He pointeth out in special the Lord's works, already wrought for his people. Whence learn, 1. Albeit the Lord worketh for the delivery of the church and his own glory, yet men are so careless to observe his works, that they can neither make use thereof for their own profit, nor for God's praise; so that there is much need to stir up our dullness to observe them and make right use thereof: *come and see the works of God.* 2. Whosoever observes the works of God, which he hath wrought for his people, shall be forced to fear and admire his wonderful acts for them, and his respect unto them : *he is terrible in his doings toward the children of men.* 3. The work of redemption of his church out of Egypt, is a work, one for all, worthy to be made use of to the end of the world, and sufficient to show that, if need be, God will invert the course of nature for the good of his people, and for their delivery out of difficulties : *he turned the sea into dry land.* 4. As the Lord will work wonders for the delivery of his people out of misery, so will he work wonders for performing promises to them, and for bringing them to the possession of what he hath given them right unto; for the drying of the river Jordan, that his people might go in to possess the promised land, was a pledge and evidence of this his purpose for all time coming: *they went through the flood on foot.* 5. As all the people of God are one body, and that which is done in one age to one generation concerneth all and every one to make use of it in their generation; so every one in after ages should reckon themselves one body with the Lord's people in former ages, and make use of God's dealing with them, as if they had been present then with them; as here the church, in the psalmist's time, joineth itself with the church in Joshua's time, rejoicing in God with them at their entering into Canaan: *there did we rejoice in him,* say they.   6. Whatsoever the Lord hath done for his people in any time bypast, he is able and ready to do the like for his people in any time to come: *he ruleth by his power for ever,* and for this cause his former acts are perpetual evidences and pledges of like acts to be done hereafter, as need is.   7. Nothing is done in any place, which the Lord is not witness unto, no plot or motion against his people which he seeth not : *his eyes behold the nations.*   8. Albeit there will be, from time to time, a generation who will not submit to this sovereign Ruler, but will stand out against him, and malign his church, yet shall they not long prosper, nor have cause of gloriation in their rebellion: *let not the rebellious exalt themselves.*

8. *O bless our God, ye people, and make the voice of his praise to be heard;*

9. *Which holdeth our soul in life, and suffereth not our feet to be moved.*

10. *For thou, O God, hast proved us : thou hast tried us, as silver is tried.*

11. *Thou broughtest us into the net; thou laidst affliction upon our loins.*

12. *Thou hast caused men to ride over our heads : we went through fire and through water ; but thou broughtest us out into a wealthy* place.

In the second part of the psalm, the psalmist exhorts the church in his time to praise God for preserving them from extirpation in the time of their fiery trial and sore affliction under the tyranny and oppression of their enemies. Whence learn, 1. The Lord's people in every age, besides all the reasons they have to praise God for his former works, want not their own particular reasons for his care, providence, and kindness to themselves in their own time, to stir up one another to bless his majesty: *O bless our God, ye people.*   2. It is the church's proper privilege, and her glory above all other incorporations and societies beside, to have special interest in God as her own: *O bless our God.*   3. It is not sufficient that the Lord's people acknowledge inwardly the mercies of God to themselves; but it is their duty in an orderly way to bring others on to the knowledge of God, and show how praiseworthy he is: *make the voice of his praise to be heard.* 4. Albeit the Lord takes many things away from his people, when he is pleased to exercise them, yet he keeps life in their soul, some sweet communion of spirit between himself and them, and suffereth not all his people to be extirpated from the earth : *which holdeth our soul in life.* 5. It is a great mercy to be kept from desperate courses in the time of sad calamities, and to be supported under burdens, that we sink not: and to be prevented from denying God or his truth in time of persecution : *he suffereth not our feet to be moved.* 6. One end of the troubles of the church, among others, is, the trial of the graces of his people, and purging them from their corruptions; for which cause the Lord useth to bring on one trouble after another, as metal is put in the fire oftener than once : *for thou, O God, hast proved us, thou hast tried us, as silver is tried.* 7. When God bringeth his church into trial there is no escaping; we must look for affliction, and not dream of declining it by our own judgment or skill : *thou broughtest us into the net, thou laidst affliction upon our loins.* 8. It is wisdom, and justice, and goodness in God, to make his people know sometimes, whether his service or men's service be most easy : *thou hast caused men to ride over our heads.* 9. When God's service and men's service are compared, the service of man is a beastly bondage in comparison; for the enemies of the church will abuse God's people like beasts, when they fall under their power : *thou hast made men ride over our heads.* 10. There is no sort of affliction, or extremity of affliction, from which the godly may secure themselves, after the time of entering into their trials, till God's time come wherein their trial is to end: *we went through fire, and through water.* 11. After troubles and trials, the Lord giveth ever an event, and a gracious delivery to his own, which bringeth as much comfort with it as their trial had grief in it : *but thou broughtest us out into a wealthy place.*

13. *I will go into thy house with burnt-offerings ; I will pay thee my vows,*

14. *Which my lips have uttered, and my mouth hath spoken, when I was in trouble.*

15. I will offer unto thee burnt-sacrifices of fatlings, with the incense of rams : I will offer bullocks with goats. Selah.

In the third and last part of the psalm, the psalmist showeth forth his thankfulness for the favours showed to himself in particular; and first, he promiseth to acknowledge his obligation to God in the place of public worship, as the Lord had required in the ceremonial law, v. 13—15. Secondly, he declareth his particular experience of God's mercy, testifying his hearing of his prayer, by his acceptance of it, v. 18, 19. And, last of all, he blesseth the Lord for the gracious answer of his prayer, v. 20.

From the promise which he maketh of public acknowledgment of the mercy, according to the prescription of the Lord's appointment, learn, 1. In common favours and deliveries granted to the visible church, each true member has his own special mercies bestowed upon him, besides the common, for which in particular, and for the common mercies also, he ought publicly to be thankful, as the psalmist is here, saying, *I will go into thy house with burnt-offerings.* 2. As it is a token of lively faith in desperate troubles to trust in God, and to hope for his deliverance, and to promise him praise before the delivery come : so it is a token of an upright heart, to be as willing to perform promises after the benefit received, as it was ready to make promises, before the benefit received : *I will pay thee my vows which my lips have uttered, and my mouth hath spoken when I was in trouble.* 3. As our persons and best services are polluted, except they be cleansed by the sacrifice of Christ : so in our approaches unto God, we should acknowledge the sinfulness of our persons and performances, and the need we stand in of Christ's mediation, and the riches of grace bestowed upon us through him, who perfumeth our persons, and prayers, and praises, as was shadowed forth in the ceremonies of the law; for this was the prophet's meaning, when he said, *I will offer unto thee burnt sacrifices of fatlings, with the incense of rams : I will offer bullocks with goats,* which were appointed in the law to be offered, partly for sin, and partly by way of thanksgiving.

16. Come and hear, all ye that fear God, and I will declare what he hath done for my soul.

17. *I cried unto him with my mouth, and he was ex-tolled with my tongue.*

From his declaration of his lately felt experience of God's mercy to him: learn, 1. As a spiritual man will not neglect outward rites of commanded public worship: so will he not rest on them, but will go about the real glorifying of God before others, as the psalmist doth here : *come and hear what the Lord hath done for my soul.* 2. The true dis-ciples of God's grace who can best discern God's works, and the experience of others, and who will be most ready to praise God with us, are those that fear God : *come and hear, all ye that fear God, I will declare what he hath done for my soul.* 3. It is no less needful for glorifying God, and the edification of others, to make the way of our coming by a benefit manifest to others—that it was by the use of holy ordinances—than to make mention of the benefit itself; *I cried unto him,* saith he; that is, I was instant in prayer for the benefit. 4. There are cases wherein the uttering of words in prayer serveth much, not only for our own up-stirring, and fixing our minds, and for others' edification; but also concerneth God's glory, on whom we profess de-pendence, and in whom we acknowledge power and good-ness to dwell : *and he was extolled with my tongue.*

18. *If I regard iniquity in my heart, the Lord will not hear* me :

19. But *verily God hath heard* me; *he hath attended to the voice of my prayer.*

From the clearing of David's sincerity in prayer, learn, 1. Sincerity of heart should be joined with the supplication of the mouth, and with self-examination, that we may be sure we pray sincerely : for, *if I regard iniquity in my heart,* imports so much in the psalmist's practice. 2. He is an up-right man in God's account, who entertaineth not affection to any known sin, but opposeth it sincerely in God's sight; for this the psalmist bringeth for the proof of his sincerity, that he did not *regard sin in his heart.* 3. Those only are sinners, whose prayer God will not hear, who live in the love of known sins, and pray for having satisfaction to their cor-rupt lusts : *if I regard iniquity in my heart, the Lord will not hear me.* 4. The lawful prayer of the upright heart shall be granted in substance, and it may be just as it was desired: which, as it is no small mercy, should be well marked, as the return of our prayer : *but verily God hath heard me, he hath attended to the voice of my supplication.*

20. *Blessed* be *God, which hath not turned away my prayer, nor his mercy from me.*

David closeth with thanksgiving for this particular experience, as an evidence of the running of the fountain of God's mercy toward him. Whence learn, 1. As it is no small mercy that our prayers are not rejected of God, albeit he should delay to answer us for a long time; so when he delayeth not to answer us, the mercy is the greater, and ought to be acknowledged in both respects : *blessed be God, which hath not turned away my prayer.* 2. The gracious answer of an upright supplication, evidenceth ready access prepared yet more for the supplicant, to the fountain of God's mercy; and this is more mercy still : *he hath not turned away my prayer, nor his mercy from me.*

PSALM LXVII.

To the chief musician on Neginoth. A psalm or song.

This psalm is a prophetical prayer for a blessing upon the church of the Jews, for the good of the Gentiles and the enlargement of the kingdom of Christ among them. The petition is propounded, v. 1, 2. In the next place, is an acclamation with the Gentiles, glorifying God at their inbringing, now foreseen that it should come most certainly, v. 3, 4. In the third place, the church of the Jews applaud the second time the conversion of the Gentiles, and their praising God, promising to themselves, that by that means the increase of God's blessing on them shall follow, and the enlarging of the kingdom of God through all the world, v. 5—7.

1. *God be merciful unto us, and bless us ;* and *cause his face to shine upon us. Selah.*

2. *That thy way may be known upon earth, thy saving health among all nations.*

This is the blessing which the Lord commanded the children of Aaron to pronounce upon the people of Israel, Numb. vi. 22, 23, which here the people turn into a prayer, for the drawing in of the Gentiles unto God's service. Whence learn, 1. It is safe to turn God's offers, promises, and forms of blessing his people into prayers; we are sure so to pray according to God's will, as the church doth here.

2. It is the duty of all citizens of the church, as lively members of that body, to' pray for the blessing of God upon all his people : *God be merciful unto us, and cause his face to shine upon us.* 3. Then are the Lord's people blessed, when God maketh them instrumental to enlarge his kingdom and to propagate the true religion, that is, the doctrine of man's salvation and God's service : and this should be the aim we shoot at in seeking any blessing to his people : *that the Lord may be known upon earth, his saving health among all nations.* 4. The world is ignorant of true religion, till God by his own instruments reveal it; and no way of religion will please God, or profit men, save God's way only, wherein he will have men to walk in the course of faith and obedience, and wherein he revealeth how he will deal with us, and how we must behave ourselves towards him; therefore say the godly, *that thy way may be known upon earth, thy saving health among all nations.*

3. *Let the people praise thee, O God; let all the people praise thee.*

4. *O let the nations be glad, and sing for joy : for thou shalt judge the people righteously, and govern the nations upon earth. Selah.*

The psalmist foreseeth by the revelation of God's Spirit, that the Gentiles shall be converted, and shall rejoice in God and praise him, and therefore will have the church of the Jews to welcome them, and to join with them in acclamation of praise to God, because of Christ's reigning among them and ruling them by his most holy laws. Whence learn, 1. The manifestation of God's freely gifted salvation in Christ, and the revealing of his manner of dealing with people, and how he will have people to deal with him, and one with another, are matters of unspeakable praise to God and joy to men, to whom this grace is revealed : *that thy saving health may be known among all nations; let the people praise thee, O God.* 2. True converts unto Christ, besides the joy they have of their own salvation, have also daily new accession of joy at the conversion of others, as they come in; and ought to bless and praise God heartily with them, when they behold their conversion; *let all the people praise thee,* do they say twice, and hereafter also the third time. 3. The conversion of the Gentiles was a thing not only wished for by the church of the Jews, but also prophesied of unto them clearly : *O let the nations be glad, and sing for joy : for thou shalt judge the people righteously, &c.* 4. The Spirit which indited the psalms, did not degrade the promised Messiah Jesus Christ from his Godhead, for his future incarnation; but speaketh of him, and to him, as " God blessed for ever;" that is, the true God to the Jewish church before his coming : and true God to the converted Gentiles after his coming in the flesh, one with the Father and holy Spirit; for six times in this psalm he is called God, and acknowledged here to be the fountain of mercy, and blessing to men, and of manifested reconciliation with men; the object of all divine honour and praise, God the Lord and lawgiver of the converted Gentiles : *thou shalt judge the people righteously, and govern the nations upon earth.* 5. The doctrine and discipline of Christ, whereby he judgeth and governeth his church, is most holy and righteous, and in as far as particular churches and Christians submit themselves to his laws, doctrine, and government, they are his true subjects, and shall find the fruit of his governing and judging : *for these shall he judge righteously,* unto these shall he do the part of a governor, even on earth : *he shall govern the nations upon earth.*

5. *Let the people praise thee, O God ; let all the people praise thee.*

6. Then *shall the earth yield her increase;* and *God, even our own God, shall bless us.*

7. *God shall bless us ; and all the ends of the earth shall fear him.*

In the last place, the Jewish church giveth a second acclamation to the incoming of the Gentiles, and promise to themselves by that means God's blessing more abundantly upon themselves, as now being one body with the Gentiles, in the same covenant of grace with them. Whence learn, 1. As the conversion of the Gentiles was esteemed by the Jews, a matter worthy to be oftener presented to God, and prayed for, and earnestly pursued by all that loved God; so was it foreseen to be a matter of growing and lasting joy to men, and growing and lasting praise to God, and to Christ, who is God, the converter of them, and the governor and teacher of them effectually, to know his name and salvation : *let all the people praise thee, O God, let all the people praise thee.* 2. The Spirit of God gave the church of the Jews to understand, that the conversion of the Gentiles, especially the conversion of the fulness of the Gentiles, (which here is prayed for, when he saith, *let all the people praise thee,*) was to be a means or a mercy antecedent unto, or nearly joined with, the bringing in and blessing of the Jewish church, and possibly in their own land : *then shall the earth yield her increase, and God even our own God shall bless us :* for, by the earth he meaneth the promised land of Canaan, which has been, and is accursed, during the time of their ejection out of it. 3. When God shall be gracious to the Jews, after the conversion and bringing in of the Gentiles, and shall renew the covenant with them in Christ, it shall fare the better with true religion, and with the Christian churches among the Gentiles; it shall be to them as a resurrection from the dead, in regard both of the purity of doctrine and worship, and the multiplication of persons converted unto Christ in all places; *God shall bless us,* saith he then; and what more ? *And all the ends of the earth shall fear him.*

PSALM LXVIII.

To the chief musician. A psalm or song of David.

This psalm is very suitable to that time when David, having gotten the victory over his enemies round about, assembled all Israel, and carried the ark of God, now returned from the land of the Philistines, triumphantly out of the house of Obed-Edom into the city of David, as a type of Christ's ascension after the work of redemption in the world. In which psalm, after the manner that Moses prayed to God, or to Christ who was to be incarnate, when the ark marched, David prayeth here, first, against the Lord's enemies, ver. 1, 2, and then for the Lord's people, ver. 3. In the next place, he exhorteth all the Lord's people to praise God, ver. 4, and giveth twelve or thirteen reasons for it; first, because of his mercy to the desolate and afflicted, ver. 5, 6; secondly, because of his wonderfulness and terribleness in delivering his people out of bondage, as appeared in his bringing his people out of Egypt and through the wilderness, ver. 7, 8; thirdly, because of his fatherly care to entertain his redeemed people, as appeared in his nourishing his church in Canaan, ver. 9, 10; fourthly, because of the victories which he giveth usually to his people when their enemies invade them, ver. 11, 12; fifthly, because of the delivery which he will give to his people out of their most sad calamities, as he hath oftentimes given proof, ver. 13, 14; sixthly, because his church is the most glorious kingdom in the world, being compared therewith, ver. 15, 16; seventhly, because Christ, the king of the church, hath all the angels at his command to serve him ; and, having ended the work of redemption, was to ascend gloriously, for sending down gifts to his church and ruling it, ver. 17, 18;

eighthly, because of God's bounty to his people, in daily renewed mercies, till he perfect the work of their salvation, ver. 19, 20; ninthly, because of his avenging himself on all his enemies, ver. 21; tenthly, because God hath undertaken to work over again in effect, as need shall require, what he hath done in bringing his people out of Egypt, and in giving them victory over the Canaanites, ver. 22, 23, whereof the experience of his power, already manifested for Israel, was a proof and pledge sufficient, ver. 24—27; eleventhly, because it was decreed by God to establish his church and to make her strong by making kings become converts, ver. 28, 29; and that, partly by treading down some of her enemies, ver. 30, and partly by making others, even some of her greatest enemies, seek reconciliation with God, even her od, ver. 31: twelfthly, he exhorteth to praise God, because of his omnipotent power, in conversion of kingdoms, ready to be let forth for the defence of his people, ver. 31—34, and ready to overthrow their enemies, and all for the strengthening of his church; for all which he exhorteth all to bless the Lord, ver. 35.

1. Let God arise, let his enemies be scattered: let them also that hate him flee before him.

2. As smoke is driven away, so drive them away: as wax melteth before the fire, so let the wicked perish at the presence of God.

3. But let the righteous be glad: let them rejoice before God; yea, let them exceedingly rejoice.

In David's prayer against his enemies and for God's people, learn, 1. Such prayers as the Spirit hath indited unto the saints in Scripture, it is lawful and expedient, for strengthening our faith, to use the same or the like words in the like case; for David prayeth here, as Moses prayed at the marching of the ark, Numb. x. 35, *let God arise, &c.* 2. As the ark was amongst the Israelites, so is Christ amongst his people; and what ground of confidence the church had, because of that pledge of God's presence at the ark, we have the same, and a more sure ground of confidence in Christ's incarnation, represented thereby; that, upon every appearance of his beginning to stir against the enemies of his work, we may say, *let God arise.* 3. The enemies of the church are the enemies of God, and esteemed haters of him because they are haters of his people; with whom, albeit the Lord doth bear for a while, yet will he take order when he pleaseth; it will not cost him much labour: only *let God arise, and let his enemies be scattered.* 4. Although all the enemies of God make head against his people, yet will they not prevail; when God appeareth, they will turn back: *let them also that hate him flee before him.* 5. Whatsoever strength of forces or number the enemies of God's people have in appearance, it is nothing before God but like smoke before the wind and wax before the fire: *as smoke is driven away, as wax melteth before the fire, so let the wicked perish at the presence of God.* 6. Albeit the Lord exercise his people with affliction and with grief for a while, yet he alloweth unto them comfort and joy, whatsoever become of their enemies: *but let the righteous be glad.* 7. The only true matter of the saint's joy are God himself and his manifested presence, and he will not be pleased except his children lift up their hearts, and comfort themselves in him above and against all grief and sense of whatsoever enemies' opposition: *let them rejoice before God; yea, let them exceedingly rejoice.*

4. *Sing unto God, sing praises to his name: extol him that rideth upon the heavens by his name JAH, and rejoice before him.*

From his exhortation of the church to praise God with the joyful voice of singing, learn, 1. Vocal singing of praises unto God is a moral duty, and a part of his holy worship, frequently called for in Scripture: *sing unto God, sing praises to his name.* 2. Our thoughts of God should not be base, but high and heavenly, lifting his name up above the most glorious creatures, all they being but his servants, as he pleaseth to make use of them; *extol him that rideth upon the heavens.* 3. The Lord is only and properly worthy of praise, because he only hath his being of himself, and giveth being to all things which are beside himself: *his name is JAH.* 4. The Lord's praises are his people's advantage, and the true matter of their confidence and joy: *sing praises unto him, and rejoice before him.*

5. *A father of the fatherless, and a judge of the widows, is God in his holy habitation.*

6. *God setteth the solitary in families: he bringeth out those which are bound with chains; but the rebellious dwell in a dry land.*

From the first reason of the exhortation to praise God, learn, 1. The Lord's highness above the heavens hindereth him not from taking notice of the lowest of his poor people: yea, the most helpless and desolate among men are the first objects of his warmest love: *a father of the fatherless, and a judge of the widows, is God.* 2. Albeit the Lord be infinite and incomprehensible by any place, yet he hath appointed a trysting-place where his people shall find him by his own ordinance; to wit, the assembly of his saints, his holy temple, shadowing forth Christ to be incarnate, who now is in heaven, now is incarnate, and sitting at the right hand of God, in whom dwells the Godhead; here, here is God to be found: *God is in his holy habitation.* 3. It is the Lord's nature, pleasure, and ordinary practice, to make up the wants, and to change to the better the disconsolate condition of his own humbled and emptied children: *God setteth the solitary in families.* 4. The souls that are most sensible of bonds and bondage lie nearest the seeking of the fruit of his redemption; yea, none in bonds have made, or shall make, use of God the Redeemer, but his bonds and fetters, hindering him from freedom of God's service, and from attaining felicity, have been, and shall be, loosed off: *he bringeth out those which are bound in chains.* 5. Such as will not be ruled by his word, according as they are disloyal rebels to him, so shall they be dealt with as rebels; that is, they shall neither have God's blessing joined with any benefit which they seem to possess, nor any spiritual comfort in their afflictions when their calamity cometh upon them: *but the rebellious dwell in a dry land.*

7. *O God, when thou wentest forth before thy people, when thou didst march through the wilderness; Selah:*

8. *The earth shook, the heavens also dropped at the presence of God: even Sinai itself was moved at the presence of God, the God of Israel.*

From the second reason of praising God, learn, 1. It is expedient for our upstirring unto thankfulness, to cast our eye upon some particulars wherein the Lord's goodness to us, and our obligation to his love, may appear, as here the psalmist leadeth us by the hand unto the Lord's particular work of redemption of Israel out of Egypt. 2. That one work of the church's delivery out of Egypt, representing the redemption of his people from the misery of sin and Satan's bondage, is a sufficient proof for ever of the Lord's love, care, power, and faithfulness, to deliver his own out of all their misery; which the church, and every member thereof, should always make use of unto the end of the world: whether we look upon that work in the type singly, or as it is a representation or pledge of the spiritual delivery of his people, this work we should often look upon, and still hold it up unto God: *O God, when thou wentest forth before thy people, when thou didst march through the wilderness.* 3. In the works of the Lord it is needful not only to look upon that which may foster faith in God and love toward him, but also to set before us what may serve to keep our hearts in fear and awe of his dreadful majesty : *the earth shook, the heavens dropped at the presence of God; even Sinai itself was moved at the presence of God, the God of Israel.*

9. *Thou, O God, didst send a plentiful rain, where-by thou didst confirm thine inheritance, when it was weary.*

10. *Thy congregation hath dwelt therein : thou, O God, hast prepared of thy goodness for the poor.*

From the third reason of God's praise, learn, 1. The ordinary sustaining of God's people bodily and spiritually, in the possession of any benefit, temporal or spiritual, given unto them, should be observed, as well as the bestowing of any benefit in an extraordinary way, as here the ordinary sustaining of Israel in Canaan, is made a part of the song of praise, no less than their miraculous delivery out of Egypt: *thou, O Lord, didst send a plentiful rain, whereby thou didst confirm thine inheritance when it was weary.* 2. The people who are in covenant with God externally, are the Lord's own peculiar, more nearly and properly than any society in the world: therefore Israel here is called by the prophet speaking to God, *thy congregation.* 3. It is for the church's cause, that the land wherein his people dwelleth, is blessed at any time by God : *thy congregation hath dwelt in it.* 4. The blessing bestowed upon the church or the place wherein they dwell, is not given for any goodness in his people, but for the goodness, grace, and good-will of God to them : *thou, O God, hast prepared of thy goodness for the poor.*

11. *The Lord gave the word; great was the company of those that published it.*

12. *Kings of armies did flee apace ; and she that tarried at home divided the spoil.*

From the fourth reason of praise, learn, 1. The Lord

will sometimes exercise his church with wars, afflictions, and trials, when he intendeth not to punish them, but to give them the victory over their enemies, and that for his own glory, as in Joshua's time and David's, whereunto the text relateth. The matter of joyful news, or the word of the church's victory over her foes, whensoever it is, proceeds from the Lord, who furnisheth matter for, and words and utterance of, joy to his people and praise to himself: *the Lord gave the word.* 2. When God will glorify himself by comforting his church, he shall not want heralds of his praise : *great was the company of those that published it.* 3. Were the enemies of the church ever so powerful, and God's people ever so far inferior unto the enemies in power, yet shall the enemy not be able to stand, when God begins to fight for his people : *kings of armies did flee apace.* 4. It is easy for the Lord to make them a prey to the weakest of his people, who set themselves to make havoc of the church, yea and to enrich his people with the spoil of such adversaries : *she that tarried at home divided the spoil.*

13. *Though ye have lien among the pots,* yet shall ye be as *the wings of a dove covered with silver, and her feathers with yellow gold.*

14. *When the Almighty scattered kings in it, it was* white *as snow in Salmon.*

From the fifth reason of praise, learn, 1. As the Lord sometimes adorneth his people with victories and wealth : so also at other times for just reasons, he will darken all their outward glory, and make them look as blacked scullions in the kitchen : *though ye have lien among the pots, &c.* 2. The Lord after the trial and hard exercises of his people for a time, will give them so glorious an event and delivery, as shall take off all the ignominy of their former affliction, and make up all their losses; yea he will cause their former-ly deforming afflictions, to serve for washing balls of soap, to make them so much the more beautiful : *though ye have lien among the pots, ye shall be as the wings of a dove co-vered with silver, and her feathers with yellow gold.* 3. Experiences of mercies shown to the Lord's people, are pledges and evidences of like mercies in time to come, as here, *when the Almighty scattered kings in the land, it was made white,* is made a proof of the promise made, v. 13.

4. As a dark, dusky mountain, whereupon groweth no green thing but black heath, is made white, when covered with snow : so is a disgraced, shamed, impoverished, enslaved land made glorious again by a merciful manner of delivery manifesting the Lord's kind respects unto it : *when the Almighty scattered kings in Judah, it was white as snow in Salmon.*

15. *The hill of God is* as *the hill of Bashan; an high hill,* as *the hill of Bashan.*

16. *Why leap ye, ye high hills?* this is *the hill* which *God desireth to dwell in ; yea, the Lord will dwell in it for ever.*

From the sixth reason of praise, learn, 1. The kingdoms of this world, especially some of more eminent sort, seem very rich and glorious in comparison of the outward appearance of the kingdom of Christ in his church, as the great, high, and fruitful hill of Bashan seemed to be more glorious, than the hill of Zion; yet, all things being compared, in special the spiritual privileges of the one, with the temporal privileges of the other, the church of God will outreach the most glorious kingdom on the earth : *the hill of God is as the hill of Bashan, an high hill as the hill of Bashan.* 2. Although the kingdoms of the world rejoice in their prerogatives, and despise the kingdom of Christ in his church, yet they have no cause to exalt themselves: *why leap ye, ye high hills?* 3. This is one privilege of the church, that it is the place of God's residence, wherein he will manifest himself familiarly and comfortably to his own, and may oversway all the excellency of all the kingdoms of the world: no kingdom which hath not God's church in it can say the like : *this is the hill which God desireth to dwell in, yea the Lord will dwell in it for ever.*

17. *The chariots of God* are *twenty thousand,* even *thousands of angels: the Lord* is *among them,* as *in Sinai, in the holy* place.

18. *Thou hast ascended on high, thou hast led captivity captive : thou hast received gifts for men ; yea,* for *the rebellious also, that the Lord God might dwell* among them.

From the seventh reason of praise, learn, 1. No kingdom hath such defence, so potent and so numerous armies to fight their battles, as the church hath: *the chariots of God are twenty thousand, even thousands of angels.* 2. The defence of angels is made fast to his church, and their power made sure to be for her, because God is in his church, even the Lord whom all angels serve and attend upon, is in his church, as appeared at his giving of the law upon mount Sinai: *the Lord is among them as in Sinai.* 3. The Lord is no less terrible against his foes in Zion, than in Sinai; and whatsoever terror the Lord showed to his church in Sinai against the violators of his law, he will manifest it for the comfort and defence of his people, who heartily embrace his gospel: *the Lord is among them,* to wit, these chariots and angels, *as in Sinai, so in the holy place.* 4. The ark was not more gloriously conveyed from the house of Obed-edom unto the city of David, than God,—that is, Christ, who is God, who descended to assume human nature, that he might therein perfect the work of redemption,—ascended gloriously into heaven, after the price of redemption was paid by him: *thou hast ascended on high,* Ephes. iv. 8—10. 5. The praises of God and joy of the church are perfected in Christ; no satisfaction in the shadows, till Christ the substance be looked unto; therefore here the Lord's Spirit led his people to look through the shadow of the ascending of the ark toward the city of David, unto the ascending of God incarnate, represented by the ark into heaven: *thou hast ascended on high.* 6. Christ did not enter into his glory without a battle going before, and that with strong and many enemies: and in his fighting he carried the victory, aud after his victory he triumphed, first in the cross and then in his ascension, over sin, Satan, the world, hell, grave, and all: *he led captivity captive.* 7. Christ as mediator and king of his church, was fully furnished with all things needful, for gathering his church, for edifying, governing, and perfecting it: *thou hast received gifts for men;* even those gifts which the apostle speaketh of, for the gathering and edifying of the body of the saints, Ephes. iv. 11, 13. 8. The gifts which Christ hath received and given forth, are not for the Jews only, or Gentiles only, for the poor only, or rich only; but for men indefinitely: *thou hast received gifts for men.* 9. As he hath received gifts for bringing on to life those that are reconciled; so also to conquer, subdue, and bring in rebels, and to reconcile enemies : *thou hast received gifts for men, yea and for the rebellious also.* 10. The end of Christ's ascension, and receiving and sending down gifts among men, is to gather and preserve and establish unto God a church in the world, wherein he may make himself manifest, and dwell and rule in the midst of his enemies : *thou hast received gifts for men, that the Lord might dwell among them.* 11. Yea, whatsoever gifts are bestowed upon unregenerate men within the visible church, or without it, which may any way be serviceable to the church, they are all bestowed on them in favour of the church, that God may dwell in his visible church, which by those gifts is edified : *thou hast received gifts for men, yea for the rebellious also, that the Lord God might dwell among them.*

19. *Blessed* be *the Lord,* who *daily loadeth us* with benefits, *even the God of our salvation. Selah.*

20. He that is *our God* is *the God of salvation; and unto God the Lord* belong *the issues from death.*

From the eighth reason of praise, learn, 1. Where the Lord will be merciful, he will be merciful, and not weary in doing good to his people in a current course of bounty; the observation whereof should stir up our hearts to thankfulness : *blessed be the Lord, who daily loadeth us with benefits.* 2. The favours and benefits which God bestoweth upon his people, come in greater number and measure unto them, than they are able to acknowledge, make use of, or be thankful for; and so, in a sort, burden the feelings of the truly godly: *blessed be God, who daily loadeth us with benefits.* 3. As all benefits flow unto God's children from the covenanted kindness of God, for giving unto them eternal salvation; so should all benefits confirm their faith in the covenant, and lead them to the hope of receiving after all other benefits, salvation also : *blessed be the Lord, who daily loadeth us with benefits, even the God of our salvation.* 4. Albeit the covenant of salvation be sure and solid in itself, yet are we slow to believe it, and weak in our laying hold of it; and have need to have the stamp and impression of it set deep upon our hearts, as here the psalmist teacheth the church by inculcating this point : *he that is our God, is the God of salvation.* 5. Temporal things which men idolize, may serve a man in this life; but at death, in death, and after death, he can have no good by them. It is God only who can deliver from death, and give an issue out of it : *unto God the Lord belong the issues from death.* 6. Let a man be once settled in the faith of his salvation, then he shall be comforted against all the troubles and dangers wherein he can fall, yea even against death itself; if he can say, *he that is our God, is the God of salvation,* he may also say with confidence, and application to himself, and comfort, *unto God the Lord belong the issues from death.*

21. *But God shall wound the head of his enemies,* and *the hairy scalp of such an one as goeth on still in his trespasses.*

From the ninth reason of God's praise, learn, 1. How great soever be the majesty of God, and the riches of bounty and grace offered in Christ, yet will men be found even within the visible church, who will wickedly refuse his grace, and oppose his kingdom, but all to their own shame and damage : *but God shall wound the head of his enemies.* 2. The character of God's irreconcilable enemies is, that they cease not to follow the course of sin : *he goeth on still in his trespasses.* 3. Though God spare his enemies long, and suffer them to grow old in the course of enmity against him, yet shall shameful, sudden, and irrecoverable judgments overtake them in their old days : *but God shall wound the hoary scalp of such a one as goeth on still in his trespasses.*

22. *The Lord said, I will bring again from Bashan; I will bring* my people *again from the depths of the sea :*

23. *That thy foot may be dipped in the blood of* thine *enemies,* and *the tongue of thy dogs in the same.*

From the tenth reason of praise, wherein the prophet promiseth in the Lord's name, that God shall work over again such works of delivery to his people, and such works of victory over their enemies as he had wrought before, learn, 1. The Lord's word is certainly sufficient for performance of his promises, and ground of comfort, and confidence, and thanksgiving, and praise to God even before the work be wrought : *the Lord said, I will bring again, &c.* 2. As the Lord will have the memory of former dangers and deliveries of his church kept in remembrance for his own glory; so will he have former dangers for his people's good to be looked upon as advertisements of what straits his church may be cast into, and his former merciful deliveries looked upon as pledges of the promises of like mercies in time to come, as need shall require : *I will bring again from Bashan, I will bring my people again from the depths of the sea*, importeth thus much. 3. As the Lord will give as great deliverances to his church when they are in straits, as ever he did before; so will he give as terrible blows to the adversaries as ever he did, according as the church's need or good shall require : *I will bring again from Bashan, &c., that thy foot may be dipped in the blood of thine enemies.* 4. Albeit neither the Lord nor his people delight in bloodshed, yet will he let his people and all men see, in the bloodshed of their enemies, how terrible he is in justice, especially against the enemies of his church, and how dear his people are to him, and that, rather than they should be overthrown, he will destroy nations for their safety, and give unto his people, in their own defence against their oppressors, notable victories : *so that thy foot may be dipped in the blood of thine enemies.* 5. When the Lord thinks it fit not to make his own people instrumental in their own delivery, then can he yoke the enemies among themselves, or raise up profane dogs like themselves, to avenge the quarrel of the Lord's people upon their enemies: *that the tongue of thy dogs may be dipped in the same ;* that is, in the blood of thine enemies.

24. *They have seen thy goings, O God ; even the goings of my God, my King, in the sanctuary.*

25. *The singers went before, the players on instruments* followed *after ; among* them were *the damsels playing with timbrels.*

To confirm what is promised, he bringeth forth old experiences acknowledged by the enemies, registered in the word of the Lord, and read in the temple. Whence learn, 1. The Lord useth to work so evidently for his people, and against his enemies, that both his people and their enemies are made witnesses, and are forced to acknowledge the Lord's work : *they have seen thy goings, O God.* 2. It is the glory of a people, when God so worketh, as he is seen to be their God, their leader, their defender, and all as in covenant with them : *they have seen thy goings, O God, even the goings of my God*, saith he. 3. That God's honour may be seen, man's honour should be laid down at his feet: and supposing a man were the greatest king, yet is it greater glory and matter of contentment to have God for his king, than to be a king without God : *they have seen thy goings, O my God, my King*, saith David, now settled in the kingdom. 4. The most clear, sure, and profitable sight of the Lord's work and ways, is to be had in the use of public ordinances, where his name, nature, covenant, and course he keepeth with all men, together with the causes, use, and ends of his works, are to be seen : *they have seen the goings of my God in the sanctuary.* 5. Where all the people receive a benefit, it becometh all the people publicly and solemnly, and with their best expression of affection, as God appointeth, to praise God, and in his worship to see that all things may be done orderly, as Israel did, when they came through the Red Sea, and at other times as the Lord gave occasion : *the singers went before, the players on instruments followed after ; amongst them*, in the middle ward, *the damsels playing with timbrels.* 6. All the powers of our souls and bodies should concur, each of them in its own order, with the best harmony of knowledge, affections, and expressions which can be attained, for setting forth the Lord's praises, and our obligation to him for his goodness to his people: and so should we march on all the days of our pilgrimage and warfare, till we come to the promised rest; for this the external ceremonies used under the pedagogy of the law, taught; which ceremonies, although they be abolished now, yet the substance and intended duties pointed at in them, being moral, still remain : *the singers went before, players on instruments followed after, &c.*

26. *Bless ye God in the congregations,* even *the Lord, from the fountain of Israel.*

27. *There* is *little Benjamin* with *their ruler, the princes of Judah* and *their council, the princes of Zebulun,* and *the princes of Naphtali.*

As the psalmist cleared the doctrine of God's dealing for his church, and against their enemies, by experiences of old; so he points here at experience later, as was to be seen by all, at the glorious triumphing of Israel over all their enemies, when they were now assembled in their several tribes, the least as well as the greatest, the most remote tribes, as well as those that were nearest hand; all of them conveying the ark of God unto the city of David, which was the type of Christ, God incarnate, ascending after his victories into heaven. Whence learn, 1. The mercies of God to his people, in special the great work of redemption, and victory over all enemies obtained by Christ in favour of his people, are abundant matter and cause to praise God, and to bless him in all the assemblies of the church: for here it is a commanded duty: *bless ye God in the congregation.* 2. Whatsoever be the part of others in discharging this duty, it is expected most at the hands of every kindly Israelite, who draws his original from the fountain of Israel, whether he be of the natural stock of Jacob, descended of him, as water out of a fountain, or have his descent of the same Spirit of regeneration with him: *bless ye God, even the Lord, from the fountain of Israel.* 3. Examples and practices of God's children at any time, are the encouragements of his people at all times thereafter: *there is little Benjamin with their ruler, &c.,* set forth here for example. 4. The piety of governors, and their precedency before, or joining with, others in the Lord's service, are more honourable unto them than their places of dignity, or their gifts of wisdom and power: *there were the princes of Judah with their council, the princes of Zebulun, and the princes of Naphtali.* 5. In the exercise of God's worship, and in spiritual privileges, the Lord joineth the smallest with the greatest, the lowest with the highest, that the lowest may glory in their exaltation, and the highest in their humiliation: *there was little Benjamin with Judah, the people with their princes and rulers.*

28. *Thy God hath commanded thy strength: strengthen, O God, that which thou hast wrought for us.*

29. *Because of thy temple at Jerusalem shall kings bring presents unto thee.*

From the eleventh reason of God's praise, learn, 1. Not in kings, or rulers, or any thing else, but in the Lord, and from the Lord, is the strength of his church, which she may expect always to be furnished with by virtue of the covenant: *thy God hath commanded thy strength,* said David to the church. 2. As the Lord hath decreed to establish his church, so hath he means and instruments in every age and place prepared for this purpose, and hath given out order by actual providence, which is always going about the work in all ages : *thy God hath commanded thy strength.* 3. The Lord's decree, and the order given forth to accomplish it, consist well with the church's using all lawful means to further that end, and in special should be joined with thankful acknowledging of what the Lord hath begun to do, or done already for it, and with earnest prayer for accomplishing what is to be further done; so teach David's example and prayer here : *strengthen, O God, that which thou hast wrought for us.* 4. The Lord's known presence in his church, maintaining and blessing his public ordinances, shall move kings at last to do homage to God incarnate, that is, to Christ represented by his dwelling in the temple of Jerusalem : *because of thy temple at Jerusalem shall kings bring presents unto thee.*

30. *Rebuke the company of spearmen, the multitude of the bulls, with the calves of the people,* till every one *submit himself with pieces of silver : scatter thou the people* that *delight in war.*

31. *Princes shall come out of Egypt ; Ethiopia shall soon stretch out her hands unto God.*

How this shall come to pass he showeth; to wit, partly by breaking the power of some of them, when they make opposition, and partly by the powerful conversion of others. Whence learn, 1. It is not against the precept of love to pray against public enemies of the church, when private spleen is not the motive, but zeal for the glory of God : *rebuke the company of spearmen.* 2. The leaders of armies, parties, and factions against God's church and cause, and the followers of such leaders, are all of them a company of beasts: *rebuke the multitude of the bulls, with the calves of the people.* 3. God is adversary to all who oppose his people and his cause in their hand, and can as easily repulse them really and overturn them, as reprove them verbally : *rebuke the spearmen, &c.* 4. The end of the church's prayer against her enemies, is, that God may be glorified, and people at least brought to outward obedience unto God, which may be a means to real conversion in God's time : *rebuke them, &c., till every one submit himself with pieces of silver ;* that is, till they offer to contribute to God's service. 5. The punishing of some of God's enemies may be a means to move others to offer obedience and submit to God, when people that delight in war are scattered: *for princes shall come out of Egypt*. 6. God will draw into subjection unto himself some of his most open and inveterate enemies : *princes shall come out of Egypt, Ethiopia shall soon stretch out her hands unto thee.*

32. *Sing unto God, ye kingdoms of the earth; O sing praises unto the Lord; Selah :*

33. *To him that rideth upon the heavens of heavens,* which were *of old ; lo, he doth send out his voice,* and that *a mighty voice.*

34. *Ascribe ye strength unto God : his excellency* is *over Israel, and his strength* is *in the clouds.*

35. *O God,* thou art *terrible out of thy holy places: the God of Israel* is *he that giveth strength and power unto* his *people. Blessed* be *God.*

From the last reason of praising God, taken from his almighty power in the conversion of kingdoms of Gentiles, ready to be put forth for the preservation of his church gathered and for the overthrow of his enemies, learn, 1. The time shall come when the kingdoms of the earth shall turn Christians in profession, in a greater measure than yet hath been seen; for, *sing unto God, ye kingdoms of the earth,* is not a simple telling of their duty, but a prophecy of their joyful joining in the worship of God, and that they shall have cause of joy within themselves to praise him : *O sing praises unto the Lord.* 2. True converts will renounce idols and false gods, and reverently worship the omnipotent Creator and Governor of heaven, the eternal God : *sing praises to God that rideth upon the heavens of heavens, that were of old.* 3. As the glorious government of heaven showeth the Lord's power ; so the thunder also showeth his power and terror, the consideration whereof is needful to dispose our stupid minds to praise him : *lo, he doth send out his voice, even a mighty voice.* 4. The right use of God's great, and sensible, and daily seen works, is to cause us to glorify the power of God, who is able to work whatsoever he pleaseth : *ascribe strength unto the Lord.* 5. The Lord's glory in his church is more excellent than all that is to be seen in the works of creation : *his excellency is over Israel.* 6. The

true worshipper must study the power and all other properties of God, both by what he hears in the society of the
church, and by what he seeth in his visible works; as well
daily transient works, such as the clouds are, as constantly
enduring works, such as the heavens are: *his excellency is
over Israel, and his strength is in the clouds.* And surely
it is no small power which beareth up such weight of mountains of snow and seas of water, and maketh them sail, as it
were, and fly with wings in the air, God dissolving them by
little and little, as we daily behold. 7. Wheresoever God
showeth his presence, whether in heaven, or in his church,
in any place of the earth, there and from thence he showeth
himself a dreadful God to such as fear him not: *O God, thou
art terrible out of thy holy places.* 8. Albeit there were no
man to hear us glorify God, or no man to take his praise
off our hand, we should acknowledge his greatness in our
heart, and before himself, who will take true worship off our
hand; for David here turneth his speech to God in the end
of the psalm, saying to him, *O God, thou art terrible out of
thy holy places.* 9. The Lord hath an everlasting interest
in the people of Israel, and they in him, for the election's
cause; and every true Israelite hath an everlasting interest
in God: he is *the God of Israel.* 10. What the Lord hath
is forthcoming to his people's support, as they have need:
*the God of Israel is he that giveth power and strength to his
people.* 11. It is reason that at all the several remembrances
of God's mercy to us, we should acknowledge his blessedness
and his blessing of us, and this is all we can do, and that also
we cannot do, except he strengthen and enable us for praise;
for, *blessed be God,* saith the prophet, for this very reason,
after he hath spoken of his giving *power to his people.*

PSALM LXIX.

To the chief musician upon Shoshannim.   A psalm of David.

David, as a type of Christ, earnestly dealeth with God for a delivery from
his perplexed condition, and from the malice of his adversaries, and
findeth a comfortable event.   There are three parts of the psalm.   In
the first part is his prayer, six times presented, and strengthened with
new reasons, to ver. 22; in the second, is his imprecation of ten plagues
against his enemies, with some reasons added, showing the justice of
inflicting the plagues, mentioned ver. 29; in the third, are four evidences of his victory, from ver. 29 to the end.   In all which, whatsoever
is proper to the type, is to be referred to the type only; and whatsoever

is fit also to be applied unto Christ, the antitype, must be referred to him only in that sense which is suitable to his majesty.

His prayer, at first, is propounded in few words: *save me*. The reasons are four. The first is, from the danger he was in, ver. 1, 2; the next, from his long and patient waiting for an answer to his prayer, ver. 3; the third, from the multitude, and malice, and iniquity of his enemies, ver. 4; the fourth is by way of attestation of God, that he was innocent of that whereof he was charged by his enemies, joined in with his humble acknowledging of whatsoever other sins justice could charge upon him in any other respect, ver. 5.

1. *Save me, O God; for the waters are come in unto* my *soul.*

2. *I sink in deep mire, where* there is *no standing; I am come into deep waters, where the floods overflow me.*

His first petition is to be saved, and the first reason of it is because of the danger he was in. Whence learn, 1. A child of God may, in his own sense, be very near to perishing, and yet must not, in the most desperate condition, cease to pray, nor cease to hope for delivery prayed for: *save me, O God.* 2. With danger of bodily death a child of God may have in his spirit a sore conflict with the sense of wrath, like to swallow up his soul, as deep waters do a drowning man: *the waters are come in unto my soul.* 3. The condition of a soul exercised with the sense of wrath threateneth no less than perdition, certain, inevitable, without any outgate, and endless, whereof the bodily danger of a drowning man is but a shadow: *I sink in deep mire, where there is no standing: I am come into deep waters, where the floods overflow me.*

3. *I am weary of my crying; my throat is dried: mine eyes fail while I wait for my God.*

The second reason of the first petition is, because he had long and patiently waited on God. Whence learn, 1. Faith in hard exercises ceaseth not for appearances of perdition, knowing that what is impossible in man's sight, is not impossible to God; for David, as a believer and a type of Christ, prayeth still for all this, although he find no delivery: *I am weary of my crying.* 2. Prayer put up in faith to God keepeth in life, and is like a man's drawing breath in the water, when the head is lifted up above the floods; for here, although the floods overflowed the psalmist, yet he is able to show this to God, and to cry till he be *weary of crying*. 3. For exercising faith and making patience to have her perfect work, it is no strange thing for God to delay relief unto an earnest supplicant till he be like to give over, till his case seem desperate and his relief hopeless : *mine eyes fail while I wait for my God.* 4. Though the flesh of the regenerate man be weak, yet the spirit is ready, and will never give over calling on God, depending on him, holding fast the covenant and the hope of deliverance; for the spirit will make this a new ground of speech unto God that it is not able to speak any thing, and a new ground of laying hold on God and hoping for help from him, because its hope is failing, as here: *I am weary of my crying, my throat is dried; mine eyes fail while I wait for my God.*

4. *They that hate me without a cause are more than the hairs of mine head: they that would destroy me,* being *mine enemies wrongfully, are mighty; then I restored* that *which I took not away.*

The third reason of the first petition is, because his enemies were many, mighty, and malicious. Whence learn, 1. Holiness and integrity cannot ward off the enmity of a wicked world; for the enemies of David, who was a well-deserving man, and Christ, (whose type he was,) much more beneficial to men, had foes innumerable : *they that hate me without cause are more than the hairs of my head.* 2. Albeit many aggravate their own grief foolishly, when they suffer hurt of them whom they did not injure or provoke; yet the conscience of harmless men toward such as wish harm to them, is a great support of their confidence when they are injuriously dealt with : *they hate me without a cause.* 3. It is no strange matter to see truly godly men to be out of credit and affection with men who are in power and authority in the world: *they that would destroy me, being mine enemies wrongfully, are mighty.* 4. He that is most just may be troubled and hated without a cause, and may be dealt with as a thief, being verily an honest man : *then I restored that which I took not away.*

5. *O God, thou knowest my foolishness; and my sins are not hid from thee.*

The fourth reason of the first petition is, because God was witness to his disposition and carriage. Whence learn, When we are condemned of men unjustly we have God to appeal to; and although there may be sins upon us in our private reckoning with God, yet, being free of what men lay to our charge, we may appeal to God in the controversy betwixt our enemies and us, and when we have acknowledged what sins are in reckoning betwixt God and us, our supplication to God shall not be cast back for our sins; for this is the force of the psalmist's reasoning, for the strengthening of his own faith in prayer, saying, *O God, thou knowest my foolishness, and my sins are not hid from thee;* that is, whether I be so foolish and injurious to my persecutors as they say or not, thou, Lord, knowest; and, whatsoever other sins may be imputed unto me upon any other score, I refuse not to reckon for them, but I am free, thou knowest, of what I am charged with.   This is applicable also in some sort unto Christ, who was most free of what men laid to his charge, although in another reckoning all the iniquities of the elect were charged upon him by imputation, according to his transaction with the Father about our debt.

6. *Let not them that wait on thee, O Lord God of hosts, be ashamed for my sake; let not those that seek thee be confounded for my sake, O God of Israel.*

The second petition is, that the godly may not be hurt by his manner of exercise, which he strengthens by four reasons.   First, because his sufferings were for God's cause, v. 7; secondly, because he was cast off by his friends, v. 8; thirdly, because he laid God's honour deeply to heart, v. 9; fourthly, because his holy and religious carriage was mocked, and, both by high and low, by honourable and base rascals, he was opposed and persecuted, v. 10—12.

From the second petition, learn, 1. The property of the godly is to seek communion with God, and patiently to attend his answer for the time, manner, and measure of it; for they are here described: *they that wait on thee, O Lord, those that seek thee.*   2. When one of God's children is persecuted for righteousness, all the rest are waiting to see the event, and it cannot but be a great dash to them to see the righteous lie under, or a good cause lie long oppressed; which inconvenience we should request the Lord to prevent: *let not them that wait on thee be ashamed; let not those that seek thee be confounded.*   3. It is a kindly mark and property of a godly person to be a lover of the good of all God's children, and to be careful that no cause or occasion of stumbling be furnished unto them by him : *let them not be ashamed for my sake ; let them not be confounded for my sake.* 4. Faith sets its eyes in prayer upon those titles of God which serve most for its purpose, as here the psalmist hath to do with enemies—*O Lord God of hosts* will do his turn against them: he is praying for the good of God's children, and, *O God of Israel,* speaketh to that point.

7. *Because for thy sake I have borne reproach ; shame hath covered my face.*

The first reason of the second petition is, because his sufferings were for God's cause. Whence learn, 1. Though suffering for God's cause in maintenance of his truth, be a glorious sort of suffering, wherein a man may go unto God confidently ; yet it may be accompanied with shame from men of this world, and the godly for a time may be so delayed in point of relief, that they know not what to say to their scorners, but may be forced to hang the head for a while : *for thy cause I have borne reproach.* 2. He that suffers shame for God's cause, shall neither have cause at length to be ashamed of his suffering, nor shall any other have cause to be ashamed for him : *let them not be confounded for my sake, because for thy sake I have borne reproach.*

8. *I am become a stranger unto my brethren, and an alien unto my mother's children.*

The second reason of the second petition is, because his friends had cast him off. Whence learn, 1. In affliction for God's cause friends will more readily forsake a sufferer, than in his affliction for a civil cause : *I am become a stranger to my brethren.* 2. The power of religion in the godly, is stronger than the bonds of blood with their kinsmen, and it will make them cleave to God, when their kindred cast them off : *I am an alien unto my mother's children.*

9. *For the zeal of thine house hath eaten me up ; and the reproaches of them that reproached thee are fallen upon me.*

The third reason of the second petition is, because he was deeply affected with the dishonour done to God. Whence learn, 1. It is not enough to love God, and his ordinances and kingdom, and his people's good ; but it is required also that we be zealous here : *the zeal of thine house hath eaten me up.* 2. Spiritual affections and passions will no less affect and trouble the body, than natural affections and passions : *the zeal of thine house hath eaten me up.* 3. Injuries done to God and religion, and to the godly, should affect us no less nearly, and be laid to heart, than injuries personally concerning us : *the reproaches of them that reproached thee, have fallen upon me.*

10. *When I wept,* and chastened *my soul with fasting, that was to my reproach.*

11. *I made sackcloth also my garment ; and I became a proverb to them.*

12. *They that sit in the gate speak against me ; and I was the song of the drunkards.*

The fourth reason of the second petition, is, because he was greatly mocked of all sorts for his holy carriage. Whence learn, 1. True zeal is ruled by knowledge, joined with humility in the man's self, and tempered with love to men, even toward persecutors; such was David's zeal: but Christ's zeal was perfectly such : *I wept and chastened my soul.* 2. Fasting in earnest is not so much the abstinence from meat, as it is the afflicting of the soul : *when I chastened my soul with fasting.* 3. The godly behaviour of the righteous is subject to horrible misconstruction; yet must they not desist from duties for all this : *fasting was to my reproach ; I made sackcloth also my garment, and I became a proverb to them.* 4. It is a sore affliction to the godly to be condemned by magistrates and judges, and yet the truly religious, even Christ and his followers, were, and are, subject to this exercise : *they that sit in the gate* (or in the courts of justice, which were erected at the entry of the parts of cities) *do speak against me.* 5. Righteousness and truth are not the worse for their being condemned by civil judges; God will not disclaim his own cause for that, but will hear such complaints as this is in this case : *they that sit in the gate speak against me.* 6. When magistrates discountenance true religion, then it becometh a matter of derision to rascals, and to every base villain without controlment, and a table-talk to every tippler : *I was a song of the drunkards.* 7. The shame of the cross is more grievous than the rest of the trouble of it. This is the fourth time that the shame of the cross is presented unto God, in these last four verses ; *I was a song of the drunkards* after complaining of his being reproached, and *being made a proverb.*

13. *But as for me, my prayer is unto thee, O Lord,* in *an acceptable time : O God, in the multitude of thy mercy hear me, in the truth of thy salvation.*

This is the third petition for deliverance, or for granting his prayer, or the third time he presenteth it; whereunto he addeth reasons taken from the time of presenting it, the multitude of God's mercies, and the truth of his promises, or covenant of salvation. Whence learn, 1. The best way to bear out the persecution of the mighty and the mockery of the base multitude, is to be frequent in prayer to God for our part : *but as for me, my prayer is unto thee, O Lord.* 2. So long as God offereth a gracious ear to supplicants, a man may be confident that petitions of grace shall have ready **access** and answer : *my prayer is unto thee in an acceptable time.* 3. The largeness of God's mercy is a sufficient encouragement for the afflicted to come and take the benefit thereof : *in the multitude of thy mercies hear thou me.* 4. When, besides the mercifulness of God, we have also his covenant and promise of salvation, we may upon these two pillars lean and roll over, and rest our faith : *hear me in the truth of thy salvation.*

14. *Deliver me out of the mire, and let me not sink : let me be delivered from them that hate me, and out of the deep waters.*

15. *Let not the water-flood overflow me, neither let the deep swallow me up, and let not the pit shut her mouth upon me.*

The fourth petition for delivery, or fourth time he presenteth it, whereunto he addeth reasons taken from the danger he was in. Whence learn, 1. Faith useth to correct the expressions of sense; and as faith gathereth strength, a man's condition groweth clearer : it was the expression of sense, v. 2, *I sink in deep mire,* and here the fear is something lessened, because faith is something more cleared : *deliver me out of the mire, let me not sink.* 2. The man that loveth truth better than worldly prosperity, and maketh the Lord his refuge, shall not faint under persecution, but shall be borne through all troubles, and delivered : *let me be delivered from them that hate me, and out of the deep waters.* 3. Faith in God giveth hope to be helped, and is half a delivery, before the full delivery come; for the psalmist is now with his head above the water, and not so afraid as when he began the psalm; for here he saith, *let not the water-floods overflow me, neither let the deep swallow me up.*　4. As the sense of danger sharpens prayer, so the greatness of it is a ground of hope, that the evil which is feared shall not prevail over us; for albeit the Lord suffer the danger to be great, yet will he not leave us in a case desperate : *let not the pit shut her mouth upon me.*

16. *Hear me, O Lord ; for thy loving-kindness is good : turn unto me according to the multitude of thy tender mercies.*

17. *And hide not thy face from thy servant ; for I am in trouble : hear me speedily.*

The fifth petition for delivery, or fifth time he presenteth it, whereunto he addeth reasons taken from the multitude of God's mercies, consciousness of his uprightness, and the greatness of his trouble. Whence learn, 1. Albeit God should give no answer for a time, faith will still press for an answer, for it knoweth it hath to do with the hearer of prayer : *hear me*, said he before and here over again, *hear me, O Lord.*　2. Faith seeth what is in God's heart, whatsoever it findeth or misseth in his hand; it fastens on love, and draweth hope and love from that : *hear me, for thy loving-kindness is good.*　3. Though a believing soul find itself deserted of God in some respects; yet, while it holds fast on his merciful nature, it may be sure to meet with a change of dispensation more comfortable : *turn unto me according to the multitude of thy tender mercies.*　4. When a believer is persecuted by man for righteousness, and friends and families turn their backs upon him; it is not strange that God, for the man's trial, should seem to hide his countenance from him also; which trial the believer counteth more heavy than all the rest, and can be content to want all the creature's kindness so he may find the Lord's kindness; for he cannot endure long to want God's presence : *hide not thy face from thy servant.*　5. The conscience of endeavour to serve God, giveth hope of comfort in time of trouble, and not so much the sooner, if the trouble be great, and perdition apparently near : *hide not thy face from thy servant, for I am in trouble, hear me speedily.*　6. An upright servant, albeit he be troubled for God's cause, and miss comfort from God, yet will he not change his master, nor despair of his favour :

P

hide not thy face from thy servant, for I am in trouble. 7. It is no limitation of God, to press his hasting to help, when trouble presseth us so sore, as we seem near to perish, if he speedily prevent not : *hear me speedily.*

18. *Draw nigh unto my soul,* and *redeem it : deliver me, because of mine enemies.*

19. *Thou hast known my reproach, and my shame, and my dishonour : mine adversaries are all before thee.*

20. *Reproach hath broken my heart, and I am full of heaviness : and I looked* for some *to take pity, but* there was *none ; and for comforters, but I found none.*

21. *They gave me also gall for my meat; and in my thirst they gave me vinegar to drink.*

In the sixth petition, or sixth time, he prayeth for obtaining delivery, whereunto he addeth reasons taken from the inhumanity and cruelty of his enemies, and desertion of his friends, and want of comfort from all men. Whence learn, 1. As straits serve to drive the godly nearer and nearer to God ; so they serve to prepare men for a renewed sense of communion with God, or for God's sensible drawing nearer to them : *draw nigh unto my soul,* saith he. 2. A new manifestation of God's love to a soul, is present relief and delivery, whatsoever be the trouble : *draw nigh to my soul, and redeem me.* 3. In the delivery of God's children from the hand of persecutors, the Lord looketh, not only to the necessity of his children, but also to the insolent pride of the enemies, in case they should prevail : *deliver me, because of mine enemies.* 4. The consideration of God's being witness to all the sufferings of the saints, is a ground of patience under trouble, and of hope to be delivered : *thou hast known my reproach, and my shame, and my dishonour : mine adversaries are all before thee.* 5. Before a believer once entered into sufferings, and put upon his trials, be delivered, he shall be made very sensible of the weight of trouble, especially of reproaches, and of his own weakness to bear the burden of the cross alone : *reproach hath broken my heart, and I am full of heaviness.* 6. As a persecuted saint may possibly be deprived of all common comfort, pity, and help from men; so the less his comfort is on earth, he may look for the more and readier comfort from God : *I looked for some to take pity, and there was none ; and for comforters, but I found none.* 7. As the wicked are ready to add affliction to affliction unto the godly, so must the godly ever look for it: yea, they must not think it strange to find the means of natural life, and ordinary refreshments of the body, made bitter to them by persecution: *they gave me gall for my meat;* that is, they made my natural refreshments taste-less, yea and bitter to me: they gave me cause of grief, in-stead of comforting me. 8. As all the sufferings of the saints are but shadows of the sufferings of Christ: so are they all mitigated and sanctified in the sufferings of Christ, upon whom all the sufferings mentioned in this psalm, it was foretold, should fall, for expiation of the sin, and sanctifying the crosses of all his followers: *in my thirst they gave me vinegar to drink,* was a prophecy of Christ's suffer-ing on the cross.

22. *Let their table become a snare before them: and* that which should have been *for* their *welfare,* let it become *a trap.*

23. *Let their eyes be darkened, that they see not; and make their loins continually to shake.*

24. *Pour out thine indignation upon them, and let thy wrathful anger take hold of them.*

25. *Let their habitation be desolate,* and *let none dwell in their tents.*

This is the second part of the psalm; wherein the pro-phet, as a type of Christ, by way of imprecation against his malicious enemies, prophesieth of the vengeance of God against all obstinate adversaries, and malicious persecutors of him, whether in his own person or in his members; and denounceth ten plagues, or effects of God's wrath, to come upon them for their wickedness. The first whereof is this, God shall curse all the comforts of this life unto the obstin-ate adversaries of Christ, and of his followers: all these comforts shall serve to harden their hearts in sin, and length-en their life therein, till they fill up the measure of their iniquities: *let their table become a snare before them.* The second plague is, all the means appointed for men's conver-sion and salvation shall turn for the aggravating of their sin and just damnation: and as all things work together for the good of those that love God, so shall all things work for the woe and torment of God's enemies: *that which should have been for their welfare, let it become a trap.* The third plague is, they shall not perceive the true intent of God's work, nor consider the day of their visitation: *let their eyes be darkened, that they see not.* The fourth plague is, there shall be no peace to the wicked, but as even in laughter their heart shall be sorrowful; so also their conscience for fear shall never dare to abide the light of the Lord's word, to be examined by it; and even in their greatest prosperity they shall have perpetual secret fear, smother it as they will: *make their loins continually to shake.* The fifth plague is, the threatened wrath of God shall be fully executed against them, and never depart from them when it is once poured out: *pour out thy indignation on them, and let thy wrathful anger take hold of them.* The sixth plague is, the curse of God shall be on their houses and posterity, and the place they have dwelt in shall be abhorred: *let their habitation be desolate, and let none dwell in their tents.*

26. *For they persecute him whom thou hast smitten; and they talk to the grief of those whom thou hast wounded.*

He giveth a reason of those fearful imprecations on Christ's adversaries, because they were cruel in their persecution of him and of the godly, even in the time of their affliction, otherwise sent by God. Whence learn, 1. It consisteth well with the love of God to his children, (even his only begotten Son Jesus Christ not being excepted,) to exercise them with sad calamities, for bringing to pass the work of man's redemption by Christ, and for perfecting the sanctification and salvation of the redeemed by Christ; of all of whom now and then it may be said to God, *thou hast smitten him, and they are those whom thou hast wounded.* 2. Whatsoever may be the reason of the Lord's smiting and wounding his own children, yet their wicked enemies have no just reason to malign them, or to trouble them, and therefore their troubling of God's children is persecution: *they persecute him whom thou hast smitten.* 3. The very talking and venting of ill speeches, to the prejudice of Christ's cause and truth, and true holiness in his saints, especially when they are under sufferings and afflictions whatsoever, is a high provocation of God's wrath: *they talk to the grief of those whom thou hast wounded.* 4. The persecution of God's children for righteousness, is a sufficient ditty for all the forenamed damnation in the preceding verses: this is the reason of the justice of the imprecation : *for they persecute him whom thou hast smitten.* 5. Without breach of duty to men, the church may sing and rejoice in these fearful imprecations against the malicious enemies of Christ and his church; first, as lovers of God more than of men : secondly, as followers, not of their own quarrel, but of the controversy of the Lord of hosts, whose soldiers they are against all his enemies whatsoever : thirdly, as subscribers to the justice of God, who will not suffer malicious cruelty to be unpunished : and fourthly, as rejoicers in God's love to his people, who owns the wrongs done to his church and servants therein, as done to himself, and will be avenged upon their adversaries; and having decreed doom against the adversaries of his church, will have his children to be ministers under the great Judge, to pronounce the sentence against his and their enemies, and, as it were, to give out order for execution of the sentence, saying, *let their table, let their eyes, let their habitation be so and so disposed of.*

27. *Add iniquity unto their iniquity; and let them not come into thy righteousness.*

28. *Let them be blotted out of the book of the living, and not be written with the righteous.*

The seventh plague of the enemies of Christ and his church, is this: howsoever ignorant zealots, some of them may find mercy; yet malicious persecutors of truth and piety grow worse and worse, and, being entered into the course of persecution, cannot go off, but draw deeper and deeper in guiltiness, and that in God's righteous judgment, punishing sin by sin : they *add iniquity unto their iniquity.* The eighth plague is, they are given over to a reprobate mind, so as they cannot lay their own sins to heart, and cannot therefore see the necessity of the remission of sin, nor put a price upon the purchase of justification unto sinners by Christ the redeemer, nor be found among the persons justified by faith in him : *let them not come into thy righteousness.* The ninth plague is this : albeit the enemies of Christ and his people may pretend to be among the number of his friends, and to have their names written in great letters, in the catalogue of the visible church, yet God shall disclaim them one day as none of his, and thrust them from him as workers of iniquity : *let them be blotted out of the book of the living.* The tenth plague is this: as the visible church hath an open book, wherein all within the external covenant are written, as saints by calling, and co-venanters with God for life and salvation, out of which book God dashes the names of his wicked enemies; so God hath a secret book and roll, as it were, wherein he enrolleth all the regenerate, all the justified; and among the names of this sort or among the names of the true members of the in-visible church of the regenerate, none of the names of Christ's malicious enemies shall be written : *let them not be written with the righteous.*

29. *But I am poor and sorrowful: let thy salvation, O God, set me up on high.*

The third and last part of the psalm, wherein is set down the glorious event of this sad exercise in four evidences of victory of his faith over this assault. The first whereof is in his confident prayer, not only to be delivered, but also to be exalted, v. 29. The second evidence is, in his hearty promise of thanksgiving, v. 30, 31. The third evidence is in a prophecy of the fruit of this exercise which the believ-ers shall have by it, v. 32, 33. The fourth is a thanks-giving for mercies foreseen, which shall come to the church, and in special to the church of Israel, v. 34—36. All which, in as far as they concern David the type, are but little in comparison of Christ the antitype. From the first evidence of the victory of his faith, appearing in his confi-dent prayer, learn, 1. It is no strange thing to see pov-erty of spirit and sad afflictions joined, the one to help and season the other : *but I am poor and sorrowful.* 2. There is as sure ground of hope of deliverance out of every trouble wherein the children of God can fall, as there is ground of hope of the overturning of the most settled worldly pros-perity of their enemies; for the forenamed curses shall come on the enemies of the godly, but the child of God in the mean time may expect salvation, and to be set on high, which he confidently prayeth for : *but I am poor and sor-rowful, let thy salvation, O God, set me up.* 3. The con-science of humiliation under God's hand, is a great evidence of delivery out of whatsoever trouble; if a man in a right-eous cause be emptied of self-conceit and carnal confidence, and brought down to poverty of spirit, and affected with the sense of sin and misery following upon it, and withal go to God in this condition, he may be sure to be helped; the poor in spirit are freed from the curse : *but I am poor and sorrowful*, saith the psalmist here, *let thy salvation set me up on high*. 4. The man afflicted and persecuted for righteousness, humbled in himself, and drawn to God for relief, shall not only be delivered, but also shall be as much exalted after his delivery, as ever he was cast down : *let thy salvation, O God, set me up on high*. 5. The kindly sufferer of righteousness, will have no deliverance, but such as God will allow him, as God shall bring unto him; and as he looketh not for delivery another way, so he looketh for a glorious delivery this way; *let thy salvation, O God, set me up on high*.

30. *I will praise the name of God with a song, and will magnify him with thanksgiving.*

31. This *also shall please the Lord better than an ox or bullock that hath horns and hoofs.*

From the second evidence of the victory of David's faith in his promised thanksgiving learn, 1. When the Lord comforts the heart of a sufferer for his cause, he can make him glad before the delivery come, by giving him the assurance that it shall come; and can engage his heart to solemn thanksgiving in the midst of trouble; for poverty of spirit will esteem the far foresight of delivery at last, as a rich mercy, and matter of a song : *I will praise the name of God, with a song*. 2. The Lord in the delivering of his children out of their troubles, will give evidence of his greatness, as well as of his goodness, of his power as well as of his mercy to them, that he may have the more glory and thanks for his work : *I will magnify him with thanksgiving*. 3. Moral worship offered in spirit and truth, in the meanest degree of sincerity, is more acceptable to God than the most pompous ceremonial service, which can be done to him without spirit and truth : *this also shall please the Lord better than an ox or bullock, that hath horns and hoofs :* that is, which is perfect and wanteth nothing in the external part of commanded service. 4. What we know shall be most acceptable to God, we ought to study and follow most, that we may walk before God unto all well-pleasing, in special to praise him in affliction, and to praise him from a contrite spirit : *this also shall please the Lord better than, &c.*

32. *The humble shall see* this, and *be glad : and your heart shall live that seek God.*

33. *For the Lord heareth the poor, and despiseth not his prisoners.*

From the third evidence of the victory of David's faith, in the prophecy of the fruits of his sufferings, mainly, as he was a type of Christ, who here is most intended, learn, 1. The trial of the saints set down in Scripture, also the trial of David and of Christ represented by him, were foretold, that they would be of great use to the church of God in after-times, as now we see in effect : *the humble shall see this, and be glad.* 2. The humble soul is most capable of divine knowledge and comfort : *the humble shall see this.* 3. The escape of our Lord Jesus out of his sufferings for us, and the escape of his afflicted children out of their sufferings through faith in him, is a matter of instruction, comfort, and joy to every humbled believer : *the humble shall see this, and be glad.* 4. As those who are pure in spirit and truly humbled, live upon God's alms, and are daily at his doors for relief of their necessities, and for communion with his gracious goodness ; so shall they thrive well in this trade : *your heart shall live that seek God.* 5. The Lord's children have a life beyond the children of men, which is able to quicken them in their deepest troubles, and to make them blessed in their delivery out of troubles; a life moral and spiritual, whereby their conscience is comforted : *your heart shall live that seek God.* 6. The right way for the godly afflicted to have the benefit of the troubles and events which Christ and his followers have had experience of, is to comfort themselves in hope of the like event and success in seeking God as they did : *the humble shall see this and be glad, and your heart shall live that seek God.* 7. As the Lord's poor men are much in prayer, so shall they be rich in good answers : *for the Lord heareth the poor.* 8. Whoever, in defence of any point of God's truth, are put to trouble, either in body or mind, by men, or Satan, or both, are all sufferers for God; they are all prisoners who, howsoever they may be misregarded by men, shall be of much price in God's eyes : *he despiseth not his prisoners.*

34. *Let the heaven and earth praise him, the seas, and every thing that moveth therein :*

35. *For God will save Zion, and will build the cities of Judah; that they may dwell there, and have it in possession.*

36. *The seed also of his servants shall inherit it ; and they that love his name shall dwell therein.*

From the last evidence of the victory of faith, set down in a prophetical thanksgiving for the foreseen mercies which were to come to the church by Christ's procurement, and specially to the Jews, learn, 1. Large sense of troubles maketh way for large observation, and a corresponding sense of mercies. The evil of the deepest afflictions the Lord can recompense with highest consolation, as the beginning and ending of this psalm giveth evidence. 2. The soul that seeth the mercy of God toward itself, seeth also the mercy of God upon the same grounds to all others his people in Zion, his church in every place and time; seeth the benefits of Christ's sufferings to be matter of praise unto God, able to fill the whole world; seeth its own insufficiency for praising God also, and that all the creatures are few enough, when they all concur in this song: *let the heaven and the earth praise him, and the seas and every thing that moveth therein.* 3. Whatsoever condition of God's people can be represented by the various condition, motion, settlement, or commotion of heaven, earth, and seas, and things therein, cannot but furnish matter of joyful praise to God, and come up to contribute to God's praises: *let the heaven and earth, the seas, and every thing that moveth therein, praise him.* 4. Every delivery of every believer, and above all the delivery of Christ as man from his expiatory sufferings, are earnests and pledges of the delivery of the church militant out of all its troubles : *for God will save Zion,* saith the psalmist, being now delivered out of his trouble. 5. As the Lord will ever maintain his church, his Zion and his Judah, so hath he a purpose to give a special evidence of this his care among the Jews, how far soever they may sometimes be from all appearance of his respect to them; for in the promise he keepeth expressly the name of Judah : *he will build the cities of Judah.* 6. What outward testimonies of God's respect to the Jews for Christ's sake shall be given unto them, after the destruction of their cities here presupposed, we must leave to God, to be in due time by his own works interpreted, and to be made out according to what here is said : *that the cities of Judah shall be builded, that they may dwell there and have it* (to wit, the promised land) *in possession, the seed also of his servants shall inherit it, and they that love his name shall dwell therein.* Only let us observe, that the duty of the true citizens of the church is, to transmit true religion to their posterity, and that this is the best and only way to transmit also the blessing of God, and the constant possession thereof unto them : *the seed also of his servants shall inherit it, and they that love his name. &c.*

PSALM LXX.

To the chief musician. A psalm of David, to bring to remembrance.

This psalm is almost one in words with the latter end of psalm xl. wherein David, being in present danger of his life by his enemies, prayeth, first, for speedy delivery, v. 1 ; next, for shameful disappointment to his enemies, v. 2, 3 ; and thirdly, for a comfortable life to all the godly, v. 4 ; from which condition albeit he himself was very far for the present, yet he professeth he relieth on God by faith, and prayeth for a timous delivery, v. 5.

From the inscription, learn, 1. Our most notable dangers and deliveries should most carefully be observed and remembered, and made use of : *this is a psalm to bring to remembrance.* 2. What hard condition we have been in before, we may fall into the like again; and the same gracious means we have used before, in seeking our relief of God, we should use again; and what words of prayer we have used before, we may use again, without any either needless affectation of other words, or superstitious tying of ourselves to the same words, as the example of David teacheth us, when we compare the end of the xl. psalm with this psalm.

1. Make haste, *O God, to deliver me ; make haste to help me, O Lord.*

From the first petition, learn, 1. Though death, or danger of it, were never so near, God can come quickly and prevent it; and prayer is a swift messenger, which in the twinkling of an eye can go and return with an answer from heaven, as this abrupt beginning of his prayer teacheth us : *O Lord, to deliver me.* These words, *make haste*, are not expressed in the original: for the haste was so great as he could not express it till he drew his breath. 2. As we have need of help, God will make haste unto our help: *make haste to help me, O Lord.*

2. *Let them be ashamed and confounded that seek after my soul: let them be turned backward, and put to confusion, that desire my hurt.*

3. *Let them be turned back for a reward of their shame that say, Aha, aha!*

From the second petition, learn, 1. The more that the enemies of God's people promise to themselves certainly to destroy such of the saints as they pitch upon, when their plot shall be ripe and fixed, when God disappointeth them they are the more confounded and ashamed: *let them be ashamed and confounded that seek after my soul,* or my life. 2. All the enemies of God's children, shall at last think shame of their injuries done to them, and evils which they have wished to them: to wit, when they shall know whose children they are, and what interest God hath in them; then at last shall they flee and hide themselves for shame: *let them be turned backward, and put to confusion, that desire my hurt.* 3. The damage of the godly is the delight of the wicked; and an enemy to the godly, is he that laughs and scorns at the misery of the godly: *they say,* when they see them in trouble, *Aha, aha.* 4. Albeit what shame the wicked put upon the godly for righteousness, or for their sufferings for righteousness, is not the shame of the godly, but the shame of the enemies, who do what they can to expose the godly to shame; yet shall the enemies have shame still more for their pains, and the terrible wrath of God shall chase them out of God's presence: *let them be turned back for a reward of their shame that say, Aha, aha!*

4. *Let all those that seek thee rejoice and be glad in thee: and let such as love thy salvation say continual-ly, Let God be magnified.*

From the third petition, learn, 1. Whatsoever be our own hard condition at any time, we should seek the welfare and prosperity of the rest of God's children, and it is the property of each of the godly in their trouble, to wish all the rest to be partakers of the blessedness which their own souls seek after, but not to be like to them in trouble or

bonds : *let all those that seek thee rejoice and be glad in thee.*
2. If one of the godly be delivered out of his troubles, all
the rest, who prayed for the delivery should rejoice in God
also as for a benefit given to themselves : *let all those
that seek thee, rejoice and be glad in thee.* 3. The godly
do not desire deliverance to themselves or their fellows except in God's way, in a cleanly and holy way : and the more
of God that is seen in the delivery of his servants, the more
are they glad in the Lord : *they are those that love God's
salvation.* 4. It is a most suitable service for the saints,
to be always praising God : *let those that love thy salvation, say continually, The Lord be magnified.*

5. *But I am poor and needy ; make haste unto me,
O God : thou art my help and my deliverer : O Lord
make no tarrying.*

From the fifth petition, learn, 1. Albeit we be not in
such a condition, as we wish all the godly men were in, yet
let us lay out that condition before a pitiful God, and submit ourselves to him in the condition wherein we are : *but I
am poor and needy.* 2. The sense of a hard condition, is
a preparation and a ground of hope to be brought out of
it to a better : *I am poor and needy, make haste unto me, O
God.* 3. Whatsoever dispensation we shall meet with, we
should hold fast the claim of faith, and of our interest in
God: *thou art my help, and my deliverer.* 4. Having settled our dependence upon God, we may, without being mistaken by God, speak all our desires to him; and, having
done so, should leave our supplication and case at his feet
with confidence : *O Lord, make no tarrying.*

PSALM LXXI.

This psalm is a prayer of David in his old age, requesting delivery from
the conspiracy of Absalom, wherein he wrestleth with the Lord by fervent supplication, in seven petitions, all tending to this purpose, that
he may be delivered, to v. 14; and, from v. 14 to the end, we have his
confidence to be delivered set forth in four evidences thereof. Absalom
is not named here, nor is the particular case set down, otherwise than
in general expressions, that so it may serve the better for the larger
use of the church of God, and of the particular members thereof in
their afflictions.

1. *In thee, O Lord, do I put my trust ; let me never
be put to confusion.*

The first petition is general, wherein he professeth his

confidence in God, and prayeth that he be not put to confusion. Whence learn, 1. As long as a child of God liveth in the world, he must look for new afflictions, as here the experience of the psalmist tossed in his old age, warneth us. 2. Look how many new troubles befall God's servants; so many new messengers are sent of God to call them to him: so many new errands are furnished unto them; so many new petitions are put into their mouth; and so many pressing necessities are sent to make them earnest in their supplication, and frugal in making use of their interest in God by faith, as here and elsewhere appeareth. 3. He that cometh to God must believe in him, and fasten his faith on God, and avow it, how weak soever he find it to be: *in thee, O Lord, do I put my trust.* 4. Albeit such as believe in God, may have many temptations to mistrust God, and great fears that they shall be disappointed of their hopes, and for a time may seem to be disappointed and put to confusion, yet it shall not be for ever; if they do not take shame unto them by distrust, they shall never have cause to be ashamed : *let me never be put to confusion.*

2. *Deliver me in thy righteousness, and cause me to escape ; incline thine ear unto me, and save me.*

The second petition is more special for safety and delivery from his enemies. Whence learn, 1. The righteousness of God is a pledge to the godly that their lawful petitions shall be granted, and especially when they seek delivery from their ungodly adversaries : *deliver me in thy righteousness, and cause me to escape.* 2. When the Lord giveth a heart to a believer to pray, he will also grant him audience and a good answer: *incline thine ear unto me, and save me.*

3. *Be thou my strong habitation, whereunto I may continually resort : thou hast given commandment to save me ; for thou* art *my rock and my fortress.*

The third petition is, that the Lord would show himself to him in effect, what he hath engaged himself to be unto believers according to the covenant. Whence learn, 1. What the Lord is to his people by covenant, he will be to them the same effectually and in deed, as their need shall require, and as they shall employ him : *be thou my strong habitation.* 2. The goodness of God covenanted to his people, is not for one good turn, but for every good which they need; not for one day, but for daily use-making, and constant enjoying of it : *be thou my strong habitation, whereunto continually I may resort.* 3. As the Lord hath all second causes, all creatures at his command, being Lord of hosts, to execute whatever he giveth order to be done; so hath he really set his active providence on work, to accomplish what he hath covenanted to every believer : *thou hast given commandment to save me, for thou art my rock nd fortress :* he giveth his believing in God who is his rock, as a reason of his saying, that God was about to save him.

4. *Deliver me, O my God, out of the hand of the wicked ; out of the hand of the unrighteous and cruel man.*

5. *For thou art my hope, O Lord God :* thou art *my trust from my youth.*

6. *By thee have I been holden up from the womb : thou art he that took me out of my mother's bowels : my praise* shall be *continually of thee.*

The fourth petition for delivery is strengthened by reasons taken from the wickedness of the enemy, v. 4; from his own confidence in God, v. 5; and from his own experience of God's kindness unto him in time past, v. 6. Whence learn, 1. It is a great advantage to be a confederate with God, when we have to deal with his enemies and ours in any debate : *deliver me O God,* saith he, *out of the hand of the wicked.* 2. The integrity of the believer in a good cause, and the iniquity of his adversaries in their ill cause, are good tokens of the believer's victory over them : *deliver me out of the hand of the unrighteous and cruel man.* 3. Confidence in God avowed against all temptations in God's presence, and specially when it is of long standing, is so strong an argument of being heard in a lawful petition, that it may persuade the believer he shall speed : *deliver me, for thou art my hope, O Lord God, thou art my trust from my youth.* 4. True thankfulness will not pass by common benefits, and true faith will read special love in common and ordinary favours, and make use thereof among other experiences for strengthening faith : *by thee have I been holden up from the womb, thou art he that took me out of my mother's bowels.* 5. The forming of us in the belly, and the common benefit of birth and bringing forth quick into the world, is a smothered wonder, and so glorious a work of God, that he deserveth perpetual praise from us for that one work : *thou art he that took me out of my mother's belly.*

7. *I am as a wonder unto many : but thou art my strong refuge.*

8. *Let my mouth be filled* with *thy praise* and with *thy honour all the day.*

The fifth petition is strengthened by reasons taken from his hard condition, and from the opportunity of God's having glory by his delivery out of it. Whence learn, 1. The exercise of the Lord's children is sometimes so strange to the beholder, as the world wondereth at them : *I am as a wonder unto many.* 2. Knowledge of God's word and ways, and faith in his name, make a believer not think strange, whatsoever fiery trial come upon him, but to rest on God's will, whatsoever befall him; *I am as a wonder unto many, but thou art my strong refuge ;* for faith judgeth not of itself, as the world judgeth, but as God hath judged and spoken of it in his word. 3. The more strange the exercise of the godly be, the more glorious is the Lord's upholding of them in it, and delivering of them out of it; and, for the hope of the glory which shall redound to God by such exercises, the hardship should be the more patiently borne, and the delivery sought and expected more confidently, that it shall come when it may be most for God's praise : *I am a wonder unto many, let my mouth be filled with thy praise, and with thy honour all the day.*

9. *Cast me not off in the time of old age : forsake me not when my strength faileth.*

10. *For mine enemies speak against me ; and they that lay wait for my soul take counsel together,*

11. *Saying, God hath forsaken him : persecute and take him ; for* there is *none to deliver* him.

The sixth petition is strengthened with reasons taken from his own old age and weakness, and from his enemies' malice. Whence learn, 1. Such as have been the Lord's servants in their youth, may be sure to find God a good and kind master to them in their old age : *cast me not off in the time of old age.* 2. Infirmities in God's children shall not move loathing and casting off, but pitying and cherishing them, that they may be supported in their weakness: *forsake me not when my strength faileth.* 3. The world conceiveth that God casteth off his children, when he bringeth them under any sad calamity, and by this means think that they have not to do with God's children when they persecute his dearest servants; yea and they encourage themselves to persecute them the more that God afflicteth them: *mine enemies speak against me, and they that lay wait for my soul take counsel together, saying, God hath forsaken him, persecute and take him, for there is none to deliver him.* 4. The misconstructions of the world, their plots and conspiracies against the godly, their evil speeches of them, their resolved cruelty to undo them, are so many arguments of good hope that God shall deliver them: *forsake me not, for mine enemies speak against me, &c.*

12. *O God, be not far from me: O my God, make haste for my help.*

13. *Let them be confounded* and *consumed that are adversaries to my soul; let them be covered* with *reproach and dishonour that seek my hurt.*

The seventh petition for delivery and disappointing of his enemies, is strengthened by reasons taken from the covenant between God and him, and from the glory which God shall have by shaming his enemies. Whence learn, 1. When temptations are most, dangers greatest, and the assault is strongest, then the believer draweth nearest unto God, and holdeth him most closely: *O God be not far from me, &c.* 2. Relying upon and avowing of the covenant between God and the soul of a believer is able to bear the greatest stress whereunto temptations and troubles can drive him: *O my God, make haste for my help.* 3. God, for the glory of his justice against the wicked, and the glory of his grace to his own, shall pour confusion, consumption, reproach, and dishonour upon persecutors of righteousness, and adversaries of his suffering servants: *let them be confounded and consumed, that are adversaries to my soul; let them be covered with reproach and dishonour that seek my hurt.*

14. *But I will hope continually, and will yet praise thee more and more.*

15. *My mouth shall shew forth thy righteousness* and

thy salvation all the day; for I know not the numbers thereof.

16. *I will go in the strength of the Lord God : I will make mention of thy righteousness,* even *of thine only.*

In the latter part of the psalm is the psalmist's confidence to be delivered set forth in four evidences thereof. The first is his resolution to persevere in hope to be helped, and in praising God and relying only on the Lord's power and righteousness, and not on his own strength. Whence learn, 1. He that is resolved to persevere in hope, may be sure of a gracious deliverance out of his trouble : *but I will hope continually.* 2. Resolute hope comforteth, enlargeth, and stirreth up the heart unto more and more praising and thanksgiving: *I will hope continually, and I will yet praise thee more and more.* 3. The matter of the continual praise of God, is partly his righteousness, whereby he keepeth his promise, not only according to, but also above condition, and giveth also remission of sins, which deserved wrath; and partly his deliverances, which he giveth to his children, out of danger of body and soul: *my mouth shall show forth thy righteousness, and thy salvation all the day ; for I know not the numbers thereof.* 4. Because in troubles a man's own strength will fail him, and fail him also in commanded duties, therefore the believer must renounce confidence in his own ability in both cases, and lean on the support of God : *I will go in the strength of the Lord God.* 5. Because the conscience of sins and sinfulness still stareth the believer in the face, and all to discourage him; the believer must renounce all confidence in his own holiness, and rely upon the imputed righteousness of Christ only, which is called the righteousness of God by faith, being witnessed unto both by the law and the prophets, Rom. iii. 21. *I will make mention of thy righteousness, even of thine only ;* for, in the point of justification and absolving of us from sin, this righteousness of God only hath place.

17. *O God, thou hast taught me from my youth : and hitherto have I declared thy wondrous works.*

18. *Now also, when I am old and gray-headed, O God, forsake me not, until I have shewed thy strength unto* this *generation,* and *thy power to every one* that is *to come.*

The second evidence of the prophet's confidence to be delivered, is the experience of God's kindness for time past, making him, with comfortable assurance of being heard, to pray for the continuance of that same kindness for time to come. Whence learn, 1. We are all of us ignorant of God and his ways, till he teach us by his word, and by his Spirit, and by his giving to us experimental knowledge thereof: *O God, thou hast taught me from my youth.* 2. The consciousness of sincere endeavour to make use of God's gifts to us for the glory of God, and edification of others, according to our place, is very sweet and comfortable in the day of trouble, and giveth much encouragement in approaching to God : *hitherto have I declared thy wondrous works.* 3. He that hath had long experience of God's mercy to himself, and thankfully acknowledgeth the same, may assure himself that the course of God's kindness to him shall not be broken off : *O God, thou hast taught me from my youth, now also when I am old and gray-headed, forsake me not, O Lord.* 4. It is a noble design for a man who hath received gifts, whereby he may glorify God and edify his people, to destinate all the days he hath to live, to serve his own generation and their posterity, in communicating to them what he knoweth of the Lord's all-sufficiency, and not to love to live in this world, except for this end : *forsake me not until I have shewed thy strength to this generation, and thy power to every one that is to come.*

19. *Thy righteousness also, O God, is very high, who hast done great things : O God, who is like unto thee ?*

20. Thou, *which hast shewed me great and sore troubles, shalt quicken me again, and shalt bring me up again from the depths of the earth.*

21. *Thou shalt increase my greatness, and comfort me on every side.*

The third evidence of his confidence to be delivered, is his looking to the unsearchable fountain of God's wisdom, faithfulness, and omnipotency, and his expecting from this wellspring, that as large consolation shall come forth to him, as he hath had a large measure of troubles. Whence learn, 1. Albeit the effects of God's wisdom, faithfulness, and omnipotence, be near to us and fall under our sense in his daily operations; yet the fountain thereof, which is God's own perfection, is unsearchable, incomprehensible, and incomparably great : *thy righteousness, O God, is very high, who hast done great things : O God, who is like unto thee?* 2. That which we see of the Lord's works, may lead us up to know what is not seen in relation to difficulties and power of men, and to see what he is able to do; and when we see the invisible God, we cannot but admire his majesty, and exalt him as sovereign over all; and then, and not till then, that we give him the honour of omnipotence and faithfulness, can the heart rest and be quiet : *thy righteousness, O·God, is very high, who hast done great things : who is like to thee?* 3. He that acknowledgeth God's justice and wisdom in his troubles, may look to see God's power and grace no less evident in his delivery and consolation : and he who in trouble hath seen his own infirmity, emptiness, and death, may look to see God's power and life in raising him out of the grave of his trouble : *thou which hast showed me great and sore troubles, shalt quicken me again ; and shalt bring me up again from the depths of the earth.* 4. As trouble humbleth and abaseth a man before the world : so the Lord's delivering of him, and showing his respect to him, honour the man again, and exalt him before men : *thou shalt increase my greatness.* 5. As no trouble cometh alone, but multitudes of troubles joined together, when the Lord will humble and try a man; so no comfort cometh single or alone, when the Lord will change the man's exercise, but a multitude of comforts joined together : *thou wilt comfort me on every side.* 6. Losses are made lighter, and comforts weightier, when God is seen and acknowledged in them : *thou which hast showed me sore troubles,* (it is but a view of trouble what we have felt, when troubles are seen to come from God's hand,) *thou shalt increase my greatness, and comfort me on every side.*

22. *I will also praise thee with the psaltery,* even *thy truth, O my God : unto thee will I sing with the harp, O thou Holy One of Israel.*

23. *My lips shall greatly rejoice when I sing unto thee ; and my soul, which thou hast redeemed.*

24. *My tongue also shall talk of thy righteousness*

all the day long : for they are confounded, for they are brought unto shame, that seek my hurt.

The fourth and last evidence of his confidence, is his promise of joyful thanksgiving, by way of a begun song, and that for the foresight of his own delivery, and of his enemies' overthrow. Whence learn, 1. Faith is so satisfied with God's promise, that it can praise heartily for what is promised, before it find performance ? *I will praise thee with the psaltery, even thy truth.* 2. It is our interest in the covenant, which makes us have interest in particular promises : *I will praise thy truth, O my God.* 3. A soul sensible of God's kindness, and by faith sure of the performance of his faithful promises, cannot satisfy itself in praising God, it hath so high estimation of his fidelity, power, and love : therefore, after he hath said, *I will praise thee,* he addeth, *unto thee will I sing with the harp.* 4. How hardly soever a soul hath been exercised with troubles for a while, so soon as it seeth by faith the Lord's prepared event, it will regard all the passages of God's providence, as just and wise and good, and in a word, as holy in all respects : *to thee will I sing, O holy One of Israel.* 5. Singing with our voice unto the Lord, is a part of moral worship, as well as prayer with the voice, when his honour, and our upstirring, and others' edifying call for it : *my lips shall greatly rejoice when I sing unto thee.* 6. As the work of praising God requireth sincerity, earnestness, and cheerfulness; so the work thus done, becometh not only honourable to God, but also refreshful to the worshipper : *my lips shall greatly rejoice when I sing unto thee.* 7. Dangers and distresses, how grievous soever they be for the time, yet furnish matter of praise to God, and joy to the party troubled afterward when the delivery cometh : *my lips shall rejoice, and my soul which thou hast redeemed.* 8. Beside, singing of psalms unto God, speaking of his praise in all companies and upon all occasions, are parts of our bounden duty of thankfulness for making his word good to us in the overthrow of our enemies and delivering us : *my tongue also shall talk of thy righteousness all the day long.* 9. The overthrow of the enemies of the godly is as certain to come, as if we saw it with our eyes already come to pass. The same word of God, the same light and persuasion of spirit, manifest the delivery of the godly, and the destruction of their enemies: *for they are confounded, for they are brought to shame, that seek my hurt.*

PSALM LXXII.

A psalm for Solomon.

In this psalm, under the shadow of king Solomon's reign, Christ's gracious government is praised. And, first, the church is taught to pray for a blessing on king David and his son's government, including Christ's, v. 1. Next, the answer is given by the Spirit of the Lord in a prophecy of the blessedness of the reign and kingdom of Christ the Son of David, from v. 2 to v. 18. Thirdly, the use hereof is set down in thanksgiving unto God, v. 18, 19; and herein is the accomplishment of all the desires of David, obtained by this satisfactory answer, v. 20.

From the inscription and prayer, learn, A king may command within his kingdom many things, but he cannot command a blessing on his own government; he must make suit for this to God. He may leave a kingdom to his child; but because a kingdom is nothing without God's blessing, he must pray for this blessing, and seek the assistance of the prayers of the church for this intent: and this duty kings may crave of the church, and God's people should not refuse it; *a psalm for Solomon.*

1. *Give the king thy judgments, O God, and thy righteousness unto the king's son.*

From the prayer of the church, learn, 1. Gifts from God are necessary to fit a man for an office; and it is not every gift which maketh fit for a particular office, but such gifts specially as are for the discharge of the place a man hath, and those must be asked from, and granted by God, and by this means sanctified: *give the king thy judgments, O God.* 2. Nothing is more conducible to make a king's government prosperous and blessed than equity and justice, according to the revealed will of God: *give the king thy judgments, and thy righteousness unto the king's son.*

2. *He shall judge thy people with righteousness, and thy poor with judgment.*

3. *The mountains shall bring peace to the people, and the little hills, by righteousness.*

4. *He shall judge the poor of the people, he shall save the children of the needy, and shall break in pieces the oppressor.*

5. *They shall fear thee as long as the sun and moon endure, throughout all generations.*

6. *He shall come down like rain upon the mown grass; as showers* that *water the earth.*

7. *In his days shall the righteous flourish; and abundance of peace so long as the moon endureth.*

8. *He shall have dominion also from sea to sea, and from the river unto the ends of the earth.*

9. *They that dwell in the wilderness shall bow before him; and his enemies shall lick the dust.*

10. *The kings of Tarshish and of the isles shall bring presents: the kings of Sheba and Seba shall offer gifts.*

11. *Yea, all kings shall fall down before him; all nations shall serve him.*

12. *For he shall deliver the needy when he crieth; the poor also, and* him *that hath no helper.*

13. *He shall spare the poor and needy, and shall save the souls of the needy.*

14. *He shall redeem their soul from deceit and violence: and precious shall their blood be in his sight.*

15. *And he shall live, and to him shall be given of the gold of Sheba: prayer also shall be made for him continually; and daily shall he be praised.*

16. *There shall be an handful of corn in the earth upon the top of the mountains; the fruit thereof shall shake like Lebanon: and* they *of the city shall flourish like grass of the earth.*

17. *His name shall endure for ever: his name shall be continued as long as the sun; and* men *shall be blessed in him: all nations shall call him blessed.*

The prophetical answer given here to the church's prayer promiseth above twenty benefits of Christ's government, all of them tending to the glory of the king and good of the subjects; the shadow whereof was to be seen in David and Solomon's reigns, joined with many imperfections, but the real accomplishment is only in Christ. The first is, Christ's subjects shall have good rules how to carry themselves in all duties, how to behave themselves righteously, and how to be made righteous, by his direction and conduct: *he shall*

judge thy people with righteousness. The second benefit of
commendation is, Christ will see the necessities of his subjects, his humble ones, his afflicted ones, to be supplied most
discreetly, and the wrongs done unto them repaired : *he shall
judge thy poor with judgment,* v. 3. The third benefit is,
Christ is not to take away civil governors' or potentates'
places, nor the several orders and ranks of greatness of superior and inferior powers, rulers, and judges; all these are
to be fixed rather by him for the good of the people : the
superior as *mountains,* and the inferior as *little hills,* shall
stand in their places for him. The fourth benefit is, Christ
shall make such magistrates as embrace him for their Lord
and Governor, a blessing to the people under them; for, by
their righteous government the people shall live quiet and
safe in God's service under them : *the mountains shall bring
peace to the people, and the little hills;* but how shall the
mountains and little hills do this ? *by righteousness,* v. 4.
The fifth benefit is, albeit Christ suffer his subjects to be
brought low, in the sense of their own weakness, and in
danger of being swallowed up by their persecutors, yet shall
he take their controversy to his cognition, and deliver his
people out of the hands of their adversaries : *he shall judge
the poor of the people; he shall save the children of the needy;
he shall break in pieces the oppressors,* v. 5. The sixth benefit is, Christ, the true king of Israel, shall never want a kingdom, he shall never want subjects, but shall always have a
church of such as shall worship and fear him, and do homage
unto him, so long as the world standeth, amidst all changes
and revolutions that can come : *they shall fear thee as long
as the sun and moon endure, throughout all generations,* v. 6.
The seventh benefit is, whatsoever sad condition his people,
shall be in, how far soever spoiled of their lustre and glory
in the world, or in any other respects whatsoever, they shall
be made as a mown down meadow possibly, yet Christ, by
his word, Spirit, and effectual blessing, shall revive and recover them ; as grass cut down, being watered by rain, is
made to grow again : *he shall come down like rain upon the
mown grass, as showers that water the earth,* v. 7. The
eighth benefit is, all the true subjects of Christ are justified
persons, and devoted in their hearts to righteousness, in the
obedience of God's will, and such as endeavour to abound
in the fruits of righteousness: *the righteous shall flourish in*

his day. The ninth benefit is, Christ's justified subjects and students of holiness shall have peace with God, peace abounding and passing all understanding, *lasting peace,* without end, in all his revolution of conditions : *the righteous shall flourish, and have abundant peace, so long as the world endureth,* v. 8. The tenth benefit of Christ's government is, the enlargement of the church and the number of his subjects, according to the length and breadth of God's promises made to his people Israel, whether Israel in the letter or in the spirit : *he shall have dominion also from sea to sea, and from the river unto the ends of the earth,* v. 9. The eleventh benefit of Christ's government is more special: whomsoever he pleaseth to make subject unto himself, how wild and savage soever they be, yea, how great enemies soever they have been to his kingdom, he shall tame them, bring them in subjection to himself, and to most humble submission unto his commands : *they that dwell in the dust shall bow before him, and his enemies shall lick the dust,* v. 10. The twelfth benefit is yet more special: the kings and rulers of the Gentiles shall find it a blessing to themselves and to their dominions to be under Christ's government, and shall effectually contribute their riches, power, and authority, to advance the kingdom of Christ, their sovereign Lord and protector: *the kings of Tarshish and of the isles shall bring presents; the kings of Sheba and Seba shall offer gifts,* v. 11. The thirteenth benefit of Christ's government, is so great an enlargement of his kingdom, by bringing all kingdoms and nations some way under his sceptre, that the prophecy of John the Divine, Rev. xi. 15, shall be acknowledged to be fulfilled: *all the kingdoms of the earth are become the Lord's and his Son Christ's,* how improbable soever this may seem; for answerably hereunto is it said here, *yea, all kings shall fall down before him, all nations shall serve him,* v. 12. The fourteenth benefit serving for the commendation of his government, is, by way of giving a reason of the marvellous enlargement of his kingdom, from his care of the meanest of his subjects, from his effectual pity toward them, love and estimation of them. The care Christ hath of his subjects is such, that there is not one so mean in all his kingdom, of whom, and whose necessities, and of whose particular petitions, he taketh not most particular and exact knowledge, whose petitions, being presented in the sense of their need,

he granteth not : *he shall deliver the needy when he crieth.*
There needeth no mediator between him and his subjects :
he heareth the needy when they cry. The man that hath
nothing within him or without him to commend him to
Christ, to assist, help, relieve, or comfort him, in heaven
or earth, is not despised by Christ, but delivered from that
which he feareth : *he shall deliver the poor, and him also
that hath no helper;* and this he doth by teaching his subjects to bear troubles, by strengthening them for the burden,
by comforting them in their grief, by giving a delivery to
their spirits by faith, and a full delivery at last, v. 13. The
fifteenth benefit and commendation of Christ's government
is, he exacteth from his subjects but that which he offereth
to furnish and enable them to discharge : he lets none be
tempted above his strength; he taketh small beginnings in
good part, he spareth the rod in a great measure, mitigates
the correction, and, in midst of wrath, he remembereth
mercy : *he shall spare the poor and needy;* whatsoever hard
exercise he put them to, he will give them their soul for a
prey : they shall not perish, who, in the sense of their need,
depend upon him : *he shall save the souls of the needy,* v. 14.
The sixteenth benefit and commendation of Christ's kingdom is, albeit the Lord suffer his subjects to be tried with
heresies and seducers, by oppressors and persecutors, yet
he will assist them in the trial and bring them out of it : *he
shall redeem their soul from deceit and violence;* and if, for
his own glory, he put any of them to lay down their life for
his cause, it shall be a point of special honouring of them,
as of precious sons whom he esteemeth much, both living
and dead : *precious shall their blood be in his sight,* v. 15.
The seventeenth benefit and commendation of Christ's government is from its everlasting endurance ; albeit other
kings die and leave their kingdoms to their successors, yet
it is not so with Christ; he endureth for ever : his death,
for paying the ransom of our sins, did not interrupt his reign,
but made way for his more glorious reigning, after his resurrection: he hath life in himself, as in the fountain : *he
shall live,* he shall live conquering and bringing in more
subjects, who shall pay tribute unto him : *to him shall be
given of the gold of Sheba.* The eighteenth benefit and
commendation of Christ's kingdom is, Christ shall be well-
beloved of all his subjects, whose exercise it shall be to wish

and pray for the prosperity of his kingdom, church, and mystical body, and who shall commend and praise his glorious and lovely majesty : *prayer also shall be made for him continually, and daily shall he be praised,* v. 16. The nineteenth benefit and commendation of Christ's government is, that a little seed of his precious word sown among men, of whose conversion there might be least hope, like a handful of corn sown upon the mountains or most barren ground, shall have a glorious increase in the conversion of many notable saints, like as corn in a barren place should grow up like cedar-trees : *there shall be an handful of corn in the earth, on the top of the mountains, the fruit thereof shall shake like Lebanon :* and this blessing of the gospel he can make to be without prejudice of the manured land of churches already planted, which are as cities inhabited; those he can bless, and will bless at his pleasure, with the abundant growth of grace amongst them: *and they of the city shall flourish as the grass of the earth,* v. 17. The last commendation and benefit of Christ's government summeth up all that can be said in these four generals : 1. That Christ's name, fame, and honour, shall be perpetuated from one generation to another, for the running of his benefits to his subjects, and for the course of his judgments on his enemies : *his name shall endure for ever ; his name shall be continued as long as the sun.* 2. His gospel shall spread further and further among men, to deliver his own from the curse due for sin, to make them partakers of the blessing of full felicity : *men shall be blessed in him.* 3. It shall be in vain to seek blessedness any where, except in him only who is the procurer, applier, and maintainer of true blessedness, the way whereunto is, to come to God in and through Christ : *in him men shall be blessed.* And, 4. Such a fulness of converted Gentiles at length shall be brought in, that the blessedness of the gospel of Christ and of spiritual communion with him, and the riches of his goodness and grace shall generally be acknowledged in all the world : *all nations shall call him blessed.*

18. *Blessed be the Lord God, the God of Israel, who only doeth wondrous things.*

19. *And blessed be his glorious name for ever : and let the whole earth be filled with his glory. Amen, and Amen.*

After this gracious answer of the church's prayer in so glorious a prophecy of Christ, thanksgiving and praise are indited unto the church, to be offered up to God for this mercy. Whence learn, 1. When the heart hath believed what the ear hath heard of the blessedness to be found in Christ, the mouth should be opened to praise and bless God: *blessed be the Lord God, the God of Israel.* 2. As the keeping of the race of David till the coming of Christ, distinct from other families, in so many revolutions of affairs, as were between David's reign and Christ's coming, is very wonderful: so the enlarging of the kingdom of Christ, since he came, is full of wonder also, whether we look to the King, or to the subjects converted, or the way of converting them, by the preaching of his word, or the preservation or continuing of Christ's kingdom in the world amongst so many devils and wicked adversaries, all his subjects being so weak and sinful as they are; it is a matter of great wonder indeed. *Blessed be the God of Israel, who only doeth wondrous things.* There are no wonders like the wonders done in the redemption of men by Christ, yea there is no other who can work any wonders, but by Christ alone. 3. As the blessings of Christ are everlasting, so should the thanksgiving for them be; and no less can content the heart of a true believer, who, the more he thinks of Christ, the more glory he seeth in him : *and blessed be his glorious name for ever,* saith he. 4. Before Christ puts an end to his work, and gives up the kingdom to the Father, his glory shall shine in all parts of the world, for the prayers indited to the church are not vanishing wishes, but real promises and certain prophecies : *let the whole earth be filled with his glory.* 5. As faith sets to its seal unto the truth of God's word, in special what concerneth the salvation of men and the glory of God in Christ; so love, both to the glory of God, and salvation of souls, sets to its seal also; or both faith and love subscribe the same truth of God in both respects, again and again : *amen, and amen.*

20. *The prayers of David the son of Jesse are ended.*

This closure of the psalm is added by the psalmist David himself, and is a part of the text; serving, first, to show, that this was the last of the psalms, indited by the Spirit to him a little before his death, when Solomon was now reigning: howsoever in the order of providence it be not in the hind-most place of this book of the psalms. And next, it serveth to show, that in this answer made to his prayer set down in this psalm, all his desires were granted, both concerning himself and his house; for he could wish no more. And, thirdly, it serveth to show his mean estimation of himself, not-withstanding the Lord's lifting of him up so high, that so the grace of God in him may be the more conspicuous; for which causes he calleth himself, *the son of Jesse.* Whence learn, 1. As a man liveth, so readily he dieth. David was a worshipper of God all his life, and now when he hath given over the kingdom to his son, and is going on his way, he is upon the same work of praying and singing psalms, for God's glory and the edification of his church. 2. Meditation on Christ, contemplation of his glory, seek-ing after and foreseeing the enlargement of his kingdom, from a noble and comfortable closing of a man's life, as here we see. 3. It is the mark of true humility and sincere love to God, to abase ourselves, and acknowledge our low condition, wherein God found us when he let forth his love to us, that thereby we may commend the riches of God's goodness and grace unto us, as appeareth here in David.

PSALM LXXIII.

A psalm of Asaph.

The psalmist setteth down here the doctrine of God's goodness to the faithful, however he seem to deal with them, v. 1, and cleareth it by his own experience. Wherein, first, after he had stumbled to see the wicked prosper in the world, comparing his own calamities with their prosperity, v. 2—12; he was like to be overcome with the temptation, and to forsake the course of godliness, v. 13, 14; next with this temp-tation he wrestles, v. 15, 16; and, thirdly, he getteth the victory, con-sulting the word of God, v. 17—20; in the last place, he maketh a fourfold use of this experience; the first whereof is, the acknowledging of his own weakness under the temptation, v. 21, 22; the next, the confessing of God's kindness to him in the time of temptation, v. 23; the third, the confirming of his own faith for time to come, v. 24—26; the fourth, his resolution to draw more near to God hereafter, v. 27, 28.

1. *Truly God* is *good to Israel,* even *to such as are of a clean heart.*

The doctrine set down in this verse, is the result of As-aph's sad trial after he had gotten the victory of the temp-tation which called in question the blessedness of believers, whensoever their outward condition should be found more miserable than the condition of the wicked. Whence learn, 1. As the temptations of Satan aim at the weakening of our believing of saving doctrine, so our trials, our experi-ences of conflicts against temptation, and our victories over it, should strengthen our faith so much the more, to hold fast that truth which the temptation opposed. After this experience, the prophet not only holds forth this doctrine, *that God is good*, but also prefixeth unto it, *truly, yet, or notwithstanding*. 2. However the Lord seem to deal more hardly with humble believers and worshippers of him, than with the wicked, yet is his dispensation toward them always for their welfare: *truly, God is good to Israel*. 3. Those persons are true Israelites, who not only cleanse their con-science by the blood of the Lamb of God, but also study to be holy in soul and body in the sincerity of their heart. This is the cleanness of heart which the Scripture teach-eth. *God is good to Israel, even to such as are of a clean heart.*

2. *But as for me, my feet were almost gone; my steps had well nigh slipped.*

3. *For I was envious at the foolish, when I saw the prosperity of the wicked.*

The psalmist compareth his late carriage under a temp-tation with the rule of this doctrine, and acknowledgeth that he did not hold it so firmly as he should have done, but was almost driven from maintaining it. Whence learn, 1. In the time of adversity, a believer may prove weak in the faith of that truth which was not questioned by him in prosperity, and be near hand unto the quitting and re-nouncing of it: *but as for me my feet were almost gone, my steps had well nigh slipped*. 2. Albeit the Lord so far decy-pher the weakness of his own children, as to let them be brought to the very brink of misbelieving a necessary and saving truth, yet he preventeth their quitting it altogether; they may be very near the fall, and not fall altogether: *my feet were almost gone, my steps had well nigh slipped*. 3. The godly will not hesitate to confess to their own shame their own weakness, when it may serve to strengthen others and give warning to prevent the fall of others, or any way prove profitable to others, as in this example we see. 4. The measure of our faith or love to God and religion, the measure of our faith to obey known truth, is best known in time of temptation, when the object is in our eye, and the tempter is making use of it to insnare us : *I was envious at the foolish, when I saw the prosperity of the wicked.* 5. If the prosperity of the wicked, and trouble of the godly be looked upon, in respect of their outward worldly estate only; it cannot but trouble a man's thoughts : *I was envious at the foolish, when I saw the prosperity of the wicked.*

4. *For* there are *no bands in their death; but their strength* is *firm.*

5. *They* are *not in trouble* as other *men; neither are they plagued like* other *men.*

6. *Therefore pride compasseth them about as a chain; violence covereth them as a garment.*

7. *Their eyes stand out with fatness: they have more than heart could wish.*

8. *They are corrupt, and speak wickedly* concerning *oppression: they speak loftily.*

9. *They set their mouth against the heavens; and their tongue walketh through the earth.*

10. *Therefore his people return hither; and waters of a full* cup *are wrung out to them :*

What was the prosperity of the wicked, which stumbled the psalmist, he setteth down in particular in these verses. Whence learn, 1. Albeit the great multitude of the wicked are subject to such outward miseries as others are; yet to some of them, yea and to some of the worst of them, God for his own holy ends useth to give health of body, long life, little sickness, and a quiet death, when the time of it is come, and in their death to keep them from many troubles which others are subject unto : yet God doth not love them, nor approve any whit more of them for this: *there are no bands in their death, but their strength is firm; they are not in trouble as other men, &c.* 2. The more liberally the Lord deals with the wicked, they are the more insolent, and proud, and vain-glorious; they are the more unjust and violent oppressors of others : their prosperity blindeth them, and serveth to increase their wickedness : *therefore pride compasseth them as a chain ; violence covereth them as a garment.* They glory in their oppression. 3. Albeit God bestow riches on the wicked, and more than they could reasonably wish, and give them health of body to make use of their riches as they please, so that they swell for fatness, (which abundance should oblige a man to serve the Lord more heartily:) yet the recompense they render to God is, that they become more and more vicious in their own persons, and threaten more and more injuries to their neighbours : *they are corrupt, and speak wickedly concerning oppression.* They stand in awe neither of God nor man, but openly in their speeches they despise all authority over them. *they speak loftily :* they scoff and mock religion, and speak blasphemously of God and his providence. *They set their mouth against the heavens :* they speak as they please of all things, and all men, not caring against whom they speak, or what they speak to any man's prejudice. *Their tongue walketh through the earth :* not caring whom it tread upon, or whom it abuse. 4. The prosperity of the wicked, and their thriving in an ill course, insnare many inconsiderate people, even members of the visible church, and move them to follow the evil ways of the openly wicked, and to make defection from their own professed duties : *therefore his people return hither,* saith he. 5. When men stumble at righteousness because of trouble, and follow the course of the wicked for love of worldly advantage; it is righteousness with God to give both the bait for a while to such changelings, and the hook also, for hardening them in their own wicked choice; *and waters of a full cup,* saith he, *are wrung out unto them :* that is, they find some worldly commodity by their defection. 6. There is a threefold temptation to draw a man from the course of holiness unto looseness and profanity; one, when the wicked are observed to prosper in the world; another, when multitudes turn off a good course and follow the example of the wicked : and a third, when those backsliders also seem to prosper after their defection, as here. 1. The wicked calumniate every good course, and they prosper. 2. God's people return hither for love of prosperity. 3. *Then waters of a full*

cup are wrung out unto them. All these things may concur, and the way meantime be most damnable notwithstanding.

11. *And they say, How doth God know? and is
there knowledge in the most High?*

12. *Behold, these* are *the ungodly, who prosper in the
world: they increase* in *riches.*

Here Asaph bringeth in the poor deluded people defending their defection, and their following the example of the
ungodly, and hardening themselves in their evil course: saying in substance, that if God disliked the ungodly, he would
not let them prosper so in the world, and heap riches upon
them as he doth; and this is in substance to blaspheme God
as an ignorant Governor of the world, or a misregarder how
men carry themselves. Whence learn, 1. When men are
once insnared in an ill course, they will seek reasons to justify themselves; those thoughts which insnared them also
hold them; for they to whom *waters of a full cup are wrung
out do say, How doth God know?* 2. Men are ready to
reproach the Lord if he do not guide the world to their
fancy, yea, and to blaspheme God rather than blame themselves for their faults, as these words import: *how doth God
know?* that is, how can it be that God taketh notice of such
men's ways as wrong, seeing he prospereth them? 3. To
think that God is well pleased with the way of the wicked,
because they prosper, and that he respects not his saints,
because he afflicteth them more than the wicked, is as much
as in effect to say, The Lord is not wise that doeth so well
to his foes, and dealeth so hardly with his friends; for so
here is it interpreted by the world: *is there knowledge in the
most High?* 4. It seemeth very reasonable to carnal reason, that if God hate ungodliness, he should not suffer the
ungodly to prosper in the world; and if he suffer them to
prosper, then he doth not hate ungodliness; and therefore
when it is clear to all men that the ungodly prosper, they
conclude, *that God knoweth not;* taketh no notice of ungodliness, or is not displeased with it: for here is their proof:
behold, say they, *these are the ungodly who prosper in the
world, they increase in riches.* 5. The thing that deceiveth
the ungodly and the misbelieving world about God's dispensations is, that they look only to that which is done by God

in this world; no punishment after death, or felicity after death do they think upon : *these are the ungodly*, say they, *who prosper in the world.*   6. In the very temptation whereby the wicked are ensnared, the worm of their gourd, and the stain of their felicity are discovered; their felicity is but in their riches, and their prosperity is but in this present world : *they prosper in the world*, say they.

13. *Verily I have cleansed my heart* in *vain, and washed my hands in innocency.*

14. *For all the day long have I been plagued, and chastened every morning.*

Here is the well near slipping of the psalmist's feet, set down in his begun yielding unto the devil's temptation, forcibly borne in upon him, and repeated over by him, after the manner of a resolute conclusion, condemning all his former course of godliness upon this one poor pretence, because he seemed to himself more miserable than the wicked were. Whence learn, 1. A temptation sometimes may be so powerfully borne in upon the spirit of a child of God, as it may seem to be admitted, yielded unto, and subscribed unto as truth, as here we see : *verily I have cleansed in vain, &c.* 2. The true course of sanctification consists in the study of cleansing a man from all pollution, both of soul and body, or *in cleansing the heart and the hands*, as here is set down. The heart is cleansed by the blood of the expiatory sacrifice laid hold on by faith, and by the begun works of the Lord's Spirit manifested in the hearty resolution, purpose, and study of holiness; the hands are cleansed by a blameless and harmless conversation or course of life and actions : *I have cleansed my heart and hands in innocency.* 3. When a man is under a temptation, or in a fleshly temper of spirit, for the present he putteth a high price upon any good he hath done, and forgetteth by what strength he did it; he forgetteth God's part, and his glory in it; for the psalmist's part was the consenter's part, the instrument's part, and he was in the point of action only a subordinate agent, and co-worker at the best by a borrowed strength; and yet as if all the work had been his work alone, *in vain*, saith he, *have I cleansed my heart, and washed my hands in innocency.* 4. That which is the break-neck of the wicked, may readily be a stumbling-stone for a time to the godly; that which is

the irrecoverable deadly sickness of the wicked, may be the
hot fever or distemper of the godly for a season. In special,
as the wicked man at all times looketh only to this present
world, and to what may make him prosperous or miserable
in this present life, so it may befall the godly man also in a
fit, at a time, to look only upon temporal prosperity and
trouble, as here we see the psalmist looketh only to his present troubles : *for all the day long I have been plagued ;*
never a word here of his sweet consolations and manifold
benefits bestowed on him. 5. To find some new cross daily,
either from God immediately, or from the world, or from
Satan, or from our own corruption, is no strange thing to
the godly : *all the day long I have been plagued, and chastened every morning*, saith the psalmist, even when he was
daily cleansing his heart and washing his hands; so doth
divine wisdom see it fit for the good of his children and glorifying of his own name.

15. *If I say, I will speak thus ; behold, I should offend* against *the generation of thy children.*

Thus have we seen the psalmist's temptation. In the next
place, we have his wrestling with it, by bringing the conclusion suggested by Satan to a further examination; and
first, of human reason, whereby he perceiveth that if this
conclusion should be maintained, then the church of God in
all ages, and all the godly from the beginning of the world
would be condemned as miserable souls; which consequence
he thinketh to be a rash condemning of the constant resolution of the godly wise in all ages past. Whence learn, 1.
Temptations driving at the subversion of faith in Christ and
holiness of life, find resistance in the heart of a renewed man,
how far soever they seem to prevail at first. The seed of
God remaineth in him, the principles of spiritual life, the
infused habits of saving grace, the new creature by God's
upstirring, make opposition, as in this example we see.
2. The way to take up and decipher Satan's temptations, is
to consider what they aim at, tend unto, drive at, what may
be the consequence thereof : *if I say, I will speak thus,*
then such a thing will follow. 3. So long as a temptation
remaineth under dispute, and is not come to a settled decree
and resolved practice, it hath not obtained full victory; it
is with the psalmist here, for all that was suggested and

seemingly yielded, no more yet, but, *if I say, I will speak thus.* 4. Whosoever condemneth piety and holy conversation, because the world doth so, or because trouble followeth such a course, he doth a high injury to all the saints from the beginning of the world, and to God the author of all holiness: *if I should speak thus, behold, I should offend against the generation of thy children.* 5. The godly are not the authors of their own spiritual being, the making them new creatures is the work of God, they are the children of God, begotten of him by his word and Spirit, and resemble their father in wisdom and righteousness; so the psalmist styleth them in the time of his hard trial here, *the generation of God's children.* 6. In our disputing with temptations by the weapons of reason, we shall do well to make God moderator of the disputants, and to look to God in our reasoning, that we may, by his testimonies, rectify every thing, lest we reason amiss, as here the psalmist doth : *I should offend against the generation of thy children.* We ought to reverence the judgment of the godly; and the more universally their judgment is one, and agreeing in a point of controversy, the more fear should we have to dissent from them, as the psalmist's example teacheth us.

16. *When I thought to know this, it was too painful for me.*

17. *Until I went into the sanctuary of God; then understood I their end.*

18. *Surely thou didst set them in slippery places, thou castedst them down into destruction.*

19. *How are they* brought *into desolation, as in a moment! they are utterly consumed with terrors.*

20. *As a dream when one awaketh ; so, O Lord, when thou awakest, thou shalt despise their image.*

In the third place, finding himself not yet satisfied, the psalmist consulteth the oracle of God, revealed in his Scripture, and the ordinances of his house, and so he findeth his doubt resolved, and victory over his bitter temptation granted unto him. Whence learn, 1. When a man seeth himself in a mist, and out of the Lord's way, he is not able by himself to find it again; for the strongest of human testimonies will not settle him and make him quiet : *when I thought to know this, it was too painful.* 2. The last refuge of brangled

faith, is God himself manifesting his will in his word and
ordinances; no settling or satisfaction of doubts in divinity
but by the Scriptures: *it was too painful for me until I
went unto the sanctuary of God;* that is, till I consulted the
Scriptures, and considered what God had revealed in his
church by his ordinances: this satisfied and settled him.
3. The Lord hath revealed in Scripture what shall be the
end and close of men's course, who study not to walk according to his direction, how prosperous soever they may
seem to be; and because the felicity of men is not to be
known by God's outward dispensation of worldly comforts
or crosses, therefore man's end must determine the difference: *then understood I their end.* 4. Whatsoever alterations and changes the godly man be subject unto in his temporal condition, bodily or spiritual, yet his felicity is settled
unto him on the rock; but the felicity of the wicked is built
on the sand; the higher they are lifted up in that earthly
felicity, which alone they affect, the nearer are they to a
fall and fearful ruin: *thou hast set them upon slippery places.*
5. Whatsoever may seem to the wicked themselves, or to the
world, or to the godly who look upon the wicked, how little
appearance soever there be of their fall; yet it is decreed it
shall be: for, notwithstanding all appearances, it is said,
surely thou hast set them in slippery places. 6. As the
wicked do not rise unto any greatness or power in the world
by themselves, but the Lord is he that setteth them up for his
own glory; so they do not fall of their own accord, but the
Lord casteth them down; beside their own weight, they have
the throw of the right hand of the Lord, who showeth his
power in the overthrow, and driveth them to more deaths than
one: *thou castedst them down into destruction.* 7. The wicked
perish suddenly, when neither they themselves nor others are
looking for their ruin, in a way much more wonderful than
their lifting up was: *they are destroyed; how are they brought
into desolation as in a moment?* 8. The destruction of the
wicked is full of terror, how senselessly soever some of them
go away; all their riches, honour, and prosperity are pulled
from them, and in great wrath they are sent out of the world,
never to see any token of favour again; they are adjudged
to irrecoverable perdition of soul and body for ever: *they
are utterly consumed with terrors.* 9. When the wicked are
flourishing in wealth, ease, and honour, men think that God

is, as it were, sleeping; but the truth is, both the wicked themselves, and all who look upon them, and judge them to be happy, are in a dream, as they shall see when the Lord's time is come to execute judgment on them; for then all their riches, honour, pleasure, and contentment shall be found nothing but a despicable picture of these things : *as a dream when one awaketh; so, O Lord, when thou awakest, thou shalt despise their image.*

21. *Thus my heart was grieved, and I was pricked in my reins.*

22. *So foolish* was *I, and ignorant : I was* as *a beast before thee.*

In the fourth place, the psalmist makes a sixfold use of this experience. The first is this, that by it he is taught how weak and foolish he is in himself, and how unable to stand in time of trial and temptation.   Whence learn, 1. Hardly will a man discern a powerful temptation, when he is under it.   The best sight to be had of the danger of a temptation is, when it is overcome and gone; and look how well pleased a man is, when the temptation is beautified with specious colours of carnal reason, so much will he be displeased with it when it is seen, and discerned by spiritual light, as here we see in the psalmist's experience.   2. Much trouble do we bring to our own spirits, when we examine God's dispensations by carnal reason, and not by the Scriptures; and we may thank ourselves for the misery which we draw upon ourselves, as here the psalmist doth : *thus my heart was grieved, and I was pricked in my reins.*   3. So soon as the godly can perceive their own error, they will no longer maintain it, and no man will more sharply censure them for their fault than they will do themselves. This is a part of their uprightness and ingenuous honesty of heart : *so foolish was I and ignorant.* 4. The sin of envy and malcontent with God's afflicting us and sparing the wicked, hath its own judgment bound upon the back of it : for as a sour-leavened vessel turneth all things put into it unto sourness, so envy of the prosperity of others maketh all the good that the Lord doeth to ourselves, uncomfortable and unpleasant to us : for the phrase, *my heart was grieved,* is in the force of the original, *my heart was imbittered, made sour, and leavened.* 5. Perplexity of mind, arising from the mistaking of God's providence, is like the pain of the gravel in the reins, very troublesome till we

be rid of it : *I was pricked in my reins*, is a similitude borrowed from the bodily pain of the gravel.   6. Carnal reason
not corrected by God's word, is beastly ignorance : it may
bear some show of reason among foolish men, but indeed it
is nothing before God, but brutish folly : *I was as a beast
before thee.*

23. *Nevertheless I* am *continually with thee ; thou
hast holden* me *by my right hand.*

The second use of this exercise, is the acknowledgment
that his standing in grace and God's obedience, depended
only upon the Lord, by whose powerful sustaining of him he
was kept from being utterly overcome by the temptations of
Satan, and falling from the way of God by the temptation.
Whence learn, 1. The perseverance of the saints, is not of
themselves, but of the Lord, who forsaketh them not, when
they of themselves are ready to forsake him, but by his power
secretly upholdeth them, and keepeth them fast to himself.
This the psalmist here acknowledgeth : *nevertheless I am
continually with thee.* 2. When we have gotten proof of our
own folly and weakness, and ill-deserving, then we most
clearly see and confess God's grace and power in preserving
us : *thou hast holden me by my right hand.*

24. *Thou shalt guide me with thy counsel, and afterward receive me* to *glory.*

The third use is the confirmation of his faith and hope in
God for time to come. Whence learn, 1. The believer, how
sensible soever he be of his own weakness, may be persuaded
of his own perseverance, by looking on God's constancy, and
felt experience of his work of grace in him in time past :
thou wilt guide me with thy counsel, &c. 2. There is an inseparable connexion between walking by God's direction in
the time of this life, and our reception into heaven after this
life : and he who is resolved to walk by the rule of God's direction, may promise to himself to be received into glory immediately after his journey in this life is ended : *thou shalt
guide me with thy counsel, and afterward receive me to glory.*
3. Albeit the believer may meet with many doubts and difficulties in his way, yet hath he a guide to direct him, and a
rule to walk by, to wit, the word of God revealed in the
church or sanctuary; whereby he may be advised effectually
how to walk on his way to heaven : *thou wilt guide me with
thy counsel.*

25. *Whom have I in heaven but thee ? and there is none upon earth that I desire besides thee.*

26. *My flesh and my heart faileth : but God is the strength of my heart, and my portion for ever.*

The fourth use of this exercise is, the settling of his affection and confidence on God, as the matter of his satisfactory contentment and upholding, when all creatures failed him. Whence learn, 1. As nothing can give true contentment, except God : so God will have us to loose our heart from all creatures, and expect no contentment in any of them, but in himself : *whom have I in heaven but thee ? and there is none upon earth that I desire besides thee.* 2. He that seeth God's sufficiency, seeth also the emptiness of the creatures, and nothing to be in them, but what they have of God. A believer may see that he needeth nothing in heaven or earth, but communion with God, to make him fully blessed : *whom have I in heaven but thee ? and there is none upon earth that I desire besides thee.* 3. As to find all things to fail us, ex-cept God, in the time of trial, serveth to loose our affections and confidence off them : so to find help in God when all things fail, serveth to tie the heart of a believer strongly to the Lord : *my heart and my flesh fail me, but God is the strength of my heart.* 4. When the believer hath seen his own strength fail him, and yet believeth not the less in God, he shall find his failing heart and fainting courage upholden, and his own exhausted strength supplied with a greater strength from God : *my heart and my flesh fail me, but God is the strength of my heart.* 5. Every man seeketh some-thing for his portion; some one thing in the creature, some another, but the believer's portion is the Lord himself, and no less will content him: *the Lord is the strength of my heart, and my portion.* 6. This is the believer's advantage above all that seek their blessedness in the creature; for his person is the eternal God, and he is made an everlasting enjoyer of him: *God is my portion for ever.*

27. *For, lo, they that are far from thee shall perish : thou hast destroyed all them that go a-whoring from thee.*

The fifth use is the psalmist's resolution to draw nearer unto God. The reasons of which resolution are two; the one, because they perish who draw not near to God v. 27;

the other, because great advantage is to be had by drawing near to him, v. 28. Whence learn, 1. The Lord's child profiteth by hardest exercises, and his temptations, being resisted by faith, leave him in better case than they found him : his knowledge of God's ways, his faith, his love to God and hatred of wicked courses are augmented, as in this example is to be seen. 2. They whose confidence, affections, course of life and actions run toward and cleave unto the creature depart from God more and more; for here they are said to be far from God : and they that depart from God draw near to eternal perdition : *they that are far from thee shall perish.* And howsoever this truth be not believed, yet it is as sure and certain, as if it were seen with our eyes : *for lo, they that are far from thee shall perish.* 3. A chaste soul hath no choice, no love to delight itself in contentedly, except God : no confidence to rest itself upon, but God. And whosoever seek their delight and satisfaction in the creature, especially if they be members of the visible church, in covenant with God, are adulterers : *they go a-whoring from God :* and they shall not find felicity in the creatures, but perdition, no less certainly, than if it were already past : *thou hast destroyed all them that go a-whoring from thee.*

28. *But* it is *good for me to draw near to God : I have put my trust in the Lord God, that I may declare all thy works.*

In this verse, the psalmist giveth the other reason of his adherence unto God, from the advantage he findeth by so doing, and closeth the psalm with the sixth use of his experience, which is the fixing of his faith on God, that his experiences may be more and more frequent, and he may be a fitter instrument to glorify God. Whence learn, 1. The right use of the perishing of the wicked, is to be more holy, and to seek nearer communion with God, as our only blessedness, how many soever depart from him : *they shall perish who are far from thee ; but it is good for me to draw near to God.* 2. No man is so near in communion with God in this life, but there is a further degree to be aimed at, and possibly to be found; as there are degrees of departing from God; so also are there degrees of coming near unto him; and the better for us, the nearer we draw : *it is good for me to draw near to God.* 3. The use of all assaults against our faith, is more and more to fix our faith and confidence on God; for this is the use the psalmist maketh of the assault spoken of in this psalm : *I have put my trust in the Lord God.* 4. None but a deliverer can discern the Lord's working; it is only faith that giveth a right construction unto all the Lord's works ; faith alone makes men fit instruments to glorify God : *I put my trust in the Lord God, that I may declare all thy works.* 5. As the believer is the best observer of God's works, and fittest to set them forth before others; so he is the man of greatest experience; and he of all men is filled with most matter of God's praise : for the Lord never disappoints the believer, but makes him have new proofs of his wonderful wisdom, power, and goodness; so doth the psalmist lay his reckoning : *I have put my trust in the Lord God, that I may declare all thy works.*

PSALM LXXIV.

Maschil of Asaph.

Of this psalm there are three parts. In the first part is the pitiful lamentation of the church presented unto God, because of the destruction of Jerusalem, and burning of the temple by the Chaldeans, to v. 11. In the next is the strengthening of the faith and hope of God's people, that God would send a delivery, to v. 18. In the third, there are sundry petitions for relief of his people, restitution of his own work, and suppression of his enemies, to the end of the psalm.

1. *O God, why hast thou cast* us *off for ever?* why *doth thine anger smoke against the sheep of thy pasture?*

2. *Remember thy congregation,* which *thou hast purchased of old ; the rod of thine inheritance,* which *thou hast redeemed ; this mount Zion, wherein thou hast dwelt.*

In the first part of the psalm there are a lamentation and prayer for relief in general, v. 1, 2; secondly, a complaint against the enemy, laying forth before God the desolation which the Chaldeans had made, especially in destroying the temple, v. 3—9; and, thirdly, a prayer unto God for vengeance upon them for their pains, v. 10, 11.

From the lamentation and prayer for relief in general, learn, 1. In all judgments, inflicted by whatsoever instruments, the Lord's people must look first to God; and albeit wrath, and fear of utter wrath stare them in the face, as hardly it can be otherwise when God putteth hand in his own temple, and taketh away all the tokens of his presence from among a people, and seemeth to cast them utterly off; yet must they make their address to God, how angry soever he seem to be; as here the church under this sad judgment doth, saying, *O God, why hast thou cast us off?* 2. In the point of casting off, and fear of casting off for ever, the Lord craveth no yielding and submission to the pressing thoughts thereof, but will allow us to call in question every appearance of any such purpose of God, and to debate that point with him, and not to endure utter casting off, yea and to say, *Why hast thou cast us off for ever?* whether it be our own particular case, or the case of the visible church, ours and others' case with us, we cannot endure to be separate from God. 3. When the wrath of the Lord is kindled against his people, all that they see seemeth to be but the beginning of more wrath, as smoke is but the beginning of burning : *why doth thine anger smoke against thy sheep?* 4. Albeit we by our sins have provoked the Lord to fall upon us, as his enemies; yet must we not quit the least relation, no, not of the external covenant between God and us, but make use of it for supporting our faith in him, as here : *why doth thine anger smoke against the sheep of thy pasture?* that is, thy church and people, the care of whom thou hast taken, as a shepherd over his flock. 5. The believer's asking *why?* is no quarrelling : nor is any speech of the saints unto God a quarrelling, which endeth or resolveth in petition and supplication, as this doth : wherein after their asking *why?* they turn themselves to supplication, and pray, *remember thy congregation.* 6. Let the Lord do to his people what he pleaseth, they must pray unto him, and make use of all the bonds between him and them, as here the church doth; pleading, 1. That they are by outward covenant his church, consecrated unto him : *remember thy congregation.* And, 2. That they are his purchase by paying price, and conquest : *thy congregation which thou hast purchased.* And, 3. That they have been in his possession for a long time : *which thou hast purchased of old.* And, 4. That the Lord had taken them into cultivation, as a piece of land measured out by line or rod, and his inheritance, not to dispose or put away : *the rod of thine inheritance.* And, 5. That he had granted deliverances out of straits before : *the inheritance which thou hast redeemed.* And, 6. That he had taken up house amongst them in his public ordinances: *this mount Zion, wherein thou hast dwelt.*

3. *Lift up thy feet unto the perpetual desolations,* even *all* that *the enemy hath done wickedly in the sanctuary.*

4. *Thine enemies roar in the midst of thy congregations; they set up their ensigns* for *signs.*

5. *A man was famous according as he had lifted up axes upon the thick trees.*

6. *But now they break down the carved work thereof at once with axes and hammers.*

7. *They have cast fire into thy sanctuary; they have defiled* by casting down *the dwelling-place of thy name to the ground.*

8. *They said in their hearts, Let us destroy them together: they have burnt up all the synagogues of God in the land.*

9. *We see not our signs:* there is *no more any prophet: neither* is there *among us any that knoweth how long.*

In the complaint, the psalmist desireth the Lord to come and see, and to take order with the desolation made by the enemies in his land, and specially in the temple, v. 3; what insolent domineering of them was over his people, yea, over God himself, so far as their lifted up banner against him could do, v. 4; each of them thinking it as great matter of commendation to him to throw down the temple, as ever it was for any man to build it, or prepare materials for it, v. 5, 6: how they had burned and demolished the Lord's house, v. 7, with a resolution to root out his people, according as they had burned all their synagogues in the land, v. 8; and how there was no appearance of comfort or delivery from this calamity, v. 9. Whence learn, 1. All the evils which the enemy doth unto God's church, proceed from the Lord's desertion of, and departing from his people, who have provoked him to wrath; for this prayer, *Lift up thy feet,* or come and see, importeth his departure, and leaving his people naked without his protection. 2. Albeit the Lord seemeth to turn his back, and depart far away from his own people, when they provoke him to anger, and to let their enemies do unto them what they please; yet will he be entreated by his people to come again, and see, and pity the desolation brought upon them, and punish the instruments of it: *lift up thy feet unto the perpetual desolations;* that is, Lord, come speedily, and see what desolations thy enemies have made amongst us, and pity and relieve us by thy manifested presence. 3. Amongst all the calamities of God's people, nothing afflicteth them so much as the insolent profanation of the worship and name of God among them; for here, in the first petition, they lament the abusing of the temple : *even all that the enemies have done wickedly in the sanctuary*—and then insist most upon this. 4. When the wicked are let loose upon God's people, they are most insolent, cruel, and savage in their carriage toward them : *thy enemies roar in the midst of thy congregations.* 5. It will not suffice the enemies of the church to insult over God's people, but they will insult over their way of religion, and over God whom they worship : *they set up their ensigns for signs;* they display their banner upon the ruins of the temple, as signs of their victory over that religion which is professed there, and over God's worship there. 6. When God's people abuse religion, and mock God in their profession of worship, and dishonour him by their carriage and conversation, it is justice with God to give over his people, and all the means of religion, into the hands of his enemies, to be abused by them, rather than to suffer his own people to mock him continually, as in this example is to be seen. 7. It is matter of a man's commendation to contribute any way to the setting up of God's worship and ordinances in a land : *a man was famous according as he had lifted up axes upon the thick trees;* that is, as he had cut down timber out of Lebanon, wood to build the Lord's temple withal. 8. When the Lord is provoked by his people's evil carriage towards him, no wonder he let the work of edification or reformation of religion go as fast down amongst them as ever it rose up, as the church of the Jews felt by experience, when *now the enemies did break down the carved work of the temple at once, with axes and hammers,* much more speedily than it was built : *they have cast fire into the sanctuary, they have defiled by casting down the dwelling-place of thy name to the ground.* This the Lord chose to permit, rather than suffer his people still to mock religion, and still to abuse the temple, and make it a shelter for them to trust in against all God's threatenings, so long as it stood. 9. Albeit the Lord's mind be only to correct his people, by letting them see their provocation in the judgments brought upon them; yet the enemies whom he useth as instruments in their correction, intend their utter destruction, and the rooting them out of the world: *they say in their hearts, Let us destroy them.* 10. When the enemies of religion cannot kill all the worshippers of God, yet will they labour to mar the means of their assembling for public worship so far as they can: for, after they have said, *Let us destroy them together*, it is subjoined, *they have burnt up all the synagogues of God in the land ;* that is, all the houses built for the weekly assembling of the people unto public worship in their several divisions through the land. 11. Houses built for meetings of the Lord's people to public worship, albeit they be not typically holy, as the temple at Jerusalem was, yet they belong to God, as means dedicated for maintaining his service, and when they are marred, it is a wrong done to God, and a cause of complaint to God against the sacrilegious spoilers thereof, as here we see. 12. External troubles are much lighter when the public ordinances and signs of God's presence in a land may be had for spiritual comfort; but when those are removed, every trouble is the more heavy: *we see not our signs, there is no more any prophet, neither any among us that knoweth how long ;* that is, public means, ordinary and extraordinary, which may give us comfort, now cease. If it be asked, how can this be applied unto the time of the captivity, seeing Jeremiah, Ezekiel, Daniel, and the prophet who wrote this psalm by inspiration, were living at the beginning of the captivity, and after the burning of the temple? it may be answered, that Jeremiah was carried away to Egypt, and the people could not have use of his ministry; Ezekiel and Daniel were carried away to Babylon, and the poor which remained in the land had none of the prophets to comfort them; yea Ezekiel and Daniel were but now and then employed of God to utter their prophecies, and the multitude of the captives, who were to make use of this psalm, were scattered in sundry places, and could not have the benefit of their or of any others' ministry, as they were wont to have. And this in special maketh the lamentation to have a ground, that the table was drawn from the children; the people had not that access which they enjoyed before, unto means either extraordinary or ordinary; they had not their former allowance; and howsoever in the copies of Jeremiah's prophecy, seventy years were determined for the people's captivity, yet none of the prophets, at the time of writing this, told, or could tell them, how long time would pass before their desolation would be repaired; how long it would be ere the temple would be rebuilt; and the prophet, by whom this psalm was indited, had no further commission than he speaketh of; and so these foresaid expressions may stand with the time of the beginning of the captivity of Babylon.

10. *O God, how long shall the adversary reproach? shall the enemy blaspheme thy name for ever?*

11. *Why withdrawest thou thy hand, even thy right hand? pluck it out of thy bosom.*

After the lamentation is subjoined an imprecation against the enemies, that God would not defer to punish them. Whence learn, 1. Men's patience is much short of God's long-suffering and forbearance: for here it is the speech of a suffering people: *O God, how long shall the adversary reproach?* when with God it is not yet time to fall upon them. 2. The Lord's long-suffering patience greatly hardeneth the adversaries in their insolent mocking of God's people; for, instead of saying, Lord, how long wilt thou bear with them? he saith, *O God, how long shall the adversaries reproach?* 3. The truly godly can endure their own troubles better than they can bear the open dishonouring and blaspheming of God, by occasion of their trouble: therefore this expression, from the deepest sense of his heart, breaketh forth: *shall the enemy blaspheme thy name for ever?* 4. Albeit temptations from carnal sense represent God as if he were idle when he suffers his enemies to trample on his people, and on his glorious name; yet faith will not admit of such a thought, but dealeth with God by prayer, to let his strength and power be so manifest, that the world may not think his hand is in his bosom: *why withdrawest thou thy hand, even thy right hand? pluck it out of thy bosom.* This he believeth the Lord shall do, and giveth reasons for his hope in what followeth.

12. *For God* is *my King of old, working salvation in the midst of the earth.*

13. *Thou didst divide the sea by thy strength : thou brakest the heads of the dragons in the waters.*

14. *Thou brakest the heads of leviathan in pieces,* and *gavest him* to be *meat to the people inhabiting the wilderness.*

15. *Thou didst cleave the fountain and the flood: thou driedst up mighty rivers.*

16. *The day* is *thine, the night also* is *thine : thou hast prepared the light and the sun.*

17. *Thou hast set all the borders of the earth : thou hast made summer and winter.*

In the second part of the psalm, the psalmist confirmeth his own and other believers' faith that God would undoubtedly deliver his people, and take order with their enemies; first, from the interest they have in God, and God in them; secondly, from the experience of sensible deliveries past of his people, v. 12; thirdly, from the great work of redemption of his people from Pharoah's tyranny, v. 13, 14; fourthly, from the Lord's feeding his people in the wilderness, v. 15; fifthly, from the Lord's sovereignty and disposing of all creatures in the world, v. 16, 17. Whence learn, 1. Relations between God and his church, and in special this, that he hath made himself King thereof, are pledges of God's defending his kingdom and injured subjects, and punishing his enemies; for here the church giveth it for a reason of her hope of delivery: *God is my King.* 2. The more that is past since God avowed himself King of his church, the more confident may later generations of the church be, to find new evidences of his royal actions for them, and against their enemies: *God is my King of old.* 3. New troubles must not make us forget old mercies, but rather call them to memory, to be made use of afresh, as pledges that what he hath done before, he will do the like again; *God is my King of old, working salvation in the earth :* that is, such deliverances of his church as all the earth was witness of. 4. The delivery of Israel out of Egypt, and the destruction of the Egyptians, is a pledge unto the church in every age after, that God will destroy their enemies, how strong and terrible soever they be, and will deliver his church: *thou didst divide the sea by thy strength, thou brakest the heads of the dragons in the waters.* 5. As all the enemies of the church are no less cruel and savage against the Lord's people, than unreasonable sea-beasts and sea-monsters; so can he make their carcases a prey to unreasonable beasts, as he made Pharaoh and his captains become food to the beasts of the wilderness, when the sea did cast up their carcases on the shore, like sea wreck : *thou brakest the heads of leviathan in pieces, and gavest him to be meat to the people inhabiting the wilderness.* 6. The Lord will not fail to provide consolation to his church in her necessity, though no probable means appear, as he furnished his people with drink from the flinty rock in the wilderness : *thou didst cleave the fountain.* 7. The Lord can and will remove all impediments out of the way of his people which may hinder them from the possession of promises, as he did to Israel : *thou didst cleave the fountain and the flood, thou driedst up mighty rivers.* 8. Faith is so thrifty as not to let the works of creation and common providence pass by, without use-making thereof : *the day is thine, the night also is thine, &c.* 9. As God hath appointed vicissitudes of day and night, light and darkness, summer and winter; so hath he no less resolvedly, wisely, and graciously appointed vicissitudes of dangers and deliverances, of grief and consolation to his people, for their good : *the day is thine, the night also is thine : thou hast prepared the light and the sun.* 10. As the Lord hath set bounds to the sea, bounds and borders to every kingdom, to summer's heat and to winter's cold : so can he do, and so hath he done, and so will he do unto all the troubles of his own, to all the rage, power, plots, and purposes of their enemies : *thou hast set all the borders of the earth, thou hast made summer and winter.*

18. *Remember this,* that *the enemy hath reproached, O Lord, and* that *the foolish people have blasphemed thy name.*

19. *O deliver not the soul of thy turtle-dove unto the multitude* of the wicked : *forget not the congregation of thy poor for ever.*

20. *Have respect unto the covenant : for the dark places of the earth are full of the habitations of cruelty.*

21. *O let not the oppressed return ashamed : let the poor and needy praise thy name.*

22. *Arise, O God, plead thine own cause: remember how the foolish man reproacheth thee daily.*

23. *Forget not the voice of thine enemies : the tumult of those that rise up against thee increaseth continually.*

In the third part of the psalm, the psalmist returneth to prayer, and redoubleth his requests for delivery to the church; taking arguments, first, from the injuries done to God by the enemy, v. 18; secondly, from the danger and weakness of God's people, v. 19; thirdly, from covenanted help in time of need, v. 20, 21; fourthly, from the Lord's interest in his own quarrel against the growing insolency of his despiteful enemies, v. 22, 23. Whence learn, 1. Although sins, especially persecution of God's people, and blasphemy against God, be not presently punished, yet shall they not be forgiven: *remember this, that the enemy hath reproached, O Lord.* 2. All sins, but in special blasphemy of God's name, are aggravated by the naughtiness of the sinner, and excellency of God : *the foolish people have blasphemed thy name.* 3. The church of God, in comparison of her many and strong enemies, is like a solitary, weak, desolate turtle dove, harmless, meek, lowly, patient in desolation, easing her grief by sighing, and exposed to a multitude of ravenous birds: *O deliver not the soul of thy turtle dove.* 4. How weak soever the church be, and how many and strong soever the enemies be, yet cannot they all devour the church, except the Lord should deliver his church over into their hands, against which evil the church hath ground of confidence to pray, *O deliver not the soul of thy turtle dove, unto the multitude of the wicked;* for he hath given his church wings, and a hiding-place too, as the comparison importeth, if he please to give her the use thereof also. 5. The church is the Lord's hospital, where his poor ones are sustained upon his provision and furniture, and he will not neglect them : *O forget not the congregation of thy poor for ever.* 6. Albeit the Lord's people deserve to be secluded many times from the covenant of grace, yet the Lord will never debar them from their right unto it, when they in their need draw near to him, and plead for the benefit of it : *have respect,* saith he, *to the covenant.* 7. Such places as want the light of the Lord's presence in his ordinances, are but dark and uncomfortable places, where there is no less hazard for the people of God to remain, than for sheep to be in the midst of the dens of cruel lions and ravenous beasts. And when it pleaseth God to cast his people by captivity or exile into such places, there is much need to make use of God's covenant for preservation : *have respect unto the covenant ; for the dark places of the earth are full of the habitations of cruelty.* 8. The emptied supplicant coming to God, especially when overloaden with troubles, shall find comfort, and shall not be disappointed of his hope : *O let not the oppressed return ashamed.* 9. The sense of need and emptiness, is the best disposition for prayer, and best preparation for praises also : and such as are poor in their prayers, shall be rich in their praises : *let the poor and needy praise thy name.* 10. The church's cause is the Lord's cause; for the wicked do not malign the godly for their sins, but for righteousness, and so the quarrel is the Lord's, which he will and must maintain, though he seem to sit still a while : *arise, O Lord, plead thine own cause.* 11. The Lord's enemies are all foolish men; for they beat out their brains upon the church's bulwark : because the Lord forbeareth for a time, they go on to blaspheme him daily to his face, but shall find at length, that God hath all their reproaches upon record : *remember how the foolish man reproacheth thee daily.* 12. Every sin, and in special enmity against God and his church, is fearful; but open gloriation therein is worse, which God will take knowledge of, and punish : for so much is imported in this prayer, *forget not the voice of thine enemies.* 13. Sin, and in special persecution, gloried in, groweth daily more and more; and the growing of sin, and in special of persecution, hasteneth the delivery of the godly, and the destruction of the enemies : *the tumult of those that arise against thee, increaseth continually.*

PSALM LXXV.

To the chief musician, Altaschith. A psalm or song of Asaph.

This psalm well agreeth with the time of David's entry into the kingdom after Saul's death, before he was established king over all the tribes; wherein he, with the church, first thanketh God for bringing him wonderfully to a begun possession of a part of the kingdom, ver. 1; secondly, he promiseth that when the Lord shall give him the rest of the kingdom in possession, to employ his power for righteously governing and settling it, after it shall be put once in a right frame, ver. 2, 3; thirdly, he begins to triumph over the wicked that followed Saul, bringing to their mind the advertisement he had given them not to be proud in their places, ver. 4, 5; partly because God had the disposing of preferments in his own hand, ver. 6, 7, and partly because albeit God gave to all his own children a taste of troubles as he saw fit, yet the dregs of wrath were reserved for the wicked, ver. 8; fourthly, he promiseth to praise God continually, for casting down the wicked and exalting the godly, ver. 9, 10.

1. *Unto thee, O God, do we give thanks,* unto thee *do we give thanks : for* that *thy name* is *near thy wondrous works declare.*

From his thanksgiving, learn, 1. The church of God should take out of his hand every beginning of mercies and deliverances with affectionate and frequent thanksgiving : *unto thee, O Lord, do we give thanks, unto thee do we give thanks.* 2. As the Lord is described in his word, so will he be found in his works; to wit, near at hand and ready to help his people as they stand in need : *we do give thanks, because thy name is near;* for this is the nearness of God's name, when his powerful, gracious, felt presence is answerable to what is said of him in his word. 3. Whensoever the Lord showeth himself for his church's comfort, he doth it by some wonderful means, in one respect or other; that is, a far other way than any could have expected : *that thy name is near thy wondrous works declare.*

2. *When I shall receive the congregation I will judge uprightly.*

3. *The earth and all the inhabitants thereof are dissolved : I bear up the pillars of it. Selah.*

From David's undertaking to govern the kingdom well when it came all into his power, learn, 1. Possession in part of promises made to us, giveth good hope to have the whole of what is promised in possession also; for, *when I shall receive the congregation,* presupposeth his certain hope and expectation to have it. 2. He that is advanced to a civil kingdom consisting of people in covenant with God, hath gotten charge to nourish the church, and to procure whatsoever a king civilly can procure to a church, that his subjects may be all of them God's church : therefore David saith not, *when I receive the kingdom, but when I receive the congregation,* or the church. 3. Foresight of a charge whereunto a man is likely to be called should make him prepare himself, and resolve beforehand on doing the duties of that calling, as David did before he was possessed of the king-dom: *when I shall receive the congregation I will judge uprightly.* 4. When a land is destitute of godly and gra-cious governors, the whole country is left loose, both in the matter of religion and civil justice, as was seen in Saul's time before David was settled: *the earth and all the inhabi-tants thereof are dissolved.* 5. Kingdoms and common-wealths have their pillars whereupon they should stand, to wit, religious and righteous government: for, *I will judge uprightly,* in the second verse, is as good as, *I will bear up the pillars thereof,* in the third verse. 6. Those that mind the reformation of a land should be sensible of the desolation of it, and have not only will, but also skill and place of power, to set matters in a right frame, as here the psalmist, after saying, *the land and all the inhabitants thereof are dissolved,* addeth, *I bear up, or shall bear up the pillars of it.* And here, whatsoever David speaketh, or could say, was but a shadow of what is to be found in Christ, of whom he is a type: for the kingdom and country is ill guided where Christ reigneth not; but when people subject themselves to him, he sets the kingdom or country upon true pillars, and sus-taineth all by his power.

4. *I said unto the fools, Deal not foolishly; and to the wicked, Lift not up the horn:*

5. *Lift not up your horn on high: speak not with a stiff neck.*

In the third place, he calleth to mind his own prophecy of the change of affairs, and advertisement given by him before to his adversaries not to behave so insolently as they did. Whence learn, 1. Even in time of trouble the godly, by the light of God's word, may be enabled to foresee and prophesy of the overturning of the wicked from the top of their preferment: *I said unto the fools, Deal not so foolishly,* saith the psalmist. 2. When the prophecy, uttered accord-ing to God's word, is like to take effect, it is no small com-fort for believers to call to remembrance acts of their believ-ing beforehand, what they saw in their own time: *I said to the foolish, Deal not so foolishly,* is a sort of triumph over his enemies here. 3. Such as are acquainted with true wisdom justly account all wicked men to be fools, forsakers of God's teaching, and followers of their own wit and will, to the ruin of their own bodies, souls, houses, and fame : *I said unto the fools.* 4. The fruits of a wicked man's prosperity are pride, vain-glory, audacious boasting against the godly, wherein they grow more and more insolent against all warnings of God's word, as this reproof importeth: *deal not foolishly, lift not up the horn : lift it not on high, speak not with a stiff neck.*

6. *For promotion* cometh *neither from the east, nor from the west, nor from the south.*

7. *But God* is *the judge : he putteth down one and setteth up another.*

From the first reason of his admonition unto the wicked, learn, 1. As the cause of men's pride in a wicked course is the forgetting of God and of his government in the world, on the one hand, and a strong conceit of their own ability to compass their designs by their own wit, power, and industry, on the other hand; so the way of wisdom to remedy the evil, is to consider that God governeth the world, and that men are nothing but what he pleaseth to make them: *promotion cometh neither from the east, nor from the west, nor from the south ;* that is, howsoever, or from whence soever, preferment to places of power in the world seemeth to come, yet the disposing of places is from a higher hand. 2. Places of power and preferment are disposed of only by the wise and righteous pleasure, and determination of the supreme Ruler of the world : *but God is judge.* He opposeth God the judge's determination to all appearances from second causes. 3. As God hath a mind, for the glory of his grace, to try, or to correct, or to comfort and employ some men in his service, so he putteth them down or setteth them up; and as he hath a mind to have the glory of his justice displayed on others, so he setteth them up or putteth them down: *God is judge ; he putteth down one, and setteth up another.*

8. *For in the hand of the Lord there is a cup, and the wine is red ; it is full of mixture ; and he poureth out of the same : but the dregs thereof, all the wicked of the earth shall wring them out,* and *drink them.*

From the second reason of the admonition given to the wicked, learn, 1. As the Lord wisely distributeth his benefits and temporal comforts among men, to testify his goodness to his creatures; so also afflictions and calamities are measured out by him unto men, to testify his justice and indignation against sin : *for in the hand of the Lord is a cup ;* that is, a measure of affliction proportioned unto them for whom it is prepared. 2. This measure of affliction ordained for each man, is prepared for the time appointed, like drink, ready for the mouth of him to whose head the cup shall be put : it is a cup with *wine* in it, *in God's hand,* ready to be set to any man's head he pleaseth. 3. The affliction is like strong wine, quickly piercing through all the man's veins who drinketh it, and cleaving fast unto him : *the wine is red.* 4. The Lord hath, as it were, both hot and cooling waters, whereby he mitigateth the cup of calamities to some, and increaseth the sense of his fiery indignation to others : *it is full of mixture ;* or it is perfectly mixed as the case requireth. 5. What is each man's measure of calamities, however mixed when it is executed, all is in God's dispensation : *he poureth forth of the same* into the mouth and belly of every person as he pleaseth. 6. The calamities of the wicked follow ofttimes after the godly have drunk the first draughts of the Lord's cup. It is toward the bottom and dregs when the wicked drink; the hottest wrath and heaviest indignation is reserved for them, and none of them shall escape, how long soever their judgment shall be delayed : *but the dregs thereof all the wicked of the earth shall drink.* 7. The wicked shall be no less accessory to the drawing on of their own calamities, than he that wringeth the dregs to draw out more liquor for himself to drink is accessory to his own drunkenness and damage : *the dregs thereof all the wicked of the earth shall wring them out, and drink them ;* their vanity, pride, greediness, lust, ambition, envy, and pleasant courses of sinning, wherein they delight themselves whilst they are drinking in iniquity as an ox doth water, shall be their destruction, as in point of merit, so also in point of the means of their own overthrow.

9. *But I will declare for ever ; I will sing praises to the God of Jacob.*

10. *All the horns of the wicked also will I cut off ; but the horns of the righteous shall be exalted.*

In the last place, David promiseth to make this holy and

wise dispensation of justice upon the wicked and mercy toward the godly, the matter of his song in God's praise.
Whence learn, 1. However matters seem to go, how deep
soever the godly drink of the cup of calamities, yet the believers in God shall ever have matter of joy in God and of
praising him: *but I will declare for ever*, saith the psalmist,
I will sing praises to the God of Jacob; yea, sanctified
affliction shall be a part of their joy and praising of God.
2. It delighteth the godly to be in the same covenant, and
of the same faith, with those that are commended by God in
the Scriptures: *I will sing praises*, saith he, *to the God of
Jacob.* 3. As a sincere heart resolveth never to be weary
in God's service, so may it be assured never to want matter
of great joy; for, after he hath said, *I will declare for ever*,
he then addeth, *I will sing praises to the God of Jacob.* 4.
It is the magistrates' part, as they have authority in their
supreme or subordinate places, to cut short the power of
wicked men: *all the horns of the wicked also will I cut off*,
saith David; which promise he did not cease to execute, by
turning every man, indifferently, whom he did not judge to
be regenerated, out of his place, and by taking course how
every man whom he found in place, should be bound to apply
his power for the good of religion and justice, as the history
of the Scripture showeth; and by this means especially David
reformed the church of Israel, and this was the way of his
true policy, to cut off *all the horns of the wicked:* not to
kill, or banish, or forfeit, or put from all place of power and
trust, all those leading men who opposed and maligned him
under king Saul; but by causing them all to concur with
him to set up true religion, and bring up the ark to mount
Zion, and to administer justice to the subjects in their several
places. Thus, by binding all men to religion and justice,
and ordaining that wickedness should have no horn or power
for it, but all bound to be against it, *he cut off all the horns
of the wicked.* And because the civil magistrate or ecclesiastical governors are able to do in their courts externally
not so much as were needful, the real effecting of what here
is undertaken by David belongeth to the antitype, Christ;
for he only can say, and make his words good : *all the horns
of the wicked will I cut off.* 5. The godly shall be victorious over all their wicked opposers, and righteousness shall
bear them better out, and shall purchase more help and power

unto them, than any course the wicked take to have their power established against them: *the horns of the righteous shall be exalted.*

PSALM LXXVI.

To the chief musician on Neginoth.   A psalm or song of Asaph.

This psalm of praise was given forth upon occasion of some great deliverance of the church, such as that was when Sennacherib's host was destroyed, or some other like overthrow given to the enemy.

The sum of the psalm is this: The Lord is glorious in his church, and greatly to be praised by his people, set down ver. 1, 2. The reasons given for this are six: the first, ver. 3; the second, ver. 4; the third, ver. 5, 6; the fourth, ver. 7; the fifth, ver. 8, 9; the sixth, ver. 10; the use whereof, with a reason for it, is set down ver. 11, 12.

From the inscription, learn, 1. The visible church hath need to be stirred up to the work of thanksgiving unto, and praising of God, no less than to any other duty; for this duty is no less needful, no less spiritual, no less difficult and disagreeable to our carnal and corrupt natural inclination than any other duty; and usually is more neglected and more slighted than any point of worship, although frequent occasion and cause be given unto it; therefore it is oftenest called for of any.   If we compare this title with others, this is *a song, a psalm,* taught to the church, to stir her up to the praising of God.   2. God had more psalmists, more sweet singers in Israel, than one; David's name is not prefixed here, and the matter is more suitable to a later time than his.   3. We are not to be curious about the penmen of canonical Scripture.   The first author is he to whom we must look most, and on whom we must rest; for, concerning all the Hebrew Bible, we are taught by Christ and his apostles that it was all given by inspiration, and that the holy writers spake as they were moved by the Holy Spirit; for here it is not certain whether Asaph was the name of the writer of it, or whether Asaph be the name of the order of such of Aaron's posterity as were precentors to the church, and had the charge of the music, to whom this psalm was committed for the church's use, as many more psalms in David's time, and after it also, were.   *A psalm or song of Asaph,* or *to Asaph;* the words may bear both alike.

1. *In Judah* is *God known ; his name* is *great in Israel.*

2. In Salem also is his tabernacle, and his dwelling-place in Zion.

From the sum and scope of the psalm set down here, learn, 1. Albeit God be in some sort known in all the world, because of the works of creation, manifesting some way the invisible excellencies of God, yet is he most of all made manifest to his visible church, where his word soundeth, and his works are best interpreted: *in Judah God is known.* 2. Where the knowledge of God's name is most revealed, there should he of duty be most glorified; for albeit Israel many times did not understand, did not acknowledge him, but were more ignorant and neglective of him than the ox or ass were of their owner and master's crib, yet daily among them he manifested his great majesty, and sometimes he made them all acknowledge it, and of duty always they should have magnified his majesty, and so *his name is great in Israel.* 3. The Lord provideth always a place where his church may visibly profess his name and worship him: he will not want a place where he hath a people in covenant bond unto him: *in Salem is his tabernacle.* 4. It is a great glory to the place where God is worshipped, for there also he maketh his residence: *in Salem also, or Jerusalem, is his tabernacle, and his dwelling-place in Zion.* 5. It is not for the worthiness of any people or place, that the Lord is among them, or manifested there; but it is his own free choice, among whom, and where he will reside. The place where the vile Canaanite had been, and the place longest possessed and abused by the Canaanite, will he choose for his chief dwellings; he will turn the Canaanite's Salem to be Jerusalem: and the stronghold of the Jebusites to be the place of his temple; therefore, saith he, *in Salem* rather than *Jerusalem is his tabernacle, and his dwelling-place in Zion.*

3. There brake he the arrows of the bow, the shield, and the sword, and the battle. Selah.

The first reason of God's praise is taken from the Lord's fighting at Jerusalem against the enemies of the church, and discomfiting them. Whence learn, 1. The greatest overthrow given to armies will be found in their fighting against God's church : there in special manner *brake he the arrows of the bow, &c.* 2. In the deliverance of the church the Lord will be seen to do all the work: *there brake he the arrows.* 3. As there are no means or instruments fit to destroy men which the enemy will not make use of against the church : so there is no weapon formed against her which shall prosper when she relieth on her Lord : *there brake he the arrows of the bow, the shield, and the sword, and the battle.*

4. *Thou* art *more glorious* and *excellent than the mountains of prey.*

The second reason of God's praise is, because he is more glorious then all the kings and kingdoms of the world, wherein the cruel and beastly raging enemies of his church have their strength and strongholds. Whence learn, 1. Those kingdoms and powers which do not subject themselves to God or Christ the king of saints, are to be esteemed as mountains where wild and ravenous beasts lie, all of them according as they are more mighty, oppressing the weaker; for they are called here, mountains of prey, or powers maintaining all oppression, as mountains give shelter to ravenous beasts, which live upon prey. 2. Whatsoever excellency is to be found in the kingdoms of the world, wherein men glory, as wisdom, riches, strength, multitude, courage, or what else can be imagined, is all nothing to the matter of gloriation which the church hath in God : *thou,* saith the psalmist unto God, *art more glorious than the mountains of prey.*

5. *The stout-hearted are spoiled, they have slept their sleep ; and none of the men of might have found their hands.*

6. *At thy rebuke, O God of Jacob, both the chariot and horse are cast into a dead sleep.*

The third reason of God's praise is, because he evacuated, and made of no use unto the enemy, whatsoever they put their confidence in. Whence learn, 1. Whatsoever strength, courage, wit, or any other point of perfection any man hath, God who gave it, can take it away when he pleaseth; yea, can make it a means of hardening his heart in carnal confidence, to engage him in a business for a mischief to him, that he may lose all whereunto he leaned : *the stout-hearted are spoiled, they have slept their sleep, and none of the men of might have found their hands ;* that is, God hath made the

courageous and strong to be found feeble and weak, and unable to save their own goods or lives. 2. Albeit the church
hath no strength in herself, yet the Lord can with a word
of his mouth do all her work, and defeat her enemies : *at
thy rebuke, O God of Jacob, they are cast into a dead sleep.*
3. The more powerful, wise, and stout the enemies of God's
church be, the more should the church rely upon God, and
the more glory doth the Lord get in overthrowing them :
therefore *the stout-hearted men of might, chariots and horse*
are here mentioned.

7. *Thou, even thou, art to be feared ; and who may
stand in thy sight when once thou art angry?*

The fourth reason of God's praise is, because he is so terrible that none can stand before him when he is angry.
Whence learn, 1. When the Lord smiteth the wicked, he warneth his own people to stand in awe; therefore the church
maketh use of what is set down before : *thou, even thou art
to be feared.* 2. Only God is to be feared lest we offend
him, and no man's anger is to be feared in comparison of
provoking God to anger : *thou, even thou art to be feared ;*
and no regard is to be paid to, nor mention made of, any
other to be feared in comparison of him. 3. Man against
man may stand, and wicked men in the time of God's patience may stand : but when the time cometh of God's judging and letting forth his wrath upon his enemies, none can
escape his hand: *who may stand in thy sight, when once thou
art angry ?* 4. The terror of the Lord against his foes, is
the comfort of his people, and the matter as of his praise, so
of their singing and rejoicing, as here is to be seen.

8. *Thou didst cause judgment to be heard from heaven ; the earth feared, and was still,*

9. *When God arose to judgment, to save all the meek
of the earth. Selah.*

The fifth reason of God's praise is, from the experience
of fearful judgments on God's enemies, when he was about
to deliver his people from their oppression. Whence learn,
1. Late mercies and deliverances given to the church, should
renew the thankful memory of old deliveries, as here is done.
2. When ordinary means and advertisements do not make the
persecutors of the church cease, God hath extraordinary
judgments from heaven, whereby he will speak unto his ad-

versaries : *thou didst cause judgments to be heard from heaven.* 3. If by one sort of more mild advertisement or rebuke men cannot be brought into order, by another and more terrible rebuke they shall be made quiet : *thou didst cause judgment to be heard from heaven ; the earth feared and was still.* 4. The property of the Lord's people is to be so acquainted with afflictions, and so sensible of their own sinfulness, that they do not impatiently fret at God's dispensation, even when they are oppressed by men; but study submission unto God, and commit their cause to him : therefore are they called *the meek of the earth.* 5. When the Lord's meek ones are in danger to be swallowed up and destroyed by their oppressors, the Lord, who is the sovereign judge to decide controversies, and to determine who is in the wrong, albeit he be silent for a while, yet will arise in due time, and speak from heaven by judgments, to the terrifying and silencing of proud oppressors : *the earth feared and was still, when God arose to judgment, to save all the meek of the earth.* 6. When the Lord ariseth to save the meek in one place and of one generation, it is an evidence and earnest that he shall arise to save at length all and every one of the meek in every place, in all times after; because his arising for his people, which was now past, is said here to be *to save all the meek of the earth.*

10. *Surely the wrath of man shall praise thee ; the remainder of wrath shalt thou restrain.*

The sixth reason of God's praise is, that he shall make the malice of the adversaries of his people contribute to his glory. Whence learn, 1. Albeit the rage and cruelty of men against the Lord's meek ones, may seem for the present to obscure God's glory, and to tend to his dishonour; yet, when he hath humbled, tried, purified his own, and done his work in mount Zion, all the rage of persecutors shall turn to God's glory undoubtedly : *surely the wrath of man shall praise thee.* 2. When God hath glorified himself in purging his saints and punishing their persecutors, yet the enmity of the wicked world against God's people will not cease; there will be still, as here is presupposed, a remainder of wrath. 3. Let the wrath of the wicked against the godly be ever so great, inveterate, lasting, and unquenchable, yet it shall vent itself only as the Lord sees fitting : he shall moderate the outletting of it, as he seeth expedient for his people's good; it shall not break out to the destruction of the people : *the remainder of wrath shalt thou restrain.*

11. *Vow, and pay unto the Lord your God : let all that be round about him bring presents unto him that ought to be feared.*

12. *He shall cut off the spirit of princes :* he is *terrible to the kings of the earth.*

The use of the former doctrine is, to teach God's people to give unto God that respect and praise which are due to him from them, and to exhort all nations without the compass of the visible church to submit themselves unto him, lest he cut off fearfully the chiefest of them. Whence learn, 1. The use of the Lord's deliverances of his church, which the people of God should make, is to call on God in their troubles, engage themselves to glorify him in word and deed for his mercies, and to entertain the consciousness of their obligation : *vow and pay unto the Lord.* 2. It is not enough to discharge a promised duty to God in outward formality, as the Philistines made their offering to the ark of God, but the godly must do what service they do to God, as to their God, reconciled unto them, and in covenant with them : *vow and pay unto the Lord your God.* 3. The Lord is to be feared and honoured of all that are near to him in covenant or profession, yea or in vicinity of place unto his people and church, where the Lord manifested himself in his ordinances : *let all that be round about him, bring presents to him that ought to be feared.* 4. How terrible soever the power of princes and great men seem unto the Lord's people, when they engage themselves and their subjects against the church; yet, ere they bring forth the ripe grapes of their designs and plots against God's people, God can and will cut off their wisdom, courage, and life, as easily as the branches of a vine tree : *he shall cut off the spirit of princes.* 5. There is greater cause why princes should be afraid of God, than why God's people should be afraid of princes: princes cannot do so much to any one of God's people, as God can do to the highest princes on earth; God can make their fall great according to the height of their place; he can root them out and their posterity, not only from all places of power, but also from all being on the earth; he can make them a terror to themselves; he can destroy them, soul and body; yea, he useth to do this to his adversaries : *he is terrible to the kings of the earth.*

PSALM LXXVII.

To the chief musician, to Jeduthun.   A psalm of Asaph.

This psalm expresseth the deep exercise of the psalmist, troubled with the sense of God's displeasure, and how he wrestled under this condition, and had deliverance from it, which is summarily propounded, v. 1, and made plain more particularly in the rest of the psalm. For, first, he setteth down his trouble of mind, v. 2—4; secondly, his wrestling with the sense of felt wrath, v. 5—9; thirdly, his begun victory by faith, v. 10—12; fourthly, the settling of his mind by consideration of God's manner of dealing with his church of old, to the end of the psalm.

1. *I cried unto God with my voice,* even *unto God with my voice ; and he gave ear unto me.*

In this summary proposition of the psalmist's sad exercise of spirit, and of his delivery out of that condition, learn, That as there are many troubles whereunto God's children are subject (whereof this is one of the most heavy, to be under the sense of the wrath of God, and fear of final cutting off) ; so God hath set down examples of this exercise in some of his dear children, for preparation of those who have not yet been acquainted with the like, and to teach patience and furnish consolation to those who are under such exercises; for here is one of the saints telling us, 1. That his own trouble in this kind was so pressing, as it made him cry. 2. Showing the course he took—*he cried to God,* and put the whole powers of soul and body to a bensal, in seeking God : *I cried to God with my voice.* 3. That he saw there was no remedy for this evil, save from God above, to whom he made his address with resolution to hold unto God only : *even unto God with my voice I cried.* 4. That at length he prevailed and received his request, graciously granted unto him : *and he gave ear to me ;* and so he was relieved.

2. *In the day of my trouble I sought the Lord : my sore ran in the night, and ceased not: my soul refused to be comforted.*

3. *I remembered God, and was troubled : I complained, and my spirit was overwhelmed.   Selah.*

4. *Thou holdest mine eyes waking : I am so troubled that I cannot speak.*

Asaph declareth this his sad exercise more specially; and, first, how great his trouble was. Whence learn, 1. The fearing and feeling the sense of God's wrath and displeasure, are of all troubles the chief; and challenge to themselves most deservedly the name of trouble, or straitening affliction, as if the psalmist had never known any trouble in comparison of them. 2. Albeit the sense of God's wrath and displeasure, while it lasteth, seemeth a sort of eternity, as, *shall I never be remembered?* and such like expressions declare; yet, when the trouble is gone, it is counted but a short time, but a day : *in the day of my trouble,* saith he, now being relieved. 3. As in this trouble most of God's face or comfortable presence is withdrawn; so nothing in this case can content a godly soul, till he find the Lord reconciled, and his gracious face shining again toward him : *in the day of my trouble I sought the Lord.* The wicked, in such a case, will, either not seek God at all, but some earthly comfort, or but take an essay what they can have by calling on God : they will not make it their work to seek him. 4. The sense of wrath giveth a sore wound unto a man's spirit, like to a wound in the body, which is like to bleed unto death : *my sore ran in the night.* 5. Trouble of conscience, as it is like a deadly wound; so is it also like a filthy boil, venting rotten issue : for many are the sins which the conscience casteth up in this case, which to look upon, causeth pain and loathing : *my sore,* or my plague, my stroke by thy hand, *ran in the night.* 6. There is no healing of this wound, no easing of this sore, no cleansing of the conscience, no quieting of a man's spirit, till God whom the soul seeketh, show himself physician; the evil continueth still and groweth : *my sore ran in the night, and ceased not.* 7. Where misery seemeth remediless, there the sad soul fitteth itself to endless sorrow : and as it is hopeless of relief, so it is heartless to seek comfort, yea what earthly comforts are offered for the relief of a spiritual wound, are but a burden to a broken spirit : *my soul refused to be comforted.* Nothing can satisfy a soul which is sensible of God's displeasure, save the sense of God's favour. 8. A troubled spirit hath many thoughts; for it runs out in meditation, calleth for the records of the memory, but can find nothing to fix upon, save God himself : *I remembered God.* 9. It is possible that the matter of

most comfort at some time may give no ease; the sweet
promises of grace, when a soul is not able to apply them,
yea, the thought of God himself and his goodness, may augment grief, when the conscience presenteth his abused favours as the cause of God's present felt wrath : *I remembered God and was troubled.*   10. Lamentation and complaints, when vented and not eased with following comfort,
but double the grief : *I complained, and my spirit was overwhelmed.*   11. Redoubled thoughts of a perplexed soul, cast
it over into confusion, and a sort of wound : *I complained,
and my spirit was overwhelmed.*   12. A wounded spirit is
able to bereave a man of the night's rest, and affect the
body with a share of its miserable condition : *thou holdest
mine eyes waking.*   13. When a soul could possibly desire
to ease its grief with a little forgetting of it, and seek a
sleep when the body is now weary; it may fall out, that
even thus much ease may be refused to a saint for a time,
which must be looked on as God's hand, for the further exercise of the Lord's sick child : *thou holdest mine eyes waking.*   14. Trouble not lenified nor mitigated, groweth to
such a height, that it stops the use of natural powers: *I am
so troubled, that I cannot speak.*   The sorrows of a soul
sensible of God's wrath, are unspeakable, neither can the
tongue utter them, nor the mind indite to the tongue what
it feeleth.

5. *I have considered the days of old, the years of
ancient times.*

6. *I call to remembrance my song in the night: I
commune with mine own heart; and my spirit made
diligent search.*

7. *Will the Lord cast off for ever? and will he be
favourable no more?*

8. *Is his mercy clean gone for ever? doth his promise fail for evermore?*

9. *Hath God forgotten to be gracious? hath he in
anger shut up his tender mercies?   Selah.*

In the second place, the psalmist setteth down his wrestling, and how, after he was overwhelmed, he fell again about
the using of all means to be relieved, considering the Lord's
work of old with others of his children, and his own exper-

ience, and what could be the cause of the change, v. 6, and how the Lord's unchangeableness in his loving-kindness towards his own, might help him, v. 7—9. Whence learn, 1. Were our cause ever so desperate, yet must we not give over, but gather strength after swounding, and use all means of relief, as the psalmist here doth. 2. To cast an eye upon the Lord's manner of dealing with his saints, mentioned in Scripture, as the psalmist did, who had the books of Moses and Job at least to make use of, is one chief means of comforting a troubled sinner, and of strengthening the faith of a weak wrestler: *I have considered the days of old, and the years of ancient times.* 3. To call to mind its own experiences of deliveries and consolations received after trouble, and its own observations made upon its own experiences, is also a good means for gathering strength and comfort for a soul under the sense of wrath : *I call to remembrance my song in the night.* 4. To search our ways, and to seek out diligently what cause in us we can find, which might procure such desertion and sense of wrath that we lie under, is a third holy means for deliverance from the straits of a troubled conscience; *I communed with my own heart, and my spirit made diligent search.* 5. Albeit it be possible, when all the former means are used, and diligent search is made by our conscience, what may be the reason of our hard exercise, that for all that we find no consolation, no ease, nor relief; yet the use of these means will witness for our wise and upright dealing, and be evidences of our endeavour and diligence in duties, as here we see the prophet making mention of his diligence for this end. 6. Albeit it be no strange thing for a wounded spirit to have suggestions cast in for the overthrow of faith, yea to have a sense of wrath speaking no less than what the temptation unto desperation allegeth; yet the nature of faith is such, that it cannot yield, but must fight against the temptation, as a thing which cannot be true, cannot be admitted, as this disputation of the psalmist giveth evidence : *will the Lord cast off for ever? and will he be favourable no more?* 7. The Lord may seem to cast a man off, and to stop the course of his wonted favour toward him, but this exercise is only for a time. It is not possible that God should cast off for ever the soul that cannot endure to be thrust from him: it is not possible that God should not be

R

favourable to such as have had experience of his favour, and long to have new proofs thereof : *will the Lord cast off for ever ? will he be favourable no more ?* Which question, *will he do so and so*, is this much in effect, as if he had said, it is not possible that the Lord should do so, albeit it seem he will do so.   8. When the consciousness of sin maketh objection against faith, then faith makes its defence in God's mercy, and the constancy of the course of mercy, where grace is begun to run; yea faith will not yield to a contrary thought : *is his mercy clean gone for ever ?*   9. The troubled conscience hungering after the sense of mercy, hath not only God's merciful nature and God's constancy in his good-will, but also his promises to lean to, for supporting itself.   Therefore after mention made of God's favour and mercy, he mentioneth here his promise also.   10. It is possible that for a time no promise may occur to a wounded spirit, which is fit for its present condition; at least no promise which it dare or is able to apply; yea it is possible that the conditional frame of the promises being made to such as are so and so qualified, may seem to pertain nothing to the troubled conscience, yet faith will not quit its interest in the promise, but will expect good according to the promise at last : *doth his promise fail for evermore ?*   11. As it is the Lord's nature to be gracious to such as come to him in the sense of their unworthiness; so faith layeth hold on him as gracious, and will never admit a suggestion of any change in him, whatsoever seem to be in his dispensation : *hath God forgotten to be gracious ?* this is to faith an absurdity and impossibility.   12. The compassions of God toward the miserable when they come before him are like a running fountain, that cannot restrain itself; yet may it seem to be shut up, and wrath and displeasure to run in the place thereof, when God is pleased to exercise his child with the sense of wrath against sin; but faith will not admit this seeming for a certainty : *hath he in anger shut up his tender mercies ?*   This is a saying which a believer must abhor to give way unto, and yet may be assaulted with, and brangled, and weakened by the temptation of it.

10. *And I said, This* is *my infirmity :* but I will remember *the years of the right hand of the most High.*

11. *I will remember the works of the Lord: surely I will remember thy wonders of old.*

12. *I will meditate also of all thy work, and talk of thy doings.*

In the third place is set down the begun victory of faith, wherein the believer checketh himself for hearkening so much unto sense, for admitting the suggestions of misbelief into a disputation, and resolveth to make use of the grounds of faith and of his former comfortable experiences, v. 10, and of the wonderful dealing of God with others of his saints before, v. 11, and to settle his faith on God's word, confirmed by his works, and to set himself to give glory unto God, v. 12. Whence learn, 1. In the inward exercise of God's children, after a while's darkness cometh light; after grief, comfort; and after wrestling, cometh victory, as here we see. 2. The trouble and disquietness which arise from fear of utter rejection by God, are from the root of natural unbelief and inlack of the strength of faith : *this is my infirmity*, saith he, as being now assured that matters were not as they seemed to him, concerning God's merciful affection to him. 3. Weakness of faith, and fear of utter wrath, are sicknesses whereunto God's children are subject, but whereof they will certainly recover : sicknesses not unto death : *this is my infirmity.* 4. Our outgate from inward trouble, and our victory over it, begin at the right side of our own weakness, of our own faults, and of a right judging of ourselves for them : *and, I said this is my infirmity.* 5. The remembrance of the experiences of former changes which we have found wrought by God's great power, serveth to make us both patient under a sad condition, and hopeful to come out of it: *I will remember the years of the right hand of God.* 6. Albeit we do not see how our comfort, delivery, and outgate from trouble shall come, yet may we find solid ground to expect that it shall come, if we consider aright God's sovereignty over all creatures, that he is *most high*, and the omnipotency of his right hand, and his continuance, being the eternal, unchangeable one, and the same from year to year, from age to age : *I will remember the years of the right hand of the most High.* From this ground he expecteth that he shall yet have experience of the omnipotency of a sovereign and constant God, working for his consolation. 7. When faith beginneth to recover after its infirmity or sickness, it will make use of memory, meditation, judgment, and speech, which were all bound up before : *I will remember, meditate, and talk.*   8. We must not think to come out of perplexity, out of sense of wrath, out of trouble of conscience, out of hard exercises of faith by having great consolations, high and ravishing joys of the Spirit at the first hand; but must be content to come creeping out of trouble by little and little: for here the psalmist under the deepest sense of God's displeasure, must use all ordinary means, and wrestle with bitter temptations, till he come to such height as is expressed, v. 7—9, and, for an outgate, must begin and reprove his own misbelief, dispute for the help of his faith, taking argument from his experience of God's power and goodwill, and God's dealing with others before him.   9. The works of God, when they are looked on cursorily, or lightly past by, cannot be discerned, but when they are well considered, they will be found wonderful : *I will remember the works of the Lord, surely I will remember thy wonders of old.*   10. It is good for a soul in a hard exercise, to raise itself from thinking of God and of his works, speaking unto God directly; no ease or relief will be found, till address be made unto himself, till we turn our face toward him, and direct our speech unto him, as here the psalmist doth, from the midst of the eleventh verse to the end of the psalm. 11. Estimation of any of God's works, and good gotten by meditation on some of his works, are able to engage the heart to a deeper consideration of all his works : *I will meditate also of all thy works,* saith he.   12. He that would have profit by God's works, must bridle the levity of his own mind, which cannot stay fixed in the consideration, till it be tied in meditation: *I will meditate of all thy works.* 13. When we have fed our own souls upon God's works, we should study to make use of what we have learned thereby, to the good of others and the glory of God : *I will meditate of all thy works, and talk of all thy doings.*

13. *Thy way, O God,* is *in the sanctuary ; who* is so *great a God as* our *God ?*

14. *Thou* art *the God that doest wonders ; thou hast declared thy strength among the people.*

In the last place, the psalmist confirmeth his faith, and settleth his mind, by consideration of the Lord's dealing with his people, recorded in holy Scripture, whereof he speaketh; first, in general, v. 13, 14, then more specially, of the bringing of his people out of Egypt through the wilderness, terribly discomfiting their enemies, and tenderly leading them, as his own flock, by weak and few instruments. Whence learn, 1. When the heart of a man is turned toward the Lord, then the veil of darkness, confusion, and misbelief is removed; he can justify the Lord in all that he doeth, as most holy and just; as here we see in the psalmist, who, since he began to direct himself toward God, can now say to him, *thy way, O God, is in the sanctuary.* 2. There is no understanding of God's dealing with us, nor can any right construction be made of his exercising us, except we come to the Lord's ordinances, where his word, his oracles of Scripture, expound his works perfectly: *thy way, O God, is in the sanctuary.* 3. When the works and ways of God are looked upon by the light of the word, in his sanctuary or church, and God is looked to through his works and word, then is a soul forced to admire his holiness, wisdom, justice, power, and goodness, above all comparison: *who is so great a God as our God?* 4. The trial of the believer's conscience with fears and suspicions of God's affection unto him, endeth in admiration and exaltation of God, in believing more firmly in him, in magnifying the grace of his being in covenant with him, in acknowledging his own blessedness and the blessedness of all other believers, for having him for their God: *who is so great a God as our God?* 5. So much in general may be seen of God's dealing with his people, as may quiet a man in his own particular case, who is troubled about God's dispensation toward him: for when Israel in Egypt was put to such straits, that they saw nothing but rooting of them out with cruelty and oppression, God wrought so well, so wisely, so powerfully, and so graciously for them, that all their hard exercise was turned to their great comfort, and God's greater glory. This, in general, is the use that the psalmist maketh of God's dealing with his people, and he findeth it applicable to his own condition: *thou art the God that doest wonders.* 6. When we cannot see how it is likely or possible that we can be extricated out of the difficulties we are cast into, especi-

ally in our spiritual condition, we are obliged to give unto
God the glory of doing above all things we can conceive,
for the good of those that desire to be his subjects: *thou art
the God that doest wonders.* 7. What God hath convinced
the world of already, concerning what he can do for his
people, may satisfy every particular soul of his wisdom,
power, and goodness toward itself, when it draweth toward
him, as one of his people; for this use the psalmist maketh
of God's doing for his people: *thou hast declared thy strength
among thy people.*

15. *Thou hast with* thine *arm redeemed thy people,
the sons of Jacob and Joseph. Selah.*

16. *The waters saw thee, O God, the waters saw
thee ; they were afraid : the depths also were troubled.*

17. *The clouds poured out water ; the skies sent out
a sound : thine arrows also went abroad.*

18. *The voice of thy thunder* was *in the heaven : the
lightnings lightened the world : the earth trembled and
shook.*

The psalmist descendeth more specially to the consideration of the redemption of Israel out of Egypt, (which is a
representation of the spiritual redemption of his people,)
whom, at the time when they were in the deepest misery,
and least able to help themselves, were most oppressed by
the enemies, and, for their own disposition, were in a most
sinful condition, and in a desperate mood against the means
and instruments of their delivery ; God delivered : he removed all the difficulties which might hinder their outgate
and escape from misery ; whence he might strongly reason
for his own comfort, that God would not fail to deal graciously with his soul, who was seeking favour from God, and
a renewed sense of reconciliation with him. Hence learn,
1. That no soul can be under such sense of wrath and desolation, but he may draw comfort from the great work of
the redemption of lost sinners : for, if, when we were enemies,
we were reconciled to God by the death of his Son, much
more being reconciled, we shall be saved from wrath by his
life. And this spiritual redemption was figured by the
bodily delivery of Israel out of Egypt : *thou hast with thine
arm redeemed thy people, the sons of Jacob and Joseph.*

2. It is by reason of the covenant that people receive deliverances, and consolations, and proofs of God's power working for them : therefore doth he style them sons of Jacob from their interest in God, and God's interest in them by covenant : *thou hast redeemed thy people.* 3. No obstacle, how great soever, can stand in the way of the delivery and comfort of God's people, but God can and will remove it; were it as the Red sea, so soon as he manifests himself, it will get out of the way as affrighted at his majesty : *the waters saw thee, O God, the waters saw thee; they were afraid : the depths also were troubled.* 4. The commotions which God hath made in heaven by rain, hailstone, thunder, fire, and lightning, when he would show himself for his people and against their enemies, testify sufficiently what God can and will do for his own children, who draw near unto him ; and how he will rebuke every adverse power which is against them: *the clouds poured out water, the skies sent out a sound ; thine arrows went abroad, the voice of thy thunder was in heaven; the lightnings lightened the world, the earth trembled and shook.* Whether we refer these words to what God did in plaguing Egypt, before he brought out his people ; or after, when he showed his anger in pursuing the Egyptians in their flight, when they were seeking to escape out of the Red sea ; or to what the Lord did in fighting for his people against the Canaanites, they teach the same doctrine to us.

19. *Thy way is in the sea, and thy path in the great waters, and thy footsteps are not known.*

20. *Thou leddest thy people like a flock by the hand of Moses and Aaron.*

He closeth his meditation with two observations. One is, that the Lord's ways are past finding out, which he indicateth by *making a way through the Red sea*, where never one went before, and never one could follow after ; the other observation is, that God can save his people by how few and weak instruments he pleaseth. Whence learn, 1. The Lord draweth deep in the working out the delivery and salvation of his own people, bringing them first unto extremity of danger, and then making a plain and clear escape from all their straits: *thy way is in the sea*, where no man can wade, except God be before him, and where any man may walk, if God take him by the hand, and lead him through. 2. What God is in working, when he engages his children in dangers, and which way he is going when he leads them into overflowing troubles and deep waters, they cannot understand, till he hath done his work : *thy path is in the great waters*. 3. A particular reason of every thing that God doeth, can no man find out : for the which cause the Lord craveth submission of all his children in their exercises, as he did of Job: *thy footsteps are not known*. 4. Whether men see the reasons of God's dealing with them or not, the Lord hath a care of his weak and witless people, as a shepherd hath of his flock, and is a gracious leader of his people that follow him : *thou leadest thy people like a flock*. 5. The Lord hath his means and instruments, of whose ministry he maketh use : and those, albeit they be few and weak, yet shall he do his greatest works by them, according as he doth employ them : *thou leddest thy people as a flock, by the hand of Moses and Aaron*.

END OF FIRST VOLUME.

A COMMENTARY ON THE PSALMS

VOLUME II

BRIEF

EXPLICATION OF THE PSALMS.

PSALM LXXVIII.

Maschil of Asaph.

In this psalm the Lord's Spirit stirreth up his people to make a right use of the Lord's works of justice and mercy set down in Holy Scripture; and to this end he giveth account of God's dealing very mercifully with his people, and never in justice, but when mercy was abused : and he showeth also the people's dealing with God unthankfully and deceitfully, whether he dealt mercifully or in justice with them.

This psalm may be divided thus: After a preface to prepare the hearer for attention and observation of what he was to deliver, v. 1—4, he bringeth forth, first, the evidence of God's gracious care of his people, in giving them his blessed word, to teach them faith and obedience, v. 5—8; secondly, the evidence of God's judgment against his people, who were put to flight before their foes, when they believed not the Lord, and made no use of his works among them, v. 9—11; thirdly, he setteth down how great things God did for them in Egypt, and in the wilderness, v. 12—16; fourthly, how they made no better use of these mercies, than to tempt God and provoke him to wrath, v. 17—20; fifthly, how for their tempting God, he was angry at them for their unbelief, and not considering the miraculous feeding of them with manna, v. 21—25, and how in wrath he satisfied their lust by sending quails, for them to eat of flesh their fill, v. 26—29; sixthly, how because they repented not of their provocation, the Lord plagued them, and they went on in their misbelief and disobedience, and God went on in the course of multiplying judgments on them, and cutting off multitudes of them, v. 30—33; seventhly, how they at last made a fashion of repenting and seeking God, but proved in effect nothing but flattering and dissembling hypocrites, inconstant in the covenant, v. 34—37; eighthly, how the Lord in mercy pitied and spared them many a time, notwithstanding all their provocations of his justice against them, v. 38—41; ninthly, he setteth down the prime cause of all this their sin and misery—because they marked not, or made no use of the difference that God put between the Egyptians and them ; nor how for their cause he had plagued the Egyptians with plague after plague, v. 42—51, and brought their fathers safely out of Egypt when their enemies were drowned before their eyes, v. 52, 53; tenthly, he setteth down how the Lord perfected their journey to Canaan, and brought them to the possession of it, thrusting out the Canaanites, that they might have place, v. 54, 55; eleventhly, how they for all this, provoked God to anger with their idolatry and superstition, v. 56—58 ; twelfthly, how the Lord for this their oft-repeated provocation, miserably vexed them in the days of Eli and Samuel, giving over his ark into the Philistines' hand, and plaguing their country with a variety of plagues, v. 59—64; thirteenthly, how God of his free mercy put his enemies to shame, and restored religion and liberties to church and kingdom, v. 65, 66; and, last of all, how he brought them to a settled condition under David, who was a type of Christ, v. 67—72.

1. *Give ear, O my people, to my law : incline your ears to the words of my mouth.*

2. *I will open my mouth in a parable ; I will utter dark sayings of old ;*

3. *Which we have heard and known, and our fathers have told us.*

4. *We will not hide* them *from their children, shewing to the generations to come the praises of the Lord, and his strength, and his wonderful works that he hath done.*

In the preface, the Spirit of the Lord calleth for attention unto the doctrine which he is to deliver, for four reasons. The first, because it was his law, and the words of his mouth directed to his covenanted people, v. 1; the next, because this doctrine was mysterious and full of hidden wisdom, v. 2; the third, because it is an ancient doctrine delivered to the church of old, and transmitted unto them that succeeded, v. 3; the fourth, because it must be known and transmitted to the succeeding posterity, and following generations of the church, for the glory of God's wonderful working for his church, v. 4. Whence learn, 1. Such is our dullness and slowness of heart to understand and believe what the Lord saith to us, that we have great need to be admonished and stirred up to attention and hearing with faith : *give ear, O my people,* saith the Spirit by his prophet. 2. The authority of divine doctrine should tie our ears to hear it reverently, believingly, and obediently; it is the Lord's law, and the words of his mouth, speaking by his prophet to us: *give ear, O my people, to my law, incline your ears to the words of my mouth.* 3. Albeit the word of the Lord be plain to the attentive believer, yet to the inattentive misbeliever it is a hidden mystery; and for this reason we have need to hear attentively and believingly : *I will open my mouth in a parable, I will utter dark sayings.* 4. The word of the Lord hath true antiquity with it; divine doctrine is no new doctrine; and for this reason should we hear it attentively and believingly : *I will utter dark sayings of old.* 5. Albeit the word of the Lord be a mystery, and dark sayings to the misbelieving multitude of the world, yet it is understood, received, and believed by the true members of the church from age to age; therefore the prophet, speaking of himself and of the godly in his time, saith of their parables and dark speeches : *which we have heard and known, and our fathers have told us.* 6. Those are worthy of the name of fathers in the church, in relation to posterity, who transmit the truth of God contained in Scripture, such as here is set down in this psalm; and this is the only infallible sort of tradition which delivereth to posterity what God delivered to the prophets, or their predecessors by Scripture, such as is the doctrine delivered in this psalm : *which we,* saith he, *have heard and known, and our fathers have told us, we will not hide from our children.* 7. The godly in every age ought to have the same care to transmit the word of truth to their posterity, which their ancestors had to transmit it to them, and to pay the debt they owe to their faithful ancestors unto succeeding generations : *we will not hide them from their children, showing to the generations to come, &c.* 8. The subject-matter of sound and saving doctrine, is the setting forth the glory of God in his attributes, and wonderful operations for his people : *showing to the generations to come the praises of the Lord, and his wonderful works that he hath done.*

5. *For he established a testimony in Jacob, and appointed a law in Israel, which he commanded our fathers, that they should make them known to their children ;*

6. *That the generation to come might know* them, even *the children* which *should be born,* who *should arise and declare* them *to their children ;*

7. *That they might set their hope in God, and not forget the works of God, but keep his commandments :*

8. *And might not be as their fathers, a stubborn and rebellious generation ; a generation* that *set not their heart aright ; and whose spirit was not steadfast with God.*

After the preface, the psalmist bringeth forth a notable evidence of the Lord's care of his church, in giving them his Scriptures and revealed rule of faith and obedience, to be transmitted from one generation to another, v. 5, 6, that they may have faith and hope in God, and obey his commands, v. 7, and not be like such of their predecessors as

were rebellious hypocrites, and backsliders from their covenanted duties, v. 8. Whence learn, 1. One of the chiefest
mercies that can be bestowed on a people, is the giving the
holy Scriptures to them, and revealing to them the way of
salvation, and of the service which God requireth; this is
put in the first room here: *for he established a testimony
in Jacob, and appointed a law in Israel.* 2. God's words
and ordinances appointed in Scripture, are witnesses for
him, of his wisdom, power, holiness, mercy, and justice
against such as do not make use thereof, and a fixed rule
for men's faith and obedience; therefore it is said, *he established a testimony in Jacob, and appointed a law in Israel.*
3. The Scriptures were appointed for a rule, not only for
those to whom they were first directed, but also for the use
of the church in all ages following, which every man must
both study to understand and obey himself, and also teach
his children and those under his charge to understand and
obey, according to his place: he gave a testimony and a
law to the fathers, *that they should make them known to their
children, that the generation to come might know them, even
the children which should be born, who should arise, and declare them to their children.* 4. The end of revealing and
teaching God's word, is to beget and increase men's faith in
God, and dependence on him, as here is set down: the word
was to be declared to their children, *that they might set their
hope in God.* 5. The way to foster faith and hope in God,
is to mark, consider, and keep in a sanctified memory, how
God hath already confirmed his word by his works, and by
pledges both of his power and purpose to perform what he
hath said; therefore he joineth unto the duty of setting their
hope in God, the duty of not *forgetting his works:* intimating that if his works were forgotten, his word would not be
believed, and faith and hope in God would not remain constantly fixed on God. 6. The faith and hope which God
craves of his people to be fixed on him, are such as may
bring forth obedience to his precepts: therefore unto hoping
in God, and not forgetting his works, he addeth, *but keep
his commandments:* so, to have faith in God, upon the terms
of grace offered unto us through a Redeemer, to hope for
and expect the accomplishment of all his promises, to foster
our faith and hope by the consideration of what he hath done
for his people, and uprightly to set ourselves to keep his

commandments, are the sum of true religion. 7. The example of fathers is not to be followed, except wherein they
follow the Lord; where their practice is not conformable to
God's word, we must not be like them : therefore, saith he,
and might not be as their fathers were, stubborn. 8. This
is the natural inclination of corrupt mankind, to go on in
our sinful course obstinately, howsoever God discharge us:
to come contrary to his commands, and flatly to refuse to
obey him; and, if we at any time seem to do him service, to
do it from corrupt principles, and for corrupt ends, still remaining unreconciled to him; and whatsoever we tie ourselves to by covenant, as double-hearted persons, to deal
deceitfully therein, and turn back from it: such were all
the unrenewed Israelites : *a stubborn and rebellious generation, a generation that set not their hearts aright, and whose
spirit was not steadfast with God.* 9. Nothing is able to
bring us off this our natural course and sinful inclination,
unless faith and hope in God, and obedience to his commands, be begun and entertained in us by the word of God;
as the connexion of these duties here, and the order they are
set down in, teach. 10. The Lord will have his people
obediently to hearken to his reproofs, and not reject his
yoke, and meekly to submit to his government, and not re-
bel; to study sincerity of affection toward God, and steadfastness in his covenant, as his condemning these carnal Israelites
for the contrary faults teacheth us.

9. *The children of Ephraim, being armed, and carrying bows, turned back in the day of battle.*
10. *They kept not the covenant of God, and refused
to walk in his law;*
11. *And forgat his works, and his wonders that he
had shewed them.*
In the second place, under the name of Ephraim, as the
most mighty and numerous tribe of all the rest, the psalmist
understandeth all Israel, and shows that the reason of the
Lord's many a time deserting Israel from age to age in the
day of battle, was their carnal confidence in their own strength,
and their not believing in God, their not regarding the covenant they were entered into with God, their disobedience to
his commands, and their not making use of his wonderful
works amongst them. Whence learn, 1. When men are

under greatest guiltiness, and at greatest distance from God, they are least sensible of their sin, least afraid of God's wrath, and most confident of their own abilities, Ephraim and Israel many times lying under breach of covenant and rebellion against God, *being armed, and carrying bows,* think themselves sufficient to encounter their enemies. 2. Multitude of men and arms will not avail a people in the day of battle, when God is against them; God can take wisdom, and courage, and strength, and good success from them : *the children of Ephraim being armed, and carrying bows, turned back in the day of battle.* 3. The cause of general calamities coming upon God's people, will be found in their sins, which have provoked the Lord against them, whereof God will convince them by judgments, when they will not be convinced otherwise : *they turned back in the day of battle;* how came this ? *they kept not the covenant of God.* 4. The Lord was wont, by his word in the mouth of his messengers, to convince his backsliding people of their defection, and to press upon them to return to the rule, and walk in his obedience; but when this admonition and offer are refused, then no wonder judgment come : for here, *they turn back in the day of battle :* when, and wherefore ? *they refused to walk in his law.* 5. As the sanctified and thankful remembrance of God's dealing with his people, is the way to keep the heart in the love, faith, and obedience of God; so the letting of his works, and specially the most remarkable and wonderful works, to slide out of their memory and affection, is the fountain of defection from God, and the cause of falling into carnal courses and confidences, and drawing God's judgments on themselves : *they forgat his works, and his wonders that he had showed them.*

12. *Marvellous things did he in the sight of their fathers, in the land of Egypt,* in *the field of Zoan.*

13. *He divided the sea, and caused them to pass through ; and he made the waters to stand as an heap.*

14. *In the daytime also he led them with a cloud, and all the night with a light of fire.*

15. *He clave the rocks in the wilderness, and gave them drink as* out of *the great depths.*

16. *He brought streams also out of the rock, and caused waters to run down like rivers.*

In the third place, the psalmist setteth down some of those wonderful works done for his people, which should have tied their faith, love, and obedience to the Lord; in special the great work of redemption and delivery of his people out of Egypt; (representing the spiritual redemption and delivery of his own out of the bonds of sin, Satan, and wrath,) how God plagued the Egyptians with wonderful plagues, in the sight of their king and princes in Zoan, the most famous city of Egypt, v. 12; how he dried the Red sea, and made his people go through between mountains of liquid water on both hands, v. 13; how he directed them and refreshed them by a pillar of fire by night, and by a cooling cloud by day, v. 14; and how he furnished them with drink out of the flinty rock in the wilderness, v. 15, 16. Whence learn, 1. The great work of bodily redemption of God's people out of Egypt, and the spiritual redemption of his people from the bondage of sin and misery by Christ, represented thereby, should be inducements to, and props of, faith in God, to all who seek life in him, and a sufficient motive unto love and obedience to him to the world's end; for this end he declared his love, care, and power to save them who enter into covenant with him to be his people: *marvellous things did he, &c.* 2. The works of God done for his people in any former age, oblige those of that age, and all the succeeding ages to make use thereof, for the increase of faith in God, and of love and obedience to God, and answerably aggravate the contrary sins, when they are not so made use of: for, *marvellous things did he in the sight of their fathers,* is the ground of challenging posterity for their defection. 3. The plagues of Egypt should serve for the comfort of God's oppressed people, and for terror to their enemies in all ages: *marvellous things did he in the sight of their fathers, in the land of Egypt.* 4. As the Lord avoweth his people, and owns their quarrel most openly in the sight of king's courts and royal cities; so should his people avow their loyalty to God before all men : otherwise, the more evidently God hath appeared for his people, the more heavy is the challenge of unthankful disobedience; as here it is made the challenge of backsliding Israel, that God in the most open theatre of the kingdom of Egypt, (whereby the fame of his works might go into all the world,) wrought for them and their fathers : *marvellous things did God for them in the field of Zoan,* whence

passage was to many countries.   5. The Lord's making a
way through the Red sea for his people's delivery, is an evidence and pledge once for all, of his power and purpose to
make a way for his own to escape, how great soever their
straits shall be : *he divided the Red sea, and caused them to
pass through.*   6. The Lord's causing the liquid waters to
stand as a wall, heaped up contrary to the nature thereof, is
a pledge of his power and purpose to make the creatures,
which by nature should devour, to be not only harmless,
but helpful also to his people, as need requireth : *he made the
waters to stand as an heap.*   7. The Lord's bringing his
people, both out of Egypt and out of the sea, is a pledge of
his power and purpose to bring his people through all hazards
whatsoever, wherein others shall perish : *he caused his people to pass through.*   8. The Lord's leading on his people
night and day, is a pledge of his constant love to his own
people, and of his power and purpose never to leave nor forsake such as love to have his guiding and conduct : *in the
daytime also he led them.*   9. The Lord's covering of the
host of his people with a cool and comfortable cloud all the
day long, to keep them from the scorching heat of the sun
in the dry and hot wilderness, is a pledge of his kind care of
his people, and constant purpose to give refreshment in the
time of persecution, or whatsoever troubles they shall be exercised with : *in the daytime also he led them with a cloud.*
10. The Lord's making a pillar of fire to burn and shine all
night, for tempering the cold of the night and directing
Israel's steps, when they were to march in the night, is a
pledge of his love, power, and purpose to furnish the light of
direction and consolation unto his own people, as they have
need : *he led them all the night with a light of fire.*   11. As
the Lord's people wanting water in the wilderness through
which their way lay, teacheth us that we may be reduced to
great straits in this life, both bodily and spiritual; so the
Lord's furnishing unto them drink, teacheth, that the Lord
both can and will furnish his people in their necessities, bodily and spiritual : *he clave the rocks in the wilderness, and
gave them drink, as out of the great depths; he brought
streams also out of the rock, and caused waters to run down
like rivers.*

   17. *And they sinned yet more against him, by provoking the most High in the wilderness.*

18. *And they tempted God in their heart, by asking meat for their lust.*

19. *Yea, they spake against God: they said, Can God furnish a table in the wilderness?*

20. *Behold, he smote the rock, that the waters gushed out, and the streams overflowed; can he give bread also? can he provide flesh for his people?*

In the fourth place, the psalmist setteth down how the people made no better use of the foresaid mercies, than to tempt God and provoke him to wrath, by seeking satisfaction to their carnal lusts, and questioning whether or not God was able to satisfy their desires. Whence learn, 1. Unrenewed nature is strongly inclined to meet the Lord's goodness with more and more ingratitude, and to sin over and over again the same sins, when new benefits and old faults being well considered, might teach more wisdom and thankfulness: *they sinned yet more against him.* 2. We are so foolish in our sinning, that we do not consider what we ourselves are, how great a majesty we offend, and what may be the consequence thereof: *they sinned yet more by provoking the most High.* O how unreasonable, uncircumspect, indiscreet, and blind fools are men in their sinning! 3. Albeit we have no outward enticements; albeit the place of our sojourning here should warn us as strangers and pilgrims to abstain from fleshly lusts; albeit we have the word and works of God as witnesses of God, and evidences of his beholding us; yet so pregnant are we in wickedness, so beastly passionate in our carnal affections, and so gross in atheism, that naturally we run on in our own ways, as the horse rusheth into the battle : *they provoked the most High in the wilderness.* 4. When God giveth sufficiently to supply necessities, and we seek to satisfy our lusts; when God hath said and done abundantly already for evidencing his power, justice, truth, and care of our welfare, and we will not rest on him, except he give such other new and extraordinary proofs of his properties, as we prescribe; then do we tempt God, and highly provoke him, by seeking thus to subject him to our direction, will, and carnal affections : *and they tempted God in their heart, by asking meat for their lust.* 5. When the sinful motions of the mind and heart are not controlled, the sin will break forth openly to outward acts tending to God's

dishonour and the evil example of others : *they tempted God
in their heart*, and then *they spake against God.* 6. Words
of misbelief, not disputing against temptations, but in effect
calling in question God's truth, power, care of, or his good-
will to us, are in effect slandering God and bearing false
witness against him: *they spake against God : they said,
Can God furnish, &c.?* 7. The carnal ungodly man hath no
esteem for God, or any of his spiritual benefits, but setteth
him a task of satisfying his fleshly conceits and affections,
which, if God answer not, he misregardeth God : *they said,
Can God furnish a table in the wilderness?* 8. Albeit the
unbeliever be convinced of God's power and goodness to his
people by his works for time past, yet he is not the wiser afterward, when it cometh to the giving credit unto God in
another work : yea, the work which God hath wrought, is
esteemed by him as nothing, except God do farther as the
unbeliever shall prescribe : *behold*, say they, *he smote the
rock, that waters gushed out : but can he give bread also?
can he provide flesh for his people?*

21. *Therefore the Lord heard* this, *and was wroth :
so a fire was kindled against Jacob, and anger also
came up against Israel ;*

22. *Because they believed not in God, and trusted not
in his salvation.*

23. *Though he had commanded the clouds from
above, and opened the doors of heaven,*

24. *And had rained down manna upon them to eat,
and had given them of the corn of heaven.*

25. *Men did eat angels' food : he sent them meat to
the full.*

In the fifth place, the psalmist setteth down how God was
wroth for their unbelief and for their not having a due estimation of the miraculous feeding of them with manna.
Whence learn, 1. Sins continued in, and in special, expressions to the dishonouring of God flowing from misbelief, have
a loud cry in God's ears, and he taketh notice of them for
executing judgment : *therefore the Lord heard this, and was
wroth.* 2. When God is openly dishonoured, the Lord by
open judgment will sanctify his own name on the sinner,
whatsoever be his privilege, and though he were ever so near
to God in external privileges : *so a fire was kindled against*

Jacob, and anger also came up against Israel. 3. Misbelief is a more grievous sin than men esteem it; for it calleth
God's truth, mercy, goodness, power, constancy, and all in
question; even his justice amongst the rest, which if the misbeliever considered, he would not provoke justice against himself by this sin : *wrath came up against Israel, because they
believed not in God.* 4. They do not believe in God, who
study not to depend upon him for salvation, and for whatsoever is necessary to them for salvation : yea they who believe not that the Lord shall bring them out of every strait,
in a way most serving to their welfare, and for his own honour; believe not in him for salvation so solidly as he requireth of them : *they believed not in God,* saith he, *and
trusted not in God's salvation.* 5. The more means, encouragements, helps, and props to support a man's faith are furnished by God, the greater is the sin of unbelief in him : as
the Israelites' misbelief was the greater, for God's miraculous
bringing water out of the rock and manna from the clouds,
so here the Israelites' misbelief is aggravated thus : *they
trusted not in his salvation, though he had commanded the
clouds, and rained down manna.* 6. Man liveth not by
bread, but by the efficacious word of God. It is as easy for
God to rain down victuals out of the clouds, as to make them
grow out of the ground; let him say the word, and it is done :
*he commanded the clouds, and opened the doors of heaven, and
rained down manna on them to eat.* 7. The Lord provideth
well for his own redeemed people; what the earth yieldeth
not to them, he maketh the heaven one way or other to furnish : as, when the Israelites wanted the corn of the earth,
*the Lord gave them of the corn of heaven, so that man did eat
angels' food :* not that there is corn in heaven, or that angels
eat any corporeal food; but manna is so called for the excellency of the food, for it might have served as food to angels, if they had any need of food. 8. The more excellent
the benefit is which God giveth, the greater is the ingratitude
of him who esteemeth and useth it not as becometh; as we
see in Israel's sin, who did not esteem manna, as they should
have done: had the Lord fed them with dust of the earth, or
roots of grass, or any other mean thing, they would have
had no reason to complain: but when he giveth them a new
food, created every morning for their cause, sent down from
heaven as fresh furniture every day, of such excellent colour,

taste, smell, and wholesomeness: what a provocation of God was it, not to be content now; in special, when he gave them abundantly of it ? *He sent them meat to the full.*

26. *He caused an east wind to blow in the heaven ; and by his power he brought in the south wind.*

27. *He rained flesh also upon them as dust, and feathered fowls like as the sand of the sea ;*

28. *And he let it fall in the midst of their camp, round about their habitations.*

29. *So they did eat, and were well filled : for he gave them their own desire ;*

Here the Lord being tempted by a murmuring and unthankful people, to refute their suspicion of his power, sendeth them the most delicate flesh that could be found in the world, quails in abundance, till they were all filled. Whence learn, 1. The Lord, that he may show what regard he hath to satisfy good and lawful desires, sometimes granteth to men their unlawful and unreasonable desires, that holy desires may be the better entertained, and constantly followed till they be granted : as appeareth by the Lord's granting the unreasonable desire of the Israelites after flesh. The Lord hath the commandment of the winds, to make them blow from what airth, and in what measure he pleaseth : *he caused an east wind to blow in the heaven, and by his power he brought in the south wind.* 2. The Lord can gather as many creatures as he mindeth to make use of, at his pleasure; he can gather birds and fowls, make their flight longer or shorter as he pleaseth, make them light and fall where he pleaseth, and bring near to man's hand what he hath a mind to give unto him : *he rained flesh also upon them as dust, and feathered fowls like as the sand of the sea; and he let them fall in the midst of their camp, round about their habitations.* 3. As the Lord granteth lawful desires in mercy, so also he granteth sinful desires in wrath : *so they did eat and were filled, for he gave them their own desire.* 4. When the carnal heart meeteth with the object of his lust, he falleth upon it as a beast doth, without fear of God, or moderation of affection : *they did eat and were filled, for he gave them their own desire.*

30. *They were not estranged from their lust: but while their meat* was *yet in their mouths,*

31. *The wrath of God came upon them, and slew the fattest of them, and smote down the chosen* men *of Israel.*

32. *For all this they sinned still, and believed not for his wondrous works.*

33. *Therefore their days did he consume in vanity, and their years in trouble.*

In the sixth place, the psalmist setteth down their impenitency continued in, and the Lord's judgments poured out, one after another, upon them. Whence learn, 1. Sinful lust is insatiable, even when the body is overcharged with the service of it. To lust sinfully is a snare, but to continue in the slavery of lust, is a selling of a man's self, and a wedding of him unto that lust. Such was the sin of the carnal Israelites: they continued in their lusting and repented not, albeit they got time to repent, they and their lust did not discord: *they were not estranged from their lust.* 2. When men will not be enemies to their own sinful lusts, they provoke the Lord to become an enemy to them, and to pour wrath on them in the very act of their sinning: *while their meat was yet in their mouths, the wrath of God came upon them.* 3. Such as are most headstrong in sin, and take to themselves most liberty to sin, and give example most unto others to sin, shall be most signally punished. High places and eminency in power, as they lessen not sin, but aggravate it; so they exempt not from judgment, but procure that it should be augmented rather, as is to be seen here in the punishment of the nobles and great men in the camp of Israel: *the wrath of God came upon them, and slew the fattest of them, and smote down the chosen men of Israel.* 4. Such is the perverseness of our natural inclination, that, neither by God's gentle dealing with us, nor by his sad judgments on others or on ourselves, can we be amended, as is to be seen in unrenewed Israelites: *for all this they sinned still.* 5. Neither extraordinary works of mercy, nor judgment, nor miracles, are able to convert men, or turn them from their evil ways, or beget saving faith in them, with whom ordinary means do not prevail: *for all this they sinned still, and believed not for his won-*

drous works. 6. When all means are essayed, and none
prevail to bring men to repentance and reconciliation with
God through faith, no wonder God in his righteous judgment should cut off the impenitent as an unfruitful and evil
tree is cut down and cast away: *they sinned still, therefore
their days did he consume in vanity, and their years in
trouble.* 7. By following lusts, and not seeking felicity in
God, men both miss the good they hoped to have by sinning,
and find nothing in their good but vanity, and also meet
with trouble and torment, which they did not fear: *they
sinned still, and believed not, therefore their days did God
consume in vanity, and their years in trouble.*

34. *When he slew them, then they sought him; and
they returned and enquired early after God:*

35. *And they remembered that God was their Rock,
and the high God their Redeemer.*

36. *Nevertheless they did flatter him with their
mouth, and they lied unto him with their tongues.*

37. *For their heart was not right with him, neither
were they steadfast in his covenant.*

In the seventh place, the psalmist describeth some fits of
their temporary faith, and repentance, v. 3—5, which in
effect proved to be but flattery or hypocrisy, and ended in
backsliding and apostasy, v. 36, 37. Whence learn, 1.
When men, neither by the Lord's liberality nor lighter chastisements, can be moved to repent, it is righteousness with
God, by fearful judgments to cut off a number, and to put
the rest in fear of present cutting off, and so to waken them
out of security; as here when the carnal Israelites went out
in their provocations, *the Lord slew them.* 2. The sense
of present devouring wrath, and the terror of an angry God,
may drive men to a temporary repentance, and to seeking
friendship and favour with God, for sparing them from
wrath and present plagues, and all this may be without serious repenting of sin, without flying to a mediator by saving faith, without minding hearty and solid reconciliation:
and may proceed only from the natural principle of fear of
death, and love of self-preservation: as here, *when he slew
them, then they sought him.* 3. Temporary repentance, may
make a temporary change of a man's course of life and car-

riage, from the worse to the better; may make him leave off his way of provocation, and seek after God for a time with some diligence in the outward form of religion: as here, *they returned, and enquired after God early.* 4. As there is a temporary repentance, moving from sin upon temporary grounds, so there is a temporary faith in many, moving toward God upon temporary considerations; that is, drawing toward God to obtain of him sparing of their life and temporal benefits, and making use of God's goodness and bounty, as much as serveth to a man's purpose : as here, *they remembered that God was their Rock.* 5. Temporary faith may make use of redemption, so far as may serve for deliverance from, or recovery out of, temporal trouble, such as present danger of wrath and plagues : as here, *they remembered that the high God was their Redeemer.* 6. Acts of faith and repentance, extracted by sore judgments, fear of wrath, and desire of temporal deliverance, may be found to be the fruits of flattery, and not of saving faith : *nevertheless they flattered him with their lips.* 7. Profession of faith and repentance, which forsaketh sin and seeketh God only for temporal reasons, is but a flying unto God in effect, howsoever the temporary believer and repenter may judge himself sound enough, as here: *and they lied unto him with their tongues.* 8. When the heart or affections of a man are not set sincerely against sin, and for God, or toward God; all the outward profession is but hypocrisy in effect, and a lie, as here : *they lied unto him with their tongues, for their heart was not right with him.* 9. Temporary faith can produce no steadfastness in the covenant, or covenanted duties, but make a man only a temporizer therein, as outward motives lead him toward duties, or from them : *their heart was not right with God, neither were they steadfast in the covenant.*

38. *But he, being full of compassion, forgave their iniquity, and destroyed them not; yea, many a time turned he his anger away, and did not stir up all his wrath.*

39. *For he remembered that they were but flesh ; a wind that passeth away, and cometh not again.*

40. *How oft did they provoke him in the wilderness, and grieve him in the desert !*

41. *Yea, they turned back, and tempted God, and limited the Holy One of Israel.*

In the eighth place, he showeth the Lord's merciful sparing of his people many a time, and pitying of their natural frailty, because if he should have killed them, they were not to live again in this world, v. 38, 39, notwithstanding their frequent provocations in the wilderness, their limiting God, and taking upon them to direct him what he should do unto them, v. 40, 41. Whence learn, 1. There is a remission of sin in regard only of temporal judgment, Lev. iv. 20, which is in effect only the not inflicting temporal punishment upon the sinner, or the not destroying of the sinner presently, the persons remaining the same impenitent sinners; such as was God's pardoning here impenitent Israel, flattering and false-hearted Israel : *but he forgave their iniquity.* 2. It is not any good in the sinner, but pity in God, which is the cause of sparing sinners from present perdition, when they provoke the Lord : *but he being full of compassion, forgave their iniquity, and destroyed them not.* 3. The Lord evidenceth his mercy and pity toward sinners, partly by his often sparing to strike, and turning away his wrath ready to break out against them; and partly by mitigating his anger, and not suffering it to break out in full force : *many a time he turned his anger away, and did not stir up all his wrath.* 4. Let men conceit of their own natural strength as they list, yet the truth is, their frailty is great : *they are but flesh, and a vapour that passeth away, and cometh not again.* 5. When no good at all is found in man for which God should spare him, he taketh occasion of his frailty and misery, whereunto man is subject, to pity him : *for he remembered that they were flesh, a wind that passeth away, and cometh not again.* 6. The oftener sin be repeated, the greater is the provocation, and the greater is the mercy that so often forbeareth to destroy; and when the frequency of sinning, and frequency of sparing are numbered, the reckoning will not be easily ended, nor the number condescended upon : *how oft did they provoke him in the wilderness ?* 7. The sins of God's people greatly displease him, and that so much the more as they are oftener repeated, and committed contrary to what God's kindness and care merit of them : *how oft did they provoke him in the wilderness, and grieve him in the desert ?* where

God gave his daily presence, led them, fed them, and protected them miraculously.　8. Amongst other aggravations
of sin, this is not the least, after conviction and correction,
and promise of amendment, resolutely to go back again to
their vomit : *yea, they turned back, and tempted God.*　9.
The Lord cannot endure that his people, who ought wholly
to depend upon, submit unto, and be ruled by him, should
prescribe, as they please, how and when he should help them,
or set bounds unto his power, truth, wisdom, or mercy, as
if he could do no more than they conceive to be probable;
therefore it is put amongst the highest aggravations of their
sins : *they tempted and limited the Holy One of Israel.*

42. *They remembered not his hand,* nor *the day when
he delivered them from the enemy :*

43. *How he had wrought his signs in Egypt, and
his wonders in the field of Zoan :*

In the ninth place, from this to v. 54, he setteth down
the prime cause of all their sin and misery, which followed
upon it; to wit, they marked not, nor made use of, the difference which God put between them and the Egyptians,
whom he plagued for their cause, while he delivered them.
Whence learn, 1. When the merciful proofs of God's respect
to us, do not confirm our faith in God, and tie us to love
and obedience to him, these experiences will soon wear out,
if not of common memory, yet out of estimative and affectionate memory : as here, *they remembered not his hand, nor
the day when he delivered them from the enemy.*　2. As the
right remembrance of former mercies may be a bridle from
all sin, and a confirmation of faith against all doubtings and
suspicions of God's good-will to us; so, the not rightly remembering experiences of God's respect shown to us, proveth an inlet to many wicked mistakings of God and disobe-
diences to him : for here the cause of the former sins and
plagues is rendered to be this : *they remembered not his hand,
nor the day when he delivered them from the enemy.*　3. Not
remembering the Lord's word and works affectionately, and
with purpose and endeavour to make right use thereof, is
in the Lord's estimation no remembrance of him in effect;
for, of this people, who could well tell the story of their
coming out of Egypt, and so had a common remembrance
thereof, the Lord saith, *they remembered not his hand, nor*

the day when he delivered them from the enemy. 4. Signs and wonders once done for confirmation of the doctrine of the true God, and his covenant, and true religion, should suffice in all times and ages after, for that end; and it is not lawful to tempt God still to do more wonders for confirmation of that truth: *they remembered not how he had wrought his signs in Egypt, and his wonders in the field of Zoan.* 5. The Lord's plagues on the enemies of the church, being rightly remembered, should warn God's people to stand in awe of him, depend upon him, submit unto him, and be wary to contend with him; when this use is not made of them, it giveth a ground of challenge: *they remembered not how he had wrought his signs in Egypt, and his wonders in the field of Zoan.*

44. *And had turned their rivers into blood; and their floods, that they could not drink.*

45. *He sent divers sorts of flies among them, which devoured them ; and frogs, which destroyed them.*

46. *He gave also their increase unto the caterpillar, and their labour unto the locust.*

47. *He destroyed their vines with hail, and their sycamore-trees with frost.*

48. *He gave up their cattle also to the hail, and their flocks to hot thunder-bolts.*

49. *He cast upon them the fierceness of his anger, wrath, and indignation, and trouble, by sending evil angels* among them.

50. *He made a way to his anger; he spared not their soul from death, but gave their life over to the pestilence;*

51. *And smote all the first-born in Egypt; the chief of* their *strength in the tabernacles of Ham:*

The psalmist numbereth out sundry plagues poured out upon the Egyptians, whereby the Israelites should have been wise. From v. 44, learn, 1. The means of men's life, comfort, wealth, and defence, can stand them in no stead when God hath a controversy against them. The Lord can deprive them of the benefit thereof, and turn benefits into the means of their grief and vexation, as he did the waters of Egypt, which were the means of life and wealth unto them: *he turned their rivers into blood; and their floods, that they could not drink.* 2. By what means people sin and provoke the Lord to wrath, he can by the same means punish them. As the Egyptians had defiled their rivers with the blood of the infants of Israel, so did God make their river speak their sin and threaten their death: *he turned their rivers into blood, and their floods, that they could not drink.*

From v. 45, learn, 1. The meanest and basest of the creatures declare the power of the Lord, and are so far from being useless that they lie, as it were, in garrison among men, to be sent out in parties upon service, as the God of hosts is pleased to give orders: *he sent divers sorts of flies among them, and frogs.* 2. Flies and frogs, and every meanest vermin, are too sore for man, when God armeth them to avenge his quarrel: *he sent out flies which devoured them, and frogs which destroyed them;* that is, which were about to destroy them, and were able enough for the work, and were acknowledged to be so by the Egyptians, who reckoned themselves lost men if these armies were not taken off them.

From v. 46—48, learn, 1. When God is not acknowledged to be the giver of corn, and cattle, and fruits of the ground, by a right using of them, he will be known to be the giver thereof by removing them: *he destroyed their increase, labour, vines, and cattle.* 2. The Lord hath means how to destroy and take away the fruits of the ground, and other serviceable creatures at his pleasure: *the caterpillar, the locust, hail, frost, and thunder-bolts.*

From v. 49, learn, 1. The plagues of God's enemies are out of mere justice, and not from fatherly love, as the strokes of his own chosen are : *he cast upon the Egyptians the fierceness of his anger.* 2. Trouble of itself is not so heavy as when indignation and wrath are joined with it, or send it forth : *he cast upon them the fierceness of his anger, wrath, and indignation, and trouble.* 3. As the Lord hath good angels, by whom he can work his own will; so hath he also evil angels, whose service he can use holily to his own purpose : *he cast the fierceness of his wrath upon them, by sending evil angels among them.*

From v. 50, 51, learn, 1. When the Lord's judgments, lighting upon men's houses, corn, cattle, and fruit-trees, do not humble men, the Lord maketh his judgment light upon their own persons; and when lighter judgments on their persons do not humble them, then God will destroy their lives, and their last plagues shall be heavier than their first; as here, when former plagues did not the turn, the Lord laid aside former pitying and long-suffering; and so *he made a way for his anger, he spared not their soul from death, but gave their life over to the pestilence.* 2. As the persecutors of God's people smite that which God loveth best, so God smiteth that which persecutors love best: *he smote all the first-born in Egypt.* 3. The curse of God coming upon the Egyptians, the posterity of Ham, commendeth the grace of God toward the Israelites, the posterity of Shem, his brother: therefore, in opposition to the tabernacles of the Israelites in the land of Goshen, it is said, *he smote the chief of their strength in the tabernacles of Ham.*

52. *But made his own people to go forth like sheep, and guided them in the wilderness like a flock.*

53. *And he led them on safely, so that they feared not; but the sea overwhelmed their enemies.*

This was the Lord's dealing with the enemies of Israel, whereof the Israelites made no right use. Now the psalmist setteth down the Lord's different dealing with Israel, whereof also they made no right use; when he had plagued and drowned the Egyptians, he gave Israel safe passage and conduct through the sea. Whence learn, 1. Whatsoever be the unworthiness of God's confederate people, yet the Lord putteth a difference between them and their enemies, and testifieth his respect to the one above the other; the Egyptians he plagued divers ways: *but he made his own people go forth like sheep.* 2. Though the Lord's people be both weak and witless, yet God careth for them, as a shepherd doth for his flock: *he made his own people to go forth as sheep, and guided them in the wilderness as a flock.* 3. Albeit the Lord putteth difference between such as are in covenant with him in the letter only, and those that are in covenant with him in the spirit also, when he compareth the sheep with the goats; yet, when he compareth the whole bulk of his people with the rest of the world, and in special with their enemies, he putteth a peculiar respect upon them all, and avoweth his interest in them all above all people in the world, and doeth for them as for his own: *he made his own people to go forth.* 4. Whatsoever fear may possibly fall upon God's people when they are following his directions, yet their course is safe and without just cause of fear, and if sometimes fear surprise them, yet the Lord so cleareth their way after, that they are out of fear: *he led them on safely, so that they feared not.* 5. The perdition of the world and wicked enemies maketh the safety of those that are saved so much the greater benefit: *his people feared not, but the sea overwhelmed his enemies.*

54. *And he brought them to the border of his sanctuary,* even to *this mountain* which *his right hand had purchased.*

55. *He cast out the heathen also before them, and divided them an inheritance by line, and made the tribes of Israel to dwell in their tents.*

In the tenth place, the psalmist pointeth at the perfecting of their journey through the wilderness, and possessing them of Canaan, with the casting out of the Canaanites. Whence learn, 1. Whatsoever become of particular persons in the visible church, the Lord followeth on the course of his care and kindness unto the church, and increaseth the obligation of the incorporation in the succeeding ages, partly by what he doeth for their predecessors, and partly by what he doeth for themselves, as we see in the church of Israel: whatsoever became of misbelievers in the wilderness, he brought his own people *to the border of his sanctuary.* 2. Albeit we should fight for the liberty of a place where God's ordinances may be publicly celebrated, and shed our blood in coming by it; yet is the commodity not ours but the Lord's purchase, and his gift to us: *he brought them to this mountain which his right hand hath purchased.* 3. Success in war is the Lord's work, and such as are dispossessed of their inheritance have God to crave for it: *he cast out the heathen also before them.* It is neither the stoutness of the one nor the feebleness of the other, but God's hand or power which doeth the business. 4. The settling of a people in a peaceable possession, so as every man may without contention enjoy what is allowed him of God, is no small benefit and obligation of a people so dealt with by God: *he divided them an inheritance by lot, and made the tribes of Israel dwell in their tents.*

56. *Yet they tempted and provoked the most high God, and kept not his testimonies;*

S

57. *But turned back, and dealt unfaithfully like their fathers: they were turned aside like a deceitful bow.*

58. *For they provoked him to anger with their high places, and moved him to jealousy with their graven images.*

In the eleventh place, he setteth down how this people yet again provoked the Lord to anger with their idolatry and superstition, their high places and their graven images: for, when God had appointed one place for their solemn worship, to wit, his tabernacle, where his ark and mercy seat were, signifying the necessity of worshipping him through the promised mediator Jesus Christ, in whom alone he would be sought and found; and in whom he would have all his people agreeing, and attending his appointment, and not devising ways of pleasing God of themselves. They would have a place of their own for public worship, high places, or hills and groves, which pleased them better than mount Zion, or the place where the tabernacle was pitched. They would have representations of their own devising, and loved them better than the ark of the covenant, to wit, graven images, which God had forbidden in the moral law, and so they provoked him to anger. Whence learn, 1. Such is the wickedness of natural men, that neither for judgments nor for favour shown to them, will they subject themselves to God's direction, but will take upon them to set rules unto God one way or other. This the prophet showeth in the example of the Israelites: *yet they tempted and provoked the most high God.* 2. When God giveth his word and ordinances for his worship to a people, and they cast away this rule, and make another to themselves, it is a tempting of God, and striving with the most high God, whether he shall direct them, or they shall direct him in the means of his worship: *they provoked the most high God;* How? *They kept not his testimonies.* 3. Altering, or changing the form of worship, which God hath appointed, is a relinquishing of God and his way, a point of treachery against him, and a notable breach of covenant: *they kept not his testimonies, but turned back and dealt unfaithfully.* 4. Following of antiquity in an error is so far from excusing sin, that it makes the children liable to their fathers'

debt and deserved punishment, because they approve their
fathers and their deeds, above God and God's testimonies :
they dealt unfaithfully like their fathers. 5. The service of
the wicked is like a bow; they will do nothing commanded
but by compulsion; and, like a *deceitful bow*, which, as it hath
a cast or throw in it, and shifteth the arrow aside from the
mark whereunto it is directed, so they will aim at another
mark than God directeth them to : *they were turned aside
like a deceitful bow.* 6. The alteration of the rule of worship prescribed by God, is a provocation of God to anger,
were it but in a circumstance: *they provoked him to anger
with their high places.* 7. Such as take liberty to themselves to depart from the ordinances of God in the less, will
depart also from him in the greater : *they provoked God to
anger with their high places, and moved him to jealousy
with their graven images.* 8. Howsoever men dream that
they may make good use of pictures and graven images, to
further them in devotion and the service of God, who is represented thereby, and that they mind not to communicate
any of his worship to the images; yet the Lord counteth
that religious use of images no less than adultery, and matter of bitter provocation, as the word imports : partly, because it is impossible not to communicate divine worship to
the images before which a man boweth himself, of purpose to
be stirred up by it, to worship God represented by it; partly,
because the deviser and user of this sort of relative worship,
hath thrust himself into the Lord's place, to whom only it
belongeth to prescribe how he will be worshipped; or at
least he hath admitted another Lord than God, in appointing
the means of religion; and partly, because the Lord expressly declareth, that by graven images he is provoked
justly to jealousy : *therefore,* saith he, *they moved him to
jealousy with their graven images.*

59. *When God heard* this, *he was wroth, and greatly abhorred Israel :*

60. *So that he forsook the tabernacle of Shiloh, the
tent* which *he placed among men ;*

61. *And delivered his strength into captivity, and
his glory into the enemy's hand.*

62. *He gave his people over also unto the sword ;
and was wroth with his inheritance.*

63. *The fire consumed their young men; and their maidens were not given to marriage.*

64. *Their priests fell by the sword; and their widows made no lamentation.*

In the twelfth place, the psalmist declareth how the Lord's wrath was kindled, v. 59, and how he took his ark from Shiloh, where it was abused in Eli's time, v. 60, and gave his ark (the sign of his strength or powerful presence among them,) into the Philistines' hands, v. 61, and made his people fall in battle, v. 62; the young men died in battle, and so maids wanted matches, v. 63; their priests were slain, and their wives made no lamentation for them, 1 Sam. 4. 22, in comparison of greater losses, v. 64. Whence learn, 1. The corrupting of God's worship and ordinances, is a sin crying for judgment, which voice God will answer: *when God heard this, he was wroth.* 2. The Lord goeth not rashly to judgment, but as it were, after perfect understanding of the cause : *when God heard this, he was wroth.* 3. Were a people or person ever so dear to God, superstition and imagery, and abusing his public worship, will provoke him to jealousy against them, and draw forth such judgments as will speak the Lord's abhorring them for that sin : *and he greatly abhorred Israel.*

From v. 60, learn, 1. When the public ordinances, the tokens of the Lord's presence, are removed from any place, the Lord removeth, and forsaketh that place : *so that he forsook the tabernacle of Shiloh,* where the ark had been till Elias' death. 2. It is in vain for any to boast of God's presence in any place, when once his public ordinances are polluted : *he forsook Shiloh the tent which he placed among men.*

From v. 61, learn, 1. When God's people abuse religion, and pollute his ordinances, no wonder he makes their open enemies to deprive them thereof, as here we see. 2. The Lord's people cannot promise unto themselves the continuance of the manifestation of the Lord's strength, and the Lord's glory among them, longer than they esteem him, and advance him as their glory, and their strength; for when Israel tempted God, kept not his testimonies, and moved him to jealousy, *he delivered over his strength into captivity, and his glory into the enemies' hands.*

From v. 62, learn, When enemies get advantage against God's people by reason of their provocation of God, and when the enemies of religion get power over God's people, so far as to deprive them of the means of religion; the Lord's anger will be more against his people, who were the causes of this wrath, than against the enemies who were the instruments of the execution of the wrath; and therefore, beside the taking away of his ordinances from his people, he will send his vengeance upon them also : *he gave his people over also unto the sword, and was wroth with his inheritance.*

From v. 63, learn, 1. When the Lord sendeth the sword on a land, he can soon consume the flower of the youth as with a fire: *the fire consumed the young men.* 2. When religion is overthrown among God's people, let not the commonwealth think to stand: when God gave his glory into the enemy's hand, *he gave his people over also unto the sword, and the fire consumed their young men.* 3. When God's people by abusing religion provoke God against them, it shall be no wonder if God give them such sad blows by their enemies, that there shall be no hope for one age at least to recover their estate; and no wonder if there be fearful appearance also of cutting off the posterity : *the fire consumed their young men, and their maidens were not given to marriage.*

From v. 64, learn, 1. It is amongst the most fearful tokens of God's displeasure against a land, when he removeth his ministers from them, especially when the good are taken away with the bad : *their priests fell by the sword.* 2. When the ministers are the abusers of religion, and chief in the provocation, no wonder to see them so exemplarily punished; for as *Hophni* and *Phinehas* made the sacrifice to be snuffed at, so God made their carcasses fall in the battle : *their priests fell by the sword.* 3. When God's wrath breaks forth against his own people for their provocations, he can make public calamities so great, as they shall swallow up domestic miseries : yea, he can make those that live, and are reserved from the sword, so weary of their lives, that they shall reckon the dead to be more happy than the living : *their priests fell by the sword, and their widows made no lamentation.*

65. *Then the Lord awaked as one out of sleep,* and *like a mighty man that shouteth by reason of wine.*

66. *And he smote his enemies in the hinder parts; he put them to a perpetual reproach.*

In the thirteenth place, the psalmist showeth how, notwithstanding all the former provocations and sore judgments, the Lord of his own free grace, by taking vengeance upon his enemies, restored his people to the privileges of church and kingdom. Whence learn, 1. Howsoever the Lord's people draw judgments on themselves, and deserve to be left in their miseries; yet God of his free and constant love to them, sendeth relief when they least expect it, as here is to be seen : when his people is in a most desperate condition, *then the Lord awaketh.* 2. As people sleep securely in their sin, when God calleth them to repentance : so it is justice with God to misken them in their calamity, and to be unto them as one asleep, as here he is described. 3. God doth not so far wink at the troubles of his own people, but the cry of their misery, and the insolency of the enemy against them, will awake him. When Israel were now as a lost people, and their enemies had taken God's ark, *then the Lord awaked as one out of sleep, and like a mighty man that shouted because of wine.* 4. Whatsoever weak similitude the Scripture useth to make us conceive somewhat of the Lord's operations, yet must we always think of him as beseemeth the glory of his majesty, leaving the imperfection of the creature, (from which the similitude is borrowed,) as the dregs of the comparison, to rest with the creature itself, as here we are led to do, except we should think blasphemous thoughts of God. 5. Albeit the enemies of God's people may be at ease, when his people are in trouble, and lying under their feet, yet God will arise in due time and punish them : *the Lord awaked, and smote his enemies in the hinder parts.* 6. The dishonour done to God, and to God's people, is but for a time, and is shortly removed; but the recompense of the enemies who dishonour God, is perpetual and everlasting : *he smote his enemies in the hinder parts,* to wit, with emerods and a bloody flux; *and so he put them to a perpetual reproach.*

67. *Moreover, he refused the tabernacle of Joseph, and chose not the tribe of Ephraim ;*

68. *But chose the tribe of Judah, the mount Zion which he loved.*

69. *And he built his sanctuary like high* palaces, *like the earth which he hath established for ever.*

70. *He chose David also his servant, and took him from the sheep-folds :*

71. *From following the ewes great with young, he brought him to feed Jacob his people, and Israel his inheritance.*

72. *So he fed them according to the integrity of his heart; and guided them by the skilfulness of his hands.*

In the last place is set down, how, albeit the Lord returned not to Shiloh with his ark, v. 67, yet he stayed in the land among his people, placed his ark in Jerusalem, built himself a glorious temple and sanctuary on Zion, v. 68, 69, and settled his people under the government of David, a type of Christ, exalted from an humble and low condition to be king of Israel, v. 70, 71, by whom the people were well governed, v. 72.

From v. 67, 68, learn, 1. The Lord can so temper his justice and mercy in his dealing with his people, as the effects of both shall be manifest. Because he was so dishonoured in Shiloh, he will have his justice seen, in not suffering his ark to come there again any more: *moreover, he refused the tabernacle of Joseph, and chose not the tribe of Ephraim ;* to wit, for the tribe that he would most respect, or where he would have the residence of his ark to be; there is his justice. Again, he will not forsake the land, or the people of Israel altogether, but will dwell in some other part of the land, and will take another tribe to have the chief evidence of his respect shown unto them : *but he chose the tribe of Judah :* here is his mercy, with an intimation of the main means of the mercy, which is the coming of Christ in the flesh, out of the tribe of Judah. Thus God will not depart from Israel, and yet he will not be found save in the tribe of Judah, out of which came Christ, the root and fountain of mercy to all Israel who should seek God through him. 2. Whatsoever be the privilege of the church universal, yet no particular place is so privileged, but God will leave it, and take another to dwell in, when he is provoked in any particular place to forsake it : for the dishonour done to his majesty in Shiloh, *he refused the tabernacle of Joseph*: he refused that his ark, the chief sign of his presence, should have its residence any more in the bounds of Ephraim or Manasseh, the sons of Joseph. 3. The cause why God chooseth, to any privilege, one tribe more than another, or one person more than another, or one place more than another, is only his own free will, grace, and love: *he chose the tribe of Judah, the mount Zion which he loved.*

From v. 69, learn, 1, In the type of building the temple on mount Zion, we are taught that the church of God is his own edifice, whoever be the workmen whom he in his providence employeth to build it: therefore it is said, *he built his sanctuary like high palaces.* 2. Albeit the Lord's church may have many troubles and commotions in it, yet shall it endure, and not be overthrown utterly for ever: *he built his sanctuary as the earth, which he hath established for ever.*

From v. 70, 71, learn, 1. The church shall not want a king to defend and protect her; for God hath his own chosen servant appointed for the purpose. As for the typical kingdom of Israel, he had David; so for the church universal, represented by the type, he hath appointed Christ the eternal Son of God, who took his human nature of the lineage of David, to be king mystical in Zion for ever; to be a type of whom, *he did choose David his servant.* 2. The Lord, to the intent he may not only show his sovereign power, whereby he can raise the meanest of men, and exalt them how high soever he pleaseth; but also to represent from how low a degree of humiliation, Christ incarnate was to be raised to the government of his church and kingdom, he setteth down the mean condition of life, wherefrom David was raised to the royal dignity of governing Israel: *he took him from the sheep-folds, from following the ewes great with young: he brought him to feed Jacob his people, and Israel his inheritance.*

From v. 72, learn, The duties and properties of a good king are these: First, he must resolve to be God's servant in his charge, as David was. Secondly, all his subjects, and in special the Lord's people must be cared for by him in a civil way, as a flock of sheep is cared for by the pastor: *David fed them.* Thirdly, a king's heart must be set uprightly for God's honour, and for his subjects' welfare in the whole course of his government: *he fed them according to the integrity of his heart.* Fourthly, a king must deal prudently with his subjects, accommodating the whole course of his dealing with them, as their several conditions require : *he guided them by the skilfulness of his hands.* And whatsoever measure David had of those properties, was but a shadow of the perfections of Christ in his government. Fifthly, neither laws, nor teaching, nor miracles, nor benefits, nor judgments can avail for the salvation of a people or person, till put under the hand and guiding of Christ; as we are taught here in the example and representation of the Lord's dealing with Israel in this psalm; wherein, when God hath tried his people with oft repeated mercies and judgments, they come to no settled state, till they be put under the government of David, who in this is a type of Christ; for he closeth with this : *he guided them by the skilfulness of his hands.*

PSALM LXXIX.

A psalm of Asaph.

The scattered and captive people of God, after the destruction of Jerusalem and the temple, put up a pitiful complaint unto God, to v. 6, and pray for a merciful relief to his church, and for avenging their blood upon their enemies. As for the complaint, in it they lament four things: first, the profanation and desolation of the Lord's inheritance and temple by the heathen their enemies, v. 1; secondly, the barbarous cruelty and inhumanity used against them, v. 2, 3 ; thirdly, the contempt and mocking of their wicked neighbours in their misery, v. 4; fourthly, as they acknowledge this to proceed from God's displeasure, so they lament that it is like to be everlasting, v. 5.

In their prayer, in the latter part of the psalm, the Jews crave, first, justice upon their enemies, v. 6, 7 ; secondly, pardon of their own sins, and deliverance out of their misery for sundry reasons, v. 8—11 ; thirdly, that God would reward their inhuman neighbours who mocked at their misery, v. 12; and they close their petition with a promise of praise and thanks unto God by the church in all succeeding ages. Whence learn in general. 1. The church of God may be brought so low, as here we see once it was. 2. So many of God's people as live to see such public calamities and misery, must not despair of a recovery, but should and may run to God and pray for the church in affliction, expecting order after confusion, and after dissipation, to see a gathering of God's people again ; and after apparent overthrow of religion, a restoring of God's public worship, as the example of the psalmist in this psalm teacheth, whose courage and confidence in God for relief of the Lord's people are wonderful, as the state of the church at that time, seemed to be desperate. As the holy Ghost, the inditer of this psalm, giveth warning here to all ages to beware to provoke the Lord unto wrath, lest he deal with them as he dealt with those Israelites, so he giveth warrant to all afflicted churches to follow the example of this afflicted church, to run to God for help ; for which cause he hath given this psalm to be made use of by the church : a psalm of Asaph.

1. *O God, the heathen are come into thine inheritance ; thy holy temple have they defiled ; they have laid
Jerusalem on heaps.*

In the first part of this lamentation learn, 1. Albeit there
be no place, nor person, how near and dear soever to God,
exempted from judgment, when they are polluted, yet the
wicked instruments of the judgment poured out upon the
place and persons consecrated to God, may justly be complained of, as here we see : *O God, the heathen are come
into thine inheritance.* 2. When God's people, who should
be holy, defile themselves and God's ordinances, it is no
wonder that by profane persons they be punished, and their
holy things polluted : *thy holy temple have they defiled ;*
that is, they have abused it, dealt with it as with a vile and
profane thing. 3. Albeit people in covenant with God have
disgraced their holy profession, and polluted his ordinances,
and be justly plagued by seeing holy ordinances put over
into the hands of profane men for their cause; yet neither
will the Lord disclaim his interest in his own ordinances, nor
do his people lose right and interest in God and his ordinances, when they take with their punishment, and make
their address to God for relief : *thy holy temple have they
defiled.* 4. When God giveth over religious ordinances into
the hands of profane men to be abused, no wonder if they
are the cause of this, and also suffer in their civil state, no
wonder the city suffer with the temple : *Jerusalem have
they laid on heaps.*

2. *The dead bodies of thy servants have they given
to be meat unto the fowls of the heaven, the flesh of thy
saints unto the beasts of the earth.*

3. *Their blood have they shed like water round about
Jerusalem ; and there was none to bury them.*

From the second part of the lamentation and complaint,
learn, 1. Falling in battle before the enemies may prove that
God hath a just cause against the party overcome; but cannot prove that the victor's cause is good, presuppose both
parties had appealed to God; for here the heathen overcome, and the Lord's servants and saints are slain, and they
who are left alive complain of the victors, and take with their
punishment at God's hand, who followeth his own quarrel
as he pleaseth, and will not at men's pleasure sit down and

decide appellations, when they call to him; or stand unto
the time set down by men to him, to determine their controversy : *O God, the heathen are come into thine inheritance, &c. The dead bodies of thy servants have they
given to be meat to the fowls.* 2. Heavy and fearful are
the temporal judgments which may come upon God's people, when they have provoked God to wrath against them
for their sins, even such as are here set down; to wit, overturning the outward face of religion; destruction of their
lands, cities, and estate; killing of them in abundance, and
want of burial when they are dead. 3. As not by outward
prosperity, so also not by outward calamities, is the love or
hatred of God to be known; the same sort of outward dispensation may befall both : *the dead bodies of thy servants
they have given to be meat to the fowls of heaven.* 4. No
temporal wrath, no calamities whatsoever can separate the
Lord's children from God's love and estimation of them, nor
untie the relation between God and them; for here, albeit
their carcasses fall, and be devoured by the fowls of heaven
and beasts of the earth, yet remain they the Lord's servants
and saints under these sufferings : *the dead bodies of thy
servants, &c., the flesh of thy saints.* 5. The slaughter
of the Lord's people, and the scattering of such of them as
escape may be so great, when his anger is kindled against
them, that none may be found to bury the slain, but the
dead may lie unburied : *their blood have they shed like
water round about Jerusalem, and there was none to
bury them.* 6. Nothing is to be expected of God's enemies
towards God's people, when they fall into their hands, but
savage cruelty and barbarous inhumanity, for which they are
to answer to God, to whom the complaint of the living, and
the cry of the blood of the slain call for vengeance, as the
experience of the Lord's people in this place teacheth.

4. *We are become a reproach to our neighbours, a
scorn and derision to them that are round about us.*

From the third part of the complaint and lamentation,
learn, 1. In the day of God's displeasure against his people,
yea in the day of the trial of the faith and patience of his people, no wonder that such as should most pity our calamity,
and be comfortable unto us, rejoice to see us in misery, yea,
and make our calamity a matter of reproach to us, a
matter of scorn and derision of us; for here it is said, *we*

are become a reproach to our neighbours, a scorn and derision to them that are round about us. 2. When God afflicteth his people, all their privileges, and the religion they profess, become contemptible and ridiculous to the ungodly, who do not esteem either God's ordinances or his people, but when they are adorned with outward prosperity. The Lord's people were feared and honoured by them that were about them, when God fought for them and countenanced them; but now they lament, *we are become a reproach to our neighbours, a scorn and derision to them that are round about us.* 3. To be mocked in misery, and specially of them by whom we should be comforted, is amongst the saddest passages of our affliction; therefore here is this part of their lamentation set down, after the formerly mentioned misery, as a load above a burden, and that which embittered their sorrow most of all, because it reflected upon their religion, their faith, their interest in God, as if all had been ridiculous.

5. *How long, Lord? wilt thou be angry for ever? shall thy jealousy burn like fire?*

From the fourth part of the lamentation, learn, 1. The Lord's displeasure and anger against his people, are more heavy to them than all the calamities which have lighted on them: *how long wilt thou be angry?* putteth the copestone on their prison-house. 2. Guilty consciences cannot but apprehend wrath, when their plagues are heavy; yea, they cannot escape a conflict with the fear of everlasting wrath, when God's hand lieth long upon them: *how long, Lord? wilt thou be angry for ever?* 3. When God's people fall from their matrimonial covenant with God, and their heart and eyes go a-whoring after idols, no wonder the Lord be jealous, and his wrath for this be most hot, and be like to devour unto utter destruction: *shall thy jealousy burn like fire?* 4. Whatsoever hath been our calamity, whosoever have been the instruments of our misery, yea how great soever our provocation of God's anger hath been ; it is wisdom, as to expound all the malice and cruelty of men to be the effects of God's anger and jealousy, and that his anger and jealousy are kindled by our sins, so to run to God, and lament the whole matter before him, and deprecate his wrath, as the church doth here : *how long, Lord? wilt thou be angry for ever?*

6. *Pour out thy wrath upon the heathen that have not known thee, and upon the kingdoms that have not called upon thy name:*

7. *For they have devoured Jacob, and laid waste his dwelling-place.*

In the latter part of the psalm is the godly's prayer; and first, for justice and vengeance on their enemies. Whence learn, 1. Albeit it be not lawful for us, in our own quarrel, to pray against our enemies, yet, in the church's quarrel, in the Lord's quarrel, it is lawful to pray in general against the incorrigible and desperate enemies of God and his people, as here the church is taught. 2. Albeit temporal judgments may overtake God's visible church, when the open enemies of God's people and of his true worship are spared, yet at length the fulness of wrath is reserved for the ungodly, one and all : *pour out thy wrath upon the heathen that have not known thee.* 3. Prayer to God, and invocation of his name upon all occasions, as God's honour and men's necessities, and duties public, private, and secret call them to come before him, is a mark differencing God's people from the ungodly, whether professed or real heathens, and a mark of such as shall find mercy distinguishing them from the objects of God's wrath : *pour out thy wrath upon the kingdoms that have not called on thy name.* 4. Unto the right worshipping of God the true knowledge of God is required; for how shall men call upon God in whom they believe not, whom they know not, or whom to know they care not ? therefore, such as are strangers from God here are described by this : *they have not known thee, they have not called on thy name.* 5. The members of a visible church may be scattered one from another, so that they cannot in one place, jointly and professedly, enjoy public ordinances : as here, *Jacob is devoured, and his dwelling-place laid waste.* 6. The heaviest article in the ditty of the ungodly is their being accessory to, or active in, the overthrow of God's people : *pour out thy wrath upon them; for they have devoured Jacob, and laid waste his dwelling-place.*

8. *O remember not against us former iniquities : let thy tender mercies speedily prevent us ; for we are brought very low.*

9. *Help us, O God of our salvation, for the glory of thy name; and deliver us, and purge away our sins, for thy name's sake.*

10. *Wherefore should the heathen say, Where is their God? let him be known among the heathen in our sight* by *the revenging of the blood of thy servants* which is *shed.*

11. *Let the sighing of the prisoner come before thee; according to the greatness of thy power preserve thou those that are appointed to die;*

Secondly, the godly pray for pardon of their sins, and delivery from the misery which their sins had procured: unto which petitions sundry reasons are added for strengthening the faith of the church. Whence learn, 1. The sense of sin maketh the afflicted to be patient, and submissive unto God without murmuring, and their lamentation for their misery endeth in prayer, and in a prayer for remission of sin : *O remember not against us former iniquities.* 2. The only right way to remedy a miserable condition is to sue for remission of sins, and for the renewed evidence of reconciliation; for, before the church here ask any thing for their outward delivery, they pray, *O remember not against us former iniquities.* 3. A people's long continuance in sin furnisheth ground for fear of the long continuing of begun wrath and judgment upon them, and therefore they pray for the forgetting of their sin, that the quarrel bringing the judgment may be removed : *O remember not against us our former iniquities.* 4. When wrath and justice are like to consume us and quickly make an end of us, a refuge is open to us in God's tender mercies who cannot destroy utterly a sinner fleeing to his mercy : *let thy tender mercies speedily prevent us, for we are brought very low.* 5. When the Lord's people are brought low, let them not look for a lifting up or relief except from God only; therefore say they here, *help us, O Lord.* 6. Such as have laid hold on God for salvation promised in the covenant, may also look for particular deliveries out of particular troubles, as appendages of the main benefit of salvation : therefore, *help us, O God of our salvation,* say they. 7. When men ask any thing the granting whereof may glorify God, they may confidently expect to have it; and in special, when God may

be so glorified as his people may also be preserved and comforted: *help us,* say they, *for the glory of thy name, and
deliver us.* 8. As the conscience of sin useth to step in
oftener between us and mercy, so must we call oftener for
remission of sin; for earnest affection can double and treble
the same petition without babbling: *deliver us, and purge
away our sins.* 9. It is the glory of the Lord to forget
sin, and when remission of sin is prayed for according to
God's promise, the Lord's glory is engaged for the helping
of faith to obtain: *purge away our sin for thy name's
sake.* 10. Idolaters are ready to insult over God's people
and their religion, and over God also, when the church is
afflicted, and this dishonour of God true saints cannot endure: *wherefore should the heathen say, Where is their
God?* 11. Howsoever the Lord will punish his own people
for their sins in the sight of the heathen, yet will he not
suffer the heathen long to insult over his people or over
true religion; but, by showing kindness to his people, will
have the heathen to know that he is their God, who will
answer for himself, and for his people and their religion also:
wherefore should the heathen say, Where is their God?
12. As it belongeth to God's honour to deliver his people
in their distress, so also to punish the persecutors of his
church and blasphemers of his name: *let him be known
among the heathen in our sight, by avenging the blood
of thy servants.* 13. It is a comfort and encouragement
to living saints to see God avenge the blood of dead saints
slain by their enemies: *let him be known in our sight, by
avenging the blood of thy servants.* 14. As it is no wonder
to see grief and sighing to be the cheer of God's people when
the Lord hath scattered them, and they are captive prisoners under their oppressors; so may we be sure their tears
and sighing shall not be misregarded by God: *let the sighing of the prisoner come before thee.* 15. Albeit it seem impossible to deliver God's people, when they are as condemned
prisoners, destined by their enemies to destruction; yet faith
seeth delivery very possible to God's omnipotency: *according to the greatness of thy power, preserve thou those
that are appointed to die.*

12. *And render unto our neighbours sevenfold into
their bosom their reproach, wherewith they have reproached thee, O Lord.*

13. *So we thy people, and sheep of thy pasture, will give thee thanks for ever : we will shew forth thy praise to all generations.*

In the last place, the godly pray for vengeance on their wicked neighbours, who mocked them and their religion in the time of their calamity; and thus they close their prayer with a promise to praise God for granting their petitions. Whence learn, 1. Such as rejoice at the calamity of God's people, and mock them in their misery, especially neighbours who should be most comfortable, as they are in some respect more guilty than open oppressors, so shall they be most severely plagued of God for their cruelty : *render unto our neighbours sevenfold into their bosom their reproach.* 2. The mocking of God's people in their misery, especially for their religion, is the mocking of God and reproaching of Him whose servants they are: *render them the reproach wherewith they have reproached thee, O Lord.* 3. When God taketh vengeance on the enemies of the church, then is it seen what interest God hath in that despised company; for the church here is confident that then their relations unto God, and God's care of them, shall be evident : *so we thy people and sheep of thy pasture shall give thee thanks ;* that is, we shall come out of distress, and gather ourselves together, and profess ourselves to be thy people and chosen flock, and shall praise thee. 4. The troubles of the Lord's people and their mourning are but temporal and of short endurance; but their deliverance and comfort, when their troubles are ended, are everlasting; and no less than everlasting duration can suffice them, to praise God and thank him for his kindness: *so we thy people will give thee thanks for ever.* 5. As the Lord's work for his distressed people calleth for thanks at their hands, so also doth it call for praise at their hands who shall hear of it; and they whose duty it is to give thanks, ought also, according to their power, to stir up others to praise God with themselves, and to stir up also the posterity in all succeeding ages, as the church here promiseth : *we will shew forth thy praise to all generations.*

.PSALM LXXX.

To the chief musician upon Shoshannim-eduth.　A psalm of Asaph.

This psalm given the church to be made use of, is of the like sad subject with the former, and may be applied to the time of carrying away the ten tribes out of the holy land, while Judah was yet in possession of it, and the temple was yet standing, and the Lord was dwelling between the cherubim in the sanctuary, where the ark and mercy-seat were yet remaining; or to the time of the begun desolation of the land by Nebuchadnezzar, or to any other desolation which threatened their final rooting out. The sum of the psalm is a lamenting of the miserable condition of the Israelites, and an earnest entreating of the Lord to give them repentance and delivery. In the first place, the church maketh her address to God, and propoundeth the main petition, ver. 1—3; in the second place, the Israelites lament their misery, and repeat the same petition, ver. 4—7; in the third place, they call to mind the Lord's care to plant his people in the land as a vine tree, and lament the doleful change of their happy condition into that of their present misery, ver. 8—13; in the fourth place, they pray for God's mercy and pity toward his desolate people, ver. 14—16; in the last place, they pray for the standing of the tribe of Judah, and that for Christ's cause, who was to take his human nature of this tribe, and close the psalm with repeating the third time their special petition for repentance and delivery to be granted unto them, ver. 17—19.

1. *Give ear, O Shepherd of Israel, thou that leadest Joseph like a flock ; thou that dwellest* between *the cherubims, shine forth.*

Many sweet fruits hath the Lord drawn forth from the bitter afflictions of his people, and this psalm among the rest; wherein, first, the church beggeth from God audience for the relations between God and them, v. 1, and then prayeth for salvation, v. 2, and to this end maketh request for the gracious gift of repentance to his people, that they might be saved, v. 3.

From the first verse, learn, 1. When our heart is full of grief, or of any holy affection, which we desire to lay forth before the Lord, we may call for, and expect, audience at the Lord's hands, as the church doth here, saying to the Lord, *give ear*. 2. He that would speak to God in the day of calamity had need to fasten faith on God, and should go about it, how grievous soever his rod seem, as here the church is taught by the psalmist to do. 3. Albeit faith will find small strength from any thing in the supplicant, yet on God's part it cannot miss solid ground to fix upon, according to the tenor of the covenant of grace, such as is Christ's prophetical and kingly office, whereby the Lord taketh on him to lead and feed his people; to govern and protect them, as a shepherd doth his flock : as here the church doth, *O shepherd of Israel.* This is one consideration. Another is, the constant experiment and proof given of his actual exercising of this office : *thou that leadest Joseph like a flock :* and unto the former they join the free offer of grace to all that seek for mercy from God through the mediator, Christ : *thou that dwellest between the cherubim.* 4. Albeit sin overcloudeth the manifesting of God's favour and lovingkindness towards his people, yet the prayer of faith upon the grounds of the covenant may expect the clearing up of his countenance again : *O shepherd of Israel, shine forth.*

2. *Before Ephraim, and Benjamin, and Manasseh, stir up thy strength, and come* and *save us.*

For understanding the second verse we must remember, that when the ark of the covenant rested or marched in the wilderness, these three tribes, *Ephraim, Benjamin, and Manasseh,* were in the rearward of the host of Israel, or on the west side thereof, as is set down, Numb. ii. 18, 19, &c.; when the host marched and the ark set forward, Moses said to the Lord, *rise up, Lord, and let thine enemies be scattered; and let them that hate thee flee before thee :* answerable to this doth the sixty-eighth psalm begin, when the ark removed, and was carried up to mount Zion. Now the people of God being in distress here, call those days to remembrance, and request the Lord, that, as he had in the eyesight of those three tribes here mentioned manifested himself many a time to be the leader and defender of his people; so he would now, also, in this their lamentable condition, stir up himself for their relief and safety. Whence learn, 1. The remembrance of the Lord's humbling himself to be familiar with his people, and how sweet and glorious communion his people have had with him, may and should encourage believers in him to seek and expect new experience of the like mercy in their need, as here the Israelites pray for new proof of that favour which their ancestors found sometimes : *before Ephraim, Benjamin, and Manasseh, stir up thy strength, and come and save us.* 2. The posterity of those who have been in fellowship with God, should pray for themselves and be prayed for by the church, that they may have room in the Lord's host, and have God their leader, as their godly fathers had before them : *before Ephraim, Benjamin, and Manasseh, stir up thy strength.*

3. *Turn us again, O God, and cause thy face to shine; and we shall be saved.*

This is the special petition most insisted upon, that God, by giving repentance, would reclaim his people from their apostasy, and grant the evidence of his former favour unto them, and so deliver and save them.　Whence learn, 1. As the apostasy of God's people from God, is the fountain of all their calamity; so their repentance and returning unto God is the first step unto their relief and delivery from procured misery of captivity, or any other calamity, as the prayer here importeth : *turn us again, O Lord.*　2. Conversion of people from their sin unto God, and leading them back from the misery drawn on by sin, is the work of God, which no man can work of himself, or in himself, or in others, till God begin, and enable to return, and lead them on in their turning; therefore, saith the psalmist, *turn us again, O Lord :* thus they say, as unable to turn again of themselves.　3. When a people or person turn unto God, repenting their sin or blacksliding from him, they may expect the Lord will show them evidences of his reconciliation and favour toward them : *turn us again, and cause thy face to shine upon us.*　4. It is to God's children very salvation to be in favour with God, and to be assured of reconciliation with him: *turn us again, cause thy face to shine, and so shall we be saved.*

4. *O Lord God of hosts, how long wilt thou be angry against the prayer of thy people ?*
5. *Thou feedest them with the bread of tears ; and givest them tears to drink in great measure.*
6. *Thou makest us a strife unto our neighbours ; and our enemies laugh among themselves.*
7. *Turn us again, O God of hosts, and cause thy face to shine ; and we shall be saved.*

In the second place, the church lamenteth the Lord's wrath; manifested, first, in answering their prayers with indignation, v. 4 ; secondly, by increasing their woful misery without consolation, v. 5 ; and thirdly, by making them the matter of their enemies' strife among themselves, which of them should have meanest Hebrews to be their slaves, and the object of their enemies' sport, when they had parted the prey among them, v. 6. After which he repeateth the former prayer for repentance, and for delivery, v. 7.

From the first part of their complaint and lamentation, set down, v. 4, learn, 1. The people of God may in their affliction put up prayers to God, which he will not accept, to wit, prayers for the removing of judgment, when they have not repented the sins which drew on the judgments; yea, they may prolong, and be instant in such prayers, and not receive a comfortable answer; yea, they may find their prayers answered with evidencing of God's disliking such prayers: *how long wilt thou be angry against the prayers of thy people?* 2. When God answereth not the prayers of his people in affliction, the afflicted must not cease to pray on still, neither may the truly godly among them cease to deal with God for his afflicted people, joined in external covenant with them, but must continue and be still instant with God, as here they do: for *how long wilt thou be angry against the prayers of thy people?* is a part of their prayer, notwithstanding that God seemeth angry at their prayers. 3. As God's supremacy over all the hosts of the creatures maketh his wrath more terrible to the supplicant, so should it make the supplicant more instant in prayer, and more loath to take a refusal to his supplication, as here it doth: *O Lord God of hosts, how long wilt thou be angry against the prayers of thy people?* 4. We are not always to look after a present answer to our prayers, but must wait on so long as God pleaseth not to answer: yea, it is possible, that after a believer hath begun to humble himself, God may send messenger after messenger of more and more appearance of wrath; but we must resolve, as to wrestle with all difficulties, so also with the sense of God's anger against us, yea, and that against our prayers: *how long wilt thou be angry against the prayers of thy people?*

From the second part of the lamentation, v. 5, learn, 1. When God's people will not mourn for sin in time, as penitents, no wonder he drive them to mourn for the fruit of their sin in sad affliction: *thou feedest them with the bread of tears.* 2. We are more sensible of the evil of trouble, than of the evil of sin; the tears of repentance are very rare, and soon dried up, but the tears of sorrow for affliction easily flow, as affliction increaseth or continueth,

and that, in God's wise dispensation, worldly sorrow for affliction, may drive us to godly sorrow for offending God :
thou feedest them with the bread of tears. 3. The comfort of the creatures, yea of necessary food, many be overcome and swallowed up by trouble and worldly sorrow, and
that in God's wise dispensation, that men may learn to hunger and thirst for heavenly and strong consolation: as it
befell this people, who were taken up so with weeping,
as they forgot their ordinary meals, and when they eat and
drank, and drenched their food with tears: *thou feedest
them with the bread of tears, and givest them tears to
drink in great measure.*

From the third part of the lamentation, v. 6, learn, 1.
It is righteousness for God to make his people find the bitterness of men's hatred and enmity, when they have slighted his friendship and favour; as here, he gave Israel over
into the hands of their enemies, when they had provoked
him : *thou makest us a strife to our neighbours, and
our enemies laugh.* 2. When the Lord lets the wicked
world loose upon his people, they find as many neighbours,
as enemies, who make havoc of them, and strive amongst
themselves who shall do them most harm, and serve themselves most of their persons and goods; and this is the
Lord's wise dispensation, to let his own know, what his
protection is worth : *thou makest us a strife unto our
neighbours.* 3. The grief and trouble of the Lord's people, is the joy of the wicked, and it is the property of an
enemy to rejoice at their calamity; and God in his most
wise dispensation will give his people a taste of this, that
they may know the fruit of their rejoicing in that which
offended God, and what they may expect of the world, if
they fall out of his favour : *thou makest us a strife to our
neighbours, and our enemies laugh among themselves.*

From the repetition of the same prayer for giving them
repentance, reconciliation, and salvation, v. 7, learn, 1.
Ardency of affection maketh the repetition of the same
prayer not to be babbling : *turn us again O God,* is now
the second time propounded. 2. The way to remedy all
the evil, both of sin and punishment, lying upon God's people, is to repent of their sins, and to seek reconciliation with
God; if his people would repent, then would not the Lord
be angry with their prayers; then affliction would either

be removed, or made light to them : for, to remedy all the lamented evils, they pray, *turn us again, O God.*   3. A praying people's case cannot be so dark and desperate, but looking to God's power shall give light and hope of relief : *turn us again, O God of hosts,* saith he; nothing is too hard for him to do.   4. God's people cannot dispense with the want of his manifested good-will to them : *turn us, and cause thy face to shine upon us,* is their fixed petition. 5. Salvation may be certainly expected in God's order; and if we labour to be sure of our turning to God, and living in the sense of communion with him, we need not make question of salvation; for that shall follow infallibly on the former two : *turn us again, O God of hosts, and cause thy face to shine upon us, so shall we be saved.* The last is not put up by way of prayer here, but promised to themselves, and put out of question, that it shall follow : *turn us, so shall we be saved,* say they.

8. *Thou hast brought a vine out of Egypt; thou hast cast out the heathen and planted it.*

9. *Thou preparedst* room *before it, and didst cause it to take deep root, and it filled the land.*

10. *The hills were covered with the shadow of it, and the boughs thereof* were like *the goodly cedars.*

11. *She sent out her boughs unto the sea, and her branches unto the river.*

In the third place, they renew their lamentation, by comparing the former blessed condition of the church of Israel, with the present miserable condition they are now in.   In former times Israel was a fruitful vineyard, v. 8—11, but now the Lord's protection is removed, and they are made a prey to every beastly enemy, v. 12, 13.   Whence learn, 1. Adversity bringeth to mind neglected prosperity in time past, and the distress of a church deprived of former favours, putteth a price upon, and giveth lustre unto, abused mercies looked back upon : as here, the calamity of the ten tribes, or of the whole twelve tribes cast out of their land, maketh their delivery out of Egypt, their planting in Canaan, and the mercies which they felt in that land, to appear very glorious; and setteth up that their former condition in the similitude of a fruitful vineyard.   2. There is no fitter similitude than a vine tree and a vineyard to represent the weakness of God's church and people, and God's care of them, to have fruits of faith and obedience from them : therefore here and elsewhere is this comparison made use of. 3. It serveth much to help the faith of God's people in their calamity, to call to mind God's begun work among them, and in them, and for them: for when his people claim wonted kindness, the Lord is ready to make his mercy run in the former channel. This is the ground of the church's reasoning here, in her supplication to God. 4. It is not enough lightly to mention a course of kindness shown to us of God, but every part and passage of it is worthy to be marked and prized highly; as here, 1. Israel's bringing out of Egypt is observed, and compared to the bringing of a noble plant out of a far country in the Lord's own hand : *thou hast brought a vine out of Egypt.* 2. The casting out of the Canaanites, is compared to the purging of the ground from stones, and thorns, and blocks, in comparison of Israel, to be planted there : *thou hast cast out the heathen, and planted it.* 3. They observe the benefit of enlarging their dwelling for commodious habitation : *thou preparedst room for it.* 4. And their settling in the land : *thou causedst it to take deep root.* 5. And their multiplying in it : *it filled the land.* 6. And their riches, and power, and glory in the land, comparable to a wood of cedars : *the hills were covered with the shadow of it, and the boughs thereof were like the goodly cedars.* 7. And the spreading of their authority and government according to the bounds set to their promised possession, Gen. xv. 18, from the Mediterranean sea westward, to the river Euphrates eastward : *she sent out her boughs to the sea, and her branches to the river.* Thus a well-ordered church is like a pleasant and fruitful vineyard.

12. *Why hast thou* then *broken down her hedges, so that all they which pass by the way do pluck her ?*

13. *The boar out of the wood doth waste it, and the wild beast of the field doth devour it.*

After calling to mind this glorious condition they were in' the church, in a weeping and lamentable manner, compare their present misery with what happiness once they had, and lay it forth before the pitiful eyes of the Lord. Whence learn, 1. As present felt misery commendeth prosperity past, so past prosperity augmenteth present misery, where the two conditions are compared, as in this comparison is held forth.   2. The most glorious and best planted church may for its unfruitfulness, and provocation of God by its ill fruits, be plucked up again, and the hedge of discipline, the hedge of civil government, and the hedge of God's protection, may all be removed suddenly from it, as here we see : *why hast thou broken down the hedges ?*   3. It is a wonderful and astonishing judgment, to see the Lord casting down the work of reformation once begun by him, and plucking up the plantation of his church once made by him; and yet the provocation of a wicked generation may procure this evil, which hardly can be believed till it come, and even then it is wonderful, and should send men unto God, to make them see rightly the causes thereof, as this interrogation importeth : *why hast thou broken down her hedges ?* 4. When God removeth his hedges from about his people, for their provocation of him, then any body that pleaseth may make a prey of them : *so that all they who pass by the way do pluck her.*   5. If God remove the hedge of his protection from about his people, no wonder they fall into the hands of the most savage, cruel, and beastly sort of men, as did befall Israel : *the boar out of the wood doth waste it, and the wild beast out of the field doth devour it.*   6. When the Lord's church is in the worst condition, she is not so wasted and destroyed, but a remnant is left to present by prayer her condition unto God, to deal with him for her restoration, as the case in hand here and elsewhere showeth.

14. *Return, we beseech thee, O God of hosts: look down from heaven, and behold, and visit this vine ;*

15. *And the vineyard which thy right hand hath planted, and the branch* that *thou madest strong for thyself.*

16. It is *burnt with fire ;* it is *cut down : they perish at the rebuke of thy countenance.*

In the fourth place, they pray that God, who was departed from them, would return and have compassion on the desolate condition of his church. Whence learn, 1. Although the Lord seem to depart from his church, yet he is within cry, and may be recalled by prayer, and may by his power set all right again : *return, we beseech thee, O God of hosts.* 2. Although no hope of help or possibility of relief can be seen on earth, yet there is hope of help from heaven: *look down from heaven.* 3. In the least degree of God's respect and kindness to a desolate church, begun to be manifested after pouring out judgments on it, faith will read hopes of relief and restoration of it: *behold and visit this vine :* for to *come and see,* is all to them which they crave. 4. The labour and care which God hath bestowed on his church, for setting up, and settling it in any place, may give hope to those who pray for it, that albeit the Lord afflict it heavily, yet he will not lose his labour : *visit this vine, and the vineyard which thy right hand hath planted.* 5. There was a branch to come of the stock of Israel, for whose cause the nation of the Israelites could not be utterly forsaken and destroyed, and this was the Messiah, Christ Jesus (promised to come of Abraham, Isaac, Jacob, Judah, David), of whose coming, because God had a special care that the stock should be underpropped and upheld, and made strong till this branch came forth, the church of Israel might be confident not to be utterly cast off, and therefore in their prayer they made mention of him ; *visit the vineyard and the branch* (to wit, of the house of David) *that thou madest strong for thyself.* In the Hebrew, it is the Son whom thou madest strong, even Christ, who is the true Son of God, the true vine tree, John xv. 1, whereabout the Father's husbandry is in a special way employed. 6. The visible church or people of God by covenant, sometimes may be so far from a glorious and flourishing condition of prosperity, that, on the contrary, in outward appearance she may be almost destroyed, and like to perish utterly : as here of the Lord's vineyard, or the whole visible church we read, *it is burnt with fire, it is cut down :* he meaneth God's people; *they perish,* saith the psalmist, *at the rebuke. of thy countenance.* 7. We are to look, not so much to instruments of the church's desolation, as to the people's sins procuring it, and to God's wrath causing it: *they perish at the rebuke of thy countenance.*

17. *Let thy hand be upon the Man of thy right hand, upon the Son of man* whom *thou madest strong for thyself.*

18. *So will not we go back from thee : quicken us,
and we will call upon thy name.*

19. *Turn us again, O Lord God of hosts, cause
thy face to shine; and we shall be saved.*

In the last place, they put up three requests. In the
first, they insist upon that point of their prayer, v. 15,
which concerneth the branch of the vineyard of Israel, the
promised Messiah, Christ the Redeemer : and make request
over again, that the stock and lineage of David, whereof
Christ was to come, might be kept to the time, till he should
assume human nature, and become the Son of man, according to the solid grounds which God had laid down to bring
this promise to pass. For the substance of the prayer is
this : seeing thou hast made one branch of this vine, which
thou broughtest out of Egypt, strong for thyself, or for
thy own purpose, namely, the man of thy right hand, the
Son of man, the promised Messiah, God to be incarnate :
let thy hand or power be employed for bringing this to pass,
that he who is at thy right hand, thy equal, may be made
man, the man of thy right hand, the Son of man : *so will
will not we go back from thee;* that is, by him we thy redeemed shall be preserved from apostasy and separation
from thee. In the second request, they pray for the pouring forth of the Spirit upon his dead people, that, having
spiritual life communicated unto them, they may worship
God in spirit and truth : *quicken us, and we will call upon thy name,* say they. In the third request, they repeat
the third time that prayer for repentance and reconciliation,
to be manifested to his people.

From the first request, v. 17, learn, 1. The refuge, rest,
consolation, and confidence of a distressed church or person is Christ; and toward him must the afflicted cast their
eye for relief, as here the church in her deepest desolation
doth. 2. Christ is always at the right hand of the Father,
in regard of power and glory; and it is for him no robbery
to be equal with God the Father, Phil. ii. 16, and his human nature assumed doth not degrade him from the glory
which he had with the Father before the world began,
John, xvii. 5. *He is the man of God's right hand,* in a
singular manner. 3. Christ and his kingdom are established before God for ever, for bringing to pass the purpose

and service of God in the redemption of his elect; *he is the man whom the Father hath made strong for himself:* for his human nature is united with his divine nature in one person; his incarnation was made sure by the eternal and immutable decree of the covenant of redemption, wherein the elect were given over to Christ, and grace was granted and given to them, in Christ Jesus, before the world began. 2. Tim. i. 9. And as his incarnation was made sure by decree, so also is it made sure by many times repeated promises in the law and prophets, beginning at Gen. iii. 15, where it is promised, that *the seed of the woman should tread down the head of the serpent,* all along the Scripture unto Malachi, iii. 1, where it is revealed, that Christ's messenger, to wit, John Baptist, in the power of Elias should come before him : and straightway after he himself should show himself, as did come to pass: *this is the Son of man,* saith he, *whom thou hast made strong for thyself.* 4. To bring this promise to effect and accomplishment, the almighty power of God did set on work, and never drew back from operation, till his purpose was brought to pass, for, after the time that the man Abraham was designed, of whose seed he was to take flesh, the Scripture showeth what care the Lord had of Isaac and Jacob, and the patriarchs in Egypt; and about the bringing of their posterity out of it to Canaan, till David's family is designed for his stock : and when the ten tribes were scattered abroad, *he preserved Judah to the fore :* and when that tribe also was thrust out into captivity, he brought it back again, and preserved David's race, and the tribe of Judah under civil government till Christ came; and this the prayer here propounded made request for : *let thy hand be upon the man of thy right hand.* 5. Neither the church, nor any member thereof needeth any more security for their stability and perpetuation, but Christ : for now when the vineyard is burnt, and the visible church defaced, the remnant are content to rest satisfied with this, which also they take for granted, and subscribe unto : *let thy hand be upon the man of thy right hand; upon the Son of man, whom thou hast made strong for thyself.* 6. The consanguinity of Christ with the believer, and his humiliation in his human nature, are strong supporters of the faith and comfort of his people that seek salvation through him :

therefore the faithful here fix themselves on this, that as he is God's Son, so he is a branch of their vineyard also; that as he is at the right hand of the Father as God, so he is *the man of his right hand also :* the Son of man, or of Adam, partaker of flesh and blood with us, of the same stock that we are of, in all things like to us, except sin : for the *Son of man* is the style, whereby Christ styled himself in his humiliation. 7. The perpetuity of the church, and the perseverance of the saints, are founded upon the sufficiency of Christ : and the unfeigned believer may assure himself, as of the continuance of the church, so of his own perseverance and constant communion with God through him : *let thy hand be upon the man of thy right hand, &c., so will not we go back from thee.*

From the second request, v. 18, learn, 1. As there is a death of alienation from the life of God in the unregenerate, and a death of disability, discomfort, and discouragement found in the regenerate in Scripture; so there is a quickening which giveth spiritual life to those that are yet dead in their sins and trespasses; and a quickening which giveth strength and comfort to the weak, disconsolate, and discouraged souls of God's children : for the first sort of quickening every regenerate man should pray, in behalf of all the elect in the visible church who are not as yet converted; and for quickening in other respects they should pray in behalf of themselves, and other afflicted spirits of the godly, as here the believers do pray : *quicken us.* 2. The honouring of God in spiritual worship should be the end of our petitions which we make for any good to our selves : *quicken us, and we shall call upon thy name.* 3. Albeit the work of calling on God's name, and worshipping God in spirit and truth, be the work of the regenerate man; yet the spiritual life, and the motion or stirring up of the regenerate man unto this work, the enabling of the man unto it, and in it, and the cheering up of his heart to do it affectionately, are the work of the Lord : for these the psalmist here distinguisheth; first, he sets down God's part : *quicken thou us ;* and then our part : *and we shall call upon thy name.*

From the third request, v. 19, repeated now the third time, learn, 1. In what respects soever the church of the Jewish nation may seem to be alienated from God, yet there is hope of their repentance and returning, and reconciliation unto God; for there is a petition of the Lord's inditing standing here, thrice repeated in their favour, to be granted in due time by God, to whom nothing is hard : and here, in the third repetition of this prayer, the name of God Jehovah, whereby he told Israel that he would be known to them to be the performer of promises, is added expressly : *turn us again, O Jehovah, God of hosts.* 2. Albeit we ourselves breed the mist and clouds which hide from us the shining of God's favour towards us, build the partition walls, and raise up mountains of transgressions which separate between God and us; yet it is the Lord himself only, who, of his own free grace and by his own power, dissolveth these clouds, and removeth these impediments out of his own way towards us : *turn us again, and cause thy face to shine.* 3. So oft as we are burdened with the same pressure, and straitened with the same necessity; so oft we may and should have recourse to God for relief by prayer : for this staff hath God put in faith's hand, to help the believer in every step of his journey, till he come home to the Lord, and be past all peril : *turn us again, cause thy face to shine.* 4. As the sight of our distance from God, and sense of his displeasure, and fear of perdition, serve to be a spur to our prayer; so desire of reconciliation, desire and purpose of repenting, and hope of salvation, serve to encourage us to persevere in prayer, till we have what we ask perfected to us : *turn us again, cause thy face to shine, so shall we be saved.*

PSALM LXXXI.

To the chief musician upon Gittith. A psalm of Asaph.

This psalm was appointed to be sung in the Jews' solemn feasts, new moons, and feast of tabernacles; in special, for a testimony of God's gracious and bountiful dealing with his people on the one hand, and of their provocation of God on the other hand, moving him to change his dispensation toward them, and to withhold many benefits from them, which otherwise they might have had, if they had not rejected God's counsel, and chosen their own ways: that by this psalm his people might learn to be wiser.

The parts of the psalm are three. The first is a preface, wherein there is a mutual stirring up of the church's members, to keep the solemn feasts, and blowing of trumpets, ver. 1—3, and a reason of this mutual exhortation, taken from God's institution of this ordinance when he brought his people out of Egypt from the service of strangers, ver. 4, 5.

In the second part is set down, how God delivered them from bondage in Egypt, and from troubles in their journey, ver. 6, 7, and how reasonable commands the Lord gave unto them : which commands are all summed up in this one : That God should be their God alone, ver. 8—10.

In the third part is set down : first, how they rejected God and his counsel, ver. 11 ; next, how therefore they were plagued, by being given over to their own lusts, ver. 12 ; thirdly, how they deprived themselves of God's benefits, which, by following God's counsel, they might have enjoyed, ver. 13—15.

1. *Sing aloud unto God our strength : make a joyful noise unto the God of Jacob.*

2. *Take a psalm, and bring hither the timbrel, the pleasant harp with the psaltery.*

3. *Blow up the trumpet in the new-moon, in the time appointed, on our solemn feast-day.*

From their mutual stirring up of one another to rejoice in God, commanded here by the psalmist in the Lord's name, learn, 1. That whatsoever may be our own private condition, it is our duty ever, and in all things, to give glory to God, to rejoice in him, to profess and avow his name : *sing aloud unto God.* 2. The Lord's people have the fulfilling, supplying, and supporting of their emptiness, wants, and weakness in God, whose sufficiency they ought to make use of, and rejoice therein : *sing unto God our strength.* 3. It is the covenant of grace, whereby God becometh our God, which entitleth us, and giveth us interest in, and right unto, his all-sufficiency, which we should entertain joyfully in our communion with God, praising him, and thanking him for it, and delighting in his presence, because of it : *make a joyful noise unto the God of Jacob;* for God was Jacob's God, because God was by covenant Abraham and his children's God, whose children also we are, who are Christ's, Gal. iii. 29.

From the use and variety of musical instruments called for, v. 2, 3, learn, 1. Albeit the external melody of musical instruments in the Lord's public worship, with the rest of the pedagogy, and shadowing dark figures of the ceremonial law, be abolished, now when the Lord, the Sun of righteousness is come; yet the moral duties represented by them are still to be acknowledged and followed by us, to wit, that the praises of the Lord are inexpressible by us, and that we are insufficient of ourselves to set forth the same, that we have matter of unspeakable joy in God our Redeemer, and should stir up all the powers of our soul to this part of his spiritual service: for this those musical instruments taught: *take a psalm, and bring hither the timbrel, the pleasant harp with the psaltery.* 2. We ought to acknowledge the stately magnificence of our exalted Lord, and our dulness and slowness to praise him: and what need we had to be stirred up, and to stir up one another to this duty: for this was pointed at in the use of the trumpets: *blow up the trumpet.* 3. We ought to acknowledge that we are subject to various changes, and to alteration of conditions in this life, that all these changes are sanctified unto the Lord's people, and that new consolations may be expected from God, one after another, to season the darkness and nights of our affliction: and we should consecrate ourselves anew from time to time to God, and give him the first part and flower of our time; yea, should study that all our time, in all changes whatsoever, may be spent in his service: for thus much did the solemnities in their new moons hold forth: *blow up the trumpet in the new moon.* 4. We ought to acknowledge that we are strangers here in the world, and have no certain dwelling-place, but that we are in our sojourning depending upon God's provision for us, and protecting of us, excepting the time when we shall appear before him, and shall be put in possession of those mansion-places prepared for us, wherein we shall have fulness of joy, and God constantly present with us; and that in the mean time we should study to rejoice in the riches of the Lord's goodness to us in our Redeemer; for this in substance was held forth in the solemn feasts, and in special, in the feast of tabernacles: *blow the trumpets in the time appointed, on our solemn feast-day.*

4. *For this* was *a statute for Israel,* and *a law of the God of Jacob.*

5. *This he ordained in Joseph* for *a testimony, when he went out through the land of Egypt;* where *I heard a language* that *I understood not.*

The church giveth two reasons of the exhortation cheerfully to glorify God in the observation of his appointed or-

dinances and solemn convocations. One is, because God
instituted and commanded this solemn rejoicing in him,
v. 4. The other is, because he appointed it after bestowing
on them great deliverance out of Egypt from their bondage
under strangers and people of an uncouth language, v. 5.
From the first reason, learn, 1. It is a sufficient motive
for observation of any religious action, that God hath ordained it; and no less authority than divine can warrant a
man in matters of religion: therefore it is said here, *for
this was a statute for Israel, and a law of the God of
Jacob.* As none may appoint acts of religious worship,
but God : so also none may alter or abrogate them, except
God himself only : *for they are statutes and laws of the
God of Jacob.* 2. The ordinances of religion appointed
of God, as they are witnesses of his will, how he shall
be served, and witnesses of his good-will toward us, and
care of us to have us saved : so also are they witnesses
of our faith and obedience, to testify for us or against us,
as we make use of them : *this he ordained in Joseph for
a testimony.* 3. The greatness of the work of redemption,
the powerful manner of bringing it to pass, and the misery
wherein we were before we were delivered, should augment
our joy and thankfulness to God, and straiten our tie to his
worship and service, as the force of the church's reasoning
here teacheth : for the Lord went through the Egyptians,
and over their belly, as a mighty conqueror, when he redeemed his people and delivered them from the servitude of
a people of a strange language; therefore they were bound
joyfully to keep his solemn ordinance: *he ordained this
for a testimony,* saith the church, *when he went through
the land of Egypt, where I heard a language which I
understood not.*

6. *I removed his shoulder from the burden : his
hands were delivered from the pots.*

7. *Thou calledst in trouble, and I delivered thee; I
answered thee in the secret place of thunder; I proved
thee at the waters of Meribah. Selah.*

In the second part the Lord speaketh, and putteth his
people in mind of his kindness to them in their delivery
from Egypt, v. 6, and of his wise care of them in the
wilderness, v. 7, and how he craved nothing of them, but

that they should keep close to him, and not go after idols, v. 8, 9. First, because he is God all-sufficient. Next, because he had entered into covenant to be their God. Thirdly, because he had given proof what he could do for them by their delivery out of Egypt. And lastly, because he was ready to make them fully blessed upon their willingness to receive his offered goodness, v. 10. And then he shows what an evil meeting they gave him.

From renewing the memory of their delivery out of Egypt, v. 6, learn, 1. For right taking up of the benefit of our redemption, whether spiritual or bodily, the heaviness of our yoke and baseness of our slavery must be called to mind : *I removed his shoulder from the burden, and his hands were delivered from the pots;* for Israel were as pioneers and scullions in Egypt, basely employed in carrying straw and mortar to make brick, as most abject slaves : and this resembleth the condition we are in by nature, under the slavery and burden of sin and misery. 2. God only is the redeemer of men from whatsoever evil condition; no instruments which God useth, must intercept his glory : none can ease our burden or cleanse our hands but God only : *I,* saith the Lord, *removed his shoulder from the burden, and hands from the pots.*

From the Lord's wise care of them, when they were come out of Egypt, v. 7, learn, 1. After delivery of us out of the state of misery, other particular troublesome passages may meet us, as met Israel at the Red sea, when they came out of Egypt, and we may fall into new troubles, for a little as they did. 2. God who delivereth us from the state of misery, must also deliver us from particular miserable cases, or miserable conditions; yea, and being called upon by us in our misery, he will deliver us as he did Israel : *thou calledst in trouble, and I delivered thee.* 3. It is God's wise disposing, that new trouble should bring to mind our former delivery and our deliverer, and should press us to pray to God, and make way for a new experience of delivery, as here we see. 4. The more the Lord manifesteth himself from heaven for us, and against our enemies, the greater is our obligation; as Israel's obligation was augmented, when, at their prayer in the Red sea, the Lord by thunder out of the black cloud against the Egyptians following them, declared himself for Israel : *I answered thee*

T

in the secret place of thunder. 5. It is an evidence of the Lord's care of his people, to put them to the trial of their faith and sincerity of affection to God, that so they may either find their former profession and opinion of themselves solid and upright, or, finding it otherwise, may be humbled and repent, and become more sincere; therefore is the trial of Israel after their coming out of the Red sea numbered among the evidences of God's care of them: *I proved thee at the waters of Meribah.* 6. Calling to mind our misbelief made manifest unto us in the day of our trial, should make us more humble and wary to depart from God thereafter, for this is the lesson which Israel's striving with God at the waters of Meribah should have taught them: *I have proved thee at the waters of Meribah,* or waters of strife.

8. *Hear, O my people, and I will testify unto thee: O Israel, if thou wilt hearken unto me;*

9. *There shall no strange god be in thee; neither shalt thou worship any strange god.*

10. *I am the Lord thy God, which brought thee out of the land of Egypt: open thy mouth wide, and I will fill it.*

We have heard of God's gracious dealing with Israel, in the point of doing for them. Now the Lord declareth what thankfulness he required of them, and how reasonable and equitable his demands were; unto the consideration whereof he awakeneth them up, v. 8; summeth up all in the first command of the moral law, v. 9; giveth reasons to move them to this, v. 10.

From his awaking them to hear, v. 8, learn, 1. When the Lord's word is to be delivered unto us, we should have our minds gathered in, and humbled and fixed unto a reverent attention, hearty belief, and humbled obedience; therefore, saith he, *hear, O Israel, and I will testify unto thee.* 2. When the Lord speaketh, whether for conviction of duty to be done, or duty not discharged, there needeth no other witness beside himself to convince the conscience, his speech is so clear, so full of truth and authority: *hear, and I will testify unto thee.* 3. Both the Lord and we ourselves have just reason to question our willingness to hear God's word inculcated unto us; because it will be found that we have proved misbelieving and rebellious hearers before, and because it is our natural disposition to be averse from all God's commands; therefore, saith the Lord, *O Israel, if thou wilt hearken unto me.* 4. The Lord requireth his people to be a willing people, and nothing can be more forcible to make us willing and obedient to God, than to understand that God is willing to teach, direct, and bless us: *hear, O Israel, if thou wilt, or shalt hearken unto me.*

From the sum of that service which God requireth of us, v. 9, learn, 1. The sum of God's law is comprised in the first command; for, as God is feared, delighted in, submitted unto, and made our God in effect, so are all the commandments kept: *there shall be no strange God in thee.* 2. As soundness in religion, and cleaving close to our only one God (as he hath revealed himself to be the Father, Son, and Holy Ghost, of whom, and through whom, and for whom are all things,) are the fountains of all obedience and keeping communion with God; so the corrupting of religion, and departing from this ground in any sort, are the fountains of all following misbehaviour, and discommunion with God: *there shall no strange God be in thee, neither shalt thou worship any strange god.*

From the reasons of this duty set down, v. 10, learn, 1. The consideration of having our life, and motion, and being of God, and that he will give to all his promises and threatenings certain performance, should move us to believe in him, adhere unto him, and serve him only: *I am the Lord, I am Jehovah.* 2. The covenant of grace, wherein the Lord hath drawn us, who profess ourselves to be his in Christ, should move us to depend on him for righteousness and life, and to study in his strength to please him: *I am the Lord thy God.* 3. The great work of our redemption, and all the benefits bestowed upon us, in relation to our bringing out of the slavery of idolatry and Egyptian darkness, to the beholding of the marvellous light and kingdom of his dear Son, represented by the delivery of his people out of Egypt, should move us to adhere to our Redeemer, and to aim at his service singly: *I am thy God who brought thee out of the land of Egypt.* 4. The fair allowance which God bestoweth upon his servants, to wit, " Ask and have," should tie our hearts to such a potent, all-sufficient, and gracious

God: *open thy mouth wide, and I will fill it.* 5. It is the narrowness of our faith, and of our spiritual desire which hindereth our felicity; we are not straitened in God, but in ourselves: for his offer is, *open thy mouth wide and I will fill it.* The Lord will give grace and glory, and will withhold no good thing from them that walk uprightly; and for this end he calleth for the enlarging of our desires, and of our belief to receive satisfaction, that we may have in him full contentment, and not be allured from him to vanities which cannot profit us.

11. *But my people would not hearken to my voice ; and Israel would none of me.*

In the third part of the psalm is set down how Israel, to their own detriment, and depriving themselves of great happiness, rejected the Lord's command, and the offer of his grace. Whence learn, 1. The people to whom the Lord is most liberal are not always most thankful; his people by external covenant are not always obedient to him, but readily give him the worst meeting: *but my people would not hearken unto my voice.* 2. The cause of not hearkening to, and obeying God's commands, is our not believing in God, not taking satisfaction, pleasure, and delight in God; for how came it that God's people by covenant did not obey his voice? It may serve for an answer: *and Israel would none of me,* or rested not on me, or had no pleasure in me.

12. *So I gave them up unto their own hearts' lust: and they walked in their own counsels.*

Here is shown how fearful was Israel's plague for their not delighting in God; they were given over to follow their own will unto their own perdition. Whence learn, 1. The idols which come in competition with God, are a man's own carnal lusts and affections, as here appeareth. 2. If these idols be adhered to, when God offereth himself for giving a man contentment, it is justice with God to take a refusal at the man's hands, and to cease to deal with his heart any more, but to give him over to the service of his idol: *they would none of me, so I gave them up unto their own hearts' lust.* 3. Whosoever refuse to serve God, shall not eschew to serve a worse master, to wit, their own beastly affections, and Satan, who ruleth men by their lusts: *they would have none of me, so I gave them up to their own*

hearts' lust; and this of all judgments is the heaviest.
4. When God leaveth a man to himself, there is no restraint
to keep him from going to mischief and perdition, as here
we see: *I gave them up, and they walked in the counsel
of their own hearts.*

13. *Oh that my people had hearkened unto me,* and
Israel had walked in my ways!

Last of all is set down, by way of God's lamenting for his
people, what felicity they lost by this their refusing to make
God their delight, and his voice their rule to walk by. First,
if they had obeyed God, their enemies would not have been
their masters, but they would have been made victorious
over their adversaries, v. 13—15. Next, they would have
been satisfied with all contentments abundantly, set forth
under the terms of feeding them with fine wheat and honey.
This lamenting of God for his people's misery, is borrowed
from the manner of men, lamenting the misery which their
disobedient children have brought upon themselves; and is
not to be taken so, as if there were in God any passion or
perturbation, or miserable lamentation; but this speech is to
be conceived, as other like speeches in Scripture, which are
borrowed from the affections of men, and are framed to move
some holy affection in men, suitable to that affection from
which the Lord taketh the similitude; and so, *O that my
people had hearkened unto me,* serveth to move his people
(who should hear this expression,) to repent and lament their
not hearkening unto God; and to study in all time to come
to be more obedient unto him, even as they would eschew
the curse which came upon misbelieving and disobedient Israel, and as they desired to obtain the blessings whereof carnal Israelites came short, and deprived themselves. And if
it be asked, what may be imported by this speech properly?
we answer, *O that my people had hearkened unto me, &c.,*
showeth these six things: First, what order the Lord hath set
in giving blessings to his visible church; namely, that they
begin and believe in him, and study to obey him, and that
they, by means appointed by him, should look to have such
blessings as he hath promised to believers, and to obedient
people. Next, this manner of speech showeth how acceptable and pleasant unto God it is to see the faith, obedience,
and welfare of his people, all joined together in his appointed

order.   Thirdly, that the meritorious and culpable cause
of men's misery is not in God but in man, who by his sin
deserveth it, and draweth it on himself. Fourthly, that God
delighteth not in the death or destruction of his people, but
that they should repent and live.   Fifthly, that this is his
will, that whosoever shall hear of the evil meeting which the
Israelites gave to God, and of the judgment which they drew
upon themselves, may be made wise by this lamentation
made by God for Israel's destruction; and so may rather
choose to hearken to God, as they did not, than to be given
over in his wrath to their own lusts, and to perish in his
indignation, as befell them.   Sixthly, that God requireth a
suitable meeting of his people to his dispensations, that is,
that they may be so willing to hearken to his voice, and so
loath to offend him, as he manifesteth by words and works
his willingness to save them, and his loathness to destroy
them.

From the Lord's lamenting, learn further, 1. As, on the
one hand, the miscarriage and misery of others before us
should make us wise to eschew the evil which befell them,
and to obtain the good whereof they, by their disobedience,
were deprived; so, on the other hand, the willingness of
God to bless those who follow his direction, should make us
diligent to understand what course God hath prescribed,
and should make us confident to obtain blessedness in our
endeavour to follow it: for, *O that my people had hearkened unto me, &c.*, teacheth us so much.   2. They may
be in the number and estimation of God's people, by virtue
of church covenant, who, for refusing to follow God's counsel, may come short of God's blessings; for, *O that my
people had hearkened unto me, &c.*, maketh this evident.
3. He who heareth God uttering his wishes for the conversion of his people, and lamenting that his word is not believed, and that his offer of grace is not received, giveth
God an evil meeting, and neither believeth God's goodness
nor careth for his own salvation, except he join with God,
lamenting his own misbelief in time past, and wish heartily
the same wish with God for his own conversion for time to
come; for this speech, *O that my people had hearkened
unto me, &c.*, is framed to this very end, to make the hearer
willing, and so to convert him, or else to convict him, if he
take not hold of the offer.   4. Whatsoever be the Lord's

secret decrees concerning the salvation of some and condemnation of others in the visible church; yet the means of
execution of those decrees are so holy and just, and wisely
carried on, as those decrees shall not be particularly revealed
to the stumbling of any man, but the offer of grace and
declaration of God's goodness so laid out in common, that
whosoever embraceth not the same, is made inexcusable; for
when God saith, *O that my people had hearkened unto me*,
he that doth not answer the Lord, with, *O that thou wouldst
frame this heart of mine to the obedience of faith*, hath
nothing to say, if he be damned, for his slighting the offer
so freely held forth unto him and pressed upon him.

14. *I should soon have subdued their enemies, and
turned my hand against their adversaries.*

15. *The haters of the Lord should have submitted
themselves unto him: but their time should have endured
for ever.*

16. *He should have fed them also with the finest of
the wheat: and with honey out of the rock should I have
satisfied thee.*

From the good which should have come to his people,
set down, v. 14—16, learn, 1. God's blessings are not to be
looked after, except in the ways of God; and if any man
come short of God's blessing, he beareth the blame himself:
*O that Israel had walked in my ways, I should soon have
subdued their enemies, &c.* 2. If the Lord's people have
provoked him to let loose their enemies upon them, and to
prevail over them, the only way to have affairs changed, is
to turn to God, and to walk in his ways: *if Israel had
walked in my ways, I should have turned my hand against
their adversaries.* 3. They that are enemies to the Lord's
people are haters of the Lord; and where the profession of
true religion and righteousness is hated, there the quarrel
is common to God with his people, for their enemies are
here called *haters of God.* 4. It is a benefit to God's people,
and a point of glory to God, when God's enemies and theirs
submit themselves to God, albeit but feignedly; which good
God's people hinder when they walk not in his ways: *if
Israel had walked in my ways, the haters of the Lord
should have submitted themselves, or lied unto him;* as
the word will bear. 5. There is no means to perpetuate a

visible church in any place, but to walk in the Lord's ways: *if Israel had walked in my ways, &c., their time should have endured for ever.* 6. Obeying the voice of God, that is, embracing the offer of grace and reconciliation with God through the sacrifice of the Messiah, Christ, and studying to walk holily, as persons reconciled, are the only ways of coming by true felicity, the only ways of being furnished with all things necessary for life and salvation, the only ways of having large allowance from God of sweet and satisfactory food for entertaining spiritual life and communion with God, promised here under the similitude of earthly food: *he should have fed them with the finest of the wheat: and with honey out of the rock should I have satisfied thee.*

PSALM LXXXII.

A psalm of Asaph.

This psalm ⸱ ⸱eeth with the time of David's persecution by Saul and his counsellors, he peers of the land; wherein the psalmist comforteth himself in God's supremacy, and his judging all judges on the earth; for executing whereof God cometh unto their meeting, ver. 1; then challengeth them for their injustice and oppression, ver. 2; thirdly, readeth the law and rule of their duty unto them, ver. 3, 4; fourthly, condemneth them as guilty, ver. 5; fifthly, pronounceth sentence of doom upon them, ver. 6, 7; and then the psalmist closeth the psalm with prayer, ver. 8.

1. *God standeth in the congregation of the mighty; he judgeth among the gods.*

From the Lord's presence in the assembly of judges, learn, 1. The name of a congregation or church is given, in Scripture, to the orderly meeting of rulers and governors, met for the execution of their office; as here, *God standeth in the congregation or church of the mighty.* 2. No judge is absolute lord over a people, but is in subordination to God, who is judge above all judges, and will judge of all the decrees of judges under him: *God standeth in the congregation of the mighty: he judgeth.* 3. God putteth his name upon civil magistrates, and hath clothed them with honour; that as their eminency is a part of his image, so their decrees should be such as God will own: *he judgeth among the gods.*

2. *How long will ye judge unjustly, and accept the persons of the wicked? Selah.*

From the Lord's challenging them for their partiality and injustice, learn, 1. Men in honour and power readily forget God, their Master and sovereign Lord, and neglect to do justice according to their office; the splendour of their power maketh them to forget their duty to God above them, and to their subjects under them, as the instance of the rulers of Israel showeth, who had God's express law instead of acts of Parliament; and God dwelling in the midst of them in a wonderful manner, for direction in extraordinary cases: even *they did judge unjustly.* 2. Corrupt judges are inclined to show favour only to the wicked, and are partial when the cause of the wicked cometh before them : *ye accept the persons of the wicked.* 3. Albeit the Lord keep peace for a while, yet will he not always be silent, but at length will call them to an account: *how long will ye judge unjustly?*

3. *Defend the poor and fatherless; do justice to the afflicted and needy.*

4. *Deliver the poor and needy : rid them out of the hand of the wicked.*

From the rule of justice which is set to magistrates, learn, 1. The touchstone of magistrates' justice is in the causes and cases of the poor, fatherless, afflicted, and needy, who are not able to attend long their suits of law, and have no friends nor money to deal for them; to whom, therefore, the mighty should be eyes to direct them, and a staff to their weakness, to support and help them to their right : *defend the poor and fatherless ; do justice to the afflicted and needy.* 2. As the poor and afflicted have need of the judge's help to clear their right, when they seek justice; so also when they are unjustly drawn to the bar, or any way oppressed, the mighty, or judges, should interpose for their relief, and rescue the oppressed from the oppressor: *deliver the poor and needy, rid them out of the hand of the wicked.*

5. *They know not, neither will they understand ; they walk on in darkness : all the foundations of the earth are out of course.*

From the condemnatory sentence for their guiltiness, learn, 1. It is a great fault in a judge not to know the duty of his office, or not to acquaint himself with the solid rules of justice; for upon this ground are they here pronounced guilty : *they know not.* 2. It is a great fault when a judge is ignorant to refuse instruction, information, and direction offered from the Lord's word, as here: *neither will they understand.* 3. It is the most culpable of all, for any man, but to judges in special, to go on still in a sinful course: *they walk on in darkness.* 4. When justice and judgment-seats are corrupted, and judges do not mind justice in their places, then the pillars of that land or kingdom must stagger, and all matters go to ruin or a perilous alteration: *all the foundations of the earth,* or of the land, *are out of course,* saith the Lord, where the foresaid injustice or faults in governors are found.

6. *I have said, Ye are gods; and all of you are children of the most High:*

7. *But ye shall die like men, and fall like one of the princes.*

From the sentence of doom pronounced against them, learn, 1. Princes, magistrates, chief rulers, and judges, have allowance from God, of honour, power, and strength, tribute and revenues, for the better discharge of their office under him: *I have said, Ye are gods, and all of you are children of the most High;* that is, I have put the image of my superiority on you, and given you pre-eminence of place, power, and gifts, over others in my name. 2. Great places among men do not exempt any man from God's power, justice, and judgment; but all men, great men no less than others, must die and come to judgment, as hath befallen others before them. A prince among God's people who executeth not justice, as becometh God's servant, shall be punished, as profane persons are who rule without the pale of God's church: *but ye shall die like men, and fall like one of the princes.* 3. The meditation of death and judgment following on it, is a pressing motive to amendment of life; for this is set before men of high places who do not stand in fear of their subjects: *ye shall die like men, and fall like one of the princes.*

8. *Arise, O God, judge the earth: for thou shalt inherit all nations.*

From the close of the psalm by this short prayer, wherein the oppressed servant of God prayeth that God would put order under the government of his people, and redress the wrongs done to them, learn, 1. Albeit the oppressed servants

of God cannot find justice at men's hands, yet there is help
to be had from God, and by prayer, shorter or longer; as
the Lord furnisheth unto them, must they seek their ease
of mind and comfort: *arise, O God, judge the earth.* 2.
When magistrates or rulers oppress God's people, private
persons may not go beyond their bounds, but must have their
recourse to God, that he may set matters that are wrong in
a better condition, as here the psalmist doth. 3. As the
church of God among the Jews was acquainted with the
prophecies of the enlargement of the church and kingdom
of God among the Gentiles, and upon this ground prayed
that he would not suffer his interest in his people then to
decay by the malice of men; so may the Lord's church, in
any place or time, upon the same ground, pray for the like
mercy; for still the reason holdeth, that God, who is about
to enlarge his kingdom, will not lose what he hath already;
and so to pray: *arise, O Lord, judge the earth; for thou
shalt inherit all nations.* Amen.

PSALM LXXXIII.

A song or psalm of Asaph.

This psalm agreeth with such a condition of the church as we read of in
the days of Jehoshaphat, 2 Chron. xx., and serveth to comfort the church
in the greatest conspiracies of her enemies against her. The psalm
hath two parts. In the former, the church crieth to God to show himself for his people, ver. 1, and complaineth of their conspiracy and preparation to come against her, ver. 2, 3, and of their purpose to root out
the Lord's people, ver. 4, 5, specifying a number of nations who were
upon the plot, ver. 6—8. In the latter part, they pray that judgment
may so befall them as befell other such enemies before, who undertook
the same enterprise, ver. 9—12. In particular, that the whole host
may be overturned and consumed, ver. 13, 14, and the remnant may
be chased and scattered, ver. 15, and ashamed and confounded for ever,
ver. 16, 17, that so God may have the more glory among them, ver. 18.

1. *Keep not thou silence, O God: hold not thy peace,
and be not still, O God.*

From his cry to God to let forth a word for his people in
this strait, learn, 1. The church may be in such a strait as,
if God do not speedily interpose himself, she cannot but be
swallowed up of her enemies quickly, as here we see. 2.
Sense of danger putteth an edge on prayer, and kindleth
affection in it: *keep not silence, O God, hold not thy peace;
and again, O God be not still.* 3. The Lord uttering a

word of comfort to his people, and of terror to his enemies, in the extremity of danger, will satisfy his church, and do all her work: *be not silent, hold not thy peace, be not still,* is the sum of all she craveth; for let him speak, and it shall be done.

2. *For, lo, thine enemies make a tumult; and they that hate thee have lifted up the head.*

3. *They have taken crafty counsel against thy people, and consulted against thy hidden ones.*

From their complaint of their enemies' preparation to come against them, learn, 1. The enemies of God's church are the enemies of God, bearing the same affection to God and to them that are reconciled to him: *for, lo, thine enemies that hate thee make a tumult.*   2. The more din the enemy makes, the more insolent he is, the higher he lifteth his head, he is the more near to be knocked down by God's appearing for his people against him: *keep not silence, for thine enemies make a tumult, they have lifted up the head.* 3. The chief enemies of the church are not the silly and simple sort of people, but the most subtle politicians usually, whose heads are most fit for Satan's devices against God's people: *they have taken crafty counsel against thy people.* 4. The true children of God, his secret ones, who, in the sense of their own weakness, shelter themselves under God's wings and glory in him, are the special objects of the malice of Satan and of his wicked servants: *they have consulted against thy hidden ones.*   5. Against the craft and policy of enemies the church hath nothing in herself to oppose, but runneth to God, who can easily disappoint all the enemies' plots, as here we see, v. 4, 5.

4. *They have said, Come, and let us cut them off from* being *a nation; that the name of Israel may be no more in remembrance.*

5. *For they have consulted together with one consent: they are confederate against thee:*

From their purpose to root out God's people, learn, 1. No less will satisfy the enemies of God's church than extirpation and abolishing of the church: *let us cut them off from being a nation; that the name of Israel may be no more in remembrance.* 2. When the church is least united, and least able to defend herself, the wicked encourage and strengthen one another in an evil course against her: *they have said,* one to another, *come, let us cut them off.* 3. Although the wicked be at enmity one against another, yet they will all agree together to overthrow the church: *they have consulted together with one consent,* saith he, *they are confederate against thee.* 4. This consideration, that the conspiracy against the church is a conspiracy against God, whose people the church is, is very comfortable in the church's extremity: *they are confederate against thee.*

6. *The tabernacles of Edom, and the Ishmaelites; of Moab, and the Hagarenes;*

7. *Gebal, and Ammon, and Amalek; the Philistines, with the inhabitants of Tyre;*

8. *Assur also is joined with them: they have holpen the children of Lot. Selah.*

In the reckoning up of the several nations conspired against Israel, learn, 1. When the church looketh upon the multitude of her enemies, and their confederacy, and their resolution to destroy her, she should gather grounds of hope, to be helped so much the more, and so much the sooner; for this is the church's argument of hope to be helped here. 2. In the persecution of the church, no wonder to see false brethren the chief leaders, whoever be followers and assistants: for here the church complaineth of it, *they have helped the children of Lot,* which importeth, that Moab and Ammon, their bastard brethren, were first in the enmity. 3. It is no wonder, nor strange thing, to see many nations on all hands invade the Lord's people at once; for here are ten nations coming all together against Israel.

9. *Do unto them as* unto *the Midianites; as to Sisera, as to Jabin, at the brook of Kison:*

10. Which *perished at En-dor; they become* as *dung for the earth.*

11. *Make their nobles like Oreb and like Zeeb; yea, all their princes as Zeba and as Zalmunna;*

12. *Who said, Let us take to ourselves the houses of God in possession.*

In the latter part of the psalm, is the church's prayer to God that he would be party against her enemies, and plague

them. There are sundry branches of the malediction, which
the church imprecateth against the enemies. The first is,
that God would destroy them, as he destroyed others before
them, who were upon such a wicked plot of rooting out
God's people. Whence learn. 1. When the church hath to
do with her enemies, she should look what in Scripture the
Lord did for her in times past; for so the church looketh
here to what the Lord did to his enemies, Judg. vii. 22,
and iv. 15, 24, and vii. 25, and viii. 21.   2. It is lawful to
pray for judgments upon the enemies of the church, provided it be of public spirit, and not out of private malice or
revenge; in which case the prayers of the church are more
forcible for the overthrow of their enemies, than all her
external force is: *do unto them as unto the Midianites*, is
a hard charge against them. 3. Former plagues poured
out upon the church's enemies, are pledges of the Lord's
bringing like judgments on their enemies afterward, and of
giving like preservation unto the church as before : *do unto
them as unto the Midianites* in Gideon's time, *and to Sisera and Jabin* in Deborah's time, when small means were
sufficient for a great overthrow of the enemy. 4. The
dead bodies of God's enemies shall not only be contemptible
before men, which is incident to the bodies of the saints
sometimes, but also contemptible before God, as here we
see : *their enemies perish at Endor, and became as dung
for the earth.* 5. The nobles, leaders, and chief amongst
God's enemies, may look for most signal judgment: *make
their nobles like Oreb and Zeeb, yea all their princes like
Zeba and Zalmunna.* 6. It is all one for their enemies to
resolve to spoil God's church, and to rob God of his habitation; specially so long as God's people love to have God
dwelling among them; for the injuries done to the church
redound to the contumely of God, who hath taken the maintenance of them: they say, *let us take to ourselves the
houses of God in possession.*

13. *O my God, make them like a wheel ; as the stubble before the wind.*

14. *As the fire burneth a wood, and as the flame set-
eth the mountains on fire ;*

15. *So persecute them with thy tempest, and make
them afraid with thy storm :*

16. *Fill their faces with shame ; that they may seek thy name, O Lord.*

17. *Let them be confounded and troubled for ever ; yea, let them be put to shame, and perish :*

From the rest of the branches of the imprecation, wherein sundry similitudes are looked unto, for showing forth the effects of God's wrath upon the enemies of the church, learn, 1. Use is to be made of our covenant with God, as well against our enemies as for ourselves : for, *O my God,* saith he now, when he is about to curse the enemy. 2. The enemies of God's church have many a mischief waiting on them, of which, if they escape one, another shall overtake them : yea, no one similitude can set forth what misery is prepared for them : no peace, no rest for them, no standing in any stablished prosperity, but they shall be rolled as a bowl turned upside down, or as a wheel : *make them like a wheel.* 3. They shall have no strength to resist the blast of God's wrath : *make them as stubble,* or chaff, *before the wind.* 4. The Lord's indignation against them shall burn them as flame doth a forest; let them be consumed, *as fire burneth a wood,* which is the greatest flame we can easily conceive ; or when a mountain of sulphur or coals is kindled, *as the flame sets the mountains on fire,* where fire above the earth and under it meet. 5. If they escape for a while, yet judgments shall follow, overtake, and toss them, and turn them in a circle till they be giddy : *so persecute them with thy tempest,* or whirlwind. 6. Beside what torment their present plague shall bring unto them, horror and fear of worse to come shall vex them : *make them afraid with thy storm.* 7. At last they shall be ashamed, when they shall be disappointed both of what they intended against the godly, and also meet with the misery which they least feared : *fill their faces with shame.* 8. If any of the enemies of God's people belong to God's election, the church's prayer against them giveth way to their conversion, and seeketh no more than that the judgment should follow them, only till they acknowledge their sin, turn, and seek God : *fill their faces with shame, that they may seek thy name, O Lord.* 9. For the rest of the wicked, irreconcilable adversaries, when shame of disappointment and temporal judgments are come upon them, the worst of all yet followeth, even everlasting perdition : *let them be con-founded and troubled for ever : yea, let them be put to shame and perish.*

18. *That* men *may know that thou, whose name alone* is *Jehovah,* art *the most High over all the earth.*

The psalmist closeth the psalm with showing the end of all this complaint and imprecation. Whence learn, 1. The end of all cursing of the wicked enemies of the church, is not to satisfy private revenge, but that God may be glorified: *let them perish, that men may know that thou art he whose name is Jehovah.* 2. The name Jehovah signifying God's being of himself, and the cause of the being of all things created, is incommunicable to any creature, and in Scripture is given only to the three persons of the Godhead, the Father, the Word, and the Spirit, whose essence is one, as is here taught, *that men may know, that thou art he whose name alone is Jehovah.* 3. If men will not acknowledge the true God to be the supreme and only governor of all the world, they shall by his heavy judgments, either upon others or upon themselves, be made to know it; for the church here declareth, that they use this heavy imprecation against God's enemies : *that men may know,* say they, *that thou whose name alone is Jehovah, art the most High over all the earth.*

PSALM LXXXIV.

To the chief musician upon Gitteth.　A psalm for the sons of Korah.

This psalm is on the same subject with psalms xlii. and psalm lxiii. In it the psalmist lamenteth his banishment from the temple and the public ordinances of religion, to v. 8, and, in the rest of the psalm, then prayeth for his restoration to that privilege. This psalm agreeth well with the time of David's parting with the ark, when he fled from Absalom.

In his lamentation, first, he commendeth the place of public worship, v. 1; then showeth his longing after it, v. 2; thirdly, wisheth to be as a sparrow, in the meanest condition partaker of that privilege, v. 3; fourthly, proclaimeth the blessedness of all the Lord's ministers, who may always be there, v. 4; fifthly, calleth them blessed who have liberty to come on foot from any part of the country, to keep at least the solemn feasts, v. 5—7. In his prayer, he requests, in general terms, to be restored to the Lord's worship, v. 8, 9, for two reasons. One reason is, because he preferreth the meanest officer's condition in God's house to the most quiet dwelling among the wicked, v. 10. Another is, because felicity is to be found in God, by means of his ordinances, v. 11; and meantime, while his prayer should be granted, he resteth by faith on God, in whom believers are made blessed, where- ever they be.

1. *How amiable* are *thy tabernacles, O Lord of hosts!*

The psalmist being now in exile, casteth his eyes upon his own country, wherein throughout all the land the Lord was worshipped in their several synagogues, but most so- lemnly in Zion, the place where the ark and the tabernacle were; and, putting a difference between the holy ordinances of God's worship, and the multitude of profane mixed among the godly, who joined in the worship, he beholdeth the glo- rious beauty of the holy service, and places where the oc- casion thereof was offered, and so breaketh out in commen- dation and admiration of their loveliness. Whence learn, 1. As God is glorious in all his hosts, who all are very ready as soldiers to fight for him at his command, so is he most glorious in the camp of the visible church militant; for here his authority, justice, mercy, grace, wisdom, and power are most of all manifested for overthrowing the kingdom of sin and Satan : therefore, saith he, *how amiable are thy ta- bernacles, O Lord of hosts!* 2. This beauty of the Lord's churches and places of residence, as it is not discerned by the blind world, but only by such as are illuminated with hea- venly light, so it is highly prized, loved, and admired by them only : for it is the sweet singer of Israel who saith, *how amiable are thy tabernacles, O Lord of hosts!* 3. Al- beit the world will not believe what is here said, nor take this praising of the loveliness of God's public worship from the hand of the godly, yet the Lord will receive this testi- mony unto the beauty of his ordinances from such as pre- sent it before him; therefore the psalmist most confidently directeth his speech to God himself here ; *how amiable are thy tabernacles, O Lord!*

2. *My soul longeth, yea, even fainteth for the courts of the Lord; my heart and my flesh crieth out for the living God.*

In the next place, the psalmist professeth his longing after liberty to enjoy the privileges of the public ordinances, albeit he was to have it nowise, but in the society of such people as were then in the visible church, of whose wickedness he had sufficient experience, they being now in arms against him, following Absalom. Whence learn, 1. The beauty and loveliness of God's public ordinances, are best discerned, and love and longing after them most stirred up, when a man is deprived of them for a time : *my soul longeth, yea, even fainteth for the courts of the Lord.* 2. Bodily affliction sharpeneth the sense of spiritual wants, and the sense of want of spiritual means of comfort augmenteth bodily affliction : *my soul fainteth, my heart and my flesh crieth out.* 3. It is not the public ordinances alone, to be enjoyed in an outward formality, which saints seek after, but it is to find God in, and by the means; it is to find the Lord's lively operation on their hearts, which they long after : *my heart and my flesh crieth out for the living God.*

3. *Yea, the sparrow hath found an house, and the swallow a nest for herself, where she may lay her young,* even *thine altars, O Lord of hosts, my King, and my God.*

In the third place, the psalmist wisheth to be partaker of the public worship, were it in ever so mean and despicable a condition. So he may enjoy God's presence in his ordinances, he is content to creep into any corner of God's house, and go out and seek his meat, and return like a sparrow or swallow. Whence learn, 1. A soul which loveth communion with God indeed, will choose any temporal condition of life, how poor soever, how despised soever, rather than be deprived of what may make better for his spiritual condition, as appeareth in the psalmist, who wished to have the *place of a sparrow,* or of *a swallow;* any residence near God's altar. 2. The soul which craveth lively communion with God, should cleave close unto the title and interest which he hath in God by covenant ; as the psalmist doth here : *thine altar,* saith he, *my King and my God.*

4. *Blessed* are *they that dwell in thy house ; they will be still praising thee. Selah.*

In the fourth place, the psalmist proclaimeth the priests and Levites, the Lord's ministers, to be blessed men, for their privilege and opportunity to serve the Lord. Whence learn, 1. Albeit many who have the means and opportunity of profiting by public ordinances, consider not the day of their visitation, to make use of the means while they have them; yet the godly who are deprived of the means, and behold the fair occasions of grace offered to them, count them blessed, as here: *blessed are they that dwell in thy house.* 2. It is a blessed thing indeed to have the occasion of communion with God in public ordinances, and to make use thereof in setting forth the Lord's glory; and in this respect there are no men in the world more blessed than faithful ministers: *blessed are they that dwell in thy house; they will be still praising thee.*

5 Blessed is *the man whose strength* is *in thee; in whose heart* are *the ways* of them.

6. Who *passing through the valley of Baca make it a well; the rain also filleth the pools.*

7. *They go from strength to strength;* every one of them *in Zion appeareth before God.*

In the fifth place, the psalmist looketh upon their condition who dwell far off from the tabernacle, who might at least thrice a year come from the farthest corner of the land to keep the solemnities appointed by God; and he counteth them blessed, albeit in their voyage they should endure ever so much toil in travelling, and should with difficulty drink their water, either rained down from the clouds, or drawn from a well or cistern digged with much labour. For albeit they should sustain toil and drought in their way, yet having refreshments one after another, and renewed strength for their journey, they should all come at last to the place of public ordinances in Zion. And here he describeth the true and blessed Israelites, whether proselytes or born Jews, resolved to come and appear before the Lord in the appointed solemnities, by these six properties: First, they encourage themselves for the journey, by hope in God to be furnished with strength: *blessed is the man,* saith he, *whose strength is in thee.* Next, they are resolved in their heart for all the inconveniences they may meet with in the journey, to hold on their course: *in whose heart are the ways of them.* Thirdly, they hold on their course through dry and comfortless places, which may be called places of *Baca,* or weeping: *they pass through the valley af Baca.* Fourthly, they overcome this difficulty of wantiug water, either by digging a well, where they may find water, or by finding some already digged cistern, wherein God's providence had reserved some quantity of rain-water for them : *who passing through the valley of Baca, make it a well : the rain also filleth the pools.* Fifthly, after refreshment found in their journey, they are encouraged to go on their way, till they need and find some new refreshment, and reparation of their strength : *they go from strength to strength.* Sixthly, these godly travellers all come at length to the place they aimed at, to Zion, where they appear before God in the holy feast, cheerful and joyful souls : *every one of them in Zion appeareth before God.* And therefore he calleth them blessed, because at length they come through all difficulties to have sweet communion with God.

These two decrees of blessed Israelites, are so painted out in figurative terms, as they may most easily lead the spiritual eye to the blessedness which the figure is fit to represent, so that the typical words cannot be well understood, except the spiritual blessedness be taken along : for there are two degrees of really blessed persons. Some are at home already dwelling with God, of whom it may be most solidly said, *blessed are they that dwell in thy house, they will be still praising thee,* which is their perpetual exercise. Others are travellers, who are in their way toward heaven, the Lord's house; who indeed despair of their own strength to make out their journey, but their confidence is in God's strength, and their encouragement to set forward is this, that of them it may be well said, *blessed is the man whose strength is in thee :* such men's journey taketh up their heart, the stream of their affections runneth thitherward : *in whose heart are the ways of them.* Those travellers have a wilderness to go through, a comfortless valley wherein they find matter of mourning, and no solid consolation, save that which God provideth, beyond the nature of the place, which God, one way or other, furnisheth to them, that they shall not fail to have a timous consolation : *who passing through the valley of Baca, make it a well : the rain also filleth the pools.* So that albeit God suffer them to thirst, yet he suffereth them not to want a sufficient measure for bringing them on their way; a strengthening them to go forward : if they miss a well, they shall have a cistern filled with rain from heaven ; the measure furnished unto them, reneweth their strength after weariness, and sufficeth them till they need, and meet with another renovation of their strength : *they go from strength to strength.* Not one of those resolute travellers, or self-denying persons, relying on God's strength and support, perisheth by the way —all are upheld and brought forward, till they come where they would be, to enjoy God's presence in Zion which is above : *every one of them,* without exception, *in Zion appeareth before God.*

8. *O Lord God of hosts, hear my prayer : give ear, O God of Jacob. Selah.*

9. *Behold, O God our shield, and look upon the face of thine anointed.*

In the latter part of the psalm is the psalmist's prayer, wherein he maketh request for communion with God, both in the outward type, and in the spiritual truth. Whence learn, 1. The godly man's holy wishes and desires do not vanish and die, but are recommended to God in prayer. What the psalmist longed for in the former part of the psalm, in the latter part he prayeth for. 2. The earnest supplicant hath no will to be refused, but fasteneth his hope to speed on God's power and covenant, and doubleth his petitions in the Lord's bosom : *O Lord of hosts, hear my prayer : give ear, O God of Jacob.* 3. Albeit the believer be separate in place from the communion of saints in public worship, yet he will find a conjunction with them in affection and prayer at the throne of God's grace, and claim the same interest with them in God for protection and comfort : *behold, O God,* saith he, *our shield.* 4. How little appearance soever of possession, or performance of promises the believer hath, yet must he claim his right and titles, which shall bring him to possession : *look upon the face of thine anointed.* He counteth himself king in regard of his right to the crown, because God had caused Samuel to anoint him to be king. 5. He who hath right to a principal mercy, may pray and look for every accessory mercy, which is presupposed in the principal, or annexed unto it, as here upon the promise of the kingdom, David prayeth for the liberty of the temple, which behoved to follow upon his repossession in the kingdom; and here also he looks through his own anointing unto the Messiah Christ, of whom he knew himself to be a type : and for the Messiah Christ, he seeketh to have his petition granted, through whom alone every good thing is purchased, and must be conveyed unto us : *look*, saith he, *upon the face of thine anointed.*

10. *For a day in thy courts is better than a thousand. I had rather be a door-keeper in the house of my God, than to dwell in the tents of wickedness.*

This is the first reason why he desireth to have the privileges of the public ordinances restored unto him. Whence learn, 1. Whatsoever may be a means to bring us to the fruition of God, is incomparably better than any earthly thing, and one hour spent in the means of eternal felicity, is worth a thousand spent otherwise : *for a day in thy courts is better than a thousand.* 2. The lowest and most painful condition of life, joined with any measure of communion with God, is better than the most quiet, easy, and plentiful condition of life without communion with God : *to be a door-keeper in the house of the Lord*, is better *than to dwell in the tents of wickedness.* 3. The godly man, whose judgment is rectified about things spiritual, is the only right estimator of states and conditions of life in this world : for that is best to him (if he may choose) wherein he may be most serviceable to God, and best helped to heaven. He for his part had rather have the meanest condition of life, joined with the benefit of the public ordinances, than live without them more plentifully among the wicked : *I had rather*, saith he, *be a door-keeper in the house of my God, than dwell in the tents of wickedness.*

11. *For the Lord God is a sun and shield; the Lord will give grace and glory: no good thing will he withhold from them that walk uprightly.*

The second reason why the psalmist so loveth the public ordinances is, because by this means he getteth access to the fountain of all felicity, who wardeth off all evil from the upright believer, and giveth unto him whatsoever is good for his soul or body in this life and in the life to come. Whence learn, 1. The godly have need of light and di-

rection, life, vigour, strength, and consolation; and all this
in God, or what more can be imported in the similitude is
taken from the sun, in relation to earthly creatures : *for
the Lord God is a sun.* 2. The godly are subject to dangers and perils from without, especially from enemies bodily
and spiritual, and have need of preservation and defence
from all adverse power, malice, and craftiness, and this pro
tection only God is able to give : *the Lord is a sun and a
shield.* 3. The believer is burdened with the body of sin,
and borne down frequently with the sense of his own unworthiness, witlessness, and weakness, and in God is the perfect remedy of all those evils : *the Lord will give grace.*
4. Albeit the beauty of godliness be much obscured in this
life, with crosses and afflictions from God, with calumnies
and persecutions from men, and the godly must lie in the
grave, and suffer corruption of their flesh, as others; yet
the remedy of this also shall be found in God to the believer : *he will give grace and glory;* grace in this life, and
glory after it, without fail. 5. Albeit the Lord seem to
keep the godly in great scarcity sometimes of things comfortable in this life, and of spiritual consolations also for a
time, yet he so disposeth of their entertainment in all respects, as every thing shall work together for their good :
*for no good thing will he withhold from them that walk
uprightly.*

12. *O Lord of hosts, blessed* is *the man that trusteth
in thee.*

When the psalmist hath lamented his exile from the public ordinances, and prayed to be restored to that privilege,
he comforteth himself in the mean time, by the consideration of God's grace and power to supply all wants, even
that of public ordinances, when it cannot without hazard of
life be had by the believer. Whence learn, 1. How hard
soever the Lord's dispensation be to his own children, yet
must we ever continue to trust in God, as the psalmist's
example here teacheth. 2. God can supply the want of
the public ordinances, and be a little sanctuary to his children, and make them quiet; yea, and blessed in believing
in him : *O Lord of hosts, blessed is the man that trusteth
in thee :* for in the beginning of the psalm his heart breaketh for the longing after the public ordinances; he counteth

the ministers of God's house blessed; he counteth every man who may be in any corner of God's house happy: he counteth the travelling Israelite coming to the ordinances blessed; and at length pronounceth every believer blessed, and so himself to be blessed also.

PSALM LXXXV.

To the chief musician.   A psalm for the sons of Korah.

This psalm agreeth well with the condition of the church of the Jews, now fallen into new troubles, after their return from the captivity of Babylon. In the former part whereof they pray for a new proof and experience of God's mercy, to ver. 8. In the latter part is set down a comfortable answer to their prayer, and for the help of their faith in their prayer. First, they make mention of their gracious delivery from the captivity, ver. 1—3. Next, they pray for repentance, and removing of the tokens of God's wrath, ver. 4, 5. Thirdly, they pray for restoration of their miserable and dead condition wherein they were lying, by some merciful deliverance, ver. 6, 7.
As for the answer in the latter part, he prepareth himself to receive it from the Lord, and by inspiration receiveth indeed a comfortable prophecy of five notable fruits of mercy. The first is, of peace to God's people, ver. 8. The next is, of deliverance and salvation to his servants, ver. 9. The third is, of the grace of Christ unto justification, and the fruits of it, ver. 10, 11. The fourth is, of temporal blessings, upon the place where the Lord's people dwell, and that for his people's comfort, ver. 12. The fifth is, of the grace of Christ unto sanctification, ver. 13.

1. *Lord, thou hast been favourable unto thy land: thou hast brought back the captivity of Jacob.*

2. *Thou hast forgiven the iniquity of thy people; thou hast covered all their sin. Selah.*

3. *Thou hast taken away all thy wrath: thou hast turned* thyself *from the fierceness of thine anger.*

After the church of the Jews had been delivered from captivity, they fell into new troubles, because of their sin and new provocations of God, and in this psalm they cry to God for mercy, and for strengthening of their faith. They acknowledge the Lord's favour in loosing their captivity, v. 1, and in forgiving their sins, v. 2, and in removing all the tokens of his wrath from them, v. 3. Whence learn, 1. After great mercies shown to God's people, new provocations draw on new judgments, as appeareth in the change of the condition of the church here represented.

2. Neither old sins nor late, neither old judgments nor presently lying under wrath, must keep back God's people from running unto God by prayer, for obtaining favour of God again, as the example of the church here teacheth. 3. As no sins can make the Lord so forget his covenant with his people, as mercy should not be let forth to penitent sinners suing for grace, so no wrath is so great, as shall debar poor supplicants from access unto God, when they come to seek mercy. 4. As new necessities call to mind old supplies received from God; so they who would have any new benefit from the Lord, should thankfully remember the old, and take encouragement from those to hope for further; *Lord, thou hast been favourable to thy land ; thou hast brought back the captivity of Jacob.* 5. As grace is the only ground of God's bounty to his people, so is it the only ground of his people's prayer for new experiences of his grace; as here, God's favour is acknowledged to be the cause of bringing back the people from captivity, and the ground whereupon the psalmist foundeth his prayer: *thou hast been favourable to thy land.* 6. As that is a benefit indeed, which is given with remission of sins; so every one who seeketh a benefit, should desire to have the benefit which they come to seek, joined with remission of their sins : as the psalmist here maketh the bringing back from captivity a complete favour, because joined with remission of sins: without which it had been the less comfortable : *thou hast forgiven the iniquity of thy people.* 7. The way of God's forgiving sins is, by not imputing them, not bringing them forth to be reckoned, but hiding them from justice's view, and covering them with the imputation of the righteousness of the Redeemer : *thou hast covered all their sin.* 8. As, while sin unrepented and unforgiven remaineth, wrath also remaineth; so when sin is taken away, God's wrath also is taken away; when God forgiveth sin, he taketh away its punishment; for, after he hath said, *thou hast covered all their sin,* he subjoineth, *thou hast taken away all thy wrath ; thou hast turned from the fierceness of thine anger.* 9. As the consciousness of sin, and feeling of wrath lying on, and fearing the growth of it, hinder much the guilty from confident approach unto God : so the seen experiences of God's drawing off those bars in former times, open the door for afflicted sinners confidently

to come and seek mercy, as here the psalmist teacheth us, in his making of this preface to his following prayer.

4. *Turn us, O God of our salvation, and cause thine anger toward us to cease.*

5. *Wilt thou be angry with us for ever? wilt thou draw out thine anger to all generations?*

In the next place, upon the foresaid grounds, the church afflicted prayeth for grace to repent, that so remission of sin and removing of wrath may follow. Whence learn, 1. Whosoever in an afflicted church are sensible of their own and the church's sins, should deal with God for giving repentance to his backsliding people, and to increase their own repentance, before they seek removal of the tokens of wrath, as here the godly pray, in the first place, *turn us, O God.* 2. The Lord's covenant with his people for everlasting salvation, is a ground to pray and hope for temporal deliverance from God, who hath power and ways of his own how to save, when we see no event: *turn us,* saith he, *O God of our salvation.* 3. When God giveth grace to a people to repent and turn to him, the tokens of his wrath will be removed also: or be so changed, as they shall be no more the effects of wrath; therefore joineth he with, *turn us,* this petition also, *and cause thine anger toward us to cease.* 4. The anger of the Lord toward his people, is but temporal and for a moment in comparison of deservings, albeit it seem to endure long: and the believer may be persuaded, that it shall not continue against supplicants long; for, *wilt thou be angry with us for ever? wilt thou draw out thine anger to all generations?* doth import, that his anger could not be perpetual.

6. *Wilt thou not revive us again, that thy people may rejoice in thee.*

7. *Shew us thy mercy, O Lord, and grant us thy salvation.*

In the third place, the church prayeth for some relief from the distress wherein they were for the time, and putteth their petition out of question, by this interrogation. because God's purpose and pleasure were that his people should have joy in their God, and thereupon request new tokens of mercy, from the ground of his covenant with them

for salvation. Whence learn, 1. As it is a death to be
deprived so much as of the evidence and sense of God's favour, so it is life to be clear that we are in favour with God;
and as such who have had the sense of God's favour, cannot
endure to want it; so shall they have it restored : *wilt thou
not revive us again ?* 2. Because plagues and wrath upon
God's people are temporal, they may look certainly for a
change to the better; and after they have smarted for their
sins for a while, may yet expect to be restored to joy and
comfort again : *wilt thou not revive us again, that thy
people may rejoice in thee ?* 3. When God changeth
the cheer of his people, their joy should not be in the gift,
but in the giver : *that thy people may rejoice in thee.* 4.
Albeit the dear children of God, for whom mercy and salvation are appointed, may be destitute of the sight and evidence of both, yet must they believe both, claim both, and
hope for the manifestation of both unto them : *shew us thy
mercy, O Lord, &c., grant us thy salvation.* 5. As
mercy is the cause of salvation temporal and eternal, and
no merit in us; so must he who looks for salvation of either
sort make mercy his plea, and no good in himself : *shew
us thy mercy, O Lord, and grant us thy salvation.*

8. *I will hear what God the Lord will speak : for
he will speak peace unto his people, and to his saints ;
but let them not turn again to folly.*

In the latter part of the psalm is the answer of this prayer,
which the psalmist expecteth and receiveth by way of prophecy, of five sweet effects of God's mercy to his people :
whereof the first are peace and reconciliation and removing
the tokens of his wrath. Whence learn, 1. The prayer
of a believer put up to our ever living Lord, is not a vain
work of pouring out words in the air, but a profitable
exercise of faith, grounded upon God's word and goodness, whereof he may expect certainly a return : *I will
hear what the Lord will say.* 2. Comfortable promises will suffice the believer, who, if he know what the
Lord sayeth, will be clear also what the Lord will do : *I
will hear what the Lord will say.* 3. Albeit God's
people be under the sense of wrath, yet the Lord
will comfort them after seeking grace of him : *he will
speak peace to his people.* 4. Those who indeed mind

true holiness, are God's people, to whom the Lord will
speak peace ; and for whose cause the society wherein they
are, shall partake of the fruits of God's favour to them: *he
will speak peace to his people and to his saints.* 5. As
the interruption of our peace with God is procured by our
folly, or foolish following of the vanities which allure to sin,
and divert us from communion with God, so the restoring
of us to peace must come by our forsaking those sinful and
foolish courses which have procured wrath; and the way to
keep us in that peace, is not to return to these courses
again; and this is the very end both of God's correcting
us, and of his restoring us to peace, that we sin not as before : *he will speak peace to his saints ; but let them not
return again to folly.*

9. *Surely his salvation* is *nigh them that fear him ;
that glory may dwell in our land.*

The second effect of mercy to God's saints, is the nearness of free salvation in Christ, who is the glory of the land
of Judah, where he was born, and the glory of that land,
whatsoever it is, wherein his saints, and he among his saints,
dwell. Whence learn, 1. The heirs of the promises are only
such as study to please God, and to eschew provoking him;
for the answer of the former prayer, and the word of promise and prophecy here, are made in favour only of *them
that fear him.* 2. There is no satisfactory deliverance to
the afflicted believer, labouring under the sense of wrath,
except Christ Jesus, who is really the only complete salvation of God, alone able to answer fully to that name, and
who was known to the church before his coming in the
flesh by that name; as we may understand by the words of
Simeon, Luke ii., who was waiting for the consolation of Israel, and had a promise that he should not see death before
he had seen the Lord's Christ, v. 25, 26. And when he
had Christ in his arms he saith, *Lord, now lettest thou thy
servant depart in peace, according to thy word, for mine
eyes have seen thy salvation,* v. 30. Here is the name
whereby Christ was of old known to the church, among
many other titles; he is God's salvation, as he is called here.
3. Consolation and deliverance, and salvation in Christ, are
near hand to every upright afflicted believer, whether the
afflicted see it comfortably for the time or not : *surely God's*

salvation is near them that fear him. 4. What land the true church of Christ, the saints, and they that fear God dwell in, there glory dwelleth; there God, there Christ by his Spirit bringing righteousness and salvation to such a society, is glorious; and for his presence the people are glorious, and the land glorious above all other lands whatsoever: *surely his salvation is near them that fear him, that glory may dwell in our land.* This commendation, for many reasons, the land of Judea might claim far above all others.

10. *Mercy and truth are met together; righteousness and peace have kissed each other.*

11. *Truth shall spring out of the earth; and righteousness shall look down from heaven.*

The third effect of mercy is the grace of Christ unto justification, and the fruits thereof bestowed upon them that are justified by faith. There are here three conjunctions, or couples, sweetly agreeing together; one is, of *mercy and truth;* another is, of *righteousness and peace;* and the third is, *of truth and righteousness.* For the first couple, *mercy and truth,* may be referred either to God bestowing something on his people—and so God's mercy pitieth, spareth, and pardoneth his sinful people, and his truth performeth all the good things which in his word he promised; and this couple indeed most eminently met, when Christ, the salvation of God, came in the flesh, for Christ's coming is the highest manifestation of mercy that ever was heard tell of, when God, out of love, and pity, and mercy, gave his Son to redeem sinners: and this also was the most glorious performance of the richest and the noblest promise that ever was made to man; for in the sending of Christ promised, all the promises are made *yea and amen;* for the way is made sure now to perform all the rest of the promises—or *mercy and truth* may be referred, the one, namely *mercy,* to God; and the other, to wit *truth,* may be referred to men, to whom God will show mercy. And in this consideration we are given to understand, that as a merciful God and misbelieving sinners are separated, and stand at a great distance, the one departing more and more from the other, so a merciful God and a believer are surely reconciled, and quickly meet together, for God in Christ holdeth forth mercy to the sinner, and mercy bestoweth faith upon the redeemed, and faith layeth hold on mercy, and so *mercy and truth are met together*. Mercy calleth for faith, and createth it, and faith calleth for mercy, and so this couple meet together.

As for the second couple, of *righteousness and peace*, both of them are the effects of the meeting of *mercy* and *truth* together, or of *mercy* and *faith* saying *amen* to *mercy's* offer; for *faith* laying hold on *mercy*, bringeth down from God *righteousness*, or justification by *faith;* and we, being justified by faith, have both peace with God and our own consciences, at least in the point of right and privilege, albeit sense, and possession of the sense of this *peace* may be interrupted. Whence learn, In whomsoever *mercy*, or the offer of grace, and *faith* receiving the offer meet, justification also, or imputed *righteousness* and *peace* with God, meet: then *righteousness and peace have kissed each other*.

The third couple is of *truth*, or true faith in man on earth, and *righteousness* from God in heaven: faith springing out of the earth, as the plantation of *mercy*, in the sensible fruits thereof, that is, in the true effects of sincere love to God and man; and the *righteousness* of God from heaven shining down as the sun, for nourishing and protecting his own plantation, and performing all promises to the believer. Whence learn, As *mercy* in God and true *faith* in man meeting together, are followed with righteousness of justification and peace with God; so, true faith in man is followed with fruits; for it cannot be idle, but must be operative in bringing forth the effects of faith or truth: *truth shall spring out of the earth*, and *righteousness* from heaven is followed with active influence upon springing faith, for defending, and increasing, and blessing it, as the sun fostereth and refresheth the fruits of the ground: *truth shall spring out of the earth, and righteousness shall look down from heaven*.

12. *Yea, the Lord shall give that which is good; and our land shall yield her increase.*

The fourth fruit of mercy is that of giving temporal benefits to the believer, and blessing the land where believers dwell. Whence learn, 1. The things of this life are appendages to the chief mercies of the gospel, which reconciled people may expect to receive of God, as their need and good require : *yea, the Lord shall give that which is good.* 2. As the place, or land, where the Lord's people dwell, beareth the tokens of God's displeasure when they provoke him; so shall the land be sensibly blessed when his people are reconciled unto him : *and our land shall yield her increase.*

13. *Righteousness shall go before him, and shall set us in the way of his steps.*

The fifth fruit of mercy is, the grace of Christ for directing and furthering believers in the way of sanctification. Christ shall be their leader, and righteousness imputed unto believers from Christ, (in the grace of conversion or holy inclination, and of perfect direction by the word and Spirit,) shall make believers follow Christ's ways, and go on in the paths of his obedience. Whence learn, 1. Christ is the captain of his redeemed and reconciled people, or the shepherd of his purchased flock; for he and his people here are walking in one way, wherein he goeth before his people that they may follow his steps, and behind them also to bring them up, and to set them forward in the way, so that none may fall off, as the similitude importeth. 2. As Christ is the leader of his people, so righteousness is the preparer of his people to follow him; first, in the work of conversion or regeneration, wherein the mind is illuminated to behold, and the heart inclined to follow righteousness; secondly, in the work of daily direction, by his word and Spirit : *righteousness shall go before him.* 3. As the way that the believer must walk in is that which is prescribed by the Lord his leader; so the effectual mover of the believer unto sanctification is the grace of righteousness or sanctification, which Christ the leader sendeth forth into his people's heart, to make them follow the direction given unto them : for, *righteousness shall go before him, and set us in the way of his steps.*

PSALM LXXXVI.

A psalm of David.

This psalm agreeth well with the time when David was in trouble, being persecuted by Saul. The sum of it was a prayer for relief, consisting of seven petitions; some of them more generally, some of them more particularly, expressing his trouble and his desire of relief; all which petitions have reasons joined to them, serving to strengthen the faith of the supplicant.

1. *Bow down thine ear, O Lord, hear me; for I am poor and needy.*

The first petition is for audience, and the reason of his hope to be heard is, because of his necessity to be helped. Whence learn, 1. When a believer hath any petition to present unto God, he may expect access unto God, and audience, and acceptance of his person and prayer : *O Lord, hear me.* 2. Albeit the supplicant be on earth and God be found in heaven; albeit the supplicant be mean and base, both in his own eyes and in effect, and God be the high and lofty One that inhabiteth eternity, yet will he humble himself to take notice of the supplication of a believing supplicant : *bow down thine ear, O Lord.* 3. Of that whereof misbelief would make use unto discouragement and desperation, faith maketh a ground of hope to be helped; for affliction and weakness, and want of all help and comfort from man, are the Lord's forerunners to advertise the believer, that the Lord is coming : *O Lord, hear me, for I am poor and needy.*

2. *Preserve my soul, for I am holy : O thou my God, save thy servant that trusteth in thee.*

The second petition is for protection of his life, and the reasons of his hope are taken from the qualities of such a person as hath right to expect God's protection. Whence learn, 1. The bodies and souls of God's children have snares laid for them by enemies, bodily and spiritual, from which they cannot deliver themselves, except they commit the custody thereof unto God, as the prophet doth, saying, *preserve my soul :* our wit, our prudence, our power, our fighting, our fleeing, or whatsoever means we can use under heaven, are little worth, if God do not preserve us. 2. That man hath a ground of hope to be preserved by God, who, being pursued for his life by malicious persecutors, for falsely alleged wrongs done by him, can attest God for his innocency, in the particular whereof he is charged, as here David doth : *preserve my soul, for I am holy*; that is, free from the fault whereof I am charged, for I am a favourite of thine, or a man who hath been bountiful in doing good to him that pursueth me; for thus much also will the word bear. 3. The consciousness of studying to please God is very sweet in time of trouble, and especially when trouble falleth on for God's service: *O my God, save thy servant.* 4. Innocency in a particular cause is not sufficient to bear us out, nor yet the consciousness of our good service done to God; but we must make use of the covenant, and put our trust in God's goodness, whensoever we expect any good from God: *O my God, save thy servant that trusteth in thee.*

3. *Be merciful unto me, O Lord: for I cry unto thee daily.*

The third petition is for mercy and forgiveness of sin; and the reason of hope is, because he is a daily supplicant. Whence learn, 1. Innocency in our carriage toward men, and the goodness of the cause which we defend, may leave us in the mire in time of trouble, because of our sins, whereof we are guilty in other respects, except we flee to God's mercy; therefore, when sin is objected, mercy must be our refuge and plea: *be merciful unto me, O Lord.* 2. Assiduity and earnestness in prayer promise certainly a good answer after asking, seeking, and knocking: *be merciful to me. for I cry unto thee.*

4. *Rejoice the soul of thy servant; for unto thee, O Lord, do I lift up my soul.*

5. *For thou, Lord, art good, and ready to forgive: and plenteous in mercy unto all them that call upon thee.*

The fourth petition is for comfort. The reasons of his hope are, first, because he seeketh his comfort nowhere else but in God; next, because God is gracious to all supplicants. Whence learn, 1. As the Lord burdeneth his own children sometimes with affliction and sorrow, for their humiliation and trial of faith; so will he also comfort them in due time, and give them cause of joy in himself, for the strengthening of their faith, and they may pray for this and expect it: *rejoice the soul of thy servant.* 2. He that would have comfort from God must set himself to seek it in him only, and not look after it elsewhere under the heaven; and in this way he may pray for it and expect it, as the psalmist doth here: *for I lift up my soul unto thee, O Lord.* 3. The knowledge of God's goodness and mercy is the life of faith, the fountain of consolation, and ground of prayer: *rejoice*

U

the heart of thy servant, for thou, O Lord, art good. 4.
Whatsoever evil the sinner findeth in himself, there is a remedy in God for it; if he lack any good thing, God hath it,
and is ready to communicate it: *for thou, Lord, art good.*
If the sinner be smitten with the consciousness of sin and deserving of wrath, *the Lord is ready to forgive;* if a man's
sins seem so many and heinous that he dare not approach,
the Lord is plenteous in mercy. 5. He who desireth to
partake of God's goodness and mercy, must resolve to worship the Lord, to believe in him, and to pray to him; and
whosoever taketh this course, whatsoever he be, without
exception, he shall find the Lord *to be good, and ready to
forgive, and plenteous in mercy to all them that call upon
him.*

6. *Give ear, O Lord, unto my prayer; and attend to
the voice of my supplications.*

7. *In the day of my trouble I will call upon thee: for
thou wilt answer me.*

8. *Among the gods* there is *none like unto thee, O
Lord; neither* are there any works *like unto thy works.*

9. *All nations whom thou hast made shall come and
worship before thee, O Lord; and shall glorify thy
name.*

10. *For thou* art *great, and doest wondrous things:
thou* art *God alone.*

The fifth petition is for relief and deliverance out of his
present distress, propounded in the general terms of granting his supplication. The first reason of his hope to be
heard is, because he is resolved to make use of the Lord's
promise, that he will answer when one calleth on him in
trouble, v. 7. The next reason is, because there is not a
God beside God; and he alone is able to work wonders, v. 8.
The third is, because the Lord is to let all nations know
him, and to gain them to his worship, by his great power
and wonderful working, as the only true God, v. 9, 10; and
therefore able and willing to give him a new experience of
his power. Whence learn, 1. When God delayeth to answer
supplicants, they must not faint in prayer, but continue instant and be importunate: *Give ear, O Lord, unto my
prayer,* saith he now over again. 2. Albeit the supplicant
meet with doubts whether his petition be regarded or not,

yet must he not yield to them, but pray directly against them, as here we are taught: *attend unto the voice of my supplication.* 3. Every man should so make use of, and apply to himself, the general command of God to call upon him in trouble, with a promise of deliverance, as his faith may be most strengthened by it; for so the psalmist doth here: *in the day of my trouble I will call upon thee; for thou wilt answer me.* And this relateth to that which is said Psal. l. 15: *call upon me in the day of thy trouble.* 4. He that hath found the fruit of true religion, and hath experience of the gracious work of God upon his own spirit, will set at nought all idolatry and false religion: *among the gods there is none like unto thee, O God.* 5. The works of God working according to his word, are such as may prove him to be the true God, with whose works no creature's works can be compared. Where is such a work of power as the creation of the world and preservation of it? where is there such a work of grace as the work of redemption? and who can work any thing like the least of the works of the Lord, in his making and upholding the meanest creature? *neither are there any works like thy works.* 6. The consideration of the largeness of God's grace and power, which he hath manifested in the conversion of nations, and is to manifest yet more and more in his own due time, may encourage any man to come and worship God, and expect grace from him for his own particular case; he will not refuse alms to any beggar, who is about to gather all poor beggars to receive his alms: *all nations shall come and worship before thee, O Lord, and glorify thy name.* Whatsoever is already done for accomplishing this prophecy, more is to be done ere the Lord close the course of time; and whatsoever shall be done by way of conversion, before the last day, we are sure that at least, by way of conviction and extorted acknowledgment, all this shall be done at the last day: for the Lord hath sworn, *that every knee shall bow to him, and every tongue shall confess to his name.* 7. It is the cognizance of a kindly subject of God's kingdom, to delight in the increase and glory of it; and he that findeth in his heart to love the enlargement of God's glory, may expect the benefit of a kindly subject, as the psalmist doth here. 8. The omnipotency of God, and the wondrous works which God hath already done, may loose all doubts about the accomplishment of all his promises, how great soever: *all nations shall come and worship before thee; for thou art great,* saith he, *and doest wondrous things.* 9. All idols and idolatry must at length be defaced, and be found to be vanity, and God at length must be known to be the only true God: *all nations shall glorify thy name, for thou art God alone.*

11. *Teach me thy way, O Lord; I will walk in thy truth: unite my heart to fear thy name.*

The sixth petition is, to be kept from following any sinful course, specially now in this his trial and temptation, v. 11. And this he hopeth shall be granted to God's glory, v. 12; first, because he had experience of God's mercy before, v. 13; next, because he had to do with proud and godless enemies, v. 14; thirdly, because God was exceedingly gracious and merciful, v. 15.

As for the petition to be saved from all sinful courses, it hath two branches. One is, to be instructed in God's way; the other, that his heart may be made to follow that way, and to stand in awe to offend. Whence learn, 1. The Lord's children, under trouble and persecution, are in danger to be driven by temptation to some sinful course; and this they should pray against, and be no less afraid for, than for any bodily trouble; as here the example of David teacheth us. 2. It is necessary for eschewing sin, to know how God useth to deal with his own children, lest we think that some strange thing hath befallen us, when we fall into trouble; and it is necessary to know also how we ought to carry ourselves in every passage of our trouble and trial, lest we neglect our duty, or do contrary to it: *teach me thy way, O God.* 3. Beside the information of the mind concerning the duty in general, which God giveth by the ministry of his word, and common operation of his Spirit, there is a more special, lively, efficacious teaching of a man, whereby he is fitted to make particular practical application of the general rule to particular circumstances of time and place; and for this we must pray to God also, after we are taught to know the duty in general: *teach me thy way, O Lord.* 4. No man must count any way to be of God's teaching, but that which is warranted by his word; and no man can walk safely, except he that followeth the Lord's truth: *teach me, and I will walk in thy truth.* 5. Whosoever would have God to inform them of his will, must first resolve sincerely to follow his will when he hath shown it, for so doth David : *teach me thy way, and I will walk in thy truth.* 6. To make instruction effectual, not only must the mind be informed, but the heart also must be wrought upon, and framed unto obedience : *unite my heart.* 7. It is the natural disease of sinful men's hearts, to be loosed from God, and scattered and distracted about a variety of vain objects, which are offered unto them to follow; and this disease God alone can cure: *unite my heart.* 8. It is not sufficient for a man once to resign over his heart to God in his conversion, but this resignation of the heart must be renewed upon all occasions into God's hand, that he may tie the affections to himself and to his holy law, and reclaim the heart from ranging and going a-whoring from him after sinful objects; for this prayer for uniting the heart is David's prayer, who long before was converted. 9. Then is the heart united and fixed, when the fear of God ruleth it; that is, when after it is informed of God's will, it feareth to omit what he commandeth, and to do what he forbiddeth : *unite my heart to fear thy name.*

12. *I will praise thee, O Lord my God, with all my heart ; and I will glorify thy name for evermore.*

13. *For great is thy mercy toward me ; and thou hast delivered my soul from the lowest hell.*

Here David hopeth to be heard, and promiseth praise to God, both for his bypast and also for his foreseen deliverance, flowing from the greatness of God's mercy to him. Whence learn, 1. He who prayeth according to God's will, may promise to himself satisfaction, and unto God thanks for granting his requests : *I will praise thee, O Lord my God.* 2. The thanksgiving of the godly, especially when the heart is enlarged, is very hearty, joined with great delight, and constant purpose of glorifying God constantly : *I will praise thee, O Lord my God, with all my heart, and I will glorify thy name for evermore.* 3. When a man seeth his sins great, his deserving great, his danger and delivery great, he must also see God's mercy toward him great, and his obligation to thanksgiving great : *I will glorify thy name for evermore ; for great is thy mercy toward me.* 4. Preventing mercy keeping us from the evil we are in danger to fall into, is to be esteemed by us, as delivering mercy, bringing us out of the evil wherein we were lying. The Lord's keeping us from falling into hell, should be accounted by us no less mercy, than if we had been in hell, and had been brought back out of it by him : *thou hast delivered my soul from the lowest hell.* The same may be said of other particulars; and when our eyes are open to see the evils from which the Lord hath kept us, when we were in danger of them, we shall be forced so to judge.

14. *O God, the proud are risen against me, and the assemblies of violent* men *have sought after my soul : and have not set thee before them.*

15. *But thou, O Lord,* art *a God full of compassion, and gracious, long-suffering, and plenteous in mercy and truth.*

Here are other reasons of his hope to be delivered, taken from the pride and oppression of the godless enemy, and from God's pity and compassion. Whence learn, 1. Proud, violent, cruel, and godless men, are the readiest instruments which can be found unto Satan for persecuting God's children. Such were the enemies of David, a type of Christ, and an example to his persecuted followers : *the proud are risen against me.* 2. Whatsoever wicked man pleaseth to make head against the godly, he will readily find multitudes to follow him : *the proud are risen against me, and the assemblies of violent men have sought after my soul.* 3. When men reject the fear of God, there is no wickedness so great which they will not commit : *they have sought after my soul, and have not set thee, O God, before them ;* that is, they neither fear thy judgments, nor care for what may please thee. 4. The more violent, cruel, profane, and ungodly our persecutors are, the more hope is there of God's pity toward us, as the psalmist reasoneth : *but thou, O Lord, art a God full of compassion.* 5. Whatsoever objections may arise from our unworthiness, from our former sinful provocations of God, and the multitude and greatness of our former sins, to hinder our hope that God shall pity us in our affliction, they are all answered and taken away by consideration of the unspeakable greatness of God's goodness: *for in God is compassion, he is full*

of compassion, a God full of compassion ; that is, infinitely compassionate, and, as it were, affected with our
misery. *He is gracious,* though we be unworthy: he *is
long-suffering,* although we be given to strife and provocation of him; and how great soever our misdeservings have
been, *he is plenteous in mercy ;* and howsoever we have
forfeited our interest in his promises, yet he will not follow
the forfeiture, but will keep up our right unto his promises
still : *he is plenteous in truth ;* great is his faithfulness
who keepeth promises, albeit he might justly reject them.

16. *O turn unto me, and have mercy upon me : give
thy strength unto thy servant, and save the son of thine
handmaid.*

17. *Shew me a token for good ; that they which hate
me may see* it, *and be ashamed; because thou, Lord,
hast holpen me, and comforted me.*

The seventh petition is for strength to stand out, till such
a clear delivery should come to him from God as might put
his enemies to confusion, when they should see it. Whence
learn, 1. Whosoever considereth well the riches of God's grace
and goodness, may confidently pray for a proof of it, in the
changing of a miserable condition into a better, even when
God seemeth angry and averse: *thou art plenteous in mercy and truth ; O turn unto me, and have mercy upon
me.* 2. It is no small mercy to have strength from God to
subsist under troubles, till the delivery come; and for this
strength the man emptied of self-confidence may call, and
should be content with supporting strength till the Lord's
time of deliverance come : *give thy strength unto thy servant.* 3. The longer course the kindness of the Lord hath
had toward us, and the more relations are between God and
us, we may expect the more confidently further effects and
fruit of his kindness for our deliverance; for David here
reckoneth from his being born within the covenant, born as
a domestic, as a child of the church, who belonged to God's
protection and care, as the son of the handmaid belonged to
the care of the master of the family : *save the son of thy
handmaid.* 4. As the wicked delight to see the godly in
misery, that they may insult over godliness, so the godly desire deliverance, that in their person godliness may not suffer,
nor wicked men be hardened in their insolence : *shew me a*

token for good, that they who hate me may see it. 5. The good success and delivery of some of the saints out of their troubles and trials, is a good token, both to themselves and to all other godly persons, of a blessed outgate to them from all their troubles: therefore David prayeth for it : *shew me a token for good.* 6. As the good outgate of the godly from their troubles is matter of joy and gloriation unto the godly, so is it also matter of shame and confusion to the wicked who hate them : *shew me a token for good, that they who hate me may see it, and be ashamed, because thou, Lord, hast holpen me, and comforted me.*

PSALM LXXXVII.

A psalm or song for the sons of Korah.

When God loosed the captivity of the Jews by Cyrus, few of them returned from Babylon ; the work of reparation of church and state, temple and city, had few to assist it. Their enemies were many, they were straitened with poverty and famine, and the hearts and hands of the godly were weakened ; they were like to faint and despair, that either church or state should flourish any more amongst them. For comfort in such a time was this psalm fitted, leading the Lord's people to live by faith, and to work on in the building of the Lord's house, and reparation of the city, looking to God the builder of his church, and maintainer of his people. To which purpose the psalmist giveth them seven consolations, opposite to so many temptations to discouragement. The first is, that they should look to God who had founded his own temple solidly, and so not faint for the weakness and fewness of the builders, v. 1. The second is, that they should look to God's love and good-will, and not be troubled for want of external power and riches, v. 2. The third is, that they should look to the prophecies concerning the church, and not be troubled for what present outward appearance and carnal reason represented, v 3. The fourth is, that they should not be troubled by the multitude of their foes for the present time, but look to the multitude of friends and converts which they would have hereafter, v. 4, 5. The fifth is, that they should not be troubled with the fear of the ruin of the church, but look to Almighty God, who would establish her so, that no power could overturn her, v. 5. The sixth is, that they should not be troubled with the present contempt under which they lay ; but look to the glory and estimation which God should put in his own time on the church and her children, v. 6. The seventh is, that they should not be troubled with the present grief they were in, but should look to the spiritual joy, and causes thereof, which the Lord was to furnish to his people, v. 7.

1. *His foundation* is *in the holy mountains.*

The first comfort of the afflicted Jews, troubled for the hindering of the building of God's temple, is, that God had by his decree and promise made the mountains of Zion and Moriah the place of his rest amongst his people, till the

Messiah should come, in whom these types were to be accomplished, and for whose cause they were to be preserved
till he came, who is the only solid rock whereupon the church
is built. Whence learn, 1. When the builders of the Lord's
church are few and weak, his people had need to be comforted against their fears and doubts, as here we see : and
the way to be comforted in such hard times, is to look by
faith to God, as the builder of his own house, who hath laid
the foundation upon solid grounds, that every believer who
trusteth in him, may be as mount Zion, which cannot be
removed : *his foundation is on the holy mountains.*

2. *The Lord loveth the gates of Zion, more than all
the dwellings of Jacob.*

The second comfort is, that God hath chosen Zion above
all other places to be his rest, and loved there to dwell rather
than elsewhere. Whence learn, 1. The dignity of any
place, person, or society, proceedeth not from any thing in
the place or society, but from the Lord's election and free
love : *the Lord loveth the gates of Zion, more than all
the dwellings of Jacob.* 2. The love of the Lord to his
chosen church, is a solid ground of assurance of her continuance, as here in the figure we are taught.

3. *Glorious things are spoken of thee, O city of
God. Selah.*

The third comfort is, from the prophecies past about the
church, and promises made unto her in figurative terms.
Whence learn, 1. The church is the incorporation in which
the Lord reigneth, ruleth, and resideth : *it is the city of
God.* 2. The privileges of the church are very glorious;
the glory of kings, crowns, and diadems is nothing to them
but bodily and temporal shadows of what is spiritually and
everlastingly bestowed on the church : *glorious things are
spoken of thee.* 3. Albeit glorious things are bestowed
of the church, yet it is not so much any thing already done,
as what is to be done, which maketh the church blessed :
it is not present possession but hope, nor sight but faith,
which maketh the church blessed; and the Scriptures are a
sufficient surety to us for all blessings to come : *glorious
things are spoken of thee, O city of God.*

4. *I will make mention of Rahab and Babylon to*

*them that know me: behold Philistia, and Tyre, with
Ethiopia; this man was born there.*

5. *And of Zion it shall be said, This and that man
was born in her; and the Highest himself shall establish her.*

The fourth comfort is, that the church's chiefest enemies
should be converted to the faith, and should count it their
greatest honour so to be. Whence learn, 1. It is among
the troubles of the church that she hath so many enemies,
and those so mighty and potent as the Egyptians and Babylonians : *I will make mention of Rahab;* that is, Egypt,
and Babylon, and Palestina, and Tyre, and Ethiopia, which
are here named as the most eminent oppressors of the
church, among all other kingdoms. 2. It should comfort
the church, that God is able to make her chiefest enemies
become converts, and that he hath done it sundry times, and
will yet do it more; and that he can take order with those
enemies which shall not be converted, as he did with Rahab
and Babylon : for, *I will make mention of Rahab and
Babylon, to them that know me,* signifieth a mention-
making of them; viz., to the edification of the church's
children, both concerning what God had done in those nations in justice, and what he would do to them in mercy, or
unto other enemies like them. 3. As it is the glory and
comfort of the church to have her enemies made converts;
so is it honourable to the enemies, were they ever so potent
in the world, to be citizens of the city of God : *I will make
mention of them, that this man was born there,* that is, in
the city of God. 4. The conversion of men from paganism
and idolatry unto fellowship in the covenant with the church,
is a sort of new birth to the externally converted, from
which their new birth and new being are to be reckoned :
this man was born there. 5. As whatsoever honour men
have in the world is not to be compared with the honour
of regeneration and being born citizens of the church : so
whatsoever contempt the members of the church suffer from
the world is made up by the honour of being born in the
church : for, *of Zion it shall be said, This and that man
were born in her.* 6. There is no reason to fear the ruin
of the church, or the not continuing of her from age to
age, to be a mother and receptacle of converts: *for the*

Highest himself shall establish her, and this is the fifth comfort of the favourers of the church in the time of trouble.

6. *The Lord shall count, when he writeth up the people,* that *this* man *was born there. Selah.*

The sixth comfort is, from God's estimation which he hath of every one of the true citizens of his church. Whence learn, 1. As all the elect, all the regenerate are taken notice of by God no less particularly than if their names were all written up in a book, one by one: so there is a time when he manifesteth his enrolling them; partly to themselves, by his witnessing to them that they are his children; partly to the world, by sustaining them in their trials and troubles; and partly by a full delivery of them and confessing their names before men and angels at the great day : *the Lord shall count when he writeth up the people;* that is, in his own time when he seeth it fit to manifest his respect to his own. 2. The converts among the nations shall be reckoned up among the converts of the Lord's people of the Jews : *the Lord shall count when he writeth up the people, that this man was born there ;* that is, whatsoever man he be, who is converted out of any country, tongue, or language, he shall be counted a member of the church of Israel.

7. *As well the singers as the players on instruments* shall be there : *all my springs* are *in thee.*

The last comfort is, from the joy spiritual, and the everlasting springs, fountains, and causes of joy, which God furnisheth and will furnish to his church. Whence learn, 1. As the church is subject to her own griefs in the world, so also is she sure of abundant consolation to be had and laid up in store for her, expressed here in terms of typical joy, appointed in solemn festivals : *as well the singers as the players on instruments shall be there.* 2. The causes of the joy of the saints are everlasting, comparable to wells and springs of living water : *all my springs shall be in thee.* 3. Such saints as have had their senses exercised are able to subscribe the truth of promises by their own experience, and in special, that there is no joy nor comfort, no gift nor grace, no refreshment nor delectation worthy to be named, except that which they have by church privileges and communion of saints, as here the psalmist confesseth : *all my springs are in thee,* saith he, speaking to the church, or to God dwelling in his church.

PSALM LXXXVIII.

A song or psalm for the sons of Korah. To the chief musician upon Mahalah Leannoth, Maschil of Heman the Ezrahite.

This Heman the Ezrahite, was one of those four wisest men in all Israel, next after Solomon, who is preferred above them all, 1 Kings iv. 31. The exercise of this wise and holy man is set down here under the heaviest condition of a wounded spirit, of any that we read of; wherein first, he prayeth for comfort to his soul, now afflicted under the sense of sad wrath and long desertion, v. 1, 2. In the second place, he poureth out his soul to God, and layeth before him a most pitiful lamentation of his distressed condition, v. 3—8. In the third place, he wrestleth by faith in his prayer to God for comfort, v. 9—14. And lastly, finding no comfort, he reneweth his lamentation, leaveth his prayer before the Lord, and writeth it for the edification of the church in all time coming, as the matter of a joyful song.

From the inscription, learn, 1. David was not the only man acquainted with sad exercise and affliction of spirit, for here is another, to wit, Heman the Ezrahite, as deep in trouble of spirit as he or any other beside. 2. They are not all men of weak minds and shallow wits who are acquainted with trouble of spirit, and borne down with the sense of God's wrath; for here is Heman, one amongst the wisest of all Israel, and inferior to none for wisdom, except to Solomon alone, under the heaviest exercise we can imagine possible for a saint. 3. When it pleaseth God to exercise a man of parts, of great gifts and graces, he can make his burthen proportionable to his strength, and give him as much to do with the difficulties he puts him to, as a weaker man shall find in his exercise, as appeareth in the experience of Heman. 4. Wise men in their trouble must take the same course with the simpler sort of men; that is, they must run to God as others do, and seek relief only in his grace, who, as he distributeth the measures of trouble, can also give comfort, ease, and deliverance from them, as the practice of Heman teacheth us. 5. What trouble of wounded spirit some of God's children have felt in former times, others dear to God may find the like in after ages, and all men ought to prepare for the like, and should not think the exercise strange when it cometh, but must comfort themselves in this, that other saints whose names are recorded in Scripture, have been under like affliction; for the psalm is appointed to give instruction : it is *Maschil of Heman.* 6. What is at one time matter of mourning to one of God's

children, may become matter of joy and singing afterward,
both to himself and to others, as this sad anguish of spirit
in Heman is made a song of joy unto God's glory, and the
comfort of all afflicted souls, labouring under the sense of
sin and felt wrath of God, to the world's end : it is *a song,
a psalm for the sons of Korah.* 7. Such as are most
heartily afflicted in spirit, and flee to God for reconciliation
and consolation through Christ, have no reason to suspect
themselves, that they are not esteemed, and loved as dear
children, because they feel so much of God's wrath: for
here is a saint who hath drunken of that cup, (as deep as
any who shall read this psalm,) here is one so much loved
and honoured of God, as to be a penman of holy Scripture,
and a pattern of faith and patience unto others; even *Heman the Ezrahite.*

1. *O Lord God of my salvation, I have cried day*
and *night before thee.*

2. *Let my prayer come before thee : incline thine
ear unto my cry ;*

In the first place, the psalmist fasteneth his faith and resolution to pray constantly to God, till he receive answer;
and requesteth comfort now at last.　　Whence learn, 1.
Whosoever have fled to God for grace, and have received
the offer of reconciliation made to the church in the Messiah, are entered into covenant with God for their everlasting
salvation, and ought to stand fast in the holding of this
covenant, whatsoever hard condition they may fall into, as
Heman doth here, saying to God, *O Lord God of my salvation.* 2. When a soul hath received the offer of grace
made to the church, in the common tender of the covenant
of grace, he is entered into covenant with God so particularly, as if the indenture were passed between God and that
soul by name, so that the believer may read his own name
in God's everlasting styles and titles, and may read in himself the mark of God's interest in him, and the mark of
his interest in God for evermore: for, *O God of my salvation* importeth no less. 3. When a believer hath laid
hold on eternal life, he may by the same right ask and expect comfort in, and deliverance out of every trouble, as an
appendix of the great salvation, which is coming unto him,
as here Heman doth. 4. God can love a man, and keep

him in faith and exercise of prayer a long time, without a comfortable answer, and all in love, wise love : *I have cried day and night before thee*, saith Heman, and the answer is not come yet. 5. There is a difference of the lamentation of the worldly man, and of the believer. The worldly man sighs and cries, and he knows not to whom, but the godly present themselves in their lamentations to God; *I have cried day and night before thee; as his dolor cleaved unto him, or was renewed upon him, so he had his recourse to God at all times. 6. Albeit our prayer, being presented before God, seem to us not to have been admitted, yet must our bill lie still, and be put up to God again and again, till it be received to our sense and knowledge : *let my prayer come before thee.* 7. The believer may be sure to have a good answer at length, but he must be instant, and deal still with God for it, and press it hard, and patiently wait for it, as Heman here doth : *incline thine ear unto my cry.*

3. *For my soul is full of troubles, and my life draweth nigh unto the grave.*

In the second place, the psalmist layeth out his trouble before God in nine degrees thereof, each of them superadding something to the former : under which he is not only wonderfully upheld, but also he maketh use of this lamentation, and long catalogue of miseries, as a ground of his hope, to have a gracious answer at last; which came to pass, as the turning of this lamentation into a song, to the comfort of others in the church that should feel the like in any measure thereafter, showeth; for his condition he setteth down under the name of *trouble*, soul-trouble; more troubles than one or two : and the first degree thereof is, that his soul is full of troubles, replenished so as it can hold no more. Whence learn, 1. Albeit we had nothing to bring before God but our grief and misery, we want not matter of confidence to find favour from our pitiful God, as this example teacheth us: *incline thine ear, for my soul is full of troubles.* 2. If the godly should smother their grief, and not go to God with it, then sorrow were able to choke them; but it is no small ease to them that they have God to go to, to whom they may freely vent their mind, as here we see. 3. Soul-troubles are the most pressing troubles, and with those readily will the Lord exercise his children, when he mindeth to try their faith, making their spirits to smart with trouble after trouble, with a number of troubles, which they are neither able to reckon nor to bear : *my soul is full of troubles.* 4. The dolors of the mind are able to waste away the body, which cannot but shrink and pine away when the soul is sick with anguish : *my life draweth near to the grave,* saith he; and this is the second degree of his trouble.

4. *I am counted with them that go down into the pit: I am as a man that hath no strength.*

The third degree of the psalmist's trouble is, that, in the judgment of those who knew his condition and possibly lamented it, he was counted a lost man; yea, and he himself found no strength to bear out, or to recover himself. Whence learn, 1. It is no small temptation and vexation of spirit to the godly believer, to be in the judgment of beholders a lost man, because of the seeming desperate condition of his soul, and yet it may befall a dear child of God : *I am counted with them that go down to the pit.* 2. Albeit God hath by grace severed death from hell unto the believer, yet the connexion of these two, if justice were not satisfied in the Redeemer, would never be forgotten, as the Scriptures giving the same name unto death, grave, and hell, may teach us : *I am counted with them that go down to the pit,* or grave, or hell. 3. Whatsoever strength of soul or body a man hath in his possession, shall be soon emptied when God putteth him in distress, except new furniture be supplied unto him, and that no less than unto the weakest : *I am as a man that hath no strength.*

5. *Free among the dead, like the slain that lie in the grave, whom thou rememberest no more : and they are cut off from thy hand.*

The fourth degree of his trouble is, that he is like the leper in the law, shut out from the living, and put among the dead, and no more fit for any duty of the living; which teacheth us, that the believer in God may sometimes be so burdened with trouble of spirit, as he can neither think nor speak, nor go about any duty of the living for a time : *I am,* or I am counted, saith he, *as one free among the dead,* or shut out, and separate among the dead.

The fifth degree of his trouble is, he is a man whose life is violently plucked from him; who gets not liberty to die at leisure or in peace, but is thrust out of the world suddenly with a deadly wound; and such may the condition of a soul dear to God seem to itself to be: *I am like the slain that lie in the grave.*

The sixth degree of his trouble is, he seemeth to be deprived of the comfortable vicissitude of the common benefits of life, and of those changes which ordinarily God's visitations make, as if he were left under the power of death, there to lie without a change of that condition for ever : and such may the case of a beloved saint seem to be, both to himself and to others; *I am as one in the grave, whom thou rememberest no more;* yea, the believer at a time may lose the sight of everlasting promises, and seem to himself to be rejected of God : *I am as they that are cut off from thy hand.*

6. *Thou hast laid me in the lowest pit, in darkness, in the deeps.*

The seventh degree of his trouble is, he seemeth as a man already condemned and possessed of the torment of hell, in the inextricable misery of the damned, deprived of all light of consolation in the gulf of desperation, wherein a man cannot find ground, nor deliverance from it. Whence learn, 1. That this also may be the case of a believer in his own sense : *thou hast laid me in the lowest pit, in darkness, in the deeps.* 2. Whatsoever trouble we are in, or how great danger soever we seem to ourselves to be in, it is the believer's wisdom still to look to God, as our party with whom we have to do, and to lay it forth before him : for albeit this may augment grief and fear on the one hand, yet it prepareth way for the remedy, and keepeth the believer in terms with God on the other hand, as this example teacheth us : *thou hast laid me in the lowest pit, in darkness, in the deeps.*

7. *Thy wrath lieth hard upon me, and thou hast afflicted me with all thy waves.   Selah.*

The eighth degree of his trouble is, the felt wrath of God pursuing him, overtaking him, lying heavy upon him, tossing him with new affrightments and assaults, as the waves of the sea do, when they come one after another, and beat with endless dashing upon what they find in their way; and such may be the case of a beloved soul in its own sense, which when we consider, we may say, How gentle is the ordinary exercise of weak believers, when this exercise is looked upon ? *Thy wrath lieth hard upon me, and thou hast afflicted me with all thy waves.*

8. *Thou hast put away mine acquaintance far from me; thou hast made me an abomination unto them : I am shut up, and I cannot come forth.*

The ninth degree of his trouble is, that, beside all the burden of the foresaid vexation, the Lord deprived him of all comfort, and bestowed not upon him so much as any consolation from his friends, or from the fellowship of the godly wise; but, by God's providence, they left him as a man desperate, yea, as a man whose condition they were afraid to look upon; yea, they abhorred his case and forsook him : and he, being thus in appearance shut out from heaven and followed with wrath from God, was not only left comfortless among men, but also was looked upon by his friends as a damned and abominable reprobate; dealt with as a man shut up for the plague or pestilence, so that he kept his chamber, and could not come abroad to look any man in the face : and this also may be the case of a soul precious in God's eyes, beloved and accepted of him in the very mean time of all this hard exercise : *thou hast put away my acquaintance far from me; thou hast made me an abomination to them : I am shut up, and cannot come forth.*

9. *Mine eye mourneth by reason of affliction : Lord, I have called daily upon thee; I have stretched out my hands unto thee.*

In the third place, the psalmist wrestleth by prayer with God for comfort, using for this end four reasons to strengthen his faith and hope to be comforted. The first is, from the consciousness of his earnest seeking his comfort and relief from his trouble only in God. Whence learn, 1. Godliness maketh not men senseless of grief, nor doth it hinder tears or mourning, or any other effects of sorrow to be seen in their body : *mine eye mourneth because of affliction.* 2. Sorrow should neither hinder the godly to seek God, nor move them to seek their consolation elsewhere : *Lord, I have called daily upon thee.* 3. It is possible that a godly man may be instant daily with God, praying with tears for comfort, and yet not obtain for a long time, as this example teacheth. 4. As in serious prayer, specially in secret, the affections of the heart utter themselves in the answerable gestures of the body, as well as in the voice and words of the mouth; so those gestures have their own speech unto God, no less than the words of the mouth have : as here, *I have stretched out my hands unto thee,* is brought forth to express his submissive rendering up of himself unto God, and his dependence upon him.

10. *Wilt thou shew wonders to the dead ? shall the dead arise* and *praise thee ? Selah.*

11. *Shall thy loving-kindness be declared in the grave ?* or *thy faithfulness in destruction ?*

12. *Shall thy wonders be known in the dark ? and thy righteousness in the land of forgetfulness ?*

The second reason is, because if God do not shortly answer him (as he thinks) he cannot but die, and then it will not be time to give answer to his prayer, for the edification of others, and glorifying of his name among men in this world, by relieving a poor supplicant, such as he was, except he would raise him up again after he is dead, extraordinarily and miraculously, which he cannot look for, and therefore he hopeth and prayeth to be comforted in time : wherein he puts it out of question, that he cannot but die quickly, if the Lord comfort him not shortly. Here he speaketh his own sense, hasteneth a little to be comforted, somewhat indirectly setteth a time to the Lord's manifesting himself, and showeth some human infirmity, yet such as the Lord useth not to quarrel for with his children in their lamentations. Meantime in this he showeth himself a noble wrestler; first, because he assureth himself that God would not fail to comfort him before he died; and again, that the Lord would rather miraculously raise him from the dead, than not glorify himself in his deliverance : and in this also he taketh a safe course to seek for what he might expect, rather in an ordinary way, than to look for miracles. Whence learn, 1. When the Lord delayeth to comfort a believing supplicant, he calleth him to wrestle in prayer, and to exercise his faith so much the more, as here we find this saint to do, expounding God's dispensation, and bending his spirit in his supplication to wrestle for comfort, as those often interrogations make evident. 2. When faith is fixed upon the covenant, and promises, and power, and goodness of God, it will expect miracles, rather than fear breach of God's promise: as, *wilt thou shew wonders to the dead* doth import. 3. A true believer should love to be comforted, yea and to live in the world, not so much for his own satisfaction, as that he may glorify God in his life : as, *shall the dead rise and praise thee* doth import. 4. It will not content a believer to have the use of any benefit unto himself alone, but he resolveth to make it forthcoming; as to the glory of God, so also to the edification of others; and therefore he loveth to have the benefits which he seeketh mainly for that end: as, *shall thy loving-kindness be declared in the grave* doth import. 5. The only time to glorify God, so as others may be edified, is this present life. After death a man may praise God in heaven, but shall not instruct any ignorant person there by his example or counsel; as, *shall thy faithfulness be declared in destruction* doth import : and that which followeth also showeth the same : *shall thy wonders be known in the dark, and thy righteousness in the land of forgetfulness ?* 6. There is no commerce between the living and the dead; the dead know not what men are doing on the earth, for death is the *land of forgetfulness*, wherein the living and dead so part and go asunder, as those do who forget one another. 7. A soul acquainted with God, hath no will to die, till the sense of wrath be removed, and the feeling of the sense of reconciliation be granted, as this example showeth: and no wonder in this, for it is a fearful thing to have the terror both of temporal and eternal death to encounter at once.

13. *But unto thee have I cried, O Lord ; and in the morning shall my prayer prevent thee.*

The third reason of his hope to have his request granted is, from his resolution never to give over praying, but as he had done before, so to continue still in his supplication. Whence learn, 1. Instancy in prayer and resolution never to give over, as they argue solid and strong faith, so they give good ground of hope to be heard, as in this example of the prophet may be seen.   2. Albeit we do not find an answer to our warrantable prayers so soon as we would, yet we must not conclude that our bypast prayer hath been amiss, but rather must avow our bypast exercise, and resolve to continue as the psalmist doth here: *but unto thee have I cried, O Lord, and in the morning shall my prayer prevent thee.*

14. *Lord, why castest thou off my soul?* why *hidest thou thy face from me?*

The fourth reason is, from the impossibility of his being a castaway, albeit it seemed so, or that God should aways hide his face from him, albeit it seemed so; as his asking *why*, in the reasoning of faith against sense and outward appearance, showeth to be his meaning, especially if these words be compared with the preceding verse.   Whence learn, 1. As the faith of God's dear children may be assaulted with suggestions moving them to suspect their rejection from God, so is it the nature of faith, and the duty of believers, to reject those thoughts, to lay them out before God, and to dispute against them: *Lord, why castest thou off my soul?*   2. When God hideth the sensible signs of his favour toward us, we are allowed to deal with God to remove the veil: *why hidest thou thy face from me?*   3. A glimpse of God's face, or of his sensibly manifested love, may mitigate the sorest trouble of a sad soul and satisfy the afflicted, as the petition involved in this speech, *why hidest thou thy face from me*, importeth: for, if he could have found any glimpse of favour, he would not have so complained.

15. *I am afflicted and ready to die from my youth up:* while *I suffer thy terrors I am distracted.*

In the last part of the psalm, the prophet, finding no consolation, returneth to his lamentation, by which he made way to his wrestling in prayer, from v. 3 to 9, and layeth down his misery at the Lord's feet, as the object of the bowels of his pity; in which misery he is persuaded that he could not but feel the effects of the Lord's compassion in due time. The parts of the lamentation are three.   The first is, for the long continuance of his sad exercise, even *from his youth up.*   Wherein he showeth, first, that he was *afflicted,* that is, put to great straits by calamities; secondly, that he was *ready to die,* as a man overset and able to bear no more; thirdly, that he was as much vexed with what he feared to come as he was troubled with what he felt—*he suffered the terrors of the Lord;* fourthly, that he was exercised frequently and a long time that way—*from his youth up;* fifthly, that, by the hard exercise and returning terrors of God upon him, he was so rent and perplexed that ofttimes he could not make use of his natural reason, as he reckoned. Whence learn, 1. When we have essayed all means for having comfort of God, it is safest for us to lay our grief before God till he be pleased to show pity : the child of God hath no oratory but mourning to his Father, as here we see. 2. A grieved mind can reckon all its afflic- tions, and call to remembrance those troubles that are long since past, as here we see. 3. It is an ordinary doctrine, but hardly believed when it cometh to application, *that God loveth them whom he chastiseth,* as the prophet's lamenta- tion and wrestlings teach us. 4. In a thorough trial the Lord bringeth the soul to the brink of death : *I am ready to die.* 5. The weight of present troubles is accompanied readily with the fear of worse to come, and the fear of evil to come doubleth the weight of evil that is present; for the Lord's *terrors* here are reckoned as his saddest sufferings. 6. Some of God's children are more exercised in their con- sciences than some others, yea, some souls may all their days be frequented with the terrors of the Lord and fears of his wrath; as this example of Heman exercised from his *youth up* showeth. 7. Sore trials may put faith sometimes to stagger with doubting, and by perplexity put a man's reason to a stand, and make him many times like a man beside himself: *I am distracted.* 8. Albeit the godly may be put to doubt, yet are they not driven to despair; albeit they be cast down, yet they are not *destroyed,* as here we see.

16. *Thy fierce wrath goeth over me ; thy terrors have cut me off.*

17. *They came round about me daily like water; they compassed me about together.*

The second part of the lamentation is for the feeling of the apparent effects of God's wrath—*fierce* wrath, *over- whelming* wrath going over him—*fears and terrors* of more and heavy wrath coming—*affrighting* wrath in appearance,

surrounding wrath and terror compassing about, like deep
waters, from which no outgate can be seen. Whence learn,
1. Trouble hath its own weight but wrath maketh it insupportable. The wrath of a father, when it is seen, is terrible; but the fierce wrath of a judge, when it appeareth, is
unspeakable: it overwhelmeth, swalloweth up; and yet this
may be the exercise of a child of God: *thy fierce wrath
goeth over me.* 2. Albeit the exercise of a child of God
may seem to himself to be the very case of a damned reprobate, yet, in the midst of it, the footsteps of grace and
evidence of faith may be seen by a beholder, as in the experience of Heman, who, in his deepest trouble, adhered to
God: for, (1.) The fear which set upon him is called the
terror of God, which importeth not only wrath, present
wrath, but also irresistible wrath, yea, and growing of God's
wrath, coming apace upon him, for *terror* importeth this.
(2.) The terrors of God (in the plural number) are upon him;
that is, frequent terrors and multiplied terrors. 3. The
effect of those terrors as they seemed—they were affrighting
terrors, which threatened to separate his soul from God utterly, altogether, and for ever, to his sense and likelihood;
they spake no less than that he was to be found a castaway:
thy terrors, saith he, *have cut me off*. 4. Last of all, for
the manner of the assault made by those terrors upon his
poor soul, they are compared to waters enclosing a man
before he be aware, compassing him so about that he can
find no outgate, and, like the returning of the tide, compassing him daily; yea, like contrary tides, one of them
thrusting another, and setting upon him on all hands together, whereby the inexpressible trouble of a soul under
the sense of God's wrath is described, but so as none can
understand it, except he who, either in lesser or greater
measure, hath felt it; and all this may befall a child of light:
*thy fierce wrath goeth over me; thy terrors have cut me
off: they came round about me daily like water; they
compassed me about together.*

18. *Lover and friend hast thou put far from me,* and
mine acquaintance into darkness.

The third and last part of the lamentation is repeated
from v. 8—that there was no man compassionate toward
him, none to pity him, none to counsel or comfort him, none

to whom he might impart his mind fully for easing him; but his old friends, and such as loved him before, failed him and forsook him, and God made it manifest that he thrust them away from him; none were to bear him company, but he demeaned himself to sit solitary in darkness. So, then, learn, 1. Albeit a friend be made for the day of trouble, and albeit it would have been an ease to have had any friend's company for means of comfort, yet he could find none; God withheld them all for the trial of his servant here, and such a heavy and comfortless condition may be the lot of a beloved child: *lover and friend hast thou put far from me, and mine acquaintance into darkness.* 2. In that he endeth the psalm without any comfort for the time, it maketh this psalm no less comfortable than any other psalm, because it showeth that he was supported insensibly for the time, and had comfort given him thereafter, so much as to make this sad complaint to be turned into a song both to himself and to the church. It also teacheth that, seeing God can sustain a soul by secretly supporting a man's faith without comfortable sense, yea, and that under the saddest sense of wrath, therefore a believer in God must lay hold on God's goodness, promise, and covenant, and must trust still in the Lord, albeit he should seem to slay him; as the example of Heman the Ezrahite here teacheth us.

PSALM LXXXIX.
Maschil of Ethan the Ezrahite.

This psalm is entitled *Maschil*, or a psalm written for instruction of Ethan the Ezrahite, who, after Solomon, was another of the four wisest men in Israel. This man, surviving the glory of Solomon's kingdom, and beholding the diminishing of the glory of David's house, lamenteth the desolation thereof unto God.

The psalm hath three parts. In the first part, he setteth his faith upon God, and laboureth to strengthen it against the temptation which was boiling in his breast, ver. 19. In the second part, he expoundeth the sum of the covenant of grace, made between God and Christ, typified by David; wherein indeed, albeit David hath his own interest, yet the substance was to be found only in Christ, who came of David according to the flesh, from ver. 19 to 38. In the third part is a lamentation of the apparent dissolving of this covenant with David's posterity, and a prayer for repairing the ruins of that kingdom, for the glory of God; which prayer he assureth himself shall be granted.

From the inscription, learn, 1. Wisdom exempteth not a man from grief and anguish, from temptation of faith and hard exercise of mind ; for here is another example beside

Heman, to wit, Ethan the Ezrahite, a man of the same family with Heman. 2. The Lord distributeth to men their inward exercises, that one may have his trouble for one cause and another have it for another cause, as it pleaseth him to measure out in his wisdom; for Heman's trouble is made about his own private condition, but Ethan's trouble is about the public calamity of church and kingdom. Not that we think Heman was insensible of the public calamity, or Ethan not acquainted with trouble in his own particular case; but because the Lord would have the one exemplary in the one sort of exercise, and the other exemplary in the other sort of exercise, and will have the exercise of both to be the instruction of his people: *Maschil of both Heman and Ethan.*

1. *I will sing of the mercies of the Lord for ever : with my mouth will I make known thy faithfulness to all generations.*

Before he utter his temptation, or bring forth his lamentation for the apparently dissolved covenant between God and David, the psalmist obligeth himself to maintain the glory of the mercy and faithfulness of God, v. 1, 2, in relation to the stability of the covenant made with David particularly, ver. 3, 4, and to this end he strengtheneth his faith by a number of reasons to v. 19. The first is, from his resolution to hold fast the belief of God's mercy and faithfulness, notwithstanding it at this time seemed that God had dissolved the covenant with David's house. Whence learn, 1. Whatsoever promise the Lord hath made to his people, they must not wonder albeit sometimes he make it very improbable to carnal sense and reason that ever it shall be performed; because this is needful for the exercise of faith, as in this example we see. 2. In the conflict of faith with misbelief, it is wisdom for the believer to suppress the suggestions of unbelief, to take part with faith, to break through the throng of desperate thoughts, and without disputation close with the mercy of God and the faithfulness of his word, to avow faith, and engage himself to maintain it, before he utter his temptation unto misbelief, or suffer it to vent itself; as here the psalmist teacheth by his example, saying, *I will sing of the mercies of the Lord for ever, &c.* 3. The mercies of God and his faithfulness, are two strong pillars of confidence in God; mercy to take away sin and misery, and faithfulness to perform all the promises of every good unto the believer : *I will sing of the mercies of the Lord for ever : with my mouth will I make known thy faithfulness to all generations.*

2. *For I have said, Mercy shall be built up for ever ; thy faithfulness shalt thou establish in the very heavens.*

The psalmist addeth a reason for his resolution to give the glory of mercy and truth unto God, which was his persuasion that the work of God's mercy, promised to David in the Messiah, should go on, be perfected, and settled for ever, and that the evidence of God's faithful promise should be manifested from heaven, albeit sometimes it should disappear on the earth. Whence learn, 1. It is believing with the heart, which sealeth God's truth, and maketh the mouth confess unto God : *with my mouth will I make known thy faithfulness, for I have said, Mercy shall be built up for ever.* 2. The sure mercies promised to David, in special concerning the Redeemer's taking flesh of his stock, are like a building which hath a foundation already laid by a wise and powerful builder, and shall come up certainly to perfection, and endure for ever : *I have said, that mercy shall be built up for ever.* 3. When the effect of God's truth disappeareth on earth, it is to be found in heaven in God's decree, good-will, power, and faithfulness, whence it will not fail to manifest itself in due time : *thy faithfulness shalt thou establish in the very heavens.*

3. *I have made a covenant with my chosen, I have sworn unto David my servant,*

4. *Thy seed will I establish for ever, and build up thy throne to all generations. Selah.*

That which he meaneth by the Lord's truth and faithfulness in general, he expoundeth in particular to be in relation to the Lord's promise made to David concerning the perpetuity of the kingdom in his posterity for the good of the church; which promise hath accomplishment in Christ, the Son of David according to the flesh. Whence learn, 1. As all the Lord's promises, so especially those which concern Christ, and all saving graces in him, (which are called the sure mercies of David,) should be narrowly looked upon, that nothing be passed by, whereof faith may take advantage; for what is promised concerning Christ, concerneth all believers in him to the world's end; and this the example of the psalmist here teacheth us : for he observeth the promise-maker, *I the Lord ;* and the qualification of the receiver of the promise, clothed with the styles of Christ, whom David represented, and in whose favour chiefly the promise is made : *thy chosen servant ;* and the nature of the promise by way of solemn *covenant ;* and the confirmation of it by an oath : *I have sworn ;* and the substance of the promise that one should come of David, who should be of everlasting continuance, established by divine power for ever, to wit, Christ the Lord; and that the kingdom of Israel, called David's throne, which was erected for governing the people of God, as it was now well founded upon the decree of God, and began to be built already, should be builded up, and grow to a perspicuous perfection from one generation to another, and be perpetuated for ever : *thy seed will I establish for ever, and build up thy throne to all generations.* 2. When disappearance of hoped good things brangleth faith, then the word of God and his promises must be called to memory, upon which faith must fix itself, as this example teacheth. 3. The mercy and faithfulness of God, which are the common grounds of the stability of all the Lord's promises, being delivered in the general, should be applied particularly to every promise, as we have need thereof, that we may strengthen our faith by reasoning from this ground, thus : God's mercy and faithfulness make all his promises fast, and therefore make fast this particular promise also, whereupon I now pitch, as the example of the psalmist teacheth us. 4. As all the promises of God are worthy to be taken notice of, so in special those promises that are made to Christ in favour of believers, who are the subjects of his kingdom, in whom all the promises are made *yea and amen,* to the benefit of the subjects; for this are we taught to do by the example of the psalmist, who, when desolation was like to swallow up both church and kingdom, maketh fast to his own faith the promise of Christ, and of the stability of his kingdom; which promise being sure, of necessity the tribe of Judah, and the posterity of David behoved to be preserved, and continue till Christ came.

5. And the heavens shall praise thy wonders, O Lord ; thy faithfulness also in the congregation of the saints.

The psalmist laboureth to strengthen his faith in this promise by ten reasons further. The first whereof is this : The heavens are an evidence both of God's power to work wonders for his people, and of his faithfulness to perform promises unto the church; therefore will he say, I have reason for me to believe this promise made to David concerning Christ's kingdom. Whence learn, 1. The consideration of the power of God manifested in the works of creation. To be able to perform whatsoever he promiseth, were it never so wonderful, may and should confirm our faith in his promise, how improbable soever it appear : for *the heavens shall praise thy wonders, O Lord.* 2. As the heavens are a pledge of God's power, in respect of his first framing them out of nothing, so are they a pattern of God's faithfulness, in their constant and orderly motion according to his word since their framing : *the heavens shall praise thy faithfulness also.* 3. However the power and faithfulness of God may be seen and heard in the work and speech of the heavens by all men, yet are they not observed and hearkened unto, except in the church by God's children : therefore saith he, *they shall praise thy faithfulness also in the congregation of the saints.*

6. For who in the heaven can be compared unto the Lord? who among the sons of the mighty can be likened unto the Lord?

The second reason to confirm the psalmist's faith is this : God is above all angels in heaven and men on earth, and hath them all under him, to perfect by them what work he pleaseth; and presuppose they had a mind to hinder any purpose of God concerning performance of his promise, they could not hinder him, they being infinitely inferior in all excellencies unto God, and no way to be compared with him; therefore will he say, I have reason to believe his promise concerning the stability of Christ's kingdom. Whence learn, 1. The height of God's excellency is above the reach of our thoughts, and we cannot take him up otherwise than by climbing up on the shoulders and tops of all created eminency, and there proclaiming God to be greater than them all : for, *who in heaven can be compared unto the Lord?* *who among the sons of the mighty can be likened unto the Lord?* 2. God hath given power natural, most of all to angels; and power accessory, most of all to princes and magistrates, and potentates in the earth, whom here he calleth the sons of the mighty; in whose power and authority we may see somewhat of God, if they be for God; and may see princes to be nothing, if they be against God : for, *who in heaven can be compared unto the Lord? who among the sons of the mighty can be likened unto the Lord?*

7. *God is greatly to be feared in the assembly of the saints, and to be had in reverence of all* them that are *about him.*

A third reason to confirm his faith, is this : God is terrible, and to be stood in awe of by all his people, and it were a fearful injury for his saints not to give him the glory of his power and fidelity; therefore will he say, I have reason to believe what he hath promised concerning the kingdom of Christ. Whence learn, 1. Holy angels and sanctified men, of all creatures have nearest access to God, and are most like to the domestics and courtiers of a king, who attend him daily, and wait upon him; for they are here said to be *about him.* 2. The fear and reverence of God imprinted on angels and saints, evidence the greatness of God's power, excellency, and majesty : *God is greatly to be feared in the assembly of the saints.* 3. The terribleness of God's holy majesty, and the reverence due to him from all his saints, should make us afraid to misbelieve his word and promises; for this is made a reason of the psalmist's believing the Lord's word : *God is greatly to be feared in the assembly of the saints, and to be had in reverence by all them that are about him.*

8. *O Lord God of hosts, who is a strong Lord like unto thee? or to thy faithfulness round about thee?*

A fourth reason to confirm his faith, is this : God is Lord of hosts, and incomparable in strength and faithfulness, whereby he is compassed on all hands round about; therefore will he say, I have reason to believe his promise concerning Christ's kingdom. Whence learn, 1. As the Lord only knoweth perfectly his own omnipotency, and his own excellency in all perfections; so we know God best when we come to him and acknowledge that he only knoweth himself fully, and so give unto him this glory, as the psalmist's directing his speech to God immediately teacheth us : *O Lord God of hosts, who is a strong Lord like unto thee?* 2. The same power which serveth to humble a man by afflicting him, serveth also to comfort him and strengthen his faith in affliction, when he draweth near unto God; for the psalmist maketh use of the same style here, both to direct his faith, and to keep down his pride, his fretting, and repining against God, saying, *O Lord God of hosts.* 3. As the Lord is, as it were, compassed about on all hands with power, and is incomparably strong in all difference of time past, present, and to come, above all his creatures; so also first and last in all difference of time, he is incomparably faithful above all his creatures: *O Lord God of hosts, who is a strong Lord like unto thee ? or to thy faithfulness round about thee ?*

9. *Thou rulest the raging of the sea: when the waves thereof arise, thou stillest them.*

A fifth reason to strengthen his faith, is : the Lord, who ruleth the raging sea, is able to suppress and compose all tumults and troubles, whatsoever are raised, or shall be raised against his church; therefore I have cause, will he say, to believe his promise concerning Christ's kingdom. Whence learn, That the power of God in ruling and calming the raging sea, may strengthen the faith of his children amidst all the tumults of people against Christ's kingdom.

10. *Thou hast broken Rahab in pieces, as one that is slain : thou hast scattered thine enemies with thy strong arm.*

The sixth reason is this : God hath done as much already for delivering his church, by destroying Rahab or the Egyptians, and scattering his enemies from time to time, as may assure me both what he can, and what he will do for his people; therefore I may be quiet. Whence learn, 1. Faith may, and should, make use of every example of God's working for his people in all times after, and in special the overthrow of the Egyptians, as a perpetual pledge of God's promise to tread down and destroy all the enemies of his church and kingdom : for, *thou hast broken Rdhab in pieces*, is here and elsewhere frequently called to remembrance for this end. 2. It is as easy for God to destroy a nation of enemies, were they ever so many or powerful, as to wound or kill one man: *thou hast broken Rahab in pieces, as one that is slain: thou hast scattered thine enemies with thy strong hand.*

11. *The heavens* are *thine, the earth also* is *thine:* as for *the world, and the fulness thereof, thou hast founded them.*

12. *The north and the south thou hast created them: Tabor and Hermon shall rejoice in thy name.*

The seventh reason for confirmation of his faith, is: heaven and earth, and all creatures in all corners of the world, are the Lord's work, sustained by him, and cared for by him; and there is not a mountain or hill, greater or lesser, such as Tabor or Hermon, which bear grass, or corn, or herbs, or trees, or whatsoever may make them look, as it were, cheerfully, and rejoice, but it is by the power of God's name; therefore I may be sure, God will much more care for his church, and for the stability of the kingdom of Christ. Whence learn, 1. The heaven and earth, and fulness thereof, belong to the Lord by due right, and are cared for by him as his own possession: *the heavens are thine, the earth also is thine; as for the world, and the fulness thereof, thou hast founded them.* 2. The making and governing of the world, which is made and is governed for the use of man, may give assurance that his church and people, (for whose cause especially all was made,) shall be continued from age to age, so long as heaven and earth remain; and shall be more particularly cared for than any other part or piece of his workmanship; for to this end doth the psalmist make mention of other creatures appointed to serve man. 3. Seeing the Lord maketh the hills and mountains, after winter blasts of frost and snow, to change their countenance, and, as it were, look joyfully, and rejoice, we may be persuaded that his church after troubles shall much more change its countenance, and rejoice in God's name: for to this end is it said that these mountains *Tabor and Hermon shall rejoice in thy name.*

13. *Thou hast a mighty arm: strong is thy hand, and high is thy right hand.*

The eighth reason is taken from the exceeding great power of God to do more than ever he hath done for his church. Whence learn, If a greater work than the making and upholding of the world, or if a greater work than anything which is done by God hitherto, were needful to be done for the good of the church, there is power enough, infinite power in God to effect it : *thou hast a mighty arm : strong is thy hand, and high is thy right hand.*

14. *Justice and judgment* are *the habitation of thy throne : mercy and truth shall go before thy face.*

The ninth reason for strengthening his faith, taken from the properties and attendants of God's kingdom, is this : justice and judgment are the supporters of his throne, and mercy and truth are his officers, preparing way for the Lord, when he is about to do justice in favour of his people; therefore I need not fear that the promise of Christ's kingdom shall fail. Whence learn, 1. Whatsoever oppression or desolation the Lord's people may be under, the unalterable righteousness of God cannot fail to execute justice and judgment for punishing the oppressor and relieving his people: for, *justice and judgment are the habitation of his throne,* or the base whereupon his throne is settled. 2. Albeit the sins of the Lord's people might stop the way of relief coming to them, or prejudice them of having any benefit from justice; yet mercy and truth are ready at hand, to prepare the way by pardon of their sins, and performing all promises unto them: *mercy and truth shall go before thy face.*

15. *Blessed* is *the people that know the joyful sound : they shall walk, O Lord, in the light of thy countenance.*

16. *In thy name shall they rejoice all the day ; and in thy righteousness shall they be exalted.*

17. *For thou* art *the glory of their strength ; and in thy favour our horn shall be exalted.*

18. *For the Lord* is *our defence; and the Holy One of Israel* is *our King.*

The tenth reason for strengthening his faith is taken from the blessedness of believers in God, whose properties and privileges are set down in order, six : all of them proving

God's people to be blessed. Whence learn, 1. Whatsoever are the afflictions of the Lord's people, and in what danger and difficulty soever they be, yet are they certainly blessed: *blessed is the people that know the joyful sound.* 2. Those are to be accounted God's people who, with a good heart, join with others, at God's command, in the worship and service of God: *blessed is the people that know the joyful sound;* for the joyful sound was the sound of the silver trumpets which were blown at the joining battle in their wars, or for their journeys, or gathering of assemblies, or intimation of solemn feasts, and at the offering of the sacrifices of Israel, Psal lxxxi., Numb. x., Joel ii.; and the knowing of this joyful sound signifieth the alacrity of God's people to serve and obey the Lord, as he, in his ordinances, should warn, direct, and guide them. 3. The properties and privileges of believers in God make sure proof of their blessedness, for they live in grace and favour with God whether they sensibly feel it or not; as their persons, so also their carriage in faith and upright endeavour to please God, are always acceptable to God. And this is the first privilege of God's people: *they shall walk, O Lord, in the light of thy countenance.* 4. Believers have matter and just cause to rejoice in God for their interest in him, whatsoever be their present condition: *in thy name shall they rejoice all the day.* This is another privilege of God's people. 5. The joy of believers is underpropped and enlarged, when they consider that God's righteousness (which is by faith in Christ) is imputed unto them, and God's righteousness in performing his promises is set on work for their direction, encouragement, reformation, and defence: *and in thy righteousness shall they be exalted.* This is the third privilege of believers. 6. Albeit the godly find no power in themselves, either to do or suffer, no power either to defend themselves or oppose their enemies; yet they want not strength, either employed for them, or furnished, as they need, unto them, by God, in a glorious manner, as they will see, if his helping of them be rightly looked upon: *for thou, Lord,* saith he, *art the glory of their strength,* wherein they may glory in their weakest condition. And this is the fourth privilege of God's people. 7. The free grace and love of God graciously tendered to believers, are the ground of their strength, comfort, confidence, and gloriation; because they are the fountain of all their felicity, and well-spring of life to them, to look unto this, that they are in favour with God : *and in thy favour our horn shall be exalted.* And this is the fifth privilege of the Lord's people. 8. Albeit believers be destitute of help from men, yet they are neither left without protection nor without government, because God, or Christ who is God, is the church's King, to protect, guide, and govern her ; for *the Lord is our defence* or *shield; and the Holy One of Israel is our King.* The original also will bear, *of and to : the Lord is our defence of and to,* the *Holy One of Israel is our King;* whereby what may be said of the typical king, David, and of the true king, Christ, considered as man, may give assurance that God would be their defence and King, because David, and Christ as man, were God's kings, and kings for God's service and honour, authorized of God and devoted to him. And this is the sixth privilege of God's people. All which privileges are so many proofs of the blessedness of the believers in whatsoever condition they are. 9. It is wisdom for every believer, when he is about to reckon the riches of God's people, and to set forth their privileges, to make application thereof to himself amongst the rest of that number, as the example of the psalmist here teacheth us, who in the latter part of this computation doth so : *in thy favour our horn shall be exalted, the Lord is our defence, our King.*

19. *Then thou spakest in vision to thy Holy One, and saidst, I have laid help upon* one that is *mighty ; I have exalted* one *chosen out of the people.*

20. *I have found David my servant: with my holy oil have I anointed him.*

In the second part, for the further comfort of the church in her saddest condition, and to strengthen yet more the godly in their troubles, the psalmist, 1. Expoundeth the covenant of grace made with Christ, represented typically by David, because he must be looked upon only as the shadow, but Christ as the chief party, and as he in whom the real substance is accomplished perfectly; therefore shall we speak of both, as the word relateth to the one or to the other, or to both in several respects. And, first, of the circumstances of the covenant, and then of the several ar-

x

ticles thereof; for the psalmist marketh, 1. The time of revealing the covenant; *then*, to wit, when it pleased God to
let it be known, that he purposed to take a course for the
comfortable governing of his church and people. 2. He
observeth the way of revealing it, which he showeth to be
by *vision ;* he spake to his *holy servant*, to wit, Samuel or
Nathan. 3. He commendeth the man who was to rule,
as fit and able to be helpful to his people: *I have laid
help upon one that is mighty.* 4. He showeth the cause
of his preferment to be his own free love and good-will: *I
have exalted one chosen out of the people.* 5. He nameth
him and his office: *I have found David my servant.* 6.
He telleth of his spiritual furniture, figured forth by anointing: *with my holy oil have I anointed him.* Whence
learn, 1. Albeit the Lord hath always a special care of the
governing of his people, yet doth he not at all times alike
clearly make manifest this care, by giving comfortable governors: he hath his own times, as to hide his face in this
particular, so his own *then* also, when to show his love:
then thou spakest. 2. The Lord's mind is not to be found
by conjectures, but by his word revealed to his holy prophets: *then thou spakest to thy Holy One in vision, and
saidst.* 3. As the Lord's people stand in need of a good
king, a man of power, able and willing to be helpful to the
subjects and not hurtful; so, God must be the enabler of
him, and designer of him after the way he pleaseth, and the
maker of him to be effectually helpful: *I have laid help
upon one that is mighty.* 4. It is conducible to the intent a rule may be helpful to the subjects, that there be some
natural tie between him and them; for this God did provide
for in appointing comfortable governors over his own people: *I have exalted one chosen out of the people.* 5. That
one is preferred before another, or advanced to any place of
power or trust over others in mercy, it is of God's grace,
free choice, and good-will: *I have exalted one chosen out
of the people.* 6. The man who must, in his government,
do good to God's people, must be a man for God, God's
servant, not by office and duty only, but of a set purpose
also: *I have found David my servant.* 7. The man whom
God employeth in government for his people must be furnished with gifts and graces of his Spirit, figured by holy
oil: *with holy oil have I anointed him.* 8. As David was

in type, so Christ is in truth, and in all respects, more eminently than David, a strong helper, mighty to save, appointed
of the Father to help us in all cases, and to whom we are
directed to go, that we may find help, on whom help lieth
and in whom we shall surely find help; he is one of our
kind, taken out from among the people, acquainted with the
meanest condition his subjects can be in, exalted to be a
Prince and Saviour, chosen and predestinated, as man, for
the office before the world was, devoted to the service of the
redemption, sanctification, government, and salvation of his
people, and filled, as man, with the Holy Ghost above measure, that out of his fulness we may all receive grace for
grace : of whom it is most really true, *with my holy oil
have I anointed him.*

21. *With whom my hand shall be established; mine
arm also shall strengthen him.*

From this verse to the 38th, the psalmist bringeth forth
ten promises, as so many heads and articles of this covenant,
whereof this is the first, concerning assistance to be given to
David in type, and to Christ more substantially and in more
eminent effects. Whence learn, 1. As to David in his kingdom, so Christ, as man, in his kingdom, God hath engaged
his outwardly assisting power constantly : *with whom my
hand shall be established.* 2. As to David, so to Christ,
full possession of power for all the parts of government, is
promised in favour of all the subjects of his kingdom: *mine
arm also shall strengthen him :* as the work is great or
difficult, divine strength shall enable him to go about it and
do it.

22. *The enemy shall not exact upon him, nor the son
of wickedness afflict him.*

The second promise is, that, as David's subjects, albeit
they had many battles, yet were they not subdued in his
time, nor made tributaries to their enemies, nor made miserable by them; so shall Christ's subjects and kindly converts
unto him be found during his time, which is from generation to generation, and for ever; albeit troubled by the spiritual enemies of his kingdom, yet they shall not be made
tributaries, voluntary servants, or miserable slaves to them;
for sin shall not have dominion over them, nor shall Satan
or persecutors have such power as to drive them away from

their liege Lord, Jesus Christ, the true David, the true king of the Israel of God : *the enemy shall not exact upon him, nor the son of wickedness afflict him,* or make him really miserable; for all things shall work together for their good.

23. *And I will beat down his foes before his face, and plague them that hate him.*

The third promise is of destroying the enemies of David's and Christ's kingdom, which albeit they should not want enemies; both open enemies, openly invading the kingdom, or opposing to it their power, and inward, secret enemies, who in heart should wish the hurt and harm of their kingdom, yet God should destroy, as David's enemies, so far as might serve the type, so Christ's enemies more eminently, and in a more complete manner and measure : *I will beat down his enemies before his face*, this is for open enemies: *I will plague them that hate him*, this is for secret intestine enemies in special. Both these sorts shall be permitted to exercise Christ's subjects, but shall at length be fully destroyed.

24. *But my faithfulness and my mercy* shall be *with him ; and in my name shall his horn be exalted.*

The fourth promise is, for removing all difficulties and impediments which might hinder the growing of Christ's kingdom and of his subjects unto full glory; for here the promise, as it relates to the type, hath not the accomplishment clearly and fully. Whence learn, 1. There are two things which oppugn and assault faith; the one is the greatness of the work and benefit promised, the other is the sin of those for whose behoof the promise is made. But God's *faithfulness* and *mercy*, promised to be with Christ for the benefit of his subjects, remove both those obstacles; for God's promise must be accomplished—how great things soever he hath promised, there is nothing too hard for him— and God's mercy taketh away the obstacle of unworthiness and ill-deserving by reason of sin. *Mercy* holdeth truth on the course thereof toward us, when justice otherwise might break it off from us : *but my faithfulness and my mercy shall be with him.* 2. The subjects of Christ's kingdom want not matter of gloriation, albeit they have nothing in themselves to boast of. God's power, wisdom, goodness, and mercy, manifested in the word, are the only ground of

their gloriation : *in thy name shall his horn be exalted;*
for, when Christ's subjects glory in God through him,
Christ's glory is exalted in God's name.

25. *I will set his hand also in the sea, and his right
hand in the rivers.*

The fifth promise made to David in the shadow, but to
Christ in the most real substance, is the enlarging of his
kingdom through the world, by sea and land, continent and
isles; and so Christ's kingdom must not be confined to more
narrow bounds than his charter beareth him, but must be
stretched out to the due length and breadth, even to whithersoever he sendeth out his gospel, and extendeth his hand to
subdue and conquer subjects unto himself, and to bring them
within the visible church; for, *I will set his hand also in
the sea, and his right hand in the rivers,* showeth that
the kingdom must reach beyond the bounds of Canaan.
Whether we look to David the type, or to Christ the antitype, we are led by this speech to the largeness of this kingdom.

26. *He shall cry unto me, Thou* art *my Father, my
God, and the Rock of my salvation.*

The sixth promise properly belonging to Christ, according as it is declared by the apostle, Heb. i. 4, from this
place, and from 2 Sam. xxii. 2: for, albeit David and Solomon were God's sons by adoption, office, government, and
chosen types, yet Christ (who came of David according to
the flesh) was God's Son by personal union of the human
nature with the Word, or second person of the Trinity.
And here he is promised as Head and Prince of the covenant of salvation made in favour of the elect, only Mediator
and Intercessor for all the redeemed. Whence learn, 1.
The covenant of grace is consolidated in Christ our Head;
and he hath the first right, as man, to say unto his Father
that which is here said, as Intercessor and Mediator for the
elect : *he shall cry unto me, Thou art my Father, my
God, and the Rock of my salvation.* 2. Hereby it is in-
timated, also, that both Christ, in his own person, and the
persons of his redeemed ones also, (in whose name Christ
taketh the right of what is promised to his subjects,) was
to be exercised with trouble, and was to be put to it, to
make use of the covenant, and of the privileges and pro-

mises of it, for sustentation and salvation: *thou art my Father, my God, and the Rock of my salvation.*

27. *Also I will make him my first-born, higher than the kings of the earth.*

The seventh promise most proper also to Christ, who, in respect of human nature, personally united with the divine nature of the eternal, only-begotten Son, is made, and declared to be, the Father's first-born, and more excellent than all the kings of the earth, how despicable soever his kingdom seem; for all earthly kings are under his footstool, and of them none can make or preserve the life of one of his subjects, nor his own: *also I will make him my first-born, higher than the kings of the earth.* David's prerogative above other kings was but a shadow of this, and of short continuance.

28. *My mercy will I keep for him for evermore, and my covenant shall stand fast with him.*

The eighth promise is of everlasting mercy to Christ's subjects, to be kept in store for Christ's dispensing forth thereof: *my mercy will I keep for him for ever:* and this is the ground of the covenant, and the sweetest consolation of the covenant, which shall never be disannulled, because established in Christ, and to him for our behoof: *my covenant shall stand fast with him.*

29. *His seed also will I make* to endure *for ever, and his throne as the days of heaven.*

The ninth promise is, of the continuance and increase of his offspring and kingdom while the world standeth, which cannot be fulfilled but in Christ. Whence learn, 1. Christ hath, from age to age, a succession of children, whom he, by his word and Spirit, begetteth unto a spiritual life; and this succession shall not be cut off, but one generation shall follow another: *his seed also will I make to endure for ever.* 2. As Christ shall not want subjects in any age, so shall he not cease to govern his people in any age: *his throne shall be as the days of heaven.*

30. *If his children forsake my law, and walk not in my judgments;*

31. *If they break my statutes, and keep not my commandments;*

32. *Then will I visit their transgression with the rod, and their iniquity with stripes.*

33. *Nevertheless my loving-kindness will I not utterly take from him, nor suffer my faithfulness to fail.*

The tenth promise is of a merciful manner of dealing with Christ's subjects, (that is, with persons regenerate and reconciled with God,) by correcting them with temporal rods, when they break forth into offences, and turn back, or go aside from obedience to God's law, that, being corrected, they may repent, and so be saved. Whence learn, 1. The covenant here made with David in type, and with Christ, the antitype, is for the behoof and benefit of the children, as this article maketh evident : *if his children forsake my law.* 2. There is a provision in the covenant, against the sins which may fall out in the persons covenanted, and might mar all our comfort if remission were not covenanted : *if his children forsake my law.* 3. If the Lord's children watch not over their own corrupt nature and against temptations, they are in danger of falling, and certainly will fall, into fits of fearful sinning against God's revealed will, both by way of commission and omission, so as they may seem not renewed, as here is presupposed : *if his children forsake my law, and walk not in my judgments : if they break my statutes and keep not my commandments.* 4. The Lord alloweth not sin in his own children more than in others, but will testify his indignation against the sins of his own children with sad judgments : *if they keep not my commandments, then will I visit their transgressions with the rod, and their iniquity with stripes.* 5. The sharpest rods and sorest stripes wherewith God visiteth the children of Christ, may, and do, harmonize with loving-kindness to them; for they are fatherly corrections, medicinal preservatives against sinning afterward, and tokens of God's hating sin—not of rejection of their persons, but rather effects of his love to the persons corrected : *nevertheless my loving-kindness will I not utterly take from him.* 6. The mercy shown to the children, is with respect to the Father with whom the covenant is made in favour of the children : *my loving-kindness will I not utterly take from him :* that is, from David as type, and Christ as antitype, for whose sake the kindness is derived to the children.   7. Except the covenant of grace had this article in it, for remission of sin, and for fatherly direction, to drive to repentance, that the penitent person, coming to God by faith, might have sin forgiven him and loving-kindness shown to him, this covenant would fail us no less than the covenant of works: *my loving-kindness will I not utterly take from him, nor suffer my faithfulness to fail.*

34. *My covenant will I not break, nor alter the thing* that is *gone out of my lips.*

35. *Once have I sworn by my holiness, that I will not lie unto David.*

36. *His seed shall endure for ever, and his throne as the sun before me.*

37. *It shall be established for ever as the moon, and* as *a faithful witness in heaven. Selah.*

After the articles of the covenant, the psalmist subjoineth the confirmation of it; first, by the subscribed promise of God, for evidencing the immutability of it, v. 34; secondly, by ratification of his oath formerly made for the stability of it, v. 35; thirdly, by witness and pledges of the continuance of it, to wit, the sun and the moon, v. 36, 37. Whence learn, 1. Albeit the sins of God's children break the covenant on their part, yet they dissolve not the covenant on God's part, nor make God to break his part of the covenant, which is to correct and chastise the sinner, and bring him back by repentance, and not take away his loving-kindness from the sinner : *my covenant will I not break.* 2. The covenant of grace is that which is revealed in the gospel for remedy of sin, and relief from wrath; and what is revealed we may be sure shall not be altered : *my covenant will I not break, nor alter the thing that is gone out of my mouth.* 3. As we are declared to be naturally averse from believing God, who stand in need of confirmation by his oath; so God, by ratification of his promise by oath, declareth his will to the uttermost, that we should believe in him, and rest upon his covenant, and so make an end of controverting with him any more, by our misbelief in this matter : *once have I sworn.* 4. There can be no greater security than the true Christian hath for his salvation; for God hath pledged his truth and his holiness, which are the glory of all his attributes, that he will not take his loving-kindness away from any of Christ's children : *once have I sworn by my holiness, that I will not lie unto David.* 5. The stability of David's seed, which is Christ, and the perpetuity of his kingdom for the comfort of all his subjects, as it is confirmed by an oath, and by pledges laid down for assurance thereof, so hath the Lord taken the sun and the moon to be witnesses of this covenant of grace, as the rainbow is witness of that covenant for not destroying the world with a flood : *his seed shall endure for ever, and his throne as the sun before me.* 6. As the witnesses of the covenant, the sun and moon remain in heaven, whatsoever change seem in them, and howsoever both of them disappear every day once, and the moon every day and every month seemeth to change something in the measure of her light, yet there is no question made that they shall appear again in due season; so the covenant of grace made with us in Christ, (whatever alterations seem to come therein, and howsoever it disappear sometimes,) should not be called in question, but esteemed faithful as the witnesses of it are : *it shall be established for ever as the moon, and as a faithful witness in heaven.*

38. *But thou hast cast off and abhorred, thou hast been wroth with thine anointed.*

39. *Thou hast made void the covenant of thy servant; thou hast profaned his crown,* by casting it *to the ground.*

40. *Thou hast broken down all his hedges ; thou hast brought his strongholds to ruin.*

41. *All that pass by the way spoil him : he is a reproach to his neighbours.*

42. *Thou hast set up the right hand of his adversaries ; thou hast made all his enemies to rejoice.*

43. *Thou hast also turned the edge of his sword, and hast not made him to stand in the battle.*

44. *Thou hast made his glory to cease, and cast his throne down to the ground.*

45. *The days of his youth hast thou shortened : thou hast covered him with shame.   Selah.*

In the third part of the psalm he falleth upon a sad lamentation, and representeth the affairs and kingdom of David as in appearance quite contrary to the covenant, v. 46; where he taketh up himself, and prayeth to God for remedy of all those evils, closing the psalm with thanksgiving and praise.

In his lamentation he bemoaneth, first, as it seemed to him, that David and his house were rejected of God, and that in wrath, v. 48: next, that the covenant was dissolved, and the kingdom and crown ruined altogether, v. 39; thirdly, that all defences and strongholds were removed and thrown down, v. 40; fourthly, that he was made a prey to any that pleased to spoil him, and a reproach to his neighbours, v. 41; fifthly, that his enemies were assisted of God, and he being deserted in battle was put to flight, v. 42, 43; sixthly, that all the privileges and prerogatives of his kingdom were abolished, v. 44; seventhly, that the happiness of his kingdom had lasted a very short time, and that all expectation of hoped for blessings were blasted, and turned to matter of shame and confusion, v. 45. Whence learn, 1. From the order and place of the lamentation, it is not time for us to enter the lists with temptations and doubts, till first we have fixed our hearts by faith on the Lord's promises against all temptations, and doubts, and fears, and appearances of evil, as the psalmist doth here. 2. The state of Christ's, no less than of David's kingdom, may sometimes seem to human sense in a condition quite contrary to what is promised concerning it; as this lamentation, wherein the hopes of Christ's kingdom are questioned by the psalmist's temptation, maketh evident. 3. The only relief to God's distressed people at such a time, is to follow the example of the psalmist, that is, to strengthen their faith, contrary to what appeareth outwardly to sense, and then lay out the doubts, fears, and temptations before God, to be answered by him, as here the prophet doth. 4. All those calamities might come upon David's civil kingdom, and yet this covenant made with him, as the type of Christ, not be dissolved, as experience hath proved; because the covenant was not made to exempt him, or his family, or kingdom, from the rods of men, in case by their miscarriage and transgressions they should provoke the Lord; for the last article in the covenant, in v. 30—32, expressly holdeth out the contrary. Secondly, because the covenant in the main scope belonged to Christ and his spiritual kingdom; to David, and his children and kingdom, as types and shadows of Christ and his kingdom, or as they were members of Christ's kingdom for their spiritual good. 5. Sense and carnal reason may misrepresent the Lord's dispensation, as if it were contrary to his covenant promise, and contrary to what the godly believe according to God's word; as here we see, comparing this lamentation with the former part of the psalm. 6. If the godly hold fast to the word of God, and believe what the Lord hath promised, whatsoever appear to the contrary, then may they with great freedom, (yea, and they should of duty and wisdom,) lay forth all their temptations, and what carnal reason and sense speak to them before the Lord, who is able to solve all doubts, and satisfy faith, without fear of being mistaken, as this lamentation, compared with what precedeth, maketh manifest. 7. Whatsoever calamity shall cross the believer's hope, God still must be esteemed and held the sender out of the calamity, as well as the author of the promise, which the dispensation seemeth to cross, that the glory, both of justice wounding his child, and of mercy healing him, may be given to the Lord; as the example of the psalmist teacheth, who in all the complaint fasteneth all the branches of the calamity upon God's doing.

46. *How long, Lord? wilt thou hide thyself for ever? shall thy wrath burn like fire?*

47. *Remember how short my time is: wherefore hast thou made all men in vain?*

48. *What man* is *he that liveth, and shall not see death? shall he deliver his soul from the hand of the grave? Selah.*

49. *Lord, where* are *thy former loving-kindnesses,* which *thou swarest unto David in thy truth?*

50. *Remember, Lord, the reproach of thy servants;* how *I do bear in my bosom* the reproach of *all the mighty people;*

51. *Wherewith thine enemies have reproached,* O *Lord; wherewith they have reproached the footsteps of thine anointed.*

52. *Blessed* be *the Lord for evermore. Amen, and Amen.*

Here the psalmist turneth his complaint into prayer for remedy, to show that he did not fret, but believe, that the Lord both could and would give relief. The reasons for strengthening his faith are four: First, because the wrath of God against his people cannot be everlasting, v. 46. The second, because the Lord's afflicted people were of a short life, and expected comfort before they died, v. 47, 48. The third, because former experience and God's sworn covenant behoved to have evident comfortable effects, v. 49. The fourth, because the mockery of the enemy against God's people and Christ's kingdom was insupportable, v. 50, 51. After which, as being assured of a good answer, he closeth the psalm with prayer and thanksgiving. Whence learn, 1. From the first reason, the children of God are more affected with God's displeasure than with the trouble they are put to : *how long, Lord, wilt thou hide thy face?* This showeth their chief wound. 2. Whatsoever be the Lord's purpose in afflicting, yet sore trouble always speaketh the wrath of God to the apprehension of the afflicted : *shall thy wrath burn like fire?* 3. As God cannot be angry for ever with his people, so his people cannot endure any appearance of everlasting wrath and utter destruction : *how long, Lord? wilt thou hide thy face for ever? shall thy wrath burn like fire?*

From the second reason to confirm his hope to be heard, set down, v. 47, 48, learn, 1. As our life is short, and the shortness of it should be a spur to seek the sense of God's good-will to us while we are in this life, so may all God's children expect, how short soever their life be, to find sensible proofs in this life of God's love to them, and care of them; for, *remember how short my time is,* importeth so much in the psalmist's reasoning. 2. Albeit God hath created no man in vain, but for his own glory one way or other, yet God's children have little or no estimation of this life, except that they therein may find God reconciled, and have communion with him in this life; for this passionate expression, *wherefore hast thou made all men in vain?* importeth as much as we count our life in vain, and nothing worth to us, if thou shalt not be reconciled unto us. 3. Albeit our words in prayer should be well weighed, yet in sad affliction and grief of heart words sometimes may escape a saint, which cannot be justified, as here this speech giveth us an instance; for this is a limiting of God to crave comfort in this life to the afflicted, at the time when they shall prescribe, or else to make all their formerly received comforts, and life itself, to be in vain given unto them : for, presuppose a man should suffer God's terror from his youth up, as Heman did, and be as a distracted man because of the terror of God, and should end his life, as Heman doth the preceding psalm, without comfort, yet life eternal might make up the troubles of the wrestling of such a man's faith, and soon recompense the loss of comfort in this life; and yet such is the weakness of champions like Ethan, as to vent some passionate expressions in their trouble : *why hast thou made all men in vain ?*   4. Mortality and shortness of life are common to all men; but to be stirred up thereby to the more earnest seeking of spiritual comfort, and preparation for eternal life, is the property of a child of God only, such as the psalmist is, who for this very end, that he might have spiritual comfort, draweth an argument from mortality : *what man is he that liveth, and shall not see death ?*

From the third reason, set down v. 49, taken from the experience of mercies and sworn promises made to David, learn, 1. Albeit a man were in ever so hard a condition for his own case, or the case of other godly persons, yet that which God hath done and promised to do unto any believer, may sustain him when he misseth all comfort or appearance of it : *Lord, where are thy former loving-kindnesses unto David ?*   2. When the believer misseth the comfort which he or any other hath gotten of God, he should go to the same fountain to have some new experience thereof, as the psalmist's example teacheth.   3. The believer taketh God's part against all doubts, and disappearances of the performing of his promises, as we see in the psalmist, who, when he is missing God's former loving-kindness, the continuance whereof was promised and sworn, assureth the truth of the promise, saying, *which thou swarest unto David in thy truth.*

From the fourth reason of his hope to have a gracious answer to his prayer, taken from the reproaching of the enemies, as it is set down, v. 50, 51, learn, 1. Beside inward temptations unto misbelief in the day of trouble, the Lord's people are wont to meet with the mockings of the wicked, insolently scorning their faith in God, which as it vexeth the godly, so is it taken notice of by God: *remember, Lord, the reproach of thy servants*. 2. The mocking of religion in the day of the church's calamity, is so much the more a terrible temptation, as the adversaries who insult over religion, are many and powerful to annoy God's people, and tread down religion: *remember the reproach of all the mighty people*. 3. The reproach of religion and of the godly lieth near, and should lie near, the heart of every lively member of the church: *remember the reproach which I do bear in my bosom*. 4. Such as reproach religion and the godly in their calamity are God's enemies, and against them God is engaged: *remember the reproaches wherewith the enemies have reproached, O Lord*. 5. The blasphemies which strike against God's promised salvation in Christ and the progress of his kingdom, are of all temptations most heavy, and are resented of God most deeply: *remember the reproaches wherewith they have reproached the footsteps of thine anointed;* for, as David's posterity and succession went on, one generation after another, so Christ made his approaches nearer to his incarnation; and when the family of David seemed to grow weak, the godly were assaulted with fears and doubts about the coming of the Messiah, and the ungodly mocked the matter of Christ's coming altogether, and reproached the promise of his progress.

From the close of the psalm, v. 52, learn, 1. Presuppose a believer should not find present comfort in his sad condition, yet it is an ease to have poured out his complaint before the Lord: and this liberty of speech is a gift worthy of thanksgiving; for, *blessed be the Lord*, the prophet addeth, when he hath said all he would say. 2. We should close and leave our prayer before God in good terms, however he shall answer us, or seem to dispose of matters towards us: and we should bless him, do what he pleaseth, as the psalmist doth here: *blessed be the Lord for evermore*. 3. The believer may be sure to have his lawful requests granted unto him, and may set to his seal to God's promises without fear, as the psalmist teacheth us in his saying *Amen*. Yea, the more temptation driveth us unto misbelief the more should faith look for a deliverance, and adhere to the truth of God's covenant, as here the prophet by doubling his seal, saith *Amen* and *Amen*.

PSALM XC.

A prayer of Moses, the Man of God.

This psalm agreeth well with the latter end of Moses' life, when he, being now to remove, presented this prayer to God, and delivered it unto the church, for their comfort and direction, how to carry themselves towards God in their short and sorrowful life.

The psalm may be divided into three parts. In the first part is the church's fourfold comfort against temporal troubles and miseries in this world. The first is taken from the Lord's kindness to his people in all ages, ver. 1. The second is taken from the decree of their election, ver. 2. The third from the hope of their resurrection, ver. 3. The fourth from the shortness of time unto it, ver. 4. In the second part, the shortness and misery of life procured by sin, are lamentably set forth before the Lord, who is full of pity, ver, 5—11. In the last part are six petitions, some whereof are for the right use of the shortness and sorrows of this life, and some of them for a gracious deliverance from them, ver. 12—17.

From the inscription, learn, 1. A teacher of God's people should earnestly intercede by prayer for them, as Moses did. This is *a prayer of Moses.* 2. He that sitteth in Moses' chair should be furnished with gifts for the ministry, called of God, consecrated unto God in his heart for this purpose, and altogether set for God in his practice; for so Moses was, *a man of God.* 3. As the consciousness of being *a man of God* is a singular comfort and encouragement to a minister in his lifetime; so is it a singular honour to him, living and dead, before God and men, to be in effect *a man of God*, as here it is to Moses, who is called, *a man of God*, to his commendation, because he was faithful in all the house of God.

1. *Lord, thou hast been our dwelling-place in all generations.*

The first comfort of the Lord's people, against the miseries of this life is from the Lord's kindness to his people in all ages. Whence learn, 1. There is no dealing with God in prayer, except we lay hold on the offer of God's kindness, according to the covenant of grace, and look upon God as gracious to us in Christ. Therefore here and else-where, supplicants begin with renewed acts and expressions of saving faith. 2. God's people in every place and age, are one incorporation with God's people in all ages preceding and following, and may lay claim to all the privileges of God's people before them, as here the church in Moses' time joineth itself with all the Lord's people in former times, for the use of succeeding ages which were to come : *Lord, thou hast been our dwelling-place in all generations.* 3. Albeit the Lord's people be strangers in the earth; partly, because they have no certain residence in this world; partly, because they are evilly entertained by men of this world; but specially, because in their affections they are pilgrims in this world : yet they want not a resting-place, and a dwelling in heaven, even God himself, in whom they dwell by faith, and find rest, and food, and protection, and comfort; yea, and in his heart they have had a lodging in all generations: *Lord, thou hast been our dwelling-place in all generations.* 4. Troubles and miseries in this life make the godly search out their interest in God, and in another life, as here and elsewhere we may perceive in the exercise of God's children : their straits on earth make them seek enlargement in heaven.

2. *Before the mountains were brought forth, or ever thou hadst formed the earth and the world, even from everlasting to everlasting thou art God.*

The second comfort of the believer against the miseries of this short life, is taken from the decree of their election, and the eternal covenant of redemption of them, settled in the purpose and counsel of the blessed Trinity for their behoof, wherein it was agreed before the world was, that the *Word* to be incarnate, should be the Saviour of the Elect : for here the asserting of the eternity of God, is with relation to his own chosen people; for, *thou hast been our dwelling-place in all generations, and thou art God from everlasting to everlasting,* is in substance thus much : thou art, from everlasting to everlasting, the same unchangeable God in purpose and affection toward us thy people, and so thou art *our God* from everlasting, in regard of thy eternal purpose of love, electing us, and in regard of thy appointing redemption for us by the Redeemer. Whence learn, 1. From God's good-will to us in time, we may rise to God's good-will to us before time; and from grace showed to us in time, we may conclude grace and good-will purposed toward us, and ordained for us before time. Thus the psalmist teacheth us to climb; for after he hath said, *from generation to generation, thou hast been our dwell-*

ing-place, that is, in all time past thou hast been our God, he subjoineth, *before the mountains were brought forth, ere ever thou hadst formed the earth and the world, thou art God :* that is, the same God unchangeable in thy purpose and love toward us before time, from everlasting. 2. From special love shown to us in time, we may conclude love toward us, not only before time, from everlasting, but also that it shall continue toward us after time for ever : *even from everlasting to everlasting, thou art God,* saith he; that is, the same strong God immutable in thy purpose and love toward us first and last: and indeed faith cannot fix itself, till, by the warrant of God's word, and feeling of his gracious working in us in time, it join God's work of grace and his purpose of grace together. Therefore the apostle, Ephes. 1., leadeth the believer in Christ, to election in Christ before the world was, and to predestination unto adoption by Jesus Christ, according to the good pleasure of his will before the world was, v. 3—5. And, 2 Tim. 1. 9, he leadeth us to a completed covenant before the world was made, between God the Father and God the Son, according whereunto all conditions required of the Redeemer are settled; and all the elect, all the redeemed are delivered over to the Son, the *Word* to be incarnate, designed Redeemer; and all saving grace is given over into Christ's hand, for behoof of the elect, to be let forth unto them in due time : for there it is said, *that grace was given to us in Christ Jesus, before the world began.* 3. The nature of God, which is to be one and the same, unchangeable from everlasting to everlasting, is the solid ground of the reasoning of faith after this manner, as here we are taught : *from everlasting to everlasting, thou art God.* 4. The knowledge of God's eternal good-will to us, is a sufficient cordial to soften and sweeten all our grief and affliction in this life : for the very end why this doctrine is prefixed to what is following about temporal misery, is, to comfort the Lord's people against all the troubles of this life.

　3. *Thou turnest man to ·destruction ; and sayest, Return, ye children of men.*

　A third comfort is from the resurrection of the dead. Whence learn, 1. Albeit God executeth the decree which hath appointed all men once to die, yet he hath appointed also a resurrection, whereby he is powerfully to recall and make return from death all the posterity of Adam : *thou turnest man to destruction*, and so all men must die; *and sayest, Return, ye children of men,* and so all men must rise again. 2. It will cost the Lord but a word to make the dead rise again, or to make them that are destroyed return again : *thou sayest, Return, ye children of men.* His word is already past forth in the doctrine of the Resurrection, and is altogether operative, and shall prove fully effectual at length.

4. *For a thousand years in thy sight* are but *as yesterday when it is past, and* as *a watch in the night.*

The fourth comfort is from the shortness of the time between a man's death and his returning from it in the resurrection set down by way of answering an objection, which might be moved concerning the long time since the resurrection was promised, till the time that it be really accomplished. Whence learn, 1. Albeit it may seem a long time between a man's death and his resurrection, yet is it before God but a short time; yea and in effect it is nothing in comparison of eternity : *for a thousand years in thy sight are but as yesterday when it is past, and as a watch in the night.* 2. Except we reckon time as God reckoneth it, we cannot but be weary and think long, and wonder at the delay of the performance of promises, and so fall into temptation of unbelief, as we are taught by the obviating of the objection, and comparing of *a thousand years in God's sight,* with *yesterday when it is past,* and with *a watch in the night.*

5. *Thou carriest them away as with a flood; they are* as *a sleep : in the morning* they are *like grass* which *groweth up.*

6. *In the morning it flourisheth, and groweth up; in the evening it is cut down, and withereth.*

In the second part of the psalm Moses setteth forth the shortness and miseries of this life; first in general, v. 5, 6, and then the miseries of the people of Israel in special, to v. 12. As for the first, he sets forth the mortality and misery of men, under the similitude of men overflowed with a flood, and in the similitude of a sleep, and of grass or flowers, which flourish in the daytime, and at even are cut down and wither. Whence learn, 1. Mortality is like a flood, growing greater and greater, compassing some sooner, others later, and at last overflowing all men without exception: as the deluge in Noah's days once overflowed all the earth, so doth death : which similitude giveth all men advertisement in time to prepare for an ark, that death may not drown both soul and body : *thou carriest them away as with a flood.* 2. This mortal life is like a sleep, wherein men dream that they have riches, honour, strength, and pleasure; but when they awake, these things will be found but dreams and shadows; and it is like a sleep, whether we look to the time of abiding in the world, or to the time between death and resurrection; it is but a sleep, wherein time is not observed for shortness: *they are,* saith he, *like a sleep.* 3. This mortal life is like grass, or flowers, which have small beginnings; at their best they are but weak, and after a short season wither; and like grass and flowers, whereupon the mower falleth with his scythe or hook, and cutteth it down in the vigour of it: *they are like grass which groweth : in the morning it flourisheth and groweth up, in the evening it is cut down and withereth.*

7. *For we are consumed by thine anger, and by thy wrath are we troubled.*

8. *Thou hast set our iniquities before thee, our secret* sins *in the light of thy countenance.*

9. *For all our days are passed away in thy wrath; we spend our years as a tale that is told.*

10. *The days of our years* are *threescore years and ten ; and if by reason of strength* they be *fourscore years, yet* is *their strength labour and sorrow : for it is soon cut off, and we fly away.*

Moses descendeth now to the mortality and calamities of the people of Israel which he had observed in his own time; they were consumed in wrath for their sins, and had their lives cut short and replenished with miseries while they lasted; whereby he pointeth forth the power of the Lord's anger, which few considered. Whence learn, 1. Common calamities and worldly miseries may be found as evidently in God's visible church, and among God's people, as in any incorporation in the world; for here is the theatre of God's judgments as well as of his mercies, and when God's people provoke him, his judgments begin at his own house: *we are consumed by thine anger.* 2. The effects of God's anger are very terrible, and able to astonish the beholder: *by thy wrath are we troubled.* 3. In the time of God's forbearance usually men's sins lie hid in atheism, ignorance, oblivion, and careless security; but God's judgments draw them forth to the light, and make it appear that God hath observed them all: *thou hast set our iniquities before thee, our secret sins in the light of thy countenance.* 4. The misbelief and disobedience of God's visible church make their life both short and miserable, as the experience of the Israelites showeth: *for all our days are passed away in thy wrath, we spend our life like a tale that is told.* 5. The more we study to see the length of man's life, it appeareth the shorter; the more we look upon man's strength, and beauty, and glory, we find him the weaker, the vainer, and the naughtier: *the days of our years are threescore years and ten; and if by reason of strength they be fourscore years, yet is their strength labour and sorrow: for it is soon cut off, and we fly away.* 6. If our infancy, and ordinary sicknesses, and casualties of incident griefs and sorrows, sometimes for one cause, and sometimes for another, be considered, the life of man hath little in it, except trouble and grief: *their strength is labour and sorrow.* 7. If any man seem to have less trouble and sorrow, or more strength than others, it is nothing to count upon; the shortness of it maketh it to lose worth and estimation: for, *it is soon cut off, and we fly away.*

11. *Who knoweth the power of thine anger? even according to thy fear,* so is *thy wrath.*

In the calamities of the Israelites he observeth how terrible the Lord's wrath is, which albeit few consider, yet might men see it in his fearful threatenings and judgments. Whence learn, 1. Albeit the misery and short life of sinful man speak somewhat of the terribleness and power of God's anger, yet is it taken notice of by few; *who knoweth the power of thine anger?* 2. The wrath of God may be known by the fear and terror of God, which his severe justice, almighty power, terrible threatenings, and fearful judgments executed against sin teach men to know : *even according to thy fear, so is thy wrath.* Seeing men know not the power of God's wrath till it break forth upon them, it is wisdom to study his fear, that wrath may be prevented, and to take the measure of the power of God's wrath, by measuring his dreadful fear and terrible terror, and to stand in awe of him in time : *who knoweth the power of thine anger ? even according to thy fear, so is thy wrath.*

12. *So teach* us *to number our days, that we may apply* our *hearts unto wisdom.*

In the third part of this psalm, he putteth up six petitions for the right use and gracious seasoning of the short and sorrowful life of the Lord's people. The first petition is for wisdom to provide in time for the remedy of sin and of everlasting misery, before this short and uncertain life be ended. Whence learn, 1. Albeit our life be both short and uncertain how soon it may end, yet we look upon the indefiniteness of the time of continuance of it, as if the duration of it were infinite, and our years were innumerable : for, *teach us to number our days,* importeth some acknowledgment of this fault. 2. Albeit it be easy for us to consider how many of our days are already past, and how few those that are to come must be by course of nature, or may be few in the way of God's ordinary providence : yet this lesson, how easy soever, must be taught of God before we can profitably consider it : *so teach us to number our days, as we may apply our hearts unto wisdom.* 3. The only remedy of sin, and of the wrath of God, and misery of mortal men for sin, is the wisdom which is taught of God in the Scriptures; to wit, that sinners should seek reconciliation with God, through the sacrifice and obedience of Christ, and study to keep friendship with God by the power of his Spirit : *so teach us to number our days, as we may apply our hearts unto wisdom.* 4. The right use of the sin, wrath, and judgments which we see in our time manifested, is to deal with God by prayer that not only he would inform us of our danger and duty, not only reveal to our minds the mystery of grace and reconciliation, but also that he would effectually move our will, heart, and affections, by faith which worketh by love, to make application of the remedy of those evils to ourselves : *so teach us to number our days, as we may apply our hearts unto wisdom.*

13. *Return, O Lord, how long? and let it repent thee concerning thy servants.*

The second petition is, that God would not only remove the tokens of his displeasure against his people, but also now at length would show himself reconciled, by changing his dispensation toward them in a course of comfort. Whence learn, 1. Albeit the Lord goeth not away from his people, but ever remaineth with them in some one or other gracious operation; yet in respect of a comfortable presence he may turn away till his people request him to return, as here : *return, O Lord.* 2. The Lord's withdrawing of his comfortable presence from his people, for how short a time soever, seemeth a long time to us in this short life : *return, O Lord, how long ?* 3. Albeit the Lord change not his affection and repent like a man, yet he can change his operation like a father, who commiserates his child's affliction, and goeth about to cherish him after correction : *let it repent thee concerning thy servants.* 4. Albeit we be but very slight servants, and be sore smitten for our disobedience, yet should we not cast away our calling, nor suffer our relations unto God to be dissolved, but should adhere unto them by any means; as here they call themselves still servants: *let it repent thee concerning thy servants.*

14. *O satisfy us early with thy mercy; that we may rejoice and be glad all our days.*

15. *Make us glad according to the days* wherein *thou hast afflicted us,* and *the years* wherein *we have seen evil.*

The third petition is for some spiritual comfort and refreshment to their spirits, which might keep them in heart and hope of eternal salvation. Whence learn, 1. A soul sensible of wrath, hath as great hunger for spiritual comfort, as a famished man hath for meat: *O satisfy us.* 2. The renewed intimation of God's mercy, pardoning sin and making clear our reconciliation, is able to comfort us in our greatest sorrow : *O satisfy us with thy mercy.* 3. As bodily hunger cannot suffer delay, so neither can sense of wrath, and desire of favourable acceptation long endure the want of consolation; but after a night of trouble, earnestly expecteth a morning of comfort: *O satisfy us early with thy mercy.* 4. A poor hungry soul lying under sense of wrath, will promise to itself happiness for ever, if it can but once again find what it hath sometimes felt; that is, one sweet fill of God's sensible mercy towards it : *O satisfy us, that we may rejoice and be glad all our days.* 5. Were our troubles ever so great, and of long continuance, the renewed intimation of God's reconciliation to us, shall season and sweeten all our trouble, recompense all our losses, and make our condition in this short and miserable life tolerable; yea, in God very comfortable : *make us glad according to the days wherein thou hast afflicted us, and the years wherein we have seen evil.*

16. *Let thy work appear unto thy servants : and thy glory unto their children.*

The fourth petition is, that God would continue the work of building and enlarging his own church, and glorifying himself in their sight, and in the sight of posterity from generation to generation. Whence learn, 1. The building, purging, enlarging, propagating of the church, and manifesting of God's care for it, are the Lord's own proper works, which he will not leave off, but albeit he hide his working for a time, yet is he on his work, and his people shall pray for, and may expect the manifestation of it : *let thy work appear unto thy servants.* 2. As it is the glory of the Lord to manifest his grace and mercy toward his people or visible church, so the desire of his people is to have the Lord glorified no less than to have themselves preserved or comforted : *let thy work appear to thy servants, and thy glory to their children.* 3. The church in every age should have a care, that posterity may be partakers of the same merciful work of God, which they in their time have had experience of; and that their children may profit by the corrections of their predecessors : *let thy work appear to thy servants, and thy glory to their children.*

17. *And let the beauty of the Lord our God be upon us : and establish thou the work of our hands upon us; yea, the work of our hands establish thou it.*

In this last verse are the two heads of his prayer. The first petition is, that God would beautify his people with his

holy ordinances, with order, and unity, and peace, with a
holy conversation, and the evidences of his dwelling among
them, as his own confederate people, proper subjects of his
kingdom, and domestics of his own family.   Whence learn,
1. As God is the glory of his own people, in whom are
their beauty and ornament, whereby they are made honourable in the sight of all nations, as the bride is made comely
by the attire and ornaments put upon her: so should his
people esteem him, affect and love him, remember him, and
seek their beauty in him: *let the beauty of the Lord be
upon us.* 2. The beauty of the Lord is upon his people, and seen to be on them, when they behave themselves
as his covenanted people, walking in faith and obedience
before him, and he showeth himself their covenanted God,
protecting and blessing them: *let the beauty of the Lord
our God be upon us;* and this petition was granted all
the days of Joshua, and of the elders that outlived Joshua.

The sixth petition is, that God would bless the endeavours of his people in promoting God's work among them,
and for transmitting his ordinances and his truth to posterity.   Whence learn, 1. Whosoever pray for the advancing
of the Lord's work in his church, must resolve not to be
idle, but to engage themselves to endeavour in their places
and callings according to their power, the promoting of his
work, as becometh his servants and instruments : *establish
thou the work of our hands.* 2. Whosoever go about
the building of the Lord's church, and promoting of religion, must acknowledge that the success of their labour
dependeth only upon God, who must be entreated for the
blessing: *establish thou the work of thy hands.* 3. In
respect that our work is so mixed and defiled with imperfections and sins, that God may justly withdraw himself
from it, we must the more earnestly deal with God, to keep
his own hand about his work, and about our hands in it,
as the twice repeating of the petition importeth : *yea, the
work of our hands establish thou it.*

PSALM XCI.

Albeit this psalm hath no inscription, not the name of the penman who
wrote it, yet Satan could not deny it to be the Lord's word, for out of
this psalm he brought one of his darts against our Saviour, Matth. iv ;

and the promises which are made here to the believer, are so much more strongly ours, as Christ, head of all his people, hath interest therein as a man, and hath taken them to him in our name.

1. *He that dwelleth in the secret place of the most High, shall abide under the shadow of the Almighty.*

The sum of the psalm is, an encouragement to believe in God by nine motives or inducements, most of them being precious promises, whereunto Christ our Lord hath the first right and title; and we only in and through him. The first motive is, because the believer shall have the warm and comfortable protection of God Almighty. Whence learn, 1. Trusting in God, is the means of entertaining constant conjunction and communion with God; for he that is a believer, *dwelleth in the secret place of the most High.* 2. The unsearchable depths of the riches of God's truth, grace, power, and goodness, and of his other attributes, whereupon faith fixeth itself, are a mystery to the world which carnal reason knoweth not, nor how to make use thereof; and therefore is well compared to a secret place : *he that dwelleth in the secret place of the most High.* 3. In the most High is whatsoever the believer standeth in need of—a habitation, well furnished with ease, comfort, peace, refreshment, protection, and whatsoever else a soul could wish; for, *the secret place of the most High*, where the believer may and must dwell, are God's truth and love; and unto him that dwelleth here is the promise made. 4. The believer is not exempted by his faith from trouble, (yea, trouble and exercise from his enemies he may surely expect,) but he is exempted from being taken, overcome, and destroyed by them : for a refuge, *even the secret place of the most High,* here is provided for him. 5. He that betaketh himself unto God for refuge, and will make his refuge his habitation, shall not be refused lodging, nor be thrust out when he is entered : *he shall abide in the shadow of the Almighty.* 6. The scorching heat of persecution shall not prevail against the believer, for God's omnipotency shall be employed for his protection and consolation : *he shall abide in the shadow of the Almighty.*

2. *I will say of the Lord,* He is *my refuge, and my fortress : my God ; in him will I trust.*

The second motive is the psalmist's example, who in his

own experience having felt the good of trusting in God in hardest straits, resolveth to believe in him still. Whence learn, 1. He that hath experience of the fruit of faith, is the fittest man to bear witness of it, and most able to speak from his own persuasion to the persuasion of others : *I will say of the Lord, He is my refuge and my fortress.* 2. The duty of the believer is to go on and grow in faith; and the right use of his experiences is the confirmation of him in the faith of the covenant, and resolution to grow therein in measure of strength and sincerity: *he is my God, in him will I trust.*

3. *Surely he shall deliver thee from the snare of the fowler, and from the noisome pestilence.*

The third motive to believe in God, is a promise of deliverance out of danger, which by human wit could not be eschewed, which he expresseth under the similitude of snares and pestilence, that overtake a man before he be aware. Whence learn, 1. A kindly believer should love to have others believing in God, as he himself doth, and should leave nothing undone to persuade others to believe, as his calling requireth; for the example of the psalmist teacheth us so. 2. There are many temptations whereby Satan (as a fowler laying snares,) catcheth poor foolish sinners, and there is much contagion of sin, whereby albeit men are infected one by another, and many perish, yet the believer in God is either preserved from falling into the snare, and from being corrupted with contagion of others' ill speeches and manners, or else he is rid and delivered out of the danger: *surely he shall deliver thee from the snare of the fowler, and from the noisome pestilence.* 3. As there are dangers in relation to our spiritual condition unavoidable, if God do not deliver us, so are there dangers of plots and conspiracies by wicked enemies in relation to bodily dangers also, from which the wisdom of believers could not deliver them; but God hath promised a deliverance, or a good escape from them all, so as the believer shall be no loser: *surely he shall deliver thee from the snare of the fowler, &c.*

4. *He shall cover thee with his feathers, and under his wings shalt thou trust: his truth shall be thy shield and buckler.*

A fourth motive is, a promise of comfortable and sure defence against the invasion of the enemies, set forth under sundry similitudes usual in Scripture. Whence learn, 1. The care and watchfulness of God over his own is such as neither nature nor art can yield sufficient similitudes to express it; as the borrowing of more similitudes, some from one thing, and some from another, here showeth. The watchfulness of the bird over her young ones, and the care that a man hath in battle to preserve his own body from hurt, are but imperfect shadows to represent the watching care of God for a believer. 2. As the Lord descendeth unto our capacity in such low similitudes of protection and comfort, so he requireth of us, that by those we should ascend in our faith to rely confidently and lovingly upon him : *he shall cover thee with his feathers, and under his wings shalt thou trust.* 3. That which we must oppose to all perils is the word of God; so long as we keep that, and ward off darts and swords by that means, we shall not be overcome : *his truth shall be thy shield and buckler.*

5. *Thou shalt not be afraid for the terror by night;* nor *for the arrow* that *flieth by day;*

6. Nor *for the pestilence* that *walketh in darkness;* nor *for the destruction* that *wasteth at noon-day.*

7. *A thousand shall fall at thy side, and ten thousand at thy right hand;* but *it shall not come nigh thee.*

A fifth motive to believe, is from a more particular promise of safety unto the believer from all sort of deadly enemies and dangers, whereinto when many fall, the believer shall stand. Whence learn, 1. The true remedy against tormenting fear, is faith in God; for many terrible things may befall men when they are most secure, like those that befall men in the night; but for any harm which may befall the believer this way, the Lord here willeth him to be nothing afraid : *thou shalt not be afraid for the terror by night.* 2. Many sudden accidents may befall men when they are most watching, and upon their guard, but the Lord willeth the believer to be confident that he shall not be harmed this way: *thou shalt not be afraid for the arrow that flieth by day.* 3. Many evils are men subject unto, which come upon them they cannot tell how, but from such evils the Lord assureth the believer he shall have no harm : *thou shalt not be afraid of the pestilence which walketh in darkness.* 4. Men are subject to many evils which come upon them openly, and not unawares, such as are calamities from enemies and oppressors; the Lord willeth the believer to be confident that he shall not be harmed this way: *thou shalt not be afraid for the destruction which walketh at noon-day.* 5. When trials and temptations come upon the world to try the children of men, albeit many fall by those temptations, yet the man who believeth in God shall stand, whether the temptation come upon the left hand, with less appearance of good offered in it, or upon the right hand, with fair pretences of lawfulness and holiness in a sinful course, whereunto the temptation driveth; albeit a thousand shall fall by the temptation on the one hand, and ten times more on the other hand, yet the believer in God, going upon the grounds of God's word shall not fall; those evils wherein others fall and perish, shall not come near him, as to the point of harming him, or of destroying him : *a thousand shall fall at thy side, and ten thousand at thy right hand ; but it shall not come near thee.* 6. The Lord will not only one way be helpful to the believer, but so many ways as he can be in danger; as the enumeration of so many sundry cases, wherein he promiseth deliverance, teacheth us. 7. The only persons who are hurt by judgments and temptations, are' such unfenced souls as believe not in God, are not reconciled with him, and stand at a distance opposite to him as the objects of his wrath; for none have right to the former promises except the believer only; as all the text holdeth forth.

8. *Only with thine eyes shalt thou behold and see the reward of the wicked.*

He answereth an objection. It may be said, that the former mentioned evils, temptations, and calamities, come very near the godly, for they are ofttimes no less deep in them than others are. He answereth, that the Lord may well acquaint them with the danger, and with the sense of their own weakness; but for the point of harm from those evils, or for the point of destruction by those evils, which is the reward of the wicked, the godly have no more but a discovery of, to see it, wherein they might have fallen, if God had not preserved them, and wherein the wicked fall and

perish. Whence learn, 1. Albeit the same external calamities may befall the believer and the wicked, yet the close of
their course, the reward of their works shall put the difference : for the godly *shall only behold the reward of the
wicked.* 2. Albeit the believer may be exercised with the
fear of destruction, yet he shall be free from falling into it:
*only with thine eyes shalt thou behold and see the reward
of the wicked.*

9. *Because thou hast made the Lord,* which is *my
refuge,* even *the most High, thy habitation;*

10. *There shall no evil befall thee, neither shall any
plague come nigh thy dwelling.*

  A sixth motive to believe in God, is a promise in general
to be delivered from all evil, that nothing shall harm him,
but all things shall rather work together for his good.
Whence learn, 1. All believers have one object of their faith,
one relief in their troubles, one retreat from the vexations
which assault them in this world, even God : *thou hast made
the Lord who is my refuge, even the most High, thy habitation.* 2. One believer may and should encourage other
believers by the same motives whereby he himself is encouraged, as here : *because thou hast made the Lord, who is
my refuge, to be thy habitation,* therefore such and such
blessings shall come upon thee, saith he. 3. The nature of
true faith is to make use of God in all conditions; in peace
and war, in prosperity and adversity, as here he is both a
refuge and a habitation. 4. As we have need to have the
same promises repeated unto us, and inculcated upon us,
so slow and dull are we to receive them, so the Lord repeateth and urgeth the receiving thereof, with an enlarging
and not abridging of what once he promised, as this general
promise teacheth : *there shall no evil befall thee, nor any
plague come near thy tabernacle,* to wit, to harm thee;
for God, who is the believer's habitation, interposeth himself, and turneth the calamity to his good, if it be suffered
to come on, that it come not near to his disadvantage.

11. *For he shall give his angels charge over thee, to
keep thee in all thy ways.*

12. *They shall bear thee up in their hands, lest thou
dash thy foot against a stone.*

  A seventh motive to believe in God, is a promise of making angels wait upon the believer, and carefully to attend his motions in all his lawful affairs, lest he should stumble and suffer harm; which promise even Satan acknowledgeth to belong to Christ, and Christ owneth it, being taken in a right sense, Matt. iv. Whence learn, 1. Such is the indulgent love of God towards his own, that he obviateth all doubts, which from any hand might hinder them to believe in him: if the severity and justice of God terrify, the Lord offereth himself as a bird with stretched out wings to receive the supplicant, v. 2. If enemies, who are too strong, pursue, the Lord openeth his bosom as a refuge, v. 3. If the child be assaulted, he becometh a fortress, v. 3. If he be hotly pursued and inquired after, the Lord becometh a secret place to hide his child; if persecution be hot, God giveth himself for a shadow; if potentates and mighty rulers turn enemies, the Lord interposeth as the most High and Almighty Saviour, v. 1. If his adversaries be crafty like fowlers or hunters, the Lord promiseth to prevent and break the snares, v. 3. Whether evils come upon the believer night or day, secretly or openly, to destroy him, the Lord preserveth his child from destruction; and if stumbling-blocks be laid in his child's way, he hath his instruments, his servants, his angels prepared to keep the believer that he stumble not: *he shall give his angels charge over thee;* not one angel only, but all of them, or a number of them. 2. The angels are ministering spirits, sent forth to minister for every believer: *he shall give his angels charge over thee, to keep thee in all thy ways.* 3. Promises are not made to foster men in their turning after folly, but to encourage them in the course of obedience in their several callings: they have *charge to keep thee in all thy ways.* 4. Albeit stumbling-stones be laid in the way of God's child, yet while he behaveth himself as a believer in God, he shall not stumble. Great peace have they who love God's law, and nothing shall stumble them, Psal. cxix. 165: *they shall bear thee up in their hands, lest thou dash thy foot against a stone.*

13. *Thou shalt tread upon the lion and adder; the young lion and the dragon shalt thou trample under feet.*

The eighth motive to believe, is a promise of victory over

every enemy of his salvation, how fierce, strong, and cruel soever he be; how crafty, malicious, and dangerous soever he be: *thou shalt tread upon the lion and adder.* God shall put Satan under his feet; tyrants and bloody persecutors, heretics and seducers shall not prevail over the believer: *the young lion and the dragon shalt thou trample under feet.*

14. *Because he hath set his love upon me, therefore will I deliver him : I will set him on high, because he hath known my name.*

15. *He shall call upon me, and I will answer him : I* will be *with him in trouble ; I will deliver him, and honour him.*

16. *With long life will I satisfy him, and shew him my salvation.*

The ninth motive to believe in God, is taken from a bundle of five or six promises, as spoken immediately by God the Father, of his Son Jesus Christ as man, and of every believer and true member of his mystical body. The first promise is of delivering the believer from whatsoever trouble or danger he can be presupposed to fall into: *I will deliver him,* saith the Lord. 2. For trial of true faith, the unquestionable property of a believer, and the evidence of a sound and saving faith in God, is fixed love toward God : *because he hath set his love upon me.* 3. As there is a because and a therefore in the process of the law, in concluding death for sin, so there is a because and a therefore in the process of grace, and of the gospel, which reasoneth from one grace given to infer another grace to be given, even grace for grace; and such is this here : *because he hath set his love on me, I will deliver him.* 4. Sound love to God floweth from, and is joined with, sound knowledge of God, as his majesty is declared unto us in Scripture : the believer who hath set his love upon God, *hath known my name,* saith he. 5. As the believer is highly privileged and honoured of God, being made a son and an heir, and co-heir with Christ, so shall he be made also more than a conqueror over all his enemies, through Christ: *I will set him on high, because he hath known my name ;* this is the second promise. 6. The third promise is, the Lord will give the spirit of supplication to the believer, and also a satisfactory answer unto his prayer; for, as when a man giveth way to misbelief, he cannot pray any more, so when he entertaineth faith, it maketh him eloquent and instant in prayer, till he receive what he seeketh : *he shall call on me, and I will answer him.* 7. As it is not to be expected, that the man who believeth in God shall want trouble, so the believer may be sure that God, who exerciseth him with trouble, shall bear him company in his trouble, shall direct him how to behave himself in it, strengthen, support, and comfort him under it, and give him delivery out of all his trouble; not only put respect upon him in the sight of those who beheld his exercise, but also at last shall glorify him before men and angels; and this is the fourth promise: *I will be with him in trouble, I will deliver him, and honour him.* 8. While others either want submission unto God, at God's pleasure to live in trouble, or want submission to die at God's pleasure, if they be not in trouble; the believer only hath satisfaction in the length of his life, to die or live as the Lord liketh, and he only departeth contentedly, and entereth into a life everlasting: *with long life will I satisfy him ;* and this is the fifth promise. 9. When the believer hath received of God satisfaction in the length of life in this world, God will enter him into the possession of blessedness, of everlasting salvation in the world to come; which is worthily called the salvation of God: *with long life will I satisfy him ;* and what then shall become of him? *and I will show him my salvation ;* and this is the sixth promise. Above all which promises, what can be more added, to induce a soul to embrace the free offer of grace in Christ, tendered in the gospel to sinners, or to move him to entertain friendship with God, by still believing in him, and resting on him?

PSALM XCII.

A psalm or *song for the Sabbath-day.*

This psalm is entitled, A psalm for the Sabbath-day; wherein the church is stirred up to praise God, by sundry reasons, v. 1—3, but specially for these three causes: First, for the great work of creation, sustentation, and wise governing of the creatures, v. 4, 5. The second cause is for his wisdom and justice in punishing the wicked, v. 6—9. The third is, for his grace and goodness toward believers, v. 10—15.

From the inscription, learn, 1. The Lord hath had a

special care of sanctifying the sabbath, as the appointing of this psalm for that day, may, amongst other things, give evidence: *a psalm, a song for the sabbath-day*. 2. For the sanctification of the sabbath, it is not sufficient to rest from our own bodily, servile, distractive works, but we must rest and cease from our own works, and be employed in religious service and worship, and exercises suitable for that day, whereof singing of psalms to the honour of God, is one: *this is a song for the sabbath-day*. 3. God hath appointed that the church should have solemn meetings on the sabbath, wherein God may, by his own ordinances, be publicly honoured, and the congregation edified in their most holy faith: for this psalm is given to the church with this title and inscription, *a psalm or song for the sabbath-day*, to be sung in the assemblies.

1. It is a *good* thing *to give thanks unto the Lord, and to sing praises unto thy name, O most High:*

2. *To shew forth thy loving-kindness in the morning, and thy faithfulness every night,*

3. *Upon an instrument of ten strings, and upon the psaltery; upon the harp with a solemn sound.*

From the exhortation unto praising of God and thanksgiving, with the reasons thereof, learn, 1. Albeit we be daily receiving more and more benefits from God, yet are we slow to acknowledge this, or to give thanks unto him, and have need to be stirred up to the duty, as this exhortation importeth. 2. Not only do we discharge a piece of our duty in thanksgiving unto God, but we also receive a new benefit by doing this duty: *it is a good thing* (pleasant to God and profitable to us and others) *to give thanks unto the Lord*. 3. Albeit we cannot give thanks unto God as we desire, or as he deserveth; yet to acknowledge and confess to God our debt, and what we have received of him, shall be accounted thanksgiving; for the word in the original giveth ground for this. 4. Approving ourselves to God in sincerity of affection, when we are about the Lord's praises, is no less profitable to us, than it is pleasant to God: *it is a good thing to sing praises to thy name, O most High.* 5. It is not enough to praise God in and with the church publicly assembled; but also it is a duty to be performed daily by every family and person, according

Y

to their place and power, as fit occasion is offered, morning and evening: *it is good to show forth thy kindness in the morning, and thy faithfulness every night.* 6. The matter of God's praise and our rejoicing, are chiefly the Lord's mercy and truth, in pitying and pardoning, and lovingly entreating sinful men, and performing the promises of the covenant to his people, contrary to their deserving: *it is good to show forth thy loving-kindness and thy faithfulness.* 7. As it is the duty of every one to study to observe and believe, and to be sensibly affected with the Lord's mercy and truth; so also to express their belief and sense thereof cheerfully and joyfully, according as the signification of typical ceremonies of musical instruments under the pedagogy of the law required: *it is good to show forth thy loving-kindness, &c., upon an instrument of ten strings, and upon the psaltery, upon the harp with a solemn sound.*

4. *For thou, Lord, hast made me glad through thy work; I will triumph in the works of thy hands.*

5. *O Lord, how great are thy works! and thy thoughts are very deep.*

The psalmist descendeth more specially to the works of creation and common providence, which are the first special matter for God's praise, and the worshipper's joy, wherein he setteth forth the glory and greatness of God's works, and the deepness of his wisdom and counsel. Whence learn, 1. One of the parts of the well-spending of the sabbath, is the looking upon, and consideration of, the works of creation: *I will triumph in the works of thy hands.* 2. The consideration of the Lord's works is a matter full of sweet refreshment and joy, when God blesseth our meditation; which blessing as we should call and look for at his hands, so should we acknowledge it thankfully, when we find it bestowed on us, and lift up our hearts in his way, being so encouraged: *Lord, thou hast made me glad by thy works; I will triumph in the works of thy hands.* 3. All the works of the Lord in their own order and degree, even the least of them bear the impression of wonderful greatness, and shall be acknowledged to be such by the man that seeth them rightly: *O Lord, how great are thy works!* 4. There is as great wisdom of God in ruling and disposing the creatures, as there is power in making them; and as the power in making is wonderfully great, so is his wisdom also in governing them passing deep : *and thy thoughts are very deep.*

6. *A brutish man knoweth not; neither doth a fool understand this.*

7. *When the wicked spring as the grass, and when all the workers of iniquity do flourish; it is that they shall be destroyed for ever.*

8. *But thou, Lord, art most high for evermore.*

9. *For, lo, thine enemies, O Lord, for, lo, thine enemies shall perish ; all the workers of iniquity shall be scattered.*

The second special matter of God's praise, is his just and wise providence in dealing with the wicked, whom the Lord punisheth and overturneth by their temporal prosperity which they seek so much after, as if it were their happiness. Whence learn, 1. Albeit wicked men seem rational, yet are they indeed beastly slaves to their sensual lusts, and therefore are called here brutish men; back and belly are what they most care for : and albeit they seem very wise, yet are they indeed fools, because they choose temporal things rather than everlasting, and lose themselves in seeking worldly gain, and therefore are called here fools. 2. The wicked may for a time spring up, flourish in worldly prosperity, as here is presupposed; but this springing up and flourishing is of short continuance, and subject to sudden alteration : *they spring up, and flourish as the grass.* 3. The end of the temporal prosperity of the ungodly, is perdition : *they shall be destroyed for ever,* yea, their very prosperity (by its fomenting their sinful lusts, and hardening their hearts against God's word,) becometh a means to draw on their everlasting perdition, and that in God's righteous judgment against those who have preferred earth to heaven, their bodily lusts unto the salvation of their souls and bodies : for, *when the wicked spring up as the grass, and when all the workers of iniquity do flourish, it is that they shall be destroyed for ever.* 4. The ungodly are so besotted with the love of the world, and possession of things temporal, that they neither do know, nor will know, nor can know this mystery, except God supernaturally reveal it to them, and give them spiritual wisdom : *a brutish man knoweth not ; neither doth a fool understand this.* 5. Albeit the wicked be in power and high place, and there be little appearance of their overthrow, yet God is higher than they, and so able according to his place to take order with them; and albeit they seem to live long, yet God endureth for ever, and so is able to cut them off when he pleaseth, and to perpetuate their torment for ever : *but thou, Lord, art most high for evermore.* 6. To acknowledge God, is sufficient ground to quiet our minds, however matters seem to go : for, because he is the sovereign Ruler of all the world, and the eternal God, he cannot but govern all things well and wisely, and will not fail to do as he hath said in his word, to punish the wicked, how great soever prosperity he grant them for a time: for the believer from his doctrine draweth light to show him the mystery of the perdition of the wicked, by the means of their prosperity, which the foolish and wicked man cannot consider : *but thou, Lord, art most high for evermore : for lo, thine enemies, O Lord, shall perish.* 7. Workers of iniquity, pretend what they please, are God's enemies, and, seeing they are God's enemies, they cannot but perish : *for lo, thine enemies, O Lord; and the second time, for lo, thine enemies shall perish.* 8. The wicked who now combine, shall be separated from God, and from the society of the blessed company of the righteous, and shall not be able to help one another in the day that God shall bring judgment upon them : *all the workers of iniquity shall be scattered ;* and this is another part of the right-spending of the sabbath, to learn this lesson well.

10. *But my horn shalt thou exalt like* the horn of *an unicorn : I shall be anointed with fresh oil.*

11. *Mine eye also shall see* my desire *on mine enemies;* and *mine ears shall hear* my desire *of the wicked that rise up against me.*

The third special reason and matter of God's praise, are his grace and goodness to believers, wherein the psalmist speaketh first with relation to his own particular case, ver. 10, 11, and then in general of all the godly, from what he believeth toward himself, as serving to teach every one to make application of the doctrine to their own use. Learn,

1. The same supremacy of God over all creatures, which giveth assurance of the overthrow of the wicked, giveth also assurance of the welfare and felicity of the godly : for, from ver. 8, he deduceth this also : *but my horn shalt thou exalt.* 2. The best condition of the godly, is not in what they are for the present, but in what they shall be hereafter : for, albeit they be now under, they shall have dominion at length, expressed here under the term, exalting the horn, which is the emblem of dignity, and power, and victory : *my horn shalt thou exalt like the horn of the unicorn.* 3. That general doctrine may be comfortable, it must be applied, as the psalmist's example teacheth here. 4. Whatsoever weakness or grief the godly lie under for a while, they shall have in due time festival refreshment, comfort, and encouragement from God's Spirit and powerful providence, and that renewed unto them from time to time, as need requireth; *I shall be anointed with oil, with fresh oil.* 5. Whatsoever might be the psalmist's persuasion of victory over his particular enemies : yet, as a type of Christ, and as one of the believers having an interest in Christ, and in all blessings purchased by him, he might by faith see and hear in the Lord's word the overthrow of all the enemies of his welfare; and so may every believer be persuaded : *mine eye also shall see my desire upon mine enemies ; and mine ears shall hear my desire of the wicked that rise up against me.*

12. *The righteous shall flourish like the palm-tree ; he shall grow like a cedar in Lebanon.*

13. *Those that be planted in the house of the Lord shall flourish in the courts of our God.*

14. *They shall still bring forth fruit in old age ; they shall be fat and flourishing ;*

15. *To shew that the Lord* is *upright* : he is *my rock, and* there is *no unrighteousness in him.*

From the Lord's goodness to all believers in general, learn, 1. The promises and comforts given unto any one believer, are not proper to him only, but common to all believers; and the man who can apply these promises to himself, is the fittest man to bear witness of the interest which others have therein : for what the psalmist hath applied to himself, he extendeth to all in substance : *the righteous shall flourish.* 2. The godly shall get up their head, not-withstanding whatsoever weight of troubles may be laid upon them, and they shall constantly grow up to the full stature of perfection, whatsoever opposition may be made : *they shall flourish like the palm-tree, he shall grow like a cedar in Lebanon.* 3. The Lord's children are like trees which do not grow in every soil, are not nourished with every moisture; the place of their planting, growth, and flourishing is the house of the Lord, where the word and Spirit of the Lord, joined with the holy ordinances, may be had for food : *they are planted in the house of the Lord, and flourish in the courts of our God.* 4. Not every barren tree or weed, not every one who is in the visible court of God's church, groweth and flourisheth, or is made partaker of the spiritual grace and blessing of the ordi-nances; but only planted ones, that is, such plants as the heavenly Father hath planted : for to those only who by covenant have embraced God, is the promise made : *those that be planted in the house of the Lord, shall flourish in the courts of our God.* 5. True believers shall still persevere, and the decay of the outward man shall not hin-der the renewing of their inward man day by day, and their last works shall be better than their first : *they shall still bring forth fruit in old age, they shall be fat and flour-ishing.* 6. The end of the Lord's destroying the wicked, and of his blessing the true believer with the growth of grace, and perseverance to the end, is the glory of God's righteousness, singleness in covenant-making, and constant affection to uprightness; for these threatenings and promises shall be made good, *to show that the Lord is upright.* 7. Whosoever neglect to give glory unto God, the believer will not fail to lay his own weight upon God, and build all his felicity on him, being assured that he will neither flee from, nor fail the godly : *he is my rock.* 8. Let the Lord do what he pleaseth, let the wicked prosper for a while, and the godly be troubled for a while; yet God is wise, and just, and holy : and that man hath profited well in the school of God, who giveth this glory unto God constantly, as the psalmist doth here : *he is my rock, and there is no un-righteousness in him.*

PSALM XCIII.

In this psalm, for the comfort of God's people, against the multitude and power of their enemies, and the greatness of kings and potentates in the world, who ofttimes are like to overflow, devour, and drown the church, the glory of the Lord is described, in whom is the church's defence, comfort, and victory. For this end, first, the praises of God for the church's comfort are set down absolutely, ver. 1, 2; then the opposition of the enemies of the church is compared to the growing flood and raging sea, ver. 3; and, thirdly, the praises of God are set down in opposition to their power, ver. 4, 5, with the use of this doctrine, ver. 5.

1. *The Lord reigneth ; he is clothed with majesty; the Lord is clothed with strength,* wherewith *he hath girded himself: the world also is stablished, that it cannot be moved.*

2. *Thy throne* is *established of old ; thou* art *from everlasting.*

From the praises of God absolutely set down for the comfort of the church in all respects, and for strengthening of her faith, specially against all her enemies, learn, 1. Howsoever matters concerning the church or any member thereof shall go; whatsoever he be that hath power for troubling the church, God is he who is great governor of all; and this is one ground of confidence and comfort to the Lord's people : *the Lord reigneth.* 2. The outward splendour of earthly kings and potentates in the world, opposite to Christ's kingdom, is no small temptation to God's people, but the believer must oppose unto this the glorious government of God : *he is clothed with majesty.* 3. How strong soever the adverse powers of the world seem, it must not terrify the believer in following the Lord's cause, but his strength must be opposed thereunto, and that so much the more comfortably, as God's strength is not borrowed from any, as the strength of the creature is : *the Lord is clothed with strength, wherewith he hath girded himself.* 4. The beholding of the constant guiding of the world showeth the power and wisdom of God, employed much more in settling the work of his church, for whose cause the world was made, and is upheld and established : *the world also is established, that it cannot be moved.* 5. The Lord's kingdom in his church is not like the new upstarts in this world, which are of short standing and un-

stable.   If any king be kind to his church, his people have
reason to thank God, but they must not lean to such a king,
his reign shall be but short: and if any king be froward,
and oppose himself to the church, we must not be too much
afraid for him, because his kingdom is but lately begun,
and is of short continuance: but the kingdom of the Lord
is an ancient kingdom and well settled: *thy throne is established of old.*   6. The eternity of God is the ground
of the immutability of his kingdom, and of the perpetual
comfort of the church against all opposers: *thou art from
everlasting.*

3. *The floods have lifted up, O Lord, the floods
have lifted up their voice ; the floods lift up their waves.*

In the second place, is the temptation of the church.
She is like to be overflowed as with a deluge, by the multitude of powerful enemies, whereof she complaineth unto
God.   Whence learn, 1. It is no wonder to see the world
rising up tumultuously to overthrow the church, and as it
were a deluge coming to drown and devour all: no wonder
to hear the enemies threatening destruction to the church,
like to the noise of waters after rain coming down the mountains upon them which are not able to flee: *the floods
have lifted up, the floods have lifted up their voice,* and
the third time, *the floods lift up their waves.*   2. The
best way to encounter threatenings and fears, is to oppose
God unto them, and to lay them forth before the Lord, that
he may answer them, as here the psalmist doth: *the floods
have lifted up, O Lord,* saith he, *&c.*

4. *The Lord on high* is *mightier than the noise of
many waters,* yea, than *the mighty waves of the sea.*

In the third place, he setteth down the power of God, in
opposition to all the brags, and malice, and power of the
enemies, as very far above their power, and more mighty
for the defence of the church than the enemy is powerful
to oppose it.   Whence learn, 1. Heavenly help and comfort
from above are alone able to quiet our minds in time of persecution against the fears of enemies here beneath: *the
Lord on high* is here opposed to the roaring of the floods
and waters dashing against the church.   2. We can neither
glorify God, nor comfort ourselves against the power of the
enemies of the church, except we lift up the Lord's power

above them all : *the Lord on high is mightier than the noise of many waters.* 3. The Lord is above all terrible things, to bridle them at his pleasure, and by his power able to terrify those that terrify his church : *the Lord is mightier than the noise of many waters, yea than the mighty waves of the sea.*

5. *Thy testimonies are very sure : holiness becometh thine house, O Lord, for ever.*

The uses of this doctrine concerning the Lord's power and good-will to defend his church, are two. The one is, that as the word of the Lord is sure and true in itself, so we should acknowledge it to be sure, and should set to our seal unto it, as the psalmist doth here : *thy testimonies are very sure.* The other use is, that such as love to have the benefit of the protection which is promised here, should labour to be holy. Whence learn, 1. Whatsoever is said in the Scripture, needeth no probation; for it is the deposition of God, declaring truth in every thing which it determineth; therefore are his promises called here, *his testimonies.* 2. By giving credit to the truth of the Scriptures, or to the Lord's testimony expressed therein, no man can be deceived : for when we have his word, our minds may be quiet and at rest : *thy testimonies are very sure.* 3. The honour, strength, and happiness of the Lord's people are, that they are the Lord's habitation and place of residence, dedicated and consecrated to him : *holiness becometh thine house,* that is, thy church and people, whereof the temple was only a shadow. 4. God will be sanctified of all that draw near unto him : and whosoever love to enjoy the preservation and privileges promised to the church, must study holiness, which is the duty of the members of the church also : *holiness becometh thy house.* 5. The dignity, duty, and privileges of God's people, and especially this of consecration, sanctification in affection and carriage, and vindication from sin and misery, belong not to any one time or age, but are perpetual, belonging to all such as study to be approved unto God, protected and made blessed by God, in all times and ages, in all places and company, all the days of their life : for, *holiness becometh thine house for evermore.*

PSALM XCIV.

This psalm is a prayer and complaint of the church unto God in the time
of her oppression by intestine enemies, in special by unjust and cruel
rulers, whereunto sundry grounds of comfort to the godly in this hard
condition are subjoined. The prayer and complaint reach unto ver. 8.
The grounds of comfort are four. The first is the consideration of
God's wisdom in the permission of this sore trouble of his people, with
a check to the oppressors for their atheism, ver. 8—11. The second
is, the consideration of the profit which God's people shall have by this
exercise, ver. 12, 13. The third is, from a promise that God shall
change the face of affairs to the joy of the godly, ver. 14, 15. The
fourth is, from the experience which the psalmist had of God's helping
him in this case, set down at large to the end of the psalm.

1. *O Lord God, to whom vengeance belongeth; O
God, to whom vengeance belongeth, shew thyself.*

2. *Lift up thyself, thou Judge of the earth; render
a reward to the proud.*

In the prayer, the church requesteth the Lord to be
avenged on intestine enemies, her proud oppressors. Whence
learn, 1. The Lord's people are subject to trouble and oppression, as from foreign, so also from intestine enemies, as
by-past experience showeth and this psalm presupposeth,
being set forth for her comfort in such cases in time to come.
2. The Lord's people may find as bitter affliction from domestic enemies as from foreign, as the doubling of the
prayer unto God the avenger, to rise and take order with
their oppressors importeth. 3. God will not fail to be
avenged on the enemies of his people, for, *he is the Lord
God to whom vengeance belongeth.* 4. Albeit for a while
the Lord suffer the troublers of his people to go on in their
persecution, yet he will show himself a righteous judge in
due time: *O God, to whom vengeance belongeth, shew
thyself.* 5. The Lord will sometimes, as it were, hide
himself, and not appear in the execution of his judgments
against wicked oppressors, till his people come crying unto
him for justice, as is imported in this prayer: *lift up thyself, thou Judge of the earth.* 6. The Lord's people are
not troubled by humble souls, sensible of their own sinfulness and frailty, but by those who little know how it fares
with the Lord's hidden ones, and afflicted children; for the
oppressors are here called the *proud.* 7. The Lord will
give the proud oppressors of his people a meeting, and
grieve them as they have grieved his saints: *render a re-*

ward to the proud. 8. When the cause is not our private quarrel, but concerneth God in his glory, and the church in her safety, such complaints as are here, are lawful: for this psalm is put in the church's hand in such cases.

3. *Lord, how long shall the wicked, how long shall the wicked triumph ?*

4. How long *shall they utter* and *speak hard things ? and all the workers of iniquity boast themselves ?*

The psalmist complaineth, first, of the long continuance of the insolent triumphing and boasting of these intestine enemies. Whence learn, 1. When the wicked go away unpunished, they think their cause right, and the cause of the godly who lie under their feet to be wrong, and thereupon insult over the godly, and boast of their purpose to do them more and more mischief: for here, *they triumph, they utter, and speak hard things, they boast themselves.* 2. The Lord may delay execution of judgment on the wicked so long, till his children may begin to wonder how his justice can endure it: *Lord, how long shall the wicked, how long shall the wicked triumph ? How long shall they utter and speak hard things ?* 3. When the godly are borne down by oppressors being in power, all the ungodly of all ranks become insolently bold also against them: *how long shall the workers of iniquity boast themselves ?* 4. As the injuries done to the godly, force them to complain; so the working of iniquity by persecutors, provoketh God to punish their oppressors. This the psalmist holdeth forth, when he giveth the adversary this description: *how long shall the wicked, how long shall the wicked triumph; and all the workers of iniquity boast themselves ?*

5. *They break in pieces thy people, O Lord, and afflict thine heritage :*

6. *They slay the widow and the stranger, and murder the fatherless.*

7. *Yet they say, The Lord shall not see, neither shall the God of Jacob regard it.*

The wickedness of the oppressors is here described more particularly, by their cruelty against such as humanity would spare; such as are the Lord's harmless people, the widow, fatherless, and stranger, whom the oppressors abuse with-

out all fear of God who beholdeth them.   Whence learn, 1.
When wicked men, haters of piety within the church, get
power in their hand, they will be more cruel enemies than
men use to be, who have only humanity and civility, and
want profession of religion : *they break in pieces thy
people, O Lord, and afflict thine heritage : they slay the
widow and the stranger, and murder the fatherless.*
2. The more relations a people hath unto God, it is the
more wickedness to oppress them, and the more dangerous
for the oppressors, for they have an owner which others
have not, even the Lord : *they break in pieces thy people,
and afflict thine heritage.*   3. It is not profession, but
practice which witnesseth what impression the Deity hath
upon men's spirits : oppression of such as God hath promised to protect, speaketh blasphemy of God in effect :
they say, the Lord shall not see.   4. Oppression of the
just cauterizeth the conscience, extinguisheth the sense of a
Deity, and maketh the oppressor secure and fearless of
judgment : *they say, the Lord shall not see, neither shall
the God of Jacob regard it.*

8. *Understand, ye brutish among the people ; and
ye fools, when will ye be wise ?*

9.   *He that planted the ear, shall he not hear ? he
that formed the eye, shall he not see ?*

10. *He that chastiseth the heathen, shall not he correct ? he that teacheth man knowledge,* shall not he
know?

11. *The Lord knoweth the thoughts of man, that
they* are *vanity.*

By way of rebuking the atheism of the oppressor, v. 8,
he giveth the first ground of comfort unto the godly, from
the attributes of God, as God's wisdom, v. 9, and from his
justice against offenders, his care of instructing his people
to be wise by all means, v. 10, and his disestimation of men's
vain thoughts, v. 11.   Whence learn, 1. The wisdom of
wicked oppressors is brutish folly, however they themselves
or others esteem them : and whatsoever high thoughts the
wicked have of themselves, or others have of them for their
high place, yet they are, notwithstanding all their honour,
nothing in God's estimation, but as the meanest of the
people, yea, as the beasts that perish : *understand, ye*

brutish among the people. 2. The wicked within the visible church have this advantage over those that are without, that in God's long-suffering they have time to repent, and admonition to be wise for gaining their souls, or clearing God's justice in their condemnation : for here they are spoken to, *ye fools, when will ye be wise ?* 3. The knowledge which wicked men seem to have, or pretend to have of God, is nothing but a base conceit of God, as if he were a dead idol, which neither heareth nor seeth : for this the psalmist's instruction given to them importeth, *he that planted the ear, shall he not hear ?* 4. Beside what the word teacheth of God, his works also teach convincingly what he is : *he that planted the ear, shall he not hear ? he that formed the eye, shall he not see ?* 5. The Lord ruleth among the heathen, and chastiseth them when they sin against the law written in their hearts : *he chastiseth the heathen.* 6. The judgments which the Lord executeth among the heathen, are a sufficient evidence of his purpose to execute judgment on oppressors within the visible church which draweth much nearer to him : *he that chastiseth the heathen, shall he not correct?* 7. The diverse measures of wit, learning, prudence, and wisdom, which God bestoweth upon men, are sufficient to prove how incomprehensible his own fountain wisdom is : *he that teacheth man knowledge, shall not he know ?* 8. It is a matter of great consolation to the godly in their oppression to know that their oppressors are fools; and that God in his wisdom is overruling all confusions, and leading them and their thoughts unto wise ends, as here the psalmist teacheth the church : *the Lord knoweth the thoughts of man.* 9. The enemies of godliness and persecutors of the godly, are at a threefold disadvantage. First, they do not put God upon their counsel, and yet he knoweth their thoughts. Next, they hope to make their own standing fast, and herein they are disappointed. Thirdly, they think that they are able to suppress piety, and that by this means they shall establish themselves; and here also are they fools and deceive themselves : *the Lord knoweth the thoughts of man, that they are vanity.* And this is the first consolation of the godly oppressed.

12. *Blessed* is *the man whom thou chastenest, O Lord, and teachest him out of thy law;*

13. *That thou mayest give him rest from the days of adversity, until the pit be digged for the wicked.*

The second consolation is, from the benefit which cometh to the godly by their exercise under the cross, their temporal trouble serveth to prepare them for everlasting rest. Whence learn, 1. The persecution of the godly by the wicked must be expounded, as it is indeed, the Lord's chastening of the godly by such a rod. This trouble whereof they complain here, is called *the Lord's chastening*. 2. Suffering for righteousness is no token of God's displeasure against a man, nor part of his misery, if it be well considered; for, *blessed is the man whom thou chastenest, O Lord.* 3. The exposition of a man's exercise and the meaning of the rod must be taken from God's word, and God only can effectually teach men to carry themselves in trouble holily and righteously in all patience: *blessed is the man whom thou chastenest, O Lord, and teachest him out of thy law.* 4. When God teacheth his child by his word to possess his soul in patience under the cross, then he also giveth him a sort of deliverance from the trouble; yea, the Lord's chastening of his own, and his teaching them out of his law to make the right use of it, are the means whereby he saveth his own, that they perish not with the world in his wrath: *whom thou chastenest, and teachest out of thy law, that thou mayest give him rest from the days of adversity.* 5. As condemned men are suffered to live till their gallows and grave be made ready, that, after their execution, they may be thrust into it, so are wicked men suffered to live till they fill the cup of their iniquity, and till God have filled the cup of his wrath for them; and this is the term-day of the saints' patience: *that thou mayest give him rest, until the pit be digged for the wicked.*

14. *For the Lord will not cast off his people, neither will he forsake his inheritance :*

15. *But judgment shall return unto righteousness; and all the upright in heart shall follow it.*

The third consolation is, that the Lord's people shall not be always under the feet of oppressors; but, because the Lord will not forsake his people, therefore such a change of affairs shall come as the godly shall have comfort and encouragement from authority which shall countenance and

encourage them to righteousness and piety. Whence learn,
1. Albeit men ofttimes cast off God's people as unworthy
to be members either of church or any civil incorporation,
yet God will not cast them off: *the Lord will not cast off
his people.* 2. Albeit the Lord may seem for a while to
hide himself from his people, when he suffereth the wicked
to persecute and oppress them; yet, because of their relation
to him as his people, and for his interest in them, as his own
inheritance, he will not suffer himself to be bereft of them:
*he will not cast off his people, neither will he forsake his
inheritance.* 3. It cometh to pass sundry times that righteousness and judgment are parted asunder for a while, partly
by earthly judges refusing to do justice and judgment for
God's people, and partly by the righteous Judge of the
world suspending, for a time, to manifest his judgment for
the godly, and against their oppressors, and that for his
own wise and holy reasons. This was the case of the godly
in this psalm, who were waiting for the *returning of judgment unto righteousness.* 4. Righteousness, and righteous
judgment executed in favour of it, shall not long be separated; for God shall either raise up righteous judges to
favour righteousness, or he shall make his righteous judgments testify for the godly and against their oppressors, or
he shall do both these: for *God will not forsake his people,
but judgment shall return to righteousness.* 5. When the
Lord maketh judges and courts of justice to favour righteousness, then the righteous have a banner lifted up for
them, to gather those together again who before were scattered in persecution, to encourage and countenance them in
their godliness and righteous ways: *judgment shall return
to righteousness, and all the upright in heart shall follow it.*

16. *Who will rise up for me against the evil-doers?*
or *who will stand up for me against the workers of
iniquity?*

The fourth consolation is from the example and experience of the psalmist, who, in his righteous cause, sought
assistance from men in a lawful way when he was oppressed,
v. 16, but found none to help him, except God only, who
was his supporter and comforter, v. 17, which he thankfully
acknowledgeth and praiseth God for, v. 18, 19; believing

that, as God was displeased with unrighteous judges and
their cruelty against the righteous, v. 20, 21, so he would
certainly defend him against their oppression, v. 22, and cut
them off, v. 23; and this his experience and example he propoundeth to the church, both to comfort them in their oppression, and to direct them in their behaviour, till the relief
should come.

From his seeking assistance against oppression, learn, 1.
There is a lawful defence of the godly, while they are oppressed by their superiors, which is nowise injurious to authority; such as is to bear witness for the godly, to speak and
make request unto the rulers for them, as Jonathan did for
David and Ebedmelech for Jeremiah; to countenance and
assist them in their appearances for defence of the truth, as
Paul's companions should have done when he was brought
before Nero, and such as here was sought after by the psalmist: *who will rise up for me against the evil doers? who
will stand up for me against the workers of iniquity?*
2. When the godly suffer injury by their own rulers, who
should maintain them, few or none possibly will be found to
countenance them in their righteous cause; for this saying,
who will arise for me, showeth that none offered themselves, and he knew none, when he thus missed all help. 3.
Before the godly complain of wrongs done to them by their
superiors, they should be first sure that they have done no
wrong, or any thing which rulers may justly punish, and
that their rulers are not only injurious to them in particular
but evil-doers also, and open enemies to equity: *who will
rise up for me against the evil-doers? or who will stand
up for me against the workers of iniquity?* 4. Rulers
should be wary that they force not the righteous to complain to God and man of them; for, if they do, the oppressed
may readily fall upon the psalmist's outcry, and that is not
safe for the magistrate, that any should have cause to cry,
who will rise up for me against the evil-doers?

17. *Unless the Lord* had been *my help, my soul had
almost dwelt in silence.*

The psalmist showeth what success his seeking of help
from men had, and that was none at all; for, if God had not
helped him, he should have perished before help had been
given to him from men. Whence learn, 1. Whosoever en-

gage in any cause, were it ever so just, with confidence in man, or with hopes to carry it on and go through with it by man's assistance, need not wonder if they be disappointed : *unless the Lord had been my help, my soul had almost dwelt in silence.* 2. Whatsoever lawful means the righteous man useth for his own relief may fail, if he lean to them, and not to God only; but if he rely upon the Lord, he shall be relieved : *unless the Lord had been my help, my soul had almost dwelt in silence.*

18. *When I said, My foot slippeth; thy mercy, O Lord, held me up.*

The psalmist showeth how he received help of God, to wit, by acknowledging unto God the danger he was in, and his own weakness to relieve himself, whereby he found support from the Lord's mercy. Whence learn, 1. Such as are put upon the trial of their faith and obedience to God by persecution, are in danger either to fall into sin or present trouble, yea, possibly also to lose their life, like unto men driven to the edge of a very steep place, as the similitude of *my foot slippeth,* importeth. 2. In time of trial and temptation, as ordinarily God maketh men's own wisdom, courage, and strength fail them, that they may distrust themselves and come to him; so should they acknowledge their own weakness, and lay it out, with the danger they are in, before God : *I said, My foot slippeth.* 3. The sense of our own weakness, presented to God in prayer, is a forerunner of God's relief coming to us: *when I said, My foot slippeth, thy mercy held me up.* 4. As it is our duty to acknowledge God's power and mercy in our supplications, so also it is our duty to glorify the mercy of God after the felt experience of it : *thy mercy, O Lord, held me up.*

19. *In the multitude of my thoughts within me thy comforts delight my soul.*

The inspired penman setteth down here a further benefit of his faith in God; to wit, that by what he saw in God, he found comfort and joy in all his perplexities. Whence learn, 1. In the time of danger, or of narrow trial, many questions, and doubts, and discourses of mind, use to arise, which appear not in time of ease; and these multiplied thoughts breed perplexity, anxiety, and grief, which call for comfort, as the experience of the psalmist teacheth : *in the multitude of my thoughts within me, &c.* 2. No ease for a perplexed soul till it go to God in Christ, the resting-stone in Zion; and in him support is to be found under burdens and comfort against whatsoever cause of grief, yea, and more also, joy and delight swallowing up all grievances, as the psalmist by experience usually found : *in the multitude of my thoughts within me thy comforts delight my soul;* now, God's comforts are gospel comforts.

20. *Shall the throne of iniquity have fellowship with thee, which frameth mischief by a law?*

21. *They gather themselves together against the soul of the righteous, and condemn the innocent blood.*

The inspired writer showeth what use he made of the oppressors' wickedness for supporting his own faith; to wit, that he was persuaded that God allowed not their mischievous courses, howsoever they pretended to do what they did by a law, because, not the good of the subject, but the overthrow of the godly, was intended by them. Whence learn, 1. The fear of justice, within the visible church, may possibly turn enemies to piety and righteousness and to those that follow God's word; in which case the grief, temptation, wrestling, and trial of the godly are not small, as the psalmist's experience teacheth us, who here cometh to God with a question, *shall the throne of iniquity have fellowship with thee?* 2. As the thrones of justice are honourable, are countenanced and protected by God, when they decree and execute righteousness; so they lose their reputation, and are denuded of God's approbation, comfort, and defence, when they decree and execute iniquity : *shall the throne of iniquity have fellowship with thee?* 3. Albeit wicked men ofttimes love to have the appearance and shadow of equity, yet unrighteousness, impiety, oppression, are not the more justifiable that they be covered with the authority of a law, but rather God will abhor that wickedness which is enjoined by a law so much the more as it hath pretence of law : *shall the throne of iniquity have fellowship with thee, that forgeth mischief by a law?* 4. The iniquity of persecutors is the matter of confidence for the oppressed; for, if our adversaries be against God and against us also, then have we fellowship with God in a common cause : *shall the throne of iniquity have fellowship with thee?* saith he. 5. When mischief is enacted by law, then shortly may the godly be paneled as criminally guilty, and they who allow the law shall be found ready to sit upon assizes to condemn the righteous, as the experience of the psalmist showeth : *they gather themselves together against the soul of the righteous, and condemn the innocent blood.*

22. *But the Lord is my defence; and my God is the rock of my refuge.*

23. *And he shall bring upon them their own iniquity, and shall cut them off in their own wickedness;* yea, *the Lord our God shall cut them off.*

From this consideration the psalmist draweth two con- clusions, one assuring him of his own protection, v. 22, another assuring him of the destruction of the adversary, v. 23. Whence learn, 1. As nothing save faith in God can uphold a man in time of persecution; so, by persecution and trouble, God useth to cause his own to make use of faith and to draw nearer hand unto him, as the psalmist found by experience, saying, *but the Lord is my defence.* 2. It is needful that he who would have God's help and protection in a particular good cause, should see that the reconciliation of his person be solidly grounded on the covenant of God's grace : *my God is the rock of my refuge.* 3. The godly may, from God's word, give out damnatory decrees against their persecutors, which surely shall be executed; as here thrice destruction is pronounced by the psalmist against the oppressors. 4. The destruction intended against the godly by their oppressors, is as ready as any thing to be the trap to take themselves in : *God shall bring upon them their own iniquity, and shall cut them off in their own wickedness.* 5. How little appearance soever there be of the vengeance of God upon wicked rulers abusing their power against the godly for their righteousness and piety, yet the overthrow of them must not be doubted of, because of the covenant passed between God and his ser- vants, who serve him in suffering for righteousness; for the repeating of the sentence of destruction the third time against such oppressors teacheth so much : *yea, the Lord our God shall cut them off.*

PSALM XCV.

This psalm is applied to Christ by the apostle, Heb. iii. 7—11; whereof there are two parts. In the first is an exhortation to worship God in Christ, or Christ God, with the Father and Holy Spirit, dwelling among them in the temple, and representing unto them the future incarnation, and the execution of his offices in types and figures. The arguments of praising and worshipping him are five. The first, because he is the Rock of our salvation, ver. 1, 2; the second, because of his greatness, ver. 3; the third, for his power, ver. 4; the fourth, because he created all things, and us his people, ver. 5, 6. The latter part of the psalm is another exhortation unto the visible church to evidence their obedience of faith, and not to harden their heart in the time of God's dealing with them by his word, as their fathers did, who perished in the wilderness for their provocation, ver. 8—12.

1. *O come, let us sing unto the Lord; let us make a joyful noise to the Rock of our salvation.*

2. *Let us come before his presence with thanksgiving, and make a joyful noise unto him with psalms.*

From the first exhortation unto a cheerful praising and worshipping of God, manifesting himself in Christ to his church, and unto joyful thanksgiving for salvation offered and granted to us in him, which is the first reason to move them to the duty, learn, 1. As the necessity and acceptableness of the duty of praising God and thanksgiving unto him are very remarkable, so are our unreadiness to the duty and uncheerfulness in it observable also; for the frequent and pressing exhortations thereunto intimate so much unto us: *O come, let us sing unto the Lord; let us make a noise, let us come before him.* 2. Every one, but especially the Lord's ministers, should stir up their people and others also to this duty, to discharge it not only in secret, but also publicly in their congregations, and that with cheerfulness, with heart and voice, whatsoever shall be their private grievances and burdens: *let us come before his presence with thanksgiving, and make a joyful noise unto him with psalms.* 3. Whatsoever evil or grief trouble us there is reason of joy, and praise, and thanks, when we look to Jesus Christ and his benefits: *make a joyful noise unto the Rock of our salvation.* From him is our full deliverance, and upon him lieth our victory over sin, Satan, death, hell, and all enmity, founded as upon a rock. 4. It is time to come before God for mercy to prevent justice, while yet we are spared, and he has not come to us in judgment; for so the word in the original giveth ground, signifying coming speedily and with prevention : *let us speedily come before his presence,* or preoccupy his presence. 5. He that cometh to God in Christ meeteth with his reconciled face; for the coming to the tabernacle, the ark, and mercy-seat, signified and promised so much : and therefore it is said, *let us come before his presence,* or *before his face.* 6. Singing of psalms should be done as a matter of honouring God, and not as a matter of pleasing our own ears or the ears of others : *let us come with thanksgiving,* or confession and praising, *and make a joyful noise unto him with psalms.*

3. *For the Lord* is *a great God, and a great King above all gods.*

Another reason of praising Christ are his greatness and supremacy above all rulers and above all imaginable excellency. Whence learn, 1. He that hath a mind to praise God shall not want matter of praise, as they who come before princes do, who, for want of true grounds of praise in them, give them flattering words : *for the Lord is a great God,* for power and pre-eminency, for strength and continuance. 2. Except we put all things that bear the name of excellency under God's feet, whether they be angels or princes, or whatsoever the world maketh their god, we do not give him his due honour : *he is a great King above all gods.*

4. *In his hand* are *the deep places of the earth ; the strength of the hills* is *his also.*

A third reason of his praise is this : He is strong, sustaining by his power sea and earth, and all things of weight. Whence learn, 1. Whatsoever is most secret and remote from men's power, or from our sight and knowledge, God hath it at his disposing; for he sustaineth it and maketh it subsist : *in his hand are the deep places of the earth.* 2. There is nothing of any strength among all the creatures which hath not its strength borrowed from God : *the strength of the hills is his also.*

5. *The sea* is *his, and he made it ; and his hands formed the dry* land.

6. *O come, let us worship and bow down; let us kneel before the Lord our Maker.*

A fourth reason of Christ's praise is, because he is the

Creator of all things, and to be worshipped by us as our
Creator. That Christ as God, or God to be incarnate,
one with the Father and holy Spirit, is here intended, appeareth by the command given to the worshippers to present themselves in the temple, and to kneel down toward the
place of the ark before God dwelling between the cherubim;
that is, before Christ, God to be incarnate. Whence learn,
1. All things were made by Christ, whether high or low,
Coloss. i. xvi. And it was meet that our Saviour should
be no other than he by whom sea and dry land were made,
so great is the work which the Mediator hath in his hands:
*the sea is his, and he made it; and his hands formed
the dry land.* 2. Christ, as he is one with the Father and
holy Spirit in greatness and power, in respect of his godhead and divine nature, so is he one with the Father and
holy Spirit in the capacity of divine honour: *O come, let
us worship and bow down.* 3. Religious kneeling is a
part of divine worship, whereby we testify our absolute submission unto, and highest giving of honour to, God in soul
and body; and this honour is incommunicable to any creature: *come, let us worship and bow down ; let us kneel
before the Lord our Maker.*

7. *For he* is *our God ; and we* are *the people of his
pasture, and the sheep of his hand. To-day if ye will
hear his voice,*

The fifth reason of Christ's praise is, because he is our
God, and pastor of his church, by office of his mediatorship.
Whence learn, 1. God deserveth praise of all the world; but
specially of his church, because of the near relation of covenant between God and his church: *let us worship and bow
down ; for he is our God.* 2. The good shepherd of the
church, who layeth down his life for his sheep, the great
doctor and prophet of the church, the Mediator of the covenant of grace, and covenanted spouse of the church, is very
God, and was known, believed on, and worshipped as very
God before his incarnation: *he is our God, and we are the
people of his pasture.* 3. Christ the maker, the God, the
mediator and pastor of the church, not only effectually feedeth his people by teaching, but also effectually governeth
and defendeth his church by his omnipotent power: *we are
the people of his pasture, and the sheep of his hand,*

whom his almighty hand and power govern and protect in all ages.

8. *Harden not your heart, as in the provocation,* and *as in the day of temptation in the wilderness.*

9. *When your fathers tempted me, proved me, and saw my work.*

10. *Forty years long was I grieved with* this *generation, and said, It* is *a people that do err in their heart, and they have not known my ways* :

In the latter part of the psalm, which beginneth in the former verse, *to-day if you will hear his voice, harden not your heart,* giveth another exhortation to his church visible, to believe and obey the voice of our great prophet Jesus Christ, as the apostle, Heb. iii. 7—11, teacheth us to expound it. The main argument to enforce the exhortation is, lest the curse of God should overtake the disobedient, and they should be debarred from heaven and happiness, as the misbelieving Israelites were secluded from Canaan, and from heaven signified by it. The history may be seen, Exod. xvii. Whence learn, 1. The voice of God in the Scriptures, in the gospel appointed to be preached by sent ministers, is the voice of God the Father, God the Son, and God the holy Spirit, one God in three persons; for, all who grant the Scriptures to be divine, acknowledge also that the Scriptures are the voice of God the Father, and this psalm the apostle, Heb. iii. 7, calleth the saying of the holy Ghost: and in that same place he expoundeth his voice, of whom this place speaketh, to be the voice of the Son, Jesus Christ; and so the voice of God in the Scriptures, in the gospel appointed to be preached by sent messengers, is the voice of God the Father, Son, and holy Spirit, as David also teacheth us, 2 Sam. xxii. 2, 3. *The Spirit of the Lord spake by me,* there is the person of the Holy Spirit : *the God of Israel said,* there is the ordinary designation of the person of the Father without excluding the Word or Spirit : *the Rock of Israel spake to me,* there is the description of the person of the Son, who is the builder of the church, his house, and the foundation whereupon his church is built, against which the gates of hell shall not prevail. 2. The visible catholic church, which hath the word of God preached unto her, and is in covenant with him, is the people of

Christ's pasture, and sheep of his hand, wherein may be found many such as harden their heart and perish, and so are not all of them elect persons; for, *to-day if ye will hear his voice*, is spoken to all to whom the word of God cometh, and bringeth them in the bond of the covenant to hear his voice.   3. Of such as are in covenant with God in Christ, to believe and obey his voice, those only are actually true disciples, who have this property—to love, to believe, and obey God's voice, to yield the heart to the Lord's word : *to-day if ye will hear his voice*, is here the probation of their covenanted profession.   4. The present time only is the opportunity of salvation, of embracing the offer of God's grace, and testifying our obedience of faith; we are not sure how long the world shall remain with us, or we with it : *to-day if ye will hear his voice*.   5. How ignorant, weak, and unable soever a man be by nature, to believe and obey the voice of God, yet, seeing God offereth himself by his word to cure him of all his evils, he cannot endure that a man should wittingly and willingly reject the counsel of the Lord, and resolutely strengthen himself in his natural misbelief and disobedience, for this were to harden his own heart yet more, which here is forbidden : *to-day if ye will hear his voice, harden not your hearts*.   6. The example of other men's sins should be made use of, to make us wise for eschewing the like, as the history of the people's murmuring against God and his ministers is for this end recorded from Exod. xvii. 3, 4, concerning their *temptation of God, and provocation of him in the wilderness*. 7. It is to good purpose that we look upon the sins of our forefathers, and upon God's judgments on them for their sins, that we may be humbled and made watchful against hereditary sins: to this end is the time told them: *when your fathers tempted me, proved me*.   8. He that maketh question either of God's power or good-will, after he hath had experience and proof thereof, burieth unthankfully the Lord's bounty, and draweth a great deal deeper in the sin: for this aggravateth the provocation of God by the carnal Israelites here, that they had often proof what God could do: *they saw my works*, saith he.   9. The Lord not only marketh men's sins, but also reckoneth how long they continue in them : *forty years long was I grieved*.   10. Misbelieving God, and not submitting ourselves to his government, are a vexing of his Spirit, and a provocation of him to reject the sinner: *forty years long was I grieved with this generation.* 11. The errors of the mind are dangerous, but the errors of the heart are yet more dangerous; for the faults of the mind, simply considered, are ignorance and error, but the fault of the heart is a loving of darkness and error : the error of the mind saith, I knew not, I did not understand such a duty; but the error of the heart saith no less than I will not know, I desire not to hear of, I care not for such a duty : *I said, it is a people that do err in their heart, and they have not known my ways ;* that is, they have not regarded my ways, have not allowed them, nor loved them; for otherwise they were not simply ignorant of them; they heard his words, and *saw his works.* 12. Not to subject ourselves to such and such particular hard exercises, difficulties, straits, and sad dispensations, as it pleases God to put us under, is a not knowing, and a disapproving of the ways of God, which he followeth in dealing with his people, and is no less than if we took upon us to be wiser than he, and to counsel and direct him how to govern the world, and our particulars, better than he doth : *they err in heart, and have not known my ways.*

11. *Unto whom I sware in my wrath, that they should not enter into my rest.*

To enforce the exhortation, the Lord repeateth the doom pronounced upon such as harden their own hearts in their unbelief and disobedience of the voice of God; to wit, he sware that so many of them as continued in this sin of hardening their hearts against the voice of God, should not enter into his rest, that is, they should not enter into the rest of reconciliation and peace with God, which is a part of the believer's rest, whereof the apostle speaketh, commenting on this place, Heb. iv. 3, nor into the rest of Canaan, the type of heaven, for they died in the wilderness; nor into the rest of heaven signified by Canaan. Whence learn, 1. There is a rest of God ordained for believers who give up their hearts to the impression of God's voice in the obedience of faith; to wit, the rest of justification, reconciliation, and peace with God; the rest of begun sanctification, and ceasing from their own works; and the rest of everlasting refreshment, begun in this life, and perfected in the life to come; for this is the rest which God calleth here his rest : *they shall not enter into my rest.* 2. As all sin hath judgment following after it, as the shadow followeth the body, so hardening of the heart against God's word in special, hath wrath annexed to it : *to whom I sware in my wrath.* 3. Obstinate hardeners of their heart in unbelief, and disobedience against God's word, are near to the curse; and whosoever continue to the end, shall be found reprobates justly damned to the eternal torment of restlessness, against whom God standeth sworn to condemn them and destroy them : *unto whom I sware in my wrath, that they should not enter into my rest.* 4. The most fearful curses and threatenings pronounced against sinners by God, and the most terrible judgments which have been executed upon disobedient unbelievers of God's word, are merciful and fatherly warnings of God's children, to eschew such sins as carefully and really as they abhor the punishment inflicted for them; for the Lord's making use of his wrath against the misbelieving and disobedient Israelites here, teacheth us so much.

PSALM XCVI.

We find, 1 Chron. xvi. 23, a part of this psalm, sung at the bringing up of the ark to Zion, to be in substance, and almost in words also, one and the same with this which is here; for as there, so here the prophet foreseeth in the Spirit the spreading of the kingdom of Christ among the nations. First, therefore, he exhorteth all people heartily to receive Christ, and propagate his glory, v. 1—3, and giveth reasons for it, v. 4—6. Then he repeateth and enlargeth the exhortation to glorify God, and to rejoice in him, because Christ was indeed to come among the Gentiles, to reign among them righteously, v. 7—13.

1. *O sing unto the Lord a new song ; sing unto the Lord, all the earth.*

2. *Sing unto the Lord, bless his name ; shew forth his salvation from day to day.*

3. *Declare his glory among the heathen, his wonders among all people.*

From the exhortation given to all nations to rejoice for Christ's coming among them, learn, 1. As sadness and sorrow, misery and mourning, are the condition of all people, till Christ, the true ark of the covenant, come unto them, so Christ coming among them is the matter of the greatest joy that ever sinners heard of; for, upon this ground are all here exhorted to rejoice: *O sing unto the Lord.* 2. As the matter of joy in Christ is everlasting, and shall never decay, so the reason of praising God for salvation in him is everlasting also, new and fresh matter being always offered of joy to us, and praise to God, which shall never vanish and wax old: *sing unto the Lord a new song.* 3. All the earth hath interest in this song, and is obliged to the duty of joy and praise, because out of all people, tongues, and languages, God is to gather a people to be saved: *sing unto the Lord all the earth.* 4. We have need again and again to be stirred up to joy in Christ, to praise him; for we are dull, and the work excellent, and no man dischargeth the duty sufficiently: therefore is it said the third time, *sing unto the Lord.* 5. The grace offered in Jesus Christ, is a perpetual reason of declaring the goodness of God, and that Christ is the fountain of all blessedness to them who receive him; for, *bless his name,* importeth so much. 6. The salvation which cometh through Christ, ought to be commended as God's salvation indeed, because he devised and purchased it, and applieth it to us, and maketh us partakers of it: *shew forth his salvation.* 7. The doctrine of salvation by Christ is the common good of mankind, and ought not to be concealed, but set forth to all, preached, and proclaimed, and spoken of by all, according to their vocation and ability: *shew forth his salvation from day to day.* 8. It is a part of the commission given to the ministers of the gospel, not only to teach their congregations concerning Christ, but also to have a care that they who never have heard of him, may know what he is, what he hath done and suffered, and what good may be done by his mediation: *declare his glory among the heathen.* 9. Nothing so glorious to God, nothing so wonderful in itself, as is the salvation of man by Christ: to behold God saving his enemies, by the incarnation, sufferings, and obedience of Christ, the eternal Son of God: *declare his glory among the heathen, his wonders among all people.*

4. *For the Lord* is *great, and greatly to be praised: he* is *to be feared above all gods.*

5. *For all the gods of the nations are idols: but the Lord made the heavens.*

6. *Honour and majesty* are *before him; strength and beauty* are *in his sanctuary.*

The reasons of the exhortation are, because God is sovereign above all, v. 4, and all other gods beside God are idols, v. 5, and whatsoever is glorious is to be found in him only, v. 6. Whence learn, 1. None can praise God till they consider his excellency, and that his wisdom, power, and empire are above all created or imaginable greatness : for, *the Lord is great and greatly to be praised.* 2. As the Lord is praiseworthy for his goodness and readiness to communicate his riches to all his creatures, and most of all to his servants; so is he able to punish his adversaries, and all that contemn his authority, which no creature is able to do : *he is to be feared above all gods.* 3. Whosoever submit not themselves to God, and worship and obey him, shall be found to serve idols and vanities, whereby they can have no good, but disappointment of hopes: for, *all the gods of the nations are idols.* 4. The framing of heaven and earth, and the upholding and governing of all the creatures, proveth, that the maker thereof is God alone, and that there neither is, nor can be any beside him; all others who have the name of gods are idols : *all the gods of the heathen are idols ; but the Lord made the heavens.* 5. Before a man can come to the knowledge of God, he must first meet with the shining beams of his honour and majesty in his word, and in his works; for these are apparitors and harbingers going before him: *honour and majesty shall go before him.* 6. The power and glory of God are not rightly seen either to God's praise or a man's salvation, except by his own ordinances in his church, where he himself is both teacher, and the substance also of what is taught: *strength and beauty are in his sanctuary.*

7. *Give unto the Lord, O ye kindreds of the people, give unto the Lord glory and strength.*

Here the psalmist repeateth and dilateth the exhortation in four branches. In the first, he exhorteth to acknowledge that glory and power belong to God, both in decreeing wisely, and in executing timously and powerfully his own decrees; in special the work of redemption and conversion of the Gentiles by Christ. Whence learn, As it is the sinful sickness of natural men, to take to themselves, or to give unto the creatures the glory of every excellent work, which is properly due to God alone: so is it the part of a renewed soul, to give the glory of every thing which is praiseworthy unto God alone, which glory God expecteth, and shall have it of the Gentiles reconciled and instructed by the gospel: *give unto the Lord, O ye kindreds of the people, give unto the Lord glory and strength.*

8. *Give unto the Lord the glory* due unto *his name: bring an offering, and come into his courts.*

In the second branch, the psalmist exhorteth all to acknowledge the Lord, as they who are worshippers of him, and who are taught by his word, should do. Whence learn, 1. It was foretold, that as the church of Israel was taught by the Lord's word to know him; so should the Gentiles be taught also: for, *give unto him the glory due unto his name*, presupposeth and importeth, that they should have his name set forth in his word, and should be instructed to know him, and how to worship him acceptably. 2. Whatsoever point of glory the Scripture giveth unto God, it may not be withdrawn from him, nor communicated to any other beside him, for it is his own proper due: *give unto the Lord the glory due to his name.* 3. It is the manner of the Scriptures of the Old Testament, to express the spiritual service of the gospel in the terms of the service of the law: *bring an offering, and come into his courts.* 4. Albeit bodily sacrifices and oblations, and the material temple of Jerusalem be taken away, yet the moral duties shadowed forth in them, are still necessary to be done. We must not come for fashion, empty and vain before God, but with the calves of our lips, offering up ourselves in a living sacrifice, holy and acceptable to him: *bring an offering to him.* 5. The church of the Gentiles makes up one church with the Jews, and is of the same incorporation and holy society, and partaker of the privileges of the church with them: *bring an offering, and come into his courts.*

9. *O worship the Lord in the beauty of holiness; fear before him, all the earth.*

In the third branch, the psalmist exhorteth more particularly all the Gentiles to worship and fear the same God as the church of the Jews. Whence learn, 1. True converts must submit themselves absolutely unto Christ's govern-

ment, in soul and body; for, *O worship the Lord*, importeth so much.   2. Then are a man's worship and submission
sanctified, and made acceptable, when it is offered in and
through Christ, and in society with his church represented
by the sanctuary, here called the beauty of holiness : *worship the Lord in the beauty of holiness*. 3. Among all
God's works, nothing so beautiful as his ordinances, rightly
made use of in his church : *worship the Lord in the
beauty of holiness*. 4. All our worship must be seasoned
with fear, lest we swerve on either hand from the rule prescribed by God : *fear before him all the earth*.

10. *Say among the heathen, that the Lord reigneth :
the world also shall be established that it shall not be
moved : he shall judge the people righteously.*

11. *Let the heavens rejoice, and let the earth be glad;
let the sea roar, and the fulness thereof.*

12. *Let the field be joyful, and all that is therein ;
then shall all the trees of the wood rejoice*

13. *Before the Lord ; for he cometh, for he cometh to
judge the earth : he shall judge the world with righteousness, and the people with his truth.*

In the fourth place, the psalmist exhorteth the Lord's
ministers, his called messengers, everywhere to proclaim
Christ King in his own church, and to declare the benefits
of his reigning; in special these three.   1. The putting of
all things which are in disorder and confusion in the world
by sin, into their own order again; and settling all things
to the perpetual benefit of his subjects.   2. Christ's righteous governing and defending of his subjects.   3. The inexpressible joy which Christ bringeth to his people, for setting forth whereof all the reasonable and understanding
creatures are unable.   Whence learn, 1. Wheresoever the
gospel is preached, there without injury to magistrates
Christ may and should be declared King, sovereign Lord
and Lawgiver in all matters of religion, and whatsoever
concerneth the salvation of men and service of God : *say
among the heathen, that the Lord reigneth*. 2. Before
Christ come to a people, men neither know God nor themselves, what is their profit, nor what is their loss. For, before Christ reveal himself to a man, things earthly and
temporal are put in the room of things heavenly and ever-

lasting, the creatures and lusts of men are put in the room of God, and the sinner is made a slave to his own lusts and unclean spirits; but when Christ cometh, who is the light of the world, and the life of men, and convinceth men of sin, and righteousness, and judgment, then is the sinner humbled, and God exalted, and every thing is put in its own place, and a solid state of grace and glory is founded by his word and working, and is settled by his decree for the bene- fit of the world of his elect and regenerate people : for, by Christ's governing, *the world also shall be established.* 3. The kingdom of Christ is a kingdom which cannot be moved, and they who are his subjects, receive this kingdom in title and right, and begun possession, which cannot be taken from them again : *the world also shall be established that it cannot be moved.* 4. The government of Christ's kingdom is so well and wisely carried by him, that right is done to God and man, to friends and foes, and no injury to any party is allowed, and course is taken to give effectu- ally to every man according as his work shall be : *he shall judge the people righteously.* 5. There is no true rejoic- ing for sinners in heaven or earth, except in and through Jesus Christ alone : all joy of sinners without him is mad- ness, and in him men have cause of rejoicing, whatsoever condition they shall be in : *let the heaven rejoice, and let the earth be glad; let the sea roar, and the fulness thereof, &c.* 6. The joy which Christ bringeth to his peo- ple is such, that men and angels are not able to express it; and if all the dumb creatures had minds and mouths to set it forth, it were a task and more for them to undertake it : *let the heavens rejoice, and the earth be glad; let the sea roar, and the fulness thereof, &c.* 7. As all the creatures are in a sort of bondage and subjection unto vanity through the sins of men; so have they their own re- demption and freedom from vanity in relation to Christ, and the service which they do unto the saints, who make right use of them; and at 'length the creature shall be fully de- livered from the bondage of corruption, and in its own kind have cause of rejoicing: *let the heaven, earth, sea, and fields rejoice, &c.* 8. All the creatures are at enmity with man, before he be reconciled to God in Christ, but when peace is made by Jesus Christ, they look upon man, all of them, with another countenance, as servants unto, and children of their Lord, who is Father of the reconciled, and governor of all for their good : *let the fields be joyful, and all that is therein ; then shall all the trees of the wood rejoice.* They shall look upon a reconciled man walking in the light of God's countenance as a paradise. 9. The first and second coming of Christ to show himself King of his church, are ground and cause of all joy to his subjects: *let them and all the creatures rejoice before the Lord, for he cometh* for this, *for he cometh* (twice said) *to judge the earth,* is given for a reason of the exhortation. 10. By Christ's government, every poor and needy subject is helped, supplied, comforted, and provided for, as their case requireth : all the subjects are justified by the imputation of the righteousness of Christ, all of them are renewed and begun to be sanctified, and made to aim at righteousness more and more in their ways; all the proud and the adversaries of his subjects are declared against; course is laid down in the word of truth for a full delivery of his people from all injuries and oppression, from all misery and sin, with the full punishment of their enemies : *he shall judge the world with righteousness, and the people with his truth.*

PSALM XCVII.

This psalm containeth a prophecy of the spiritual glory of Christ's kingdom, to ver. 8, and the use of the doctrine to the end of the psalm. The comfort of Christ's kingdom in relation to his church is set down, ver. 1, 2; and the terribleness thereof in relation to his enemies, ver. 3—6, with a curse upon image-worshippers, ver. 7. The uses of the doctrine are four. The first is, that all excellency, and whatsoever is honourable in the world, should do homage to him, set down in the end of ver. 7. The second is, that the true church should be glad at the hearing and seeing of the execution of God's judgments upon idolaters, with a reason for it, ver. 8, 9. The third use is, a direction to the saints to beware of sin, with some reasons for it, ver. 10, 11. The fourth use is, that the righteous should rejoice, and thank God upon all occasions, ver. 12.

1. *The Lord reigneth ; let the earth rejoice ; let the multitude of isles be glad* thereof.

2. *Clouds and darkness* are *round about him: righteousness and judgment* are *the habitation of his throne.*

The psalmist proclaimeth Christ King among the Gentiles, and commendeth his kingdom to them, as full of joy,

full of majesty, and full of righteousness. Whence learn,
1. Beside the sovereignty which God hath over all people,
he hath a special kingdom, wherein he reigneth by the
Gospel of Christ : this is it whereof here he speaketh, saying, *the Lord reigneth.* 2. Comfort against all grief from
sin or misery, true matter of joy and full felicity, is to be
had by the coming of this kingdom : *the Lord reigneth,
let the earth rejoice.* 3. The isles of the sea are in Christ's
charter, and have their share of the joy which is to be had
in Christ : *let the multitude of the isles be glad thereof.*
4. How despicable soever Christ's kingdom may seem to
the world, yet it is full of heavenly majesty : *clouds and
darkness are round about him.* 5. The glory of Christ's
kingdom is unsearchable, and hid from the eyes of the
world, who cannot take up the things of God, except he
reveal himself to them, and open the eyes of their understanding: *clouds and darkness are round about him.* 6.
The kingdom of Christ giveth no liberty unto sin, but is
altogether for righteousness and judgment; for therein
righteousness is taught to sinners, and they made righteous,
and kept in the course of righteousness, and defended from
the harm of their adversaries, and rewarded according to
their righteousness, and all the unrighteous are adjudged to
punishment according to their works : *righteousness and
judgment are the habitation of his throne.*

3. *A fire goeth before him, and burneth up his enemies round about.*

4. *His lightnings enlightened the world: the earth
saw, and trembled.*

5. *The hills melted like wax at the presence of the
Lord, at the presence of the Lord of the whole earth.*

6. *The heavens declare his righteousness, and all
the people see his glory.*

After the psalmist hath set down how comfortable Christ
is to his subjects, he showeth how terrible he is to his enemies. Whence learn, 1. Albeit the kingdom of Christ be
a kingdom for righteousness, and a fountain of joy to all
who receive him; yet such is the natural wickedness of men,
that he shall not want enemies, as here is imported plainly.
2. There is no less, but rather more, wrath attending the
despisers of the gospel, than attended the giving out of the

Z

law, Heb. xii. 29: *a fire goeth before him.* 3. Albeit the enemies of Christ were ever so many, environing his flock round about; yet shall he reign in the midst of them, and consume all his adversaries: *a fire goeth before him, and burneth up his enemies round about.* 4. He letteth forth his wrath, not all at once, but by degrees; lighter judgments, and foregoing terrors come before destruction: *his lightnings lightened the world: the earth saw, and trembled.* 5. Christ shall utterly undo the greatest potentates on earth, if they stand in his way and oppose him: *the hills melted like wax at the presence of the Lord.* 6. There is no comparison between Christ and his enemies; how great monarchs soever they be, they cannot stand before his presence: for he is *the Lord of the whole earth.* 7. Our Lord shall not want preachers of his righteousness: for, beside the word of God, blessings from heaven upon his friends, and judgments from heaven upon his enemies, according to the word, shall testify for Christ: *the heavens declare his righteousness.* 8. The judgments of God upon the enemies of the church, and his blessings upon his church, shall be so evident, as beholders shall be forced to acknowledge God in them, manifesting himself for Christ's kingdom: *and all the people shall see his glory.*

7. Confounded be all they that serve graven images, that boast themselves of idols: worship him, all ye *gods.*

The psalmist setteth down God's curse upon idolaters, or image-worshippers, and then showeth the uses of the former doctrine, for further setting forth the glory of Christ's kingdom. Whence learn, 1. All they who either serve or worship graven images, are reckoned by God enemies to God, and to Christ; and it is a part of Christ's glory to abolish images, and all worship and service unto images out of his church: *confounded be all they that serve graven images.* 2. Albeit such as are lovers of imagery, not only serve images, but also will defend the use of images in that exercise of religion, and glory in them; yet shall they at length be ashamed of their boasting: *confounded be all they that serve graven images, that boast themselves of idols.* 3. God will not have such relative worship as men would give him, by serving or worshipping him in, at, or before images. The way God will be served, is by a direct and immediate worshipping of him, without the meditation or intervening of any thing which may intercept his worship: for, in opposition to relative worship in the in the service of graven images, he saith, *worship him;* importing that when images are worshipped, God is not worshipped at all, whatsoever the image-worshipper intendeth. 4. Whatsoever creature hath excellency in heaven or earth, or can pretend to any eminency or excellency, of whatsoever sort, must do homage unto Christ: *worship him all ye gods,* and this is the first use of the former doctrine.

8. *Zion heard, and was glad; and the daughters of Judah rejoiced because of thy judgments, O Lord.*

9. *For thou, Lord, art high above all the earth: thou art exalted far above all gods.*

The second use is to comfort all true worshippers; partly, because they hear God's wrath threatened and executed against idolaters, and partly, because they have hereby a clear evidence of Christ's supremacy over all creatures. Whence learn, 1. The condemnation of imagery, and of all service and worship to graven images, is a doctrine comfortable to the true members of the church: *Zion heard,* (to wit, this curse against idolatry,) *and was glad.* 2. The true church, considered in her collective incorporation, as the mother Zion, and, in her particular branches and subdivisions, as daughters of Judah depending upon Christ the vine-tree of Judah, have the same reasons of joy, and the same grounds of edification by God's word and works of judgment, wrought for clearing of true religion, and shaming false worship: *Zion heard, and was glad; and the daughters of Judah rejoiced, because of thy judgments, O Lord.* 3. The manifestation of the gospel of Christ, is the exaltation of God, and manifestation of his excellency, whose dishonour as it should be the matter of our grief, so his manifested glory should be our joy, as the reason here given of the joy of the saints teacheth us: *for thou Lord, art high above all the earth: thou art exalted far above all gods.*

10. *Ye that love the Lord, hate evil: he preserveth*

the souls of his saints; he delivereth them out of the hand of the wicked.

11. *Light* is *sown for the righteous, and gladness for the upright in heart.*

The third use of the doctrine, is an exhortation to the faithful to study holiness, and to eschew the fellowship of sin, whatsoever may be the danger; partly, because the Lord will deliver his own out of the hands of their enemies, partly, because God hath appointed comfort unto them, both in and after their afflictions. Whence learn, 1. A believer in God, or a true worshipper of God in Christ, is a lover of God; for thus are they described here: *ye that love the Lord.* 2. The love of God must be joined with, and manifested by the study of a holy life; and with not only abstaining from, but also with hating and abhorring of, that which is sinful: *ye that love the Lord, hate evil.* 3. Albeit the hating of evil and loving of God, may readily make a man the object of malice and persecution from wicked men, yet shall the godly have their souls saved; yea, and at length be fully delivered from the harm which Satan and the wicked intend to bring upon the godly for that cause: *he preserveth the souls of his saints: he delivereth them out of the hand of the wicked.* 4. All the exercises of the godly, and specially their troubles for righteousness, are but the seed of their joy and consolation, which God is to bring forth unto them out of these troubles: *light is sown for the righteous.* 5. The Lord's children, who love him and hate evil, must not think to have the fruit of their righteousness presently in possession, but must give a time unto it, as is given to corn that is cast into the ground; and as after a time the corn springeth, and cometh to a ripe harvest; so shall the troubles of the godly have a comfortable issue: *light is sown for the righteous.* 6. In reckoning of the righteous, the Lord counteth men by their hearts: and so many as by faith in Christ have purified their hearts unto the unfeigned study of holiness, are righteous before God, albeit their infirmities be many; and whatsoever fit of grief and interruption of joy, such men be subject unto for a time, yet at length their portion shall be a full harvest of gladness: *light is sown for the righteous,* and who these are, he showeth; *and gladness for the upright in heart.*

12. *Rejoice in the Lord, ye righteous; and give thanks at the remembrance of his holiness.*

The fourth use of the doctrine, is an exhortation unto believers, to be joyful and thankful, whatsoever be their condition in the present life, because of the salvation manifested in Christ. Whence learn, 1. Whatsoever may be the tribulation of the faithful in the world, they have matter of joy in the Lord, and they should stir up themselves to rejoice, and make conscience of the commandment : *rejoice, ye righteous, in the Lord.* 2. Whatever can be taken from the godly, their right and interest in Christ can never be taken from them, and so there is cause to give thanks for this gift for ever : *and give thanks at the remembrance of his holiness, or confess to the remembrance of his holiness;* that is, acknowledge to his glory the benefit which you have by being a subject to this king. 3. Whatsoever word or work of Christ bringeth us to the remembrance of his name, should bring us also to the consideration and remembrance of his holiness, which is the untainted glory of all his attributes; wisdom, justice, goodness, power, mercy, truth, &c.—and is the untainted glory of his word, works, and purchase unto us : *give thanks at the remembrance of his holiness.*

PSALM XCVIII.

This psalm is an exhortation to Jew and Gentile, to rejoice and bless the Lord for Christ's coming to set up his kingdom in the world. The exhortation is thrice pressed, 1. In proper terms, requiring the church to sing for joy, with reasons adjoined, ver. 1—3. Then it is repeated, and musical instruments called for, to show that by human voice the matter of the joy which is in Jesus Christ, is inexpressible, ver. 4—6. 3. To show that neither voice of man, nor musical instruments are sufficient to express the joy which cometh by Christ's kingdom, the whole creatures, are called unto this work of rejoicing, and setting forth his glory, ver. 7, 8. And the reason is given, because Christ cometh to set up and exercise his kingdom in righteousness, ver. 9.

1. *O sing unto the Lord a new song; for he hath done marvellous things: his right hand, and his holy arm, hath gotten him the victory.*

2. *The Lord hath made known his salvation: his righteousness hath he openly shewed in the sight of the heathen.*

3. He hath remembered his mercy and his truth toward the house of Israel: all the ends of the earth have seen the salvation of our God.

The exhortation to sing unto the Lord, who is Christ, hath five reasons adjoined. The first is, because he hath wrought the work of redemption wonderfully; the next, because he hath done his work by conflict with his enemies, and hath gotten the victory, v. 1; the third, because he hath caused to preach his salvation to the Gentiles, v. 2; the fourth, because he hath performed his promises made to the Jews; and the fifth, because he hath made all the earth to see the salvation which God in covenant with his church hath wrought for his people, v. 3. Whence learn, 1. The joy which Christ bringeth, can never wax old : but because mercies through him are everlasting, and the persons who have share in this joy, are made new, and all things unto them are made new; therefore the song and joy also shall be made new : *O sing unto the Lord a new song.* 2. Salvation brought by Christ, and the work of redemption wrought by him, is a most wonderful work; for it is brought about by the incarnation of God, by the painful suffering and shameful death of God incarnate; by whose stripes we are healed, and by whose death and resurrection we have life and immortality given unto us : *for he hath done marvellous things.* 3. It is by battle against the enemies of our salvation that we are delivered : for Christ hath wrestled with the guiltiness, demerit, and punishment of our sins; wrestled with the curse of the law, with Satan, death, and hell, and whatsoever could hinder our redemption and salvation, and hath gotten unto himself the victory to our advantage : *his right hand and his holy arm hath gotten him the victory.* 4. No creature's help hath our Lord used in this work, but he has done all immediately by his own divine power, being God omnipotent : *his right hand, and his holy arm, hath gotten him the victory.* 5. The glory of the salvation of man, by this means is most justly to be ascribed to him alone, and to be called his salvation; because he devised it, and brought it about immediately by himself, and causeth to proclaim it in his own name to the world by the preaching of the gospel : so it is in all these respects his salvation : *the Lord hath made known his salvation.* 6. The way how Christ maketh known his salvation, and maketh us partakers of his salvation, is by making known *his righteousness,* or the righteousness of faith, and making us partakers thereof by the preaching of it among the Gentiles : *his righteousness hath he openly shown in the sight of the heathen.* 7. Whatsoever promise he hath made to the Jews, he doth not forget it: but whatsoever cloud is come upon that nation, all the mercies and promises made to them shall be performed : *he hath remembered his mercy and his truth toward the house of Israel.* 8. The fulness of the Gentiles shall be made partakers of the covenant of grace, with the true church of the Jews : *all the ends of the earth have seen the salvation of our God.*

4. *Make a joyful noise unto the Lord, all the earth: make a loud noise, and rejoice, and sing praise.*

5. *Sing unto the Lord with the harp ; with the harp, and the voice of a psalm.*

6. *With trumpets, and sound of cornet, make a joyful noise before the Lord the King.*

From the repeating of the exhortation to the whole earth, Jews and Gentiles, and calling for musical instruments to express this joy, whereby the pedagogy of the church under the ceremonial law, (which is now abolished,) taught them the greatness of the spiritual joy of Christ's coming, learn, 1. The joy of faith, the joy allowed unto believers in Jesus Christ, is unspeakable and full of glory, which cannot be expressed by words or human voice; for this the variety of musical instruments in God's praise, at the offering of the sacrifices, shadowed forth under the law; and here it is signified by this exhortation, to sing *with the harp, trumpet, and cornet ;* and that with special relation to Christ as King in Zion: *make a joyful noise before the Lord the King.*

7. *Let the sea roar, and the fulness thereof; the world, and they that dwell therein.*

8. *Let the floods clap* their *hands : let the hills be joyful together.*

In the exhortation directed to the dumb creatures, sea, floods, and hills, that they should utter songs of joy, learn,

1. The setting forth the praise of Christ for the redemption of sinners, may not only furnish work to all reasonable creatures, but also if every drop of water in the sea, and in every river and flood, every fish in the sea, every fowl of the air, every living creature on the earth, and whatsoever else is in the world : if they all had reason and ability to express themselves; yea, and if all the hills were able by motion and gesticulation to communicate their joy one to another; there is work for them all to set out the praise of Christ : for, *let the sea roar, and the fulness thereof ; the world, and all that dwell therein ; let the floods clap their hands,* &c., importeth so much. 2. As the Lord can never be sufficiently praised for salvation through Christ; so cannot any hearers dutifully and as becomes them hear them, hear this doctrine, without great joy or stirring up themselves to rejoice therein : for, if senseless creatures in their own kind be called upon to rejoice, much more sinful men to whom the grace of Christ is offered, and for whom the work of redemption is wrought.

9. *Before the Lord: for he cometh to judge the earth ; with righteousness shall he judge the world, and the people with equity.*

The reason of all this joy is rendered in this, that Christ is coming to judge the earth and the world righteously, and to judge his own people in special. Whence learn, 1. All the joy conceived for the redemption and salvation wrought by Christ, and all the joy which floweth from his righteous government, should be offered unto God in sincerity, as a part of worship and thankful acknowledgment of his gracious gift : for the exhortation is not to rejoice simply, but *to rejoice before the Lord.* 2. Christ is very God, essentially Jehovah before he be incarnate, and when he cometh into the world, by assuming our nature, he is the same : *rejoice before the Lord,* or *Jehovah, for he cometh to judge the earth ;* that is, *Christ, who is Jehovah, cometh to judge the earth.* 3. It was foretold that the work of governing the church, and of ruling the whole earth for the church's behoof, is committed unto Christ incarnate, or to Christ coming into the world : *he cometh to judge the earth.* 4. Christ shall guide the whole world, so as all wrongs shall be condemned, and be taken order with :

his own people shall have injuries done to them avenged, and themselves directed, protected, and comforted: *with righteousness shall he judge the world.* 5. As Christ shall reward every man according as his works have been, and do no man wrong; so shall he make his own people righteous, and followers of the rule of equity : *with righteousness shall he judge the world, and the people with equity.*

PSALM XCIX.

For the comfort of the church against a multitude of enemies round about her, there is in this psalm a declaration of the kingdom of Christ, reigning as God, one with the Father and Holy Spirit in the church of Israel, before his incarnation, and a fourfold exhortation to all who shall hear of him. The first exhortation is to stand in awe of him, because of his great majesty manifested in Zion, ver. 1, 2; another exhortation is to praise him for his greatness, terribleness, holiness, and righteousness, ver. 3, 4; a third exhortation is, to glorify and worship him for sundry reasons, ver. 5—8; for which he repeateth the exhortation the fourth time, ver. 9.

1. *The Lord reigneth; let the people tremble : he sitteth* between *the cherubims; let the earth be moved.*

2. *The Lord* is *great in Zion ; and he* is *high above all people.*

From the first exhortation to fear Christ and to stand in awe of him, learn, 1. Christ was King in his church before his incarnation, and reigned in the sight of his saints from the beginning of the world : for, as the Father, from the beginning, was in Christ his Son, the Mediator, reconciling the world to himself, not imputing their trespasses unto them; so Christ, the eternal Son, was in the Father, and with the Father and Holy Spirit, gathering and governing his church all the time before his incarnation ; for it is Christ of whom here the psalmist speaketh, and calleth him Jehovah, King in Zion : *the Lord reigneth.* 2. Albeit the church be compassed about with enemies, as the lily among the thorns, yet, because her Lord reigneth in the midst of her, she hath reason not only to comfort herself in him, but also hath ground of defying her enemies and boasting against them : *the Lord reigneth, let the people,* or nations, *tremble.* 3. The Lord's people do not worship an unknown God, they know who he is and where to find him; to wit, in his ordinances, on the throne of grace, reconciling himself to the world in Christ: *he sitteth* between *the cherubims.* 4. Whosoever seek God in Christ have the angels attending on Christ, to go forth for the service and safety of the believer and worshipper, for this the ceremonial figure signified: *he sitteth* between *the cherubims.* 5. As Christ is attended by angels to the comfort of his church, so also for the terror and punishment of all adversaries in the world: *he sitteth* between *the cherubims, let the earth be moved.* 6. Albeit the Lord be great in his works everywhere, yet is his greatness most manifest to his church by his word and works to her and for her: *the Lord is great in Zion.* 7. There is no opposition which can be made against the church, no power or multitude of people able to prevail by counsel, device, plot, or practice, against his Zion or his church; for, *he is high above all people,* to dissipate their devices, bridle their fury, and destroy them at his pleasure.

3. *Let them praise thy great and terrible name; for it is holy.*

4. *The king's strength also loveth judgment: thou dost establish equity, thou executest judgment and righteousness in Jacob.*

The second exhortation is to praise Christ the King of his church for his greatness, terror, holiness, moderation of power, and love of justice. Whence learn, 1. Whatsoever we know or understand of God, we should not only by faith subscribe to it and seal it, and praise God for it ourselves, but should also commend it to others, and wish the like should be done by all men: *let them praise thy name.* 2. As the greatness of God in Christ, on the one hand, should induce men, so the terror of our God, who is a consuming fire to his adversaries, on the other hand, should press men to praise him: *let them praise thy great and terrible name.* 3. Whatsoever in Scripture is said of Christ will be found to be really in him; he will answer to his name perfectly in all things, without stain or blot: *let them praise thy great and terrible name, for it is holy.* 4. Albeit the enemies of Christ despise the weakness and simplicity of his government, yet he is a powerful and strong King, both in himself, and in and for all who believe in him; for here the church praiseth *the King's strength.* 5. Christ moder-

ateth his power, specially in relation to his subjects, and
doeth not what he may; dealeth not in the rigour of justice
with his people; layeth no more on them than they are able
to bear. His yoke is easy and his burden is light: yea, he
suffereth them not to be tempted above their strength, but
dealeth discreetly with them—moderation and discretion
please him : *the King's strength loveth judgment.* 6.
The course which our God hath set down for comforting
the afflicted, relieving the oppressed, taking order with hypocrites and obstinate offenders, is very equitable, and a course
which he will not alter nor change: for, *he loveth judgment, and thou dost establish equity,* saith he. 7. Christ's
actions and dispensations are answerable to his laws and his
revealed word; he teacheth his subjects righteousness, he
maketh them righteous, performeth his promises, and exe-
cutes his threatenings in his church, according to his sacred
word : *thou executest judgment and righteousness in
Jacob.*

5. *Exalt ye the Lord our God, and worship at his
footstool ; for he is holy.*

A third exhortation, wherein he presseth the same duty
of glorifying God, the third time, by three reasons. One
is, because he is holy, v. 5; another is, from the example of
the Lord's most approved servants, who subjected themselves
unto the Lord's ordinances, to their own and others' advantage, v. 6, 7; a third reason, from the example of the church
both in the wilderness and in after times, who, as they found
the benefit of obedience of the ordinances of God, when they
worshipped God as he commanded them; so they smarted
for their disobedience when they followed their own inventions, v. 8; whereupon he repeateth the exhortation the
fourth time, v. 9.

Whence learn, 1. God is rightly acknowledged when his
covenant of grace, offered in Christ, is embraced, when
men join themselves to the true God of Israel, and when
they esteem and acknowledge God as supreme Lord and
King over all : *exalt ye the Lord our God.* 2. God will
be worshipped when, and where, and how he pleaseth to
command, and will not be worshipped but in Christ, figured
by the temple and ark of the testimony in it : *worship at,*
or *before, his footstool.* 3. The worshippers of God under

the Old Testament were taught to lift their minds above all earthly things, and loose their minds from all limitation of God unto any corporal presence in the sanctuary or ark, and to worship him as Solomon did, to wit, as God incomprehensible, everywhere present, and to be sought in heaven and adored in a spiritual manner; for the temple and ark were but as his footstool, 1 Kings xviii. 27 : *exalt the Lord our God, and worship at his footstool.* 4. Holiness is the Lord's property: he is holy in himself, holy in appointing his ordinances, and holy in receiving worship; rejecting all worship but what he commandeth and calleth for, and he will be acknowledged holy by all that worship him; and worthy is he so to be esteemed, for *he is holy.* And this is the first reason.

6. *Moses and Aaron among his priests, and Samuel among them that call upon his name; they called upon the Lord, and he answered them.*

7. *He spake unto them in the cloudy pillar: they kept his testimonies, and the ordinance* that *he gave them.*

The next reason is from the example of holy men of God —Moses and Aaron, priests or chief officers, and Samuel, a priest, prophet, and ruler of the Lord's people, who all of them subjected themselves to the ordinances of God, and worshipped him to their own great utility, and advantage also of them with and for whom they prayed unto and worshipped God. Whence learn, 1. The examples of holy men of God commended in Scripture unto us, serve for inducement and encouragement to us to believe in God, to worship and obey him : *Moses and Aaron among his priests,* or chief officers, *and Samuel among them that call upon his name.* 2. Because the holiest men of God that ever were in the church stood in need of the ordinary means of grace and worship, and subjected themselves unto ordinances : the Lord will have none of his people to neglect ordinances or lift themselves above them; for *Moses, Aaron, and Samuel, were among them that call upon his name.* 3. Whoever worship God and obey his ordinances uprightly, are enrolled in the catalogue with the chiefest saints, worshippers of God : *Moses, Aaron, and Samuel, among them that call upon his name.* 4. The prayers of the faithful are not frustrated, but have a good answer; and the answer

of the holiest supplicants is set forth to encourage the meanest of believers to call upon God also, as the impartial hearer
of the prayers of all that call upon God in truth : for he is
no respecter of persons; and to show this, it is said here,
they called upon the Lord, and he heard them. 5. The
more evidences we have of God's presence, and the more
familiarly he condescendeth to teach us, the more humble
and observant should we be of his ordinances and commands : *he spake unto them in the cloudy pillar : they
kept his testimonies, and the ordinances which he gave
them.*

8. *Thou answeredst them, O Lord our God : thou
wast a God that forgavest them, though thou tookest
vengeance of their inventions.*

The third reason to move all to the duty of worship and
obedience, is from the example of the mercy of God toward
sincere worshippers, on the one hand, and justice toward
them that followed men's inventions in religion in the wilderness, or afterwards, on the other hand. Whence learn, 1.
The same God, the same Mediator, the same covenant of
grace, belong to the true church both in former and later
ages : *thou answeredst them, O Lord our God.* 2. Albeit
the Lord give forth his ordinances most holy and perfect to
direct men in their worshipping, yet so perverse is men's
corrupt nature, as, from time to time, they are contriving
devices, and following their own inventions, as here is imported. 3. As the Lord is very merciful to his people,
when they continue in his fear, so is he just to correct them
when they pollute religion: *thou tookest vengeance of their
inventions.* 4. Penitent sinners, although plagued for their
sin, yet were never refused forgiveness of sin when they prayed
and beseeched God for it : *thou wast a God that forgavest
them, though thou tookest vengeance of their inventions.*
5. Plagues inflicted for sin upon God's people are not punishments satisfactory to justice, but means of correction,
serving to drive men to repentance and to seeking of mercy,
and may well harmonize with forgiveness of sins; for God
can both plague sinners to drive them to repentance, and
forgive their sin when they repent: *thou wast a God that
forgavest them, though thou tookest vengeance of their
inventions.*

9. *Exalt the Lord our God, and worship at his holy hill: for the Lord our God is holy.*

The fourth exhortation to glorify God, wherein he expoundeth what he meaneth by the footstool of the Lord, spoken of v. 5, to wit, mount Zion, the holy hill where the ark was; adding the same reason of the exhortation which was before, *because the Lord our God is holy.* Whence learn, 1. It is a part of our exalting the true God, to join with his true church, and to offer unto him, with others, such worship as he prescribeth: *exalt the Lord our God, and worship at his holy hill.* 2. The Lord's holiness requireth of all men the exaltation of his name and subjection to his ordinances; neither can his holiness suffer any other worship than what he himself appointeth: *worship at his holy hill, for the Lord our God is holy.* 3. The holiness of God, and the untainted glory of all his attributes, are both the glory and comfort of his people who are in covenant with him, and a motive also to them to invite all men to the fellowship of his service with themselves: *exalt the Lord our God, for the Lord our God is holy.*

PSALM C.

A psalm of praise.

The title of the psalm showeth the sum and scope thereof to be for stirring up the whole church to praise God cheerfully; unto which duty all are exhorted once, ver. 1, 2, for three reasons. First, because he is God; secondly, because we are his creatures; thirdly, because we are his covenanted people, or members of the visible church, whereof he taketh care as a pastor doth of his own flock, ver. 3. And again, all are exhorted to thank, praise, and bless him, ver. 4, and that for his goodness, mercy, and truth, ver. 5.

1. *Make a joyful noise unto the Lord, all ye lands.*
2. *Serve the Lord with gladness; come before his presence with singing.*

From the first exhortation to praise God, learn, 1. The duty of the visible church, in all her particular meetings in every place, how largely soever God shall extend it, is to accept the offer of the grace of God joyfully, and to acknowledge the glorious riches of the grace of God, which he offereth unto them in the gospel: *make a joyful noise unto the Lord, all ye lands*, or, *all the earth.* 2. As we ought to accept of the offer of the grace of God joyfully, so should we also dedicate ourselves to God's service heartily, as he calleth for it; because, according to the gospel, our persons and services are accepted, imperfections pitied, our sins pardoned, and our holy endeavours are graciously rewarded: *serve the Lord with gladness.* 3. Our joy should be stirred up and expressed by singing psalms, especially when we come to the assemblies or public meetings, wherein the Lord hath promised to give his presence with his own ordinances: *come before his presence with singing.*

3. *Know ye that the Lord he is God: it is he that hath made us, and not we ourselves: we are his people, and the sheep of his pasture.*

From the reasons of this exhortation, learn, 1. Such is our natural atheism that we have need again and again to be instructed *that the Lord is God;* of whom, and through whom, and for whom are all things: *know ye that the Lord he is God.* 2. If we consider well that we are God's creatures, it were a forcible motive to us to employ in God's service whatsoever we have of God—life, motion, being, and gifts, and to beware to make any thing we have of God a weapon of unrighteousness for fighting against him; and of this consideration we have need to be put in mind, and to be stirred up to the duty: *he it is that hath made us.* 3. The glory of our regeneration or new creation belongeth unto God, no less than the glory of our creation and natural birth: and it is no less madness to ascribe the work of our regeneration to our own power than to ascribe our first creation to ourselves, for in both respects here it is said that *it is he that made us, and not we ourselves.* 4. As the Lord's people should stir up themselves to more thankful service to God, as their relations unto God and obligations to him as their king and pastor, are joined; so may they expect from God, for their encouragement, whatsoever is needful to a people or a flock to have from a good king and faithful pastor: *we are his people, and the sheep of his pasture.*

4. *Enter into his gates with thanksgiving,* and *into his courts with praise: be thankful unto him,* and *bless his name.*

From the repetition of the exhortation, learn, 1. It is our duty in our approaches to God, specially for any solemn service, to consider what rich benefits we have from him, that thereby we may be stirred up unto the more hearty acknowledgment of his favours: *enter into his gates with thanksgiving.* 2. As the Lord's benefits to us should be looked upon in our addresses unto him; so also his glorious attributes, and his works answerable thereto, should be considered, whereby we may be the better disposed to give unto him glory in all respects: *enter into his courts with praise.* 3. The more we look upon God's praises, the more shall we see our own riches and the solidity of our blessedness in him, and the reasons to move us to thank and bless him: *be thankful unto him, and bless his name.*

5. *For the Lord* is *good; his mercy* is *everlasting; and his truth* endureth *to all generations.*

From the reasons subjoined to the second exhortation to praise the Lord, learn, 1. It is a matter of perpetual praise to God, and of thanksgiving and blessing of him, that, as he is all-sufficient in himself, so he is also communicative of his riches unto his creatures, and to his own people most of all: *bless his name, for the Lord is good.* 2. Albeit we be sinful, and deserve to be cut off in justice from the benefits which God's goodness might bestow upon us; yet the course of his pardoning mercy, renewing the remission of sin to us as oft as we come to him in his Christ, keepeth the channel of his goodness open and clear to us, that it may run toward us for ever: *his mercy is everlasting.* 3. The covenant of grace, set down in the Scriptures of the Old and New Testaments, with the legacy of so many rich promises, serving to strengthen the faith of every weak believer, maketh the matter of God's praise and of his people's joys so sure, that, how sad soever our spirits may be, when we look to ourselves, yet we shall have matter of praising, thanking, and blessing God, when we look to his goodness and mercy, and to what he hath for our comfort said in the word of his everlasting truth: *be thankful unto him, and bless his name: for the Lord is good; his mercy is everlasting; and his truth endureth to all generations.*

PSALM CI.

A psalm of David.

David, not being as yet entered into possession of his kingdom, by direction of the holy Spirit, falleth upon a consideration of the duties of a righteous prince, which he setteth down as a rule to be followed by himself and all magistrates, obliging himself to endeavour to conform his government thereto: wherein he is but a type and shadow of Christ, in whom alone the perfect performance of the duties here promised are to be found. The principal duties which David undertaketh to discharge, may be, for order's sake, reduced to the number of eight, according to the number of the verses.

1. *I will sing of mercy and judgment : unto thee, O Lord, will I sing.*

The first duty which he undertaketh, is to delight himself in all royal virtues, required for the government of good or bad subjects; to make those duties his song; and to approve himself to God for the sincerity of his intention in this undertaking. Whence learn, 1. All the duties of righteous government may be comprehended under these two heads, *mercy and judgment* ; for, *mercy* taketh in the care of the poor, needy, oppressed, or injured, and *judgment* taketh in the care of equity and righteous dealing among his subjects, with the rewarding of the good, and punishing of evil doers. *Mercy* provideth for all good things which the subject needeth, and *judgment* provideth for security, and for removing whatsoever evil may trouble them: *I will sing*, saith he, *of mercy and judgment.* 2. Such as are designed unto any calling, especially any public charge, should prepare themselves for it; partly, by laying before themselves the duties belonging to the right discharge of such a calling, and partly by bending their hearts, and laying engagements on their spirits, for the faithful discharge thereof: for so much David's example here teacheth us. 3. Duties of a man's calling should both be studied and discharged with some cheerfulness and readiness of mind: for, *I will sing of mercy and judgment*, importeth so much. 4. As it is expedient for the people's better acceptance of a man to a public charge, that his purpose to discharge his duty therein be published; so also it is expedient for the man's stirring up and fastening to his duty, that he engage his heart unto God; for so David's example teacheth us: *unto thee, O Lord, will I sing.*

2. *I will behave myself wisely in a perfect way. O*

*when wilt thou come unto me? I will walk within my
house with a perfect heart.*

The second duty which he undertaketh, when God shall
come unto him to perform his promise, and put him in possession of the kingdom, is, that he will cast a copy to all the
subjects, of godly and wise behaviour in his own person and
family, according to the rule of God's word. Whence learn,
1. He that purposeth to carry a public charge well, must
discharge the duty of a private man well in his own person,
and make his own personal carriage exemplary to all who
shall hear of him; for so David's undertaking here teacheth us. 2. It is necessary for our personal carriage, and
conversing with others, that we make the Lord's commands
our rule; for that is a perfect way; and that we study to
make application of general rules prudently, according to
the circumstances of time, place, and person; for this is wisdom, as David's example teacheth: *I will behave myself
wisely in a perfect way.* 3. Such as believe God's promises, long to have the performance of them, as we see in
David, who had a promise of the kingdom, and looked long
for it: *O when wilt thou come unto me?* 4. In the performance of promises, the Lord maketh his approaches
nearer and nearer unto the believer, and then shall be the
nearest communion, when God shall perform all that he
hath promised us: for David calleth the giving to him the
possession of the promised kingdom God's coming unto him:
O when wilt thou come unto me? 5. A man's holiness,
righteousness, and wisdom, are put to proof by his behaviour to his domestics, with whom he most frequently and
entirely converseth; for herein David promiseth to give evidence of his walking wisely in a perfect way: *I will walk
within my house with a perfect heart.* 6. To complete
a man's sincerity, it is necessary not only that he have a
perfect way, and a prudent carriage in it, but also that he
be upright in his heart, intentions, ends, and motives: therefore David addeth, *I will walk with a perfect heart.*

3. *I will set no wicked thing before mine eyes: I hate
the work of them that turn aside; it shall not cleave to
me.*

The third duty undertaken is, that David will be far from
plotting any wicked thing, and far from communion with

any persons in any evil course, which is a proof of the uprightness of his heart, undertaken in the former verses. Whence learn, 1. A wicked design is inconsistent with uprightness of heart, which hath an aim at pleasing God, and at nothing else but what he will allow : *I will set no wicked thing before mine eyes.* 2. A man can hardly be free of an evil course, if he shall be tempted to it, except he hate and abhor such courses in other men's practices; for he who is resolved to be upright should say truly, *I hate the work of them that turn aside.* 3. Albeit an upright heart may be at unawares entangled in a sinful course, yet so soon as he perceiveth it to be such he will quit it; therefore, after David hath said, *he hateth the work of them that turn aside*, he addeth, *it shall not cleave to me.*

4. *A froward heart shall depart from me; I will not know a wicked* person.

The fourth duty undertaken, is in relation to the court and places of trust : he will not have in his company, or countenance a perverse or wicked person. Whence learn, 1. Among the vices of the heart, frowardness, perverseness, and wickedness, are most of all to be eschewed and abhorred, because those evils harden the heart against admonition, and make it incorrigible in an evil course, albeit a better course be shown; therefore David denounceth war against such a disposition : *a froward heart shall depart from me.* 2. It is good for a king, for his court, for his subjects, and for the standing of his kingdom, that wicked, perverse, and impious men be out of credit in the court, and not admitted to places of power or trust; for nothing can be more acceptable to God in the point of government, or more amiable to the subjects than this : for which cause David promiseth to the subjects beforehand, *I will not know a wicked person;* much more will Christ not know, but disclaim such a person.

5. *Whoso privily slandereth his neighbour, him will I cut off : him that hath an high look and a proud heart will not I suffer.*

The fifth duty undertaken, is the curbing of our outbreaking wickedness, especially of that which most hindereth the peace and welfare of the subjects, such as is privy slander, and open insolence. Whence learn, 1. There is no sort

of persons more pernicious to a king, or to his subjects, than
is a privy slanderer, having credit in court; for he is able
to murder any subject, and ruin his state, by secret and
false reports of him, while the innocent is ignorant of it,
and wanteth all opportunity to defend himself; therefore
this evil is to be severely punished by the magistrate: *whoso privily slandereth his neighbour, him will I cut off.*
2. A kingdom is not well ruled, except proud and insolent
spirits, whose behaviour speaketh prodigality, strife, emulation, and oppression, be taken order with and borne down :
*him that hath an high look and a proud heart will not I
suffer.* Such, if they escape men's judgments, will not be
winked at by Christ, in whom the truth of types is accomplished.

6. *Mine eyes* shall be *upon the faithful of the land,
that they may dwell with me: he that walketh in a perfect way, he shall serve me.*

The sixth duty undertaken, is countenancing, and encouraging the godly of the land. Whence learn, 1. The
magistrate should have a special care to countenance upright men, and such as fear God : *mine eyes shall be upon
the faithful of the land.* 2. It is good policy for kings to
have in their court and council such as are faithful: *mine
eyes shall be upon the faithful of the land, that they may
dwell with me.* 3. He is to be held in our estimation for
a faithful man, who walketh after the rule of God's commandments; for such as he called faithful before, he expoundeth here to be such as walk in a perfect way; whether
his heart be upright or not, belongeth to God to judge.
4. As it is good policy in a state to have about the king, or
supreme magistrate, such as are professors of true religion,
and of an honest conversation, so it is good thrift and husbandry for every man to choose such for his servants in
the family: *he that walketh in a perfect way, he shall
serve me.*

7. *He that worketh deceit shall not dwell within my
house: he that telleth lies shall not tarry in my sight.*

The third duty undertaken is the purging out of discovered
hypocrites, if they shall creep into credit or trust. Whence
learn, 1. Deceitful and false men, and counterfeit hypocrites
may escape men's observation, and creep into the fellowship

of the godly, and climb up to the court, and get place in king's houses: for so David presupposeth here.   2. When men are discovered, and found to be deceitful workers and liars, then such as have power should purge them out: *he that worketh deceit shall not dwell within my house ; he that telleth lies shall not tarry in my sight*.

8. *I will early destroy all the wicked of the land; that I may cut off all wicked doers from the city of the Lord*.

The eighth duty undertaken, is to suppress all ungodliness in the land, and that for the good of religion, and furtherance of the welfare of the church.   Whence learn, 1. The duty of magistrates is to suppress all the wicked in their kingdom, lest by indulgence shown to them they multiply, and so bear down the godly : *I will destroy all the wicked of the land*.   2. The more timously the magistrate declareth himself against all wickedness, the more doeth he what belongeth to his duty: *I will early destroy all the wicked of the land*.   3. Albeit it be not possible for any magistrate, corporally to destroy all the wicked in the land; partly, because it is impossible to find out every one; partly, because the number of the righteous and sound-hearted is few, and their power weak; and partly, because none can determine who they are in particular : yet a godly magistrate may civilly destroy them all, by causing civil punishments to be executed, and ecclesiastical discipline to be exercised against all those who do not submit themselves to God's laws, till all men yield outward obedience; and unto this duty should every magistrate set himself: *I will early destroy all the wicked in the land*.   4. The magistrate's duty is, by his power and by punishment of evil doers, to endeavour the welfare of God's church within his bounds, as the minister of God appointed for that end : for David saith, *I will early destroy all the wicked of the land, that I may cut off all the wicked doers from the city of the Lord*.   If the magistrate shall punish open transgressions, the church will be in better case.   This was David's resolution as a type of Christ, and howsoever in execution much was wanting in the type, yet Christ will perform all this exactly in his own appointed time, and in his own order, partly in this life, partly at men's death, and partly at the last day.

PSALM CII.

A prayer of the afflicted, when he is overwhelmed, and poureth out his complaint before the Lord.

This psalm agreeth well with the time of the Babylonish captivity of the Jews, about the end whereof the seventy years being now nigh expired, the weight of the misery of God's people, and the mockery of the heathen, and the people's longing for delivery, so afflicted the prophet, that in compassion towards the scattered church, he poureth out his prayer, and communicateth it, at the Lord's direction, to all other feeling members of the body, to be made use of for waking up their affections, and strengthening their hope of delivery. The parts of it are three. In the first part, he craveth audience to his prayer because of his sad condition, wherein he sympathizeth with the church in affliction, to v. 12. In the second, he encourageth himself in the hope of being heard in behalf of the church, to v. 23. In the third, he layeth forth the occasion of all this grief, which was the fear he had of the cutting off of the church of the Jews before the coming of the Messiah, and showeth how he strengthened himself in prayer against this temptation.

From the inscription, learn, 1. It is no strange thing for the dear children of God to be under heavy affliction; for here it is presupposed that they might be afflicted, yea, and overwhelmed. 2. The consideration of the condition wherein the church is, serveth to assuage and mitigate the private calamities of any particular person at any time; for this prayer giveth direction to the afflicted, whatsoever be his affliction, to look upon the condition of the church in the mean time, that it may ease his private grief if it be well with the church; and again, that it may either ease his private grief, or turn it to run in the right channel, if the church be in a hard condition, as here it is held forth; for the most kindly grief of a lively member of the church is that grief wherein he sympathizeth with the calamity of the body, and this wisdom is propounded in this psalm, and recommended to God's people to be made use of. 3. The affliction of the saints before us, may and should be the matter of our comfort and song to God, and hope of help to us in our prayers; for this the inscription and psalm teach us. 4. The way for a man afflicted and overwhelmed to have ease, comfort, and deliverance, is, *to pour out his soul before the Lord ;* for so much is here imported. 5. Albeit a person afflicted cannot fill up the words of this psalm in his own proper present feeling, yet may he make good use of this prayer, which teacheth him how to wrestle for a deliverance; for the general title prefixed to the psalm teacheth so much.

1. *Hear my prayer, O Lord, and let my cry come unto thee.*

2. *Hide not thy face from me in the day when I am in trouble ; incline thine ear unto me : in the day when I call answer me speedily.*

In the first part of the psalm, the psalmist prayeth for ready access and audience to his prayer, because of his heavy affliction, which is set down more generally, v. 1, 2, and more particularly branched forth in the nine following verses. From his petition for audience, learn, 1. A soul afflicted, seeking relief and comfort in God, may both confidently pray for, and certainly expect, audience and acceptance of its prayer: *hear my prayer, O God.* 2. The earnest prayer of an humble supplicant cannot be kept out from God, by whatsoever objected impediment; for, *let my cry come unto thee,* is thus much, *let nothing hold out my prayer.* 3. Albeit it is not any strange thing to see a soul in trouble, and God to seem to be displeased with it also, yet the want of God's consolation, and sense of his displeasure, are more heavy than the trouble, and are what the godly can least endure : *hide not thy face from me, in the day when I am in trouble.* 4. The Lord suffereth his babbling children to speak to him in their own form of speech, (albeit the terms which they use, be not fitted for his spiritual, invisible, and incomprehensible majesty,) such as are, *hear me, hide not thy face, incline thine ear unto me,* and such like other speeches. 5. A soul perplexed and overwhelmed with trouble, cannot long endure the Lord's withdrawing of his presence from it : *in the day when I call answer me speedily.*

3. *For my days are consumed like smoke, and my bones are burned as an hearth.*

4. *My heart is smitten, and withered like grass ; so that I forget to eat my bread.*

5. *By reason of the voice of my groaning my bones cleave to my skin.*

6. *I am like a pelican of the wilderness ; I am like an owl of the desert.*

7. *I watch, and am as a sparrow alone upon the house-top.*

The prophet setteth down his affliction more particularly; first, in the effects and signs of his sorrow to be seen in his body, to v. 8; then in the causes thereof, to v. 11; thirdly, in the consequence and chief effect thereof repeated, which is the apparent utter undoing of him, v. 11. As for the first, we may take the signs of sorrow expressed in a number of similitudes, to describe both the condition of the prophet's natural body, and also the condition of the body politic, of the tribe of Judah now in captivity. Whence learn, 1. The Lord's children are subject to such sad conditions, as may bring their very natural body to a sort of decay, as those similitudes here used express. 2. The condition of a visible church, may seem, and really be in its own kind, in such a weak, sorry, and sick condition, as the comparisons here hold forth. 3. As smoke is extracted by fire out of a moist body, and vanisheth when it is evaporated: so may the life and vigour of a saint's body be spent and consumed by trouble and sense of God's withdrawing, or of his wrath : *my days are consumed like smoke.* 4. As fire heateth the hearth, and the hearth, once hot with fire, is able to kindle and burn timber or coals, or any combustible matter cast on it; so is the sense of God's wrath in long-lasting trouble, able to spend the strength of the strongest man : *my bones are burnt as an hearth.* 5. As grass withereth when it is cut; so is the courage of a man cast down, when he findeth God's anger pursuing his church or himself : *my heart is smitten, and withered as grass.* 6. When God is seen to be angry, the comforts of this life are tasteless, and can yield no pleasure: *I forget to eat my bread.* 7. Heavenly sorrow can hardly be suppressed, sighs and groans must of necessity give some vent to it : for, here is *the voice of groaning.* 8. The exercise of the spirit of God's dearest children may endure long, even till their flesh fail them, and their leanness may be such as here is spoken of: *my bones cleave to my skin.* 9. As in sad troubles familiars use to draw back from, and leave a man alone; so also a sad soul loveth to be alone, rather than to be a spectacle of misery to others: *I am like a pelican in the wilderness, I am like an owl in the desert.* 10. Trouble of mind is able to bereave a man of night's rest, and then his readiest ease of mind, is to vent his grief heaven-ward : *I watch, and am as a sparrow alone on the house-top,* chirping.

8. *Mine enemies reproach me all the day ; and they that are mad against me are sworn against me.*

The causes of his grief are three. First, the reproach and desperate cruelty of the enemy against the church, v. 8. Secondly, the sense of God's anger appearing in his dispensation, which drew him not only to frequent fasting and tears, but also to an uncomfortable life. Thirdly, the comparison of times of the former prosperity of the church with the present adversity, v. 7, 10. Whence learn, 1. The men of this world use to meet with pity in their calamity, but the godly are subject to reproaches in their troubles, which mockery and calamity double their misery : *mine enemies reproach me all the day.* 2. The enemies of God's people are reasonless and implacable in their indignation against the godly : *they are mad against me.* 3. Albeit the miseries of God's people may be such, as the wicked enemy of religion, when he would curse any person, shall wish no worse to them than to say, Let him be like such a people, and such a godly person, yet will the wicked not be satiated with this, except he bring more mischief upon the godly : *they that are mad against me, do curse by me,* or *are sworn against me.*

9. *For I have eaten ashes like bread, and mingled my drink with weeping.*

10. *Because of thine indignation and thy wrath : for thou hast lifted me up, and cast me down.*

The second cause of his grief, were the signs of God's indignation appearing in the church's misery, which made him sit desolate many times in the dust, weeping when he should have taken some refreshment to his body. Whence learn, 1. The condition of the godly may sometimes make them miserable, not only in the eyes of the world, but also in their own eyes for a time : *I have eaten ashes like bread, &c.* 2. Not only may the godly be driven to frequent fasting and prayer, but also to have grey dusty bread for their ordinary diet, and that joined with such grief, that they can take no food with comfort : *I have eaten ashes like bread, and mingled my drink with weeping.* 3. The sharpest ingredient in the trouble of the godly, is the sense of God's indignation : *I mingled my drink with weeping, because of thy indignation.* 4. The troubles which the Lord bringeth upon his own children, shall lead them to a sense of their sin, and of God's just displeasure against them for the same : *I mingled my drink with weeping, because of thy indignation and wrath.* 5. As it is the Lord which maketh changes of condition, and giveth now prosperity in his indulgence, and anon adversity for the abuse of prosperity; so should he be acknowledged in his bounty and justice good and holy : *for thou hast lifted me up, and cast me down.* 6. Comparison of past prosperity with present adversity, maketh the present afflicted condition the heavier, and God's just indignation the more evident; for thus doth the psalmist prove God's wrath pursuing him and the church : *for thou hast lifted me up, and cast me down.*

11. *My days are like a shadow that declineth ; and I am withered like grass.*

Here the prophet repeateth the apparent sad consequence and effect of his own and the church's affliction; he and the church of the Jews now in captivity, were like to be cut off without comfort or hope of deliverance. Whence learn, 1. Not only the visible face of a church, but also the scattered parts thereof, may be near to disappearing, and to utter decaying under long continued trouble : *my days are like a shadow that declineth ; and I am withered like grass.* 2. The miseries of the godly, and the extreme danger of the church, being laid forth before God, are good arguments of hope that God shall shortly help; for therefore is it repeated, and laid down here for the last part of pouring out his soul : *my days are like a shadow that declineth ; and I am withered like grass.*

12. *But thou, O Lord, shalt endure for ever, and thy remembrance unto all generations.*

In the second part of the psalm, he striveth to comfort himself, in the hope of grace to be shown to the church, by seven arguments. The first is, because God hath purposed to perpetuate the memorial of himself unto all generations, and endureth for ever to see it done. Whence learn, 1. There is ground of hope to believers in the saddest condition of the church; for albeit believers be mortal, yet God in whom their life is hid, is eternal : *but thou, O Lord, shalt endure for ever.* 2. Because God will have his

name known in all generations, and will have his word and
ordinances of religion made use of among men, for preserving the memory of his attributes, works, and will, therefore the church must continue from age to age: *thou shalt
endure for ever, and thy remembrance unto all generations.*

13. *Thou shalt arise,* and *have mercy upon Zion :
for the time to favour her, yea, the set time, is come.*

The second argument of hope, that God will shortly have
mercy on his church, is, because the time of the seventy
years set for their captivity, was now almost expired. Whence
learn, 1. It is good reasoning from God's unchangeableness,
to conclude a change of the sad condition of the church
afflicted, from a worse unto a better: *thou shalt endure
for ever,* and therefore, *thou shalt arise, and have mercy
upon Zion.* 2. As the Lord hath set times for exercising
his people with affliction; so also he hath set times for comforting them again: and when these times are come, God
will have mercy on them whom he hath afflicted: *thou
shalt arise and have mercy upon Zion; for the set time
to favour her, yea, the set time, is come.*

14. *For thy servants take pleasure in her stones,
and favour the dust thereof.*

The third argument is, because the Lord's people had a
great desire to re-build the temple, lying now ruined.
Whence learn, 1. It is no new thing to see the outward face
of religion, and holy ordinances defaced; for the temple of
Jerusalem is here lying in the dust of a ruinous heap. 2.
The ordinances of religion shall not be utterly abolished,
but so much thereof shall be preserved, as may serve for
the furtherance of reformation, and re-edification of his
church, in God's appointed time; as here the temple is ruined; but there are *stones* reserved for a new building. 3.
When the ordinances of God are at the lowest, and most
deformed in the eyes of the world, they are and should be
most lovely, and looked upon with most estimation and affection by God's people : *thy servants take pleasure in
her stones, and favour the dust thereof.* 4. It is a good
ground of hope that God will shortly repair the ruins of
religion, when he provides builders, and putteth into their

hearts a love to set upon the work of reformation, as the psalmist's reasoning here teacheth us.

15. *So the heathen shall fear the name of the Lord, and all the kings of the earth thy glory.*

The fourth argument of hope is, from the promised conversion of the Gentiles, to whom the true religion was to be transmitted in God's own time, by the means of restoring the church of the Jews to their wonted privilege. Whence learn, 1. The enlargement of the knowledge and fear of God among them that know him not, should be the aim and encouragement of zealous reformers, to use all means which may conduce to reformation; for so much are we taught in the psalmist's example, desiring the restoration of the church of the Jews, that the Gentiles might be brought in; and by the hope of the conversion of the Gentiles, giving hope of restoration to the scattered church of the Jews: for, *so the heathen shall fear thy name*, is the reasoning of the psalmist. 2. When the Lord is pleased to arise, for restoring his afflicted people to comfort, and religion to its own beauty, he can work so as kings shall fear and tremble, to see God's care of his own despised people; for so, saith he, *the heathen shall fear thy name, and all the kings of the earth thy glory.*

16. *When the Lord shall build up Zion, he shall appear in his glory.*

The fifth argument of hope is, from the glory which God should have in restoring his church. Whence learn, 1. Whatsoever instruments the Lord useth in the gathering of his church, he will have himself seen to be the builder thereof; for it is the Lord here, *that shall build up Zion.* 2. As the glory of the Lord is obscured when his church is scattered; so when he sets up his own ordinances again, his glory appeareth, yea, and that more than if his church had not been scattered: *when the Lord shall build up Zion, he shall appear in glory.* 3. The connexion of God's glory with the salvation of his church, is a comfortable ground of hope, that, howsoever the church be demolished, yet it shall be restored and repaired again: for, *when the Lord shall build up Zion, he shall appear in glory*, importeth so much.

17. *He will regard the prayer of the destitute, and not despise their prayer.*

The sixth argument of hope is, from the Lord's respect to the prayers of his people. Whence learn, 1. The Lord's people reckon themselves destitute and desolate, when they have not the face of a church, and want the public ordinances of religion, which are the tokens of the Lord's presence among them : for, especially in relation to their scattering from Jerusalem and the temple, the psalmist here calleth them destitute or desolate. 2. When the Lord's people are scattered one from another, they can trust one another, and meet together at the throne of grace, by their prayer presented before God, as here the faithful scattered in captivity, meet in a joint petition for the building up of Zion; the destitute have their prayer put up in God's hearing : *he will regard the prayer of the destitute.* 3. Albeit the Lord's people be desolate and destitute of all earthly comfort and help, and be despised by the world, yet their persons and prayer are in estimation with God : *he will regard the prayer of the destitute, and not despise their prayer.*

18. *This shall be written for the generation to come : and the people which shall be created shall praise the Lord.*

19. *For he hath looked down from the height of his sanctuary ; from heaven did the Lord behold the earth ;*

20. *To hear the groaning of the prisoner; to loose those that are appointed to death ;*

21. *To declare the name of the Lord in Zion, and his praise in Jerusalem ;*

22. *When the people are gathered together, and the kingdoms, to serve the Lord.*

The seventh argument of hope to be heard, is, from the assurance, that as their calamity was foretold in Scripture, so their delivery promised should be recorded in Scripture also, to the praise of God, to the edification and consolation of the church of God in their solemn meetings, in whatsoever kingdoms they lived. Whence learn, 1. The more glory we foresee shall come to God by the granting of our prayers, the more confidence may we conceive to have our petition granted, as the psalmist's example teacheth us. 2. God hath so provided, that the exercise and experience of the church, in former times, should serve to manifest his glory, and edify posterity in after times: *this shall be written for the generation to come.* 3. The Lord hath determined by holy Scripture to propagate true religion, whereby he may be glorified, and his church edified, from generation to generation: *this shall be written for the generation to come.* 4. The gathering together again of a scattered church, the conversion of more sinners, and drawing them into the church, and the perpetuation of the church from age to age, is a creation or work of the omnipotent Creator: *the people which shall be created shall praise the Lord.* 5. The Lord should be praised, as for all his work, so in special for the delivery of his church; and praised not only by them who see his present work, and are partakers in their own persons of the gift, but also by all them that shall hear of the delivery in after times: *the people which shall be created shall praise the Lord.* 6. The Lord so maketh manifest his particular and active providence about his people, that all ages shall acknowledge his care for them; for posterity shall say, *he hath looked down from the height of his sanctuary, &c.* 7. Howsoever the Lord speak of his dwelling in his sanctuary, or in his church here on earth, yet must we conceive none but heavenly thoughts of him, as present at once both in heaven and earth, to hear and see the condition and carriage of every one: *he looked down from the height of his sanctuary, from heaven did the Lord behold the earth, to hear, &c.* 8. The Lord's heavenly majesty doth not hinder him to humble himself to behold even the most contemptible things upon the earth, but rather he will thus raise his praise among men: *from heaven did the Lord behold the earth, to hear the groaning of the prisoner.* 9. Albeit the Lord's people may be prisoners, and put to silence among men; yet their sighs and groans have a loud speech in the ears of the Lord: *he beholdeth the earth, to hear the groans of the prisoner.* 10. Albeit the Lord suffer his children to be imprisoned and condemned to die, yet he can interpose himself (if he please) for their delivery, before the purpose of their enemies be executed: *he beholdeth the earth, to loose those that are appointed to death.*

11. The end both of the sufferings and deliverances of the saints is the glorifying of God: and as their danger groweth, so the matter of God's praise in doing for them groweth up also : *for he beholds the earth, to hear the sighs of the prisoner, and to loose them that are appointed to death; to declare the name of the Lord in Zion, and his praise in Jerusalem.* 12. The time of glorifying God for his works done for the church of the Jews, is in a special manner to be under the gospel, in the assemblies of the churches of the Gentiles : for, *he loosed those that were appointed to death, to declare the name of the Lord in Zion, when the people are gathered together, and the kingdoms to serve the Lord :* that is, in the time when Christ shall make the kingdoms of the earth subject to him.

23. *He weakened my strength in the way; he short-ened my days.*

The third part of the psalm, wherein the prophet declareth the cause of his sorrow, v. 23; and his wrestling against it, v. 24—27; and his victory over the temptation, v. 28. As for the first, the prophet compareth the case of the church unto his own personal condition; for as he, in the flower of his age, was like to die by reason of grief for the church, so was the church like to perish in their captivity, and not to go on unto the hoped-for coming of the Messiah, and calling in of the Gentiles, which was necessary for the perpetuation of the church unto the end of the world. Whence learn, 1. There is such a strait union between the church of one age and another, that the whole church is as one man—the church of the Jews is as one Israel—and there is such a union between the church and every member thereof, that every member may and should take and esteem the condition of the church as his own personal condition, and may speak of it so, especially if he be the mouth of the body, a prophet or minister of the corporation of the church; for so much the prophet's example here teacheth us. 2. The church of Israel, from Abraham forward, was like a man entered on his journey, and, as it were by so many steps, from one generation to another, walking on to the coming and receiving of Jesus Christ, the promised Messiah, who was to come of them, as the form of speech here, borrowed from a wayfaring man, giveth us to understand. 3. When the Lord scattered the ten tribes, and after that also led into captivity the other two to Babylon, it seemed unto Israel a stopping of them from going on their appointed journey to the coming of Christ, and a making the tribe of Judah so weak as there was no appearance of the possibility of their endurance, or making progress to their desired end; for so much is imported in the words of the prophet, taking on the person of Israel: *he weakened my strength in the way.* 4. Yea, there was fear of cutting off that tribe, and of the abolishing of Israel, and that the Messiah coming of them should not appear—and this was the exercise of the church scattered in the Babylonish captivity—and the fear and the temptation wherewith the church and the prophet, about the end of the captivity, were wrestling, as is expressed in these words, *he shortened my days;* that is, to appearance, saith Israel by the prophet's mouth, I was cut off from being as a church or tribe, for any such use as I expected.   5. The desire after Christ and communion with him which the church and every believer have, is like the longing which a man hath to be at his journey's end, and the impediments which seem to hinder their communion with him are like the taking away of their life from them : *he hath shortened my days*, saith Israel.

24. *I said, O my God, take me not away in the midst of my days : thy years* are *throughout all generations.*

25. *Of old hast thou laid the foundation of the earth ; and the heavens* are *the work of thy hands.*

26. *They shall perish, but thou shalt endure; yea, all of them shall wax old like a garment : as a vesture shalt thou change them, and they shall be changed :*

27. *But thou* art *the same, and thy years shall have no end.*

Against this temptation the church, or the prophet in the church's name, wrestleth in prayer, and strengtheneth his faith by sundry arguments taken from God's, to wit, Christ's eternity, omnipotency, and immutability, Heb. i. 11, 12.   Whence learn, 1. The church, and any member thereof, may possibly sometimes be put in fear of being cut off before they can attain their desired end : as here, *take me not away in the midst of my days*, importeth.   2. Faith taketh God for the party to deal with, whatsoever strait it shall be brought into; God is the doer of what is done, saith the believer, and so he dealeth with God by prayer for relief : *I said, O God, take me not away.* 3. Appearance of perishing should not hinder us to pray, but sharpen us rather in our duty, and when God's promises and his dispensation seem to disagree, we may press the covenant, and not displease God by so doing : *I said, O my God, take me not away, &c.* 4. The eternity of Christ is the consolation of the believer in his mortality; and the eternity of Christ, as God, is the pledge of his preservation, and of the performance of God's promises unto him : *thy years are throughout all generations.* 5. The omnipotency of God, even Christ, which may be seen in the works of creation, is a rock for the believer who is in covenant with God to rest upon; for what can He not do who hath made all things of nothing? *of old hast thou laid the foundation of the earth, and the heavens are the work of thy hands.* 6. The immutability of God is a notable comfort to his afflicted people, who, because he is not changed, shall therefore not be consumed : *heaven and earth shall perish, but thou shalt endure, &c., but thou art the same.* 7. As the heavens and the earth are subject to vanity on man's account, and so, in regard of the condition wherein they are now, shall perish; so also they shall not simply and altogether perish, but be changed as a garment for man's cause, Rom. viii. 2 : *they all shall wax old as doth a garment ; and as a vesture shalt thou fold them up, and they shall be changed : but thou art the same, and thy years shall not fail,* Heb. i. 11, 12, which refers to Christ.

28. *The children of thy servants shall continue, and their seed shall be established before thee.*

Here is his victory over the temptation, and a solid assurance of the perpetuity of the church, from one generation to another, grounded upon the foresaid attributes of Christ. Whence learn, 1. He that is sorry for the affliction of the church shall have consolation from God, and a gracious answer to his prayer, as the experience of the prophet here teacheth us. 2. The perpetuity of the church and establishing of it may be solidly concluded from the unchangeableness and eternity of God, for thus the prophet reasoneth. 3. The church shall never be barren, but from age to age

AA

bring forth children unto God : *the children of thy servants shall continue, and their seed.* 4. The true members of the church are not the children of the flesh simply, but the children of the same faith and obedience with the godly teachers and servants of God; for so are they who have the promises here described : *the children of thy servants shall continue.* 5. Whatsoever change may befall the visible church before the world, yet before God she is fixed and stable, as a house built upon a rock : *the seed of thy servants shall be established before thee.*

PSALM CIII.

A psalm of David.

This is a psalm of praise and thanksgiving to God for his grace to his people, wherein the believer stirreth up himself, and, by his own example, others also, to praise God, ver. 1, 2; and that for seventeen reasons or arguments of praise: some of them taken from mercies shown to himself, some from mercies to all believers, and some taken from his sovereign dominion over all, unto ver. 20. And in the last three verses there is an exhortation to all the creatures to join in God's praises with the prophet.

1. *Bless the Lord, O my soul; and all that is within me,* bless *his holy name.*

2. *Bless the Lord, O my soul, and forget not all his benefits:*

In the prophet's stirring up of himself to praise God, learn, 1. The sense of God's goodness to a believer is very blessedness felt, flowing from God the fountain and cause of blessedness : *bless the Lord, O my soul.* 2. When a believer is satisfied with God's goodness, he cannot satisfy himself in the expression of his sense of it, or of his discharge of thankfulness for it; but stirreth up his own dull spirit to the work of praise : *bless the Lord, O my soul.* 3. In praising God special care is to be had of the sincerity of our heart and affections : *all that is within me, bless his holy name.* 4. Whatsoever is said of God will be found really to be true of him, and the believer will subscribe unto the unstained glory of his name, and may say, *all that is within me, bless his holy name.* 5. Albeit we obtain not of our heart at first what we would, yet must we still insist on the stirring up of the grace of God in us for any service we are about: *bless the Lord, O my soul,* saith he the second time. 6. God hath put so many obligations upon

every believer as may furnish reasons of praise and thanksgiving : *bless the Lord, O my soul, and forget not all his
benefits.* 7. As oblivion is always unthankful, so the remembrance of what the Lord hath bestowed upon us, with
a due estimation of the meanest benefit, is a point of upright thankfulness : *bless the Lord, O my soul, and forget not all his benefits ;* that is, forget not any of his
benefits, as the form of speech in the original importeth.

3. *Who forgiveth all thine iniquities; who healeth all
thy diseases ;*

The first reason of thanksgiving is for remission of sins;
the second reason is for healing, specially of spiritual maladies. Whence learn, 1. Saving grace bestowed upon us
should have the first room in our thanksgiving unto God,
because it is the evidence of God's special love to us; for
this the order of the prophet's thanksgiving teacheth us. 2.
The most holy of God's servants are not justified by their
good works, but by gracious remission of their evil works :
bless the Lord, who forgiveth thy iniquities. 3. The remission of sin is a perfect taking away of the guiltiness, not
of some only, but of all sins : *who forgiveth all thine iniquities.* 4. After remission of sin and justification of our
persons, there remain much inbred corruption, and many,
not only bodily, but also and especially, sinful infirmities,
diseases, and maladies of our souls, whereby we become unable to do the good which we would, or to eschew the evil
which we would not do; and of these diseases God becometh
a physician to heal them all, by his Spirit of sanctification
bestowed upon all whom he justifieth : *who healeth all thy
diseases.*

4. *Who redeemeth thy life from destruction ; who
crowneth thee with loving-kindness and tender mercies ;*

The third reason of thanksgiving is for delivering the
prophet graciously from perishing; and the fourth reason is
for giving unto him mercifully many good things. By *destruction* here, he meaneth not only the danger of being
killed by his enemies, but also, and especially, the state of
condemnation and perishing in God's wrath, from which the
man justified is redeemed by the Mediator. Whence learn,
1. The benefit of preservation from eternal death is given
unto the man to whom all iniquity is forgiven, for here these

benefits are joined the one with the other. 2. The deliverances which are given to believers, as well bodily as spiritual,
temporal as well as everlasting, come to us in the way of
redemption, made by our kind and faithful kinsman, Jesus
Christ : *who redeemeth thy life from destruction.* 3. A
man must be sensible of the merit of sin, and see himself in
the state of perdition for sin, before he can put a right estimation upon his delivery; he must count himself a lost man
till the LORD's Redeemer deliver him, as we may perceive
in the prophet, saying, *he hath redeemed thy life from
destruction.* 4. The favour which God bestoweth upon a
believer is not in giving him one or two, or some few evidences of his love and mercy, but in a constant compassing
of him on every hand, in every thing; so that, turn him
about to what act he will, he is encircled with love and
mercy, supplying wants, preventing, or mitigating and seasoning his troubles, reclaiming him from sin and directing
him in God's way : *who crowneth thee with loving-kindness and tender mercies.* 5. The evidences of God's kindness and mercy to a man are not only means to glorify God,
but also means to put respect and honour, yea, and a crown
of glory on the head of the believer, in the sight of all who
look upon him: therefore, saith he, *who crowneth thee
with loving-kindness and tender mercies.*

5. *Who satisfieth thy mouth with good* things; so
that *thy youth is renewed like the eagle's.*

The prophet's fifth reason of thanksgiving is not only for
God's blessing the use of the creatures to him, but also,
and especially, for feeding him with spiritual food, and giving comfortable refreshments to his church, set forth under
the similitude of corporeal feeding upon dainties. The sixth
reason is for comforting his spirit, and reviving it in his
dead condition, as the eagle is revived and renewed after
casting her bill. Whence learn, 1. The blessing of God
upon the believer makes the use of God's benefits, and his
ordinary meals and morsels, savoury and sweet, because he
hath all that is given to him with God's allowance and good-
will : *who satisfieth thy mouth with good things.* 2. The
Lord, after spiritual hunger and thirst, giveth such satisfaction to the soul of the believer as banquet-cheer and dainties
give to a hungry and thirsty man, as the similitude here

showeth: *who satisfieth thy mouth with good things.* 3.
As the eagle decayeth and groweth lean when her bill, or
beak, groweth so long and crooked that she cannot eat for
it, and when she casteth her bill, and her beak is now fitted
better to take her food, then she is revived and strengthened, and, as it were, groweth young again; so fareth it
with the soul of the believer, which sometimes is so exercised and troubled, as it refuseth comfort, and lieth in a
dead condition; but when the Lord reneweth the sense of
his love it is a new life, and the inner man is revived again :
thy youth is renewed as the eagle. 4. It is an act of
thanksgiving to God to give account to ourselves, and to
reckon over to our own souls what the Lord hath bestowed
on us and done for us, as appeareth in the prophet's practice here, speaking all this to his own soul in reckoning over
the benefits.

6. *The Lord executeth righteousness and judgment
for all* that are *oppressed.*

The prophet goeth on in his thanksgiving, and ascendeth
from the mercies shown to himself to the praising of God's
righteousness and mercifulness toward all believers, as well
as toward himself, according as every one's need requireth :
and here is the seventh reason of God's praise, for maintaining the cause of all his oppressed people. Whence learn,
1. The sight of God's goodness towards ourselves should
lead us to the observation of God's goodness to all his children in common, and unto his righteous, holy, and gracious
nature, as the example of the psalmist teacheth us. 2. As
to be oppressed was not David's lot alone, but is the common condition whereunto the godly in all ages are subject;
so, to have God the defender and the avenger of those that
oppress them was not the privilege of David alone, but common to him and all God's children : *for the Lord executeth
righteousness and judgment for all that are oppressed.*

7. *He made known his ways unto Moses, his acts
unto the children of Israel.*

The eighth reason of God's praise is, for revealing his
will and works to his prophet Moses, and to the people of
Israel. Whence learn, 1. The knowledge of God's will, of
his way of dealing with men, and of his works, are mysteries
which men cannot understand till the Lord reveal all to

them : *it is he who maketh his ways known.* 2. As God
hath the choosing of people to whom, so also of the men
by whom, he will reveal himself and his ways : *he made
known his ways unto Moses, his acts to the children of
Israel.* 3. As the revealing of God's way wherein he will
walk with us, and of his way wherein he will have us to
walk before him, is no small mercy to his church; so is it
no small obligation put upon his people, and matter of
praise and thanks unto God; for this is made here the matter of the church's thanks and God's praise, *that he made
known his ways to Moses,* and made Israel to see that he
wrought as he had spoken: *he made known his acts to
the children of Israel.*

8. *The Lord* is *merciful and gracious, slow to anger, and plenteous in mercy.*

The ninth reason of God's praise is, for his merciful and
gracious nature expressed in sundry titles. Whence learn,
1. The Lord is compassionate to us in our mercies, and
ready to pardon our sins : *the Lord is merciful.* 2. The
Lord is not hindered by our unworthiness to do us good,
when we come unto him, but is ready to show favour to
such as acknowledge themselves to be unworthy, and seek
nothing but of his free love: *the Lord is gracious.* 3. The
Lord easily letteth not forth the evidence of his anger, even
when he is provoked : *he is slow to anger.* 4. Even in
wrath he remembereth mercy, and letteth not forth the effects of his wrath in full measure, but tempereth his chastisements so as we may endure them, and mixeth mitiga-
tions in the most bitter cups : *he is plenteous in mercy.*

9. *He will not always chide; neither will he keep
his anger for ever.*

The tenth reason of praise is, for the short continuance
of the effects of his wrath. Whence learn, 1. Albeit the
Lord be ready to live as a reconciled God and father with
us his children, yet we are given to strife, and frequently
offend and grieve him, and give reason to him to rebuke
us, as his *not chiding* of us importeth. 2. When he hath
debated his controversy by words, and by the rod, and hath
made our conscience challenge and chide us, he prolongeth
not the controversy: *he will not always chide.* 3. Albeit
the tokens of God's anger endure longer than we would,

yet shall they be removed at length: he will not pursue his quarrel further than our real humiliation : *neither will he keep his anger for ever.*

10. *He hath not dealt with us after our sins, nor rewarded us according to our iniquities.*

The eleventh reason of God's praise is, for the common experience which the saints have had already of his mercy. Whence learn, 1. What the word saith of God's grace, mercy, long-suffering, and other titles of his goodness, the common experience of his children, yea, and of all the members of the visible church, may bear witness unto : *he hath not dealt with us after our sins.* 2. The felt mercies of the Lord should not extenuate our sins, but rather make us aggravate our faults, and weigh our misdeservings in the balance of the sanctuary; for, not by the weight of judgments, (which ofttimes are laid aside, or are gently inflicted,) but by the word must we judge of our iniquities : *for he hath not rewarded us according to our iniquities.*

11. *For as the heaven is high above the earth,* so *great is his mercy toward them that fear him.*

The twelfth reason of God's praise is, for the unmeasurableness of his mercy towards his servants, compared with the unmeasurable height of the heaven above the earth. Whence learn, 1. Our mind cannot find out a comparison too large for expressing the superabundant mercy of the Lord toward his people : *for as the heaven is high above the earth, so great is his mercy toward them that fear him.* 2. Those are the children of God, who, howsoever they are not free of sin, yet they are careful to please God, and loth to offend him : they are persons *that fear him.* 3. The consolations of God, and the riches of his mercy, are not appointed to foster sin or security in any man, but to cherish the hearts of those that stand in awe to offend God, and study to please him : *great is his mercy to them that fear him.*

12. *As far as the east is from the west,* so *far hath he removed our transgressions from us.*

The thirteenth reason of God's praise is, for complete fullness of remission of sin unto the believer in him. Whence learn, 1. Albeit sins hinder our access unto God, yet they do not hinder God's approaching unto them on whom he will have mercy; for sin is not removed till Christ come to the sinner, as here is imported. 2. Remission of sin is a gift, full and complete, given by God unto every believer in Christ; and the guiltiness and debt of sin are so far and so fully removed, that it can never be imputed unto the believer, nor come near to hurt him: *as far as the east is from the west, so far hath he removed our transgressions from us.* Understand this of the believer, who doth not turn the grace of God into wantonness, but maketh use of grace to strengthen him in his battle against the body of sin in himself.

13. *Like as a father pitieth* his *children,* so *the Lord pitieth them that fear him.*

The fourteenth reason of God's praise is, for his fatherly pity toward all his weak children, who would heartily serve him better than they do. Whence learn, 1. The course of renewed pardon of sin, and daily removing of sin from the penitent believer, floweth from the Lord's adopting believers to be his children, as the similitude taken from a father showeth unto us. 2. The love which nature teacheth a father to bear toward his obedient children, is but a shadow of the love of God to believers: *like as a father pitieth his children, so the Lord pitieth them that fear him.* 3. As none of the Lord's children want their own infirmities, shortcomings in duties, and fallings into transgressions, so all of them are looked on by God in as tender pity as ever father showed to children: *like as a father pitieth his children, so the Lord pitieth them that fear him.* Understand this of such as esteem their sinful inclination their greatest misery.

14. *For he knoweth our frame ; he remembereth that we* are *dust.*

The fifteenth reason of God's praise is, his discretion in moderating his dealing with us, so as our weakness may bear; and this reason serveth to clear and confirm the former. Whence learn, 1. There is no more strength in man of himself than there is in the matter he was made of : *we are but dust.* 2. The Lord knoweth our weakness perfectly, and what we are able to endure : *he knoweth our frame,* what stuff we are made of, and how frail our natural constitution is. 3. It is not for any worthiness in us that God dealeth gently with us, but out of his own goodness, free love, and pity : *he pitieth them that fear him, for he knoweth our frame.*

15. As for *man, his days* are *as grass ; as a flower of the field, so he flourisheth :*

16. *For the wind passeth over it, and it is gone; and the place thereof shall know it no more.*

17. *But the mercy of the Lord* is *from everlasting to everlasting upon them that fear him, and his righteousness unto children's children ;*

18. *To such as keep his covenant, and to those that remember his commandments to do them.*

The sixteenth reason of God's praise is, for his everlasting mercy, and constant fidelity in performing whatsoever he hath promised to every sincere believer. Whence learn, 1. All the glory of man in his natural condition, when he is adorned at the best with learning, wisdom, beauty, strength, riches, honour, and whatsoever other ornaments he can have, is but like the glory of grass and flowers, which are very tender, and subject to many hazards, and easily broken down or blasted; and albeit no harm should come to them from without, yet of themselves they endure but a very short season, and then fade away : *as for man, his days are as grass, as a flower of the field so he flourisheth ; for the wind passeth over it, and it is gone, &c.* 2. Human infirmities, and mortality serve indeed to humble a man, but do not hinder the humbled man to come and receive of God complete mercy, that is, pardon of sins, supply of all wants, and life everlasting : *man's days are as a flower, the wind goeth over it, and it is gone, and the place thereof shall know it no more ; but the mercy of the Lord is from everlasting to everlasting.* 3. The true believer and the heir of the promises, is he who, in his greatest confidence in God's everlasting mercy, standeth in awe to offend God : *the mercy of the Lord is upon them that fear him.* 4. As mercy is decreed and prepared before the beginning of the world, for the believer who feareth God, so is it let forth in actual application unto him in this life, and for evermore after this life is gone: *the mercy of the Lord is from everlasting to everlasting to them that fear him.* 5. Such as out of love to God are loth to offend him, and out of faith in God's mercy study to please him, shall have justice to be their friend, to themselves and to their children who follow their footsteps, from one generation to another: the Lord's righteousness shall be for them, and not against them; all that is promised to the saints shall be done to them, and for them: *his righteousness shall be unto his children's children.* 6. As God hath given the offer of his grace by covenant, for reconciliation of enemies, so hath he given his law and commandments for a rule to lead the reconciled man unto salvation, and he only is the heir of the promise of everlasting mercy and righteousness, who studieth to prove the sincerity of his faith, by his endeavouring of obedience: for the promise here is made *to such as keep his covenants, and to those that remember his commandments to do them.*

19. *The Lord hath prepared his throne in the heavens; and his kingdom ruleth over all.*

The last reason of God's praise is, his universal dominion over all the creatures, whereby a strong obligation is put upon angels and men to glorify him. Whence learn, 1. What God giveth to believers he is able to preserve to them; what he promiseth he is able to perform to them; whatsoever power in earth or in hell be against them, he is able to defend his church and every member of it: *the Lord hath prepared his throne in heaven.* 2. Whatsoever praise we owe to God for benefits which we have received from him, fewer or more, greater or less, we must remember to praise him also for his glorious and great majesty, and transcendent excellency over all the creatures: *he hath established his throne in heaven, and his dominion is over all.* 3. Whatsoever confusions appear on earth, whatsoever revolutions fall in church or state, whatsoever hardships God's children meet with, God guideth the whole business very orderly and well, and performeth all his own good pleasure: *his kingdom ruleth over all.*

20. *Bless the Lord, ye his angels, that excel in strength, that do his commandments, hearkening unto the voice of his word.*

21. *Bless ye the Lord, all ye his hosts; ye ministers of his, that do his pleasure.*

22. *Bless the Lord, all his works, in all places of his dominion: bless the Lord, O my soul.*

In the last three verses, the prophet inviteth angels, and men, and all creatures to join with his soul in praising God. True it is, that the angels need not be exhorted to bless God, and many of the Lord's hosts and works are not capable of our exhortations ; yet this form of speech signifieth, that all of them in their own kind, and materially at least, show forth the blessedness of God; and that if they were all endued with reason, able and fitted formally, expressly, and directly to glorify God, they were all too few for the work, and could not, either severally or jointly, glorify the Lord, as his deserving is. Whence learn, 1. The weight of the offering of praise unto God, is too heavy for men to lift, and as for angels, it will take up all their strength, and their best abilities to go about it : *bless the Lord, ye his angels that excel in strength.* 2. It is the commendation of angels, that they obey all God's commands readily, and we should follow their example, and aim at their perfection in service, that the will of God may be done on earth, as it is in heaven : *for they do his commandments, hearkening to the voice of his word.* 3. All the several ranks of creatures, are so many mustered hosts, ready to execute all God's judgments, as they are directed; and are always in their kind setting forth on all hands, the glory and goodness of God : *bless the Lord, all ye his hosts.* 4. The family of believers, the servants of the Lord, who know his will, and study to do it; and in special, his ministers in the church, servants in state, pastors and teachers of God's people, have a special obligation lying on them to bless the Lord, who has intrusted them in his service, and made them do his will : *bless the Lord, ye ministers of his that do his pleasure* 5. There is none of God's works in any part of the world; nothing which his hands hath made, how base and mean soever it may seem, which contributeth not matter to the song of God's praise, and furnisheth not reasons to glorify and bless the maker : *bless ye the Lord, all his works, in all places of his dominion.* 6. When the believer looketh on all the creatures in their own kind, as contributors to glorify God, he shall find his own particular obligation for special mercies bestowed on himself, calling for particular praise and thanks at his hands; as David doth here, who, when he had set all the creatures on work to bless God, concluded thus; *bless the Lord, O my soul.*

PSALM CIV.

As in the former psalm, the prophet stirred up himself, and all others to glorify God, specially for the works of grace; so here he stirreth up himself and others to glorify God, specially for the works of creation and providence. And, in the first place, he showeth the scope of all the psalm, v. 1. In the second place, he bringeth arguments for pressing the duty of praising God, from the first day's work of creation, to wit, the light; from the second day's work in spreading forth the heavens, v. 2—4; from the third day's work of bringing forth the earth, the sea, the floods, and plants, for the use of man and beast, which were the work of the sixth day, v. 5—18; from the works of the fourth day, sun and moon, v. 19—24; and from the works of the fifth day, fishes greater and smaller, v. 25, 26. In the third place, he bringeth arguments of God's praise, from the preservation, specially of living creatures, v. 27—30. In the fourth place, is the conclusion of the psalm, with some further reasons for praising God, v. 31—35.

1. *Bless the Lord, O my soul. O Lord my God, thou art very great; thou art clothed with honour and majesty:*

Here is the scope of the whole psalm, wherein he stirreth up his own soul, and, by his own example, all others that have ears to hear, to glorify our God for his greatness and majesty, manifested in his works of creation and providence. Whence learn, 1. The Lord is to be praised by his children, not only for benefits bestowed upon them, but also for his own glorious majesty and greatness; not only is he to be praised for the works of redemption and grace to his elect children, but also for the works of creation and what he hath bestowed upon the creatures, as this psalm compared with the former teacheth us. 2. Because men have ofttimes the words of praise in their mouth, and care little to have their affection suitable to the work in their hand; therefore when we go about to praise God, we should stir up our spirits unto a religious disposition, as David doth here, saying, *bless the Lord, O my soul.* 3. When we go about the work of God's praise, we should consider his majesty, how great he is, and worthy to be praised: *O Lord, thou art very great.* 4. The heart is best fitted

for God's praises, when the soul that is about the work of
praise, apprehendeth its interest in God, and looketh upon
him as reconciled, and in covenant with itself: *O Lord my
God, thou art very great.* 5. The praises of God depend
not upon the man that praiseth him, but are fixed in God, and
flow forth from himself so clearly, that none can be excused
for ingratitude, who do not acknowledge his glory: *thou
art clothed with honour and majesty.* 6. Albeit God be
invisible, and unsearchable; yet his honour and majesty may
be seen in his works, which are as a garment, both to hide
him in one respect, and hold him forth in another to be seen:
thou art clothed with honour and majesty.

2. *Who coverest* thyself *with light as* with *a garment; who stretchest out the heavens like a curtain;*

3. *Who layeth the beams of his chambers in the waters; who maketh the clouds his chariot; who walketh
upon the wings of the wind;*

4. *Who maketh his angels spirits; his ministers a
flaming fire.*

In the second place are set down the arguments for praising God, taken from the works of creation, such as were
wrought the first and second day, whereof only so much is
spoken as may lead us to what more is said thereof in the history written by Moses. Whence learn, 1. The works of
creation, besides their natural use, serve for spiritual uses
also; to wit, to furnish unto us the knowledge of God, to
edify us in faith, and stir us up to glorify the maker, as
here appeareth. 2. Among all the sensible creatures
of God, the creation of the light hath the first place, for
manifestation of his glory; whether we look unto the brightness and admirable purity of it, which cannot be polluted by any filthiness whereupon it shines, or the use it
hath in operation upon, and setting forth of, the beauty of
the rest of the creatures; therefore he beginneth at it here.
3. Our thoughts of God should be higher, larger, more
purified from bodily apprehensions and all imperfections,
than our thoughts of created light are, when we look upon
the light illuminating all the world at once; for as the garment of a king showeth his majesty, and yet is no part of
his substance or essence, and in its nature is much inferior

to his worth; so is the light nothing but God's creature, serving to show forth his glory, and is infinitely inferior to him, *who covereth himself with light, as a garment.* 4. As light filling the world, is nothing but as the garment of the glorious Creator, manifesting himself within the compass of the world to his creatures; so the heavens in their largest circle, are but the canopy cast about the seat of a king: *for he stretcheth out the heavens like a curtain.* 5. This world is like a stately house, which is divided into upper or lower rooms, by joists, beams, and planks put between the lower rooms and the higher, and the firmament sustaining the clouds, is the first division : *who layeth the beams of his chambers in the waters ;* or in the second region of the air where the waters in the clouds are gathered, and stored up as it were in their distinct chambers, for the several uses which God hath for them. 6. As the glory of kings is to be seen when they go in coaches with their train following them, or when they ride on horseback with their followers attending them; so is the glory of the Lord seen, when he maketh the weighty clouds, having in them floods of water, to move from place to place, as chariots above our heads, and not fall down at once: *he maketh the clouds his chariot.* 7. The swift and unperceivable motion of the winds, being raised by God, from all parts in all places of the world, serveth as a shadow to point out the everywhere presence of God, *who walketh upon the wings of the wind.* 8. The angels are the Lord's creatures, and serve him at his pleasure, as the winds and flaming fire do, swiftly going where he commandeth them, and in the fervour of their love to him, despatching every business committed to them : *who maketh his angels spirits, and his ministers a flame of fire.* 9. Great and glorious must our Lord Jesus be, who is the Creator and Lord of angels, *and maketh his angels spirits.*

5. Who *laid the foundations of the earth*, that *it should not be removed for ever.*

6. *Thou coveredst it with the deep as* with *a garment: the waters stood above the mountains.*

7. *At thy rebuke they fled ; at the voice of thy thunder they hasted away.*

8. *They go up by the mountains; they go down by*

the valleys unto the place which thou hast founded for them.

9. *Thou hast set a bound that they may not pass over ; that they turn not again to cover the earth.*

From this to the 19th verse, he describeth the third day's work of the creation, prepared for the use of man and beast, which were the sixth day's work. The preparation of the dwelling-house of man and beast, and other living creatures above the earth, is set down in these five verses. Whence learn, 1. The settling of the earth in a like distance on all hands from the circle of heaven, compassing it round about, and hanging of the earth in the midst of the globe, and fixing it by his sole command, where it is now fixed, declareth the unsearchable power of God, and glory of his workmanship : *he laid the foundations of the earth, that it should not be moved for ever.* 2. The natural place of the element of water is to be above all the earth on all parts round about : *he covereth the earth with the deep as a garment, and the waters stood above the mountains.* 3. That a dwelling-house might be fitted and prepared for man not as yet created, the Lord by his powerful command, made the waters go off so much of the earth as might serve for man's use; and straightway, as if the waters had been driven and chased, they ran away hastily from off the bounds allotted to them as it were terrified at the thundering, imperious, and effectual command of God : *at thy rebuke they fled, at the voice of thy thunder they hasted away.* 4. If a man had been present when God commanded the seas to retreat from the earth, he might have seen both a terrible and a joyful spectacle of a wonderfully hasty chase and flight of the waters running fiercely over the mountains, and when no more mountains were in their way, gliding down through the valleys into the place wherein they are now : *they go up by the mountains, they go down by the valleys, unto the place which thou hast founded for them.* 5. The waters of the sea, albeit they be higher than the earth, yet are they bound in the place wherein they are, that without command given to them from God, they may not pass over the bounds prescribed unto them, but stay within the sea-mark, and there lay down their proud boasting waves : *thou hast set a bound that they may not pass over, that they turn not again to cover the earth :* which they would infallibly do by their own natural motion, if this miraculous standing command were not constantly in force, as was to be seen in the flood of Noah, when the boundaries were loosed for a year, till God executed vengeance on the wicked world, and thereafter they were sent back never to come again for such an universal judgment.

10. *He sendeth the springs into the valleys,* which *run among the hills.*

11. *They give drink to every beast of the field : the wild asses quench their thirst.*

12. *By them shall the fowls of the heaven have their habitation,* which *sing among the branches.*

13. *He watereth the hills from his chambers : the earth is satisfied with the fruit of thy works.*

14. *He causeth the grass to grow for the cattle, and herb for the service of man : that he may bring forth food out of the earth ;*

15. *And wine* that *maketh glad the heart of man,* and *oil to make* his *face to shine, and bread* which *strengtheneth man's heart.*

16. *The trees of the Lord are full* of sap ; *the cedars of Lebanon, which he hath planted ;*

17. *Where the₄ birds make their nests :* as for *the stork, the fir-trees* are *her house.*

18. *The high hills* are *a refuge for the wild goats,* and *the rocks for the conies.*

Thus the ground of man's habitation is swept; now here it is replenished and furnished with all necessaries serving for man's use, and to fowls and beasts for man's sake. Whence learn, 1. Because the use of fresh water was necessary for man, and necessary it was that man should have it nigh hand unto him, for the more commodious use, the Lord broke up wells of water in several places, and made brooks, and waters, and rivers, and floods, like veins in a man's body, to carry from them water along to all habitable places of the earth, where God had appointed men to dwell: *he sendeth the springs into the valleys, which run among the hills.* 2. Not only where men dwell, but also where men's ordinary resort is not, the Lord hath set drinking vessels full of water, for the use of travelling men, and other creatures appointed to attend man, and some way to serve his use: *he sendeth the springs into the valleys, which run among the hills.* 3. For the furnishing of man's house on earth, God hath provided him with parks for beasts to feed in, and trees for fowls and birds to live in, and ponds for fishes, as we will hear afterward; and these beasts, and fowls, and singing birds have their drinking vessels set for them : *they give drink to every beast of the field, the wild asses quench their thirst.* 4. The Lord hath adorned the habitation of man with trees, growing beside the waters, not only for his own proper use, but also for the use of fowls and singing birds : *by them shall the fowls of heaven have their habitation, which sing among the branches.* 5. Where wells and rivers are not, as in hills and high places it is seen for the most part, there the Lord supplieth the inlack of waters by rain from the clouds : *he watereth the hills from his chambers,* that is, from the clouds, wherein as in chambers he hath stored up great waters. 6. The Lord dissolveth not the clouds all at once, but by little and little maketh them distil smaller or greater drops only: *he watereth the hills from his chambers.* 7. There is no part of the earth whereupon God bestoweth not so much of the fruit of his operation, as may fill it full of his glory : *the earth is satisfied with the fruits of thy works.* 8. The grass and herbs, and the divers sorts of them, serving for the use of beasts and men, are worthy of a room in our meditation of God's provident care for man and beast : *he causeth the grass to grow for the cattle, and herbs for the service of man, that he may bring forth food out of the earth.* 9. The Lord's allowance for man is very large, not only for necessity, but also for delectation : for he hath provided *wine, and oil, and bread.* 10. The right use of God's creatures is not to surfeit, and bury the memory of God, and of the excellency of man above beasts, in gluttony and drunkenness; but to give him strength and gladness in such a measure as may encourage him cheerfully to serve his maker : *and wine that maketh glad the heart of man, and oil to make his face to shine, and bread which strengtheneth man's heart.* 11. God will have his excellency taken notice of in every thing which is great, notable, and excellent : upon which ground great trees are called here, *the trees of the Lord.* 12. The Lord hath furnished trees not only with so much sap as might make them grow, but also with so much sap as might serve man for meat and drink, and medicine, and other uses : *the trees of the Lord are full of sap.* 13. Among the trees, the Lord will have us take notice of the cedars, as of a special plant of his husbandry on the earth, for their height and greatness, and durableness of the timber, and namely of those of Lebanon, designed for the use of his people : of which he saith, *the cedars of Lebanon which he hath planted.* 14. It is worthy of our marking, that for the nests of birds he hath provided high trees, where they might breed and lodge, and bring forth their young more safely and securely: *where the birds make their nests : as for the stork, the fir-trees are her house.* 15. It is worthy of our observation for glorifying God, that God hath taught weak creatures naturally to draw themselves to strong defences, and sundry sorts of them to have their several sorts of refuge : *the high hills are a refuge for the wild goats, and the rocks for the conies.*

19. *He appointed the moon for seasons ; the sun knoweth his going down.*

20. *Thou makest darkness, and it is night; wherein all the beasts of the forest do creep* forth.

21. *The young lions roar after their prey, and seek their meat from God.*

22. *The sun ariseth, they gather themselves together, and lay them down in their dens.*

23. *Man goeth forth unto his work, and to his labour, until the evening.*

24. *O Lord, how manifold are thy works ! in wisdom hast thou made them all : the earth is full of thy riches.*

Here the psalmist bringeth arguments of praise from the works of creation on the fourth day, and showeth the uses thereof. Whence learn, 1. The mind of man is not able to overtake all God's works at once, whether in their number, or order, or properties, or uses, as the prophet's pitching upon some of them only teacheth us. 2. The making of two great lights, the sun and the moon, is worthy of our special observation; for, by them the glory of the rest of the works is much manifested : *he appointed the moon for seasons, &c.* 3. The making of two lights to move about the earth, the one to supply in a sort the other's absence, is a reason of God's praise: *he made the moon and the sun.* 4. The dividing of time into nights and days, and sundry seasons, that the continuance thereof might not be irksome unto man, but the more acceptable by their interchanges and vicissitudes, is a reason for magnifying God's wisdom and goodness to man : *he appointed the moon for seasons, the sun knoweth his going down.* 5. The Lord hath so wisely mixed the motion of the sun and moon, that a sweeter temper is not imaginable; for if their motion had been the same, and they moved near together, then the use of the moon had been less; if the moon had been always punctually opposite to the sun, then she would have been in a perpetual eclipse; if the course of the sun had not been complete once a-year, and the course of the moon once every month, the earth could not have had so great service of both : but *God hath appointed the moon for seasons, and the sun knoweth his going down ;* each of them exactly keeping their course as God hath ordained. 6. As God's wisdom and goodness are to be seen in the light, so also in the vicissitude of darkness between day and night; for darkness intervening between days maketh light every day a new gift, and darkness calleth man from his labour and travail unto rest, that he may be refreshed therewith, and with sleep : *thou makest darkness, and it is night.* 7. It is a remarkable providence, that ravenous beasts for the most part are kept in their dens all day, and not let loose for seeking their prey *till night, wherein all the beasts of the forest creep forth.* 8. None of the ravenous beasts find their prey till God bring it unto them: for *the young lions* for hunger *roar after their prey.* 9. The natural cries of the distressed creatures are in substance nature's prayer to its Maker for relief and help : *the young lions by their roaring seek their meat from God.* 10. It is a matter of praise to God, that the daylight is made a natural terror to cruel beasts, or that any measure of being feared by man is left in them : *the sun ariseth, they gather themselves together, and lay them down in their dens.* 11. It is the Lord's praise that he giveth daily new use of the light of the sun to man, that he may follow his work and business the better till the evening, and suffereth it to remain only so long a time as weak bodies may endure moderate travail: *man goeth forth to his work and labour until the evening.* 12. The more men meditate on God's works, the more do they find a bottomless deep, and the number and variety of them more and more unsearchable: *O Lord, how manifold are thy works !* Thus much may be learned of God's works, that they are all excellently well, and wisely wrought and ordered, and that the riches of God's bounty to man, and to the creatures, filleth all the earth: *in wisdom hast thou made them all, the earth is full of thy riches.*

25. So is *this great and wide sea, wherein* are *things creeping innumerable, both small and great beasts.*

26. *There go the ships;* there is *that leviathan,* whom *thou hast made to play therein.*

The prophet cometh now to the works of the fifth day, specially the furnishing of the sea as a fish-pond for man's use, and making it portable for ships to sail in. Whence learn, 1. The greatness and wideness of the sea, the ebbing and flowing thereof, the motion and saltness of it to keep it from rotting, speak the glory of God, no less than the ornament and rich furniture of the earth do: *for as the earth is full of riches, so is the great and wide sea.* 2. The diversity and number of great and small fishes in the sea, speak much of God's power, wisdom, and bounty: *wherein are things creeping innumerable, both small and great beasts.* 3. The making of the sea for the use of navigation, that men, who cannot fly nor swim, might the more commodiously keep commerce one with another in all parts of the world, is a point of God's praise: *there go the ships.* 4. Albeit all and every one of God's works set forth God's power, yet some of them do it more eminently than other some, for making men see God's glory the more in the rest, yea, and in the meanest of his works. Such, for example, are the elephant on earth, and the whale and other great monsters in the sea: *that leviathan whom thou hast made to play therein.*

27. *These wait all upon thee, that thou mayest give* them *their meat in due season.*

28. That *thou givest them they gather : thou openest thine hand, they are filled with good.*

29. *Thou hidest thy face, they are troubled: thou takest away their breath, they die, and return to their dust.*

30. *Thou sendest forth thy spirit, they are created; and thou renewest the face of the earth.*

In the third place, the prophet bringeth forth arguments of God's praise from the care the Lord hath of the preservation of his works, which most appeareth in the feeding of all living creatures, and propagation of the kind; for, when some of the kind are dying, from time to time, others are quickened and put in their room. Whence learn, 1. There is a natural instinct in all the living creatures in their want, to wait on God's providence, which men may observe in them; although the brute creatures know not this, and cannot reflect upon their own inclinations: for the psalmist, speaking of all living creatures no less than of the fishes, saith, *these all wait on thee, that thou mayest give them their meat.* 2. So long as God will have any creature to live, he provideth timously enough for its food : *they wait for thee, that thou mayest give them their meat in due season.* 3. God's providence reacheth to the least bit of food which any living creature meeteth with: *that thou givest them, they gather.* 4. The Lord is liberal in his dispensation, and feedeth all the creatures abundantly, so long as he will have them to live : *thou openest thy hand, they are filled with good.* 5. The Lord demonstrates himself to be the fountain of life, and that the living creatures hold their life of him, as well by the sickening and weakening of the living creatures, as by the feeding and strengthening of them. For when God withdraweth in any measure the wonted influence of his power from them, then they find a change to the worse : *thou hidest thy face from them, they are troubled.* 6. God hath no less special hand in removing life than in giving it : *thou takest away their breath, they die and return to their dust.* 7. Albeit the Lord taketh away the life of all individual living creatures, yet he preserveth the species and kind of every living creature, by making new ones, and raising them up in the room of those that are taken away: *thou sendest forth thy Spi-*

rit, they are created. 8. The same Spirit which created the world in the beginning, worketh yet powerfully in forming new creatures continually : *thou sendest out thy Spirit, they are created.* 9. The Lord puts a new face, as it were, upon the earth from time to time, partly by spring-time and summer every year, partly by young living creatures, in their several generations, one after another, and all these things contribute to his renewed praise : *thou renewest the face of the earth.*

31. *The glory of the Lord shall endure for ever : the Lord shall rejoice in his works.*

32. *He looketh on the earth, and it trembleth; he toucheth the hills, and they smoke.*

In the last place is the conclusion, wherein he addeth yet more reasons for praising God, and then maketh sundry uses of the former doctrine. He taketh up all that he would say, in this : that God shall have perpetual glory from the works of his goodness and power. Whence learn, 1. The end of all the workmanship of God is God's glory, and he is worthy of glory for his work, and shall not want his glory from his works for ever : *the glory of the Lord shall endure for ever.* 2. As the Lord saw all his work in the beginning to be good, so, in the closing thereof, he shall see all that he hath done to be good, and nothing properly to be repented of whatsoever he hath done : *the Lord shall rejoice in his works.* 3. As the Lord is bountiful to his creatures, so also is he terrible to the strongest of them, that he may be feared as well as loved and praised : *he looketh on the earth, and it trembleth ; he toucheth the hills, and they smoke.* 4. The signs of his terrible power which he hath actually manifested, in shaking the earth and kindling the mountains, bear witness how powerful and terrible the Lord is : *he looketh on the earth, and it trembleth ; he toucheth the hills, and they smoke.*

33. *I will sing unto the Lord as long as I live; I will sing praise to my God while I have my being.*

34. *My meditation of him shall be sweet; I will be glad in the Lord.*

35. *Let the sinners be consumed out of the earth, and let the wicked be no more. Bless thou the Lord, O my soul. Praise ye the Lord.*

Here the prophet setteth down the uses of this doctrine, which are five, teaching us so many doctrines. For the first use, here he bindeth upon himself an obligation joyfully to praise God for ever; teaching us to do the same when we consider the Lord's works: *I will sing unto the Lord so long as I live; I will sing praise to my God while I have my being.* 2. For the second use of this doctrine, he promiseth to himself joy and gladness in the discharge of the work of God's praise; which teacheth us how profitable it is to ourselves to praise God. Nothing more sweet to a believer than to be about the glorifying of God and beholding the matter of his praise : *my meditation of him shall be sweet : I will be glad in the Lord.* 3. For the third use, he denounceth wrath and destruction unto the contemners of God, who do not regard his glory, but stand out as common enemies of God and of all his workmanship; which teacheth us, that such as do not join with God's children in glorifying God, but go on in transgressing his commands and abusing his creatures, shall be separated from the society of God's servants; unto which judgment every believer must subscribe as very righteous : *let the sinners be consumed out of the earth, and let the wicked be no more.* 4. For the fourth use, he stirreth up himself to bless the Lord for his own particular case, who had found favour to be no more of the number of God's enemies but among the Lord's servants, whereby he teacheth those whom God has called from the state of sin unto his holy service, to stir up themselves to thanksgiving : *bless thou the Lord, O my soul.* 5. For the fifth use, he calleth upon all other believers and exhorteth them to praise God, and teacheth us that every one, according to his place, should stir up another unto the honouring of God : *praise ye the Lord.*

PSALM CV.

The first part of this psalm was sung at the carrying up of the ark of God to the city of David, 1 Chron. xvi. 8. The whole psalm containeth an exhortation to the church of Israel to praise God for his mercies shown towards them, with reasons serving to press the duty. The exhortation is set down, ver. 1—6. The reasons are more particularly expressed in the rest of the psalm : the first rank whereof is taken from the Lord's covenanting with Abraham, Isaac, and Jacob, and the care which the Lord had of their persons, ver. 7—15. The second rank is taken from the care the Lord had of their posterity, when he sent them down into Egypt, and all the while they were there, ver. 17—25. The third rank is taken from the manner of their delivery out of Egypt, when they were oppressed, and from the plaguing of the Egyptians for their sake, ver. 26—37. The fourth rank is taken from the Lord's care in leading them through the wilderness, from ver. 37 to 43. And the last rank of reasons is taken from the Lord's placing them in Canaan, where they might serve God according to his law, ver. 44, 45.

1. *O give thanks unto the Lord ; call upon his name : make known his deeds among the people.*

The prophet's exhortation to thankfulness is branched forth in ten particulars, whereof three are in this verse set down in order. Whence learn, 1. As in the matter of glorifying God there are several motives, so should there be several considerations of those motives, and acts of praising the Lord conform thereto; and namely, in relation to benefits received, the gifts should be acknowledged and confessed to his praise : *O give thanks unto the Lord.* 2. In relation to benefits to be received, or to evils to be removed, prayer to God is a part of praise : *call on his name.* 3. It is a part of true thankfulness unto God to make the world know what God hath done to and for his church : *make known his deeds among the people.*

2. *Sing unto him, sing psalms unto him : talk ye of all his wondrous works.*

The fourth, fifth, and sixth branches of the exhortation to thanksgiving, are set down in this verse. Wherein learn, 1. The Lord requireth, as a part of his praise and of our thankfulness, that we rejoice in him, and express our joy by singing : *sing unto him.* 2. It is not sufficient to offer the empty vessel of our joy unto God, or our singing voice in musical tune only; but it is also required that we fill our joyful voice with holy matter and good purpose, whereby God only may be reasonably praised : *sing psalms unto him.* 3. Albeit we have nothing to speak of God's wonderful works but what is known to any neighbour as well as to ourselves, yet it is a part of God's praise, and of our thankfulness, to make his known works the matter of our talk and ordinary conference, as we get occasion : *talk ye of all his wondrous works.*

3. *Glory ye in his holy name : let the heart of them rejoice that seek the Lord.*

The seventh and eighth branches of the exhortation are set down in this verse. Wherein learn, 1. It is a part of

God's praise and of our thankfulness to him, to make our boast of God, and rejoice because of our interest in him, and to proclaim ourselves blessed because of our communion with him: *glory ye in his holy name.* 2. Our gloriation in God should be holy, joined with a low estimation of ourselves, and with great reverence toward our most holy God: *glory ye in his holy name.* 3. It is a part of God's praise and of our thankfulness, to profess our need of God, and in the consciousness of our emptiness and his unsearchable riches, to seek our supply in him: for here the seeking of God is recommended unto us. 4. As seeking communion with God is a mark of a child of God, so it is also a reason of gladness and joy, because it both declares that we are of the number of converts and true worshippers of God, and also that joy is reserved for us: *let the heart of them rejoice that seek thee.*

4. *Seek the Lord, and his strength; seek his face evermore.*

The ninth branch of the exhortation is here set down, directing the people where, and how, and for what cause, to seek God; to wit, in his own ordinances before the ark, which was the figure of Christ to be incarnate, and is called here the *Lord's strength*, because it was a pledge of God's powerful presence with them who come to God through Christ; as also it is called *God's face*, because God is reconciled and favourable to all that seek him in Christ, who was signified by the ark and mercy-seat. Whence learn, 1. It is not unusual for the Scripture to give the name of the thing signified to the sign appointed of God to represent or shadow it forth, because of the judicial union of the sign and thing signified and exhibited to the believer by the appointment and institution of God, the supreme Judge and Lawgiver; so here the ark of the covenant is called *the Lord*, and *the Lord's strength*, and *the Lord's face*, because the believer, seeking God according to his ordinance, met by faith with the Lord, and his strength, and face, or good-will, engaged to the true worshipper. 2. Whensoever the believer maketh use of holy signs of God's presence, it is not the sign, but God or Christ signified by the sign, which the believer fixes his heart upon; as here, he that looked toward the ark, which was the sign of God in Christ

reconciling himself to the world, not imputing their trespasses unto them, is commanded to seek the thing signified:
seek the Lord, seek his strength, seek his face. 3. None
seek the Lord so earnestly but they have need of stirring
up to seek him more earnestly, neither have any attained
to such a measure of communion with God but they have
need to seek for a further measure : therefore is it said,
seek the Lord, seek his strength, seek his face evermore.

5. *Remember his marvellous works that he hath done ;
his wonders, and the judgments of his mouth;*

6. *O ye seed of Abraham his servant, ye children of
Jacob his chosen.*

The tenth branch of the exhortation is directed, together
with all the former branches, toward the seed of *Abraham.*
Whence learn, 1. It is a part of God's praise and of our
thankfulness, to entertain the memory of the Lord and of
his works and words : *remember his marvellous works that
he hath done.* 2. The remembrance of the Lord's wonderful works and gracious words is to be joined with seeking
his face, as a special help of us to this duty, as the conjunction of the parts of the exhortation teacheth us. 3. The
words of God in holy Scripture, whether law or gospel, are
to be looked upon as decrees given by the great Judge of
the world, whereupon certain execution is to follow according as it is foretold : *remember*, saith he, *the judgments of
his mouth.* 4. It is wisdom to join the remembrance of the
Lord's works and words, and to compare the one with the
other, that we may the better conceive of both, and discern
both the words and the works to be the Lord's works and
words : *remember*, saith he, *his wonders, and the judgments of his mouth.* 5. Because we are dull in appre-
hending God's ordinary working, he worketh sometimes
marvels and wonders, that by them we may the better take
up his power in his ordinary works; and therefore, for this
end, so much the more should the wonders be remembered :
*remember his marvellous works that he hath done, and
his wonders.* 6. The praise of God which is called for at
the church's hand, is expected only of believers, the spiritual children of Abraham and Jacob's faith and obedience :
*O ye seed of Abraham his servant, ye children of Jacob
his chosen.* 7. As the consideration of God's grace, be-

stowing spiritual privileges on us, obligeth us to praise and
serve God, so also it serveth to stir us up to the duty; for
therefore are the faithful called *the seed of Abraham his
servant, the children of Jacob his chosen.*

7. *He* is *the Lord our God ; his judgments* are *in
all the earth.*

8. *He hath remembered his covenant for ever, the
word* which *he commanded to a thousand generations :*

9. *Which* covenant *he made with Abraham, and
his oath unto Isaac ;*

10. *And confirmed the same unto Jacob for a law,*
and *to Israel* for *an everlasting covenant ;*

11. *Saying, Unto thee will I give the land of Canaan, the lot of your inheritance :*

In the first rank of reasons taken from the Lord's covenant with Abraham, Isaac, and Jacob, and from his care of
their persons, learn, 1. Our privilege to be in covenant with
God, is a special reason of thanks and praise to him : *he
is the Lord our God.*   2. The Lord's sovereignty without
the church, in all nations of the world, and in exercising
justice among all men, is the Lord's praise and the church's
profit; so it is the church's obligation unto the thankful acknowledging thereof : for the greatness of God's dominion
over all the earth, commendeth the specialty of his respect
to his church : *his judgments are in all the earth.*   3.
As the covenant of God is not for a day, or for temporal
favours only, but also and especially for spiritual and everlasting mercies; so the Lord forgetteth neither less nor more
of that which he hath promised, but albeit long time may
intervene before the performance of his promise, yet, nevertheless, he remembereth it still till it be fufilled : *he hath
remembered his covenant for ever.*   4. The experience of
every age and proof had of God's faithfulness, should force
men in every age to bear witness to the Lord's steadfastness
in his covenant: *he hath remembered his covenant for
ever, the word which he hath commanded to a thousand
generations.*   5. The word which the Lord hath said he
will do; in special his promises shall certainly take effect in
due time, and order given by magistrates for executing their
decrees, is but a shadow of the effectual accomplishment of
God's promises, which are called here, *a word which he*

commanded to a thousand generations. 6. God's co-venant made with our fathers in our name, is to be laid hold on by us their children, as the example of the Israelites here teacheth us: *which covenant he made with Abra-ham.* 7. For further engaging and confirming the chil-dren of covenanters, there is need to repeat and apply the covenant to their children and posterity: *for he gave his oath unto Isaac, and confirmed the same unto Jacob.* 8. The covenant of grace is an everlasting covenant with all who embrace it: for, *the covenant made with Abra-ham was an oath unto Isaac.* 9. It is not free for the children of covenanters to embrace or reject, as they please, the covenant of God made with their fathers, because the Lord imposed the covenant upon the posterity, as a duty whereunto they were obliged from generation to generation: *for he confirmed the same unto Jacob for a law, and to Israel for an everlasting covenant.* 10. The covenant of grace made with Abraham, Isaac, and Jacob, and with believers after them, consisted in promises made by God, and embraced of them by faith, as here it is described; for the everlasting covenant is expounded to be the Lord's, say-ing, *unto thee will I give the land of Canaan, the lot of thy inheritance;* which promise being received by faith, became a covenant with the believer. 11. The everlasting covenant of grace, propounded in whatsoever expressions, was one and the same in substance to the believers: for these promises,—to wit, *In thee shall all the families of the earth be blessed,* Gen. xii. 3; and again, *Tell the stars, so shall thy seed be:* which promise Abraham receiving, *be-lieved in the Lord, and he counted it unto him for right-eousness,* Gen. xv. 6. *And I will be a God unto thee, and to thy seed after thee,* Gen. xvii. 7. *And I will give unto thee, and to thy seed after thee, the land wherein thou art a stranger, all the land of Canaan for an ever-lasting possession, and I will be their God,* Gen. xvii. 8, whereunto this place doth relate—are all taken up here in the free and gracious promise, of giving everlasting life to the believers, shadowed forth in the typical terms of giving *the land of Canaan for the lot of their inheritance.*

12. *When they were* but *a few men in number; yea, very few, and strangers in it.*

13. *When they went from one nation to another, from* one *kingdom to another people,*

14. *He suffered no man to do them wrong ; yea, he reproved kings for their sakes ;*

15. Saying, *Touch not mine anointed, and do my prophets no harm.*

In the care which God had of the persons of Abraham, Isaac, and Jacob, who were in covenant with him, learn, 1. They who are in covenant with God, may be found sometimes but a small number : *they were but a few men in number : yea, very few.* 2. They who are in covenant with God for a promised blessing, may be far from appearance of the possible possession of what is promised, as Abraham, Isaac, and Jacob were a *very few men, and strangers in the land of promise.* 3. As the paucity, meanness, low condition, unworthiness, and weakness of men, hinder not God to enter into covenant with them, but rather by this means, he commendeth the freedom and riches of his grace to them; so is it requisite that they who enter into covenant with God, be stripped bare of all conceit of both their own and their fathers' worthiness, and yet not be hindered thereby from believing, embracing, and holding fast the covenant; for this did Abraham, Isaac, and Jacob, *when they were very few, and strangers in the land* promised to them. 4. They who have the promises, both of this life and the life to come, may be pilgrims and sojourners without any dwelling-place in the world : the patriarchs *went from one nation to another, from one kingdom to another people.* 5. In whatsoever worldly condition believers are, and whatsoever they want in things earthly, yet they want not the love and good-will of God; they have always the defence and protection of God, as his federates : *he suffered no man to do them wrong.* 6. No power or place how high soever, no worldly authority on earth, no law nor privilege of any person or kingdom, is a sufficient plea for troubling God's servants, walking in his service : *he reproved kings for their sakes.* 7. The person of every believer walking in God's way, is sacred, sanctified, and set apart for God's peculiar service : *they are the Lord's anointed.* 8. They who, both by covenant and special calling to the holy ministry, have charge to declare the Lord's will to the world, are owned of God as his prophets, and are fenced with a strict caveat given to all men by God, how great soever, that they harm them not : *touch not mine anointed, and do my prophets no harm.* And upon all these aforesaid considerations, God is to be thanked and praised by his people.

16. *Moreover, he called for a famine upon the land; he brake the whole staff of bread.*

17. *He sent a man before them,* even *Joseph,* who *was sold for a servant;*

18. *Whose feet they hurt with fetters: he was laid in iron:*

19. *Until the time that his word came: the word of the Lord tried him.*

20. *The king sent and loosed him;* even *the ruler of the people, and let him go free.*

21. *He made him lord of his house, and ruler of all his substance;*

22. *To bind his princes at his pleasure, and teach his senators wisdom.*

In the second rank of reasons for God's praise, taken from the care the Lord had of the posterity of *Abraham, Isaac,* and *Jacob,* in bringing them into *Egypt,* and preserving them there, learn, 1. Every plague, and in special famine, is a servant of God, ready at a call to come forth and execute his judgment : *moreover, he called for a famine upon the land.* 2. No food can be had except God furnish it, and no food, when it is given, can feed, except God give a powerful blessing with it; when that is removed, bread feedeth not : *he brake the whole staff of bread.* 3. The way of the Lord's performing his covenant is not such as carnal reason would prescribe, by giving probable means of bringing it to pass; but the way he chooseth is such as may try the faith of his children, to wit, by seeming to do the contrary. As here the patriarchs having the promise of the land of *Canaan,* shall not be suffered to be so much as sojourners in it, but must leave it and go elsewhere : *he called for a famine upon that land,* which might seem to make it in less request, and by the famine also he forced them to go where they might find bread. 4. Whensoever the Lord bringeth his children into straits and difficulties, he maketh provision for their sustenance in their straits, and deliverance from the same. When the Lord was to bring his people into *Egypt,* he provided so as they should have a friend at court before they came : *he sent a man before them,* even *Joseph.* 5. Whatsoever may be the intent of men or devils in troubling God's children, God hath a hand in every thing which befalleth them, how accidentally soever it may seem to come. *Joseph's* coming down to *Egypt* is called God's message : *he sent a man before them,* even *Joseph.* 6. What men do sinfully, for satisfaction of their own lusts, God doeth holily and wisely for his own ends : by *Joseph's* brethren selling their brother, to be rid of him, God sendeth *Joseph* into *Egypt* to provide for their livelihood : *he sent a man before them,* even *Joseph,* who *was sold for a servant.* 7. It is not strange to see the man whom the Lord mindeth to exalt most humbled before he be exalted, and cast into prison before he be lifted up to liberty : *Joseph was sold for a servant, whose feet they hurt with fetters.* 8. When the Lord's servants are entered into the trial of their faith, they may look to be soundly searched before they have ended their trials, and that by sharp affliction, as *Joseph* was tried : *whose feet they hurt with fetters : he was laid in iron.* 9. The afflictions and trials of God's children will not end when they wish, but they have a set measure and time determined of God : *he was laid in irons until the time came, &c.* 10. There is a secret word of God's decree and providence for ending the affliction of God's children, which God bringeth forth to light in his own time; and, until this come, his servants must lie in bonds, as *Joseph lay in iron till the time that his word came;* that is, till God made his decree manifest about the loosing of him. 11. Before affliction shall end, the manifested work of God's providence in affliction must put the afflicted to the trial of all that is in him, and trial must go before deliverance : *the word of the Lord tried him.* 12. The time appointed in God's decree to send delivery to his afflicted children is made manifest in the effectual moving of instruments and means of delivery; and in this case, if need be, kings shall be set on work for the delivery of the Lord's children : *the king sent and loosed him.* 13. Such as are bound ignominiously for righteousness, shall be one way or other loosed honourably : *the ru-ler of the people let him go free.* 14. When the Lord's people are humbled sufficiently, God raiseth them up, and sometimes even in a visible manner before the world,—as here *Joseph* is by the king of *Egypt made lord of his house, and ruler of all his substance.* 15. As God's children are exalted for the benefit of those over whom they are set, so should they manage and maintain their honour and power by doing good to their inferiors, as *Joseph* did who was exalted,—*to bind Pharaoh's princes at his pleasure, and teach his senators wisdom.*

23. *Israel also came into Egypt ; and Jacob sojourn-ed in the land of Ham.*

24. *And he increased his people greatly, and made them stronger than their enemies.*

25. *He turned their heart to hate his people, to deal subtilely with his servants.*

After *Joseph,* the rest of the family is brought down in-to *Egypt,* who sojourned there, and were preserved till they grew a strong people, and then began their afflictions, as a preparation to their out-bringing. Whence learn, 1. Albeit a man hath wrestled with God in prayer, and gotten his blessing, yet may he be tossed in the world by troubles : *Israel also came into Egypt.* 2. The heirs of the pro-mise and the Lord's dearest children may be made sojourn-ers among wicked people, even in their old age, when they need most to be at rest : *Jacob sojourned in the land of Ham.* 3. As when the Lord's people grow up to any con-siderable number among idolaters, it is no strange thing if they find enmity; so it is no strange thing in God's way to make them grow the more in number and power, the more they be oppressed; yea, and to make them under oppression and persecution to become mightier than their adversaries : *he increased his people greatly, and made them stronger than their enemies.* 4. The hearts of all men are in God's hand, to turn them whither he pleaseth, to love or hate, as their affections may serve best his holy purposes: *he turned their heart to hate his people.* 5. The trouble and ex-ercise of God's people, by whatsoever instruments it be mov-ed, is of the Lord, and he will own the evil of trouble which is in the city or country whatsoever : *he turned their heart to hate his people.* 6. In the most sinful affections, plots, and actions of the wicked against God's people and servants, God hath a holy hand, and is not the cause of their sin : for all the motions of the creatures which live, and move, and have their being of God, are made use of by the Creator as instruments whereby he worketh his own just and holy work for his own ends : but, when men are about that same work for their sinful ends, what is holy on God's part, becometh sinful in them, as the crucifying of Christ was most holy on God's part, and most sinful on his enemies' part : *he turned their heart to hate his people : to deal subtilely with his servants.*

26. *He sent Moses his servant,* and *Aaron whom he had chosen.*

27. *They shewed his signs among them, and wonders in the land of Ham.*

In the third rank of reasons, taken from God's delivering of his people out of *Egypt,* and plaguing of the Egyptians, learn, 1. When, by the malice of enemies, God's people are brought to greatest straits, then is deliverance near to be sent from God unto them ; *they dealt subtilely with his servants ; he sent Moses his servant.* 2. As it is the Lord who bringeth his own people into trouble and straits, so it is he who delivereth them again, and provideth instruments for the doing thereof : *he sent Moses his servant.* 3. As whosoever serve God's church to any good purpose, do it not of themselves, but by stirring up or commission from God; so whosoever are about to do the church good, should do it of intention, as doing him service : *he sent Moses his servant, and Aaron his chosen.* 4. As to the end, that God may have his own glory in every good work, his part is to be distinguished from his servants' part : so when his servants do the servants' duty faithfully, God will have them commended and approved for it among men : *Moses* therefore is called *God's servant, and Aaron his chosen.* 5. The signs and wonders are called the Lord's signs and wonders, and *Moses* and *Aaron's* service is called their showing of his signs : *they showed his signs among them, and wonders in the land of Ham.*

28. *He sent darkness, and made it dark ; and they rebelled not against his word.*

BB

29. *He turned their waters into blood, and slew their fish.*

30. *Their land brought forth frogs in abundance in the chambers of their kings.*

31. *He spake, and their came divers sorts of flies,* and *lice in all their coasts.*

32. *He gave them hail for rain,* and *flaming fire in their land.*

33. *He smote their vines also and their fig-trees, and brake the trees of their coasts.*

34. *He spake, and the locusts came, and caterpillars, and that without number,*

35. *And did eat up all the herbs in their land, and devoured the fruit of their ground.*

36. *He smote also all the first-born in their land, the chief of all their strength.*

The psalmist reckoneth sundry plagues brought upon Egypt, which are sufficient for his purpose to bring the whole history to mind. Whence learn, 1. The sun cannot expel darkness in the air but as God maketh way for it; for God can turn the day into palpable darkness when and where he pleaseth. He can make the sun to shine in one place, and take the comfortable use of it away in another place, as he thinks good; he can put his enemies under darkness when his people have light : *he sent darkness, and made it dark.* 2. It is a piece of glory unto God, when either his brute creatures or his rational servants do what he commandeth : *and they rebelled not against his word.* 3. God can make the most useful creatures become noisome : *he turned their waters into blood.* 4. God can plague men in the matter of their meat as well as in their drink; and when the Lord doth plague in the one, it is not strange if he shall plague in the other also : *he turned their waters into blood, and slew their fish.* 5. God can daunt the pride of the stoutest of his enemies by his meanest creatures : *the land brought forth frogs in abundance, in the chambers of their kings.* 6. As the Lord speaketh, so shall it be found in due time, he needeth not to make much ado in any business, but speak the word, and it shall be done : *he spake, and there came divers sorts of flies.* 7.

When the proud strive against God, they gain nothing but more and more shameful abasement : *he brought lice in all their coasts.* 8. The clouds are at God's command, to send down soft rain, or hard and heavy hailstones : *he gave them hail for rain.* 9. Although fire and hailstones are most contrary in their natures, yet they can agree well in the work of God's service, when he employeth them : *he gave them hail for rain and flaming fire in their land.* 10. When lighter judgments do not move men, God will send more heavy plagues, which shall leave their impression behind them: *he smote their vines also, and their fig-trees, and brake the trees of their coasts.* 11. When God fights against a people, all the creatures are ready to fight against them also, as they are called forth : *he spake, and the locusts came, and caterpillars, and that without number.* 12. Whatsoever hath escaped the dint of one plague, God can overtake it by another plague : *they did eat up all the herbs in the land, and devoured the fruit of their ground.* 13. When God smiteth the creatures which serve for man's use, he showeth his long-suffering and patience towards man, and his lothness to destroy him, as we see in the order of God's proceeding with Egypt. 14. When warning given unto man moveth him not to repentance, then the Lord layeth his hand on that which is most precious to him : *he smote also all the first-born in their land.* 15. When the Lord pleaseth to put forth his hand, they that are naturally strongest and most lively, are no less near to death, than they who are naturally weaker : *he smote all their first-born, the chief of all their strength.*

37. *He brought them forth also with silver and gold; and* there was *not one feeble* person *among their tribes.*

38. *Egypt was glad when they departed ; for the fear of them fell upon them.*

39. *He spread a cloud for a covering, and fire to give light in the night.*

40. *The* people *asked, and he brought quails, and satisfied them with the bread of heaven.*

41. *He opened the rock, and the waters gushed out ; they ran in the dry places* like *a river.*

42. *For he remembered his holy promise,* and *Abraham his servant.*

In the Lord's bringing his people out of Egypt, and through the wilderness, learn, 1. Albeit there may be many impediments to the delivery of God's people out of their trouble, and from their persecutors, yet the work of delivery is perfected at length; for when God had smitten Egypt in favour of his own people, *he brought his people forth.* 2. All riches that men have are at God's disposing, to transfer the right and possession thereof to whom he pleaseth, and the Lord's special and express warrant gave title to the Israelites, to retain the Egyptians' borrowed jewels: *he brought them forth also with silver and gold.* 3. When God grants a delivery, or any sort of benefit, it is a new gift to enable a man to make use of the offered delivery or bestowed benefit: such was the benefit bestowed on Israel, when God brought his people out of Egypt: *there was not one feeble person among their tribes.* 4. The Lord can make bloody persecutors of his people to cease from their persecution, and to contribute to their delivery; and to be desirous to be rid of them: *Egypt was glad when they departed.* 5. God can make his persecuted people terrible to their persecutors, which is no less a wonder than to make the wolf tremble for fear of the lambs: *Egypt was glad when they departed, for the fear of them fell upon them.* 6. Except the Lord take the guiding and protecting of his own people, they will perish many ways, after their delivery out of trouble; but whom he delivereth he taketh care of, as he did of Israel, for whom he provided the pillar of cloud, to temper unto them the heat of the day: and the pillar of fire to temper unto them the darkness and cold of the night, and made both of them to direct their journey: *he spread a cloud for a covering, and fire to give light in the night.* 7. Sometimes the Lord will give unto his people, at their earnest desire, that which is not good for them, and so he may give them evidence of his readiness, much more to give them what is good for them, when they earnestly ask it: *the people asked, and he brought quails.* 8. When ordinary means of the preservation of God's people fail, God will provide for them wonderfully, as he gave his people manna in the wilderness, *and satisfied them*

with the bread of heaven. 9. As the fountain of the
feeding of God's people, is not in the creatures, but in God;
so should the eye of his people be carried above the creatures, unto heaven for preservation of this life, as well temporal as spiritual: for this end it is said, *he satisfied them
with the bread of heaven.* 10. God can bring consolation unexpected, and that by means most unlikely to yield
it : *he opened the rock, and the waters gushed out.* 11.
There is no scarcity in God, of what the Lord's people stand
in need of; he both can and doth furnish plenteously, and
makes the opportunity of having the use of his provision
follow his people whithersoever he leadeth them : *the waters out of the rock ran in the dry places as a river.*
12. What the Lord doeth to his people, is for his covenant's sake; as here, *he remembered his holy promise.*
13. How many years soever intervene between God's pro-
mise-making, and the performance, the Lord forgetteth not
his promise, as here we see after four hundred and thirty
years : *he remembereth his holy promise, and Abraham
his servant.*

43. *And he brought forth his people with joy,* and
his chosen with gladness;

44. *And gave them the lands of the heathen; and
they inherited the labour of the people;*

45. *That they might observe his statutes, and keep
his laws.   Praise ye the Lord.*

From the manner of the Lord's bringing his people out
of Egypt, and planting them in Canaan, learn, 1. Whatsoever bondage the Lord's people fall into, the Lord in due
time will bring them out of it, *as he brought forth his
people* from the bondage of Egypt. 2. How much soever
sorrow his people may find in the expectation of delivery,
so much joy shall they have in the performance of the
Lord's promise : *he brought forth his people with joy,
and his chosen with gladness.* 3. The Lord leaveth not
his people, till he put them to some rest after their troubles;
as he gave rest to his people Israel, whom, when he carried
them through the wilderness, he gave the possession of Canaan : *he gave them the lands of the heathen.* 4. The
Lord maketh no end of multiplying obligations on his people; he maintains them in their possession of what he giv-

eth them: *they inherited the labour of the people.* 5.
The end of the Lord's liberality, is to engage the hearts of
his people more and more to the obedience of his ordinances,
as he did all this to Israel, *that they might observe his sta-*
tutes. 6. There is no rule for serving God acceptably,
except his own commands; for Israel's rule was, *to observe*
his statutes, and keep his laws. 7. The right use which
we should make of whatsoever good was done to the Lord's
people, is to glorify God when we hear of it, or read of it,
as here we are directed: *praise ye the Lord.*

PSALM CVI.

The sum of this psalm is to teach the godly in the time of calamity, lying upon the church, or upon themselves, first, to glorify God by faith
in him; secondly, to reckon up for their encouragement, the frequent
forgiveness of grievous sins to his people in former times; and thirdly,
to pray for the like favour to themselves, and in hope to have their
prayer granted, to give thanks to God. There are three parts of the
psalm answerable thereunto. The first part is the prophet's strengthening his own faith, ver. 1—5. The second part is the confession of
our sins in general, ver. 6, and in special of eight or nine gross provocations, which the Lord after correction pardoned, and gave comfort to
his people, to ver. 46, which are so many arguments of hope to find
the like mercy to the church in this time. The first sin, with the forgiveness of it, is set down from ver. 7—13; the second sin, v. 13—15;
the third sin, ver. 17, 18; the fourth sin, ver. 19—23; the fifth sin,
ver. 24—27; the sixth sin, ver. 28—31; the seventh sin, ver. 32, 33;
the eighth sin, from ver. 34—43; the ninth point of confession is of
a general heap of sins, ofttimes repeated and all pardoned, with pity
manifested to God's people, ver. 43—46. The third part of the psalm,
is a prayer for new experience of like mercy, and a close of the psalm
with praise and thanksgiving, ver. 47, 48.

1. *Praise ye the Lord. O give thanks unto the*
Lord; for he is *good: for his mercy* endureth *for*
ever.

The psalmist stirreth up himself and others four ways to
glorify God under sad afflictions, by believing on him.
First, by exhorting all to praise and thank the Lord for his
goodness. Whence learn, 1. The exercise of praising and
thanking the Lord, is very fit for a soul lying under the
sense of affliction and guiltiness: for that which serveth
for the Lord's praise, serveth also for the comfort and encouragement of humbled sinners: therefore, saith he,
praise ye the Lord. 2. The meditation of God's goodness and readiness to communicate his bounty to men, is fit

to furnish matter of his praise: *praise ye the Lord, for he is good.* 3. Albeit a man be conscious of his much abusing God's goodness, and so might find this to be the matter of his grief, yet mercy answereth all objections, everlasting mercy looseth all doubts, and giveth fresh encouragement to the humbled sinner to draw near, and make yet again use of his goodness: *for his mercy endureth for ever.*

2. *Who can utter the mighty acts of the Lord? who can shew forth all his praise?*

The next means which he useth, to stir up himself and others to glorify God in believing on him, is wondering at the Lord's works, and innumerable causes of praise. Whence learn, 1. It is a disposition fit for praising God, to be sensible of our inability and unfitness for so great a work, as the prophet showeth in this example, saying, *who can utter the mighty acts of the Lord?* 2. There is such an impression of God's omnipotence on all his works, and in special on those works wherein he hath been pleased most clearly to manifest his power, that no man can comprehend or express it: *who can utter the mighty acts of the Lord?* 3. Albeit the praises of the Lord surpass all men's ability to declare them, yet neither must the greatness of the work nor the weakness and unworthiness of the servant of God, hinder him to praise as he is able; for even this is a part of praising God, to confess and say, *who can show forth all his praise?*

3. *Blessed* are *they that keep judgment,* and *he that doeth righteousness at all times.*

The third means whereby he stirreth up himself to glorify God by believing in him, is a declaring how blessed the believer is. Whence learn, 1. The consideration of the blessing of God upon every true believer, is a notable encouragement to put confidence in God: *blessed are they that keep judgment, &c.* 2. The evidence of a sincere believer, is not only to keep judgment, that is, to receive, respect, and entertain the word of God, as a decree wisely given forth by him, but also to study to obey it in practice constantly upon all occasions: *blessed are they that keep judgment, and he that doeth righteousness at all times.*

4. *Remember me, O Lord, with the favour* that thou bearest unto *thy people : O visit me with thy salvation ;*

5. *That I may see the good of thy chosen, that I may rejoice in the gladness of thy nation, that I may glory with thine inheritance.*

The fourth means of stirring up himself and others to believe in God, especially in the time of the presupposed calamity of the church, and of the supplicant, is prayer to God for a new proof of the loving-kindness which God beareth to his people in all ages. Whence learn, 1. Whatsoever be the outwardly afflicted state of God's people, yet they are still beloved, still in favour, even when tokens of anger by public calamities are manifested against them : *remember me with the favour which thou bearest unto thy people.* 2. There needeth no more felicity unto any man, save to be one of God's people : it may content any man to have his lot with the children of God, in whatsoever condition they are put into : for the psalmist craveth no more, but, *remember me, O Lord, with the favour which thou bearest unto thy people.* 3. Albeit the Lord's people seem to be forgotten, yet the Lord will make evident that he doth not forget them, nor any one of them : *remember me, O Lord, with the favour which thou bearest unto thy people.* 4. Such as share with God's people in their grief shall be partakers also of their consolation, deliverance, and salvation, which God hath wisely prepared for them : therefore prayeth the psalmist, *O visit me with thy salvation, &c.* 5. As there are times wherein God declareth his displeasure against the sins of his people, so there are times when he removeth the tokens of his displeasure, and letteth forth the evidence of his love and respect to them, in doing them good, making them glad, and causing them to glory in him; this is it which the psalmist looketh after : *visit me with thy salvation, that I may see the good of thy chosen, that I may rejoice in the gladness of thy nation, that I may glory with thine inheritance.* 6. The near interest which God hath in his people, and which they have in him, is a solid ground of hope of good, and gladness, joy and gloriation reserved for them; for they are God's *chosen*, God's *nation*, appropriate unto him : and his *inheritance*, to remain in his possession from generation to generation; whereupon the psalmist assureth himself and the church of his hope of good, reserved for the church: *that I may see the good of thy chosen, &c.*

6. *We have sinned with our fathers, we have committed iniquity, we have done wickedly.*

In the second place is the confession of sins, for which God justly might afflict the supplicants, but in his mercy could forgive them also, as he had done to his people in former generations. The force of his reasoning is this: Many times thou showedst mercy to our fathers in their afflictions, notwithstanding their grievous provocations, therefore we must entreat thee, yea, and hope also for the like mercy in our time. Whence learn, 1. It is not for nought that the Lord bringeth calamity on his people, he is provoked so to do by their grievous offences: *we have sinned.* 2. As judgments are set to convince of sin, and to draw forth the acknowledgment thereof; so there is no readier way to remove the sin and judgment also, than by confession thereof: *we have sinned.* 3. As God, when he punisheth his people, reckoneth with them, both for their own, and also for their fathers' faults, whose footsteps they have followed; so must the penitent reckon with God for their own faults, and for their fathers' sins whereunto they have accession: *we have sinned with our fathers, &c.* 4. Confession of sins must not be slighted, but seriously gone about, and aggravated duly: *we have sinned, we have committed iniquity, we have done wickedly.* 5. True penitents will neither excuse their sins by the example of their fathers, nor justify themselves, how holy soever they be, when God is pleading with his church, but will join in confession with the multitude, as here the holy prophet doth: *we have sinned with our fathers, we have committed iniquity, we have done wickedly.*

7. *Our fathers understood not thy wonders in Egypt: they remembered not the multitude of thy mercies; but provoked him at the sea, even at the Red sea.*

The first particular sin which he confesseth is rebellion at the Red sea, Exod. xiv. 10—12; which sin was so much the greater, as the wonders done in Egypt for them were great and many. Whence learn, 1. Albeit God manifest himself in extraordinary working in the sight of misbelievers, yet will they remain blind ignorants, and brutish beholders of his operations: *our fathers understood not thy wonders in Egypt.* 2. Albeit the Lord should often convince a misbeliever, both of his justice and mercy, yet the Lord's works make no lasting impression upon his mind: *they re-membered not thy mercies.* 3. One sin is a degree to another more heinous, for *not observing,* is followed with *not remembering,* and *forgetfulness* of duty draweth on *disobedience* and rebellion: *our fathers understood not thy wonders in Egypt, they remembered not the multi-tude of thy mercies, but provoked him at the sea, even at the Red sea.*

8. *Nevertheless he saved them for his name's sake, that he might make his mighty power to be known.*

9. *He rebuked the Red sea also, and it was dried up: so he led them through the depths, as through the wilderness.*

10. *And he saved them from the hand of him that hated them, and redeemed them from the hand of the enemy.*

11. *And the waters covered their enemies; there was not one of them left.*

12. *Then believed they his words; they sang his praise.*

As he observed their sin, so he observeth God's mercy to his people; for, notwithstanding their provocation, he brought them through the Red sea, and destroyed their enemies. Whence learn, 1. The evil deservings of God's people do not always interrupt the course of God's good-ness toward them; for, *nevertheless* of the aforesaid provo-cation, he *saved* them. 2. As the Lord's goodness aggra-vateth men's sins, so men's sins amplify God's grace, and make his goodness to the unworthy to appear the more: *nevertheless he saved them.* 3. The Lord hath other things to look to, when he hath to do with his people, than presently to fall upon punishing their wickedness and mis-deservings, even when they are found delinquents: he useth to respect the glory of his mercy toward his people, and the declaration of his power against his enemies in favour of his people : *nevertheless he saved them for his name's sake, that he might make his mighty power to be known.* 4. The manner and circumstances of God's working, are as well to be considered as the matter, and how easily he bringeth the greatest works to pass : *he rebuked the Red sea also, and it was dried up.* 5. The Lord can make a danger to turn into a delivery, and a peril wherein a man was like to perish, to be a means of preservation : *so he led them through the depths, as through the wilderness.* 6. In any one mercy unfolded, we may take up more mercies than one, and each particular part of the mercy, when it is discovered, will appear no less glorious than the whole mercy looked upon confusedly and in gross, as here in the delivery at the Red sea, the delivery from Pharaoh, which is but a part of the work pitched upon : *and he saved them from the hand of him that hated them, and redeemed them from the hand of the enemy.* 7. The comparing of God's dealing with his own people, and with their enemies, amplifieth God's goodness to his people, and their obligation unto him : *he redeemed them from the hand of the enemy, and the waters covered their enemies.* 8. When the Lord's time cometh to enter into judgment with the foes of his church, he will not miss one whom he mindeth to overtake, as here : *there was not one of them left.* 9. The Lord sometimes worketh so clearly for convincing of the misbeliever, that the most blind and obstinate infidel shall be forced to acknowledge his works : *when the waters covered their enemies, then believed they his words.* 10. It serveth much for God's glory, when he extorteth credit to his words by wonderful works, but little to the commendation of the believers who give credit to God's word upon that ground only, as here we see; for not before, but *then did they believe his words;* which importeth their preceding misbelief, and that their duty was to believe his word, whatsoever appearance might be to the contrary. 11. A temporary belief extorted by some extraordinary work, may have joined with it a temporary joy, and praising of God for a time, without any root of saving grace in the heart: *then they believed his words, they sang his praise.*

13. *They soon forgat his works; they waited not for his counsel;*

14. *But lusted exceedingly in the wilderness, and tempted God in the desert.*

15. *And he gave them their request; but sent leanness unto their soul.*

The second sin confessed here is the Jews' murmuring for want, not of water but of flesh, Numb. xi. 4—6; which lust God satisfied in his wrath to them. Whence learn, 1. Temporary faith, with the fruits thereof, lasteth no longer than a new temptation assaulteth; and faith grounded, not on the word or truth of it, but only on God's sensible works, is ready to vanish when the work is a little past and gone : *they soon forgat his works.* 2. If God's works be not remembered with estimation of, and affection to, God the worker, and with some use-making thereof in the obedience of faith, God esteemeth them to be forgotten, as here : for this cause, he saith, *they soon forgat his works.* 3. What the Lord withholdeth from his people, or doeth unto them, he doeth it for good purpose, resolvedly to train his people unto obedience, and to try them whether they will follow their own will or his *counsel,* as is here insinuated. 4. Misbelievers take the ruling of themselves into their own hand, and will not stay upon God's provision for them, but must needs prescribe what they love to have done, and murmur if their carnal desires be not satisfied, as here the sin marked in the Israelites showeth : *they waited not for his counsel, but lusted.* 5. When men wait not on God's direction, lusts become their leaders; yea, furious drivers of them, as poor slaves, to all unreasonable appetites: *they lusted exceedingly.* 6. When God, by circumstances of time and place, calleth for moderation of carnal appetite, the transgression is the more heinous and offensive to God: *they lusted exceedingly in the wilderness,* where they should have contented themselves with any sort of provision. 7. They that do not make use of the life and welfare which God alloweth and provideth, but prescribe unto God what they would have done to them, tempt God: *they tempted God in the desert.* 8. Importunity and excessive affection to any unnecessary worldly thing, may draw out of God's hand that which is good: *they lusted, and God gave them their request,* to wit, *flesh in abundance.* 9. As lawful means are attended with God's blessing, so unlawful means are

followed by God's curse : *he gave them their request, but
sent leanness into their soul.*

16. *They envied Moses also in the camp,* and *Aaron
the saint of the Lord.*

17. *The earth opened and swallowed up Dathan, and
covered the company of Abiram.*

18. *And a fire was kindled in their company ; the
flame burnt up the wicked.*

The third sin confessed is sedition, which broke forth in
Korah and his accomplices, and was fearfully punished,
Numb. xvi. 1—3, &c. Whence learn, 1. The manner of
the Lord's governing his people, how gentle soever it be, is,
notwithstanding, to wicked men a thing insupportable, as
appeareth in the people's not enduring the Lord's meek
governing of them by Moses and Aaron. 2. Rebellion
against God's manner of governing, howsoever it be indeed
against God, yet pretendeth to be only against men : *they
envied Moses in the camp.* 3. Ministers are to be looked
to as men consecrated unto God, and injuries done to them
are against the Lord : *they envied Aaron the saint of the
Lord.* 4. Whatsoever open wicked course is set on foot by
ringleaders to any mischief, and is not disclaimed by the
body of the people, may justly be charged upon all, albeit
not in the same degree of guiltiness, as here Korah and his
accomplices' fault is charged upon the people : *they envied
Moses in the camp.* 5. Authors of sedition in the state
and of schism in the church, highly provoke God to punish
them exemplarily, as appeareth here : *the earth opened
and swallowed up Dathan, and covered the company of
Abiram.* 6. Such as will not be warned to eschew sin by
judgments poured forth upon others, provoke God to make
themselves spectacles of wrath in the sight of others : *a fire
was kindled in their company, the fire burnt up the
wicked.*

19. *They made a calf in Horeb, and worshipped the
molten image.*

20. *Thus they changed their glory into the similitude
of an ox that eateth grass.*

21. *They forgat God their Saviour, which had done
great things in Egypt ;*

22. *Wondrous works in the land of Ham,* and *terrible things by the Red sea.*

23. *Therefore he said that he would destroy them, had not Moses his chosen stood before him in the breach, to turn away his wrath, lest he should destroy* them.

The fourth sin confessed is the idolatry of the golden calf, which sin is aggravated, and the danger of their destruction for it, till Moses interceded for them, is briefly set down here, but more largely expressed, Exod. xxxii. and Deut. ix. Whence learn, 1. They that are ready to change the government of the church which God hath appointed, will be ready also to change the worship of God, as experience in the Israelites teacheth, who are charged with the one fault, v. 16, and with the other here : *they made a calf in Horeb, and worshipped the molten image.* 2. Idolaters are so bewitched with the opinion of the lawfulness of idolatry, as they dare both devise and practise it in God's presence : *they made a calf in mount Horeb,* the mountain where the Lord showed himself terrible. 3. Albeit image-making in the matter of religion, and image-worshipping be an old sin, yet this relative worship offered unto God before an image, is always rejected of God, as no worship done to him, but only to the image; for God expoundeth not communion of worship to an image, or relative worship before an image, according to the intention of the worshipper, but according to the nature of the action which is discharged in the second command of the moral law : Israel intended to offer the holiday to the Lord, and appointed the worship toward the golden image for him, as the history showeth, Exod. xxxii. 4, 5—*to-morrow is a feast of the Lord*—yet here the Lord's Spirit declareth this to be a worship, not of God, but of the image : *they worshipped the molten image.* 4. Making images to represent God, or any of the persons of the holy Trinity, is but a vilifying of the glory of God and giving it to the image of a creature; yea, the making of an image to represent God is the changing of the glory of God into a vile image of some base creature, and the placing of the one in the other's stead and room : for so God judgeth, saying, *thus they changed their glory into the similitude of an ox that eateth grass.* 5. To have God for our God, and to have him alone for our God, and the only object of our worship, without any mixture of human devices, is our glory, and to do otherwise is the shame of the worshipper: *they changed their glory into the similitude of an ox.* 6. To devise images and pictures to put us in mind of God, is a very forgetting, both of God's nature and of his authority discharging such devices, for so the Lord expoundeth it: *they forgat God their Saviour.* 7. Whatsoever works God hath wrought for making people know him, are all forgotten as well as God is forgotten, whensoever men may make devices of their own for memorials of God: *they forgat God their Saviour, which had done great things in Egypt ; wondrous things in the land of Ham, and terrible things by the Red sea.* 8. Idolatry openly committed in a land is a cause sufficient to destroy the nation which is guilty of that sin; for, *therefore the Lord said he would destroy them.* 9. As they who fear God in a land should deprecate God's wrath that it fall not on it, and should stand in the gap to divert the Lord's wrath: so is their intercession acceptable to God, and a hopeful means to divert wrath, as is to be seen in Moses, *who stood up before him to turn away his wrath, lest he should destroy them.* 10. When God is glorified in a people's obedience to him, he is a wall about them to save them from harm; but when he is provoked by open idolatry or avowed sin, then is a gap made in the wall of his protection, that mischief may enter now in upon them at the breach : *he said he would destroy them, had not Moses his chosen stood before him in the breach.*

24. *Yea, they despised the pleasant land; they believed not his word;*

25. *But murmured in their tents,* and *hearkened not unto the voice of the Lord.*

26. *Therefore he lifted up his hand against them, to overthrow them in the wilderness :*

27. *To overthrow their seed also among the nations, and to scatter them in the lands.*

The fifth sin confessed is the contempt of God's most precious promises, figured out in the despising of the promise of Canaan unto them; which, as it flowed from misbelief of God's word, so it brought forth murmuring against his dispensation, which put them in hazard of dissipation and destruction, as is set down more largely, Numb. xiii. 14. Whence learn, 1. When the promised inheritance of heaven (which was figured by the pleasant *land of promise*) is not counted worthy of all the pains and difficulties which can be sustained and met with in the way of going toward it: the promised inheritance is but little esteemed, as appeareth in the Israelites, who, for love of ease and fear of the Canaanites, were ready to turn back to Egypt: *they despised the pleasant land.* 2. Misbelieving of God's word is the cause of disesteeming his precious promises, as here is shown: *they believed not his word.* 3. Disestimation of God's precious promises maketh men quarrel with God's providence when he is leading them to the possession thereof; for this made the Israelites malcontent with all that God had done for them : *they murmured in their tents.* 4. When God's dispensation pleaseth not men, they will not fail to take a course of their own, and misregard what God commandeth them : *they murmured in their tents, and hearkened not unto the voice of the Lord.* 5. The faithless man is secluded from heaven and from God's rest by an oath : *they hearkened not unto the voice of the Lord, therefore he lifted up his hand against them*; that is, not only began to smite them, but also, as it is in Heb. iv. 3, *he sware they should not enter into his rest.* 6. We should " fear, lest, a promise being left us of entering into his rest, any of us should seem to come short of it," Heb. iv. 1; and we should " labour to enter into that rest, lest any man fall after the same example of unbelief," Heb. iv. 11, because against unbelieving Israelites, *God lifted up his hand to overthrow them in the wilderness.* 7. The Lord's vengeance against unbelievers, and despisers of the gospel and of the precious promises thereof, readily followeth the posterity of unbelievers, as here the vengeance reached *to overthrow their seed also among the nations, and to scatter them in the lands.* 8. As the Lord's threatenings go forth for sure execution, so they leave room to repentance and intercession, and make both the man that perisheth inexcusable and the man that is spared to know the wrath which he hath deserved; for God lifted up his hand to destroy the unbelievers in the wilderness before he destroyed them, and threatened the posterity before the execution came; for this the apostle, Heb. iv., teacheth us, from the example of God's dealing with the Israelites.

28. *They joined themselves also to Baal-peor, and ate the sacrifices of the dead.*

29. *Thus they provoked* him *to anger with their inventions ; and the plague brake in upon them.*

30. *Then stood up Phinehas, and executed judgment : and* so *the plague was stayed.*

31. *And that was counted unto him for righteousness unto all generations for evermore.*

The sixth sin confessed, is the mixing themselves in fornication, bodily and spiritual, in open idolatry with the Moabites, for which they were plagued, till Phinehas interceded for them, Numb. xxv. Whence learn, 1. Unbelievers are easily induced to change their religion, and to make defection from God, as is evident in the Israelites, who, by the lust of their flesh, mixed themselves with the daughters of Moab, and then joined with them in their idolatry : *they joined themselves also to Baal-peor.* 2. Idolatry is a breach of wedlock with God, and an adulterous joining of a man's soul to an idol : *they joined themselves to Baal-peor.* 3. Communion with idolaters in worship, or in ceremonies and appendicles of idolatrous worship, proveth the communicants to be guilty of idolatry : *they ate the sacrifices of the dead.* 4. Such as fall from true religion to idolatry, make an ill bargain; they go from the living God to dead idols, and deadly idolatry : *they ate the sacrifices of the dead.* 5. Men's devices in religion, and God's acceptable ordinances, stand in opposition, one to another ; because men's inventions cannot please God : *for thus they provoked him with their inventions.* 6. Nothing draweth on more sudden and sore judgment than change of the true worship of God for men's inventions : *they provoked him to anger with their inventions ; and the plague brake in upon them.* 7. Such as have warrant from God to punish open sin, should not delay justice; for thus much doth the extraordinary service of Phinehas teach unto the ordinary magistrate, who beareth the sword by office : *then stood up Phinehas to execute judgment.* 8. As the Lord is loth to strike when he is provoked, so he is ready to hold his hand, and cease upon any convenient occasion : *Phinehas*

*stood up to execute judgment, and so the plague was
stayed.*   9. The rule and order which God hath appointed
men to follow, hindereth not God to give extraordinary
commission to whom he pleaseth, for any extraordinary
piece of service, as appeareth in this instance of Phinehas.
10. What God setteth men at work to do by inward and
immediate inspiration, that he maketh manifest to the church
by his revealed word of approbation, as the inspired command given to Phinehas was justified by God's revealed will
to the church : I say, by inspiration, because impressions
on men's spirits, or instigations to that which the revealed
will of God alloweth not, or secret impulses unto unlawful
actions are one thing, and inspiration of God's extraordinary direction to any special work is another thing; for inspiration from God was the way of shunning God's revealed
will, which was to be communicated to the church by a
moral way of command given to the prophet; such as was
that inspiration whereby God used sometimes to reveal his
will to the church, before the writing of the Scripture was
fully closed.   Thus God revealed his will expressly to Abraham concerning the offering of his son Isaac.   Thus God
gave order to Moses for the Israelites borrowing the jewels
of the Egyptians, upon the right and title which he hath to
all creatures to dispose of them at his pleasure.   Thus the
whole Scripture was not of private interpretation, but the
holy men of God spake as they were inspired and moved
by the Holy Ghost.   And thus was Phinehas instructed for
the particular service; but impressions, impulsions, instigations, which are not according to the revealed rule of God's
word, which now is fully set down in Scripture, as they want
God's moral direction to teach them, so also they want God's
moral approbation : I say moral direction, because providential leading a man to any action is one thing, and moral
direction is another thing.   In the way of providential leading, a man may be led in God's justice, by his own lusts and
Satan's impulse, into temptation, against which evil Christ
directeth us to pray, " lead us not into temptation, but deliver us from that evil," or the evil one.   But where moral
direction is, the man hath his manifested commission, and
knoweth formally the warrant of his action, and so sinneth
not herein; in providential leading, a man is only a brute
instrument, as the Assyrians and Nebuchadnezzar were,

whom God made use of as of a rod of his indignation, and he knew it not; but in moral direction, the man is a rational servant, as knowing what he doeth to be warrantable service; and so was Moses in all the house of God a faithful servant, doing all as God commanded him; and so was Phinehas here God's servant, following morally a clear divine inspiration, a clear command and direction, and therefore had he also God's moral approbation: *for it was counted to him for righteousness.* 11. As there is a justification of a man's person, which is only by faith in Jesus Christ, so is there a justification of a certain deed or action, when it is accepted by God for service; and of this sort is the justification of Phinehas' zealous act: for this act was *imputed unto him for righteousness*, or for a righteous piece of service. 12. What God justifieth, whether it be a man, or a man's action, no man may condemn it, for it standeth absolved, as in this may be seen: *it was imputed unto him for righteousness, unto all generations for evermore.*

32. *They angered him also at the waters of strife, so that it went ill with Moses for their sakes:*

33. *Because they provoked his spirit, so that he spake unadvisedly with his lips.*

The seventh sin confessed, is murmuring at Meribah for want of water, whereby meek Moses was drawn into the snare of a rash speech, and of a notable inconvenience, Numb. xx. Whence learn, 1. Oft-repeated sin obstinately persisted in, cannot but provoke God to anger; for, as before they had murmured, so also now murmuring again, *they angered God at the waters of strife.* 2. When the Lord's servants in doing their calling are striven against, there God is also striven against; for this cause the place where the people strove with Moses is called the waters of strife; to wit, with God, because they strove with Moses. 3. The Lord's servants are in danger to be drawn into sundry temptations and snares, by the evil carriage of the people over whom they have charge, as by occasion of the people's murmuring, *it went ill with Moses for their sakes.* 4. Albeit men are to be pitied who are provoked to sin, yet the provocation excuseth not the sinner, but it aggravateth the sin of the provoker: as here, *it went ill with Moses for their sakes, because they provoked his spirit.* 5. In the holiest of men, there are reliques of sin unmortified, and such weakness as they may readily fall into sin in an hour of temptation : *for Moses spake unadvisedly with his lips.* 6. It is a dangerous case to come to the Lord's holy service with any passion or carnal perturbation, or to mingle God's public service with our passions, as appeareth in the case of Moses. 7. The leading of a holy life in the former time of a man's life, cannot justify or excuse an ill action thereafter, or hinder God's wrath when the sin breaketh forth, as is to be seen in Moses' case, *with whom it went ill, because he spake unadvisedly with his lips.*

34. *They did not destroy the nations, concerning whom the Lord commanded them.*

The eighth sin is their disobedience to God's command, after they were placed in the land of *Canaan*, which is set down in sundry particulars. The first is, their sparing of the Canaanites, whom God commanded them to destroy. Whence learn, 1. Neglect and omission of that which God commandeth to be done, bring men under guiltiness, challenge, and wrath, and prove the fountain of more mischief afterwards than men are aware of, as here appeareth: *they did not destroy the nations, concerning whom the Lord commanded them.* 2. Men should not spare the lives of those whom God commandeth to destroy, lest God make a quarrel of it, as here he doth against the Israelites.

35. *But were mingled among the heathen, and learned their works.*

36. *And they served their idols : which were a snare unto them.*

The next particulars following the former sparing of the Canaanites, are forbidden marriages with them and contagion of their ill manners. Whence learn, 1. Sins of omission make way for, and draw on, sins of commission, as here we see. 2. Unequal matching with open idolaters draweth on contagion of idolatry : *they were mingled among the heathen, and learned their works. And they served their idols.* 3. Making of images, in the matter of religion, is a work of the heathen; for so it is here reckoned, and called *their work.* 4. Idolatry is a sin that is easily learned, the contagion whereof spreadeth quickly : for the Canaanites' *idols were a snare* to the Israelites. 5. Service to images

is condemned by God as worship of images is condemned;
yea, God comprehendeth under service, all and whatsoever
respect done to images, as an abominable and damnable sin:
for, *they served their idols*, is here the challenge. 6. How
pleasant soever, delectable, and profitable, men plead images
to be, yet God esteemeth them as doleful inventions, which
bring no profit to their servants and worshippers save grief;
for so much the word in the original giveth us to understand. 7. Whatsoever fair pretences men suffer themselves
to be led away with, unto the fellowship of idolaters and service of images, are nothing but deluding deceits, which shall
bring on the contrary evils undoubtedly: *they served their
idols, which were a snare to them.*

37. *Yea, they sacrificed their sons and their daughters unto devils,*

38. *And shed innocent blood,* even *the blood of their
sons and of their daughters, whom they sacrificed unto
the idols of Canaan: and the land was polluted with
blood.*

39. *Thus were they defiled with their own works,
and went a-whoring with their own inventions.*

Another particular of their disobedience in *Canaan*, is
their sacrificing their children to idols, whereby the land
was fearfully polluted. Whence learn, 1. When men depart from the rule of God's worship, there is no stay nor
standing till they fall into the grossest idolatry, whereunto
they are tempted: *yea*, saith he, *they sacrificed their sons
and daughters*. 2. The rage of idolatry is such that it
will not spare whatsoever is dearest; even the lives of children and friends, to maintain it: *they sacrificed their
sons and daughters*. 3. The service done to idols and
images of man's devising, is not done to God, as men pretend who worship them, but to devils, who are the devisers,
suggesters, and enticers of men to all sort of unlawful worship; and who are served and obeyed in effect by false religion, Deut. xxxii. 17. 2 Chron. xi. 15. 1 Cor. x. 20:
*they sacrificed their sons and daughters unto devils,
whom they sacrificed unto the idols of* Canaan. 4. Idolaters are blood-thirsty, and respect not the innocence of any
party or person, by whose bloodshed the idol may be honoured and Satan pleased, who is a liar and murderer from

the beginning : *they shed innocent blood, even the blood of their sons and daughters, whom they sacrificed to the idols of* Canaan. 5. When innocent blood is shed, the land is polluted, whatsoever be the cause which is pretended : *they shed innocent blood, and the land was polluted with blood.* 6. The highest point of holiness in a false religion, is but filthiness and pollution ; and no invention of man can make the followers thereof more holy by observation thereof, but polluteth them still, the more they follow them : *for thus were they defiled with their own works.* 7. Following men's inventions in religion, is idolatry, or spiritual adultery, because God is forsaken in so far, and another god and lord in religion is received in God's stead : for so much saith the text, *they went a-whoring with their own inventions.*

40. *Therefore was the wrath of the Lord kindled against his people, insomuch that he abhorred his own inheritance.*

41. *And he gave them into the hand of the heathen ; and they that hated them ruled over them.*

42. *Their enemies also oppressed them, and they were brought into subjection under their hand.*

Here is shown what followed on their following their own inventions, to wit, slavery and subjection to men, in God's indignation. Whence learn, 1. When men follow sin and their own ways, wrath follows them : *for therefore was the wrath of God kindled against his own people.* 2. When from the word of the Lord men will not believe how odious superstition is to him, he will make them find it by his plagues : *for therefore was the wrath of the Lord kindled.* 3. No privilege can make men so lovely before God, as the love of idols and images in the matter of religion maketh them to be loathed of him : *his wrath was kindled, even against his own people, insomuch that he abhorred his own inheritance.* 4. When God's people follow the superstition of idolaters, either by complying to gratify them, or in way of pleasing themselves, it is justice with God to make idolaters their masters, and to make his people lose the benefit hoped for by compliance : *and he gave them into the hand of the heathen.* 5. It is righteousness with God to put his people under the yoke of men that hate

them, when they have cast off the easy yoke of God who
loveth them: and when men follow ways which God abhorreth, God justly makes them suffer what they most
abhor: *he gave them over into the hand of the heathen;
and they that hated them, ruled over them.* 6. The sins
of God's people make open way for their enemies, and put
strength, courage, and victory into their hands; and lest
the Lord's people should not be moved by that change of
government, he makes their burden under their enemies
unsupportable: *their enemies also oppressed them.* 7.
When the people will not humble themselves in the way of
repentance, it is righteousness with God to bring them low
by judgments, as here is seen: the Israelites repented not
of their sins, *and they were brought into subjection under their enemies' hand.*

43. *Many times did he deliver them; but they provoked* him *with their counsel, and were brought low for
their iniquity.*

44. *Nevertheless he regarded their affliction, when
he heard their cry:*

45. *And he remembered for them his covenant, and
repented according to the multitude of his mercies.*

46. *He made them also to be pitied of all those that
carried them captives.*

The ninth, and last point of confession, is of a heap of
manifold sins often repeated; notwithstanding which, God
showed pity to his people for his covenant's cause. Whence
learn, 1. The Lord leaveth no means unessayed to gain his
people; sometimes he puts them to sore trouble, sometimes
he delivereth them, and exerciseth them with the vicissitudes
of calamities and deliveries, if by any means they may be
saved: *many times did he deliver them.* 2. Such is our
wickedness and perverse nature that still we give the Lord
a bad meeting for his mercies, and, instead of thankfulness, provoke him by doing and following what we ourselves
think fittest, as is to be seen in the Israelites: *many times
did God deliver them, but they provoked him with their
counsel.* 3. Men, in the course of their sins, have high
and self-pleasing conceits of themselves, and no impenitency
is without pride; but by sad judgments God many times
maketh those lie low in affliction who do not walk humbly

in the way of obedience, as here we see the Israelites *provoked God by their counsel*; that is, by their own devices, conceits, and inventions : *but they were made low by their iniquities.* 4. Albeit God's people ofttimes provoke him, and in their prosperity regard not God or his commands, yet God regards them so as both, after a while's prosperity, to correct them, and, after a while's adversity, to comfort them : *nevertheless he regarded their affliction.* 5. God, by heavy affliction, moveth men to cry unto him who otherwise would not have called upon him at all, as his dealing with proud provoking Israel here showeth, who in affliction are made *to cry.* 6. Albeit there be commonly great unsoundness in the cry of oppressed people, yet God will hear that cry and help them out of a temporal trouble, as here : *he regarded their affliction, when he heard their cry.* 7. As when God's people abuse his grace and forget his covenant, and are plagued for their sins, the good of the covenant, and confederacy with God are obscured, buried, and, as it were, forgotten; so, when the Lord changeth his dispensation, the benefit of the covenant is brought to light again; for then God taketh occasion to show that, albeit his people forget the covenant, yet he forgets it not : *for he remembered for them,* or, for their behalf, *his covenant.* 8. The unchangeableness of God's merciful nature and love to his people maketh him change the course of justice into mercy, and no other change, except of this dispensation, is meant by God's repentance, when it is said, *and he repented according to the multitude of his mercies.* 9. The mercy of the Lord is so large that the multitude of former sins and abused bypast favours cannot hinder the sinner once again to come to the inexhaustible fountain of grace, and cannot hinder God once more to show mercy to a sinner; yea, albeit God hath entered into judgment with the sinner, and hath begun to pour out deserved wrath upon him—even justice, thus begun to be executed, cannot hinder God to hold his hand and show mercy once again to the sinner; for here experience teacheth that, ofttimes when he had entered into judgment with Israel, *he repented according to the multitude of his mercies.* 10. God hath the ruling of all men's affections, to make them turn as he pleaseth. God mixeth the most bitter cup of judgment given to his people to drink, with the ingredients *of compassion;* and what pity his people find from any hand, it is the fruit, effect, and evidence of God's pity toward them : *he made them also to be pitied of all those that carried them captive.*

47. *Save us, O Lord our God, and gather us from among the heathen, to give thanks unto thy holy name,* and *to triumph in thy praise.*

48. *Blessed* be *the Lord God of Israel from ever-lasting to everlasting : and let all the people say, Amen. Praise ye the Lord.*

This is the last part of the psalm, wherein the psalmist draweth two conclusions from what he hath been speaking, and teacheth the church to do the same in their sad afflictions. The one is a prayer for the fresh experience of the like mercy unto the church, and to every member thereof in his time, v. 47 ; the other is a praising of God in assurance of faith, that he would certainly do so, v. 48. Whence learn, 1. The right use of the history of God's mercies to his church is to go to God in humility, and to encourage ourselves to seek and expect the like to ourselves : *save us* also, saith the church here. 2. Seeing God, in showing mercy to his people, always respecteth the covenant, it is good for the sinner not to quit his interest therein, but to claim new experience of mercy, according to the tenor thereof; for this the church prayeth here : *save us, O Lord our God.* 3. The visible church may be so defaced for a time, that, howsoever the visible members thereof can never cease to be, but one generation shall follow another; yet the outward societies and solemn assemblies of the church may be dissolved and disappear by being scattered, as this part of their prayer, *gather us,* importeth. 4. It is a heavy affliction for the godly to live in the company of enemies, and of men of a false religion; from this evil they desire to be delivered : *gather us from among the heathen.* 5. The face of a visible church, wherein we may have the communion of saints, and occasions to associate with them, and enjoy the public and free use of religion, is a great mercy, and worthy that God should be entreated for it : *gather us from among the heathen, to give thanks to thy holy name.* 6. The Lord's people are allowed to glory in the Lord and to boast in his praise; and the end of their seeking the liberty of freely assembling themselves should be, that they may declare the Lord's praise, and glory in him: *gather us, to give thanks to thy holy name, and to triumph in thy praise.* 7. When we have prayed according to God's will we should take our prayer for granted, and leave it lying at God's feet, as the church doth here. 8. Let the Lord do to his covenanted people what he pleaseth, they shall never want reason to praise, thank, and bless him; for the closing of this psalm teacheth us so much: *blessed be the Lord God of Israel.* 9. The Lord is the ever-living fountain of spiritual and everlasting blessings to his own people; and whatsoever becomes of temporal things, there is reason to bless God for spiritual and everlasting mercies, and to say, *blessed be the Lord God of Israel from everlasting to everlasting.* 10. When the Spirit of the Lord raiseth the song of the praises of God by his prophets and ministers, it is the bride's part, and the part of every member of the church, to join in the thanksgiving, and subscribe, with acclamation, unto the blessing of God: *and let all the people say, Amen.* 11. When the believer hath, in his own person, given thanks to God, he should stir up others, according as his station calleth him to it, to praise the Lord also, as here is done: *praise ye the Lord.*

PSALM CVII.

This is a psalm of praise for God's gracious and wise dispensations towards men. In the first part the psalmist reckoneth four exercises of God's people by God's justice bringing them to straits, and by his mercy delivering them again. The first exercise is by banishment, and by the Lord's bringing them back from it, to ver. 10; the second is by captivity and imprisonment, and delivery out of it, to ver. 17; the third is by bodily sickness, and recovery from it, to ver. 23; the fourth is through danger by sea, and the delivery out of it, to ver. 33.

In the latter part of the psalm he praiseth God for his wise dealing with people and nations, in changes made among them, in their lands, persons, goods, and estates, for the good of his own and overthrow of the proud. One change is of a fertile land into a barren wilderness, for the inhabitants' sins, ver. 33, 34; another change is of a barren land into a fertile and plentiful soil, well-peopled, to ver. 39; a third change is, wasting and spoiling a well-peopled and fertile country, ver. 39; a fourth change is, pulling down princes and statesmen, and confounding them so that they know not what to do or whither to go, ver. 40; the fifth change is, the lifting up of the poor and desolate, and enlarging them in all respects, ver. 41. The best witnesses of which changes are the godly and wise observers of God's providence, who, for a reward of their observation, shall have comfortable use and benefit of all God's dispensations, ver. 42, 43.

1. *O give thanks unto the Lord, for he is good; for his mercy endureth for ever.*

2. *Let the redeemed of the Lord say so, whom he hath redeemed from the hand of the enemy;*

3. *And gathered them out of the lands, from the east, and from the west, from the north, and from the south.*

The psalmist exhorteth all to give thanks unto the Lord, and specially the Lord's redeemed ones, brought back from exile out of all countries where they wandered. Whence learn, 1. Unto no duty do we feel more dull and untoward, than to the praise of God, and thanksgiving unto him; neither is there any duty whereunto there is more need that we should be stirred up, as this earnest exhortation importeth : *O give thanks unto the Lord.* 2. Whether men acknowledge the grace and bounty of the Lord or not, he is worthy to be thanked and praised; partly because of his liberal and ready communicating his goodness freely, not only to not deserving, but also to ill deserving persons, and that out of mere mercy; partly, because he followeth the man who hath found mercy, with mercy more and more; and partly, because he refuseth to no man mercy who seeketh it, or shall seek it of him, at what time soever, to the world's end; for so much saith the reason of the exhortation, *for he is good, for his mercy endureth for ever.* 3. Every man hath matter, reason, and obligation lying on him, to praise God; but specially such as have more particular, oftener, and greater experience of mercies than others have had : *let the redeemed of the Lord say so.* 4. Redemption made by Christ of his own elect, is the fountain of every particular benefit bestowed upon them; for the elect are called the redeemed of the Lord here, before the particular delivery from banishment be specified, and that delivery is called a redeeming of them : *whom he hath redeemed from the hand of the enemy,* as flowing from the great redemption. 5. So oft as men have received deliverances, they owe unto God so many lives, and God hath so many titles of right unto them, as they have received preservations; and those will the Lord have to be witnesses of his mercy before the rest of the world : *let the redeemed of the Lord say so, whom he hath redeemed from the hand of the enemy.* 6. As the Lord's children may be scattered into all the corners of

the world, and excluded from the external communion of
the saints, so none of them return from exile, to join in the
use of religion and holy ordinances, except by God's special
hand gathering them: *for he gathered them out of the
lands, from the east, and from the west, from the north,
and from the south.*

4. *They wandered in the wilderness in a solitary
way; they found no city to dwell in.*

5. *Hungry and thirsty, their soul fainted in them.*

Here is described, first the distress of the redeemed in
their exile, v. 4, 5; then their exercise in calling unto God;
and, thirdly, their bringing home, v. 6, 7. Whence the
psalmist inferreth the duty of thanksgiving, whereunto he
had before exhorted, v. 8, 9. From their distress, learn,
1. Such as the Lord hath a purpose to draw into the fellowship of himself and his saints, are subject to wandering and
exile, both bodily and spiritual, as the exercise of exiled Israelites showeth: *they wandered in the wilderness.* 2. The
Lord's exiled ones find no home, till they be brought to the
fellowship of the saints: *they wandered in the wilderness,
in a solitary way: they found no city to dwell in.* 3. The
Lord's exiles may be in danger of famine, both bodily and
spiritual, and like to faint for lack of food, bodily or spiritual, or both sorts, as the banished here *were hungry and
thirsty, and their soul fainted in them.*

6. *Then they cried unto the Lord in their trouble,*
and *he delivered them out of their distresses.*

7. *And he led them forth by the right way, that they
might go to a city of habitation.*

From their exercise in their double distress of banishment
and famine, and from their delivery, learn, 1. Straits put
men to seek God in a serious manner: *then they cried unto
the Lord in their trouble.* 2. The earnest prayer of God's
distressed children wanteth not a good answer: *and he delivered them out of their distresses.* 3. When the Lord
will comfort a supplicant, he will deliver him from so many
parts of his trouble as may serve to lead him on his journey; he will furnish food, and direction, both whither to go,
and by what way to go: *and he led them by the right way,
that they might go to a city of habitation.* 4. To be directed by God what to do, whether it be in relation to mat-

ters temporal or spiritual, is a special benefit, and a fair fruit of prayer; for he whom the Lord guideth shall walk safely, and prosper in his way : *he led them by the right way, that they might go to a city of habitation.*

8. *Oh that* men *would praise the Lord* for *his goodness, and* for *his wonderful works to the children of men !*

9. *For he satisfieth the longing soul, and filleth the hungry soul with goodness.*

From the duty required of the exile now returned home, learn, 1. The mercies of the Lord showed to his own, call for praising God by themselves and all beholders; they call for praise, both in secret and in society : *Oh that men would praise the Lord for his goodness.* 2. The Lord's manner of delivering his own out of their great troubles, whether bodily or spiritual, hath ordinarily some observable wonder in it : *Oh that men would praise the Lord for his wonderful works to the children of men.* 3. The poor and needy supplicants live upon God's support; he is a provider for such, and letteth them want nothing, but satisfieth them sufficiently; and this is no small comfort unto us, and matter of praise unto God : *for he satisfieth the longing soul, and filleth the hungry soul with goodness.*

10. *Such as sit in darkness, and in the shadow of death,* being *bound in affliction and iron ;*

11. *Because they rebelled against the words of God, and contemned the counsel of the most High ;*

12. *Therefore he brought down their heart with labour : they fell down, and* there was *none to help.*

13. *Then they cried unto the Lord in their trouble,* and *he saved them out of their distresses.*

14. *He brought them out of darkness and the shadow of death, and brake their bands in sunder.*

15. *Oh that* men *would praise the Lord* for *his goodness, and* for *his wonderful works to the children of men !*

16. *For he hath broken the gates of brass, and cut the bars of iron in sunder.*

Here is set down the second exercise of God's people, to

wit, by captivity and imprisonment, brought upon them for
their sins, and their delivery from it, upon their turning to
God, with the use thereof. Whence learn, 1. As liberty of
our persons to go about our callings freely is no small benefit, so imprisonment is a sore affliction, even a sort of living
death, and a form of burial of the quick: *for they sit in
darkness, and in the shadow of death.* 2. Bonds and
chains put upon the prisoner, add much weight to the heavy
condition of the imprisoned, and yet the Lord's people are
subject to both: for here is presupposed, that *they may be
bound in affliction and iron* in their prison. 3. It is above
all the affliction of imprisonment and bonds, when the cause
of the imprisonment is not righteousness, but *because they
have rebelled against the word of God, and contemned
the counsel of the most High.* 4. The not bearing the
easy yoke of obedience, may bring the heavier yoke of iron,
bonds, and imprisonment upon us, as here is expressed.
5. The greatness of the majesty of God, aggravateth the sin
of despising his word: *they contemned the counsel of the
most High.* 6. As the word of the Lord is both deep counsel for wisdom, and also profitable advice for us, so the con-
temning of it is so much the greater sin, and draweth on the
greater wrath: *they were bound in affliction and·iron,
because they rebelled against the words of God, and contemned the counsel of the most High.* 7. The Lord
bringeth men into sore distresses, to make them sensible of
their despising his authority, to break their natural pride
and stoutness of heart against him, and to show them the
vanity of all their former fleshly confidence: *therefore he
brought down their heart with labour.* 8. Affliction is
then come to the height, and its complete measure, when
the sinner is made sensible of his own weakness, and seeth
that there is no help for him save in God alone: *they fell
down, and there was none to help.* 9. When all help and
comfort under heaven fail, relief may be found in God for
those that cry to him for it: *there was none to help, then
they cried to the Lord in their trouble.* 10. The Lord will
not only hear and help those who are unjustly imprisoned,
but those also who for their sins are so punished: *they cried,
and he saved them out of their distresses.* 11. It matters
not how deep the danger be wherein a man is, when he turneth to God for relief; for so great as his distress is, so great

shall be his delivery: *he brought them out of darkness and the shadow of death, and brake their bonds in sunder.* 12. The end of the delivery of poor sinners is, that they may glorify the Lord, and may invite others to do the like; for this here is a part of the thankful man's ditty: *Oh that men would praise the Lord for his goodness, and for his wonderful works to the children of men.* 13. No power of man, no bonds, no opposition which any creature is able to make, can hinder the delivery of the man whom God will own: *he hath broken the gates of brass, and cut the bars of iron in sunder.*

17. *Fools, because of their transgression, and because of their iniquities, are afflicted:*

18. *Their soul abhorreth all manner of meat; and they draw near unto the gates of death.*

19. *Then they cry unto the Lord in their trouble, and he saveth them out of their distresses.*

20. *He sent his word, and healed them, and delivered them from their destructions.*

21. *Oh that men would praise the Lord for his goodness, and for his wonderful works to the children of men!*

22. *And let them sacrifice the sacrifices of thanksgiving, and declare his works with rejoicing.*

The third exercise of God's people, is by sickness of body; the drawing on whereof he showeth to be by sin, v. 17, 18; the means of delivery to be by prayer, v. 19; whereupon they are recovered as God giveth order, v. 20; and the use of this is set down, v. 21, 22. Whence learn, 1. As other troubles come for sinning against God, so sickness cometh among the rest: *fools, because of their transgression, and because of their iniquities, are afflicted.* 2. Sin blindeth sinners, and bereaveth them of the right use of their season, and maketh them choose trifles, with the loss of what should be most precious: therefore they are justly called fools. 3. Natural means of life and refreshment are unsavoury and unable to refresh, except God give the man ability to make use of them, and put his blessing into them: *their soul abhorreth all manner of meat.* 4. As in other troubles, so in sickness, men are not easily brought to the sense of their sin, till trouble be at the height, and the man made low : *their soul abhorreth all manner of meat, and they draw near to the gates of death.* 5. Great is the stupidity of a sleeping conscience, which cannot be wakened up to seek God till extremity come : *they draw near to the gates of death, then they cry unto the Lord in their trouble.* 6. When men are brought to the sense of their sins and misdeservings, of their danger and their own weakness, and thereby made to seek the Lord, the mercy and relief are near at hand : *then they cried unto the Lord in their trouble, so he saved them out of their distresses :* and here are to be seen mercy and goodness in God, to cause sicknesses as his sergeants and messengers to lay hold on the fugitive sinner. 7. Neither sickness, nor health comes or goes, but God giveth order to them, as to his own servants. He saith to sickness, go from a man; and to health, return to him : *he sent his word, and healed them.* 8. When trouble showeth wrath, and that wakeneth the sense of sin, and sense of sin sends the man to seek mercy, then God will readily remove all his troubles together: *he sent his word and healed them, and delivered them from their destructions.* 9. As men have found mercies of God, so should they study to be thankful, and specially in such a way as may be most profitable to others: *Oh that men would praise the Lord for his goodness, and for his wonderful works to the children of men !* 10. Moral and spiritual service is more acceptable to God than any ceremonial performance; the sacrifice of thanks is more than the sacrifice of an ox : *let them sacrifice the sacrifices of thanksgiving.* 11. The special matter of joy in receiving a benefit, is the manifestation of God's respect to us, in his working for us : *and let them declare his works, with rejoicing.*

23. *They that go down to the sea in ships, that do business in great waters ;*

24. *These see the works of the Lord, and his wonders in the deep.*

25. *For he commandeth, and raiseth the stormy wind, which lifteth up the waves thereof.*

26. *They mount up to the heaven, they go down again to the depths ; their soul is melted because of trouble.*

27. *They reel to and fro, and stagger like a drunken man, and are at their wit's end.*

The fourth exercise of God's children, is by their danger in sea, and their delivery from their danger. Whence learn, 1. The art of navigation and following the merchant trade by sea, how dangerous soever they be, yet are lawful and allowed of God, for compassing men's affairs, in commerce between nation and nation : for this is set down here as the vocation and occupation of some men, to wit, of *those that go down to the sea in ships, that do business in great waters.* 2. Some persons have more occasion of observa-- tion, and experience of remarkable passages of providence in preserving men's lives, than others have; and these most of all should bear witness of God's work according to their experience : *these see the works of the Lord, and his wonders in the deep.* 3. There is no storm or motion in the sea, or blowing of the winds out of any airth, but as God actually raiseth them : *for he commandeth, and raiseth the stormy wind, which lifteth up the waters thereof.* 4. When God will try a man by trouble, he will not leave him till he make him sensible of his frailty, weakness, and inability to overcome dangers : *they mount up to the hea-ven, they go down again to the depths ; their soul is melted because of trouble. They reel to and fro, and stagger like a drunken men, &c.*

28. *Then they cry unto the Lord in their trouble, and he bringeth them out of their distresses.*

29. *He maketh the storm a calm, so that the waves thereof are still.*

30. *Then are they glad because they be quiet; so he bringeth them unto their desired haven.*

In their delivery from the storm, learn, 1. Albeit the Lord delivereth many from shipwreck by sea, yet he takes none of them for witnesses of his mercy, but such as had recourse to him in their strait by prayer : *then they cry unto the Lord in their trouble ;* those are the men whom the Lord remarketh. 2. The fervent prayer of the Lord's redeemed, who at length, at least make God their refuge in trouble, has deliverance for the fruit following upon it : *they cry, and he bringeth them out of their distresses.*

3. As the raising of a storm is from the Lord, so the quieting of it again is his work also; and both the one and the other work hath the time and measure of it so disposed, as may best serve his purpose: *he maketh the storm a calm; so that the waters thereof are still.* **4.** According as is men's grief in trouble, so is, or should be, the greatness of their joy in their delivery: *then are they glad because they be quiet.* **5.** So many sea voyages, are so many evidences of God's so oft conducting and conveying seamen to and fro: *so he bringeth them to their desired haven.*

31. *Oh that* men *would praise the Lord* for *his goodness, and* for *his wonderful works to the children of men!*

32. *Let them exalt him also in the congregation of the people, and praise him in the assembly of the elders.*

From the use of this exercise here required, learn, 1. That it is the part of every man, who comes to the knowledge of any experience or new proof of God's mercy, in special to any of his people, not only to acknowledge God's goodness by himself, but also to wish that the reason of his praises were known to all men, and that all men might praise God for it: *Oh that men would praise the Lord for his goodness.* 2. It is the duty of a thankful man, not only to praise God for the experience he hath had of God's goodness in his own person; but also to praise God upon that occasion, for any other wonderful works which the Lord worketh daily for the children of men: *Oh that men would praise the Lord for his wonderful works to the children of men.* 3. After returning home, seamen should carefully observe the meetings of the church, as for other reasons, so because they have been withdrawn so long from those assemblies, while their voyage lasted: *and let them exalt him also in the congregation of the people.* 4. Beside the assembly of the whole congregation, the Scripture maketh mention of the church or congregation, or assembly of the elders, who had the oversight and governing of the particular synagogues and churches of the people: for here and elsewhere, beside the congregation of the people, there is mention made of the assembly of the elders, as distinguished from the assembly of the people: *and let them praise him in the assembly of the elders.* 5. As prayers are or should be made in the congregation for such of the flock as are in any special danger of their lives; so duty requireth that praises should be offered for the remarkable deliveries, or recoveries out of those dangers: for of such as are delivered from shipwreck, it is said, *let them exalt him also in the congregation of the people.* 6. As it is a part of the people's duty, to acquaint the elders of the congregation with such passages of God's most remarkable providence about them, as may be most glorifying to God, and for the people's edifying; so it is a part of the work of the eldership to take notice of, and make the best use in their prudence of, what falleth out among their flocks, whereby all may be edified: for, as the right judging of God's works of providence requireth prudence and wisdom; so they who are set over the congregation, as most eminent therein for their wisdom and prudence should go about this part of their charge among other duties; for it is said, *and let them praise him in the assembly of the elders.*

33. *He turneth rivers into a wilderness, and the water-springs into dry ground;*

34. *A fruitful land into barrenness, for the wickedness of them that dwell therein.*

In the latter part of the psalm, the Lord is praised for his wisdom, in making changes upon countries and nations, men's persons and estates, some in justice, some in mercy, as he seeth fit: of which changes he reckoneth up five. The first whereof is, the turning of a fertile land into barrenness for the inhabitants' sins. Whence learn, 1. When a fertile land becometh barren, and men are cut short of their commodities by sea or land, by the creatures not yielding service, as they were wont to do, men should lift their eyes above all second causes, and fix them on God, who what way he thinketh best bringeth the change: *he turneth rivers into a wilderness, and the water-springs into dry ground;* that is to say, *a fruitful land into barrenness.* 2. The proper meritorious cause of God's cursing a fertile land, are the sins of the inhabitants, whom God will have so answered in their labours on the ground, as they answer the Lord in his husbandry and pains taken upon them; and whom God will chastise for their sin, and so move them to repent: *he turneth a fruitful land into barrenness, for the wickedness of them that dwell therein.*

35. *He turneth the wilderness into a standing water, and dry ground into water-springs.*

36. *And there he maketh the hungry to dwell, that they may prepare a city for habitation;*

37. *And sow the fields, and plant vineyards, which may yield fruits of increase.*

38. *He blesseth them also, so that they are multiplied greatly, and suffereth not their cattle to decrease.*

The second change mentioned, is of a barren land into fertility. Whence learn, 1. The fertility of land is not to be attributed to men's industry, but to God: *he turneth the wilderness into a standing water, and dry ground into water-springs.* 2. If God afflict, his justice findeth the cause of it in a man: but if he do good to any man, it is of his own good pleasure, without any cause in man: therefore no reason is given here of this change, as was of the former, but simply, *he turneth dry ground into water-springs.* 3. The Lord taketh pleasure to provide for the needy, and they shall be forced to acknowledge his goodness in his provision for them: *and there he maketh the hungry to dwell, that they may prepare a city for habitation.* 4. When God openeth a door for blessing men, he will have it improved, and ordinary means diligently used, as here, *he will have them sow the fields, and plant vineyards, which may yield fruits of increase.* 5. When the Lord is pleased to bless men, he will bless them largely in the growth of their families and substance, and will extend his care even to their beasts: *he blessed them also, so that they are multiplied greatly, and suffereth not their cattle to decrease.*

39. *Again, they are minished, and brought low through oppression, affliction, and sorrow.*

The third change is by spoiling a populous and well planted country. Whence learn, 1. Such as have been raised from a low condition, can hardly bear prosperity, but are readily puffed up with it, as their change presupposeth. 2. God can bring down such as abuse prosperity, and make them as base as ever they were: *again, they are minished and brought low.* 3. The Lord hath more ways than one to spoil a fertile country; for , albeit he make it continue fertile, yet he can bring the sword of the enemy on it: *they are brought low through oppression, affliction, and sorrow.*

40. *He poureth contempt upon princes, and causeth them to wander in the wilderness,* where there is *no way.*

A fourth change is, in pulling down princes, and putting statesmen to perplexity. Whence learn, 1. As kings and rulers keep not their place, power, and estimation among men, but by God's investing them with dignity, so when they lose their dignity and are despised, they must look to God as the doer, and search the quarrel: for God will honour them that honour him, and they who despise him shall be lightly esteemed : *he poureth contempt upon princes.* 2. It is God who giveth wisdom and prudence to men, for ruling states; and when their wit is employed for their own earthly interest, he can take their wisdom from them, and give them a cup of giddy wine, and put them in such perplexity, as they know not what to do; he can banish them out of their country, and send them as vagabonds through the earth : *he caused them to wander in the wilderness, where there is no way.*

41. *Yet setteth he the poor on high from affliction, and maketh* him *families like a flock.*

The fifth change is, in comforting the afflicted, and raising them out of the dust to a better condition, after they are humbled in the sense of their own poverty. Whence learn, 1. Albeit the Lord casteth down the mighty, and putteth the wise to perplexity; yet he will pursue them no farther than into humiliation. If so be they take with their sins, and seek reconciliation with God as his word prescribeth, and depend upon God as needy poor souls, he will lift them up again : *yet setteth he the poor on high from affliction.* 2. As pride and self-estimation, because of riches, or power, or wisdom, or any other earthly rea-

son, go before ruin; so lowliness of mind, humiliation in
the sense of sin and unworthiness, and of weakness and
witlessness, driving a man to depend on God, as a beggar
for alms, goeth before exaltation: *he setteth the poor on
high from affliction, and maketh him families like a
flock.*

42. *The righteous shall see* it, *and rejoice; and all
iniquity shall stop her mouth.*

43. *Whoso* is *wise, and will observe these* things,
*even they shall understand the loving-kindness of the
Lord.*

The psalmist closeth the psalm with two promises; the
one of performing what is here said, to the comfort of the
righteous and shame of the misbelieving proud sinner; the
other of manifesting his loving-kindness to such as observe
and make use of God's providence.   Whence learn, 1. Such
as, being justified by faith, endeavour to order their conversation righteously, shall be witnesses of the Lord's performing his word : *the righteous shall see it.*   2. As there
is joy in believing the Lord's word, so there is yet more
joy in beholding the performance of his word : *the righteous shall see it, and rejoice.*   3. Among other mercies
bestowed upon the righteous man, this is one, that the
Lord putteth him upon the counsel of his working, expoundeth his providence to him by his word, teacheth him
to compare God's word and his works, and maketh him
witness that God is as good as his word: *the righteous
shall see it, and rejoice.*   4. The wicked shall be disappointed of his expectation, in regard of the good which he
hoped to himself, and shall find himself mistaken about the
godly, whose ways he counted to be folly : *the righteous
shall rejoice; and all iniquity shall stop her mouth.*   5.
As the works of the Lord's goodness, justice, and mercy,
are wrought in the sight of men, that they may observe
his way, and keep the observation thereof in memory; so
are they the wisest men, who observe God's providence best,
and compare it with the Lord's word, that they may understand it rightly : *whoso is wise, and will observe these
things.*   The wise man, and the observer of God's ways toward the children of men here, are one.   6. Albeit there
be very few wise observers of God's proceeding with men

in justice or mercy, yet so many as are his disciples, students of his word, and walk answerably thereunto, shall never want matter of observation of God's kindness toward themselves: *for whoso is wise, even they shall understand the loving-kindness of the Lord.*

PSALM CVIII.

A song or psalm of David.

This psalm is composed of a part of the fifty-seventh psalm, from ver. 7, to the end, and of a part of the sixtieth psalm, from ver. 5, to the end, but in a diverse notion; for, in the fifty-seventh and sixtieth psalms, David is praying for experience of the truth of the promise made to him concerning the kingdom of Israel, and victory over his enemies on all sides, being now in hazard by them: but here he is making use of the experience received, and of victory obtained over enemies within and without the kingdom of Israel, for the encouragement of the church militant to the end of the world, against all intestine and foreign enemies whatsoever. Again, in these two former psalms, whence he repeateth the words of this psalm, he had his own interest to plead, beside what was typical in his exercise. Here, his own interest being settled, and the promise made to himself performed; he recommendeth this experience of his on a more abstract notion from his own particular, and in a more typical way of a pledge of the victory of the true church militant, under her Head and Lord, over all both her intestine and foreign enemies, without the verge of the visible profession, that in the faith of Christ, and hope of his prevailing in the work of enlarging and reforming the visible catholic church, and overthrowing the open enemies of Christ's kingdom, typified under the exercise of David, the true subjects of Christ might go on in their warfare with the greater confidence.

This psalm hath two parts. In the former is the thanksgiving of faith, and promise of praise, in hope of obtaining all which the church is here to pray, v. 1—5. In the latter part is the prayer for preservation of the church, v. 6, with confidence to be heard and helped, whatsoever impediment appear, against all who stand out against Christ's kingdom, whether within the visible church, v. 7, 8, or whether without, such as are professed enemies unto it, v. 9—11; which prayer is followed forth, v. 12, and comfortably closed with assurance of the church's victory by the assistance of God, v. 13.

1. *O God, my heart is fixed; I will sing and give praise, even with my glory.*

2. *Awake, psaltery and harp; I myself will awake early.*

In the thanksgiving of faith and promise of praise, he composeth himself in the best frame of spirit for the work, and fitteth himself by all means to it. Whence learn, 1. It is our duty, especially when we are about any piece of immediate spiritual worship, to take heed what we are doing, what the work is about which we are going, who the Lord is with whom we have to do and, how our heart is disposed, that so we may approve ourselves to God with the more comfort: for this the psalmist's example teacheth us: *O God, my heart is fixed, I will sing.* 2. In God's worship it is very needful we should have our minds present without diversion, and our affections composed, and set rightly toward the Lord, and the work in hand, as here: *my heart is fixed.* 3. As a man first tuneth his instrument, and then playeth on it; so should the holy servant of God first labour to bring his spirit, heart, and affections into a solid and settled frame for worship, and then go to work: *my heart is fixed,* or prepared firmly, *I will sing and give praise.* 4. As the glory of man above the brute creatures, is, that from a reasonable mind he can express what is his will by his tongue; so the glory of the saints above other men, is to have a tongue directed by the heart, for expressing God's praise: *I will sing and give praise, even with my glory.* 5. That only is our glory wherein and whereby we most glorify God: for this cause the tongue directed by a holy heart, is here called David's glory: *I will sing and give praise, even with my glory.* 6. Under typical terms we are taught to make use of all sanctified means, for stirring us up to God's service: for this the psalmist intendeth, when he saith, *awake psaltery and harp.* 7. We ourselves must first be stirred up to make right use of the means before the means can be fit to stir us up; therefore saith he, *I myself will awake early.*

3. *I will praise thee, O Lord, among the people: and I will sing praises unto thee among the nations.*

4. *For thy mercy is great above the heavens, and thy truth reacheth unto the clouds.*

5. *Be thou exalted, O God, above the heavens; and thy glory above all the earth;*

Here is the praise of God, and the reasons thereof. Whence learn, 1. It is no small help for the discharge of a duty, to engage the heart to God for its performance; for in effect that is the most we can attain to in this life; but in the next life we shall have full vent for our will to praise God, and shall follow our purpose with perpetual perseverance : *I will praise thee, O Lord, among the people.* 2. Sincerity hath confidence to profess its purpose before the Lord : *I will praise thee, O Lord.* 3. As it is the duty and desire also of a true worshipper, that all the world should be stirred up to praise the Lord, so it was the comfort of the church of the Jews to foresee the joining of the Gentiles in the song, and to see the Gentiles stirred up by the song of the Jewish church: *I will praise thee, O Lord, among the people, and will sing praises unto thee among the nations.* 4. The matter and reasons of God's praise, are higher than the worshipper can reach, and larger than he can fathom; and in special, the mercy of the Lord toward his people is larger than the wide circle of heaven : *thy mercy is great above the heavens.* 5. There is more stuff and substance of good in the Lord's promises, than the sharpest-sighted saint ever did or can perceive; for, when we have followed the promise, to find out all the truth which is in it, we meet with a cloud of unsearchable riches, and are forced to leave it there : for so much is included in this, *thy truth reacheth unto the clouds.* 6. The height of our praising God, is to put the work of praising God upon himself, and to point him out unto others as going about the magnifying of his own name, and to be glad for it, as here : *be thou exalted, O God, above the heavens, and thy glory above all the earth.*

6. *That thy beloved may be delivered: save* with *thy right hand, and answer me.*

After the praise of God from faith, followeth the prayer of faith. Wherein learn, 1. The church is the Lord's beloved, or the incorporation more loved than any thing else in the world : therefore it is here called, *thy beloved.* 2. Because the church is God's beloved, the care of it should be most in our mind, and the love of the preservation of it should draw forth our prayer most in favour of it : *that thy beloved may be delivered, save.* 3. Whosoever is intrusted with any public charge, civil or ecclesiastic, in a special manner should make the preservation and welfare of

God's people their chief aim, and the chief matter of their prayer, and the greatest satisfaction of their desires, as is here done: *that thy beloved may be delivered, save, and answer me.* 4. As it is presupposed that the church shall be frequently in danger, so it is certain that her delivery and preservation must be brought about by God in his way, and by his power, and God must be trusted with this work: therefore saith he, *that thy beloved may be delivered, save with thy right hand.*

7. *God hath spoken in his holiness; I will rejoice, I will divide Shechem, and mete out the valley of Succoth.*

8. *Gilead* is *mine; Manasseh* is *mine; Ephraim also* is *the strength of mine head; Judah* is *my lawgiver;*

Here the psalmist looketh unto the word of promise for his answer, Whence learn, 1. Suppliants must take the answer of their prayers from the word of promise; for he who findeth his warrant to pray, hath his answer before he begin to pray, for he prayeth according to the will of God, and so he hath his petition; so David teacheth: *God hath spoken in his holiness.* 2. Faith closing with a promise, will furnish joy to the believer, before he enjoy the performance of it: *God hath spoken,* saith he, *I will rejoice.* 3. The believer of a general promise may branch out the particulars in it, which are to be performed no less clearly than if they had been particularly expressed: for so the psalmist teacheth, saying, *I will divide Shechem, and mete out the valley of Succoth;* which thing came to pass as he believed, and the whole kingdom under him was now settled for his particular interest, when this psalm was composed; but as it typified the reducing of the distracted parts of Christ's kingdom into the unity of reformation, and joint subjection to his government, it was to be performed no less certainly than the distracted parts of the typical kingdom of Israel was to be joined in uniform subjection under David, who here saith, *Gilead is mine, Manasseh is mine, Ephraim also is the strength of my head, Judah is my lawgiver.*

9. *Moab* is *my wash-pot; over Edom will I cast out my shoe; over Philistia will I triumph.*

After composing of the tribes of Israel, representing the visible church, he turneth him to the foreign enemies of the kingdom, and assureth the church of victory over them also. Whence learn, 1. As in the typical victories of David, so in the conquest which Christ maketh, some are more sincere and cordial subjects, some feign subjection out of constraint or carnal motives, and as in David's, so in Christ's victories, some are vessels of dishonour—all serving for the use of the great house : *Moab is my wash-pot, over Edom will I cast out my shoe, over Philistia will I triumph.* 2. When faith looketh through the prospect of God's word and promises, it will discover afar off many advantages, as here we see.

10. *Who will bring me into the strong city ? who will lead me into Edom ?*

11. Wilt *not* thou, O God, who *hast cast us off ? and wilt not thou, O God, go forth with our hosts ?*

In the war against Edom, the difficulties are represented, which the church militant shall meet with in her battles against open enemies, which difficulties are here overcome by faith encouraging her against all impediments. Whence learn, 1. The church of believers may find, and shall find in some passages of their exercise, some main difficulties meeting them in their progress, and some enemies harder to overcome than others, some devils stronger in their possession than others, represented here by the strongest city of Edom : *who will bring me into the strong city ?* 2. When we meet with any difficulty greater than any former hath been, faith must give more employment to God, and put in to him for more assistance and strength : *who will lead me into Edom ? wilt not thou, O God ?* 3. Faith must not be discouraged in her warfare, from any tokens of God's displeasure formerly let forth against his people, but rather must draw encouragement from these, taking all the executions of threatenings for so many pledges of the performing of promises, as the psalmist doth here : *wilt not thou who hast cast us off ? and wilt not thou go forth with our hosts ?*

12. *Give us help from trouble ; for vain* is *the help of man.*

He repeateth his prayer, and insisteth upon his request. Whence learn, 1. When the believer findeth his faith weakest, he must make use of prayer, as the infirm man doth of a staff in his walking : *give us help from trouble.* 2. He who would have God's help in any business, must quit confidence in man's help; and the seeing of the vanity of man's help, must make the believer to trust the more to, and expect the more confidently God's help, as here is done : *give us help from trouble, for vain is the help of man.*

13. *Through God we shall do valiantly : for he* it is that *shall tread down our enemies.*

The psalmist closeth the psalm comfortably, in assurance of the church's victory. Whence learn, 1. Whatsoever may be the variety of the exercises of faith, victory and triumph shall close the war, and crown the wrestler : *through God we shall do valiantly.* 2. Albeit the means be nothing but vanity without God, yet they must be used, for they are something when they are used by us, and put in God's hand : for, *through God we shall do valiantly.* 3. What the Lord doeth by the believer as his servant, or by any other instrument, God must have the glory of it : *through God,* saith he, *we shall do valiantly.* 4. The faith of the church's victory over her enemies, is grounded upon God's engaging in the war for the church and against her enemies : *for he it is that shall tread down all our enemies.*

PSALM CIX.

To the chief musician. A psalm of David.

David, as a type of Christ, hath here to do with his and the Lord's desperate enemies. The psalm hath three parts. In the first part, he complaineth against them unto God, v. 1—5. In the second, he pronounceth the fearful vengeance of God against them, by way of imprecation in the spirit of prophecy, to v. 21. In the third part, he putteth up a prayer to God for himself, and is comforted. In all which he is a type of Christ, and hath an eye to Christ's kingdom, and to the desperate enemies thereof, as the Apostle Peter teacheth us in his application of of what is here spoken, as a prophecy to be in part completed in Judas, Acts i. 20. And so David here is not satisfying his own private revenge against Ahithophel, or any other such like traitor, but as a prophet foretelling what judgment was to fall on the desperate enemies of God, and as a saint subscribing to God's righteous judgments for the terror of all opposers of Christ's kingdom.

1. *Hold not thy peace, O God of my praise ;*

2. *For the mouth of the wicked, and the mouth of the deceitful, are opened against me : they have spoken against me with a lying tongue.*

3. *They compassed me about also with words of hatred ; and fought against me without a cause.*

4. *For my love they are my adversaries ; but I* give myself unto *prayer.*

5. *And they have rewarded me evil for good, and hatred for my love.*

In his complaint, the psalmist prayeth the Lord to show himself in justice against his desperate enemies, and chargeth them for false and malicious calumnies, and wicked ingratitude against him.   Whence learn, 1. As the most innocent and holy servants of God are subject to heavy slanders and false calumnies raised against them, so the best remedy and relief in this case is to go to God with the matter, as here the psalmist doth. 2. The Lord will bear witness in due time to the innocency of his oppressed and unjustly defamed servants, as here the prophet prayeth for in his prayer, and expecteth it : *hold not thy peace, O God.* 3. A good conscience may be sure to be cleared from false imputations, and should comfort itself with God's approbation in the mean time; because whatsoever infamy the believer lieth under, the Lord will bring forth his innocence and commendation : for this reason, among others, the prophet calleth the Lord, *O God of my praise.* 4. Impudent backbiters will put such a face upon the most wicked calumny and slander of an innocent servant of God, and will avow it openly in his face, as if it were truth, as here we see: *for the mouth of the wicked, and the mouth of the deceitful are opened against me, they have spoken against me with a lying tongue.* 5. An innocent man may be so circumvented with calumnies and lies forged against him, that he shall be unable to find out any way to clear himself, as here we see: *they compassed me about also with words of hatred.* 6. Albeit when an innocent man hath to do with a wicked and impudent slanderer, he may be put to no less hard exercise than if he were yoked in a combat to fight for his life; yet it is comfort when God and his own conscience know that he suffereth unjustly : *they fought against me without a cause.* 7. Innocence, kindness, and good deeds, done by the godly to the wicked instruments of Satan, will not exempt them from their malicious calumniating of them; yea, no man is more subject to this requital, than they who deserve best of the wicked world, even Christ and his servants are of all men most traduced : *for my love they are my adversaries*, saith the type of Christ, and Christ in him. 8. To render reviling for reviling, or to loose the tongue to evil words, is not the way to overcome the calumnies of the wicked; but the only way to overcome all, is, to go to God as supplicants, as here the psalmist did : *but I gave myself to prayer.* 9. When malicious lips against a man are joined with the ingratitude of the calumniator, it maketh up a fearful ditty against the slanderer, as here: *and they have rewarded me evil for good, and hatred for my love.*

6. *Set thou a wicked man over him; and let Satan stand at his right hand.*

7. *When he shall be judged, let him be condemned; and let his prayer become sin.*

8. *Let his days be few;* and *let another take his office.*

9. *Let his children be fatherless, and his wife a widow.*

10. *Let his children be continually vagabonds, and beg: let them seek* their bread *also out of their desolate places.*

11. *Let the extortioner catch all that he hath; and let the stranger spoil his labour.*

12. *Let there be none to extend mercy unto him; neither let there be any to favour his fatherless children.*

13. *Let his posterity be cut off;* and *in the generation following let their name be blotted out.*

14. *Let the iniquity of his fathers be remembered with the Lord; and let not the sin of his mother be blotted out.*

15. *Let them be before the Lord continually, that he may cut off the memory of them from the earth.*

16. *Because that he remembered not to show mercy, but persecuted the poor and needy man, that he might even slay the broken in heart.*

17. *As he loved cursing, so let it come unto him ; as he delighted not in blessing, so let it be far from him.*

18. *As he clothed himself with cursing like as with his garment, so let it come into his bowels like water, and like oil into his bones.*

19. *Let it be unto him as the garment* which *cover-eth him, and for a girdle wherewith he is girded continually.*

20. Let *this* be *the reward of mine adversaries from the Lord, and of them that speak evil against my soul.*

In this second part of this psalm the psalmist pronounceth the most fearful vengeance of God upon malicious calumniators, and that as a prophet and the messenger of God, to show the wrath of God against such wicked persons in general, and especially against the enemies of the gospel; for he speaketh here as the type of Christ, as Peter showeth, applying this prophecy to Judas by name, Acts ii. 20. Whence learn, 1. Albeit it be not lawful for any man to use such imprecations, out of private revenge, or against any man in particular, as David doth, who was led as a prophet by the Spirit of God; yet this showeth us that fearful and heavy are those judgments which attend ungrateful calumniators of honest men, and in special all such as are enemies to Christ, his gospel, faithful ministers, or those in whom the work of God's grace appeareth; and that in special for their devising and fostering lies and slanders against those that profess God's truth, on purpose to make them, and the truth which they maintain, and all of their kind, to be the more hated and despised among men; for what is written here shall be their judgment, according as they draw deeper in this sort of transgression and approach Judas's treachery. 2. More specially, these are the wages and reward of the desperate enemies of Christ, the gospel, and Christ's servants. First, all sorts of mischief shall come upon such a man's own person from men, from devils, from judicatories, and from heaven. Wrath shall be on him, in relation to his liberty, his enterprises, his suits of law, and his exercises of religion, till he be cut off from the world and rooted from his place, v. 6, 7, 8. Secondly, mischief shall be on his family, wife and children, goods and estate—whereof his children shall have no benefit, but be exposed to all misery without pity, v. 9—12. Thirdly, mischief shall be upon his posterity till they be rooted out, with infamy to him of whom they came, being pursued in wrath to the third and fourth generation, as the children of him that hated God, till his fame and memory perish, v. 13—15; and that for his merciless persecuting of the Lord's poor children, v. 16. Fourthly, the curse of God, without hope of God's blessing, shall pursue his graceless and cursed disposition, to the vexation of his soul and body, and it shall be fastened on him on all hands perpetually, v. 17—19, as the just reward of the deadly enemies of the Lord and of the salvation of his people, v. 20. And this is set down as a part of a psalm of David, to be sung to God's praise, allowed and said *amen* unto, by all the people of God, against the desperate and irreconcilable enemies of Christ and of his true servants, whereby the church of God may be edified and kept fast in the faith and profession of Christ, and free from persecution of his faithful servants.

21. *But do thou for me, O God the Lord, for thy name's sake; because thy mercy* is *good, deliver thou me.*

22. *For I* am *poor and needy, and my heart is wounded within me.*

23. *I am gone like the shadow when it declineth: I am tossed up and down as the locust.*

24. *My knees are weak through fasting; and my flesh faileth of fatness.*

25. *I became also a reproach unto them:* when *they looked upon me they shaked their heads.*

The third part of the psalm, wherein the persecuted saint putteth up prayer to God for comfort to himself and for delivery, using sundry reasons for strengthening his faith, to v. 26, where he repeateth his prayer, with other reasons to enforce it, to v. 29, and, having found comfort and victory, he closeth the psalm with thanksgiving, v. 30, 31.

From his first prayer and the reason thereof, learn, 1. Whatsoever mischief be appointed for the enemies of God and his Son Jesus Christ, it shall not prejudice the godly persecuted, nor hinder their access unto God, or God's befriending them; for so teacheth the psalmist: *but do thou for me, O God the Lord.* 2. It concerneth God in his glory, as to punish his foes, so to defend his friends and children: *do thou for me for thy name's sake.* 3. The plea of the believer is not his own goodness, but the readiness of God's mercy to supplicants: *because thy mercy is good, deliver thou me.* 4. Because God is good and merciful, therefore he will not suffer his own to perish in their affliction: *because thy mercy is good, deliver thou me.* 5. Before the Lord comfort his children in their affliction, he bringeth them to the sense of their own insufficiency and need of his help; and when this poverty of spirit is given, it is a forerunner of delivery: *deliver thou me, for I am poor and needy.* 6. As the Lord by affliction wakeneth the sense of sin and woundeth the impenitent man's spirit, so is he a ready physician to the contrite: *deliver thou me, for my heart is wounded within me.* 7. This mortal life is like a shadow, and when affliction is superadded to mortality, man's life is like the shadow of the evening, which is speedily stretched forth till it vanish; and when a saint is in this condition, he may expect the fruit of God's compassion, as here, *deliver me, for I am gone like a shadow when it declineth.* 8. The children of God must not look for any certain dwelling-place, but to be driven to and fro by persecution, as the wind maketh the locust to leap from place to place: *I am tossed up and down as the locust.* 9. The grief of the godly under persecution may overcome the natural comfort of meat and drink, and bring their body to wasting leanness: *my knees are weak through fasting, and my flesh faileth of fatness.* 10. As it is usual for the wicked to mock the godly, being brought low by persecution, so there is no part of the cross more heavy to the godly than derision: *I became also a reproach unto them when they looked upon me.* 11. What God threateneth for a curse on the wicked may, for the point of outward calamity, fall upon God's dearest children, as what is threatened, Deut. xxviii, in sundry things, is here found on the persecuted child of God: *I became a reproach unto them, they shaked their heads.*

26. *Help me, O Lord my God: O save me according to thy mercy;*

27. *That they may know that this is thy hand; that thou, Lord, hast done it.*

28. *Let them curse, but bless thou: when they arise, let them be ashamed; but let thy servant rejoice.*

29. *Let mine adversaries be clothed with shame; and let them cover themselves with their own confusion, as with a mantle.*

He prayeth again for help, and addeth more reasons, especially this reason, that so the difference of God's dealing with his servants and with his foes may the better appear. Whence learn, 1. As trouble is lengthened and lieth on, so must prayer be repeated and insisted in, as here: *help me, O Lord my God, and save me according to thy mercy*. 2. When the Lord's children perceive that God's honour is obscured by their suffering, they become no less desirous to have God restored to his honour, than to have themselves delivered from trouble : *save me, that they may know that this is thy hand, and that thou, Lord, hast done it*. 3. Albeit the Lord be the inflicter of the troubles of the godly for their trial, and for manifestation of his truth toward them and grace in them, yet the world cannot perceive this, till God lift up the head of his own out of trouble : *save me, that they may know that this is thy hand, and that thou, Lord, hast done it*. 4. When God showeth himself reconciled to a soul, light ariseth in trouble, to let them see both their own relief and the overthrow of their adversaries, as here is shown in the proposition of the condition of the godly and their enemies. 5. It matters not what the enemy speak against the godly, so long as God approveth them; yea, the more the enemy be despiteful the more will the Lord be kind to his servants : *let them curse, but bless thou*. 6. When the controversy between the godly and the persecutors cometh before the Lord to be judged, shame shall cover the face of the persecutor, and God's child shall rejoice : *when they arise*, (to wit, to plead their cause,) *let them be ashamed, but let thy servant rejoice*. 7. The pretences whereby the wicked deceive their own consciences in persecuting the saints, shall be their sin, and their shame and confusion: *let mine adversaries be clothed with shame, and let them cover themselves with their confusion as with a mantle*.

30. *I will greatly praise the Lord with my mouth; yea, I will praise him among the multitude.*

31. *For he shall stand at the right hand of the poor, to save* him *from those that condemn his soul.*

The psalmist closeth his prayer and the psalm comfortably. Whence we learn, 1. Albeit the persecuted children of God be put to mourning and prayer for a time, yet the issue of their exercise shall be joy and praise : *for, I will greatly praise*, saith the supplicant here. 2. It is not unusual for God to make the delivery of his children manifest before the people, who were witnesses of their hard usage by the wicked, and to make his servants proclaim his praise with their own mouth : *I will greatly praise the Lord with my mouth, yea, I will praise him among the multitude.* 3. As Satan, v. 6, shall stand at the right hand of the persecutor, both to drive him on to perdition in his sin, and then to accuse him and torment him for it; so shall the Lord stand at the right hand of his persecuted servants in their lowest condition, to strengthen them under their trouble, and to deliver them out of it : *for he shall stand at the right hand of the poor, to save him from them that condemn his soul.* 4. Albeit the experience of the promised delivery be not yet come, yet the foresight of it by faith in God's word and gracious nature, is sufficient cause of joy to the persecuted saint, and matter of praise to God : *I will greatly praise the Lord with my mouth, for he shall stand at the right hand of the poor to save him.*

PSALM CX.

A psalm of David.

This psalm containeth the doctrine of Christ, God and man in one person, concerning his everlasting kingdom and priesthood, whose kingdom, albeit begun to be manifested among the Jews, yet was to be extended to the Gentiles with great success, v. 1—3. As for his priesthood, he is settled therein for ever by an oath, v. 4, and that with the overthrow of his enemies, how great or many soever, v. 5, 6, yet not without Christ's sufferings, by which he was first to be humbled, and then to be exalted, v. 7.

1. *The Lord said unto my Lord, Sit thou at my right hand, until I make thine enemies thy footstool.*

In the first place, the prophet being taught of God, describes the person of Christ, in both his natures, and in his kingly office, which he exerciseth in heaven from the beginning of the world to the end thereof, until all his enemies shall be destroyed. Whence learn, 1. Albeit the understanding of Christ's person and offices be necessary to the church, yet none know the Son save the Father, and they to whom he will reveal him : for David knew Christ only by the Father's teaching : *the Lord said*, saith he. 2. Christ is David's Son, and David's Lord also : David's Son, in as much as Christ assumed his human nature of David's seed; and David's Lord, because he is God, very God and very man in one person : *the Lord said to my Lord*, that is, God the Father revealed to me concerning God the Son, my Lord and Redeemer. 3. Christ in his kingly office is exalted to the fellowship of glory and power with the Father, authorized by him in his kingdom, and established therein by divine decree : *the Lord said to my Lord*. 4. Christ since the beginning of the world hath had, and to the end of the world shall have, enemies to his kingdom, who shall fight against him, but he shall prevail over them completely and gloriously, to their shame and confusion : *sit thou at my right hand, until I make thine enemies thy footstool*. 5. No less than divine power is able to subdue the enemies of Christ's kingdom; for devils and wicked men, sin, death, and hell, are opposite to his throne : *sit here, until I make thine enemies thy footstool*. 6. Albeit this victory is not fully obtained, till the end of the world, because of the renewing of the battle by new instruments, from generation to generation; yet till then and for ever Christ the King enjoyeth his glory in heaven, and sitteth judging and ruling powerfully all things for the good of his church : *sit thou at my right hand, until I make thine enemies thy footstool*.

2. *The Lord shall send the rod of thy strength out of Zion : rule thou in the midst of thine enemies.*

In the second place, he showeth the means and manner of his conquest and governing, to wit, by the preaching of the gospel. Whence learn, 1. Christ wanteth not a rod and sceptre whereby to govern, but he hath the word of God preached for the ensign of his princely power or pre-eminence, which is the arm and power of God unto salvation to every one that believeth, and which is able to throw down every stronghold exalted against the knowledge of him : *this is the rod of thy strength*. 2. Christ was King in his church, and was in exercise of his office before his incarnation, and that by his word preached, which is the rod of his mouth, Isa. xi. 4 : *for he shall send the rod of thy strength out of Zion,* presupposeth the rod of his strength in Zion. 3. It was decreed that Christ's kingdom, howsoever first and most clearly manifested among the Jews, yet should not be limited within Judea, but should go forth to the Gentiles for subduing them : *the Lord shall send the rod of thy strength out of Zion.* 4. How many enemies soever shall oppose the kingdom of Christ, and how powerful soever they shall be, yet Christ shall bear rule, enjoy his kingdom, maintain his subjects, and go on in his conquests : *rule thou in the midst of thine enemies.*

3. *Thy people* shall be *willing in the day of thy power, in the beauties of holiness from the womb of the morning : thou hast the dew of thy youth.*

In the third place, the prophet showeth what success Christ shall have ; for he shall have abundance of converts, who shall come to his church offering themselves, as the free-will offerings were brought to the beautiful holy temple, and that in such multitudes and confluence, as his young converts shall be innumerable, like the dew upon the grass, which dew issueth forth as it were from the morning's womb as its daily birth. Whence learn, 1. Whatsoever course our Lord shall take, for inviting and compelling guests to come to his feast and to the society of his visible church, yet only his elect, his redeemed ones, all of them are made most willing converts by his omnipotent power effectually inclining their hearts, and making them willing : *thy people shall be willing in the day of thy power.* 2. Christ's church, by the administration of holy ordinances, by setting forth the Lord's holiness, by teaching and persuading effectually to the duties of holiness, is exceedingly beautiful in the eyes of God and spiritual beholders: *thy people shall be willing in the beauties of holiness.* 3. True converts by the power of the gospel are Christ's children and offspring, who shall grow up before him in simplicity and harmlessness as the youth in each generation grow, and shall be for multitude as the stars of heaven, as the sand on the sea-shore, or as the morning dew descending from heaven : *from the womb of the morning, thou hast the dew of thy youth.*

4. *The Lord hath sworn, and will not repent, Thou art a priest for ever after the order of Melchisedec.*

In the fourth place, is his priesthood settled. Whence learn, 1. As Christ is king of his church, so is he priest also, for the teaching of God's will to his subjects, for reconciling them to God by his propitiatory sacrifices, for sanctifying them, for making their services acceptable, for bearing the iniquity of their holy things, for interceding always for them, and blessing them effectually in the name of the Lord : *thou art a priest,* saith the Lord unto our Lord. 2. Christ is an everlasting priest, who liveth for ever to make intercession for us, and neither needeth nor can admit any successor, or suffragan to himself in his office : *thou art a priest for ever.* 3. Christ in his office is no usurper, for he is called to it; his priesthood is unchangeable, confirmed by an oath, having the glory of God as a pledge of its stability and continuation without change : *the Lord hath sworn, and will not repent, thou art a priest for ever.* 4. *Aaron's* order was not confirmed by an oath, but was an imperfect type of Christ's priesthood, to endure only till the Lord came, till the time of reformation came, and was to be changed at Christ's coming ; for, seeing a change behoved to be made of the priesthood, a change behoved also to be made of the Levitical law : *thou art a priest for ever,* (not after the order of *Aaron,* but) *after the order of Melchisedec.* 5. *Melchisedec's* order was not the pattern, but a type and shadowing resemblance of Christ's priesthood ; for, as *Melchisedec* in his scriptural being is mentioned and brought in, without showing who was his father or mother, and had both the offices of king and priest joined in his person, and was first king of righteousness, and then king of peace, as is more largely described by the apostle in his epistle to the Hebrews ; so is Christ really without beginning and ending, both king and priest, who bringeth perfect righteousness and peace to his subjects : *thou art a priest for ever, after the order of Melchisedec.*

5. *The Lord at thy right hand shall strike through kings in the day of his wrath.*

6. *He shall judge among the heathen, he shall fill*

the places *with the dead bodies: he shall wound the heads over many countries.*

In the fifth place is set down the victory of Christ over his enemies. Whence learn, 1. Christ the mediator, and king of his church, and every believer in him, have God ready at hand in all that they have to do ; for, as Christ is at the right hand of the Father for glory, so the Father is at Christ's right hand for co-operation and assistance: *the Lord at thy right hand,* saith he. 2. As the kings and rulers of the earth are usually great enemies to Christ's kingdom, so he is the hardest party that ever they shall meet with : *the Lord at thy right hand shall strike through kings.* 3. The Lord hath a time of patience wherein he beareth with his enemies, and a day of wrath when he will break forth against his adversaries : *he shall strike through kings in the day of his wrath.* 4. Christ's government is wise and just, convincing some of sin, and pardoning the penitent; convincing others of sin, and sealing them up to condemnation ; casting down the proud, and comforting the cast down ; and doing all good things for the good of the subjects most discreetly : *he shall judge among the heathen.* 5. Were there ever so many enemies to Christ, they are all dead men before him, whom he will kill, and will cast their carcasses into the ditches of their own camps : *he shall fill the places with dead bodies.* 6. As he will punish the multitudes of people, who under wicked commanders oppose his kingdom ; so will he in special punish wicked rulers, that lead on their people against him, how many soever they be who are joined in conspiracy : *he shall wound the heads over many countries.*

7. *He shall drink of the brook in the way: therefore shall he lift up the head.*

In the last place is set down the manner of Christ's carrying on his kingdom and priesthood in his church ; to wit, by suffering and enduring hardship as a good soldier pursuing the victory : for which humiliation it is promised he shall be exalted. Whence learn, 1. It behoved Christ first to suffer, and then enter into joy : *he shall drink of the brook in the way;* or, he shall partake of the waters of affliction. 2. Whatsoever a good soldier doeth or suffereth in his warfare against, and in pursuit of his enemies, Christ did and suffered in pursuing his enemies in his own person, and shall do and suffer in his mystical body. *He shall drink of the brook*, that is, content himself with any obvious entertainment which he meeteth with in the chase of his enemies, and not be retarded with any care of better fare than what may further his purpose. 3. As Christ's personal sufferings were not to endure any longer than the time he was on his way to glory, so neither are the sufferings of his soldiers, or his church militant, his mystical body, to endure any longer than they are in their way to the triumph; that is, during this short life: *he shall drink of the brook in the way.* 4. As Christ in his person was exalted after his sufferings, as victor, and entered into his glory, so shall he exalt every member of his mystical body after their suffering, and lift up their head : for it is appointed even for them, through many afflictions to enter into glory : *therefore shall he lift up the head.*

PSALM CXI.

The scope of this psalm is to stir up all to praise God, and that for so many reasons as there are verses in the psalm. The exhortation is in the first words: *praise ye the Lord.* The reasons follow in order. The psalm is composed so after the order of the Hebrew alphabet, as every sentence or half verse beginneth with a several letter of the A B C in order, and all the psalm is of praise only. Whence we learn in general, 1. Sometimes it is expedient to set all other things apart, and employ ourselves expressly to proclaim the praises of the Lord only: for so is done in this psalm. 2. The praises of the Lord are able to fill all the letters and words composed of letters, in all their possible junctures of composition; for so much the going through all the letters of the A B C pointeth out to us : he is Alpha and Omega, and all the middle letters of the A B C of praise. 3. The praises of the Lord are worthy to be kept in memory: for, that this psalm may be the better remembered, it is composed after the manner of the A B C, and so it insinuateth thus much to us.

1. *Praise ye the Lord. I will praise the Lord with* my *whole heart, in the assembly of the upright, and in the congregation.*

The psalmist setteth down the scope of the psalm in a word of exhortation to praise the Lord, and then annexeth ten reasons and motives thereunto. The first motive is from his own example. Whence learn, 1. When we are about any part of divine worship, it is good to set our eye mainly upon the scope which we propound to ourselves therein; for so, with less wavering thoughts and more fixed presence of mind, we shall follow our purpose. Thus much the psalmist's example here teacheth us, setting down all he purposeth to aim at in this sentence: *praise ye the Lord.* 2. The pastor of the congregation, being about to stir up others to this or any other spiritual duty, should go before them in his own example, and stir up himself to that same end: for so teacheth the psalmist, saying, *I will praise the Lord.* 3. As the Lord is worthy of hearty praises, so should we with our heart take up this song, and bear out the work: *I will praise the Lord with my whole heart.* 4. Solemn meetings of God's children for his public worship and furthering one another therein, are ordinances of God appointed for that end: *I will praise—in the assembly, and in the congregation.* 5. Albeit the true members of the church invisible be only they who are justified and regenerate, and who are students of sanctity and righteousness; and albeit such only are fittest hearers, discerners, and joiners in the Lord's worship, yet must the whole congregation, or visible members of the church, whatsoever they be before God, be admitted to the fellowship of hearing God praised; for thereby the elect unconverted may be regenerate : so when the psalmist hath said, *I will praise the Lord in the assembly of the upright,* he subjoineth also, *and in the congregation.*

2. *The works of the Lord are great, sought out of all them that have pleasure therein.*

The second reason of the exhortation to praise God, is from the greatness and excellency of God's works. Whence learn, 1. We need not go far to seek matter for praising the Lord; his works are at our hand to furnish matter; and albeit the Lord's works in comparison one with another, be some of them greater, some of them lesser, yet all and every one of them being looked upon severally are great: *the works of the Lord are great.* 2. Whatsoever glory appeareth in God's works, there is more hid treasure and excellency therein to be sought out; and if men see not much in God's works, it is because they do not seek them out: *the works of the Lord are great, sought out of all them, &c.* 3. It is a mark of a wise child of God to take pleasure in God's work, and to take pleasure to see ch and see God's praise therein, and such alone reap the right use and benefit thereof: *they are sought out of all them that have pleasure therein.*

3. *His work is honourable and glorious; and his righteousness endureth for ever.*

The third reason of praise, is the glory and honour of God to be seen in his works. Whence learn, 1. The glory of God's wisdom, power, justice, or mercy, or some of his attributes, is stamped upon his works of creation and providence, and they who have an open eye to look upon them rightly, will acknowledge it: *his work is honourable and glorious.* 2. When the rays of God's wisdom, power, goodness, or any attribute, are perceived in his work, they cause an honourable estimation of God and of his work also; and a right estimation of God's work cannot be attained till his glory be seen in it: *his work is honourable and glorious.* 3. Albeit the world always, yea, and God's children also, often misconstrue the Lord's work and dealing with themselves and others, yet there is no wrong therein; there was never any wrong, nor ever shall there be any the least point of injustice in his dealing: *his righteousness endureth for ever.*

4. *He hath made his wonderful works to be remembered: the Lord is gracious, and full of compassion.*

The fourth motive to praise God, is the course he taketh to make his works remembered, mixing mercy and compassion in all his providence towards men, and specially his own people. Whence learn, 1. What the Lord hath done for his church, he hath ordained that it should be remembered; and this he procureth, partly by printing upon his works the large impression of his power and goodness; partly by doing the like works when the church standeth in need thereof; and partly by his ordinances, commanding them to be remembered: *he hath made his wonderful works to be remembered.* 2. As the grace and loving pity of God towards his church are the cause of the wonderful working of God for his church; so are they strong motives to cause his works to be remembered unto his praise: for, *the Lord is gracious, and full of compassion,* doth here infer so much.

5. *He hath given meat unto them that fear him: he will ever be mindful of his covenant.*

The fifth motive to praise God, is, because God according to his covenant, provideth for the necessities of his people. Whence learn, 1. The Lord in all ages hath carefully furnished maintenance for the life, both bodily and spiritual, of his own people : *he hath given meat to them that fear him.* 2. As what good the Lord doeth unto his people, is because of his covenant with them, so what is to be done for them, he will do for his covenant's sake also, without being wearied : *he will ever be mindful of his covenant.*

6. *He hath shewed his people the power of his works, that he may give them the heritage of the heathen.*

The sixth motive to God's praise, is the proof which he gave of his power for, and good-will to this people, in bringing them out of Egypt, and into Canaan. Whence learn, 1. The Lord's working wonderfully and extraordinarily for his people, were it but once and at one time, as it is a sufficient reason of praising him ordinarily at all times thereafter, so it is a sufficient prop to the faith of his people at all times : for this use are we taught to make of the Lord's working for his people, *in giving them the heritage of the heathen.* 2. As the Lord's working for his people at one time, giveth evidence of what he can do for them at any time; so will he have his own people in special, spectators, observers, and witnesses of his working at any time, that they may make use thereof at all times: *he hath shewed his people the power of his works, that he may give them the heritage of the heathen.*

7. *The works of his hands are verity and judgment : all his commandments are sure.*

8. *They stand fast for ever and ever,* and are *done in truth and uprightness.*

The seventh and eighth motives to God's praise, are the suitableness of his work to his word, and the stability of his word and works in truth and uprightness. Whence learn, 1. The works of the Lord done for his church, and in his church, to his people for their correction or comfort, and against their enemies for their overthrow, prove the Lord to be true and faithful in his promises and threatenings : *the works of the Lord are verity and judgment.* 2. As the words and the workings of the Lord agree, so should they be esteemed, acknowledged, and commended by us: *the works of the Lord are verity and judgment.* 3. The whole word of God, all which he hath commanded us to observe and make use of, is worthy of all commendation, and of perpetual use; for all the parts of it agree one with another, suitable to the condition of his people in all ages, good and profitable to them. It is clear and plain, when it is rightly considered and compared with itself: for even the ceremonial law, albeit abolished for the outward observation of the carnal ceremony, which figured forth Christ to come, yet endureth for ever in the real signification of substance, benefits, and duties thereby shadowed forth; and the moral law, howsoever it serveth to condemn men for their sins, is also a pedagogy to draw and drive condemned men to seek righteousness and life in Christ, and to lead the believer along in his hand to heaven : *all his commandments are sure, they stand fast for ever and ever, and are done in truth and uprightness.*

9. *He sent redemption unto his people ; he hath commanded his covenant for ever : holy and reverend is his name.*

The ninth motive to God's praise, is the course which he hath taken for man's salvation, and for his divine honour. Whence learn, 1. The Lord hath made redemption ready for men, and hath given forth a commission for making it, and for applying it to the benefit of the believer: *he sent redemption to his people.* 2. Whosoever receive the message of redemption sent unto them, God is entered with them into an everlasting and unchangeable covenant, for grace and salvation unto them : *he hath commanded his covenant for ever.* 3. Whereinsoever God hath engaged himself by covenant, we must not suspect him to be otherwise minded than he hath spoken, but must in faith and fear subscribe to this declaration, lest we take his name in vain : *for holy and reverend is his name.*

10. *The fear of the Lord is the beginning of wisdom : a good understanding have all they that do* his commandments : *his praise endureth for ever.*

The tenth motive to praise God, is, from the fruit of believing and obeying him. Whence learn, 1. As it is true wisdom to know the Lord's will, and to observe it, so men begin to give proof of wisdom in them, when they begin to make conscience of the obedience of faith, and to stand in awe to misbelieve God's word, or disobey his commands: *for the fear of the Lord is the beginning of wisdom.* 2. Howsoever the wicked, who follow their own counsel, may seem wise to worldlings, and the Lord's children simple and witless; yet in effect, the man that studieth constantly unto the obedience of faith, is the only wise man: *a good understanding have all they that do his commandments.* 3. Albeit many neglect to praise God, yet he shall not want praise, for the matter of his praise shall endure, and he shall provide such as shall praise him, from generation to generation, and for evermore: *his praise endureth for ever.*

PSALM CXII.

1. *Praise ye the Lord. Blessed* is *the man* that *feareth the Lord,* that *delighteth greatly in his commandments.*

This psalm is a praising of God for blessing believers; and the whole psalm proveth that the believer is blessed : which proposition is set down, v. 1, and confirmed with as many reasons as there are verses following. Whence learn, 1. Albeit in singing of some certain psalm, or part thereof, there be nothing directly spoken of the Lord, or to the Lord, yet he is praised when his truth is our song, or when his works and doctrine are our songs, as here it is said, *praise ye the Lord.* And thereafter the blessedness of the believer taketh up all the psalm. 2. It is the Lord's praise, that his servants are the only blessed people in the world : *praise ye the Lord* : why ? because, *blessed is the man that feareth the Lord.* 3. He is not the blessed man who is most observant to catch all opportunities to have pleasure, profit, and worldly preferment, and careth not how he cometh by them : but he is the blessed man, who is most observant of God's will, and careful to follow it : *blessed is the man that feareth the Lord.* 4. As there is matter of great delight and contentment in God's word, unto all those who fear God; so the true mark of a sound believer and fearer of God, is delighting to know, believe, and obey God's word: for so he describeth the man that feareth God : *he delighteth greatly in his command-ments.*

2. *His seed shall be mighty upon earth : the gen-eration of the upright shall be blessed.*

The first proof of the believer's blessedness, is the bless-ing of his children, (if God shall see it good to give him sons and daughters of his body,) or the blessing of those that by his teaching and example follow the footsteps of his faith and obedience. Whence learn, 1. Albeit we are bound to serve God, whether he give unto us benefits or not; albeit our service at the best be but a very weak en-deavour, and many ways tainted; and albeit we be unpro-fitable servants, presupposing we could so serve as we should give perfect obedience, and do all that is command-ed; yet it pleaseth God to allure us into his service, by pro-pounding rewards and encouragements to us, as we see in this psalm. 2. The best way to bring a blessing on our children and posterity, is to fear God, and, by our instruction and example, to teach them to follow us in the Lord's fear: *for their seed shall be mighty upon earth,* even kings and priests unto God, whatsoever shall be their worldly portion. 3. Albeit few believe, yet is it true, that upright dealing hath better fruits than witty projecting and cunning catch-ing : *the generation of the upright shall be blessed.*

3. *Wealth and riches* shall be *in his house; and his righteousness endureth for ever.*

The second proof of the believer's felicity, is the blessing of him in his outward estate. Whence learn, 1. Whether God shall give more or less to the upright man, one way or other it shall be more useful to him than all the wealth of the wicked can be to them : *wealth and riches shall be in his house.* 2. Besides the temporal commodity and fruits in this life of the believer's righteous carriage, gracious re-wards are laid up for him in another life for ever : *his righteousness endureth for ever.*

4. *Unto the upright there ariseth light in the dark-ness :* he is *gracious, and full of compassion, and right-eous.*

The third proof of the believer's blessedness is comfort in all troubles, and deliverance out of all difficulties, as the fruit of God's grace enduring in him. Whence learn, 1. Albeit the Lord will not exempt the believer from dark passages of his providence, or from affliction and perplexity, yet he will make him sure of comfort, direction, and a good event : *unto the upright there ariseth light in darkness.* 2. The light and comfort which are bestowed upon the upright, are the fruit of God's grace toward him and of the junction of saving graces in him; for the words may be extended both to God and to the believer by God's donation : *he is gracious and full of compassion, and righteous;* which is true of the believer in some degree, and of God it is true absolutely and infinitely.

5. *A good man sheweth favour, and lendeth : he will guide his affairs with discretion.*

A fourth proof of the believer's blessedness is, from his properties or the fruitfulness of his faith, in the works of justice and mercy, dispensed with discretion. Whence learn, 1. The believer to whom God hath extended favour and kindness, will be good to them among whom he liveth, and, by the fruits of equity, love, kindness, and mercy, will give evidence of God's grace dwelling in him; for here the believer is called *a good man, who showeth mercy, and lendeth.* 2. Grace and godliness, sound and fruitful faith, do not make men fools without discretion, but consist well with prudence and discretion, in ordering their affairs wisely, and teach them to give, when, what, and to whom they should give, as the circumstances of time, place, and person, need of the party, and their own ability require : *he will guide his affairs with discretion.*

6. *Surely he shall not be moved for ever : the righteous shall be in everlasting remembrance.*

A fifth proof of the believer's blessedness, is the promise of his stability in grace and estimation with God for ever. Whence learn, 1. No man shall serve God for nought; the grace bestowed upon him, causing him to abound in well-doing, shall be followed with more grace, rewarding and crowning grace in him, and in special he shall be settled in the state of grace, whatsoever temporal changes of inward or outward condition he may suffer : *surely he shall not be moved for ever.* 2. Albeit the world may misregard the believer, and traduce him while he liveth, and calumniate him when he is dead, yet his memory shall remain fresh and fragrant before God, angels, and good men who know him: *the righteous shall be in everlasting remembrance.*

7. *He shall not be afraid of evil tidings: his heart is fixed, trusting in the Lord.*

A sixth proof of the believer's blessedness is from the peace of God guarding his heart against the fear of evil. Whence learn, 1. Albeit the believer wanteth not his own infirmities and fears, yet he is not overcome of fears, as the wicked and incredulous are: *he shall not be afraid of evil tidings*. 2. The guard of the godly man's heart is not confidence in his own wisdom or strength, natural courage, or any earthly thing, but that which settleth him is faith in God: *his heart is fixed, trusting in the Lord.*

8. *His heart* is *established, he shall not be afraid, until he see* his desire *upon his enemies.*

The seventh proof of the believer's blessedness is his security from his enemies. Whence learn, 1. Albeit the believer be not exempted from having enemies, yea, and those mighty and terrible, and such as will be studying a mischief against him and breathing out terrors, yet faith in God will guard his heart so, that he shall not be moved from the course of God's obedience for all that the enemy can do: *his heart is established, he shall not be afraid.* 2. The light of God's word showeth the believer both his own delivery and the overthrow of his enemies, which, if he do not see in full effect in his own time, yet he shall foresee in the predictions of God's word: *he shall not be afraid, until he see his desire upon his enemies.*

9. *He hath dispersed, he hath given to the poor; his righteousness endureth for ever; his horn shall be exalted with honour.*

The eighth proof of the believer's blessedness is from his constant course in fruitfulness of faith, and from the fruits thereof. Whence learn, 1. The works of mercy to the distressed are a special fruit and commendation of the faith of the believer: *he hath dispersed, he hath given to the poor.* 2. The believer so giveth as he may be still able to give to many: *he hath dispersed.* 3. As the believer's righteousness by justification, so his endeavour to be righteous in the effect of sanctification, is not by fits, but constant and permanent : *his righteousness endureth for ever.* 4. Albeit the righteous may have their reputation blasted among men, yet God, in due time, shall make them honourable : *his horn shall be exalted with honour.*

10. *The wicked shall see* it *and be grieved ; he shall gnash with his teeth, and melt away; the desire of the wicked shall perish.*

The last proof of the blessedness of the believer, is, that his enemies shall envy his happiness, when they shall see the godly in good case and themselves miserable. Whence learn, 1. Sometimes, even in this life, the Lord so exalteth the believer, that his enemies are made witnesses thereof to their grief; yet, however, at length, at the great day, they shall see the believer's joy clearly, to the increase of their own sorrow : *the wicked shall see it, and be grieved.* 2. The more the wicked envies the good of the godly, the more miserable he makes himself : *he shall gnash with his teeth, and melt away.* 3. As the seeming good which the wicked doeth shall be consumed and vanish, so the good which he hoped and desired to have shall never come to be enjoyed by him, but shall vanish : *he shall melt away; the desire of the wicked shall perish.*

PSALM CXIII.

This also is a psalm of praise, wherein, first, the proposition that God is to be praised by all, is set down, ver. 1—3. In the next place, are the reasons taken from his incomparable majesty, ver. 4, 5. In the third place, are the reasons of his praise, taken from his bounty towards men, in raising the afflicted to an honourable condition, ver. 6—8, and enlarging desolate families, ver. 9.

1. *Praise ye the Lord. Praise, O ye servants of the Lord, praise the name of the Lord.*

2. *Blessed be the name of the Lord from this time forth and for evermore.*

3. *From the rising of the sun, unto the going down of the same, the Lord's name* is *to be praised.*

From the exhortation to praise, and declaration of his deserving to be praised, learn, 1. As it is all men's duty to praise the Lord, so in special it is the duty of his ministers and officers of his house. First, because their office calleth for the discharge of it publicly; next, because, as they should be the best judges of the reasons of his praise, so also should they be the fittest instruments to declare it; and, lastly, because the ungodly are deaf to the exhortation, and dumb in the obedience of it : therefore, when he hath said, *praise ye the Lord*, he subjoineth, *praise, O ye servants of the Lord.* 2. As the Lord will not be known but as he declareth himself in his word, so he will not be praised save as he hath declared himself: *praise the name of the Lord.* 3. The time of the exercise of God's' praise and the continuation of the service hath no term set to it, but shall endure all our life, and for ever after : *blessed be the name of the Lord from this time forth and for evermore.* 4. The praise of the Lord is not to be confined to any place, people, or nation; but course should be taken that it may be extended from one end of heaven to the other, from east to west, on both hands, south and north : *from the rising of the sun unto the going down of the same, the Lord's name is to be praised;* for everywhere there is matter for it.

4. *The Lord* is *high above all nations,* and *his glory above the heavens.*

5. *Who* is *like unto the Lord our God, who dwelleth on high?*

In the reasons taken from the Lord's majesty, learn, 1. God must be exalted above whatsoever excellence is to be seen in kings and people in all the earth : *for the Lord is high above all nations.* 2. God must be exalted above whatsoever glory is to be seen in the fabric of heaven, and more glory must be given to him than what all the creatures can express : for heaven and earth, and all things which he hath made, are but the effects of some few words of the Lord : *his glory is above the heavens.* 3. Of any, or of all things which we see or hear of, or can imagine, there is no comparison to be made with God, who hath set his throne above all creatures : *who is like unto the Lord our God, who dwelleth on high?*

6. *Who humbleth* himself *to behold* the things that are *in heaven, and in the earth!*

7. *He raiseth up the poor out of the dust,* and *lifteth the needy out of the dunghill ;*

8. *That he may set* him *with princes,* even *with the princes of his people.*

9. *He maketh the barren woman to keep house,* and to be a *joyful mother of children. Praise ye the Lord.*

In the reasons taken from the Lord's gracious providence, in the revolutions of kingdoms and families, learn, 1. As the excellence and majesty of God are so great, that in regard of his own all-sufficiency he might justly despise the excellence of angels and men, whereof he standeth in no need; so the Lord's taking any notice of men or angels, is a point of humbling himself, a point of love to the creature, making him stoop so low as to look toward them : *for he humbleth himself to behold the things that are in heaven, and in the earth.* 2. As the Lord declareth himself wonderful in the works of creation, so also in the works of providence, in changing the public affairs of kingdoms, above and contrary to all probability and expectation of men: *he raiseth the poor out of the dust, and lifteth the needy out of the dunghill.* 3. Preferment to high places cometh neither from the east, nor from the west, but as God casteth down some, so he raiseth other some : *that he may set them with princes, even with the princes of his people.* 4. God's way manifested in Scripture, is contrary to the course of levelling, for he will have some to be in a mean place, and some to be princes, even among his own people, as this text showeth. 5. Howsoever the Lord be no less conspicuous in throwing down the mighty, than in raising the poor, yet will he rather take his praise here from his lifting up of the needy and poor, than from casting down the mighty, that so he may give comfort and hope to the dejected, who depend on him : *he lifteth the needy out of the dunghill, that he may set them with princes.* 6. It is no small benefit, yea, it is the greatest dignity in the world, to be advanced, not in wrath, but in mercy, to rule over the Lord's people : for so God here commendeth his bounty to the needy : *that he makes them sit with the princes of his people.* 7. All changes in men's families are of God, no less than the changes of state : *he maketh the barren woman to keep house.* 8. It is the special blessing of a family to increase in number: for the Lord's making the barren bear a number of children, is here made the example of the most comfortable change of a distressed house: *he maketh the barren to be a joyful mother of children.* 9. The very hearing what comfortable changes the Lord can and doth make the afflicted to find, is a matter of refreshment to all, and of praise to God from all: *praise ye the Lord.*

PSALM CXIV.

This psalm is a praising of God, for the gracious and glorious work of delivering his people out of Egypt, and bringing them into Canaan, and that for six reasons. The first whereof is, v. 1; the next, v. 2; the third, v. 3; the fourth, v. 4; the fifth, with the special use thereof, v. 5—7; the sixth, v. 8.

1. *When Israel went out of Egypt, the house of Jacob from a people of strange language.*

From the matter of praise here specified, learn, 1. The Lord's most glorious work done for his people, in special the work of redemption, should be oftenest remembered, as the mention-making here and elsewhere *by the time when Israel came out of Egypt,* showeth. 2. Redemption is best esteemed, when the miserable condition wherein we were is called to mind, as here Israel's redemption is commended from the state they were in, in Egypt: *the house of Jacob went from a people of a strange language.* And this is the first reason of commending this work of God.

2. *Judah was his sanctuary,* and *Israel his dominion.*

The next reason for commending this glorious work, is the joining of delivered Israel in a near fellowship with God. Whence learn, 1. People redeemed by God, are no more their own, but are the Lord's purchase, redeemed for his service: *Judah was his sanctuary, and Israel his dominion.* 2. The title and interest which God justly claimeth in his people is, that they may be consecrated to him in holiness, and subject themselves as his loyal subjects to his government: *Judah was his sanctuary, and Israel was his dominion.* 3. All the consecration and sanctification of Israel are comprehended in and flow from what was to be found in the tribe of Judah, and that is in Christ Jesus, the flower of his tribe : *all Israel is his dominion, but Judah is his sanctuary.*

3. *The sea saw it, and fled; Jordan was driven back.*

The third reason of God's praise for this work, is from the drying of the Red sea, and of Jordan, that his people might pass out of Egypt, and into Canaan. Whence learn, 1. God's dealing for his people whom he ransomed, proveth his wonderful power for them, and love towards them, as the two miracles of drying the sea and Jordan commend the redemption of Israel. 2. When God will deliver his people, no oppression can hinder ; and when he will possess them of what he promised, no impediment can withstand him : *the sea saw it, and fled, and Jordan was driven back.*

4. *The mountains skipped like rams,* and *the little hills like lambs.*

The fourth reason of God's praise, is the causing mount Horeb and other hills (in the way to Canaan) to tremble and quake, when he put forth his power on them in the sight of his people. Whence learn, 1. There is no power in the earth which God cannot overtop when he pleaseth, even though like the strong mountains: for, as he can shake the earth, so can he move and remove any power on earth, as he gave evidence when he made the mountains by earthquake *to skip like rams, and the little hills like lambs.*

5. *What* ailed *thee, O thou sea, that thou fleddest? thou Jordan, that thou wast driven back?*

6. *Ye mountains, that ye skipped like rams;* and *ye little hills, like lambs?*

7. *Tremble, thou earth, at the presence of the Lord, at the presence of the God of Jacob.*

The fifth reason of God's praise, is the evidence of his power put forth before his people, in so wonderful and miraculous a manner, as no cause can be given of the works wrought for his people in their coming out from Egypt, their entry into Canaan and the wilderness, except only God's extraordinary manifestation of his presence

amongst his 'people, and for them : which the psalmist
bringeth forth by asking the cause of these miracles, and
answering the question by the terrible presence of God.
Whence learn, 1. The Lord can work so clearly for his people, that the most stupid and brute souls shall be convinced
of his respect to his children, as experience showeth. 2. If
atheism and unbelief in men could find any natural reason,
or any pretence of reason, whereby they might obscure the
glory of God's doing for his people, they would not fail to
do it, as this interrogation teacheth : *what ailed thee, O
thou sea, &c.?* 3. The more narrowly the works of the
Lord are looked to, the more evidently his power and
presence appear in working them, as the answer to the
question and holding forth the Lord's presence twice, for
the cause of such changes on the creatures, show. 4. The
end and use of God's power manifested in favour of his
people; first, that all flesh should fear God, and stand in awe
of him : and next, that his covenanted people should loo
upon his terror as their bulwark : *tremble thou earth at
the presence of the Lord, at the presence of the God of
Jacob.*

8. *Which turned the rock* into *a standing water,
the flint into a fountain of waters.*

The sixth reason of God's praise, in the work of delivery
of his people out of Egypt, is his wonderful provision for
their drink in the dry wilderness, by dissolving the flinty rock
into water. Whence learn, 1. For whomsoever the Lord
redeemeth, and setteth on their way to heaven, he will provide whatsoever is necessary for their sustentation and
comfort in their journey, as his providing of drink for the
camp of Israel giveth proof. 2. We being called of God
to follow our Redeemer, till we be put in possession of promises, must not stand for any difficulty, or disappearance of
means for our sustentation and comforts, for God can work
his purpose by contrary-like means : *he turned the rock
into a standing water, the flint into a fountain of
waters.*

PSALM CXV.

The church of Israel being under the power of the heathen, and unable
to help themselves, flee to God for relief; and in the former part of the
psalm they pray for delivery, strengthening their hope to be heard by
four arguments, to v. 9. In the latter part, the church is encouraged
to trust in God, and to expect deliverance in due time, by several reasons, all serving to confirm their faith, unto the end of the psalm.

1. *Not unto us, O Lord, not unto us, but unto thy
name give glory, for thy mercy,* and *for thy truth's
sake.*

In praying for relief from the bondage of idolaters, they
reject all confidence in themselves, and bring arguments of
their hope to be helped from other grounds. Whence learn,
1. It is no strange thing to see God's people, for their chastisement, or trial, put under the power of idolaters, as this
experience of Israel showeth. 2. When we seek any thing
from God, we ought to acknowledge our own unworthiness
and ill deserving, and to renounce all confidence in ourselves: *not unto us give the glory,* saith the church here.
3. Albeit the Lord's afflicted people may want all ground
of hope from their own behaviour, yet grounds of hope can
never be wanting, when they look to God's mercy and truth,
and the glory of his grace in helping them : *not unto us,
O Lord, not unto us, but unto thy name give glory : for
thy mercy, and for thy truth's sake.*

2. *Wherefore should the heathen say, Where* is *now
their God?*

The second reason of hope to have their petition granted,
is because, if the Lord do not deliver them, idolaters, under
whose power they lie, will continue to blaspheme the true
religion, and the true God whom the true church worshippeth. Whence learn, 1. The enemies of the church are
ready to blaspheme the true religion, when the Lord's people are brought into straits, and under their power, as here :
the heathen say, Where is now their God? 2. When we
have brought ourselves into misery, and our religion in danger of disgrace, we ought to be more careful to have the
Lord restored to his honour, and true religion restored to
its own beauty, than to be freed from misery; for the church
here cannot endure the dishonour of God in their affliction :
*wherefore should the heathen say, Where is now their
God?*

3. But our God is in the heavens; he hath done whatsoever he hath pleased.

The third reason of hope to be heard is, because God is omnipotent, and supreme governor of all things, and his authority is, as his power, absolute to do what he pleaseth: and this reason strengthens also the former reason. Whence learn, 1. The more the wicked oppose God and true religion, the more should his servants assert his glory and truth, as the church doth here, saying, *but our God is in heaven.* 2. The consideration of God's absolute power and authority, exalteth God above all idols, stoppeth all murmuration against his dispensations towards his people and their enemies; closeth all disputation against his revealed will, and looseth all objections arising from difficulties and impediments, which might hinder hope to be helped out of misery, as here we see: *our God is in heaven, he doeth whatsoever he pleaseth.*

4. Their idols are silver and gold, the work of men's hands.

5. They have mouths, but they speak not; eyes have they, but they see not;

6. They have ears, but they hear not; noses have they, but they smell not;

7. They have hands, but they handle not; feet have they, but they walk not; neither speak they through their throat.

A fourth reason of hope that the church shall be delivered from the power of idolaters, is, because there is no other God to deliver them, save the Lord. Idols can neither help their worshippers, nor hurt God's people who despise them, and therefore his people will hope in their own true God, and despise both idolaters and their idols. Whence learn, 1. Images, in the matter of religion, whatsoever they seem to be, or represent, are but idols, for so are they called here. 2. Images in religion profit nothing, but bring trouble to men, as their name in the original importeth. 3. Albeit idolaters bestow largely upon their idols, and put upon them artificially some shape, to represent some perfections by them, yet the riches of the matter can give them no excellency: they are but silver and gold at the best, their forgers

and authors are but men; for it is sufficient to disgrace any
point of religion, if it be of man's devising : *they are the
work of men's hands.* 4. So many members as the images
have, serving to represent some perfections by them, are so
many lies : *for they have mouths, but they speak not ;
eyes have they, but they see not ; they have ears, but
they hear not ; noses have they, but they smell not ;
they have hands, but they handle not ; feet have they,
but they walk not ; neither speak they through their
throat.*

8. *They that make them are like unto them ;* so is
every one that trusteth in them.

For closing this reason, he turneth the reproach which
idolaters cast upon the true God and his worship, over on
themselves. Whence learn, 1. Albeit the Lord be angry at
his own people, yet must not they forsake him and go after
idols to be helped by them; for so the church here teacheth
us. 2. The consideration of the folly of false religion,
should make us cleave the closer to the true religion,
and to abhor the errors of human devising; for so are we
taught by this example. 3. As it is an honour to be of the
true religion, so it is the greatest disgrace a man can have,
to be an idolater; for the disgrace of the idol falleth upon
the worshipper thereof, as here we see. 4. All idolaters are
brutish, the makers of idols, authorizers of them, worshippers and servers of them, are all like reasonless and senseless blocks, in this matter like the idols which they make :
they that make them are like unto them ; that is, *they have
eyes, and see not, &c.* 5. Whosoever expect any good by
making or worshipping images, join the inward worshipping of them with the outward; and, in their expecting any
good by that means, they prove themselves like reasonless
blocks, as void of true wisdom in this point as images are
of sense and motion : *so is every one that trusteth in them.*

9. *O Israel, trust thou in the Lord ; he* is *their help
and their shield.*

10. *O house of Aaron, trust in the Lord ; he* is *their
help and their shield.*

11. *Ye that fear the Lord, trust in the Lord ; he* is
their help and their shield.

In the latter part of the psalm the church is encouraged to trust in the Lord, and so to expect deliverance according to the petition set down, v. 1; and that by seven reasons. The exhortation to trust in God is threefold; one directed to Israel, v. 9; another to the priests and Levites, v. 10; the third to all that fear God, v. 11 : unto which exhortation the first reason of encouragement is added and repeated again and again. Whence learn, 1. No trial of affliction should drive us from expecting relief in trouble, and trusting in God for it; for, notwithstanding the church here is under the feet of the heathen, yet all are exhorted to trust in God: *O Israel, trust thou in the Lord.* 2. Whosoever in their trouble trust in God may be assured to be delivered, and guarded against all evils which may mar their blessedness : *trust in the Lord, for he is their help and shield.* 3. The ministers of God's house should go before the Lord's people in trusting in God and adhering to him, specially in time of trouble : *O house of Aaron, trust in the Lord.* 4. Such promises as are made in common to the house of Israel, are sufficient to support the faith of public ministers of the Lord's house, as here we see: *he is their help and shield.* 5. As every one that feareth God is of the number of true Israelites, so, trusting in the Lord, he may be no less confident of the consolation and protection of God than the public ministers of the Lord's house : *ye that fear the Lord, trust in the Lord, he is their help and their shield.* And this is the first reason of encouragement to trust in God.

12. *The Lord hath been mindful of us; he will bless us: he will bless the house of Israel; he will bless the house of Aaron:*

13. *He will bless them that fear the Lord,* both *small and great.*

The second reason of encouragement is taken from former experience of God's respect to the people who fear him, and the third is taken from the promise of blessing them in time to come. Whence learn, 1. Albeit the Lord useth to afflict his people, yet he forgetteth them not nor layeth aside affection for them : *the Lord hath been mindful of us.* 2. The right use of bypast experience of God's care of us in affliction and trials, is to put trust in God in after-times of new trial and affliction : as here, *the Lord*

hath been mindful of us, is made use of to this end.   3.
As the duty of trusting in the Lord is common to all sorts
of persons, so the blessing of faith is common, and belongeth to all sorts of believers, great and small : *he will bless
us, he will bless the house of Aaron, he will bless them
that fear the Lord, both small and great.*

14. *The Lord shall increase you more and more, you
and your children.*

The fourth reason of encouragement to trust in the
Lord, is, because the number of believers shall be multiplied.   Whence learn, Albeit the church be driven to deep
affliction and distress, yet the number of believers in God
shall increase, the measure of God's graces in his people
shall be augmented, no age, even unto the last, shall want
a posterity of believers, and God will make no end of blessing them—which is no small encouragement to believers :
*the Lord shall increase you more and more, you and
your children.*

15. *Ye* are *blessed of the Lord, which made heaven
and earth.*

The fifth reason of encouragement is, because God omnipotent hath pronounced believers to be blessed, how miserable soever they may seem to themselves and others.   Whence
learn, 1. Whatsoever distress believers may fall into, yet can
they never be accursed nor deprived of the blessing of righteousness and eternal life; for, it is said to them all, *you are
blessed of the Lord*, who calleth things that are not, and
maketh them to be.   2. The sight of the Lord's work in
making heaven and earth of nothing, should strengthen us
to apprehend how richly the Lord can and will perfect what
he saith of blessing his people: *you are blessed of the
Lord, who made heaven and earth.*

16. *The heaven, even the heavens, are the Lord's ;
but the earth hath he given to the children of men.*

The sixth reason of encouragement to trust in God, is,
that albeit the Lord be abundantly satisfied in himself, and
needeth nothing from the world, yet men have need to depend upon his goodness, and trust in him who hath given
unto them the use of his creatures on the earth.   Whence
learn, 1. As it is no need of any creature which hath moved
God to make a world, but rather his superabundant self·

sufficiency hath made the heavens and the earth, in order
that therein he may show forth his all-sufficiency to the
creatures; so, it was not need of man's service which prompt-
ed him to create a people and crave service of them; for he
could be served with what he hath in heaven : *the heaven,
even the heavens are the Lord's.* 2. Albeit God hath no
need of men, and can live without dependence on man, yet
man cannot live without dependence on God and use of his
creatures in the world : *the heaven is the Lord's, but the
earth hath he given to the children of men,* wherein they
may dwell and be sustained by what he bestoweth on them
there. 3. As the abundance of the earth's riches is a pledge
of the Lord's readiness to give better things to man; so it is
an evidence of man's poverty, and need of the service of so
many of God's creatures, and of his obligation to trust in
and depend on God : *the heaven is the Lord's, but the
earth hath he given to the children of men.*

17. *The dead praise not the Lord, neither any that
go down into silence.*

18. *But we will bless the Lord from this time forth
and for evermore. Praise the Lord.*

The seventh reason of encouragement to trust in God,
is, because the church of believers shall be continued from
generation to generation, and shall never want reason to
praise and bless God, from this time forth and for ever;
therefore, in confidence of this mercy, let them trust in
him and praise him. This reason he maketh clear thus :
the dead spiritually cannot praise the Lord, and if the succession of the church of believers should be now cut off with
this afflicted generation, neither could we who live praise
God on the earth longer than we live on it, nor should there
be any church after us to discharge this duty among the
children of men; but this is impossible, for God shall not
want a generation of living believers to praise and bless him
for his goodness, to the world's end; therefore we shall live
and come forth of this present affliction, and, ere we die, another generation of believers shall take this work off our hand,
and so shall we that are the church of God, *bless him from
this time forth and for evermore.* Whereupon he exhorteth all men in this confidence to praise the Lord, and closeth
the psalm. Whence learn, 1. If there were not a church of

believers, God would want his praise on the earth; for the dead, to wit spiritually, do not praise the Lord. 2. And if, in any time of affliction, while the world standeth, there were not a deliverance unto the church, so that one generation of believers might not follow another, then should God's praise among the children of men be abolished from the world; for, as the dead spiritually cannot praise the Lord, so neither can the dead bodily praise him among them that know him not; that is, on the earth, where God's praise is to be taught to men : for *the dead praise not the Lord, neither any that go down into silence.* 3. Because God shall never want living men on earth to praise and bless him for his goodness, therefore the church of believers shall be continued from one generation to another, that they may bless and praise the Lord in every age, as here is said : *but we shall praise the Lord, from this time forth and for evermore.* 4. The church's affliction cannot be so heavy but they shall have cause to bless the Lord for his goodness, and to stir up others to praise God with them; for the prophet closeth the psalm, made in deep affliction of the church, with, *praise the Lord.*

PSALM CXVI.

This psalm is a threefold engagement of the psalmist to thanksgiving unto God for his mercy to him, and in particular for some notable delivery of him from death, both bodily and spiritual. The first engagement is, that he shall, out of love, have his recourse to God always by prayer, ver. 1, 2; the reasons and motives whereof are set down, because of his delivery out of a great strait, ver. 3—8; the second engagement is to a holy conversation, ver. 9,[the motives and reasons whereof are set down, ver. 10—12; the third engagement is to promised praises, or paying of praises and vows before the church, with the reasons thereof, ver. 13—19.

1. *I love the Lord, because he hath heard my voice* and *my supplications.*

2. *Because he hath inclined his ear unto me, therefore will I call upon* him *as long as I live.*

In his first engagement to a constant dependence on God and calling on him by prayer, learn, 1. As it is among the wise purposes of God to put his children to straits that they may call on him, and he, by granting their petition, may give them a new proof of his love to them, and so stir up

their love to him; so it is the duty of his children to stir
up their love to God upon every fresh experience of his respect to them, for this the example of the prophet teacheth
us : *I love the Lord, because he hath heard my prayer.*
2. Not God's benefits, but God himself, is the satisfactory
object of our complacency and love, wherein we may acquiesce : *I love the Lord,* saith the prophet, after he had
perceived the benefit. 3. To love God for himself, and to
love him for his favour and benefits bestowed upon us, consist well together; for the loving him for favour bestowed
on us, leadeth us to love him for himself : *I love the Lord
because he hath heard my voice, and my supplications.*
4. The root of thanksgiving is love to God, therefore love
is professed before thanksgiving be promised : *I love the
Lord,* is first set down, and then a promise to call on him
in all straits thereafter. 5. It is no small comfort and obligation put upon a man, to have experience of God's regarding his prayer and granting his request, as the psalmist's twice mentioning it showeth——once, v. 1, and here again :
because he hath inclined his ear unto me. 6. One proof
of God's hearing our prayer may, and should, stir us up to
believe in, worship, and have our recourse by prayer to him
all the rest of our life : *because he hath inclined his ear
unto me, therefore will I call upon him as long as I live.*

3. *The sorrows of death compassed me, and the
pains of hell gat hold upon me : I found trouble and
sorrow.*

The sum of the reasons of this engagement, is set down
in his late experience, containing his deep trouble, v. 3; his
calling to God for relief, v. 4; and God's grace and mercy
usually extended to poor supplicants, which helped him
out of his low condition, v. 5, 6. The use whereof, namely, to rest on God who had delivered him, is in v. 7, 8.

From his trouble and danger wherein he was, learn, 1.
It is no strange thing to see a godly person in fear of
death, bodily and spiritual, temporal and everlasting, at one
time : *the sorrows of death compassed me, and the pains
of hell gat hold upon me.* 2. The trouble of mind and
conscience also, whereunto God's children are subject, as
it is found in its several degrees, cannot easily be expressed,
therefore here are divers words used : *sorrows of death,
pains of hell, trouble and felt sorrow.* 3. The greatness

of the trouble, danger, misery, and straits, whereunto the Lord casteth his own, layeth a greater obligation on those who are delivered from these evils, and maketh God's glory to be the more manifested in their recovery, as the scope of the psalmist's narration of his troubles here teacheth us.

4. *Then I called upon the name of the Lord: O Lord, I beseech thee, deliver my soul.*

From the course taken to have relief by calling on God, learn, 1. The only true remedy of a grieved soul, is God being called upon by prayer; for he is a strong refuge whereunto the humble soul may flee, and be exalted: *I called upon the name of the Lord.* 2. There is a place and time for prayer, even when the danger seemeth greatest, and the condition of the party supplicant appeareth desperate, as here we see: *when the pains of hell caught hold upon me, then called I on the name of the Lord.* 3. Whether our desires be laid open before God in many words, or few, it is not material before God: such a hearty speech as this will pass before God for prayer, *O Lord, I beseech thee, deliver my soul.*

5. *Gracious is the Lord, and righteous; yea, our God is merciful.*

6. *The Lord preserveth the simple: I was brought low, and he helped me.*

From the fountain of grace and mercy, when he was helped, learn, 1. God's gracious and merciful actions give evidence of his gracious nature, and his readiness to show favour to all men, who, according to the tenor of the covenant of grace, call on him; as here the psalmist, to show the cause of his receiving actually a good answer, saith, *gracious is the Lord, and righteous, yea, our God is merciful.* 2. There is nothing wanting in God's attributes which may give assurance to the believing supplicant that his request will be granted: he is *gracious*, and standeth not for the person's unworthiness; he is just and *righteous*, and will not fail to keep covenant and perform all promises; he is *merciful*, and is not unwilling to pardon sin, iniquity, and transgressions: *gracious is the Lord, and righteous*; *yea, our God is merciful.* 3. The Lord's children commonly are not the most worldly-wise people, but for the most part are of mean worldly-wit, and whosoever of them hath any measure of prudence, are for the course which they keep in trials and troubles, accounted foolish; yea, and in their own estimation they are very witless, and dare not lean to their own understanding, but seek to be directed by God; therefore they are here and elsewhere called *simple*. 4. Such as are emptied of conceit of their own wisdom, and seek their direction, protection, and preservation from God, lie nearest to the fountain of God's mercy and help in every difficulty: *for the Lord preserveth the simple*. 5. Any one example of God's grace and mercy to any believer, is sufficient to prove God's nature, inclination, readiness, and good-will to every believer that calleth on him; so reasoneth the psalmist: *I was brought low, and he helped me*.

7. *Return unto thy rest, O my soul ; for the Lord hath dealt bountifully with thee.*

8. *For thou hast delivered my soul from death, mine eyes from tears,* and *my feet from falling.*

Here is a twofold use of this experience—one to settle his confidence on God, another to praise God for the experience of so great a delivery. Whence learn, 1. The general use of all the experiences of God's favour which we find, is the strengthening of our faith in God, as here we are taught. 2. Albeit trouble and temptations overcome not our faith, yet they may and usually perturb, if not the peace of our conscience, at least the peace of our mind, and sometimes the peace of both : for, *O my soul, return to thy rest,* imports a disquieting of him from his rest. 3. As we should study, not only to lay hold on God by faith, but also to rest and acquiesce in his love and truth confidently, so should we take advantage of every fresh experience of God's favour whereby we encourage ourselves to rely upon God's grace and mercy, as here the psalmist doth : *return unto thy rest, O my soul, for the Lord hath dealt bountifully with thee.* 4. Meditation on God's goodness to us, and speaking of it in the third person, are ready ways to bring us to nearer access unto God, and to speak unto his majesty in the second person, as here we see: *for thou hast delivered my soul from death,* saith he, directing his speech to God. 5. When outward trouble and inward temptations set upon a soul at one time, when men show their wrath, and God hideth his face, it is a sad condition, able to draw tears from the stoutest, and to put him in hazard of sinning, and in peril to perish : *thou hast delivered my soul from death, mine eyes from tears, and my feet from falling.* 6. As an humble and sensible soul will bind up many troubles into one, so a thankful soul will branch one mercy into sundry branches, as here the psalmist distinguisheth the delivery *of his soul from death, of his eyes from tears, and of his feet from falling.*

9. *I will walk before the Lord in the land of the living.*

The second engagement, by way of thankfulness, is to a more holy way of walking with God, whereunto, as his faith made him confident that he should attain, v. 10, so his recovery from desperation made him a debtor to pursue the duty, v. 11, and a debtor in so high a measure, as he knew not how to be thankful, v. 12.

From his hopeful engagement to a holy carriage before God and his church, learn, 1. To engage and oblige ourselves to a more sure and holy ordering of our ways, as the psalmist doth, is a good use of experiences of God's goodness : *I will walk before the Lord.* 2. As our lifetime is the proper opportunity of showing our thankfulness to God, so the visible church is the fittest society we can live in for expressing our thankfulness; for, while we are living, and that among the godly (beside whose society the rest of the world is as a company of dead corpses), we have time and place for manifesting our obedience to God : *I will walk before the Lord, in the land of the living.* 3. As a sincere deportment hath God and men for witnesses, so should the upright servant of God study to approve himself to both, as the psalmist doth : *I will walk before the Lord, in the land of the living.*

10. *I believed, therefore have I spoken : I was greatly afflicted.*

11. *I said in my haste, All men are liars.*

12. *What shall I render unto the Lord for all his benefits toward me ?*

The psalmist addeth motives to this his confident and hopeful engagement. Whence learn, 1. Faith giveth boldness to promise to and of ourselves, what the Lord's word

giveth warrant for : *I believed, therefore have I spoken.*
2. Faith is our surest holding of God's blessings—more
sure than present sense, past experience, or begun profession; for all these may be interrupted and overclouded, but
faith, laying hold on God's word, holds fast when all things
else fail : *I believed, therefore have I spoken.* 3. Our
comfort, confidence, quietness, and delivery are so much
the sweeter, as heavy troubles and temptations have gone
before them, as here the engagement is more cheerful, and
the confidence more precious, *because,* saith he, *I was
greatly afflicted,* and more specially, *I said in my haste,
all men are liars :* which if we understand of David, showeth that he doubted of the performance of the promise of
the kingdom made in God's name to him by Samuel, and
therefore he was so much the more comforted, when he saw
the truth of it appear again. 4. The servants of God
hesitate not to confess their faults and infirmities to their
own shame, when thereby God may be glorified : as here the
psalmist saith, *I said in my haste, &c.* 5. Misbelief may
sometimes so far prevail, as it may seem to reign, and as a
judge to sit down, and give out decrees : *I said in my haste,*
that is, I gave it forth as a conclusion or decree. 6. As
hastiness is the proper companion of misbelief, so it cannot
endure long in a believer, but only during the time of an
inconsiderate passion, and fit of temptation : *I said in my
haste.* 7. When misbelief dares not directly vent itself
against God, or God's express word, it falls to quarrel with
the messenger, and his fidelity in his commission : *I said
in my haste, all men are liars.* 8. He that seeth God's
benefits rightly, shall see himself unable to give thanks as
becomes him, and shall be forced to say, *What shall I
render unto the Lord?* Yea, one benefit well considered,
shall call to mind many other bypast and present mercies,
as this one delivery maketh the psalmist say, *what shall I
render to the Lord for all his benefits towards me ?* 9.
The seen impossibility to render due thanks and praise to
God for his mercies to us, should not hinder us, but rather
stir us up to aim at the duty, as we are enabled, as here
it doth the psalmist.

13. *I will take the cup of salvation, and call upon
the name of the Lord.*

14. *I will pay my vows unto the Lord now in the presence of all his people.*

The third engagement is to express praising of God before the congregation, as he had vowed, v. 13, 14; the reason whereof is given, v. 15, 16; and the engagement repeated, v. 17—19.

In his promising to pay his vows, and to give thanks publicly, he alluded to the form of the Levitical ceremony, used in drink-offerings, as 1 Cor. x. 16. Whence learn, 1. All that we can do when God hath bestowed upon us all that can be desired, is to acknowledge the goodness of God, and to thank him for it; and this must also be presented unto God by our high priest Jesus Christ, and so it is accepted: *I will take the cup of salvation;* or, I will take the cup of blessing, and thanksgiving for salvation granted to me for the true sacrifice's sake. 2. It is reckoned by God as a point of thankfulness for benefits already received, to come to God, and seek yet more benefits of him, as our need requireth, as here we see: *I will take the cup of salvation, and call upon the name of the Lord.* 3. For strengthening our faith, and binding us the more firmly to give thanks to God in the time of straits, it is lawful to make a vow to God that we will praise him, provided we vow nothing but what God alloweth, and provided we do not intend to put an obligation upon God to help us by that means: as here, *I will pay my vows unto the Lord, now in presence of all his people.* 4. When a lawful vow is made, we should be mindful to perform it truly, as the psalmist's example here teacheth us.

15. *Precious in the sight of the Lord* is *the death of his saints.*

16. *O Lord, truly I* am *thy servant; I* am *thy servant,* and *the son of thine handmaid: thou hast loosed my bonds.*

The motives of this engagement are: First, because God valueth much the blood of his servants, v. 15; next, because God had used him as one of his own family, and made him as a free-born child, to be set at liberty from the bondage he was in, v. 16. Whence learn, 1. God's children are, and should study to be more and more good, merciful, and meek: for thus much the word *saints* in the original signifieth. 2. Albeit the Lord's children are very precious in his eyes, yet he puts them to sufferings and hazard of life, but lets them not be killed, except he sees it for his own honour and theirs also; and in that case, howsoever the world shall esteem their death, yet shall it be dear and precious in God's eyes: *precious in the eyes of the Lord is the death of his saints.* 3. What estimation God manifesteth himself to have of any of his saints, he hath the same estimation of all: and what proof he giveth of his estimation of them, in the preservation of any one of them in time of danger and suffering, it may serve to clear his care of all: for the psalmist intending to praise God for the care he had of him, draweth up the praise with respect to all the saints: *precious in the sight of the Lord, is the death of his saints,* without exception. 4. What privileges we believe to belong to God's children, we may and should apply to ourselves, as the psalmist doth here: after the general doctrine of God's estimation of his saints, he subjoineth and assumeth to himself in particular, saying, *O Lord, truly I am thy servant.* 5. He who feareth or doubteth to apply the privileges of God's children to himself under some higher title, may and should apply them to himself under some other title more suitable to his condition and measure: as here, albeit the psalmist says not, *O Lord, I am a saint,* yet he saith it in substance, in a more humble-like title, *O Lord, I am thy servant, and the son of thine handmaid;* that is, a born servant within the house, as the child of the bond maid under the law, was born a bond servant to the master of the family. 6. How unworthy soever we find ourselves of the meanest styles of the Lord's children, yet must we join ourselves to that number under some title, and not suffer ourselves to be put out of that society; as here the psalmist, albeit conscious of his own unworthiness and infirmity in service, yet being conscious also to an honest purpose and endeavour to serve God, averreth and asserteth his interest in God as a servant, and doubleth and trebleth the asseveration: *truly I am thy servant;* and again, *I am thy servant;* and the third time, *the son of thine handmaid;* because born within the visible church, a child of the covenant, claiming right to God's family by it. 7. Albeit we can speak little of our doing service to God, yet if we can speak of God's doing to us and for us, as for his own children, delivering us from the bonds of sin, Satan, hell, and hellish torments of conscience, we shall prove the point of our interest in God, as here the psalmist, for proof that his death was precious in God's eyes, and that he was cared for as a child of his family, saith, *thou hast loosed my bonds*, and so proveth his point.

17. *I will offer to thee the sacrifice of thanksgiving, and will call upon the name of the Lord.*

18. *I will pay my vows unto the Lord now in the presence of all his people,*

19. *In the courts of the Lord's house, in the midst of thee, O Jerusalem. Praise ye the Lord.*

The psalmist repeateth the third engagement to the solemn praising of God, and with this also, the first engagement to dependence on God, by worshipping and invocating his name. Whence learn, 1. Believers in the church of Israel before Christ, rested not upon the external ceremonies, but looked through them to the spiritual intent and signification of the ceremonies; for moral and spiritual service is here promised by the psalmist : *I will offer to thee the sacrifice of thanksgiving, and will call upon the name of the Lord.* 2. Believers in the church of Israel knew that even no moral, nor spiritual service was acceptable to God, except through the intercession, suffering, and oblation of Christ, signified by the sacrifices, for, therefore he calleth his praising of God a sacrifice : *I will offer unto thee the sacrifice of thanksgiving.* 3. The promises and vows of the sincere servant of God should not be fleeting motions, and rash expressions, but resolute and fixed purposes of the heart, which a man need not repent nor alter, as the repeating of the former encouragement here teacheth us : *I will pay my vows, &c.,* is repeated in the same words. 4. Public assemblies of God's people, and places to meet in are needful, that by this means God may be more solemnly glorified, and his people edified and strengthened in the service of God, and profession of his truth : *I will pay my vows in the courts of the Lord's house, in the midst of thee, O Jerusalem.* 5. When a man hath said all he can for God's praise, he must acknowledge that it is a work which requireth more hands than his own to lift such a weighty sacrifice; for this the prophet's example teacheth us; closing this psalm with *praise ye the Lord.*

PSALM CXVII.

1. *O praise the Lord, all ye nations: praise him, all ye people.*

2. *For his merciful kindness is great toward us: and the truth of the Lord endureth for ever. Praise ye the Lord.*

This psalm is an exhortation to the Gentiles to praise God, v. 1, for his mercy and truth towards his people, v. 2. Whence learn, 1. In God's worship it is not always necessary to be long; few words sometimes say what is sufficient, as this short psalm giveth us to understand. 2. The conversion of the Gentiles was foreseen and foretold long before the Jews were rejected, as this exhortation, directed to them and prophesying of their praising God, giveth evidence. 3. Invitation of any to the fellowship of God's worship, and in special to praise and thanksgiving, is an invitation of them to renounce their sinful course, and to subject themselves to God in Christ, and to embrace the offer of his grace, that so they may join with the church in the song of praises, for all the nations are invited to come unto the society of the church in these words: *O praise the Lord, all ye nations.* 4. Yea, this invitation of all the nations to praise God set down in Scripture, is a prophecy which was to take effect in all the elect Gentiles of all nations, for so reasoneth the Apostle, Rom. xv. 11, from this place: *praise him, all ye people.* 5. Albeit there be matter of praise to God in himself, though we should not be partakers of any benefit from him, yet the Lord giveth his people cause to praise him for favours to them in their own particular case: *for his merciful kindness is great towards us.* 6. There is no less reason to praise God for what he hath promised, than for what he hath given already: *for the truth of the Lord endureth for ever,* is made a reason of his praise. 7. As God's kindness and truth are the pillars of our salvation, so also are they the matter of our praise, which always go together, and run in the same channel toward the same per-

sons, and run abundantly and for ever together : *his kindness is great towards us, and the truth of the Lord endureth for ever.* 8. All they who hear of God, are bound
to praise God : *praise ye the Lord.*

PSALM CXVIII.

The psalmist in this thanksgiving for bringing him so wonderfully to the
kingdom, prophesieth in this psalm of Christ's troubles by his enemies, and of his victories over them, both in his own person, and in his
mystical body. This psalm hath such an eye and respect to Christ and
his church, that, whatsoever shadow of these things may be found in
David, the main substance and accomplishment of all things herein
contained, are to be found most clearly and fully in Christ's wrestling
with his enemies, and his triumphing over them for the comfort of the
church, and glory of the Father : and this the church of Israel perceived and acknowledged ; as appeareth by their acclamation taken out
of this psalm, and made to Christ at his coming into Jerusalem, as
king riding, and by Christ's interpretation, and appropriating it unto
himself, Mat. xxi. 9—42. For this cause also the psalmist does not pre-
fix his name to this psalm, whatsoever might be fit for his particular
experience in it, but leaveth it to run the more clearly and directly toward the Messiah, or Christ, who is here mainly intended.
The psalm may be divided into three parts. In the first part, the psalmist, and Christ represented by him, exhorteth the church to praise
God, and giveth sundry reasons for it, to v. 14. In the second, he reneweth the song of God's praise, and giveth new reasons for the same,
to v. 19. In the third, Christ's triumph is set down wherein he goeth
into the temple and solemn assembly of the church : and here Christ
by his rejoicing stirreth up the church to rejoice, and the church giveth
acclamation to him as their Lord and King, and all the company rejoice
together, and priests and people stir up one another to praise the Lord,
to the end of the psalm.

1. *O give thanks unto the Lord; for* he is *good : because his mercy* endureth *for ever.*

2. *Let Israel now say, that his mercy* endureth *for
ever.*

3. *Let the house of Aaron now say, that his mercy*
endureth *for ever.*

4. *Let them now that fear the Lord say, that his
mercy* endureth *for ever.*

The exhortation is to the visible church in general, to
thank God for his everlasting mercy, to the house of Aaron,
and to those that fear God more specially, to praise him for
that same cause. Whence learn, 1. Upon all occasions we
ought to glorify God, and to stir up others to do so, especially when we consider what God doeth for the kingdom of

Christ; and here let us say, *O give thanks unto the Lord.*
2. Albeit the wisdom, power, and justice of God, be glorious matter for praising him, yet none can heartily glorify him for these reasons, till they first have experience of the sweetness of his goodness and mercy : *give thanks, for he is good, for his mercy endureth for ever.* 3. Such as are partakers of the goodness which is purchased by Christ, may lay hold on everlasting mercies, and give thanks for those: *because his mercy endureth for ever.* 4. Albeit all the elect have interest in God's praise, for mercies purchased by Christ to them, yet the elect of Israel have the first room in the song: for Christ is first promised to them, and came of them according to the flesh, and will be most marvellous about them: *let Israel now say, that his mercy endureth for ever.* 5. Men who have more gifts, higher place, and in special they who are ministers of God's house, should go before others in glorifying God's mercy manifested in Christ : *let the house of Aaron now say, that his mercy endureth for ever.* 6. Whatsoever others do, such as worship God in their spirits sincerely, should let forth their thankfulness for God's grace manifested to them through Christ : *let them now that fear the Lord say, that his mercy endureth for ever.* 7. As the salvation of the elect is one, and the love of God to them one, so should their song be one : as here four several times it is said, *his mercy endureth for ever.* 8. Christ being come at length into the world, in the fulness of time, and having ended his sufferings, and entered into his kingdom, notwithstanding all the provocations of men to move God to cut short this mercy, hath given proof once for all of his everlasting goodness and mercy : therefore it is said, *let Israel now, let Aaron now, let them that fear God now, say, that his mercy endureth for ever.* And this is one reason of his praises.

5. *I called upon the Lord in distress : the Lord answered me, and set me in a large place.*

Another reason of this thanksgiving is, the psalmist's experience, representing Christ's suffering and victory : he called to God, and was delivered. Whence learn, 1. As the deliverance which David had out of his troubles, was a reason of joy to all the kingdom of Israel, because of the benefits which they enjoyed under his government; so the deliverance which Christ had out of his sufferings, is a reason for joy, thanksgiving, and glorifying God to all his subjects : *I called upon the Lord in distress, he answered me, and set me in a large place.* 2. Albeit the Lord bring his children into straits, yet he will not leave them in distress, but will bring them forth into a large place, as this experience of the psalmist, and of Christ our Head, both distressed and delivered for our sake, giveth assurance. 3. The distress of the Lord's children is not so bitter, as the delivery and enlargement out of it is sweet: *for he answered me, and set me in a large place,* is here the matter of victorious joy, and of God's high praises. 4. Delivery out of any great danger, is a matter of glorifying God, especially when it is the return of prayer, as here : *I called on the Lord, and he answered me, &c.*

6. *The Lord is on my side; I will not fear : what can man do unto me?*

7. *The Lord taketh my part with them that help me: therefore shall I see my desire upon them that hate me.*

A third reason of praise is, because the psalmist hath by this experience received such confirmation of God's respect to him, as made him fearless for time to come, and assured of the overthrow of his enemies. Whence learn, 1. Experience of hearing our prayer should confirm us about God's friendship, as here from his late experience he draweth this conclusion : *the Lord is on my side.* 2. God's favour and friendship believed should free us from the fear of men ; *the Lord is on my side, I will not fear.* 3. Albeit the power of man be an ordinary temptation to divert the godly from their duty, yet when God's favour and displeasure are well weighed, and compared with man's hatred and favour, it shall be found to be but little which either man's terror or allurement can do, as this interrogation speaketh : *what can man do unto me?* 4. Faith obtaineth more good by deliveries, than it findeth hurt by assaults; and then is true faith victorious, when God's friendship is opposed to whatsoever the wrath of the creature can do, as here is seen. 5. Albeit we have got some notable victories against our enemies, yet we must know our warfare is not ended; for so much the psalmist insinuateth, when he goeth to make party against his enemies : *the Lord is on my side, the Lord taketh my part.* 6. Albeit the Lord's people despise not means and helpers, yet they rely not on them, but on God's help, who can bless the means : *the Lord taketh my part with them that help me.* 7. Faith, in its own victory by God's assistance, seeth also the overthrow of the adversaries : *the Lord taketh my part, therefore shall I see my desire on them that hate me.* 8. Many good uses may a believer make of one benefit one victory, one experience, as here the psalmist doth. He confirmeth himself in his reconciliation and friendship with God, encourageth himself against dangers to come, exalteth God, and esteemeth as nothing the hatred and favour of man, and resolveth to use means, and to expect the blessing from God, with other sundry good uses which follow hereafter.

8. It is *better to trust in the Lord than to put confidence in man :*

9. It is *better to trust in the Lord than to put confidence in princes.*

A fourth reason of praise and thanks to God, is for blessing the course of faith, and making it better than the course of policy or carnal reason. Whence learn, 1. As faith gathereth strength, when it seeth what blessing followeth on believing, so God getteth praise by blessing the obedience of faith : *it is better to trust in the Lord than to put confidence in men.* 2. Such as believe in God, in whatsoever mean condition they may be, are in better case than the minions of kings, who lean only to men's favour; and time will prove this to be true : *that it is better to trust in the Lord, than to put confidence in princes.*

10. *All nations compassed me about : but in the name of the Lord will I destroy them.*

11. *They compassed me about; yea, they compassed me about : but in the name of the Lord I will destroy them.*

12. *They compassed me about like bees; they are quenched as the fire of thorns : for in the name of the Lord I will destroy them.*

A fifth reason of thanks to God, is David's victory in the type, and Christ's victory signified, begun, and made sure to be perfected over a world of adversaries. Whence learn, 1. Many adversaries had David, but Christ hath more; for all the world are deadly adversaries to him: *all nations compassed me about.* 2. The church and kingdom of Christ hath neither power to defend itself, nor way in this world to escape from its enemies: *all nations compassed me about,* is thrice expressed. 3. Christ's enemies are so despiteful, that in fighting against his kingdom, they regard not what become of themselves, so be they may hurt his people; but as the bee undoeth herself in stinging, and loseth her life or her power with her sting, so do they: *they compassed me about like bees.* 4. All that the enemies of Christ's church can do against his people, is but to trouble them externally; their wounds are like the sting of a bee, that is, in pain and swelling, and a short trouble only, but are not deadly: *they compassed me about like bees.* 5. The power whereby victory is obtained over the enemies of Christ and his people, is merely divine, even the omnipotency of the Godhead of our Lord, who fighteth all his own battles and ours: *in the name of the Lord I will destroy them,* thrice expressed. 6. Particular victories now and then, give ground of hope of complete victory over all enemies; for Christ hath undertaken here to destroy them all: *in the name of the Lord I will destroy them.* 7. The rejoicing of the enemies, and the putting forth their malice against the church, are but for a short time, and all to destroy themselves: *they are quenched as the fire of thorns.*

13. *Thou hast thrust sore at me, that I might fall: but the Lord helped me.*

A sixth reason of thanks is, for delivery to Christ mystical, from the chief ruler of the adverse powers; that is, from Satan. Whence learn, 1. Whosoever be the instruments of the persecution of Christ in his members, Satan is the prime agent, the captain of these cursed soldiers; for toward him mainly is this speech directed: *thou hast thrust sore at me.* 2. The aim of Satan in his opposition to the church, is to drive them from their station which they have by faith in God, that they may despair and sin: *thou hast thrust sore at me that I might fall.* 3. How weak soever the Lord's persecuted children are, when Satan raiseth persecution against them, and driveth his darts at them, yet he prevaileth not, because God assisteth them: *but the Lord helped me.* 4. The Lord's servants, being assisted in their trials, shall have such deliverances, as shall give them reason to exult, time out of mind, over Satan and all their enemies, as here the psalmist, as a type and soldier of Christ, and Christ our chieftain do.

14. *The Lord* is *my strength and song, and is become my salvation.*

This we make the second part of the psalm, wherein the song of praise and thanksgiving is renewed, and four new reasons are added. And, first, he giveth all the glory of his victory to God, his strength and salvation. Whence learn, 1. As human strength is not sufficient to overcome Satan, so must the wrestler be emptied of the conceit of his own abilities, and betake himself to God, as the complete furnisher of him, as this example teacheth us. 2. He that hath renounced confidence in created strength, and hath betaken himself to God's support, promised in his word, shall have cause to sing, *the Lord is my strength and song.* 3. Experimental proof of the truth of God's promises, is a new impression of believed truth, and a new taking up of it, which maketh a man say, I perceive of a truth that God is such as he calleth himself: *he is become my salvation,* importeth so much; and this is the first reason of his renewed song.

15. *The voice of rejoicing and salvation* is *in the tabernacles of the righteous: the right hand of the Lord doeth valiantly.*

16. *The right hand of the Lord is exalted; the right hand of the Lord doeth valiantly.*

The second reason for praise and thanksgiving is from the joy which cometh to the justified through faith in Christ, for the certainty of their salvation purchased by his sufferings and battles. Whence learn, 1. Such as believe in Christ, and endeavour new obedience, as they are the persons for whom Christ hath purchased salvation, so shall they find the joy of the purchase, and acknowledge it to God's glory: *the voice of rejoicing and salvation is in the tabernacles of the righteous.* 2. Albeit the righteous be pilgrims and have no settled dwelling-place, yet are their pilgrimage and private tabernacles made refreshful to them by the joy of their salvation: *the voice of rejoicing and salvation is in the tabernacles of the righteous.* 3. The matter of the joy of the righteous, is the sight of God's power employed for their safety, and victoriously working out their salvation and his own glory: *the right hand of the Lord doeth valiantly; the right hand of the Lord is exalted; the right hand of the Lord doeth valiantly.*

17. *I shall not die, but live, and declare the works of the Lord.*

The third reason of thanksgiving, is assurance of complete victory, and employment of all gifts given to him in God's service. Whence learn, 1. The believer may be assured, that death shall not prevent him, till he have ended his appointed service; and that, as death had not dominion over Christ, so shall it not have lasting dominion over him: *I shall not die, but live, and declare the works of the Lord.* 2. To honour and praise God in this life, should be life to the believer, and dearer to him than life, in regard he loveth this life, and the next also, mainly because he shall therein praise God: *I shall not die, but live, and declare the works of the Lord.*

18. *The Lord hath chastened me sore: but he hath not given me over unto death.*

The fourth reason of thanksgiving, is the Lord's moderating all chastisements, so that the psalmist is not destroyed by them. Whence learn, 1. As Christ our Head was chastised for our peace, and tasted of death, but was not given over to it; so his servants, albeit not exempted from chastisements, yet shall not be destroyed by them: *the Lord hath chastened me sore, yet he hath not given me over unto death,* saith the type of Christ, speaking history of himself and prophecy of Christ. 2. The moderation of chastisements and salvation wrought by them, should swallow up the grief of them, and make them the matter of our song, as here we are taught: *the Lord hath chastened me sore, yet he hath not given me over unto death.* 3. It is wisdom to observe the moderation of chastisements, as well as their sharpness and weight, and to remember that when adversaries trouble us, and would destroy us, God is about only to correct us, and do us good : as here is observed.

19. *Open to me the gates of righteousness : I will go in to them,* and *I will praise the Lord :*

20. *This gate of the Lord into which the righteous shall enter.*

The third part of the psalm, wherein is set down the royal triumph of the psalmist, as the type of Christ. First, his marching up to the sanctuary, v. 19, 20; then, his beginning the song of praise, and exhorting all the church to rejoice with him, v. 21—24; thirdly, the church's acclamation to her triumphing king, v. 25—27; fourthly, the psalmist, as a type of Christ, glorifieth God reconciled by covenant to the church, promiseth to praise him still, and closeth the psalm with an exhortation to thanksgiving, as he began, v. 28, 29.

As for the first, the psalmist as the type of Christ, commands to make way for his entering into the Lord's temple and assembly of the saints, where he may praise the Lord. Whence learn, 1. The place of Christ's and the believer's triumphing on the earth, is the assembly of the church, and they who are touched with the feeling of God's grace and salvation, have and should have a great desire to have God glorified in the holy assemblies : *open to me the gates of righteousness.* 2. As the material temple of Jerusalem was, so every visible assembly of the saints is the place where the righteousness of faith and obedience is to be preached, where the saints are to be edified in the course of righteousness, and toward which the truly righteous have, and should have, great desire to frequent and honour these meetings : *open to me the gates of righteousness,* into which the righteous enter : *I will go in to them.* 3. The exercise of the church met together, is mainly to proclaim the Lord's praise : *I will go in to them, and praise the Lord.* 4. The church's assembly is the convenient place, where the Lord and the righteous meet : *this is the gate of the Lord, into which the righteous shall enter.* And this is the first part of the description of the triumph.

21. *I will praise thee : for thou hast heard me, and art become my salvation.*

22. *The stone* which *the builders refused is become the head* stone *of the corner.*

23. *This is the Lord's doing; it* is *marvellous in our eyes.*

24. *This* is *the day* which *the Lord hath made ; we will rejoice and be glad in it.*

The second part of the description of the triumph, hath the song of the psalmist, as the type of Christ's song of praise, wherein he in his own name and in the name of all believers praiseth God for hearing the intercession made for the church, and for granting salvation to them. Whence learn, 1. The intercession of Christ, and the prayers also of the saints put up in his name, are all granted, and thereby God is greatly glorified : *I will praise thee, for thou hast heard me.* 2. The several victories of Christ, and of his militant members, are the fruits of Christ's intercession, and the evidence of salvation to his mystical members : *thou hast heard me, and art become my salvation.* 3. As David the type, so Christ represented by him was first despised and set at nought by the chief rulers, before he was exalted; for he was indeed that precious stone set at nought by men : *the stone which the builders refused.* 4. Men may have high place in the visible church, who cannot take up Christ when he showeth himself, who have little skill to embrace Christ and apply him to themselves or others; as the builders of the church—priests, scribes, and pharisees—refused to acknowledge Christ so much as for a true member of the church : *he is that stone which the builders refused.* 5. Albeit men misregard Christ offering himself in his doctrine and ordinances, yet he is the rock whereon the church is built, the foundation whereupon to settle it, the corner stone to hold the building compact together, and the head stone of the corner for adorning and perfecting the building gloriously, Matt. xxi. 9, 15, 42 : *he is become the head stone of the corner.* 6. In nothing more do the wisdom, grace, and power of God appear, than in the magnifying of Jesus Christ, and building of his church: *this is the work of the Lord.* 7. When the weakness of the church in herself, the power of her manifold enemies, and the impediments of this work, are looked upon, it is a wonder of wonders to see the going on of God's work in it :

this is the work of the Lord, and it is marvellous in our eyes.   8. Albeit there be no day which God hath not made, yet in the day of the manifestation of righteousness and life immortal through Christ, the time of the gospel, and most specially the day of the resurrection of Christ from the dead, wherein Christ was declared victoriously the only begotten Son of God, is made a day of light and gladness to poor self-condemned sinners : *this is the day which the Lord hath made.*   9. Christ alloweth joy and gladness to every believer and true member of his church, and willeth them to glorify God in this holy joy, wherein he will join with them : *we will rejoice and be glad in it.*

25. **Save** now, *I beseech thee, O Lord : O Lord, I beseech thee, send now prosperity.*

26. **Blessed** be *he that cometh in the name of the Lord : we have blessed you out of the house of the Lord.*

27. **God** is *the Lord, which hath showed us light : bind the sacrifice with cords,* even *unto the horns of the altar.*

This is the third part of the triumph, wherein the church makes her Lord welcome, and congratulateth his victory, prayeth for a blessing upon his kingdom, prophesieth of the blessings, and sets herself to offer the sacrifices of praise and thanksgiving to God for it.   Whence learn, 1. As it is the duty, so it is the hearty desire of every believer to welcome Christ offering himself as our victorious mediator and king : for he is worthy, to whom *hosanna* (as it is written, Matth. 21 should be sung.   2. Where Christ cometh, salvation also and spiritual prosperity come, which were promised before, and shadowed forth in types : for, *save now, I beseech thee, send now prosperity,* is a promising prayer.   3. Albeit Christ hath no need of our prayers for advancing his own kingdom; yet will he have us to pray for his people's sake, that his kingdom may come, and will have all believers, in testimony of their love to his honour, to draw the chariot of his triumph, that it may ride prosperously, saying, *save now, I beseech thee, O Lord, send now prosperity.*   4. Christ is not come unsent into the world, but with commission to save his people from their sins : *he cometh in the name of the Lord.* 5. Together with Christ all blessings come, which every believer should heartily acknowledge and proclaim: *blessed be he that cometh in the name of the Lord.* 6. The priests and ministers of the Lord have warrant from the Lord to bless all them that bless Jesus Christ; for, after the acclamation which the people give to Christ, the ministers of the Lord pronounce so many of the people as heartily receive him for their king, to be blessed: *we have blessed you,* say they to the people, *out of the house of the Lord.* 7. Comfort against all sin and misery is brought to the church by Christ, and they who sat in darkness, in him have seen a great light, which should be acknowledged, as here: *God is the Lord who hath shown unto us light.* 8. As the ministers of the Lord preach that believers in Christ are blessed, so should they set them all on work, and themselves also with them, to express by all means their thankfulness to God for the great grace sent by him: *bind the sacrifice with cords, even unto the horns of the altar.*

28. *Thou art my God, and I will praise thee;* thou art *my God, I will exalt thee.*

In the last place, the psalmist, as a type of Christ, proclaimeth the covenant between the Father and Christ, and between God and himself in Christ, as a settled and ratified bargain, and exhorteth the church to thanksgiving, as he began : for we understand this as the speech of Christ triumphing in his church. We learn, 1. The Father and Christ, both before he was incarnate and after, stand agreed in the covenant of redemption : for Christ saith here to the Father, *Thou art my God.* 2. By virtue of the covenant of redemption between God and Christ the mediator, all sufferings and battles for the elect are undertaken, and such deliverance is given from all troubles and victory over all enemies obtained, as the mediator is satisfied about it, and praiseth God : *thou art my God, and I will praise thee;* and over again, *thou art my God, and I will exalt thee.* 3. By virtue of the covenant of redemption, God is the believer's God also, and ought to be praised, and more and more exalted in our hearts, and outwardly by us; for, as Christ called God his Father, and our Father, his God and our God, so every one who believeth in him may say to

God, *Thou art my God, and I will praise thee : thou art my God, and I will exalt thee.* 4. The goodness of the Lord in sending Christ a saviour to us, and the constancy of his mercy to us in him, calls for everlasting praise and thanks to God from us: *O give thanks unto the Lord, for he is good, for his mercy endureth for ever.*

29. *O give thanks unto the Lord ; for he is good : for his mercy endureth for ever.*

PSALM CXIX.

We read of no man who had more troubles and exercises of conscience, greater vicissitude of changes outward and inward, more frequent experiences of his own weakness, witlessness, and sinfulness, or of God's merciful direction, consolation, and deliverance, than *David.* This man the Lord fitted, by the immediate inspiration of the Holy Ghost, for the edification of the church, to express his exercises and good deliverances from them all : and in this psalm, as in a bundle, he hath collected the sum of his holy meditations, and of the profitable uses which he made of the revealed will of God in Scripture, in all the conditions wherein he was, to teach all the faithful after him, to have the word of God in special regard, and to have respect to it, as the only rule whereby they might find direction, consolation, and salvation, however matters went. To this end, for memory's sake, he hath filled the Hebrew alphabet with twenty-two meditations, every one of them beginning with a several letter of the alphabet, and every section having eight verses, beginning with the same letter, and every verse almost of every section under some expression, making mention of the Scripture.

The words wherein the Scripture, or revealed will of God in Scripture, is here expressed are one of these ten. 1. The *law* or *doctrine,* which signifieth the Lord's will to be taught by God, that all men should learn it. 2. *Statutes,* which signify that this revealed will of God containeth the duties which God hath appointed and prescribed for our rule. 3. *Precepts,* which signify that this will of God is imposed by the authority of our sovereign lawgiver. 4. *Commands,* which signify that this revealed will is committed to our trust to be kept. 5. *Testimonies,* which signify that this revealed will of God testifieth of our duty and our doings, whether conform or not to the rule; and testifieth also what event may be expected by our believing or misbelieving, by our obedience or disobedience thereof. 6. *Judgments,* which signify the Scripture to be God's judicial decree, ordaining how our words, deeds, and thoughts shall be ordered, and what shall be the execution of his will answerable thereto. 7. *Ora-*

cle or speech, because the Scripture proceedeth, as it were, from the mouth of God. 8. The *word,* which signifieth God's expounding his mind to us, as if he were speaking to us. 9. The *way of God,* which signifieth the Lord's giving direction for our several actions how we should walk, as by so many steps to the kingdom of heaven. 10. *Righteousness,* which signifieth that the word of God showeth the way how a man shall be justified, to wit by faith, and how a justified man should approve himself to God and man, as justified by faith; and that every son of wisdom, must and will justify this word of God, as the perfect rule of righteousness.

ALEPH.

In the first section, he describeth the blessed men to be they only who walk in the obedience of faith, as God's word prescribeth, v. 1—3, and then he maketh application of this doctrine to himself, v. 4—8.

1. *Blessed* are *the undefiled in the way, who walk in the law of the Lord.*

2. *Blessed* are *they that keep his testimonies,* and that *seek him with the whole heart.*

3. *They also do no iniquity : they walk in his ways.*

In the description of the truly blessed man, learn, 1. This is the first lesson for the direction of a man's life, to know wherein true blessedness consisteth, and who is the blessed man; for the beginning of this psalm with this doctrine insinuateth so much. 2. Albeit every man confusedly desireth happiness, yet it is the property of the children of God, effectually and in earnest to seek true happiness; as the description of the blessed man showeth. 3. As the word of God alone revealeth true happiness, and the way to it, so they alone are blessed, who choose the clear way of God's word to direct them to blessedness, and make conscience sincerely to put this doctrine into practice: *blessed are the undefiled in the way, who walk in the law of the Lord.* 4. God hath testified in his word, how a man shall be pardoned of his sins, reconciled to God, and have right to eternal life, to wit, by faith in the Messiah, Jesus Christ, and that blessed is the man who holdeth this way fast : *blessed are they that keep his testimonies.* 6. The true believer of God's testimonies concerning the way of true blessedness, studieth to have communion with God, and to grow in the fellowship of his grace sincerely: *they seek the Lord with their whole heart.* 6. As the blessed man holds fast the Lord's testimonies for reconciliation and communion with God, so he ordereth his conversation in the way which God in his word hath prescribed, eschewing sin, and studying to please God: *they also do no iniquity;* that is, they are not workers of iniquity: *they walk in his way;* that is, they aim and endeavour to follow the course which God prescribeth. 7. Albeit there be no man who sinneth not, yet such as flee to God's grace offered in Christ for daily pardon, and set themselves to obey God's directions set down in his word, are esteemed to be no workers of iniquity, but men going homeward to God, howsoever clogged with infirmities: *they also do no iniquity.* How so? *They walk in his ways.*

4. *Thou hast commanded* us *to keep thy precepts diligently.*

This doctrine the psalmist applieth to himself, and first acknowledgeth his obligation to follow the direction of the Lord in the obedience of faith, v. 4; and then he wisheth to have grace to obey, v. 5—7; and, thirdly, engageth himself to follow this course by promise and prayer, v. 8. From the acknowledgment of his obligation to obey God's word, learn, 1. The doctrine of faith and obedience set down in Scripture, is not left to our arbitrament, but is enjoined on us by divine authority. There is a command given forth to us to believe in the Son of God, and a command to follow the duties of love to God and man: *thou hast commanded us to keep thy precepts.* 2. Albeit the obedience of God's word had no promise of reward, and albeit felicity were not proposed to us, as the gracious reward of the obedience of faith; yet the very command itself, and the authority of God should be sufficient motives to it; which obligation as we should acknowledge, so should we subject ourselves to it, and say, *thou hast commanded us to keep thy precepts.* 3. Howsoever there be great weakness, even in reconciled souls, and albeit there be some strong relics of corrupt nature in them, hindering them to do as they would, yet God will have them aiming to keep his precepts, diligently making conscience of all duties to God and man, of

the smaller duties as well as of the greater, and that on all
occasions, in all times, places, and companies, with their
best affection and strength: *thou hast commanded us to
keep thy precepts diligently.*

5. *O that my ways were directed to keep thy statutes!*

6. *Then shall I not be ashamed, when I have respect unto all thy commandments.*

7. *I will praise thee with uprightness of heart, when
I shall have learned thy righteous judgments.*

The psalmist wisheth to have grace to obey; 1. because
so he would not be ashamed nor disappointed of his hope,
v. 6, and also, so he should be enabled to glorify and praise
God more perfectly, v. 7. Whence learn, 1. The commandments of God are not grievous to the honest heart; for, albeit he be unable to do what he should, yet it is the desire
of his heart to do what is commanded: *O that my ways
were directed to keep thy statutes,* is his hearty wish.
2. When we have received the general direction of God's
word, we have need of the effectual direction of God's Spirit
to apply the word rightly to our particular actions: *O that
my ways were directed,* saith he. 3. The holiest man is
most sensible of his coming short in understanding, and of
his weakness to keep God's commands, and most desirous
of God's help, as this example teacheth us. 4. No man
shall ever have cause to repent of a sincere endeavour to
obey God's revealed will; for, howsoever he may suffer hard
things from men, and be mocked for his sincerity, yet shall
he not be disappointed of his hopes, nor be confounded before God: *then shall I not be ashamed, when I have respect to all thy commandments.* 5. Sincerity must aim at
universal obedience; for, to pretend to keep one command,
and to be found a misregarder of other commands, is a matter of shame, and a mark of unsoundness: *for then shall I
not be ashamed when I have respect to all thy commandments.* 6. As God's word and commands are all righteous
decrees in themselves, and unalterable by men, so are they
seen to be such by those who know them best: *even God's
righteous judgments.* 7. Men praise God uprightly, only in
the measure that they are careful to frame their life to God's
will; for honour given to God with the mouth, agreeth not
with dishonour done to him in deeds in a man's life and con-

versation : *I will praise thee with uprightness of heart, when I have learned thy righteous judgments.* 8. Sound praises of God are the fruit of soundness in piety and righteousness; and the holiest of God's servants are but scholars and students in the knowledge and obedience of both : *I will praise thee with uprightness of heart, when I shall have learned thy righteous judgments.*

8. *I will keep thy statutes : O forsake me not utterly.*

From his engagements to observe this course, learn, 1. Albeit our resolutions and purposes have no strength of themselves, yet God requireth of us that we should with full purpose of heart cleave unto his service, and this course he will bless, for so this practice teacheth us : *I will keep thy statutes ;* that is, I resolve to aim at upright obedience to thy word; for, to endeavour to obey them, is the keeping of God's statutes. 2. As he who is most upright in his resolution, is most diffident of his own strength to perform his resolution, so is he also most earnest with God in prayer, to enable him to do as he resolveth, as this example teacheth us : *I will keep thy statutes, O forsake me not.* 3. Albeit no man can be exempted from temporal desertions, whereby his Christian graces may be tried, and his corruptions mortified, yet the believer may both pray and expect that he shall not be deserted, so as his faith should fail, and his course of obedience should be cut off : for so much this prayer promiseth : *O forsake me not utterly.*

BETH.

In this section, first he propounds this doctrine : The word of God is the only rule and effectual instrument of renewing and sanctifying an unrenewed man, and the only way to find the efficacy of the word, is to study to conform a man's mind, will, and actions thereunto, v. 1. And then, in the next place, to the end he may teach men to make use of this doctrine by his example, he showeth the sincerity of his own endeavour, by seven evidences in the seven following verses.

9. *Wherewithal shall a young man cleanse his way ? By taking heed* thereto *according to thy word.*

In the doctrine about the means of regeneration and reformation of life, learn, 1. As all men are from the birth polluted with sin, so should they early and timously be sensible of this evil, and seek for the remedy of the running issues of sin : for here it is presupposed, *that a young man shall cleanse his way*.   2. Seeing death is uncertain, and sin groweth stronger through custom ; seeing justice is the more provoked, the longer men continue in sin; seeing no age is fitter to serve Satan than youth—inclined to take liberty to be headstrong, self-willed, and given to despise grave admonition—and no age hath more excuses to continue in sin to its own perdition, therefore no age hath more need of remedy from God than youth hath, and this is imported in the question, *wherewith shall a young man cleanse his way ?*   3. Seeing youth is loose, inconsiderate, and inattentive ; seeing the way of obedience is slippery, and many by-paths are offered to the way-faring man; seeing danger of perishing is great, and many are the enemies of man's salvation, who are always seeking whom they may devour ; and seeing no reconciliation can be made with God, no forgiveness of sin can be obtained, no solid sanctification and salvation can be had, except the word of God be held for the only rule of direction, faith, and conversation : therefore there can be no means *to cleanse the young man's way, but by taking heed thereto, according to that word.*

10. *With my whole heart have I sought thee : O let me not wander from thy commandments.*

After the psalmist hath set down the rule of a young man's conversion and conversation, he offereth himself as an example to follow this rule : and here are the first and second evidences of his sincerity in aiming at this way.   The first is, the conscience of his upright seeking of God : and the second evidence is, his prayer to be preserved from wandering from the way of God's obedience.   Whence learn, 1. The sight of what others have attained, is a great encouragement to young scholars in God's school : for, to encourage the young man, the psalmist showeth here his own profiting in his study.   2. Sensibleness of a man's own imperfections, sins, and dangers, and seeking God all-sufficient for relief of sin and misery, and for a daily nearer and nearer communion with God, are marks of sincerity in religion : *with my whole heart have I sought thee.*   3. The more experience a man hath in the ways of God, the more sensible is he of his own readiness to wander insensibly, by ignorance and inadvertency from the ways of God; but the young soldier dares to run hazards to ride into his adversary's camp, and talk with temptations, being confident he cannot easily go wrong : he is not so afraid, as David here, crying, *O let me not wander.* 4. To be diffident of our own wit and strength, and to depend upon God, instantly praying to be kept in and recalled from wandering, prove the sincerity of the purpose of holiness : *O let me not wander from thy commandments.* 5. The going on of the believer in the course of obedience, and his living the life of God, is not from what he hath received before, but must flow from the present influence of grace, sustaining what was given before, and from grace furnishing fresh supply drawn forth by prayer; as this prayer, *O let me not wander*, testifieth.

11. *Thy word have I hid in mine heart, that I might not sin against thee.*

The third evidence of David's endeavour to cleanse his way, by taking heed thereto according to God's word, is, the laying up of the word by faith in his heart. Whence learn, 1. It is not sufficient to have the word of God in brain-knowledge and common memory, for, not wit and memory, but the heart is the chest to keep it in : *I hid thy word in my heart.* 2. Seeing it is impossible to keep sin out of the heart void of the word of God, it is necessary for the servant of God to lay up the Lord's word in his heart by faith and honest affection to it : *thy word have I hid in my heart, that I should not sin against thee.* 3. It is a proof of our sincere endeavour to profit by the word of God in the course of sanctification, to be careful that we let not the word of God slide from us, that we be not spoiled of it by fear of men, or force of temptation : that we be not deceived by Satan's wiles, that we suffer it not to go by our negligence and forgetfulness of it, and that we be careful to approve ourselves to God, in our love to the Lord's word, and estimation of it, as of a most precious jewel, as here we see : *thy word have I hid in my heart, that I should not sin against thee.*

12. *Blessed* art *thou, O Lord: teach me thy statutes.*

A fourth evidence of David's sincerity, in making use of the word of God, is his blessing God for the knowledge he hath received of it, joined with prayer for increasing the measure thereof. Whence learn, 1. It is a mark of sincerity of obedience, to be thankful for what measure we have received, and to be seeking to increase, as young birds receive their food and cry for more : *blessed art thou, O Lord : teach me thy statutes.* 2. Beside all external teaching, we have need of inward and effectual teaching from God, to make knowledge lively and fruitful : *teach me thy statutes.* 3. The goodness of God, and his readiness to bless more and more, are grounds of encouragement to seek a greater measure of his blessing : *blessed art thou, O Lord : teach me thy statutes.*

13. *With my lips have I declared all the judgments of thy mouth.*

A fifth evidence of David's sincere endeavour to make use of God's word, is his care to edify others, and glorify God by the knowledge and experience which he had of it. Whence learn, 1. The revealed will of God in Scripture should be the matter of our speech and conference with others : *with my lips have I declared all the judgments of thy mouth.* 2. The word of God in Scripture should be looked upon as the sentence of the supreme Judge, uncontrollable and unalterable by any creature, and whereby men must judge of all truth, looked to be judged by it ; for therefore is it called, *the judgment of his mouth.* 3. As the conscience of communicating our knowledge and our spiritual gifts is a means of encouragement to seek a greater measure ; so it is an evidence of the sincerity and fruitfulness of what knowledge we have : *teach me thy statutes; with my lips have I declared all the judgments of thy mouth.*

14. *I have rejoiced in the way of thy testimonies, as much as in all riches.*

The sixth evidence of David's sincere endeavour to conform his way to God's word, is his joy in God's service. Whence learn, 1. Delight in God's service and worship, is a mark of sincere obedience to his word : *I have rejoiced in the way of thy testimonies.* 2. Spiritual joy

in spiritual objects far exceedeth any joy in worldly possessions : *I have rejoiced in the way of thy testimonies, more than in all riches.* 3. It is a most sure joy,
which ariseth from the conscience of practical obedience,
and not from contemplation only : *I have rejoiced in the
way of thy testimonies.*

15. *I will meditate in thy precepts, and have respect
unto thy ways.*

16. *I will delight myself in thy statutes : I will not
forget thy word.*

The seventh evidence of David's sincere endeavour to
conform his way to God's word, is his engagement to set
his heart toward God's word in time to come, and not to
rest upon any thing already past and done. Whence learn,
1. Sincerity of our obedience, present and past, is proved
best, by joining our hearty resolution and purpose to go on
for time to come : *I have rejoiced, I will meditate, I will
delight in thy statutes.* 2. It is a profitable means to grow
in grace, to meditate on God's word : *I will meditate on
thy precepts.* 3. Meditation is fruitful, when in our conversation we have respect to the ways of God set down in
his word whereupon we have meditated : *I will have respect unto thy ways.* 4. In meditation on the word, and
endeavour to make use of it in our life, we will easily wax
weary, except we make this course our delight : *I will delight myself in thy statutes.* 5. Meditation will fail, and
delectation will wax cold, except the word be treasured up
in a sanctified memory : *I will not forget thy word.* Thus
a copy is cast for a young man to cleanse his way, and to
make his life comfortable.

GIMEL.

In this section the psalmist prayeth the Lord for continuance of his life,
that he may have occasion of further service, which he desireth may be
done by him, and for this end also he prayeth, that he may have a
deeper insight in the mysteries of God's word, v. 17, 18. And these
two petitions he presseth by three reasons v. 19—21. He prayeth also
for clearing of his innocency, and for removing reproach from him, for
other three reasons, v. 22—24.

17. *Deal bountifully with thy servant,* that *I may
live, and keep thy word.*

18. *Open thou mine eyes, that I may behold wondrous things out of thy law.*

From the first two petitions, learn, 1. As lengthening of life is the good gift of God in itself, and no small benefit to the man who purposeth to employ it well; so life may be lawfully prayed for: *deal bountifully with thy servant, that I may live.* 2. As the end of our life should be, that God may be served; so life should not be desired nor loved, except for that end, but willingly laid down, rather than we should forsake his command: *deal bountifully with thy servant, that I may live and keep thy word.* 3. A faithful servant should count his by-past service richly rewarded, by being employed yet more in further service, as this prayer teacheth: *deal bountifully with thy servant, that I may live and keep thy word.* 4. The whole word of God is a law, a canon, or rule, whereby we should square our faith and conversation, for it is here called also, *thy law.* 5. We by nature are blind, and cannot see the light which shineth in the word of God, till he open our eyes to behold it: therefore prayeth he, *open thou mine eyes.* 6. The word of God is full of wonders, high and heavenly mysteries, and he who seeth them best, wondereth most: *open thou mine eyes, that I may behold wondrous things out of thy law.*

19. *I* am *a stranger in the earth ; hide not thy commandments from me.*

20. *My soul breaketh for the longing* that it hath *unto thy judgments at all times.*

21. *Thou hast rebuked the proud* that are *cursed, which do err from thy commandments.*

Of the three reasons of David's petition, one is, because he is but a stranger here, except for service; another is, because he longeth much to know more of God's word; the third is, because he seeth God's vengeance following those who study not to serve God. Whence learn, 1. Albeit the believer live on the earth, yet he is not at home, so long as he is on the earth: *I am a stranger in the earth.* 2. Whatsoever possession a godly man hath in the earth, were it a kingdom, he should be a stranger for the matter of estimation of, or affection to, any thing on earth: *I am a stranger in the earth.* 3. Acquaintance with the word of God, is able to make up all the losses of the pilgrim, and to season all his griefs; it is able to supply the room of friends and counsellors, to furnish light, joy, strength, food, armour, and defence, and whatsoever else the pilgrim needeth : for the Lord's word shall either bring all these good things to the pilgrim, or lead him to God, where he shall find them all : *I am a stranger in the earth, hide not thy commandments from me.* 4. There is a hiding of the word of God, when means to hear it explained by preachers, are wanting; and there is a hiding of the comfortable and lively sight of the Spirit, who must quicken the word in us; and from both these evils may we, and should we pray to be saved : *hide not thy commandments from me.* 5. Albeit the godly be the dearest souls to God of all men in the world, yet will he exercise them with heart-breaking, especially for spiritual causes, that so he may raise in them an estimation of his own presence, and furnish work in the mean time to their faith : *my heart breaketh for the longing which it hath unto thy judgments.* 6. It is not every faint and cold wish, which maketh a believer profit in God's school; there must be some heat and earnestness in holy desires; and this affection, as it may not be cold, so neither must it be fleeting, but constant : *my heart breaketh for the longing which it hath at all times.* 7. Those who are not penitent for their sin, are proud men before God, and are not subjected to his obedience : for so they are here called. 8. The word of God condemneth the proud, and pronounceth a curse upon them, so long as they continue proud and impenitent : *thou hast rebuked the proud that are cursed.* 9. To dare to wander after a man's own will, and go away from the direction which God giveth us, is pride indeed, and a bold hazarding where God commandeth to fear : *the proud err from thy commandments.*

22. *Remove from me reproach and contempt; for I have kept thy testimonies.*

23. *Princes also did sit* and *speak against me :* but *thy servant did meditate in thy statutes.*

24. *Thy testimonies also* are *my delight,* and *my counsellors.*

The psalmist prayeth also to be cleared in his innocence, and that his reproach may be removed, and giveth three reasons thereof. One is, because he was indeed innocent in the point wherein he was challenged by his enemies; another, because he had sustained the wrath of princes, for his obedience to God; and the third, because he had chosen God's word for counsellors and comforters. Whence learn, 1. As it is no strange exercise for the godly, to be traduced, calumniated, and reproached; so it is no light burden to bear it, but such as the godly have cause to seek the removal of it : *remove from me reproach and contempt.* 2. A good conscience is a ground of comfort in the case of being reproached, and a ground of confidence to seek of God relief from it : *remove contempt, for I have kept thy testimonies.* 3. It is not strange to see, not only the wicked multitude, but also judges and rulers who should defend the godly, act as their enemies : *princes also did sit, and speak against me.* 4. Troubles will try men whether they fear God or men most, and, except the godly take heed to God's word, they cannot stand under the temptations wherewith they may meet : *princes did speak against me, but thy servant did meditate in thy statutes.* 5. The word of God is able, not only to uphold a man in his trouble, but also to make him rejoice in his trouble : *thy testimonies are my delight.* 6. A king with his cabinet council, shall not be so well furnished to persecute the innocent, as the godly patient shall be advised by the word of God, how to answer and carry himself in his trouble : *thy testimonies are my delight, and my counsellors.*

DALETH.

25. *My soul cleaveth unto the dust : quicken thou me according to thy word.*

In this section there are six petitions with their several reasons annexed to them; some of them set down before, some of them set down after, the petition. The first petition is for comfort, because of his heavy condition. Whence learn, 1. Beside the outward trouble from men which the godly ofttimes feel, it pleaseth God to exercise them also sometimes with trouble of mind, immediately from his own hand : *my soul cleaveth unto the dust.* 2. Albeit the Lord suffer his own to lie so long low in their heavy condition of spirit that they may seem dead, yet, by faith in his word, he keepeth in so much life as furnisheth to them prayer to God for comfort: *quicken thou me according to thy word.*

26. *I have declared my ways, and thou heardest me: teach me thy statutes.*

Another petition is for direction and power to obey God's word, because he hath laid open before God all his own course, and confessed what he knew of his own way. Whence learn, 1. When we are deserted in the point of consolation, it is wisdom to search our way, if any thing in it possibly hath grieved God's Spirit; and what we find right, or wrong, or doubtful, it is our wisdom to lay it out before the Lord in sincerity, as here: *I have declared my ways.* 2. As we have found audience and comfort after confession in former times, so may we expect to find the like again: *I have declared my ways, and thou heardest me.* 3. The end of our exercise is to make us study to walk with God more holily, and to feel his direction and guiding more effectually: *teach me thy statutes.*

27. *Make me to understand the way of thy precepts: so shall I talk of thy wondrous works.*

A third petition is, for increase of understanding of the mysteries of God's word, that thereby he might edify others. Whence learn, 1. Great is our natural blindness in God's matters, and the disease is obstinate, and therefore the petition for light is so much the more to be insisted in: *make me to understand.* 2. It is not sufficient to know the meaning of the word, except we know also the way of practising it prudently: *make me to understand the way of thy precepts.* 3. Desire of knowledge should not be for satisfying curiosity, for ostentation, or for worldly gain, but to edify ourselves and others in wisdom: *so shall I talk of thy works.* 4. It is good first to understand, and then to talk of and express truth formerly meditated and digested, as the order of these two teacheth us. 5. The works of creation, redemption, and providence, either set down in Scripture or observed in our own experience, transcend our capacity, and cannot but draw forth admiration from those that contemplate aright: *I shall talk of thy wondrous works.*

28. *My soul melteth for heaviness: strengthen thou me according unto thy word.*

A fourth petition is for strength and consolation in his felt fainting. Whence learn, 1. The Lord's children find both supernatural joys and sorrows which the natural man, who wanteth experience of spiritual exercise, understandeth not, as this expression showeth : *my soul melteth for heaviness.* 2. No natural means can be a remedy for a spiritual disease, but the word of God alone, being quickened by himself, is the proper cure: *strengthen thou me according to thy word.* 3. Spiritual exercise giveth to the saints the clearest discerning of their own weakness and need of support from God : *my heart melteth, strengthen thou me.* 4. Whatsoever the believer needeth, God by the word supplieth to him; as *light,* that he may not wander; *life,* that he die not; *comfort,* that he faint not; and *strength,* that he fall not: *strengthen me according to thy word.*

29. *Remove from me the way of lying; and grant me thy law graciously.*

A fifth petition is, to be freed from the course of sinning in general, and from the course of lying in particular, that so he might neither deceive others nor be deceived himself, but directed by God's law, which can deceive no man. Whence learn, 1. All sinful courses in life or religion are ways of lying, because they cannot but deceive a man, whatsoever pretences they carry : *remove from me the way of lying.* 2. As lying in special, and all sinful courses are natural to us, and cleave to us; so should we pray the more against them to God who alone can remove them : *remove from me the way of lying.* 3. Nothing can decipher unto us a lying way nor guard us from it but God's law, which is the only true way; therefore, saith he, *grant me thy law.* 4. Not only are we inclined naturally to lying, but also we have so foully defiled ourselves with the lying way of sinning, that it is so much the more grace to find any deliverance from it: *grant me thy law graciously.*

30. *I have chosen the way of truth ; thy judgments have I laid* before me.

31. *I have stuck unto thy testimonies: O Lord, put me not to shame.*

32. *I will run the way of thy commandments, when thou shalt enlarge my heart.*

A sixth petition is, to be saved from shame, and comforted, with the reason thereof—because he had adhered to the obedience of the word, and hoped to go on cheerfully in the obedience thereof, if God should be pleased, by the removal of his dreaded reproach, to comfort and enlarge his heart. Whence learn, 1. When a man is about to resolve upon the manner of his carriage, in general or particular, many rules and counsels will be suggested and offered to him, each of them having a pretence of some good, so as a man had need to be well advised what course he chooseth, and then only doth a man resolve rightly when he chooseth the way of obedience to God's word, which cannot deceive him : *I have chosen the way of thy truth.* 2. He that would have special direction in any particular trial, must be a man resolved to follow the rule of God's word, in all his ways in general; for, otherwise he may be left without direction when he hath most need, except he may say for the whole course of his life, *I have chosen the way of truth.* 3. The solid consideration, that God's word is God's decree, may guard a believer against men's terrors and allurements, and fix him in his right choice, as here : *thy judgments I have laid before me.* 4. As he who hath been most steadfast in trials, is not past danger of being driven from God's word; so of all men it is the greatest shame for such a man in trials to quit his hold : *I have stuck to thy testimonies : O Lord, put me not to shame.* 5. In the trial of our steadfast obedience to God, there is no way to persevere, except, in the sense of our weakness and faith of God's goodness, we shall call on God to save us, who will not suffer us to be confounded : *O Lord, put me not to shame.* 6. The child of God is subject to bondage of spirit, even after regeneration, in sundry cases, especially when God bringeth troubles upon him, hideth his comfort from him, and letteth forth appearance of wrath upon him; as the straitening of David's heart here importeth. 7. As when a man's spirit is in bonds, he can hardly walk in God's service cheerfully; so when God showeth his countenance and comforteth a man, then all God's service is easy : *I will run the way of thy commandments, when thou hast enlarged my heart.* 8. When the Lord giveth large comfort, and looseth a man's affection from the spirit of bondage, he useth to give also large measure of strength and activity in his service, albeit

not so large as the man's affection is : *I will run the way
of thy commandments, when thou hast enlarged my
heart.*

HE.

33. *Teach me, O Lord, the way of thy statutes, and
I shall keep it* unto *the end.*

In this section there are eight petitions, according to the
number of the verses. From the first, learn, 1. The narrow way of God's obedience is hard to be found, hardly
kept, and easily mistaken, except God teach us daily by his
Spirit, what he at any time teacheth us by his word : therefore we have need again and again to pray, *Teach me, O
Lord, the way of thy statutes.* 2. As the Lord requireth our perseverance in his service, so our perseverance
dependeth on his continued direction and assistance, which
the believer and daily supplicant for grace may promise to
himself in God's name : *teach me, O Lord, the way of
thy statutes, and I shall keep it unto the end.*

34. *Give me understanding, and I shall keep thy
law ; yea, I shall observe it with* my *whole heart.*

From the second petition, learn, 1. There is no true
wisdom, except by the knowledge of God's will revealed in
Scripture and applied by him, and this we should always
pray for: *give me understanding.* 2. Where God becometh teacher, the disciple may promise obedience : *give
me understanding, and I shall keep thy law.* 3. As no
service pleaseth God, but that which a man desireth, at
least, to do heartily, so he that purposeth to persevere, must
purpose also to serve God affectionately : *yea, I shall observe it with my whole heart.*

35. *Make me to go in the path of thy commandments ;
for therein do I delight.*

From the third petition, learn, 1. Because there are innumerable by-paths from terrors and allurements without,
to make us swerve from the obedience of God, and we of
ourselves are both weak and subject to errors within us,
therefore should we be the more instant in prayer : *make
me to go in the path of thy commandments.* 2. As it is
a fair grace of God to have pleasure in God's service, so he
who hath gotten of God this grace, may expect also direc-

tion and strength to go on in the path of God's obedience : *for therein do I delight*, is given as a reason of his praying, *make me to go in the path of thy commandments.*

36. *Incline my heart unto thy testimonies, and not to covetousness.*

From the fourth petition, learn, 1. As the most holy of God's servants have in them the remainder of their natural stiffness and averseness from the obedience of God's word; so are they of all men most sensible of this sickness, and most instant with God, the only physician, to heal it : *incline my heart unto thy testimonies.* 2. The heart cannot want some object whereunto it must cleave; a man must love something; and if the heart be not set on things spiritual and heavenly, it will not fail to fix upon things base and earthly, as here is insinuated by opposition of *covetousness* to God's *testimonies.* 3. The love of God's testimonies, or of obedience to God's word, and the love of base objects, as the lust of the eye, the lust of the flesh, and the pride of life, are inconsistent, for the one is contrary to the other, as here is shown : *incline my heart unto thy testimonies, and not unto covetousness.*

37. *Turn away mine eyes from beholding vanity ;* and *quicken thou me in thy way.*

From the fifth petition, learn, 1. The sinful concupiscence of the heart hath defiled the external senses, and made them servants unto itself, except God heal both the heart and the senses, as the petition, *turn away mine eyes,* importeth. 2. Albeit the corruption of the heart be deadly wounded, yet it may soon recover life and strength by the external objects of the senses, if watching over the external man be neglected, as, *turn away mine eye from beholding vanity,* importeth. 3. Whatsoever draweth away the heart from God's obedience, is but deceit and folly, whatsoever it may seem to the beholder : *turn away mine eyes from beholding vanity.* 4. Albeit we know that the outward allurements of sin be nothing but vanity, yet we cannot beware of them, nor renounce them, except the Lord help us when the bait is offered : therefore is it needful to pray, *turn away mine eyes from beholding vanity.* 5. As God setteth a watch over the senses, and keepeth the covenant between the renewed heart and the eyes, and reneweth the vigour of the life of grace, so is the inward corruption suppressed and mortified : for the dying of sin, is, by the quickening of gracious habits in the heart into actual exercise, as, *quicken thou me in thy way*, importeth.

38. *Stablish thy word unto thy servant, who* is devoted *to thy fear.*

In the sixth petition he prayeth for the fruit of God's promises for circumcising and purifying his heart, and that by experience he may be settled in the faith of the promises. Whence learn, 1. Faith purifieth the heart by laying hold on the promises of sanctification, and urging God by prayer to the performance of them : *stablish thy word unto thy servant.* 2. Albeit the promise be sure in itself, and sure unto faith also, yet when experimental performance cometh, the truth of it is much more confirmed to us : *stablish thy word unto thy servant.* 3. We believe the promises, when we take them as made, not only to others but also to ourselves by name, as this prayer showeth : *stablish thy word to me thy servant,* (to wit, the promise of sanctification made to believers) and so, *to me thy servant.* 4. He who prayeth for the performance of promises, should resolve to be a servant, and careful to observe precepts : *stablish thy word to thy servant.* 5. That man is indeed God's servant, how weak soever he be in practice, who is devoted to God's fear : for he proveth himself to be a servant by this, *because I am devoted to thy fear.*

39. *Turn away my reproach which I fear ; for thy judgments* are *good.*

From the seventh petition, learn, 1. As the godly are subject to sinful outbreakings, which may bring reproach on them, and on their profession; so are they also jealous of themselves as unable to keep themselves, except God prevent them from giving scandal : *turn away my reproach which I fear.* 2. The way to be kept blameless, is, to fear to offend, to pray to God for preservation, and to watch over our hearts, as we are taught here : *turn away my reproach which I fear.* 3. As the fear of dishonouring our profession by sin, is a guard on the one hand; so esteem and love of prescribed holiness, as of a good and profitable thing, are a guard against sin on the other hand : *turn away my reproach which I fear, for thy judgments are good.*

40. *Behold, I have longed after thy precepts ; quicken me in thy righteousness.*

From the eighth petition, learn, 1. Sincerity loveth to come to the light, and offereth itself to be approved by God : *behold, I have longed after thy precepts.* 2. To love and long for sanctified subjection to God's word, is a proof of sincerity : *I have longed after thy precepts.* 3. A saint may have a great desire to believe and obey God's word, and yet in his own sense, feel much deadness in his affections for a time : *I have longed, quicken me.* 4. They who bewail their own deadness to God, shall find, according to his righteous promises, life spiritual recovered and quickened : *quicken me according to thy righteousness.*

VAU.

41. *Let thy mercies come also unto me, O Lord,* even *thy salvation, according to thy word.*

42. *So shall I have wherewith to answer him that reproacheth me : for I trust in thy word.*

In this section the psalmist prayeth, first, for deliverance out of his hard condition, and giveth reasons for strengthening his hope in this prayer, v. 41, 42 ; next, he prayeth for grace to confess God's truth openly, till the deliverance come; and he strengthens his hope by six or seven reasons in the rest of the section.

From his first petition, and the reasons of it, learn, 1. The believer must lay hold on mercies not seen, and must not rest till he draw them forth by prayer : *let thy mercies come also unto me, O Lord.* 2. Whatsoever may remove our sins and evil merits, and make way for performance of promises, is mercy in effect, and must be sought no less than inward quickening and consolation : *let thy mercies come also unto me.* 3. As perils and hazards of life must be anticipated by God's servant, so deliverances one after another, and salvation may be surely expected : *let thy mercies come unto me, even thy salvation.* 4. It is not any sort of delivery by any means which the servant of God being in straits calleth for, or desireth, but such a deliverance as God will allow, and be pleased to give in a holy way : *let thy salvation come.* 5. As the word of promise is the rule of our petition, so is it a pledge of the thing promised, and must be held fast till the performance come: *let thy salvation come, according to thy word;* and this is one reason of the petition. 6. As the Lord's delivering of his people from the hand of persecutors stoppeth the mouths of their enemies, who say of them that they are in a wrong course, and that God is not their friend; so the believer desireth the Lord to appear for him, to this very end, that the mouth of the enemy may be stopped: *so shall I have wherewithal to answer him that reproacheth me:* and this is another reason of his petition. 7. Whatsoever be our encouragements in our sufferings, the word of God received by faith must be the ground of our comfort and confidence, or else the work will not be sound: *for I trust in thy word* is the ground of *David's* comfort.

43. *And take not the word of truth utterly out of my mouth; for I have hoped in thy judgments.*

44. *So shall I keep thy law continually for ever and ever.*

45. *And I will walk at liberty: for I seek thy precepts.*

46. *I will speak of thy testimonies also before kings, and will not be ashamed.*

47. *And I will delight myself in thy commandments, which I have loved.*

48. *My hands also will I lift up unto thy commandments, which I have loved; and I will meditate in thy statutes.*

From the next petition, and the seven reasons added thereunto, learn, 1. It is not sufficient for God's glory that we believe the word of God in our heart, but we must also confess it with our mouth in the time of trial: *take not thy word out of my mouth.* 2. As God may justly for our sins desert us in the time of trial, when his glory and our duty call for a testimony ; so we must, in the sense of our ill-deserving, flee to God's grace by prayer, and say with confidence, *take not thy word out of my mouth.* 3. If it shall please God, for humbling us, to desert us in some passage of our trial, yet let us believe in him, and deal with him not to forsake us altogether in our trial: *take not the word of truth utterly out of my mouth.* 4. Where the

belief of God's executing his word of threatening and promise hath place with God's children, there is hope that neither men's terror nor allurement shall overcome them in
their trials : *for I have hoped in thy judgments* is set
down here for the first reason of his hope to obtain his petition. 5. The Lord's keeping our heart in faith, and our
mouth and outward man in the course of confession and
obedience, is the cause of our perseverance : *so shall I
keep thy law continually for ever and ever :* and this is
the second reason of his petition. 6. As he who departs
from confessing God's truth casteth himself in straits, in
danger, and bonds; so he that beareth out the confession of
the truth, walketh as a free man, the truth doth set him
free : *and I will walk at liberty ;* which is the third
reason of his petition. 7. Even the consciousness of
honest endeavour to obey the word hath the promise of
not being utterly deserted in the day of trial : *for I have
sought thy precepts* is the fourth reason of the petition. 8. The terror of kings and of men in power is an
ordinary hindrance of free confession of God's truth in time
of persecution ; but faith in the truth sustained in the heart
by God is able to bring forth a confession upon all hazards :
I will speak of thy testimonies before kings. 9. He that
is resolved to confess the questioned truth of God, whosoever mock at it, shall not be ashamed of his confession, but
rather shall have credit by it : *I will speak of thy testimonies also before kings, and will not be ashamed :* and
this is the fifth reason of the petition. 10. The more men
know the excellency of God's truth, and feel the power of
God's hand sustaining them in the faith and confession of
it, the more will they love and delight in the word of the
Lord : *I will delight myself in thy commandments which
I have loved :* which is the sixth reason of his petition. 11.
He that findeth himself borne out in the confession of the
truth in time of trial, should, in all time after so much the
more as his experience is greater, embrace heartily the
Lord's commands as precious gifts, and should give up himself absolutely to be governed thereby : for the *lifting up
of his hands to the Lord's commandments* importeth so
much. 12. He who, out of love to God's commandments,
hath endured trial by trouble, and hath overcome temptations, may comfortably approve himself in his former loving

of the Lord's commands, and thereby renew and increase his love to obedience of them : for, after he hath said, *I will lift up my hands to thy commandments*, he showeth that he will do so, with a ratification and approbation of his love to them, by adding, *thy commandments which I have loved*. 13. The experience of the worth of divine truth, which is able to bear out itself, and the man also who confesseth it, should set a believer on a more and more earnest study to know the mind of God revealed therein, as the prophet resolveth to do : *and I will meditate in thy statutes :* and this engagement is the last reason of the petition.

ZAIN.

49. *Remember the word unto thy servant, upon which thou hast caused me to hope.*

In this section, David prayeth for the performance of the promise which he hath believed, and whereof he hath found the fruits already in a good measure. Whence learn, 1. The promises of the gospel and grace of God, give liberty and confidence to the believer to draw near to God, to seek the full performance thereof: as here, *remember the word wherein thou hast caused me to hope.* 2. The general offer of the gospel, and the promises made to the believer, are addressed to every individual in particular, no less than if his name were inserted in the promise, or written in the Bible : *remember the word spoken unto thy servant,* or promised to me, 3. God, that maketh the offer of the word, is he who also worketh faith in the believer, and moveth him to apply it, and trust in it; the acknowledging whereof, as it is God's glory, so it is the believer's profit : *remember the word, upon which thou hast caused me to hope ;* for faith and hope are not of ourselves, they are the gift of God.

50. *This* is *my comfort in my affliction : for thy word hath quickened me.*

51. *The proud have had me greatly in derision : yet have I not declined from thy law.*

52. *I remembered thy judgments of old, O Lord ; and have comforted myself.*

53. *Horror hath taken hold upon me, because of the wicked that forsake thy law.*

54. *Thy statutes have been my songs in the house of my pilgrimage.*

55. *I have remembered thy name, O Lord, in the night, and have kept thy law.*

56. *This I had, because I kept thy precepts.*

The fruits which he hath found already by his faith in the word, are seven, all in order set down in the rest of the verses of this section.   Whence learn, 1. Faith and hope in God exempt not God's children from trouble, but comfort them in it, so as all other consolations are nought in comparison : *this is my consolation in my affliction.* 2. When the believer is damped with trouble, and sometimes as it were dead in regard to spiritual operations, motions, and affections, faith draweth life again out of the word of promise : *for thy word hath quickened me :* and this is the first fruit of faith in God's word. 3. Albeit impenitent, graceless men mock grace, mock faith and obedience in the godly, and (in Satan's drift and theirs) to the intent they may make the godly forsake God's law; yet faith in the word is able to bear the believer up against derision, as experience showeth : *the proud have had me greatly in derision, yet have I not declined from thy law :* and this is the second felt fruit of his faith. 4. It is good to have a number of examples of God's dealing with his servants, and with his adversaries, laid up in the storehouse of a sanctified memory, that thereby faith may be strengthened in the day of affliction; for so are we here taught : *I remembered thy judgments of old, O Lord.* 5. Faith draweth comfort out of the execution of God's word of promise, and of threatening also in former times : *I remembered thy judgments of old, O Lord, and was comforted :* and this is the third felt fruit of his faith. 6. To see wrath and judgment in the face of sin, and to be diverted from sinning by the sight of God's judgments threatened and executed upon the wicked, are an evidence of sincerity in God's service : *terror hath taken hold upon me, because of the wicked that forsake thy law :* and this is the fourth felt fruit of his faith. 7. As God's children are in this world strangers and pilgrims in affection, and dealt with as strangers where they live, so also are they ofttimes banished from their native country : *thy statutes have been my songs in the house of my pil-*

grimage. 8. Wheresoever the believer is, and whatsoever be his outward condition, the word of God received by faith, shall bear him company, and furnish him with matter of comfort and rejoicing : *thy statutes have been my songs in the house of my pilgrimage :* and this is the fifth felt fruit of his faith. 9. The knowledge and deep impression of the majesty of God, as he revealeth himself in his works and word, are powerful means to strengthen us in the obedience of faith : *I have remembered thy name, O Lord, and have kept thy law :* and this is the sixth felt fruit of his faith. 10. Well-spent time in secret when we are solitary, shall be rewarded openly by a good carriage in society and company : *I remembered thy name in the night, I have kept thy law.* 11. It is no small benefit to see and observe what good we have had by our obedience to God, and how grace hath been rewarded by grace in our persons : *this I had* (to wit, all the former fruits,) *because I kept thy precepts :* and this is the seventh felt fruit of faith, that a man may enjoy the approbation and comfort of the fruits of faith. 12. Those are reckoned keepers of God's precepts, not who have no sin in them, but who study to be free of sin, and to do God's will : *this I had, because I kept thy precepts.* 13. It is wisdom to reckon what good we have by faith in God, and to endeavour to please him, rather than to reckon our temporary and light afflictions in our service, as here we are taught.

CHETH.

57. Thou art *my portion, O Lord : I have said that I would keep thy words.*

58. *I entreated thy favour with* my *whole heart : be merciful unto me according to thy word.*

59. *I thought on my ways, and turned my feet unto thy testimonies.*

60. *I made haste, and delayed not to keep thy commandments.*

61. *The bands of the wicked have robbed me :* but *I have not forgotten thy law.*

62. *At midnight I will rise to give thanks unto thee because of thy righteous judgments.*

63. *I* am *a companion of all* them *that fear thee, and of them that keep thy precepts.*

64. *The earth, O Lord, is full of thy mercy: teach me thy statutes.*

In this section, the psalmist laboureth to confirm his faith, and to comfort himself in the certainty of his regeneration, by eight properties of a sound believer, or eight marks of a new creature; the first whereof is his choosing God for his portion. Whence learn, 1. Such as God hath chosen and effectually called, get grace to make God their choice, delight, and portion : and such as have chosen God for their portion, have an evidence of their regeneration and election also; for here David maketh this a mark of his regeneration : *thou art my portion, O Lord.* 2. It is another mark of regeneration, after believing in God, and choosing him for our portion, to resolve to bring out the fruits of faith in new obedience, as David did : *I have said, that I will keep thy words.* 3. As it is usual for God's children, now and then because of sin falling out, to be exercised with the sense of God's displeasure; so it is a mark of a new creature, not to lie stupid and senseless under this exercise, but to deal with God earnestly, for restoring the sense of reconciliation, and giving new experience of his mercy, as the psalmist did : *I entreated thy favour with my whole heart :* and this is the third evidence of a new creature. 4. The penitent believer hath the word of grace and the covenant of God for his assurance to be heard, when he seeketh mercy: *be merciful to me according to thy word.* 5. The searching in what condition we are, the examination of our ways according to the word, and renewing of repentance with an endeavour of amendment, are a fourth mark of a new creature: *I thought on my ways, and turned my feet unto thy testimonies.* 6. When we see our sin, we are naturally slow to amend our doings, but the sooner we turn us to the way of God's obedience, we speed the better; and the more speedy the reforming of our life is, the more sound mark it is of a new creature: *I made haste, and delayed not to keep thy commandments.* 7. Enduring persecution and spoiling of our goods for adhering to God's word, without forsaking our cause, is a fifth mark of a new creature: *the bands*

*of the wicked have robbed me, but I have not forgotten
thy law.* 8. As it is the lot of God's children who resolve
to be godly, to suffer persecution, and to be forced either
to lose their temporal goods, or else to lose a good cause
and a good conscience; so it is the wisdom of the godly to
remember what the Lord's word requireth of us, and
speaketh to us, and this shall comfort our conscience more
than the loss of things temporal can trouble our minds:
*the bands of the wicked robbed me, but I have not for-
gotten thy law.* 9. A sixth mark of a new creature, is to
be so far from fretting under hard exercise, as to thank
God in secret cheerfully for his gracious word, and for all
the passages of his providence, where none seeth us, and
where there is no hazard of ostentation : *at midnight I
will rise to give thanks unto thee, because of thy righteous judgments.* 10. A seventh mark of a renewed creature, is, to associate ourselves, and keep communion with,
such as are truly gracious and fear God indeed, as we are
able to discern them : *I am a companion of them that
fear thee.* 11. The fear of God is evidenced by believing
and obeying the doctrine and direction of the Scripture, and
no other ways : *I am a companion of all them that fear
thee, and of them that keep thy precepts.* 12. The
eighth mark of a new creature, is, not to rest in any measure of renovation, but earnestly to deal with God for the
increase of saving knowledge, and fruitful obedience: for,
teach me thy statutes, is the prayer of the man of God, in
whom all the former marks are found. 13. As the whole
creatures are witnesses of God's bounty to man, and partakers of that bounty themselves; so are they pledges of God's
pleasure to bestow upon his servants greater gifts than
these, even the increase of sanctification, in further illumination of mind and reformation of life : for this the psalmist useth for an argument, to be more and more sanctified :
*the whole earth is full of thy bounty, O Lord; teach
me thy statutes.*

TETH.

65. *Thou hast dealt well with thy servant, O Lord,
according unto thy word.*

In this section he gives eight marks of a thankful soul,
delivered from heavy trouble for a time. The first mark is

his hearty acknowledgment of God's goodness toward himself. Whence learn, 1. There is a time to acknowledge mercies received, as well as to pray for good things not as yet received; and as it is the duty of a believer to pray in his need, so it is the duty of the thankful man to confess what he hath received for supplying it : *thou hast dealt well with thy servant*. 2. The Lord will so perform his promise, as he shall make the believing supplicant witness of his fidelity : *thou hast dealt well with thy servant, according to thy word*. 3. As gifts prayed for, so also gifts received, ought to be examined, whether they be given to us, or to servants of God, and according to the promises made to his servants in the word, or not; otherwise a man can neither make right use of them, nor be thankful for them, as the psalmist doth here, who saith, *thou hast dealt well with thy servant, according to thy word*.

66. *Teach me good judgment and knowledge: for I have believed thy commandments.*

Another mark of David's thankfulness, is his seeking the increase of wisdom and discretion, for enabling him to serve God better in time to come. Whence learn, 1. Beside the knowledge of the general rule of God's will, it is necessary to have the gift of discretion, to know our duty when particulars, clothed with circumstances, come to be tried by the rule ; and this the thankful man should pray for : *teach me good judgment and knowledge*. 2. He that would be directed in the faith and obedience of God's word in particular, ought to be clear in general of his estimation and belief of all God's word in Scripture : *teach me good judgment*, saith he, *for I have believed thy commandments*.

67. *Before I was afflicted, I went astray : but now have I kept thy word.*

The third mark of David's thankfulness, is, his acknowledgment of the wisdom and goodness of God, manifested in, and wrought by afflicting him. Whence learn, 1. So perverse are we by nature, that we are the worse ofttimes by prosperity : *before I was afflicted, I went astray*. 2. When prosperity is abused, it is God's mercy to us, to visit us with the rod of affliction, and by it to drive us to make better use of his word: *but now have I kept thy word*. 3. When affliction is sanctified, and found in the fruits thereof, it is no less sweet when it is past, than it was bitter when it was present; as the comparison of times here showeth.

68. *Thou* art *good, and doest good : teach me thy statutes.*

The fourth mark of David's thankfulness, now being comforted after trouble, is, his acknowledgment of the goodness of God's nature and working, and his drawing from this fountain more sanctification. Whence learn, 1. As goodness is God's nature, and good is his work; so it is the thankful man's part to observe it, acknowledge it, and heartily to praise him for it, especially when he is called to this by late favours, as the psalmist doeth here: *thou art good, and doest good.* 2. When the goodness of God is solidly apprehended, it furnisheth ground of great confidence to seek further fruits thereof towards us : as here the psalmist doeth. 3. Of all the fruits of God's goodness which a thankful man can crave to himself, none is fitter to be sought than the growth of the grace of sanctification : as here, *teach me thy statutes.*

69. *The proud have forged a lie against me :* but *I will keep thy precepts with* my *whole heart.*

A fifth mark of a thankful man comforted, is his renewed purpose not to sin, for fear of the malice or craft of any persecutors. Whence learn, 1. Beside violence and cruelty, we shall find lies and false calumnies to be the weapons of the wicked against the godly: *the proud have forged a lie against me.* 2. The slanders and calumnies of the wicked against the godly, are so trimmed and dressed up with much artifice, as if they were cast in a mould : *the proud have forged a lie against me.* 3. The only way of resisting and overcoming this temptation, is by sincerely adhering to God in the faith and obedience of his word : *but I will keep thy precepts with my whole heart.*

70. *Their heart is as fat as grease :* but *I delight in thy law.*

The sixth mark of a thankful man comforted after affliction and persecution, is his despising the prosperity of the wicked, in comparison of the benefit of a good conscience, and joy in God. Whence learn, 1. It is the prosperity of the proud, which encourageth them to persecute the godly, yea their prosperity so benumbeth their consciences, that they may not fear to persecute: *their heart is as fat as grease*. 2. As a benumbed and seared conscience is a sin annexed to the sin of persecution, so is it also the plague of God upon them ordinarily, that they should not repent: *their heart is as fat as grease*. 3. The comfort of a good conscience, and the comfort of delighting in the obedience of faith, is a greater welfare to the godly than prosperity, how great soever it can be to the wicked; and so the godly need not envy the proud and prosperous man: *their heart is as fat as grease; but I delight in thy law.*

71. It is *good for me that I have been afflicted; that I might learn thy statutes.*

The seventh mark of a thankful mind comforted after affliction, is his estimation, that holiness wrought by affliction bringeth more pleasure and gain than affliction brought with it loss or pain. Whence learn, 1. The godly have as evil natures as the wicked have, which cannot be subdued and beaten down, except by affliction, as appeareth by this experience of the psalmist. 2. Albeit no affliction for the present be pleasant, yet afterward it proveth medicine to the godly, whose wisdom it is to observe all the advantages which come thereby, as the psalmist doeth here: *it is good for me that I was afflicted.* 3. Profiting in sanctification, is more than may recompense all the trouble which we are put to in learning it: *it is good for me that I have been afflicted, that I might learn thy statutes.*

72. *The law of thy mouth is better unto me than thousands of gold and silver.*

The eighth mark of a thankful mind comforted after affliction, is preferring the advantage of the written word of God to all riches. Whence learn, 1. No affection to the word of God can be in a man, till it be esteemed by him, as it is indeed, the word of God's mouth, as it were breathed out by himself speaking it: for it is called here, *the law of thy mouth*, to direct and enforce our obedience. 2. The spiritual advantage which a holy man maketh of God's word, is more worth than all earthly riches: *the law of thy mouth is better unto me than thousands of gold and silver.*

JOD.

73. *Thy hands have made me, and fashioned me:
give me understanding, that I may learn thy commandments.*

74. *They that fear thee will be glad when they see
me: because I have hoped in thy word.*

In this section is set down the example of the right carriage of a believer, brought out of one calamity and cast
into another.   His good behaviour consisteth in these six
duties.   The first is, to guard well against sin, by seeking
wisdom from God to bear well the temptation of new trouble.
Whence learn, 1. Albeit nothing can satisfy misbelief, yet
true faith will make use of the most common benefit of creation to strengthen itself : *thine hands have made me and
fashioned me.* 2. It is a good way of reasoning with God,
to ask another gift because we have received one; and because he hath given common benefits, to ask that he would
give us also saving graces: *thy hands have made me
and fashioned me : give me understanding that I may
learn thy commandments.* 3. Seeing God is our Creator,
and that the end of our creation is to serve God, we may
confidently ask whatsoever grace may enable us to serve
him, as the psalmist's example teacheth us.   4. As the afflicted petitioner for grace to obey God's commandments,
is strengthened in his faith by the hope of the glory which
may come to God by his holy behaviour; so also is he
strengthened in his prayer, by the hope of the edification
which others of the Lord's children may have by beholding
his carriage ; *they that fear thee will be glad when they
see me.*   5. It should be the joy of all believers, to see one
of their number sustained and borne out in his sufferings;
for, in the proof and example of one sufferer, a pledge is
given to all the rest, that God will help them in the like
case: *they that fear thee will be glad when they see me.*
6 The Lord shall so work for the man that hopes in his
word, that both he and others shall have cause to be glad,
for the grace of faith and hope bestowed on him : *they shall
be glad when they see me, because I hoped in thy word.*

75. *I know, O Lord, that thy judgments* are *right,
and* that *thou in faithfulness hast afflicted me.*

The second duty of the suffering believer is to justify God in afflicting him. Whence learn, 1. Albeit we see not the particular reasons of God's dispensation, yet the belief of the Lord's righteousness and wisdom should quiet our minds from all murmuring and disputation, and suspicion about the Lord's doing, as here is done: *I know, O Lord, that thy judgments are right.* 2. It is not sufficient that we justify God and forbear to murmur against his afflicting us, but we must believe that God out of love afflicteth us, by way of performing his covenant to us: *I know that thou in thy faithfulness hast afflicted me.*

76. *Let, I pray thee, thy merciful kindness be for my comfort, according to thy word unto thy servant.*

77. *Let thy tender mercies come unto me, that I may live: for thy law is my delight.*

The third duty of the afflicted servant of God is to seek comfort from God according to his promise. Whence learn, 1. Albeit we know that our sins have drawn on our affliction, yet that must not hinder us to seek comfort from God in that affliction; and nothing can comfort the afflicted, except the sense of God's kindness and mercy to him: *let, I pray thee, thy merciful kindness be for my comfort.* 2. Albeit full remedy be promised in the word, and albeit salve for every sore be treasured up there, yet the sweet effect of those promises we cannot have, without dealing with God by prayer, to apply in particular what faith in the word believeth in general: *let thy merciful kindnesses be for my comfort according to thy word.* 3. To the end we may have the benefit of the promise, it is wisdom to thrust in ourselves among those to whom the promise is made, under one title or other as we can, and to put our name in God's writ: *let comfort come unto me, according unto thy word, to thy servant;* that is, the word of promise which is made to servants, and so to me, and so let it come to me. 4. The sense of God's tender mercy to the believer is the very life of the believer—it is death to him to want it: *let thy tender mercies come unto me, that I may live.* 5. As we love the sense of God's mercy, so must we love God's word, and study the obedience of faith, and he who hath the one may pray and hope for the other: *let thy tender mercies come unto me, for thy law is my delight.*

78. *Let the proud be ashamed ; for they dealt per-*
versely with me without a cause : but *I will meditate*
in thy precepts.

The fourth duty of the afflicted servant of God, especially by persecution, is to pray against his enemies, and
then go on in his way of serving God.   Whence learn, 1.
Proud, graceless, impenitent men, will not prove friends to
the godly, but unreasonable persecutors of them, as they
find occasion : *the proud have dealt perversely with me*
without a cause.   2. When the proud and wicked in the
world are our party, God will be a friend to us who seek
for relief from him, and will disappoint them of their plots
against us : *let the proud be ashamed, for they dealt per-*
versely with me without a cause.   3. Persecution by the
wicked maketh, and should make, the godly study to understand the word of God more clearly and fully than before :
let the proud be ashamed, but I will meditate in thy pre-
cepts.   4. The best defence against persecution is to stand
fast in a good cause, and study obedience to God's word;
for, by this means the afflicted remain God's servants, and
the Lord is engaged to do for them as his servants : for this
is the course the psalmist taketh.

79. *Let those that fear thee turn unto me, and those*
that have known thy testimonies.

The fifth duty of the afflicted and persecuted, is to labour
to have friendship and fellowship with others who are godly,
which may both strengthen themselves and others.   Whence
learn, 1. As it should not seem strange unto us if the godly
forsake our fellowship when we are persecuted, seeing God
suffereth this for humbling, and trying, and turning us
to believe in God alone; so it is our duty to recover those
who have deserted us, to draw them to us again, and to
pray to God to further us : *let those that fear thee turn*
unto me, teacheth all this.   2. As God, when he pleaseth,
diverts the comfort of the fellowship of godly friends, so he
can bring them back again to us, as the prayer importeth.
3. Only they who, with fear to offend God, have the sound
knowledge of God's word, are fit comforters and strength-
eners of the godly under persecution : *let those that fear*
thee turn unto me, and those that keep thy testimonies.

FF

80. *Let my heart be sound in thy statutes, that I be not ashamed.*

The sixth duty of the afflicted, is to study, above all things, to be sincere in his carriage and in his defence of a good cause; uprightly aiming to do what is right rightly, and for the right ends. Whence learn, 1. Mind and heart, in the best men, are so perverted by natural corruption, (which is not fully abolished in any,) that not man's free will, but God's free grace must help this evil : for this prayer, *let my heart be sound in thy statutes*, importeth so much. 2. Sound knowledge of the statutes, sound affection towards them, and a sound purpose in following them, must be joined together in the Lord's martyrs : *let my heart be sound in thy statutes.* 3. As the unsound heart will not bear out the good cause, nor keep up with the godly in their good way, but will fall off to his own shame ; so the upright man fleeing to God in the fear of his own weakness and suspicion of the deceit of his own heart, shall be preserved from shame, as this prayer importeth, *let my heart be sound in thy statutes, that I be not ashamed.*

CAPH.

In the first four verses of this section is shown how deep the persecuted servant of God may draw in his affliction, before God give him comfort; and, in the last four, how he should behave himself in that sad condition.

81. *My soul fainteth for thy salvation :* but *I hope in thy word.*

82. *Mine eyes fail for thy word : saying, When wilt thou comfort me ?*

83. *For I am become* like *a bottle in the smoke:* yet do *I not forget thy statutes.*

84. *How many* are *the days of thy servant ? when wilt thou execute judgment on them that persecute me ?*

As for the first, there are four degrees of his deepness in distress, to wit, fainting of faith, almost failing of hope, failing of the body, and longing for death. Whence learn, 1. It is not strange to see God breaking the heart of his own child with affliction, even when he is suffering persecution, that so his faith may be tried and trained to more strength : *my soul fainteth.* 2. A believer in God, how afflicted soever he be, seeketh not to be delivered, but in a way allowed by God : *my soul fainteth for thy salvation:* or, till thou deliver me in thy good way. 3. The strength of the faith of the strongest of God's servants will prove but small, when affliction is great, and God's help is delayed : *my soul fainteth for thy salvation.* 4. Albeit the faith of the Lord's children seem to faint, yet it cannot die, it cannot fail altogether ; for it looketh to the word, and thereby gathereth strength and hope : *my soul fainteth, but I hope in thy word.* 5. Albeit hope keepeth the eye of the mind so fixed upon the promise, that it is ever looking for deliverance, yet long delay of help maketh hope weak and ready to faint : *mine eyes fail for thy word.* 6. Hope, patience, and complaining to God may stand altogether, but they must never be severed from prayer : *mine eyes fail for thy word, saying, When wilt thou comfort me ?* 7. Longer exercise by trouble may affect the body of God's dearest children, so that wasting leanness may be seen on it : *I am become as a skin bottle dried in the smoke.* 8. No trouble should drive us to sin, but we should choose rather to pine away in affliction, than to be freed from it with sin : *I am become like a bottle in the smoke, yet I do not forget thy statutes.* 9. It is good, in time of every persecution or affliction, to have an eye both on the promises, and on the precepts : for the looking to the promise encourageth to hope, and the eying of the precepts proveth the hope to be sound ; the psalmist *hoped in the word,* v. 81, and v. 83, *he forgat not the statutes.* 10. Albeit long affliction be able to make the believer weary of life, and desire to die, yet must he yield to God, to live so long as he pleaseth : *how many are the days of thy servant ?* 11. The delivery of the persecuted is ordinarily joined with the punishment of the persecutors, and the afflicted must wait till their cup be full : *when wilt thou execute judgment on them that persecute me ?*

85. *The proud have digged pits for me, which are not after thy law.*

86. *All thy commandments are faithful : they persecute me wrongfully ; help thou me.*

87. *They had almost consumed me upon earth : but I forsook not thy precepts.*

88. *Quicken me after thy loving-kindness ; so shall I keep the testimony of thy mouth.*

The psalmist showeth yet further how he carried himself in this condition : he layeth out his enemies' carriage before God, v. 85, 86, and his own steadfastness in extreme danger, v. 87 ; and prayeth for comfort, that he may in his trial bear out, v. 88. Whence learn, 1. The course of persecutors is full of traps and snares, whereby they study to overtake the godly, without fear of sinning in so doing : *the proud have digged pits for me, which are not after thy law.* 2. As the common quarrel of the wicked against the godly is for keeping God's commands ; so the common comfort of the godly is, that they have a good cause to defend : *all thy commandments are faithful, they persecute me wrongfully.* 3. The worse the cause and course are, which our adversaries follow, the more hopeful may we be to be helped of God : *they persecute me wrongfully, help thou me.* 4. It is a good means of courage, and comfort, and strength in persecution, to lay the carriage and cause of us and our adversaries before our eyes, and compare them together by the word, and then lay them forth before God, as the psalmist doeth here. 5. Albeit the godly may run the hazard of losing all things they may have on earth, yet that is the height of their hazard in defence of God's truth, for what they have in heaven cannot be taken from them : *they had almost consumed me upon earth.* 6. No hazard of whatsoever we have in the world— life, lands, goods, friends, liberty, or what else—can warrant a man to depart from the obedience of God's command controverted between the persecutor and him : *they had almost consumed me upon earth, but I forsook not thy precepts.* 7. Through the infirmity of the flesh, the feeling of the comforts of religion, and the freedom of following God's service cheerfully, may be interrupted, as, *quicken me,* here importeth. 8. Whatsoever measure of spiritual life, strength, or comfort can be abated and diminished by affliction, the renewed sense of God's love and friendship to us, (which we should seek after always) can easily restore and recompense it : *quicken me after thy loving-kindness, so shall I keep the testimonies of thy mouth.*

LAMED.

In this section the psalmist showeth, first, how he was comforted under persecution by faith in God's word ; and to this end he commends the worth of the word of God, or of the Scripture, for four reasons :—The first is, because of the stability of it in heaven, v. 89; the next, for the durable usefulness of it in every age of the church, v. 90; the third, because by God's word the earth is established, v. 90, 91; the fourth, because of his own experience of comfort and strength by it in his affliction, v. 92; and, in the next part, he expresseth his thankfulness in the rest of the verses of this section.

89. *For ever, O Lord, thy word is settled in heaven.*

90. *Thy faithfulness is unto all generations : thou hast established the earth, and it abideth.*

91. *They continue this day according to thine ordinances : for all* are *thy servants.*

92. *Unless thy law* had been *my delights, I should then have perished in mine affliction.*

In setting down the comfort which *David* had by faith in the word, and what estimation he had of the Scripture, let us learn, 1. God hath given us his word to bear up our faith in every the hardest condition, and it is a sure rock which will not fail us, whatsoever appear, or howsoever we fail or faint : *for ever, O Lord, thy word is established.* 2. Albeit the effect of God's word appeareth not sometimes, but is overclouded with trouble and temptations; yet it is sure and fixed by God's decree, unalterable in heaven, and cannot want the effect in due time : *for ever, O Lord, thy word is settled in heaven.* 3. The stability of the Lord's word depends upon the stability of God's truth and faithfulness, which, because he is absolutely unchangeable, his word is so also : *thy faithfulness is unto all generations.* 4. The truth of God is not always hidden in heaven, but in all generations the truth of the word and the faithfulness of God who hath spoken it, are from age to age made manifest amongst men : *thy faithfulness is unto all genera-*

tions. 5. The stability of the earth is nothing but the effect of God's word, and the stability of the earth and frame of the world is a pledge of the stability of God's word : *thou hast established the earth, and it abideth.* 6. As heaven and earth continue in their motion and station, and serve God as his word hath ordained ; so should we : *they continue this day according to thine ordinances, for all are thy servants.* 7. Affliction draweth forth the worth of God's word, which otherwise could not be known, and lets it be seen that the word of God is able to save a sinking man in tribulation: *unless thy law had been my delight, I should then have perished in my affliction.* 8. The word of God, being received by faith, is able not only to save the believer from desperation in trouble, but also to make him rejoice, as he who is feeding on delicates, as experience hath proved: *unless thy law had been my delight, I should have perished in mine affliction.*

93. *I will never forget thy precepts : for with them thou hast quickened me.*

94. *I am thine, save me : for I have sought thy precepts.*

95. *The wicked have waited for me to destroy me : but I will consider thy testimonies.*

96. *I have seen an end of all perfection,* but *thy commandment* is *exceeding broad.*

In the latter part of the section, the psalmist showeth his thankfulness : first, by engaging his heart to the faith and obedience of the word, v. 93; then, by dedication of himself to God as his servant, to be saved by him, v. 94; thirdly, by engagement of his heart to continue against all persecution, in the obedience of the word, v. 95; and, fourthly, by commendation of the word above all things in the world, v. 96. Whence learn, 1. The worth of the word of God is found so excellent in the experience of believers, that their experience fixeth and settleth their estimation of it, love to it, and purpose to make use of it always : *I will never forget thy precepts, for with them thou hast quickened me.* 2. The believer is the Lord's peculiar servant, bound to him by the bonds of creation, redemption, and covenant; and it is his duty thankfully to reckon on his interest

and right in God, and God's interest in him, for his own
encouragement and for God's praise : *I am thine.* 3.
When a man's faith is strengthened about his own interest
in God, then may he be confident to pray to God, and to
expect ·salvation, temporal and eternal, from him : *I am
thine, save me.* 4. Honest endeavour to obey God's commands, how weak soever, proveth the believer's interest in
God, and confirmeth his hope to be saved by him : *I am
thine, save me, for I have sought thy precepts.* 5. Persecutors of God's servants for obedience to God's word, are
in effect murderers both of soul and body, in driving them
to forsake God's commands : *the wicked have waited for
me to destroy me.* 6. The trouble which the godly sustain
by persecutors, should drive them to search more deeply
into the word of God, and to harden themselves against all
that the persecutors can do; and every comfort given to
them from the word should do the same : *but I will consider thy testimonies.* 7. The use of all things visible is
temporal, but the benefit of the Scripture is everlasting.
All things visible have their own perfections in their own
kind, and extend some of them to one temporal use, others
to another; but the word of God extendeth in its kind to
all uses which may bring blessedness in this life, and in the
world to come. A man may satisfy himself in the contemplation of the worth and virtue of any thing which is visible in the world, but the riches of the word of God are unsearchable—the deep wisdom of God in the Scriptures is
unsearchable, and the perfection of the Scripture is above
all comparison : *I have seen,* saith he, *an end of all perfection, but thy commandment is exceeding broad.*

MEM.

97. *O how love I thy law ! it* is *my meditation all
the day.*

The psalmist goeth on in this section to commend the
word of God, and to show his estimation of it for eight rea·
sons. The first is, because it hath gained the affection of
his heart, so that he cannot but continually dwell upon the
meditation of it. Whence learn, 1. As the Scripture in itself is most lovely for the author, matter, and use thereof ;
so is it most affectionately loved by the believer, and none
can either express or judge how great is his affection to it,

except God only : *O how love I thy law !* **2.** True love to the Scripture causeth good memory of it, and frequent meditation of it also : *it is my meditation all the day.*

98. *Thou, through thy commandments, hast made me wiser than mine enemies; for they* are *ever with me.*

The second reason of commending the Scripture, is the wisdom which it teacheth against enemies. Whence learn, 1. Holiness is great wisdom; for, albeit learning, malice, and long experience may teach persecutors much, yet wisdom from the word of God teacheth the persecuted believer far more : *through thy commandments thou hast made me wiser than mine enemies.* **2.** Such as derive their wisdom, not from the word of God, but from the counsel of flesh and blood, within or without themselves, cannot have their counsellors always with them to consult with; but he that seeketh his wisdom from God and his word, hath his counsel always present with him to bring to his remembrance what he hath learned, and to teach him to make use of it : *for thy commandments are ever with me.* **3.** Whatsoever use or benefit we make by the word of God, all the glory thereof belongeth to the Lord : *for thou through thy commandments hast made me wiser than mine enemies.*

99. *I have more understanding than all my teachers : for thy testimonies* are *my meditation.*

The third reason of commending the Scripture, is, because the believer thereby is made wiser than his teachers. Whence learn, 1. Wisdom is not so tied to teachers, but God is free to give as much and more to those that are taught : *I have more understanding than my teachers.* **2.** Though the teacher give forth the general doctrine of faith and manners, yet there is a more particular application of the word to the hearers, which God alone furnisheth to the believer by the word : and in this respect the believer may say, *I have more understanding than my teachers.* **3.** The special application of the word to our several necessities, cometh by joining private means with the public, such as are reading, praying, and meditation : *for thy testimonies are my meditation.*

100. *I understand more than the ancients, because I keep thy precepts.*

The fourth reason for commending the word, is, because it is able to make a man more wise than old age, and long experience of the affairs of men in the world can do. Whence learn, 1. Old age and experience in common affairs, are not effectual to direct men in the course of God's obedience, especially when they have to do with persecutors, but God's special wisdom by the word must come in here and teach : *I understand more than the ancients.* 2. To keep close to the direction of God's word is safer than to follow the mind of antiquity departing from the word, or the authority of men : *I have more understanding than the ancients, because I keep thy precepts.*

101. *I have refrained my feet from every evil way, that I might keep thy word.*

The fifth reason of David's commendation of the Scripture, which is also an evidence of his respect for it, is, because for the love of understanding, and keeping it, he hath abandoned every sinful course, how pleasant and how profitable soever it seemed to be. Whence learn, He that would be a wise disciple of God's word, must beware to follow sinful courses; for so he shall grieve God's Spirit, who must make the word clear to him; neither is it sufficient to abstain from notorious sins only, but also from every evil way, for the same reason : *I have restrained my feet from every evil way, that I may keep thy word.*

102. *I have not departed from thy judgments : for thou hast taught me.*

The sixth reason of his commending the word, is, because he was enabled by it to overcome all temptations which tended to divert him from obedience thereof. Whence learn, 1. As there are not wanting temptations on all hands, to divert men from obedience to the word, specially in time of persecution; so there is great need of adhering to it always, and specially in time of trouble, as the psalmist did : *I have not departed from thy judgments.* 2. He who hath stood fast in his obedience in the day of trouble, may lawfully take comfort in it afterward, but must give the glory thereof to God, as here : *I have not departed from thy judgments, for thou hast taught me.*

103. *How sweet are thy words unto my taste !* yea, sweeter *than honey to my mouth !*

The seventh reason of David's commending the Scripture, is because of felt sweetness in it. Whence learn, 1. There is delight to be found in hearing, reading, speaking, and meditating on God's word; yet the believer alone can discern it : *how sweet are thy words to my taste!* 2. Spiritual pleasure far surmounteth earthly and carnal pleasure : *thy words are sweeter than honey to my mouth.*

104. *Through thy precepts I get understanding : therefore I hate every false way.*

The eighth reason of his commending the word, is, because he is made wise to sanctification by it, and made to hate all sin for it. Whence learn, 1. As men are involved in error, because they understand not the Scripture; so, by the knowledge of it they are delivered from error, and made wise against seducers : *through thy precepts I get understanding.* 2. He that rightly understandeth the Scripture, as he cannot but love and commend it, so he cannot but hate every course contrary to it: *therefore I hate every false way.* 3. Because every sinful way is false, and cannot but deceive the man that walketh therein, therefore we must hate it, and that from the fountain of love to the word of God : *through thy precepts I get understanding, therefore I hate every false way.*

NUN.

105. *Thy word* is *a lamp unto my feet, and a light unto my path.*

As in the former section, the psalmist gave evidences of his love and respect to the word of God, so in this section he giveth eight evidences of his sincere purpose to make use of it in his practice for time to come. The first is, his resolution to make it his light to direct him in all his actions. Whence learn, 1. A man's ways are all in darkness, except in so far as he followeth the direction of Scripture; but he that followeth the rule of the word, knoweth whither he goeth, and what he doeth: *thy word is a lamp unto my feet.* 2. The light of Scripture is able not only to give a man general rules for ordering his life, but also to direct every particular action : *thy word is a light unto my path.* 3. Love to the word, and estimation of it, (which is the duty set forth in the former section,) are best evidenced by making practical use of it in a man's conversation, which is the duty set down in this section: and whosoever loveth it, and that so as to obey it, shall find a sweet, lively, and comfortable light in it, to carry him through all the dark passages of this miserable and sinful life, that he shall have cause to say, *the word is a lamp unto my feet, &c.*

106. *I have sworn, and I will perform* it, *that I will keep thy righteous judgments.*

The second evidence of David's purpose to conform his life to the rule of the word, is the tying himself by an oath to endeavour to keep it. Whence learn, 1. The upright man is willing to be bound to the obedience of God's word, not only with the necessary bond of God's command, and of his natural duty to his sovereign, but also by the straitest voluntary bonds he can, and he will not repent his resolution for ever: *I have sworn and will perform it, that I will keep thy righteous judgments.* 2. Vows, covenants, and oaths to tie us to the faith, profession, and obedience of the true religion set down in Scripture, are lawful and sanctified means to help us to be constant: *I have vowed and will perform it, that I will keep thy righteous judgments.* 3. The equity of all the commands of God should be a great motive to fasten us to the obedience thereof: *I will keep thy righteous judgments.*

107. *I am afflicted very much : quicken me, O Lord, according unto thy word.*

A third evidence of David's purpose to make use of God's word, is his seeking nothing for his comfort and encouragement in the greatest affliction, except the quickening of spiritual life in himself by the word. Whence learn, 1. It is no strange thing for the most holy men to be acquainted with the saddest sort of affliction, bodily and spiritual: *I am afflicted very much.* 2. Whencesoever affliction cometh, faith goeth to God only for comfort, as here: *quicken me, O Lord.* 3. When God is pleased to make the word of promise lively, or to perform what the promise alloweth us to expect, such a consolation is a sufficient antidote to the heaviest affliction: *quicken me, O Lord, according to thy word.*

108. *Accept, I beseech thee, the free-will offerings of my mouth, O Lord, and teach me thy judgments.*

A fourth evidence of David's purpose to make use of
God's word, is his present practice of it, in offering spiritual sacrifices of confession, praise, and prayer, that his service may be acceptable, and that he may be taught yet more
in the obedience of the word. Whence learn, 1. It was
spiritual, moral service, which the Lord, by the ceremonial
law, taught his people of old to offer him, through Christ;
and the godly in the Jewish church were not ignorant of
this; for here the psalmist prayeth, *accept, I beseech thee,
the free-will offerings of my mouth.* 2. Albeit our best
service be unworthy, of itself, to be presented to God, but
must have weight by God's gracious acceptation, yet must
we offer it, and have hope, through Christ's sacrifice, that
it shall be accepted : *accept, I beseech thee, the free-will
offering of my mouth.* 3. Together with the offer of
present service, it is good to join the purpose of growing
in obedience, and prayer for grace to do so still: *accept, I
beseech thee, the free-will offerings of my mouth, and
teach me thy judgments.*

109. *My soul* is *continually in my hand : yet do I
not forget thy law.*

The fifth evidence of David's purpose to practice God's
word, is his resolution on all hazards, even of his life, to
keep affectionate memory of, and actual respect for God's
revealed will. Whence learn, Whosoever will live godly,
must resolve to run hazard of life daily in the time of persecution, and he who layeth his reckoning so, hath evidence
in himself of his upright purpose to follow God's word: *my
soul,* or my life, *is continually in my hand,* as ready to
be laid down for maintaining righteousness : *yet do I not
forget thy law.*

110. *The wicked have laid a snare for me : yet
erred I not from thy precepts.*

The sixth evidence of his purpose of constancy in God's
service, is his approving of his former carriage in his by-
past trial, which showeth that he is resolved so to do also
for time to come. Whence learn, 1. It is usual with persecutors to make acts and statutes, or to broach some danger, one or other, which shall either force the godly to go

off the right way of obedience to God's word, or to fall into the snare : *the wicked have laid a snare for me.* 2. The godly must hold on the royal way of God's commands, whether he fall into the snare of worldly inconvenience or not, as the psalmist did : *yet I erred not from thy precepts.* 3. He who hath kept the highway, and hath trodden upon snares, and regretteth not his course, giveth evidence of his sincere purpose to follow the Lord thereafter also, through all dangers, as this example teacheth us.

111. *Thy testimonies have I taken as an heritage for ever : for they are the rejoicing of my heart.*

A seventh evidence of David's purpose to adhere to God's word, is, his placing his riches and pleasure in his adhering to it. Whence learn, 1. The word of God believed is the surest riches of the saints, which, when all things fail, maintaineth and holdeth up their right to God and eternal life ; and so should it be looked upon by the believer : *thy testimonies have I taken as my heritage for ever.* 2. The felt benefit of the word of God, furnishing spiritual light, comfort, peace, strength, meat, drink, clothing, and whatsoever commodities an inheritance can yield, is and should be the joy of the believer, and a tie upon his heart to make him stick close to it : *thy testimonies have I taken as my heritage for ever, for they are the rejoicing of my heart.*

112. *I have inclined mine heart to perform thy statutes alway,* even unto *the end.*

The eighth evidence of his purpose to practise the word of God, is the bent of his heart carrying him on to perform whatsoever God commandeth all the days of his life. Whence learn, 1. Albeit it be God's work alone to incline the heart to his testimonies, as we see, v. 36, yet when God hath made the change, and his child is content to follow the direction of God's word, this inclination of the heart is counted also the man's own work: as here, *I have inclined my heart.* 2. As only hearty service pleaseth the Lord, so that only is sincere and constant, which proceeds from the heart : and he who findeth this inclination, hath in himself the witness of his sincerity : *I have inclined my heart to perform thy statutes always even to the end.*

SAMECH.

113. *I hate* vain *thoughts : but thy law do I love.*

114. *Thou* art *my hiding-place and my shield : I hope in thy word.*

As *David* gave before evidences of his affection to the Scripture, and of his purpose to obey it in practice; so in this section he giveth six evidences of his hatred of the evil that is contrary to the good which is promised and commanded in the Scripture. The first evidence is his hatred of the most secret and meanest degrees of actual breaches of the Lord's law : and for this protestation he giveth three reasons. Whence learn, 1. With sincere love to good, hatred of evil must necessarily be joined, as the connexion of these duties in several sections teacheth. 2. Every dislike of evil is not sufficient, but perfect hatred is required of us against all sorts and degrees of sin : *I hate vain thoughts.* 3. All sinful courses in religion or conversation (such as are all those that are not warrantable by God's word) are unprofitable, and shall disappoint all those who follow them : *I hate vain thoughts.* 4. Hatred of sin is acceptable to God, when it floweth from the love of God's word set down in Scripture : *but thy law do I love.* And this is the first reason of his protestation. 5. The protection which is to be found in God against the evil of trouble, should strengthen the believer in the hatred of the evil of sin, as here it doth : *thou art my hiding-place and my shield :* and this is the second reason of his protestation. 6. Faith in God's word is the fountain of the hating of sin, and confiding in God : *I hope in thy word :* and this is the third reason of his protestation.

115. *Depart from me, ye evil doers : for I will keep the commandments of my God.*

A second evidence of his hatred of sin is his renouncing all fellowship in sinning with whatsoever person or persons; let them seek associates where they list, he would have no fellowship with them in the unfruitful works of darkness. Whence learn, 1. He that would eschew sin, must beware of complying with wicked men in their wicked courses, and in this respect must separate from them—not altogether from conversing with them, for then a man must go out of the world, but from fellowship with them in evil-doing; for, in this respect is it that he saith, *depart from me, ye evil doers.* 2. Nothing can save a man from complying with sinners, but sincere resolution to keep covenant and communion with God, and not to displease him: *for I will keep the commandments of my God.*

116. *Uphold me according unto thy word, that I may live: and let me not be ashamed of my hope.*

The third evidence of *David's* hatred of sin is partly his estimation of it as a shameful thing, and partly his prayer to be preserved from the shame which sin draweth after it. Whence learn, 1. The believer leaneth not to his own strength or holy purpose, but is sensible that he shall easily fall into sin, except God preserve spiritual life in him; and therefore he prayeth, *uphold me that I may live.* 2. Albeit a believer be not able in himself to persevere, yet, because of God's promise to hold up the weak who cleave to him, he may be confident to stand: *uphold me, according to thy word, that I may live.* 3. Sin should therefore be hateful, because it bringeth shame to the sinner of itself, and shameful disappointment of his hoped for felicity: *uphold me, and let me not be disappointed of my hope.*

117. *Hold thou me up, and I shall be safe: and I will have respect unto thy statutes continually.*

The fourth evidence of his hatred of sin is his fear of mischief and perishing, which he cannot eschew, except by God's preserving him in the course of his obedience. Whence learn, 1. The strongest believer is most sensible of his own weakness, most afraid to sin, and most apprehensive of the evil of sinning, and the good of persevering in the obedience of God: therefore again he prayeth, *hold thou me up, and I shall be safe.* 2. God's preserving a man from sinful courses giveth great encouragement to him to persevere sincerely in the obedience of all God's commands: *hold thou me up, and I will have respect unto thy statutes continually.* 3. The believer may undertake any duty, provided he take God for the surety of his performance, who, if he be sought by prayer, and relied upon in the use of means, will not refuse to enable us to perform whatsoever duty we shall undertake: *hold thou me up, and I will have respect unto thy statutes continually.*

118. *Thou hast trodden down all them that err from thy statutes : for their deceit* is *falsehood.*

119. *Thou puttest away all the wicked of the earth* like *dross : therefore I love thy testimonies.*

The fifth evidence of *David's* hatred of sin is his observation of the mischief decreed and begun to be executed against evil-doers. Whence learn, 1. To observe the mischief which followeth thereupon, is a special means to preserve us from sinful courses: *thou hast trodden down all them that err from thy statutes.* 2. Only they who fear to sin see the evil of other folks sinning, and only they can make good use of God's judgment on others who are sensible of the merit of sin, if they should fall into it themselves : for this is the observation of a believer. 3. Albeit the wicked hold their head high, and lift up themselves in their sinful courses against God, yet he hath already trodden down many such persons, and hath decreed to tread down all of that sort: *thou hast trodden down all them, &c.* 4. Not only such as are openly and grossly wicked and profane, but also all they who please themselves in the by-paths of their own wandering, and care not for pleasing God, shall perish : *thou hast trodden down all them that err from thy statutes.* 5. Whatsoever be the baits of pleasure, profit, and preferment which draw men from the obedience of God, and whatsoever be the excuses, pretences, and confidences which secure impenitent sinners' consciences, all will be found to be self-deceit, lies, and vanity : *for their deceit is falsehood.* 6. The godly and wicked live together in the visible church, as dross and good metal, but God, who is the purger of his church, will not fail, by diversity of trials and judgments, to put difference between them, and at last will make a perfect separation of them, and cast away the wicked as refuse : *thou puttest away all the wicked of the earth as dross.* 7. The destruction of evil-doers, as it should make us hate sin, so should it move us to love the course of holiness : *thou puttest the wicked away, therefore I love thy testimonies.*

120. *My flesh trembleth for fear of thee; and I am afraid of thy judgments.*

The sixth evidence of David's hatred of sin, is the fear he hath of God's threatening wrath, and judgments.

Whence learn, 1. A tender heart is easily affected, as with God's mercies, so also with God's judgments : *my flesh trembleth*. 2. The godly, because of the remainder of sin in them and their natural frailty, are not exempted from the sense of the terror of God, yea, it is needful they be now and then exercised therewith, that so they may be kept in awe, their joy tempered with fear and trembling, their prayer sharpened, and they kept watchful, and thus their obedience furthered : *my flesh trembleth for fear of thee, and I am afraid of thy judgments*.

AIN.

121. *I have done judgment and justice : leave me not to mine oppressors.*

In this section the psalmist prayeth to be directed, comforted, and upheld against his oppressors, for six reasons. The first whereof, is because his carriage and cause were righteous. Whence learn, 1. It is no strange thing to see godly innocent men troubled, persecuted, and oppressed : for here is one oppressed, who saith truly, *I have done judgment and justice*. 2. A believer put in the power of oppressors for a good cause, may call for, and look for God's assistance and presence, and not to be given over to the will of the persecutors : *leave me not to mine oppressors*.

122. *Be surety for thy servant for good : let not the proud oppress me.*

Another reason of David's petition, is because he hath ground by the covenant of grace, to request God to engage for him, that he shall not be oppressed utterly. Whence learn, 1. Seeing the Lord is obliged to his people by covenant, to defend his servants against their enemies, and that all things shall turn to their good, the believer hath warrant to employ God in his need, to interpose himself for the relief of his servant, that he be not distressed : *be surety for thy servant for good, and let not the proud oppress me*. 2. Before men turn persecutors of the godly, they forget both God and their own condition, and become proud : *let not the proud oppress me*.

123. *Mine eyes fail for thy salvation, and for the word of thy righteousness.*

A third reason, is because he is like to faint and lose hope by the Lord's long delaying delivery. Whence learn, 1. As men have received a greater measure of faith, so they usually get a greater measure of trial, as here this champion is suffered to lie in trouble till he be like to sink under it: *mine eyes fail for thy salvation.* 2. Albeit the words of promise be neither performed, nor like to be performed, yet faith should justify the promise, as true and faithful: *mine eyes fail for the word of thy righteousness.*

124. *Deal with thy servant according unto thy mercy, and teach me thy statutes.*

125. *I am thy servant; give me understanding, that I may know thy testimonies.*

The fourth reason of David's petition for delivery and help, and for direction how to carry himself in trouble in the mean time, till delivery come, is because the Lord usually deals with his servants, not in justice but in mercy. Whence learn, 1. The course of God's dealing with his children, is not the rule of strict justice, or the covenant of works, but the way of mercy: *deal with thy servant according to thy mercy.* 2. It should satisfy the request of the child of God under persecution, if God shall direct him to walk holily and righteously till the delivery come, and to profit in sanctification: *deal with thy servant according to thy mercy, and teach me thy statutes.* 3. When temptation to unbelief opposeth our petition, or the reasons thereof, it is wisdom to resist it, and to assert our interest in the promise, whatsoever be opposed, and to pursue our petition: *I am thy servant, give me understanding, that I may know thy testimonies.*

126. It is *time for* thee, *Lord, to work;* for *they have made void thy law.*

The fifth reason of David's petition, is because the persecutors were come to the height of sin, and stood in no awe of God or his word, but rejected the word as a thing of nought. Whence learn, 1. As sinners grow in sin till they trample God's law under their feet, so according as they grow in their sin, the time of God's manifesting his justice draweth near: *it is time for thee, Lord, to work.* 2. What persecutors intend, yea, and what their work of

persecution driveth at, and intendeth, is put upon the persecutors' score: *for they have made void thy law*, is
charged upon them for their contravening it so grossly, as
if they had intended to abolish it.

127. *Therefore I love thy commandments above gold,
yea, above fine gold.*   •

128. *Therefore I esteem all* thy *precepts* concerning
all things to be *right ;* and *I hate every false way.*

The sixth reason of David's petition, is because the more
the persecutors go about to make God's law void, the
psalmist was the more zealous for it, loved, esteemed, and
justified it, and hated whatsoever was contrary to it so much
the more. Whence learn, The hatred of holiness and
God's truth, perceived in the persecutors, should stir up
the love of the godly to the truth so much the more : *therefore I love thy commandments.* The more that the wicked despise God's word, we should esteem it the more : *I love
thy commandments above gold, yea, above fine gold.*
The more they wrangle, and wrest it in any point, the
more should we defend and justify it in every point: *therefore I esteem thy precepts concerning all things to be
right.* And the more the wicked love wickedness, we
should the more hate it, and all the branches of it : *I hate
every false way.*

PE.

In this section, the psalmist professeth his high estimation of, and affection to, the word of God, v. 129—131, and prayeth for the benefits
which are offered, and may be had in it, in the rest of the section.

129. *Thy testimonies* are *wonderful : therefore doth
.my soul keep them.*

130. *The entrance of thy words giveth light ; it giveth understanding unto the simple.*

131. *I opened my mouth, and panted : for I longed
for thy commandments.*

The psalmist falleth here into a new admiration of the excellency of the word of God, and into a vehement passion of
love toward it. Whence learn, 1. As the word of God in Scripture is wonderful in itself, and wonderful in the operation
thereof; so, when it is best seen, it is most admired, and every
new looking upon it raiseth new admiration of it : *thy testi-*

monies are wonderful. 2. The more the word is admired, the more is it loved and submitted to, and more earnest desires are kindled to make use thereof in practice: *therefore doth my soul keep them.* 3. The innermost cabinet of a man's soul, is the proper case wherein to put the knowledge of faith, love, and purpose of obedience to God's testimonies: *my soul doth keep them.* 4. Albeit the word of God in Scripture be full of high mysteries, yet (which is indeed wonderful) it may be read with profit by simple people, or any who desire knowledge; and it is so plain to every one who will be God's disciple, that it giveth light and direction presently to the reader, in the main points of salvation and commanded duties: *the entrance of thy word giveth light.* 5. An humble soul, loving to be instructed, albeit weak in natural judgment, shall be made wise to salvation by it: *it giveth understanding to the simple.* 6. The more a man knows the wonderful excellency, use, and benefit of the Scripture, the more will he love it, and long to understand more of it, as here the psalmist's experience teacheth: *I opened my mouth, I panted for, I longed for thy commandments.* 7. Common and ordinary affection, or desire after, the saving knowledge of the Scripture, is not sufficient, but affection earnestly bended is necessary according as the excellency of the wisdom in it requireth: *I opened my mouth, and panted.* 8. The word of God is no less necessary and comfortable to a man's soul, than meat is to the hungry, drink to the thirsty, or cool air to the weary: *I opened my mouth and panted.* 9. When a man's affection and love to religion are kindled, he hath great need to study hard, to have sound knowledge and understanding of the Scripture, lest his zeal and affection miscarry: *I longed for thy commandments.*

132. *Look thou upon me, and be merciful unto me, as thou usest to do unto those that love thy name.*

Unto this profession of his estimation of and affection for Scripture, David subjoineth four petitions for the right use and benefit thereof. The first is the sense of that mercy which is promised and usually bestowed upon such as love the Lord. Whence learn, 1. The Lord bestoweth on his servants but a short glimpse of his favour and reconciliation, that they may find their need to have that sense often re-

newed : *look thou upon me, and be merciful unto me.*
2. As it is a mark of God's child to find in himself a love of
God's name, so it is a mark put upon him, to be visited by
God with a glimpse of kindness and mercy : *look upon me,
and be merciful unto me, as thou usest to do unto those
that love thy name.* 3. As it is good to mark God's usual
dealing with his own children, so it is good to study conformity with God's children in our affection to God, that we
may find conformity with them in consolation : for so doth the
psalmist here. 4. It is wisdom for us not to affect singu-
larity of divine dispensations toward us, but to be content
to be dealt with as others of God's children before us have
been dealt with : *be merciful to me, as thou usest to do
unto those that love thy name.*

133. *Order my steps in thy word : and let not any
iniquity have dominion over me.*

The second petition is for sanctification of his actions, and
for mortification of sin. Whence learn, 1. Albeit we have
the word of God for our perfect rule, yet we have need that
God should fit us and strengthen us for obedience to it :
order my steps in thy word. 2. Albeit by nature we are
ignorant and erroneous, uncertain and unstable in the way
of God's obedience, yet, in the sense of our sin and weakness, we may pray to God with confidence to be heard : *direct, order, and establish my steps in thy word ;* for so
much the original importeth. 3. Albeit by nature we are
slaves to sin, and any sin may bring us into subjection, yet
when, in the sense of our weakness, we have recourse to
God to be helped, we may pray with hope to be heard : *let
not any iniquity have dominion over me.*

134. *Deliver me from the oppression of man : so
will I keep thy precepts.*

The third petition is for delivery from the oppression of
persecutors, that they may not be able to drive us from the
belief and obedience of God's word. Whence learn, 1. Beside the body of sin and inward temptations, the godly have
the persecution of the wicked without to drive them from
God's service, as this prayer importeth. 2. When the Lord's
servants, in the sense of their weakness, seek help against
persecutors, he both can and will deliver them, either by
breaking the yoke of the oppressor, or by giving strength

to them to bear out in holy obedience of God's word under
the burden : *deliver me from the oppression of man.*
3. The end of our seeking to be free from bodily bondage
and trouble from men should be, that we may serve God
the more cheerfully : *deliver me, so will I keep thy statutes.*

135. *Make thy face to shine upon thy servant : and
teach me thy statutes.*

The fourth petition is for spiritual consolation, and increase of sanctification.   Whence learn, 1. Albeit the sense
of God's favour to us may be withdrawn for a time, yet the
right which we have to God reconciled to us in Christ, may
bear us out in the hope of having it renewed to us in his
service: *make thy face to shine upon thy servant.* 2. Because the Lord useth, with the light of consolation, to give
also the light of direction, in duties we should seek both
and wait for both from the Lord : *make thy face to shine,
and teach me thy statutes.* 3. As there are degrees of
God's manifesting his favour, and degrees of profiting in
the obedience of God's word; so should we seek the increase
of both, and no measure received should hinder the seeking
of a greater measure, as the often repeating of the same
petitions in effect showeth : *make thy face to shine upon
thy servant, and teach me thy statutes.*

136. *Rivers of waters run down mine eyes, because
they keep not thy law.*

David addeth a reason to this last petition, because it
grieved him much to see God dishonoured by those among
whom he lived, and to see them, by not obeying God's statutes, draw upon themselves God's wrath.   Whence learn,
1. He who is sorrowful for displeasure and dishonour done
to God, may look to be comforted by God, as the connexion
of this reason with the former petition teacheth.   2. True
zeal is so far from private revenge of personal injuries received by persecutors, that it can pity their miserable case,
and mourn for them : *rivers of waters run down mine
eyes, because they keep not thy law.* 3. Godly affections
are larger than bodily expressions can set forth, and that
which bodily expressions set forth, signifieth a will to vent
much more than the body could furnish : *rivers of waters
run down mine eyes, because they keep not thy law.*

TZADDI.

137. *Righteous* art *thou, O Lord, and upright* are *thy judgments.*

In the last verse of this section the psalmist prayeth for a greater measure of the saving knowledge of the Scripture, most ardently, and premiseth eight reasons before the prayer, from which he inferreth his petition as a conclusion. The first reason of this petition, is from the righteousness of God, which appeareth in the Scripture; and in the execution of God's word. Whence learn, 1. The way set down in Scripture for justifying and sanctifying men, and for saving such as follow the way prescribed by God for salvation, and punishing such as despise the way of life prescribed, is very righteous when well considered: *upright are thy judgments.* 2. The way of righteousness set down in Scripture, and of execution made according to it, may be demonstrated by the essential righteousness of God's nature, because as he is righteous so must his word and working conform thereto be righteous also: *righteous art thou, O Lord, and upright are thy judgments.*

138. *Thy testimonies* that *thou hast commanded* are *righteous and very faithful.*

The second reason of the petition is, because the testimonies of Scripture which God hath commanded us to believe and obey, are not only righteous but also very faithful, and can never fail a man that believeth and obeyeth them. Whence learn, 1. To the end that our faith and obedience may be solidly grounded, we must hold for a foundation, that the Scriptures are righteous and true, and that every truth revealed therein, includeth a command to believe it; and every duty of men declared therein, includeth a command to obey it : *thy testimonies which thou hast commanded, are righteous and very faithful.* 2. It is needful for a believer to labour to have the impression of the truth and righteousness of the word of God in Scripture stamped on his own heart by frequent meditation and acknowledgment thereof, as the psalmist's example here teacheth us.

139. *My zeal hath consumed me ; because mine enemies have forgotten thy words.*

The third reason of the petition is, because David's zeal

for the commands of God was so great, that the opposition which his enemies made to them tormented him, and such zeal required growing knowledge. Whence learn, 1. Zeal had great need of sound knowledge, that it miscarry not, and he that findeth zeal kindled in his breast, should labour to inform himself well, as the psalmist doth, v. 144, and here : *my zeal hath consumed me, because mine enemies have forgotten thy word.* 2. Holy affections are able to work upon the body, no less than common and natural affections : *my zeal hath consumed me.* 3. The contempt and misregard of the word of God, perceived, and especially in professors within the visible church, are a just reason of zeal, a just cause of grief and anger against such workers of iniquity : *my zeal hath consumed me, because mine enemies have forgotten thy word.*

140. *Thy word is very pure : therefore thy servant loveth it.*

The fourth reason of David's petition is, because he seeth such holiness and unmixed truth in God's word, that he cannot but love it, and therefore must pray that he may know more of it. Whence learn, 1. The word of God is a word pure from all mixture of flattery or falsehood, proved to be true in the experience of all ages: *thy word is very pure.* 2. New contemplations of the excellency of the word of the Lord, draw forth new commendations of it, and raise fresh affection of love to it: *thy word is very pure, therefore thy servant loveth it.*

141. *I am small and despised ; yet do not I forget thy precepts.*

The fifth reason of his petition is, because the word of God held up his heart, and comforted him against all the contempt of men. Whence learn, 1. The godly may readily lose reputation at wicked men's hands, when they will not comply with their wickedness : *I am small and despised.* 2. Albeit we lose estimation for adhering to the word of God, yet the word should not lose estimation for that with us: *I am despised, yet do not I forget thy precepts.*

142. *Thy righteousness is an everlasting righteousness, and thy law is the truth.*

The sixth reason of his petition is, because everlasting righteousness and everlasting truth are in God's word, and may be found in experience by it. Whence learn, 1. The excellency of the law of God above all the laws of men, is that not only is it righteous at the first giving out, but also in all ages and times : *thy righteousness is an everlasting righteousness, and thy law is truth*. 2. The righteousness which God hath devised and set down in his word to justify sinful men, is an everlasting righteousness, even the righteousness by faith in Jesus Christ, borne witness to by the law and the prophets : *thy righteousness is an everlasting righteousness, and thy law is truth*. 3. It is good for settling and strengthening the holds of our faith, to consider again and again, what excellent profit may be had by it, and how true it is, as here the psalmist doth.

143. *Trouble and anguish have taken hold on me ; yet thy commandments are my delights.*

The seventh reason of his petition is, because the word of God hath been his delight, when trouble and vexation befell him for obedience to it. Whence learn, 1. The believer is not exempted from outward trouble for righteousness, nor from the vexation and inward anguish of spirit which may follow it : *trouble and anguish have taken hold on me.* 2. After the believer hath felt his own weakness, and the force of trouble, he may expect victory over trouble, to be rid from the vexation of it, and brought even to rejoicing in tribulation : *yet thy commandments are my delight.*

144. *The righteousness of thy testimonies is everlasting : give me understanding, and I shall live.*

The eighth reason of his petition is, because life everlasting is to be had by the everlasting righteousness set down in God's word; therefore he prayeth to have more understanding thereof, that is, to have more clear knowledge and more strong faith in God's testimonies. Whence learn, 1. This is the main doctrine in all the word of God, to teach men concerning everlasting righteousness, or how a man is justified before God; therefore is this again repeated : *thy righteousness*, or, *the righteousness of thy testimonies is everlasting*. 2. The belief or saving understanding of this doctrine bringeth eternal life to the believer, and for this end, being joined as the last reason with the former seven reasons, it should make a man seek to grow in the faith, or in the saving knowledge of the testimonies of God set down in his word : *give me understanding, and I shall live.*

145. *I cried with* my *whole heart; hear me, O Lord : I will keep thy statutes.*

In this section the psalmist falleth on another main petition to God, for restoring to him, and increasing in him, the vigour of spiritual life by his word, v. 149; and to press this petition he useth four arguments, some going before, some following after it. The first argument hath four branches. The first is, because he hath prayed earnestly before for the quickening of him, that so he might be enabled to serve God. Whence learn, 1. When the world is crying, Who will show us any good thing ?—this man wishing for pleasure, and that man for riches, he for honour, and he for preferment, the Lord's children should be seeking grace to serve God, as the psalmist did : *I cried with my whole heart, hear me, O Lord, and I will keep thy statutes.* 2. When the conscience can bear witness to the hearty seeking of grace to serve God, the supplicant may confidently call for, and expect comfortable quickening of his spirit for God's service, as the comparison of this verse with the 149 verse showeth. 3. Whatsoever spiritual grace we seek of God, we should seek it earnestly; for if we seek it so as if we did not regard whether we obtained our request or not, such seeking will undervalue the grace which we seek; *I cried with my whole heart.*

146. *I cried unto thee ; save me, and I shall keep thy testimonies.*

Another branch of the argument is, because he did not pray for delivery out of his trouble, for satisfaction of his natural desire, but that he might give further proof of his purpose to obey God's word. Whence learn, The consciousness of a sincere purpose to seek God, may encourage us to seek both consolation and a lively ability to serve him : *I cried unto thee, save me, and I shall keep thy testimonies.*

147. *I prevented the dawning of the morning, and cried: I hoped in thy word.*

A third branch of the argument is, because out of hope to find the fruit of God's promises, he had been early about the duty of prayer. Whence learn, 1. Prayer should be earnestly followed and with no small diligence in using the means, specially of prayer, so that the Lord's children may come by their holy desires, as here we see: *I prevented the dawning of the morning, and cried.* 2. Looking unto the word furnisheth faith and hope, and faith and hope furnish prayer, or else the supplicant might soon faint: *I cried, I hoped in thy word.*

148. *Mine eyes prevent the* night-*watches, that I might meditate in thy word.*

A fourth branch of the argument is, because when David's night's rest was broken by troubles, he meditated on God's word when his persecutors were securely sleeping. Whence learn, 1. The difficulty wherein the Lord's children are cast many times, bereaveth them of their night's rest: *mine eyes prevent the night watches.* 2. The time which solicitude taketh from our sleep, is to be spent upon prayer and meditation of God's word, and not upon perplexing thoughts: *mine eyes prevent the night watches, that I might meditate in thy word.*

149. *Hear my voice, according unto thy loving-kindness: O Lord, quicken me according to thy judgment.*

This is the main petition in this section, put up for renewing and increasing in him the vigour of spiritual life by faith in the word, wherein he giveth a second reason of this his prayer, taken from God's kindness expressed in his promises. Whence learn, 1. Albeit a man had no special promise of help in a particular exercise of trouble, yet the consideration of God's mercy and loving-kindness, manifested in general in his word, is a sufficient ground to strengthen his hope to be helped: *hear my voice, according to thy loving-kindness ; O quicken me according to thy judgments.* 2. As the feeling of spiritual deadness argueth life and sense in God's children, so it fitteth a man for renewed influence and sense of spiritual life: *O Lord, quicken me according to thy testimonies.*

150. *They draw nigh that follow after mischief: they are far from thy law.*

151. *Thou* art *near, O Lord; and all thy command-ments* are *truth.*

The third reason of David's petition is, because his ene-mies were ready to do him a mischief, and were far from regarding God's law; but he believed God was the nearer to deliver him, and that this word was true, and therefore he desireth renewed vigour of spiritual life. Whence learn, 1. The nearer that danger is, the more ground of con-fidence have God's children in their danger, to call and hope for the influence of his Spirit: *they draw near that follow after mischief.* 2. The further the enemies of the godly are from God's law, and the nearer they are to do a mischief, the nearer are God's children to find the com-munion of the life of God: *they draw near that follow after mischief, they are far from thy law.* 3. For the consolation of a sufferer for righteousness, it is necessary to believe God's readiness to deliver him, and to believe the truth of God's word, whereby his cause is justified; for the following of God's command is a pledge of God's assist-ing him, and delivery also, no less than a promise: *thou art near, and all thy commandments are truth.*

152. *Concerning thy testimonies, I have known of old that thou hast founded them for ever.*

A fourth reason of the petition is, because David had long since experience of the everlasting stability of God's testimonies, and therefore craveth to be quickened accord-ing to them. Whence learn, 1. The faith of the stability and unchangeableness of God's word in general, is a good means of applying and making use of the passages thereof in particular: *concerning thy testimonies, I know that thou hast founded them for ever.* 2. Bypast experience of the truth of God's word, is an encouragement to hope for help in like trials afterward: *concerning thy testi-monies, I know of old that thou hast founded them for ever.*

RESH.

153. *Consider mine affliction, and deliver me: for I do not forget thy law.*

In this section the psalmist prayeth for delivery out of his affliction, and for the quickening of him by consolation and spiritual ability to serve God till the delivery came; and to strengthen himself in the hope of obtaining this, he bringeth forth eight reasons for his petition. The first is, the consciousness of his adherence to, and endeavour to obey, the Lord's word. Whence learn, 1. Albeit the Lord cannot but see and consider our trouble, yet we can hardly rest satisfied till he by real effect make it evident that he pitieth us in our affliction, and delivereth us out of it: *consider mine affliction, and deliver me.* 2. As no trouble or temptation should drive us from the obedience of God's word; so the more closely we adhere to the word in the obedience of faith, the more may we be assured to be delivered: *deliver me, for I do not forget thy law.*

154. *Plead my cause, and deliver me : quicken me according to thy word.*

David urgeth the same petition, and insinuateth a second reason for it, from the Lord's engagement, by his word, to be advocate for him, to deliver him, and to quicken him. Whence learn, 1. Albeit the godly under persecution have a good cause, yet they cannot plead it, except God their Redeemer show himself as advocate for them ; therefore prayeth the psalmist, *plead my cause.* 2. When God the Redeemer pleadeth a man's cause, he doeth it to purpose, really and effectually : *plead my cause and deliver me.* 3. Except the Lord's clients shall find new influence from God from time to time in their troubles, they are but as dead men in their exercise : for, *quicken me,* importeth this. 4. Till we find lively encouragement given to us in trouble, we must adhere to the word of promise : *quicken me according to thy word.* 5. What the believer hath need of, that God hath not only a will to supply, but also an office to attend it, and power to effectuate it; as here he hath the office of an *Advocate,* and of a powerful *Redeemer* also, wherein the believer may confidently give him daily employment, as he needeth : *plead my cause, and deliver me, quicken me according to thy word.*

155. *Salvation* is *far from the wicked : for they seek not thy statutes.*

A third reason of David's petition for delivery is, because the wicked who misregard God's commands, when

they fall into trouble, are far from delivery. Whence learn,
1. The wicked have neither right to salvation nor to temporal delivery from trouble when they fall into it: *salvation
is far from the wicked*. 2. It is the mark of a wicked
person to misregard, or not to care to know and obey God's
word : *salvation is far from the wicked, for they seek
not thy statutes*. 3. Salvation is near to those that make
conscience to obey God's word, how strait soever their condition shall seem, for so much the force of this reason importeth.

156. *Great are thy tender mercies, O Lord: quicken
me according to thy judgments.*

A fourth reason of his petition is, because God's tender
mercies are great, and therefore the psalmist may expect
the influence of life till he be delivered. Whence learn, 1.
When the godly think or speak of the damnable condition
of the wicked, they should not be senseless of their own deserving, nor of God's grace, which hath made the difference between the wicked and them : *great are thy tender
mercies, O Lord*. 2. As the mercies of the Lord, which
are the fountain of all the benefits the believer asketh,
are very excellent in themselves; so are they in the estimation of the believer, when he looketh upon them ; they are
many and mother-like, tender and great: *great are thy
tender mercies, O Lord*. 3. Spiritual life is subject to
often fainting, and hath need frequently to be supported
and restored by the believer's looking to the promise, and
presenting his case to God on the one hand, and by God's
granting of the petition on the other hand : *quicken me
according to thy judgments*.

157. *Many are my persecutors and mine enemies ;
yet do I not decline from thy testimonies.*

A fifth reason of his petition is, because he had many persecutors, and yet adhered to God's word. Whence learn,
1. As it is no strange thing to see the godliest men exposed
most to persecution ; so it is no small measure of grace
which God bestoweth on them to bear out the truth against
all opposition : *many are my persecutors and mine enemies, yet do I not decline from thy testimonies*. 2. He
who continueth in the faith and obedience of the word
against persecution, may expect sustenance and consolation

in his trouble, and delivery out of it : for this is the force of the reason.

158. *I beheld the transgressors, and was grieved ; because they kept not thy word.*

A sixth reason of his petition is, because he was sorrowful to see his enemies provoke God by their transgressions. Whence learn, 1. Anger, grief, indignation, and loathing (which the word in the original beareth) are lawful in God's quarrel against sin : *I beheld the transgressors, and was grieved, because they kept not thy word.* 2. He who is affected with grief, anger, and vexation for God's cause, when he seeth God provoked by transgressors, may expect consolation and strength to himself in the defence of God's cause; as the force of the reason importeth.

159. *Consider how I love thy precepts : quicken me, O Lord, according to thy loving-kindness.*

A seventh reason of David's petition is, because he sincerely loved the Lord's word, and therefore expected to be quickened in the sense of God's kindness. Whence learn, 1. It is a mark of true zeal for God, which floweth from love of the Lord's word; and he who findeth this mark in himself, may offer it to God for a proof of his sincerity : *consider how I love thy precepts.* 2. He who can prove his love to God's word, and his zeal for God to be sincere, may expect consolation and strength from God in his need, as the reason proveth. 3. So oft as we find deadness in our spirits, so oft should we run to God's kindness, the fountain of life, to repair it : *quicken me, O Lord, according to thy loving-kindness.*

160. *Thy word is true from the beginning : and every one of thy righteous judgments endureth for ever.*

The eighth reason of his petition is, because the word of God, and every part of it, according whereunto he craved comfort and delivery out of his trouble, was true and unchangeable for ever. Whence learn, 1. Such is the excellency of the word of God, that it can neither be sufficiently commended, nor the believer satisfy himself in commendation thereof, as this among many commendations testifieth. 2. Truth, and all truth is the short sum of the whole Scripture; from the beginning to the ending of it nothing but truth; nothing allowed in it but righteousness : *thy word is true from the beginning, and every one of thy righteous judgments endure for ever.* 3. He who foundeth his prayer for comfort and delivery on the rock of God's faithful and righteous word, may be sure to obtain his request : as the force of this reason evidenceth.

SCHIN.

161. *Princes have persecuted me without a cause: but my heart standeth in awe of thy word.*

In this section the psalmist taketh comfort by six approved evidences of saving grace felt in himself, which he presenteth to God to be sealed by him. The first evidence is his adherence to the obedience of faith, notwithstanding of his being persecuted by princes. Whence learn, 1. It is a sore temptation when the godly are persecuted for righteousness by their governors, by whom they should be encouraged and defended, and yet this exercise of the godly is no strange matter : *princes have persecuted me without a cause.* 2. As it is an ease and a piece of comfort to the godly that they have not deserved persecution; so their innocence is an aggravation of the sin of the persecutor, as here : *they have persecuted me without a cause.* 3. There is no means to save us from sinning for fear of men, but the fear of the supreme power of the Almighty : *but my heart standeth in awe of thy word,* which is all the same as to stand in awe of God. 4. To bear out persecution of princes, out of respect to the obedience of God's word, and fear to offend God, is a mark of saving grace, as here it is brought forth.

162. *I rejoice at thy word, as one that findeth great spoil.*

The second evidence of saving grace in David is a greater joy felt in God's word, than in any thing in this world, yea, such a joy, as the greatest joy of worldly men is but a shadowing similitude of it. Whence learn, 1. He that feareth to offend God more than he feareth to fall into any worldly inconvenience, may rejoice in the obedience of faith more than in any worldly advantage, as the experience of the psalmist teacheth, who saith, *my heart stood in awe of thy word, when princes did persecute me,* and subjoineth,

I rejoice in thy word, as one that findeth great spoil.
2. The joy of a believer, which he findeth in the obedience
of faith, is as great, as the joy which a victor in battle
findeth in the spoil of his defeated enemies, which is but a
shadow of it, albeit the joy of delivery from death, the joy
of victory, the joy of riches, honour, peace, and ease are
joined in the victor's breast altogether on a sudden : *I rejoiced at thy word, as one that findeth great spoil.* 3.
The junction of fear to offend God and joy in obedience to
him, is a mark of a gracious spirit, as the psalmist's producing it as a mark of grace in him maketh evident.

163. *I hate and abhor lying :* but *thy law do I
love.*

The third evidence of saving grace in the psalmist, is his
joint hating and abhorring of all sin, and loving the obedience of God's word.　Whence learn, 1. As the speaking
of untruth, or the concealing of truth which should be confessed, is lying; so every contravening of professed obedience to God s word, is a work of lying and self-deceiving,
which a believer should hate and eschew : *I hate and
abhor lying.* 2. Slight hatred of a sinful course is not sufficient to guard a man against it : for, where the enmity is
not great, the man's agreement with sin may soon be made,
but such abhorring and deadly hatred of sin is required, as
cannot admit reconciliation : *I hate and abhor lying.*
3. Hating and abhorring of all sin arising from, and joined
with, the love of God's word, is a solid mark of saving
grace : for, abhorring of some sin, and of all sin, for temporary reasons, may prove unsound; but this is sincerity
when a man can say, *I hate and abhor lying, but thy law
do I love.*

164. *Seven times a day do I praise thee, because of
thy righteous judgments.*

The fourth evidence of saving grace in the psalmist is
the frequent admiration of the goodness of God to man, set
forth in God's word, with hearty praising of God for it.
Whence learn, 1. As the studying of the word of God
bringeth the believer to see his own blessedness revealed in
it ; so it bringeth him also to admire and praise God for
that and for all his righteousness declared in it : *seven*

*times a day do I praise thee, because of thy righteous
judgments.* 2. The more a man discovers God's glory in
the word, and is inspired with the love and admiration of
God by what he seeth, and maketh use of God's word to
God's praise ; the more clear evidence hath he of the work
of saving grace in himself, as here the psalmist maketh use
of the mark : *seven times a day do I praise thee, because
of thy righteous judgments.*

165. *Great peace have they which love thy law;
and nothing shall offend them.*

For confirmation of the former marks of saving grace,
David commendeth the love of God's word, by two notable
effects. One is, that it bringeth a glorious peace with it;
another, that it maketh a man hold on the way of God's
obedience, whatsoever impediments or stumbling-blocks shall
be cast in his way. Whence learn, 1. The receiving of the
truth of God in love, giveth great peace, peace passing
understanding : for the law of works showeth a man's debt
and danger, and the believer subscribeth lovingly to the
justice thereof ; and the law of saving faith showeth remission of sin, righteousness, and eternal life, through the
Messiah Jesus Christ, and the believer embraceth the offer
heartily : and the law of new obedience directeth the justified man how to go on to the full possession of blessedness,
and the believer heartily taketh this holy yoke upon
him, and so walketh as a man reconciled with God, and
at peace with him : *great peace have they who love thy
law.* 2. Albeit there be many stumbling-blocks and impediments to divert the believer, from the obedience of
God's word, arising from the terror and allurements of the
world, from the troubles and exercises of the godly, from
the scandals given by professors, and such like, yet the love
of God's word is able to carry a man straight on his way
to heaven without stumbling or turning aside to the one
hand or the other : *great peace have they who love thy
law, and nothing shall offend them.*

166. *Lord, I have hoped for thy salvation, and done
thy commandments.*

The fifth evidence of saving grace in the psalmist, is, the
consciousness of his sound faith and obedience. Whence learn,
1. Sound hope of salvation is joined with the care of keeping

the commandments; for he who hath this hope purifieth himself that he may be holy : *Lord, I have hoped for thy salvation, and done thy commandments.* 2. As none can have heart or hand to keep God's commands, except he have hope to be helped out of every trouble whereinto he may fall, and to be fully saved at last; so he who hath the hope of salvation, hath great encouragement to obedience, and where the conjunction of these two is found, the man hath evidence of saving grace, and boldness to go to God in this confidence, as the psalmist doeth : *Lord, I have hoped for thy salvation, and done thy commandments.*

167. *My soul hath kept thy testimonies ; and I love them exceedingly.*

168. *I have kept thy precepts and thy testimonies : for all my ways* are *before thee.*

The sixth evidence of saving grace, is the approved testimony of his conscience concerning the sincerity of his heart, and that after a new examination of the soundness of former marks, which are here looked upon over again, and presented to God with other three marks of sincerity, to wit, spiritualness in obedience, exceeding love to the word, and daily walking as in the sight of God. Whence learn, 1. After a believer hath found marks of saving grace in himself, it is wisdom for him to examine these marks over again, whether they be in him in deed and in truth; for, if they be indeed in him, how weak soever they be, and albeit joined with imperfections, if compared with the perfection of the moral law, yet will they bear weight in the balance of the gospel (where any measure of uprightness passeth for perfection) : as here the example of the psalmist teacheth. 2. Where the soul, or the renewed part of the man is for the obedience of faith, there is a sincere keeping of the commands : *my soul hath kept thy testimonies.* 3. Where love to God's word, and obedience thereto exceed man's love to any thing which might divert him, there is a sincerity in keeping the word : *I love thy testimonies exceedingly.* 4. As the looking always to God's all-seeing eye, is a special means to make a man keep his commands, so the consciousness of his endeavour so to do, testifieth sincerity *I have kept thy precepts and thy testimonies, for all my ways are before thee.*

TAU.

169. *Let my cry come near before thee, O Lord : give me understanding according to thy word.*

In this last section, the psalmist closeth all the former sweet meditations, and comfortable expressions concerning his faith and love, and the fruits thereof, with five petitions. The first is, for the increase of saving knowledge of the Scriptures. Whence learn, 1. Nothing is so necessary to be sought from God as practical knowledge, whereby a man may know how to behave himself toward God and man in every estate, according to the rule of Scripture : *give me understanding according to thy word.* 2. If God delay to answer us in this petition or in any other, or seem to hide himself from us, let us follow hard after him with earnest supplication, as the psalmist teacheth us : *let my cry come near before thee, O Lord.* 2. The promises of God's word are sufficient to give us breath in crying, hope to have a good answer, and patience till it come: *give me understanding according to thy word.*

170. *Let my supplication come before thee: deliver me according to thy word.*

The next petition is for deliverance out of his trouble. Whence learn, 1. Albeit the believer is not exempted from trouble, but rather engaged to bear the cross, till he come to the crown, yet is he privileged to have access to God in prayer for comfort, strength, and deliverance from it : *let my supplication come before thee : deliver me according to thy word.* 2. The believer craveth nothing but what is promised, and as that may, so it doth satisfy him: *deliver me according to thy word.*

171. *My lips shall utter praise, when thou hast taught me thy statutes.*

172. *My tongue shall speak of thy word: for all thy commandments* are *righteousness.*

David strengthens his hope in these two prayers, by a promise of thankfulness for any measure of a gracious answer. Whence learn, 1. As the end of our petitions should be, that we may be enabled to praise God really, so the use of granting our petitions should be thanks and praise : *my lips shall utter thy praise, when thou hast taught me thy*

statutes. 2. Thanksgiving in words best beseemeth the man
who is indeed obedient to God in his life; and as no man
can obey God in his deeds, but he that is taught of God, so
he that is taught of God to obey in deeds, may well promise
upon that condition to praise God in words also : *my lips
shall utter praise when thou hast taught me thy statutes.*
3. To teach others the ways of God, requireth that we ourselves be taught of God : *when thou hast taught me thy
statutes, my tongue shall speak of thy word.* 4. There
is no ground for edifying ourselves and others, and of glorifying God, but from the word of the Lord : *my tongue
shall speak of thy word.* 5. True righteousness is to be
found only in the word of God; and nothing is approved in
it, or recommended to us by it, save righteousness only,
which should move us the more to study it ourselves, and
then to communicate it to others: *for all thy commandments are righteousness.*

173. *Let thine hand help me : for I have chosen thy
precepts.*

174. *I have longed for thy salvation, O Lord; and
thy law is my delight.*

A third petition is for assistance in trouble, till God send
full delivery to him, whereof three reasons are subjoined.
One, from his making choice of the word above all earthly
things; another, from his longing and expecting deliverance
according to it; and the third, from his delight in the word.
Whence learn, 1. As they who are resolved to serve God
may be sure of opposition, and of adversaries, and trouble
from them; so may they be persuaded to find God's help
in all their troubles against adversaries : for thus much is
imported in these words, *let thy hand help me.* 2. Albeit
allurements to divert the believer from God's obedience, be
offered unto him, yet must he reject them, and deliberately
prefer God's obedience to them all; for thus much is imported in the psalmist's practice : *for I have chosen thy
precepts.* 3. He who hath preferred obedience to the baits
of sin, and hath resolved rather to suffer than to sin, may
look for God's assistance to sustain him in his trouble, that
he shall never have cause to repent him of his choice : *help
me, for I have chosen thy precepts.* 4. Albeit it be natural to seek deliverance out of trouble, yet it is proper for

the godly to love no deliverance but such as God sendeth by his own means, in his own time, and in this mind to wait for this sort of deliverance in the way of God's obedience: *for I have longed for thy salvation, O Lord*, was the psalmist's way to be delivered. 5. The believer is not comfortless in his trouble; he hath his own spiritual comfort and delight in God's truth, or in God manifested therein: *thy law is my delight*, saith the psalmist in trouble.

175. *Let my soul live, and it shall praise thee; and let thy judgments help me.*

A fourth petition is for continuation of David's life for honouring God. Whence learn, 1. As the godly have no will to fall into the hands of men, or to lose their life by murderers; so do they not love life, but for further glorifying God : *let my soul live, and it shall praise thee.* 2. Whosoever have a design to honour God in their life, which they have not as yet attained, may lawfully pray for prolonging their life a while : *let my soul live, and it shall praise thee.* 3. As the word of God hath pronounced sentence already for sustaining his suffering servants, and for taking order with their persecutors; so may the godly pray and expect to be helped : *let thy judgments help me.*

176. *I have gone astray like a lost sheep : seek thy servant; for I do not forget thy commandments.*

The fifth and last petition is, that the Lord would recall the psalmist, now being a banished exile, and bring him home to the communion of his people, as a wandering sheep is brought home to the flock by a kindly shepherd. Whence learn, 1. As the believer is always a pilgrim in his affection toward this earth; so also he may be corporally banished from his native country, and thrust out from the fellowship of the church, as the experience of the psalmist teacheth, who lamenteh his case, saying, *I have gone astray like a lost sheep*, driven out by storm or dark day, or by the hunting of the dogs, chased out from the rest of the flock. 2. Albeit the banished believer be separated from the fellowship of the church, and from his friends, yet not from communion with God, the good shepherd, who heareth the bleating of the poor wandering sheep wherever it be, and will take care of it, and seek it out : *seek thy servant*, saith the exiled psalmist to the Lord. 3. The way for the

believer to keep communion with God in his trouble of
banishment or whatsoever other trouble, is to remember the
direction of God in his word, for going on in the way of
faith and obedience, and he may assure himself that the
good shepherd shall not forget him : *seek thy servant, for
I do not forget thy commandments.*

PSALM CXX.

A Song of Degrees.

The scope of this psalm is, by the experience of the psalmist, to teach and
comfort such as shall be traduced, and falsely slandered.   His exercise
and deliverance are set down summarily, v. 1; and his prayer in his
distress, more largely in the rest of the psalm.

1. *In my distress ᵉI cried unto the Lord, and he
heard me.*

From the psalmist's exercise in general, and deliverance,
learn, 1. The godly are ofttimes put to straits and perplexities, so that they know not what to do till they go to
God by prayer : *in my distress I called unto the Lord.*
2. Distress is a means to make prayer fervent; and fervent
prayer wanteth not a good answer : *I cried unto the Lord,
and he heard me.*

2. *Deliver my soul, O Lord, from lying lips,* and
from a deceitful tongue.

In the rest of the psalm, the psalmist first puts up his
petition to be saved from the bloody tongue of the calumniator, v. 2; and then denounceth God's judgment against
him, v. 3, 4; and closeth with a lamentation, v. 5—7.

From his particular petition, learn, 1. How innocently
soever the godly shall behave themselves, yet are they subject to the bitter backbiting of bloody calumniators, traduc-
ing them and forging lies against them, to make their
governors and judges fall upon them, as the psalmist's experience showeth : *deliver my soul,* or my life, *O Lord,
from lying lips, and from a deceitful tongue.* 2. Albeit the innocent believer can find no means to refute the
calumny, nor is he able to eschew the danger whereinto
he is cast thereby; yet God can find a way for clearing his
name and saving his person, as the prayer teacheth : *deliver
my soul, O Lord, from lying lips.*

3. *What shall be given unto thee? or what shall be done unto thee, thou false tongue?*

4. *Sharp arrows of the mighty, with coals of juniper.*

The psalmist denounceth God's judgment against the calumniator, however the matter shall go. Whence learn, 1. The calumniator hath as little advantage by his sin, as any sort of sinner, but he is sure of the judgment of God: for *what shall be given unto thee, thou false tongue?* 2. The traducer of the godly hath exquisite vengeance waiting for him, which he never dreamed of, and which no tongue can sufficiently express: *what shall be done unto thee, thou false tongue?* 3. As calumnies hurt the name of the godly suddenly before he can be aware, and the wound remaineth long, as arrows shot against them; and as the coals of juniper have the greatest heat, and burn long ere they are quenched; so shall the judgment of the calumniator be: *sharp arrows of the mighty*, or shot by a strong man, *and coals of juniper.*

5. *Woe is me, that I sojourn in Mesech,* that *I dwell in the tents of Kedar!*

6. *My soul hath long dwelt with him that hateth peace.*

7. *I* am for *peace: but when I speak they* are *for war.*

In his lamentation, learn, 1. False brethren, counterfeit professors of religion, rotten members of the visible church, are no better neighbours than savage and wild barbarians, robbers, Muscovites, and Arabians, men of Mesech and Kedar, without the verge of the visible church. 2. It is a woful condition to dwell among the wicked, and yet the godly cannot eschew it; they may well lament it: *wo is me that I sojourn in Mesech, that I dwell in the tents of Kedar.* 3. So long as the godly live among wicked calumniators, they reckon themselves as banished men living in a foreign country, and are made ofttimes to lament their condition: *wo is me that I sojourn in Mesech, and dwell in the tents of Kedar.* 4. A man should have great cause of lamenting before he give vent to his woe; his patience should do its part for a sufficiently long time, in hope to have the evil remedied; for the psalmist breaketh not forth at first, but saith, *my soul hath long dwelt with him that hateth peace.*   5. It is not sufficient to live innocently with the wicked, but duty requireth that we should labour to mitigate the fury of adversaries, as the psalmist did : *I am for peace.*   6. If peace be studied with those among whom we live, and we obtain it not, yet shall the ditty of the wicked be so much the more augmented thereby; *when I speak they are for war.*

PSALM CXXI.

A Song of Degrees.

The scope of this psalm is to show, that, howsoever we are ready to seek help anywhere else, rather than in God, yet no help is to be had except from God : perfect help and full delivery are to be had in him undoubtedly, as the psalmist's experience and example of faith teach : wherein the psalmist, leaving all other confidences beside God, betaketh himself to God Almighty only, v. 1, 2 ; and, from his own experience, giveth encouragement to all God's people to place their confidence in God alone, by six promises, in the six verses following, to the end of the psalm.

1. *I will lift up mine eyes unto the hills, from whence cometh my help.*

2. *My help* cometh *from the Lord, which made heaven and earth.*

From the psalmist's example and exercise, learn, 1. The Lord usually bringeth such trouble upon his own children as shall make them sensible of their own weakness, and of their need of help ; for, otherwise we are ready to encounter with smaller troubles in our own strength : *I will lift up mine eyes to the hills, from whence cometh my help.*   2. Some one earthly power or other is the first refuge which naturally we look to, to see what help may be found there : which, our natural inclination, the psalmist taxeth indirectly in the name of *lifting the eyes to the hills,* to wit, to the powers of the world, rather than to the heavenly hills of God's omnipotency : *I lift up mine eyes unto the hills ;* not these earthly ones, will he say, which I see cannot help me, but to hills higher than the highest earthly help, as afterward he maketh clear.   3. Nothing can satisfy faith except the all-sufficiency of God, who made heaven and earth of nothing, and can give help where there is no appearance of relief : *my help cometh from the Lord, which made heaven and earth.*

3. He will not suffer thy foot to be moved : he that keepeth thee will not slumber.

For the confirmation of his own faith and the faith of others, that they may rest on God and depend on him only for relief in their straits, whether they have means of delivery or not, he brings forth six promises of God to the believer : for, our faith being weak, hath need to have the promises of God branched into small parts, and multiplied in particulars, that so they may be the more easily applied. The first promise is in this verse. Whence learn, 1. Albeit the believer be of himself weak and ready to fall, yet the Lord will save him from ruin, and keep him fast in the defence of the truth for which he is put in straits : *he will not suffer thy foot to be moved.* 2. The providence of God is so vigilant for the safety of the believer, that the believer needeth not to fear lest he suffer any inconvenience by God's oversight : for, *he that keepeth thee will not slumber.*

4. Behold, he that keepeth Israel shall neither slumber nor sleep.

A second promise made to all God's people, which also confirmeth the former promise. Whence learn, 1. The Lord is keeper and watchman over his church, and every member thereof, and this is his style and memorial in all ages : *behold, he that keepeth Israel shall neither slumber nor sleep.* 2. The right which particular believers have to promises belongeth to them, because they are made to the church, over which the Lord taketh such care, that he never in any moment of time faileth in attending the church, and every particular member thereof : *he that keepeth Israel shall neither slumber nor sleep.*

5. The Lord is thy keeper ; the Lord is thy shade upon thy right hand.

The third promise particularly directed to the believer, including the psalmist himself. Whence learn, 1. Albeit the believer hath not a promise to be free from trouble and persecution, yet he hath a promise of consolation in it, and of defence from the hurt of it : *the Lord is thy keeper, the Lord is thy shade.* 2. When trouble cometh, the Lord is not far to seek, but is ready to be found for protection and consolation : *the Lord is thy shade upon thy right hand.*

6. *The sun shall not smite thee by day, nor the moon by night.*

The fourth promise made with allusion to, and application of, that care which God had over his people when he brought them out of *Egypt* through the wilderness, when he guarded them from the heat of the sun with a cloud by day, and from the cold and moistness of the night and moon with a pillar of fire by night. Whence learn, 1. Albeit the believer be subject to sundry perils from adversity and prosperity, from one adverse power at one time, and from another adverse power at another; yet the Lord so careth for him, and so tempereth and moderateth his exercises, that he shall be sure not to be harmed, in order and relation to the carrying on of his felicity : *the sun shall not smite thee by day, nor the moon by night.* 2. What care the Lord had over his people in the wilderness, the same hath he still over every believer, as the application of the like mercy showeth : *the sun shall not smite thee by day, &c.*

7. *The Lord shall preserve thee from all evil; he shall preserve thy soul.*

From the fifth promise, learn, 1 Whatsoever trouble shall befall the believer, he shall be freed from the evil of it, because God shall make all troubles work together for his good : *the Lord shall preserve thee from all evil.* 2. If the believer lose any thing by trouble, he shall not lose what is most precious; the Lord shall save his soul, and, so long as it is expedient, his bodily life also : *he shall preserve thy soul.*

8. *The Lord shall preserve thy going out, and thy coming in, from this time forth, and even for evermore.*

From the sixth promise, learn, 1. Albeit all men have need to have their carriage in all their affairs directed by God, yet none hath the promise of direction and success save the believer only, to whom it is said here, *the Lord shall preserve thy going out and thy coming in.* 2. The Lord so taketh his own by the hand to care for them, that he leaveth them not, nor forsaketh them afterward, but goeth along with them for ever : *the Lord shall preserve thy going out and thy coming in, from this time forth, and even for evermore.*

PSALM CXXII.

A Song of Degrees of David.

The ark of God had for a long time moved from place to place. At length the Lord revealeth unto David the place whereof Moses hath spoken, to be Zion where the ark should rest, and there David set up the ark, having revealed to the people the oracle : whereupon the people heartily embraced the will of God, came to that place appointed for public worship, and invited one another to go up to worship. In this psalm, we have first David's joy for the people's willingness to assemble in the Lord's house, v. 1, 2. In the next place, he praises Jerusalem, v. 3—5. In the third place, he exhorteth all to pray for the peace of Jerusalem, representing the universal church, and useth some reasons to set them forward on the duty, v. 6—9.

1. *I was glad when they said unto me, Let us go into the house of the Lord.*

2. *Our feet shall stand within thy gates, O Jerusalem.*

From the joy which David had in the people's willingness to join in the public worship of the Lord, learn, 1. Sometimes the message of the Lord's servants is well taken at their hand, and the fruit of the labour is returned upon them, to their no small joy ; and here David professeth in his experience, *that he was glad when they said unto him, Let us go.* 2. As people lawfully may, yea and should, not only stir up one another, by their example and mutual private exhortation, to the service of God, but also stir up their teachers and rulers ; so teachers and rulers should think it no encroachment upon their office, nor disparagement to their person, or gifts, or place, to be stirred up to their duties by the people, but should rather cherish and foster the people's holy zeal, as here we are taught by David's practice : *I was glad when they said unto me, Let us go into the house of the Lord.* 3. As it is no small benefit to have a settled place for public assemblies unto God's worship ; so should it be thankfully acknowledged when it is bestowed and resolutely made use of, as here we see the people did : *our feet shall stand within thy gates, O Jerusalem.*

3. *Jerusalem is builded as a city that is compact together :*

4. *Whither the tribes go up, the tribes of the Lord, unto the testimony of Israel, to give thanks unto the name of the Lord.*

5. *For there are set thrones of judgment, the thrones of the house of David.*

David commendeth Jerusalem, the figure of the church of God and of the corporation of his people, first, as a city for a community ; secondly, as the place of God's public assemblies for religious worship ; thirdly, as the place of public judicatories, for governing the Lord's people under David, the type of Christ. Whence learn, 1. The church of God is not without cause compared to a city, and especially to Jerusalem, because of the union, concord, community of laws, mutual commodities, and conjunction of strength, which should be among God's people : *Jerusalem is builded as a city that is compact together.* 2. What commendeth a place most of any thing, is the erecting of the Lord's banner of love in it, and making it a place for his people to meet together for his worship : *Jerusalem is a city where the tribes go up.* 3. Whatsoever civil distinction God's children have among themselves, and howsoever they dwell scattered in several places of the earth ; yet as they are the Lord's people, they should entertain a communion and conjunction among themselves as members of one universal church, as the signification of the people's meeting thrice in the year at Jerusalem taught : *whither the tribes did go up, the tribes of the Lord.* 4. As the tribes, so all particular churches, how far soever scattered, have one Lord, one covenant, one law and scripture, signified by the tribes going up to the testimony of Israel, or to the ark of the covenant or testimony, where the whole ordinances of God were to be exercised. 5. The end of the ordinances of Gôd, of holy covenanting and communion, and joining in public worship, is to acknowledge the grace and goodness of God, and to glorify him ; for the tribes went up *to give thanks unto the name of the Lord.* 6. The church of God wanteth not the government and governors, courts and judicatories, belonging to Christ and his church, as the erecting of ecclesiastic judicatories in Jerusalem signified and taught : *for there are set thrones of judgments.* 7. The civil governors, in their civil power, should contribute what their power can, to the furtherance of the church government, and the courts thereof as the thrones of the house of David, joining their assistance in Jerusalem unto the ecclesiastic courts, did signify and teach : *there are set the thrones of the house of David.*

6. *Pray for the peace of Jerusalem : they shall pros-per that love thee.*

7. *Peace be within thy walls,* and *prosperity within thy palaces.*

8. *For my brethren and companions' sakes, I will now say, Peace* be *within thee.*

9. *Because of the house of the Lord our God I will seek thy good.*

In the last place David exhorteth all to pray for the peace of *Jerusalem,* or of the church signified by it, and joineth four motives to it. One motive because, as it was a proof of love to the church, so it had a promise of a blessing, v. 6 ; another, from his own example, praying for it, v. 7 ; a third, because so love to the brethren required, v. 8; a fourth, because so respect and love to the church or house of God required, v. 9. Whence learn, 1. The universal church mi-litant, should be dear to every member thereof, and prayed for, that it may prosper : *pray for the peace of Jerusalem.* 2. As none can pray for the welfare of the church heartily, except they love her ; so none shall love her and seek her welfare, but shall fare the better for it : for it is promised here, *they shall prosper that love thee.* 3. The church is a war town, and a walled town which is situated among ene-mies, and may not trust those without, but must be upon its keeping, as the type thereof, *Jerusalem,* with her walls and towers, shadowed forth : *peace be within thy walls.* 4 Peace within the church is no less needful than pros-perity within it ; and if peace be within the church, it mat-ters the less what enemies she have without : *peace be within thy walls, and prosperity within thy palaces,* importeth or insinuateth so much. 5. All the members of the church militant should be affected one to another as brethren, as fellow-partners in loss and gain, for the relation which they have to one Father the Lord, and one mother the universal church : *for my brethren and companions' sake, I will now say, Peace be within thee.* 6. Seeing the church is the Lord's dwelling-house in this world, whosoever loveth the Lord must not only inwardly affect, but also effectually by all means endeavour to promote the good of the church ; that is to say, every true member of the church must do what in him lieth, and as his calling will suffer, to have re-ligion established, God's ordinances obeyed, public worship

erected, the word truly preached, sacraments rightly ad-
ministered, and church government according to the word
of God exercised: for so teacheth this example ; *because of
the house of the Lord my God, I will seek thy good.*

PSALM CXXIII.

A song of degrees.

The scope of this psalm is to teach the Lord's people, how to carry themselves when they are oppressed by the tyranny of their proud adversaries, and are destitute of all help under heaven, wherein the psalmist
maketh his address to God, in patience, humility, and hope, v. 1, 2;
and prayeth for comfort under, and relief from, the contempt of the
proud adversaries, v. 3, 4.

1. *Unto thee lift I up mine eyes, O thou that dwellest
in the heavens.*

2. *Behold, as the eyes of servants* look *unto the hand
of their masters,* and *as the eyes of a maiden unto the
hand of her mistress; so our eyes* wait *upon the Lord
our God, until that he have mercy upon us.*

From the psalmist's address to God, by this short prayer,
under the oppression of the church, learn, 1. The force of
prayer consisteth not in the multitude of words, but in faith,
and fervent laying forth of desires before the Lord, as here
we see. 2. It is not strange to see God's children oppressed, and despised, and destitute of all relief, except of what
may be expected from heaven, as this case here set down
showeth. 3. Albeit the Lord seem to hide himself from all
manifestation of his kind respects to his people on earth,
yet he will be found in heaven, and there must we betake
ourselves in hardest straits : *unto thee lift I up mine eyes,
O thou that dwellest in the heavens.* 4. The very lifting
up of the bodily eye of the believer toward God in his trouble, hath its own use and force with God : *unto thee lift I
up mine eyes.* 5. As servants of old were in their condition slaves, deprived of the common comfort of liberty,
might wear no weapons, were exposed to all injuries, and
had no help or comfort, except the favour of their master
or mistress ; so fares it ofttimes with the believer for his
outward condition, as the similitude and present case of the
church here teacheth : *behold, as the eyes of servants look
unto the hand of their masters.* 6. It is fitting that the
persecuted believer have a low estimation of himself before

God, be patient under his hand, submissive to his dispensations, and hopeful of help in his address to God ; for so
much the similitude from servants' behaviour toward their
master and mistress teacheth : *as the eyes of a maiden unto
the hand of her mistress, so our eyes wait upon the Lord.*
7. The interest which the believer hath in God under any
relation, hath comfort sufficient included in it, as here the
Lord's being *Master*, is sufficient to sweeten bondage of
servant and *handmaid*, but covenant interest sweeteneth it
much more : *our eyes are upon the Lord our God.* 8.
As masters and mistresses are taught to show pity, mercy,
bounty, and protection to their servants, on the one hand,
and servants are here taught, on the other hand, by their
good behaviour, not to mar their favour ; so the believer is
taught to behave himself before God, as a *servant* indeed,
by endeavouring indeed to obey God. 9. The term of the
saint's patience and waiting, is till God show mercy : *behold,
as the eyes of the servants, &c., so our eyes wait on the
Lord our God, until that he have mercy on us.*

3. *Have mercy upon us, O Lord, have mercy upon
us : for we are exceedingly filled with contempt.*
4. *Our soul is exceedingly filled with the scorning
of those that are at ease, and with the contempt of the
proud.*

From the psalmist's prayer for comfort and relief, learn,
1. Whatsoever aileth the church, the Lord's mercy is the
remedy : *have mercy.* 2. Each member of the church
should be sensible of the trouble of the whole body, and deal
for it as for himself : *have mercy upon us, O Lord.* 3.
As misery is more pressing, so should petitions be doubled
and poured forth before the Lord : *have mercy, have mercy
upon us.* 4. Contempt, disdain, and derision of God's suffering servants, form the heaviest and most grievous part of
their affliction : *have mercy upon us, for we are exceedingly filled with contempt.* 5. They that prosper in wickedness, are ready instruments to afflict the godly, to persecute them for righteousness, and to mock them in their
misery, when they have wrongfully troubled them : *our
soul is exceedingly filled with the scorning of them that
are at ease.* 6. So long as the persecutors and oppressors
of God's church prosper, and find success in their ways,

they will not cease to please themselves in their wicked course, and despise both the persons and the cause of God's people, whatsoever be said against them : *our soul is filled with the contempt of the proud.*

PSALM CXXIV.

A Song of Degrees of David.

The scope of this psalm is, first, to acknowledge the delivery of the church to be evidently the Lord's own work, the danger being so great out of which they were lately delivered, v. 1—5; and, next, to bless the Lord for their preservation, v. 6—8.

1. *If* it had not been *the Lord who was on our side, now may Israel say ;*

2. *If* it had not been *the Lord who was on our side, when men rose up against us :*

3. *Then they had swallowed us up quick, when their wrath was kindled against us :*

4. *Then the waters had overwhelmed us, the stream had gone over our soul:*

5. *Then the proud waters had gone over our soul.*

In the acknowledgment of their wonderful delivery, the psalmist showeth that their adversaries, on the one hand, were so strong, so many, so crafty, so cruel, and malicious, and the Lord's people, on the other hand, were so weak, and so destitute of all counsel and help, that their deliverance could be ascribed to no cause, save God's strong power assisting his own. Whence learn, 1. Albeit the Lord suffer his church sundry times to be brought near to destruction, yet always he proveth himself the church's friend and helper against their enemies: *if it had not been the Lord who was on our side.* 2. The Lord so helpeth his people, that he draweth forth the acknowledgment of their weakness to help themselves, and of utter impossibility to be safe without his assistance : *if the Lord had not been on our side, may Israel now say.* 3. After we are delivered out of a danger, we should study to contemplate it with no less liveliness than when we are in the danger, and that so much the more as we are naturally disposed to the contrary, as the repeating and new representing of the danger they were in importeth and teacheth. 4. Men in the state of nature are ready to be party adversaries to the church : *if the Lord had not been on our side, when men rose up against us.* 5. The wicked have an appetite after the blood of God's people, as wild beasts have after their prey : *then they had swallowed us up quick.* 6. If God bridle not the fury of the wicked against his people, the worldly strength of the godly to defend themselves is nothing : *then they had swallowed us up quick, when their wrath was kindled against us.* 7. If the wickedness of the world were let loose against God's people, it would run as violently against the church, as floods of water against those that are within the channel : *then the waters had overwhelmed us, the stream had gone over our soul.* 8. The more the matter of the church's delivery is looked upon, the danger is the better seen, and the greatness of their delivery also, as the insisting in the similitude teacheth : *then the proud waters had gone over our soul.*

6. *Blessed* be *the Lord, who hath not given us as a prey to their teeth.*

7. *Our soul is escaped as a bird out of the snare of the fowlers : the snare is broken, and we are escaped.*

8. *Our help* is *in the name of the Lord, who made heaven and earth.*

In the church's thanksgiving for their delivery, they make a threefold use of their experience. First, they praise and bless God's goodness, v. 6. Secondly, they make much of the benefit, and rejoice therein, v. 7. And, thirdly, they strengthen their faith in God for time to come, v. 8. Whence learn, 1. It is our duty after delivery from dangers, to acknowledge not only God's power for us, but his goodness also toward us, and to acknowledge him the fountain of all blessedness upon that occasion : *blessed be the Lord who hath not given us as a prey to their teeth.* 2. As the church's enemies are superior to her in worldly strength, so also in policy, craftiness, and worldly wit, as the fowler is craftier than the bird : *our soul is escaped as a bird out of the snare of the fowlers.* 3. According as the danger is fearful, so is the delivery sweet and joyful : *the snare is broken, and we are escaped.* 4. It is as easy for God to deliver his people out of their enemies' hands, even when they have the godly in their power, as to break a net made of thread or yarn, wherewith birds are taken : *blessed be the Lord, the snare is broken, and we are escaped.* 5. The fairest fruits of our bypast experience is to glorify God by confidence in him for time to come, as here : *our help is in the name of the Lord.* 6. Our confidence in God to be delivered from evil is well bottomed, when we consider the Lord's omnipotence manifested in the creation of the world, and held out by his word to us; for so much the psalmist teacheth when he maketh mention of the name of the Lord, and the work of the Lord, in professing his confidence : *our help is in the name of the Lord, who made heaven and earth.*

PSALM CXXV.
A Song of Degrees.

The scope of this psalm is to confirm the faith of the believer, persecuted and oppressed by the wicked, that he may hold out, walking in the straight way of God's obedience; and to this end the psalmist useth four arguments. The first is from the stability of the believer's felicity, v. 1, 2. The second is from the short time of his trouble, which he shall suffer by persecutors, v. 3. The third is from the goodness which God will manifest toward him, set down in the psalmist's prayer, v. 4. The fourth is from the Lord's judgments upon backsliding hypocrites, who make shift for themselves to be freed from trouble by unlawful means, v. 5.

1. *They that trust in the Lord* shall be *as mount Zion,* which *cannot be removed,* but *abideth for ever.*

2. As *the mountains* are *round about Jerusalem, so the Lord* is *round about his people from henceforth, even for ever.*

From the first encouragement to trust in God in the time of trial, learn, 1. There is no service more acceptable to God, or more profitable to us, than glorifying God, by faith in him, when temptations assault us; as the professing of the duty, and the motives which are here used teach us. 2. Seeing the happiness of the believer is so established that he cannot be deprived of it, he may the more cheerfully hazard in God's service all things temporal and movable, trusting in the Lord : *they that trust in the Lord shall be as mount Zion, which cannot be removed, but abideth for ever.* 3. The preservation of the believer, and the stability of his blessedness floweth not from any strength in himself, but from the Lord's guarding him: *as the mountains are round about Jerusalem, so is the Lord round about his people.*

3. *For the rod of the wicked shall not rest upon the lot of the righteous; lest the righteous put forth their hands unto iniquity.*

From the second encouragement of the believer to trust in God in the time of trial, learn, 1. No promise made to the believer, must secure him from being exercised with trouble, but rather must forewarn him of, and forearm him against trouble; for here it is presupposed he may be burdened by *the rod of the wicked.* 2. It is a sore trial for the godly, to have their rulers their persecutors for righteousness, but this exercise shall not last long: *for the rod* (which is the sign of power) *of the wicked shall not rest on the lot of the righteous.* 3. Because there is hazard lest the believer should faint in trouble, therefore the Lord will not try his own who believe in him above their strength, but will give them a deliverance that they may escape: *the rod of the wicked shall not rest on the lot of the righteous, lest the righteous put forth their hands unto iniquity.*

4. *Do good, O Lord, unto those that be good, and to them that are upright in their hearts.*

From the third motive to believe in God, in time of trial especially, learn, 1. The true believer is a good man, harmless, bountiful, delighting to do good to all men, and to do wrong to no man, for here he is so called: *do good, O Lord, to those that be good.* 2. Albeit the believer seem to be hardly handled by afflictions, yet shall it afterward appear that God hath thereby been working for his welfare; for the prayer of the psalmist indited by God promiseth so much: *do good, O Lord, unto those that be good.* 3. As a man that trusts in God is honest in his heart, how weak soever in doing the good he would, and he taketh care not only to cleanse his life, but also to purify his heart; so shall he be dealt with by God as a good man, whatsoever be his own estimation of himself: *do good to those that are good, and unto them that are upright in their heart.*

5. *As for such as turn aside unto their crooked ways, the Lord shall lead them forth with the workers of iniquity:* but *peace* shall be *upon Israel.*

From the fourth motive to believe in God for bearing out in trial, learn, 1. In the time of trial, sundry will be found hypocrites, counterfeit dealers, misbelievers, who will shift for themselves, and turn aside from the obedience of faith, by their own crooked courses, as here is insinuated : *as for such as turn aside unto their crooked ways.* 2. God will decipher hypocrites, who do not trust God, or do not adhere to the obedience of faith in time of trouble and trials and will put them as compliers with the wicked, in the same reckoning with his open enemies : *the Lord will lead them forth with the workers of iniquity.* 3. To look upon the judgments of God, pursuing backsliding misbelievers in time of persecution, should be a strong motive, to make professors constant in the obedience of faith, on all hazards in time of trial; for the punishment of the wily misbeliever is set down here, to teach men to be honest and stout in the faith and obedience of God : *for such as turn aside unto their crooked ways, the Lord shall lead them forth with the workers of iniquity.* 4. Whatsoever trouble the Lord's people shall be put to in the time of trial, they shall still remain in God's favour and grace; and when the Lord hath purged his church in some measure, by winnowing corrupt hypocrites out from among his people, the church shall be restored to her peace : *but peace shall be upon Israel.*

PSALM CXXVI.
A Song of Degrees.

This is the church's song of thanksgiving for her delivery from the captivity of Babylon, wherein first the greatness of the mercy is set down, v. 1—3; then a prayer to God for enlarging the benefit, by making many embrace the offer of delivery, v. 4; and thirdly, an encouraging consolation to such as had returned or should return from Babylon to their own land, v. 5, 6.

1. *When the Lord turned again the captivity of Zion, we were like them that dream.*

2. *Then was our mouth filled with laughter, and our tongue with singing : then said they among the heathen, the Lord hath done great things for them.*

3. *The Lord hath done great things for us,* whereof *we are glad.*

In the thanksgiving the mercy is magnified; first, because it was above all their expectation, v. 1; secondly, because it not only rejoiced God's people, but also convinced the heathen of God's power for, and goodness toward his people, v. 2; thirdly, because it was in itself a mercy worthy to be praised and rejoiced for, v. 3. Whence learn, 1. As the Lord sometimes giveth evidence of his justice in afflict-ing his church; so also sometimes he giveth evidence of his mercy to his people, by delivering, restoring, and comfort-ing them : as this psalm holdeth forth. 2. Whosoever be the instruments of the delivery and consolation of the church, the Lord will so order matters as he shall be seen to be the worker of the work himself; therefore it is said here, *when the Lord turned again the captivity of Zion.* 3. The performance of God's promises is more glorious than the believer can perceive or apprehend before he see it : *when the Lord turned again the captivity of Zion, we were like them that dream.* 4. The delivery and con-solation of God's church is no less matter of joy and glad-ness, and praising God, than their affliction is of sorrow : *then was our mouth filled with laughter, and our tongue with singing.* 5. In the delivery of the church the Lord usually works so evidently for his people, that their adver-saries are forced to acknowledge it : *then said they among the heathen, the Lord hath done great things for them.* 6. Inward joy in God, and outward acknowledgment of God's working for his people, are the duty of every true member of the church, and are all which can be done at the first receipt of the mercy by way of thankfulness : *the Lord hath done great things for us.* 7. There is a special eminence in the Lord's working for his people, above what he worketh in governing the rest of the world : *the Lord hath done great things,* say both the heathen and the church. 8. There is this great difference between the praise which the heathen are forced to give to God, and that which the Lord's people heartily offer him. The one speaketh as having no interest or share in the mercy; the other speak as they for whom the mercy is intended, and wherein they have their portion with others : *he hath done great things for them,* say the heathen : but, *he hath done great things for us,* say the Lord's people.

4. *Turn again our captivity, O Lord, as the streams in the south.*

From the prayer, learn, 1. The offer and opportunity

given of a mercy, is one benefit, and the embracing of the offer, and taking the opportunity to make use of it, are another benefit: many have the one who receive not the other, as many had the liberty of returning from the captivity of Babylon, who made no use thereof, but preferred the ease and pleasures of Babylon, to the prerogatives of Zion : as this prayer importeth. 2. It is no less mercy to give people a heart to embrace and make use of offered mercy, than it is to purchase the means, and proclaim the offer of it in their audience : as this prayer importeth. 3. Such as have found grace to embrace the offer of God's mercy should pity and pray for others, that they may find the like mercy also : *turn again our captivity, O Lord.* 4. As the restoration of the church is no less comfortable, than is the making of a river run in a dry land; so is the one no less possible to God than the other : *turn again our captivity as the rivers of the south,* or droughty lands.

5. *They that sow in tears shall reap in joy.*

6. *He that goeth forth and weepeth, bearing precious seed, shall doubtless come again with rejoicing, bringing his sheaves* with him.

From the encouraging consolation of all the Lord's afflicted people, learn, 1. As the Lord hath appointed harvest to follow the seed-time, so hath he appointed the consolation of his own church to follow after their afflictions : this the similitude importeth. 2. As the husbandman hath first toiling, labour, and great expenses, and a time to endure in patience, till he find the fruit of his labours; so fareth it with God's children, who may be in great grief for a time before they find the good of religion : this also the similitude holdeth forth. There is a difference between the husbandman and the Lord's afflicted child. The husbandman may have an ill harvest, but the child of God afflicted, and using the means, shall never have an ill harvest; his labour shall not be in vain in the Lord : his sorrow shall be turned into joy, and his fruit shall be multiplied to him abundantly : *for they that sow in tears, shall reap in joy : he that goeth forth, and weepeth, bearing precious seed, shall undoubtedly come again with rejoicing, bringing his sheaves with him.* His consolation shall be sweeter than his affliction was bitter.

PSALM CXXVII.

A Song of Degrees for Solomon.

The scope of the psalm is to show, first, that the defence of our persons and success in our affairs depend upon God's blessing on the means used, v. 1, 2; next, to show that the multitude of God's children is God's blessing also, v. 3—5. The psalm is entitled for Solomon, who was to build the house of God, and to enlarge the kingdom of Israel. Whence learn, 1. All truth of God must be studied, but specially that part whereof we may have special use in our life and exercise of our calling, as this doctrine here commended to Solomon teacheth. 2. Neither Solomon, nor the wisest and most active among men, must ascribe more to themselves in compassing their affairs than other men may do: for this doctrine is taught to Solomon. 3. Of whatsoever we have, do, purchase, or can achieve, by whatsoever lawful means, God must be acknowledged as the giver, doer, and the blesser of us therein : for the scope of this psalm is to teach this lesson to Solomon, and to the whole church.

1. *Except the Lord build the house, they labour in vain that build it : except the Lord keep the city, the watchman waketh* but *in vain.*

2. It is *vain for you to rise up early, to sit up late, to eat the bread of sorrows :* for *so he giveth his beloved sleep.*

From the first doctrine, showing that the defence of our persons and success in our affairs depend on God's blessing, learn, 1. We are subject to a twofold practical error. One is, we ordinarily look first to means, to our own strength, or to appearances of accomplishing our designs, and in the confidence of these we follow our business. Another is, when any success is found, we are ready to sacrifice to our own nets, and to intercept the praise due to God, as this doctrine presupposeth. 2. To correct our natural error, it is wisdom to consider that many men have had plenty of means, and have managed them skilfully and carefully, and yet without success : *for except the Lord build the house, they labour in vain that build it.* 3. As it is a duty for men to provide for their own commodious living, and their families' well-being by allowed means, and in their incorporations to provide for magistrates, rulers, and other things needful for the defence and welfare of the incorporation, and not to neglect the means; so must God be looked to, believed in, and depended on, because he only can give the blessing; he can work without means, but the means can effect nothing without him : *except the Lord keep the city, the watchman doth watch but in vain.* 4. The Lord justly plagueth the anxiety of some, who toil like infidels in the use of the means, whereby the truth of the doctrine appeareth : *it is vain for you to rise up early, to sit up late, and to eat the bread of sorrows,* that is, sparingly to feed upon coarse morsels to eschew expenses. 5. The only way for having a quiet mind and good success, is to use the means without anxiety, and to commit the success to God : and this wisdom is the peculiar gift of God's chosen children : *for so he giveth his beloved sleep.*

3. *Lo, children* are *an heritage of the Lord :* and *the fruit of the womb* is his *reward.*

4. *As arrows* are *in the hand of a mighty man ; so* are *children of the youth.*

5. *Happy* is *the man that hath his quiver full of them : they shall not be ashamed, but they shall speak with the enemies in the gate.*

From the second doctrine, learn, 1. The Lord will be seen in a special manner in withholding or giving children to married persons, and will have the benefit acknowledged when he bestoweth it : *lo, children are an heritage of the Lord, and the fruit of the womb is his reward.* 2. When God giveth children for a blessing, he giveth grace as to the parents to bring them well up, so to the children to be kind to their parents, and to go about their parents' business as readily as arrows out of the bow : *as arrows are in the hand of a mighty man, so are children of the youth.* 3. In peace and war, dutiful children will do for their parents, and for their pastors, magistrates, rulers, as their fathers and mothers : for the parents who have such children *shall not be ashamed, but shall speak with the enemies in the gate.* 4. Temporal benefits are evidences of happiness, when the man is a believer in God, a depender upon him, and blessed spiritually by God : for of such only doth the psalmist say, *happy is the man that hath his quiver full of such arrows,* as gracious children or gracious subjects are.

PSALM CXXVIII.

A Song of Degrees.

The scope of this psalm is to show the blessedness of the man that feareth God. This appeareth, first, in the temporal blessing of him in his calling, v. 1, 2; secondly, in his family, v. 3, 4; thirdly, in pouring spiritual blessings upon him, v. 5, 6.

1. *Blessed* is *every one that feareth the Lord : that walketh in his ways.*

2. *For thou shalt eat the labour of thine hands : happy* shalt *thou* be, *and* it shall be *well with thee.*

From the doctrine of the blessedness of the man that feareth God, learn, 1. That the sure evidence of a sound believer, and truly blessed man, is the true fear of God, keeping him in the awe and reverent obedience of God : *blessed is every one that feareth the Lord.* 2. He is not the man that feareth God, whose fear is taught by the precepts of men, or who deviseth to himself ways of God's service, and bindeth superstitious bonds upon his own conscience, but he that walketh in the prescribed paths of the obedience of God's commands : only he feareth God, *that walketh in his ways.* 3. The fear of God consisteth not with an idle life, but requireth that a man according to his abilities should be employed in some lawful exercise profitable for the use of the incorporation where he liveth : for here the labour of his hands is presupposed, whereby God's blessing of him may be derived to him : *thou shalt eat the labour of thine hands.* 4. It is no small favour from God, to have the right and comfortable use of his benefits given us, and only the godly man who is diligent in his calling, hath the promise of this: *happy shalt thou be, and it shall be well with thee.*

3. *Thy wife* shall be *as a fruitful vine by the sides of thine house : thy children like olive-plants round about thy table.*

4. *Behold, that thus the man shall be blessed that feareth the Lord.*

From the second evidence, which is God's blessing of his family, learn, 1. Marriage is a state of life, well beseeming the godly man, and it neither hindereth the fear of God, nor the man's felicity, but consisteth well therewith: *thy wife shall be as a fruitful vine.* 2. Godliness is great gain; it hath the promise of this life, (so far as is good for us,) and of the life to come: wife and children, and a table with maintenance competent for the sustenance of the family, are branches of blessedness, when bestowed upon a godly man, and should be so looked upon: *thy wife shall be as a fruitful vine by the sides of thy house, thy children like olive-plants round about thy table.* 3. There is a reward for the righteous, even in this life, and albeit it be not always discerned, yet he who shall behold and consider God's providence about the godly man, shall see this temporal favour, or the equivalent granted him: therefore is it said, *behold, thus* (that is, in this or the equivalent benefit,) *shall the man be blessed that feareth the Lord.*

5. *The Lord shall bless thee out of Zion ; and thou shalt see the good of Jerusalem all the days of thy life.*

6. *Yea, thou shalt see thy children's children;* and *peace upon Israel.*

From the third evidence of God's blessing the true believer and fearer of his name, by giving him things spiritual, learn, 1. What measure soever of things temporal the Lord shall give to the man that feareth him, he reserveth unto him all the promises of righteousness and life, which the Lord's word holdeth forth to the church, and of those he shall be sure: *the Lord shall bless thee out of Zion.* 2. The godly man shall not want succession, if God see it good for him, or if not children of his body, yet followers of his faith and footsteps in piety, whom he hath been instrumental to convert: *thou shalt see thy children's children.* 3. Whatsoever estate the church of God be in, during the godly man's lifetime, he shall behold in the mirror of the Lord's word, and in the sensible feeling of his own experience he shall perceive and take up the blessed condition of the true church of God, and rejoice therein all his days: *thou shalt see the good of Jerusalem all the days of thy life, thou shalt see peace upon Israel.*

PSALM CXXIX.

A Song of Degrees.

The scope of this psalm is to confirm the faith of God's people against persecution. The parts thereof are two. The first is praise to God for delivering many times his church from the oppression of persecutors, v. 1—4. The other hath a prophetical curse against the enemies of the church, v. 5—8.

1. *Many a time have they afflicted me from my youth, may Israel now say:*

2. *Many a time have they afflicted me from my youth ; yet they have not prevailed against me.*

In praising God for the church's delivery lately granted to her, the psalmist calleth to mind many bypast persecutions, wherein the Lord had preserved his church from overthrow. Whence learn, 1. The visible church from the beginning of the world is one body, and as it were one man, growing up from infancy to riper age ; for so speaketh the church here: *many a time have they afflicted me from my youth.* 2. The wicked enemies of the church are also one body, one adverse army, from the beginning of the world continuing war against the church : *many a time have they afflicted me from my youth.* 3. As the former injuries done to the church, are owned by the church in after ages, as done against the same body, so also the persecution of former enemies is imputed and put upon the score of present persecutors : *many a time have they afflicted me from my youth, may Israel now say.* 4. New experience of persecution, when the righteous call to mind the exercise of the church in former ages, serve much for encouragement and consolation in troubles : *many a time have they afflicted me, may Israel now say.* 5. Albeit in all ages it hath been the endeavour of the wicked to destroy the church, yet God hath still preserved her from age to age : *yet they have not prevailed.*

3. *The plowers plowed upon my back ; they made long their furrows.*

4. *The Lord is righteous : he hath cut asunder the cords of the wicked.*

He repeateth the same praise of God in delivering his church from oppression of the enemy, under the similitude of cutting the cords of the plough, which tilleth up another man's field. Whence learn, 1. The enemies of the church no more regard her, than they do the earth under their feet, and seek to make their own advantage of her, as usurpers usually do in possessing and labouring another man's field : *the plowers plowed upon my back*. 2. The Lord usually suffers his enemies to break up the fallow ground of his people's proud and stiff hearts with the plough of persecution, and to draw deep and long furrows on them : *they made long their furrows*. 3. What the enemies do against the church, the Lord maketh use of for manuring the church, which is his field ; albeit they intend no good to God's church, yet they serve in God's wisdom to prepare the Lord's people for receiving the seed of God's word ; for the similitude speaketh of their tilling the church, but nothing of their sowing, that being reserved for the Lord himself, who is owner of the field. 4. When the wicked have plowed so much of God's husbandry, as he thinketh good to suffer them, then he stoppeth their design, and looseth their plow : *he hath cut asunder the cords of the wicked*. 5. In all the exercise of the church, and in all God's patience towards the persecutors thereof, and in his delivering the church and punishing the wicked, the Lord is upon a laudable work of chastising, humbling, trying, and training his people to better service, and showing his mercy on his people, when they are humbled, and his justice against the wicked : *the Lord is righteous, he hath cut asunder the cords of the wicked*.

5. *Let them all be confounded and turned back that hate Zion :*

6. *Let them be as the grass* upon *the house-tops, which withereth afore it groweth up ;*

7. *Wherewith the mower filleth not his hand : nor he that bindeth sheaves his bosom.*

8. *Neither do they which go by say, The blessing of the Lord be upon you : we bless you in the name of the Lord.*

In the latter part of the psalm he prayeth against all the enemies of the church, and curseth them. Whence learn, 1. All those are the enemies of the church who love her not, who seek not her welfare, who are glad when it goeth ill with her, and envy her prosperity : *they hate Zion*.

2. Confusion of face and destruction shall be their portion, who are enemies to God's people, and the church may lawfully pray for it in the general: *let them all be confounded, and turned back, who hate Zion.* 3. Albeit the trouble of the church, which she sustaineth by persecution, seem long, yet the time of the persecutors is but short, like the time of *grass on the house top which withereth ere it grow up;* their glory is but a vain show, like the greenness of *grass on the house top;* their high place is their ruin, as the house top exposeth the *grass* on it, to the greater heat of the sun; their strength wanteth root, *like the grass on the house top, which withereth before it grow up, wherewith the mower filleth not his hand, nor he that bindeth sheaves his bosom.* 4. To salute the reapers of the field, or any within the visible church, whom we find about their lawful labour or employment, and to pray God to speed them and bless them, is not unlawful, nor a taking of God's name in vain, when done honestly; for, in the psalmist's days, it was the laudable custom of God's people, as they went by the reapers of the field, to say, *The blessing of the Lord be upon you, we bless you in the name of the Lord.* 5. It is no small loss, which the wicked persecutors of the church sustain by this, that their work is not blessed unto them by the Lord, and that they should want the benefit of the prayers of the church: for *they shall be as the grass,* which cometh to no ripeness nor good fruit, whereupon any man can crave a blessing from God unto them: they who go by them at this their work, shall not say, *The blessing of the Lord be upon you, we bless you in the name of the Lord.*

PSALM CXXX.

A Song of Degrees.

This psalm containeth the exercise of the psalmist, wrestling under the sense of sin with fearful temptations, which were like to overcome him, wherein he prayeth for relief, v. 1, 2; opposeth God's mercy to his justice, v. 3, 4; and waiteth for comfort, v. 5, 6; then he bringeth forth the use which he maketh of the relief and comfort which God gave him, by encouraging the church to trust in God's mercy, because he will deliver his people from all trouble and sin, v. 7, 8.

1. *Out of the depths have I cried unto thee, O Lord.*

2. *Lord, hear my voice ; let thine ears be attentive to the voice of my supplications.*

In the first two verses we have his distress, and prayer for relief in general terms. Whence learn, 1. The dearest saints of God have been hardly exercised by trouble in their spirits, and brought into danger of desperation sometimes, while they seemed to themselves to be in a lost condition, like a man ready to drown in deep waters: *out of the depths did I cry unto thee, O Lord.* 2. How desperate soever our condition, or the case of our soul seem to us to be, yet should we not cease from prayer unto God : *out of the depths have I cried unto thee, O Lord.* 3. Albeit our prayers seem to us sometimes to be misregarded by God, and neglected, yet should we not give way to such thoughts as those, but should double our petitions so much the more, that temptations dissuade us to pray, as the psalmist did : *Lord, hear my voice, let thine ears be attentive to the voice of my supplications.*

3. *If thou, Lord, shouldest mark iniquities, O Lord, who shall stand?*

4. *But* there is *forgiveness with thee, that thou mayest be feared.*

In these two verses, we have the objection made against his prayer, from the consciousness of his sins, according to the law, and his answer to the objection from the mercy of God, according to the grounds of the gospel. Whence learn, 1. Sin furnisheth ground to all our vexations, temptations, and objections made against our prayers, our comfort, and our faith : as the experience of the psalmist teacheth us, against whom the iniquities here stood up, to hinder his answer from God. 2. In the case of conscience, wherein sin is justly charged upon us, there is no shift for us to deny or excuse sin : it must be confessed and laid open before God, as the psalmist doth here. 3. If the Lord should deal with supplicants in the way of strict justice, according to the tenor of the law, or covenant of works, no man could escape condemnation and the curse: *if thou, Lord, shouldest mark iniquities, O Lord, who shall stand?* that is, no man shall stand. 4. He who is fled for refuge to God's mercy according to the covenant of grace in Christ Jesus, may decline judgment according to the covenant of works, and betake himself to the way of justification by faith, according to the covenant of grace, whereby remission of sin is promised to the believer : *if thou, Lord, shouldest mark iniquities, O Lord, who shall stand? but there is forgiveness with thee.* 5. The belief of God's mercifulness openeth our mouth in prayer, and encourageth us to the hearty worship, service, and obedience of God, whereunto otherwise we could never have heart nor hand : *but forgiveness is with thee, that thou mayest be feared.* 6. Grace and mercy in God are rightly made use of, when we fear to offend God, so much the more as we believe him to be gracious to forgive the penitent supplicant : *forgiveness is with thee, that thou mayest be feared.*

5. *I wait upon the Lord, my soul doth wait; and in his word do I hope.*

6. *My soul waiteth for the Lord, more than they that watch for the morning;* I say, more than *they that watch for the morning.*

Having prayed and wrestled by faith against the terror of God's justice, the psalmist waiteth for a good answer, and for consolation. Whence learn, 1. Albeit the Lord doth not at first heal the conscience of sin, and the smart of it, yet the believer may surely expect comfort from him : *I wait for the Lord.* 2. Faith doeth its own part when it frameth the heart to patient waiting on God, and hope in him : *my soul doth wait.* 3. He that waiteth for a good answer from the Lord, must have the word of promise made in the gospel to such as seek mercy from God, for the warrant of his hope : *my soul doth wait, and in his word do I hope.* 4. He that waiteth on God for comfort, should persuade himself of his speeding, and must not slack his hope for a delay, but grow in desire after the Lord, more than the watchman waiteth for the morning : *my soul waiteth for the Lord more than they that watch for the morning ; I say, more than they that watch for the morning.*

7. *Let Israel hope in the Lord : for with the Lord* there is *mercy, and with him* is *plenteous redemption.*

8. *And he shall redeem Israel from all his iniquities.*

In the latter part of the psalm, it is presupposed he hath gotten comfort, and here he exhorteth all the Lord's people to follow his example in the day of their outward trouble and perplexity of conscience, assuring them of grace to be found in God to their full satisfaction. Whence learn, 1. When God hath delivered us out of straits, it is our duty to extend the fruit of that mercy as far as we may, and to exhort others according to our place to follow the way of faith in God : *let Israel hope in the Lord.* 2. Mercy, according to the covenant of grace, giveth the same ground of hope to every one within the church, which it giveth to the psalmist, or to a writer of the Scripture : *let Israel hope in the Lord, for with the Lord there is mercy,* saith the psalmist from his own experience. 3. So many straits as the Lord's people can fall into, so many escapes and deliveries hath the Lord in store for them : *with him is plenteous redemption.* 4. As sin is the root of all trouble, and the chief evil of God's people; so the remission of sin is the chief cure of all their trouble, and this the believer may be sure of : *he shall redeem Israel from iniquities.* 5. When the Lord forgiveth sin to his own, he forgiveth all sin, less and more, whereof his believing child is guilty : *he shall redeem Israel from all his iniquities.* 6. The delivery of God's people from sin and trouble floweth all from the covenant of redemption, and every delivery of them is a part of the execution of that covenant : *with him is plenteous redemption, and he shall redeem Israel from all his iniquities.*

PSALM CXXXI.

A Song of Degrees of David.

1. *Lord, my heart is not haughty, nor mine eyes lofty ; neither do I exercise myself in great matters, or in things too high for me.*

2. *Surely I have behaved and quieted myself, as a child that is weaned of his mother : my soul is even as a weaned child.*

3. *Let Israel hope in the Lord from henceforth and for ever.*

HH

In this psalm, the prophet, minding to teach the godly to be humble before God, however matters go with them, propoundeth his own example, v. 1, 2; so that the believer may persevere in hope, v. 3. He proveth his humility by lowliness of heart, sobriety of carriage, and keeping himself within his vocation, v. 1 ; and, by the submission of his will to God's dispensation, v. 2, the use and profit whereof, as he had found in his own experience, so he recommendeth the following of his example to all God's people, as the way to be constant in their hope, v. 3. Whence learn, 1. Albeit pride be a rife vice, which attendeth vain man in every degree of excellence and supposed worth in him, yet the grace of God is able to keep humble a wise, rich, and potent man, yea, to keep humble a king and conqueror; for it is David who saith here, *Lord, my heart is not haughty.* 2. He who will approve himself to God in his humility, must purge from pride his heart as the fountain, and his eyes and outward carriage also, that they be not the signs and tokens of pride, and must watch over his actions, that they go not without the bounds of his calling and the commission given him in God's word : *Lord, my heart is not haughty, nor mine eyes lofty, neither do I exercise myself in great matters, or in things too high for me.* 3. Albeit the most excellent of men are but witless, weak, and unclean things, comparable to young children lately weaned from the breasts, yet it is the property of the godly to know this, and acknowledge himself to be *as a child that is weaned of his mother.* 4. The Lord is as a mother, wise and tender toward his children, dealing with them as their age, weakness, witlessness, and other necessities require : for so much the similitude leadeth us to. 5. The godly must not look to be satisfied in their childish will and appetite, but must resolve to be deprived of their carnal comforts, which naturally they most affect, as a child weaned is put from the breast to a more hard diet : this the comparison importeth. 6. The humble man must be content to be handled and dealt with as the Lord pleaseth, and to submit himself absolutely to God's dispensation ; he must depend upon his care and favour, and wait for the manifesting of it, when and how it shall please God to dispose, and this most of all proveth humility : *my soul is even as a weaned child.* 7. The peace and quiet comfort of humility is such, that the humble man from his own experience may encourage every man to follow that way, with confidence to find the benefit of it: for, *let Israel hope in the Lord,* saith the psalmist here, from his own experience. 8. The servant of God who desireth to persevere to the end, must wait on God in the way of humility, and hope in him unto the end: *let Israel hope in the Lord, from henceforth and for ever.*

From this doctrine we may have the description both of a proud and a humble man. He is a proud man, who, being ignorant or insensible of his sinfulness and infirmities, lifteth up himself in vain confidence to follow some unwarrantable course for satisfying his own mind, and who will not submit himself to God's dispensation. Again, he is a humble man, who, in the sense of his sins and infirmities, standeth in awe of God, keepeth himself within the bounds of his calling and commission, renounceth all confidence in his own wit, and submitteth to God's dealing, in hope to be helped by God in all things, as he standeth in need.

PSALM CXXXII.

A Song of Degrees.

In this psalm the church is taught to pray, according to the covenant made with David, representing Christ, first, for the maintenance of true religion, to v. 10; next, for the continuing of the kingdom in his race, and the preservation of the church of Israel, and so of the kingdom and church of Christ figured by it. In the first petition he prayeth for the Lord's affectionate and effectual remembrance of David, and of the sufferings undergone by David for maintaining his covenant with God, v. 1. Then he calleth to mind the care which David had in settling the place of God's worship, v. 2—5. Thirdly, he showeth how, after the Lord's departing from Shiloh, his ark was found in Kirjath-jearim, and thence brought up to the city of David, v. 6. Fourthly, the church professeth her willingness and purpose to worship the Lord, now ascended to mount Zion, v. 7, 8. And fifthly, the psalmist prayeth for holiness of doctrine in the Lord's ministers, and joy to the godly in obeying them, v. 9. In the next petition, first, the church prayeth for the covenant's sake made with David, that the Lord would not withdraw countenance from his offspring, v. 10. Then, to strengthen her faith in the petition, she repeateth the covenant of God made with David, as we have it, Psal. lxxxix, concerning his offspring, and mainly concerning Christ, v. 11, 12. Then she prayeth concerning the temple and city of Jerusalem, representing the universal church, v. 13, 14; concerning his ministry, v. 15, 16; and concerning the increase of Christ's kingdom, and for confusion of his enemies, v. 17, 18. For we must not conceive this prayer delivered to the church for the use of all ages, to have its full accomplishment, except Christ, his church, and kingdom be mainly comprehended and aimed at in it.

From the whole psalm in general, learn, 1. There is a perpetual kingdom and priesthood appointed to be established among the people of God in his church, as the prayer given to the church, to be applied and made use of in all ages, giveth us to understand : and this is the kingdom and priesthood of Christ. 2. As the evident appearing of this kingdom and priesthood of Christ should be dear to the hearts of all God's children, so should supplication daily be made to God, that this his kingdom may come, with its own blessing following upon it, as the church is taught here.

1. *Lord, remember David,* and *all his afflictions :*

In the first petition, learn, 1. Seeing the covenant made with David, especially concerning sure mercies, was known mainly to belong to Christ, and to concern the church and every member thereof ; it is wisdom for the church in all ages to look to her interest in this covenant, and to hold up before God the memory and use thereof, as here the church is taught to do : *Lord, remember David,* that is, remember the covenant made with David in type, and with Christ represented by him. 2. Albeit the Lord can properly forget nothing, yet he is said to remember, when he by effectual working testifieth his not forgetting ; this is the remembrance which the saints here pray for : *Lord, remember David.* 3. The covenant made with David and with Christ, consisteth well with afflictions probatory on David's part, and expiatory on Christ's part ; and neither the one sort nor the other wanted their own weight with God; but Christ's afflictions, being redemptory and meritorious, are most to be heeded by the church : *remember David, and all his afflictions.* 4. Whatsoever care the godly have to promote God's honour; whatsoever grief and sorrow they bear when they find opposition, or want success in this their endeavour ; whatsoever trouble and persecution they suffer in maintaining or promoting God's cause—all is reckoned up to them as parts of service, which God will not forget to follow with mercy to them, and to theirs after them : *Lord, remember David, and all his afflictions.*

2. *How he sware unto the Lord,* and *vowed unto the mighty* God *of Jacob ;*

3. *Surely I will not come into the tabernacle of my house, nor go up into my bed;*

4. *I will not give sleep to mine eyes, or slumber to mine eyelids,*

5. *Until I find out a place for the Lord, an habitation for the mighty God of Jacob.*

In the second place is set down the care which David had to settle the worship of God in the land. What time this vow or oath was made by David, is not specified in any other place of Scripture, neither is it needful for us to be curious about the time or form of words : for the meaning is not as if David on a certain day, being ignorant of the place of settling God's ark and building the temple, limited God to reveal it to him ere night came; but the meaning is, that David swore to have a care of the settling of God's ark before he settled his own house, and that he would not enjoy the commodities which his royal palace (not as yet built) might yield him, before he saw the ark settled in the place where the temple should be built. Whence learn, 1. It is lawful to tie ourselves by an oath to that duty, whereunto we were absolutely tied by law before; yea, and it may sometimes be expedient to tie ourselves to a duty by swearing, for evidencing our hearty purpose to follow that duty cheerfully, and for stirring up ourselves so much the more to follow it, as we are conscious of our slackness in it, or feebleness to resist temptations; for here David *sware unto the Lord,* that he would discharge such a duty. 2. A lawful vow is a part of divine worship, due to be made to God alone; for David offered this religious worship to God only : *he vowed unto the mighty God of Jacob.* 3. The omnipotence of God is the treasure of the church's strength, wherein every believer hath an interest : *he is that mighty one of Jacob.* 4. The care of God's public worship, and of establishing religion where we have place and power, should be more earnest and greater in every true subject of God's kingdom, than the care of his own private affairs; and in case of competition and comparison, the settling of God's worship should be preferred before our settling in any worldly commodity : as the example of David here teacheth us.

6. *Lo, we heard of it at Ephratah ; we found it in the fields of the wood.*

In the third place, the church speaketh and compareth the settled condition of the ark now with the fleeting condition wherein it was before. For it was some time in Shiloh, in the tribe of Ephraim, and now it is said, *lo, we heard of it at Ephratah :* and when it was in a manner lost, being taken by the Philistines, it is said, the church found as a thing once lost, the ark in Kirjath-jearim, or city of the woods: *we found it in the fields of the wood ;* and now it is settled, it will be said, we know where to find it established. That this is the church's meaning is given us to understand in the next verse, wherein it is said, *we will go up into his tabernacles.* Whence learn, 1. The presence of the Lord in his ordinances was never so fixed in any place, but that mercy may be turned into a story of it : *it was or hath been :* if it be abused, as what the Lord did to his house in Shiloh was a history in the days of the kings, *lo, we have heard of it* (that is, of the ark of the covenant) *at Ephratah.* 2. When once the Lord hath flitted the tokens of his presence far out of a land, it is a rare mercy and unexpected, and no less than is the finding of a treasure, or of a lost jewel, to see the restoring of his ordinances again, as was to be seen when God brought back the ark from the Philistines to Kirjath-jearim; which mercy the church here acknowledgeth : *we found it in the fields of the wood.* 3. The way of God, about the showing of his presence in his holy ordinances in any place, is not as men may expect, but as God seeth good to dispose, as the church's speech giveth us to understand : *we found the ark in the fields of the wood.*

7. *We will go into his tabernacles ; we will worship at his footstool.*

8 *Arise, O Lord, into thy rest ; thou, and the ark of thy strength.*

In the fourth place, the church stirreth up herself to worship God in Zion, where the ark representing Christ was placed, praying now for the benefit of God's presence, as Moses prayed at the marching and settling of the ark. Whence learn, 1. When God hath revealed his will in any point of religion, we should without delay or dispute follow his direction, as the church doth here, when the ark is settled in Zion: *we will go into his tabernacles.* 2. Where the Lord hath promised to be found, there must we come and keep trust with him, and worship him : *we will go into his tabernacles, we will worship at his footstool* 3. The true worshipper must lift his mind above every external and visible ordinance of God, and seek him in heaven where his glory shineth most, counting all things on the earth no more but as his footstool; for so was the church of old directed to do, when they had the Lord most sensibly manifesting himself in his tabernacle and temple: *we will worship at his footstool.* 4. The church in after ages may call for, and expect the like benefit of God's presence with his ordinances, which his church in former ages hath found, as the prayer of the church here, being one with the prayer of the church in the wilderness, teacheth us : " arise, O Lord," as Moses said when the ark removed. 5. The ark of the covenant was the figure of God incarnate, the type of Christ in whom the fulness of the Godhead dwelleth bodily, and therefore, after the manner of sacraments, the sign receiveth the name of the thing signified : *arise, O Lord, thou and the ark of thy strength.*

9. *Let thy priests be clothed with righteousness; and let thy saints shout for joy.*

Now the psalmist closeth the first petition with a prayer for God's blessing his ministers, and their ministry among the people. Whence learn, 1. Where the Lord is received, he must have ministers, men set apart for his public worship and service, as the prayer for the priests presupposeth. 2. The chief badge and cognizance of the Lord's minister, is the true doctrine of justification and obedience of faith in a holy conversation : *let thy priests be clothed with righteousness.* 3. People have reason to rejoice, who have the benefit of such approved ministers ; and whosoever really embrace the true doctrine of justification by grace, whereby men justified by faith become the servants of righteousness in their life, are indeed saints, and are called to rejoice : *let thy priests be clothed with righteousness, and let thy saints shout for joy.* 4. It is the duty of the whole church to pray for such a ministry, and for such effectual blessing following on it, as may make sinners become saints, and sad souls to sing for joy, as here is prayed for.

10. *For thy servant David's sake turn not away the face of thine anointed.*

The second main petition is for the manifestation of God's respect to David's offspring, wherein, under the figure of David's successors in the kingdom, he prayeth for the kingdom of Christ, as before he prayed for his priesthood. Whence learn, 1. Every faithful member of the church should pray, as for the church's welfare, so also for the welfare of the supreme magistrate, and of the civil state whereof they are members; for so runneth the prayer here in the figure: *turn not away the face of thine anointed;* to wit, the king of Israel, for whom they pray, that he be not put to shame by disappointment of his hopes. 2. The Lord's anointed, or the supreme ruler of the Lord's people, should be a daily supplicant unto God, and a depender upon him; for the petition presupposeth that his face was toward the Lord praying to him and waiting for good from him: *turn not away the face of thine anointed.* 3. The Lord's covenant is of great respect with God, and should be made much use of by us, as here we are taught: *for thy servant David's sake, turn not away the face of thine anointed,* that is, for the covenant's sake made with David in the type, and with Christ represented by him, refuse not his lawful petitions. 4. The truth intended in the type, teacheth us that the intercession of Christ for his subjects shall never miscarry, nor shall Christ be refused in what he willeth to be done to or for his subjects; for in him the prayer is surely heard; Christ, that anointed one, cannot be refused, nor any who truly pray in his name.

11. *The Lord hath sworn* in *truth unto David; he will not turn from it; Of the fruit of thy body will I set upon thy throne.*

12. *If thy children will keep my covenant and my testimony that I shall teach them, their children shall also sit upon thy throne for evermore.*

From strengthening of faith in this petition, the psalmist calleth to mind more particularly the covenant of God with David. Whence learn, 1. Every word and circumstance of God's promise is worthy to be looked upon and well considered, as this example teacheth us. 2. Whosoever seek a benefit, according to God's word, ought firmly to believe the promise of it, and to rest upon the stability of the promise, as here we find the example: *the Lord hath sworn, he will not turn from it.* 3. Albeit the promise that Christ should come of David be absolute, and settled with an oath, yet the promises of temporal things made to David, are conditional; as God should see fit to give them, and as his children should carry themselves in God's obedience, so should they have temporal benefits, and succeed him in the temporal throne: *if thy children will keep my covenant and my testimonies, thy children also shall sit upon thy throne for evermore.*

13. *For the Lord hath chosen Zion ; he hath desired* it *for his habitation.*

14. *This* is *my rest for ever : here will I dwell ; for I have desired it.*

He giveth a reason for the absolute promise of Christ's coming to rule the spiritual kingdom of Israel, or the church, because the Lord hath chosen Zion in the type, and the universal church under the figure, to be his chosen temple and habitation, wherein he delighted.　Whence learn, 1. Where God will settle his sanctuary there will he settle his kingdom also : Zion must not want a king; for the reason here, why the Lord will with an oath set up one who shall be the fruit of David's body upon the throne, is, *because he had chosen Zion.* 2. The Lord's pitching upon any place to dwell in, or persons to dwell among, cometh not of the worthiness of the place or persons, but from God's good pleasure alone; *for the Lord hath chosen Zion, he hath desired it for his habitation.* 3. The Lord resteth in his love toward his church, accepting the persons, prayers, and services of his chosen people : he smelleth a sweet savour of Christ here, and his love maketh his fear among his people steadfast : *this is my rest, I have desired it.* 4. What is promised under typical figures, is really everlasting, not in regard of the figure, but in regard of the signification : *for this is my rest for ever,* is true only in respect of the church, represented by Zion. 5. No reason is to be craved for God's everlasting good-will to any person or incorporation; his pleasure may suffice for a cause: *this is my rest for ever, here will I dwell, for I have desired it, or have pleasure in it.*

15. *I will abundantly bless her provision : I will satisfy her poor with bread.*

16. *I will also clothe her priests with salvation; and her saints shall shout aloud for joy.*

The rest of the articles of the Lord's covenant with David, are so many promises which the Lord maketh concerning the blessing of the ministers of Christ unto the church's good, and the increase of Christ's kingdom, in despite of his enemies, in the last verses.

From the promise made concerning the blessing of the ministry for the people's good, learn, 1. The true subjects of Christ, shall not want the means of spiritual life, spiritual meat, drink, clothing, and whatsoever is necessary for their salvation : *I will abundantly bless her provision.* 2. The dispensation of good things to God's children, is such as shall make them sensible of their own insufficiency ; they are not exempted from feeling their wants, and being in straits, but as they feel their need, so shall they be provided for : every evil which they feel, shall have a perfect remedy in Christ, and in his word which shall satisfy the needy soul : *I will satisfy her poor with bread.* 3. Christ's church shall neither want ministers, nor shall his sent ministers want commission for teaching saving truth, but shall be clothed with authority to preach and proclaim salvation to the believers : *I will also clothe her priests with salvation.* 4. The ministers of righteousness teaching the true way of justification, and obedience of faith, are also the ministers of salvation : for *clothing of her priests with righteousness,* v. 9, is here, *the clothing of them with salvation.* 5. Comfort and joy shall the Lord's people have, who embrace a ministry clothed with commission to hold forth to them righteousness and salvation in Christ: *her saints shall shout aloud for joy.*

17. *There will I make the horn of David to bud : I have ordained a lamp for mine anointed.*

18. *His enemies will I clothe with shame : but upon himself shall his crown flourish.*

From the promise made in favour of Christ's kingdom, learn, 1. As Zion in the type was the place where Christ manifested himself king of Israel, so also the church mainly signified by it, is the place and incorporation, wherein Christ is to be seen manifestly to be king : *there will I make the horn of David to bud.* 2. The glory of typical David's

kingdom, was revived in Christ the true David; the budding of Christ's kingdom in Jerusalem, was the budding
of David's kingdom in a more glorious way than ever his
temporal kingdom flourished : *there will I make the horn
of David to bud.* 3. That she hath Christ for her king,
is the crown and accomplishment of the church's felicity :
there will I make the horn of David to bud. 4. How
low soever Christ's kingdom can be brought in the world,
yet it is fixed as a well rooted tree, it is rooted as the horn
of a unicorn; although it may seem gone, or so weak as
it cannot subsist, yet it shall bud and grow in despite of all
opposition : *there will I make the horn of David to bud.*
5. It is no wonder to see adversaries opposing Christ's kingdom, for it is here foretold and presupposed, *his enemies
will I clothe with shame.* 6. Albeit the enemies of Christ
promise to themselves advantage, by their opposition made
to Christ, and hope to overturn his kingdom; yet have
they all been, and shall be ashamed for ever of their expectation, whosoever hate his kingdom : *his enemies will I
clothe with shame,* which they shall not be able to hide,
but must put on and walk therein, as a man doth in his
garments. 7. The more Christ is opposed, the more shall
his splendour and glory grow in the world : *but upon himself shall his crown flourish.*

PSALM CXXXIII.
A Song of Degrees of David.

1. *Behold, how good and how pleasant* it is *for
brethren to dwell together in unity !*

2. It is *like the precious ointment upon the head, that
ran down upon the beard,* even *Aaron's beard ; that
went down to the skirts of his garments ;*

3. *As the dew of Hermon,* and as the dew *that descended upon the mountains of Zion : for there the Lord
commanded the blessing,* even *life for evermore.*

This psalm fitteth the condition of God's people, in
David's time, when after their civil wars they were brought
to a happy unity in religion and civil government. This
sort of concord and communion of saints is here commended
to the church as both pleasant and profitable. The goodness of it is spoken of, v. 1; the pleasantness of it, v. 2;

the profitableness of it, *v.* 3.   Whence learn, 1. Those are most fit to put a price and right estimation upon peace and concord, who have seen and felt the evil of discord and contention, as David's experience proveth; for this is a psalm of David, who had proof both of war and peace.   2. The fruits of peace in the reformation of religion and civil judicatories, so redound to the comfort of all families and private persons, that the good of concord may be demonstrated sensibly : *behold, how good it is!*   3. Such a concord is genuine, and worthy of the name, which uniteth the members of the visible church, as brethren, or children of one father, in the true religion, for the mutual discharge of all the duties of love : *how good is it for brethren to dwell together in unity!*   4. Some things are pleasant and not profitable, and some are profitable and not pleasant, but the concord of God's people, or holy peace within the visible church in any place, is both pleasant and profitable : *behold, how good and how pleasant it is, for brethren to dwell together in unity!*   5. This blessing is not to be expected by any, but through Christ, on whom the oil of gladness, and all the graces of the Spirit are first poured out, and then from him are carried to the meanest member of his body; as Aaron's head being anointed with oil, the benefit of it extended itself to the uttermost borders of his garments; for the similitude borrowed from Aaron's anointing, as the type of Christ, teacheth us so much : *it is like the precious ointment, &c.* And this similitude representeth the pleasantness of concord, the sweet smell whereof refresheth all that have any spiritual sense.   6. As dew maketh the herbs and trees to flourish, for the use of man; so is concord profitable to Church and State : *as the dew of Hermon, or dew that descended upon the mountains of Zion.*   7. Where holy concord maketh its residence among brethren dwelling together in unity, there the blessing of the God of peace in this life, and for the life to come, makes its residence also : *there the Lord commanded the blessing, even life for evermore.*   8. This blessing of brethren living in the unity of the Spirit and bond of peace, is not promised only, but there also is an everlasting order given forth from the supreme Ruler of all things, for forthwith applying the blessing effectually to those that thus live together : *there the Lord commanded the blessing, even life for evermore.*

PSALM CXXXIV.

A Song of Degrees.

In this short psalm, the Spirit of the Lord, by the mouth of the psalmist, exhorteth the Lord's ministers to go about the exercise of their public ministry, in praying, preaching, and praising God, v. 1, 2; and in blessing the congregation met together, v. 3.

1. *Behold, bless ye the Lord, all* ye *servants of the Lord, which by night stand in the house of the Lord.*

2. *Lift up your hands* in *the sanctuary, and bless the Lord.*

From the exhortation of the Lord's ministers, learn, 1. The public worship of God is to be carefully looked to : and all men, but especially ministers, had need to be stirred up to take heed to themselves, and to the work of God's public worship when they go about it : for so much, *behold,* in this place importeth. 2. The scope and special end of public worship, are to set forth the blessedness of God in himself, and in his operation for and toward his church : for all the parts of public worship and service, in prayer, reading of Scripture, preaching, praising, and thanksgiving, singing of psalms, and blessing the people, aim at this : *behold, bless ye the Lord.* 3. The discharging of the public worship of God, requireth that there be public ministers, appointed by God, and separated unto this holy function : *bless ye the Lord, all ye servants of the Lord.* 4. It was commanded in the law, Exod. xxvii. 20, 21, that so soon as daylight began to fall at even, lamps should be lighted, and shine all night in the tabernacle, till the morning ; and that the priests and Levites should in course wait upon his service, that there might not be darkness in the Lord's house, but light always night and day. Whereby was signified, that howsoever the world lieth in the darkness of ignorance, of sin and misery, yet in the Lord's church remedy against all those evils, and relief from them is to be had; and that God hath ordained ministers and public officers, to entertain and hold forth the shining of the light to the church; and for this end not to hesitate to break their night's rest, when the service calleth for it : *bless the Lord, all ye servants of the Lord, which by night stand in the house of the Lord.* 5. Prayer to God, as the mouth of the people, is a part of the office of the Lord's ministers; for so much is imported by pointing at the gesture of the supplicant : *lift up your hands in the sanctuary,* that is, in the place where the people assemble. 6. To praise the Lord, and to teach the people what the Lord is, what blessedness is to be found in him, and how they should acknowledge this, and make use of it, is another part of the minister's office : *lift up your hands in the sanctuary and bless the Lord.*

3. *The Lord, that made heaven and earth, bless thee out of Zion.*

In this verse the Lord's ministers, as directed, go about to bless the people out of *Zion,* in the name of the Lord : *out of Zion,* because there was the ark of the covenant, the figure of Christ, God incarnate, through whom alone the Lord's blessing is derived to his church. Whence learn, 1. All men lie under the curse, till God bring them into the fellowship of his church, and pronounce them blessed by his word, as *the Lord bless thee,* importeth. 2. It is a part of the office of the Lord's ministers, to pronounce with authority God's blessing upon his people, which is no more than a wish or prayer for them ; for they are sent of God with commission to say, *the Lord bless thee.* 3. No blessing is to be expected but from Christ, represented by the ark of the covenant, which was in *Zion : the Lord bless thee out of Zion.* 4. The confidence of the believer to obtain whatsoever is promised in the Lord's word, is built on the covenant and omnipotence of God : and what can a soul stand in need of, which this fountain cannot yield ? *the Lord that made heaven and earth, bless thee out of Zion.*

PSALM CXXXV.

The scope of this psalm is to set forth the praises of the Lord: wherein there is an earnest exhortation to all the church and all the Lord's ministers to praise God, v. 1—3 ; whereunto are added seven motives or reasons, from v. 3 to 12. In the next place, the psalmist turneth his speech towards the Lord, and praiseth him; and giveth two reasons more for praising God, v. 13—18. In the third place, more specially he exhorteth the ministers, and every particular member of the church, to praise God, and so closeth with blessing him.

1. *Praise ye the Lord. Praise ye the name of the Lord ; praise* him, *O ye servants of the Lord.*

2. *Ye that stand in the house of the Lord, in the courts of the house of our God.*

In the exhortation directed to the whole church, and to the ministers, learn, 1. The work of praising God should be gone about affectionately, and unto it should we stir up ourselves and others, with all our might : as this manifold exhortation *to praise the Lord, and sing praise*, teacheth us. 2. That which is spoken or manifested by God, must be carefully taken notice of, that he may be praised out of knowledge : for he will not have praises, but as his word directeth : for this, *praise the name of the Lord*, importeth. 3. The public ministers of God's house, who are set apart for teaching and leading the people in his service, by reason of their office and employment, stir up themselves to this work of praising God, whatsoever may be their own private condition, sad or joyful ; for their obligation so to do is greatest : *praise him, O ye saints of the Lord, O ye servants of the Lord.* 4. As our privileges are more than the rest of the world, by being in covenant with God and admitted to have room in the holy assemblies of his people, so should our care to praise God be the greater : *ye that stand in the house of the Lord, in the courts of the house of our God.*

3. *Praise the Lord; for the Lord* is *good; sing praises unto his name ; for* it is *pleasant.*

The psalmist insisteth in the exhortation, and beginneth to give reasons to move us to praise God. Whence learn, 1. The Lord is worthy to be praised, not only for his essential goodness, but also for bestowing it on his creatures, and, most of all, on his people : *praise the Lord, for the Lord is good :* and this is the first reason or motive to praise. 2. Singing the Lord's praises is a part of the moral worship of God, and should be done with cheerfulness of heart, as a work wherein we rejoice to be employed : *sing praises unto his name.* 3. The work of praising God hath a sort of reward joined with it : when we praise God most, we get much benefit by so doing : it is so comely in itself, so pleasant to God, and so profitable to the person that offereth praises—so fit to cheer up his spirit, and strengthen his faith in God, whose praises are the pillars of the believer's confidence and comfort—that a man should be allured thereunto: *sing praises unto his name, for it is pleasant*; and this is the second motive or reason to praise God.

4. *For the Lord hath chosen Jacob unto himself,* and *Israel for his peculiar treasure.*

The third reason of praising God is, because he hath, by electing *Israel*, put a great respect and price upon his people. Whence learn, 1. The Jews have distinguished honour put upon them, (how unworthy soever they have proved themselves of it many times,) above all the nations of the world, in that God hath chosen them to be his people, among whom he will always have a chosen number, which of no other nation can be said: *for the Lord hath chosen Jacob unto himself.* 2. The Lord's covenanted people are no less precious in his eyes, than a peculiar treasure is in a man's eyes: *he hath chosen Israel for his peculiar treasure.*

5. *For I know that the Lord* is *great, and* that *our Lord* is *above all gods.*

The fourth reason of God's praise, is, because the Lord is greater than all earthly, yea than all imaginable excellences in the world—the church both believeth and knoweth by experience. Whence learn, 1. The largeness of God's dominion over all nations, and over all imagined excellency of the idols of the Gentiles, commendeth the mercy of God to that nation which he preferreth to the rest, by taking them into covenant with himself: *the Lord is great, and our Lord is above all gods.* 2. As the Lord, by his extraordinary working for his people, maketh manifest his glorious and great majesty to them, so should they so much the more for their experience praise him before all the world: *for I know that the Lord is great, and our Lord is above all gods,* importeth not only the psalmist's belief of the point, and experience of the truth thereof, but also his practice of the duty.

6. *Whatsoever the Lord pleased,* that *did he in*

*heaven, and in earth, and in the seas, and in all deep
places.*

The fifth reason of God's praise, serving also to confirm
the former reason, is, because God is the omnipotent Creator, and absolute Governor of all things, disposing of them
as he pleaseth. Whence learn, 1. The great works of creation, sustentation, and governing all things, show the Lord's
greatness, and furnish matter of his praise : *whatsoever the
Lord pleased, that did he in heaven and in earth, in the
sea, and in all deep places.* 2. The Lord's will and pleasure are the measure of the extending of his omnipotence,
and no further must we extend his power unto action, than
his revealed will giveth warrant : *whatsoever the Lord
pleased, that did he.* 3. The Lord's will is the sovereign
and absolute cause of all his working, and that whereon all
men's faith and reason must rest : *whatsoever he pleased,
he did.*

7. *He causeth the vapours to ascend from the ends
of the earth : he maketh lightnings for the rain : he
bringeth the wind out of his treasuries.*

The sixth reason of God's praise, is, because there is no
motion in the clouds or in the air, but what he maketh.
Whence learn, There are none of the motions of the creatures so light or variable, which are not wrought by God,
and wherein his providence putteth not actually forth itself
in vapours, clouds, rain, lightnings, winds, and all : *he
causeth the vapours to ascend from the ends of the
earth, he maketh lightnings for the rain, he bringeth the
winds out of his treasuries.*

8. *Who smote the first-born of Egypt, both of man
and beast.*

9. *Who sent tokens and wonders into the midst of
thee, O Egypt, upon Pharaoh, and upon all his servants.*

10. *Who smote great nations, and slew mighty
kings ;*

11. *Sihon king of the Amorites, and Og king of
Bashan, and all the kingdoms of Canaan :*

12. *And gave their land* for *an heritage, an heritage unto Israel his people.*

The seventh reason of God's praise is for his wonderful redemption of his people out of Egypt, powerful overthrow of the Canaanites, and placing his people in their room. Whence learn, 1. The Lord's working for his church in former times, is matter of praising God in all after ages: as this example of mentioning so oft the *slaughter of the first-born of Egypt, both man and beast,* teacheth. 2. God's working for his people is such, that their enemies being posed, must acknowledge his wonderful acts: *he sent tokens and wonders in the midst of thee, O Egypt, upon Pharaoh and all his servants.* 3. When God engageth for his people, he will overtop the mightiest kings and kingdoms, and tread them under in favour of his church: *who smote great nations, and slew mighty kings, Sihon king of the Amorites, and Og king of Bashan, and all the kingdoms of Canaan.* 4. The care of God for his people is indefatigable ; he ceaseth not to prosecute begun favours, till he bring them to an end ; he followeth Israel's redemption out of Egypt, till he give them possession of Canaan. 5. Albeit there be difficulties and opposition to the settling of God's people in their possession, yet the work goeth on, and must be perfected; and the close of God's work is no less glorious than the beginning of it : *he gave their land for an heritage, an heritage unto Israel his people.*

13. *Thy name, O Lord,* endureth *for ever ;* and *thy memorial, O Lord, throughout all generations.*

In the second place, the psalmist turneth his speech toward the Lord, and praiseth him yet more: and then, in the following verses addeth other two reasons for his praising God. From this verse, learn, 1. What the Lord declareth himself to be in one generation toward his church, may and should be a means to know what he will do in all time to come for his people, as need shall require : *thy name, O Lord, endureth for ever, and thy memorial, O Lord, throughout all generations.* 2. As the constancy of God's love toward, and care for his people, is a matter of high praise to God; so it is a matter of sweet refreshing joy to the believer, which maketh him look up kindly to

God, and praise him ; as here the psalmist in praising God's constancy, turneth his speech twice toward him : *O Lord, O Lord.*

14. *For the Lord will judge his people, and he will repent himself concerning his servants.*

The first new reason of God's praise, is the hope that the Lord will plead the cause of his afflicted people, and comfort them. Whence learn, 1. Bypast mercies of God are rightly made use of, when they strengthen faith and hope in God for mercies to come : as here we see the Lord's memorial made use of, for the church's present comfort. 2. Wheresoever God's people are oppressed by their enemies, howsoever God hath just quarrel against his people, yet will he examine what moved his enemies to trouble them : and albeit he at first give not out sentence, yet he will execute justice in favour of his people in due time : *for the Lord will judge his people*, by pleading their cause against their enemies. 3. The constancy of God's love to his people, makes the change of his sad dispensations into more comfortable ones certain : and therefore God's afflicting of his people, is a work wherein he will not continue, because his mercy toward his people is everlasting : *for the Lord will judge his people, and he will repent himself concerning his servants.* 4. As it is a sort of grief to God to afflict his people, so it is a sort of comfort to him to comfort his people, by delivering them from their sad affliction ; for the words, *repent himself*, signify in the original also *to comfort himself.*

15. *The idols of the heathen* are *silver and gold, the work of men's hands.*

16. *They have mouths, but they speak not : eyes have they, but they see not :*

17. *They have ears, but they hear not ; neither is there any breath in their mouths.*

18. *They that make them are like unto them :* so is *every one that trusteth in them.*

The second new reason of God's praise is taken from the baseness of all idols compared with God, and of all idolaters compared with his servants. Whence learn, 1. True worshippers of God detest images and idols, and all false religions, how gorgeously soever they be decked up by idolaters : *the idols of the heathen are silver and gold, the work of men's hands.* 2. How delectable soever the invention of images, or worshipping of idols seem to be, yet these vanities bring nothing to the worshippers save grief and vexation : for so their name in the original importeth. 3. Worshippers of images are not esteemed according to their intention and profession, when they say they worship the thing represented by them, but are to be judged by God's verdict of them, who hath pronounced their gods to be no other thing than their images, which are shaped by the artificer like a man : *they have mouths, but they speak not, &c.* 4. Idolatry is a benumbing sin, which bereaveth the idolater of the right use of his senses and reason : *they that make them are like to them.* 5. Beside outward worship offered by idolaters to their images, they are found to offer them also the inward worship of their souls : *they trust in them ;* and, by trusting in them, or looking for any good from them, they are but brutish, or like senseless blocks ; *so is every one that trusteth in them.*

19. *Bless the Lord, O house of Israel : bless the Lord, O house of Aaron :*

20. *Bless the Lord, O house of Levi : ye that fear the Lord, bless the Lord.*

21. *Blessed be the Lord out of Zion, which dwelleth at Jerusalem. Praise ye the Lord.*

In the close of the psalm, the psalmist exhorteth all ranks of the godly, both public officers and private members of the church, to bless God, and giveth example of obedience in his own person. Whence learn, 1. As the whole incorporation of the church receiveth common benefits from God more than any incorporation beside, and as every rank and order of people receiveth benefits more particularly to itself; so should the whole incorporation together, and every one of every rank give praise unto God, and set forth his blessedness before others, as their vocation permitteth : for, *bless the Lord, O house of Israel,* is spoken to the whole incorporation ; *bless the Lord, O house of Aaron,* speaketh to the priests; and, *bless the Lord, O house of Levi,* is directed to the under officers of God's house. 2. Albeit all men be exhorted, and each person in his own place called upon, yet they only who fear God will discharge the duty conscientiously; therefore, after all it is said, *ye that fear the Lord, bless the Lord.* 3. The true worshipper of God draweth this special point of God's praise from God's manifesting himself to his church in, and through, and for Christ : for this is signified by the types, figures, and tokens of his presence in Zion and Jerusalem: *blessed be the Lord out of Zion, which dwelleth at Jerusalem.* 4. When the song of praise is sung to God, the work of his praise is not ended, but must be continued, renewed, and followed still : *praise ye the Lord.*

PSALM CXXXVI.

This psalm is an exhortation to confess God's goodness and mercy, and to praise and thank him for the manifestation thereof, in so many sundry works of his : upon this ground, because the fountain of his mercy, whence his works flowed, ran still, and endureth for ever, to the benefit of his own people in special. The reasons of the exhortation to thanks and praise are set down in order, so many in number as the verses are, to every one whereof is added one common reason, from the everlasting endurance of his mercy. In the first place, the exhortation is thrice propounded, with reasons taken from the Lord's attributes or names, v. 1—3. In the second place, reasons are given from his works, and in special from the work of creation, v. 4—13. In the third place, reasons are given from the work of the redemption of Israel, bringing them forth out of Egypt, and planting them in Canaan, from v. 10 to 23. In the fourth place, reasons of thanks are given from his late mercy to the church in the psalmist's time, v. 23, 24. And, last of all, a reason is given from his goodness to all living creatures, v. 25; whereupon he closeth with an exhortation unto thanksgiving to the God of heaven, v. 26.

1. *O give thanks unto the Lord ; for* he is *good: for his mercy* endureth *for ever.*

2. *O give thanks unto the God of gods : for his mercy* endureth *for ever.*

3. *O give thanks to the Lord of lords : for his mercy* endureth *for ever.*

From the threefold exhortation to give thanks, with the reasons subjoined thereto, learn, 1. When we have praised God for what reasons we have offered unto us in one psalm, we must begin again, and praise for other reasons; and, when

we have done so, we have not overtaken our task; the duty
lieth still at our door to be discharged afresh, as this psalm
showeth. 2. God is to be acknowledged and praised as the
fountain of the being, continuance, and preservation of all
things that are in the world, and as the performer of all his
promises : *O give thanks unto the Lord Jehovah.* 3. The
knowledge of God's attributes, properties, or name, and in
special of his goodness, is able to draw forth the praise to
God from every believer : *O give thanks unto the Lord,
for he is good.* 4. Neither is God weary of doing good,
nor is his mercy spent, by what he hath already let forth of
it, but it continueth as a river still running : *for his mercy
endureth for ever.* 5. Whatsoever is the Lord's praise is
for our profit and advantage, and so is a matter of thanks
from us to his majesty : *O give thanks unto the Lord, for
he is good.* 6. The Lord is more excellent than all the magistrates, rulers, princes, and kings in the world; yea, he
hath all those perfections joined in one in him, which idolaters feign to be scattered among their idols, of which they
conceive one to excel in one thing, and another in another
thing : *O give thanks to the God of gods.* 7. To whom
the Lord is God by covenant, he is always and for ever their
God : *for his mercy endureth for ever.* 8. God is the
only sovereign Lord of all things, and the only potentate
who hath absolute right, and absolute power to do what he
pleaseth, and can, when he will, overtop all principalities
and powers, to the benefit of his followers : *O give thanks
to the Lord of lords.* 9. The perpetuity of God's mercy
maketh the benefit of God's sovereignty forthcoming for
ever to the believer, and to stand as a matter of constant
praise and thanksgiving to him : *give thanks to the Lord
of lords ; for his mercy endureth for ever.*

4. *To him who alone doeth great wonders : for his
mercy* endureth *for ever.*

5. *To him that by wisdom made the heavens : for his
mercy* endureth *for ever.*

6. *To him that stretched out the earth above the waters : for his mercy* endureth *for ever.*

7. *To him that made great lights : for his mercy*
endureth *for ever.*

8. *The sun to rule by day : for his mercy* endureth *for ever.*

9. *The moon and stars to rule by night: for his mercy* endureth *for ever.*

From the reasons of praise and thanks to be given to God, which are taken from his works of creation, learn, 1. Every work of God is wonderful, and able to make a man astonished, if it be well considered : *to him who doeth great wonders.* 2. Whatsoever instruments 'the Lord is pleased to use in any of his wonderful works, he alone is the worker, and will not communicate the glory of the work to any creature : *to him who alone doeth great wonders.* 3. The constancy of God's mercy to his own, maketh the use of God's wonderful power constantly forthcoming to them, as their need requireth : *for his mercy endureth for ever.* 4. The making of the heaven, as it is a wonderful work, and a matter of constant praise to God, so is it a wondrous benefit unto his people in many respects : *to him that made the heavens.* 5. The wisdom of God appearing in the fabric of heaven, as it is worthy to be praised, because it is of so large a compass, that the motion of it shall be in no way troublesome to man: the stars, so glorious an ornament, so useful to man, and so regular in their motion as is wonderful : *to him that by wisdom made the heavens.* 6. It is the mercy of God that the heavens continue their service to sinful men : *for his mercy endureth for ever.* 7. The earth's standing up above the waters, (which by course of nature should be above the earth,) is a standing miracle for the use of man, that he might have a pleasant dwelling while in the world : *to him that stretched forth the earth above the waters.* 8. It is the mercy of God that the waters do not return to their natural course to cover the earth, as they did in the flood of Noah : *for his mercy endureth for ever.* 9. The illumination of the world by so great lights, as might at once shine upon the one half of the earth, (which otherwise would be in darkness for the most part,) is matter of God's praise and man's profit, deserving thanks from man to God : *to him who made great lights.* 10. It is of the Lord's mercy that he hath not changed this course, nor removed this much abused benefit from us : *for his mercy endureth for ever.* 11. The making the sun to be the fixed fountain of daylight, rather than to serve the world with the light which shined the first three days of the creation, is for the greater benefit of man, as for many other reasons, so for this, that every part of the day might be better distinguished, according to the motion of the body of the sun: *the sun to rule the day*. 12. That God hath not discharged the sun to shine upon sinful men, who deserve to live in darkness, is a proof of his endless mercy to his own: *for his mercy endureth for eper*. 13. The tempering of the darkness of the night by the moon's light, and by the light of the stars in their courses, is matter of God's praise and man's comfort; and the continuing of this favour still, is the evidence of his mercy to his people: *he maketh the moon and stars to rule by night, for his mercy endureth for ever*.

10. *To him that smote Egypt in their first-born : for his mercy* endureth *for ever :*

11. *And brought out Israel from among them : for his mercy* endureth *for ever :*

12. *With a strong hand, and with a stretched-out arm : for his mercy* endureth *for ever.*

13. *To him which divided the Red sea into parts : for his mercy* endureth *for ever.*

14. *And made Israel to pass through the midst of it : for his mercy* endureth *for ever.*

15. *But overthrew Pharaoh and his host in the Red sea : for his mercy* endureth *for ever.*

16. *To him which led his people through the wilderness : for his mercy* endureth *for ever.*

17. *To him which smote great kings : for his mercy* endureth *for ever.*

18. *And slew famous kings : for his mercy* endureth *for ever.*

19. *Sihon king of the Amorites : for his mercy* endureth *for ever.*

20. *And Og the king of Bashan : for his mercy* endureth *for ever.*

21. *And gave their land for an heritage : for his mercy* endureth *for ever.*

22. Even *an heritage unto Israel his servant : for his mercy* endureth *for ever.*

In the reasons of God's praise, taken from the delivery of Israel out of Egypt, conveying them through the wilderness, and planting them in Canaan, learn, 1. The Lord should be praised for the works of creation, as by all men, so especially by those who are partakers of the benefit of redemption; and those only who are sensible of the benefit of redemption, will give him praise for the works of creation and common providence, the fastening of the duty of praise, especially upon Israel, here teacheth us. 2. The Lord's preserving his church from the beginning concerneth the true members of the church in all times after, to be thankful for it, no less than for continuing the course of the heavens, sun, moon, and stars; as the context of the psalm holdeth forth. 3. The Lord's punishing the enemies of his church in Egypt, is an obligation on the church to praise him for ever; and his constant mercy giveth assurance, that he will avenge the quarrel of his oppressed people in all ages : *to him that smote Egypt in their first-born, for his mercy endureth for ever.* 4. The delivery of Israel from the bondage of Egypt, is matter of God's perpetual praise ; and it is a pledge of God's mercy to his church in all ages : *he brought out Israel from amongst them; for his mercy endureth for ever.* 5. As the work of the church's delivery is more difficult, so the Lord putteth forth more clearly his omnipotence for perfecting it, as appeared in Israel's bringing forth out of Egypt, *with a strong hand, and out-stretched arm.* 6. One proof of God's power manifested for his church, is a pledge of his purpose to give so oft proof as need shall be, of his power for his people's relief : *for his mercy endureth for ever.* 7. The most improbable deliverances from danger, are very possible to God, who can turn the sea into dry land for his people's escaping : *to him which divided the sea into parts.* 8. The constancy of God's mercy to his church, maketh his dividing of the sea a pledge of his power and purpose to deliver his church, how great soever her straits shall be : *for his mercy endureth for ever.* 9. To give his people grace to make use of an offered means of delivery is a work of no less mercy and power, than to prepare the deliverance for them; but the constancy of God's mercy doth not only provide the means, but also giveth his people grace to make use thereof in all ages: *he made Israel to pass through the midst of it, for his mercy endureth for ever.* 10. God can make that means which proveth effectual for the safety of his people, to prove a snare to the wicked for their destruction, as the Red sea was a snare to the Egyptians: *but he overthrew Pharaoh and his host in the Red sea.* 11. The constancy of God's mercy toward his people, is a pledge of the constant course of his justice against their enemies: *for his mercy endureth for ever.* 12. As thankfulness maketh search of many mercies in the bosom of one, so the innumerable multitude of God's mercies forceth the thankful man to sum up many mercies in one: as here all the mercies in the forty years' journeying in the wilderness are drawn up in a word: *to him that led his people through the wilderness.* 13. It is the constancy of God's mercy, which maketh him continue the conduct of his people, and bear with their manners, till he put an end to their journey: *he led his people through the wilderness, for his mercy endureth for ever.* 14. The people of God may meet with no less difficulties in their way to heaven, than they have found hindrances to their conversion, as the typical example of Israel's meeting with opposition before they entered Canaan showeth. 15. Albeit kings and potent powers should oppose the settling of God's church in any place where he pleaseth to plant it, yet they shall not be able to hinder his work: for his mercy is forthcoming in one age as well as in another, that praise and thanks may always be given unto him *who smote great kings, for his mercy endureth for ever.* 16. Men of renown lose their credit when they meddle with the Lord's church, and readily they lose their lives also: this should be a document to all mighty men, and a matter of comfort to God's people: *he slew famous kings, for his mercy endureth for ever.* 17. The Lord will have the first opposers of the settling of his people exemplarily punished, and their punishment made no less famous than their sin hath been: *he slew Sihon king of the Amorites:* and the like will the Lord do in all ages against the chief adversaries of his people: *for his mercy endureth for ever.* 18. When judgment upon one enemy

terrifieth not others of them from opposing God's people,
the like destruction shall fall upon those that make head
against the church : *and he slew Og king of Bashan.*
19. The slaughter of the enemies of God's people is the
work of the Lord, whosoever be the instruments ; for it is
not here said that the Israelites slew Sihon and Og, *but the
Lord slew them;* and the like mercy may the church look
for in all ages : *for his mercy endureth for ever.* 20. It
is the Lord who gave heritages at his pleasure, and who
can dispossess such men of their lands, who will not suffer
the Lord's people to inherit the land the Lord hath given
them : *he slew Sihon and Og, and gave their land for
an heritage ;* and the like mercy may the church look for
in all ages, as it shall be found good for her : *for his mercy
endureth for ever.* 21. When the Lord puts down the
enemies, and puts his servants in their place, it is a double
mercy : *he gave the lands of Sihon and Og to be an
heritage unto Israel his servants.* 22. There can no
cause be found in God's people why God should do good to
them, or why he hath done good to them, but the constancy of his own mercy only : *for his mercy endureth for
ever.*

23. *Who remembered us in our low estate : for his
mercy* endureth *for ever.*

24. *And hath redeemed us from our enemies : for
his mercy* endureth *for ever.*

In the reasons for God's praise taken from the late experience of the church in the days of the psalmist, learn,
1. Unto whatsoever praise we can give to God for what he
hath done before our time, we should add praises also for
what the Lord hath done for us in our time, as here the
church in the psalmist's days to all the former addeth this :
who remembered us in our low estate. 2. The season
and ordinary time of the Lord's manifesting himself for his
people is, when they are brought low, and emptied of their
own strength, and of all hope of worldly assistance : *who
remembered us in our low estate.* 3. The Lord's presence, help, and assistance, good-will, and respect to us, is
better observed by afflicted people than by prosperous : for
troubles, necessities, and straits are means to open men's
eyes, and waken up their senses, to take up the worth of
the Lord's working : *he remembered us in our low estate.*

4. The mercy of the Lord is set on work for his people, both to sustain them in adversity, and raise them out of it; and to maintain them in prosperity, and teach them the good use of it, in looking wisely on God's dealing with them in both conditions: *he remembered us in our low estate, for his mercy endureth for ever.* 5. Albeit the proud enemies of the church may prevail, and bring the church into bondage for a time, yet the Lord will not suffer the enemy to oppress, nor his people to be oppressed always, but will deliver his own in due time, as here: *he hath redeemed us from our enemies.* 6. The same reason and cause is to be found of the delivery of Israel out of Egypt, and of the delivery of the church at any time from their enemies, and that is mercy only: *for his mercy endureth for ever.*

25. *Who giveth food to all flesh: for his mercy* endureth *for ever.*

In the reason of God's praise taken from his goodness to all living creatures, learn, 1. The Lord's goodness and fatherly care of all living creatures, is worthy to be marked and made use of for his praise, in special the giving to all living creatures their own food convenient for them, and that in due season every day: *who giveth food to all flesh.* 2. The mercy of the Lord toward his children, is the cause of his care and respect to such other creatures as man hath need of: *for his mercy endureth for ever.* 3. The care which God hath of all flesh to give them their food, is a ground of assurance to the people of his far greater care of them: *for his mercy endureth for ever,* to them.

26. *O give thanks unto the God of heaven: for his mercy* endureth *for ever.*

From the close of the psalm, learn, 1. Heaven and heavenly gifts are the height of all the felicity of the saints, and the flower of all God's benefits to his children, for which above all other favours he is to be thanked and praised by his people: *O give thanks unto the God of heaven.* 2. God is the strong God of heaven, not only because he made the heaven, and showeth his glory most there, but especially because he hath promised to give heaven, and all spiritual graces with eternal life in heaven, to his own people by an everlasting covenant; of which heaven and heavenly mercies he is God: *O give thanks unto the*

God of heaven. 3. As mercy hath entitled the saints to heaven, so mercy preserveth them in their right, and will preserve them in the possession thereof for ever: *for his mercy endureth for ever.*

PSALM CXXXVII.

This psalm may be divided into three parts. In the first part, is set down the lamentable condition wherein the Lord's people were in their captivity in Babylon, ver. 1—3. In the next, is their constancy in religion, ver. 4—6. In the third, is their denouncing of judgment by way of imprecation against the instruments and chief authors of their calamity, ver. 7—9.

1. *By the rivers of Babylon, there we sat down; yea, we wept, when we remembered Zion.*

In the first part, wherein the sorrowful condition of the captive church of God is set down, learn, 1. The people of God by their sins may procure the taking away of the face of a visible church from them, and the taking away of their civil liberties, and may procure banishment from their own country among idolaters, as the captivity of the Jews in Babylon showeth. 2. When men do not make use of the privileges of God's public worship, it is righteousness with God to remove those much abused favours, and to cast the abusers thereof out among idolaters, as here the Jews were, who, because they made not use of Jerusalem, the vision of peace, are thrust out into Babylon, a place of all confusion. 3. When the Lord's people provoke God against them, the wickedest wretches and vilest idolaters in the world may overcome them in a battle, and rule over them as over slaves: as the experience of the Jews proveth. 4. When desolation is brought upon God's people, it is no wonder to see them remain in that condition for a time, and not delivered immediately out of it: *by the rivers of Babylon there we sat down.* 5. The public miseries of the church, are causes of heaviness to the true members thereof, and motives of mourning: *there we sat down, yea, we wept.* 6. Comparison of a prosperous condition bypast, with adversity present, augmenteth misery and increaseth grief, especially when bypast mercies abused are compared with just judgments inflicted in the place thereof: *we wept*

when we remembered Zion. 7. They who will not esteem
the privileges of Zion when they have them, will be forced
to acknowledge the worth thereof with sorrow when they
want them : *we wept, when we remembered Zion.*

2. *We hanged our harps upon the willows in the
midst thereof.*

The Lord's people carried with them into their captivity
their harps; first, as means of stirring up their affections,
in their private worship of God; secondly, in hope to have
some use of them afterward in the Lord's worship, in their
own land; and, thirdly, that thereby they might make profession before their oppressors of religion, and of their hope
of restitution in God's appointed time, albeit they could not
frame their heart for the present to rejoice as they were
wont to do. Whence learn, 1. Means to help in private
devotion must be the more made use of, that public means
are wanting : for the Jews, debarred from the temple, carry
their harps with them into their scattering and captivity.
2. In the midst of our calamity, we ought both to have hope
of deliverance out of our trouble, and to profess it before
those that have us under their power; for so did the captive Jews in their captivity : they carried their harps into
Babylon. 3. There are times when the signs of our joy
may be suppressed, and the signs of our sorrow expressed :
we hanged our harps on the willows. 4. The most lawful and commendable sorrow, is that which is felt for the dishonour of God and the desolation of the church : *when we
remembered Zion, we hanged our harps.* 5. No natural
comfort, nor invitation to carnal joy can counterbalance the
causes of spiritual grief ; neither rivers, nor the shadow of
willows, nor any thing else can stay the godly grief of God's
captive people : *we hanged our harps upon the willows,
in the midst thereof.*

3. *For there they that carried us away captive required of us a song, and they that wasted us required
of us mirth,* saying, *Sing us* one *of the songs of Zion.*

Their affliction was augmented by the insulting of the
Babylonians over them, calling for a song from the Jews, to
feed their godless mirth. Whence learn, 1. Ofttimes sorrows go not single, but one grief is joined to another, one

deep calleth to another : as here, insultation of the Babylonians is joined with the bondage and captivity of God's
people. 2. As the sorrow of the godly is the matter of the
laughter and joy of their enemies, and no sport to the wicked
is so relishing as a jest broken upon true religion; so no
affliction is so heavy to the godly, as to find their own sin
drawing not only misery on themselves, but also dishonour
upon their religion : as here we see, the Jews hung up
their harps, and why ? *for they that carried us away captive, required of us a song : and they that wasted us,
required of us mirth, saying, Sing us one of the songs
of Zion.* 3. Corrupt nature maketh no other use of spiritual things, than thereby to satisfy their sensual desires : as
here, it is mirth and singing only, for which the Babylonians
seek to hear a psalm sung : *sing us one of the ;songs of
Zion.*

4. *How shall we sing the Lord's song in a strange
land?*

5. *If I forget thee, O Jerusalem, let my right hand
forget her cunning.*

6. *If I do not remember thee, let my tongue cleave
to the roof of my mouth ; if I prefer not Jerusalem above
my chief joy.*

In the second place, wherein the Jews' constant profess-
sion of their religion is set down, and their refusing to satisfy their enemies' desire, in prostituting the Lord's worship to their carnal pleasure, learn, 1. Albeit we be under
the feet of our enemies, and albeit we have drawn on our
misery by our sinning, yet must we neither deny our religion, nor any part thereof, for fear of man, nor subject it
to men's pleasure, as they think good to direct us in it,
whatsoever may be the danger ; for so the example of the
captive people of God teacheth us, refusing to sing psalms
at the desire of the Babylonians : *how shall we sing the
Lord's song in a strange land?* 2. The place where
God is not worshipped, should be a strange land to us his
people, and no place should be kindly or comfortable to us,
but where the Lord's people may enjoy the liberty of public worship, and the communion of saints: *how shall we
sing the Lord's song in a strange land?* 3. Whatsoever
be our own private condition, worse or better, it must not

take up the room in our affection which is due to the church; it must not make us forget the affliction of *Joseph*, for that were to provoke God to make those benefits useless to us, that diverted us from sympathy with the church : *if I forget thee, O Jerusalem, let my right hand forget her cunning;* or if the church of God, and the good of it, be not preferred above our own private gratification, it shall be righteousness with God to turn the means of our private pleasure to be the means of our private grief : *if I do not remember thee, let my tongue cleave to the roof of my mouth, if I prefer not Jerusalem above my chief joy.* 4. To seek men's favour to the detriment of any point of religion, or to consent to men's encroachment upon matters of religion, that we may have their favour, or that we may be freed from their trouble, or sit at more ease under them, is to forget God and his church, and the respect we owe to God and his church : as we are taught by the example of the Jews, refusing to sing psalms at the Babylonians' desire or direction, and expounding their obedience to the Babylonians in this point, to be nothing else but a forgetting of *Jerusalem*, and a denying of their religion, if they had yielded.

7. *Remember, O Lord, the children of Edom in the day of Jerusalem; who said, Rase it, rase it, even to the foundation thereof.*

8. *O daughter of Babylon, who art to be destroyed; happy shall he be that rewardeth thee as thou hast served us.*

9. *Happy shall he be that taketh and dasheth thy little ones against the stones.*

In the imprecation used against the enemies of the church, and in particular against their false brethren, the Edomites, who helped on their affliction, and against the Babylonians, who were the chief oppressors of them, learn, 1. False brethren are the chief instruments of persecution of the true members of the church, wheresoever they find occasion, as the Edomites, the posterity of *Esau*, proved in the destruction of *Jerusalem : remember, O Lord, the children of Edom.* 2. Whosoever delight in the church's calamity, and attempt the church's ruin by word or deed ; by their stirring up others to afflict her ; or by any oppression, which may tend to the church's prejudice, when the Lord is visiting her, their sin shall not be forgotten by God in the day when the Lord judgeth his people, but shall be severely punished: *remember, O Lord, the children of Edom, in the day of Jerusalem.*   3. No less will suffice the adversaries of the church than the utter ruin, and rasing of her to the ground: *who said of Jerusalem, Rase it, rase it, even to the foundation thereof.*   4. The state of the church at the worst is better than that of *Babylon,* or any state of her adversaries, how prosperous soever, at the best ; for, albeit the church be in captivity and oppressed, yet she shall not be destroyed, but it is not so with her adversaries: but, *O daughter of Babylon, who art to be destroyed.* 5. Faith is neither blinded by the prosperity of the wicked, nor by the adversity of the church, but seeth through the prospect of the Lord's word, both the approaching delivery of the church, and the ruin of her enemies : for, *O daughter of Babylon, who art to be destroyed,* showeth the captive Jews so much.   6. As the enemies of God's church have measured out to the Lord's people, so shall it be measured back again and more, for a reward to her adversaries: *happy shall he be that rewardeth thee as thou hast served us.*   7. There is a happiness, wherein blessedness consisteth not, which is neither a part nor branch of blessedness, nor a proper mark of blessedness, but only signifieth some happiness in consequence of man's work, tending to the glory of God and good of his church; and such is the happiness of the Medes and Persians here spoken of, who, whatsoever were their corrupt intentions in their war, albeit not as religious servants, yet as God's instruments, a good work of justice on the oppressors of God's people, and a good work of delivery of the Lord's people : *happy shall he be that taketh and dasheth thy little ones against the stones.*   8. Albeit it be a sinful thing to satisfy our carnal affection in the misery of any man ; yet it is lawful in God's cause to wish that God be glorified, albeit in the confusion of his enemies : and here there is great need to have the heart well guarded with the fear of God, for, otherwise to allow *the dashing of little ones against the stones,* might make a man guilty of savage cruelty.

II

PSALM CXXXVIII.
A Psalm of David.

This psalm is David's thanksgiving to God, and praising of him for the
experience he had of his love and faithfulness. The promise of praise
or thanksgiving, is set down, v. 1; and six reasons are subjoined in the
verses following, which are closed with a prayer in the end of the psalm.

1. *I will praise thee with my whole heart: before
the gods will I sing praise unto thee.*

In the promise of praising God, learn, 1. It is a part of
our thankfulness, to engage our heart to praise God for
after time, when we find that all the thanks we can give for
the present, are short of our duty or desire to praise him :
I will praise thee, saith *David.* 2. As the believer will
sometimes find his heart set at liberty in God's worship,
which at another time he will find to be in bands, so should
he take the opportunity of an enlarged heart, to run in the
way of God's service, as *David* doth here : *I will praise
thee with my whole heart.* 3. Albeit the faces of princes,
rulers, and magistrates, usually in some measure restrain
the liberty of speech which men usually take before mean
persons, and albeit princes ordinarily love rather to hear
themselves praised by flatterers, than to hear either God or
man magnified in their audience; yet a heart enlarged with
the sense of God's majesty, greatness, and goodness, will
not hesitate to confess and proclaim God's truth, greatness,
and goodness, and other points of his praise, in the audience
of the greatest men on earth, although they should think
themselves cried down, and more lightly esteemed, by this
means : *before the Lord will I sing praise to thee.*

2. *I will worship toward thy holy temple, and praise
thy name for thy loving-kindness, and for thy truth :
for thou hast magnified thy word above all thy name.*

The psalmist engageth himself also to the public ordinary
worship of God, according to God's command, and then
giveth the reasons of his engagement. Whence learn, 1.
Worship of God in secret is indeed necessary, but it is not
sufficient for the man who mindeth thankfulness to God,
except he follow the public means also, and that after the
way which is prescribed by God, directing all his service to
be offered to God through Christ : for this is imported in

David's worshipping toward the ark, which was placed in the tabernacle or temple : *I will worship toward the holy temple, and praise thy name.* 2. The experience of the Lord's kindness and faithfulness in his promises made to the people, is a lively motive to believers to praise him : *I will praise thy name for thy loving-kindness and thy truth.* 3. There is more to be seen and felt in the experience of God's children, than they could promise to themselves out of God's word ; for they find that God in effect is better in his payment than in his promises ; for thus much this commendation importeth : *thou hast magnified thy word above all thy name* ; that is, I have found more effect in the performance of thy promise, than the promise seemed to me to hold forth in thy name, and this is the first reason of David's engagement to thankfulness.

3. *In the day when I cried thou answeredst me,* and *strengthenedst me* with *strength in my soul.*

The second reason of David's thanksgiving is more special, because God had upheld him by his inward comfort in the time of his trouble, and had answered his prayer graciously. Whence learn, 1. The Lord usually puts his children to straits before he deliver them, that he may be seen more clearly to be their deliverer : for, David cried to the Lord, before the answer of his ordinary and daily prayer was given him : *in the day when I cried,* saith he. 2. To be supported in trouble, and to have strength to bear out in trouble, till the full delivery come, is a real and remarkable answer from God to his people's prayers : *in the day when I cried, thou answeredst me, and strengthenedst me with strength in my soul.* 3. Albeit before the outward and complete delivery come, the passages of God's secretly sustaining a man be not well marked, yet when they are looked back upon in the clear light of accomplished deliverance, the least degrees of delivery and secret support of the man under trouble, will appear clearly to be answers of prayer, and begun delivery ; as David here observeth, and giveth account thereof : *in the day when I cried, thou answeredst me, and strengthenedst me with strength in my soul.*

4. *All the kings of the earth shall praise thee, O Lord, when they hear the words of thy mouth.*

5. *Yea, they shall sing in the ways of the Lord: for great is the glory of the Lord.*

The third reason of David's thanksgiving is, because he foreseeth, in the spirit of prophecy, how great glory, praise, and thanks the Lord shall have when he shall convert the Gentiles, and reveal his words and works to them. Whence learn, 1. The foresight of the glory which God shall have in the world before its end, by the promised propagation of his gospel, should stir up all who believe the approaching glory of God to magnify and praise him in their own time : for the foresight of the glory of God to be manifested among the Gentiles is here the matter of the song of David and the church of the Jews : *all the kings of the earth shall praise thee, O Lord.*   2. When the glory of the Lord is seen, it outshineth all the glory in the world : for kings, when they see God's glory, shall fall down and praise God : *all the kings of the earth shall praise thee, O Lord.*   3. It is the word of God mainly which showeth forth the glory of the Lord, and maketh his works wonderful : *all the kings of the earth shall praise thee, when they hear the words of thy mouth.*   4. Albeit the knowledge of God, which cometh only by his works, be able to convince even the heathen of the Lord's care over his people, and to astonish them ; yet not the knowledge of the Lord which cometh by his works, but that which cometh by the hearing of the word of the Lord, is able to convert a man, make him walk in the obedience of faith, rejoice in God, and sing his praises cheerfully : *when they hear the words of my mouth, they shall sing in the ways of the Lord.*   5. The glory of the Lord which is manifested in his word, is the highest glory which is manifested to the world ; for, after all the glory of his works of creation and providence, which the word holdeth forth, it showeth forth the glory of God's grace and mercy to the self-condemned sinner, which mercy to the penitent soul, in some respect, is above all God's works : for, in this respect it is here said, *great is the glory of the Lord.*

6. *Though the Lord be high, yet hath he respect unto the lowly : but the proud he knoweth afar off.*

A fourth reason of David's thanksgiving and praising
God is for his different dealing with the humble and proud.
Whence learn, 1. Albeit the Lord be so highly exalted above
all the creatures, as it is a sort of humbling himself to behold his creatures, even in the heavens, yet he is so good
and gracious, that his superlative grandeur hindereth not
his taking notice of the meanest lost sinner who humbleth
himself before him : *though the Lord be high, yet hath
he respect unto the lowly.* 2. The greatness of the majesty of God commendeth his humility, and the Lord's looking low for the good of the poor supplicant, commendeth
his greatness, and maketh it more lovely : for it is here put
for a point of his praise, *that though the Lord be high,
yet hath he respect unto the lowly.* 3. The Lord observeth the disposition of men who are proud and who are humble before him; for this the text pointeth at. 4. The humble lose nothing by their humility, nor do the proud gain
any thing by their pride; but, on the contrary, the humble
find grace, and the proud are resisted by God : *he hath
respect to the lowly, but the proud he knoweth afar off.*
5. Pride excludeth a man from access to God, and a proud
man cannot have communion with God : *he knoweth the
proud afar off.*

7. *Though I walk in the midst of trouble, thou wilt
revive me : thou shalt stretch forth thine hand against
the wrath of mine enemies, and thy right hand shall
save me.*

The sixth reason of David's giving thanks and praise to
God, is his confidence that whatsoever trouble he shall fall
into hereafter by his enemies, the Lord will sustain him under it, and deliver him out of it. Whence learn, 1. It is a
good use of bypast experience to cherish hope to be helped
of God in time to come; as the example of David here
teacheth us. 2. Whatsoever trouble a man hath been in,
he may fall into as great or greater afterward; yea, he may
possibly be in a comfortless condition, and helpless and
hopeless for anything that can be seen, yea, and be compassed about with trouble on all hands, yea, he may faint
under the burden, and be as a dead man; for thus much
David presupposeth may be his condition afterward: *though
I walk in the midst of trouble.* 3. How great soever,

and how many soever straits and difficulties the believer can forecast and foresee, he may promise to himself as great and as many supplies of strength, and deliveries from God : *though I walk in the midst of troubles, thou wilt revive me*, that is, thou wilt put new life and comfort in me. 4. Against the power and wrath of adversaries, God's power and good-will are a sufficient guard, succour, and relief : *thou shalt stretch forth thine hand against the wrath of mine enemies, and thy right hand shall save me.*

8. *The Lord will perfect* that which *concerneth me : thy mercy, O Lord,* endureth *for ever : forsake not the works of thine own hands.*

The sixth reason of his giving thanks and praise, is his confidence of the Lord's constantly continuing with him, and making him persevere in God's obedience to the end, which he closeth with a prayer that he may persevere. Whence learn, 1. The believer's heart cannot be quiet till it be sure of perseverance, and of this he may be made assured : for the same Spirit of grace which hath made him see the Lord's engagement for him in time past, can give certainty of the continuing of God's grace in time to come : *the Lord will perfect that which concerneth me :* he findeth a work of God's love to him already begun, and then gathers hence that the Lord will perfect that work of grace which he hath begun. 2. The believer buildeth not his hope of perseverance upon any strength or constancy in himself, but upon the unchangeableness of God's everlasting mercy, as here David showeth us : *the Lord will perfect that which concerneth me,* why, and upon what ground is he so confident ? *Thy mercy, O Lord, endureth for ever.* 3. True assurance of perseverance must be joined with the sense of a man's own weakness, and unworthiness, and ill-deserving (if God should deal with him in justice); yea, it must be joined with dependence upon God in faith and prayer, and use of the means; for such was the assurance which David had, who, after he had said, *the Lord will perfect that which concerneth me,* subjoineth, *forsake not the work of thine own hands,* which importeth so much. 4. Faith hath always, for its own strengthening, to make use of all bonds betwixt God and itself as a creature, and in special as a new creature, so that, seeing his calling and gifts are without repentance, he may make out the work of grace and salvation, where he hath begun it, as David teacheth us : *forsake not the work of thine own hands.*

PSALM CXXXIX.

A Psalm of David.

David being wickedly slandered and persecuted by his adversaries, findeth his zeal kindled against them : and, lest his own heart's corruption should deceive him, as being carnal in this matter, he presenteth his heart to God, the all-seeing and everywhere-present judge of the secrets of all hearts; and he presenteth also his adversaries, both persons and cause, with his own carriage toward them to be tried by God, praying that himself may be directed toward life everlasting.

In the first place, the omniscience of God is declared, v. 1—6. In the next, the omnipresence of God, with his omniscience, is set forth, v. 7—12. In the third place, the reason is given of God's very exact knowledge of all the secrets of his heart, which is because the Lord formed and fashioned him, in so wonderfully wise and powerful a way, as he could neither express nor comprehend, v. 13—18. In the fourth place, he confesseth to God his judgment of wicked men, and his hatred of their ways, making God, who is the searcher of hearts, witness and judge of his sincerity, corrector and director of his course toward everlasting life, v. 19—24.

1. *O Lord, thou hast searched me, and known* me

2. *Thou knowest my down-sitting and mine up-rising : thou understandest my thought afar off.*

3. *Thou compassest my path, and my lying down, and art acquainted* with *all my ways.*

4. *For* there is *not a word in my tongue, but, lo, O Lord, thou knowest it altogether.*

5. *Thou hast beset me behind and before, and laid thine hand upon me.*

6. Such *knowledge* is *too wonderful for me ; it is high, I cannot* attain *unto it.*

In David's acknowledgment of God's omniscience and perfect knowledge of every thing in him, and in his betaking himself to God, for clearing him, comforting him, and bearing him through all calumnies and reproaches, learn, 1. The godly may sometimes be so overclouded with calumnies and reproaches, that they cannot find a way to clear themselves before men, but must comfort themselves with the testimony of a good conscience, and with God's approbation of their integrity, as David doth here, saying, *O Lord, thou hast searched me and known me.* 2. As the knowledge which the Lord hath of us is most accurate, having, as it were, a perfect searching joined with it; so the belief of this point is necessarily to be applied to ourselves, that it may rule our conversation, impart to us comfort and peace, and confidence in our approaches to God, whosoever be against us, as David's example here teacheth us. 3. The Lord is acquainted with all the motions of the external man; the meanest gesture of the body falleth under his cognition and observation : *thou knowest my down-sitting and my up-rising.* 4. Whatever advisements we are upon, whatever consultations and deliberations we are about, the Lord knoweth all perfectly before we conclude anything : *thou understandest my thoughts afar off.* 5 The Lord not only observeth our aim and scope, but also how we purpose to convey out matters, and how we go on and proceed in accomplishing our purposes—what rule we follow or reject, from the morning to the evening : *thou compassest my path, and my lying down.* 6. The Lord knoweth us so well, that the best knowledge which our entire friend can have of us, to whom we communicate our mind, and who knoweth all our design and way to go about it, is but a shadowing similitude of God's knowledge of us : *thou art acquainted with all my ways.* 7. There is not a word which we speak, either idle or to purpose, but the Lord considereth it perfectly : *for there is not a word in our tongue, but lo, O Lord, thou knowest it altogether.* 8. We are so enclosed within the view of God's eye, so compassed by his providence, and so powerfully ruled by his power, that we cannot turn this way or that way, but we are still in his sight, and under his disposal : *thou hast beset me behind and before, and laid thy hand upon me.* 9. The knowledge which God hath of us and our ways, is so minute and perfect, so far above our capacity, that we cannot comprehend the manner of it : *such knowledge is too wonderful for me.* 10. When we are about to look upon God's perfections, we should observe our own imperfections, and thereby learn to be the more modest in our searching into God's unsearchable perfection : *such knowledge* saith David, *is too high for me, I cannot attain unto it.* 11. We see most of God, when we view him as incomprehensible, and see ourselves swallowed up in the thoughts of his perfection, and are forced to fall into admiration of God, as here : *such knowledge is too wonderful for me, it is high, I cannot attain unto it.*

7. *Whither shall I go from thy Spirit? or whither shall I flee from thy presence?*

8. *If I ascend up into heaven, thou* art *there : if I make my bed in hell, behold, thou* art there.

9. If *I take the wings of the morning,* and *dwell in the uttermost parts of the sea ;*

10. *Even there shall thy hand lead me, and thy right hand shall hold me.*

11. *If I say, Surely the darkness shall cover me ; even the night shall be light about me.*

12. *Yea, the darkness hideth not from thee ; but the night shineth as the day : the darkness and the light* are *both alike* to thee.

In David's setting forth the Lord's omnipresence and omniscience to be such that he cannot escape his sight and power, learn, 1. The right making use of God's all-seeing providence, and everywhere presence, is, to consider our duty to walk before God, as in his sight always, and not to seek to hide ourselves, or our counsel from him, as David doth here : *whither shall I go from thy Spirit, or whither shall I flee from thy presence?* 2. Whosoever walk in the darkness of their own devices, and misregard God in their ways, as if they might escape his sight, or eschew his hand, are much mistaken; for there is no place of refuge from his pursuing : *whither shall I go from thy Spirit, or whither shall I flee from thy presence?* 3. Neither men's presumption and blessing themselves in courses not allowed by God, nor their estimation of high preferment in church or state, (which are a sort of a man's lifting up himself to heaven,) can avail a man, when he cometh to be tried before God : *if I ascend to heaven, thou art there ;* where fugitives from God cannot have place. 4. A man's base condition and meanness in the world, or his desperate resolution to perish, provided he can have his will for a time, yea, his desperate despatching himself when he is incurably miserable, will not avail a man, nor carry him through; for God fastening the man in the misery which he hath resolved to endure, will make him find that he hath too sore a party: *if I make my bed in hell, behold, thou art there.*   5. Changing from place to place, and fleeing from one country to another, or going to such solitary places where no man resorteth, cannot deliver a man from God's pursuing and overtaking him: *if I take the wings of the morning and dwell in the uttermost parts of the sea, even there shall thy hand lead me, and thy right hand hold me.*   6. Whithersoever a man shall go, he must be furnished with power and strength from God to go thither: for, *there shall thy hand lead me,* importeth so much.   7. God's power and justice shall ever be a man's master, go whithersoever he may: *thy right hand shall hold me.* 8. The fugitive sinner hath many devices in his head, to elude God's sight and justice, and all to deceive himself, and will run from one shift to another before he turn to God; and his thoughts of God's presence are so gross, as, among other thoughts, to think himself hid in the night from God; but in all, poor fool, he is deceived: *for if I say S urely the darkness shall cover me, even the night shall be light about me ; yea, the darkness hideth not from thee, but the night shineth as the day, the darkness and the night are both alike to thee.*

13. *For thou hast possessed my reins: thou hast covered me in my mother's womb.*

14. *I will praise thee ; for I am fearfully* and *wonderfully made ; marvellous* are *thy works; and* that *my soul knoweth right well.*

15. *My substance was not hid from thee, when I was made in secret,* and *curiously wrought in the lowest parts of the earth.*

16. *Thine eyes did see my substance, yet being unperfect ; and in thy book all* my members *were written,* which *in continuance were fashioned, when* as yet there was *none of them.*

17. *How precious also are thy thoughts unto me, O God ! how great is the sum of them !*

18. If *I should count them, they are more in number than the sand : when I awake, I am still with thee.*

In the third place, where the psalmist giveth a reason for God's exact knowledge of, and power over him, because he hath formed him in the belly wonderfully, learn, 1. Since God hath made us in the womb, and we live, and move, and subsist by his power, God must know our words, works, and thoughts, and all—and have us always in his sight and under his power: *for thou hast possessed my reins, thou hast covered me in my mother's womb.* 2. The knowledge of God, and his government of the creature, is not like a man's, who setteth himself for a while on this object, and then turneth off to another object, but God's knowledge and government are a settled possessing of his own workmanship, by a constant beholding, by a settled ruling of his work, by a constant maintaining and judging of the most secret motion of a man's spirit : *for thou hast possessed my reins, thou hast covered me in my mother's womb.* 3. In framing our bodies in our mother's womb, the Lord covered his tender work with his mighty power from all inconveniences, as with a shield : *thou hast covered me in my mother's womb.* 4. The right sight of God's workmanship in our very bodies, will force us to praise God's unspeakable wisdom : *I will praise thee; for I am fearfully made.* 5. When God is seen in his glory in anything, his majesty becometh terrible to the beholder, his glory is so bright: *I am fearfully made.* 6. As the Lord's rare works, without considerance, look to a man very common-like ; so his common works, being well considered, become very wonderful : *I am wonderfully made.* 7. The right sight of any one of God's works, giveth light to all his works, showing them all wondrous : *marvellous are thy works.* 8. The consideration of God's work in our bodies, well digested, is profitable for our souls : *and that my soul knoweth right well.* 9. As the Lord acquainteth us with his works, we should observe them well, and bear witness to what we observe for his glory, as David doth, saying, *and that my soul knoweth right well.* 10. In framing our bodies God knoweth what he is making ; neither darkness nor distance of heaven from earth, nor any other impediment, hindereth him in his working: *my substance was not hid from thee, when I was made in secret.* 11. The making of a man's body of so many bones, arteries, veins, sinews, &c., is a most curious piece of work: *I was curiously wrought in the lowest parts of the earth.* 12. God seeth things before they are made, and his purpose to make hath no less clearness of knowledge of the thing to be made, than the substance of it, when it is made, can give ; and God in his decree to do, knoweth the thing to be done, as fully as when it is done : *thine eyes did see my substance, yet being unperfect, and in thy book all my members were written, which in continuance were fashioned, when as yet there was none of them.* 13. The Lord's decrees of things to be done, are so clear, so determinate, so certain, as if the description and history of the thing already come to pass were written in a book : for so much the comparison, taken from a written book to show the nature of God's decrees, importeth : *in thy book all my members were written, which in continuance were fashioned, when as yet there was none of them.* 14. There is rare wisdom to be learned out of God's decrees and works : *how precious are thy thoughts unto me ?*   15. What pains a man taketh in the searching thereof, is well recompensed with pleasure and profit, as David's experience teacheth. 16. We should study this wisdom till we find it sweet, and then lay it up as a precious jewel in our mind, when we have found it : *how precious also are thy thoughts unto me, O God ?*   17. All God's revealed decrees, are the matter of the believer's comfort and his joy, how harsh soever they seem to the unbeliever and unrenewed man : *how precious also are thy thoughts unto me, O God ?*   18. The particulars of God's purpose and decreed will toward his own children, which from time to time come to light, as they are revealed by the daily execution of them, are innumerable : *how great is the sum of them ? if I should count them, they are more in number than the sand.* 19. Albeit the most vigilant of the saints sometimes fall into drowsiness and sleepiness of spirit, so that they cannot perceive God's presence with them, care of them, and love to them, yet, when the Lord wakeneth up their souls, and reneweth their spiritual senses, they are forced to see and acknowledge that the Lord never leaveth them, even when they least perceive his presence ; *for when I am awake, I am still with thee,* importeth all this.

19. *Surely thou wilt slay the wicked, O God: de-*
part from me therefore, ye bloody men.

20. *For they speak against thee wickedly,* and *thine*
enemies take thy name *in vain.*

In the last place, the psalmist confesseth his judgment of,
and affection toward, his adversaries, and offereth all to be
searched and approved of God, and himself to be directed
thereafter unto life everlasting: and, first, he showeth his
judgment of his adversaries, and the reason of his abhorring
the fellowship of their courses. Whence learn, 1. Where we
perceive wickedness reigning, there we may be assured destruction will follow : *surely thou wilt slay the wicked, O*
God. 2. When we pass our judgment of men's persons
and conduct, we had need to conform our judgment to
what we know the Lord will allow, as here the psalmist
doth, directing his speech to God. 3. When the Lord will
comfort his servants under persecution, he will let them see,
not only their own blessedness in himself, but also the destruction of their enemies approaching, as here we see. 4.
When we see destruction attending upon the way wherein
others are walking, we ought to keep off from fellowship
with their unfruitful works of darkness ; for, otherwise,
whatsoever duties any special relations call for at our hands,
David was very observant of, toward his greatest enemies,
but he separated from them only as wicked and as bloody,
and as they were on a course of perdition : *depart from*
me, therefore, ye bloody men. 5. When we have a controversy with the wicked, we should take heed that private
spleen do not rule us, but that only our interest in God's
quarrel with them move us, as the psalmist doth here: *for*
they speak against thee wickedly. 6. What the wicked
do or speak against God's servants for righteousness' sake,
it is against God in effect: *they speak against thee, and*
are thy enemies. 7. Such as profess themselves the people of God, and yet persecute the godly unjustly, under the
colour of law, or some specious pretences, in effect take
God's name in vain : *thine enemies take thy name in vain.*

21. *Do not I hate them, O Lord, that hate thee ?*
and am not I grieved with those that rise up against
thee ?

22. I hate them with perfect hatred ; I count them mine enemies.

After declaring his judgment of his enemies, David professeth his hatred to their persons, qualified with wickedness, as is said. Whence learn, 1. There are some men, who, beside the common enmity which is in all men against God, oppose themselves in an eminent way against God and godliness, as *haters* of God; for this the text presupposeth. 2. Such as are perceived open enemies of God, we may lawfully hate, without breach of the law of love; for the love which we owe to God absolutely, giveth warrant to hate those who oppose God comparatively : *do I not hate them that hate thee ?* 3. Injuries done against God should touch and affect us no less nearly than injuries done to ourselves : *and am not I grieved with those that rise up against thee ?* 4. When God is injured by our enemies, we had great need to look to the sincerity of our affection, that our hatred against them, and our zeal for God and his truth be upright, so as we may say with David, *I hate them with a perfect hatred, I count them mine enemies.*

23. Search me, O God, and know my heart; try me, and know my thoughts ;

24. And see if there be any wicked way in me, and lead me in the way everlasting.

When David hath searched himself, and is approved of his own conscience, he offereth himself over again to be searched by God. Whence learn, 1. As we have need to try our zeal when God's quarrel and our interest are joined, that there be not some dregs of our ill-humours mixed therewith ; so must we not rest upon the testimony of our own conscience in this case, but must offer our heart to be searched by God over and over again, and must entreat him to purge us of every corrupt mixture, as David doth : *search me, O God, and know my heart, try me, and know my thoughts.* 2. He had need to be sincere in all his ways who craveth God's approbation in any one of his ways; for, if a man be corrupt in any of his ways, he may deceive his own heart in all his other ways : this David importeth when he saith, *and see if there be any wicked way in me.* 3. Every wicked way is a way of grief, trouble, and sorrow; for so imports the name given to it in the original. 4. The good way allowed of God is a lasting way appointed by God of old, and will be approved by him for ever: *lead me in the way everlasting.* 5. We cannot walk in the ways of God without his actually and effectually leading us therein, beside his direction given in common by his word; and therefore we had need to pray with David, *lead me in the way everlasting.*

PSALM CXL.

To the chief musician.　A Psalm of David.

David being pursued for his life, and loaded with false calumnies of wicked men, prayeth, first, for deliverance from them, v. 1—7; secondly, he prayeth against them, v. 8—11; and, thirdly, he declareth the Lord's gracious answer, v. 12, 13.

1. *Deliver me, O Lord, from the evil man : preserve me from the violent man ;*

2. *Which imagine mischiefs in* their *heart : continually are they gathered together* for *war.*

3. *They have sharpened their tongues like a serpent : adders' poison* is *under their lips.　Selah.*

In his prayer for deliverance, first, David requesteth preservation from their cruel devices and slanders, v. 1—3 ; then repeateth his prayer for preservation from the present dangers wherein he was, by reason of the snares laid for him, v. 4, 5; thirdly, he repeateth his petitions with some special grounds of confidence and hope to be relieved, v. 6.

From the first request, learn, That most innocent and godly men, by the calumnies of the wicked, are sometimes cast into great dangers, whence they see no way of deliverance for clearing their name, or saving their life, except God find it out : and in this case God is and should be their refuge *deliver me, O Lord, from the evil man.* 2. How wicked soever, how violent soever the enemies of God's children be, God can rescue his servants out of their hands : *preserve me from the violent man.* 3. Such as, not only in a fit of passion, but also in cold blood, resolve to do mischief to the godly, may justly be esteemed evil men, violent men, for so are they here described : *which imagine mischief in their hearts.* 4. When wicked men have devised what they can by themselves against the righteous, they cannot trust their own wits, as able to make the plot fast, except they consult one with another frequently, that they may join their counsels and their forces together, to make the snare sure: *continually they are gathered together for war.* 5. That wicked men may the better carry on their design against the godly, they possess the simple people with prejudices against them, devising and spreading malicious lies, and bloody calumnies of them, contrived with great cunning, and made very probable in appearance, lest any should pity them when they are cut off: *they have sharpened their tongue like a serpent.* 6. When the wicked have vented deadly lies of the godly, they have in readiness new slanders and capital crimes to charge them with falsely: *adders' poison is under their lips.*

4. *Keep me, O Lord, from the hands of the wicked; preserve me from the violent man, who have purposed to overthrow my goings.*

5. *The proud have hid a snare for me, and cords: they have spread a net by the way-side; they have set gins for me.   Selah.*

In his repeated petition for preservation, learn, 1. It will not suffice the wicked to defame the godly, and murder them in heart and tongue, but they also seek to have them in their grips, except God interpose himself for their safety: *keep me, O Lord, from the hands of the wicked.* 2. The desperate resolution of the wicked to overcome the godly, must not discourage the godly, but sharpen their prayer: *preserve me from the violent man, who has purposed to overthrow my goings.* 3. Hunters and fowlers never went more cunningly to work, by snares, nets, and traps, to catch their prey, than the wicked go about to have the advantage of the godly, to bring their life under their power: *the proud have laid a snare for me, and cords: they have spread a net by the way-side, they have set gins for me.*

6. *I said unto the Lord, Thou art my God: hear the voice of my supplications, O Lord.*

7. *O God the Lord, the strength of my salvation, thou hast covered my head in the day of battle.*

In David's repeating his petition the third time, with reasons of hope to be helped, learn, 1. The malice of men should move the believer to make use of God's favour and friendship, and of the covenant with him: *I said unto the Lord, thou art my God.* 2. The claim which faith layeth to God, should proceed from a fixed purpose to stand to its right and interest in God : *I said unto the Lord, thou art my God.* 3. When faith findeth the covenant fixed, then prayer findeth vent, and the man poureth forth his desire with hope, as here : *hear the voice of my supplications, O Lord.* 4. When misbelief presenteth to the godly the greatness of the danger, the man's own weakness, and the power of the adversary, faith should present, in opposition to these, the strength of God and his power for salvation, as engaged by covenant to the behoof of the believer : *O God, the Lord, the strength of my salvation.* 5. As present straits should bring to mind bygone dangers and deliverance, so bygone experience of delivery should strengthen faith for the present : for this use David maketh of his present and bygone exercise. 6. In time of danger God usually interposes himself for the preservation of his own servant, more nearly and closely than a helmet cleaves to a man's head in the day of battle, and wardeth off a blow better than any piece of armour can do; as David's experience teacheth : *thou hast covered my head in the day of battle.*

8. *Grant not, O Lord, the desires of the wicked : further not his wicked device,* lest *they exalt themselves. Selah.*

9. As for *the head of those that compass me about, let the mischief of their own lips cover them.*

10. *Let burning coals fall upon them : let them be cast into the fire ; into deep pits, that they rise not up again.*

11. *Let not an evil speaker be established in the earth : evil shall hunt the violent man to overthrow* him.

In the second part of the psalm, wherein David prayeth against his enemies, learn, 1. God can overthrow all the devices of the wicked, and the wicked can effect nothing against the godly, except God grant them their desire; for so much this prayer importeth : *grant not, O Lord, the desires of the wicked.* 2. The prayer of the godly against the plots of the wicked, hath more power to overturn them than the wicked have wit or strength to promote them : *further not his wicked device.* 3. When one of the wicked findeth success in his wicked devices, all of them grow proud, and misken God for that cause : *further not his wicked device, lest they exalt themselves.* 4. God will not give always success to the wicked oppressors of his people, were there no other reason for it but this one —to crush the pride of his enemies, and to make it cease : *further not his wicked device, lest they exalt themselves.* 5. What mischief the wicked have threatened to bring upon the godly shall fall upon themselves, and bitter as gall shall their part be (as the word in the original will bear,) who are chief ringleaders of the persecution of the godly : *as for the head of them that compass me about, let the mischief of their own lips cover them.* 6. The overthrow of the wicked shall come upon them as the ruin of a wall, covering them and smothering them : *let mischief cover them ;* their torment shall be piercing and intolerable, like the perdition of Sodom: *let burning coals fall upon them ;* no escaping for them : *let them be cast into the fire ;* no getting out of the torment, no recovery for them : *let them be cast into deep pits, that they rise not again.* 7. Backbiters and calumniators shall not only be debarred from heaven, but also God's curse shall follow them on earth, and not suffer them nor their posterity to enjoy quiet prosperity in the world : *let not an evil speaker be established in the earth.* 8. When oppression hath cried to God against the oppressor, it is sent forth as a serjeant to follow him at the heels wherever he go, till it overtake him, and throw him headlong into destruction : *evil shall hunt the violent man to overthrow him.*

12. *I know that God will maintain the cause of the afflicted,* and *the right of the poor.*

13. *Surely the righteous shall give thanks unto thy name ; the upright shall dwell in thy presence.*

In the third part of the psalm, is the answer of the psalmist's prayer, in a comfortable persuasion of God's maintaining his persecuted children, and delivering his own afflicted servants out of all their troubles. Whence learn, 1. Whosoever shall persecute and oppress the righteous, shall find God their party, joined in the cause with the afflicted : *the Lord will maintain the cause of the afflicted.* 2. The faith of God's assistance is a sufficient comfort to the godly, to uphold them till the deliverance come, and this persuasion God useth to give his persecuted servants for their upholding : *I know that the Lord will maintain the cause of the afflicted.* 3. The main thing which the Lord's servants care for, is their cause and their right, that, whatsoever they shall suffer, their cause may go free and be justified; and this the Lord secureth here: *the Lord will maintain the cause of the afflicted, and the right of the poor.* 4. Whatsoever hardship the godly meet with in their exercise, joy and deliverance shall close their troubles, and whatsoever prayer and mourning they shall be driven to by persecution, praise and thanksgiving shall be the last part of their trial; and this the Lord will have his people persuaded of : *surely the righteous shall give thanks unto thy name.* 5. Whatsoever imperfections the believer shall find in himself, yet his upright and sincere dealing with God, by the daily acknowledgment of what is amiss in him, and by his making use of the remedy held forth in the gospel, shall prove him to be a righteous man; for the righteous and the upright man here is one. 6. Beside all the comfortable blinks of God's kindness in this world, granted to the believer, he hath assurance of perseverance, and of everlasting fellowship with God : *the upright shall dwell in thy presence.*

PSALM CXLI.

A Psalm of David.

The psalmist, being in distress by the malicious persecution of his adversaries, prayeth for relief, and for a holy carriage under his trouble, till his own full delivery, and till his enemies' destruction should come. The petitions are seven. The first is general, for acceptation of his person, and granting his prayer, v. 1, 2. The next is, for direction of his speeches, v. 3. The third is, for guiding his heart and actions, v. 4. The fourth is, for the benefit of the fellowship of the saints, by their wholesome counsel and admonition, v. 5: with the reasons thereof, v. 6, 7. The fifth is, for the comfort of spiritual communion with God, v. 8. The sixth is, for preservation from the plots of the enemies, v. 9. The seventh is, for the overthrow of his enemies, v. 10.

1. *Lord, I cry unto thee : make haste unto me ; give ear unto my voice, when I cry unto thee.*

2. *Let my prayer be set forth before thee* as *incense,* and *the lifting up of my hands* as *the evening sacrifice.*

In the first petition, which is general, for granting his prayer, and accepting his person in his prayer, learn, 1. Misbelief seeketh many ways for delivery from trouble, but faith hath but one way to go to God, to wit, by prayer, for whatsoever is needful: *Lord, I cry unto thee.* 2. Present danger, or long continuance of trouble, putteth an edge upon the devotion of the believer : *Lord, I cry unto thee.* 3. Albeit the godly dare not set a time to God, when he shall come, yet they may declare the strait they find themselves in, and what need they have of speedy help : *make haste unto me.* 4. As it is an ordinary temptation suggested to the godly in time of trouble, when they pray and receive not an answer, that their supplication is misregarded; so should it be repelled by renewing our petition so oft as it is offered, as this example teacheth : *give ear unto my voice, when I cry unto thee.* 5. The prayer of God's children is very sweet-smelled and acceptable to God, through the mediation of Christ, as the ceremonial offering of incense and sacrifice, (whereunto David here alludeth) signifieth : *let my prayer be set forth before thee as incense, and the lifting up of my hands as the evening sacrifice.* 6. Our prayers to God should be joined with submissiveness of spirit, self-denial, and hopeful dependence on God; for so much the gesture of lifting up the hands in prayer of its own nature signifieth, and therefore here the gesture is put for the prayer, which should be joined with such an inward disposition : *let the lifting up of my hands be as evening sacrifice.*

3. *Set a watch, O Lord, before my mouth ; keep the door of my lips.*

In the second petition, which is more special, for direction of his speeches, learn, 1. The godly in their trouble, especially by persecution, are under temptation to hurt their own cause by unadvised and passionate speeches ; for this the prayer importeth. 2. As words of passion, from our muddy affection, are ready to break out in time of trouble, so should we, in the sense of our own inability to suppress them, entreat God to bridle our tongue, that nothing break forth to his dishonour : *set a watch, O Lord, before my mouth ; keep the door of my lips.*

4. *Incline not my heart to* any *evil thing, to practise wicked works with men that work iniquity : and let me not eat of their dainties.*

In the third petition, for guiding David's heart and actions, learn, 1. The godly are subject also to another temptation under persecution, to be driven to some unlawful way of revenge, or some sinful compliance with the wicked, either by terror or allurement : as this petition importeth. 2. The holiest of God's servants have reason to pray to God, *lead us not into temptation,* when they consider that their daily sinning may open a door to justice, to give over their hearts, for a time, to its own natural wicked inclination : for, in the sense of this danger, David prayeth, *incline not my heart to any evil thing.* 3. As to meet injuries with injuries, is not a means to be rid of trouble, but a means to involve us in further trouble ; so also, to comply with workers of iniquity, for fear of danger from them, is not a means to eschew trouble, but rather a means to draw down God's wrath : *incline not my heart to any evil thing, to practise wicked works with them that work iniquity.* 4. As the Lord is the only sovereign over the heart, in whose hand the heart is, to turn it where he pleaseth, so will he, being entreated by prayer, set it right : *incline not my heart to any evil thing.* 5. The present pleasure and commodity of sin is in high estimation with the sinner, and much sweeter to him than what he may lawfully enjoy : *the pleasures of sin are his delicacies.* 6. No man can keep himself from being taken with the allurements of a sinful course except the Lord preserve him: *let me not eat of their dainties.* 7. The holiest men in Scripture have been most sensible of the importance of their own free will and inability to resist temptations, or to bring forth the habits of grace into action ; most diffident of themselves, most dependent upon God, most careful to make use of means, and conscientious in following ordinances, as their prayers testify : *incline not my heart to any evil thing, let me not eat of their dainties.*

5. *Let the righteous smite me,* it shall be *a kindness; and let him reprove me,* it shall be *an excellent oil,* which *shall not break my head : for yet my prayer also* shall be *in their calamities.*

The fourth petition is for the benefit of the communion of saints, wherein David, perceiving the mischief which unhappy flatterers about the king procured to him and the godly in the land, prayeth to God to grant him such godly men about him as would never consent to any wrong deed of his, but would dissuade him, differ from him, yea, reprove and rebuke him rather, if need were : which sort of friendly smiting of him, he promiseth shall be acceptable to him, and for this giveth four reasons : the first whereof is, because he had so much love to his enemies as to pity them in their calamities, and to pray for them. Whence learn, 1. As flatterers are a plague to princes, especially when they are upon unjust courses; so righteous and faithful admonishers of us, in whatsoever place we are, are a notable blessing, and worthy to be prayed for : *let the righteous smite me.* 2. According as a man hateth sin, and loveth righteousness, so he hateth flattery, and loveth to be freely dealt with, and reproved or admonished : for it is the love of righteousness, and hatred of sin, which make David say, *let the righteous smite me.* 3. No man is so far mortified but a reproof will be a wound to his proud flesh : *let the righteous smite me.* 4. Free dealing and plain reproof are fruits of love unfeigned : *let the righteous smite me, it shall be a kindness.* 5. As most precious oil is to the body, so are the counsel, admonition, and reproof of the righteous to the soul; for the fruit of both is health and gladness : *let him reprove me ; it shall be an excellent oil, which shall not break my head.* 6. The godly, when they are persecuted, need not to seek private revenge; for calamities abide their persecutors, which they by faith in God's word may clearly foresee ; as David here presupposeth unquestionably that their calamities were coming : *my prayer shall be in their calamities.* 7. The Lord's children should be so far from private revenge, and so ready to abandon that course, if they be tempted to it, that they should keep so much love to their adversaries as may make them discharge all commanded duties toward them, as David here is disposed, whose words import thus much: if I were upon private revenge, Lord, let me find a friend to hinder me, because I resolve to follow the duties of commanded love toward mine adversaries: *for yet my prayer, also shall be in their calamities.* And this is the first reason of the fourth petition.

6. *When their judges are overthrown in stony places, they shall hear my words: for they are sweet.*

The second reason is, from David's purpose to deal with the simple people, (who now persecuted him, by the misleading of their corrupt rulers) as with his kindly subjects, disciples, or children, and he hopeth to find them tractable. Whence learn, 1. Difference must be put between ringleaders in an evil course, and those that follow it in simplicity; for so the prophet here putteth difference betwixt the people and their corrupt and wicked judges. 2. Wicked rulers and misleaders of the people, shall be fearfully punished, as they who are cast down from a steep place, and fall among stones: *their judges shall be overthrown in stony places.* 3. Misled people should be kindly entertained, and instructed in the truth of God's word, as disciples and children, so soon as the Lord offereth opportunity: *when their judges shall be thrown in stony places, they shall hear my words.* 4. As the doctrine of grace and godliness is sweet and pleasant in itself, so should it be esteemed by the preachers, so recommended to the people, and so handled in the way of preaching it, that it may be acknowledged by the people to be such. This it shall be esteemed, if, with the deciphering of sin and the curse, the remedy constantly be holden forth in Christ; if, with the doctrine of all moral duties, people be directed to draw strength from Christ to obey them, and to seek to have their service acceptable through Christ; for thus shall the words of the Lord be both pleasant and profitable to the people: this course David resolved: *they shall hear my words, for they are sweet.*

7. *Our bones are scattered at the grave's mouth, as when one cutteth and cleaveth wood upon the earth.*

This is a third reason, not only of the fourth petition, but also and mainly in the whole prayer, for comfort and deliverance from persecution, wherein many of the Lord's priests were slain, and many others of David's friends were undone, and no more regard had of their lives and bones, than the hewer of wood hath regard to the chips which fall off in hewing: wherein David and his followers were a type of Christ and his followers, whose persecution is here represented and prophesied of. Whence learn, 1. Albeit the death of the Lord's servants be dear unto him, yet their lives, and the burial of their bones, are no more regarded by the wicked, than so many chips of wood, which the hewer of wood heweth off with his axe: *our bones are scattered at the grave's mouth, as when one cutteth and cleaveth wood upon the earth.* 2. When Christ's subjects are so entertained, (as here is set forth) their case being presented to God, hath no small force to draw down delivery, and to bring a change of the affairs of their foes, as the force of the reason annexed to the prayer teacheth.

8. *But mine eyes* are *unto thee, O God the Lord: in thee is my trust; leave not my soul destitute.*

The fourth reason of the petition, relating mainly to the prayer for delivery: after which is subjoined the fifth petition, including the substance of all his prayer. Whence learn, 1. How great soever the darkness of his calamities may be, and how thick soever the clouds of present trouble are, to hide from us the Lord's care of us, and his loving-kindness to us, yet faith must look and pierce through them all to God, and to his power and constancy of truth and love: *but mine eyes are unto thee.* 2. Whensoever faith turns toward the Lord, it seeth sufficiency in God to help, as the man hath need: *mine eyes are toward thee, O God the Lord.* 3. As it is good to believe in God in time of greatest straits, so it is good to avow our belief before God, and to observe this for our further strengthening, that we may have obtained mercy to believe, as here David doth: *mine eyes are toward thee: in thee is my trust.* 4. A soul which hath God for a covering of protection and comfort, hath also every condition it can be in, well seasoned; but the soul that lacketh this covering is bare, and naked, and destitute, without guard against any evil which may fall upon it: against this evil we have great need to pray, *leave not my soul destitute.* And this is the fifth petition in this prayer.

9. *Keep me from the snares* which *they have laid for me, and the gins of the workers of iniquity.*

The sixth petition, is, to be saved from the privy plots which his enemies had laid against him. Whence learn, 1. The adversaries of God's people, or persecutors of the righteous for righteousness' sake, are workers of iniquity, let them pretend to godliness, laws, or justice, as they please, for so are they here described. 2. Persecutors of the righteous do not usually go so openly to work, as to persecute them directly for righteousness, but make plausible laws and statutes, which may seem reasonable to the world, and yet such laws as the godly cannot without sin obey, and so their commands ensnare the godly, as here they are called *snares and gins*. 3. From the plots of persecutors, and in special from iniquity established by a law, none can deliver the godly so as they shall neither sin nor suffer the penalty, except God alone: *keep me from the snares which they have laid for me, and the gins of the workers of iniquity.*

10. *Let the wicked fall into their own nets, whilst that I withal escape.*

The seventh petition is, as for his own delivery, so also for the overthrow of obstinate enemies, who cannot be reclaimed. Whence learn, 1. The prayers against persecutors which are indited by the penmen of the Scripture, are prophecies of their punishment, and decrees whereunto the church may subscribe in the general: and this prayer is one among the rest. 2. When persecutors lay plots and snares against the righteous, they lay plots against themselves; and there is no need of another plot for their ruin, save that which is of their own devising: *let the wicked fall into their own net*. 3. It is not unusual to see the overthrow of persecutors, and the delivery of the righteous, wrought by one and the self same means, and brought about at one time: *let the wicked fall into their own net, whilst that I withal escape.*

PSALM CXLII.

Maschil of David, &c.

This psalm showeth what was David's exercise, when he was in the cave
of one of the mountains of Engedi, (1 Sam. xxiv.) flying from Saul.
He first setteth down his betaking himself to prayer in general, v. 1, 2;
secondly, the straits wherein he was for the time, v. 3, 4; thirdly, what
were the especial petitions of his prayer, with the reasons thereof,
v. 5—7.

From the inscription, learn, 1. That when the Lord putteth any of his
children in straits and difficulties, he is providing instruction, and wise
direction to them and others, by this means; for this danger bringeth
forth a psalm of instruction: maschil of David. 2. The profit which
followeth upon sharp exercises, is able to recompense all the pains
whereunto they are put in trouble: as this particular instance showeth.
3. It is wisdom for us to mark the special dangers whereinto we fall,
and how we have behaved ourselves therein, and to see what use we
should make thereof; as this example of David's calling to mind the
danger he was in, in the cave, teacheth us.

1. *I cried unto the Lord with my voice : with my
voice unto the Lord did I make my supplication.*

2. *I poured out my complaint before him ; I shewed
before him my trouble.*

In the setting down of his exercise in this danger, and
how he made God his refuge by prayer, learn, 1. The grace
of God can so calm a man's mind in the deepest danger of
present death that he may confidently put up his desire for
delivery; and no danger can be so desperate, but a man may
by prayer be delivered out of it, one way or other, as David's experience teacheth : *I cried unto the Lord,* saith
David, being in the cave, half buried as in a grave; Saul
and his host being at the mouth of it. 2. He that is acquainted with God, and seeketh his presence by prayer, ordinarily will find a ready way to God, in an extraordinary
danger, whereof David in this difficulty, showeth his experience. 3. The uttering of right words with the voice in
prayer, in the time of perplexity, is a work of faith, presuppose there were so much inward confusion and multitude of thoughts in the mind, as might call in question
whether the supplication of so perplexed a mind could be
an acceptable prayer : therefore David twice mentioneth
the uttering of his voice : *I cried with my voice, with my
voice.* 4. It is a sweet mercy to have grace to pray to God,
and is not only profitable for the present, but also the me-

mory of this mercy is refreshful afterward, as experience here showeth. 5. It may be an ease to our minds, when we are full of perplexity, grief, and fear, to tell the Lord what aileth us: *I poured out my complaint before him.* 6. To present our confusion, perplexity, and trouble of mind, to be looked upon by God and to be read by him, is a real prayer or supplication: *I showed before him my trouble.*

3. *When my spirit was overwhelmed within me, then thou knewest my path : in the way wherein I walked have they privily laid a snare for me.*

4. *I looked on* my *right hand, and beheld, but* there was *no man that would know me : refuge failed me; no man cared for my soul.*

The strait wherein David was, made his wit fail him, so that he knew not what to do; for, albeit his cause and carriage in it was approved of God, yet his enemies hunted him so hard, that they had very nigh catched him in the snare; his soldiers, who were with him fainted, and were ready to shift for themselves and give up David, if the army had approached the cave; no man cared for his life, none would stand to his defence. Whence learn, 1. Trouble and danger in extremity, put a man's wit on work to think upon all means of possible delivery, and when none can be found, the mind is involved in perplexity, and falleth down as it were in a swoon : *my spirit was overwhelmed within me.* 2. Whatsoever danger we may fall into, it is good that our cause and carriage be such as God will allow. This was David's advantage here: *when my spirit was overwhelmed within me, then thou knewest my path;* that is, thou approvedst my part, who was unjustly pursued. 3. How innocently soever we behave ourselves, yet persecutors will not cease to hunt us, till they take us in the snare, if they can : *in the way wherein I walked have they privily laid a snare for me.* 4. When great straits come, worldly friends and all who may be in danger from helping us, will readily forsake us : and this is the lot of Christ and his servants, who, in suffering for righteousness, are left alone without all comfort or encouragement from men : *I looked on my right hand, and beheld, but there was no man that would know me: refuge failed me ; no man cared for my soul.*   5. It is lawful for a believer to make use of lawful means for his delivery, and to call for assistance from such as are bound to assist him, albeit he may suspect to be refused, as David did here.

5. *I cried unto thee, O Lord: I said, Thou* art *my refuge* and *my portion in the land of the living.*

6. *Attend unto my cry ; for I am brought very low : deliver me from my persecutors ; for they are stronger than I.*

7. *Bring my soul out of prison, that I may praise thy name : the righteous shall compass me about ; for thou shalt deal bountifully with me.*

In the last place, David setteth down his last refuge, and the words of his prayer, with the reasons to help his hope to be heard. Whence learn, 1. Albeit all men, and all means of delivery in the world should fail us, yet must we not give over, but pray to God, and depend upon him who never faileth his supplicants that seek him, as David did : *I cried unto thee, O Lord.* 2. The less comfort we find in the creature, we should trust the more in God, as David did, who, when all forsook him, said, O God, *thou art my refuge.* 3. God alone being with us may suffice us in every condition, as he did David : *thou art my portion in the land of the living.* 4. As the sense of our weakness and our adversaries' power, is a good whetstone to sharpen our prayer; so the lower we are brought and emptied of carnal confidence, we may expect the more confidently help from God, as here David reasoneth : *attend unto my cry ; for I am brought very low : deliver me from my persecutors ; for they are stronger than I.* 5. So long as the godly man is debarred from the benefit of God's public worship and ordinances, he is but in a prison in his own estimation : *bring my soul out of prison.* 6. The end of our prayer for delivery out of trouble, should be, that we may the more freely and fruitfully serve the Lord : *bring my life out of prison, that I may praise thy name.* 7. When any one of God's persecuted servants is delivered, it is a matter of comfort, joy, and encouragement, and of mutual congratulation to all the godly, who have interest in their righteous cause any way : *the righteous shall compass me about.* 8. Before a bodily delivery come, the Lord sometimes giveth inward assurance that it shall come; thus, *thou shalt deal bountifully with me ;* for David's words, being taken as spoken in the cave, show so much.

PSALM CXLIII.

A psalm of David.

David being in great trouble of mind, for the long continuance of his persecution by his enemies, and also under some exercise of conscience, through the sense of his sin, prayeth in this psalm for deliverance in general, from the twofold trouble, v. 1, 2, because of his pitiful condition set down, v. 3—6. Then he presseth his prayer in nine more special petitions, in the rest of the psalm.

1. *Hear my prayer, O Lord; give ear to my supplications : in thy faithfulness answer me,* and *in thy righteousness.*

2. *And enter not into judgment with thy servant: for in thy sight shall no man living be justified.*

In the prayer, as it is generally propounded, learn, 1. Outward bodily trouble is able to raise trouble of mind, and trouble of conscience also, especially when outward trouble continueth long, and God seemeth to debar prayer from access, or not to give answer thereto, as this experience of David showeth. 2. Whatsoever be the trouble of a man's mind, and from what cause soever it ariseth, prayer is the first and readiest means of ease and quietness, as here we see in David : *hear my prayer, O Lord, and give ear to my supplication.* 3. The Lord's faithfulness and righteousness, which serve to terrify a natural man, are props and pillars of comfort and encouragement to the believer, who has fled to the throne of grace : *in thy faithfulness answer me, and in thy righteousness.* 4. When the conscience of sin opposeth our prayer, or our hope of delivery out of trouble, it must be answered by flying to God's grace : and when justice seemeth to pursue us, then the prayer of faith changeth the court of justice into the court of grace : for albeit the sins of the godly may take peace of conscience from them for a time, yet they cannot debar them from seeking favour and pardon, according to the covenant of grace; especially when they are studying to serve God, as this example teacheth us : *and enter not into judgment with thy servant.* 5. There is no way of justification by the works of the law, neither before regeneration nor after, except by grace; for David, a man of singular holiness, saith, *enter not into judgment with thy servant, for in thy sight shall no one living be justified :* to wit, if thou enter into judgment with me according to the law of works.

3. *For the enemy hath persecuted my soul ; he hath smitten my life down to the ground : he hath made me to dwell in darkness, as those that have been long dead.*

4. *Therefore is my spirit overwhelmed within me ; my heart within me is desolate.*

The reasons of his prayer are two. The first is taken from the miserable condition, whereinto the violence and oppression of the enemy hath driven him. v. 3, 4; the other is from his careful use of the means for finding grace, v. 5, 6. In the first reason, learn, 1. After we have fled to God's mercy, according to the covenant of grace for remission of sin, we may confidently lay forth all our worldly trouble before God, and hope for relief, as here David doth. 2. It is not strange to see the godly in a manner wracked by their persecutors, and undone in their worldly condition, for so was David served : *the enemy hath persecuted my soul, he hath smitten my life down to the ground : he hath made me to dwell in darkness, as those that have been long dead :* and this he speaketh in regard to his being hunted from place to place, and forced to hide himself in the wilderness, at length take banishment upon him, and live among idolaters in the land of darkness. 3. Troubles, when they are long continued, are able to daunt the natural courage of the stoutest of God's servants; for God, to empty his own children of self-conceit, and humble them in the sense of their own weakness, usually suffers trouble to have more weight than they could beforehand apprehend, as here : *therefore is my spirit overwhelmed within me, my heart within me is desolated.* 4. How heavy soever trouble be found, and how unable soever we find ourselves to bear it any longer, yet must we not succumb nor give over wrestling, but must present our case to the Lord, as his example teacheth us.

5. *I remember the days of old; I meditate on all thy works; I muse on the work of thy hands.*

6. *I stretch forth my hands unto thee : my soul* thirsteth *after thee, as a thirsty land. Selah.*

From the second reason of his prayer, taken from the consciousness of his diligent use of the ordinary means for finding comfort and relief, learn, 1. The remembrance of our own former experience, and of the experience of others of the saints set down in Scripture, (which should have force to support our faith, albeit we have nothing of our own experience,) is a fit exercise for a fainting soul under trouble, as here we see : *I remember the days of old, I meditate on all thy works.* 2. Meditation on the works of creation and providence, is a fit means also to support our faith in God's word, albeit we have no example nor experience of any who had been in the like condition before us ; for therein we shall find the evidence of what the wisdom and omnipotence of God can do, in performing promises : *I muse on the works of thy hands.* 3. Before we can draw profit from the pledges of God's power apparent in his works, we must resolve to meditate and muse upon them at leisure; for a slight look of these will not draw forth the profitable use of them : *I remembered, I meditated, I mused,* saith David. 4. With meditation upon God's works, earnest prayer must be joined : *I stretch forth my hands unto thee.* 5. When faith seeth not only a promise of help, but also, by the experience of others who have been helped, a probability also of its coming speed, it raiseth a longing for the fruit of the promise, and keepeth the eye fixed on God, without looking for relief anywhere else : *my soul thirsteth after thee, as a thirsty land.*

7. *Hear me speedily, O Lord; my spirit faileth: hide not thy face from me, lest I be like unto them that go down into the pit.*

In the rest of the psalm, the psalmist presseth this prayer more particularly in nine petitions. The first is for speedy deliverance ; the second for some blink of favour ; and both these have their reasons adjoined in this verse. Whence learn, 1. Sore trouble and long delaying of God's help, are

able to shake faith and weaken courage : *hear me speedily,
O Lord, my spirit faileth.* 2. The believer must never
give over seeking God's help, how nigh soever he be to
failing and falling off : *hear me, O Lord, my spirit faileth
me.* 3. Faith maketh use of extreme dangers and instant
destruction, as of wings to mount itself up to God ; for
death and destruction cannot be so nigh, but faith findeth
time to flee to its refuge and run to God, to interpose himself before destruction be executed : *hear me speedily, my
spirit faileth.* 4. The Lord's displeasure, apprehended in
trouble, is more terrible than the trouble itself, and the least
intimation of his favour, is very life and delivery ; for, *hide
not thy face from me,* was here David's deepest distress,
and the showing of the least blink of God's favour should
have relieved him. 5. The Lord will not suffer his children's faith to be overset, albeit he suffer it to be hardly
assaulted : *hide not thy face from me, lest I be like to
them that go down to the pit,* or lest I be like to them
that perish. 6. The sense of trouble and weakness in God's
children acknowledged before God, is more able to bear
them through under their troubles, than all the stupid
stoutness of contumacious minds, as the experience of this
champion David showeth.

8. *Cause me to hear thy loving-kindness in the
morning ; for in thee do I trust : cause me to know the
way wherein I should walk ; for I lift up my soul unto
thee.*

The third petition is for timous comfort in the word of
promise ; and the fourth is, for direction in the way of God's
obedience—both these have their reasons adjoined in this
verse. Whence learn, 1. The consolation which the believer
seeketh is that which is promised in the word ; and he will
content himself with the comfort which cometh by hearing,
till the full effect of the promise come : *cause me to hear
thy loving-kindness.* 2. That comfort is indeed early,
and sufficiently timous, which cometh before we perish or
despair : *cause me to hear thy loving-kindness in the
morning.* 3. Trusting in God without comfort, is a reason
to persuade us that we shall have comfort, and the readiest
way that can be to come by it : *cause me to hear thy
loving-kindness : for in thee do I trust.* 4. As it is the

believer's trouble to be in such perplexity, as not to know how to behave himself in it ; so it is a part of his comfort and delivery to understand what to do next, and how to behave himself: *cause me to know the way wherein I should walk.* 5. He who seeketh direction from God, must lift up his heart off all diversions, and depend on God only: for, *I lift up my soul to thee,* is the reason of his petition to be directed.

9. *Deliver me, O Lord, from mine enemies : I flee unto thee to hide me.*

The fifth petition is for delivery from his enemies, whereunto a reason is added here. Whence learn, 1. As there are no enemies from whom the Lord cannot deliver a man who is reconciled, how potent soever the enemies be; so deliverance from our enemies is a fruit of our friendship with God : *deliver me from mine enemies.* 2. Albeit our enemies had compassed us so, as there were no apparent escape, yet the believer may find a hiding-place in God : *I flee unto thee to hide me.*

10. *Teach me to do thy will ; for thou art my God : thy Spirit is good ; lead me into the land of uprightness.*

The sixth petition of the psalmist is for grace to walk righteously and holily, till he came to heaven, which he called the land of uprightness. Whence learn, 1. In time of trials and troubles, men are in no less danger of sinning and soul-losing than they are to fall into further bodily dangers and inconveniences, and have need, in the sense of their inability, to walk circumspectly, and seek direction from God : *teach me to do thy will.* 2. The covenant of grace whereinto the believer is entered, giveth ground to pray and hope for the growth of sanctification : *teach me to do thy will, for thou art my God.* 3. We have need of such teaching as hath with it leading, such direction as hath with it strengthening unto obedience, such information as directeth us, not only in the general rule, but also how to apply it in the particular actions, and which doth not leave us to ourselves in any part of our duty: *teach me, lead me.* 4. Heaven is the land of uprightness, and we must have the Lord's constant teaching, and his constant leading of us, till we be possessed of it : *lead me into the land of upright-*

KK

ness. **5.** The teacher and leader of believers, in the obedience of God's word and will, is the Spirit of God, whose goodness must be opposed to our natural sinfulness and ill-deserving: *thy Spirit is good; lead me into the land of uprightness.*

11. *Quicken me, O Lord, for thy name's sake: for thy righteousness' sake bring my soul out of trouble.*

The seventh petition is for some reviving of his damped and dead spirit, and the eighth is for ending the course of the enemies' persecution of him; and reasons are subjoined to both. Whence learn, 1. Albeit believers be subject to soul-fainting and deadness, yet they retain spiritual life in such a measure as maketh them still sensible of their own weakness, and able to bemoan themselves to God, who is able to revive them: *quicken me, O Lord.* 2. It concerneth God in his honour, to revive the spirits of the contrite ones, when they have their recourse to him: *quicken me, O Lord, for thy name's sake.* 3. Albeit the Lord acquaint his children with trouble, yet he will not suffer them to lie still in trouble, but will in due time set them free: *bring my soul out of trouble.* 4. The Lord will have his justice not terrible to his children in trouble, but comfortable and a pledge of their delivery from their oppressors: *for thy righteousness' sake, bring my soul out of trouble.*

12. *And of thy mercy cut off mine enemies, and destroy all them that afflict my soul: for I am thy servant.*

The ninth petition is for the overthrow of the psalmist's desperate enemies, whereunto reasons are added. Whence learn, 1. The enemies of the righteous who are persecuted for righteousness, shall perish: *cut off mine enemies, destroy them all.* 2. Mercy to the Lord's oppressed children, and justice against their enemies, go together; and the work of justice on persecutors, is a work of mercy to the oppressed: *of thy mercy cut off mine enemies.* 3. As the consciousness of endeavours to serve God, giveth sweet refreshment in time of trouble; so our short-coming must not deprive us of the title of servants, but we must assert our interest in God our Master and Lord, so long as we love to do his will, as David doth here: for, *I am thy servant.*

PSALM CXLIV.

A Psalm of David.

David being now king, but not yet fully settled on his throne, in this psalm giveth thanks to God for the work already wrought, v. 1—4; prayeth for completing the deliverance and settling him in his kingdom, v. 5—8, and, in hope to be heard, promiseth praise to God, v. 9, 10; and, in the last place, repeateth his petition, with reasons taken from the benefit which should redound to the Lord's people, by settling him in his kingdom, v. 11—14.

1. *Blessed* be *the Lord my strength, which teacheth my hands to war,* and *my fingers to fight.*

2. *My goodness, and my fortress; my high tower, and my deliverer; my shield, and he in whom I trust; who subdueth my people under me.*

3. *Lord, what is man, that thou takest knowledge of him! or the son of man, that thou makest account of him!*

4. *Man is like to vanity: his days are as a shadow that passeth away.*

In David's thanksgiving for what the Lord had done for him, learn, 1. As we are to praise God for mercies received, when we would have new mercies; so we are to strengthen our faith for receiving new benefits, by looking what we have received already, as David doth here. 2. The believer hath all his abilities and support, not so much in what is received already in himself, as without himself in God: *blessed be the Lord my strength.* 3. As what skill, what measure of strength, what success a man hath in any thing, is of the Lord; so the acknowledgment thereof, is both a part of his thankfulness to God, and a means of the confirmation of his own faith: *blessed be the Lord my strength, which teacheth my hands to war, and my fingers to fight.* 4. What the Lord is in his own nature, he is in his goodwill, covenant, and operation toward the believer, and thus appropriate to the believer as his own treasure, out of which he is furnished in all things: therefore David calleth him, *his goodness.* 5. Many evils are ready to rush in upon the believer, which the Lord as a bulwark wardeth off: and upon this account David saith, *my fortress.* 6. When trouble from the world and inferior creatures fight against the believer, the Lord lifteth him up above all, and compasseth him about with defence: for this David saith, *my high tower*. 7. Albeit it please the Lord sometimes to let trouble in upon the believer, yet he suffereth not the believer to perish therein, nor the trouble to harm him more than if it had been kept off: for this cause David calleth God, his *deliverer*. 8. Albeit the Lord will guard the believer on all hands when he is to enter the lists with an enemy, yet will he be employed for this end: for this cause David compareth the Lord to a shield or buckler, and calleth him his *shield*. 9. The multitude of ways, how God is and may be a support to us, serveth to make use of him by faith, according to our several necessities, as David teacheth, saying, *It is he in whom I trust*. 10. As the light of faith showeth what God is to us by right and covenant; so also it showeth us what are his operations and particular benefits bestowed upon us: *it is he*, saith David, *who subdueth my people under me*. 11. God's mercies are most highly esteemed when the believer is humble in the sense of his own in particular: *Lord, what is man that thou takest knowledge of him*. 12. It is a mercy to be wondered at, that the unworthiness of man neither hindereth God to love him, nor to esteem him: *what is the son of man that thou makest account of him*. 13. There is nothing in a man wherein he can glory, nothing which can deserve any thing at God's hand, and all natural perfections are but the shadow of something in effect: *man is like to vanity*. 14. Were there no more to abase a man, than what he may have in this world, his mortality and shortness of life are a sufficient reason for it: *his days are as a shadow that passeth away*—and all this commendeth the riches of God's grace and good-will to man, and helpeth the believer's faith against the enemy of man.

5. *Bow thy heavens, O Lord, and come down: touch the mountains, and they shall smoke.*

6. *Cast forth lightning, and scatter them: shoot out thine arrows, and destroy them.*

7. *Send thine hand from above; rid me, and deliver me out of great waters, from the hand of strange children;*

8. *Whose mouth speaketh vanity; and their right hand* is *a right hand of falsehood.*

In the next place, the psalmist prayeth to God to let forth his power, for subduing the rest of the kingdom under him, by repressing his enemies, and saving him from their contention and conspiracies against him. Whence learn, 1. How unworthy soever a man may be in his own eyes, he may seek great things of God, according to the estimation and respect he hath in God's eyes: for, upon this account, David prayeth, *that God would bow the heavens, and come down* for his help ; that is, would humble himself so far as to own his own *servant*. 2. If God please to manifest himself for any of his servants against the highest powers on earth, they shall soon feel the force of his wrath, like fire taking hold on them : *touch the mountains, and they shall smoke*. 3. No man can stand against him who hath thunder and lightning at his command, and arrows of destruction to shoot as he pleaseth : *cast forth thy lightnings, and scatter them ; shoot out thine arrows, and destroy them*. 4. Whatsoever the power of adversaries may be, or the difficulty or danger the believer can be in, if he shall oppose God's good-will and omnipotence for him, against the difficulty, he shall be master over it : *send thine hand from above, rid me, and deliver me out of great waters*. 5. The enmity of false brethren, counterfeit professors of religion, whose words, oaths, and covenants, cannot bind them, nor secure the godly whom they malign, is no less dangerous than deep and raging waters are, out of which God only can deliver a man : for, *deliver me out of great waters*, is expounded here, *deliver me from the hands of strange children, whose mouth speaketh vanity, and their right hand is a right hand of falsehood*.

9. *I will sing a new song unto thee, O God : upon a psaltery*, and *an instrument of ten strings, will I sing praises unto thee*.

10. It is he *that giveth salvation unto kings : who delivereth David his servant from the hurtful sword*.

David addeth his purpose and promise to praise God for the benefit which he prayeth for, as a reason of his hope to be heard. Whence learn, 1. The Lord in wisdom giveth deliverance out of trouble, by parts and degrees, and so dispenseth his benefits, that he may give his children occasion, both of oftener prayer and of oftener new praises, as

David's experience showeth; who, having given thanks for the bringing of him to the kingdom in part, prayeth for the enlargement of the benefit, promising upon this account a new thanksgiving: *I will sing a new song unto thee, O God.* 2. The upright engaging of our heart to praise God for the benefit we pray for, is an argument of hope that we shall have it, as here David useth it: *I will sing a new song unto thee, O God.* 3. According as a benefit not yet received hath lustre, and shineth in our eye, so are we content to be in God's debt for thanksgiving, if he shall grant it; (let the performance thereof prove as it may,) as we see here in David, who, because the adding of the government of the eleven tribes to his dominion over the tribes of Judah, seemed to be a great accession to his present possession, if God should give them to him, promiseth large thanks: *upon a psaltery, and an instrument of ten strings, will I sing praises unto thee:* which imports the highest measure of praising God that he could imagine; and to this his promise, he subjoineth the form of thanksgiving which he purposed to use. 4. It is not the place or power of a man, how great soever he be, which preserveth him, but the greatest of men must be preserved by God, no less than the meanest: *it is he that giveth salvation unto kings.* 5. One experience is sufficient to a believer, for confirming his faith in any general doctrine, as here: *he who delivereth David his servant from the hurtful sword,* is sufficient to make him subscribe, that *it is he that giveth salvation to kings.*

11. *Rid me, and deliver me from the hand of strange children, whose mouth speaketh vanity, and their right hand* is *a right hand of falsehood:*

12. *That our sons* may be *as plants grown up in their youth;* that *our daughters* may be *as cornerstones, polished* after *the similitude of a palace;*

13. That *our garners* may be *full, affording all manner of store;* that *our sheep may bring forth thousands and ten thousands in our streets.*

14. That *our oxen* may be *strong to labour;* that there be *no breaking in, nor going out; that* there be *no complaining in our streets.*

David repeateth his prayer for delivery from false and treacherous enemies, whom neither word nor writ, neither oath nor covenant could bind, and addeth yet more reasons for enlarging his kingdom, from the benefits which might come to the Lord's people thereby. Whence learn, 1. As the greatness of a benefit, so also the greatness of the difficulties which may hinder that benefit, being foreseen, should sharpen prayer for the benefit, and against the impediments thereof, as here the repetition of, *rid me, and deliver me*, &c., teacheth us. 2. He that is called to public employment, or the office of governing a people, should seek all things of God, for the public good of the people mainly, and should make the holy peace and prosperity of the people their main aim ; as David here craveth deliverance from his enemies, and the enlargement of his power, that the people might prosper and flourish, both in children and riches: *that our sons may be as plants*, &c. 3. Godly magistrates are a special means of peace and prosperity to the subjects, and should be careful, as in training up young men in grace and virtue, so they may be fruitful instruments of the public good, *as plants grown up in their youth ;* so also in training young women, that they may be beautified with all endowments that may make them godly mothers of the succeeding age: *our daughters may be as cornerstones, polished after the similitude of a palace.* 4. Peace and plenty of corn and cattle, and other things needful for this present life, are benefits of God in themselves, very helpful for the standing of a kingdom, and training up the youth in goodness and virtue, and worthy to be prayed for : *that our garners may be full, affording all manner of store, that our sheep may bring forth thousands and ten thousands in our streets.* 5. For the continuance of prosperity and peace in a land, industry in every man's vocation is requisite, and such righteous behaviour of the people, as may prevent not only war offensive and defensive, but also may prevent any vagabond beggars being suffered, or indigent persons forced, to complain in the streets : for so much is imported, while he saith, *that our oxen may be strong to labour ; that there be no breaking in*, to wit, of foreign enemies ; *nor going out*, to wit, of the people to invade other nations; *that there be no complaining in our streets*, for want of justice or necessary maintenance.

15. *Happy* is that *people that is in such a case;* yea, *happy* is that *people whose God* is *the Lord.*

David closeth the psalm with the commendation of such a condition of a well-governed people, but with a provision, that they be in covenant with God, and believe in him. Whence learn, 1. A people is happy which is so governed and cared for, and blessed of God, as Israel was under the reign of David, the servant of the Lord: *happy is that people that is in such a case,* as is here described. 2. A people's happiness is not solid where true religion is not settled; where the people is not in a covenant of grace and reconciliation with God, whatsoever worldly prosperity they may have: but so many as are in favour with God, and walk in friendship with him, are blessed, whatsoever be their outward condition: *happy is that people, whose God is the Lord.*

PSALM CXLV.

David's psalm of praise.

This psalm consists altogether of praises, every verse beginning with a several letter of the Hebrew alphabet, from the first to the last. Here David stirreth up himself to the work of God's praise somewhat more generally, from the beginning to verse 8; and from the eighth verse, he praiseth God more particularly, giving ten arguments for praise, to the last verse; and he closeth the psalm with engaging himself anew again, and exhorting others to follow the song for ever.

From the inscription, which is, A psalm of praise, learn, 1. It is our duty, and a point of spiritual wisdom, to set aside all particulars of our own, and go about the work of praising God only, as this psalm teacheth us. 2. The praises of God are able to fill all the volumes in the world, and what composition of letters can be made in any language: and this the going through all the letters in the Hebrew alphabet giveth us to understand. 3. It is expedient to commit to memory some select psalms, especially about God's praises, to help memory: the wisdom of God hath ordered this, and some other psalms, so that the order of the letters of the Hebrew alphabet may help the memory not a little.

1. *I will extol thee, my God, O King; and I will bless thy name for ever and ever.*

2. *Every day will I bless thee; and I will praise thy name for ever and ever.*

David engageth himself to the work of praising God twice: once in the former part of the psalm, v. 1, 2—and of this he giveth a reason, and prophesieth that the praise of the Lord shall be perpetuated throughout all ages, v. 3, 4—then he engageth himself the second time, and prophesies of the church's holding up this song, v. 5—7.

In David's first engaging himself to praise, learn, 1. The man who can heartily praise God, is he that is reconciled to God ; a man in covenant of grace, reconciliation, and friendship with God, as David was : *I will extol thee, my God.* 2. God is praised, when the man who giveth him praise is humble before him, and all things created are put under God's feet, and God lifted up in estimation above all : *I will extol thee.* 3. Every king should do homage to God, as King over him, as David doth : *I will extol thee, my King.* 4. Praise should so be given to God, that the man who praiseth, may approve himself to God, for sincerity of purpose, as to a present hearer of those praises : *I will extol thee, I will bless thy name.* 5. He who will praise God, must know him as he hath revealed himself, and praise him according to that rule : *I will bless thy name.* 6. Seeing God is essentially blessedness in itself, and the fountain of blessing to his worshippers, it is a point of our thankfulness and praise of him, to acknowledge so much : *I will bless thy name.* 7. As an upright worshipper of God hath no time set to his purpose of service, so no time shall end his task : *I will bless thy name for ever and ever.* 8. Praising of God is not a work for solemn days only, but also must be ordinarily discharged : for every day giveth new reasons for it : *every day will I bless thee.*

3. *Great is the Lord, and greatly to be praised ; and his greatness is unsearchable.*

4. *One generation shall praise thy works to another, and shall declare thy mighty acts.*

From the reasons of this engagement taken from God's greatness, and from the prophecy of the continual proclamation of it to be in the church, learn, 1. The greatness of God manifested in his work ; partly in the manner of manifestation of his presence now and then, by apparitions ; partly in the amplitude of his dominion, power, wisdom, and providence, &c., is worthy of our meditation, and to be acknowledged by us ; and the Lord himself is worthy to be praised for this his greatness : *great is the Lord, and greatly to be praised.* 2. When we have searched what we can, and have meditated till we be faint, there is no finding out the Lord's greatness: *his greatness is unsearchable*. 3. As it is the duty of the church in every age to praise God, and to transmit the praises of God to posterity, so it is the Lord's purpose to have a care that this duty be done in all ages; for it is prophesied, *one generation shall praise thy works to another*. 4. Every age shall have their own addition of God's mighty acts in their time, to what he hath done formerly: *they shall declare thy mighty acts*.

5. *I will speak of the glorious honour of thy majesty, and of thy wondrous works.*

6. *And* men *shall speak of the might of thy terrible acts; and I will declare thy greatness.*

7. *They shall abundantly utter the memory of thy great goodness, and shall sing of thy righteousness.*

In David's engaging himself the second time to praise God, and in his prophesying of the church's holding up the song, learn, 1. In God, and in his works and ways, there is a wonderful beauty and comeliness, a splendour of glory, and a shining majesty to be seen; and that should be observed and talked of by the observers, unto the edification of others: *I will speak of the glorious honour of thy majesty*. 2. There is no looking in upon God immediately, but men must behold him as he letteth forth himself in his word and works to be seen: for, *I will speak of thy wondrous works*, is subjoined to the talking of God's glorious honour and majesty. 3. When men mark not his works of mercy and bounty, the Lord will show them works of justice, that is, terrible works, and give them matter of talking on this account: *and men shall speak of the might of thy terrible acts*. 4. He who knoweth most of God, or hath seen and observed best his operations, should labour most to set forth his praise; whoever cometh short in the duty, such a man should not fail, as David teacheth us, saying, *I will declare thy greatness*. 5. Albeit every work of God be matter of his praise, yet the works of mercy and truth to and for his church is the special theme which the Lord giveth his people to study and declare: *they shall abundantly utter the memory of thy great goodness*. 6. The righteousness of God, whereby he justifieth sinners, sanctifieth the justified, and executeth judgment for his reconciled people, is the sweetest object of the church's joy: *they shall sing of thy righteousness.*

8. *The Lord is gracious, and full of compassion ; slow to anger, and of great mercy.*

In the second place, David praiseth God more particular-ly, and giveth ten reasons or arguments for his praise. The first is from his grace towards sinners. Whence learn, 1. Unworthiness and ill-deserving should not hinder sinners to come to receive mercy and reconciliation: *the Lord is gracious.* 2. Albeit the sinner hath drawn much misery on himself, and justice hath seized upon him for his sins, yet may he be relieved and brought out of his misery if he seek the Lord : *for the Lord is full of compassion.* 3. Al-beit the Lord be sundry ways provoked to visit with the rod, yet he gives time to repent before he declareth his wrath : *he is slow to anger.* 4. The Lord's anger endureth not long-er than that his people may be humbled in the sense of their provocation ; and, when they seek pardon, he is ready to grant it : *he is of great mercy.*

9. *The Lord is good to all ; and his tender mercies are over all his works.*

The second reason for God's praise is his bounty gener-ally to all the creatures, and that for man's sake. Whence learn, 1. The Lord is good and kind to all men, even the wicked not excepted : *the Lord is good to all.* 2. God's mercy may be seen toward man in the continuation of the whole race of the creatures, which, being defiled by man's sin, he might in justice have abolished, or made them either useless to man, or else instruments of his grief : *his tender mercies are over all his works.*

10. *All thy works shall praise thee, O Lord ; and thy saints shall bless thee.*

The third reason for God's praise is the glory of his works, which furnish matter to the saints to bless God. Whence learn, 1. Albeit all men were silent, the Lord's works, one and all, shall speak, each of them in its own kind, to the praise of God : *all thy works shall praise thee, O God.* 2. Albeit every man maketh not use of God's goodness and works, but most men smother the glory of God in their atheism ; yet the Lord hath a number who have found grace in his eyes, who shall observe God's goodness, both to the creatures and to themselves, and shall bless him on that account : *and thy saints shall bless thee.*

11. *They shalt speak of the glory of thy kingdom, and talk of thy power ;*

12. *To make known to the sons of men his mighty acts, and the glorious majesty of his kingdom.*

The fourth reason for God's praise is from the Lord's dominion and power, whereof the saints are both observers and heralds. Whence learn, 1. There is no less matter for praising God for upholding and governing the creatures, than for making them : *they shall speak of the glory of thy kingdom, and talk of thy power.* 2. The Lord will have his saints to instruct such as are not converted to know his glory, power, and majesty, that they may be brought in, and made subjects of his special kingdom of grace : *thy saints shall speak of the glory of thy kingdom, and talk of thy power, to make known to the sons of men his mighty acts, and the glorious majesty of his kingdom.*

13. *Thy kingdom is an everlasting kingdom, and thy dominion endureth throughout all generations.*

The fifth reason for God's praise is from the perpetual endurance of his kingdom. Whence learn, 1. Earthly kings, as they have but few subjects, so they live but a short while in their kingdom; but the kingdom of God—both that general kingdom which he hath over all the creatures, and that special kingdom over the saints in his church—is from age to age perpetual : *thy kingdom is an everlasting kingdom, and thy dominion endureth throughout all generations.*

14. *The Lord upholdeth all that fall, and raiseth up all those that be bowed down.*

The sixth reason for God's praise is from his carefully sustaining the weakest of the subjects of the kingdom of grace. Whence learn, 1. Albeit none of the subjects of the kingdom of grace are freed from the danger of falling into sin and trouble; yet they are preserved that they fall not so deep as the bottom of sinning unto death, or perishing in their troubles ; for God interposeth himself to prevent their perdition : *the Lord upholdeth all that fall.* 2. So many of the subjects of the kingdom of grace as feel their own weakness and inability to stand under the burden either of sin or trouble, or both, find God a supporter, comforter, and deliverer of them : *he raiseth up all them that be bowed down.*

15. *The eyes of all wait upon thee : and thou givest them their meat in due season.*

16. *Thou openest thine hand, and satisfiest the desire of every living thing.*

The seventh reason for God's praise, is his particular care to maintain the life of every living creature so long as he pleaseth to lend it. Whence learn, 1. The Lord casteth not off the care of any living creature which he hath made; but keepeth so constant an eye of providence upon it, as maketh every living creature, in its own kind, turn the eye of it toward him : *the eyes of all wait upon thee.* 2. There is a secret instinct of nature in all living creatures, which leadeth them toward their Maker, in their danger to cry, and in their hunger to bestir themselves; and the business which they make of going to and fro to seek their meat, is a kind of hoping and waiting to find some sustenance of their life, provided by their Maker, in one place or another : *they wait upon thee.* 3. God frustrateth not the natural expectation of hungry creatures, but giveth to every one of them that sort of food which is fit for them : *thou givest them their meat.* 4. As in the variety of meat, suitable to the variety of living creatures; so also in the time and season of giving it, the wisdom, riches, and goodness of God appear : *thou givest them their meat in due season.* 5. As in the meat, and in the time of bestowing it, so also in the measure bestowed, the Lord's goodness and rich bounty are to be seen toward the basest of living creatures : *thou openest thy hand, and satisfiest the desire of every living creature.*

17. *The Lord is righteous in all his ways, and holy in all his works.*

The eighth reason for God's praise, is, from his righteousness and holiness, in all his proceedings and works.

Whence learn, 1. As the providence of God about the creatures in common, is to be marked, so also and especially
his dealing with man, according to the rule of equity and
justice : *the Lord is righteous,* saith he, *and holy.* 2. Albeit the Lord deal otherwise in many things than we could
have expected, and otherwise sometimes than we can see
the reason of his doing, yet is he always just and holy in
his proceedings: *the Lord is righteous in his ways, and
holy in his works.* 3. It is not sufficient for us to give the
glory of righteousness and holiness to God, only in some of
his ways and works, or in his ways toward others, and not
towards ourselves, or in his dealing with some persons, and
not with all persons; but we must justify the Lord in our
hearts and words always, and in all things, toward all men,
for ever : *the Lord is righteous in all his ways, and holy
in all his works.*

18. *The Lord* is *nigh unto all them that call upon
him, to all that call upon him in truth.*

19. *He will fulfil the desire of them that fear him :
he also will hear their cry, and will save them.*

The ninth reason for God's praise, is, for his hearing the
prayer of needy supplicants. Whence learn, 1. The Lord
loveth the praise which ariseth to him, from his goodness to
his people and the citizens of his church, more than any
other points of his praise : as the frequent repetition of
praise to God on this ground showeth. 2. Albeit God be
everywhere present, yet there is a sort of more friendly
presence, which God giveth to them that worship him, than
what is his common presence everywhere; and this is the
nearness of grace and friendship : *the Lord is nigh to
them that call on him.* 3. As God will have his gracious
presence laid open, and manifested to his worshippers by
prayer; so will he have this favour alike patent to all that
pray to him, and seek him, without exception of persons :
the Lord is nigh to all them that call upon him. 4. Because there is a counterfeit and false sort of worshipping
and calling upon God, which is debarred from the benefit of
this promise, to wit, when the party supplicant is not reconciled, nor seeking reconciliation through Christ the Mediator,
or is seeking something not promised, or something for a carnal end, that he may bestow it on his lusts; therefore he

who hath right unto this promise, must be a worshipper of God in faith, and sincere intention; and to such the Lord will show himself nigh : *he is nigh to all them that call upon him, to all that call upon him in truth.*   5. Those are worshippers of God in truth, who fear him; and such men's holy desires are prayers which the Lord will not refuse, but answer : *he will fulfil the desire of them that fear him.*   6. If the Lord answer not the prayer of the man that feareth him at first, yet when he calleth in earnest, when he is in trouble, in straits and hazard, he will answer him, and close his exercise with salvation : *he also will hear their cry, and will save them.*

20. *The Lord preserveth all them that love him : but all the wicked will he destroy.*

The tenth reason for God's praise, is from his different dealing with his friends and with his foes.   Whence learn, 1. True worshippers and true fearers of God, are persons who love God, and such persons shall be sure, that all things shall work to their welfare, nothing shall hurt them : *the Lord preserveth all them that love him.*   2. All such as love not God, but love to lie still in sin, and to follow their own lusts, shall be as certainly without exception destroyed, as the lovers of God shall be preserved : *the Lord preserveth all them that fear him, but all the wicked will he destroy.*

21. *My mouth shall speak the praise of the Lord : and let all flesh bless his holy name for ever and ever.*

David closeth the psalm with a promise to praise the Lord yet more, and exhorteth all men to bless him for ever. Whence learn, 1. When a man hath said all that he can in God's praise, he shall find himself come short of his duty, and his obligation to praise God, to be still lying on him, as this example of David in the close of the psalm showeth us. 2. The Lord will be praised in our spirits, and outwardly in our words and external expressions also : *my mouth shall speak the praises of the Lord.*   3. Some duties belong to some persons, and other duties belong to other persons; but the duty of praising the Lord, is the duty of every man, albeit only the believer giveth obedience to this : *let all flesh bless him.*   4. It is needful that every worshipper of God in the discharge of praise, remember their own frailty and be humbled : *let all flesh bless him.* 5. The duty of praising and blessing God must be so holily discharged, as the Lord may be honoured in effect : *let all flesh bless his holy name.* 6. Such as praise God, and bless him heartily, shall follow his exercise for ever : *let all flesh bless his holy name for ever and ever.*

PSALM CXLVI.

This psalm is a psalm of praise wholly, wherein, when the psalmist hath exhorted all men to praise the Lord, he engaged himself to the work, v. 1, 2. Then he teacheth the way how to praise God in effect, to wit, by renouncing all carnal confidence, and trusting only in the Lord, v. 3—5. Thirdly, he giveth reasons, both of trusting in God, and praising him: and he closeth as he began, with the same exhortation to praise God.

1. *Praise ye the Lord. Praise the Lord, O my soul.*

2. *While I live will I praise the Lord ; I will sing praises unto my God while I have any being.*

From the stirring up of others and himself to praise God, learn, 1. The duty of praising God is so necessary, so deserved by God, so profitable to us, and so spiritual, that we had need frequently to stir up ourselves and others to it : *praise ye the Lord.* 2. For discharging the duty of praise, all the powers of the soul must be stirred up ; the mind, to meditate ; the memory, to bring forth former observations ; the heart and affections, for discharging the duty of praise in the best manner : *praise the Lord, O my soul.* 3. Whatsoever concurrence we find of others in the work of praise, less or more, let us set ourselves seriously and heartily to it, and engage our own heart for it : *while I live, I will praise the Lord.* 4. There can be little heartiness in this work, till the soul lay hold on God by faith, embrace the covenant of grace, and so find its own interest in God ; then the soul will praise in earnest, as the psalmist's example may show us : *I will sing praises to my God while I have any being.*

3. *Put not your trust in princes, nor in the son of man, in whom there is no help.*

4. *His breath goeth forth, he returneth to his earth : in that very day his thoughts perish.*

The psalmist showeth the way how to praise God really, to wit, by renunciation of all earthly confidence, and fixing faith and trust on God alone. For renouncing all confidence in creatures, he giveth reasons, v. 3, 4 ; and for trusting in God, he giveth reasons, by praising God, to the end of the psalm.

In the forbidding of carnal confidence, learn, 1. What a man trusteth most in, that he esteemeth most, and praiseth most in his heart. The psalmist setteth us upon God, therefore, as the right object of trust, and diverteth us from the wrong, that he may teach us to make God the only object of praise. 2. Because the main object of our carnal confidence naturally is man in power, who seemeth able to do for us, able to promote us to dignity and riches, and to keep us up in some state in the world, therefore must we throw down this idol in particular, that we may place our confidence in God the better: *put not your trust in princes.* 3. To cut off carnal confidence in man, that neither mean men may trust in great men, nor great men may trust in the multitude of mean men, we must remember, that no man is naturally better than his progenitors, but such as his fathers were, such is he ; that is, a sinful, weak, and inconstant creature : *put not your trust in princes, nor in the son of man.* 4. The reason why we must not put trust in man, is, because he can neither help himself, nor the man that trusteth in him, when there is most need : *in whom there is no help.* 5. He that cannot deliver himself from death, is not to be trusted in, because it is uncertain how soon death shall seize upon him : *his breath goeth forth, he returneth to his earth.* 6. Whatsoever the good-will, or purpose, or promise of any man can give assurance of, all vanish when the man dieth : *in that very day his thoughts perish.*

5. *Happy* is he *that* hath *the God of Jacob for his help, whose hope* is *in the Lord his God;*

In exhorting us to trust in God, he giveth this encouragement to it, that he who trusteth in God may look for help and happiness in him. Whence learn, 1. The only true object of our faith and confidence is God, as he is revealed by his word to his church, to wit, *the God of Jacob, the God of Israel.* 2. Faith in God bringeth true felicity with it, and help in time of need : *happy is he that hath the God of Jacob for his help.* 3. Hope of help and happiness, from trust and confidence in God, must be grounded upon the Lord's entering into covenant with us, and becoming ours through the Mediator : *whose hope is in the Lord his God.*

6. *Which made heaven and earth, the sea, and all that therein* is; *which keepeth truth for ever ;*

7. *Which executeth judgment for the oppressed : which giveth food to the hungry. The Lord looseth the prisoners :*

8. *The Lord openeth* the eyes of *the blind : the Lord raiseth* them that are *bowed down : the Lord loveth the righteous.*

9. *The Lord preserveth the strangers ; he relieveth the fatherless and widow ; but the way of the wicked he turneth upside down.*

10. *The Lord shall reign for ever,* even *thy God, O Zion, unto all generations. Praise ye the Lord.*

For encouraging us yet more to believe in God, who offereth himself to be reconciled with us, and to be our God in Christ, the psalmist giveth other ten motives; and, as every one of them is a point of God's praise, so it is a prop and pillar to support the believer's faith. The first motive to believe in God, and the first reason for God's praise, is his omnipotence and all-sufficiency, made manifest by the work of creation, and the preservation of all creatures: *which made the heaven and the earth, the sea, and all that therein is.* 2. The second motive to believe in God, is another point for God's praise, to wit, his faithfulness in making and keeping covenant, and performing his promises unto everlasting : *which keepeth truth for ever.* 3. The third point for God's praise and for a prop of faith, is this, that, albeit the Lord, for the glory of his name, and good of his own people, suffer the godly to be persecuted and oppressed also, yet he will plead the cause and controversy of the believer, deliver the oppressed, and punish the oppressor : *which executeth judgment for the oppressed.* 4. The fourth point for God's praise, and pillar of faith, is this, that albeit the Lord suffer the believer to feel the need of what is needful for soul or body, yet he suffereth him not to starve for want of what is necessary: *he giveth food to the hungry*. 5. The fifth point for God's praise is, that, albeit the believer may, for his sins or for trial of his faith, be cast in prison, and brought into bondage, yet the Lord will loose his bonds: *the Lord looseth the prisoners.* 6. The sixth point for God's praise is, that albeit the believer may be in darkness of trouble, and anxiety of mind for a time, and knoweth not what to do, yet the Lord will show him deliverance, and give him direction and comfort: *the Lord openeth the eyes of the blind.* 7. The seventh reason for God's praise, and encouragement to trust in him, is, that, howsoever the burden of trouble may overpower the believer, and make him walk heavily under discouragement, yet the Lord will renew strength, and comfort, and delivery to him: *the Lord raiseth them that are bowed down*. 8. The eighth reason to praise God, and the eighth encouragement to trust in him, is, that the believer who has fled to the righteousness of the Mediator for his justification, and studieth to maintain a holy and righteous conversation, may be sure that he is free from the curse, approved of God, and shall find the fruits of God's good-will to him: *the Lord loveth the righteous.* 9. The ninth reason for God's praise, and encouragement to trust in him, is, from the Lord's different manner of dealing on the one hand, with the poor and needy believer, who hath none to do for him: and, on the other hand, with the proud and powerful man of this world, who trusteth to carry his business by means of the creature, and misregardeth the Lord; he preserveth the one and destroyeth the other: *the Lord preserveth the stranger, and relieveth the fatherless and the widow ; but the way of the wicked he turneth upside down.* 10. The tenth reason for God's praise, and the last encouragement of the believer to trust in him, and not to put confidence in princes, is, that the Lord is the only sovereign king, who liveth for ever, and hath engaged himself to the church and every believer in every age, therefore he only is worthy to be trusted in, and worthy to be praised: *the Lord shall reign for ever, even thy God, O Zion, unto all generations. Praise ye the Lord.*

PSALM CXLVII.

This psalm is for stirring up the church to praise and thanksgiving. The
exhortation is threefold. The first is, v. 1, and six reasons for it, or
motives to it, are set down, v. 2—6. The second exhortation is, v. 7,
and three reasons for it, v. 8—11. The third is, v. 12, and six reasons
for it, to the end.

1. *Praise ye the Lord: for* it is *good to sing
praises unto our God; for* it is *pleasant;* and *praise
is comely.*

In the first exhortation, learn, 1. There is no part of
God's worship whereunto we are more indisposed, or need
more stirring up, than to praise God, as the frequently repeated exhortations import. 2. The first motive is this,
all the encouragements which can be imagined to any work
concur here: it is profitable to praise God ; *for it is good
to sing praises to our God.* 3. All God's praises are the
believer's advantage and storehouse ; and *it is pleasant ;*
full of sweet refreshment, as when a man vieweth his own
rich and well situate inheritance. It is honourable to be
about the employment of angels, to be heralds of the Lord's
glory: *praise is comely.*

2. *The Lord doth build up Jerusalem : he gathereth
together the outcasts of Israel.*

The second reason for God's praise, is his care over his
church. Whence learn, 1. The church is the Lord's special
handywork ; he is the builder, upholder, and restorer of
any breach in it: *the Lord doth build up Jerusalem.*
2. The members of the true church are ofttimes scattered,
one from another, not only by common judgments, but also
by persecution and schisms, that they cannot keep that
sweet communion, one with another, which is to be wished,
but God is the only gatherer and uniter of them, after
whatsoever sort of scattering: *he gathereth together the
outcasts of Israel.*

3. *He healeth the broken in heart, and bindeth up
their wounds.*

The third reason for God's praise, is his care of the afflicted believer, when, by trouble outward, or inward, or
both, he is wounded in spirit, broken, and brought down,

made sickly and weakened : *he healeth the broken in heart, and bindeth up their wounds,* as a tender chirurgeon or physician doth the wound of his patient.

4. *He telleth the number of the stars ; he calleth them all by* their *names.*

The fourth reason for the exhortation to praise God, is his particular knowledge of every thing which transcendeth the capacity of men, and to them is impossible.: *he telleth the number of the stars ; he calleth them all by their names.* In which similitude he showeth also, that albeit Abraham could not comprehend the multitude of the children, either of his faith, or of the flesh, more than he could count the number of the stars; yet the Lord knoweth every believer by name, as he knoweth every star, and can tell every *one by their names.*

5. *Great* is *our Lord, and of great power :* his *understanding is infinite.*

The fifth reason for God's praise, is, because in his attributes he is incomprehensible, namely, in his dominion over all, in his power to do all, and in his wisdom to contrive whatever we stand in need of, so that nothing can be against us, but he is above it ; nothing can be needful for us, but his wisdom can devise the means to bring it to us, and his power putteth his will in execution for our good : *great is the Lord, his power is great, his understanding is infinite.*

6. *The Lord lifteth up the meek : he casteth the wicked down to the ground.*

The sixth reason is from his different dealing with the godly and the wicked : as for the godly, who in the meekness of a subdued spirit, submit themselves under the mighty hand of God, he comforteth them and relieveth them ; but he abaseth the proud who do not stand in awe of his majesty : *the Lord lifteth up the meek, but he casteth the wicked down to the ground.*

7. *Sing unto the Lord with thanksgiving; sing praise upon the harp unto our God :*

The second exhortation to praise and thanksgiving, in

cheerfulness and joy, is expressed with three reasons. In the exhortation, learn, The whole works of God, each of them in its own way, call, as it were, for our estimation and praise of the workmanship which we see : they call for our answer, as it were, and our duty requireth of us joyfully to make answer to the call (as the word importeth) in praising the Maker, and thanking him for the use and benefit which we have of his works : *sing unto the Lord with thanksgiving, sing praise upon the harp unto our God.*

8. *Who covereth the heaven with clouds, who prepareth rain for the earth, who maketh grass to grow upon the mountains.*

The first reason, from the second exhortation, is his wise disposing of the clouds. Whence learn, 1. Sometimes the Lord hideth the glory of the open heaven with clouds, that it may appear again with so much more new, fresh, and pleasant lustre : *he covereth the heaven with clouds.* 2. The change which God maketh upon the face of the heaven by dark clouds, is for advantage to the inhabitants of the earth : *he prepareth rain for the earth.* 3. The Lord taketh care of the most barren parts of the earth, to make them by raining on them, more pleasant and profitable, than otherwise they could be : *he maketh grass to grow upon the mountains.*

9. *He giveth to the beast his food,* and *to the young ravens which cry.*

The second reason of the second exhortation to praise God, is, from the Lord's care of beasts and fowls; whereby he giveth men to understand, that he hath a far greater care of them : *he giveth to the beast his food, and to the young ravens which cry.*

10. *He delighteth not in the strength of the horse ; he taketh not pleasure in the legs of a man.*

11. *The Lord taketh pleasure in them that fear him, in those that hope in his mercy.*

The third reason of the second exhortation is, because God esteemeth very little those things wherein men natur-

ally put confidence, whether their own strength or the
strength of any creatures, such as horses are, whereof men
make most use ; but he taketh pleasure in the godly, who
fear him, and hope in him.   Whence learn, 1. Men have
more objects of carnal confidence than the idol of the power
of princes, or of the multitude of followers : for, before man
will want an idol, he will idolize his own strength, or the
strength of a horse, and put confidence therein : as the
slight estimation which God hath of these confidences, and
the discharge from putting confidence in them, insinuate.
2. Whereinsoever a man delighteth most, and puts most
confidence, that is the man's idol, and that which the man
bringeth into competition with God, as the Lord's discharging from taking delectation or pleasure in the creature, instead of discharging to esteem it, or put trust in it, importeth.   3. God esteemeth no man for his riches, honour, command of horse and foot, or for his bodily strength : *he delighteth not in the strength of the horse* ; *he taketh not
pleasure in the legs of a man.*   4. The only right object
of our joy, pleasure, and confidence is God himself, as the
opposition teacheth us : such as both believe in God, and
fear to offend him, are the only men acceptable to God, in
whom God delighteth, and taketh pleasure to keep communion with them : *the Lord taketh pleasure in them that
fear him, in those that hope in his mercy ;* and, by consequence, such as fear him not, and who, when they are
overtaken in a transgression, run not to him for pardon in
the hope of mercy, *he taketh no pleasure in.*

12. *Praise the Lord, O Jerusalem ; praise thy God,
O Zion :*

In the third exhortation to praise God, expressly directed
to Jerusalem and Zion, representing the church in all ages,
learn, 1. Albeit all the earth be obliged to praise God, yet
only the Lord's people are the right estimators of his glory,
and the fit proclaimers of his praise : *praise the Lord, O
Jerusalem.*   2. Albeit all the creatures are the Lord's, yet
the church is the Lord's in a more nigh relation : for the
church may claim interest in God as her own by covenant :
praise thy God, O Zion.

13. *For he hath strengthened the bars of thy gates ;
he hath blessed thy children within thee.*

14. *He maketh peace* in *thy borders, and filleth thee with the finest of the wheat.*

The reasons of the third exhortation are six; whereof four are in these verses. The first is, the Lord had fenced his church with walls, gates, and bars, that the gates of hell cannot prevail against it : *he hath strengthened the bars of the gates ;* to wit, by interposing his omnipotent power for her preservation. 2. The second reason of praise is, that he maketh one generation to follow another in his church, and the children to be in greater number than their forefathers, by adding daily to the church such as are to be saved : *he hath blessed thy children within thee ;* not only in regard to multiplication of them, but also by making them to abound in all knowledge and grace. 3. The third reason of praise, is, that the true members of the church have peace with God, and among themselves, in that measure which is expedient for her good : *he maketh peace in thy borders.* 4. The fourth reason is, because he feedeth his people with food convenient, but especially in regard to their spiritual nourishment, in giving them the bread of life, whereof the finest flour is but a similitude : *he filleth thee with the finest of the wheat.*

15. *He sendeth forth his commandment* upon *earth : his word runneth very swiftly.*

16. *He giveth snow like wool : he scattereth the hoar-frost like ashes.*

17. *He casteth forth his ice like morsels ; who can stand before his cold ?*

18. *He sendeth out his word, and melteth them : he causeth his wind to blow, and the waters flow.*

The fifth reason of the third exhortation to God's praise, is taken from God's powerful ruling of the least changes in the clouds, and in the air, in making foul weather and fair, frost and fresh weather, as he pleaseth, by which similitude he will have his people to understand, that the Lord ruleth with a more special eye all the changes which fall out in the external condition of the church. Whence learn, 1. The course of the creatures, and the changes in them, even unto the least meteor or change which is to be seen in the clouds, or in the air, is particularly directed and governed by God, whose will is a law to the creature, and whose command hath ready execution : *he sendeth forth his commandment upon earth ; his word runneth very swiftly* 2. The least change of weather, by snow or frost, or ice, is by God's dispensation and appointment, much more any change of affairs in his church : *he giveth snow like wool, he scattereth the hoar-frost like ashes ; he casteth forth his ice like morsels.* 3. The consequences and effects of the changes which God maketh, as well in one case as in another, could not be endured, if God should not temper them, and provide some remedy against them, as appeareth in the making of frost : *who can stand before his cold ?* 4. Before any change from frost to fair weather can be made, a new order must come forth from the Lord, and when that cometh, air and water return to that former course, and so it is in any other change in the world, especially in the affairs of the church : *he sendeth out his word, and melteth them : he causeth the wind to blow, and the waters flow.*

19. *He showeth his word unto Jacob, his statutes and his judgments unto Israel.*

20. *He hath not dealt so with any nation : and* as for his *judgments, they have not known them. Praise ye the Lord.*

The sixth reason of the third exhortation to praise God, is, from the different dealing of God with his church, and with the rest of the people of the world. Whence learn, 1. The benefit of the Scriptures, and the laying open and application of them, to the edification of the hearers, is a precious gift of God : and this benefit the Lord hath bestowed on his church, called by the name of Jacob or Israel : *he showeth his word unto Jacob, his statutes and his judgments unto Israel.* 2. The benefit of the Scriptures, and revealing the word of life to the church, make God's people in a better condition, and more excellent than any other incorporation can be in : *he hath not dealt so with any nation.* 3. Where the word of God in his Scriptures is not laid open, there the Lord's dealing with men in justice and mercy, and the way which the Lord keepeth in ruling the world, is not understood, but the people there live in deadly darkness : *as for his judg-*

ments, they have not known them. 4. As the benefits bestowed upon the church are most excellent, so the church is most bound to praise God, both for those mercies, and for all other his glorious works : *praise ye the Lord.*

PSALM CXLVIII.

In this psalm, the church is stirred up to praise God, because of the incomparable excellency of his glory and majesty, appearing, first, in the heavens above, v. 1—6; secondly, in the earth and sea beneath, and lower parts under the heaven, v. 7—10; thirdly, in governing men, and all sorts and ranks of men, but especially in doing for his church, v. 11—14. In all which, as he showeth how the world is full of God's glory, so he pointeth at matter of his praise, whithersoever we turn our eyes.

1. *Praise ye the Lord. Praise ye the Lord from the heavens : praise him in the heights.*

2. *Praise ye him, all his angels : praise ye him, all his hosts.*

3. *Praise ye him, sun and moon : praise him, all ye stars of light.*

4. *Praise him, ye heavens of heavens, and ye waters that* be *above the heavens.*

5. *Let them praise the name of the Lord : for he commanded, and they were created.*

6. *He hath also stablished them for ever and ever : he hath made a decree which shall not pass.*

In the exhortation to praise God because of his glory shining in the heavens, learn, 1. Howsoever the glory of the Lord shineth in all his works, yet there are degrees of the shining of it, and the chiefest glory is from celestial creatures, and from the consideration of what is in heaven : *praise ye the Lord, praise ye the Lord from the heavens.* 2. As God is praised in heaven by the blessed spirits there, so the true worshipper should join with those that praise him there : *praise him in the heights,* or high places. 3. Albeit the angels have the first place in the song of God's praise, and need not to be stirred up to the work of praise by us, yet it is a part of our praising God, to consent to their song, and account their work well bestowed on the Lord their Maker, holding their example before our eyes, aiming to do God's will on earth, as it is done in hea-

ven : *praise him, all ye angels.* 4. The Lord hath at his
hand swift servants not a few, to go in what message he
pleaseth to direct them, and they are ministering spirits for
the good of his church : *praise ye him, all ye his angels,*
or his messengers. 5. The Lord is also well furnished with
soldiers, for all his creatures are ready at his command, to
fight in God's quarrel, in defence of his friends, and pursuit
of his foes : *praise ye him, all his hosts.* 6. The Lord's
armies are not idle, but are still on their work of praising,
doing the works of peace even in the midst of war : *praise
him, all his hosts.* 7. Beside the common song of praise
which all things have as they are creatures, every one of
the creatures has its own proper part in the song : the sun
in his particular virtue and motion, the moon in hers, and
the stars in theirs, every one by themselves, and these also
jointly make up a sweet and harmonious melody, to the
praise of God : *praise ye him, sun and moon ; praise ye
him, all ye stars of light.* 8. The variety and difference
of place and distance from the earth, of sun, moon, and
stars, some of them being lower, some of them higher, as
the eclipses of sun and moon, and the diverse positions of
the stars show, are all matters of God's praise : for the
lowest region of the air is here called heaven ; and the
place where the sun, moon, and stars are set, is called
heaven, and the heaven of heavens, the third heaven, where
angels and the spirits of just men made perfect remain,
each and all of them serve for God's praise : *praise him, ye
heavens of heavens.* 9. The bottles of waters in the clouds,
flying above the lowest region of air, ready to be dissolved
here and there, as God pleaseth to water the earth, serve
as matter, both of wondering at God's work, and of praising him : *praise him ye waters that be above the heavens.*
10. Praise is due to God, not only for making the heavens,
but also for making them of nothing, by the sole word of
command, which produced them, by saying, *let them be ;
let them praise the name of the Lord ; for he commanded, and they were created.* 11. The speechless
creatures have their own way of praising God, and men
have their way of praising : speechless creatures praise God
in their own kind, when they hold forth, as in a table, the
matter and reason of praising God, and men praise God,
when they observe and acknowledge, and proclaim one to

another, the reasons for God's praise, and these exhortations import both: *let them praise the name of the Lord.* 12. The course and appointed motions of the heavens, are so settled during the standing of the world, that they shall not fail to go on according to God's decree, which, as it is a matter for God's praise, so also for man's comfort, who shall have the use and benefit thereof from generation to generation : *he hath also established them for ever and ever : he hath made a decree which shall not pass.*

7. *Praise the Lord from the earth, ye dragons and all deeps :*

8. *Fire and hail ; snow and vapour ; stormy wind fulfilling his word :*

9. *Mountains, and all hills ; fruitful trees, and all cedars :*

10. *Beasts, and all cattle ; creeping things, and flying fowl.*

In the exhortation made, in the second place, to the creatures under heaven, learn, 1. As the heavens, so also the earth and the deep sea, are filled with the matter of God's praise: *praise the Lord from the earth, ye dragons and all deeps.* 2. The most terrible creatures serve to set forth God's glory, as well as the most useful and comfortable : *ye dragons and all deeps.* 3. The changes which are made in the clouds or in the air, by storms or tempests, or whatsoever way, come not by chance, but are all directed forth by God, for some intent of his : and, in what work he employeth them, they fail not to execute his will: *fire and hail, snow and vapour, stormy wind, fulfilling his word:* and out of those changes praises arise unto God. 4. The diversifying of the face of the earth with higher and lower parts, with mountains, hills, and valleys, and the adorning of the face thereof with trees, some taller, some lower and smaller, some barren, some fruitful, contributeth much to the praise of God : *mountains and all hills, fruitful trees and all cedars.* 5. Besides all that is said in the variety of things living on the earth, each of them contends with the other, which of them shall show forth more of God's wisdom, power, and goodness ; *beasts and all cattle, creeping things and flying fowl :* all those creatures offer matter of praise to God, that men may take the song off their hand, and directly, formally, and properly, praise God for his glorious properties evinced by them.

11. *Kings of the earth, and all people ; princes, and all judges of the earth :*

12. *Both young men and maidens ; old men and children :*

13. *Let them praise the name of the Lord ; for his name alone is excellent : his glory* is *above the earth and heaven.*

Having gone through other creatures, the psalmist cometh to man, who is the chief, both matter and instrument of God's praise. Whence learn, 1. The Lord is glorious in his workmanship and government of all the creatures, but most of all in men, whom he calleth to be factors, collectors, and chamberlains, as it were, to gather to him the rent of praise and glory, from all other creatures, and then to pay praises for their own part also : *kings of the earth, and all people let them praise,* &c. 2. God is no leveller of men's estates and outward condition in the world, or allower of levelling, but, for his own praise and men's good, he hath ordained distinction of men in kings and subject people, princes and judges, and people to be judged in all parts of the earth : *kings of the earth and all people, princes and all judges of the earth.* 3. As civil government is appointed by God, so they who are advanced to this dignity, are first in the obligement to the duty of setting forth God's praise, and yet subjects here also must contribute, according to their place and ability : *kings of the earth and all people, princes and all judges of the earth.* 4. It should qualify the minds of men who are in honour, that their preferment is but on earth, and their time no longer than while they are on the earth ; that they are under a king and judge whose dominion is heavenly and everlasting ; therefore he joineth this addition : *kings of the earth, princes and judges of the earth.* 5. As distinguishing men in regard to estate, so distinguishing of sex and age offereth much matter of praise, when particulars are considered ; and for the very distinction in sex and age, God is to be praised : *both young men and maidens, old men and children, let them praise.* 6. There is much matter of God's glory in

the earth, and more in the heavens, but the glory of himself and of his properties, is more than all that either is or
can be seen, or found or expressed in or by the creature :
*let them praise the name of the Lord ; for his name
alone is excellent, his glory is above the earth and the
heavens.*

14. *He also exalteth the horn of his people, the praise
of all his saints ; even of the children of Israel, a
people near unto him.   Praise ye the Lord.*

In the last place, the psalmist pointeth at the glory of
God manifested to the church, for which all God's people
are bound to praise him.   Whence learn, 1. The praise of
God for what he doeth to and for his church is above all the
rest of his praises, from the rest of his works, as far as the
work of redemption, grace, and salvation to sinners, is
above the works of creation and worthy to put the cape-
stone upon the rest of the work of his praises, as here it is
placed.   2. Beside all the use and benefit which the Lord's
people have of the whole works of God's hands, he lifteth them
up in strength, victory, and glory over all their enemies, and
over all other incorporations in the world, who are but slaves
to sin and Satan in comparison of them : *he also exalteth
the horn of his people*.   3. The exalting of the strength,
victory, and glory of the church, standeth mainly in exalting the Messiah, or the kingdom of the Messiah represented
by the exalting of David ; for Christ is the horn of his people, in whom their victory and glory are obtained, and maintained to them; and therefore the horn of his people is expounded here to be, *the praise of the saints*.   4. Those
are the true children of Israel, who glory in Christ as their
strength, victory, and glory, and study to be in effect saints :
for, his people, and his saints, are here expounded to be,
even the children of Israel.   5. Students of holiness, who
glory and rejoice in Jesus as their strength, victory, righteousness, and salvation, and who are wrestlers for the blessing as true Israelites, are the Lord's people in a more strait
union with God, than any other people in the world; *a
people near unto him :* and that in regard of their covenant with God, their incorporation in Christ, the inhabita-
tion of the holy Spirit in them, and the mutual love between God and them.   6. Of all people in the earth, people

of God have most reason to praise their Lord : *praise ye the Lord.*

PSALM CXLIX.

This psalm is a ninefold exhortation to the true members of the church, who are believers and saints in effect, to praise God for saving grace bestowed on them, and for special privileges granted them; not only above what is given to the world, but also above what is given to the visible members of the church, who are not as yet converted ; whereunto some reasons or motives to the obedience of those exhortations are added.

1. *Praise ye the Lord.   Sing unto the Lord a new song,* and *his praise in the congregation of saints.*

From the first two exhortations, learn, 1. The elect, regenerate, or true believers, have a song of their own, for mercies peculiar to them, beside the praise which they have to give for the Lord's work round about them, and therefore they have a proper reason to praise God for their own particular mercies : *praise ye the Lord.* 2. The song of the redeemed, elect, and converted, is a new song which shall never wax old, nor be cut off, an everlasting song : *sing unto the Lord a new song.* 3. It is God's ordinance, that the worshippers of the Lord should have assemblies and meetings, wherein publicly and jointly they may glorify the Lord in proclaiming cheerfully his praise : *sing his praise in the congregation of the saints.*

2. *Let Israel rejoice in him that made him : let the children of Zion be joyful in their King.*

From the third and fourth exhortation learn, 1. It is the Lord's command, that his people rejoice in himself, with a joy above all the joy which they can have in the creatures, which God hath given to them, that they may the more cheerfully praise him : *let Israel rejoice in him.* 2. The church of the elect and renewed saints, is the special workmanship of God's grace, not only as his creatures, but also as his new creatures, created in Christ Jesus to good works: *let Israel rejoice in him that made him.* 3. The church is a peculiar kingdom by itself, whereof God is king in a peculiar way, able to govern his people by his word, discipline, and Spirit, and to defend his church, and all his own ordinances therein, to the comfort of all the true members thereof: *let the children of Zion be joyful in their King.*

3. *Let them praise his name in the dance: let them sing praises unto him with the timbrel and harp.*

From the fifth and sixth exhortation to praise God, learn, 1. The joy of the believer is a great and growing joy, arising from rejoicing, in the former verse, to exalting, in this verse, signified by *dancing: let them praise his name in the dance.* 2. The joy of the godly is a complete joy, employing all, and filling all the powers of the soul, signified by musical instruments used in the pedagogy of the old church: *let them sing praises unto him with the timbrel and harp.*

4. *For the Lord taketh pleasure in his people: he will beautify the meek with salvation.*

Of these exhortations he giveth two reasons. Whence learn, 1. The Lord loveth believers and repenteth not, but resteth in his love, and taketh pleasure in his workmanship upon them: *the Lord taketh pleasure in his people.* 2. The constancy of the Lord's love towards his people, is the ground of the church's constant joy in God and perpetual praising of him: *let them sing praises to him with the timbrel and the harp:* for the Lord taketh pleasure in his people. 3. Whatsoever matter of joy believers or true saints have in God, yet they are acquainted with as much affliction in the world, as emptieth them of rejoicing in themselves, humbleth them, and subdueth their spirits, and maketh them to aim and endeavour, without fretting or grudging, to digest all the Lord's dispensations toward them; and for this cause the believers or saints, are called meek. 4. Albeit the affliction wherewith the godly are acquainted, obscureth their blessedness, and hideth the beauty thereof before the world, yet God in love to them, ofttimes wipeth off the black and blemish of affliction, by giving them glorious delivery, and at length he giveth to them full salvation: *he will beautify the meek with salvation.*

5. *Let the saints be joyful in glory: let them sing aloud upon their beds.*

6. Let *the high* praises *of God* be *in their mouth, and a two-edged sword in their hand:*

From the seventh, eighth, and ninth exhortations to praise God, learn, 1. The godly, or true members of the church, are God's favourites, endued with grace, accepted through the beloved, yea, and are good to such as they live among ; for so much the word saints imports.　2. The believer may be joyful now, for the glory hoped for, and may glory in the promised blessedness, as if it were already possessed : *let the saints be joyful in glory.*　3. The joy allowed upon the saints is a lasting joy, both day and night ; a joy which, when they are most retired, may be most enjoyed, which, being examined in secret, shall be found solid ; a joy full of quiet, rest, and peace, as if they were resting in their beds ; a joy which shall continue with them when their bodies are lying in the grave : for thus much may the words bear in divers respects : *let them sing aloud upon their beds.*　4. The praises of God set down in his word, wherein the Lord's name and attributes, the Lord's promises and glorious works, especially done in favour of his saints, are set down, are the matter of the saints' confidence, gloriation, and joy, worthy to be talked of and openly declared in the audience of others, for the glory of God and edification of his people ; for what the Lord is, to wit, wise, powerful, merciful, just, &c., that the Lord is for his people, and for every believer in him ; and, therefore, *let the high praises of the Lord be in their mouth.*　5. As the word of God, wherein God's praises are set down, is the matter and warrant of the saint's joy and confidence in God, so also is it a powerful weapon to overturn all adversaries' power whatsoever, both bodily and spiritual : *let the praises of God be a two-edged sword in their hand.*

7. *To execute vengeance upon the heathen,* and *punishments upon the people ;*

8. *To bind their kings with chains, and their nobles with fetters of iron ;*

9. *To execute upon them the judgment written : this honour have all his saints.　Praise ye the Lord.*

By way of motive to the obedience of the former exhortations to rejoice in God, and glorify him, the psalmist subjoineth a special use of the praises of God, set down in Scripture in relation to enemies and persecutors of the saints, over whom all believers have a spiritual victory by faith in God, so that, as the Lord's officers, they may pronounce doom and sentence condemnatory against all their enemies, great and small, according as the Scripture giveth them warrant. And this doom and sentence of judgment, pronounced by the believer, whether in his own mind or vocally, as occasion offereth, must have execution undoubtedly following upon it, according to what is written in the Scripture ; and this is no small honour allowed upon the saints. Whence learn, 1. The elect and regenerate, believing students of holiness, have enemies, both without the visible church and within it, both heathen and people.   2. God will be avenged upon them all, great and small ; for it is presupposed that *vengeance* must be executed upon *the heathen, and punishments upon the people.*   3. The believers are in a sort executioners of this vengeance, because they, as doomsters, take the sentence from the mouth of God, the just judge, and pronounce doom on them, whereupon, in the set time, followeth execution; the word of God falling on them in effect as a sharp sword to cut them asunder: thus the truth and justice of God, with his other attributes, all being parts of his praise, *are a two-edged sword in their hand to execute vengeance upon the heathen and punishment upon the people.*   4. The greatest monarchs, rulers, and judges among men are subjected to the word of God, and must be bound either to the belief and obedience of it, or to the punishment and vengeance pronounced against the transgressors thereof, so fast as if they were bound in strongest fetters : for the praises of God in the mouth of his saint are, *to bind their kings with chains, and their nobles with fetters of iron.*   5. The Lord's children and saints must not do wrong to kings or nobles, or to any man else ; they must neither pronounce nor execute judgment according as they please, but as the written word of God prescribeth or alloweth : for here they are tied, *to execute nothing upon them, save the judgment written.*   4. These privileges are spiritual and common to all believers, who, according to their places and callings, whether public or private, may for their own comfort and for others' edification, accordingly apply the word of God to themselves, and against their enemies : for, *this honour have all his saints*, and therefore they ought in a special manner to bless God for their privileges : *praise ye the Lord.*

PSALM CL.

A Psalm of David.

In this psalm, the Spirit of the Lord calleth upon us thirteen times to praise the Lord—each exhortation pointeth forth God as the only object of praise. The first and the last exhortation is to all, to praise God absolutely, without giving any motive more than his very name importeth, which indeed is a sufficient reason: for, seeing the Lord is God, who hath his being of himself, and all the creatures have their being of him, and dependence on him, it followeth of necessity, that he is praiseworthy in himself, and deserveth to be praised by all his creatures. The second, third, fourth, and fifth exhortations, have reasons and motives annexed to them, as the matter of his praise, v. 1, 2. The sixth, seventh, eighth, ninth, tenth, and eleventh, teach the matter of his praise under the terms of the Levitical service, v. 3—5 ; and the twelfth pointeth at the persons or special party, which must yield the praise to God, with a reason insinuated, moving thereunto, v. 6.

1. *Praise ye the Lord. Praise God in his sanctuary : praise him in the firmament of his power.*

2. *Praise him for his mighty acts : praise him according to his excellent greatness.*

From these exhortations which have motives annexed to them, learn, 1. The holiness of God (which is the unstained clearness, and untainted glory of all his attributes, such as are his wisdom, power, justice, mercy, and all the rest of his properties mentioned in Scripture,) is the subject of the saints' praising God in the church, and of spirits praising him in heaven; for the word in the original beareth, *praise the Lord in his holiness, in his sanctuary, in heaven his holy place.* 2. The holiness of God should be mainly looked to by all men, who are about to praise him, that our hearts and mouths may be rightly framed for so high a service, and we may beware to take his name in vain; for he will be sanctified of all that draw near unto him, especially in the work of praise : *praise God in his holiness.* 3. Matter of praise is furnished to us, in the wisdom and power of God, which is to be seen in the creatures, and particularly in the frame of the stories of heaven; in the first whereof, his power supports the huge weight of waters in the clouds; in the second, the stars and planets move, and make their circles constantly; and in the third, heavens, angels, and spirits of just men made perfect, praise God : *praise him in the firmament of his power.* 4. Matter of praising God is furnished by his manifold mighty acts, to be seen in the powerful sustaining, ruling, and employing of all his creatures, as he seeth fittest for his own glory, for the building of his church, delivering her from dangers, and overthrowing her enemies : *praise the Lord for his mighty acts.* 5. Matter of praising God is furnished in his wonderful greatness, and in the rays of excellence shining in all his dispensations, and manner of governing the world, sustaining some individual creatures, which are still the same from the creation, and multiplying others in their kind, to the astonishment of a serious beholder: *praise him according to his excellent greatness.*

3. *Praise him with the sound of the trumpet: praise him with the psaltery and harp.*

4. *Praise him with the timbrel and dance : praise him with stringed instruments and organs.*

5. *Praise him upon the loud cymbals : praise him upon the high-sounding cymbals.*

Here are other six exhortations, teaching the manner of praising God under the shadow of typical music, appointed in the ceremonial law. Whence learn, 1. Albeit the typical ceremonies of musical instruments in God's public worship, belonging to the pedagogy of the church, in her minority before Christ, be now abolished with the rest of the ceremonies; yet the moral duties shadowed forth by them, are still to be studied, because this duty of praising God, and praising him with all our mind, strength, and soul, is moral, whereunto we are perpetually obliged. 2. The variety of musical instruments, some of them made use of in the camp, as trumpets; some of them more suitable to a peaceable condition, as psalteries and harps; some of them sounding by blowing wind into them; some of them sounding by lighter touching of them, as stringed instruments; some of them by beating on them more sharply, as tabrets, drums,

and cymbals; some of them sounding by touching and blowing also, as organs: all of them giving some certain sound,
some more quiet, and some making more noise: some of
them having a harmony by themselves; some of them making
a concert with other instruments, or with the motions of the
body in dancing; some of them serving for one use, some of
them serving for another, and all of them serving to set
forth God's glory, and to shadow forth the duty of worshippers, and the privileges of the saints;—the plurality and
variety, I say, of these instruments, were fit to represent
divers conditions of the spiritual man, and of the greatness
of his joy to be found in God, and to teach what stirring
up should be of the affections and powers of our soul, and
one of another, unto God's worship; what harmony should
be among the worshippers of God, what melody each should
make in himself, singing to God with grace in his heart, and
to show the excellence of God's praise, which no means nor
instrument, nor any expression of the body joined thereunto,
could sufficiently set forth: and thus much is figured forth
in these exhortations to praise God with *trumpet, psaltery,
harp, timbrel, dance, stringed instruments, and organs,
loud and high sounding cymbals.*

6. *Let every thing that hath breath praise the Lord.
Praise ye the Lord.*

In the twelfth exhortation, pointing at the party called
upon to praise God, learn, 1. Living creatures, which draw
breath, give unto and take from God their life afresh every
moment in their breathing, above all visible creatures speak
most to the praise of God's wisdom and power in framing
and preserving them: *let every thing that hath breath
praise the Lord.* 2. Of all living creatures, men are most
bound to praise God, as they in whom God in the creation,
and in their several generations from age to age, did and
doth breathe the spirit of life, and of all men those are
most bound to praise God, on whom he hath bestowed his
Holy Spirit: and howsoever the Lord's works in all men
shall speak to his praise, how wicked soever men shall be,
yet only renewed souls, into whom God hath breathed his
Spirit, as the word *breath* in the original may bear, shall
voluntarily and sincerely praise God: *let every thing that
hath breath praise the Lord.* 3. The Spirit of the Lord,

when he gave the psalms to the church of the Jews, had an eye toward the rest of the world, of whom he was in his appointed time to exact this song of praise : and so we who are Gentiles, brought into the society of the church, are bound to join in the work with them ; and when we are joined, and when all who are to be converted are joined, yet are we all too few, to bear up the song of God's praise; and, therefore, to show this, it is said, *let every thing that hath breath praise the Lord.* 4. When we have said all we are able to say for God's praise, we are but to begin again anew; for this are we taught by the renewing of the exhortation, in the close of sundry psalms, and here also at the end of all the psalms : *praise ye the Lord.* And after us must all the creatures come in their own kind and order, to offer up praises also, as we are taught, Rev. v. 12, where, after that elect angels and saints, whose number was ten thousand times ten thousand, and thousands of thousands, had sung their song, saying, *with a loud voice, Worthy is the Lamb that was slain, to receive power and riches, and wisdom, and strength, and honour, and glory, and blessing ;* then it followeth, v. 13, *And every creature which is in heaven, and on the earth, and under the earth, and such as are in the sea, and all that are in them, heard I, saying, Blessing, and honour, and glory, and power be unto him that sitteth upon the throne, and to the Lamb for ever and ever.*

THE END.